Marketing

13th Edition

McGraw-Hill Series in Marketing

Marketing

13th Edition

Michael J. Etzel
University of Notre Dame

Bruce J. Walker
University of Missouri–Columbia

William J. Stanton
University of Colorado–Boulder

 Irwin

Boston Burr Ridge, IL Dubuque, IA Madison, WI New York
San Francisco St. Louis Bangkok Bogotá Caracas Kuala Lumpur
Lisbon London Madrid Mexico City Milan Montreal New Delhi
Santiago Seoul Singapore Sydney Taipei Toronto

MARKETING

Published by McGraw-Hill/Irwin, a business unit of The McGraw-Hill Companies, Inc., 1221 Avenue of the Americas, New York, NY, 10020. Copyright © 2004, 2001, 1997, 1994, 1991, 1987, 1984, 1981, 1978, 1975, 1971, 1967, 1964 by The McGraw-Hill Companies, Inc. All rights reserved. No part of this publication may be reproduced or distributed in any form or by any means, or stored in a database or retrieval system, without the prior written consent of The McGraw-Hill Companies, Inc., including, but not limited to, in any network or other electronic storage or transmission, or broadcast for distance learning.

Some ancillaries, including electronic and print components, may not be available to customers outside the United States.

This book is printed on acid-free paper.

domestic   2 3 4 5 6 7 8 9 0 QPD/QPD 0 9 8 7 6 5 4
international   2 3 4 5 6 7 8 9 0 QPD/QPD 0 9 8 7 6 5 4

ISBN 0-07-252650-5

Editor in chief: *John E Biernat*
Executive editor: *Linda Schreiber*
Developmental editor I: *Anna M. Chan*
Marketing manager: *Kim Kanakes*
Media producer: *Craig Atkins*
Project manager: *Laura Griffin*
Senior production supervisor: *Michael R. McCormick*
Designer: *Adam Rooke*
Photo research coordinator: *Judy Kausal*
Photo researcher: *Romy Charlesworth*
Lead supplement producer: *Cathy L. Tepper*
Senior digital content specialist: *Brian Nacik*
Cover design: *George Foreman grill courtesy of Salton Inc., XM radio imagery courtesy of XM Satellite Radio Inc., Enterprise logo courtesy of Enterprise Rent-A-Car, Starbucks logo courtesy of Starbucks Corporation, Palm logo courtesy of Palm, Inc., and Segway logo courtesy of Segway LLC.*
Typeface: *10/12 Sabon*
Compositor: *Carlisle Communications, Ltd.*
Printer: *Quebecor World Dubuque Inc.*

Library of Congress Cataloging in Publication Data

Etzel, Michael J.
    Marketing / Michael J. Etzel, Bruce J. Walker, William J. Stanton.–13th ed.
       p. cm.
    Includes index.
    ISBN 0-07-252650-5 (alk. paper) – ISBN 0-07-121455-0 (international : alk. paper)
    1. Marketing. I. Walker, Bruce J. II. Stanton, William J. III. Title.
  HF5415.S745 2004
  658.8—dc21

                                   2003042615

INTERNATIONAL EDITION ISBN 0-07-121455-0
Copyright 2004. Exclusive rights by The McGraw-Hill Companies, Inc. for manufacture and export. This book cannot be re-exported from the country to which it is sold by McGraw-Hill. The International Edition is not available in North America.

www.mhhe.com

About the Authors

Michael J. Etzel received his Ph.D. in marketing from the University of Colorado. Since 1980, he has been a professor of marketing at the University of Notre Dame. He also has been on the faculties at Utah State University and the University of Kentucky. He has held visiting faculty positions at the University of South Carolina and the University of Hawaii. In 1990, he was a Fulbright Fellow at the University of Innsbruck, Austria. His other overseas assignments include directing and teaching in the University of Notre Dame's program in Fremantle, Australia, in 1994, and the University's London MBA program in 1998.

Professor Etzel has taught marketing courses from the introductory through the doctoral level. He received a Kaneb undergraduate teaching award from the University of Notre Dame in 2001. His research, primarily in marketing management and buyer behavior, has appeared in the *Journal of Marketing, Journal of Marketing Research, Journal of Consumer Research,* and other publications. He is the coauthor of another college-level text, *Retailing Today.*

He has been active in many aspects of the American Marketing Association at the local and national levels. He served as chairman of AMA's board in 1996–1997.

Bruce J. Walker became professor of marketing and dean of the College of Business at the University of Missouri–Columbia in 1990. Professor Walker received his undergraduate degree in economics from Seattle University and his master's and Ph.D. degrees in business from the University of Colorado.

Professor Walker was a member of the marketing faculties at the University of Kentucky and then at Arizona State University. Dr. Walker has taught a variety of courses, including principles of marketing. His research, focusing primarily on franchising, marketing channels, and survey-research methods, has been published in the *Journal of Marketing, Journal of Marketing Research,* and other periodicals. He has also coedited or coauthored conference proceedings and books, including *Retailing Today.*

Dr. Walker has been involved with the American Marketing Association, including serving as vice president of the Education Division. Currently, he is a trustee for the International Franchise Association's Education Foundation and a member of several corporate boards including Salton, Inc., an international housewares company.

William J. Stanton is professor emeritus of marketing at the University of Colorado–Boulder. He received his Ph.D. in marketing from Northwestern University, where he was elected to Beta Gamma Sigma. He has worked in business and has taught in several management development programs for marketing executives. He has served as a consultant for various business organizations and has engaged in research projects for the federal government. Professor Stanton also has lectured at universities in Europe, Asia, Mexico, and New Zealand.

A coauthor of the leading text in sales management, Professor Stanton has also published several journal articles and monographs. *Marketing* has been translated into Spanish, and separate editions have been adapted (with coauthors) for Canada, Italy, Australia, and South Africa. In a survey of marketing educators, Professor Stanton was voted one of the leaders in marketing thought. And he is listed in *Who's Who in America* and *Who's Who in the World.*

Dedication

Mike Etzel
To Jake, Eric, and a player to be named

Bruce Walker
To Pam, and Walker, Nicole, Justin, and Aidan

Bill Stanton
To Kelley and Little Joe

Brief Contents

Contents

Part Two
Identifying and Selecting
Markets   86

4

Consumer Markets and
Buying Behavior   86
Can HARLEY-DAVIDSON Ride
Any Faster?   87

5

Business Markets and
Business Buying
Behavior   116
Can FREEMARKETS Satisfy Buyers
and Sellers?   117

6

Market Segmentation,
Targeting, and
Positioning   144
The SMART CAR Is Short and Sweet,
but Will It Sell?   145

10 Brands, Packaging, and Other Product Features   258
Is GEORGE FOREMAN the Champion in Another Ring?   259

11 Services Marketing   284
Can ENTERPRISE Rent-A-Car Stay in the Fast Lane?   285

Part Four
Price   316

12 Price Determination   316
With PRICELINE.COM, Is the Price Always Right?   317

Part Seven
Managing the Marketing Effort   568

22 Marketing and the Information Economy 620
What's the Incentive for MARITZ to Use Technology?   621

Preface

Having moved beyond the novelty and frenzy of entering another century, we can objectively examine what a new era is likely to mean for business and marketing. Surely some developments of the 20th century will continue unabated. For example, the internationalization of business, reflected in the expansion of the European Union, increasing privatization in China, and the growth of truly global corporations, is becoming the norm. Virtually all industries and careers now have an international dimension.

Technology has been an important component of business progress since the Industrial Revolution. However, the pace of technological advances has increased markedly. Two developments in communications, cellular phones and the Internet, are highly visible illustrations of how technology dramatically affects everyday life and the way we do business. In virtually every other aspect of lives from health care to entertainment, technology will continue to amaze and sometimes baffle us.

And then there is the physical environment. Always a concern, it will almost certainly take on greater significance this century. Global warming, food production, air and water quality, and waste disposal are just a few of the issues that will require significant attention in the foreseeable future.

In response to, or perhaps in anticipation of, these developments, marketers will change the ways they go about their roles. Fresh opportunities will be made possible by access to more and better data on customers and prospects. Added pressure will be exerted to consider the quality of life when developing and marketing products. New markets, both domestically and globally, will have to be assessed for their short- and long-term potential. Marketing, as an integral dimension of virtually every part of our lives, will be affected by these events. Although we may not be able to anticipate every development, it is clear that important changes are occurring and they will make marketing more challenging, dynamic, and exciting.

We have designed the 13th edition of *Marketing* to help students prepare to operate in and contribute to the 21st century. Regardless of whether a person intends to work in a business, for the government, or in a nonprofit organization, the concepts, strategies, and techniques of effective marketing are relevant.

Structure of the 13th Edition

Over several editions, we have introduced a number of changes to arrive at a structure we believe is both student- and instructor-friendly. We are gratified that so many adopters have found the sequence of topics to be effective for teaching and learning about marketing. The major features of our structure are:

- Providing seven parts to the text that logically build from fundamental concepts through the major tasks associated with marketing to the strategic role of marketing in an organization.

- Bringing early attention to the global nature of marketing by dedicating Chapter 3 to this important topic, integrating global examples throughout the book, and providing "A Global Perspective" box in almost every chapter.

- Emphasizing the similarities as well as the differences between consumer and business marketing by means of back-to-back coverage in Chapters 4 and 5.

- Combining demand forecasting with its logical antecedents—segmentation, targeting, and positioning—in Chapter 6.

- Covering marketing research in Chapter 7, after students have been exposed to consumer and business markets and segmentation.
- Making services marketing (Chapter 11) part of the product section of the book.
- Combining wholesaling and physical distribution in one chapter.
- Integrating planning, implementation, and evaluation in Chapters 20 and 21 to provide a broad strategic context after students have a grasp of what marketing entails.
- Carrying four themes throughout the book—global marketing, ethical challenges, the marketer as decision maker, and the usefulness of technology—with separate boxes interspersed throughout the chapters. These vignettes are intended to both inform students about noteworthy topics and issues and stimulate critical thinking on their part.
- Concluding with a chapter that examines the growing role that technology has—and surely will continue to have—in marketing.

Other Noteworthy Features

The changes we have made in the 13th edition are expected to make the book an even better learning device for students. Among the more noteworthy changes are:

- The text has been shortened without reducing the number of topics covered.
- The Internet's role is properly reflected throughout the book with examples, Web addresses, and boxes.
- The chapter-opening and part-ending cases, within-chapter boxes, and Interactive Marketing Exercises at the end of each chapter are useful instruments for stimulating active learning through projects, classroom discussions, and debates.
- Two appendices, one on marketing math and the other on career planning and job search, are practical tools that can be integrated into the course or used independently by students. The latter appendix can be found on the website for the text.

Chapter-Related Cases

Each chapter begins with a contemporary case that sets the stage for the upcoming material. At the conclusion of the chapter, the case is revisited and more specific information is presented about marketing-related activities associated with the organization or product that is the subject of the case. By addressing the questions at the end of the "More about . . . " part of each case, which follows the chapter text, students discover how they can apply what they have learned in the chapter to an actual marketing situation.

Some of the organizations and products that are highlighted in the cases are highly recognizable whereas others are relatively unknown or somewhat unusual. However, we have made a special effort to select cases that students will find interesting.

We have been asked, "Aren't you concerned that some of the facts in a case may become dated or firms or products may be gone by the time the case is covered in class?" Our answer is an emphatic "No." Students should be encouraged to do a little research on any case they examine and focus on the concepts, strategies, and techniques highlighted in the case. Students can learn from failures as well as successes.

Chapter-opening cases involving relatively well-known organizations and products that have significant marketing opportunities and challenges include:

- AFLAC
- Avon Products

- Enterprise Rent-A-Car
- George Foreman's Lean Mean Fat Reducing Grilling Machine
- Harley-Davidson
- Lego
- Nordstrom
- Starbucks

Another group of cases address situations in which technology, including the Internet, is an important issue. They include:

- FreeMarkets
- Maritz
- Palm
- PETsMART
- Priceline.com
- U.S. Census Bureau
- W.W. Grainger
- XM Satellite Radio

Still others deal with less familiar products and situations that have substantial marketing implications. Among these are:

- Bluefly
- The Automotive Systems Group of Johnson Controls
- Royal Caribbean International
- Segway Human Transporter
- Smart Car
- Zara

Most of the chapter-opening cases are new to the 13th edition. Any cases carried over from the 12th edition have been thoroughly updated.

Part-Ending Cases

Each of the seven parts of the text ends with two cases. All of these cases involve real organizations and products. Rather than being comprehensive, we have focused each case on the subject matter covered in that particular part of the text in order to avoid overwhelming students with the complexity of many business problems. Included among the part-ending cases are:

- Amazon.com
- Dell Computer
- eBay
- The Gap
- The Hummer
- McDonald's
- Nike
- Southwest Airlines
- Target
- Walt Disney Co.'s theme parks

Cases we have developed that focus on competitive rivalries have been well received by both students and instructors, so we have retained that feature. Part-ending cases that illustrate the competitive battles between or among companies are:

- Coca-Cola Co. versus PepsiCo
- Costco versus Sam's Club
- Nintendo versus Sony versus Microsoft in video games
- UPS versus FedEx versus USPS

Learning Aids

Given the accelerated pace of business today and the dynamic nature of marketing, we anticipate important developments related to the part-ending cases. Therefore, we will put news about major breaking developments related to the cases on the website for the 13th edition. This form of updating will keep the cases timely and interesting over the life of the edition. Students should go to the website to obtain this additional information about the organizations and products covered in the cases.

Students need to be informed about and, in turn, recognize the significance of the evolving context in which marketing is performed. We have selected three environmental dimensions—globalization, information technology, and ethics—for special attention. Examples throughout the book and boxes titled "A Global Perspective," "Marketing in the Information Economy," and "An Ethical Dilemma?" help students understand how these important dimensions affect marketing and, more broadly, business and society.

To place students in a more active role as they learn about marketing, we have incorporated "You Make the Decision" boxes throughout the text. After actual situations faced by marketers are described briefly, students are asked how they would deal with the particular challenge or opportunity.

Each chapter concludes with three learning aids in addition to the "More about . . . " part to the chapter-opening case:

- A list of Key Terms and Concepts that provides reinforcement of important vocabulary from the chapter.
- A set of Questions and Problems that stresses the application of the text material rather than memorizing or defining terms.
- Several Interactive Marketing Exercises, which require students to interact with customers and/or marketers outside the classroom. In carrying out these assignments, students will observe marketing situations, gather information firsthand, and/or utilize valuable secondary sources. The objective of these exercises is to give students a better sense of how marketing is actually carried out.

Teaching and Learning Supplements

In addition to the *Marketing* text, which serves as the primary learning instrument, several supplements facilitate the teaching and learning process. These supplements include:

- A *Student Study Guide* prepared by Dr. Tom Adams that provides chapter outlines, sample test questions, exercises, and additional real-world examples.
- An *Instructor's Manual* that includes additional lecture material, commentaries on the chapter-opening and part-ending cases, suggested answers to the chapter-ending questions and problems, and discussion material for two categories of boxes, "An Ethical Dilemma?" and "You Make the Decision."

- A *Test Bank* of over 2,500 objective questions, coded to indicate the type (definition, concept, application) and text location.

- An *Instructor's Resource CD-ROM,* containing electronic versions of the Instructor's Manual, Test Bank, and PowerPoint presentation materials.

- A *Video Program* featuring cases of real-world companies, incorporating concepts from every chapter. The 13th edition features two completely new video cases, Palm and Salton, that specifically align with the text.

- A *website* that allows instructors to access the Instructor's Manual and Power-Point materials as well as part-ending case commentaries, video segment notes, and links to professional resources. A link to McGraw-Hill's PageOut enables professors to create a course-specific website. For a student, this website features the updated Appendix B, "Careers and Marketing."

- A *Student CD-ROM,* which is new to the 13th edition, features an interactive online business case from SmartSims. The case focuses on a hypothetical company, Music2Go. This interactive simulation provides students with the opportunity and the incentive to develop strategies and make decisions related to marketing and production in a realistic, interesting business setting.

Acknowledgments

We are grateful to many people, including our teachers both in the classroom and from the world of marketing, our students, past and present colleagues, and business executives who shared their insights and experiences with us. Although too numerous to identify by name, we wish to thank all of these people who have contributed to our professional endeavors, including this text.

Special thanks are extended to Therese Basham for preparing drafts of the part-ending cases. We are also grateful to Karen Hill of Elm Street Publishing for her firm's assistance with the chapter-opening cases. A number of students who assisted with research and a variety of other tasks also deserve our thanks: Bill Bernhardt, Paul deLacy, Jake McCarthy, Jared Spader, Cristin Watson, and Xunjie Wang.

Several individuals have contributed significantly to the preparation of the supplements and learning aids, and we thank them for doing so. Dr. Tom Adams rejoined our team and prepared the Instructor's Manual and the Student Study Guide. Professors Tom and Betty Pritchett of Kennesaw State College developed the extensive set of test questions. Dr. Mary Albrecht of Maryville University prepared the PowerPoint presentation materials.

We'd like to recognize those who helped shape the previous editions, including: **Bruce L. Conners,** *Kaskaskia College;* **Carol Bienstock,** *Valdosta State University;* **Charles Prohaska,** *Central Connecticut State University;* **Craig A. Hollingshead,** *Marshall University;* **Craig A. Kelley,** *California State University–Sacramento;* **Darryl W. Miller,** *Washburn University;* **Denise M. Johnson,** *University of Louisville;* **Ed Timmerman,** *University of Tennessee;* **Irving Mason,** *Herkimer County Community College;* **Jack L. Taylor,** *Portland State University;* **Jennifer Friestad,** *Anoka Ramsey Community College;* **John Phillips,** *University of San Francisco;* **Joyce H. Wood,** *Northern Virginia Community College;* **Justin Peart,** *Florida International University;* **Keith B. Murray,** *Bryant College;* **Kenneth Laird,** *Southern Connecticut State University;* **Larry Crowson,** *Florida Institute of Technology;* **Louise Smith,** *Towson State College;* **Madeline Johnson,** *University of Houston;* **Mark Mitchell,** *University of South Carolina–Spartanburg;* **Mary Lou Lockerby,** *College of Du Page;* **Michael J. Swenson,** *Brigham Young University;* **Mort Ettinger,** *Salem State College;* **Robert E. Thompson,** *Indiana State University;* **Robert G. Roe,** *University of Wyoming;* **Ronald J. Adams,** *University of North Florida;* **Roy Cabaniss,** *Western Kentucky University;* **Sharon Wagner,** *Missouri Western State College;* **Stephen Goodwin,** *Illinois State University;* **Steven Engel,** *University of Colorado–Boulder;* **Thomas J. Adams,** *Sacramento City College;* and **Timothy L. Wilson,** *Clarion University.*

We are also very grateful to the staff at McGraw-Hill/Irwin, without whose talents, labors, and patience this book would not have been published. This team of professionals includes: Anna Chan, development editor; Romy Charlesworth, photo researcher; Laura Griffin, project manager; Barrett Koger, associate sponsoring editor; Michael McCormick, production supervisor; Adam Rooke, designer; Linda Schreiber, sponsoring editor; and Cathy Tepper, supplements producer. The individual and collective efforts of the editorial, design, and production departments at McGraw-Hill/Irwin did much to make this textbook an effective and attractive teaching and learning resource.

Michael J. Etzel

Bruce J. Walker

William J. Stanton

Guided Tour

Marketing, 13th edition, by Etzel, Walker and Stanton continues to be a popular, economy-priced, soft cover text for an introductory marketing course. This edition of the text is thoroughly revised, completely updated, and features in-text and boxed examples that highlight global issues, technology, ethics, and applied decision making, chapter-opening cases, and part-ending cases.

This edition of **Marketing** continues to take an in-depth look at current marketing issues including customer relationship management (CRM), database management, global marketing, marketing research, supply chain management, and integrated marketing communications. This complete coverage not only provides you with the tools to learn effective marketing, but you will also find some of the finest supplements available in this course area. In all, this book and its package include everything you need to enter the successful world of marketing in a modern business environment.

Chapter Opening Cases

Each chapter begins with a contemporary case that introduces some of the concepts, strategies, and tactics covered in the chapter.

Chapter 6
Market Segmentation, Targeting, and Positioning

"But it's still an open question whether U.S. consumers will take to the Smart. Daimler's marketing team launched an intensive survey of the U.S. market to determine whether to bring the little car to the United States."

The **Smart Car** Is Short and Sweet, but Will It Sell?

Can DaimlerChrysler convince U.S. consumers that a car that gets 57 miles per gallon of gas is a good deal? Can it sell them on the notion that they can change the color of this new car in a snap, with nothing more than an extra set of resilient plastic side panels? Will consumers be attracted by the car's price, starting at around $9,000? How about the fact that you can park it, literally, on a dime? Some parking garages even give it a 50% discount. After all, it's only 8 feet long.

DaimlerChrysler's tiny new Smart Car has been called an electric shaver on wheels. The three-cylinder two-seater got off to a slow start in western Europe and Japan—that's in sales, not speed; the car accelerates to 63 mph in under 20 seconds—but it's been rising in popularity since then, and the executive who heads the Smart venture has expressed high hopes for its success worldwide, including in the United States.

Begun as a cooperative effort between Swatch, the watch company, and Mercedes-Benz, the Smart Car became a project for Daimler (the maker of Mercedes) after Swatch pulled out. The car attracted a lot of attention when its first Paris dealership opened in 1998. (The name Smart is a combination of Swatch, Mercedes, and art.) But the high price, the U.S. equivalent of about $11,000, drove most prospective buyers away. To make matters worse, Mercedes took the car out of production to improve its stability and maneuverability, changes that notched the price up even higher. First-year sales were well below projections, at only 80,000 vehicles. It's been estimated that it will take until

2005, or 11 years after the car was conceived, for the Smart to make a profit.

DaimlerChrysler refused to give up, however. The company bought out Swatch's interest, hired an executive to direct the project, wrote off its losses, and forged ahead. To get the marketing on track, the sales targets were reduced to a more reasonable level and the price was reduced. The firm also opened Smart showrooms in Japan, where consumers are known for their fondness for unusual designs.

And the tide is beginning to turn. Though many early buyers are wealthy folks who like the toylike aspect of the car, Daimler plans to stay the course and hopes that the novelty appeal will eventually give way to more general respect for the car's maneuverability and fuel economy. The firm now makes right-hand drive and left-hand drive models, and the car is available as coupe or convertible in a range of colors and options. All told, 13 different models are available, and more—including one with an electric-powered engine and four seats—are on the way. Buyers can put the car on a credit card or purchase it over the Internet; leases are also available.

With all that flexibility, sales picked up 25% in 2000 and, with dealerships in Italy, France, Germany, the Netherlands, Britain, Japan, Portugal, and Sweden, they reached a new high of 110,000 vehicles in 2001. More dealerships are

www.smart.com

Thematic Boxes

Throughout the text, these boxes carry four themes that distinguish the book—**A Global Perspective, You Make the Decision, An Ethical Dilemma?, and Marketing in the Information Economy.** Intended to both inform and stimulate critical thinking, these boxes highlight the latest marketing issues and topics to keep you abreast of the latest marketing trends.

A Global Perspective boxes emphasize the global nature of marketing in highly interesting ways. These global examples provide a better understanding of how virtually all industries and careers have an international dimension.

You Make the Decision boxes present synopses of actual situations faced by marketers and allow you an opportunity to see how you would respond. The boxes move you from a passive observer of marketing to an active participant who makes decisions about marketing actions.

An Ethical Dilemma? boxes will raise your awareness of the nature and frequency of ethical challenges in marketing. They are also intended to help you formulate an ethical perspective.

Marketing in the Information Economy boxes illustrate the pervasive impact technology is having on marketing and emphasizes technology's importance as a component of business progress.

A GLOBAL PERSPECTIVE

Is western marketing changing Chinese women?

Some dramatic changes are taking place in China's consumer markets. First, there was the entrance of western brand names such as Coca-Cola and Philips, then retailers such as Wal-Mart and fast-food outlets such as KFC and McDonald's arrived on the scene. But maybe the most important development for the future of consumer marketing in China has been the change in Chinese women. The portion of females in the work force holding managerial positions more than doubled between 1990 and 2000, whereas the portion of women with professional or technical jobs rose from 17% to 23%. The impact has been twofold. First, these young women have more income to spend and, second, they have been exposed to western marketing. As a result, the appeals being made to this developing market are growing in number and changing in form. For example, a recent fashion exhibit in Shanghai attracted over 500 firms from more than 20 countries. And the advertising aimed at this group by western marketers is also changing. For example, in an ad for its Rejoice shampoo, Procter & Gamble revised the scenario from featuring an airline stewardess to one that features a woman working as a mechanical engineer. Because the average annual income in China's urban areas has more than tripled since 1990, many western firms foresee major changes in consumer behavior. However, because the annual income amounts to only the equivalent of $764, it remains to be seen how consumers will spend it.

Sources: Cris Prystay, "As China's Women Change, Marketers Notice," *The Wall Street Journal*, May 30, 2002, p. A11; "Western Fashions Hit Traditional China," Xinhua News Agency, Mar. 19, 2002; "China Attracts Well-Known Fashoin Giants," Xinhua News Agency, Apr. 25, 2002.

YOU MAKE THE DECISION

How can a firm appeal to Generation Y?

For decades, demographers and sociologists have labeled generations for various reasons, including an effort to understand their buying behavior. Rather than grouping by income or education, these cohorts are based on age and, as a result, shared historical experiences. **Baby boomers** are Americans born in the 20 years following World War II. **Generation X** refers to about 40 million people born roughly between 1966 and 1976 who, in turn, entered the workplace during a recession. Not surprisingly, "Gen X" has been labeled as cautious and somewhat pessimistic.

Generation Y represents the successors to Generation X. Gen Y is most commonly defined as those young people born between 1977 and 1994, essentially representing the children of baby boomers. (However, some experts define Gen Y differently, such as including people born through 1997.) Numbering 71 million, Gen Y is a sizable target market—three times as large as Gen X and rivaling baby boomers in size. Growing up in the best economy ever, these young adults are also relatively affluent and materialistic. Gen Y is diverse—in fact, more diverse than previous cohorts—in that about one-third are minorities, one-quarter come from a single-parent household, and three-quarters have working mothers. This diversity also manifests itself in more acceptance of sexual and racial differences, nontraditional families, and global perspectives.

Many members of Gen Y probably have vivid memories of the O. J. Simpson case, the Bill Clinton–Monica Lewinsky scandal, and the tragedy at Columbine High School. Although it's difficult (and sometimes dangerous) to generalize, Gen Y tends to be concerned about their personal safety and skeptical of the media. Further, Gen Y does not look at public figures as role models. Instead, in a recent survey, 57% of college seniors listed a parent as the person they admired and respected the most. And talk shows and reality TV have reinforced beliefs that everyone deserves to be heard and involved, that there is often more than one right answer, and that differing viewpoints should be tolerated.

No group as large as Gen Y is homogeneous and receptive to a single marketing appeal, of course. Thus companies are trying various approaches to sell goods and services to Gen Y, often using media that allow specific targeting. Marketers have tried to develop messages that take into account the values, attitudes, and life experiences of Gen Y. For instance, Sprite has been successful with its "Image is nothing, obey your thirst" campaign. In 2000, Gap's funky commercials contributed to a surge in sales. Innovative new products with the Gen Y lifestyle in mind—such as a microwave dryer big enough for just two pairs of jeans and a backpack with speakers to be used with an MP3 player—are hitting store shelves. Even automobile manufacturers have their sights on this consumer market. Toyota's new Scion, Saturn's Ion, and Honda's Element are all targeted at Gen Y members.

What marketing strategies would you suggest to a company that wants to appeal to Generation Y consumers? What strategies should be avoided?

Sources: Elliot Spagat, "Like, What's a Spin Cycle?" *The Wall Street Journal*, June 4, 2002, pp. B1, B4; Karl Greenberg, "Automakers Brake for Generation Y," *Brandweek*, Apr. 1, 2002, p. 12; Pamela Paul, "Getting Inside Gen Y," *American Demographics*, September 2001, pp. 42–49; Jim Pearse, "Gen Y Gold Mine," *Dealerscope*, September 2001, pp. 28–28; Bob Dart, "What's Your Generation?" *St. Louis Post-Dispatch*, Apr. 9, 2001, pp. G1, G3; Evan Ramstad, "Backpacks with Speakers? Electronics Makers Court Jaded Gen Y," *The Wall Street Journal*, May 18, 2000, pp. B1, B4; Maricris G. Briones, "Ad Biz Faces Technology, Gen Y and Competition," *Marketing News*, Dec. 7, 1998, pp. 2, 10; Ellen Neuborne, "Generation Y," *Business Week*, Feb. 15, 1999, pp. 81–84+; and Faye Rice, "Making Generational Marketing Come of Age," *Fortune*, June 26, 1995, pp. 110–112+.

AN ETHICAL DILEMMA?

Preschoolers watch an average of 23 hours of television a week, more than any other group of children. However, until recently most shows designed especially for them, such as *Sesame Street* and *Mister Rogers' Neighborhood*, appeared on the commercial-free Public Broadcasting System (PBS). That is changing for several reasons. First, sales of preschooler products such as stuffed toys, pajamas, and drink cups, has become big business, estimated to be $21 billion annually. Many of these items have licensing potential (charging a manufacturer a fee to incorporate the likenesses and/or names of familiar characters on the item). And the kids greatly influence what is purchased. Second, the average ratings for networks such as Nickelodeon and Disney are being dragged down by small midday audiences, and those averages affect advertising rates for the entire schedule. Preschoolers, at home during the day, can boost the ratings if the networks can attract them.

To overcome the concerns of parents, preschooler programming on commercial networks such as *Dora the Explorer* and *Blue's Clues* incorporates educational principles of learning and cognitive development, and the amount of advertising per hour is about half of what is aired at other times.

Should a commercial television network, with an organizational objective of profit, actively pursue impressionable preschoolers?

Sources: Sally Beatty, "In Battle for Toddlers, TV Networks Tout Educational Benefits," *The Wall Street Journal*, Apr. 1, 2002, pp. A1+; Donna Petrozzello, "Nickelodeon to Launch Spinoff of Animated Hit 'Rugrats,'" *New York Daily News*, Mar. 14, 2002, p. 6.

MARKETING IN THE INFORMATION ECONOMY

If it's such a great service, why did Webvan fail?

Online retailing now generates over $75 billion in sales, with annual growth rates above 20%. This track record is impressive, considering that total retail sales typically increase by about 2% to 4% annually. Yet, despite heavy financial backing, aggressive marketing campaigns, and sometimes strong growth, numerous online merchants (also called e-tailers) have failed. Etoys, pets.com, and drugstore.com are just a few of the high-profile e-tailers that had to shut their virtual doors. They had trouble making a profit on each order, let alone recouping the massive investments made in technology, warehouses, and other business components.

Webvan, which offered next-day delivery of groceries to a consumer's residence, became one of the larger and heavily publicized online failures in mid-2001. The service appeared to be made for the steadily increasing number of working women who juggle both a career and homemaking as well as other consumers who place a premium on free time. With an extensive selection, easy-to-use website, convenient delivery times where customers picked a 30-minute delivery window, and free delivery for orders over $75, Webvan had many attractive features. Customers spent an average of $110 per order, purchased frequently, and praised the service to their friends.

Despite these positives, Webvan lost a whopping $830 million from its inception in April 1999 until July 2001, when the firm shut its doors and laid off over 2,000 employees. What happened, considering that Webvan was quite satisfying to a segment of consumers? Some observers trace Webvan's failure to market factors, others point to cost factors. Evidently not enough consumers valued the service. Webvan also suffered from the expense of an enormous business operation, designed to support 26 markets, which required 4,000 orders per day per market to break even. The company invested in numerous warehouses (at $25 million apiece) as well as expensive technology. Thus Webvan needed—but didn't obtain—a very large customer base in order to cover its costly operations.

Webvan isn't the only online retailer to try to tackle the $450 billion grocery market. A few have had a measure of success. Netgrocer is still shipping groceries via FedEx, and Peapod was acquired by Royal Ahold USA, owner of chains such as Stop and Shop. Large supermarket chains are also experimenting with this type of service; Albertson's, Kroger, and Safeway all have home-delivery programs underway.

Under what circumstances, if any, could an online grocery store be successful?

Sources: Eric Hellweg, "Furniture, Food, and Other Tales of Dotcom Revival," *Business 2.0*, Apr. 17, 2002, at *www.business2.com/articles/web*; Nick Wingfield, "Online Retailing Still Growing Despite Some Losses Last Year," *The Wall Street Journal*, June 12, 2002, p. B4; Linda Himelstein, "Webvan Left the Basics on the Shelf," *Business Week*, July 23, 2001, p. 43; Mylene Mangalindan, "Webvan Joins List of Dot-Com Failures," *The Wall Street Journal*, July 10, 2001, pp. A3, A6; "Can Webvan Deliver, Financially Speaking?" *internetnews.com*, Jan. 9, 2001; and Jean Shermen Chatzky, "You've Got Groceries," *USA Weekend*, Jan. 28–30, 2000, p. 4.

Marketing, 13th edition, features some of the finest supplements available in this course area. From the free Student CD-ROM with Music2Go—a student marketing simulation program included with every new text—to the interactive text Website, this book and its package include everything you need to learn marketing functions within a dynamic business environment.

Closing Cases Commentaries

At the conclusion of each chapter, the companies featured in the opening cases are revisited in the *More about. . .* commentaries. By addressing the questions presented at the end of each case, you can apply what you learned in the chapter to the challenges and issues faced in actual marketing situations. These cases give you a glimpse into the world of marketing and an opportunity to apply what you've learned to solve a problem, develop a plan, or address a marketing issue.

More about **Harley-Davidson**

Despite at least one biker magazine describing the V-Rod's liquid-cooled engine as a shocking design misstep for Harley, the firm has big plans for the new machine. It is the first of a new family of "high-performance" motorcycles and is likely to play a big part in the company's efforts to hang onto its market share. Judging from the sold-out production run of the first model, the V-Rod is fulfilling its promise.

Harley knows, however, when the real crunch will come. "We don't need new customers today, we don't need them tomorrow. But we may 10 years from now," says the company's chief financial officer. The company also knows it could intimidate younger prospects with the cultlike devotion shown by some of its aging adherents. That's why Harley is willing to invest heavily in two new ventures that aren't making any money at the moment—the driver training program, called Rider's Edge, and a subsidiary named Buell.

When Harley engineer Erik Buell left the firm in the 1990s to start his own company, Harley funded it, and in 1998 the firm completed its acquisition of the little company. Buell manufactures a light, sleek single-cylinder bike called the Blast, with a $4,400 price tag and strong appeal

among first-time and younger riders. With design innovations like a tucked-away muffler that won't burn inexperienced riders' legs and an adjustable seat height, the Blast should appeal to more women than Harley's other bikes do; right now only 9% of riders of traditional Harley models are females.

Rider's Edge, which has trained about 4,300 people in its first two years, could also bring more women into the fold. Described as an effort to "lighten our image without losing our edge," the driver's ed program also covers how Harley bikes are made and how they are sold. It requires passing grades on the same strict written and road tests required by the Motorcycle Safety Foundation—and the bike that students train on is the Buell.[24]

1. What role do you think a rider's self-image plays in the purchase of a motorcycle? In the purchase of a Harley-Davidson motorcycle? Do you think the influence of reference groups plays any part in a Harley purchase? Why or why not?

2. Harley-Davidson's revenue and net income have climbed steadily for over 15 years. Why do you think the firm has been able to weather economic recessions much better than other major manufacturers?

...nmental forces influence an organization's marketing activities. Some ...o the firm and are largely uncontrollable by the organization. Other ...hin the firm and are generally controllable by management. Successful ...uires that a company develop and implement marketing programs that ...unt its environment. To start with, management should set up a system ...ntal monitoring—the process of gathering and evaluating environ- ...ation.

...variables constitute the external environment that generally cannot be ...an organization. Demographic factors are one of these macro influ- ...r is economic conditions such as the business cycle, inflation, and in- ...anagement also must be aware of the various types of competition and ...e structure within which its firm operates. Social and cultural forces, ...es in life-styles, values, and beliefs, must be taken into account as mar- ...s are developed. Four noteworthy sociocultural trends are the green- ...a, changing gender roles, a greater premium on time, and added em- ...ysical fitness and health. Political and legal forces, ranging from ...fiscal policies to legislation, also affect marketing. As with the other ...oenvironmental influences, technology can present both opportunities ...s for marketers.

...et of environmental factors—suppliers, marketing intermediaries, and ...elf—is also external to the firm. But these forces can be controlled to ...y the firm. Although all three of these external forces are generally un- ...they can be influenced in some situations. As such, these *micro*envi- ...ronmental forces are different from *macro*environmental forces such as economic conditions and technology.

At the same time, a set of nonmarketing resources *within* the firm—production facilities, personnel, finances, location, research and development, and company image— affects its marketing effort. These variables generally are controllable by management.

More about **XM Satellite Radio**

XM's major competitor is Sirius Satellite Radio, based in New York City. Sirius entered the market later than XM because of technical problems and a management shake-up that included the resignation of its CEO. In its first half year of operation, Sirius signed up fewer than 10,000 subscribers. Although XM got off to a faster start, Sirius is well-equipped to give the "first mover" a run for its money. In fact, Sirius' goal is to reach profitability with 2 million subscribers by 2005.

Sirius relies on three satellites, launched from a once-secret Soviet installation in Kazakhstan. Sirius' satellites orbit a little higher in the sky than XM's, but have fewer repeaters. XM says this makes a difference in sound quality; Sirius isn't commenting. The newcomer offers about the same number of channels as XM, but one-half of them are music pro-

grams and the other half are talk shows of various kinds. Sirius's carmaker deals are with BMW, Ford, and DaimlerChrysler.

Sirius is asking consumers to pay a higher price, $13 a month compared with XM's $10, but its programs will have no advertising at all. As to whether consumers will pay for what they can get for free, the CEO of Sirius observed, "TV is free, but 70% of consumers choose to pay for cable—and another 10% pay for satellite TV." Thus a prerequisite for success for satellite radio is to offer consumers more quantity and/or quality of radio programming than they can receive for free, which would emulate the approach used by both cable and satellite TV.

Receivers for each of the competing satellite–radio systems are not compatible with one another, and installation costs are high enough to make switching unlikely. So unlike traditional radio stations, each satellite radio firm will have to focus its efforts on winning the customer the first time out. But the market potential—

More about the **Smart Car**

Most of the questions Daimler's marketing executives will be asking themselves as they evaluate selling the Smart Car in the U.S. will deal with the size of its probable market segment. In the original Swatch/ Mercedes partnership, the car was designed for drivers who felt existing cars are too pricey, hard to maneuver, and expensive to operate. Management must find out whether that motivation or some other applies to a substantial segment in the U.S., where consumers have recently adopted much larger and more utilitarian vehicles in huge numbers. The Smart Car's spiffy design isn't for everyone, and the firm doesn't expect it to sell in the more conservative regions of the Midwest where trips tend to be of greater distances, for instance.

The four-seater Smart Car is unlikely to replace the minivan or SUV as a family car; two Smart Cars parked end-to-end are still 3 feet shorter than the Ford Excursion. Could it work as a family's second or third car if they already own a van? Or will the fact that its cargo space is little more than a mere shelf deter sales?

Though it has not yet been a big hit among young buyers in Europe, some industry consultants think the bug-eyed Smart Car could be a fashion statement. Will

young U.S. buyers choosing their first car, say, urban college students looking for cheap transportation that's hip and new, be attracted to its looks and fuel economy?

There are still some safety concerns about the tiny vehicle even if it's not quite the "crash helmet on wheels" that one British showroom manager claims. DaimlerChrysler has made a promotional video showing the car skittering away from a 30-mph crash with a Mercedes S-class sedan to counter some anticipated reactions, but the fact remains, the car needs upgrading to meet U.S. safety standards. And while Daimler doesn't see the car as a highway cruiser but rather as a city car for congested urban streets, it's unclear whether U.S. consumers will share that view once they get behind the wheel.

So far favorable ratings are pouring in for the car's clever design, maneuverability, comfortable interior, environmental friendliness, and low price. The executive in charge claims to be very happy about the challenge that marketing the Smart Car brings. In his view, "This is a chance to develop a brand, and you don't get to do that very often."[14]

1. Should DaimlerChrysler pursue a single-segment or multiple-segment strategy for the Smart Car in the United States?

2. As DaimlerChrysler has positioned it, with which transportation alternatives would the Smart Car likely compete in Europe? In the U.S.?

Supplements

Online Learning Center:

At this text-specific site, Instructors can access the Instructor's Manual, Digital Transparencies, PowerPoint, Mini-Lectures, part-ending case notes and commentaries, video notes, and links to professional resources. For the student, this site features an updated appendix on Careers and Marketing, which offers students guidelines on treating the job search process as a marketing effort, applying what they have learned in the course, and describes career opportunities in marketing. The site also features online quizzes, career profiles, and Internet exercises.

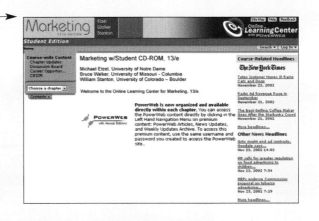

Student CD-ROM:

Completely new with the 13th edition, this disc is included free with all new copies of the text and introduces an interactive online business case from SmartSims, featuring a simulated music company Music2Go. Students compete as teams against each other online in a simulated consumer electronics industry. Students apply the concepts of market analysis, segmentation, marketing mix, and product life cycle in this realistic, interactive marketing case study. Students and instructors alike will gain the benefits of Music2Go as it helps add a new dimension, providing real understanding and appreciation of the fundamentals and dynamics of marketing.

Video Program:

Gary Ragan - Director of Marketing

Cases about real-world companies incorporate concepts from every chapter. The 13th edition features two completely new video cases that are written specifically to align with the text. These cases allow students to see how marketing concepts, strategies and techniques from the book are applied in an actual business, and how they affect its performance.

Chapter

1

The Field of Marketing

"With lavish service and the right selection of merchandise, Nordstrom built a winning—and profitable—formula."

How Durable Is the **Nordstrom** Way?

How does a retail store build an enviable reputation and nurture it successfully for generations? Nordstrom once knew the answer. The big question many are asking now is whether the upscale department store can renew itself in time to restore its sliding profitability.

Founded as a shoe store in Seattle in 1903, Nordstrom expanded its offerings to include clothing back in 1963 and has continued to add high-quality products over the years since then. Unlike its many competitors, it has been cautious about adding new stores and has retained its legendary focus on extraordinary customer service. The retailer seeks to build lasting relationships with customers by treating them very well—even pampering them.

Nordstrom's first step toward accomplishing this goal has been to maintain a large, highly trained sales staff. Equally important is its abundance of customer services, including valet parking, in-store restaurants, live piano music, free use of baby strollers, and liberal merchandise return policies. It even offers "personal shoppers" who will take your shopping list and pick suitable items for you. "We know by giving good service we sell more," says president Blake W. Nordstrom. "It's the heart and soul of our business."

With lavish service and the right selection of merchandise, Nordstrom built a winning—and profitable—formula. Its efforts won the store a loyal following among baby-boom shoppers without the need to run the frequent sales and specials on which its competitors relied to bring in business. Recently, however, the picture began to change. Profits slipped alarmingly, pulled down by a generally weakening retail environment. For the first time since 1963, Nordstrom had a fall clearance sale in 2001 and stepped up its plans to cut expenses, reduce inventories, and upgrade its inventory-tracking system. It even announced the largest layoff in its history; about 2,500 employees were let go.

But the slump in retailing wasn't the only problem Nordstrom faced. An attempt to reach younger, trendier shoppers with a campaign called "Reinvent Yourself" confused older, long-time customers and was cut short. It may even have damaged the store's standing with its core following. In addition, specialty retailers like Talbots, The Limited, and Ann Taylor grew fiercely competitive, and retail giant Neiman Marcus jumped ahead of Nordstrom in customer service rankings. Finally, customers—even those with cash to spend—learned to shop around, looking for the best prices even if they didn't always come with Nordstrom's level of service. "These are challenging times for us," Mr. Nordstrom said, "and we don't have a very clear picture for the future."

The firm will have to act quickly to decide how much to change the way it does business. After an interval in which the company was run by a CEO hired from the outside, a management shake-up returned day-to-day operations of the firm to members of the Nordstrom family, Blake and his father Bruce, who serves as

www.nordstrom.com

chairman. In the short term, markdowns helped move merchandise out of the stores, but at the cost of some profit, a situation the chain would very much like to avoid in the future. Management recognizes that frequent sales and promotions can make the glamorous store look too much like "just another department store," which could dilute its exclusive image. Other strategies include adding more lower-priced goods to Nordstrom's racks and shelves to achieve a better balance of merchandise and ensure it offers more than just the priciest items; designing layoffs to leave the sales staff intact as much as possible so as not to damage Nordstrom's reputation for superior service; and replacing an obsolete inventory management process that relied on loose-leaf binders full of handwritten notes with a computerized inventory system. Although the "Reinvent Yourself" campaign has been dropped, its theme might apply to Nordstrom itself as it reaches a turning point in its 100-year history.[1]

What role has marketing played in its past success, and how can it help the venerable retailer return to its past prominence? See www.nordstrom.com for more details.

Marketing and the Internet   The Internet is a powerful and dynamic marketing tool. Throughout the book we have included Uniform Resource Locators (or URLs, the technical term for Internet addresses), to help you find "home pages" of many organizations. We encourage you to explore these websites to learn more about how the Internet is currently being used as well as stimulate your thinking about how it can be utilized even more effectively in the future. Space limitations occasionally require us to break URLs into two lines; but when entering an Internet address always type it on one line.

Nordstrom's is an excellent example of both the rewards and challenges of marketing. It became a highly successful operation by identifying and meeting the needs of many consumers. However, maintaining a high level of success proved difficult. So Nordstrom's, like most organizations, has been faced with making adjustments in its operation that will satisfy its customers. Finding ways to satisfying customers effectively and efficiently is what marketing is all about. To understand what that means, we need to systematically examine the question, "What is marketing?"

Chapter Goals

After studying this chapter, you should be able to explain:

- The centrality of exchange to marketing.
- A definition of marketing that applies to business and nonbusiness situations.
- The way marketing has evolved in the U.S.
- The marketing concept and related issues.
- The heightened concern about ethics in marketing.
- The components of a company's marketing program.
- The many ways in which marketing affects our lives.

Nature and Scope of Marketing

Marketing can occur any time a person or organization strives to exchange something of value with another person or organization. Thus, at its core marketing is a transaction or exchange. In this broad sense, marketing consists of activities designed to generate and facilitate exchanges intended to satisfy human or organizational needs or wants.

A futures trading "pit" meets all the conditions for a market exchange. Traders, representing buyers and sellers, use eye contact, their voices, and hand signals to buy and sell agricultural and industrial commodities. One of the world's largest futures markets, the Chicago Mercantile Exchange, handles over 400 million contracts worth nearly $300 trillion a year. Fortunes can be made and lost in hours or even minutes. It is not a place for the faint of heart!

www.cme.com

Exchange as the Focus

Exchange is just one of three ways we can satisfy our needs. If you want something, you can make it yourself, acquire it by theft or some form of coercion, or you can offer something of value (perhaps your money, your services, or another good) to a person or organization that has that desired good or service and will exchange it for what you offer. Only this last alternative is an exchange in the sense that marketing is occurring.

The following conditions must exist for a marketing exchange to take place:

- Two or more people or organizations must be involved, and each must have needs or wants to be satisfied. If you are totally self-sufficient, there is no need for an exchange.

- The parties to the exchange must be involved voluntarily.

- Each party must have something of value to contribute in the exchange, and each must believe that it will benefit from the exchange.

- The parties must communicate with each other. The communication can take many forms and may even be through a third party, but without awareness and information there can be no exchange.

These exchange conditions introduce a number of terms that deserve some elaboration. First there are the parties involved in the exchange. On one side of the exchange is the marketer. *Marketers* take the initiative by trying to stimulate and facilitate exchanges. They develop marketing plans and programs and implement them in hopes of creating an exchange. In this respect, a retailer such as Nordstrom's, a college or university recruiting students, the American Cancer Society soliciting donors, and United Airlines seeking passengers are all marketers.

On the other side of the exchange is the *market,* which consists of people or organizations with needs to satisfy, money to spend, and the willingness to spend it. Marketing programs are directed at markets that either accept or reject the offer. Markets are made up of current and prospective *customers,* defined as any person or group with whom a marketer has an existing or potential exchange relationship.

The object of the exchange or what is being marketed is referred to generically as the *product*. It can be a good, service, idea, person, or place. All of these can be marketed, as we shall see.

We most often think of *something of value* as money. However, barter (trading one product for another) is still fairly common among small businesses and even between countries. Of course, many exchanges in the nonbusiness world, such as donating blood in exchange for a sense of helping others, do not involve cash.

Marketers use many forms of personal and nonpersonal *communication*, from billboards to personal selling, to inform and persuade their desired markets. Because there are so many communication methods available, selecting the most effective combination is an important marketing task.

In describing exchanges, we use the terms *needs* and *wants* interchangeably because marketing is relevant to both. Technically, needs can be viewed in a strict physiological sense (food, clothing, and shelter), with everything else defined as a want. However, from a customer's perspective, the distinction is not as clear. For example, many people consider a cellular phone or a home computer a necessity.

Definition of Marketing

This book focuses on the activities carried out by organizations to facilitate mutually beneficial exchanges. These organizations may be profit-seeking business firms, or they may have a primary objective other than profit—a university, charity, church, police department, or political party, for example. (Marketing can also be performed by individuals. As you approach graduation, you can use marketing principles to maximize the effectiveness of your job search. We have more to say about this in "Careers and Marketing" on our website www.mhhe.com/etzel04.)

Both types of organizations face essentially the same marketing challenges and opportunities. Nordstrom's, the retailer described in the chapter-opening case, must attract buyers. Initially it focused on carefully selected merchandise and personalized service. However, faced with increasing competition the firm is exploring other alternatives including price reductions and special promotions. Similarly, in an effort to attract tourists, Cedar Rapids, Iowa, is using a $2.5 million state grant to renovate a historic theater, update its arts center, and create a science museum with hands-on exhibits. The community is using a website to inform prospective visitors about the attractions. Consequently, we need a definition of marketing to guide executives in business and nonbusiness organizations in the management of their marketing efforts, and to direct our examination of the subject.

www.priority1.com

Therefore, our definition of marketing—based on the concept of exchange and applicable in any organization—is as follows: **Marketing** is a total system of business activities designed to plan, price, promote, and distribute want-satisfying products to target markets in order to achieve organizational objectives. This definition has two significant implications:

- *Focus:* The entire system of business activities should be customer-oriented. Customers' wants must be recognized and satisfied.

- *Duration:* Marketing should start with an idea about a want-satisfying product and should not end until the customers' wants are completely satisfied, which may be some time after the exchange is made.

As you will see in the discussion below, these conditions are not always met.

Evolution of Marketing

The foundations of marketing in America were laid in Colonial times, when the early settlers traded among themselves and with the Native Americans. Some settlers became retailers, wholesalers, and itinerant peddlers. However, large-scale marketing

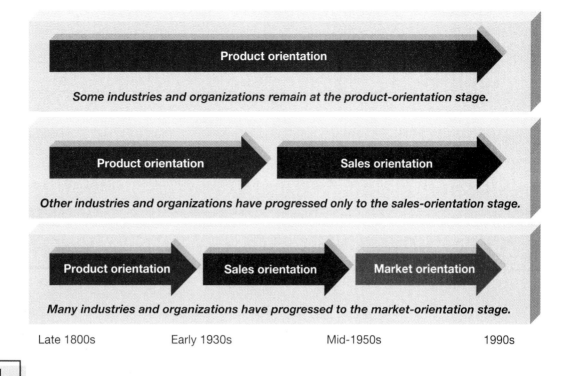

Late 1800s   Early 1930s   Mid-1950s   1990s

FIGURE 1.1

Three Stages of Marketing Evolution in the United States.

in the U.S. did not begin to take shape until the Industrial Revolution in the latter part of the 1800s. Since then, marketing has evolved through three successive stages of development: product orientation, sales orientation, and market orientation.

Our description links each stage with a period of time. But you should understand that these stages depict the general evolution of marketing and reflect states of mind as much as they do historical periods. Thus, although many firms have progressed to the market-orientation stage, some are still in the first or second stage, as shown in Figure 1.1.

Product-Orientation Stage

Manufacturers in the **product-orientation stage** typically focused on the quality and quantity of output while assuming that customers would seek out and buy reasonably priced, well-made products. Managers with backgrounds in manufacturing and engineering shaped a firm's strategy. In an era when the demand for goods generally exceeded the supply, the primary focus in business was to efficiently produce large quantities of products. Finding the customers was viewed as a relatively minor function.

Manufacturers, wholesalers, and retailers operating in this stage emphasized internal operations and focused on efficiency and cost control. There wasn't much need to worry about what customers wanted because it was highly predictable. Most people spent the vast majority of their incomes on necessities. If a firm could make a good quality shoe inexpensively, for example, a market almost certainly existed.

When this was the prevailing approach to business the term *marketing* was not in use. Instead, producers had sales departments headed by executives whose primary responsibility was to supervise a sales force. The function of the sales department was simply to carry out the transaction, at a price often dictated by the cost of production. The philosophy of the Pillsbury company in the late 1800s is characteristic of this stage: "Blessed with a supply of the finest North American Wheat, plenty of water power, and excellent milling machinery, we produce flour of the highest quality. Our basic function is to mill high-quality flour, and of course (and almost incidentally) we must hire salesmen to sell it, just as we hire accountants to keep our books."[2]

This emphasis on products and operations dominated until the early 1930s. The approach is understandable when you consider that for generations the primary concern of business was how to produce and distribute an adequate quantity of acceptable products to meet the needs of a rapidly growing population.

Sales-Orientation Stage

The world economic crisis of the late 1920s (commonly referred to as the Great Depression) changed perceptions. As the developed countries emerged from the depression it became clear that the main economic problem no longer was how to manufacture efficiently, but rather it was how to sell the resulting output. Just offering a quality product was no assurance of success. Managers began to realize that to sell their products in an environment where consumers had limited resources and numerous options required substantial postproduction effort. Thus, the **sales-orientation stage** was characterized by a heavy reliance on promotional activity to sell the products the firm wanted to make. In this stage, advertising consumed a larger share of a firm's resources and sales executives began to gain respect and responsibility from company management.

Along with responsibility came expectations for performance. Unfortunately, these pressures resulted in some managers resorting to overly aggressive selling—the "hard sell"—and unscrupulous advertising tactics. As a result, selling developed an unsavory reputation in the eyes of many. Old habits die hard, and even now some organizations believe that they must use a hard-sell approach to prosper. In the United States the sales stage was common into the 1950s, when modern marketing began to emerge.

Market-Orientation Stage

At the end of World War II there was strong pent-up demand for consumer goods created by wartime shortages. As a result, manufacturing plants turned out tremendous quantities of goods that were quickly purchased. However, the postwar surge in consumer spending slowed down as supply caught up with demand, and many firms found that they had excess production capacity.

In an attempt to stimulate sales, firms reverted to the aggressive promotional and sales activities of the sales-orientation era. However, this time consumers were less willing to be persuaded. Sellers discovered that the war years had also changed consumers. The thousands of service men and women who spent time overseas came home more sophisticated and worldly. In addition, the war effort brought many women out of the home and into the work force for the first time. Because of their experiences, consumers had become more knowledgeable, less naive, and less easily influenced. In addition, they had more choices. The technology that was developed during the war made it possible to produce a much greater variety of goods when converted to peacetime activity.

Thus the evolution of marketing continued. Many companies recognized that to put idle capacity to work they had to make available what consumers wanted to buy instead of what the businesses wanted to sell. In the **market-orientation stage,** companies identify what customers want and tailor all the activities of the firm to satisfy those needs as efficiently as possible.

In this third stage, firms are marketing rather than merely selling. Several tasks that were once associated with other business functions became the responsibility of the top marketing executive, called the marketing manager or vice president of marketing. For instance, inventory control, warehousing, and some aspects of product planning are turned over to the head of marketing as a way to serve customers better. To increase effectiveness, input from the marketplace is sought before a product is produced not just at the end of a production cycle. In addition, marketing is included in long-term as well as short-term company planning.

A market orientation is often reflected in an executive's attitude toward marketing. Philip Knight, chairman and CEO of Nike, makes this point: "For years we thought of ourselves as a production-oriented company, meaning we put all our emphasis on designing and manufacturing the product. But now we understand that the most important thing we do is market the product."[3]

We are *not* saying that marketing is more important than other business functions. They are all essential. Nor are we suggesting that marketing executives should hold the top positions in a company. But it is necessary that everyone in an organization understand the importance of the market, that is, be *market-oriented*.

Many American business firms and not-for-profit organizations are presently in this third stage in the evolution of marketing. Others may recognize the importance of a market orientation, but have difficulty implementing it. Implementation requires accepting the notion that the wants and needs of customers, not the desires of management, direct the organization. Forty-five years ago Peter Drucker, the most influential business writer of the 20th century, observed that companies exist not to make a profit, but to create and satisfy customers. In a recent interview, he commented that the statement is even more true today because the customer has the ultimate power to choose.[4]

A basic implication of a market orientation is the way an organization describes what it does. For example, Oprah Winfrey with her television show, magazine, and other enterprises has been described as being in the business of "soothing souls."[5] Table 1.1 shows how some well-known organizations might define their businesses under a product orientation and invites you to try your hand at defining them based on a market orientation.

Note that not every organization needs to be market-oriented to prosper. A monopolist selling a necessity is guaranteed of having customers. Therefore, its management should be much more concerned with low-cost, efficient production than with marketing. Such was the case for public utilities prior to deregulation. Now many electricity and natural gas providers are scrambling to find ways to satisfy customers who have alternative sources of supply. There are also instances in which the potential customers consider the product to be so superior that they will seek it out. For example, the world's best heart surgeons or particularly popular artists find a market for their services regardless of their orientations.

The Marketing Concept

Managers who adopt a market orientation recognize that marketing is vital to the success of their organizations. This realization is reflected in a fundamental approach to doing business that gives the customer the highest priority. Called the

TABLE 1.1

How Should a Business Be Defined?

(Try your hand at composing a market-oriented answer and then see note 6 for some possibilities.)[6]

Company	Product-Oriented Answer	Market-Oriented Answer
Kodak	We make cameras and film.	We help preserve beautiful memories.
Amazon.com	We sell books and recordings.	?
Hewlett-Packard	We make computer printers.	?
Nordstrom	We sell clothing for families.	?
Steelcase	We make office furniture.	?
Caterpillar	We make construction machinery.	?

marketing concept, it emphasizes customer orientation and coordination of marketing activities to achieve the organization's performance objectives.

Nature and Rationale

The marketing concept is based on three beliefs that are illustrated in Figure 1.2:

- All planning and operations should be *customer-oriented*. That is, every department and employee should be focused on contributing to the satisfaction of customers' needs. The inspiration for the "hub and spoke" concept created by FedEx was the customer need for reliable, overnight package delivery. Making it work requires the coordination provided by sophisticated information management, state-of-the-art material handling, and dedicated customer service personnel. What seemed like an impractical idea 35 years ago is now the basis for a $20 billion business that delivers 4.8 million packages a day in over 200 countries.[7]

- All marketing activities in an organization should be *coordinated*. This means that marketing efforts (product planning, pricing, distribution, and promotion) should be designed and combined in a coherent, consistent way, and that one executive should have overall authority and responsibility for the complete set of marketing activities. At Barnes & Noble stores, consumers discover a relaxing environment where they can enjoy a cup of coffee in a store that's big enough to offer a broad selection of books and small enough to provide local entertainment and children's story hours. The combination of carefully selected inventory, discount pricing, and inviting surroundings produces over $3.4 billion a year in sales for the firm.[8]

- Customer-oriented, coordinated marketing is essential to achieve the *organization's performance objectives*. The ultimate objective for a business is typically measured in terms of return on investment, stock price, and market capitalization. However, the immediate objective might be something less ambitious that will move the organization closer to its ultimate goal. For example, when H. J. Heinz Company, with annual sales of $10 billion, had two giant Heinz Ketchup bottles installed on either side of the Jumbotron screen at Heinz Field in Pittsburgh, one

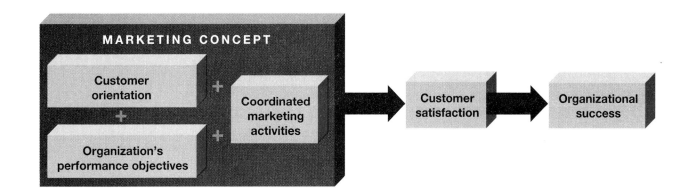

FIGURE 1.2

Components and Outcomes of the Marketing Concept.

might question how that contributes to increasing sales. However, when the bottles open and "pour" ketchup on the screen triggering an animation that generates fan support for the home team at critical points in a game, Heinz generates goodwill, reminds thousands of spectators of its product, and may even encourage the sale of a few hot dogs. This and other promotional efforts build the brand and are intended to contribute to organizational goals in the long run.[9]

Sometimes the marketing concept is simply stated as a customer orientation, as expressed in these words of the late Sam Walton, founder of Wal-Mart: "There is only one boss: the customer."[10] As important as it is to stress a customer focus, however, it should not replace achievement of objectives as the fundamental rationale for the marketing concept.

Implementing the Marketing Concept

The marketing concept is an appealing idea, but it must be converted into specific activities to be useful for managers. Over the years it has been interpreted and applied in a number of different ways. "No questions asked" return policies to satisfy customers and automated warehouses to improve efficiency and support discounted prices are examples from the past. Today the marketing concept is being applied in a number of other ways. Several of the most important developments are introduced below.

Customer Orientation

Relationships.   The value of a good relationship is not a new idea. However, it is only recently that organizations, with the benefit of extensive data, have made a concerted effort at customer relationship management (**CRM**)—establishing multidimensional connections with a customer such that the organization is seen as a partner. By sorting and analyzing data supplied by customers, gathered from third parties, and collected from previous transactions, a marketer is able to better understand a customer's needs and preferences. But there is more to relationship management than data. By examining successful partnerships in business and elsewhere, marketers have discovered that enduring relationships are built on trust and mutual commitment, require a lot of time and effort to create and maintain, and are not appropriate for every exchange situation. Applying this concept to their marketing programs, many firms are dedicating much of their marketing effort to building lasting relationships with selected customers.11

Consider, for example, what motorcycle maker Harley-Davidson has done. The firm created a club (The Harley Owners Group or HOG) for bike owners. It offers the more than 650,000 members insurance, travel planning, roadside emergency service, the Harley-Davidson magazine, free safety lessons, safe-riding competitions, and 1,150 local chapters that hold regular meetings. The Internet, with its two-way communication capability, has made it easier for firms to build relationships with customers by personalizing their interactions. On its website, Harley-Davidson has a HOG's "members only" page where Harley owners can get specific questions answered and chat with other club members.[12]

www.harleydavidson.com

What do Harley-Davidson and other firms that make these investments hope to get in return? A feeling of goodwill among their best customers and a sense that the firms care about more than making the next sale. That is, they are seeking a long-term relationship with their customers that will be mutually beneficial.

Mass Customization.   The modern marketing system was built on identifying a need experienced by a large number of people (a mass market), and using mass production techniques and mass marketing (relying heavily on network television advertising) to satisfy that need. By producing and selling large quantities of standardized products, firms were able to keep the unit costs low and offer need-satisfying products at attractive prices. However, the market has changed. Mass marketing is being challenged by **mass customization,** that is, developing, producing, and delivering affordable products with enough variety and uniqueness that nearly every potential customer can have exactly what he or she wants. Deere and Co., maker of John Deere farm machinery, produces 45 different models of seed planters with a total of 1.7 million options in order to meet the varied needs of all types of farmers. What may be more remarkable is that they can all be built on the same assembly line in Moline, Illinois.[13]

www.johndeere.com

The movement toward mass customization is made possible by the tremendous advances in information, communications, and manufacturing technology. Firms are now able to learn a lot more about their current and prospective customers, and use that information in designing products, manufacturing, and distribution. They also can advertise to very specific audiences through cable television and via the Internet. The result is a proliferation of products in many product categories. Consider, for example, the variety of dry breakfast cereals available from General Mills and the snack alternatives offered by Frito-Lay.

Marketers are coming to realize, however, that more variety is not always better. In some areas the number of choices creates as much confusion as satisfaction. Consider, for example, the number of different pain relievers available in the drugstore. Retailers are also concerned by the explosion of products because they are pressed to find shelf space for them.

Coordinated Marketing Activities

Quality.   Although most firms do not ignore quality, there is a tendency to think in terms of "acceptable" levels of quality as determined by engineers and manufacturing people. However, when some firms added quality as defined by customers as a key ingredient of their strategies, it wasn't long before consumers responded. Soon the benefits of a commitment to quality became evident in the success of firms such as Sony and Honda. Thus, beginning in the 1980s improving quality became a priority for most organizations.

Some suggest that American executives became complacent about quality. However, it is more likely that American businesspeople had come to believe that quality and cost were directly related. That is, as quality is increased, costs must go up. Although that is generally true, the relationship is not as strong as first thought. Through careful study, firms found it is possible to substantially increase quality without unacceptable cost increases by:

- Obtaining and responding to input from customers about how they define quality and what they expect in a particular product.

- Improving designs to reduce problems in manufacturing, and identifying and correcting problems early in the production process to reduce expensive reworking and waste.

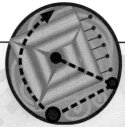
- Encouraging employees to call attention to quality problems, and empowering them to initiate action to improve quality.

Concerns about quality are not limited to manufacturing and service. Every business function has a quality component. Within marketing there are quality aspects to making sales calls, answering customers' questions, preparing advertisements, and every other activity. The breadth of quality issues, along with the realization that achieving and maintaining quality depends on the efforts of employees, led to the development of **total quality management (TQM)** in the 1980s. TQM is a system for implementing organization-wide commitment to quality that involves every employee accepting responsibility for continuous quality improvement. Despite the good intentions that surrounded TQM programs, their focus on introducing change led many proponents to overlook the costs and benefits of the changes. As a result, firms are now evaluating the impact of quality proposals on customer satisfaction, and treating quality improvements as investments. This refinement of TQM is known as a return on quality (ROQ) approach.

Value Creation. The customer's perception of all the benefits of a product weighed against all the costs of acquiring and consuming the product is its **value.**[14] The benefits can be functional (the roominess of a minivan for a large family), aesthetic (the attractiveness of the minivan), or psychological (the peace of mind that the van is designed to withstand a collision). Besides the money paid to the seller, the costs might include learning about the product, negotiating the purchase, arranging financing, learning how to use the product, and disposal of the product when it is no longer useful.

PCs were standardized, mass produced, and sold through retailers until Dell came along in 1984. The firm was founded on the revolutionary idea of allowing consumers to customize computer systems to their own specifications and purchase them direct from the manufacturer. This mass customization effort required new approaches to order taking, purchasing parts from which the products are made, delivery of the finished product, and customer service. In this photo, Dell employees assemble and test PCs, keyboards, and monitors before they are sent to consumers.

www.dell.com

Marketers are taking a closer look at what customers value in a product. As we have noted earlier, the heavy emphasis on mass production and mass marketing were largely driven by the desire to offer products at the lowest possible price. The focus on price overshadowed other benefits sought by customers. With better information about what customers desire and constant improvements in technology that make meeting those desires possible, marketers are engaging in **value creation** that extends beyond just offering the lowest possible prices.

Two points are important to note here. First, value means much more to the buyer than the amount of money charged for a product. For example, some consumers have found the Palm Pilot handheld electronic device indispensable for keeping track of appointments, phone numbers, and other day-to-day information. Second, the perception of value varies among individuals. Recently Palm initiated a marketing program aimed at corporate chief information officers when its research found that Palm has high awareness as a company that makes devices for consumers, but low awareness of the use of its devices for business applications.[15]

Organizational Objectives

Performance Metrics. Recall that one element of the marketing concept is the accomplishment of organizational goals. In the past the impact of marketing on organizational goals has been defined rather broadly. Because marketing is only one of many factors that influence how customers behave, it was assumed that a specific cause-and-effect relationship between marketing efforts and sales or profits could not be measured. As a result, marketing expenditures generally have been treated as expenses rather than investments, and managers adopted a short-term approach of trying to minimize these expenses as opposed to investing in marketing for both the short and long term. Today that thinking is changing.

Recognizing that marketing now accounts for at least 50% of all corporate costs, while manufacturing has gone from 50% to less than 30%, managers are demanding greater accountability. In response, organizations are searching for creative ways to measure marketing's effect, or the **return on the marketing investment.**

Marketers are now expected to demonstrate a link between traditional measures of marketing performance such as positive attitudes toward a brand, customer satisfaction, and customer retention to the firm's financial performance. As a result, efforts are underway in many firms to put a dollar value on their brands (referred to as brand equity)[16] and to determine the lifetime value of a customer (referred to as customer equity). Not surprisingly, these are difficult to isolate and measure. For example, estimating customer equity requires that a firm predict all future revenue from a current customer and subtract from that the marketing costs of acquiring the customer, retaining the customer, and servicing the customer.[17]

The Societal Marketing Concept.   Not long after the marketing concept became a widely accepted approach to doing business, it came under fire. For more than 40 years critics have persistently charged that marketing ignores social responsibility. That is, although the marketing concept may help an organization achieve its goals, it may at the same time encourage actions that conflict with society's best interests.

From one point of view, these charges are true. A firm may totally satisfy its customers (and in the process achieve a hefty profit), while also adversely affecting society. To illustrate, a pulp and paper mill in the Pacific Northwest might be supplying its newspaper customers with quality newsprint at a reasonable price, but to do so it might be polluting the air and water near the mill.

However, this need not be the case. A firm's social responsibility can be quite compatible with the marketing concept. Compatibility depends on two things: how

Cause-related marketing can reflect adoption of the societal marketing concept. The Breast Cancer Crusade sponsored by Avon raises funds through the sale of special Crusade products and through a series of three-day, sixty-mile fundraising walks such as the one shown here. Although the short-term business benefits of cause-related marketing are often difficult to measure directly, it suggests the sponsoring firm has adopted a broader societal perspective on the needs and wants of its customers.

www.avoncrusade.com

TABLE
1.2

America's 20 Best Corporate Citizens*

Company	Rank	Company	Rank
IBM	1	Intel Corp.	11
Hewlett-Packard	2	State Street Corp.	12
Fannie Mae	3	HB Fuller	13
St. Paul Companies	4	Timberland	14
Procter & Gamble	5	Bank of America	15
Motorola Inc.	6	Amgen	16
Cummins Engine	7	Lucent Technologies	17
Herman Miller	8	Qualcomm	18
General Mills Inc.	9	Sun Microsystems	19
Avon Products	10	Southwest Airlines	20

Source: "100 Best Corporate Citizens," *Business Ethics,* March/April 2002, pp. 10–11, *www.business-ethics.com.*

*Ranking is based on data from 1998–2000 on how well a firm serves seven stakeholder groups: stockholders, employees, the community, the environment, overseas stakeholders, minorities and women, and customers.

broadly a firm perceives its marketing goals and what the firm is willing to invest to achieve those goals. A firm that sufficiently extends the *breadth* and *commitment* dimensions of its marketing goals to fulfill its social responsibility is practicing what has become known as the **societal marketing concept.**

When the marketing concept's breadth is extended, a company recognizes that its market includes not only the buyers of its products but also anyone directly affected by its operations. In our example, the paper mill has several markets to satisfy, including (1) the newspaper publishers, (2) the consumers of the air that contains impurities given off by the mill, and (3) the recreational users of the local river where the mill releases its waste matter.

Extending the commitment dimension of its marketing goals means a firm must recognize that meeting the broader needs of society may require more time, technology, and skill than meeting just the needs of its immediate customers. Although these investments seem costly when they are made, they reflect a long-term view of customer satisfaction and performance objectives, rather than a focus only on today. For a company to prosper in the long run, it must satisfy its customers' social needs as well as their economic needs.

To draw attention to firms that have adopted a broad societal view, a ranking has been developed that equally weights seven performance indicators: profitability, as well as service to employees, the community, the environment, overseas stakeholders, minorities and women, and customers.[18] The top 20 firms are presented in Table 1.2. It is interesting to note that the top performers include both industry giants such as IBM and Procter & Gamble as well as much smaller firms.

Thus the marketing concept and a company's social responsibility are compatible if management strives over the long run to (1) satisfy the wants of its product-buying customers, (2) meet the societal needs of others affected by the firm's activities, and (3) achieve the company's performance objectives.

If the marketing concept and the refinements we've just discussed direct a modern marketer's approach to the marketing task, just what is it that marketers do? In the next section we'll describe the areas of responsibility and decision making that are generally referred to as marketing management.

A Company's Marketing Program

Recall that we said a **market** consists of people or organizations with needs to satisfy, money to spend, and the willingness to spend it. For example, many people need transportation and are willing to pay for it. However, this large group is made up of many subgroups or segments with different transportation needs. For example, among the people who want to travel long distances by air, there are some who want low prices and efficiency, whereas others are willing to pay for luxury and privacy. These subgroups or **market segments** are consumers or organizations that share similar wants, buying preferences, or product-use behaviors. If a segment is large and sufficiently distinct, firms typically respond with a specially designed offering. Thus, we often see the same basic need satisfied in very different ways. For example, Southwest Airlines, with low prices but no meals and no reserved seats, and NetJets Inc., which offers private jets on a time-share basis, are both highly successful air transportation marketers.

Ordinarily it is impractical for a firm to satisfy all or even most of the segments of a market. Instead, a company first identifies the segments and then selects one or more at which to target its efforts. Thus a **target market** refers to a market segment at which a firm directs a marketing program.

www.volvocars.com

Usually several firms are pursuing a particular target market at the same time, and each attempts to be viewed in a distinct and attractive way by prospective customers. That is, each firm uses strategies and tactics in an effort to establish a unique **position** in the prospects' minds. For example, Volvo's marketing strives to have its cars perceived by consumers as safe. Segmenting markets, selecting targets, and devising positioning strategies are fundamental marketing tasks.

Usually firms do a considerable amount of research to identify markets and define segments. Among the many questions market research seeks to answer, one of the most important is the sales potential of particular market segments. To determine sales potential, a firm must **forecast demand** (that is, sales) in its target markets. The results of demand forecasting will indicate whether the segments are worth pursuing, or whether alternatives need to be identified.

Next, management must design a **marketing mix**—the combination of a product, how it is distributed and promoted, and its price. Together, these four components of strategy must satisfy the needs of the target market(s) and, at the same time, achieve the organization's marketing objectives. Some of the challenges facing marketing managers in developing a marketing mix are:

- *Product.* Strategies are needed for deciding what products to introduce, managing existing products over time, and dropping products that are no longer viable. Strategic decisions must also be made regarding branding, packaging, and other product features such as warranties.

- *Price.* Setting the base price for a product is a marketing decision. Other necessary strategies pertain to changing price, pricing related items within a product line, terms of sale, and possible discounts. An especially challenging decision is selecting the price for a new product.

- *Distribution.* Here, strategies relate to the channel(s) by which ownership of products is transferred from producer to customer and, in many cases, the means by which goods are moved from where they are produced to where they are purchased by the final customer. In addition, any middlemen, such as wholesalers and retailers, must be selected and their roles designed.

- *Promotion.* Strategies are needed to combine individual methods such as advertising, personal selling, and sales promotion into an integrated communications campaign. In addition, promotional strategies must be adjusted as a product moves from the early stages to the later stages of its life.

The four marketing-mix elements are interrelated; decisions in one area affect actions in another. To illustrate, design of a marketing mix is certainly affected by whether a firm chooses to compete on the basis of price *or* on one or more other elements. When a firm relies on price as its primary competitive tool, the other elements must be designed to support aggressive pricing. For example, the promotional campaign likely will be built around a theme of "low, low prices." In nonprice competition, however, product, distribution, and/or promotional strategies come to the forefront. For instance, the product must have features worthy of a higher price, and promotion must create a high-quality image for the product.

Each marketing-mix element contains countless alternatives. For instance, a producer may make and market one product or many, and the products may be related or unrelated to each other. They may be distributed through wholesalers, to retailers without the benefit of wholesalers, or even directly to final customers. Ultimately, from the multitude of alternatives, management must select a combination of elements that will satisfy target markets and achieve organizational and marketing goals.

Like many areas of business, marketers sometimes face seemingly contradictory goals. The desire to satisfy customers, for example, may seem to conflict with a particular revenue or profit objective. When this occurs, ethical predicaments may arise. Thus ethics in marketing deserves our attention.

Ethics and Marketing

Marketers are responsible to a variety of groups. Certainly their customers depend on them to satisfy their needs. Also, their employers expect them to generate sales and profits, suppliers and distributors look to them for their continued business, and society expects them to be responsible citizens. The frequently divergent interests of these groups create a wide variety of ethical challenges for marketers.

What Is Ethical Behavior?

A discussion of the philosophical underpinnings of ethics is beyond the scope of this book. However, it is safe to say that there is considerable disagreement over what is and what is not ethical conduct. For example, ethics vary from society to society. Take bribery; although repugnant in most societies, it is an accepted and even necessary aspect of business behavior in many parts of the world. Thus, for our purposes it is sufficient to say that **ethics** are the standards of behavior generally accepted by a society. Note that ethics goes beyond laws, which establish the minimum rules a society agrees to follow. Thus, it is possible to behave legally but still be unethical.

The temptation to act in an ethically questionable fashion can be very strong, particularly when the behavior can be rewarding. Take, for example, a development in the drugstore business. For years it has been a common practice for suppliers to grant discounts to retailers for damaged or outdated merchandise. However, some firms appear to be taking advantage of the policy. There have been a number of mergers among retail drugstore chains, giving them substantial leverage. As suppliers have become more dependent on these chains, they charge that some chains have gotten more liberal in their interpretation of "damaged and outdated," and are taking unauthorized deductions from their invoices. Is this unethical? The suppliers think so, but others say the suppliers have had the upper hand for years. In the past they had been able to dictate terms to the retailers and now "turnabout is fair play."

Instilling an Ethical Orientation

Organizations are addressing ethical issues. For example, most firms have a code of ethics for their employees. However, as long as there are conflicting goals and the opportunity for people to make judgments, ethical failures will occur. To relieve some of the pressure on employees faced with ethical challenges and perhaps reduce the frequency and severity of ethical problems, organizations have taken several steps:

Transparency International Bribe Payers Index 2002

In order to shed some light on who uses bribery, 835 business experts in 15 leading emerging-market countries were asked, "In the business sectors with which you are most familiar, please indicate how likely companies from the following countries are to pay or offer bribes to win or retain business in this (your) country?"

A score of 10 would be perfect; that is, no perceived propensity to pay bribes. As scores decline, the use of bribery is seen as more common. Interestingly, the survey indicated that domestically owned companies in the 15 countries surveyed have a much higher propensity to pay bribes than foreign firms.

Many organizations, including the one that conducted this survey, oppose bribery because it has a corruptive influence and results in the misallocation of scarce resources in poor countries.

Are there any conditions in which bribery to obtain and/or to retain business would be ethical?

Source: Transparency International website: *www.transparency.org.* Students also may want to examine the text of the Foreign Corrupt Practices Act of 1977 that stipulates what U.S. businesses are permitted to do when conducting business internationally.

Rank	Country	Score
1	Australia	8.5
2	Sweden	8.4
	Switzerland	8.4
4	Austria	8.2
5	Canada	8.1
6	Netherlands	7.8
	Belgium	7.8
8	United Kingdom	6.9
9	Singapore	6.3
	Germany	6.3
11	Spain	5.8
12	France	5.5
13	U.S.	5.3
	Japan	5.3
15	Malaysia	4.3
	Hong Kong	4.3
17	Italy	4.1
18	South Korea	3.9
19	Taiwan	3.8
20	People's Republic of China	3.5
21	Russia	3.2
	All domestic companies	1.9

- Clearly communicating the organization's ethical standards and expectations through initial training and frequent reminders and updates.

- Ensuring that employee requirements in terms of goals, quotas, and deadlines are reasonable.

- Creating a senior-level position of "ethics officer" occupied by a person with the skill to provide advice as well as the authority to respond to complaints and inquiries.

- Commending extraordinary ethical behavior and dealing decisively with ethical violations.

The Benefits of Ethical Behavior

One could argue that ethical behavior should in itself be rewarding. However, there are tangible benefits as well. Business is built on relationships with suppliers, customers, employees, and other groups. The strength of those relationships is largely a function of the amount of trust the parties have in each other. Unethical behavior undermines trust and destroys relationships.

Issues related to ethics are often ambiguous. There are situations in which the behavior of a marketer might be judged inappropriate and unethical by some, and totally acceptable by others. It is important for you to be aware of typical ethical challenges in marketing and to consider how you would respond to them. To help you in that regard, we have included Ethical Dilemma boxes throughout the book. In most, there are no absolutely right or wrong answers. That's why we call them dilemmas. We hope you find them interesting and helpful in refining your own sense of ethics.

Importance of Marketing

It would be difficult to imagine a world without marketing. But it may be equally difficult to appreciate the importance effective marketing plays in most aspects of our lives. We take for granted the media that are largely supported by advertising, the vast assortment of goods distributed through stores close to our homes, and the ease with which we can make purchases. Let's consider for a moment how marketing plays a major role in the global economy, in the American socioeconomic system, in any individual organization, and in your life.

Globally

Until the late 1970s, American firms had a large and secure domestic market. The only significant foreign competition was in selected industries, such as agriculture, or for relatively narrow markets, such as luxury automobiles. But this changed dramatically through the 1980s as more foreign firms developed attractive products, honed their marketing expertise, and then successfully entered the U.S. market. Imported products in some industries, such as office equipment, autos, apparel, watches, semiconductors, and consumer electronics, have been very successful. As a result, in recent years the U.S. has been importing more than it exports, creating large annual trade deficits.

In the not too distant future there will be new challenges. The dramatic changes taking place in the governments and economies of eastern Europe and growing capitalism in China and the former Soviet Union will certainly create new and stronger international competitors.

Trade agreements are also altering the global business picture. The European Union, the North American Free Trade Agreement, and the Asia-Pacific Economic Cooperation forum are reducing economic barriers and liberalizing trade between their members. However, as trade agreements increase the marketing opportunities for firms within the member countries, they often result in stiffened competition for firms from outside.

In response to these developments, more and more U.S. firms are looking abroad. They are concluding that their profit and growth objectives are most likely to be achieved through a combination of domestic and international marketing, rather than solely from domestic marketing. Table 1.3 gives you some insight into how important foreign trade is for U.S. firms.

Although we don't yet know everything that will result from these developments, one thing is certain. We live in a global economy. Most nations today—regardless of their degree of economic development or their political philosophy—recognize the importance of marketing beyond their own national borders. Indeed, economic growth in the less developed nations of the world depends greatly on their ability to design effective marketing systems to produce global customers for their raw materials and industrial output. We will explore these issues in more detail throughout the book.

Domestically

Aggressive, effective marketing practices have been largely responsible for the high standard of living in the United States. The effi-

When a case of mad cow disease was detected in a cow raised in Japan, sale of all beef in that country, including imports, declined dramatically. Since Japan is the largest export market for U.S. beef, the industry was faced with a serious problem. To counteract consumers' concerns that tainted all beef, the U.S. Meat Export Federation, an industry group, launched an advertising campaign in Japan touting the safety of American beef. This ad describes how a U.S. cattle breeder cares for her cows and serves the beef to her family.

TABLE

1.3

U.S. International Trade and Major Trading Partners, 2001

Exports		Imports	
Destination	**$ Value (billions)**	**Source**	**$ Value (billions)**
Canada	179	Canada	229
Mexico	112	Japan	147
Japan	65	Mexico	136
United Kingdom	42	China	100
Germany	29	Germany	59
Total U.S. exports	1,066	Total U.S. imports	1,441

Sources: *Statistical Abstract of the United States: 2001,* 121st ed., U.S. Bureau of the Census, Washington, DC, 2001; Economic Indicators, Bureau of Economic Analysis, U.S. Department of Commerce, at *www.economicindicators.gov.*

ciency of mass marketing—extensive and rapid communication with customers through a wide variety of media and a distribution system that makes products readily available—combined with mass production brought the cost of many products within reach of most consumers. Since about 1920 (except during World War II), the available supply of products in the United States has far surpassed total demand. Making most products has been relatively easy; the real challenge has been marketing them.

Now mass customization means even more products virtually tailored to our individual tastes. As a result, the average American enjoys things that once were considered luxuries and in many countries are still available only to people earning high incomes.

Employment and Costs   We can get an idea of the significance of marketing in the U.S. economy by looking at how many of us are employed in some way in marketing and how much of what we spend covers the cost of marketing. *Between one-fourth and one-third of the U.S. civilian labor force is engaged in marketing activities.* This figure includes employees in retailing, wholesaling, transportation, warehousing, and communications industries, as well as people who work in marketing departments of manufacturers and those who work in marketing in agricultural, mining, and service industries. Furthermore, over the past century, jobs in marketing have increased at a much more rapid rate than jobs in production, reflecting marketing's expanded role in the economy. On the average, *about 50 cents of each dollar we spend as consumers goes to cover marketing costs.* The money pays for designing the products to meet our needs, making products readily available when and where we want them, and informing us about products. These activities add want-satisfying ability, or what is called utility, to products.

Creating Utility   A customer purchases a product because it provides satisfaction. The want-satisfying power of a product is called its **utility,** and it comes in many forms. It is through marketing that much of a product's utility is created.

Consider eBay as an example. Pierre Omidyar and Jeff Skoll, two San Jose, California, entrepreneurs, envisioned operating a giant auction where many buyers and sellers could gather and trade goods. But an auction in San Jose was not likely to generate the kind of crowds they desired. Faced with the challenge of how to increase access to their auction, they came upon the Internet. They wondered if the Internet could transport information from sellers about their products and bids from buyers interested in making purchases. Even if the technology could be made to work, potential buyers and sellers had to be made aware of this unique auction

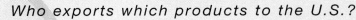
format and informed about how to use it. Excited by the possibilities, they created eBay, Inc., and the rest, as we say, is history.

Let's see what kinds of utility have been created in this process:

- *Form utility* is associated primarily with production—the physical or chemical changes that make a product more valuable. When lumber is made into furniture, form utility is created. This is production, not marketing. However, marketing contributes to decisions on the style, size, and color of the furniture. Similarly, marketing is involved in developing almost all products. In the case of eBay, an attractive, easy-to-use website had to be designed. Visitors to the site had to be able to find goods that interested them quickly and easily. These features contribute to the product's form utility.

- *Place utility* exists when a product is readily accessible to potential customers. An auction on the Internet can increase the number of buyers and sellers, but once products are purchased they still have to be delivered quickly and in good condition. Physically moving a purchased item to a successful bidder is an essential element of its value.

- *Time utility* means having a product available when you want it. In the case of eBay, this may be one of its primary attractions. Prospective buyers can visit the eBay Internet site day or night at their convenience. There's no need to have a store open or staffed.

- *Information utility* is created by informing prospective buyers that a product exists. Unless you know about a product and where you can get it, the product has no value. Advertising that describes the eBay auction concept and provides some information about how to list an item and how to make bids creates information utility. To create awareness of eBay, it had to be advertised. *Image utility* is a special type of information utility. It is the emotional or psychological value that a person attaches to a product or brand because of its reputation or social standing. Image utility is ordinarily associated with prestige or high-status products such as designer clothes, expensive foreign automobiles, or certain residential neighborhoods. However, the image-utility value of a given product may vary considerably depending on different consumers' perceptions. Shopping on the Internet using an online auction is still a novelty for many consumers. For some it may even be a status symbol that they can tell their friends about. Thus, for some consumers using eBay also provides image utility.

- *Possession utility* is created when a customer buys the product—that is, ownership is transferred to the buyer. This is a concern for eBay because there is virtually no policing of the buyers or the sellers. It's possible for sellers to misrepresent goods and for buyers to renege on paying. Clearly this is much less of an issue in face-to-face transactions. For eBay, providing possession utility is taking on growing significance as the number of users of the service increases.

Organizationally

Marketing considerations should be an integral part of all short-range and long-range planning in any company. Here's why:

- The success of any business comes from satisfying the wants of its customers, which is the social and economic basis for the existence of all organizations.
- Although many activities are essential to a company's growth, marketing is the only one that produces revenue directly.

When managers are internally focused, products are designed by designers, manufactured by manufacturing people, priced by financial managers, and then given to sales managers to sell. This approach generally won't work in today's environment of intense competition and constant change. Just making a good product will not result in sales. Two special applications, services marketing and not-for-profit marketing, are described below.

Service Marketers
The U.S. has gone from primarily a manufacturing economy to the world's first service economy. As opposed to goods, services are activities that are the object of a transaction. Examples are transportation, communications, entertainment, medical care, financial services, education, and repairs. Services account for over two-thirds of the nation's gross domestic product. Almost three-fourths of the country's nonfarm labor force is employed in service industries, and

Entertainment is an important segment of the services industry, and amusement parks make up a growing component of entertainment. There are over 320 million paid visits to amusement parks each year as operators race to see who can attract consumers with the most novel and exciting experiences.

www.rcdb.com

over one-half of all consumer expenditures are for the purchase of services. Projections indicate that services' share of all these categories (gross domestic product, employment, expenditures) will continue to grow.

Because the production of goods dominated our economy until fairly recently, most marketing knowledge was derived from experience with goods (such as groceries, clothing, machine tools, and automobiles) rather than from services. But progress in services has been rapid, and now some service sector firms such as FedEx, Disney, and Marriott Corp. are generally considered to be among the most market-oriented companies in the world.

Not-for-Profit Marketers During the 1980s and early 1990s many not-for-profit organizations realized they needed effective marketing programs to make up for shrinking government subsidies, a decrease in charitable contributions, and other unfavorable economic conditions. Colleges with declining enrollments, hospitals with empty beds, and symphony orchestras playing to vacant seats all began to understand that marketing was essential to help them turn their situations around.

Today charities, museums, and even churches—all organizations that formerly rejected any thought of marketing—are embracing it as a means of growth and, for some, survival. This trend is likely to accelerate for two reasons:

- Increasing competition among nonprofit organizations. For example, the competition among colleges and universities for students is intensifying, and the search for donors has become more intense as the number of charities has increased.

- Not-for-profit organizations need to improve their images and gain greater acceptance among donors, government agencies, news media, and of course, consumers, all of which collectively determine an organization's success.

Personally

Okay, so marketing is important globally, in our economy, and in an individual organization. But what's in it for you? Why should you study marketing? There are a number of reasons:

- Consider how many marketers view you as part of their market. With people like you in mind, firms such as Nike, VISA, Microsoft, and Kellogg's have designed products, set prices, created advertisements, and chosen the best methods of making their products available to you. In response, you watch television with its commercials, buy various articles over the Internet and in stores, and sometimes complain about prices or quality. As we said at the outset of the chapter, marketing occupies a large part of your daily life. If you doubt this, just imagine for a moment what it would be like if there were no marketing institutions—no retail stores to buy from or no advertising to give you information, for example. Clearly it is important to understand such a significant part of our society.

- Studying marketing will make you a better-informed consumer. You'll have a better appreciation for why some firms are successful and other, seemingly well-run businesses, fail. More specifically, you will discover how firms go about deciding what products to offer, and what prices to charge. Your exploration of marketing will help you understand the many forms of promotion and how they are used to inform and persuade consumers. And it will help you appreciate the modern miracle of efficient distribution that makes products available when and where buyers want them.

- Last, marketing probably relates—directly or indirectly—to your career aspirations. If you are thinking about a marketing major and employment in a marketing position, you can develop a feel for what marketing managers do. (For an introduction to the many career opportunities in the field, we especially suggest

The Cook County Illinois Sheriff's Department has developed a 3-D, virtual reality stereoscopic theatre in a trailer that visits area high schools to show students a 5-minute movie about the implications of drunk driving. With a movie produced by a professional video company and the sponsorship of several corporations, this approach indicates the sheriff's department recognizes that even important ideas require effective marketing to be accepted.

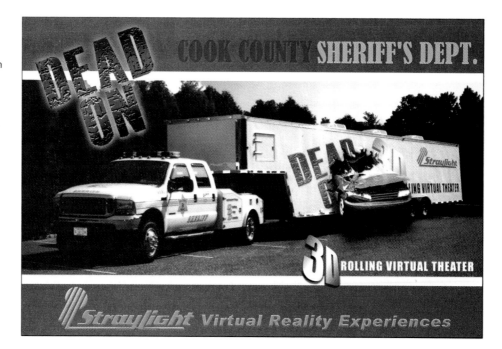

you read "Careers and Marketing" found on our website.) If you're planning a career in accounting, finance, or some other business field, you can learn how marketing affects managerial decision making in these areas. Finally, if you are thinking about a career in a nonbusiness field such as health care, government, music, or education, you will learn how to use marketing in these organizations.

Summary

The foundation of marketing is exchange, in which one party provides to another party something of value in return for something else of value. In a broad sense, marketing consists of all activities designed to generate or facilitate an exchange intended to satisfy human needs.

Business firms and nonprofit organizations engage in marketing. Products marketed include goods as well as services, ideas, people, and places. Marketing activities are targeted at markets consisting of product purchasers and also individuals and groups that influence the success of an organization.

In a business context, marketing is a total system of business activities designed to plan, price, promote, and distribute want-satisfying products to target markets in order to achieve organizational objectives.

Marketing's evolution in the United States has gone through three stages: It began with a product orientation, passed through the sales orientation, and is now in a market orientation. In this third stage a company's efforts are focused on identifying and satisfying customers' needs.

Some successful organizations remain at the first or second stage, not progressing to the market-orientation stage, because they have monopoly power or because their products are in such great demand. Other firms have difficulty accepting a market-driven approach to business or have problems implementing a market orientation.

A business philosophy called the marketing concept was developed to aid companies with supply capabilities that exceed consumer demand. According to the marketing concept, a firm is best able to achieve its performance objectives by adopting a customer orientation, coordinating all of its marketing activities, and fulfilling the organization's goals. Examples of implementation of the marketing concept include relationship building, mass customization, heightened sensitivity to quality, value creation, utilizing performance metrics, and the societal marketing concept. Ethics, the standards of behavior accepted by society, are important concerns of market-oriented organizations.

Marketing management involves segmenting markets, selecting target markets, and establishing a position in the minds of buyers. The primary focus of marketing is the marketing mix—the combination of a product, price, promotion, and distribution process to meet the needs of a targeted segment of a market.

Marketing is practiced today in all modern nations, regardless of their political philosophy. As international competition has heated up, the attention paid to marketing has increased. In the U.S. between one-fourth and one-third of the civilian work force is involved with marketing, and about one-half of consumer spending covers the cost of marketing. This investment in marketing is justified by the form, information, place, time, and possession utilities it creates.

Depending on circumstances, marketing can be vital to an organization's success. In recent years numerous service firms and nonprofit organizations have found marketing to be necessary and worthwhile. Marketing also is useful to individuals. Students particularly find marketing helpful in the search for career opportunities.

More about **Nordstrom**

One of the many ways in which Nordstrom hopes to reestablish itself as a premier retail chain, while relying on its upscale image, is by way of the Internet. Nordstrom.com was established in late 1999 in an ambitious drive to offer an online shopping experience that matches, and maybe even improves on, a visit to the actual store. Carefully planned and meticulously managed, the website draws thousands of visitors every month who browse, purchase, and even write to the store. The website's staff read and answer customer e-mails, analyze the way customers use the search engine, track fashion trends, and scan data for shopping patterns. All the information is fed back into improvements in the site's design and product offerings.

Nordstrom is very happy with the results of its Internet foray and expects the benefits to continue to grow. Because the site can do things the stores themselves can't, such as offering 30 million pairs of shoes, there's good reason to be optimistic. But no matter how well designed it is, the website will always require the special human touch that made Nordstrom's customer service a legend in the retail business long before the Internet. The website's executive vice president of marketing offered this example: "A customer who had received some smoked salmon as a wedding gift several years ago . . . sent us an e-mail to say that he had not eaten it yet and that he wanted to know if it was still good. Our personal shopper told the customer that he would get right back to him. He ran to Pike Place Fish Market here in Seattle, bought smoked salmon, shipped it off to the customer, and then sent an e-mail telling him to throw the old stuff away!"[19]

1. How can a retailer's website help it more effectively meet the conditions of the marketing concept?

2. How does the creation of customer relationships differ on the Internet from the way it is accomplished in Nordstrom's stores?

Key Terms and Concepts

The numbers next to the terms refer to the pages on which the terms and concepts are defined. In addition, the Glossary at the end of the book defines key terms and concepts.

Exchange (5)
Marketing (6)
Product-orientation stage (7)
Sales-orientation stage (8)
Market-orientation stage (8)
Marketing concept (10)
Customer relationship management (CRM) (11)

Mass customization (12)
Total quality management (TQM) (13)
Value (13)
Value creation (14)
Return on marketing investment (14)
Societal marketing concept (16)
Market (17)

Market segments (17)
Target market (17)
Position (17)
Forecast demand (17)
Marketing mix (17)
Ethics (18)
Utility (21)

Questions and Problems

1. Explain the concept of an exchange, including the conditions that must exist for an exchange to occur, and give one example each of a business exchange that does not involve money and a nonbusiness exchange.

2. Name some companies that you believe are still in the product or sales stages in the evolution of marketing. Explain why you chose each of them.

3. Describe how each of the following could go beyond an exchange situation to establishing a relationship with customers.

   a. Online fresh-cut flower retailer
   b. CPA firm
   c. Blood bank
   d. Automobile dealership
   e. University
   f. Appliance manufacturer

4. Describe how the operation of a product-oriented shoe manufacturer might be different from the operation of a market-oriented manufacturer.

5. Explain the three elements that constitute the marketing concept.

6. "The marketing concept does not imply that marketing executives will run the firm. The concept requires only that whoever is in top management be market-oriented." Give examples of how a production manager, company treasurer, or personnel manager can be market-oriented.

7. For each of the following organizations, describe the marketing mix.

   a. Luxor hotel and casino in Las Vegas
   b. Airline Pilots Association labor union
   c. Professor teaching a first-year chemistry course
   d. Police department in your city

8. One way to explain the utilities provided by marketing is to consider how we would live if there were no marketing facilities. Describe some of the ways in which your daily activities would be affected if there were no retail stores or advertising.

9. Name two service firms that, in your opinion, do a good marketing job. Then name some that you think do a poor marketing job. Explain your reasoning in each case.

Interactive Marketing Exercises

1. Select an organizational unit at your school (for example, food service, placement office, intramural sports, library), observe the operation, and interview an administrator and some customers to identify (*a*) what is being exchanged; and (*b*) whether the unit is product-, sales-, or market-oriented.

2. Visit the sites of two different online book retailers (for example, Amazon.com and Barnes & Noble.com) and request information about this book. Keep track of the length of time it takes to find the book on the site and what information the site provides about the book. Next, note what information a customer is required to provide in order to purchase the book (but don't actually order one unless you need another copy). From the perspective of a consumer seeking utility, how does the Internet search compare with visiting a bookstore?

Chapter 2

The Dynamic Marketing Environment

PART 1

"As cable was to broadcast television, we want to be the same thing to radio."

Is **XM Satellite Radio** Playing Your Song?

Are you ready to get 101 different radio stations on your car radio? XM Satellite Radio is ready to bring them to you. Called "the best thing to happen to car radio since FM," XM's satellite programming consists of 70 music stations of all kinds (33 of them commercial-free), and 30 other stations that offer news, talk, sports, and entertainment. For $120 a year in service fees, plus between $150 and $1,000 in one-time charges for the dashboard radio, trunk-mounted receiver, and roof-mounted antenna, you can select from among 11 pop music stations and 11 rock music channels as well as various stations featuring jazz, country, hip-hop, soul, world music, Latin sounds, classical selections, and music from each decade from the 1940s to the 1990s. Comedy and kids' stations and special-interest programming complete the lineup.

XM receivers are now available in three dozen General Motors, Honda, Nissan, Volkswagen, and Isuzu models, inviting buyers to enjoy satellite radio in a new car. Tests indicate that the two powerful digital signals sent by XM's satellites to blanket the continent with music and talk transmit a clear, seamless sound from coast to coast.

Besides serving the mobile consumer, XM intends to push satellite radio as suitable for in-home listening using a different receiver. Thus satellite radio could be a boon not only for truck drivers and long-distance commuters but also for rural populations and anyone who loves the sheer breadth of choice and clear reception it offers. According to XM's programming head, "This is a once-in-a-lifetime opportunity to truly reinvent radio—across America." An XM vice president added, "As cable was to broadcast television, we want to be the same thing to radio."

Radio is not new, of course, although radio in its traditional form is facing some new challenges now—notably competition from alternative products such as personal music players. In contrast, bouncing radio off satellites *is* new, and XM has exploited technological advances to create a new marketing opportunity. Its two satellites, known as Rock and Roll, were launched from a converted oil rig near the equator, from which they required less energy to get to their geostationary orbits 22,500 miles above the earth. Among the most powerful communications satellites ever built, they use a different band than satellite TV and maintain their signals even in bad weather. With the help of "repeaters" to strengthen and retransmit their signals, Rock and Roll can even surmount reception problems caused by tall buildings.

XM estimates that it will need about 4 million U.S. subscribers—about 2% of all car radios currently on the road—to make a profit. If early adopters of this new product spread the word (and the message is favorable), more drivers are likely to replace their AM-FM radios with retrofitted XM equipment. But XM has a long way to go from the 200,000 subscribers who signed on in the first 10 months of national service to reach its multimillion goal.

www.xmradio.com

It's expected that the customer base will surge as a result of GM's offering factory-installed units as options, because the cost of options is a relatively small fraction of the total price of the new car. Start-up costs of a satellite radio business are astronomical, but ongoing operating costs are low. Thus, if part of the target market of 200 million subscribers materializes, profits could soar.

Of course, advanced technology does not guarantee commercial success. It appears that the Rock and Roll satellites are going to need replacement sooner than XM anticipated. And, most fundamentally, the willingness of consumers to pay for radio at all is still an open question. In the meantime, competitors—including Internet radio—are gearing up. But for the 105 million radio listeners who live outside the country's largest radio markets, especially the 22 million who get fewer than half a dozen stations, satellite radio may be just what they want to hear.

What marketing considerations will be particularly important for XM as it tries to make subscription radio successful?[1]

As the XM Satellite Radio situation illustrates, any organization must identify and then respond to numerous environmental forces ranging from shifting consumer tastes to advancing technology. Some of these forces are external to the firm, whereas others come from within. Management can't do much about controlling the external forces, but it generally can control the internal ones.

Many of these forces influence what can and should be done in the area of marketing. Ultimately, a firm's ability to adapt to its operating environment determines, in large part, its level of business success. Thus XM, like any organization, must manage its marketing program within its combined external and internal environment.

After studying this chapter, you should be able to explain:

Chapter Goals

- The concept of environmental monitoring.

- How external environmental forces such as demographics, economic conditions, and social and cultural trends can affect an organization's marketing.

- How external factors such as markets, as well as suppliers and intermediaries that are specific to a given firm, can influence that firm's marketing.

- How nonmarketing resources within a firm can affect its marketing

Environmental Monitoring

Environmental monitoring—also called *environmental scanning*—is the process of (1) gathering information regarding a company's external environment, (2) analyzing it, and (3) forecasting the impact of whatever trends the analysis suggests. Often the word *environment* is associated with our physical environment—air quality, water pollution, solid-waste disposal, and natural-resource conservation. However, we use the term *environment* in a much broader sense in this chapter.

An organization operates within an *external* environment that it generally *cannot* control. At the same time, marketing and nonmarketing resources exist *within* the organization that generally *can* be controlled by its executives.

There are two levels of external forces:

- *Macro* influences (so called because they affect all firms) such as demographics, economic conditions, culture, and laws.

- *Micro* influences (so called because they affect a particular firm) consist of suppliers, marketing intermediaries, and customers. Micro influences, although external, are closely related to a specific company.

Successful marketing depends largely on a company's ability to manage its marketing programs within its environment. To do this, a firm's marketing executives must determine what makes up the firm's environment and then monitor it in a systematic, ongoing fashion. They must be alert to spot environmental trends that could be opportunities or problems for their organization. According to one source, "Successful trend-spotting is necessary for companies big and small . . . ; not only does being able to ride a trend boost profits for existing products, but it also can revive sales for products that are flagging." Noteworthy "waves of change" include growing interests in personal safety (no doubt magnified by the attacks on September 11, 2001) and life-long learning.[2]

How important is environmental monitoring to business success? In a word, *very.* One study of about 100 large companies concluded, "Firms having advanced systems to monitor events in the external environment exhibited higher growth and greater profitability than firms that did not have such systems."[3]

External Macroenvironment

The following external forces have considerable influence on any organization's marketing opportunities and activities (see Figure 2.1). Therefore, they are *macroenvironmental forces*:

- Demographics
- Economic conditions
- Competition

FIGURE 2.1

External Macroenvironment of a Company's Marketing Program.

Six largely uncontrollable external forces influence an organization's marketing activities.

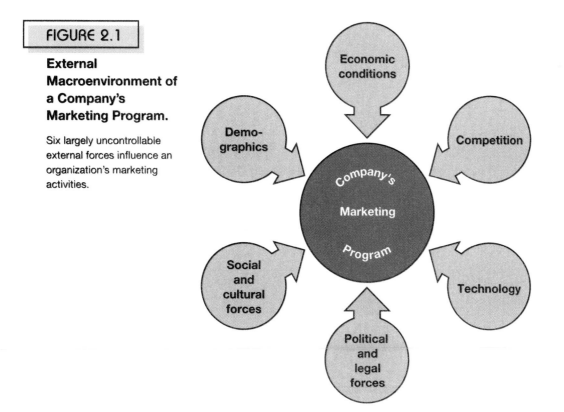

- Social and cultural forces
- Political and legal forces
- Technology

A change in any one of them can cause changes in one or more of the others. Hence, they are interrelated. One thing they all have in common is that they are dynamic forces—that is, they are subject to change *and* at an increasing rate!

These forces are largely uncontrollable by management, but they are not *totally* uncontrollable. A company may be able to influence its external environment to some extent. For instance, a firm may influence its political–legal environment by lobbying or by contributing to a legislator's campaign fund. Or, in international marketing, a company can improve its competitive position by a joint venture with a foreign firm that markets a complementary product. Coca-Cola and Swiss-owned Nestlé, the world's largest food manufacturer, joined forces to market ready-to-drink iced Nestea in the U.S. and chocolate, coffee, and tea drinks in Europe.[4]

www.celebrex.com

On the technological frontier, new-product research and development can strengthen a firm's competitive position. For instance, Pfizer and Pharmacia are enjoying a blockbuster success with their drug, Celebrex, which among other things fights pain caused by arthritis. In fact, the technology of the now merged companies is an external competitive force that affects other pharmaceutical companies.[5]

Now let's take a look at these six external forces in more detail.

Demographics

www.census.gov

Demographics refer to the characteristics of populations, including such factors as size, distribution, and growth. Because people constitute markets, demographics are of special interest to marketing executives. Here we'll just cover a few examples of how demographic factors influence marketing programs; some aspects of demographics related to consumer buying behavior will be considered in Chapter 4.

According to projections, there will be approximately 325 million Americans by the year 2020, an increase of about 40 million over the present total. Perhaps the most significant demographic trend at this time is the aging of the U.S. population, a shift that is expected to continue for a while. The statistics in Table 2.1 underscore

TABLE 2.1

Projected Changes in the Distribution of the U.S. Population

	% change	
	2000–2010	2010–2020
Under 5 years old	6.5	9.2
5–14 years old	−0.6	7.9
15–24 years old	11.5	−1.3
25–34 years old	3.8	10.1
35–44 years old	−12.1	3.2
45–54 years old	18.8	−12.1
55–64 years old	47.6	18.9
65–74 years old	16.3	48.7
Over 74 years old	11.5	20.0
Total population	8.9	8.4

Source: Adapted from U.S. Bureau of the Census, *Statistical Abstract of the United States: 2000*, p. 15, at *www.census.gov/epcd/abstract/statistical/statistical-abstract-us.html,* accessed July 24, 2002.

The U.S. population is aging, to the point that the 55-and-over group is a very attractive target market for a variety of businesses and non-business organizations. AARP, a not-for-profit entity, provides a range of services to its members, who must be at least age 50 but do not have to be retired. Over 35 million people belong to AARP, formerly called the American Association of Retired Persons. Key member benefits are travel-related discounts, the *Modern Maturity* magazine, and opportunities for service and friendships through local chapters.

www.aarp.org

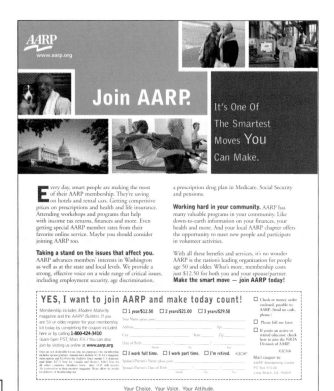

how the age distribution of the population evolves over time. Changes in the age distribution are the result of many factors, including the quality of health care and nutrition. Two key factors are the number of women who are of child-bearing age and the birthrate. The number of women of child-bearing age is a function of the births that occurred some years before and thus is highly predictable. However, the birthrate at any one point in time is influenced by a wide variety of social and economic factors that are much less predictable. For example, attitudes toward careers and family size certainly affect the birthrate.

There are several noteworthy points in Table 2.1. First, peaks and valleys in the population distribution move through time. To mention one example, the projected 12% decline in the 45 to 54 age group can be traced back to lower birthrates between 1965 and 1974. Therefore, it is possible to track changes and, to the extent that behavior is related to age, anticipate what impacts they will have. Second, even in a 10-year period, there can be quite dramatic shifts in the population. For instance, the number of people in the 65 to 74 age group will increase by nearly 50% from 2010 to 2020, which means growing markets for products such as health care and retirement communities.

Another notable demographic trend is the rapid growth of minority markets—and their buying power. In the past decade, the buying power of minorities expanded more than did the size of this population segment. For instance, Hispanics' buying power increased 118% (compared to a growth in numbers of 45%), whereas Asian Americans' buying power rose 125% (compared to 51%). Now, minorities represent about 28% of the total U.S. population; by the year 2025, the proportion is expected to increase to 38%. Between 2000 and 2020, particularly rapid growth is forecast for Asian Americans (a 74% increase) and persons of Hispanic origin (70%). As a result, Hispanics will soon surpass African Americans as the largest minority group in the U.S. Marketers are interested in these overall projections as well as the growing market potential among minority groups.[6]

None of these ethnic groups is homogeneous, however. The Hispanic market, for instance, really consists of separate markets built around subgroups of Cubans,

Puerto Ricans, Mexicans, and other Latin Americans. A simple product such as beans illustrates the differences among subgroups. Cubans prefer black beans, Mexicans eat refried beans, and Puerto Ricans go for red beans.[7] Many consumer-product companies realized only recently that they must target their products and advertising at each of the Hispanic subgroups.

Economic Conditions

People alone do not make a market. They must have money to spend and be willing to spend it. Consequently, the **economic environment** is a significant force that affects the marketing activities of just about any organization. A marketing program is affected especially by such economic factors as the current and anticipated stage of the business cycle, as well as inflation and interest rates.

Stage of the Business Cycle

The traditional **business cycle** goes through four stages—prosperity, recession, depression, and recovery—then returns full cycle to prosperity. Economic strategies adopted by the federal government have averted the depression stage in the U.S. for about 70 years. Marketing executives need to know which stage of the business cycle the economy currently is in, because a company's marketing programs usually must be changed from one stage of the business cycle to another.

Prosperity is a period of economic growth. During this stage, organizations tend to expand their marketing programs as they add new products and enter new markets.

A *recession* is a period of retrenchment for consumers and businesses—we tighten our economic belts. People can become discouraged, scared, and angry. Naturally, these feelings affect their buying behavior. For example, some consumers cut back on eating out and entertainment outside the home. As a result, firms catering to these needs face serious marketing challenges, and some may incur economic losses.

Recovery is the period when the economy is moving from recession to prosperity. The marketers' challenge is to determine how quickly prosperity will return and to what level. As unemployment declines and disposable income increases, companies expand their marketing efforts to improve sales and profits.

After prosperity for most of the 1990s, the U.S. economy slowed down and entered a recession in 2001. The downturn, which was relatively mild by historical standards, was characterized by a drop in the stock market, decreased business spending, and layoffs (especially in the technology sector). As you read this, what stage of the business cycle do you think the U.S. economy is in currently?

Inflation

A rise in the prices of goods and services represents **inflation**. When prices rise at a faster rate than personal incomes, consumer buying power declines. Inflation rates affect government policies, consumer psychology, and also marketing programs.

During the late 1970s and early 1980s, the U.S. experienced what for us was a high inflation rate—above 10%. But inflation dropped below 5% in the early 1990s and to one-half that rate since then.[8] Some countries around the world are plagued by extremely high rates of inflation—increases of 20, 30, or even 50% yearly.

Perhaps surprisingly, periods of declining prices—called *deflation*—or low inflation—sometimes termed *disinflation*—present challenges for marketers. In particular, it is very difficult for firms to raise prices because of consumer resistance. As a result, they need to cut their costs or else profits will evaporate. To do so, companies must take such steps as redesigning products to pare production costs and cutting back on coupons and other promotions that in effect lower prices.[9]

Interest Rates

Interest rates are another external economic factor that influences marketing programs. When interest rates are high, for instance, consumers tend not to make long-term purchases such as housing. Marketers sometimes offer below-market interest rates (a form of price cut) as a promotional device to increase business. Auto manufacturers use this tactic occasionally.

Competition

A company's competitive environment obviously is a major influence on its marketing programs. A firm generally faces three types of competition:

www.toysrus.com

- *Brand competition* comes from marketers of directly similar products. Despite an online partnership with Amazon.com, Toys " Я " Us has suffered as a result of growing competition from discounters such as Wal-Mart and Target.[10] VISA, MasterCard, Discover, and American Express compete internationally in the credit card field. And, yes, even the authors' three schools compete with each

A number of companies have developed software that helps firms manage their relationships with customers. Competitors engage in aggressive marketing to build their brands and gain a differential advantage. Here one competitor in this field, salesforce.com, states its case against a larger competitor, Siebel Systems.

www.salesforce.com

other for charitable contributions from business firms and from alumni who hold degrees from any pair of these schools.

- *Substitute products* satisfy the same need. During winter in Chicago, for example, the Bulls professional basketball team, the Blackhawks hockey team, the Lyric Opera, the Chicago Symphony Orchestra, and stores selling or renting videos all compete for the entertainment dollar. In recent years, a growing number of homeowners have been choosing wood flooring instead of carpeting, causing carpet sales to stagnate.[11]

- In a third, more general type of competition, *every company* is a rival for the customer's limited buying power. So the competition faced by the maker of Wilson tennis rackets might be several new pairs of Levi's Docker slacks, a Nissan repair bill, or a cash contribution to some charity.

Skillful marketing executives constantly monitor all aspects of competitors' marketing activities—their products, pricing, distribution systems, and promotional programs. Any enterprise strives to gain a **differential advantage,** which is any feature of an organization or brand that is perceived to be desirable and different from those of the competition. In contrast, this same enterprise has to work hard to avoid a differential *dis*advantage. A differential advantage attracts customers, whereas a differential disadvantage drives them away.

Social and Cultural Forces

The task facing marketing executives is becoming more complex because our sociocultural patterns—lifestyles, values, and beliefs—are changing much more quickly than they used to. Here are a few changes in **social and cultural forces** that have significant marketing implications.

How competitive do we want to be?

The North American Free Trade Agreement (NAFTA) was established in 1994 among the U.S. and its two largest trading partners, Canada and Mexico. Its purpose is to promote trade by phasing out all tariffs on goods between these countries by 2008. (Other trade agreements, linking countries in various regions, will be described in Chapter 3.)

Without tariffs, imports and exports compete on more equal footing. And, without the burden of having their goods taxed in another country, it is expected that the "best" producers (that is, those that are most efficient or effective) will rise to the top. The proponents of free trade and NAFTA assert that businesses, workers, and consumers all benefit from this increased competitiveness and efficiency. Businesses benefit through increased trade with the participating countries. Workers benefit as more jobs are created to support the increased trade. And consumers benefit from access to a wider range of competitively priced goods.

However, there is a significant issue of contention: job loss. Critics claimed that opening up borders would result in a "giant sucking sound," a term coined by NAFTA opponent H. Ross Perot. He argued that millions of jobs would move out of the U.S. to lower-wage countries. Critics further argued that other workers in the U.S. jobs would suffer from depressed wages because of the increased labor competitiveness.

NAFTA has been in effect now for about a decade, and the increase in trilateral trade has been dramatic, rising from $297 billion in 1993 to over $676 billion in 2001. Other specific outcomes include:

- U.S. exports to its two NAFTA partners increased 104% from 1993 to 2000, a growth rate twice what the U.S. experienced in other parts of the world.

- Mexico's average tariff on U.S. goods will fall from 10% pre-NAFTA to .5% in 2002.

- According to the U.S. trade representative, 900,000 jobs were created to support U.S. exports to Mexico and Canada since 1993, and the wages for these jobs were about 15% higher than the average American wage.

- Mexico's exports to the U.S. now account for 25% of its economy, almost double the pre-NAFTA level.

- About 1.75 million jobs have been created in Mexico since 1995 to support the NAFTA export boom.

- In addition to a trade boom with the U.S., two-way trade between Canada and Mexico increased from $5.6 billion in 1994 to $14.1 billion in 2000.

Of course, there are "two sides to every story," so NAFTA's critics would offer contrary statistics. In any event, it is likely that there will be more, not fewer, trade agreements in the foreseeable future. One possibility is expanding NAFTA to become an Americas and Caribbean Free Trade Agreement that would include countries throughout North, Central, and South America as well as the Caribbean region.

Sources: Roger Morton, "Missing Uncle in Between," *Transportation & Distribution*, March 2002, pp. 57–58; Office of the United States Trade Representative, "Joint Statement of the NAFTA Free Trade Commission Building on a North American Partnership," July 31, 2001, no pages given; Charles J. Whalen, "NAFTA's Scorecard: So Far, So Good," *Business Week*, July 9, 2001, pp. 54–56; Office of the United States Trade Representative, "NAFTA Partners Speed Up Elimination of Tariffs on $25 Billion in Trade," Jan. 9, 2001, no pages given; Robert P. Imbriani, "NAFTA: Past, Present and Future," *World Trade*, October 2001; pp. 24–28.

Concern about Natural Environment   Many Americans emphasize the *quality* of life rather than the *quantity* of goods consumed. The theme is "not more, but better." High on the list of what people consider integral to quality of life is the natural environment. Thus we hear concerns expressed about air and water pollution, holes in the ozone layer, acid rain, solid waste disposal, and the destruction of rainforests and other natural resources. These concerns raise the public's level of environmental consciousness.

A number of businesses noticed—and responded to—consumers' environmental consciousness. Specific efforts have focused on using resources efficiently and, in particular, conserving fossil fuels. To cite several examples:[12]

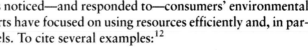

www.toyota.com/
html/shop

- Honda and Toyota introduced, respectively, Insight and Prius hybrid autos that combine traditional gas-powered engines with electric motors. In mid-2002,

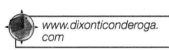

www.hondacars.com/ models

www.dixonticonderoga. com

Honda was the first automaker to receive certification to introduce a car powered by a hydrogen fuel cell.

- Dixon Ticonderoga developed a crayon using soybeans rather than paraffin wax, which is a petroleum-based product.
- Reclamere, Inc., collects old, unwanted electronic equipment such as computers and disposes of them, recycling any hazardous materials in an environmentally sound way.

By the mid-1990s, the proportion of consumers who bought environmentally friendly products approached one-half. However, relatively few consumers (29%, according to a recent survey) purchase a product strictly because it is environmentally friendly. A common mistake by companies is neglecting to mention the product's benefit to the consumer, not just to the environment.[13] To satisfy "green consumers," a product must also be competitive with alternatives on such factors as price, reliability, and convenience.

Many people who hold favorable attitudes toward environmentally friendly products do not purchase them. Further, and perhaps most perplexing, some products that consumers think are good for the environment—and that companies promote as being environmentally friendly—are more harmful than alternatives. For example, is a paper cup more environmentally friendly than a plastic cup? Actually, "a plastic cup takes half as much energy to make and results in 35% fewer pounds of toxic chemicals . . . than a paper cup does."[14]

Thus concern about the natural environment appears to be having a diminished impact on buying decisions in the U.S. However, environmental consciousness is greater in many other parts of the world—ranging from the European Union to Japan—than it is in the U.S.[15] As a result, a company must be environmentally sensitive in its marketing activities, especially product development, all around the world.

Changing Gender Roles   For many reasons (most notably the increasing number of two-income households), male–female roles related to families, jobs, recreation, and buying behavior are changing dramatically. Now, for example, more men shop for household necessities, particularly groceries, whereas more women purchase such products as cars, mutual funds, and business travel. In an interesting reversal, women are buying more athletic shoes then men are.[16] In contrast, a growing number of "house husbands" are staying home and assuming primary responsibility for child care and homemaking while their wives work full-time.

One of the most dramatic shifts in our culture has been the changing role of women. Over one-half of American women, including almost three-quarters of those in the 25 to 54 age group, are working outside the home today. According to a study by an advertising agency, women need to be segmented not just by age or employment status but also by other variables such as the father's degree of involvement in the family and the mother's interest in self-fulfillment.[17] Marketers obviously need different approaches to reach, and appeal to, women who are working full-time and/or raising children on their own versus stay-at-home mothers.

Women's attitudes toward careers, shopping, and products continue to evolve. Now, employed women are seeking a better balance between work and family. In turn, they are very interested in products that help them do that, especially by saving time. Thus working women represent a prime market for frozen and prepared food, more efficient appliances, and cleaning products and services such as house cleaning and fast food. Further, they are more likely to reward themselves by going to the beauty salon for a makeover or by buying a new CD player for their car. Seeing that, Johnson & Johnson has promoted its new Neutrogena makeup line with a "be free to spend more on yourself" theme.[18]

www.nike.com/
nikegoddess

Recognizing women's changing roles and growing economic power, many companies have developed new or altered marketing programs to reach the market of adult females. For example, for some time Nike and its competitors have been designing athletic shoes for the female market.[19] Still, some industries, such as consumer electronics and personal computers, have been slower to adapt to shifts in male–female buying patterns.[20]

Changing gender roles have affected men as well. Some men are doing more shopping and housework only because it's demanded of them, whereas other men hold more favorable attitudes toward the shift in gender roles. Research shows that "change adapters" are younger, better educated, and more affluent than the "change opposers." Marketers should be aware that these two groups of men buy different items and shop in different ways.[21]

A Premium on Time   Many Americans are working longer hours than their parents did. This has been especially true since the early 1990s, when many large companies downsized, thereby expanding the workload for the remaining employees. Further, a substantial number of people also consider it necessary to be involved in activities such as continuing education, personal fitness, and various kinds of professional or civic endeavors. In recent years, many people have also placed more emphasis on family activities.

Time-short people seek to gain more free time, if possible, and to maximize the benefit of whatever free time they have. From a marketing standpoint, this means many people, especially two-income households, with more income but less time are more willing to pay for convenience.

Every phase of a company's marketing program is affected by consumers' desire for convenience:

- Product planning should consider the opportunity to provide convenience related to a myriad of factors ranging from ease of preparation (with a food product, for example) to learning time (with a new computer, for example).

More and more women are paying attention to health and physical fitness. At the same time, many women are pressed for time as a result of their family and/or career responsibilities. Recognizing these trends, Yoplait designed a package that allows yogurt to be eaten on the go.

www.yoplaitexpresse.
com

- Distribution arrangements should offer convenient locations and store hours. Some convenience stores (such as 7-Eleven) and copy centers (such as Kinko's) responded by remaining open 24 hours a day. More and more shoppers are using the Internet to save time in purchasing a wide variety of consumer and business products. According to one study, the Internet now generates more than 5% of total sales of books, computers, event tickets, music and video products, toys, and travel.[22]

- Pricing policies should take into account the costs of providing the various kinds of convenience. A segment of convenience-conscious travelers who do not want to book their travel online has been willing to pay a special per-trip fee being charged by many travel agents. These fees have become essential revenue to travel agents as some airlines have cut their sales commissions.

- The company's commitment to saving time for consumers is a possible basis for promotion, perhaps creating a differential advantage for the firm.

MARKETING IN THE INFORMATION ECONOMY

If it's such a great service, why did Webvan fail?

Online retailing now generates over $75 billion in sales, with annual growth rates above 20%. This track record is impressive, considering that total retail sales typically increase by about 2% to 4% annually. Yet, despite heavy financial backing, aggressive marketing campaigns, and sometimes strong growth, numerous online merchants (also called e-tailers) have failed. Etoys, pets.com, and drugstore.com are just a few of the high-profile e-tailers that had to shut their virtual doors. They had trouble making a profit on each order, let alone recouping the massive investments made in technology, warehouses, and other business components.

Webvan, which offered next-day delivery of groceries to a consumer's residence, became one of the larger and heavily publicized online failures in mid-2001. The service appeared to be made for the steadily increasing number of working women who juggle both a career and homemaking as well as other consumers who place a premium on free time. With an extensive selection, easy-to-use website, convenient delivery times where customers picked a 30-minute delivery window, and free delivery for orders over $75, Webvan had many attractive features. Customers spent an average of $110 per order, purchased frequently, and praised the service to their friends.

Despite these positives, Webvan lost a whopping $830 million from its inception in April 1999 until July 2001, when the firm shut its doors and laid off over 2,000 employees. What happened, considering that

Webvan was quite satisfying to a segment of consumers? Some observers trace Webvan's failure to market factors, others point to cost factors. Evidently not enough consumers valued the service. Webvan also suffered from the expense of an enormous business operation, designed to support 26 markets, which required 4,000 orders per day per market to break even. The company invested in numerous warehouses (at $25 million apiece) as well as expensive technology. Thus Webvan needed—but didn't obtain—a very large customer base in order to cover its costly operations.

Webvan isn't the only online retailer to try to tackle the $450 billion grocery market. A few have had a measure of success. Netgrocer is still shipping groceries via FedEx, and Peapod was acquired by Royal Ahold USA, owner of chains such as Stop and Shop. Large supermarket chains are also experimenting with this type of service; Albertson's, Kroger, and Safeway all have home-delivery programs underway.

Under what circumstances, if any, could an online grocery store be successful?

Sources: Eric Hellweg, "Furniture, Food, and Other Tales of Dotcom Revival," *Business 2.0*, Apr. 17, 2002, at *www.business2.com/articles/web*; Nick Wingfield, "Online Retailing Still Growing Despite Some Losses Last Year," *The Wall Street Journal*, June 12, 2002, p. B4; Linda Himelstein, "Webvan Left the Basics on the Shelf," *Business Week*, July 23, 2001, p. 43; Mylene Mangalindan, "Webvan Joins List of Dot-Com Failures," *The Wall Street Journal*, July 10, 2001, pp. A3, A6; "Can Webvan Deliver, Financially Speaking?" *Internetnews.com*, Jan. 9, 2001; and Jean Sherman Chatzky, "You've Got Groceries," *USA Weekend*, Jan. 28–30, 2000, p. 4.

Physical Fitness and Health

Most demographic and economic segments of our society seem to reflect an increased interest in physical fitness and health. Participation in fitness activities from aerobics to yoga (we could not think of an activity beginning with a z) is on the rise. Fitness centers as well as manufacturers of exercise equipment have benefited from this trend. However, with an expanding number of competitors, there is no assurance of success for an individual firm.

Paralleling the fitness phenomenon, many Americans are changing their dietary habits. The public is constantly made aware of the relationship between diet, on the one hand, and heart disease and cancer, on the other. Consequently, a large number of consumers have become more interested in diets for weight loss; foods low in salt, additives, and cholesterol; and foods high in vitamins, minerals, and fiber content. (Some habits are hard to shake, however, so some of us still consume bacon double cheeseburgers.)

Companies need to recognize and respond to the public's growing interest in health. Thus, at the retailing level, most supermarkets now stock an assortment of health foods. At the manufacturing level, Campbell Soup Co. developed and introduced Intelligent Quisine, a line of nutrient-fortified foods. However, success of new products that try to address consumer needs is not assured. For example, even though many customers raved about the health benefits of Intelligent Quisine during market tests, the product failed because of insufficient sales. Further, initial sales of Frito-Lay's new Wow! line of fat-free salty snacks were hurt by reports that some consumers who ate them experienced digestive problems.[23]

Political and Legal Forces

Every company's conduct is influenced, often a great deal, by the political and legal processes in our society. The **political and legal forces** on marketing can be grouped into the following four categories:

- *Monetary and fiscal policies.* Marketing efforts are affected by the level of government spending, the money supply, and tax legislation.

- *Social legislation and regulations.* Legislation affecting the environment—antipollution laws, for example—and regulations set by the Environmental Protection Agency fall into this category.

- *Governmental relationships with industries.* Here we find subsidies in agriculture, shipbuilding, passenger rail transportation, and other industries. Tariffs and import quotas also affect specific industries. Government *deregulation* continues to have an effect on financial institutions and public utilities (such as electric and natural gas suppliers) as well as on the telecommunications and transportation industries.

- *Legislation related specifically to marketing.* Marketing executives do not have to be lawyers, but they should know something about laws affecting marketing—why they were passed, their main provisions, and current ground rules set by the courts and regulatory agencies for administering them.

These laws, which are summarized in Table 2.2, are designed either to regulate competition or to protect consumers. Note that there has been very little new legislation affecting marketing since 1980. However, court decisions and agency rulings based on these laws are issued quite frequently. To forestall added legislation, individual companies and perhaps even entire industries sometimes respond to government signals and modify troublesome business practices.

Occasionally, a company or even a group of companies is charged with violating a long-standing law. For example, the American Booksellers Association, on behalf of independent bookstores around the U.S., filed suits alleging that publishers give unfair discounts to giant chains ranging from Barnes & Noble to Sam's Club. The

To Regulate Competition

1. Sherman Antitrust Act (1890). Prohibits monopolies and combinations in restraint of trade.
2. Federal Trade Commission (FTC) Act (1914). Prohibits unfair competition.
3. Clayton Antitrust Act (1914). Regulates several activities, notably price discrimination.
4. State Unfair Trade Practices Acts (1930s). Prohibit "loss-leader" pricing (selling below cost). Laws still in effect in about half the states.
5. Robinson-Patman Act (1936). Amends the Clayton Act by strengthening the prohibition of price discrimination. Regulates price discounts and allowances.
6. Wheeler-Lea Act (1938). Amends the FTC Act; broadens and strengthens regulation of unfair or deceptive competition.
7. Lanham Trademark Act (1946). Regulates brands and trademarks.
8. Consumer Goods Pricing Act (1975). Repeals *federal* laws supporting *state* fair-trade laws. Does away with state laws allowing manufacturers to set retail prices.
9. Various *deregulation* laws pertaining to specific industries:
   a) Natural Gas Policy Act (1978)
   b) Airline Deregulation Act (1978)
   c) Motor Carrier Act (1980)
   d) Staggers Rail Act (1980)
   e) Depository Institutions Act (1981)
   f) Drug Price Competition and Patent Restoration Act (1984)

To Protect Consumers

1. Pure Food and Drug Act (1906). Regulates labeling of food and drugs and prohibits manufacture or marketing of adulterated food or drugs. Amended in 1938 by Food, Drug, and Cosmetics Act.
2. Automobile Information Disclosure Act (1958). Requires manufacturers to post suggested retail prices on new passenger vehicles.
3. Kefauver-Harris Drug Amendments (1962). Requires that drugs be labeled with their generic names, new drugs be pretested, and new drugs get approval of the Food and Drug Administration before being marketed.
4. National Traffic and Motor Vehicle Safety Act (1966). Provides safety standards for tires and autos.
5. Fair Packaging and Labeling Act (1966). Regulates packaging and labeling.
6. Cigarette Labeling and Advertising Acts (1966, 1969). Require manufacturers to label cigarettes as being hazardous to health and prohibit TV advertising of cigarettes.
7. Consumer Credit Protection Act (1968). The "truth in lending" law that requires full disclosure of interest rates and other financing charges on loans and credit purchases.
8. Consumer Product Safety Act (1972). Establishes the Consumer Product Safety Commission with broad powers to limit or even halt the marketing of products ruled unsafe by the commission.
9. Consumer Product Warranty Act (1975). Increases consumers' rights and sellers' responsibilities under product warranties.
10. FTC Improvement Act (1980). Limits the power of the Federal Trade Commission to set and enforce industry trade regulations. In effect, reverses the trend toward more FTC protection of consumers.
11. Nutritional Labeling and Education Act (1990). Requires that detailed nutritional information be stated on labels of most food products.
12. Children's Television Act (1990). Limits the number of minutes of advertising that can be shown on programs designed for children.

independents claimed that such discounts put small bookstores at a competitive disadvantage and violate antitrust laws.[24]

Up to this point, our discussion of political and legal forces affecting marketing has dealt essentially with the activities of the *federal* government. However, there are also strong political and legal influences at the *state and local* levels. For instance, many firms' marketing programs are affected by zoning requirements, interest-rate regulations, state and local taxes, prohibitions against unsubstantiated environmental claims, and laws affecting door-to-door selling. All of these have been put in place by numerous states and municipalities.

Technology

Technology has a tremendous impact on our lifestyles, our consumption patterns, and our economic well-being. Just think of the effect of technological developments such as the airplane, plastics, television, computers, antibiotics, lasers, and—of course—video games. Except perhaps for the airplane, all these technologies reached their major markets in your lifetime or your parents' lifetime. Think how your life in the future might be affected by cures for the common cold, development of energy sources to replace fossil fuels, low-cost methods for making ocean water drinkable, or even commercial travel to the moon.

Technological breakthroughs can affect markets in three ways:

- By starting entirely new industries, as computers, lasers, and robots have done.
- By radically altering, or virtually destroying, existing industries. When it first came out, television crippled the radio and movie industries. And computers all

Technological advances sometimes lead to products that have features not previously available. In this case, Honda developed a "hybrid" automobile powered by a combination of a gasoline engine and an electric motor. The new model has a particular appeal to environmentally conscious consumers.

It's an environmental movement all by itself.

How many cars does it take to change the world? Just one, perhaps. Especially if it's the Insight from Honda, America's first gasoline-electric hybrid automobile.

Nothing short of an engineering breakthrough, the Insight achieves a terrific 68 miles per gallon on the highway, 61 miles per gallon in the city, and an astounding 700-mile range on one tank of fuel.* How? By combining an efficient three-cylinder gasoline engine with an electric motor powered by nickel-metal hydride batteries that never need to be plugged in. Then add a world-class aerodynamic design, and an extremely lightweight body, and you have the ultra-low-emission† Insight.

It's the culmination of years of research and development into lighter, cleaner, more efficient automobiles. In other words, technology with a conscience. Then again, what else would you expect from a car powered by Honda?

HONDA
The power of dreams:

*Mileage figures based on EPA estimates for Insight with manual transmission. Actual mileage may vary. Range based on EPA highway mileage. †California Air Resources Board ULEV-certified for California and some Northeastern states. LEV-certified in rest of country. © 2001 American Honda Motor Co., Inc. honda.com but replaced typewriters, sending Smith Corona Corp. into bankruptcy protection in the mid-1990s.

- By stimulating markets and industries not related to the new technology. New home appliances and microwavable foods give people additional time in which to engage in other activities.

Advances in technology also affect how marketing is carried out. For example, breakthroughs in communications now permit people and organizations to transact business from almost any location at any time of the day. Since the late 1990s, the Internet has had a profound effect on millions of Americans as well as countless enterprises.

We should also note that technology is a mixed blessing in some ways. A new technology may improve our lives in one area while creating environmental and social problems in other areas. Television and video games provide built-in child care, but they are criticized for reducing family discussions and reading by children. The automobile is a convenient form of personal transportation, but it also creates traffic jams and air pollution. In turn, technology is expected to solve some problems it is criticized for having caused (air pollution, for example).

External Microenvironment

Three additional environmental forces are external to an organization and affect its marketing activities. These are the firm's market, suppliers, and marketing intermediaries. They represent *microenvironmental forces* for a company (see Figure 2.2). Dealing effectively with them is critical to business success. Recognizing that, many companies are using customer relationship management software to keep track of their customers' buying activities and to communicate better with them.[25]

Although all three of these external forces are generally uncontrollable, they can be influenced in some situations. As such, they are different than the *macro*environmental forces discussed previously. A marketing organization, for example, may be able to exert pressure on its suppliers or middlemen. And, through its advertising, a firm should have some influence on its market.

FIGURE 2.2

External Microenvironment of a Company's Marketing Program.

The arrows reflect the interrelationships—flows of products, payments, information, and influence—between the company and its external environment.

The Market

The market really is what marketing is all about—how to reach it and serve it profitably and in a socially responsible manner. The market should be the focus of all marketing decisions in an organization. But just what is a market? A *market* may be defined as a place where buyers and sellers meet, goods or services are offered for sale, and transfers of ownership occur. A *market* may also be defined as the demand made by a certain group of potential buyers for a good or service. For instance, there is a farm *market* for petroleum products.

These definitions are not sufficiently precise to be useful to us here. For marketing purposes, we define a **market** as people or organizations with needs to satisfy, money to spend, and the willingness to spend it. Thus, in marketing any given good or service, three specific factors need to be considered:

- People or organizations with needs,
- Their purchasing power, *and*
- Their buying behavior.

When we consider *needs,* we do so from the perspective of the dictionary definition of need as the lack of anything that is required, desired, or useful. We do not limit needs to the physiological requirements of food, clothing, and shelter essential for survival. Recall from Chapter 1 that the words *needs* and *wants* are used interchangeably in this text.

Suppliers

A business cannot sell a product without being able to make or buy it. That's why the people or firms that supply the goods or services required by a producer to make what it sells are critical to marketing success. So too are the firms that provide the merchandise a wholesaler or retailer resells. And that's why we consider a firm's **suppliers** a vital part of its marketing environment.

Marketing executives often are not concerned enough with the supply side of marketing. However, when shortages occur, they recognize the need for cooperative relationships with suppliers. Further, as online sales rise, Internet companies are paying much more attention to sources of supply and also the methods by which orders will be processed and delivered to buyers.

Marketing Intermediaries

Marketing intermediaries are independent business organizations that directly aid in the flow of goods and services between a marketing organization and its markets. There are two types of intermediaries: (1) the firms we call *middlemen*—wholesalers and retailers, and (2) various *facilitating organizations* furnishing such services as transportation, warehousing, and financing that are needed to complete exchanges between buyers and sellers. These intermediaries operate between a company and its markets and between a company and its suppliers. Thus they are part of what we call *channels of distribution.*

In some cases, it may be more efficient for a company to not use marketing intermediaries. A producer can deal *directly* with its suppliers or sell *directly* to its customers and do its own shipping, financing, and so on. But marketing intermediaries are specialists in their respective fields. They often do a better job at a lower cost than the marketing organization can do by itself.

Collectively, the company, its suppliers, and its intermediaries (both middlemen and facilitating organizations) comprise a **value chain.** That is, all of these enterprises—each in its own way—perform activities to add value to the product that is eventually bought by an individual or an organization. It's relatively easy to comprehend the value added by a manufacturer when it combines various materials to form a finished product. But it's more difficult to detect the value added by other members of the value chain. For example, consider a financial institution that agrees to provide credit to consumers who buy vehicles from an auto dealership. This facilitating organization has added value to the product, essentially by making it easier for a prospective buyer to make a purchase.

Organization's Internal Environment

An organization's marketing effort is also shaped by *internal* forces that are controllable by management. As shown in Figure 2.3, these internal influences include a firm's production, financial, and personnel activities. If the Colgate-Palmolive Co. is considering adding a new brand of soap, for example, it must determine whether existing production facilities and expertise can be used. If the new product requires a new plant or machinery, financial capability enters the picture. Although this example involves a manufacturer, we are viewing *production* in a broad sense, referring to the various activities that create the set of products an organization offers to its markets. Therefore, all concerns—retailers, wholesalers, service firms, and not-for-profit organizations—engage in production, in this broad sense.

Other nonmarketing forces are the company's location, its research and development (R&D) strength, and the overall image the firm projects to the public. For a manufacturer, plant location often determines the geographic limits of the company's market, particularly if transportation costs are high or its products are perishable. For a middleman, location of a store (in the case of a retailer) or a warehouse (in the

FIGURE 2.3

Internal Environment Affecting a Company's Marketing Activities.

A company's internal, nonmarketing resources influence and support its marketing program.

case of a wholesaler) affects the number of customers drawn to the firm as well as its operating expenses. Of course, online retailers may not have to worry about the location of physical stores, but they still need to be concerned about the location of warehouses. The R&D factor may determine whether a firm will lead or follow in its industry. An organization's image has an impact on its ability to attract capital, employees, and customers.

Another consideration in a firm's internal environment is the need to coordinate marketing and nonmarketing activities. Sometimes this can be difficult because of conflicts in goals and executive personalities. Production people, for example, like to see long production runs of standardized items. However, marketing executives may want a variety of models, sizes, and colors to satisfy different market segments. Financial executives typically want tighter credit and expense limits than the marketing people consider necessary to be competitive.

To wrap up our discussion of the marketing environment, Figure 2.4 shows how all environmental forces combine to shape an organization's marketing program. Within the framework of these constraints, management should develop a marketing program to satisfy the needs of its markets.

The Entire Operating Environment for a Company's Marketing Program.

Summary

Various environmental forces influence an organization's marketing activities. Some are external to the firm and are largely uncontrollable by the organization. Other forces are within the firm and are generally controllable by management. Successful marketing requires that a company develop and implement marketing programs that take into account its environment. To start with, management should set up a system for environmental monitoring—the process of gathering and evaluating environmental information.

Six broad variables constitute the external environment that generally cannot be controlled by an organization. Demographic factors are one of these macro influences. Another is economic conditions such as the business cycle, inflation, and interest rates. Management also must be aware of the various types of competition and the competitive structure within which its firm operates. Social and cultural forces, such as changes in lifestyles, values, and beliefs, must be taken into account as marketing programs are developed. Four noteworthy sociocultural trends are the greening of America, changing gender roles, a greater premium on time, and added emphasis on physical fitness and health. Political and legal forces, ranging from monetary and fiscal policies to legislation, also affect marketing. As with the other external macroenvironmental influences, technology can present both opportunities and challenges for marketers.

Another set of environmental factors—suppliers, marketing intermediaries, and the market itself—is also external to the firm. But these forces can be controlled to some extent by the firm. Although all three of these external forces are generally uncontrollable, they can be influenced in some situations. As such, these *micro*environmental forces are different from *macro*environmental forces such as economic conditions and technology.

At the same time, a set of nonmarketing resources *within* the firm—production facilities, personnel, finances, location, research and development, and company image—affects its marketing effort. These variables generally are controllable by management.

More about XM Satellite Radio

XM's major competitor is Sirius Satellite Radio, based in New York City. Sirius entered the market later than XM because of technical problems and a management shake-up that included the resignation of its CEO. In its first half year of operation, Sirius signed up fewer than 10,000 subscribers. Although XM got off to a faster start, Sirius is well-equipped to give the "first mover" a run for its money. In fact, Sirius's goal is to reach profitability with 2 million subscribers by 2005.

Sirius relies on three satellites, launched from a once-secret Soviet installation in Kazakhstan. Sirius's satellites orbit a little higher in the sky than XM's, but have fewer repeaters. XM says this makes a difference in sound quality; Sirius isn't commenting. The newcomer offers about the same number of channels as XM, but one-half of them are music programs and the other one-half are talk shows of various kinds. Sirius's carmaker deals are with BMW, Ford, and DaimlerChrysler.

Sirius is asking consumers to pay a higher price, $13 a month compared with XM's $10, but its programs will have no advertising at all. As to whether consumers will pay for what they can get for free, the CEO of Sirius observed, "TV is free, but 70% of consumers choose to pay for cable—and another 10% pay for satellite TV." Thus a prerequisite for success for satellite radio is to offer consumers more quantity and/or quality of radio programming than they can receive for free, which would emulate the approach used by both cable and satellite TV.

Receivers for each of the competing satellite–radio systems are not compatible with one another, and installation costs are high enough to make switching unlikely. So unlike traditional radio stations, each satellite radio firm will have to focus its efforts on winning the customer the first time out. But the market potential—revenues of up to $10 *billion* according to one analyst—is so great that the competition between Sirius and XM is likely to be aggressive and expensive.[26]

1. Does satellite radio coincide with, or run counter to, major demographic, social, and cultural trends in the U.S.?

2. What consumer needs does satellite radio fill?

3. Which firm do you think has a competitive advantage, and why?

Key Terms and Concepts

Environmental monitoring (30)
Demographics (32)
Baby boomers (34)
Generation X (34)
Generation Y (34)
Economic environment (34)

Business cycle (35)
Inflation (35)
Interest rates (35)
Differential advantage (36)
Social and cultural forces (36)
Political and legal forces (41)

Technology (43)
Market (45)
Suppliers (45)
Marketing intermediaries (45)
Value chain (46)

Questions and Problems

1. In areas where the number of college-age students is still declining, what marketing measures should a school take to adjust to this trend?

2. For each of the following companies, give some examples of how its marketing program is likely to differ during periods of prosperity as contrasted with periods of recession:
   a. Schwinn bicycles
   b. Williams-Sonoma.com (the online arm of the home-furnishings retailer)
   c. General Cinema movie theaters
   d. Salvation Army

3. What would be the likely effect of high interest rates on the market for the following goods or services?
   a. Swatch watches
   b. Building materials
   c. Nursery school programs

4. Explain the three types of competition faced by a company. What marketing strategies or programs would you recommend to meet each type?

5. Name three U.S.-manufactured products you think would be highly acceptable to "green consumers" in European markets. Name three products you think would be environmentally unacceptable.

6. Give some examples of how the changing role of women has been reflected in American marketing.

7. What are some marketing implications of the increasing public interest in physical fitness and health?

8. Using examples other than those in this chapter, explain how a firm's marketing can be influenced by the environmental factor of technology.

9. Specify some external macroenvironmental forces affecting the marketing programs of:
   a. Pizza Hut
   b. Your school
   c. Drugstore.com
   d. Clairol (hair-care products)

10. Other than technology, which macroenvironmental forces are particularly important to Internet companies?

11. Explain how each of the following resources within a company might influence its marketing program:
    a. Plant or store location
    b. Company image
    c. Financial resources
    d. Personnel capabilities

Interactive Marketing Exercises

1. Identify two controversial social or cultural issues in the community where your school is located, and explain their impact on firms that market in the community.

2. After doing some "Net surfing," identify two product categories (other than those mentioned in the chapter) that you believe can be sold well over the Internet. Then identify two categories that you think that will be hard to sell online.

"Through its steady adherence to free play, one of the company's core values, Lego managed never to lose sight of its fundamental mission—use toys to stretch the imagination."

Lego Is Still Playing, but Have the Rules Changed?

Everyone probably remembers playing with Lego bricks, those simple plastic blocks in primary colors that interlock to become almost anything a child could imagine them to be, whether it was an airplane, a castle, or a schoolhouse. Appropriately enough, the company that makes Legos has a nearly storylike history.

Begun by a carpenter more than 70 years ago in the Danish village of Billund, still the location of its world headquarters, Lego sold its first red brick in 1949, refined and patented its product in 1958, and hasn't changed so much as the recipe for the plastic in almost 40 years. That consistent approach to its product is also the reason that every toy Lego offers still requires a child's input to make it come alive.

"Free play" is an open-ended activity that requires children to use imagination to create a play scenario. It's what Legos are all about, and it is different from the directed play that typifies character dolls, licensed toys from movies and TV, and video games that all come with a prewritten "script." Through its steady adherence to free play, one of the company's core values, Lego managed never to lose sight of its fundamental mission—use toys to stretch the imagination. Evidence that the toy meets a universally recognized childhood need for unfettered play is suggested by the fact that global sales of Lego bricks have passed the *320 billion* mark, which works out to more than 50 bricks for each person on earth!

The firm has held true to other values from its past. New Legos won't make your old ones obsolete; for instance, bricks manufactured today interlock smoothly with bricks from the 1970s, and the scale and colors are all compatible. The bricks simply don't break or wear out. Nor are 20th-century weapons to be found in Lego's catalog of items, except for a special kit for building a World War I Sopwith Camel airplane. Even simple items such as those given away in McDonald's Happy Meals require some construction to encourage free play. And there still is no "right" or "wrong" way to assemble the classic blocks. Their flexibility has been earning Legos the approval of educational experts for years.

The business itself has kept things simple, too. Peter Eio, who retired as the company's U.S. head after 20 years with Lego, recalls that during the four job interviews that preceded his hiring, the word *profit* was never mentioned. Godtfred Christiansen, the owner at the time and father of the present CEO, smiled at Eio. "If we do all things right, the profit will come," he said.

But is that formula still working for this venerable Danish firm with simple values? Profits peaked in 1996 and fell sharply in 1997. In 1998 Lego survived a losing year, and in the following year it let 1,000 people go, the first big layoff in its history. Sales were off again, disastrously, in 2000. Has the entertainment economy, with its focus on television, computers, and video games,

 www.lego.com

changed childhood and the concept of play enough to make Lego's values a thing of the past?

Analysts worry, too, that Lego has confused growth with success. The company expanded dramatically in the 1980s, but it was simply expanding its conservative products worldwide, not creating many innovative new ones. Although it's true that a British association of toy retailers and *Forbes* and *Fortune* magazines all called Lego "the toy of the twentieth century," and its brand is the seventh most powerful worldwide among families with children, the simple blocks may not be flashy enough in a new world where nearly 50% of all toys are licensed.

Some newer Lego products are less committed to free play. Recent block sets are elaborate kits that come with instructions for making arctic adventures and jungle scenes with hundreds of interlocking pieces. Others feature licensed characters and their stories, such as Harry Potter, Winnie the Pooh, and most notably *Star Wars*, which became the biggest seller in the company's history with 14 different themed kits. And in 1998, Lego developed programmable Lego bricks for use with the computer. The well-designed software that drives the product called MindStorms helps the user design not only the appearance of the monster, animal, or robot but also its behavior. There are even Legoland theme parks, the first of them right next to company headquarters in Billund. And ambitious new marketing plans and partnerships with software and game producers have been formed.[1]

Lego captured a global market before many other firms had even thought about a global strategy. How can it regain its leadership in the world of play?

Lego's sustained international marketing performance is certainly impressive. But as the opening case indicates, even experienced firms such as Lego face unfamiliar challenges when they venture beyond their domestic borders. Something as basic as the marketing mix—the plans for the product, along with pricing, distribution, and promotion programs—may be more difficult in a foreign market. Complicating factors such as language, culture, business practices, and government restrictions affect the process. As a result, "going international" involves many unique strategic and tactical considerations. Given the differences from domestic marketing, we need to examine international marketing in some detail.

Chapter Goals

After studying this chapter, you should be able to explain:

- The significance of international marketing to firms and countries.
- What makes foreign markets attractive.
- Challenges in designing marketing strategies for international markets.
- Alternative organizational structures for operating in foreign markets.
- Marketing-mix issues and some concepts unique to international marketing such as countertrade and gray marketing.

The Significance of International Trade

International trade is not a new phenomenon. There is evidence that it was an important part of the lives of many ancient civilizations, including the Etruscans, Egyptians, and the Chinese. The economic reasons for international trade are:

- *Access to products otherwise unavailable.* A large number of goods, including many foodstuffs, spices, and even types of wood, are available only in certain parts of the world. Without foreign trade, consumers in other regions could not experience these products.

- *Comparative advantage.* Some countries possess unique natural or human resources that give them an edge when it comes to producing particular products. This factor, for example, explains South Africa's dominance in diamonds, and the ability of developing Asian and Central American countries with low-wage rates to compete successfully in products assembled by hand. By specializing where it has a comparative advantage and trading for other products, a country maximizes its economic prosperity.

International trade also has political and social implications. In fact, historians give trade much of the credit for the peace and well-being that existed for centuries in the far-flung Roman Empire. In today's world, the interaction fostered by trade reduces social barriers and prejudices and increases tolerance.

To get an idea of how significant international marketing has become, consider that in 2000 world exports had a value of more than $7.6 *trillion.* As the total volume suggests, trade is critical to the economies of many countries. For example, each year the U.S. exports an amount equal to about 10% of what it produces, whereas Germany and France each export an amount equal to 25% of what they produce. However, trade does not have the same impact on all countries. China, with 1.2 billion people had exports of $184 billion in 2000. In the same year, Japan with just one-tenth as many people exported more than twice as much.[2] The differences among countries are further illustrated in Table 3.1, which shows the proportion of its total domestic output each exports.

Countries use trade to hasten their economic growth. The underdeveloped countries of the world accounted for over 25% of all exports in 2000, a far higher proportion than their share of world productivity. By engaging in trade these countries provide jobs and income for their citizens.

What are the prospects for international business? At both the national and individual firm levels, international trade is important to the health of a nation. However, the relationship between how much a country imports and how much it exports has significant implications. To appreciate this, we need to examine the concepts of balance of payments and balance of trade, and we will use the U.S. as an example.

www.imf.org

TABLE 3.1   Role of Export Trade in Selected Countries

Country	Exports as a % of Gross Domestic Product	
	1992	2001
Canada	26%	43%
S. Korea	28	43
Mexico	17	28
United Kingdom	23	27
Brazil	7	13
Japan	10	11
United States	10	11

Source: *International Financial Statistics Yearbook,* International Monetary Fund, Washington, DC, 2002, www.imf.org.

This young woman is a member of the Huli tribe in the highlands of Paupau, New Guinea. Her tribe, which now numbers about 65,000, had virtually no contact with the outside world until the 1940s. As you can see from this photo, Pepsi, as well as many other Western brands, has reached some of the most remote places on earth.

A country's **balance of payments** is an accounting record of all its transactions with all the other nations of the world. The major categories of expenditures and income in a country's balance of payments are military and foreign aid, investments abroad, profits returned on foreign investments, tourism, and its trade balance. These terms are self-explanatory except for a country's **trade balance,** which is the difference between what it exports and what it imports. When exports exceed imports, the balance is positive and the country is said to have a trade *surplus.* When imports exceed exports, the balance is negative and the country has a trade *deficit.*

By definition, a country's balance of payments must balance. That is, the outflow of wealth must equal the inflow. So, for example, if the foreign tourism expenditures of a country's citizens (outflow) exceed the expenditures of tourists visiting the country (inflow), the difference must be made up by one of the other balance-of-payment categories. What happens if there is not enough surplus in the other categories to offset a deficit? Then the country must borrow to make up the difference, and that is where a problem lies. If a country's debt grows, it is faced with pressure to raise taxes and lower government spending.

Historically, the U.S. has had large expenditures in four areas that significantly affect the balance of payments: (1) military forces stationed overseas, (2) foreign aid, (3) oil imports, and (4) American tourist travel abroad. To offset these expenditures and maintain equilibrium in the U.S. balance of payments, American businesses had to generate a substantial trade surplus. That is, exports of goods and services had to greatly exceed imports. Up to about 1970, this was not a problem because the U.S. generally had a positive balance of trade. Then the balance declined to the point where it was not sufficient to offset the expenditures abroad.

Through most of the 1980s, the U.S. was in an unfavorable trade position with large trade deficits. The relationship between imports and exports improved in the late 1980s and early 1990s, with the deficit reaching a low of $31 billion in 1991, but the balance was consistently unfavorable. Since then the deficit has steadily increased, amounting to $370 billion in 2000, more than doubling in three years.[3] Large trade deficits have a direct negative effect on jobs, investment, and growth.

Several factors affect a country's balance of trade. In the case of the U.S., the most significant are:

- *Consumer preferences.* U.S. consumers have come to know and buy many imported products.
- *Technology.* The "technology gap" between the U.S. and other major industrial countries is narrowing or has disappeared entirely, so the U.S. does not enjoy the same technology advantage it once did.
- *Trade barriers.* Some countries have barriers that severely limit, or entirely prohibit, the importation of products that might compete with their domestic output.
- *Subsidized industries.* Some foreign governments aid their export trade more than the U.S. These subsidies often enable the producers to sell their products in foreign markets at prices lower than the prices of domestic producers.

- *Tax structure.* Some countries derive substantial revenue from indirect taxes, such as a value-added tax, which are often rebated when products are exported. As a result, companies in these countries have an added incentive to seek markets abroad.
- *Relative marketing capabilities.* Firms worldwide have narrowed the gap between their marketing skills and those of the more developed nations.

The foreign trade balance in the U.S. has changed from a bright spot to a problem. Imports probably will remain high because of the factors described above. Consequently, the U.S. must continue to expand its exports by:

- Offsetting higher labor costs with improved productivity.
- Adapting marketing efforts to foreign cultures to improve the attractiveness of products.
- Investing in the future by taking a longer-range view than currently is typical among most U.S. firms.

The Attraction of International Marketing

International trade describes any type of business that firms carry out beyond their domestic borders. More specific to our interests, **international marketing** takes place when an organization actively markets its products in two or more countries. For many U.S. companies, international markets account for a substantial share of their operations. For example, IBM and Boeing regularly get about half their annual sales revenues from outside the U.S. Likewise, many non–U.S. companies, such as Sony, Bic, Gucci, Toyota, Lipton, Shell Oil, and adidas, rely heavily on the U.S. market.

A firm moves beyond its domestic market into international trade for several possible reasons:

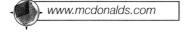

- *Potential demand in foreign markets.* There is a strong demand for a wide variety of products all over the world. Among the developing as well as the developed nations of the world, there is a demand for business products such as machine tools, construction equipment, and computers. As a result, firms can often take advantage of their specialized skills in manufacturing or distribution in new regions. For example, Hewlett-Packard, which began in 1938 manufacturing an electronic instrument to test sound equipment, now markets an array of technology goods and services to over a billion customers in 162 countries.
- *Saturation of domestic markets.* Firms—even those without international experience—look to foreign markets when domestic demand plateaus. As attractive domestic locations became harder to find in the 1970s, McDonald's opened an increasing number of outlets overseas. Now half the firm's 30,000 restaurants are outside the U.S., and expansion plans are almost exclusively focused abroad.
- *Customer expectations.* Often a firm follows its domestic customers abroad. For example, many U.S. banks found it necessary to establish branches in foreign countries because their customers were doing business internationally. Because Delco Remy, a U.S. supplier of automotive electrical equipment, finds it efficient to locate its manufacturing near automakers, it now has plants all over the world.

MARKETING IN THE INFORMATION ECONOMY

How does the Internet improve global marketing operations?

Much of the marketing potential of the Internet is managing information "behind the scenes" where consumers never see it.

Nestlé, the world's largest food and beverage company, with annual sales over $50 billion and operations around the world, is using the Internet to organize the massive amount of information necessary to run its businesses. The system will allow Nestlé employees, the company's suppliers, and its retail customers access to information that will lower costs and speed up the movement of products. For example, with over 500 production plants, Nestlé does not know how much it buys from various suppliers around the

world. With its new system, its buyers of raw materials and supplies will be able to find out instantly where supplies are available, their quality, the price, and the delivery time. Other improvements will result from retailers placing orders directly over a website, monitoring and controlling inventories on the basis of retailers' sales, and speeding up deliveries to reduce shortages and stock-outs. When fully operational, the system is expected to produce savings of nearly $2 billion a year.

Sources: William Echikson, "Nestle: An Elephant Dances," *Business Week e.Biz*, Dec. 11, 2000, pp. EB44+; "IBM Technology to Be Integral Partner in Nestlé's Landmark Global Business Transformation," IBM news release, Canadian Corporate News, March 7, 2002.

Strategic Planning for International Marketing

Firms that have been very successful in domestic marketing have no assurance whatsoever that their success will be duplicated in foreign markets. Satisfactory performance overseas is based on (1) understanding the environment of a foreign market and (2) gauging which domestic management practices and marketing-mix elements should be transferred directly to foreign markets, which ones modified, and which ones not used at all.

A **global strategy** is one in which essentially the same marketing program is employed around the world. Because it is very cost efficient, a global strategy is an ideal situation. FedEx is an example of a company that has globalized its strategy. According to a senior marketing executive, "We're the largest all-cargo carrier in the world, and as a result we've got a pretty good formula for attacking any market whether it's China or Japan or Germany, it really doesn't make any difference."[4]

In consumer product marketing, a global strategy is often more difficult to accomplish because of social and cultural differences. However, some firms have at least approached a global strategy. Dove, developed in 1957 and positioned by Unilever as a "beauty bar" rather than as a soap because it contains moisturizers, is marketed in essentially the same way in over 80 countries around the world.

www.unilever.com

When large geographic areas have much in common, but are quite distinct from other regions because of factors such as climate, custom, or taste, a firm might develop a **regional strategy.** This is what Coca-Cola has done in beverages. On its website

www.cocacola.com

Coca-Cola lists nearly 300 different beverage brands that it markets around the world. Among the most intriguing are Juggy, Samurai, North Neck, and Love Body!

In some cases markets differ so much that a firm must develop customized marketing programs for each area it enters. When a firm employs a **local strategy,** there are relatively few marketing-mix dimensions that are transferred from one market to another. Surprisingly, that can be the case even for a commodity. To market its packaged flour in India, Pillsbury had to change the ingredients (for local taste), the package size and packaging material (because of the climate), the advertising (to demonstrate local uses), and the distribution (because small retail stores carry little inventory).[5] Even in countries with quite similar cultures such as the U.S. and the United Kingdom, the flour differs in texture and additives.

To develop a strategic plan, a firm must examine the operating environment that exists in a foreign market. Several of the most important dimensions of the environment are described below.

Analysis of the Environment

Throughout the world, market demand is determined by the number of people, the ability to buy, and buying behavior. Also, human wants and needs have a universal similarity. People need food, clothing, and shelter. They seek a better quality of life in terms of lighter workloads, more leisure time, and social recognition and acceptance. But at about this point, the similarities in foreign and domestic markets seem to end, and the differences in culture, the economic environment, and political and legal forces must be considered.

Social and Cultural Forces

Culture is a set of shared values passed down from generation to generation in a society. These values determine what is socially acceptable behavior. Some of the many cultural elements that can influence a company's marketing program are described below.

Family. The priorities of families and the relationships among family members with regard to purchasing and consumption vary considerably from culture to culture. In some countries a mother would always accompany a teenager shopping for clothes, whereas in other cultures shopping "with Mom" would be avoided at all costs. In China, where one-child families are the norm, parents typically spend one-third to one-half of their disposable incomes on their children. The family situations in each country may require a distinctive type of promotion, and perhaps even different types of products.

Customs and Behavior. Some customary behavior defies explanation. For example, when it comes to medication, red is the preferred color of pills among Americans, whereas English and Dutch consumers prefer white pills. Other differences among cultures such as in eating behavior, personal space, physical contact, the degree of

The celebration of Quinceanera on a young woman's 15th birthday marking her transition from child to adult is an important custom in the Hispanic community. It involves a religious ceremony and a party with family and friends. It also provides a marketing opportunity for retailers who understand the event.

formality in social and business interactions, gift giving, and the use of gestures may be easier to anticipate but may still trip up the unwary. Wal-Mart's acquisition of the Japanese supermarket group Seiyu, poses some significant cultural challenges for the firm.[6] Japanese consumers are more sensitive than Americans to the way products are presented. Individually wrapped items and attractive packaging are much more common in Japan. As opposed to their American counterparts who eat a lot of processed foods, Japanese consumers prefer fresh food. And Japanese consumers tend to visit stores more frequently and buy in small quantities. All of these differences work against the operating efficiencies of standardization and volume that Wal-Mart has developed in its domestic operation. It remains to be seen what adjustments the firm will have to make in order to duplicate its success in the U.S.

Education.   The educational level in a country affects the literacy rate, which in turn influences advertising, branding, and labeling. The brand mark may become the dominant marketing feature if potential customers cannot read and must recognize the article by the picture on the label.

Language Differences.   Language differences pose many problems in international marketing, from being one of the primary explanations for the high failure rate of cross-border mergers to making it difficult to complete customs forms. Language is often the hurdle that discourages firms from entering foreign markets. In marketing strategy, a literal translation of advertising copy or a brand name may result in ridicule of a product, or even hostility toward it. For example, in Chinese KFC's well-known slogan "Finger lickin' good" translates as "Eat your fingers off."

Economic Environment   In international marketing a firm must closely examine the economic conditions in a particular country. A nation's infrastructure and stage of economic development are key economic factors that affect the attractiveness of a market and suggest what might be an appropriate marketing strategy.

Infrastructure.   A country's ability to provide transportation, communications, and energy is its **infrastructure**. Depending on the product and the method of marketing, an international marketer will need certain levels of infrastructure development. For example, an Internet marketer such as Amazon.com selling a low-priced product requires a warehouse and transportation system that will permit widespread distribution. How about communications? Some firms would find it impossible to do business without the availability of newspapers in which to advertise or telephones with which to contact other businesses.

There is a danger in assuming that systems a marketer takes for granted domestically will be available elsewhere. The international marketer must recognize what infrastructure is needed and what is available. For example, in France there is one phone for every two people, whereas in India there is about 1 phone for every 35 people.

Level of Economic Development.   The level of economic development of a country is a general indicator of its attractiveness as a market as well as an indicator of the types of products that are likely to be in demand. The most common criterion for assessing economic development is gross domestic product (GDP) per capita, a measure of the value of all goods and services produced in a country during a year, divided by its population. This measure, per capita GDP, has been used to produce a four-category classification of countries.[7]

Among the world's approximately 170 independent countries, about 55 have a per capita GDP of less than $800. These *preindustrial* countries account for 37% of the world's population but only about 3% of its GDP. In these countries most of the population engages in subsistence farming because they lack most of the resources for growth. These countries tend to rely heavily on foreign aid. Overpopulation is a common problem, and the governments are frequently unstable. Included in this category are Azerbaijan, Chad, Ethiopia, Haiti, Madagascar, Tanzania, and Zaire. Generally these countries provide very few market opportunities; however, some are developing a small export trade by becoming the final assembly points for such things as clothing items.

At the next level are the *less developed countries* (or LDCs), with per capita GDP between $800 and $3,000. The 60 countries in this group have 39% of the world's population and about 11% of the GDP. Included are Bolivia, Estonia, Jamaica, Lebanon, Philippines, Romania, and Thailand. These countries are just beginning the industrialization process. They have factories that produce a variety of consumer goods for their domestic market, though they still depend on imports for many consumer items. They combine an eager work force, low wages, and reasonably stable governments to produce standardized, labor-intensive products for export. Athletic shoes for companies such as Nike and adidas are produced in LDCs. These countries are attractive markets for many consumer goods as well as basic technology that will increase productivity.

About 25 countries make up the next group known as *industrializing* countries. With per capita GDP between $3,000 and $9,500, these countries account for about 7% of the world's population and a like percentage of its GDP. The population in these countries has experienced a significant shift from agriculture to urban industrialization. The levels of literacy and education are rising, along with wages. The production of goods for export are typically an important part of the economy. These countries import technology and a wide variety of consumer luxury goods. Among the countries in this group are Brazil, Hungary, Mexico, Poland, and Venezuela.

Finally, there are the *postindustrial* countries. There are about 35 countries in this group with per capita GDP over $9,500. In includes Australia, Canada, France, Japan, Singapore, and the U.S. They have well-developed infrastructures, high levels of education, constantly advancing technology, and stable governments. They are called postindustrial economies because the service sector accounts for more than 50% of GDP, and information and technology have become the primary resources. These countries are heavily involved in both importing and exporting. Although they are the wealthiest countries and therefore would appear to offer the most attractive markets, they are also the ones in which a foreign firm is likely to face the stiffest competition.

Note that a classification like this can be useful, but its simplicity may make it misleading. For example, Saudi Arabia, because of its oil revenues and small population, is in the highly industrialized group. However, Saudi Arabia's level of economic development is quite different from countries such as Japan and Switzerland. On the other hand, China, with a per capita GDP of only $930, attracts many foreign firms that see enormous potential in its huge population. Thus, when analyzing a given foreign market, management must also consider other indications of development. Common economic indicators include the (1) distribution of income, (2) rate of growth of buying power, and (3) extent of available financing. Useful noneconomic indicators are (1) infant mortality rate, (2) percent of the population that lives in urban areas, and (3) the number of daily newspapers.

Competition.   Sometimes overlooked by firms considering international opportunities are the strength and resilience of the native competition. The new entrant must have a differential advantage sufficiently strong to overcome the loyalty built up by established brands and the nationalism that may motivate buyers to support local producers.

International marketers can also expect local competitors to design strategies to protect their businesses. On discovering that a foreign competitor is entering the market, local firms often introduce new products, spruce up customer service, and increase promotion and advertising. As an alternative, the local competitor may also retaliate in the foreign competitor's home market as Kodak did by creating a Japanese subsidiary when Fuji boosted its marketing efforts in the U.S.

Political and Legal Forces

International marketers often discover regulations quite different from those experienced in domestic markets. For example, Japan regulates retail store hours and stipulates that large retailers must shut down for 20 days a year. In Greece, toys cannot be advertised on television, and in all of Europe advertising prescription drugs to consumers is banned.[8] The principal political concerns of international marketers are the stability of governments and their attitudes toward free trade. Obviously, an unstable government adds to the risk of doing business in a country. For example, the frequent coups in several central African countries make them less attractive places to do business than Southeast Asia.

An unresolved legal issue is the global regulation of electronic commerce. The challenges are formidable. For instance, in Europe disputes over cross-border consumer purchases must be resolved in the courts of the consumer's country. Unless this is changed it is likely to have a chilling effect on a large segment of electronic commerce because one of the most attractive features of the Internet is the ability to shop for goods worldwide. However, small website operators outside Europe may be deterred from doing business there if they are faced with the possibility of lawsuits that must be defended in Europe. Likewise, the international purchase of raw materials such as steel over the Internet has been hampered by the quotas, taxes, and other regulations specified by various countries.[9]

Trade Barriers. The most common legal forces affecting international marketers are barriers created by governments to restrict trade and protect domestic industries. Examples include the following:

- **Tariff**—a tax imposed on a product entering a country. Tariffs are used to protect domestic producers and/or raise revenue. To illustrate, China recently reduced tariffs on imported automobiles as much as 80%, but then offset the reduction by increasing the fees for documentation (simply a tariff by another name) by nearly 100%.

- **Import quota**—a limit on the amount of a particular product that can be brought into a country. Like tariffs, quotas can protect a country's domestic industry or can broaden access to its markets. For example, U.S. import quotas on women's lingerie ensure smaller countries such as Sri Lanka access to the American market by restricting the amount larger countries such as China are allowed to import.

- **Local-content law**—a regulation specifying the proportion of a finished product's components and labor that must be provided by the importing country. For example, to be sold in Taiwan, Japanese cars must be at least partially assembled there. To comply with a local-content law, a firm may import most of a product's parts, buy some locally, and have the final product assembled locally. These laws are used to provide jobs and protect domestic businesses.

- **Local operating laws**—a constraint on how, when, or where retailing can be conducted. These regulations, many intended to protect small businesses, are having an impact on Internet shopping. For example, in Germany the retail price of a product has to be the same for everyone. As a result, a system like Priceline.com, where consumers propose a price for an airline seat, rental car, or hotel room and the seller decides if it is acceptable, is illegal. In Austria, France, and the Netherlands publishers specify the retail price of books regardless of where or how they are sold. This prevents Internet firms, despite having a cost advantage over bookstores, from offering a lower price to consumers.

- **Standards and certification**—a requirement that a product contain or exclude certain ingredients or that it be tested and certified as meeting certain restrictive standards. European countries, for example, have restricted genetically altered corn and also beef that has been fed growth hormones.
- **Boycott**—a refusal to buy products from a particular company or country. Boycotts, also called embargoes, are used by a government to punish another country for what are perceived to be unfair importation rules.

Trade Agreements. Trade agreements reduce trade barriers by giving preferential treatment to firms in the member countries. However, they may also result in member countries establishing barriers to trade with the rest of the world. Thus they have implications for all marketers. By examining several major trade agreements, we can form an impression of the role they play in international marketing. In parentheses following the abbreviation of the trade organization is the volume of all the members' exports in 2000, and the proportion of those exports that went to other members of the trade organization.[10]

www.wto.org

- **World Trade Organization (WTO).** This organization was created in 1995, as the governing body of global commerce. It has 144-member countries that account for 90% of world trade. The members participate in periodic negotiations on issues such as tariff reductions, import restrictions, local-content rules, and subsidization of industry by government. The WTO provides a forum for airing trade disputes between countries, but it does not guarantee that solutions to disagreements will be found. Recently it has addressed the issue of safeguarding intellectual property rights.

  The WTO is the successor to the *General Agreement on Tariffs and Trade*, or GATT, founded in 1948. GATT negotiations resulted in the liberalization of trade in 50,000 products and a 40% reduction in tariffs around the world, significant decreases in the subsidies provide for firms engaged in exporting, and the extension of trading rules beyond just goods to include investments.

www.europa.eu.int

- **European Union** (EU, $2,931 billion, 73%). This political and economic alliance evolved from the Treaty of Rome in 1957 that brought together France, Italy, Belgium, West Germany (now the combined East and West Germanys), Luxembourg, and the Netherlands. It was originally called the European Common Market and later the European Community. It is now known as the European Union or EU. Over the years membership has grown to include Denmark, Great Britain, Greece, Spain, Ireland, Portugal, Austria, Sweden, and Finland (see Figure 3.1).

Recent meetings of the World Trade Organization have sparked protests. Here the demonstrators express their displeasure with the policies of the organization. Among their allegations are that in WTO decisions economic progress overshadows other issues such as the environment, and that multinational corporations in the more advanced countries are exploiting the less developed nations of the world.

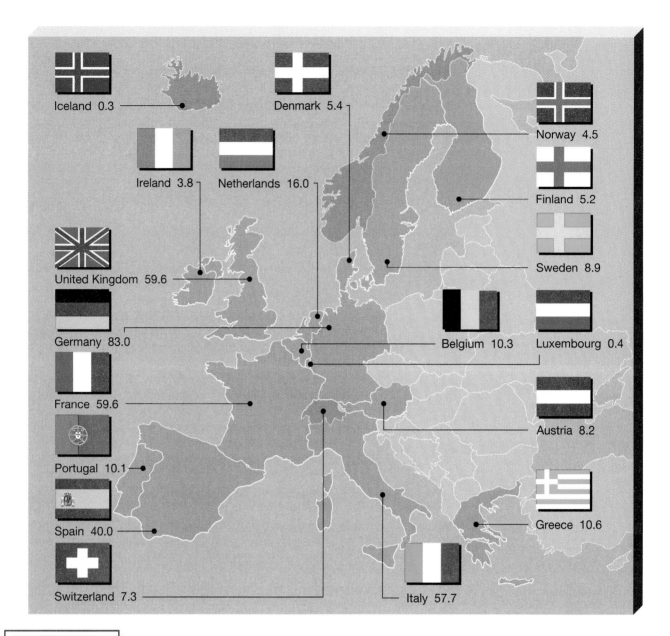

FIGURE 3.1

The European Union Countries (green) and the European Economic Area Countries (purple) in 2000 (with population figures in millions).

The EU's overriding objective is to liberalize trade among its members. More specifically, the goal is a single market for its members that would permit the free movement of goods, services, people, and capital. In addition, the members would be governed by the same set of rules for transporting goods, regulating business, and protecting the environment. Fully accomplishing these goals entails adopting a common currency, a single central bank, and a shared foreign policy, among other things.

A major milestone was accomplished in 2002 when the full adoption of the euro as the official currency for 12 of the members was completed (Sweden, Denmark, and the United Kingdom declined to participate). Given the history of animosities and rivalries that exist among European countries, the level of cooperation has been quite remarkable. In all likelihood the EU will continue to evolve, dealing with social and cultural issues as well as economic ones.

The prospect of a market with 375 million consumers with the same regulations for product ingredients, advertising, packaging, and distribution is very appealing. However, for some American firms it is creating a new reality. In the past, if products were designed to meet U.S. regulations, it generally

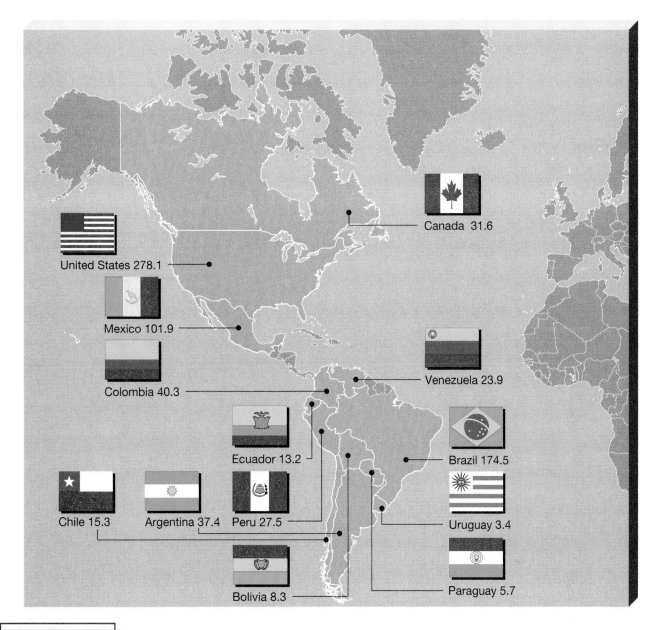

FIGURE 3.2

The Americas (with population figures in millions).

meant they would be acceptable anywhere in the world. But because many EU consumer protection standards are stricter than those in the U.S., items from promotional toys to air-conditioning compressors are being modified so they can be sold in Europe.[11]

Several European countries, notably Switzerland, Norway, and Iceland, object to certain aspects of the EU agreement and have chosen not to join at least for now. The EU will certainly continue to expand. A dozen or more central and eastern European countries are being considered for membership. These countries, which now consume very small amounts of western goods, are seen as primary growth markets.

- **North American Free Trade Agreement** (NAFTA, $1,224 billion, 56%). The U.S. and Canada forged a pact in 1989 that over a 10-year period phased out tariffs on goods traded between the two countries. The agreement was expanded in 1994 to include Mexico, creating a North American free-trade zone. Several other Western Hemisphere countries are interested in joining and may eventually become members. (See Figure 3.2.)

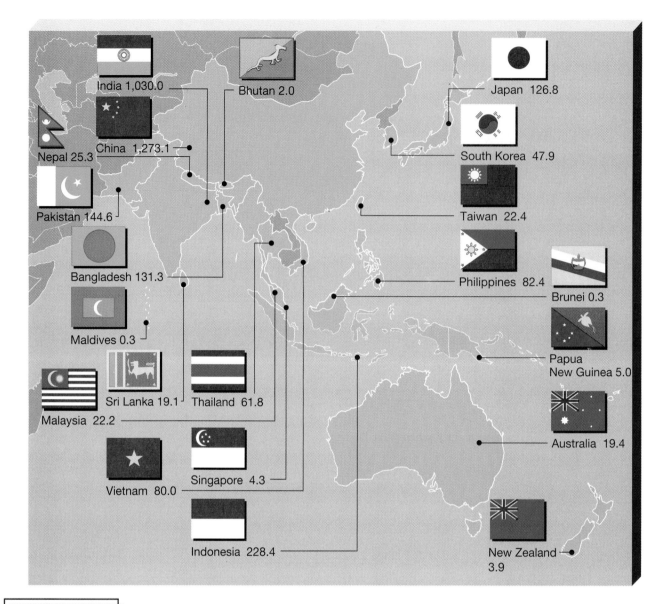

FIGURE 3.3

South Asia and the Asian Side of the Pacific Rim (with population figures in millions).

www.nafta-sec-alena.org

www.apec.org

Despite the fact that Canada and Mexico were major trading partners with the U.S. before NAFTA the agreement still has had a substantial impact. For example, U.S. exports to Mexico have increased by 170% since 1993, while Mexican exports to the U.S. have grown by nearly 250% in the same period. This growth in trade has added to the economic stability of Mexico. However, the specialization that some analysts predicted, with assembly jobs moving from the U.S. to Mexico and technical production increasing in the U.S., has been slow to materialize.[12]

- **Asia-Pacific Economic Cooperation forum** (APEC, $2,931 billion, 73%). Twenty-one Pacific Rim nations participate in this trade pact—Australia, Brunei, Canada, Chile, China, Hong Kong, Indonesia, Japan, Malaysia, Mexico, New Zealand, Papua New Guinea, the Philippines, Singapore, South Korea, Taiwan, Thailand, Peru, Russia, Taipei, Vietnam, and the U.S. The objective of the members, which account for 45% of the world's international trade, is to create a free-trade zone in the Pacific. South Asia and the Asian side of the Pacific Rim are shown in Figure 3.3. Not surprisingly, given the number of participants in APEC, progress is slow. Their representatives met for the first time in 1992, and the current goal is to have the major trade barriers substantially eliminated by 2020.

www.aseansec.org

- **Association of Southeast Asian Nations** (ASEAN, $427 billion, 24%). This pact was established in 1967 as a free-trade zone initially consisting of Indonesia, Malaysia, Philippines, Singapore, and Thailand. They were later joined by Brunei, Cambodia, Laos, Myanmar, and Vietnam. The ASEAN nations have a combined population of 500 million and a gross domestic product of $737 billion. The rapid growth and industrialization of these nations have led analysts to predict that their imports from the U.S. could soon reach $150 billion.

www.
mercosurinvestment.com

- **Common Market of the South** (MERCOSUR, $85 billion, 21%). Consisting of Argentina, Brazil, Paraguay, and Uruguay, and encompassing 190 million people, this pact permits 90% of the trade among these countries to occur tariff-free. The objectives of MERCOSUR are very similar to the EU, the elimination of tariffs among the members and the establishment of common external tariffs. A similar agreement, called the Andean Common Market (ANCOM), has reduced trade barriers among Venezuela, Colombia, Ecuador, Peru, and Bolivia.

Other trade agreements are in existence or are being developed. Seven South Asian nations—India, Pakistan, Bhutan, Bangladesh, the Maldives, Nepal, and Sri Lanka—have formed the South Asian Association for Regional Cooperation (SAARC). With a population of over a billion people, these countries acting in concert have the potential to become a global force. However, traditional rivalries and political problems have thus far hindered the implementation of an effective free-trade arrangement.

What do regional trade agreements mean for the rest of the world? Although they may eventually eliminate *internal* trade barriers among the members, trade agreements create fears that *external* barriers may restrict entry of products from outside the member countries. For example, the EU's exports to Mexico declined significantly when NAFTA opened Mexico up to U.S. and Canadian exports. Recognizing these concerns, some coalitions are undertaking efforts to build good relations with nonmember countries. For example, Mexico and the EU have reached a free-trade agreement. And the U.S. and the EU established an accord called the New Transatlantic Agenda that commits them to working toward establishing common product standards, agreement on standards for television programming, and many other trade-related issues.

It is too soon to measure the impact of trade agreements. However, the growth of regional economic trading blocs is a significant development that will create both opportunities and challenges for international marketers.

In the 21st century, perhaps the area with the greatest international marketing potential is China, with its *1.2 billion* people. Already we have seen glimpses of these possibilities. Foreign cosmetic sales in China, unheard of a few years ago, are soaring. KFC opened its first store in China in 1987. Now the firm has over 625 outlets in 150 Chinese cities with average per store sales higher than in the U.S. China also has significant potential as an exporter. By 1990, the country was a major exporter of clothing. And China is using American and European investments in a quest to become a significant international exporter of automobiles, semiconductors, and telecommunications equipment.

Organization Structures for International Markets

Having evaluated the opportunities and conditions in a foreign country, management must select an appropriate organizational structure for its marketing effort. There is a range of methods for operating in foreign markets (see Table 3.2), which represents successively greater international involvement.

TABLE
3.2

The Range of Structures for Operating in Foreign Markets

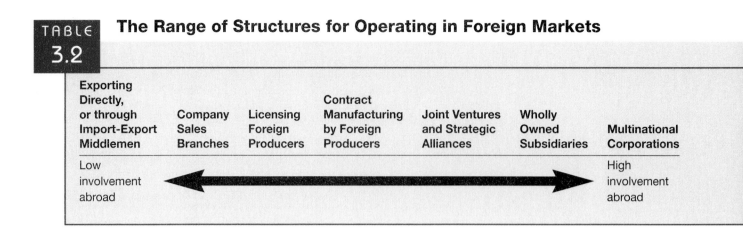

Exporting Directly, or through Import-Export Middlemen	Company Sales Branches	Licensing Foreign Producers	Contract Manufacturing by Foreign Producers	Joint Ventures and Strategic Alliances	Wholly Owned Subsidiaries	Multinational Corporations
Low involvement abroad	←				→	High involvement abroad

Exporting

The simplest way to operate in foreign markets is by **exporting:** selling goods either directly to foreign importers or through import-export middlemen. Because it is the easiest way to get into international markets, exporting is popular with small firms. The Internet has created new export opportunities for many companies. Amazon.com, the best-known online bookseller, derives 25% of its revenue from foreign customers.[13] However, using the Internet to sell directly to consumers in other countries presents some interesting challenges. There are issues of the language or languages to use on the site, the currency in which to quote prices, selection of the method of payment, and arrangements for reliable delivery of the goods.

www.amazon.com

In international markets, just as in domestic markets, middlemen may own the goods they deal in or simply bring buyers and sellers together. An **export merchant** is a middleman operating in the manufacturer's country that buys goods and exports them. Very little risk or investment on the part of the manufacturer is involved. Also, minimal time and effort are required on the part of the exporting producer. However, the exporter has little or no control over merchant middlemen.

An **export agent** may be located in either the manufacturer's country or in the destination country. The agent negotiates the sale of the product and may provide additional services such as arranging for international financing, shipping, and insurance on behalf of the manufacturer, but does not own the goods. Greater risk is involved, because the manufacturer retains title to the goods. Because they typically deal with a number of manufacturers, both types of middlemen generally are not aggressive marketers, nor do they generate a large sales volume.

To counteract some of these deficiencies, management can export through its own **company sales branches** located in foreign markets. Operating a sales branch enables a company to (1) promote its products more aggressively, (2) tailor its distribution network to the product, and (3) control its sales effort more completely. If sales people require extensive training and frequent retraining in order to provide the services customers need, as is the case with Microsoft software, sales branches in international markets are used frequently. Another situation in which sales branches may be preferable to export agents is when a firm must deal with complex local regulations as is the case for marketers of alcoholic beverages and prescription drugs.

With an international sales branch, management now has the task of managing a sales force. The difficulty is that these sales people are either employees sent from the home country who are unfamiliar with the local market, or foreign nationals who are unfamiliar with the product and the company's marketing practices.

Contracting

Contracting involves a legal relationship that allows a firm to enter a foreign market indirectly, quickly establish a market presence, and experience a limited amount of risk. Three frequently used forms of contracting are licensing, contract manufacturing, and franchising.

Licensing means granting to another producer—for some amount of compensation—the right to use one's production process, patents, trademarks, or other assets. For example, in Japan, the Suntory brewery is licensed by Anheuser-Busch to produce Budweiser beer, whereas in England, Budweiser is brewed under license by the Watney brewery. Producers run the risk of encouraging future competition by licensing. A licensee may learn all it can from the producer and then proceed independently when the licensing agreement expires.

In **contract manufacturing,** a marketer such as Sears Roebuck contracts with a foreign producer to supply products that Sears then markets in the producer's country. For example, rather than import U.S.–made tools and hardware for its department stores in Mexico, Brazil, and Spain, Sears contracts with local manufacturers to supply many of these products.

If you have traveled outside the U.S., most likely you have seen the impact of one form of contracting firsthand. **Franchising** has allowed many U.S. retailers, such as McDonald's, KFC, and Toys "Я" Us, to expand overseas rapidly and with minimal risk. Franchising combines a proven operating formula with local knowledge, financing, and entrepreneurial initiative.

Contracting offers companies flexibility with minimal investment. It allows a producer to enter a market that might otherwise be closed to it because of exchange restrictions, import quotas, or prohibitive tariffs.

Direct Investment

Another alternative is **direct foreign investment,** through which a company can build or acquire production or distribution facilities in a foreign country. U.S. firms have about $1,134 billion in direct investments around the world. In comparison, the foreign direct investment in the U.S. amounts to about $1,125 billion.[14] Table 3.3 indicates where U.S. firms have made the greatest amounts of foreign investments. Note that these are not sales figures; they are the value of the owned assets such as plants and equipment at a point in time.

Two Malaysian women in Kuala Lumpur ham it up with a statue of KFC icon, Colonel Sanders. The first KFC franchised restaurant in Malaysia was opened in 1983. Since then, the number has increased to nearly 300 in cities and towns around the country, serving 80,000 pieces of chicken daily.

TABLE 3.3 Direct Foreign Investment in Selected Countries by U.S. Firms

Country	Direct Investment in 1999 ($ billions)
United Kingdom	213
Canada	112
Netherlands	106
Switzerland	51
Germany	50
Japan	48
Bermuda	46
Brazil	35
Australia	34
Mexico	34
China	8

Source: *Statistical Abstract of the United States: 2001,* 121st ed., U.S. Bureau of the Census, Washington, DC, 2001, p. 794.

The magnitude of foreign investments is a direct reflection of the strength and stability of a country's economy in comparison to the rest of the world. The amount invested in a particular country reflects its political and social receptivity to foreign investment as well as its economic attractiveness.

Direct investment can take the form of a joint venture or a wholly owned foreign subsidiary. A **joint venture** is a partnership arrangement in which the foreign operation is owned in part by a domestic company and in part by a foreign company. General Motors has three auto-manufacturing joint ventures in China, two in Japan (with Isuzu and Suzuki), and one in South Korea (with Daewoo). The company hopes these agreements will help increase its market share in the fastest-growing region of the world.[15]

When the controlling interest (more than 50%) is owned by foreign nationals, the domestic firm has no real control over the marketing or production activities. However, a joint venture may be the only structure, other than licensing, through which a firm is legally permitted to enter some foreign markets. Joint ventures are frequently undertaken on a country-by-country basis. For example, in less than a year, Royal Crown Cola entered Mexico, Argentina, Syria, Portugal, Australia, and Indonesia on the basis of joint ventures.

Some major corporations have created a hybrid version of a joint venture called a strategic alliance. A **strategic alliance** is a formal, long-term agreement between firms to combine their capabilities and resources to accomplish global objectives without joint ownership. For example, DaimlerChrysler, Mitsubishi, and Hyundai have formed an alliance to develop a "small-car engine" that would power as many as a million of the companies' cars. Because an engine is one of the most expensive parts of a car and the profit margins on small cars are razor thin, this type of alliance provides savings for all the firms but still lets them compete on other product features.[16]

Joint ventures and alliances in international marketing are particularly attractive when:

- Local laws create barriers to foreign ownership of a business. For example, the national regulations countries impose on airlines led Lufthansa, United Airlines, and other airlines to form alliances for passenger sharing and pooling maintenance facilities.

Fourteen international airlines have formed the Star Alliance to facilitate ticketing to multiple destinations, rerouting travelers on other alliance-member airlines to avoid delays, access to airport lounges around the world, and other benefits that appeal to business travelers. Flight attendants of alliance members, which includes flights to 729 destinations in 124 countries, are shown in this photo. With this alliance each airline extends its ability to serve customers without an additional capital investment.

www.staralliance.com

- Local knowledge is especially important. Retailing in particular requires an understanding of local customs and tastes. Powerful firms like British retailer Tesco, in an alliance with Samsung when it entered South Korea, and Wal-Mart, working with Cifra in Mexico, recognized that much can be learned from established local firms.

- A firm wants access to a market but does not want to expand its resources or expertise. If the risks of a foreign venture are too great for a firm to assume or gaining the necessary expertise would be too costly or time-consuming, a joint venture may be an option. Turner Broadcasting Services joined with Philips, a Dutch electronics firm, to gain quick access to digital communications hardware.

Wholly owned subsidiaries in foreign markets are foreign-based assembly or manufacturing facilities. They are commonly used by companies that have evolved to an advanced stage of international business. Nissan built Europe's most efficient auto manufacturing plant in England, where it will make a car for the European market using a design provided by Renault.

With a wholly owned foreign subsidiary, a company has maximum control over its marketing program and production operations. To ensure that the product is made and presented according to the same standards around the world, the company makes use of subsidiaries rather than licensees. For example, adidas America, a wholly owned subsidiary of adidas-Salomon AG, produces a broad range of footwear and apparel targeted at U.S. preferences and tastes. The line includes baseball and football cleats, adventure shoes, and women's workout shoes for which there are strong U.S. markets. Because it is a subsidiary, the actions of adidas America come under the scrutiny of the parent organization. Thus, it operates with the same corporate philosophy but a somewhat different strategy. For example, adidas America places greater emphasis on fashion merchandise and has higher sales volume goals than other units of the company, reflecting the greater potential in the U.S.[17] A wholly owned subsidiary requires a substantial investment of money, labor, and managerial attention.

Multinational Corporations

We've now come to the highest level of international involvement—one reached by relatively few companies. It is the truly global enterprise—the **multinational corporation**—in which both the foreign and the domestic operations are integrated and are not separately identified except possibly for legal reasons. A regional sales office in Atlanta is basically the same as one in Paris. Business opportunities abroad are viewed in the same way as those in the home country. That is, domestic opportunities are no longer automatically considered to be more attractive. From a legal point of view, a multinational has a home country. Thus, Nestlé is a Swiss firm and Shell Oil is Dutch. However, from a strategic perspective, a true multinational firm is a worldwide enterprise and does strategic marketing planning on a global basis. The result can produce some interesting management challenges, such as the ones faced by Nestlé with its 230,000 employees, operating over 500 factories in 83 countries, producing more than 8,000 different products ranging from cat food to candy bars.

Even though we have described these operating methods as distinct, it is not uncommon for a firm to use more than one of them at the same time. To illustrate, Honda Motor Company exports cars from Japan, imports minivans to Japan from its subsidiary in Canada, and manufactures cars and trucks for the U.S. market at subsidiaries in the U.S. Likewise, Hershey exports candy to Canada, is involved in a joint venture with the largest candy company in Scandinavia, and has a wholly owned subsidiary in Germany—Gubor, a boxed-chocolate company.

Designing the Marketing Mix

As in domestic marketing, the manager must design a marketing mix that will effectively meet customers' needs and accomplish the organization's objectives. However, as the following discussion suggests, domestic practices may have to be modified or entirely replaced in international marketing.

Marketing Research

The scarcity of reliable statistical data is often a major impediment in many foreign markets. Typically, the quality of the data is related directly to a country's level of economic development. However, the nature of the data varies widely. For example, most nations (including England, Japan, France, Spain, and Italy) do not even ask their citizens for income figures in their national censuses.

Another problem is a lack of uniformity among countries in how they define basic measures such as unemployment and the cost of living. As a result, comparisons across countries are often unreliable. In some parts of the world, figures on population and production may be only crude estimates. In less developed countries, studies on such things as buying habits or newspaper readership are even less likely. It was only in the 1990s that China was able to report television audience figures, even in the largest urban areas.

Other challenges arise when collecting data directly from customers and prospects. The absence of reliable lists makes it very difficult even to select a representative sample. Telephone surveys, for example, are likely to be invalid if telephone service is not available to virtually the entire population of a country. Even conducting a focus group can be very difficult. The quality of data also depends on the willingness of people to respond accurately when researchers pose questions about attitudes or buying behavior. Gathering useful data is very difficult in societies where opinion polls are relatively uncommon or strangers are viewed with suspicion.

Product Planning

A critical question in product planning concerns the extent to which a company can market the same product in several different countries. *Product extension* describes the situation in which a standard product is sold in two or more countries. For example, Gillette sells the same razor blades worldwide, and Burger King operates 11,000 stores in 57 countries.

We can make a few broad generalizations regarding product extensions. The best bet for standardization is in the area of durable business goods. In such industries as aircraft, computers, and tractors, the worldwide market (at least among industrialized nations) is quite uniform. For example, the Boeing Company is selling its two-engine 777 airliner to both Singapore Airlines and United Airlines.

Consumer durable goods such as cameras, watches, pocket calculators, small appliances, and television sets are only slightly more difficult to extend into foreign markets virtually unchanged. The benefits of standardization are reflected in the efforts of automakers to develop "world cars."[18] If Ford is able to design cars that can be sold around the world, it estimates that its $8 billion annual product-development budget can be reduced by *billions*.[19]

The most difficult products to standardize globally are personal products such as food, health and beauty aids, and wearing apparel. This difficulty can be traced to national tastes and habits. For example, U.S. consumers eat four times as much dry cereal per capita as the French. This should come as no surprise, because even in large national markets such as the U.S., we often find strong regional differences in food and clothing preferences. Marketers frequently respond with a second product strategy option, *product adaptation,* or modifying a product that sells successfully in one market to suit the unique needs or requirements of other markets. Procter & Gamble modified its Max Factor line of cosmetics with brighter colors for Latin Americans, and its Vidal Sassoon shampoo with more conditioners for the Asian market.

The third alternative product strategy is *invention,* the development of an entirely new product for a foreign market. For example, Maybelline developed a high-humidity face makeup formula for the Asian Pacific market.

Marketers must study carefully the cultural and economic environment of any market—foreign or domestic—before planning products for that particular area. In Europe, for example, large refrigerators are popular in the north because consumers prefer to shop once a week. In contrast, southern Europeans enjoy shopping at open-air markets daily and therefore opt for small refrigerators. And in Europe, where washing machines are often in the kitchen, consumers prefer smaller, quieter versions than U.S. households.

Branding and labeling are other considerations in foreign marketing. Most firms would prefer to use the same brand name in domestic and foreign markets, because it provides greater overall familiarity and recognition and can also produce some economies in promotion. However, care must be taken with translating brand names. Clairol introduced a curling iron in Germany called the Mist Stick only to discover that mist is a German slang word for manure.

A concern of many marketers is **trademark infringement.** In many countries copyright laws are nonexistent or poorly enforced. As a result, local firms manufacture products with names and packaging very similar to well-known imported goods in hopes of deceiving consumers. For example, a Chinese food outlet apparently was trying to take advantage of the popularity of McDonald's and KFC when it named itself "McKentucky."[20] Often these products are of inferior quality, so not only do they steal business from the imported brand, they also damage its reputation.

Global pirating of computer software, music, and videos—virtually anything that can be transmitted electronically—is another serous problem. In the past, firms were provided with at least some protection from pirating by domestic laws and the physical limitations of making and shipping a video tape or CD. With those constraints reduced or eliminated, it's been suggested that the makers of these electronic products will be forced to find new ways to market their products. One approach, already used by some software firms, is to give their products away via the Internet, and generate revenue by selling advertising space on the Internet site.

Should a country or region be allowed to restrict the use of the name of a food?

Should use of the terms champagne, catfish, vidalia sweets, basmati (rice), and parmesan be limited to products produced in particular regions? Some industries and governments think so. The U.S. Congress has passed legislation that permits only fish raised in the U.S. to be sold as "catfish." A lower-priced, genetically identical product imported from Vietnam must be sold under a different name. Similarly, in an effort to protect its rice growers, the Indian government is attempting to prevent a U.S. firm from marketing a long-grained, fluffy variety of rice associated with South Asia by its regional name, "basmati."

Other regions such as Parma, Italy (with parmesan cheese), Vadalia, Georgia, in the U.S. (with onions), and Napa Valley, California (with wine), want the names restricted to locally produced products.

What effects would such restrictions have on international trade?

Sources: Desa Philadelphia, "Catfish by Any Other Name," *Time Global Business,* February 2002, pp. B14–15; "Vietnam Voices Opposition to U.S. Farm Security, Rural Investment Act," BBC Monitoring, Hanoi, May 20, 2002.

Marketers must also be alert to shifting tastes. After largely ignoring Disneyland Paris when it opened in 1992, Europeans have recently shown a great interest in U.S.–style amusement parks. There are currently nine in operation and more planned for the future. Explanations for their popularity range from European consumers having more disposable income to a trend to shorter, more frequent vacations closer to home. Whatever the reason, those quickest to act are likely to reap the most benefit.[21]

Pricing

Determining the price for a product is a complex and inexact task, frequently involving trial-and-error decision making. This process is often even more complex in international marketing. An exporter faces variables such as currency conversion, differences in what is included in the price (such as postsale service), and often a lack of control over middlemen's pricing.

Cost-plus pricing (setting price by adding an amount to provide a profit to the cost of manufacturing a product) is relatively common in export marketing. Because of additional physical distribution expenses, tariffs, and other export costs, foreign prices usually are considerably higher than domestic prices for the same product. For example, a Jeep Cherokee costs about 50% more in Japan than in the U.S. At the retail level, price bargaining is quite prevalent in many foreign markets—especially in Asia, Africa, and South America—and must be taken into consideration in setting the initial price.

Sometimes companies engage in a practice called **dumping**—selling products in foreign markets at prices below those charged for the same goods in their home markets. The price may be lowered to meet foreign competition or to dispose of slow-moving products. Recently U.S. steelmakers claimed firms in Russia, Brazil, South Africa, and China were dumping products in America.[22] Dumping, which frequently involves selling goods below cost, is viewed as an unfair business practice by most governments, and generally results in threats of tariffs or establishment of quotas.

An issue of growing concern is the **price differential** charged for an identical brand in different, often neighboring, countries. Differentials of 30 to 150% are not uncommon. Because of differences in taxes, costs of doing business, and regulations, a can of Coke costs nearly twice as much in France as in Austria. On the other hand, butter is 40% cheaper in France than in Austria.[23] European consumers will become much more aware of these differentials with the introduction of the euro as the common EU currency.

Price differences result from the strength of demand, the complexity of the distribution structures in various countries, and differences in tax systems. With the easy flow of information across borders and increased travel by consumers, price differentials add considerable complexity to the job of middlemen, especially retailers, doing business in several countries. They also encourage arbitrage—the purchase and sale of a product in different markets to benefit from the unequal prices.

Prices may be quoted in the seller's currency or in the currency of the foreign buyer. Here we encounter problems of **foreign exchange** and conversion of currencies. As a general rule, a firm engaged in foreign trade—whether it is exporting or importing—prefers to have the price quoted in its own national currency. If a seller deals in a foreign currency and that currency declines in value between the signing of a contract and the receipt of the foreign currency, the seller incurs a loss. Similarly, a buyer dealing in a foreign currency would lose money if the foreign currency increased in value before payment was made. The risks from fluctuations in foreign exchange are shifted to the other party in the transaction if a firm deals in its national currency.

An alternative to currency-based pricing is **countertrade** or **barter.** Rather than buy goods with cash, some countries arrange to trade domestically made products for imported goods. PepsiCo, for example, has traded soft drinks to Poland for wooden chairs that are used in its U.S. Pizza Hut stores. Two reasons for countertrade are:

- *Lack of hard currency.* Less developed countries may not have enough "hard" currency (the money of countries viewed in world markets as reasonably stable) to buy needed capital goods. So they trade their less-sophisticated products for equipment and technology. A Canadian firm selling steel in Indonesia was compensated in palm oil, coffee, timber, and rattan furniture.

- *Inadequate marketing structure.* Some countries do not have a marketing structure that encourages or permits international trade. Without global distribution systems, adequate promotion, or the ability to provide service, they cannot sell their domestic goods overseas. To overcome this problem, these countries may require foreign firms that import products into the country to accept local goods in total or partial payment. Both China and Romania require that importers accept countertrade.

Agreements between manufacturers and middlemen in the same industry are tolerated to a far greater extent in many foreign countries than in the U.S. They are allowed even when the avowed purpose of the combination is to restrain trade and reduce competition. Recognizing this, Congress passed the Webb-Pomerene Act in 1918. This law allows American firms to join this type of trade combination in a foreign country without being charged with violation of American antitrust laws.

The best-known of these international marketing combinations is the cartel. A **cartel** is a group of companies that produce similar products and act collectively to restrain competition in manufacturing and marketing. Cartels exist to varying degrees in steel, aluminum, fertilizers, petroleum products, rayon, and sulfur. Probably the world's best-known cartel is OPEC, the Organization of Petroleum Exporting Countries, which has tried—with varying degrees of success—to control the price of crude oil.

Distribution Systems

The different environments in foreign markets force firms to adjust their distribution systems, because marketing institutions, such as various types of retailers, are responses to the environment. They can also provide an opportunity to experiment

On January 1, 2002, 12 members of the EU replaced their national currencies with euro coins and notes. Certainly a common currency makes it easier for consumers to make price comparisons. However, shortly before the transition date, some say in anticipation of it, prices on many consumer products were raised. Interestingly, many of the changes were exactly an amount that resulted in the converted euro prices ending in a psychologically attractive "95" or "99." For example, in Germany The Lego Life on Mars spaceship was raised from 64.95 marks to 68.43 marks. In euros, that took it from 33.21 to 34.99.

Must a price increase always be justified by an increase in costs?

Sources: G. Thomas Sims, "Marketer's Friend, .99, Hits the Euro Zone," *The Wall Street Journal*, July 21, 2001, p. A14; David McHugh, "Euro May Aid Consumers," *South Bend Tribune*, Jan. 27, 2002, p. e-3; G. Thomas Sims, "Germans Come Late, but with Enthusiasm, to the Anti-Euro Party," *The Wall Street Journal*, May 30, 2002, p. A12.

with new strategies. For example, in Taiwan, General Motors owns its retail dealers. Freed of the constraint of trying to keep franchised dealers happy (as it must do in the U.S.), GM can install and test a system that allows consumers to configure, order, and buy cars on the Internet.

Middlemen and Channels of Distribution

International middlemen were introduced earlier in this chapter in connection with organizational structures for international marketing. Foreign middlemen representing importers and operating within foreign countries are, in general, less aggressive and perform fewer marketing services than their counterparts selling domestically produced products. The foreign marketing situation, however, usually argues against bypassing these middlemen. Often the demand is too small to warrant establishing a sales office or branch in the foreign country. Also, in many countries, knowledge of the market may be more important than knowledge of the product, even for high-technology products. And sometimes government controls preclude the use of a firm's sales organization abroad. Thus, middlemen in foreign countries ordinarily are a part of the channel structure.

A deceptive practice employed by some middlemen is called export diversion or **gray marketing.** When a distributor buys a product made in one country and agrees to distribute it in a second country, but instead diverts the product to a third country, gray marketing is occurring. The term used to describe the practice comes from the fact that the goods are typically sold in a reputable outlet, typically at a substantial discount, and thus do not appear on the "black market." The discounts stem from the fact that the gray marketer does not bear any of the promotional costs for the product, instead capitalizing on the promotional efforts of the authorized dealers, nor does the gray marketer provide the service and warranty protection of an authorized dealer. An investigation of a health scare associated with Coke bottled in Belgium led to the discovery that as much as 20% of all the soft drinks sold in Great Britain are diverted goods. One reason gray marketing occurs is because manufacturers selling their products in several countries often have more difficulty monitoring the activities of middlemen than they do in the domestic market.

Physical Distribution

Various aspects of physical distribution in foreign marketing are quite different from anything found on the domestic scene. Generally, physical distribution expenses account for a much larger share of the final selling price in foreign markets than in domestic markets. Problems caused by climate, pilferage, handling, and inadequate marking must be considered in international shipments. Requirements regarding commercial shipping, insurance, and government documents complicate foreign shipping. As noted earlier, one of the primary benefits of economic alliances like the EU is the efficiency they bring to physical distribution. With the free movement of goods across European borders, distribution time and expense will be drastically reduced.

Bribes, kickbacks, and sometimes even extortion payments are facts of life in international distribution. Bribery is so rooted in many cultures that it is described with special slang words. It's called *mordida* (small bite) in Latin America. The French call it *pot de vin* (jug of wine). In Italy there is *la bustarella* (the little envelope), left on a bureaucrat's desk to cut the red tape. South Koreans use *ttuk kab* (rice cake expenses).

Revelations about the amount of bribery led Congress to pass the Foreign Corrupt Practices Act in 1977. The act prohibits U.S. companies, their subsidiaries, or representatives from making payments to high-ranking foreign government officers and political parties. The law, however, does not exclude small, facilitating payments to lower-level foreign government employees who are not policymakers, because these payments are a way of life in many parts of the world.

What complicates this situation is the fact that bribery is not a sharply defined activity. Sometimes the lines are blurred among a bribe, a gift to show appreciation, a reasonable commission for services rendered, and a finder's fee to open a distribution channel. For example, businesses in South Korea make contributions to government officials to mark major holidays. According to South Korean executives, the payments are not made to obtain favors. Rather, they serve to protect a firm from punitive treatment by government bureaucrats. Realistically, in some foreign markets a seller must pay a fee or commission to an agent to get in touch with prospective buyers. Without paying such fees, there is simply no effective access to those markets.

Advertising

There are numerous advertising decisions in international marketing. The availability of media, access to consumers, choice of advertising agencies, and the design of messages are just a few examples. Rather than trying to deal with all aspects of advertising and promotion, we limit our discussion to the issue of standardizing the message to illustrate the strategic challenges faced by international marketers in communicating with customers.

In its purest form, standardization entails using the same advertisement in multiple countries. Although posed as a strategic alternative over 30 years ago, the conditions under which it is practical remains a controversial topic.[24] In recent years, interest in standardization has been spurred by the increase in international communication and entertainment. Many TV broadcasts reach worldwide audiences through satellite and cable networks. The Internet has made it possible for consumers to instantaneously visit the websites and view the messages of firms anywhere. Magazines and newspapers are widely circulated and are also globally available on the Internet. In addition, international business and pleasure travel have become quite common.

A second factor contributing to the interest in standardization is the economies it can produce. Creating quality advertising is expensive. Substantial savings can be achieved if the same advertisement can be used effectively in various parts of the world.

Despite its attractiveness, pure standardization is not typical. Rather, there are frequently efforts by international marketers to optimize their investment in advertising by adapting the same basic theme, appeal, or message in different countries. Firms that have used modified global appeals successfully include Toys "Я" Us with very similar TV ads in the U.S., Germany, and Japan, Gillette for its Sensor razor, Nike, Procter & Gamble, and Nestlé for Nescafe coffee. However, in each case the advertiser has customized the way the message is presented to fit the local market.

For international marketers, the issue is not whether to standardize, but how much and where it is possible. Advertising must capture attention and convey a message.

Advertisements do that by using a variety of communication devices such as humor, contrast, and surprise. The difficulty in standardizing international advertising is what works in one culture might take on quite a different meaning in another. For example, a Toyota ad in Italy that presented a lighthearted contrast between the Italian government's image as corrupt and the reliability of the Toyota Carina created a major controversy.

The challenge of standardization comes down to balancing efficiency by minimizing the investment in advertising with effectiveness by maximizing the fit of the ads to the particular market.

The goal of advertising is the same in any country, namely to communicate information and persuasive appeals effectively. For some products, the appeals are sufficiently universal and the markets are sufficiently homogeneous to permit the use of very similar advertising in several countries. It is only the media strategy and the details of a message that must be fine-tuned to each country's cultural, economic, and political environment. However, care must be taken to recognize when differences in national identity and characteristics are sufficient to require specialized advertising in a particular country.

Our discussion has described environmental factors, organizational arrangements, and tactical issues related to the marketing mix elements of product, price, distribution, and promotion that are fundamental to designing an international marketing strategy. There are other issues that further distinguish domestic from international or global marketing. A primary purpose of this chapter is to make you aware of the fact that along with the opportunities, marketing beyond one's domestic borders raises new and unique strategic challenges.

Summary

Countries encourage international trade for economic, social, and political reasons. In particular, it provides access to goods that otherwise would be unavailable and, because of comparative advantage, it maximizes a country's economic potential. Firms engage in international marketing because of demand abroad, the saturation of domestic markets, and to serve the international needs of their domestic customers. Many companies in the U.S. and abroad derive a substantial share of their total sales and profits from their foreign marketing operations.

Although international trade can contribute to the growth of a nation's economy, a country must be concerned about the relationship between exports and imports. For the U.S., trade surpluses are needed to offset deficits in other balance-of-payment categories. In recent years, the U.S. balance of trade has been adversely affected by consumers' preferences for imported products, entry barriers, and other policies of foreign governments, as well as the growing technological and marketing capabilities of other countries.

In terms of organizational structure, the simplest way to operate in a foreign market is to export. This can be done directly to consumers via the Internet or through middlemen specializing in foreign trade.

Another method is to export through company sales branches located in foreign countries. More involved approaches include contracting, engaging in a joint venture, or forming a wholly owned subsidiary. The most fully developed organizational structure for international marketing is the multinational corporation.

The macroenvironment faced by an international marketer in various countries will determine whether a global, regional, or local strategy is appropriate. Differences in the social and cultural environment are reflected in family values, customs, education, and language. Critical economic conditions include the infrastructure in a market and a country's stage of economic development. Political and legal forces unique to international marketing are trade barriers and international trade agreements. Organizations such as the World Trade Organization (WTO) as well as trade agreements and economic alliances in Europe (EU), North America (NAFTA), South America (MERCOSUR), Asia (ASEAN), and elsewhere in the world have implications for marketers in both member and nonmember nations.

To develop an international marketing program, a basic issue is how global or standardized the marketing can be. This is made difficult by the fact that market data may be less plentiful in many parts of the world, and conducting marketing research can be very difficult. In some cases each of the marketing-mix elements requires modification or adaptation.

Oftentimes operating in a foreign market entails accommodating unique conditions. Chief among these are dumping, foreign exchange, countertrade, price differentials, gray markets, cartels, and bribery.

More about Lego

How has the concept of play changed since the birth of Lego? Among children, and the parents who buy their toys, is there still an appreciation of open-ended creative play? Do they admire products that are not saturated with references to popular culture? Or are the original Legos now only attractive to the very young, whereas their older siblings, once part of Lego's cherished market, flock to video games, Baywatch Barbies, and action figures spun off from the entertainment industry?

These are some of the questions that Lego will have to confront as it moves ahead with its plans for MindStorms, a high-end toy with a starting price of $200 (and 700 pieces). MindStorms was an initial success, not just among children but also among teens and even technically minded adults. (It was developed in conjunction with the Massachusetts Institute of Technology.) Adults bought 70 percent of the kits the first year they were available and constitute something of a cult following for the toy. But one of the most interesting uses to which MindStorms has been put is a partnership between Lego and FIRST, a New Hampshire nonprofit group founded to get kids interested in science and engineering. FIRST sponsors Lego Leagues that run team competitions in which young teens race to build robots to complete specified tasks. General Motors, Honeywell, 3M, and NASA are among the organizations supporting leagues and teams around the country.

Lego is also looking at other markets for its venerable name. New software deals, such as with Electronic Arts, mean that at least 30 Lego-based electronic video games will soon be available for the newest game consoles.

And then there is Bionicle. Lego's latest toy venture is a line of action figures—six heroes, six wise ones, and five supervillains—who inhabit a tropical isle with meticulously planned geography. The creatures, which are to be assembled from hundreds of pieces, all have names, characters, and different "masks of power and knowledge"—and they come with specific, ready-made stories that must be known in order to play. It is all a long way from the original red plastic block. Is it too far, or not far enough?[25]

1. Considering that Lego's success has been based on global appeal of toys that stretch the imagination, will the fact that Bionicle characters come with stories already invented by the company be a handicap to sales in the toy market Lego faces today? Why or why not?

2. How do you think Lego can broaden the appeal of MindStorms? Consider its high price and complexity, the need for a computer, and the fact that most members of the Lego Leagues are boys in their early teens.

Key Terms and Concepts

Association of Southeast Asian
Nations (ASEAN) (65)
Common Market of the South
(MERCOSUR) (65)
Exporting (66)
Export merchant (66)
Export agent (66)
Company sales branch (66)
Contracting (67)

Licensing (67)
Contract manufacturing (67)
Franchising (67)
Direct foreign investment (67)
Joint venture (68)
Strategic alliance (68)
Wholly owned subsidiary (69)
Multinational corporation (69)
Trademark infringement (71)

Dumping (72)
Price differential (72)
Foreign exchange (73)
Countertrade or barter (73)
Cartel (73)
Gray marketing (74)
Bribes (75)

Questions and Problems

1. Find out which U.S. products have the largest volume of exports. (*Hint:* Check *International Financial Statistics* or *International Marketing Data and Statistics*—two publications that are likely in your school's library and on the Internet.) What explains the popularity of these products outside the U.S.?

2. What should a country such as the U.S. do to reduce its trade deficits?

3. A U.S. manufacturer of premium-quality luggage has been exporting its products to Europe. However, the firm has discovered that its luggage is often sold alongside much lower-quality products in discount stores. What approach to international marketing should the firm consider if it wants greater control over how its products are sold at retail?

4. Interview some foreign students on your campus to determine how the grocery buying behavior of people in their countries differs from yours. Consider such factors as when, where, and how people in their countries buy. What roles do various family members play in buying decisions?

5. Many countries have a low literacy rate. In what ways might a company adjust its marketing program to overcome this problem?

6. Visit the website of an international trade organization such as the EU or NAFTA. What are the major issues being addressed by the organization's governing body? Are the issues the result of the relative size of the member countries, their differing levels of industrialization, or some other factors?

7. If an American company uses foreign middlemen, it must usually stand ready to supply them with financial, technical, and promotional help. If this is the case, why is it not customary to bypass these middlemen and deal directly with the ultimate foreign buyers?

8. Examine the ads in a foreign magazine in your college or city library. Particularly note the ads for American products, and compare these with the ads for the same products in American magazines. In what respect do the foreign ads differ from the domestic ads? Are there significant similarities?

9. "Prices of American products are always higher in foreign countries than at home because of the additional risks, expenses of physical distribution, and extra middlemen involved." Discuss.

Interactive Marketing Exercises

1. Report on export marketing activities of companies in the state where your school is located. Consider such topics as the following: What products are exported? How many jobs are created by export marketing? What is the dollar value of exports? How does this figure compare with the value of foreign-made goods imported into the state?

2. Select one product—manufactured or nonmanufactured—for export, and choose the country to which you would like to export it. Examine the macroenvironmental factors described in the chapter and prepare an analysis of the market for this product in the selected country. Be sure to include the sources of information you use.

Cases for Part 1

Making a Bid to Be the Internet's Largest Marketplace

Originally called Auction Web, eBay was launched by Pierre Omidyar in 1995 to help his girlfriend sell Pez dispensers over the Internet. This simple, modest site soon attracted hundreds of other sellers wanting to hawk their wares online, and Omidyar dedicated himself to responding to their concerns and suggestions by constantly improving the site and expanding its product categories. Within four years, at a time when most dot-com businesses were burning through venture capital at an alarming rate, eBay had managed to turn a profit.

In 1998, Omidyar turned the company over to a new chief executive officer, Meg Whitman, a former executive at Hasbro. Under Whitman's direction, eBay has continued to grow and become increasingly profitable. But Whitman stunned the industry when she announced in mid-2001 that she intended to increase eBay's revenues 50% annually in order to achieve $3 billion in revenues by 2005. To achieve that target, eBay will have to triple its number of buyers and sellers to 150 million, raising concerns among some of its current customers that the company will no longer be able to maintain its unique sense of community.

Sold! On the Concept of Online Auctions

Despite its immense and increasing size, eBay's business model remains strikingly simple. Anyone with something to sell can create an electronic classified ad that is featured on eBay's website for a small fee. The ad describes the item in detail, and usually includes a digital photograph. Buyers search the website for desirable items, and can bid on them up until a time specified by the seller. When the auction is closed, the highest bidder wins the item as long as the bid meets a minimum price set by the seller. The buyer and seller make all payment and shipping arrangements, and eBay collects 1.25% to 5% of the sales price as a commission.

Because in-person auctions are lengthy, often tedious ordeals, the idea of an online auction marketplace appealed to a large number of people. The site quickly became a giant electronic flea market, with collectibles comprising the majority of items being sold. Soon, though, people began offering event tickets, fine art, travel services, cars, and even houses through eBay. One misguided gentleman even put one of his kidneys up for auction. eBay constantly monitors the items being offered, and shuts down sales they consider to be inappropriate, including firearms—and the kidney of course.

To his credit, Omidyar quickly figured out that it wasn't only the items being featured on eBay that made the company successful. It was also the extensive network of individuals that comprised eBay's unique community. After all, they were the ones doing most of the work. They handled their own inventory, shipping, pricing, and payment arrangements. So Omidyar began capturing their ideas for innovation and expansion in a number of ways. When users began overloading his e-mail inbox with suggestions and questions, he created an online bulletin board so users could interact and help each other solve problems. When fraud became a problem, Omidyar established a rating system called Feedback Forum, so that buyers and sellers could evaluate one another, and identify individuals who delivered inferior goods or who did not ship items or pay for them on time. Less than 1% of the comments are negative and sellers go to great lengths to avoid an unfavorable evaluation. "Every time you get a negative feedback, your sales go down," explains one veteran eBay merchant. Partly as a result, fraud occurs on less than .01% of eBay transactions, a rate that is nine times less than credit card fraud. Not only have these solutions increased customer satisfaction, they have lessened eBay's need for a large staff of support personnel.

Another frequent user complaint was addressed in 1999. As a result of its rapid growth, eBay began to suffer severe and frequent system crashes, some of them lasting almost an entire day. As a result, the company's computer systems were upgraded significantly and backup systems were put into place to help accommodate the higher levels of traffic. The site is now down less than 42 minutes a month.

In 1998 there were more than 150 online auction sites as many companies tried to duplicate eBay's formula for success. However, by 2002, eBay commanded more than 80% of the U.S. market. Although there were still a plethora of sites offering electronic auctions, most were small, specializing in distinct product niches. A couple of Internet heavyweights, Amazon and Yahoo!, run online auctions, but their auction services account for only a small portion of their business.

Moving Way beyond Pez Dispensers

Despite being known as a great place to get rid of that ugly lamp that's been relegated to the attic, eBay has expanded its business by adding new product categories, attracting different types of sellers and buyers, and entering foreign markets. It began auctioning used automobiles in 1999, and by 2002 it was the largest online car dealer. With sales of about $1 billion, cars comprised 16% of eBay's gross merchandise sales. eBay also teamed up with Sotheby's in early 2002 to offer fine art and antiques online. A few sellers began holding auctions for homes, and in August of 2001, eBay established a category for real estate and purchased a website that allowed prospective buyers to bid on properties in foreclosure. An average of 25 properties are sold each day, and one of them that was recently up for bid was the childhood home of Lucille Ball! In early 2002, eBay boasted a whopping 18,000 product categories.

In addition to adding new types of products, eBay is offering new ways for buyers to purchase them. In 2000, eBay bought Half.com, an online retailer that sells books and CDs for 50% or more off the typical retail price, a move that surely raised a few eyebrows at Amazon. "Half.com is bringing the Amazon buyer into person-to-person trading," explained an eBay executive. Six months later, eBay introduced a new feature called "Buy It Now." It allows sellers to list a predetermined price, and an auction automatically ends once a buyer accepts that price. eBay benefits from Buy It Now because it helps end auctions more quickly, thereby granting eBay faster payment. These methods of "fixed pricing," as opposed to auctions, appeal to buyers who are not interested in haggling, and in 2002, comprised 19% of eBay's sales.

eBay's model of person-to-person trading has evolved to include business-to-person and business-to-business trading. Disney discovered it could recycle movie props, animation cells, and a variety of other items that would normally be thrown away or put into storage, by auctioning them off on eBay. IBM sells last-generation laptops to individuals and small businesses through eBay, and was pleasantly surprised to discover that this new distribution channel did not cannibalize

sales from its own website. In fact, eBay is bringing a whole new set of customers to IBM. "We see eBay as an incredible growth engine for us," commented one IBM executive, and in early 2002, IBM was the #1 seller on eBay. Even governments are using eBay to sell foreclosed assets. Although these large entities make up less than 3% of eBay's total sales, they represent an enormous opportunity for the company that was once best known for its impressive selection of Beanie Babies. Buyers appreciate this new distribution channel as well. The chief executive of a small consulting firm procures office equipment through eBay. "It's an equivalent of on-demand purchasing," he stated. "I consider it the shopping place of first resort."

Other opportunities for growth await eBay in foreign markets, and the company is already a force in many of them. For instance, 25% of Germans who use the Internet visit eBay's website. eBay now has 27 global sites, and is the leader in Australia, Great Britain, Canada, France and Germany. In 2001, international sales were 14% of eBay's total business, a figure that is twice what it was in 2000. However, plans were announced in February of 2002 to close eBay's Japanese site after only two years of operation. Yahoo! was already an established auction site in Japan when eBay entered the market, and eBay mistakenly promoted its used collectibles categories, instead of new items favored by Japanese buyers.

Haggling over Eyeballs

From the Enron ethics manual to the infamous Palm Beach County voting machines used in the much-maligned 2000 presidential campaign, people find just about anything and everything on eBay. For example, a woman from New Jersey sells 19th-century glass eyeballs. In August of 2001, a Gulfstream jet brought in the company's highest-ever bid of $4.9 million. Three motorcycles an hour, two laptops a minute, and one book every four seconds exchange hands.

And the folks at eBay never touch any of this stuff. (And really, why would you want to touch a vintage glass eyeball?) As a result, overhead is kept to a minimum with less than 2,000 eBay employees supporting the site's 38 million users and 7 million ongoing auctions. This accounts for eBay's impressive profitability of $250 million in 2002, based on $1.2 billion in revenue. Even the terrorist attacks that took place on September 11th and the recession that followed didn't dampen eBay's prospects, as they did so many other dot–coms. "These guys have done a killer job," commented Amazon's chief financial officer. In fact, bleak economic times might even help eBay as more and more companies discover it to be a useful distribution channel for getting rid of excess inventory.

eBay is hoping to help more people discover the power of its website, and has only recently begun to more aggressively promote itself. In its early days, the company relied on word-of-mouth advertising to attract customers. Now it is advertising on television, in print ads and, of course, online. It has entered into an exclusive partnership with America Online and is sponsoring the popular PBS television program, *Antiques Roadshow*. "An association with the *Antiques Roadshow* gives more cache to the site so people will think 'antiques' instead of 'other people's junk.' It's a smart way to change the association," explained one analyst. Not everyone within the antiques business is thrilled though. There are now so many people buying and selling items that were once much harder to find, that prices have fallen by about 30% in recent years. One dealer criticized eBay by saying, "We all hate it. They leveled the playing field, but unfortunately they leveled it underwater."

Listing Users as Its Main Resource

Aside from a group of disgruntled antiques dealers, critics of eBay are in the minority. Many people appreciate this new marketplace because it allows them to purchase hard-to-find items, make a little extra cash, or even start a whole new business. One woman in Indiana began as a "weekend warrior," auctioning flea market finds on eBay, and soon realized there was an enormous need for shipping supplies within the eBay community alone. Now she buys supplies directly from a manufacturer, and has generated enough business to support her family by filling more than 150 orders a day. And her situation is not unusual. As of April 2001, there were more than 75,000 Americans making a living on eBay.

These individuals rely on eBay, and in turn, eBay relies on them. eBay's greatest resource is the energy of the people that come together on its site to transact business, and combined, these individuals generate an intangible element known as "social capital." By rating one another through the Feedback Forum, helping each other solve problems on the online bulletin board, and contributing in a multitude of other ways, eBay's users have created a unique sense of community that has helped eBay succeed and grow. However, as eBay continues to expand, this social capital becomes more and more difficult to maintain.

One threat was the addition of corporate sellers. For instance, the Disney company is given special billing over individuals and smaller companies selling Disney merchandise. According to one observer, "The general consensus of veteran sellers is that they've forsaken the people who built them in favor of corporate sellers." eBay also infuriated sellers when it decided to direct losing bidders to other auctions featuring similar merchandise. The online bulletin boards lit up with tirades of angry sellers who feared losing their customer base. One particularly irritated gentleman immediately auctioned off a rare eBay jacket and included a rather colorful attack on the new policy. This came to the attention of Whitman and Omidyar, and to their credit, they immediately arranged a meeting with the man in his hometown. Within days, the new policy had been modified, leading the irate seller to say, "No other large corporation listens nearly as well as they do."

Realizing it would be impossible to meet with each and every eBay user, the company continues to cultivate its customers' social capital in a number of ways. It regularly holds "Voice of the Customer" focus groups to capture improvement suggestions. Whitman is kept apprised daily of the hot topics on the bulletin boards. And the company has a decentralized organizational structure with managers in charge of each major product category and foreign market.

To achieve Whitman's revenue goal of $3 billion by 2005 and become "the world's most compelling commerce platform on the Internet," eBay must continue to listen and respond to its customers—all 38 million of them. Otherwise, it risks the social capital that made the company so successful. And according to Omidyar, the company's founder, "If we lose that, we've pretty much lost everything."

Questions

1. Describe the three components of the marketing concept as they apply to eBay. Which is likely to provide the greatest challenge to eBay's success?

2. Which environmental factors are working in eBay's favor? Which are likely to pose problems in the future?

3. What is necessary for eBay to continue its international expansion?

www.ebay.com

Coca-Cola Co. versus PepsiCo

Quenching Their Customers' Thirst for New Beverages

For many years, the term "cola wars" has been used to describe the hard-fought battle for market share that has been waged by Coca-Cola and Pepsi. Coke has managed to stay on top, and in 2001 boasted 43.7% of the U.S. soft drink market but consumers' tastes evolved, and sales of carbonated sodas slowed. Juices, bottled water, sports drinks, coffee beverages, and vitamin-enriched drinks are now being marketed, both by Pepsi and by Coke. Pepsi has been more proactive at introducing new types of noncarbonated beverages to a population that is increasingly health conscious and more individualistic. In fact, Pepsi is the top seller of noncarbonated beverages in the U.S. As their product mixes are expanding, Coke in particular is struggling to determine the best way to market a variety of disparate brands instead of just its powerhouse sodas.

Fizzling Soda Sales

After growing at a rate of 2% to 3% each year during the 1990s, domestic soda sales declined in 1999 and 2000. They rebounded slightly in 2001, with a small increase of 0.6%. However, the average U.S. consumer drank less soda in 2001, estimated at 55.4 gallons, as opposed to 55.7 gallons in 2000 and 55.9 gallons in 1999. These trends have had a profound impact on the top two soft drink producers.

During the 1980s and most of the 1990s, Coca-Cola's performance was excellent. Except for the embarrassing failure of "New Coke," a reformulation of its flagship cola's flavor in 1985, the company's strategy was on target. During that period, Coca-Cola had annual earnings increases that averaged at least 15% and its stock rose a dazzling 3,500%. But by 2001, the company experienced its third consecutive year of flat or declining market share in the U.S. In addition, earnings were declining, and Coca-Cola was facing serious threats on several fronts, not the least of which was from its perennial challenger, Pepsi.

After losing market share to Coca-Cola in the 1990s, Pepsi began to make small gains on Coke's share of the domestic cola market, and in 2001 claimed 32% of the $61.7 billion industry. The company began aggressively fighting with Coke for every vending machine, restaurant contract, and supermarket shelf that came available. Boosting PepsiCo's (the parent

company of Pepsi-Cola) overall health is its fast-growing snack foods division, Frito-Lay International, which comprises more than 60% of the company's sales.

Perhaps anticipating the slowdown in soda sales, Pepsi asserted its desire to become a "total beverage company" in the early 1990s and began rapidly expanding its product mix to include bottled water, juices, and much more. This plan has paid off as an aging population of consumers have become increasingly concerned about the health risks associated with caffeine, sugar, and artificial sweeteners. At the same time, recognizing that 12- to 24-year-olds drink the most soda, Pepsi revitalized its cola products with splashy ad campaigns.

Experimenting with New Flavors of Management at Coke

Maintaining a focused, coherent strategy has been difficult for Coca-Cola since the company lost its long-time and highly regarded CEO in 1997 when Roberto Goizueta died of cancer. He was replaced by Doug Ivester, a rigid and analytical executive who alienated Coke's largest bottlers and whose European expansion efforts ran into government regulatory hurdles. As a result, Coke's earnings declined despite very aggressive growth targets, and the company's advertisements and promotional strategies lost momentum.

Ivester was replaced by Douglas Daft in December of 1999, and in January of 2000, it fell to Daft to announce that Coke would lay off 6,000 employees, about 20% of its work force. He also decided to emphasize decentralized decision making to give local managers more authority over marketing strategy. "Think local, act local" was the phrase coined by Daft to describe Coke's new strategy. "No one drinks globally. Local people get thirsty and go to their retailer and buy a locally made Coke."

Daft engaged in joint ventures with Nestlé for ready-to-drink teas and coffees, and with Walt Disney for Disney-branded children's drinks. The new joint ventures and the focus on local decision making were major departures for the company that has long been known for brilliant global marketing strategies that resulted in Coke being the most recognized brand in the world.

Daft also inherited unrealistic growth expectations. Stockholders and analysts had come to expect 15% to 20% annual growth in earnings, and 7% to 8% annual increases in revenues. "For us to achieve the growth rate that people are expecting, we have to become more diversified," stated one of Coke's marketing executives in February of 2000. "We have to move beyond Coke and the carbs (other carbonated beverages)."

Juicing Up Their Product Mixes

Although soft drink sales rose a very modest 0.6% in 2001, the top two brands experienced declines. Coca-Cola Classic managed to hold onto the top spot, but its market share declined slightly, as did Pepsi-Cola's. And both products experienced diminished sales volumes.

At the same time, the noncarbonated beverages market grew 60% faster than soft drinks in 2001, and Pepsi sold more than any other company. In fact, Pepsi owns Tropicana, the #1 orange juice brand; Lipton, the #1 iced tea brand; Gatorade, the #1 sports drink brand; and Aquafina, the #1 bottled water brand. It began pouring resources into these and other noncarbonated beverages well before Coke, and its efforts have paid off.

For instance, Pepsi acquired Tropicana in 1998 to compete with Coke's Minute Maid brand. Supported by Pepsi's marketing, Tropicana captured 39% of the chilled orange juice market in 2001, and ranked #3 in sales among all supermarket beverages, trailing only Pepsi-Cola and Coca-Cola Classic. Coca-Cola responded by introducing a not-from-concentrate orange juice called Simply Orange that it claims tastes even fresher than Tropicana. It hopes the new brand will steal away some loyal Tropicana drinkers without cannibalizing any of Minute Maid's 21% market share.

Perhaps the hardest-fought recent battle waged between Coke and Pepsi has been for the acquisition of Quaker Oats, owner of the Gatorade brand. In 2000, Coke's board refused to approve a $16 billion offer for Quaker. That cleared the way for Pepsi to buy the company for $13.8 billion in 2001, giving it a commanding 78% share of the sports drink market. By comparison, Coke's Powerade has only 15%. Soon after Pepsi acquired Gatorade, Coke decided to overhaul its line of Powerade drinks. It began by repositioning the brand to appeal to people besides just the traditional athletes targeted by Gatorade, and developed ads geared toward those participating in extreme sports such as rollerblading. It also announced plans to add new Powerade products, such as a breakfast drink and beverages with herbal supplements and energy enhancements. Some analysts worry that the brand will be diluted with all these new additions. Others feel Pepsi's lead is too large to overcome. One analyst commented that, "There's a lot of brand equity in Gatorade. As the distant number two, Coke shouldn't overinvest."

Prior to its acquisition of Quaker, Pepsi also managed to outmaneuver Coke in its bid for South Beach Beverages and the SoBe brand in 2000. At the time of sale, SoBe's line included more than 30 different drinks, with more on the way. In 2001, Coke responded by supplementing its "new age" Fruitopia line of juice drinks with the purchases of Mad River Traders and Odwalla, the makers of premium juice drinks, teas, and gourmet sodas. Although both purchases were relatively small ($7 million and $181 million, respectively) they gave Coke the means to compete with Pepsi in this rapidly growing market that has gained wide appeal with younger consumers.

Coke purchased another small company called P. J. Bean in 2001. Its Planet Java bottled coffee drinks and roasted coffee were meant to take on Pepsi's Frappuccino products. Again, the company was very small (with only 100,000 cases sold in 2000), but like Odwalla and Mad River, Coke planned to rapidly increase sales by utilizing its massive distribution system.

Although most of their focus has been on expanding their domestic, noncarbonated beverage offerings in the U.S., Coke and Pepsi have recently introduced some new sodas as well. Pepsi, trying to develop a lemon–lime brand to compete with Coke's Sprite and Cadbury Schweppes' 7UP, launched Sierra Mist in 2000. Its previous lemon–lime products, Teem, Slice, and Storm were all unsuccessful, but Sierra Mist has proven to be popular with younger consumers. Pepsi also unveiled lemon-flavored Pepsi Twist and cherry-flavored Mountain Dew Code Red, and Coke countered with Diet Coke with Lemon.

On the international front, both companies have a large stable of brands that have been developed or acquired in order to appeal to local cultures and tastes. For instance, Coke markets Thums Up in India and Inca Cola in Peru. In Japan, Coke offers Marocha Green Tea, and in Brazil it has developed a carbonated soda that incorporates a locally popular flavor from guaranaberries that are found in the Amazon. But Coke is facing challenges in many foreign markets as well. Declining economies in Brazil, Japan, and Russia adversely affected Coke's sales. And in Mexico, the #2 market for Coke outside the U.S., Coke has been charged with illegally signing exclusivity agreements with its retailers, charges similar to those that have been brought against Coke in Europe.

Perhaps the most unexpected new product to be introduced by these companies has come from Coke.

Many hip Londoners are now sporting Coca-Cola Ware. The new clothing line, which features trendy sportswear, was a hit in stylish London boutiques, and has been a big seller with Coke's coveted 13- to 29-year-old audience. Coke hopes to introduce it to the rest of Europe and Eurasia by 2002, and eventually to the U.S. market.

Noncarbonated Beverage Offerings in the United States

Type of Product	Coca-Cola	PepsiCo
Bottled water	Dasani	Aquafina
Sports drink	Powerade	Gatorade
Orange and fruit juice	Simply Orange Juice, Minute Maid, Hi-C, 5-Alive	Tropicana, Dole
Coffee drinks	Planet Java	Frappucino
Tea	Nestea and Nescafe, Mad River	Lipton, SoBe
Juice drinks	Fruitopia Mad River, Odwalla	SoBe, Fruitworks

Trying to Hit the Spot with Various Ad Strategies

Despite having more than 230 brands in 200 countries, Coca-Cola soda still accounts for 60% of the company's global sales. Long recognized as "the world's most famous brand," Coca-Cola has had a string of advertising hits using taglines such as "Coke is it," "Always Coca-Cola" and "The Real Thing." And anyone old enough to recall the days of bell-bottom pants, yellow smiley faces, and peace signs will surely remember the landmark television ad that showed kids from around the world swaying while singing, "I'd like to teach the world to sing . . . I'd like to buy the world a Coke." These campaigns contributed to Coke's recognition throughout the world, but as Coca-Cola continued to diversify its product offerings, it became more difficult to advertise on a global basis. One analyst sums up this conundrum by saying, "Without the Coke name, they're just another brand on the shelf."

For this reason, Daft announced his "Think local, act local" strategy in 2000, and empowered local marketing managers to develop their own ideas for products and how to market them. Unfortunately, this led to some ads that were not considered to be appropriate by Coke's executives, and some of them even turned off consumers. In 2001, Daft announced that the corporate marketing team in Atlanta had developed the theme, "Life Tastes Good," and that

local managers were free to use this concept and further develop it to fit local cultures and sensibilities.

The theme was yanked after it proved to be only marginally successful. In addition, many local managers were frustrated by the lack of direction from corporate headquarters, and some were turning out ads that were not considered to be in keeping with Coke's wholesome image. For example, one Italian ad featured nude bathers. As a result, some analysts feared Coke was losing its well-established identity.

Coke also banked on a tie-in with the successful film, *Harry Potter and the Sorcerer's Stone* to spur sales, but Coke's placement was so minor in the ads that Coke's marketing vice president questioned the investment. In March 2002, Coke switched gears once more and abandoned the "Think local, act local" concept. According to a marketing executive at Coca-Cola, "It was pretty obvious we had lost our way." For the second time in one year, Coke began looking for a universal tagline to spur sales of its flagship cola products, although one marketing executive contends that local managers will still have some flexibility to tweak the themes so they make sense within their local markets.

While Coke searched for its next big tagline, Pepsi proclaimed, "The Joy of Cola." Long a proponent of celebrity-based ads, Pepsi hit the jackpot in 2001 with upbeat spots featuring pop-culture princess Britney Spears singing about her favorite soft drink. That same year Pepsi launched www.pepsistuff.com, an Internet site that took Pepsi's loyalty program online. PepsiStuff was a program that allowed consumers to exchange proof of purchases for items such as branded clothing, video games, and DVDs, but it required that Pepsi print 100 million 10-page catalogs. By going online, the need for the catalogs was eliminated, and Pepsi gained valuable data about more than 3.5 million consumers by requiring them to provide name, e-mail address, zip code, and date of birth. In addition to this new database, Pepsi benefited from a 5% spike in sales during the promotion.

Only time will tell whether Pepsi will be successful in its bid to take over Coke's top spot in the famous clash of the colas. But that duel may ultimately prove to be just one battle in a much larger war.

Questions

1. Describe which factors in the macroenvironment will significantly affect the future of both Coca-Cola and PepsiCo. How will each individual factor influence the companies' marketing activities?

2. What motivates a consumer's choice of a beverage? How important is a brand name?

3. Why would Coca-Cola introduce Coca-Cola Ware? If successful, do you feel it will increase the sale of its beverages in the markets in which the clothes are sold? Why or why not?

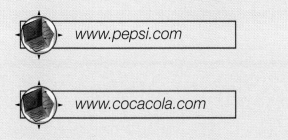

www.pepsi.com

www.cocacola.com

Sources

Case 1: eBay
Erik Schonfeld, "eBay's Secret Ingredient," *Business 2.0,* March 2002, pp. 52–58; Nick Wingfield, "eBay, Conceding Missteps, Will Close Its Site in Japan," *The Wall Street Journal,* Feb. 27, 2002, p. B4; William Hageman, "For Sale on eBay: The Enron Ethics Manual and Much More," *Chicago Tribune,* Jan. 29, 2002; Alexandra Peers and Nick Wingfield, "Sotheby's, eBay Team Up to Sell Fine Art Online," *The Wall Street Journal,* Jan. 31, 2002, p. B8; "Margaret C. Whitman," *Business Week,* Jan. 14, 2002, p. 69; Michael Totty, "The Consumers' Choice," *The Wall Street Journal,* Dec. 10, 2001, p. R6; Robert D. Hof, "The People's Company," *Business Week,* Dec. 3, 2001, pp. EB14–21; Chirsty McKerney, "Infamous Voting Machines Selling as Collector's Items," *South Florida Sun-Sentinel,* Nov. 20, 2001; Karen Bannan, "Sole Survivor," Sales & Marketing Management, July 2001, pp. 36–41; Adam Cohen, "Her Own Bubble Economy," *Time,* Apr. 30, 2001; Fred Vogelstein, "eBay," *Fortune,* Mar. 19, 2001, p. 72; Roger Taylor, "Going, Going, Gone.com," *Financial Times,* Apr. 10 and 11, 1999, p. 7; Saul Hansell, "Hackers' Bazaar," *The New York Times,* Apr. 2, 1998, p. D1.

Case 2: Coca-Cola Co. versus PepsiCo
www.pepsi.com, Apr. 14, 2002; www.cocacola.com, Apr. 14, 2002; Betsy McKay and David Luhnow, "Mexico Finds Coke and Its Bottlers Guilty of Abusing Dominant Position in Market," *The Wall Street Journal,* Mar. 8, 2002, p. B8; Betsy McKay, "Coke Hunts for Talent to Re-Establish Its Marketing Might," *The Wall Street Journal,* Mar. 6, 2002, p. B4; Betsy McKay, "PepsiCo Inc. Gains in Soda Market as Coca-Cola's Share and Sales Slip," *The Wall Street Journal,* Mar. 1, 2002, p. B5; Patricia Sellers, "Who's in Charge Here?" *Fortune,* Dec. 24, 2001; John Gaffney, "Corn Syrup, Britney, the Web, and Thou," *Business 2.0,* August/September 2001, p. 167; "Coca-Cola Expected to Disclose Purchase of Small Drinks Firm," *The Wall Street Journal,* May 11, 2001, p. B2; Betsy McKay, "Sports Drinks Refresh Rivalry for Coke, Pepsi," *The Wall Street Journal,* May 8, 2001, p. B1; Betsy McKay, "Coke Aims to Revive 'Feel Good' Factor," *The Wall Street Journal,* Apr. 20, 2001, p. B8; Betsy McKay and Daniel Machalaba, "Coke to Launch Juice Targeting Tropicana's," *The Wall Street Journal,* Mar. 15, 2001, p. A3; Richard Tomkins and Betty Liu, "Still Thirsty," *Financial Times,* Mar. 15, 2001, p. 14; Betsy McKay, "Coke's 'Think Local' Strategy Has Yet to Prove Itself," *The Wall Street Journal,* Mar. 1, 2001, p. B6; Cathleen Egan, "Coke Is Ready to Work the Runways," *The Wall Street Journal,* Feb. 12, 2001, p. A23C; Betsy McKay, "Coke to Acquire Maker of Coffee, Bottled Drinks," *The Wall Street Journal,* Jan. 12, 2001, p. B4; Betsy McKay, "Juiced Up," *The Wall Street Journal,* Nov. 6, 2000, A1; Betsy McKay and Nikhil Deogun, "Pepsi Edges Coke in Deal to Buy New Age SoBe," *The Wall Street Journal,* Oct. 30, 2000, p. B1; Betsy McKay, "Pucker Up! Pepsi's Latest Weapon Is Lemon–Lime," *The Wall Street Journal,* Oct. 13, 2000, p. B1; Dean Foust and Deborah Rubin, "Now, Coke Is No Longer It," *Business Week,* Feb. 28, 2000, pp. 148–151; Betsy McKay, "Coke's Daft Lays Out Vision for More-Nimble Soft-Drink Giant," *The Wall Street Journal,* Jan. 31, 2000, p. B2; Betsy Morris and Patricia Sellers, "What Really Happened at Coke," *Fortune,* Jan. 10, 2000, pp. 114–116; Natasha Tarpley, "Crunch Time," *Fortune,* July 19, 1999; Dean Foust, Geri Smith and David Rocks, "Man on the Spot," *Business Week,* May 3, 1999, pp. 142–151.

4

Consumer Markets and Buying Behavior

"Harley's devotees, which also include about half its 8,000 employees, are so attached to the bikes they want that the typical year-long wait for a particular model doesn't faze them."

Can **Harley-Davidson** Ride Any Faster?

You probably know what this company makes, but do you know how successful it's been? With demand running far ahead of supply, its faithful customers are willing to wait many months to get the product they want. Meanwhile the company made shareholders very happy by meeting its earnings estimates for nearly 30 consecutive quarters, and over the same period its stock price rose in value an astounding 15,000%.

Harley-Davidson, the mystique-laden U.S. motorcycle manufacturer, has rebounded strongly from a slide into near-bankruptcy that it experienced in the 1980s. It has vanquished quality problems to restore the luster of its brand and generate record earnings—as well as a customer following so diverse that its members, male and female, wear everything from leather to pinstripes and pumps to cowboy boots. Harley's devotees, which also include about half its 8,000 employees, are so attached to the bikes they want that the typical year-long wait for a particular model doesn't faze them. Meanwhile Harley's plants are running at full capacity, supplying a hefty 62% of the U.S. heavyweight motorcycle market, and 23% of the total U.S. market. Though the company says it would like to cut the wait time down to six months, it knows full well that limiting the supply of bikes only adds to the allure of its brand image.

Straddling one of the firm's massive bikes is often considered an act of rugged individualism, yet there are plenty of ways for Harley owners to "belong" to its community of riders. Harley actively caters to its customers' willingness to raise the brand to near-cult status. It runs an own-ers' group that boasts 640,000 members (called HOGs), and it maintains a 720-page parts and accessories catalog for those who can always use one more Harley item. Since its earliest days the firm has licensed its logo for use on everything from leather jackets to hats to blue jeans and even pickup trucks. The name carries such cachet that Harley owners have been known to tattoo the company logo on their bodies.

The firm has also started a 25-hour training program, run by 42 dealers in 23 states, to teach the uninitiated how to ride a motorcycle. The idea is that if they learn to ride a Harley, new bikers will want to buy one. The program has been moderately successful, with 86% of the students buying bikes, and about a quarter of them buying Harleys.

The median age of a Harley buyer has crept upward in recent years, from 37 years old in 1990 to 46 about a decade later, and because the dealers can obtain high markups on much-wanted models, today's buyers also tend to be among the more affluent. Tough competitors like Honda, Yamaha, Suzuki, and Kawasaki are taking advantage of Harley's intentional constraints on supply to pitch their products to an eager market of younger budget-minded riders. Some of these new customers are less interested in the Harley image than they are in just getting out on the road on great-looking bikes. And the competition is making headway. Harley's market share

www.harleydavidson.com

is beginning to suffer as its competitors turn out attractive and solid-looking products that buyers don't have to wait for.

Harley has a counterstrategy, however—the new V-Rod. The first small bike the company has made in more than 20 years, boasting a radically new design, the V-Rod sells for $17,000, $5,000 below the price Harley gets for its famous touring bike. Its target markets are young, hip U.S. and European bikers. The V-Rod, which weighs about 600 pounds and has been called a "piece of jewelry" made of chrome and aluminum has a 110-hp engine and a top speed of 140 miles per hour. The company isn't saying how much it spent to develop the V-Rod, but industry experts say it was more than it has spent on any other project in its history. Porsche partnered with Harley to build the V-Rod's liquid-cooled engine, an engineering first for Harley that helps boost the bike's rate of acceleration.

"The V-Rod is a signal to the world that the 100th anniversary for Harley-Davidson is not an end point, it's a milestone," says CEO Jeffrey Bleustein. And, in keeping with that long-standing Harley tradition, the V-Rod is proving very hard to get. Dealers in San Francisco, Dubuque, Gainesville, and Meredith, New Hampshire, all sold out their allocations before the new bike ever left the factory.[1]

Once again Harley buyers are willing to line up and wait. What accounts for their behavior and Harley-Davidson's success?

The market, consisting of buyers and prospective buyers, is made up of consumers and businesses. In this chapter we examine consumer markets, and in Chapter 5 we will discuss business markets. To help you understand consumers, we will first describe their demographics and highlight changes that influence marketing to them. As Harley-Davidson discovered, these changes can profoundly impact performance. Then we will examine how consumers go about making purchase decisions, a process influenced by information, social environment, psychological forces, and situational factors.

Chapter Goals

After studying this chapter, you should be able to explain:

- The factors commonly used by marketers to describe consumer markets.
- Important consumer demographic changes taking place and predicted.
- How consumers make purchase decisions.
- The information sources, psychological forces, social factors, and situational influences that affect consumers' decisions.

The Consumer Market

Ultimate consumers buy goods and services for their own personal or household use. In the U.S., there are over 290 million consumers, living in 108 million households. They spend over $5.5 trillion a year on goods and services. The efforts of many marketers are focused on these (or more likely a subset of these) potential customers.

The consumer market is not only large, it is dynamic. Consider that the U.S. is the fastest-growing industrialized nation, and that every hour there are 461 births, 274 deaths, and 122 new immigrants.[2] These statistics convert to a net change of over half a million people a month in the mix of consumers. Thus, the first challenge is to gain an understanding of what this market looks like and how it is changing. To develop an appreciation of this dynamic consumer market, we will examine its geographic distribution, several demographic dimensions, and some representative behaviors.

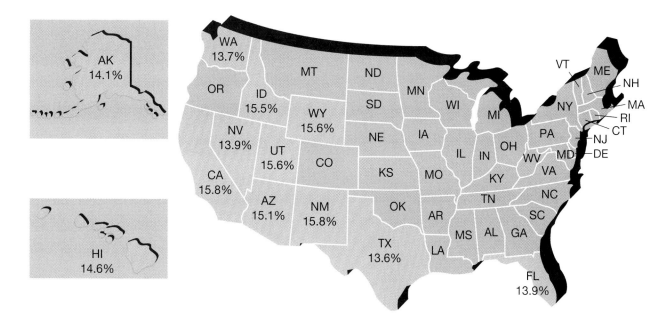

Geographic Distribution

About 16% of the U.S. population moves to a different home every year. Marketing executives monitor current patterns and projected trends in the regional distribution of the population in order to make decisions that range from where to locate retail stores to the appropriate mix of products to offer. The largest population concentrations are in the eastern half of the country, as they always have been. However, the greatest rate of population growth over the past four decades has occurred in the Southern and Western regions. Figure 4.1 shows the states projected to grow at the fastest rates between 2000 and 2010. By the year 2010, the four most populous states will be California, Texas, New York, and Florida, in that order.

The Rural Population

Rural areas of the U.S. lost population to the cities for decades, but this trend seems to have reversed. In the 1990s nearly five times as many Americans took up residence in rural areas as in the 1980s. Rural areas, although they contain only about one-fourth the total population, are now growing at nearly the same rate as cities. There are several explanations for this development. One is the growth in employment opportunities on the outer edges of large urban areas. People can take advantage of these jobs while still living in the country. Another factor is the growing number of retirees who are leaving the cities for rural areas with smaller communities and slower-paced lifestyles.

Rather than view the increasing popularity of rural living as a temporary adjustment, some see it as a gradual deconcentration of the U.S. population. With the continual growth in telecommuting (working from home), advances in communication technology, and the decline in industrial jobs, the need for people to concentrate in small areas is greatly diminished. As a result, the population may be slowly moving toward a country of smaller, more widely dispersed cities and towns.

There is also a change in the mix of the rural population. In the past, young adults migrated from rural to urban areas, and the primary source of replacements was births. Now an important source of replacements for young adults leaving rural areas is older adults moving away from urban areas. Certainly these are developments to watch because changes in the size and mix of the rural population have many implications. For example, retailers such as Wal-Mart that depend on masses of customers must consider these population shifts as store locations and the assortment of merchandise are selected. On the other hand, catalog retailers and merchants using the Internet to reach customers are likely beneficiaries of this shift.

The Urban Population   About 75% of the U.S. population lives in large urban areas. Recognizing the importance of the urban population, the federal government established a three-part classification of metropolitan areas. Observing trends within these classifications provides marketers with a means of identifying growing and declining areas. The three categories are as follows:

- The **Metropolitan Statistical Area (MSA)** is the basic urban unit. An MSA has a city with at least 50,000 residents and a total area population of at least 100,000. The boundaries of an MSA are drawn along county lines and may cross state borders. But the counties must be socially and economically integrated, and virtually all employment must be nonagricultural. There are about 260 MSAs. Not suprisingly, almost all of the MSAs projected to grow the fastest are in the West and Southwest.

- A **Primary Metropolitan Statistical Area (PMSA)** is an MSA that has a population of at least 1 million. About 73 of the largest MSAs are categorized as PMSAs.

- A **Consolidated Metropolitan Statistical Area (CMSA)** is a giant urban center consisting of two or more adjacent PMSAs. The hub of each of the 18 CMSAs is a very large city such as New York, Los Angeles, Chicago, or Philadelphia.

The Suburban Population   As metropolitan areas have grown, their composition has also changed. The central cities are growing very slowly, and in some cases older, established parts of the cities are actually losing population. In 1950, 60% of the people living in metropolitan areas lived in the central city. By 1990 that figure had been reversed, with over 65% of metropolitan residents living in the suburbs.

Most of the real growth in the last 25 years has occurred in the suburbs. As families moved to the suburbs to escape the congestion and turmoil in the cities, the economic, racial, and ethnic compositions of many cities (especially the core areas) changed. For example, 60% of African American households live in the central cities of large metro areas, but only 25% of African American households reside in the suburbs. More recently, the suburbs have expanded outward, creating "inner-ring" suburban communities that are more like the urban centers they encircle than the affluent suburbs. The changes in these areas have had several market implications.

First, suburbanites are more likely than city dwellers to have two cars because of the unavailability of mass transit. They also are inclined to spend more leisure time at home, so they are a big market for home entertainment and recreation.

Second, services providers typically locate close to their markets. That's why retail services firms such as banks, fast-food establishments, florists, and travel agents open branches or start new ventures in the suburbs. In addition, many investment and insurance brokers, realtors, physicians and dentists, and other professional service firms have left the central cities to pursue suburbanites.

The slow but steady migration of retailers to the suburbs created a void in many inner cities, and led to the assumption that inner cities have little market potential. However, that view may be changing. The Initiative for a Competitive Inner City (ICIC) has identified several advantages inner-city locations offer businesses. Of particular interest to retailers are a ready supply of employees and underserved markets. For example, inner-city residents annually spend $85 billion, but more than 25% of that spending is done with retailers outside the inner city.[3]

Stargate Industries, headquartered in Pittsburgh, PA, and pictured here, is an Internet service provider that was born out of the founder's frustrations with the poor connections and bad service of existing providers in the early 1990s. Now it's a $30+ million, nationwide business with over 370 employees. Equally important, it is located in the inner-city, providing jobs and opportunities for many people. As a result, Stargate was selected by ICIC as the #1 inner-city firm for 2002.

www.innercity100.org

Consumer Demographics

Demographics are the vital statistics that describe a population. Marketers make use of a variety of demographic characteristics including age, gender, family life cycle, education, income, and ethnicity. They are important to marketers because they are closely related to the demand for many products.

Changes in demographics signal the rise of new markets and the elimination of others. Some noteworthy demographic developments and their significance for marketers are described below.

Age
As was pointed out in Chapter 2, the U.S. population is getting older. This aging trend will continue. By 2010, there will be 23 million more consumers over the age of 50. The marketing implications are significant because this group will account for just 32% of the population, but half of all discretionary income and three-quarters of the total financial assets held by consumers. This age group spends more than younger consumers on health insurance, medical services, drugs, education (for their children), housing, and home remodeling. Other areas likely to feel the impact are the apparel industry (older consumers buy less) and the travel industry (older consumers have the income and time to travel).

Family Life Cycle
Family life-cycle stages, the various forms families can take over time, are major determinants of behavior. A single-parent family (divorced, widowed, or never married) with dependent children faces social and economic problems quite different from those of a two-parent family. Young married couples with no children typically devote large shares of their income to clothing, autos, and recreation. When children start arriving, expenditure patterns shift as many young families buy and furnish a home. Families with teenagers find larger portions of the budget going for food, clothing, and educational needs.

Researchers have identified nine distinct life-cycle stages with different buying behavior:[4]

- *Bachelor stage:* young, single people
- *Young married:* couples with no children
- *Full nest I:* young married couples with children
- *Single parents:* young or middle-aged people with dependent children
- *Divorced and alone:* divorced without dependent children
- *Middle-aged married:* middle-aged married couples without children
- *Full nest II:* middle-aged married couples with dependent children
- *Empty nest:* older married couples with no children living with them
- *Older single:* single people still working or retired

Just over 40% of adults or about 80 million people are unmarried. The living arrangements of these singles take several forms. Many live alone. For the first time the number of single-person households is greater than the number of traditional families—married couples with children. The impact that singles of either sex have on demand is demonstrated by the availability of apartments for singles, social clubs for singles, and resorts, cruises, and restaurants catering to singles. Other arrangements include single parents living with children, people living together as unmarried couples, or people sharing a house or apartment with one or more roommates.

In 2000, there were over 8 million single-parent households with children under 18, a number projected to increase to 9 million by 2010. Although they typically have less money to spend than traditional households, more purchase decisions and a greater proportion of actual purchases are made by the children in these families. As a result, advertisers that normally focus on adults are increasingly looking for ways to reach children.

The bottom line is marketers today think beyond the traditional stereotype of a household—a married couple with children—in developing marketing plans. There are two concerns in particular they must address. The first is the decision-making process in today's households. For example, it is not as apparent who are the primary decision makers and who may be the influencers. The second concern is the expected duration of the living arrangement. Young adults today are likely to have several more different household arrangements during their lives than their parents. As a result, they are likely to include the expected length of a living arrangement in the purchase decisions of durable goods such as appliances or furniture.

Education and Income

Education has a significant impact on income. A high school diploma is worth about $600,000 in additional income over a lifetime, and a college degree is worth $1.5 million. For families where both spouses work (that is, over half of all the couples in the U.S.), these earnings figures can be doubled. About 85% of Americans over 25 have completed high school, and 25% have at least a bachelor's degree. Combine these observations with the fact that 15 million Americans are enrolled in institutions of higher learning, an increase of 50% over just 20 years ago, and it suggests that the U.S. population is well educated and prosperous.

However, these figures don't represent the complete picture. In spite of the considerable increase in disposable income in the past 30 years, 32 million people (about 12% of the population) live below the government-defined poverty level. And the situation may get worse. It was recently reported that high-paying, unionized manufacturing jobs for unskilled workers are being increasingly replaced by lower-paid, nonunion service jobs.[5]

Panera Bread restaurants illustrate an appeal to changing consumer demographics and tastes. Whereas fastfood franchises such as McDonald's or Taco Bell focus on speed, price, and offerings that appeal to children, Panera represents a new category of casual dining that offers a more adult menu and atmosphere along with quick services. What changes in the population do you think Panera is responding to?

Knowing what is happening to incomes is important because spending patterns are influenced by how much income people have. Here are some findings from Department of Labor studies of consumer spending:[6]

- For all product categories, people in a given income bracket spend significantly more *total* dollars than those in lower brackets. However, the lower-income households devote a larger *percentage* of their total expenditures to some product categories, such as housing.

- In each successively higher-income group, the amount spent for food declines as a percentage of total expenditures.

- The percentage of total expenditures devoted to the total of housing, utilities, and home operation remains reasonably constant in the middle- and high-income brackets.

- The percentage of total expenditures for transportation, including the purchase of automobiles, tends to grow as incomes increase in low- and middle-income groups. The proportion levels off or drops a bit in higher-income brackets.

- In each successively higher-income group, a smaller percentage of total family expenditures goes for health care, but a higher percentage goes for insurance and pensions.

Race and Ethnicity

In many cities, the ethnic population is especially large. African Americans, Hispanics, and Asians constitute over 50% of the population in 25 of the nation's largest cities. These cities include Los Angeles, San Antonio, New Orleans, Miami, Atlanta, Baltimore, Washington, DC, Detroit, and Chicago. During the 1990s, ethnic minorities accounted for nearly 70% of total U.S. population growth, a trend that is expected to continue.

Segmenting markets based on ethnicity presents an interesting challenge. On the one hand, a company must understand an ethnic group's buying behavior and motivation. Studies by the Bureau of Labor Statistics and private research firms show that there are some distinct differences among races. For example, on average, African American and white Americans differ in income, level of education, and the likelihood of living in urban or rural areas. And data from the 2000 census of the population indicate that the racial mix of most neighborhoods did not change during the 1990s. The average white person lives in a neighborhood that is 83% white. The average black person lives in a neighborhood that is 54% black.[7]

On the other hand, ethnic markets are not homogeneous units any more than any other population segment consisting of 20 or 30 million people. This is reflected in the 2000 census in which for the first time respondents had the option of identifying themselves with more than one racial group. Given this opportunity, nearly 7 million people declared they were multiracial.[8] There is nearly as much diversity within every ethnic group as there is similarity. African American and Hispanic markets contain subgroups based on income, occupation, geographic location, and life-cycle stage. Thus, it would be a serious marketing error to be misled by aggregate figures and averages. For example, firms that make products for which skin color is a major choice determinant recognize this diversity. Prescriptives, a subsidiary of Estée Lauder cosmetic company, has a line of makeup foundations for black women with 115 different shades.

www.prescriptives.com

This broad overview of the consumer market is intended to suggest its vibrancy and diversity. It also indicates that there are many ways to describe consumers. A challenge faced by marketers, which we will discuss in detail in Chapter 6, is how to most effectively describe particular markets. But first, let's continue our examination of consumers with a look at their decision making.

Consumer Decision Making

Why is consumer marketing difficult? We've just described one reason: The mix of people in the market is constantly changing. Not only is it difficult to anticipate what marketing program will work, but what worked yesterday may not work today—or tomorrow. Another challenge is understanding how consumers make decisions. This is reflected in the chapter-opening case about Harley-Davidson. In recent years the market for motorcycles has changed substantially. It is now older, wealthier, and much more likely to include females—and we haven't yet discussed the reasons why consumers buy bikes! Thus, Harley-Davidson, as well as all other marketers, must constantly improve their understanding of consumers and adapt their strategies accordingly.

Figure 4.2 brings all the dimensions of buying behavior together in a model that provides the structure for our discussion. The model features the buying-decision process and the four primary forces that influence each stage.

The Consumer Buying-Decision Process

To deal with the marketing environment and make purchases, consumers engage in a decision process. One way to look at that process is to view it as problem solving. When faced with a problem that can be resolved through a purchase ("I'm bored. How do I satisfy my need for entertainment?"), the consumer goes through a series of logical stages to arrive at a decision.

As shown in the center of Figure 4.2, the stages of the **consumer buying-decision process** are:

1. *Need recognition.* The consumer is moved to action by a need or desire.
2. *Identification of alternatives.* The consumer identifies alternative products and brands and collects information about them.

FIGURE 4.2

The Consumer Buying-Decision Process and the Factors that Influence It.

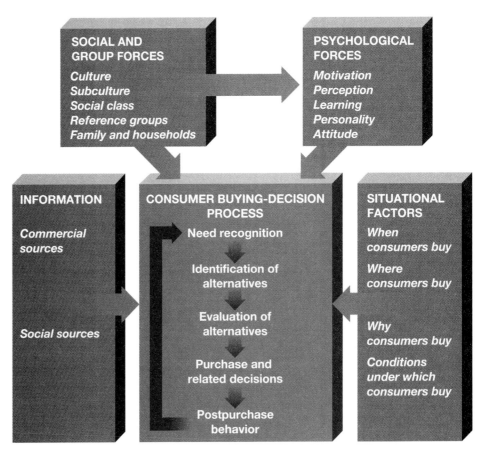

3. *Evaluation of alternatives.* The consumer weighs the pros and cons of the alternatives identified.

4. *Decisions.* The consumer decides to buy or not to buy and makes other decisions related to the purchase.

5. *Postpurchase behavior.* The consumer seeks reassurance that the choice made was the correct one.

Although this model is a useful starting point for examining purchase decisions, the process is not always as straightforward as it may appear. Consider these possible variations:

- The consumer can withdraw at any stage prior to the actual purchase if the need diminishes or no satisfactory alternatives are available.

- The stages usually are of different lengths, may overlap, and some may even be skipped.

- The consumer is often involved in several different buying decisions simultaneously, and the outcome of one can affect the others.

A significant factor influencing how consumer decisions are made is the consumer's **level of involvement**, reflected in the amount of effort that is expended in satisfying a need. Some situations are *high* involvement. That is, when a need arises a consumer decides to actively collect and evaluate information about the purchase situation. These purchases entail all five stages of the buying-decision process.

Although it is risky to generalize because consumers are so different, involvement tends to be *greater* under any of the following conditions:

- The consumer lacks information about alternatives for satisfying the need.

- The consumer considers the amount of money involved to be large.

- The product has considerable social importance.

- The product is seen as having a potential for providing significant benefits.

Most buying decisions are for relatively low-priced products that have close, acceptable substitutes and therefore do not meet any of these conditions. These are *low*-involvement situations, in which the consumer either skips or moves very quickly through stages 2 and 3 of the decision process—identification of alternatives and evaluation of alternatives. Typical examples of low-involvement situations are the majority of purchases made in supermarkets, variety stores, and hardware stores.

The notion of involvement raises two important marketing issues: loyalty and impulse purchases. **Loyalty** exists when a consumer, because of past experience, is sufficiently satisfied with a particular brand or retailer that he or she buys that brand or from that retailer when the need arises without considering other alternatives. This is low-involvement purchasing because the decision does not involve gathering and analyzing information. However, the product may be very important to the consumer.

Impulse buying, or purchasing with little or no advance planning, is also a form of low-involvement decision making. A shopper waiting in the checkout line at a grocery store who notices the headline "Plane Missing since 1939 Lands at LaGuardia" on an issue of *Weekly World News* and purchases a copy to satisfy his or her curiosity is engaging in impulse buying. Self-service, open-display retailing has conditioned shoppers to do more impulse buying. Marketing researchers have found that an increasingly large proportion of purchases are unplanned. Consider, for example, how many of your purchases are unplanned (or impulsive). Because of the growth of this type of low-involvement purchasing, greater emphasis must be placed on promotional programs such as in-store videos demonstrating product benefits. Also, displays and packages must be made appealing, because they serve as silent sales people.

In the following discussion we examine the complete five-stage process that characterizes high-involvement buying decisions. However, keep in mind that the stages may have to be adjusted to fit the circumstances of a particular purchase situation. For a wealthy person, the purchase of a country club membership could be a low-involvement experience, whereas for a person with a high need for social acceptance, purchase of toothpaste might be highly involving. Thus involvement must be viewed from the perspective of the consumer, not the product.

Recognition of an Unsatisfied Need

Everyone has unsatisfied needs and wants that create discomfort. Some needs can be satisfied by acquiring and consuming goods and services. Thus the process of deciding what to buy begins when a need that can be satisfied through consumption becomes strong enough to motivate a person. This need recognition may arise internally (for example, when you feel hungry). Or the need may be dormant until it is aroused by an external stimulus, such as an ad or the sight of a product. The decision process can also be triggered by the depletion of an existing product (your pen runs out of ink) or dissatisfaction with a product currently being used.

Becoming aware of a need, however, is not enough to generate a purchase. As consumers we have many needs and wants, but finite amounts of time and money. Thus there is competition among our needs.

Identification of Alternatives

Once a need has been recognized, the consumer must next identify the alternatives capable of satisfying the need. Typically alternative products are identified first, and then alternative brands are identified. Product and brand identification may range from a simple memory scan of previous experiences to an extensive external search.

The search for alternatives is influenced by:

- How much information the consumer already has from past experiences and other sources.
- The consumer's confidence in that information.
- The expected value of additional information or, put another way, what more information is perceived to be worth in terms of the time and money required to get it.

Evaluation of Alternatives

When a satisfactory number of alternatives have been identified, the consumer must evaluate them before making a decision. The evaluation may involve a single criterion, or several criteria, against which the alternatives are compared. For example, you might select a frozen dinner on price alone or on price, taste, and ease of preparation. When multiple criteria are involved, they typically do not carry equal weight. For example, preparation time might be more important than price.

Because experience is often limited or dated and information from sources such as advertising or friends can be biased, evaluations can be factually incorrect. That is, a consumer may believe that the price of brand A is higher than that of brand B, when in fact the opposite is true. Marketers monitor consumers to determine what choice criteria they use, to identify any changes that may be taking place in their criteria or priorities, and to correct any unfavorable misperceptions.

Purchase and Related Decisions

After searching and evaluating, the consumer must decide whether to buy. Thus the first outcome is the decision to purchase or not to purchase the alternative evaluated as most desirable. If the decision is to buy, a series of related decisions must be made regarding features, where and when to make the actual transaction, how to take delivery or possession, the method of payment, and other issues. So the decision to make a purchase is really the beginning of an entirely new series of decisions that may be as time-consuming and difficult as the initial one.

Have some firms been too successful for their own good? After achieving near cult status among consumers some brands and some retailers experience problems that are variously described as overexposure or oversaturation. Maybe consumers' tastes change, possibly they get bored with a brand or a store after awhile, or maybe when they see others not like themselves using the product they feel it no longer conveys the desired image. Whatever the reason mega brands such as Levi, Nike, and Toyota and retailers such as McDonald's and The Gap have experienced it.

When a popular brand or retailer hits a "flat spot" with customers, what should managers do? Some firms try to fight through it. Convinced that because whatever made the product successful is still there, they feel staying the course will bring the product back. Others replace the product with new or refined versions. Others add new products or models. Faced with an aging customer base (the average age of Camry buyers is nearly 50), Toyota has attempted to reach younger consumers with several new vehicles, but none has been particularly successful. The firm's latest bid is the Scion brand. An interesting marketing question is how far should the new brand distance itself from Toyota's existing offerings?

Sources: Norihiko Shirouzu, "This Is Not Your Father's Toyota," *The Wall Street Journal*, Mar. 26, 2002, pp. B1+; Sholnn Freeman, "Auto Makers Target Young Buyers with Hot Hatchbacks," *The Wall Street Journal*, Mar. 19, 2002, p. B9.

Alert marketers recognize that the outcome of these additional decisions affects satisfaction, so they find ways to help consumers make them as efficiently as possible. For example, car dealers have speeded up loan approval, streamlined the process of tracking down a car that meets the buyer's exact specifications, and, in the case of Saturn, made delivery of the car a "miniceremony" to make the customer feel important.

Selecting a source from which to make a purchase is one of the buying decisions. Sources can be as varied as Internet websites or manufacturers' outlets. The most common source is a retail store, and the reasons a consumer chooses to shop at a certain store are called **patronage buying motives.**

People want to feel comfortable when they shop. They want the assurance of being around people like themselves and in an environment that reflects their values. There are consumers, for example, who would feel uncomfortable shopping in an upscale store such as I. Magnin or Bergdorf-Goodman.

Patronage motives can range from something as simple as how easy an item is to find, to something more complex, such as the atmosphere of a restaurant. Some common patronage motives are:

- Location convenience
- Service speed
- Merchandise accessibility
- Crowding
- Prices

- Merchandise assortment
- Services offered
- Store appearance
- Sales personnel
- Mix of other shoppers

Like the criteria consumers use to choose products and brands, their patronage motives will vary depending on the purchase situation. Successful retailers evaluate their customers carefully and design their stores accordingly. For example, some shoppers might be surprised to learn that such different apparel outlets as The Limited stores, Victoria's Secret, Henri Bendel, Bath & Body Works, and Express are part of The Limited Brands Corp. A manufacturer, in turn, selects retailers with the patronage characteristics that complement its product and appeal to its market.

Firms selling on the Internet must also identify and appeal to patronage motives. For example, one of the features attributed to Internet shopping is convenience. Thus it's essential that a firm's website be easy to access and navigate. Fancy, animated graphics may be pretty, but they may not be what Internet shoppers are seeking.

Postpurchase Behavior   What a consumer learns from going through the buying process has an influence on how he or she will behave the next time the same need arises. Furthermore, new opinions and beliefs have been formed and old ones have been revised. It's this change in the consumer that is indicated by an arrow in Figure 4.2 from the *postpurchase behavior* stage of the buying-decision process model back to the need-recognition stage.

Something else often occurs following a purchase. Have you ever gone through a careful decision process for a major purchase, selected what you thought was the best alternative, but then had doubts about your choice after the purchase? What you were experiencing is **postpurchase cognitive dissonance**—a state of anxiety brought on by the difficulty of choosing from among desirable alternatives. Unfortunately for marketers, dissonance is quite common, and if the anxiety is not relieved, the consumer may be unhappy with the chosen product even if it performs as expected!

Postpurchase cognitive dissonance occurs when each of the alternatives seriously considered by the consumer has both attractive and unattractive features. For example, in purchasing a DVD player, the set selected may be the most expensive (unattractive), but provides the best sound system (attractive). The brand not chosen was recommended by a friend (attractive), but came with a very limited warranty (unattractive). After the purchase is made, the unattractive features of the product purchased grow in importance in the consumer's mind, as do the attractive features offered by the rejected alternatives. As a result, we begin to doubt the wisdom of the choice and experience anxiety over the decision. Internet shoppers may be especially prone to dissonance because they are unable to physically examine or test the product and must wait for some time after the purchase before taking possession of the product. Dissonance typically increases (1) the greater the importance of the purchase decision and (2) the greater the similarity between the item selected and item(s) rejected. Thus buying a house or car is likely to create more dissonance than buying a set of tires.

Consumers try to reduce their postpurchase anxieties. They avoid information (such as ads for the rejected products) that is likely to increase the dissonance. And they seek out information that supports their decision, such as reassurance from friends. For Internet shoppers, the use of electronic shopping agents, known as bots, to compare prices and find the best deals may reduce postpurchase dissonance. Also, prior to the purchase, putting more effort into evaluating alternatives can increase a consumer's confidence and reduce dissonance. Sellers can reduce the likelihood of dissonance with guarantees and liberal return policies, high-quality postsale service programs, and reassuring communications after the purchase.

www.botspot.com

With this background on the buying-decision process, we can examine what influences buying behavior. We'll begin with the sources and types of information used by consumers.

Information and Purchase Decisions

Purchase decisions require information. Until consumers know what products and brands are available, what features and benefits they offer, who sells them at what prices, and where they can be purchased, there won't be a decision process because there won't be any decisions to make.

As shown in Figure 4.2, there are two sources of buying information—the commercial environment and the social environment. The **commercial information environment** consists of all marketing organizations and individuals that attempt to communicate with consumers. It includes manufacturers, retailers, advertisers, and sales people whenever any of them are engaged in efforts to inform or persuade.

Advertising is the most familiar type of commercial information. In the U.S., $230 billion is spent every year on advertising of all types. It's estimated that on average, the typical adult is exposed to about 300 ad messages a day, or almost 10,000 per month. Commercial sources also include retail store clerks, business websites, and telephone solicitors as well as consumers' physical involvement with products, such as trial product use and sampling.

The **social information environment** is comprised of family, friends, and acquaintances who directly or indirectly provide information about products. To appreciate the marketing significance of these social sources, consider how often your conversations with friends or family deal with purchases you are considering or have made.

The most common kind of social information is word-of-mouth communication—two or more people discussing a product. "Chat rooms" on the Internet have become popular places for consumers with similar interests to gather and exchange information. Other social sources include observing others using products and exposure to products in the homes of others. Recognizing the power of word-of-mouth communication, marketers actively stimulate it. For example, Ford identified trendsetters in several markets and gave them each a new Ford Focus subcompact to drive for six months. Their only duty was to give away a Ford-themed trinket to anyone showing an interest in the car. Similar tactics, aimed at getting consumers to talk about products, have been employed by the marketers of Vespa Scooters, Lee Jeans, and the Harry Potter book series.[9]

When all the different types of information are considered, it becomes apparent that there is enormous competition for the consumer's attention. Consequently, the consumer's mind has to be marvelously efficient to sort and process this barrage of information. To better understand consumer behavior, we will begin by examining the social and group forces that influence the individual's psychological makeup and also play a role in specific buying decisions.

Social Influences

The ways we think, believe, and act are determined to a great extent by social forces. And our individual buying decisions—including the needs we experience, the alternatives we consider, and the ways in which we evaluate them—are affected by the social forces that surround us. To reflect this dual impact, the arrows in Figure 4.2 extend from the social forces in two directions—to the psychological makeup of the individual and to the buying-decision process. Our description begins with culture, the force with the most *general* impact, and moves to the force with the most *specific* impact, the household.

Culture   **Culture** is a set of symbols and artifacts created by a society and handed down from generation to generation as determinants and regulators of human behavior. The symbols may be intangible (attitudes, beliefs, values, language) or tangible (tools, housing, products, works of art). Although culture does not include instinctive biological acts, the way people perform instinctive acts such as eating is culturally influenced. Thus, everybody gets hungry, but what, when, and how people eat vary among cultures. For example, in the Ukraine, raw pig fat is considered a delicacy.

Cultures do change over time, as old patterns gradually give way to the new. During recent years in the U.S., cultural trends of far-reaching magnitude have occurred. Marketing executives must be alert to these changes so they can adjust their planning to be in step with, or even a little ahead of, the times. Some cultural trends affecting the buying behavior of U.S. consumers in recent years include the following:

- *Time has become as valuable as money.* Americans feel overcommitted, with more obligations and demands on their time than they can fulfill. This has contributed to the growth in time-saving services (such as home cleaning services

Is western marketing changing Chinese women?

Some dramatic changes are taking place in China's consumer markets. First, there was the entrance of western brand names such as Coca-Cola and Philips, then retailers such as Wal-Mart and fast-food outlets such as KFC and McDonald's arrived on the scene. But maybe the most important development for the future of consumer marketing in China has been the change in Chinese women. The portion of females in the work force holding managerial positions more than doubled between 1990 and 2000, whereas the portion of women with professional or technical jobs rose from 17% to 23%. The impact has been twofold. First, these young women have more income to spend and, second, they have been exposed to western marketing. As a result, the appeals being made to this developing market are growing in number and chang-

ing in form. For example, a recent fashion exhibit in Shanghai attracted over 500 firms from more than 20 countries. And the advertising aimed at this group by western marketers is also changing. For example, in an ad for its Rejoice shampoo, Procter & Gamble revised the scenario from featuring an airline stewardess to one that features a woman working as a mechanical engineer. Because the average annual income in China's urban areas has more than tripled since 1990, many western firms foresee major changes in consumer behavior. However, because the annual income amounts to only the equivalent of $764, it remains to be seen how consumers will spend it.

Sources: Cris Prystay, "As China's Women Change, Marketers Notice," *The Wall Street Journal*, May 30, 2002, p. A11; "Western Fashions Hit Traditional China," Xinhua News Agency, Mar. 19, 2002; "China Attracts Well-Known Fashoin Giants," Xinhua News Agency, Apr. 25, 2002.

and Internet shopping) and labor-saving products (such as prepared entrées in grocery store delis).

- *Two-income families are the norm.* When both adults in a household work outside the home, it affects not only the ability to buy but also the choice of products and the time in which to buy and consume them. It has also created a demand for preschools and day-care centers.

- *Gender roles are losing their identity.* This is reflected in educational opportunities, occupations, clothing styles, sports participation, and language.

- *Youthfulness is admired.* To be thought of as younger than your chronological age (once you're over 21!) is seen by most as a compliment. To retain the vigor and healthy appearance generally associated with youth, more Americans have made exercise a regular part of their lives.

Subcultures   In any society as heterogeneous as the U.S., there are bound to be subcultures. **Subcultures** are groups in a culture that exhibit characteristic behavior patterns sufficient to distinguish them from other groups within the same culture. The behavior patterns that distinguish subcultures are based on factors such as race, nationality, religion, and urban-rural identification. Some of these were discussed earlier in the chapter in the context of demographic market forces.

A subculture takes on importance in marketing if it constitutes a significant part of the population and specific purchasing patterns can be traced to it. For example, increasing attention is being paid in the U.S. to behavioral influences stemming from racial and ethnic subcultures. Early immigrants came to America primarily from Europe. Now the principal sources are Asia and Latin America. West Coast cities have had large Chinese and Japanese populations for over a century. The new wave of Asian immigrants, however, includes people from Korea, Vietnam, and Thailand. The U.S. Census Bureau has observed that over 40 separate languages are spoken by substantial segments of the Los Angeles area population. These new subcultures bring with them different beliefs, customs, and values, not to mention languages, that must be taken into consideration by firms attempting to sell to them.

To reach a teen subculture with an anti-smoking message, the American Legacy Foundation used an award-winning approach that brought music, entertainment, and fashion to concert venues, schools, and other teen hangouts. Because traditional media and standard messages are generally ignored or overlooked by this group, to be effective the message had to reflect how this subculture behaves.

Social Class

Social class is a ranking within a society determined by the members of the society. Social classes exist in virtually all societies, and people's buying behavior is often strongly influenced by the class to which they belong or to which they aspire.

Without making value judgments about whether one class is superior to or happier than another, sociologists have attempted to describe class structure in a meaningful way. One scheme useful to marketing managers is the five-class model developed by Coleman and Rainwater,[10] classifying people by education, occupation, and type of residential neighborhood.

Notice that income is not one of the classification factors. Social class is not an indication of spending capability; rather, it is an indication of preferences and life-style. For example, a young lawyer might make the same income as a middle-aged electrician, but they probably have quite different family backgrounds, tastes, and attitudes.

In the summary of the five classes in U.S. society that follows, the population percentages are only approximations and may vary from one geographic area to another.

- The *upper class*, about 2% of the population, includes two groups: (1) socially prominent "old families," often with inherited wealth, and (2) newly rich corporate executives, owners of large businesses, and professionals. They live in exclusive neighborhoods and patronize fancy shops. They buy expensive goods and services, but they do not conspicuously display their wealth.

- The *upper-middle class*, about 12% of the population, is composed of moderately successful business and professional people and owners of medium-sized companies. They are well educated, have a strong desire for success, and push their children to do well. Their purchases are more conspicuous than those of the upper class. They live well, belong to private clubs, and support the arts and various social causes.

- The *lower-middle class*, about 32% of the population, consists of office workers, most sales people, teachers, technicians, and small business owners. As a group they are often referred to as white-collar workers. They strive for respectability and buy what is popular. Their homes are well cared for, and they save money to send their children to college. They are future oriented, strive to move up to the higher social classes, have self-confidence, and are willing to take risks.

- The *upper-lower class*, about 38% of the population, is the blue-collar working class of production workers, semiskilled workers, and service personnel. These people are tied closely to family for economic and emotional support. Male-female roles are quite clearly defined. They live in smaller houses than the lower-middle class, drive larger cars, have more appliances, and watch bigger television sets. They buy American products, and stay close to home on vacations. Their orientation is short term, and they are very concerned about security.

- The *lower-lower class*, about 16% of the population, is composed of unskilled workers, the chronically unemployed, unassimilated immigrants, and people frequently on welfare. They are typically poorly educated, have low incomes, and live in substandard houses and neighborhoods. They tend not to have many opportunities; hence they focus on the present. Often their purchases are not based on economic considerations. The public tends to differentiate within this class between the "working poor" and the "welfare poor."

Marketers recognize that there are substantial differences among classes with respect to buying behavior. Because of this diversity, different social classes are likely to respond differently to a seller's marketing program. Thus, it may be necessary to design marketing programs tailored to specific social classes.

Reference Groups

Each group in a society develops its own standards of behavior that then serve as guides, or frames of reference, for the members. Families and a circle of friends are such groups. Members share values and are expected to conform to the group's behavioral patterns. But a person does not have to be a member of a group to be influenced by it. There are groups we aspire to join (a campus honor society or club) and groups we admire even though membership may be impossible (a professional athletic team). All of these are potential **reference groups**—groups of people who influence a person's attitudes, values, and behavior.

Studies have shown that personal advice in face-to-face groups is much more effective as a behavioral determinant than advertising. That is, in selecting products or changing brands, we are more likely to be influenced by word-of-mouth information from members of our reference groups than by ads or sales people. This is especially true when the information comes from someone we consider knowledgeable about the product and/or whom we trust. A research firm that tracks consumer trends reports that 83% of consumers considering a purchase ask for information from someone they know already owns the product.[11]

Advertisers are relying on reference-group influence when they use celebrity spokespersons. Professional athletes, musicians, models, and actors can influence people who would like to be associated with them in some way—for example, Alex Rodriguez of the Texas Rangers baseball team for Radio Shack, Kirstie Alley (*Cheers*) for Pier 1 Imports, and Wynonna Judd (country singer) for milk.

Reference-group influence in marketing is not limited to well-known personalities. Any group whose qualities a person admires can serve as a reference. For example, the physically fit, the socially conscious, and the professionally successful have all served as reference groups in advertising.

Families and Households

A **family** is a group of two or more people related by blood, marriage, or adoption living together in a household. During their lives many people will belong to at least two families—the one into which they are born and the one they form at marriage. The birth family primarily determines core values and attitudes. The marriage family, in contrast, has a more direct influence on specific purchases. For example, family size is important in the purchase of a car.

A household is a broader concept that relates to a dwelling rather than a relationship. A **household** consists of a single person, a family, or any group of unrelated persons who occupy a housing unit. Thus an unmarried homeowner, college

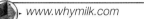

9 essential nutrients in every easy-to-open bottle.

got milk?

students sharing an off-campus apartment, and cohabiting couples are examples of households.

Average household size at the end of 2000 was 2.62 members, whereas average family size was 3.17 persons. Although household size has remained about the same since 1990, family size has been slowly declining for years. This long-term trend is due in large part to more single-parent families, childless married couples, and unmarried people living together.

Sensitivity to household and family structure is important in designing marketing strategy. It affects such dimensions as product size (How large should refrigerators be?) and the design of advertising (Who might be offended by the depiction of a "traditional" family in a TV ad?).

In addition to the impact household structure has on the purchase behavior of members, it is also interesting to consider the buying behavior of the household as a unit. Marketers should treat this issue as four separate questions, because each may call for different strategies:

- Who influences the buying decision?
- Who makes the buying decision?
- Who makes the actual purchase?
- Who uses the product?

Different household members may assume these various roles, or one individual may play several roles in a particular purchase. For example, children aged 4 to 12 influence over $187 billion in family purchases.[12] There have also been changes in who does the shopping. In families, for many years the female household head did most of the day-to-day buying. However, as was described earlier, this behavior has changed as more women have entered the work force, and men and children have assumed greater household responsibility.

Psychological Factors

In discussing the psychological influences on consumer behavior, we will continue to use the model in Figure 4.2. One or more motives within a person activate goal-oriented behavior. One such behavior is perception; that is, the collection and processing of information. Other important psychological activities that play a role in buying decisions are learning, attitude formation, personality, and self-concept.

Motivation—the Starting Point
To understand why consumers behave as they do, we must first ask why a person acts at all. The answer is, "Because he or she experiences a need." All behavior starts with a need. Security, social acceptance, and prestige are examples of needs. A need must be aroused or stimulated before it becomes a motive. Thus, a **motive** is a need sufficiently stimulated to move an individual to seek satisfaction.

We have many dormant needs that do not produce behavior because they are not sufficiently intense. Hunger strong enough to impel us to search for food and fear great enough to motivate a search for security are examples of aroused needs that become motives for behavior.

The broadest classification of motives is based on the source from which a need arises:

- Needs aroused from physiological states of tension (such as the need for sleep).
- Needs aroused from psychological states of tension (such as the needs for affection and self-respect).

A refinement of this concept was formulated by the psychologist Abraham Maslow. He identified a hierarchy of five need levels, arrayed in the order in which people seek to gratify them.[13] **Maslow's needs hierarchy** is shown in Figure 4.3. Maslow recognized that a normal person is most likely to be working toward need satisfaction on several levels at the same time, and that rarely are all needs on a given level fully satisfied. However, the hierarchy indicates that the majority of needs on a particular level must be reasonably well satisfied before a person is motivated at the next higher level.

FIGURE 4.3

Maslow's Hierarchy of Needs.

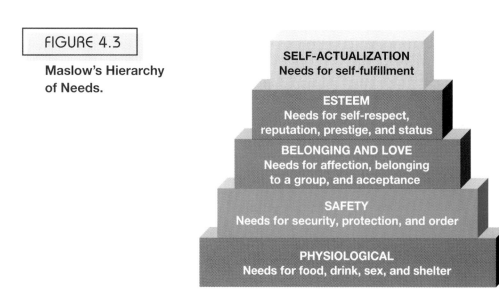

SELF-ACTUALIZATION
Needs for self-fulfillment

ESTEEM
Needs for self-respect, reputation, prestige, and status

BELONGING AND LOVE
Needs for affection, belonging to a group, and acceptance

SAFETY
Needs for security, protection, and order

PHYSIOLOGICAL
Needs for food, drink, sex, and shelter

For marketers attempting to design appealing products, persuasive ad messages, inviting retail store layouts, and the like, Maslow's five levels may be too general. Fortunately, there are continuing efforts to better understand and describe motives. For example, a recently proposed model suggests that all behavior is determined by 15 fundamental motives, and individual differences are the result of varying priorities and intensities among these motives.[14] The 15 motives are:

- Curiosity
- Rejection
- Order
- Citizenship
- Family
- Food
- Sex
- Independence
- Pain avoidance
- Social contact
- Honor
- Physical exercise
- Power
- Prestige
- Vengeance

Identifying the motive(s) for a particular action can range from simple to impossible. To illustrate, buying motives may be grouped on three different levels depending on consumers' awareness of them and their willingness to divulge them. At one level, buyers recognize, and are quite willing to talk about, their motives for buying most common, everyday products. At a second level, they are aware of their reasons for buying but will not admit them to others. Some people probably buy luxury cars to impress others. But when questioned about their motives, they may offer other reasons that they think will be more socially appropriate. The most difficult motives to uncover are those at the third level, where even the buyers cannot explain the factors motivating their buying actions. These are called unconscious or subconscious motives, and we will have more to say about them when we discuss personality.

To further complicate our understanding, a purchase is often the result of multiple motives. Moreover, various motives may conflict with one another. In buying a new suit, a young man may want to (1) feel comfortable, (2) please his girlfriend, and (3) spend as little as possible. Accomplishing all three objectives in one purchase may be truly difficult! Finally, a particular motive may produce different behavior at different times.

Despite the challenges, significant advances have been made in understanding buyer's needs. Some of the methods for gaining insights into motives will be described in Chapter 7 in the discussion of marketing research. However, because marketers are unable to precisely describe the needs operating in many purchase situations, more work needs to be done to identify consumption-specific motives and measure their strengths.

Perception   In many purchase situations, a person gathers information before making a choice. **Perception** is the process of receiving, organizing, and assigning meaning to information or stimuli detected by our five senses. It is in this way that we interpret or understand the world around us. Perception plays a major role in the stage of the buying-decision process where alternatives are identified.

What we perceive—the meaning we give something sensed—depends on the object and our experiences. In an instant the mind is capable of receiving information, comparing it to a huge store of images in memory, and providing an interpretation. Consumers make use of all five senses. Scents, for example, are powerful behavior triggers. Who can resist the aroma of popcorn in a theater or of fresh cookies in a supermarket bakery? As with all perception, memory plays a large part with aromas. Research on everyday odors found that scents such as vanilla, chocolate, cedar, lavender, and rosemary create comforting associations, and psychologists have found that the aroma of spiced apples has a calming effect on people. Marketers use this type of information to odorize products and environments to create positive perceptions. For example, Disney uses machines to introduce odors in its Magic Kingdom and Epcot Center rides to add to the experiences.[15]

AN ETHICAL DILEMMA?

Coupons to gain trial of new products or stimulate sales of existing brands are commonplace in consumer marketing. E-mail and Internet websites have been added to traditional mail, newspaper and magazine inserts, and in-store displays as methods of coupon distribution. Some pharmaceutical firms have begun using consumer coupons as part of their promotional efforts for prescription drugs. Their hope is that patients will persuade their physicians to prescribe a new medication for which they can use the coupon to obtain a free sample. The coupons appear most often for new versions of drugs about to lose patent protection. The goal is to switch users of the older version of the drug to the new formulation before generic alternatives appear and underprice the older version.

Is it ethical for a pharmaceutical firm to distribute coupons for prescription medications to consumers in hopes that they will influence their physicians' decisions about prescribing drugs?

- www.clarinex.com
- www.purplepill.com

Sources: Gardiner Harris, "Drug Makers Offer Coupons for Free Prescriptions," *The Wall Street Journal*," Mar. 13, 2002, pp. B1+; websites include *www.clarinex.com* and *www.purplepill.com*.

Every day we come in contact with an enormous number of marketing stimuli. However, with the aid of **selective perception** techniques we are able to deal with the commercial environment.

- We pay attention by exception. That is, of all the marketing stimuli our senses are exposed to, only those with the power to capture and hold our attention have the potential of being perceived. Using a somewhat insensitive analogy, an ad executive compared consumers to roaches—"you spray them and spray them and they get immune after a while."[16] This phenomenon is called *selective attention.*

- As part of perception, new information is compared with a person's existing store of knowledge, or frame of reference. If an inconsistency is discovered, the new information will likely be distorted to conform to the established beliefs. Despite the fact that most authorities claim people are not saving enough for retirement, many consumers continue to spend all or most of their discretionary income.[17] Why? One reason is because the advice is inconsistent with the way these consumers want to live now, so they distort the incoming information. For example, they may decide the authorities are simply being too conservative even though there is no evidence to support such a conclusion. This is called *selective distortion.*

- We retain only part of what we have selectively perceived. For example, nearly 80% of Americans cannot remember a typical TV commercial one day after seeing it. This is known as *selective retention.*

There are many communication implications in this selectivity process. For example, to grasp and hold attention, an ad must be involving enough to stimulate the consumer to seek more information. If the ad is too familiar, it will be ignored. On the other hand, if it is too complex, the ad will be judged not worth the time and effort to figure out. Thus, the goal is a mildly ambiguous first impression that heightens the consumer's interest.

Selective distortion tells us that marketers cannot assume that a message, even if it is factually correct, will necessarily be accepted as fact by consumers. In designing a message, the distance between the audience's current belief and the position proposed by the message must be considered. If the distance is large, a moderate claim may be more believable than a dramatic claim, and therefore more effective in moving consumers in the desired direction.

Even messages received undistorted are subject to selective retention. Consequently, ads are repeated many times. The hope is that numerous exposures will etch the message into the recipient's memory. This aim partially explains why a firm with very familiar products, such as Wrigley's, spends over $100 million a year advertising chewing gum.

Learning

Learning involves changes in behavior resulting from observation and experience. It excludes behavior that is attributable to instinct such as breathing or temporary states such as hunger or fatigue. Interpreting and predicting consumer learning enhances our understanding of buying behavior, because learning plays a role at every stage of the buying-decision process.

There is no universally accepted learning theory. However, one with direct application to marketing strategy is stimulus-response. According to **stimulus-response theory,** learning occurs as a person (1) responds to some stimulus by behaving in a particular way and (2) is rewarded for a correct response or penalized for an incorrect one. When the same correct response is repeated in reaction to the same stimulus, a behavior pattern, or learning, is established.

From a marketer's perspective, learning can be desirable or undesirable. As examples of desirable learning, marketers have "taught" consumers to respond to certain cues, such as:

- End-of-aisle displays in supermarkets suggest that the displayed item is on sale.
- "Sale" signs in store windows suggest that bargains can be found inside.
- Large type in newspaper grocery ads suggests that the item is a particularly good bargain.

On the other hand, by their own admission, U.S. automakers have contributed to some undesirable learning. Thirty years ago three auto manufacturers—General Motors, Ford, and Chrysler (now DaimlerChrysler)—accounted for the bulk of U.S. car sales. Their quality slipped badly in the 1970s, which alienated many baby boomers who were buying their first new cars at that time. According to a Ford researcher describing that period, "We taught them that we build junk (and) the lessons learned in the 1970s will stay with baby boomers the rest of their lives." Despite substantial quality improvements in subsequent years, the Big Three automakers have had a difficult time overcoming this early learning and its generalization to their later products. However, they continue to make large investments in both "hard" quality improvements—making sure things don't break or fail—and "perceived" quality improvements—making sure things consumers can see such as the quality of interior materials and the way parts fit together look and feel right, because both are critical to overcoming the undesirable learning that has taken place.[18]

Once a behavior pattern has been established it becomes a habit and replaces conscious, willful behavior. In terms of the purchase-decision process, this means when a habit is established the consumer skips several of the steps in the buying process, and usually goes directly from the recognized need to the purchase.

Learning is not a perfect predictor of behavior because a variety of other factors also influence a consumer. For example, a pattern of repeatedly purchasing the same brand may be disrupted by a person's desire for variety or novelty. Or a temporary situation such as being short of money or pressed for time may produce behavior different than a learned response. Thus a learned response does not necessarily occur every time a stimulus appears.

Personality   **Personality** is defined broadly as an individual's pattern of traits that influence behavioral responses. For example, we speak of people as being self-confident, domineering, introverted, flexible, and/or friendly, and as being influenced (but not controlled) by such personality traits in their responses to situations.

It is generally agreed that personality traits do influence consumers' perceptions and buying behavior. However, there is considerable disagreement as to the nature of this relationship—that is, *how* personality influences behavior. Many studies have been made of personality traits in relation to product and brand preferences in a wide variety of product categories, with mixed results. The findings generally have been too inconclusive to be of much practical value. Although we know, for example, that people's personalities often are reflected in the clothes they wear, the cars they drive (or whether they use a bicycle or motorcycle instead of a car), and the restaurants they eat in, researchers have not been particularly successful in predicting behavior on the basis of personality traits. The reason is simple: Many things besides personality enter into the consumer buying-decision process.

The **psychoanalytic theory** of personality, formulated by Sigmund Freud at the turn of the century and later modified by his followers and critics, has had a tremendous impact on the study of human behavior and also marketing. Freud contended that people have subconscious drives that cannot be satisfied in socially acceptable ways. As we learn that we cannot gratify these needs in a direct manner, we develop other, more subtle means of seeking satisfaction. This results in very complex reasons for some behavior.

One significant marketing implication is that a person's real motive(s) for buying a product or shopping at a certain store may be hidden. Sometimes even we ourselves do not understand why we feel or act as we do. Psychoanalytic theory has caused marketers to realize that they must appeal to buyers' dreams, hopes, fantasies, and fears. Yet at the same time they must provide buyers with socially acceptable rationalizations for many purchases. Thus, we see ads emphasizing the practicality of $60,000 cars, the comfort of fur coats, and the permanence of diamond jewelry.

Self-concept is a marketing application of personality theory. Your **self-concept,** or *self-image,* is the way you see yourself. At the same time it is the picture you think others have of you. Psychologists distinguish between the *actual self-concept*—the way you see yourself—and the *ideal self-concept*—the way you want to be seen or would like to see yourself.

Studies of purchases show that people generally prefer brands and products that are compatible with their self-concepts. However, there are mixed reports concerning the degree of influence actual and ideal self-concepts have on brand and product preferences. Some researchers contend that consumption preferences correspond to a person's actual self-concept. Others hold that the ideal self-concept is dominant in consumers' choices.

Perhaps there is no consensus here because in real life we often switch back and forth between our actual and ideal self-concepts. A middle-aged man may buy some comfortable, but not fashionable, clothing to wear at home on a weekend, where he is reflecting his actual self-concept. But he may also buy some expensive, high-fashion clothing, envisioning himself as a young, active, upwardly mobile guy (ideal self-concept).

Attitudes   An **attitude** is a learned predisposition to respond to an object or class of objects in a consistently favorable or unfavorable way.[19] In our buying-decision process model, attitudes play a major role in the evaluation of alternatives. All attitudes have the following characteristics in common:

- Attitudes are *learned.* They are formed as a result of direct experiences with a product or an idea, indirect experiences (such as reading about a product in *Consumer Reports*), and interactions with social groups. For example, the opinions expressed by a friend about diet foods plus the consumer's favorable or unfavorable experience as a result of using diet foods will contribute to an attitude toward diet foods in general.

- Attitudes have an *object.* By definition, we can hold attitudes only toward something. The object can be general (professional sports) or specific (Chicago Cubs); it can be abstract (campus life) or concrete (the computer lab). In attempting to determine consumers' attitudes, the object of the attitude must be carefully defined. This is because a person might have a favorable attitude toward the general concept (exercise), but a negative attitude toward a specific dimension of the concept (jogging).

- Attitudes have *direction* and *intensity.* Our attitudes are either favorable or unfavorable toward the object. They cannot be neutral. In addition, they have a strength. For example, you may mildly like this text or you may like it very much (we hope!). This factor is important for marketers, because both strongly held favorable and strongly held unfavorable attitudes are difficult to change.

- Finally, attitudes tend to be *stable* and *generalizable.* Once formed, attitudes usually endure, and the longer they are held, the more resistant to change they become. People also have a tendency to generalize attitudes. For instance, a person who likes the produce section in a particular supermarket has a tendency to form a favorable attitude toward the entire store.

A consumer's attitudes do not always predict purchase behavior. A person may hold very favorable attitudes toward a product but not buy it because of some inhibiting factor. Typical inhibitors are not having enough money or discovering that your preferred brand is not available when you want to buy it. For example, the sale of french fries is declining in part because many of the newer fast-food outlets such as Subway don't offer them.[20] Under such circumstances, purchase behavior may even contradict attitudes.

Changing attitudes can be difficult or impossible. When change is accomplished, it normally takes a long time and a lot of money. Consider how long it took to gain widespread acceptance of air bags in cars. They were initially ridiculed but now are demanded by car buyers. When faced with unfavorable attitudes, and recognizing how difficult changing them will be, marketers frequently alter the product to conform to the attitudes.

Situational Influences

Often the situations in which we find ourselves play a large part in determining how we behave. Students, for example, act differently in class than they do when they are in a stadium watching a football game. The same holds true of buying behavior. On spring break you might buy a souvenir that seems very strange when you get home. This is an example of **situational influence,** a temporary force associated with the immediate purchase environment that affects behavior.

Situational influences tend to be less significant when the consumer is very loyal to a brand and when the consumer is highly involved in the purchase. However, they often play a major role in buying decisions. The four categories of situational influences are related to when, where, and how consumers buy as well as the conditions under which they buy.

The Time Dimension

In designing strategy for a product, a marketer should be able to answer at least three time-related questions about consumer buying:

- How is it influenced by the season, week, day, or hour?
- What impact do past and present events have on the purchase decision?
- How much time does the consumer have to make the purchase and consume the product?

The time of day influences the demand for some products. For example, because they associate it with breakfast, Americans drink 10 times as much orange juice as the Japanese. The time dimension of buying has implications for promotion scheduling. Promotional messages must reach consumers when they are in a decision-making frame of mind. It also influences pricing decisions, as when marketers adjust prices in an attempt to even out demand. For instance, supermarkets may offer double coupons on Tuesdays, usually a slow business day.

The second question concerns the impact of past or future events. For example, the length of time since you last went out to dinner at a nice restaurant may influence a decision on whether to go to a fancy restaurant tonight. Marketers need to know enough about the recent and planned behavior of consumers to anticipate the effects of these past and future events.

The growth and popularity of fast-food restaurants, quick-service oil-change outlets, and catalog retailers such as L. L. Bean and Lands' End are marketers' responses to the time pressure experienced by consumers. A factor in the anticipated popularity of the Internet as a place to make purchases is consumers' desire to spend less time shopping. To help consumers conserve time, marketers are making large and small changes. For example, some photoprocessing operations return the developed prints by mail to eliminate the customers' second trip to pick up the pictures. To help customers locate specific products and therefore reduce shopping time, a number of supermarkets have electronic directories attached to their shopping carts.

The Surroundings

Physical surroundings are the features of a situation that are apparent to the senses, such as lighting, smells, weather, and sounds. Think of the importance of atmosphere in a restaurant or the sense of excitement and action created by the sights and sounds in a gambling casino. Music can be an important element in a store's strategy. In an experiment involving supermarket shoppers, background music apparently influenced behavior. Customers who said they liked the store's piped-in music "a lot" stayed in the store an average of nine minutes longer than other shoppers and spent on average $15 more.[21]

The social surroundings are the number, mix, and actions of other people at the purchase site. You probably would not go into a strange restaurant that has an empty parking lot at dinnertime. In a crowded store with other customers waiting, you will probably ask the clerk fewer questions and spend less time comparing products.

Terms of the Purchase

Terms and conditions of sale as well as the transaction-related activities that buyers are willing to perform affect consumer buying. For instance, for many years credit was extended only by retailers selling big-ticket items. However, today consumers can use credit cards at fast-food restaurants and grocery stores. The average household has 14 credit cards, and an average of over $8,000 in outstanding balances, an increase of 160% since 1990. Another transaction device, the debit card, is growing in popularity. A debit card looks like a credit card, but when it is used the payments are deducted directly from the consumer's checking account. Debit cards provide the convenience of making purchases without carrying cash or having to write a check. Also some consumers see them as a way of avoiding over-spending. In 2001, for the first time debit cards accounted for more in-store transactions than credit cards, a trend many feel will continue.[22]

Marketers have also experimented with transferring functions or activities to consumers. What were once called "service stations" are now called "gas stations" because you pump your own gas and wash your own windshield. Consumers have shown a willingness to assemble products, sack their own groceries, and buy in case quantities—all in exchange for lower prices.

Consumer Moods and Motives

Sometimes consumers are in a temporary state that influences their buying decisions. When you are feeling ill or late for an appointment, you may be unwilling to wait in line or to take the time or care that a particular purchase deserves. Moods can also influence purchases. Feelings such as anger or excitement can result in purchases that otherwise would not have been made. In the atmosphere accompanying a rock concert, for example, you might pay more for a commemorative T-shirt than you would under normal circumstances. Part of the success of online auctions such as eBay and television shopping networks such as QVC can be attributed to the excitement of competing against other consumers.

Marketers must also monitor long-term situational influences. The optimistic U.S. consumers of the 1990s were both free spending and apparently carefree. According to a 1998 Roper-Starch study, low inflation and a strong economy made U.S. consumers the most confident in the world going into the end of the decade. However, just three years later in 2001, a study by the same firm found that a sluggish economy had dampened consumer optimism. As the 21st century began, an increased number of consumers in the U.S. were concerned about the future of small

How long would you wait in line to visit the Louvre Museum in Paris? It is almost always crowded, but following a three-week employees' strike in 2001, the lines were even longer than normal. This situational influence probably discouraged some tourists . . . who probably chose to "settle" for visits to Notre Dame Cathedral or the Paris Opera instead.

businesses, anticipated gasoline shortages, and predicted the stock market would decline.[23] This type of uncertainty can create a more cautious mood among consumers and affect their purchasing behavior.

This chapter has dealt with the willingness to buy—part of our definition of marketing. We described the consumer market and examined the consumer's decision-making process. You should now appreciate just how difficult it is for marketers to identify needs and predict consumer buying behavior. In the next chapter we will examine the other category of buyers—the business market.

Summary

The dynamic nature of the consumer market is reflected in its geographic distribution and its demographic characteristics. The U.S. population is shifting toward the West and the South. Further, the mix of people in rural communities is changing as the out-migration of young people continues but an in-migration of older Americans increases.

Demographics are the vital statistics that describe a population. They are useful to marketers because they are related to behavior and they are relatively easy to gather. Demographics frequently used to describe consumers are age, gender, family life cycle, income, ethnicity, and other characteristics such as education, occupation, religion, and nationality.

The buying behavior of ultimate consumers is described as a five-stage buying-decision process, influenced by information, social and group forces, psychological forces, and situational factors.

The stages in the buying-decision process are need recognition, identification of alternatives, evaluation of alternatives, purchase and related decisions, and postpurchase behavior. Buying decisions are either high or low involvement. Low-involvement decisions include fewer stages; high-involvement decisions consist of all five stages. Low-involvement situations occur when the consumer views the decision as relatively minor, there is brand and store loyalty, or in impulse buying.

Information fuels the buying-decision process. Without it, there would be no decisions. There are two categories of information sources: commercial and social. Commercial sources include advertising, personal selling, selling by phone, and personal involvement with a product. Word of mouth, observation, and experience with a product owned by someone else are social sources.

Social and group forces are composed of culture, subculture, social class, reference groups, family, and households. Culture has the broadest and most general influence on buying behavior, whereas other household occupants have the most specific and immediate impact on an individual. Social and group forces have a direct impact on individual purchase decisions as well as a person's psychological makeup.

Psychological forces that impact buying decisions are motivation, perception, learning, personality, and attitudes. All behavior is motivated by some aroused need. Perception is the way we interpret the world around us and is subject to three types of selectivity: attention, distortion, and retention.

Learning is a change in behavior as a result of experience. Stimulus-response learning involves drives, cues, responses, and reinforcement. Continued positive reinforcement leads to habitual buying and brand loyalty.

Personality is the sum of an individual's traits that influence behavioral responses. The Freudian psychoanalytic theory of personality has caused marketers to realize that the true motives for behavior are often hidden. The self-concept is related to personality. Because purchasing and consumption are very expressive actions, they allow us to communicate to the world our actual and ideal self-concepts.

Attitudes are learned predispositions to respond to an object or class of objects in a consistent fashion. Besides being learned, all attitudes are directed toward an object, have direction and intensity, and tend to be stable and generalizable. Strongly held attitudes are difficult to change.

Situational influences deal with when, where, how, and why consumers buy, and the consumer's personal condition at the time of purchase. Situational influences are often so powerful that they can override all the other forces in the buying-decision process.

More about **Harley-Davidson**

Despite at least one biker magazine describing the V-Rod's liquid-cooled engine as a shocking design misstep for Harley, the firm has big plans for the new machine. It is the first of a new family of "high-performance" motorcycles and is likely to play a big part in the company's efforts to hang onto its market share. Judging from the sold-out production run of the first model, the V-Rod is fulfilling its promise.

Harley knows, however, when the real crunch will come. "We don't need new customers today, we don't need them tomorrow. But we may 10 years from now," says the company's chief financial officer. The company also knows it could intimidate younger prospects with the cultlike devotion shown by some of its aging adherents. That's why Harley is willing to invest heavily in two new ventures that aren't making any money at the moment—the driver training program, called Rider's Edge, and a subsidiary named Buell.

When Harley engineer Erik Buell left the firm in the 1990s to start his own company, Harley funded it, and in 1998 the firm completed its acquisition of the little company. Buell manufactures a light, sleek single-cylinder bike called the Blast, with a $4,400 price tag and strong appeal among first-time and younger riders. With design innovations like a tucked-away muffler that won't burn inexperienced riders' legs and an adjustable seat height, the Blast should appeal to more women than Harley's other bikes do; right now only 9% of riders of traditional Harley models are females.

Rider's Edge, which has trained about 4,300 people in its first two years, could also bring more women into the fold. Described as an effort to "lighten our image without losing our edge," the driver's ed program also covers how Harley bikes are made and how they are sold. It requires passing grades on the same strict written and road tests required by the Motorcycle Safety Foundation—and the bike that students train on is the Buell.[24]

1. What role do you think a rider's self-image plays in the purchase of a motorcycle? In the purchase of a Harley-Davidson motorcycle? Do you think the influence of reference groups plays any part in a Harley purchase? Why or why not?

2. Harley-Davidson's revenue and net income have climbed steadily for over 15 years. Why do you think the firm has been able to weather economic recessions much better than other major manufacturers?

Key Terms and Concepts

Ultimate consumers (88)
Metropolitan Statistical Area (MSA) (90)
Primary Metropolitan Statistical Area (PMSA) (90)
Consolidated Metropolitan Statistical Area (CMSA) (90)
Demographics (91)
Family life-cycle stages (91)
Consumer buying-decision process (94)
Level of involvement (95)

Loyalty (95)
Impulse buying (95)
Patronage buying motives (97)
Postpurchase cognitive dissonance (98)
Commercial information environment (98)
Social information environment (99)
Culture (99)
Subculture (100)
Social class (101)
Reference groups (102)
Family (102)

Household (102)
Motive (104)
Maslow's needs hierarchy (104)
Perception (105)
Selective perception (106)
Learning (107)
Stimulus-response theory (107)
Personality (108)
Psychoanalytic theory (108)
Self-concept (108)
Attitude (108)
Situational influence (110)

Questions and Problems

1. Give two examples of goods or services whose market demand would be particularly affected by each of the following population factors:
   a. Regional distribution
   b. Urban-rural-suburban distribution
   c. Marital status
   d. Gender
   e. Age

2. List three population trends noted in this chapter (for instance, the over-65 segment is growing). Speculate on how each of the following types of retail operations might be affected by each of the trends:
   a. Supermarket
   b. Sporting goods store
   c. Online auction
   d. Sports bar

3. Under what conditions might a relatively inexpensive purchase (under $10) be high involvement for a consumer?

4. From a consumer behavior perspective, why is it incorrect to view the European Union or the countries of Asia as single markets?

5. Provide examples of a person and a group that could serve as reference groups in the choice of the following products:
   a. Shampoo
   b. Auto tune-up

   c. Office furnishings
   d. Cellular phone service

6. What roles would you expect a husband, a wife, and their young child to play in the purchase of the following items?
   a. Preschool
   b. Choice of a fast-food outlet for dinner
   c. Personal computer
   d. Lawn-care service

7. Does the psychoanalytic theory of personality have any practical application in the marketing of cars that have a top speed of 120 mph when the speed limit on most U.S. highways is 70 mph or less?

8. Explain how self-concept might come into play in the purchase or use of the following:
   a. Eyeglasses
   b. Man's suit
   c. Online brokerage
   d. College education

9. Interview the manager of a store that sells big-ticket items (furniture, appliances, electronic equipment) about the methods, if any, the store uses to reinforce purchase decisions and to reduce the cognitive dissonance of its customers. What additional methods can you suggest?

10. What situational influences might affect a family's choice of a motel in a strange town while on vacation?

Interactive Marketing Exercises

1. Go to the Census Bureau website (www.census.gov) and open the American Fact Finder page. Select a city and examine the data on the population, economy, and geography that is available. Comment on how the data could be used by a bank marketer looking for sites for new branch locations. Comment on how any differences you find may be useful to a fast-food franchisee looking for a location for a new outlet.

2. Have a friend describe a high-involvement purchase that he or she recently made. Show how each of the five stages described in the chapter is reflected in the description. Identify the primary social influences that played a part in the decision.

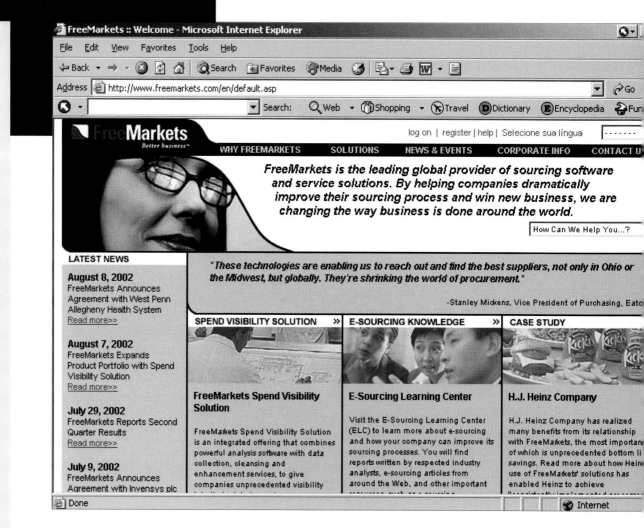

"Some suppliers dislike the system because they think it puts too much emphasis on price, discouraging consideration of other factors that may be equally important."

Can **FreeMarkets** Satisfy Buyers and Sellers?

When a manufacturer buys a large quantity of a product, for example, a component part for a personal computer, typically several potential suppliers are invited to make offers. The offers are submitted in writing, and the buyer selects the most attractive one. This, the traditional system of business buying, has worked for years, but it has left buyers with a nagging question: Am I paying the lowest possible price for the desired product? A method of buying over the Internet, called a reverse auction (because it involves sellers bidding a price *down* instead of buyers bidding a price *up*), is providing an answer.

FreeMarkets, Inc., is a firm that offers an Internet business-to-business reverse auction service. It assists buyers of materials, commodities, and service products in the identification of potential suppliers, and then conducts electronic, real-time auctions over the Internet in which the suppliers bid for the business.

The auctions are held on FreeMarkets's Internet site, so only invited suppliers are permitted to participate. At a designated time, the buyer and all the prospective suppliers log in to the site. The buyer's computer screen shows all the suppliers and all the offers. The suppliers, however, see only the lowest offer on their individual screens. The suppliers don't know the identities or the number of firms participating in the bidding. The bidding goes on for a specified time, usually two to three hours. When the auction closes, the buyer decides which bid it wants to accept. Typically the result is a price as much as 20% below what a buyer would pay under the old, single-bid process. For its service, FreeMarkets charges the buyer a fee.

Procter & Gamble, Caterpillar, and Zenith are among the major firms that have used FreeMarkets's service. United Technologies, an electronics manufacturer, purchased circuit boards for $18 million that had a list price of $24 million, a 35% savings, after three hours of bidding by 10 suppliers located on three different continents.

According to its founder, Glen Meakem, FreeMarkets provides clients with three services.

- First, it assists in identifying the best prospective suppliers. Consultants at FreeMarkets help the buyer prepare a comprehensive request for quotation (RFQ) which, depending on the product being purchased, may consist of several hundred pages of specifications. Then FreeMarkets narrows down the list of qualified suppliers on the basis of its research and the responses of potential suppliers to the RFQ.
- Second, FreeMarkets has developed a global electronic market system that allows the pre-qualified suppliers to participate in a real-time competitive bidding process. By operating on a private Internet network (or extranet) and using its proprietary software, FreeMarkets can provide privacy and security for both the buyer and the sellers.
- Third, FreeMarkets contends that it provides unequaled research on the suppliers and the industry to help the buyer evaluate bids. For example, at the end of a bidding session,

www.freemarkets.com

FreeMarkets may recommend that a buyer reject the lowest bid and accept instead a supplier with a more reliable delivery record.

Buyers like the speed of the process, and of course the lower prices. Also, using FreeMarkets allows firms that choose not to invest in creating their own electronic procurement system to enjoy the benefits of Internet bidding. However, there is concern that pitting prospective suppliers against one another in a bidding battle may undermine loyalties that can benefit a company during difficult economic times or when it needs special consideration, such as in handling a rush order.

Some suppliers dislike the system because they think it puts too much emphasis on price, discouraging consideration of other factors that may be equally important. On the other hand, they like the idea that it gives them a chance for business that they might have been closed out of because of a long-standing relationship between a buyer and a seller.

Whatever buyers and sellers think about the procedure, it's been a success for FreeMarkets. Begun in 1995 with just 13 employees, the firm has opened offices in Europe, Asia, Australia, and South America and operates in more than 30 languages. It has gone from being unprofitable in late 1999, with about 30 customers, to being on the verge of profitability with 125.[1]

How does the approach developed by FreeMarkets for the business market differ from marketing to consumers?

Although most people recognize large, technical equipment such as the robots used in assembling cars or the air-conditioning units used in office buildings as business products, many other products, like paper bags or bottle caps are easily overlooked. In fact, the business market is big, dynamic, and widely diversified. It employs millions of workers in thousands of different jobs, and is actually larger than the consumer market. And, as the chapter-opening case describing FreeMarkets, Inc., suggests, there is plenty of room for innovation in the way business products are bought and sold.

In many ways business markets are similar to the consumer markets we examined in Chapter 4, but there are also important differences. After studying this chapter, you should be able to explain:

Chapter Goals

- The nature and scope of the business market.
- The seven categories of business buyers.
- The differentiating characteristics of business markets.
- What determines business market demand.
- The buying processes in business markets.

Nature and Scope of the Business Market

The business market consists of all individuals and organizations that buy goods and services for one or more of the following purposes:

- *To make other goods and services.* Dell buys microprocessors to make computers, and Henredon buys wood to make furniture.

- *To resell to other business users or to consumers.* Toys "Я" Us buys electronic games to sell to consumers, and ReCellular, Inc., buys used cellular phones and wireless equipment to refurbish and sell to business customers.
- *To conduct the organization's operations.* Kroger buys bags to sack groceries, the University of Vermont buys office supplies and computer software for use in the registrar's office, and the Mayo Clinic buys hazardous-materials disposal services to get rid of its medical refuse.

So, any good or service purchased for a reason other than personal or household consumption is part of the **business market,** and each buyer within this market is termed a **business user.** The activity of marketing goods and services to business users, rather than to ultimate consumers, is **business marketing** and a firm performing the activity is a **business marketer.**

The distinction of whether a good or service is a consumer or business product depends on the reason it is purchased, not on the item itself. For example, a PC purchased from Dell by a small business to keep track of its orders, inventory, and accounts receivable would be a business good. The same PC (with different software), also purchased from Dell but as a family Christmas gift for educational and entertainment use at home, would be a consumer good. This is not simply a semantic distinction because, as you will see, the marketing activities in these two situations are very different.

Because the business market is largely unknown to the average consumer, it is easy to underestimate its significance. Actually, it is huge in terms of total sales volume and the number of firms involved. About 50% of all manufactured products are sold to the business market. In addition, about 80% of all farm products and virtually all mineral, forest, and sea products are business goods. These are sold to firms for further processing.[2]

The magnitude and complexity of the business market are also evident from the many transactions required to produce and market a product. Consider, for example, the business marketing transactions and total sales volume involved in getting leather workshoes to their actual users. First, cattle are sold through one or two middlemen before reaching a meatpacker. Then the hides are sold to a tanner, who in turn sells the leather to a shoe manufacturer. The shoe manufacturer may sell finished shoes to a wholesaler, who markets them to retail stores or to employers that supply shoes for their workers. Each sale in the chain is a business marketing transaction.

In addition, the shoe manufacturer buys metal eyelets, laces, thread, glue, steel safety toe plates, heels and soles, and shoe polish. Consider something as simple as the shoelaces. Other industrial firms must first buy the raw cotton. Then they must spin, weave, dye, and cut the cotton so that it becomes shoestring material. All the manufacturers involved have factories and offices with furniture, machinery, furnaces, lights, and maintenance equipment and supplies required to run them—and these also are business goods that have to be produced and marketed. In short, thousands of business products and business marketing activities come into play before almost any product—consumer good or business good—reaches its final destination.

The magnitude and complexity of the business market loom even larger when we consider all the business services involved throughout our workshoe example. Each firm engaged in any stage of the production process probably uses outside accounting and law firms. Several of the producers may use advertising agencies. And all the companies will use services of various financial institutions.

Every retail store and wholesaling establishment is a business user. Every bus company, airline, and railroad is part of this market. So is every hotel, restaurant, bank, insurance company, hospital, theater, and school. In fact, the total sales volume in the business market far surpasses total sales to consumers. This difference is due to the very many business marketing transactions that take place before a product is sold to its ultimate user.

Fashion shows such as this one in Milan, Italy, for spring and summer clothing, take place several months before the actual selling season. Buyers representing fashion retailers visit these shows, see what designers have created, and make decisions about what their stores will offer. Thus they create time and place utility for consumers.

Components of the Business Market

Traditionally, business markets were referred to as industrial markets. This caused many people to think the term referred only to manufacturing firms. But as you can see from what we just described, the business market is a lot more than that. Certainly manufacturers constitute a major portion of the business market, but there are also six other components—agriculture, reseller, government, services, nonprofit, and international. Although they may be overlooked because of the historical focus on manufacturing, each is a significant part of the business market.

The Agriculture Market

The large amount of income from the sale of agricultural products—over $190 billion in 1999, the most recent data available—gives the 2 million U.S. farmers, as a group, the purchasing power that makes them a highly attractive business market. Moreover, world population forecasts and food shortages in many countries undoubtedly will keep pressure on farmers to increase their output. Companies hoping to sell to the farm market must analyze it carefully and be aware of significant trends. For example, both the proportion of farmers in the total population and the number of farms have been decreasing and probably will continue to decline. Counterbalancing this has been an increase in large corporate farms. Even the remaining "family farms" are expanding in order to survive. Also, farming is becoming more automated and mechanized. These developments mean that capital investment in farming is increasing. **Agribusiness**—farming, food processing, and other large-scale farming-related businesses—is big business in every sense of the word.

Agriculture has become a modern industry. Like other business executives, farmers are looking for ways to increase their productivity, cut their expenses, and manage their cash flows. Technology is an important part of the process. For example, many of today's farmers are engaged in what is called precision agriculture—a term that describes a wide variety of technology products and processes designed to reduce costs and increase farm output. Yield monitoring, grid sampling, variable rate fertilization, self-guided machines, and disease tracking are examples of techniques and equipment that utilize computers, satellite-generated photographs, and sophisticated soil analysis to identify problems and opportunities.[3] Representatives of agricultural product firms such as International Mineral and Chemical Company can use this information to design unique strategies for individual farms and adapt them as necessary to best serve their customers.

The Reseller Market

Intermediaries in the American marketing system—over 500,000 wholesaling middlemen and 2.7 million retail establishments—constitute the **reseller market.** The basic activity of resellers—unlike any other business market segment—is buying products from supplier organizations and reselling these items in essentially the same form to the resellers' customers. In economic terms, resellers create time, place, information, and possession utilities, rather than form utility.

Resellers are also business users, buying many goods and services for use in operating their businesses—items such as office supplies, warehouses, materials-handling equipment, legal services, electrical services, and janitorial supplies.

It is their role as buyers for resale that differentiates resellers and attracts special marketing attention from their suppliers. To resell an item, you must please your customer. Usually it is more difficult to determine what will please an outside customer than to find out what will satisfy someone within your own organization. Consider an airline that decides to redesign the uniforms of its flight crews. Management can carefully study the conditions under which the uniforms will be worn and work closely with the people who will be wearing the uniforms to get their views. As a result, the airline should be able to select a design that will be both functional and acceptable. Contrast that with a retailer trying to anticipate what clothing fashions will be popular. The Gap, Express, and Ann Taylor have all had their ups and downs as they try to predict tastes. In both cases clothing is being purchased. However, the opportunity for interaction with the users and the greater interest by those likely to be affected by the purchase make buying for internal use less difficult and less risky than buying for resale.

Especially in a large reseller's organization, buying for resale can be a complex procedure. For a supermarket chain such as Kroger or Vons, buying is frequently done by a buying committee made up of experts on demand, supply, and prices. Timing purchasing to balance obtaining good prices with optimizing the investment in inventory often plays a major role in determing a reseller's profitability.

Resellers, also called "middlemen" or "intermediaries," are the business marketers most directly affected by electronic commerce. The growth of Internet-based selling is contributing to the replacement of some traditional intermediaries in a process that has become so commonplace it has a name—**disintermediation.** Only resellers that can create utility will continue to prosper.

The Government Market

The fantastically large **government market** includes over 87,000 federal, state, and local units that spend over $2.8 *trillion* a year buying for government institutions, such as schools, offices, hospitals, and military bases. Spending by the federal government alone accounts for almost 25% of our gross domestic product. Spending at the state and local levels accounts for another 20%.

Government procurement processes are different from those in the private sector of the business market. A unique feature of government buying is the competitive bidding system. Much government procurement, by law, must be done on a bid basis. That is, the government agency advertises for bids using a standard format called a request for proposals (RFP) that states specifications for the intended purchase. Then it must accept the lowest bid that meets these specifications. However, for some purchases the lowest bid may not be the selection criterion and the government agency may negotiate a contract with a particular supplier. This marketing practice might be

All branches and all levels of government are important markets. The National Aeronautics and Space Administration (NASA) makes some of the more dramatic purchases. For example, this Mars orbiter created business for hundreds of government contractors. Annually NASA awards over $12 billion in contracts to suppliers, with over 10% of the total going to small businesses. Learn more at NASA's website.

www.nasa.gov

www.fedbizopps.gov

used, for instance, when the Department of Defense wants to have a new weapons system developed and built and there are no comparable products on which to base bidding specifications.

A glance at an issue of *FedBizOpps/Commerce Business Daily* (formerly the *Commerce Business Daily*), a publication that describes RFPs for contracts in excess of $25,000, will give you an idea of the size and variety that exists in this market. The potential is sufficiently attractive that some firms concentrate exclusively on it, and for others it can be a springboard to additional opportunities. AM General Corporation, for example, developed the HUMMER, an all-terrain vehicle, in response to a Department of Defense RFP. The firm eventually expanded its marketing effort for the vehicle to other government agencies such as the Forest Service, and business firms such as mining and oil exploration companies. Now a civilian version of the HUMMER is being marketed by General Motors.

Despite its potential, many companies make no effort to sell to the government because they are intimidated by the red tape. There is no question that dealing with the government to any significant extent usually requires specialized marketing techniques and information. Some firms, such as ZDS (Zenith Data Systems), have established special departments to deal with government markets. Also, there are information and guidelines available from agencies such as the General Services Administration and the Small Business Administration on the proper procedures for doing business with the government.

The Services Market

Currently, firms that produce services greatly outnumber firms that produce goods. That is, there are more service firms than the total of all manufacturers, mining companies, construction firms, and enterprises engaged in farming, forestry, and fishing. The **business services market** includes purchasers of marketing research and the services of ad agencies. Also operating in this market with the products they produce are trucking companies and public utilities, as well as the many financial, insurance, investment, legal, and real estate firms. Organizations that provide such diverse services as rental housing, temporary help, repairs, and executive search services are also examples of service marketers.

Service marketers themselves constitute a huge market that buys goods and other services. Mirage resorts, for example, buys blankets and sheets from textile manufacturers. Hospitals buy supplies and medical equipment from Baxter Healthcare Corporation. The Chicago Cubs and other professional baseball teams buy their Louisville Slugger baseball bats from Hillerich and Bradsby. And all of these service firms buy legal, accounting, and consulting advice from other service marketers.

Brokerage firms that bring buyers and sellers together are important service marketers. With the growth of electronic commerce in recent years, their significance is growing. Business marketers are using Internet-based brokers to inform buyers about the goods they have available, and buyers are publicizing their needs electronically. For example, PurchasePro is an Internet service that brings together hotels and casinos with over 4,000 vendors of all types. Hilton Hotels annually buy $1.5 billion in goods and services through the site.[4] Firms in industries as diverse as paper stock and metals are finding that Internet brokers provide more alternative sources of supply while saving them time and money.

www.purchasepro.com

The "Nonbusiness" Business Market

In recent years some long-overdue marketing attention has been given to the multibillion-dollar market comprised of so-called nonbusiness or not-for-profit organizations. The **nonbusiness market** includes such diverse institutions as churches, colleges and universities, museums, hospitals and other health care institutions, political parties, labor unions, and charitable organizations. To prosper, each of these so-called nonbusiness organizations should think of itself as a business enterprise. In the past, however, our society (and the institutions themselves) did not perceive a museum or a charity as a business because its primary objective is something other than making a profit. And many people today still feel uncomfortable thinking of their church, school, or political party as a business. Nevertheless, these organizations do virtually all the things that businesses do—offer a product, collect money, make investments, hire employees—except having profit as one of their goals. Therefore, they require professional management.

Not-for-profit organizations also conduct marketing campaigns—albeit under a different name—in an effort to attract billions of dollars in donations, grants, and contributions. In turn, they spend billions of dollars buying goods and services to run their operations and to provide for their clients.

The International Market

Annual exports of goods and services by U.S. firms amount to approximately $1 trillion, a figure that has increased steadily since the mid-1980s. The biggest recent growth in the **international market** has been in medical products, scientific instruments, environmental protection systems, and consumer goods.

Many small organizations are also heavily involved in the export market. These firms benefit from help from the U.S. Commerce Department with trade fairs and "matchmaking" programs, reduced language barriers as English becomes more common in global business, and greater access to markets via the Internet. The market-expanding potential of the Internet for small businesses is unprecedented. For example, Neoforma, a medical supplies distributor in California, uses its website to conduct business with the government of Oman and other international customers it could not reach any other way.[5]

www.neoforma.com

A GLOBAL PERSPECTIVE

How can a business marketer learn about international opportunities?

Exporting has become commonplace for large firms. With the availability of the Internet it has also become an option for smaller companies. However, doing business abroad has many challenges. For U.S. firms looking for opportunities abroad and businesses in other countries considering the U.S. market, the Census Bureau provides valuable resources. At its website (www.census.gov/foreign-trade) the Foreign Trade Division of the Census Bureau provides a wealth of useful information on the export and import of specific products. For firms looking for market opportunities, trying to evaluate the competition, or assessing trade patterns over time, it is an excellent resource. Macro information available on the site about U.S. exporters include:

- Firms with 500 or more employees account for 70% of U.S. export value but less than 4% of exporters.

- Firms with less than 100 employees make up nearly 90% of exporters but only 20% of exports.

- Over 60% of exporting companies trade with only one country.

- 0.5% of exporters trade with 50 or more countries but account for one-half the total export value.

- More than twice as many companies (100,000 +) export to Canada as export to Mexico (40,000).

Source: *www.census.gov/foreign-trade.*

Another dimension of international business is foreign-based subsidiaries. Although these sales do not count as exports, they are a significant part of the operations of many firms. McDonald's domestic sales are growing, but its foreign sales are growing nearly four times as fast, and now account for half the firm's total volume. A significant number of U.S. firms receive over half their total revenue from overseas subsidiaries. Included are Exxon, IBM, Philip Morris, Procter & Gamble, and Coca-Cola.

Operating overseas has several benefits for U.S. firms:

- It gains them access to countries participating in trade agreements that restrict imports from nonmembers. For example, a joint operation between Dow Chemical and Sumitomo in Japan to make high-performance plastics gives Dow greater access to the countries of the Pacific Rim than it would otherwise have.

- Manufacturing abroad allows firms to gain a better understanding of local markets and customers. Ford could have tried to export a windshield wiper to Europe that was designed for the U.S. market. Instead, through its German subsidiary, Ford learned that it had to produce a specially designed wiper to accommodate the speeds on German autobahns (where there are no speed limits).

- Foreign operations contribute to the volume of a firm's exports. About 25% of all exports by U.S. firms are sales to affiliates located overseas.

Characteristics of Business Market Demand

Four demand characteristics differentiate the business market from the consumer market. In business markets demand is derived, demand for a product tends to be inelastic, demand is widely fluctuating, and the market is well informed.

Demand Is Derived

The demand for a business product is derived from the demand for the consumer products in which that business product is used. Thus the demand for steel depends partially on consumer demand for automobiles and refrigerators, but it also depends on the demand for butter, baseball gloves, and CD players. This is because the tools, machines, and other equipment needed to make these items are made of steel. Consequently, as the demand for baseball gloves increases, Wilson Sporting Goods may buy more sewing machines with steel components and more steel filing cabinets for an expanding managerial staff.

There are two significant marketing implications in the fact that business market demand is a derived demand. First, to estimate the demand for a product, a business marketer must be very familiar with how it is used. This is fairly easy for a company like Pratt & Whitney, a maker of jet engines. But what about the manufacturer of rubber O-rings (doughnut-shaped rings of all sizes that are used to seal connections)? Considerable research may be necessary to identify specific uses and users.

Second, the producer of a business product may find it worthwhile to engage in marketing efforts to encourage the sale of its buyers' products. For example, Intel advertises to consumers, urging them when buying PCs to ask specifically for products that contain Intel memory chips. Similarly, the NutraSweet Company ran a consumer advertising campaign designed to build consumer loyalty for products sweetened with NutraSweet. The idea, of course, is that increases in demand for these consumer products will, in turn, trigger increases in derived demand for their components or ingredients.

Demand Is Inelastic

Another characteristic of the business market is the demand elasticity of business products. **Elasticity of demand** refers to how responsive demand is to a change in the price of a product. (If you would like to review some economics relative to marketing, see Appendix A in Part 4 where demand elasticity and other concepts are explained.)

The demand for many business products is relatively inelastic, which means that the demand for a product responds very little to changes in its price. Two situations contribute to *inelasticity:*

- *If the cost of a part or of material is a small portion of the total cost of a finished product.* For example, Boeing, the maker of passenger jet airplanes, has over 1,200 suppliers. One, Huck International, produces fasteners for aerospace applications. If the price of fasteners should suddenly rise or fall considerably, how much effect would it have on the price of Boeing jets? Despite the fact that the fasteners are critical parts, they are such a small portion of a jet's cost that the price increase would not likely change the price of the plane. As a result, demand for passenger jets would remain the same, so there would be no appreciable change in the demand for fasteners either.

    Even the cost of expensive capital equipment such as a robot used in assembling automobiles, when spread over the thousands of units it helps produce, becomes a very small part of the final price of each one. As a result, when the price of the business product changes, there is very little change in the price of the related consumer products. Because there is no appreciable shift in the demand for the consumer goods, then—by virtue of the derived-demand feature—there is no change in the demand for the business product.

- *If the part or material has no close substitute.* In the mid-1990s the cost of white bond paper increased over 50% because of a shortage of supply. Because paper is a major component of catalogs and magazines, producers of these products had no alternative but to buy it. The catalog and magazine publishers were unable to pass the increase along to their customers because it would have nearly doubled the price of their publications. As a result, they were severely affected by the price change. The bond paper manufacturers, on the other hand, sold all they could produce at the higher price. However, an interesting longer-run effect was that catalog producers and other firms dependent on paper began looking at the Internet as a communication alternative sooner than they would have if paper prices had remained stable.

From a marketing point of view, three factors can moderate the inelasticity of business demand. The quantity of a product demanded is likely to be affected by a change in price:

- *If the price change occurs in a single firm.* An industry-wide increase in the price of aerospace fasteners used in jets will have little effect on the price of planes and therefore little effect on the demand for Boeing aircraft. Consequently, it will cause minimal shift in the total demand for fasteners. The pricing policy of an individual firm, however, can substantially alter the demand for its products. If one supplier raises the price of its fasteners significantly, the increase in price may shift business to competitors. Thus, in the short run, the demand curve faced by a single firm may be quite elastic.

- *If demand is viewed from a long-run time perspective.* Much of our discussion thus far applies to short-term situations. Over the long run, the demand for a given business product is more elastic. If the price of cloth for women's suits rises, there probably will be no immediate change in the price of the finished garment. However, the increase in the cost of materials could very well be reflected in a rise in suit prices for next year. This rise could then influence the demand for suits, and thus for cloth, a year or more hence.

- *If the cost of a specific business product is a significant portion of the cost of the finished good.* We may generalize to this extent: The greater the cost of a business product as a percentage of the total price of the finished good, the greater the elasticity of demand for this business product.

Demand Is Widely Fluctuating

Although the demand for many business goods does not change much in response to price changes, it does respond to other factors. In fact, market demand for most classes of business goods fluctuates considerably more than the demand for consumer products. The demand for installations—major plant equipment, factories, and so on—is especially subject to change. Substantial fluctuations also exist in the market for accessory equipment—office furniture and machinery, delivery trucks, and similar products. The fluctuating demand for finished goods tends to accentuate the swings in the demand for raw materials and fabricating parts. We can see this very clearly when changes in demand in the construction and auto industries affect suppliers of lumber, steel, and other materials and parts. For example, Navistar, the manufacturer of diesel engines for trucks, has benefited greatly from the increase in demand for vans, pickups, and sport-utility vehicles.[6]

A major reason for these fluctuations is that individual businesses are very concerned about having a shortage of inventory when consumer demand increases or, alternatively, being caught with excess inventory should consumer demand decline. Thus they tend to overreact to signals from the economy, building inventories when they see signs of growth in the economy and working inventories down when the signs suggest a downturn. When the actions of all the individual firms are combined, the effect on their suppliers is widely fluctuating demand. This is known as the *acceleration principle*. One exception to this generalization is found in agricultural products intended for processing. Because people have to eat, there is a reasonably consistent demand for animals intended for meat products, for fruits and vegetables that will be canned or frozen, and for grains and dairy products used in cereals and baked goods.

Fluctuations in the demand for business products can influence all aspects of a marketing program. In product planning, fluctuating demand may stimulate a firm to diversify into other products to ease production and marketing problems. For example, IBM moved from concentrating on large, mainframe computers to software and consulting. Distribution strategies may also be affected. When demand declines, a manufacturer may discover that selling to some resellers is unprofitable, so they are dropped as customers. In its pricing, management may attempt to stem a decline in sales by cutting prices, hoping to attract customers away from competing firms. In a long struggle with imported steel and alternative products such as aluminum and fiberglass, Bethlehem Steel repeatedly reduced its prices, eventually resulting in the firm's bankruptcy.

Buyers Are Well Informed

Typically, business buyers are better informed about what they are buying than ultimate consumers. They know more about the relative merits of alternative sources of supply and competitive products for three reasons. First, there are relatively few alternatives for a business buyer to consider. Consumers generally have many more brands and sellers from which to choose than do business buyers. Consider, for example, how many options you would have in purchasing a TV set. However, in most business situations a buyer has only a few firms that offer the particular combination of product features and service desired. Second, the responsibility of a buyer in an organization is ordinarily limited to a few products. Unlike a consumer who buys many different things, a purchasing agent's job is to be very knowledgeable about a narrowly defined set of products. Third, for most consumer purchases, an error is only a minor inconvenience. However, in business buying the cost of a mistake may be thousands of dollars or even the decision maker's job!

The importance of information in business marketing has two significant implications. For sellers of business products, it means placing greater emphasis on personal selling than do firms that market consumer products. Business sales people must be carefully selected, properly trained, and adequately compensated. They must give effective sales presentations and furnish satisfactory service both before and after each sale is made. It is increasingly common to have sales people focus on a particular industry so they can become experts on that business. For example, a sales person representing IBM mainframe computers might call on only banks or colleges and universities. Firms also identify especially important customers, called key accounts, and direct sales people to become very familiar with their businesses and give them extra attention.

For buyers and sellers, information is valuable, and the Internet has made information even more accessible. As the chapter-opening case demonstrates, FreeMarkets makes it possible for a buyer to consider the bids of many sellers in a short period of time. Thus, it and similar online auction services permit unprecedented comparison shopping. The Internet has also made it efficient for buyers to pool their purchasing power to get better prices. By combining their needs over an intranet and buying on the Internet, various divisions of General Electric have saved 20% on $1 billion in purchases of operating supplies.

Determinants of Business Market Demand

Recall from Chapter 4 that to analyze a consumer market a marketer would study the distribution of population and various demographics such as income, and then try to determine the consumers' buying motives and habits. Essentially the same type of analysis is used by a firm selling to the business market. The only difference, but a very important one, is the attributes selected for analysis. The factors affecting the market for business products include the number of potential business users and their purchasing power, their buying motives, and their buying habits. In the following discussion we'll identify several basic differences between consumer markets and business markets.

Number and Types of Business Users

Number of Buyers   The business market contains relatively few buying units compared to the consumer market. In the U.S. there are about 20 million business users, in contrast to about 290 million consumers divided among more than 100 million households. The business market is even more limited because most companies sell to only a small segment of the total market. For example, a firm that markets hard-rock coal mining equipment certainly is not interested in the total business market, or even in all 24,000 firms engaged in various forms of mining and quarrying. It won't even describe the 1,200 firms involved in coal mining as its market. Rather, it will focus on the 60 that extract anthracite coal. The point is, unlike most consumer marketers, business marketing executives in many industries are able to pinpoint their markets carefully by type of industry or geographic location, sometimes down to the level of individually identifying every prospect.

For many years marketers relied on a method for organizing industry information called the Standard Industrial Classification (SIC) system. In this system, designed by the federal government, all types of businesses in the U.S. were divided into 10 groups, with a range of two-digit code numbers assigned to each group. Then additional numbers were used to subdivide each of the major industries into smaller segments.

www/naics.html

All federal government industry data reported prior to 1997 rely on the SIC system. Subsequent data use the new **North American Industry Classification System (NAICS)**, jointly adopted by the U.S., Canada, and Mexico. The NAICS is similar to the SIC code, but has 20 (rather than 10) industry sectors, providing a more detailed and contemporary classification scheme. For example, service industries are subdivided into several sectors. These 20 NAICS groups are subdivided into 96 three-digit subsectors, 313 four-digit industry groups, and 1,170 five and six-digit industries. Table 5.1 lists the NAICS two-digit industry sector codes, and shows the breakdown for one industry, pagers—a segment of the wireless telecommunications industry— within the information sector.

Using the NAICS classification scheme, the federal government provides information on the number of establishments, number of employees, payroll, and measures of output, typically sales or the value of shipments, depending on the industry—all by geographic area. These valuable data are used by marketers to identify potential target industries and geographic markets, monitor trends in growth or decline, and benchmark the activities of other firms in an industry or area.[7]

One limitation of data reported using these codes is that a multiproduct company is listed in only its largest four-digit category. Thus, the diversity of a conglomerate such as Sara Lee, which produces bakery goods and hosiery, is hidden. Also, the government's nondisclosure rules prevent revealing information that will identify a given establishment. Consequently, four-digit detail is not available for an industry in a geographic location where this information would easily identify a particular company.

Size of Business Users   Although the business market may be limited in the total number of buyers, it is large in purchasing power. A relatively small percentage of firms account for the greatest share of the value added to products by manufacturing. **Value added** is the dollar value of a firm's output minus the value of the inputs

TABLE 5.1

NAICS Industry Sectors and the Classification of the Pager Industry

NAICS Industry Sectors	An Industry Subclassification
11 Agriculture, forestry, fishing, & hunting	
21 Mining	
22 Utilities	
23 Construction	
31–33 Manufacturing	
42 Wholesale trade	
44–45 Retail trade	513 Broadcast & telecommunications
48–49 Transportation & warehousing	
51 Information	5133 Telecommunications
52 Finance and insurance	
53 Real estate, rental, & leasing	51332 Wireless telecommunications carrier
54 Professional, scientific, & technical	
55 Management of companies	513321 Pagers
56 Waste management	
61 Education	
62 Health care	
71 Arts, entertainment, & recreation	
72 Accommodations & food services	
81 Other services	
92 Public administration	

Source: *North American Industry Classification System—United States, 1997,* U.S. Government Printing Office, Washington, DC, 1997.

it purchased from other firms. If a manufacturer buys lumber for $40 and converts it into a table that it sells for $100, the value added by the manufacturer is $60.

The marketing significance of this fact is that buying power in many business markets is highly concentrated in a relatively few firms. That is, a high percentage of industry sales are accounted for by a very small number of firms. That's obvious in some major industries such as automobiles, mainframe computers, and jet aircraft, but it is also true in many smaller industries. To illustrate, a firm that sells to U.S. manufacturers of light bulbs can cover 97% of the manufacturing capacity of the industry by contacting only 39 firms. Similarly, four firms produce 78% of all lead pencils, and eight firms make 85% of household vacuum cleaners.

When industries have such a small number of firms, suppliers have the opportunity to deal with them directly. As a result, middlemen often are not as essential in business markets as they are in the consumer market.

Of course, these statements are broad generalizations covering the total business market. They do not take into account the variation in business concentration from one industry to another. In some industries—women's dresses, upholstered furniture, natural and processed cheese, and ready-mix concrete, for example—there are many producers and, therefore, a relatively low level of concentration. Nevertheless, even a so-called low-concentration industry represents far more concentration than anything in the consumer market.

Regional Concentration of Business Users
There is substantial regional concentration in many major industries and among business users as a whole. A firm that sells products used in copper mining will find the bulk of its American market

in Utah and Arizona, and a large percentage of American-produced shoes come from the Southeast.

The eight states constituting the Middle Atlantic and East North Central census regions account for almost 40% of the total value added by manufacturing. Just 10 Standard Metropolitan Areas alone account for about 25% of the total U.S. value added by manufacturing.

Vertical and Horizontal Business Markets

For effective marketing planning, a company should know whether the market for its products is vertical or horizontal. A **vertical business market** exists when a firm's product is usable by virtually all the firms in only one or two industries. For example, aircraft landing gear is intended only for the airplane manufacturing market, but every plane maker is a potential customer. A **horizontal business market** is one in which the firm's product is usable by many industries. Some component and business supplies, such as General Electric small motors, Pennzoil lubricating oils and greases, and Weyerhauser paper products, are examples of products with horizontal markets.

A company's marketing program ordinarily is influenced by whether its markets are vertical or horizontal. In a vertical market, a product can be tailor-made to meet the specific needs of one industry. However, the industry must buy enough to support this specialization. In addition, advertising and personal selling can be directed more effectively in vertical markets. In a horizontal market, a product is developed as an all-purpose item, to reach a larger market. Because of the larger potential market, however, the product is likely to face more competition and the seller must decide how and where to focus its marketing effort.

Buying Power of Business Users

Another determinant of business market demand is the purchasing power of business customers. This can be measured either by the expenditures of business users or by their sales volume. Unfortunately, such information for individual customers is unavailable or is very difficult to estimate. In such cases purchasing power is estimated indirectly using an **activity indicator of buying power**—that is, some market factor related to sales and expenditures. One important source of data is the Economic Census conducted and reported every five years (in years ending in 2 and 7) by the U.S. Census Bureau. The results of the census are published in 18 industry reports ranging from construction to health care. Following are examples of activity indicators that give some idea of the purchasing power of business users.

www.census.gov/epcd

Measures of Manufacturing Activity

Firms that sell to manufacturers might use as activity indicators the number of employees, the number of plants, or the dollar value added by manufacturing. One firm that sells work gloves determined the relative attractiveness of various geographic areas from the number of employees in manufacturing establishments within the areas. Another company that sells a product to control stream pollution used two indicators to estimate potential demand: (1) the number of firms processing wood products (paper mills, plywood mills, and so forth) and (2) the manufacturing value added by these firms. These types of data are gathered in the Economic Census and reported in 473 manufacturing sector reports. Yearly updates are available in the *Annual Survey of Manufactures*, a report based on a sample of 55,000 manufacturing firms.

Measures of Mining Activity

The number of mines operating, the volume of their output, and the dollar value of the product as it leaves the mine may all indicate the purchasing power of mining and mining-related firms. These data are published every five years in the mining sector reports derived from the Economic Census. This information is useful to any firm marketing business products related to extracting and processing everything from aluminum to zirconium.

Measures of Agricultural Activity

A company marketing agricultural products or equipment can estimate the buying power of its farm market by studying such indicators as cash farm income, commodity prices, acreage planted, or crop yields. A chemical producer that sells to a fertilizer manufacturer might study the same indices, because the demand for chemicals in this case derives from the demand for fertilizer. These data are in the *Census of Agriculture*, conducted by the U.S. Department of Agriculture.

Measures of Construction Activity

If a business is marketing building materials, such as lumber, brick, gypsum products, or builders' hardware, its market depends on construction activity. This can be gauged by the number and value of building permits issued. Another indicator is the number of construction starts by type of structure (single-family residence, apartment, or commercial). Local data are available from county and city records, whereas regional and national statistics are found in reports from the Census Bureau's Manufacturing and Construction Division.

These sources illustrate the kinds of information available for predicting buying power of business markets. Many other public and private information sources are useful in forecasting demand. We will have more to say about forecasting in Chapter 6.

Business Buying Behavior

Business buying behavior, like consumer buying behavior, is initiated when an aroused need (a motive) is recognized. This leads to goal-oriented activity designed to satisfy the need. Once again, marketers must try to determine what motivates the buyer, and then understand the buying process and buying patterns of business organizations in their markets. The actual process is very similar to consumer decision-making, except the influences are different. Figure 5.1 summarizes the business buying-decision process and the primary influences.

The Importance of Business Buying

Top managers in most companies have come to realize that the buying decisions their organizations make are an important part of overall strategy. Securing the right products at the right time for the right price can play a major role in a firm's performance for at least three reasons:

- *Companies are making less and buying more.* For example, Toyota annually buys $15 billion worth of parts, materials, and services from hundreds of U.S. suppliers for use in its production both in the U.S. and overseas. When outside suppliers become this significant, buying becomes a prime strategic issue.

- *Firms are under intense quality and time pressures.* To reduce reworking costs and improve efficiency, firms cannot tolerate defective parts and supplies. As a result, price is only one of several decision criteria used in selecting vendors.

- *Firms are concentrating their purchases.* To get what they need, companies are dealing with fewer suppliers but are developing long-term "partnering" relationships with them. This level of involvement extends beyond a purchase to include such things as working together to develop new products and sharing information on inventories, production schedules, and costs. For example, Maytag, the appliance maker, is reducing its number of suppliers by nearly 75%, with the remaining suppliers expected to provide on-site representation at Maytag manufacturing plants, continuous cost improvements, and research and development efforts to produce new products.[8]

FIGURE 5.1

The Business Buying-Decision Process and the Factors that Influence It.

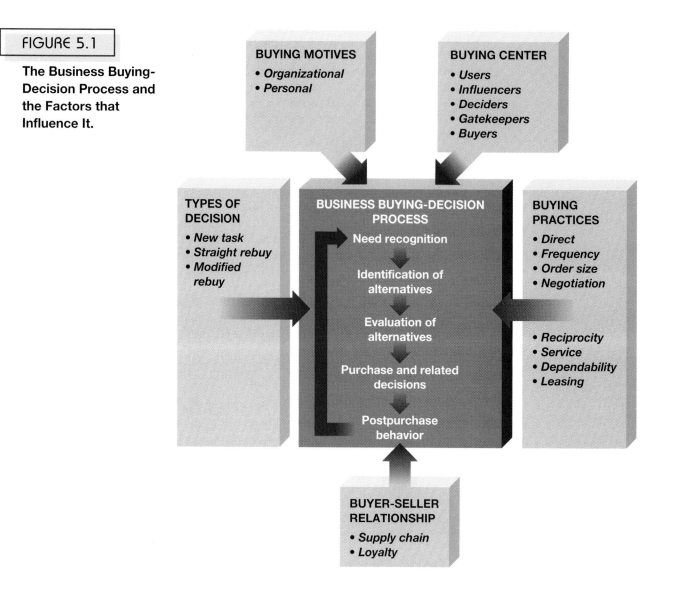

BUYING MOTIVES
- *Organizational*
- *Personal*

BUYING CENTER
- *Users*
- *Influencers*
- *Deciders*
- *Gatekeepers*
- *Buyers*

TYPES OF DECISION
- *New task*
- *Straight rebuy*
- *Modified rebuy*

BUSINESS BUYING-DECISION PROCESS
Need recognition
↓
Identification of alternatives
↓
Evaluation of alternatives
↓
Purchase and related decisions
↓
Postpurchase behavior

BUYING PRACTICES
- *Direct*
- *Frequency*
- *Order size*
- *Negotiation*

- *Reciprocity*
- *Service*
- *Dependability*
- *Leasing*

BUYER-SELLER RELATIONSHIP
- *Supply chain*
- *Loyalty*

Buying-Decision Process in Business

The buying-decision process in business markets is a sequence of five steps. It is depicted in the center of Figure 5.1. To illustrate the process, let's assume that Hershey Foods Corporation, responding to increased concerns about diet and nutrition, is considering introducing a line of confectionary goods using a sugar substitute:

- *Need recognition.* Hershey's marketing research has found that a growing number of consumers are concerned about sugar and calories in their diets. For some it is related to a medical condition such as diabetes. For others, it is simply a matter of trying to lose weight or avoid excess weight gains without changing their lifestyle. The opportunity to produce high-quality, good-tasting confections without sugar or with fewer calories is, therefore, very attractive, but finding the right sugar substitute is the challenge.

- *Identification of alternatives.* Hershey's marketing, production, and research and development managers draw up a list of product-performance specifications for the sugar-free goods. To appeal to consumers they must taste good, be competitively priced, meet their dietary needs, and have the texture or mouth-feel of sugar-based products. To satisfy production requirements the ingredient must be easy to use, available in sufficient quantities, and reasonable in cost. The R&D

staff is concerned about the stability of the finished product on the shelf, how it interacts with other ingredients, and how the human body processes it. Given the agreed-upon specifications, the purchasing department goes about identifying possible alternatives and sources of supply. Possibilities include saccharin, aspartame, sucralose, neotame, altitame, and a few others. Suppliers include such firms as Merisant Co., McNeil Specialty Products, a division of Johnson & Johnson, and Monsanto.

- *Evaluation of alternatives.* The marketing, production, and research people jointly evaluate the alternatives. Suppliers that meet some preliminary qualifications are invited to make presentations, and knowledgeable sources such as university food science researchers are contacted for information. Hershey discovers that some sugar substitutes cannot withstand high temperatures, there are differences in how well they simulate the taste and texture of sugar, and the approval from the Food & Drug Administration restricts how others can be used and must be labeled. The evaluation goes beyond performance and price to consider the suppliers' abilities to meet delivery schedules and provide consistent quality.

- *Purchase decision.* Based on the evaluation, Hershey managers decide on a specific ingredient and supplier. Next, the purchasing department negotiates the contract. Because large sums of money are involved, the contract will likely include many details. For example, it might incorporate provision of marketing support for Hershey's finished product by the producer of the sugar substitute.

- *Postpurchase behavior.* Hershey managers continue to evaluate the performance of the sugar substitute and the selected supplier to ensure that both meet expectations. Future dealings with the supplier will depend on this performance evaluation and on how well the supplier handles any problems that may arise involving its product.

In the following sections we will explore several of the differences between consumer buying behavior and business buying behavior that are reflected in this scenario.

Buying Motives of Business Users

Business **buying motives** are the needs that direct the purchasing behavior of business users. As shown in Figure 5.1, they fall into two broad categories—organizational and personal. Generally, business purchases are methodical and structured. Thus business buying motives are presumed to be, for the most part, practical and unemotional. Business buyers are assumed to be motivated to achieve organizational goals by securing the optimal combination of price, quality, and service in the products they buy.

An opposing view is that business buyers are human, and their business decisions are certainly influenced by their attitudes, perceptions, and values. In fact, many sales people would maintain that business buyers seem to be motivated more toward personal goals than organizational goals, and the two are often in conflict.

The truth is actually somewhere in between. Business buyers have two goals—to further their company's position (in profits, in acceptance by society) and to protect or improve their position in their firms (self-interest). Sometimes these goals are mutually consistent. For example, the firm's highest priority may be to save money, and the buyer expects to be rewarded for negotiating a low price. Obviously the more consistent the goals are, the better for both the organization and the individual, and the easier it is to make buying decisions.

However, there are often significant areas where the buyer's goals do not coincide with those of the firm, such as when the firm insists on dealing with the lowest-price supplier, but the buyer has developed a good relationship with another supplier and doesn't want to change. In these cases a seller must appeal to the buyer both on a rational "what's good for the firm" basis, and on a self-interest "what's in it for you" basis. Promotional appeals directed to the buyer's self-interest are particularly useful when two or more competing sellers are offering essentially the same products, prices, and postsale services.

Types of Buying Situations

In Chapter 4 we observed that consumer purchases can range from routine to complex buying decisions, termed low involvement and high involvement, respectively. In like manner the buying situations in business organizations vary widely in their complexity, number of people involved, and time required. Thus, not every purchase involves all five steps of the buying decision process.

To account for these different situations, Figure 5.1 depicts three classes of business buying situations. The three **buy classes** are new-task buying, straight rebuy, and modified rebuy:

- **New-task buying.** This is the most difficult and complex buying situation because it is a first-time purchase of a major product. Typically more people are involved in new-task buying than in the other two situations because the risk is great. Information needs are high and the evaluation of alternatives is difficult because the decision makers have little experience with the product. Sellers have the challenge of discovering the buyer's needs and communicating the product's ability to provide satisfaction. A hospital's first-time purchase of laser surgical equipment and a company buying robots for a factory (or buying the factory itself) are likely to be new-task buying conditions.

- **Straight rebuy.** This is a routine, low-involvement purchase with minimal information needs and little or no consideration of alternatives. Typically the buyer has had extensive, satisfactory experience with the seller, so there is no incentive to search. An example is the repeat purchase of linens and towels by a hospital. These buying decisions are made in the purchasing department, usually from a predetermined list of acceptable suppliers. If a supplier is not on this list, it may have difficulty even getting an opportunity to make a sales presentation to the buyer.

Recently KLM Royal Dutch Airlines announced it was dividing its purchase of new airplanes between Boeing and Airbus (a European firm). The purchase will amount to more than $4 billion. This move by KLM reflects what appears to be a growing practice among airlines of moving away from a single-manufacturer fleet of planes. A KLM spokesperson observed, "There are advantages to having a dual-vendor policy. You keep them (the suppliers) both sharp."

In contrast, Southwest Airlines attributed much of its early success to operating with only one model of plane from one supplier. The explanation is that it keeps maintenance costs down (because flight crews and maintenance people need only be familiar with one plane), reduces the needed inventory of replacement parts, and makes crews and equipment more interchangeable. Can these differing strategies be reconciled?

Sources: J. Lynn Lunsford and Daniel Michaels, "KLM to Order Planes from both Boeing , Airbus," *The Wall Street Journal*, Mar. 29, 2002, p. A2; "Boeing, Airbus Woo Thailand," *Xinhua News Agency*, June 5, 2002; "Boeing Still Bullish about Japan," *Associated Press Online*, June 4, 2002.

- **Modified rebuy.** This buying situation is somewhere between the other two in terms of time and people involved, information needed, and alternatives considered. For example, in selecting diagnostic equipment to test blood samples, a hospital would consider a small number of reputable suppliers and evaluate the new features added to the equipment since its last purchase. Similarly, a school district would have a committee review textbooks from a defined group of publishers in selecting a book to replace an outdated edition.

Understanding how the buyer views a buying situation is very important to a seller. The allocation of sales resources, the nature of the presentation made to the buyer, and even the prices offered should be influenced by the buyer's perception of the buying situation.

Multiple Buying Influences—the Buying Center

A **buying center** consists of all the individuals or groups involved in the process of making a decision to purchase. This includes the individuals within and outside an organization that influence the buying decision as well as the person ultimately responsible for the decision. Typically the members of a buying center are not formally identified. That is, there is no list of the buying center members to which a supplier or sales person can refer. One of the biggest challenges in business-to-business marketing is identifying the members of the buying center and their roles for a particular purchase.

Research suggests that the average size of a buying center ranges from three to five persons.[9] In other words, there are *multiple* buying influences, particularly in medium-sized and large firms. Even in small companies where the owner-managers make all major decisions, knowledgeable employees are usually consulted before certain purchases are made. The size and makeup of a buying center will vary depending on the product's cost, the complexity of the decision, and the stage of the buying process. The buying center for a straight rebuy of office supplies will be quite different from the center handling the purchase of a building or a fleet of trucks. Recognizing the existence of buying centers helps sellers appreciate that a successful sales effort seldom can be directed to a single individual.

As shown in Figure 5.1, a buying center includes the people who play any of the following **buying roles:**

- *Users*—the people who actually use the business product, perhaps a secretary, an executive, a production-line worker, or a truck driver.

- *Influencers*—the people who set the specifications and aspects of buying decisions because of their technical expertise, their organizational position, or even their political power in the firm.
- *Deciders*—the people who make the actual buying decision regarding the business product and the supplier. A purchasing agent may be the decider in a straight-rebuy situation. But someone in top management may make the decision regarding whether to buy an expensive computer system.
- *Gatekeepers*—the people who control the flow of purchasing information within the organization as well as between the firm and potential vendors. These people may be purchasing agents, secretaries, receptionists, or technical personnel.
- *Buyers*—the people who interact with the suppliers, arrange the terms of sale, and process the actual purchase orders. Typically this is the purchasing department's role. But again, if the purchase is an expensive, complex new buy, the buyer's role may be filled by someone in top management.

Several people in an organization may play the same role. For example, in the same firm, accountants and product designers use PCs for different purposes. As a result, they may prefer different brands. Or the same person may occupy more than one role. A secretary may be a user, an influencer, and a gatekeeper in the purchase of word processing software.

The variety of people contributing to any business buying decision, plus the differences among companies, present real challenges to sales people. As they try to determine who is performing each buying role in a buying situation, sales reps often call on the wrong people. Even knowing who the decision makers are is not enough, because these people may be very difficult to reach and people move into and out of the buying center as the purchase proceeds through the decision process. This, in part, explains why a sales person typically has only a few major accounts.

Certainly the challenges presented in the business buying-decision process should suggest the importance of coordinating the selling activities of the business marketer with the buying needs of the purchasing organization.

Buyer-Seller Relationships

A purchase can be looked upon as an isolated transaction or as part of a larger relationship that involves more parties than the buyer and seller and more interaction than the specific exchange. Figure 5.1 notes two dimensions of this relationship perspective—the supply chain and loyalty.

Rather than focus only on the immediate customer, many marketers approach marketing as a series of links between buyers and sellers. This **supply chain** approach considers the roles of suppliers, producers, distributors, and end users to see how each adds value to and benefits from the final product. This perspective leads to a recognition and understanding of the roles played by the entire value network in successfully bringing a product to market.

Business marketers are also placing greater emphasis on building repeat customers. Research has shown that it is as much as six times less expensive to make a repeat sale than it is to make a sale to a new customer. Repeat sales are often the result of **loyalty**—a willingness of the buyer to purchase from the seller without an extensive evaluation of alternatives. Loyalty requires a high level of trust on the part of the buyer. The time and effort necessary to build such trust is a major undertaking for both parties. For example, it typically entails sharing information about costs, processes, and plans for the future. The process of moving toward long-term, cost-effective, mutually beneficial trust with selected customers is known as relationship marketing, and its implementation is called **customer relationship management (CRM)**. Besides establishing criteria for selecting customers to do business with,

Recognizing that the people who actually use laptop computers may play an important role in the organizational buying decision, IBM targets them with ads for its ThinkPad. One campaign, exemplified by this ad, features successful people using ThinkPads at work. If the ads have their intended effect, more mid-level managers will become part of buying centers for laptop purchases.

CRM involves managing interactions with them. The types of interactions and the processes for effectively using them are organized into three categories:[10]

- *Operational CRM.* The objective is to make routine marketing operations such as sales calls, service programs, and customer support activities more efficient. By keeping track of a customer's purchase history, service schedule, and special requests, a firm can do a better job of anticipating the customer's needs, deciding which new products are best suited to the customer's operation, and providing preventive maintenance before problems occur.

- *Analytical CRM.* The objective is to effectively analyze all the available data about a customer. This involves merging data from internal company sources such as billing and payment histories, data generated by the customer such as average inventory amounts and reorder schedules, and data from third parties such as the government and credit bureaus. The analysis of such data helps a firm assess a customer's current and potential profitability, satisfaction, and loyalty.

www.crmguru.com

- *Collaborative CRM.* The objective is to provide mechanisms for customers to interact with the firm. Rather than the traditional one-way seller-to-buyer communication of media advertising, brochures, or printed catalogs, this is an effort to regularly tap into what the customer is thinking. Examples include incoming call centers, seller-sponsored chat rooms where customers can communicate with one another, and regular satisfaction surveys. Encouraging customer input permits a firm to identify issues before they become problems that disrupt the relationship.

The level at which CRM is conducted depends on the organization. Good sales people have always practiced some form of it, but often their efforts were informal and as a result missed important information. Today's formal CRM approaches combine sophisticated software that can link a firm with its customers, utilize the Internet to move data quickly, and employ data mining techniques that can look for patterns and meaning in databases that far exceed what the human mind can accomplish.

Several traditional business practices tend to discourage relationship building. For example, compensation plans for sales people that reward the volume of sales may result in customers' needs being overlooked. Likewise, the common accounting practice of treating each department in a firm as a cost center may cause managers

In the spring and summer of 2002, long-haul truck manufacturers experienced large increases in orders for new trucks. The reason for the surge was an environmental regulation scheduled to go into effect on October 1, 2002, reducing the permissible level of nitrogen oxide diesel engines release into the air. Nitrogen oxides have been associated with asthma and lung infections. Trucks delivered prior to the October deadline must only meet the prior environmental regulations.

Trucking companies are concerned because the technology that reduces pollutants also increases the cost of an engine by up to a third, already about $15,000. According to information filed with the Environmental Protection Agency by the engine makers, it is also likely that the new engines will consume more fuel, be costlier to maintain, and break down more often than existing versions. A spokesperson for trucking company Schneider National, which has over 13,000 truck tractors in its fleet, observed, "Our industry's scared to death about the new engines."

As a result of the buying binge, the transition to cleaner engines will be slowed, and the anticipated reduction in pollution from diesel engines (one-third by 2008), won't be accomplished until 2015.

Because the purpose of the regulation is to reduce air pollution, is it ethical for trucking companies to accelerate their purchases of new equipment and effectively delay the effects of the regulation?

Sources: Jeffery Ball, "Truck Firms Go on Buying Binge to Circumvent a New EPA Rule," *The Wall Street Journal*, May 28, 2002, p. A1+; James P. Miller, "EPA Probes Whether Truck-Engine Makers Encourage 'Pre-Buying,'" *Chicago Tribune*, May 14, 2002; Kevin Smith, "Large Trucking Firms Make Run on Current Models to Avoid EPA Regulations," *Inland Valley Daily Bulletin*, May 31, 2002.

to focus on cost minimization rather than customer service. And even the procedure of setting individual department performance goals may foster an environment of competition rather than cooperation.

Building and maintaining relationships may require changing the way business is done. For example, Apple Computer, which once relied exclusively on dealers, recognized that many of its larger customers needed specialized service. To satisfy this segment of the market and maintain strong ties to these key customers, the computer firm now has its own sales force calling directly on about 1,000 large accounts. However, many of the orders taken by the sales force are passed along to the dealers for fulfillment to ensure that they are involved as well.

Buying Practices of Business Users

Buying practices in the business market are similar to situational influences in consumer behavior. Several are shown in Figure 5.1. These practices, which are described below, stem from the nature and use of the products and characteristics of the markets.

Direct Purchase   In the consumer market, consumers rarely buy directly from the producer except in the case of services. In the business market, however, direct purchase by the business user from the producer is quite common even for goods. This is true especially when the order is large and the buyer needs much technical assistance. Makers of microprocessors and semiconductors, such as Intel Corp. and Micron Technology, deal directly with personal computer manufacturers because the memory technology is changing so rapidly. From a seller's point of view, direct sale in the business market is reasonable, especially when there are relatively few potential buyers, they are big, or they are geographically concentrated.

Frequency of Purchase   In the business market, firms buy certain products very infrequently. Large installations are purchased only once in many years. Small parts and materials to be used in the manufacture of a product may be ordered on long-term contracts, thus a selling opportunity exists as seldom as once a year. Even standard operating supplies, such as office supplies or cleaning products, may be bought only once a month. Because of this buying pattern, a great burden is placed on the personal selling programs of business sellers. The sales force must call on potential customers often enough to keep them familiar with the company's products and to know when a customer is considering a purchase.

Size of Order

The average business order is considerably larger than its counterpart in the consumer market. This fact, coupled with the infrequency of purchase, spotlights the significance of each sale in the business market. China Airlines, Taiwan's largest commercial carrier, is buying 12 wide-body jets that will have a purchase price of over $2 billion. Production and delivery of the planes will occur between 2004 and 2008. Given the relatively few number of airlines in the world buying these big jets and the impact of each purchase on the operation of the successful seller, it's clear why winning the contract is so important to a company such as Boeing.[11]

Length of Negotiation Period

The period of negotiation in a business sale is usually much longer than in a consumer transaction. Reasons for extended negotiations include:

- The number of executives participating in the buying decision.
- The large amount of money involved.
- The customization of the product to meet the buyer's needs.

Reciprocity Arrangements

There has been a significant decline, but not elimination, of reciprocity: the practice of "I'll buy from you if you'll buy from me." This decline has occurred for two reasons, one legal and the other economic. Both the Federal Trade Commission and the Antitrust Division of the Department of Justice have forbidden the practice of reciprocity in any *systematic* manner, particularly in large companies. A firm can buy from a customer, but it must be able to prove that it is not given any special privileges regarding price, quality, or service.

From an economic point of view, reciprocity may not make sense because the price, quality, or service offered by the seller may not be competitive. In addition, when a firm fails to pursue objectives that maximize profits, morale of both the sales force and the purchasing department may suffer.

Reciprocity is an area in which U.S. firms run into problems in doing business overseas. In many parts of the world, it is taken for granted that if I buy your product, you will buy mine.

Service Expectation

The user's desire for excellent service is a strong business buying motive that may determine buying practices. Frequently a firm's only differentiating feature is its service, because the product itself is so standardized that it can be purchased from any number of companies. Consider the choice of suppliers that provide elevators for a major office building or hotel. The installation of the elevators is no more important than keeping them operating safely and efficiently. Consequently, in its marketing efforts, a firm such as Montgomery Elevator emphasizes its maintenance service as much as its products.

Sellers must be ready to furnish services both before and after the sale. For example, suppliers such as Kraft Foods conduct a careful analysis of a supermarket's customers and sales performance and then suggest a product assortment and layout for the store's dairy department. In the case of office copiers, manufacturers train the buyers' office staffs in the use of the equipment and, after the machines have been installed, offer other services, such as repairs by specially trained technicians.

Market-oriented companies recognize the value of extraordinary service. For example, when a timing belt on a piece of equipment failed at a Frito-Lay processing plant, the manager contacted Motion Industries, a nearby industrial supplier, for a replacement part. Normally an emergency delivery would take an hour. However, on this particular day heavy rains had isolated the small town where the plant is located. Motion's manager rented a small plane, had the pilot fly over the Frito-Lay plant, and the needed part was dropped to the waiting maintenance manager on the ground. Motion Industries almost certainly lost money on the sale, but because it helped the plant manager save 25,000 pounds of potatoes, it may have won a customer for life.

Dependability of Supply   Another business buying practice is the user's insistence on an adequate quantity of uniform-quality products. Variations in the *quality* of materials going into finished products can cause considerable trouble for manufacturers. They may be faced with costly disruptions in their production processes if the imperfections exceed quality control limits. The emphasis on total quality has increased the significance of dependability. Because it has been established that firms can operate with virtually zero defects, buyers expect a very high standard of performance.

Adequate *quantities* are as important as good quality. A work stoppage caused by an insufficient supply of materials is just as costly as one caused by inferior quality of materials. However, firms refuse to buy well in advance of their needs, because doing so would tie up their resources in large inventories of supplies. In order for suppliers to provide sufficient quantities of a product just in time for the buyer's intended use, called just-in-time (JIT) delivery, unprecedented amounts of information must be exchanged. For example, Ford permits its automotive suppliers to have access to its detailed production schedule in order that critical parts and components can be delivered exactly when they are needed.

Leasing   Many firms in the business market lease business goods instead of buying them. In the past this practice was limited to large equipment, such as computers (IBM), packaging equipment (American Can Company), and heavy construction equipment. Presently, industrial firms are expanding leasing arrangements to include delivery trucks, automobiles used by sales people, machine tools, and other items that are generally less expensive than major installations.

Leasing has several merits for the lessor—the firm providing the equipment:

- Total net income—the income after charging off repairs and maintenance expenses—is often higher than it would be if the equipment were sold.
- The lessor's market may be expanded to include users who could not afford to buy the product, especially for large equipment.
- Leasing offers an effective method of getting users to try a new product. They may be more willing to rent a product than to buy it. If they are not satisfied, their expenditure is limited to a few monthly payments.

From the lessee's—or customer's—point of view, the benefits of leasing are:

- Leasing allows users to retain their investment capital for other purposes.
- Firms can enter a new business with less capital outlay than would be necessary if they had to buy equipment.
- Leased products are usually repaired and maintained by lessors, eliminating one headache associated with ownership.
- Leasing is particularly attractive to firms that need equipment seasonally or sporadically, as in food canning or construction.

The Impact of Electronic Commerce

The most important feature differentiating business from consumer marketing is the customization of products. Because of the significance of a purchase on the buyer's operation, business products often have to be adapted to the user's specific circum-

Are private exchanges displacing public exchanges?

Online Internet exchanges allow buyers and sellers to interact electronically. Most people are familiar with eBay, an online exchange that relies primarily on an auction format (see the case at the end of Part 1 for more details). Consumer-oriented Web-based exchanges are also offered on Yahoo.com, Amazon.com, and other sites. However, it may surprise you to learn that online exchanges account for a much larger volume of B-2-B than consumer transactions. Public sites (to which multiple businesses have access) include FreeMarkets (commodities), Covisint (auto parts), and e2open (high-tech equipment). The number of B-2-B exchanges grew rapidly in the 1990s. By 2000, over $5 billion had been invested to create more than 350 companies offering online exchanges. However, by 2002, 120 of them had been shut down as public sites or were being replaced by private exchanges. A private exchange, such as the one created by Burlington Northern Santa Fe railroad on which it recently auctioned 47 surplus locomotives in one afternoon, is controlled by a single firm. Private exchanges offer greater security, broader application than just buying and selling by linking all the members of a firm's supply chain, and less risk of a firm's purchases tipping off the competition about its plans. Wal-Mart, Dell, and Intel are some of the companies expected to conduct $2 trillion in business on their private exchanges by 2004.

Sources: David Gaffen, "The Ultimate Online Auction," *Fortune/CNET Technology Review,* Summer 2001, p. 36; Eric Young, "Web Marketplaces that Really Work," *Fortune/CNET Technology Review,* Winter 2002, pp. 78+.

---

stances. For example, Freightliner, a truck manufacturer, works with customers to design individual trucks to meet the buyer's needs. Thus, hundreds of decisions are required, all the way from the engine type and size to the configuration of the outside mirrors. Verson, a firm that makes metal presses used by appliance manufacturers and automakers, takes 18 months to build a press to meet the customized needs of a buyer. As a result, in many business marketing situations there must be a close, personal working relationship between many levels and functions of buyers and sellers.

However, there are also many business purchases of standardized products. For example, the sale of commodities such as bulk plastic, diesel fuel, and steel stock require much less buyer-seller interaction. There are also many low-technology, standardized products such as office supplies, maintenance products, and many component parts that are purchased in large quantities. An increasing number of firms are using the World Wide Web to facilitate buying these standardized products. Covisint, an auction site jointly owned by Ford, General Motors, DaimerChrysler, Renault, Nissan, and others handled $51 billion in transactions between 2,000 auto suppliers and the automakers in 2001. In a single transaction, DaimerChrysler used the site to buy 10,000 personal computers and laptops.[12]

Electronic commerce, which involves interactions and transactions over the Internet, takes many forms. The reverse auctions conducted by FreeMarkets, the subject of the chapter-opening case, is a version that is growing in popularity. Also, electronic bulletins boards (where sellers can post their offerings and prospective buyers can post their needs) are expanding rapidly. Web-based firms such as Ariba and Commerce One are giving buyers and sellers 24-hour, real time access to each other.

www.ariba.com

www.commerceone.com

Electronic commerce will not change all business marketing. There is still a need for personalized relationships in most situations. However, the impact and growth of business transactions on the Internet is a major development that requires the attention of all business marketers. Therefore, we will describe it in detail in Chapter 22.

At this point you know what marketing is and how it fits into an organization's strategy. You also appreciate the nature of consumer and business markets, and how they function. With this background, we are now ready to examine how firms identify the particular markets they wish to serve.

Summary

The business market consists of organizations that buy goods and services to produce other goods and services, to resell to other business users or consumers, or to conduct the organization's operations. It is an extremely large and complex market spanning a wide variety of business users that buy a broad array of business goods and services. Besides manufacturing, the business market includes agriculture, reseller, government, services, nonprofit, and international components.

Business market demand generally is derived, inelastic, and widely fluctuating. Business buyers usually are well informed about what they are buying. Business market demand is analyzed by evaluating the number and kinds of business users and their buying power.

Business buying, or purchasing, has taken on greater strategic importance. Organizations are buying more and making less, under intense time and quality pressures, and developing long-term partnering relationships with suppliers.

The buying-decision process in business markets may involve as many as five stages: need recognition, identification of alternatives, evaluation of alternatives, purchase decision, and postpurchase behavior. The actual number of stages in a given purchase decision depends on a number of factors including buying motives, the type of decision, the buying center, the buyer-seller relationship, and business buying patterns.

Business buying motives are focused on achieving a firm's objectives, but the business buyer's self-interest must also be considered. The types of business buying situations are new-task buy, straight rebuy, or modified rebuy.

The concept of a buying center reflects the multiple buying influences in business purchasing decisions. In a typical buying center are people playing the roles of users, influencers, deciders, gatekeepers, and buyers.

Developing a buyer-seller relationship stems from recognizing the importance of the customer's supply chain and the benefits of developing loyalty. Relationships require commitment and are built on trust and sharing of information.

Buying practices of business users often are quite different from buying practices in the consumer market. In the business market, direct purchases (that is, without middlemen) are more common, purchases are made less frequently, and orders are larger. The negotiation period usually is longer, and reciprocity arrangements sometimes exist. The demand for service is greater, and the dependability of supply is more critical. Finally, leasing (rather than product ownership) is quite common in business marketing.

Electronic commerce is having a major impact on business transactions involving standardized products. Even though it will not replace the need for personalized relationships in many situations, the Internet will affect nearly every aspect of business marketing.

More about **FreeMarkets**

Although consumer Internet auction sites like eBay and Priceline get most of the media attention, business-to-business marketers are actually much heavier users of e-commerce. FreeMarkets, for instance, has helped its customers around the world to transact more than $25 billion worth of purchases in over 190 product and service categories.

FreeMarkets intends to continue growing. Now that it has a presence in a dozen different countries around the world, it attracts bids from more than 150,000 suppliers in 17,500 different online markets. Industrial equipment accounts for a large portion of its business for clients like BP Amoco, Bombardier, United Technologies, Bayer, and Navistar. FreeMarkets has also conducted successful bidding events for a number of other major firms like General Motors, Unilever, and SmithKline Beecham, as well as for public utilities and government agencies. The state of Pennsylvania used the service to buy aluminum for license plates, saving over $250,000.

The fundamental necessities that make buying successful—information and preparation—have not changed with the introduction of the Internet. What has changed is the *amount* of information that can be gathered and processed, and the *speed* with which it can be updated and transferred. As a result, buyers and sellers who might not have known of each other's existence in the past can now become business partners. With services like FreeMarkets, they need not even be in the same country.

FreeMarkets has thus far focused on low-tech commodity products such as coal, metal, and foodstuffs, and services such as trucking, and it has zealously stressed customer service. Other reverse auction sites have taken a different approach, specializing in business markets for particular industries. For example, USBid, Inc., creates auctions for electronic products, and Seafax, Inc., serves the perishable food industry. One of FreeMarkets's biggest competitors is Ariba Inc., which markets itself as a cost-saving technology solution, and supply-chain networks in the auto industry have begun to feature online auctions.

Auctions come close to the notion of a market where the buyer has "complete information," something that previously had been only a simplifying assumption in economic models. According to Glen Meakem, founder of FreeMarkets, electronic auctions cause all suppliers to improve their businesses by forcing them to become more efficient in order to compete.[13]

1. Are there particular business-to-business purchases that are most likely to be affected by reverse auctions? Some that are least likely?

2. Which buying patterns of business users are most likely to be changed by FreeMarkets and similar business-to-business auction sites?

Key Terms and Concepts

Business market (119)
Business user (119)
Business marketing (119)
Business marketer (119)
Agribusiness (120)
Reseller market (121)
Disintermediation (121)
Government market (121)
Business services market (122)
Nonbusiness market (123)
International market (123)

Elasticity of demand (125)
North American Industry
   Classification System (NAICS) (128)
Value added (128)
Vertical business market (130)
Horizontal business market (130)
Activity indicator of buying power
   (130)
Buying motives (134)
Buy classes (134)
New-task buying (134)

Straight rebuy (134)
Modified rebuy (135)
Buying center (135)
Buying roles (135)
Supply chain (136)
Loyalty (136)
Customer relationship management
   (CRM) (136)
Electronic commerce (141)

Questions and Problems

1. What are some marketing implications in the fact that the demand for business goods:
   a. Fluctuates widely?
   b. Is inelastic?
   c. Is derived?

2. What are the marketing implications for a seller in the facts that business customers are typically geographically concentrated and limited in number?

3. What differences would you expect to find between the marketing strategies of a company that sells to horizontal business markets and those of a company that sells to vertical business markets?

4. An American manufacturer has been selling to a large oil company in Norway for 10 years. What factors might influence which of the three buy classes would best describe this buyer-seller relationship?

5. Explain how the five stages in the buying-decision process might be applied in the following buying situations:
   a. New-task buying of a conveyor belt for a soft-drink bottling plant.
   b. Straight rebuying of maintenance services for that conveyor belt.

6. How would you go about determining who occupies each of the buying-center roles in a hospital buying patient beds?

7. NCR, IBM, Xerox, and other manufacturers of office equipment make a substantial proportion of their sales directly to business users. At the same time, wholesalers of office equipment are thriving. Are these two market situations inconsistent? Explain.

Interactive Marketing Exercises

1. Find an ad for a business good or service that is directed toward the business market and another ad for the same product that is directed toward consumers (such as an ad for leasing fleets of Chevrolets and an ad for Chevrolets aimed at consumers). Discuss the buying motives appealed to in the ads.

2. Interview a purchasing agent about buying a product that would qualify as a modified rebuy. Draw a diagram that shows the purchasing agent's perceptions of (a) the stages of the decision process; (b) who was in the buying center at each stage of the decision process; and (c) what role(s) each person played at each stage of the process. Comment on how this diagram might be useful to a sales person representing the product in question.

6

Market Segmentation, Targeting, and Positioning

"Daimler's marketing team launched an intensive survey of the U.S. market to determine whether to bring the little car to the United States."

The **Smart Car** Is Short and Sweet, but Will It Sell?

Can DaimlerChrysler convince U.S. consumers that a car that gets 57 miles per gallon of gas is a good deal? Can it sell them on the notion that they can change the color of this new car in a snap, with nothing more than an extra set of resilient plastic side panels? Will consumers be attracted by the car's price, starting at around $9,000? How about the fact that you can park it, literally, on a dime? Some parking garages even give it a 50% discount. After all, it's only 8 feet long.

DaimlerChrysler's tiny new Smart Car has been called an electric shaver on wheels. The three-cylinder two-seater got off to a slow start in western Europe and Japan—that's in sales, not speed; the car accelerates to 63 mph in under 20 seconds—but it's been rising in popularity since then, and the executive who heads the Smart venture has expressed high hopes for its success worldwide, including in the U.S.

Begun as a cooperative effort between Swatch, the watch company, and Mercedes-Benz, the Smart Car became a project for Daimler (the maker of Mercedes) after Swatch pulled out. The car attracted a lot of attention when its first Paris dealership opened in 1998. (The name Smart is a combination of Swatch, Mercedes, and art.) But the high price, the U.S. equivalent of about $11,000, drove most prospective buyers away. To make matters worse, Mercedes took the car out of production to improve its stability and maneuverability, changes that notched the price up even higher. First-year sales were well below projections, at only 80,000 vehicles. It's been estimated that it will take until 2005, or 11 years after the car was conceived, for the Smart to make a profit.

DaimlerChrysler refused to give up, however. The company bought out Swatch's interest, hired an executive to direct the project, wrote off its losses, and forged ahead. To get the marketing on track, the sales targets were reduced to a more reasonable level and the price was reduced. The firm also opened Smart showrooms in Japan, where consumers are known for their fondness for unusual designs.

And the tide is beginning to turn. Though many early buyers are wealthy folks who like the toylike aspect of the car, Daimler plans to stay the course and hopes that the novelty appeal will eventually give way to more general respect for the car's maneuverability and fuel economy. The firm now makes right-hand drive and left-hand drive models, in both a coupe and convertible style, in a wide range of colors and options. All told, 13 different models are available, and more—including one with an electric-powered engine and four seats—are on the way. Buyers can put the car on a credit card or purchase it over the Internet; leases are also available.

With all that flexibility, sales picked up 25% in 2000 and, with dealerships in Italy, France, Germany, the Netherlands, Britain, Japan, Portugal, and Sweden, they reached a new high of 110,000 vehicles in 2001. More dealerships are opening in Hungary, Croatia, and Taiwan. But

www.smart.com

it's still an open question whether U.S. consumers will take to the Smart. Daimler's marketing team launched an intensive survey of the U.S. market to determine whether to bring the little car to the United States.

In the meantime, Chrysler's PT Cruiser and the return of the Volkswagen Beetle seem to be showing that small stylish cars can have wide market appeal in the United States, and BMW launched a hip new version of the Mini, popularized by the Austin Powers movies. And there may be other developments supporting small cars. In a rush to comply with California's clean-air rule, which took effect in 2003, Detroit is rolling out thousands of neighborhood electric vehicles or NEVs, which are not much more than souped-up golf carts, battery-powered to reach speeds of 25 miles an hour and run for a little longer than that before recharging. With at least three other populous states poised to adopt California's zero-emission vehicles rule, Ford, GM, and other manufacturers will all be targeting college campuses, military bases, and gated retirement communities with their NEVs.[1]

What information does DaimlerChrysler need about the U.S. market for the Smart Car, and how can it use the information to target its marketing effort?

Chapter Goals

Daimler faces a classic marketing challenge. It has a distinctive new product that is clearly not for everyone. What segments of the market will want to buy the Smart Car, and what features, price, and promotion strategy will work for each one? In this chapter, we will see why markets are segmented and how it is done. We will also consider the alternatives a firm faces in selecting which segments or target markets it wishes to pursue. Then we will introduce the concept of positioning or how a firm makes its offering attractive to a target market. Finally, we'll examine forecasting, the process of estimating the sales potential of a market. After studying this chapter, you should be able to explain:

- The related concepts of market segmentation, target marketing, and positioning.
- The process of market segmentation, including its benefits and conditions for use.
- Bases for segmenting consumer and business markets.
- Three target-market strategies: aggregation, single-segment strategy, and multiple-segment strategy.
- The three steps in developing a positioning strategy.
- The most frequently used methods of forecasting the demand of market segments.

An Overview of Market Segments and Target Markets

In Chapter 2 we defined a market as people or organizations with (1) needs to satisfy, (2) money to spend, and (3) the willingness to spend it. However, within a total market, there is always some diversity among the buyers. Not all consumers who wear pants want to wear jeans. Some vacationers take a cruise for rest and relaxation, others look for adventure and excitement. Among businesses, not all firms that use computers want the same amount of memory or speed, and not every software buyer needs the same amount of expert advice.

What we are seeing here is that within the same general market there are groups of customers—**market segments**—with different wants, buying preferences, or product-use behavior. In some markets these differences are relatively minor, and the benefits sought by consumers can be satisfied with a single marketing mix. In other markets, some customers are unwilling to make the compromises necessitated by a single marketing mix. As a result, the segments must be targeted individually with different marketing mixes. A specific market segment (people or organizations) for which the seller designs a particular marketing mix is a **target market.** Using the marketing mix, a firm attempts to establish an attractive position for its offering in the minds of the target market.

Before positions can be defined and marketing mixes designed, however, potential target markets must be identified and described. This process is called *market segmentation.*

Market Segmentation

The variation in customers' responses to a marketing mix can be traced to differences in buying habits, in ways in which the good or service is used, or in motives for buying. Customer-oriented marketers take these differences into consideration, but they usually cannot afford to design a different marketing mix for every customer. Consequently, most marketers operate between the extremes of one marketing mix for all and a different one for each customer. To do so involves **market segmentation,** a process of dividing the total market for a good or service into several smaller, internally homogeneous groups. The essence of segmentation is that the members of each group are similar with respect to the factors that influence demand. A major element in a company's success is the ability to segment its market effectively.

Benefits of Market Segmentation

Market segmentation is customer-oriented, and thus it is consistent with the marketing concept. In segmenting, we first identify the wants of customers within a submarket and then decide if it is practical to develop a marketing mix to satisfy those wants.

By tailoring marketing programs to individual market segments, any company can do a better marketing job and make more efficient use of its marketing resources. Focus is especially important for a small firm with limited resources. Such a firm might compete very effectively in one or two small market segments; however, it would likely be overwhelmed by the competition if it aimed for a major segment. For example, The Hain Celestial Group, Inc., is focusing on various segments of the U.S. and international markets for organic and natural foods. Under one of its brands, Celestial Seasonings, the firm markets specialty teas. After water, tea is the most heavily consumed drink in the world, and Hain Celestial is developing new market and distribution strategies to support new tea flavors for many different market segments.[2]

By developing strong positions in specialized market segments, medium-sized firms can grow rapidly. For example, the Oshkosh Truck Company in Wisconsin has become the world's largest producer of fire and rescue trucks for airports.

Even very large companies with the resources to engage in mass marketing supported by expensive national advertising campaigns are abandoning mass-market strategies. These companies embrace market segmentation as a more effective strategy to reach the fragments that once constituted a mass, or homogeneous, market in the U.S.

The marketing of many consumer products illustrates this approach. The typical supermarket stocks about 40,000 items, twice the number of a few years ago. Many are very similar. For example, there are 19 different types of Pert shampoos and conditioners, each purporting to offer distinctive benefits such as "deep moisturizing" or

www.the hainfood group.com

Cooking, cleaning, and shopping are chores an increasing number of consumers are paying others to perform for them. Recently there has been an increase in outsourcing another chore, pet care. Firms are providing everything from day care to birthday parties for pets. Since it's unlikely that all of the 60 million U.S. households with pets are potential customers for pet care outsourcing, how would you go about identifying an attractive market segment?

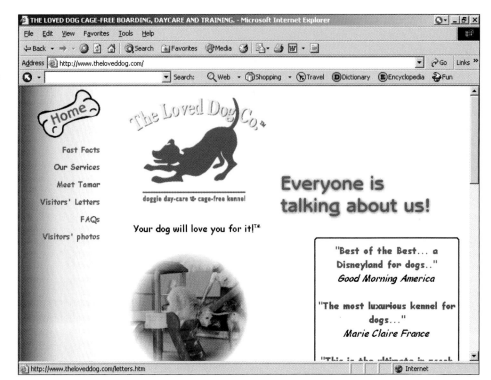

"volume." Similarly, P&G offers 72 varieties of Pantene hair-care treatments, and Kellogg's has 16 flavors of Eggo waffles.[3]

This proliferation of alternatives has a potential downside. Consumers can become frustrated by the complex decision making that is required for even a simple purchase when many similar products are available. As a result, marketers should seek a balance between meeting the specialized needs of consumers and overwhelming them with choices.

The Process of Market Segmentation

Markets are sometimes segmented intuitively; that is, a marketer relies on experience and judgment to make a decision about the segments that exist in a market and how much potential each offers. Others follow the lead of competitors or earlier market entrants. For example, Gatorade was invented by University of Florida scientists to rapidly replenish the body fluids of the school's football players. When it was later introduced as a consumer product, it met the needs of a group of beverage consumers that became known as the "sports drink" segment. As Gatorade's popularity grew, imitators such as Powerade from Coca-Cola and All Sport from Pepsi were introduced. Each has taken a small share of the market, but they did not unseat Gatorade as the brand with the largest share. And the future may get even rougher for these imitators now that Gatorade has been acquired by Pepsi, and will benefit from even broader distribution. Another alternative is to perform a structured analysis, often supported by some marketing research, in order to identify segments and measure their potential. This approach, even if done with a small budget, often produces insights and opportunities that would be overlooked otherwise.

The steps involved in segmenting a market in an organized fashion are:

1. *Identify the current and potential wants that exist within a market.* The marketer carefully examines the market to determine the specific needs being satisfied by current offerings, the needs current offerings fail to adequately satisfy, and the needs that may not yet be recognized. This step may involve interviewing and/or

observing consumers or firms to determine their behavior, levels of satisfaction, and frustrations. Within the market for wristwatches there is a shared desire among all customers to know the time, and certainly all watches must accurately tell time. But there are also customers who variously want a watch to be a fashion accessory, a status symbol, an exercise timer, or an appointment reminder. There might be others who would like a watch to function as a computer, a voice recorder, a pulse monitor, a television receiver, or a telephone. These wants individually or in some combination represent potential market segments within the wristwatch market.

2. *Identify characteristics that distinguish among the segments.* In this step the focus is on what prospects who share a particular want have in common to distinguish them from other segments in the market that have different wants. Among business firms it could be a physical feature (like size or location). Among consumers it might be an attitude or a behavior pattern. From the results of this step, potential marketing mixes (including product ideas) for the various segments can be designed. These alternatives can then be further analyzed.

3. *Determine the size of the segments and how well they are being satisfied.* The final step is to estimate how much demand (or potential sales) each segment represents and the strength of the competition. These forecasts will determine which segments are worth pursuing. American Express launched an Internet banking service that allows customers to make deposits, purchase certificates of deposit, and pay bills online. Despite the fact that online competition from conventional banks and other credit card companies is fierce, American Express' existing cardholders make up an attractive initial market segment.

A group that shares a want distinguishable from the rest of the market is a market segment. However, to be useful to marketers, results of a segmentation effort must also meet some conditions:

- The bases for segmenting—that is, the characteristics used to describe what segments customers fall into—must be *measurable,* and data describing the characteristics must be *obtainable.* The age of customers is both measurable and obtainable. On the other hand, the "desire for ecologically compatible products" may be a factor useful in segmenting the market for mulching lawn mowers. But this characteristic is not easily measured, nor can the data be easily obtained.

- The market segment should be *accessible* through existing marketing institutions—middlemen, advertising media, the company's sales force—with a minimum of cost and wasted effort. To increase the benefits of segmentation, most national magazines such as *Time* and *Sports Illustrated* and large metropolitan newspapers such as the *Chicago Tribune* publish separate geographic editions. This allows an advertiser to run a magazine ad aimed at, say, a Southern segment of the market or a newspaper ad for particular suburbs, without having to pay for exposure in other, nontargeted areas.

- Each segment should be *large enough* to be profitable. Procter & Gamble found a segment of candy consumers that wants a low-calorie product. However, it is too small to justify the investment a line of confections would require. In concept, management could treat each single customer as a separate segment. Actually, this situation, called **micromarketing,** is becoming more common in consumer markets and is quite common in some business markets, as when Freightliner custom-designs a long-haul truck for a customer, or when Citibank makes a loan to the government of Mexico or Argentina. Micromarketing occurs in selected consumer markets such as custom-designed homes. But in segmenting most consumer markets, a firm must not develop too broad an array of styles, colors, sizes, and prices, because the production and inventory costs would make it unprofitable.

Ultimate Consumers and Business Users—the First Cut

As we shall see, a company can segment its market in many different ways, and the bases for segmentation vary from one market to another. Often the first step is to divide a potential market into two broad categories: ultimate consumers and business users. Black & Decker does this, offering the DeWalt line of power tools for professionals and the Quantum line for the do-it-yourself segment.

The sole criterion for this first cut at segmenting a market is the customer's reason for buying. Recall from Chapter 4 that ultimate consumers buy goods or services for their own personal or household use and are satisfying strictly nonbusiness wants. They constitute the consumer market. Business users, described in Chapter 5, are business, industrial, or institutional organizations that buy goods or services to use in their organizations, to resell, or to make other products. Black & Decker recognized that professionals who earn their living in the building trades need durable tools that perform precisely. Do-it-yourselfers, on the other hand, use their tools less often, typically take on less complicated projects, and are satisfied with less powerful equipment. These segments were judged to be so different that they required separate marketing mixes.

Segmenting a market into these two groups—consumers and businesses—is extremely significant from a marketing point of view because the two segments buy differently. Consequently, the composition of a seller's marketing mix will depend on whether it is directed toward the consumer market or the business market.

Segmenting Consumer Markets

Dividing a total market into ultimate consumers and business users results in segments that are still too broad and varied for most products. We need to identify some characteristics within each of these segments that will enable us to divide them further into more specific targets.

As shown in Table 6.1, there are a number of ways the consumer market can be segmented. The bases for segmentation include many of the characteristics used to describe the consumer market in Chapter 4, as well as some psychological and behav-

Black & Decker recognizes that differences in the business and consumer market segments for power tools are sufficient to require different marketing programs. DeWalt is the company's professional caliber line, Quantum is for the do-it-yourself frequent tool users, and the Black & Decker brand is intended for the occasional household user. Each line has distinct features, prices, packaging, and even distribution outlets.

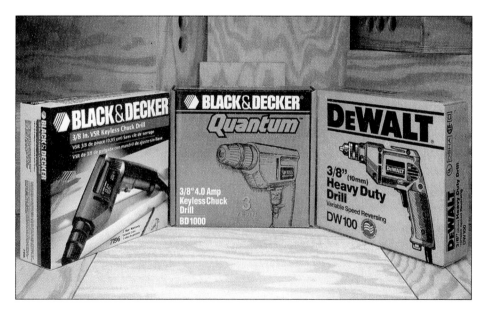

TABLE
6.1

Segmentation Bases for Consumer Markets

Segmentation Basis	Possible Market Segments
Geographic	
Region	New England, Middle Atlantic, and other census regions
City or metro-area size	Population under 25,000; 25,000–100,000; 100,001–500,000; 500,001–1,000,000; etc.
Urban–rural	Urban, suburban, rural
Climate	Hot, cold, sunny, rainy, cloudy
Demographic	
Income	Under $25,000; $25,000–$50,000; $50,001–$75,000; $75,001–$100,000; over $100,000
Age	Under 6, 6–12, 13–19, 20–34, 35–49, 50–64, 65 and over
Gender	Male, female
Family life cycle	Young, single; young, married, no children; etc.
Social class	Upper class, upper-middle, lower-middle, upper-lower, etc.
Education	Grade school only, high school graduate, college graduate
Occupation	Professional, manager, clerical, sales, student, homemaker, unemployed, etc.
Ethnic background	African, Asian, European, Hispanic, Middle Eastern, etc.
Psychographic	
Personality	Ambitious, self-confident, aggressive, introverted, extroverted, sociable, etc.
Life-style	Activities (golf, travel); interests (politics, modern art); opinions (conservation, capitalism)
Values	Values and lifestyles 2 (VALS2), list of values (LOV)
Behavioral	
Benefits desired	Examples vary widely depending on product: appliance—cost, quality, operating life; toothpaste—no cavities, plaque control, bright teeth, good taste, low price
Usage rate	Nonuser, light user, heavy user

ioral dimensions. To illustrate, we will discuss four bases for segmenting consumer markets that are used separately or in combination:

1. Geographic
2. Demographic
3. Psychographic
4. Behavioral

Geographic Segmentation

Subdividing markets into segments based on location—the regions, counties, cities, and towns where people live and work—is **geographic segmentation.** The reason for this is simply that consumers' wants and product usage often are related to one or more of these subcategories. Geographic characteristics are also measurable and accessible—two of the conditions for effective segmentation. Let's consider how the geographic distribution of population may serve as a basis for segmentation.

Regional Population Distribution   Many firms market their products in a limited number of geographic regions, or they may market nationally but prepare a separate marketing mix for each region. The regional distribution of population is important to marketers because people *within* a given region generally tend to share similar values, attitudes, and style preferences. However, significant differences often exist *among* regions because of differences in climate, social customs, and other factors. For example, Campbell Soup Company has altered some of its soup and bean recipes to suit regional tastes, and Friday's restaurants, with 345 units nationwide, allows each outlet to offer up to 30 regional items on its menu.

Many organizations segment their markets on the basis of city size or population concentration; that is, they utilize an urban-suburban-rural distribution. Toys "Я" Us, the largest chain of toy stores in the U.S., initially located stores only in metropolitan areas with populations exceeding 250,000 to ensure a sufficiently large customer base. In contrast, Wal-Mart's initial strategy was to locate only in towns of less than 35,000 people in order to minimize the amount of competition.

A popular reference source used for geographic segmentation is *Sales & Marketing Management* magazine's annual "Survey of Buying Power." This two-part report provides information on population, income, and spending behavior by state, county, major metropolitan area, television market, and newspaper market. With these data, a marketer can compare spending power and purchasing behavior across geographic areas.

Demographic Segmentation

Demographics are also a common basis for segmenting consumer markets. They are frequently used because they are often strongly related to demand and are relatively easy to measure. Recall that several demographic variables were discussed in Chapter 4 in descriptions of the consumer market. The most popular characteristics, used alone or in combination, for **demographic segmentation** are age, gender, family life-cycle stage, income, and education. For example, the average age of new Toyota buyers is 44 years old.[4] This is in large part due to the popularity of the Camry among consumers over 50. However, as a result Toyota is developing a reputation as a brand for middle-aged consumers. To dispel that image and attract younger customers, Toyota has developed models specifically for drivers in their twenties and thirties: the M2Spyder, a midengine two-seater convertible; Matrix, a five-door hatchback; and the RAV4, a mini SUV. Examples of demographic segmentation characteristics are shown in Table 6.1.

It is important to note that there are no rules for the number or breadth of categories used in a segmentation effort. The market and the need being satisfied should dictate the choices. For example, there may be a certain symmetry in an age category that includes all teenagers (and data may be available on "teens"), but the purchase behavior and motivations of 13- and 14-year-olds in a particular market may be quite different from 18- and 19-year-olds.

Social class, a composite measure made up of several demographic dimensions, illustrates this approach to segmenting a market. The most commonly used indicator of social class includes level of education, type of occupation, and the type of neighborhood a person lives in. Many consider social class a "richer" indicator than income or any of the individual social class components taken separately. They would argue that a lawyer and a plumber, for example, might have the same income but be members of different social classes. Because a person's social class—be it upper class or blue-collar working class—has a considerable influence on that person's choices in many product categories, companies frequently select one or two social classes as target markets and then develop a product and marketing mix to reach those segments.[5]

The ways in which segmentation bases can be combined is limited only by the imagination of the marketer and the availability of data. For example, an approach called geodemographic clustering is based on ZIP codes, demographic data available from the U.S. Census, and household data collected by the research firm Claritas. The trade name for the procedure is PRIZM (short for Potential Rating Index for ZIP Markets). Using Census data on education, income, occupation, housing, ethnicity, urbanization, and other variables, Claritas grouped the 36,000 U.S. ZIP codes into

www.claritas.com

62 similar clusters or segments. Each cluster then was further examined for similarities in lifestyles and consumption behavior, and given descriptive names such as "kids and cul-de-sacs," "gray power," and "shotguns and pickups." Marketers use this information to identify ZIP codes for direct-mail promotions, to select locations for retail outlets, and to determine the best mix of products and brands to offer in particular stores.

Psychographic Segmentation

Demographics are used to segment markets because these data are related to behavior and because they are relatively easy to gather. However, demographics are not in themselves the causes of behavior. Consumers don't buy windsurfing equipment because they are young. They buy it because they enjoy an active, outdoor lifestyle, and it so happens that such people are also typically younger. Thus demographics often correlate with behavior, but they do not explain it.

Marketers often go beyond demographic attributes in an effort to better understand why consumers behave as they do. They engage in what is called **psychographic segmentation**, which involves examining attributes related to how a person thinks, feels, and behaves. Frequently included in a psychographic segmentation effort are personality dimensions, life-style characteristics, and consumer values.

Personality Characteristics
An individual's **personality** is usually described in terms of traits that influence behavior. Theoretically, they would seem to be a good basis for segmenting markets. Our experience tells us that compulsive people buy differently from cautious consumers, and quiet introverts do not buy the same things or in the same way as gregarious, outgoing people.

However, personality characteristics pose problems that limit their usefulness in practical market segmentation. First, the presence and strength of these characteristics in the general population are virtually impossible to measure. For example, how would you go about measuring the number of people in the U.S. who could be classified as aggressive? Another problem is associated with the accessibility condition of segmentation. There is no advertising medium that provides unique access to a particular personality type; that is, television reaches introverts as well as extroverts, aggressive people as well as timid people. So one of the major goals of segmentation, to avoid wasted marketing effort, is not likely to be accomplished using personality.

Nevertheless, firms often tailor their advertising messages to appeal to personality traits. Even though the importance of the personality dimension in a particular decision may be unmeasurable, the seller believes that it does play an influential role. Thus, for years Hallmark promoted its greeting cards by suggesting to consumers, "When you care enough to send the very best," and L'Oréal models used the company's products "Because I'm worth it."

LifeStyle
Lifestyle relates to activities, interests, and opinions. Your lifestyle reflects how you spend your time and what your beliefs are on various social, economic, and political issues. It is a broad concept that overlaps what some consider to be personality characteristics.

People's lifestyles undoubtedly affect what products they buy and what brands they prefer. Marketers are aware of this and often design their strategies based on life-style segments. Ads for Polo clearly portray a life-style image. And the firm's website describes the strategy in the words of Ralph Lauren:[6]

> Polo has always been about selling a quality product by creating worlds and inviting our customers to be part of our dream. We were the first to create lifestyle advertisements that tell a story. We were the first to create stores that enable customers to interact with that lifestyle.

Home Depot, well-known for its warehouse-style home improvement stores aimed at the weekend do-it-yourself market, has identified another market segment based on lifestyle and income. Through its chain of stores called Expo, the company is offering design assistance, more expensive furnishing and decorations for the home, and assistance with large-scale renovations to customers who might never consider visiting a Home Depot warehouse. Compare their websites.

www.homedepot.com

www.expo.com

Although it is a valuable marketing tool, life-style segmentation has some of the same limitations as segmentation based on personality characteristics. For example, it is difficult to accurately measure the size of life-style segments in the population. For example, how many people want to reflect the "Polo life-style" in what they wear? Another problem is that a given life-style segment might not be accessible at a reasonable cost through a firm's usual distribution system or promotional program.

Values According to psychologists, **values** are a reflection of our needs adjusted for the realities of the world in which we live. Researchers at the Survey Research Center at the University of Michigan have identified nine basic values that relate to purchase behavior. The nine, which they call the list of values (LOV), are:

- Self-respect
- Security
- Excitement
- Fun and enjoyment in life
- Having warm relationships
- Self-fulfillment
- Sense of belonging
- Sense of accomplishment
- Being well respected

Although almost everyone would view all these values as desirable, their relative importance differs among people, and their relative importance affects behavior. For example, people who place a high value on fun and enjoyment are more likely to enjoy skiing, dancing, bicycling, and backpacking, whereas people who have high value for warm relationships tend to give gifts for no particular reason. Thus, the relative strength of values could be the basis for segmenting a market.

Behavioral Segmentation

Some marketers regularly attempt to segment their markets on the basis of product-related behavior—they utilize **behavioral segmentation.** In this section we briefly consider two of these approaches: the benefits desired from a product and the rate at which the consumer uses the product.

Benefits Desired From a customer-oriented perspective, the ideal method for segmenting a market is on the basis of customers' desired benefits. Certainly, using benefits to segment a market is consistent with the idea that a company should be marketing benefits and not simply the physical characteristics of a product. After all, a carpenter wants a smooth surface (benefit), not a Black & Decker electric sander (the product). In many cases, however, benefits desired by customers do not meet the first condition of segmentation described above. That is, they are not easily measured because customers are unwilling or unable to reveal them. For example, what bene-

Will "Kathy" and "Lewis" Buy the New Taurus?

To design its new Taurus sedan, Ford arranged for researchers to "live" with a sample of families, observing their behavior at home, on the road, and in the community. Called "customer immersion," the goal is to develop a detailed demographic, behavioral, and psychographic profile of targeted consumers.

Those working on the Taurus redesign used the data base to create stereotypical consumers, with names, stories about their backgrounds and families, photos from stock files that best resembled them, and descriptions of their personalities, motives, and likes and dislikes—all fictional. Even screen savers with the selected qualities were created and placed on each employee's computer.

What is Ford's vision of the next generation of sedan buyers? "Kathy" is 39 years old, married with two kids, 6 and 10. Her husband is an engineer. She's a college graduate, working as a speech pathologist. She volun-

teers at the Humane Society and plays in a recreational volleyball league. She's a little worried about time passing, but finds some adventure in juggling work and family.

"Lewis" is 41 with a 17-year-old daughter who is just starting college. He is a branch bank manager. His wife sells real estate and they live with their 14-year-old son in a suburban home they are remodeling. He's a little intimidated by the pace of change today, and is looking forward to more leisure but doesn't feel like he's earned it yet.

Time will tell if Ford's investment in information to create a virtual Kathy and Lewis will pay off in greater focus and an attractive design.

Sources: Greg Schneider, "Ford Invents the Model Two," The Washington Post, Oct. 27, 2002, pp. H01+; Rick Popley, "Ford Takes Tall Step into the Future with New Sedan Design," The Chicago Tribune, Oct. 27, 2002, p. 1+.

fits do people derive from clothing that has the label on the outside? Conversely, why do others refuse to wear such clothing?

Performing benefit segmentation is a multistep process. First, the specific benefits consumers are seeking must be identified. This typically involves several research steps, beginning with the identification of all possible benefits related to a particular product or behavior through brainstorming, observing consumers, and listening to group discussions. Then more research is conducted to screen out unlikely or unrealistic benefits and to amplify and clarify the remaining possibilities. Finally, large-scale surveys are conducted to determine how important the benefits are and how many consumers seek each one.

To illustrate, Forrester Research, Inc., surveyed 131,000 consumers about their motivations, buying habits, and financial ability to purchase technology products. The results produced 10 segments, including the career-minded "fast forwards" (the earliest adopters and biggest spenders), "new-age nurturers" (big spenders on home uses such as family PCs), "digital hopefuls" (families with limited budgets but still interested in buying new technology), and "media junkies" (those who prefer older entertainment-oriented media like TV).[7] When this information is combined with demographic profiles, marketers have a better idea how to reach particular segments and what types of messages will appeal to them.

Usage Rate   Another basis for market segmentation is the rate at which people consume a product. A popular categorization of usage rates is nonusers, light users, medium users, and heavy users. Normally a company is most interested in the heavy users of its product because fewer than 50% of all users of a product typically account for 80 to 90% of the total purchases. These heavy users are often referred to in an industry as the "heavy half" of the market. Many marketers aim their marketing efforts at retaining the consumers who make up the heavy half for their brand, and encouraging the heavy-half users of competitors' brands to switch. For example, customer service representatives at First Union Corp.'s Charlotte, North Carolina, offices can look at their computer screens at the beginning of each call to see the customer's banking profile. A tiny red square pops up next to the names of customers whose accounts are losing money for the bank. A green dot indicates those who generate substantial profits, which means they get preferential treatment. Yellow is for those in-between. The rankings are generated from a customer database that tracks account balances, number of branch visits, services purchased, and other information. First Union expects to generate about $50 million in added annual revenue from extra fees paid by the unprofitable customers and retention of preferred customers that the reps can identify and pamper.[8]

Sometimes a marketer will select as a target market the nonuser or light user, intending to woo these customers into higher usage. Or light users may constitute an attractive niche for a seller simply because they are being ignored by firms that are targeting heavy users. Once the characteristics of these light users have been identified, management can go to them directly with an introductory low-price offer. Or a seller might get consumers to increase their usage rates by (1) describing new uses for a product (baking soda as a refrigerator deodorizer, chewing gum as an alternative to cigarettes); (2) suggesting new times or places for use (soup as an after-school snack, air fresheners in school lockers); or (3) offering multiple-unit packaging (a 12-pack of soft drinks).

Segmenting Business Markets

Even though the number of buyers in a business market may be relatively few compared to a consumer market, segmentation remains important. The reason is quite simple—a highly focused marketing effort directed at meeting the specific needs of a group of similar customers is both more efficient and more likely to be successful.

In Table 6.2 examples of business market segmentation bases are grouped by customer location, customer type, and transaction conditions. Notice that many of the bases are similar to ones used for segmenting consumer markets. To provide a feel for business market segmentation, several of these bases are described in more detail.

TABLE 6.2 **Segmentation Bases for Business Markets**

Segmentation Basis	Possible Market Segments
Customer Location	
Region	Southeast Asia, Central America, Upper Midwest, Atlantic Seaboard
Locations	Single buying site, multiple buying sites
Customer Type	
Industry	Selected NAICS codes
Size	Sales volume, number of employees
Organization structure	Centralized or decentralized, group or individual decision
Purchase criteria	Quality, price, durability, lead time
Transaction Conditions	
Buying situation	Straight rebuy, modified rebuy, new buy
Usage rate	Nonuser, light user, heavy user
Purchasing procedure	Competitive bidding, lease, service contracts
Order size	Small, medium, large
Service requirements	Light, moderate, heavy

Customer Location

Business markets are frequently segmented on a geographic basis. Some industries are geographically concentrated. For example, businesses that process natural resources locate close to the source to minimize shipping costs. Other industries are geographically concentrated simply because newer firms either spun off from or chose to locate near the industry pioneers. For example, several brands of recreational vehicles, including Skyline and Monaco Coach (formerly Holiday Rambler) are manufactured in northern Indiana. Some firms that sell to this industry, such as Patrick Industries (cabinets and paneling) and LaSalle-Bristol (floor covering), have chosen to locate nearby and focus their efforts geographically.

Companies also segment international markets geographically. In considering developing countries, for example, a firm might consider the reliability of public utilities, the quality of the transportation system, and the sophistication of the distribution structure in deciding where to expand its operation.

Customer Type

Industry   Any firm that sells to business customers in a variety of industries may want to segment its market on the basis of industry. For example, a company that sells small electric motors would have a broad potential market among many different industries. However, this firm will do better by segmenting its potential market by type of customer and then specializing in order to more completely meet the needs of organizations in a limited number of these segments. The NAICS codes, described in Chapter 5, are particularly useful for this purpose because information published by the government and industry on such factors as the number of firms, their size, and their location is often organized according to this scheme.

Size   Business customer size can be estimated using such factors as sales volume, number of employees, number of production facilities, and number of sales offices. Many sellers divide their potential market into large and small accounts, using separate distribution channels to reach each segment. The seller's sales force may contact large-volume accounts directly, but to reach the smaller accounts, the seller may use a middleman or rely on the Internet or telemarketing.

Organization Structure   Firms approach buying in different ways. Some rely heavily on their purchasing departments to control the inflow of information, reduce the number of potential alternatives, and conduct negotiations. Selling to such companies would require a strong personal selling effort directed specifically at purchasing executives. It would also need excellent supporting materials if the product exceeded the technical expertise of the purchasing managers.

Other buyers opt for greater involvement in the purchase process by the people who will be directly affected by the purchase. These buyers tend to include many people in their decisions, hold meetings over a long period of time, and engage in a lot of internal communication. Government agencies are especially known for lengthy purchase decisions. For example, because of the extensive approval processes, obtaining an order to sell supplies to a prison often takes two or three years. Selling to a market segment such as this requires many, varied contacts, and often involves several people from the selling firm.

Purchase Criteria   All buyers want good quality, low prices, and on-time delivery. However, within a market there are groups for which one of these or some other purchase criterion is particularly significant. Consider the automotive business. General Motors buys over $90 *billion* in components, machinery, and equipment a year. In selecting suppliers GM has a formal process that takes into account a prospect's technical capabilities, defect rates, and delivery schedule among other criteria.

Transaction Conditions

The circumstances of the transaction can also be a basis for segmenting a market. Sellers may have to modify their marketing efforts to deal with different buying situations, usage rates, purchasing procedures, order sizes, or service requirements. To illustrate, three of these transaction conditions are described below.

Buying Situation
When United Airlines is faced with the decision of whether or not to buy Boeing's Sonic Cruiser, a plane that will hold 300 passengers and fly at near the speed of sound, it is making a new buy. The decision is quite different from the modified rebuy that occurs when United purchases additional 737s, a plane it has flown successfully for years. These buying situations, along with the straight rebuy, are sufficiently unique that a business seller might well segment its market into these three buy-class categories. Or the seller could at least set up two segments by combining new buy and modified rebuy into one segment. Different marketing programs would be developed to reach each of these two or three segments.

Usage Rate
Markets for most products can be divided among heavy users, light users, and nonusers (prospects). Heavy users appear to be the most attractive because of the volume they purchase, but they also generate the most competition. As an alternative to pursuing heavy users, some firms have found it profitable to avoid the competition by concentrating on light users.

Purchase Procedure
Products can be leased, financed, or purchased outright. A price can be simply stated, negotiated, or submitted in a sealed bid. Consider how a bidding system affects a seller. Government agencies often buy on the basis of sealed bids; that is, each prospective seller submits a confidential bid in response to a detailed description of what the agency wants to buy. When the bids are opened, the agency is typically bound by law to accept the lowest bid unless it is clearly inappropriate. How is this different from a negotiated price? For one thing, the seller has only one chance to propose a price. Also, to compete in a sealed-bid market, it is essential to have low costs. And good industry knowledge is important in order to accurately predict what other firms will bid. These differences might cause a firm to treat the government as a distinct segment.

Segmentation identifies the opportunities that exist in a market. The next step is for a firm to decide which of those opportunities to target with a marketing effort.

Target-Market Strategies

After a company has segmented a market, management must next select one or more segments as its target markets. The company can follow one of three strategies—market aggregation, single-segment concentration, or multiple-segment targeting.

Aggregation Strategy

By adopting a **market-aggregation strategy**—also known as a *mass-market strategy* or an *undifferentiated-market strategy*—a seller treats its total market as a single segment. An aggregate market's members are considered to be alike with respect to demand for the product. That is, customers are willing to make some compromises on less important dimensions in order to enjoy the primary benefit the product offers. In this situation, the total market is the firm's target. Therefore, management can develop a single marketing mix and reach most of the customers in the entire market. The company offers a single product for this mass audience; it designs one pricing structure and one distribution system for its product; and it uses a single promotional program aimed at the entire market. This is sometimes described as a "shotgun" approach (one program to reach a broad target).

When is an organization likely to adopt a market-aggregation strategy? In reality, the notion of an aggregate market is relatively uncommon. Even a commodity such as gasoline is provided at different octane levels, with or without ethanol, and with a variety of other additives. The total market for most types of products is too varied—too heterogeneous—to be considered a single, uniform entity. To speak of a market for vitamin pills, for example, is to ignore the existence of submarkets that differ significantly from one another. Because of these differences, One-A-Day vitamins are offered in 19 variations including the well-known regular formula for adults, a special women's formula, the Scooby-Doo children's formula, and also separate formulations for energy, memory, tension and mood, as well as several others.

Generally an aggregation strategy is selected after the firm has examined a market for segments and concluded that regardless of their differences, the majority of customers in the total market are likely to respond in very similar fashion to one marketing mix. This strategy would be appropriate for firms that are marketing an undifferentiated, staple product such as salt or sugar. In the eyes of many people, sugar is sugar, regardless of the brand, and all brands of table salt are pretty much alike.

The strength of a market aggregation strategy is cost minimization. It enables a company to produce, distribute, and promote its products very efficiently. Producing and marketing one product for the entire market means longer production runs at lower unit costs. Inventory costs are minimized when there is no (or a very limited) variety of colors and sizes of products. Warehousing and transportation are most efficient when one product is going to one market. Promotion costs are minimized when the same message is transmitted to all customers.

The strategy of market aggregation typically is accompanied by the strategy of product differentiation in a company's marketing program. **Product differentiation** occurs when, in the eyes of customers, one firm distinguishes its product from competitive brands offered to the same aggregate market. Through differentiation an organization creates the perception that its product is better than the competitors' brands, as when C&H Sugar advertises its product as "pure cane sugar from Hawaii." In addition to creating a preference among consumers for the seller's brand, successful product differentiation can also reduce price competition.

A seller differentiates its product either by (1) creating a distinctive appearance with the package or product shape, for example, or (2) using a promotional appeal that features a differentiating claim. For example, various brands of aspirin claim to be the most effective in relieving pain, although they all contain essentially the same ingredients.

Single-Segment Strategy

A **single-segment strategy,** also called a *concentration strategy,* involves selecting one segment from within the total market as the target market. One marketing mix is developed to reach this single segment. A company may want to concentrate on a single market segment rather than take on many competitors in the broader market.

When manufacturers of foreign automobiles first entered the U.S. market, they typically targeted a single segment. The original Volkswagen Beetle was intended for the low-price, small-car market, and Mercedes-Benz targeted the high-income market. Today, of course, most of the established foreign car marketers have moved into a multisegment strategy. Consider, for example, the Volkswagen product line. Only a few, such as Rolls-Royce and Ferrari, continue to concentrate on their original single segment.

A single-segment strategy enables a seller to penetrate one market in depth and to acquire a reputation as a specialist or an expert in this limited market. Firms that pursue single segments are often referred to as **niche marketers** and their targeted segments as **niche markets.** Niche markets are often, but not always, relatively small. Two firms recently included in a list of fast-growing companies and their niches are

Shampoos, deodorants, razors, and soaps have all been successfully gender targeted with products made especially for men or women. Toothpaste is the last "unisex" grooming product. Now Procter & Gamble is targeting women with Crest "Rejuvenating Effects." It is offered in vanilla and cinnamon flavors and contain a small amount of sparkle that women said they liked. Are there any limits to targeting?

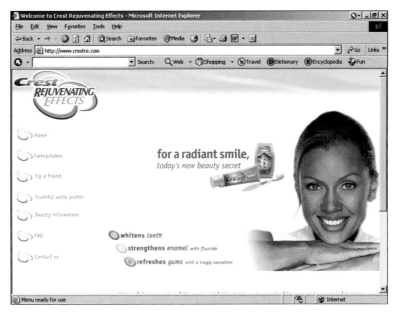

Brass Eagle, an outfitter for the sport of paintball, and Ahead Headgear, a manufacturer of golf caps.

A company can initiate a single-segment strategy with limited resources. As long as the single segment remains a small market, large competitors are likely to leave it alone. However, if the small market should show signs of becoming a large market, then the "big boys" may jump in.

The risk and limitation of a single-segment strategy is that the seller has "all its eggs in one basket." If the market potential of that single segment declines, the seller can suffer considerably. Also, a seller with a strong name and reputation in one segment may find it very difficult to expand into another segment. For example, General Motors decided to eliminate the Oldsmobile brand when it was unable to attract a younger segment of the car-buying market.

Multiple-Segment Strategy

Under a **multiple-segment strategy,** two or more different groups of potential customers are identified as target markets. A separate marketing mix is developed to reach each targeted segment. For example, the maker of Bayer aspirin offers seven variations of its pain relief product, each with its own marketing program.

In a multiple-segment strategy, a seller frequently will develop a different version of the basic product for each segment. For example, Harley-Davidson's V-rod line of high-performance motorcycles with liquid-cooled engines is viewed by Harley purists as nontraditional and therefore unappealing. This new line is faster and lighter than the familiar Harley heavyweight touring bikes and is designed to attract a younger, wealthier segment of the market.[9] However, market segmentation can also be accomplished with no change in the product, but rather with separate distribution channels or promotional appeals, each tailored to a given market segment. Wrigley's, for example, targets smokers by promoting chewing gum as an alternative in situations where smoking is unwelcome. And Evian bottled water is attempting to broaden its market beyond athletes and fitness-oriented consumers with advertising aimed at other groups, including pregnant women and environmentalists.

A multiple-segment strategy normally results in a greater sales volume than a single-segment strategy. It also is useful for a company facing seasonal demand. Because of lower summer enrollments, many universities market their empty dor-

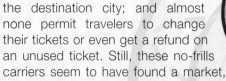

Do segments transcend borders?

The Southwest Airlines business model of keeping prices low by cutting operating costs seems to have caught on in Europe. Carriers such as Buzz, EasyJet, Go, and Ryanair, many of which are owned by larger airlines like British Air and KLM, are offering flights between European cities for previously unheard-of fares. For example, a traveler recently flew from London to Florence for $84 on Ryanair while British Airways quoted a fare of $800 for the same trip.

What customers of these airlines aren't getting are amenities. Planes are often small and cramped; most charge passengers for all refreshments, including water; others fly to secondary airports miles from the destination city; and almost none permit travelers to change their tickets or even get a refund on an unused ticket. Still, these no-frills carriers seem to have found a market, much like Southwest has done in the U.S., and are operating their flights at a healthy 75% of capacity.

Sources: Ernest Beck, "London to Frankfurt, $28," *The Wall Street Journal*, Oct. 6, 2000, p. W10; Katrina Brooker, "The Chairman of the Board Looks Back," *Fortune*, May 28, 2001, *www.fortune.com*; Michael Learmonth, "The Little Airline that Could," *The Industry Standard Magazine*, Mar. 13, 2000, *www.thestandard.com*.

mitory space to tourists—another market segment. A firm with excess production capacity may well seek additional market segments to absorb this capacity.

Multiple segments can provide benefits to an organization, but the strategy has some drawbacks with respect to costs and market coverage. In the first place, marketing to multiple segments can be expensive in both the production and marketing of products. Even with today's advances in production technology, it is obviously less expensive to produce mass quantities of one model and one color than it is to produce a variety of models, colors, and sizes. And a multiple-segment strategy increases marketing expenses in several ways. Total inventory costs grow, because adequate inventories of each style, color, and the like, must be maintained. Advertising costs go up because different ads may be required for each market segment. Distribution costs are likely to increase as efforts are made to make products available to various segments. Finally, general administrative expenses go up when management must plan and implement several different marketing programs.

Before selecting a strategy, management must determine the desirability of each of the segments it has identified. Some guidelines that are helpful in making that evaluation are discussed next.

Guidelines in Selecting a Target Market

Four guidelines govern how to determine whether a segment should be chosen as a target market. First, a target market should be compatible with the organization's goals and image. For years many manufacturers resisted distributing their products through Kmart because of the chain's discount image. However, as Kmart achieved a high level of acceptability with consumers, image concerns seemed to disappear.

A second guideline is to match the market opportunity represented by the target market with the company's resources. In examining the power tool and appliance markets, Black & Decker considered several options and chose as one of its targets the do-it-yourself home-improvement segment because of the marketing economies that could be achieved. The firm's name was well known to consumers, and the products could be sold through the retail outlets already selling Black & Decker products. Thus, entering this market was much less expensive than entering a market in which Black & Decker was inexperienced.

Over the long run, a business must generate a profit to survive. This rather obvious statement translates into our third market selection guideline. That is, an organization should seek markets that will generate sufficient sales volume at a low enough cost to result in a profit that justifies the required investment. Surprisingly, companies often have overlooked profit in their quest for high-volume markets. Their mistake is going after sales volume, not *profitable* sales volume. When the online grocery delivery service Webvan went bankrupt, costing investors hundreds of millions of dollars, it became apparent that the firm had vastly overestimated the size of the potential market. Its business model required huge, automated warehouses to stock groceries and large fleets of trucks to deliver them. But there were simply not enough consumers willing to buy groceries online to support the infrastructure.[10]

Fourth, a company ordinarily should seek a market where competitors are few and/or weak. A seller should not enter a market that is already saturated with competition unless it has some overriding advantage that will enable it to take customers from existing firms. Nobel Learning Communities is a company that operates a chain of 140 privately owned primary schools. The schools are designed to appeal to families that are dissatisfied with public schools but are unable to afford fancy private schools. The objective is to provide a solid education without frills. The advantage of these schools over traditional private schools is a lower price, while their private status gives them greater control over the students than exists in public schools. Despite these differences, Nobel Learning has had difficulty establishing itself in a market with many established competitors, notably public schools.

Positioning

Having identified the potential segments and selected one or more to target, the marketer must next decide what position to pursue. A **position** is the way a firm's product, brand, or organization is viewed relative to the competition by current and prospective customers. To establish itself in a market that was dominated by firms appealing primarily to the preferences of children, Wendy's positioned its burgers as "hot and juicy," and therefore primarily for adults. If a position is how a product is viewed, then **positioning** is a firm's use of all the elements at its disposal to create and maintain in the minds of a target market a particular image relative to competing products.

When positioning a product, the marketer wants to convey the benefit(s) most desired by the target market. A classic example of successful positioning is the original Head and Shoulders shampoo. As the first shampoo positioned as a dandruff remedy, the product's name implied the benefit, the medicinal fragrance suggested its potency, and the color (blue-green) and consistency (a paste rather than a liquid) indicated that it wasn't an ordinary shampoo.

This pocket-size video player developed by Intel will store 70 hours of video programming on a hard disk. Content can be loaded from a computer or a digital video recorder. The player's batteries last about four hours. A user cannot transfer the video files from the player to any other device, but can erase the hard disk and replace it with newer material. If there is a market for the player, how should it be positioned?

To simplify decision making, individuals formulate mental positions for products, brands, and organizations. Often these positions are based on a single attribute and/or limited experience because consumers are seldom willing to invest much time and effort in the process. Because a product's position is critical to its evaluation, firms go to great lengths to influence how positions are formed.

There are three steps in a positioning strategy:

1. *Select the positioning concept.* To position a product or an organization, a marketer needs to first determine what is important to the target market. Marketers can then conduct positioning studies to see how members of a target market view competing products or stores on the important dimensions. The results of this research can be portrayed in a perceptual map that locates the brand or organization relative to alternatives on the dimensions of interest. A hypothetical example for jeans is shown in Figure 6.1. The length of the lines (or vectors) indicate the relative importance of the attributes, and the position of a brand relative to a vector indicates how closely the brand is associated with the attribute. For example, Calvin Klein jeans are perceived as more expensive than Gap jeans but not as comfortable, whereas Wranglers are seen as durable but low in status. This map suggests that a brand offering comfort and durability at a reasonable price would have little competition from these other brands. Thus it might be an attractive option if a substantial segment of the market finds these attributes desirable.

FIGURE 6.1

A Hypothetical Perceptual Map for Jeans.

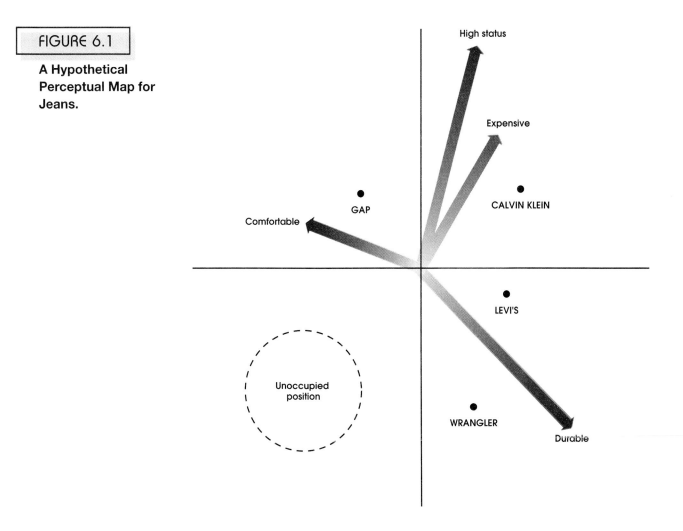

AN ETHICAL DILEMMA?

Preschoolers watch an average of 23 hours of television a week, more than any other group of children. However, until recently most shows designed especially for them, such as *Sesame Street* and *Mister Rogers' Neighborhood*, appeared on the commercial-free Public Broadcasting System (PBS). That is changing for several reasons. First, sales of preschooler products such as stuffed toys, pajamas, and drink cups, has become big business, estimated to be $21 billion annually. Many of these items have licensing potential (charging a manufacturer a fee to incorporate the likenesses and/or names of familiar characters on the item). And the kids greatly influence what is purchased. Second, the average ratings for networks such as Nickelodeon and Disney are being dragged down by small midday audiences, and those averages affect advertising rates for the entire schedule. Preschoolers, at home during the day, can boost the ratings if the networks can attract them.

To overcome the concerns of parents, preschooler programming on commercial networks such as *Dora the Explorer* and *Blue's Clues* incorporates educational principles of learning and cognitive development, and the amount of advertising per hour is about half of what is aired at other times.

Should a commercial television network, with an organizational objective of profit, actively pursue impressionable preschoolers?

Sources: Sally Beatty, "In Battle for Toddlers, TV Networks Tout Educational Benefits," *The Wall Street Journal*, Apr. 1, 2002, pp. A1+; Donna Petrozzello, "Nickelodeon to Launch Spinoff of Animated Hit 'Rugrats,'" *New York Daily News*, Mar. 14, 2002, p. 6.

2. *Design the dimension or feature that most effectively conveys the position.* A position can be communicated with a brand name, a slogan, the appearance or other features of the product, the place where it is sold, the appearance of employees, and in many other ways. However, some features are more effective than others. It is important to not overlook details. According to a consultant, chairs for customers are vital in upscale retail environments because they signal that the seller "cares." Because the marketer has limited resources, decisions have to be made on how best to convey the desired positioning concept.

3. *Coordinate the marketing mix components to convey a consistent position.* Even though one or two dimensions may be the primary position communicators, all the elements of the marketing mix—the product, price, promotion, and distribution—should complement the intended position. Many product failures are the result of inconsistent positioning that confuses consumers. For example, a compact car with a high price tag (Cadillac Cimarron), and Tetley Instant Iced Tea (in Britain, where the people take great pride in brewing tea) both flopped.

Over time a position may erode because of lack of attention, become less attractive to the market as needs or tastes change, or be usurped by a competitor. Hence positions must be regularly monitored and sometimes adjusted. For example, Quality Inns, Comfort Suites, and Sleep Inns, all brands of Choice Hotels, Inc., were losing ground and sales to competitors such as Hampton Inn and Holiday Inn. An evaluation of their position in the minds of consumers suggested they had become dated and less desirable relative to the competition. In response the firm upgraded the facilities at many of its locations and signaled the revised position with new logos and signs as well as a $35 million ad campaign.[11]

When its position has eroded, and a firm attempts to reestablish its attractiveness, it is engaging in **repositioning.** When it discovered that "oil" had a negative connotation for younger women evaluating beauty products, Procter & Gamble repositioned its venerable Oil of Olay brand with a simple name change to "Olay." The 50-year-old brand, which is not oily, generates $50 million in sales of skin-care and cosmetics products around the world. To avoid alienating existing customers, P&G did not publicize the name change. Rather, it simply introduced it with a new logo and other packaging changes.[12]

Forecasting Market Demand

Recall that one condition for useful segmentation is that the resulting segments be large enough to produce a profit. The potential of a segment is determined by forecasting how much it will buy. The process of forecasting demand is discussed next.

Demand forecasting estimates sales of a product during some defined future period. Forecasting is done to make various kinds of predictions. For example, a forecast can refer to an entire industry (such as apparel), to one firm's product line (Levi casual wear), or to an individual brand (Levi 501 jeans). Thus, for a forecast to be understood, it is important to make very clear what it describes.

Basic Forecasting Terms

In this section we'll explain some concepts so our discussion will be easier to follow.

Market Share   A term used frequently in business as a performance measure, **market share** is the proportion of total sales of a product during a stated period in a specific market that is captured by a single firm. If Almega Corp. sold $210 million worth of turbine engines in 1999, and total industry sales of turbine engines that year were $7 billion, Almega's market share was 3%.

Market share can refer to entire industries (aircraft), segments of industries (single-engine business jets), or particular geographic areas (Pacific Rim), and can also apply to past, present, or future periods. For example, the steel industry, which has a 95% market share for canned-food containers, is working to prevent a recurrence of the inroads in food packaging that were made by aluminum makers in the market for beverage cans.

Market Factor   A **market factor** is something that (1) exists in a market, (2) is measurable, and (3) is related to the demand for a product in a known way. To illustrate, the "number of cars three years old and older" is a market factor related to the demand for replacement tires. It's a market factor because the number of replacement tires that can be sold changes as the number of older cars changes.

In segmenting world markets geographically, McDonald's uses population, per capita income, and the number of people per store in the U.S. as market factors to obtain a rough forecast of the number of stores a country can support.[13] The formula looks like this:

$$\frac{\text{population of the country}}{\text{\# of people per McDonald's in U.S.}} \times \frac{\text{per capita income of the country}}{\text{per capita income of U.S.}} = \frac{\text{the number of stores the country can support}}{}$$

The formula, which produces a preliminary estimate that is adjusted for factors such as eating habits and competition, suggests the following:

Country	Market Potential (no. of outlets)
China	784
Colombia	79
Pakistan	90
South Africa	190

Market Potential, Sales Potential, and Sales Forecast

Market potential is the total sales volume that *all organizations* selling a product during a stated period of time in a specific market could expect to achieve under ideal conditions. **Sales potential** is the portion of market potential that a *specific company* could expect to achieve under ideal conditions. For example, market potential applies to all refrigerators, but sales potential refers only to a single brand of refrigerators (such as Whirlpool).

With either of these measures of potential, the market may encompass whatever group or area interests the forecaster. It could be the world, one country, or a smaller market defined by income or some other basis. For example, Whirlpool may consider the market potential for refrigerators in the New England states, or the sales potential for Whirlpool refrigerators in households with incomes of $25,000 to $50,000.

The term *potential* refers to a maximum level of sales assuming that (1) all marketing plans are sound and effectively implemented and (2) all prospective customers with the desire and ability to buy do so. Of course, few industries or companies achieve their full potential. Therefore, potential should not be the final outcome of demand forecasting. It is an intermediate step. We must move from *potential* sales to *probable* sales, which are estimated by preparing forecasts.

A **sales forecast** is an estimate of probable sales for one company's brand of a product during a stated period in a specific market, assuming a defined marketing plan is used. Like measures of potential, a sales forecast can be expressed in dollars or product units. However, whereas market potential and sales potential are estimated on the basis of general factors and market assumptions, a sales forecast is made on the basis of a specific marketing plan for the product.

A sales forecast is best prepared after market potential and sales potential have been estimated. Sales forecasts typically cover a one-year period, although many firms review and revise their forecasts quarterly or even monthly. Forecasts of less than a year may be desirable when activity in the firm's industry is so volatile that it is not feasible to look ahead an entire year. As a case in point, many retailers and producers in the fashion industry prepare forecasts for only one fashion season at a time. Hence, they prepare three or four forecasts a year.

Once a sales forecast has been prepared, it affects all departments in a company. The sales forecast is the basis for deciding how much to spend on various activities like advertising and personal selling. Planning the necessary amount of working capital, plant utilization, and warehousing facilities is accomplished on the basis of anticipated sales. Scheduling production, hiring production workers, and purchasing raw materials also depend on the sales forecast.

Methods of Forecasting Sales

There are many methods of forecasting sales. Several of the more commonly used methods are described below.

Market-Factor Analysis

In many situations, future demand for a product is related to the behavior of certain market factors. When this is true, we can forecast future sales by studying the behavior of these market factors. Basically, **market-factor analysis** entails determining what these factors are and then measuring their relationship to sales activity.

Using market-factor analysis successfully requires that the analyst (1) select the best market factors and (2) minimize the number of market factors. The best factors are ones that vary in a consistent way with the demand for the product being forecast. Fewer factors are preferable in order to simplify the data collection and analyses.

We can translate market-factor behavior into a demand forecast with the **direct-derivation method.** To illustrate, suppose a producer of automobile tires wants to know the market potential for replacement tires in the U.S. in 2002. The primary market factor is the number and age of automobiles on the road. The first step is to estimate how many cars are prospects for new tires.

Assume that the producer's studies show (1) the average car is driven 10,000 miles per year and (2) the average driver gets 30,000 miles of use from a set of tires. This means that all cars that become three years old or multiples of three years old in 2002 can be considered as comprising the potential market for replacement tires during that year. From state and county auto license agencies as well as private organizations, the producer can obtain a reasonably accurate count of the number of cars that were sold in the U.S. in 1999 and therefore will be three years old in 2002. In addition, with a little digging the producer can determine how many cars will become 6, 9, and 12 years old and still be on the road in 2002, and therefore would also be ready for another set of tires.

The number of cars in these age brackets multiplied by four (tires per car) should give the approximate market potential for replacement tires in 2002. Of course, we are dealing in averages. Not all drivers will get 30,000 miles from their tires, and not all cars will be driven 10,000 miles per year.

The direct-derivation method is simple, inexpensive, and requires little statistical analysis. Executives who are not statisticians can understand it and interpret its results. This method's main limitation is that it can be used only when it is possible to identify an easily measured market factor that affects the product's demand in a stable way.

Correlation analysis is a statistical refinement of the direct-derivation method. It is a measure of the association between potential sales of the product and the market factor affecting its sales. Detailed explanation of this statistical technique is beyond the scope of this text. However, in general, a correlation analysis measures, on a scale of 0 (no association) to 1 (perfect association), the variation between two data series. For example, one data series might be the number of residential housing starts (from government statistics), and the other the wholesale furniture sales (from industry sources) in the corresponding years. If there is a reasonably strong historical relationship between these two series, a marketer might use current housing starts to predict the demand for furniture.

Correlation analysis gives a more precise estimate of how well the market factor predicts market demand than does direct derivation. That's because in direct derivation, the association is assumed to be 1.0 (that is, perfect). But rarely is there a perfect association between a market factor and the demand for a product. Using a more sophisticated form of correlation analysis called **multiple correlation,** it is possible to include more than one market factor in the calculation.

Correlation analysis has two major limitations. For one thing, not all marketing executives understand it. For another, it can be used only when both of the following are available: (1) a sales history of the industry or firm consisting of at least 20 consecutive time periods, and (2) a corresponding history of the market factor being used to forecast demand. Last, correlation analysis depends on the assumptions, which can be quite unrealistic, that approximately the same relationship has existed between sales and the key market factor(s) during the entire period, and that this relationship will continue in the sales period being predicted.

Survey of Buyer Intentions

A **survey of buyer intentions** involves asking a sample of current or potential customers how much of a particular product they would buy at a given price during a specified future period. Some firms ask a sample of consumers from the target segment about their buying intentions and then extrapolate the result to the entire segment.

Selecting a representative sample of potential buyers can be a problem. For many consumer products, a large sample is needed because many groups with different buying patterns make up the market. Thus this method can be costly in terms of both money and time. This method has another serious limitation. Because it is one thing for prospects to *intend* to buy a product but quite another for them to *actually* buy it, surveys of buying intentions often show an inflated measure of market potential. Such surveys are probably most accurate in forecasting demand when (1) there are relatively few current or potential buyers, (2) the buyers are willing to express their buying intentions, and (3) their past records show a consistent relationship between their actual buying behavior and their stated intentions. These conditions are most likely to exist in a business market.

Test Marketing

In **test marketing** to forecast demand, a firm markets a new product in a limited geographic area, measures sales, and then—from this sample—projects the product's sales over a larger area. Test marketing is often used to determine whether there is sufficient demand for a new product to be viable. It also serves as a basis for evaluating new-product features and alternative marketing strategies. More details about test marketing, including its benefits and drawbacks, are presented in Chapter 7.

Past Sales and Trend Analysis

A popular method of forecasting is based entirely on past sales. Small retailers whose main goal is to "beat last year's figures" frequently use this technique. In **past sales analysis,** the demand forecast is simply a flat percentage change applied to the volume achieved last year or to the average volume of the past few years.

This technique is simple and inexpensive. For a firm operating in a stable market where its market share has remained constant for a period of years, past sales alone can be used to predict future volume. However, few companies operate in unchanging environments, making this method highly unreliable.

Trend analysis examines past sales data to calculate the rate of change in sales volume and uses it to forecast future sales. One type of trend analysis is a long-term projection of sales, usually computed with a statistical technique called regression. However, the statistical sophistication of long-term trend analysis does not offset the inherent weakness of basing future estimates only on past sales activity. A second type of trend analysis entails a short-term projection using a seasonal index of sales covering several months. Short-term trend analysis may be acceptable if a firm's sales follow a reliable seasonal pattern. For example, assume that the second quarter of the year historically produces sales about 50% higher than the first quarter. Hence, if sales reach 10,000 units in the first quarter, we can reasonably forecast sales of 15,000 units for the second quarter.

Sales-Force Composite

In sales forecasting, a **sales-force composite** consists of collecting from all sales people estimates of sales for their territories during the future period of interest. The total of all these estimates is the company's sales forecast.

A sales-force composite method can produce an accurate forecast if the firm has competent, well-informed sales people. Its strength is that it takes advantage of sales people's specialized knowledge of their own markets. Furthermore, it should make sales people more willing to accept their assigned sales quotas, because they participated in the process that produced the forecasts that serve as the basis for their quotas. A sales-force composite is most useful for firms selling to a market composed primarily of a few large customers where sales people work closely with them and are well informed about their plans. Thus this method would be more applicable to sales of large electrical generators to energy utilities than to sales of small general-use motors to many thousands of firms.

This method also has limitations. A sales force may not have the time or the experience to do the research needed for sales forecasting, and managers must guard against sales people who overestimate or underestimate future sales, depending on circumstances. For instance, sales people are by nature optimistic and therefore may overestimate future possibilities. Or, if compensation is based on meeting sales quotas, sales people may underestimate future sales.

Executive Judgment

Basically, **executive judgment** involves obtaining opinions from one or more executives regarding future sales. If these are well-informed opinions, based on valid measures such as market-factor analysis, then executive judgment can produce accurate forecasts. However, forecasting by executive opinion alone is risky, because such opinions are sometimes simply intuition or guesswork. Many Internet businesses were initiated on the basis of executives' guesses about potential sales and failed a year or two later when the forecasts proved to be overly optimistic.

One specialized form of executive judgment is the **Delphi method,** named after the location of an oracle in ancient Greece. Developed by the Rand Corporation for use in environmental forecasting, this technique can also be applied to sales forecasting. It is especially applicable to products that are truly innovative or are significant technological breakthroughs.

The Delphi method begins with a group of knowledgeable individuals anonymously estimating future sales. Each person makes a prediction without knowing how others in the group have responded. These estimates are summarized, and the resulting average and range of forecasts are fed back to the participants. Now, knowing how the group responded, they are asked to make another prediction on the same issue. Participants may change or stick to their original estimates. This process of estimates and feedback is continued for several rounds. In some cases—and usually in sales forecasting—the final round involves face-to-face discussions among the participants to produce a consensus sales forecast.

An advantage of the Delphi method is that the anonymity in the early rounds prevents one individual (for example, a top executive) from influencing others (a subordinate). And it permits each participant to consider the combined judgment of the group. If an individual's forecast is widely divergent from the group's average, the opportunity exists to justify or modify it in the next round. A potential disadvantage of the Delphi method—and of any executive judgment method—is that participants may lack the necessary information on which to base their judgments.

No method of sales forecasting is perfect. An executive's challenge is to choose an approach that is likely to produce the most accurate estimate of sales given the firm's particular circumstances. Because all techniques have limitations, companies should consider using a combination of forecasting methods and then reconciling any differences that are produced.

Summary

A market consists of people or organizations with wants, money to spend, and the willingness to spend it. However, within most markets the buyers' needs are not identical. Therefore, a single marketing program for an entire market is unlikely to be successful. A sound marketing program starts with identifying the differences that exist within a market, a process called market segmentation, deciding which segments will be pursued as target markets, and selecting a competitive position that will be conveyed to customers through the marketing mix.

Most marketers adopt some form of market segmentation as a compromise between the extremes of a strategy that treats the market as an aggregate, undifferentiated whole, and a strategy that views each customer as a different market. Market segmentation enables a company to make efficient use of its marketing resources. Also, it allows a small company to compete effectively by concentrating on one or two segments. The apparent drawback of market segmentation is that it will result in higher production and marketing costs than a one-product, mass-market strategy. However, if the market is correctly segmented, a better fit with customers' needs will actually result in greater efficiency. For segmentation to be effective: (1) the bases for segmentation must be measurable with obtainable data, (2) the segments identified must be accessible through existing marketing institutions, and (3) the segments must be large enough to be potentially profitable.

At the broadest level, most markets may be divided into two segments: ultimate consumers and business users. The four major bases used for further segmenting the consumer market are geographic, demographic, psychographic, and behavioral. The business market may be segmented on the basis of customer location, customer type, and transaction conditions. Normally, in either the consumer or business market, a seller will use a combination of two or more segmentation bases.

The three alternative strategies for selecting a target market are market aggregation and single-segment and multiple-segment strategies. Market-aggregation strategy involves using one marketing mix to reach a mass, undifferentiated market. With a single-segment strategy, a company still uses only one marketing mix, but it is directed at only one segment of the total market. A multiple-segment strategy entails selecting two or more segments and developing a separate marketing mix to reach each segment. The guidelines for selecting segments to target are compatibility with the firm's goals, fit with the firm's resources, profit potential, and the strength of the competition.

When targets have been selected, the organization must decide how to position the offering. Position is the way a brand or organization is viewed relative to the competition by current and prospective customers. A positioning effort should convey the benefits most desired by the target market. The three steps in positioning are (1) selecting the positioning concept, (2) designing the feature to convey the position, and (3) coordinating the marketing mix to consistently communicate the desired position.

Forecasting is essential in evaluating possible target segments. It involves estimating the demand of a market. Management usually estimates the total sales that could be expected under ideal conditions for all firms comprising the industry—market potential—and for its particular product—sales potential. The final step in estimating demand is a sales forecast, indicating probable sales for the company's brand of a particular product in a future time period and with a specified marketing program. The forecast normally covers one year.

Specific methods used to forecast sales are market-factor analysis, survey of buyer intentions, test marketing, past sales and trend analysis, sales-force composite, and executive judgment. Management's challenge is to select the techniques that are appropriate in a particular situation.

More about the **Smart Car**

Most of the questions Daimler's marketing executives will be asking themselves as they evaluate selling the Smart Car in the U.S. will deal with the size of its probable market segment. In the original Swatch/Mercedes partnership, the car was designed for drivers who felt existing cars are too pricey, hard to maneuver, and expensive to operate. Management must find out whether that motivation or some other applies to a substantial segment in the U.S., where consumers have recently adopted much larger and more utilitarian vehicles in huge numbers. The Smart Car's spiffy design isn't for everyone, and the firm doesn't expect it to sell in the more conservative regions of the Midwest where trips tend to be of greater distances, for instance.

The four-seater Smart Car is unlikely to replace the minivan or SUV as a family car; two Smart Cars parked end-to-end are still 3 feet shorter than the Ford Excursion. Could it work as a family's second or third car if they already own a van? Or will the fact that its cargo space is little more than a mere shelf deter sales?

Though it has not yet been a big hit among young buyers in Europe, some industry consultants think the bug-eyed Smart Car could be a fashion statement. Will young U.S. buyers choosing their first car, say, urban college students looking for cheap transportation that's hip and new, be attracted to its looks and fuel economy?

There are still some safety concerns about the tiny vehicle even if it's not quite the "crash helmet on wheels" that one British showroom manager claims. DaimlerChrysler has made a promotional video showing the car skittering away from a 30-mph crash with a Mercedes S-class sedan to counter some anticipated reactions, but the fact remains, the car needs upgrading to meet U.S. safety standards. And while Daimler doesn't see the car as a highway cruiser but rather as a city car for congested urban streets, it's unclear whether U.S. consumers will share that view once they get behind the wheel.

So far favorable ratings are pouring in for the car's clever design, maneuverability, comfortable interior, environmental friendliness, and low price. The executive in charge claims to be very happy about the challenge that marketing the Smart Car brings. In his view, "This is a chance to develop a brand, and you don't get to do that very often."[14]

1. Should DaimlerChrysler pursue a single-segment or multiple-segment strategy for the Smart Car in the United States?

2. As DaimlerChrysler has positioned it, with which transportation alternatives would the Smart Car likely compete in Europe? In the U.S.?

Key Terms and Concepts

Market segments (147)
Target market (147)
Market segmentation (147)
Micromarketing (149)
Geographic segmentation (151)
Demographic segmentation (152)
Psychographic segmentation (153)
Personality (153)
Lifestyle (153)
Values (154)
Behavioral segmentation (154)
Market-aggregation strategy (158)
Product differentiation (159)

Single-segment strategy (159)
Niche marketers (159)
Niche markets (159)
Multiple-segment strategy (160)
Position (162)
Positioning (162)
Repositioning (164)
Demand forecasting (165)
Market share (165)
Market factor (165)
Market potential (166)
Sales potential (166)
Sales forecast (166)

Market-factor analysis (166)
Direct-derivation method (166)
Correlation analysis (167)
Multiple correlation (167)
Survey of buyer intentions (167)
Test marketing (168)
Past sales analysis (168)
Trend analysis (168)
Sales-force composite (168)
Executive judgment (169)
Delphi method (169)

Questions and Problems

1. Give two examples of goods or services whose market demand would be particularly affected by each of the following population factors:
   a. Regional distribution
   b. Marital status
   c. Gender
   d. Age
   e. Urban-rural-suburban distribution

2. From a recent "Survey of Buying Power" (from *Sales & Marketing Management* magazine), record the available data for the county in which you live and another county with which you are familiar (maybe the one in which your school is located). Comment on how differences you find may be useful to a fast-food franchisee seeking a location for a new outlet.

3. Using the psychographic bases discussed in this chapter, describe the segment appropriate to investigate as a market for:
   a. Ski resorts
   b. Online auto sales
   c. Power hand tools
   d. Donations to United Way
   e. PC that includes Internet access

4. What user benefits in advertising for each of the following three products might lead you to conclude that the marketer is trying to appeal to each of these three market segments?

Product	Market
a. DVD player	a. Young singles
b. Toothpaste	b. Retired people
c. 10-day Caribbean cruise	c. Empty-nest couples

5. What demographic characteristics would you think are likely to describe heavy users of the following?
   a. Online investment advice and stock trading
   b. Ready-to-eat cereal
   c. Videocassette recorders
   d. Laptop computers

6. How would you segment the market for copying machines such as Xerox or Canon photocopiers?

7. How might the following organizations implement the strategy of market segmentation?
   a. Manufacturer of personal computers
   b. American Heart Association
   c. Universal Studios (Hollywood movies)
   d. Internet-only retail banking service

8. Find a magazine advertisement that communicates the position for a product in each of the following categories:
   a. Household appliance
   b. Cellular phone service
   c. Airline
   d. Hotel or motel chain

9. What market factors might you use in estimating the market potential for each of the following products?
   a. Central home air-conditioning
   b. Electric milking machines
   c. First-class airline travel
   d. Printers to accompany personal computers

10. How would you determine (a) market potential and (b) a sales forecast for a textbook for an introductory marketing course?

Interactive Marketing Excercises

1. Interview three friends or acquaintances who all own athletic shoes but differ on some demographic dimension (for example, education or age). Using the criteria of demographics, psychological variables, and behavioral variables, describe in as much detail as possible the market segment each represents.

2. Examine the annual reports (available in your library) of two consumer product marketers and two business product marketers to determine what target markets they are currently serving.

PART 2

"Though strict confidentiality of information about individual persons or businesses is maintained, national data are disaggregated to the local level, making much Census data extremely useful to marketers."

Who's Counting on the **Census Bureau?**

The need for information about its population is almost as old as the U.S. itself. The nation's founders quickly realized that the desire of their country's new states to report fewer people as a way of reducing their share of the Revolutionary war debt could only be offset by their desire to have the largest possible number of congressional representatives. Thus, the first census was undertaken in 1790, shortly after George Washington became president. It counted 3.9 million inhabitants, relying on a fairly primitive process in which U.S. marshals and their assistants had to furnish their own paper for tallies and record keeping and were required to post the results in public places.

From its beginning, the Census Bureau was mandated by law to count the U.S. population every 10 years. As the country and the population grew, new techniques and tools for collecting information came into play, and new uses for the data were found. Statistical sampling, in which certain questions are asked of only a representative sampling of the population, eased the data-gathering process beginning in the 1940s, computers came into use in the Census Bureau in the 1950s, and collecting information by mail became the norm in the 1960s.

Now an arm of the Department of Commerce, the Census Bureau gathers data not only about the population but also about housing, manufacturing, wholesaling, retailing, exports, imports, shipping, construction, transportation, and government. It also conducts specialized data-gathering operations for federal, state, and local agencies on demand. Though strict confidentiality of information about individual persons or businesses is maintained, national data are disaggregated to the local level, making much census data extremely useful to marketers.

The most recent national reckoning, Census 2000, gathered information by mail from about 95 percent of U.S. households. Questions were asked about age and sex, race, citizenship, physical or mental handicaps, type of housing, education, marital status, place of birth, income, nationality, language spoken, and such economic characteristics as their type of job, income, the way they travel to work, and employment status.

One important finding of Census 2000 was that the U.S. population has grown at a historic pace since 1990, increasing by 13% to over 281 million. Of interest to marketers is the fact that this is the largest increase in the size of the consumer market since the start of the "baby boom" in 1946. Immigrants, both legal and illegal, have arrived in numbers larger than expected, accounting for much of the increase. Census 2000 also showed population growth occurring in every state, the only time this occurred in the 20th century, though the rates varied widely by state with the greatest growth occurring in the South and West.

The number of consumers between the ages of 20 and 34 declined, whereas those between 45 and 49 and between 50 and 54 grew faster

www.census.gov

than any others. For the first time, the number of single-person households is greater than the number of married couples with children, and the number of unmarried couples and those who live with friends or roommates has also grown.

According to Census 2000, the Hispanic portion of the population grew at a staggering pace to 35.3 million people, and it now rivals the black population as the country's largest minority group. Although the heaviest concentrations of Hispanics are along the coasts and in the Southwest, substantial numbers now reside in communities across the U.S., and many marketers are reacting to these burgeoning groups of consumers.

In recognition of the fact that things can change during the 10 years between censuses of the population, the Census Bureau is implementing the American Community Survey, an ongoing project designed to provide annual estimates of demographic, housing, social, and economic characteristics for states, cities, counties, and metropolitan areas.[1]

To find out what other information of interest to marketers is available, browse the Census Bureau's website at *www.census.gov.* Be sure you click on the "American Fact Finder" link on the left side of the page. What kinds of data are available? What do you need to know in order to search for information here?

Though the census was created for governmental purposes, it soon became evident that information about the populace was valuable to business. Over the years, as the country expanded and became increasingly diverse the need for information also grew. Today more than ever, developing effective strategy requires current, accurate information about the macroenvironment, about markets, and about internal and external forces that impact organizations. The census is one resource marketers rely on. In this chapter we will examine how information essential to marketing is obtained and utilized.

Chapter Goals

After studying this chapter, you should be able to explain:

- What marketing research is, the need for it, and the variety of forms it takes.
- How information systems increase the usefulness of data.
- The growing role of technology in marketing research.
- The appropriate way to conduct a marketing research project.
- How firms gather and use information about competitors.
- How ethics enters into the performance of marketing research.
- Some threats to the future of marketing research.

The Marketing Research Function

Marketing research is needed before a product is introduced to the market, and on a regular basis throughout its life. Research is not limited to products; it is conducted to answer questions about potential market segments, entire stores, brand names, advertising, prices, and every other aspect of marketing. The challenges in every research project are to correctly define the issue to be studied, gather the appropriate data, and transform the raw data into useful information. To see how to do this, we will begin by briefly discussing where organizations use research. Then we will focus our attention on how research is performed and managed.

Uses of Marketing Research

Competitive pressure, the cost of making a strategic mistake, and the complexity of both domestic and foreign markets dictate that a firm must have access to timely information. Consider some of the marketing issues that are frequently researched:

- *Markets and market segments.* Experienced managers often suspect that a need exists in the market, but intuition is usually not sufficient to justify a decision that may require the investment of millions of dollars. Research can be used to clarify the need, identify and describe exactly who has it, and determine the strength of the need in various segments.

- *Marketing mix.* Even when a marketer is confident that a need exists, it is not always clear what form a product should take to satisfy the need, at what price it will sell, how prospects should be informed about it, or in what fashion it should be distributed. Consider that several firms are designing and testing personal delivery units that are necessary if electronic shopping is to grow. These units are storage boxes that permit deliveries to a home or office when no one is present to personally accept the merchandise. The boxes must be accessible yet secure, large enough to hold a variety of different deliveries but not obtrusive, reasonably attractive, and easy to install. Having consumers evaluate alternative designs and react to possible prices will help the makers. Then there's the question of how best to inform and persuade potential customers about a product like this. What message and media will reach the intended audience, attract their attention, and convey the desired message about a storage box? Finally, where should they be sold? Would a home improvement retail store be a better distribution route than direct sales over the Internet? These and other marketing-mix questions are addressed with marketing research.

- *Competition.* Finding out what current and potential competitors are doing and how it may affect a firm's strategy is an increasingly important dimension of marketing research.

- *Expectations and satisfaction.* It is important to know what customers expect, which is influenced by what marketers have promised in their ads, and how well those expectations are being satisfied. Surprisingly few customers volunteer information to a firm. For example, it's frequently suggested that as few as 10% of dissatisfied customers formally complain to the company responsible. However, what they do is tell their friends and take their business elsewhere. Firms need research to quickly identify problems and solve them before they result in lost business.

This is just a sample of the many types of marketing research. The 50 largest marketing research firms in the U.S. are paid over $6 *billion* a year by their clients from around the world for information to improve the quality of decision making.[2] Unaccounted for in this figure is the research done internally by firms and the hundreds of smaller marketing research companies. Obviously, research is an important part of marketing!

What Is Marketing Research?

Marketing research consists of all the activities that enable an organization to obtain the information it needs to make decisions about its environment, marketing mix, and present or potential customers. More specifically, **marketing research** is the development, interpretation, and communication of decision-oriented information to be used in all phases of the marketing process.

This definition has two important implications:

- Research plays a role in all three phases of the management process in marketing: planning, implementation, and evaluation.

- It recognizes the researcher's responsibility to develop information, which includes defining problems, gathering and analyzing data, interpreting results, and presenting the information in such a way that it is useful to managers.

Scope of Marketing Research Activities

acnielsen.com/services/retail

Depending on their needs and level of sophistication, marketing managers make use of four main sources of information. One is regularly scheduled reports that are produced and sold by research firms. These are called *syndicated services* because they are developed without a particular client in mind, but are sold to anyone interested. An example is ACNielsen's Retail Measurement Services. For over 70 years the firm has gathered data at the retail store level on product movement, market share, and prices across a wide variety of consumer packaged goods. Subscribing to this service allows a marketer to regularly monitor retail sales of its own and competitors' products by type of outlet and geographic area.

The second source is a *marketing information system,* an internally coordinated activity that provides continuous, scheduled, or on-demand standardized reports. Most marketing information systems (MkIS) rely heavily on internal data such as sales reports, inventory amounts, and production schedules, but they also often include information purchased from research firms or trade associations. An MkIS is used by both managers and sales people. For example, a sales person sitting in a customer's office can use a laptop computer and an MkIS to check on the availability of current inventory and the schedule for producing more. Other frequent applications include tracking the sales performance of products and monitoring changing consumer tastes.

A *decision support system* is the third source. It is also internal, but it is interactive. It permits a decision maker to interact directly with data through a personal computer to answer specific questions. A manager, for example, might have a decision support system that will estimate the impact of various levels of advertising on sales of a product when given specific assumptions.

The fourth source is a nonrecurring, proprietary *marketing research project,* conducted by a company's own staff or by an independent research firm to answer a specific question. For example, Toro, a manufacturer of lawn mowers, might conduct a survey of retail dealers, consumers, or both to identify the most common problems customers have with power mowers.

www.infores.com

www.marketfacts.com

There are many providers of syndicated research, the first source of information mentioned above. In fact, they account for about 40% of the total amount spent on research in the U.S.[3] However, detailing the topics and varied research methods of syndicated researchers goes beyond the scope of this discussion. (For more information and examples of syndicated research services, see the websites of Information Resources, Inc., and Market Facts, Inc.) Now, we will concentrate our discussion on the other three sources.

Marketing Information Systems

As computers became common business tools in the early 1960s, firms were able to collect, store, and manipulate larger amounts of data to aid marketing decision makers. Out of this capability developed the **marketing information system (MkIS)**—an ongoing, organized procedure to generate, analyze, disseminate, store, and retrieve information for use in making marketing decisions. Figure 7.1 illustrates the characteristics and operation of an MkIS.

The ideal MkIS:

- Includes real-time data.
- Generates regular reports and recurring studies as needed.

FIGURE 7.1

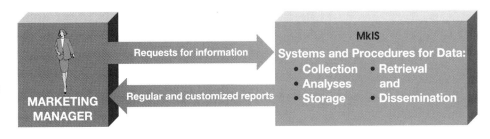

- Analyzes data using statistical analysis and mathematical models that represent the real world.
- Integrates old and new data to provide information updates and identify trends.

Designing a Marketing Information System

To build an effective MkIS, marketing managers must identify the information that will help them make better decisions. Working with researchers and systems analysts, managers then determine whether the data needed are available within the organization or must be procured, how the data should be organized, the form in which the data should be reported, and the schedule according to which the data will be delivered.

For example, the brand manager at Procter & Gamble who is responsible for Tide wants to know the retail sales of all detergent brands by geographic area on a weekly basis. The same manager may want monthly reports on the prices that competitors are charging and how much advertising they are doing. Less frequently, possibly once a year, this manager needs to know about developments in the marketplace such as demographic changes that might affect Tide in the long term. In addition to these (and probably other) regular reports, the manager may periodically request special reports that can be compiled from existing data. For example, while contemplating a proposal to introduce another version of Tide, the manager may want to see what share of the total market each detergent brand had by quarter over the last five years and a projection of how each is likely to perform over the next three years.

A well-designed MkIS can provide a continuous flow of this type of information for decision making. Collecting data on consumer purchases has been greatly facilitated by electronic cash registers and computer systems that connect retailers directly with their suppliers. The storage and retrieval dimensions of an MkIS allow a manager to examine data for trends and patterns over time. With this capability, managers can continually monitor the performance of products, markets, sales people, and other marketing units.

An MkIS is of obvious value in a large company, where information is likely to get lost or distorted as it becomes widely dispersed. However, experience shows that even relatively simple information systems can upgrade management's decision making in small and medium-sized firms. For example, a small manufacturer of electric motors that tracks sales by customer over time can use the information to divide its customers into good, better, and best categories, and allocate selling effort accordingly.

How well an MkIS functions depends on three factors:

- The nature and quality of the data available.
- The ways in which the data are processed and presented to provide usable information.
- The ability of the operators of the MkIS and the managers who use the output to work together.

Global Marketing Information Systems

As firms expand their operations beyond national borders, their needs for information also grow. Centrally managed international organizations must be informed about what is happening around the world. Thus, many companies are creating global marketing information systems. However, establishing worldwide agreement on the types and forms of information to be maintained can be challenging. For example, to maintain its prominence in food as well as home and personal-care products, Unilever keeps 90,000 of its employees in over 150 countries linked through an information system. Besides sharing information on new product research and innovation, this company with brands such as Slim-Fast, Lipton, Ragu, Dove, Vaseline, and Breyers ice cream, gathers and distributes information on product performance and best marketing practices by various units. In a typical day, Unilever employees respond to over a million electronic messages.

Clearly, designing and operating a global MkIS can be more complex than developing one at the domestic level. It requires convincing each unit of the value of timely and accurate information, accommodating differences in the operational definitions of terms, and adjusting for the use of different currencies and measures in reporting data.

The original features of an MkIS—a focus on preplanned, structured reports and centralized control over the information by computer specialists—resulted from the skills required to operate computers. Now, personal computers with greatly enlarged capacity and user-friendly software have reduced that dependency and led to the development of decision support systems.

Decision Support Systems

A **decision support system (DSS)** is a computer-based procedure that allows a manager to directly interact with data using various methods of analysis to integrate, analyze, and interpret information. Like an MkIS, the heart of a DSS is data—different types of data from a wide variety of sources. Typically, a DSS contains data describing the market, customers, competitors, economic and social trends, and the organi-

Gillette has worldwide sales of nearly $9 billion. It has 34 manufacturing operations in 15 countries, and nearly 32,000 employees worldwide. To coordinate these far-flung operations, share information, and benefit from the scale economies of marketing the same products in many countries, Gillette has invested heavily in a sophisticated global information system.

zation's performance. Also, like an MkIS, the DSS has methods for analyzing data. These methods range from simple procedures such as computing ratios or drawing graphs to sophisticated statistical techniques and mathematical models.

Where the MkIS and DSS differ is in the extent to which they permit managers to interact directly with the data. By combining personal computers and user-friendly software, the DSS allows managers to independently retrieve data, examine relationships, and even create unique reports to meet their specific needs. This interactive capability makes it possible for managers to react to what they see in a set of data by asking questions and getting immediate answers. Figure 7.2 depicts the relationships in a DSS.

Consider this example: Midway through the month, the brand manager for Sunshine brand of frozen lemonade wants to check on the performance of the product. Sitting down at her computer, she calls up the monthly forecast and the actual sales figures to date. Discovering that sales are slightly below the rate necessary to achieve the month's forecast, she commands the system to provide similar data for each of the four different package sizes of the product. Finding that three of the sizes are on target, she concludes that there is a problem with only one. Next, she asks the system to break down the total sales figure by geographic areas and discovers that the poor sales results occurred in only two of seven regions.

Suspecting competitive activity, she then has the system retrieve and compare couponing activity, advertising levels, and prices of Sunshine lemonade and competing brands in the markets where sales forecasts were achieved and where they weren't. Finding nothing out of the ordinary, she decides to examine distribution in the territories. Requesting data on stock-outs for all package sizes of the lemonade, she finds that in the two regions where sales have slipped the frequency of stock-outs is higher than elsewhere. Next, she checks production figures and warehouse inventory levels and finds the problem is not due to internal shortages. Thus she concludes there must be a problem in the distribution of the product to the retail stores. As a result, she decides to investigate the performance of distributors in the problem regions.

Notice that, with an adequate DSS, this entire task was done in a short time by simply formulating a question, requesting information, analyzing the information, and moving on to another question suggested by the analysis. Note also that to function optimally the system requires current, accurate data that can be both costly and difficult to assemble and maintain.

The DSS adds speed and flexibility to the MkIS by making the manager an active part of the research process. The increased use of desktop computers, user-friendly software, and the willingness of suppliers and customers to link their computer systems (networking) have greatly enhanced the potential of DSS.

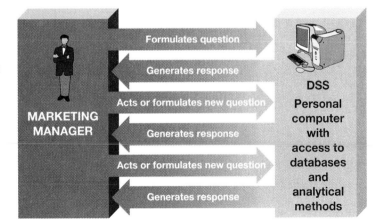

FIGURE 7.2

The Structure and Function of a Decision Support System.

Databases, Data Warehouses, and Data Mining

An MkIS or a DSS uses data from a variety of sources both within the organization and from outside suppliers. Typically these data are organized, stored, and updated in a computer. The assembled data pertinent to a particular topic—customers, market segments, competitors, or industry trends, for example—are called a **database.**

Researchers probe databases with specific questions to uncover useful relationships and developments. For example, the managers of a retail supermarket chain might want to know which items are purchased most frequently in each of its stores. By having the computer sort through the electronic records of all completed transactions, this information can be compiled quickly. The resulting tallies can be used to customize each store's layout and improve customer convenience. Databases are not new. For years managers have been monitoring their customers and the environment. Computers, with their speed and capacity, have simply made the process more manageable, efficient, and accurate.

Analyzing databases has enabled marketers to better understand marketplace behavior and, as a result, address their customers' needs more specifically. Some believe that through the management of data, marketers will eventually reach the ultimate level of personalized marketing—targeting individuals. Some large banks, for example, are moving in that direction. By comparing an individual customer's transaction pattern to a database of many customers' transactions, customers that are showing signs of closing their accounts are "red flagged." The bank managers investigate the causes and, when possible, develop individually tailored programs to solve the problem and retain the customer.

Some organizations move beyond databases to create large and complex data repositories. Acknowledging that they are more than simply a "base" of data, these collections are called data warehouses. A **data warehouse** is an enormous collection of data, from a variety of internal and external sources, compiled by a firm for its own use or for use by its clients. For example, American Express has the history of every transaction made with an American Express card—over 500 billion bits of data. Some firms make a business out of creating data warehouses. DoubleClick, a marketing services company, has pooled transactional data from over 1,800 merchants. The database includes more than 90 million households and over 3.5 billion individual transactions that DoubleClick's clients study to identify target markets.[4]

Data warehouses can be analyzed in the same way as databases, searching for predetermined patterns in the data. However, because of their size it would be a slow and cumbersome process. Fortunately, more advanced statistical and artificial intelligence techniques are now being applied to data warehouses. Called **data mining,**

As the Harrah's example in the text illustrates, when marketers can identify and track consumer purchase patterns by mining data bases, their marketing efforts can be much better focused. What other industries besides gambling could benefit from constructing and analyzing databases on customer behavior?

these techniques have the capability to identify patterns and meaningful relationships in masses of data that would be overlooked or unrecognizable to researchers. Harrah's Entertainment, owner of over two dozen casinos, is especially interested in getting a larger share of its existing customers' gambling dollars. By combining a customer identification card (a plastic card with a magnetic strip the customer voluntarily inserts into the gaming machine while gambling) with a network that links its 40,000 machines in 12 states, the company is able to collect a vast amount of data about individual customers regardless of which Harrah's casinos they visit. From the data Harrah's develops a profile of a person's gambling behavior and a profit projection that determines what promotional incentives are likely to be most effective. Harrah's data mining effort has isolated 90 demographic segments with different marketing strategies directed to each.[5]

Major Data Sources

The data used by researchers and managers in databases and data warehouses are gathered from many sources. Internally, data can come from the sales force, marketing, manufacturing, and accounting. Externally, information is available from hundreds of research suppliers. Companies such as Information Resources, Inc. (IRI), have developed computer systems to take the data captured from supermarket checkout systems to provide information on how well specific coupons work in various neighborhoods and which in-store displays are the most effective in generating sales.

Some sources provide a continuous flow—as when all transaction data for a retailer are fed into the system—whereas others are occasional or periodic providers—as when new demographic information on the population is released by the government. Some examples of especially useful data are described in more detail below.

Probably the most important data source for consumer databases is **retail scanners,** the electronic devices at retail checkouts that read the bar code on each item purchased. Scanners were originally intended to speed up checkout and reduce errors in supermarkets. By matching an item's unique code with price information stored in a computer, the scanner eliminated the need for clerks to memorize prices and reduced mistakes from hitting the wrong cash register key. However, retailers quickly discovered scanners could also produce information on purchases that could be used to improve decisions about how much of a product to keep in inventory and the appropriate amount of shelf space to allocate to each product.

Many retailers, including Kroger and Safeway, have taken scanning a step further by adding the customer's identity to the record of their purchases in what are called frequent shopper programs. Participants in the stores' frequent shopper programs are given discounts if they permit the cashier to run their membership card through a reader when they check out. This allows the store to combine data stored on the card about household demographics and lifestyle with the shopper's scanned purchases. The store is then able to relate product choices to household characteristics and adjust the product assortment and store layout to make it more appealing. At its website (*www.ncr.com*) NCR Corp., a manufacturer of the computer equipment used in these systems, provides some indications of how extensive and varied these data capture programs have become.

Linking household information to product purchases is even more valuable if you know what advertising the purchasers have been exposed to and the coupons they have used. IRI has created a database to provide this information. The firm maintains a sample of cooperating households for which it:

- Maintains an extensive demographic profile.
- Monitors television viewing electronically.
- Tracks the use of coupons.
- Records grocery purchases.

AN ETHICAL DILEMMA?

Information about you and your behavior is constantly flowing into databases to be "sliced and diced" by marketers. The results range from simple targeted direct-mail advertisements to forecasts of future behavior and strategies for speeding up purchases or discouraging defection.

In many cases not only do consumers not know how information is being used, they don't even know who is using it. For example, each year more than a million high school students complete a questionnaire for the National Research Center for College and University Admissions, providing their names, addresses, grade-point averages, race, religion, and social views. The survey form includes a statement explaining that the responses are "used by colleges, universities and other organizations to assist students and their families." The students are also informed that completing the survey will broaden their higher-education options because their names and profiles are distributed to hundreds of colleges and universities. Besides colleges and universities, the information is sold to companies that market a wide array of goods and services to the students. Though most are legitimate businesses such as Gillette, American Express, and *Seventeen* magazine, there are also instances in which illicit organizations have purchased the names, as in the case of one company convicted of mail fraud for bilking students out of thousands of dollars with offers of phony scholarships.

Should people have control over how their personal information is collected, stored, sold, or used?

Sources: Daniel Golden, "Surveyor Quietly Sells Student Information to Youth Marketer," *The Wall Street Journal*, Dec. 3, 2001, pp. A1+ ; "Selling Is Getting Personal," *Consumer Reports*, November 2000, pp. 16–20; Nicole Harris, "Data-Mining Company Helps Businesses Analyze Customers," *The Wall Street Journal*, Aug. 9, 2001, p. B10.

The result is that household demographics can be correlated to television advertising exposure, coupon usage, and product purchases. The output is called **single-source data** because all the information can be traced to individual households, providing a single source for the data.

Marketing Research Projects

Before MkIS and DSS, much of what was called marketing research consisted of projects to answer specific managerial questions. Projects, some that are nonrecurring and others that are repeated periodically, are still an important part of marketing research. The results of a project may be used to make a particular decision. They could also become part of a database to be used in an MkIS or a DSS. Examples of marketing research projects are described briefly in Table 7.1.

TABLE 7.1

Typical Marketing Research Projects

Project	Objective
Concept test	To determine if a new-product idea is attractive to potential customers
Copy test	To determine if the intended message in an advertisement is being communicated effectively
Price responsiveness	To gauge the effect a price change would have on demand for a brand
Market-share analysis	To determine a firm's proportion of the total sales of a product
Segmentation studies	To identify distinct groups within the total market for a particular product
Customer satisfaction studies	To monitor how customers feel about an organization and its products

FIGURE 7.3

Marketing Research Procedure.

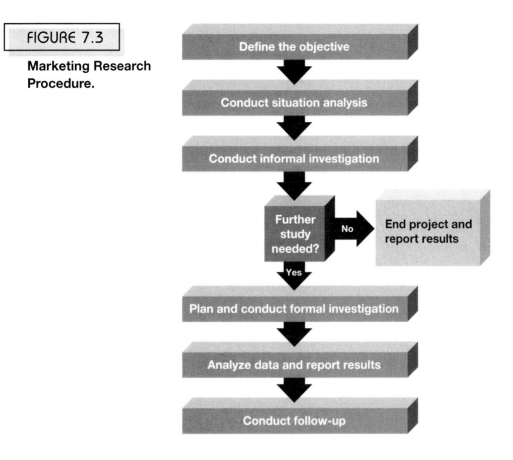

Most marketing research projects follow the procedure outlined in Figure 7.3. Let's examine what goes into conducting a marketing research project.

Define the Objective

Researchers need a clear idea of what they are trying to learn—the objective of the project. Usually the objective is to solve a problem, but this is not always so. Often the objective is to better understand or *define* a problem or opportunity.

Sometimes the objective is simply to determine if there is a problem. To illustrate, a manufacturer of commercial air-conditioning equipment had been enjoying a steady increase in sales volume over a period of years. Management decided to conduct a sales analysis. This research project uncovered the fact that, although the company's volume had been increasing, its share of the market had declined because the industry was growing even faster. In this instance, marketing research uncovered a problem that management did not know existed. After specifying the objective, the researcher is ready for the second step—the situation analysis.

Conduct a Situation Analysis

Next, the researchers try to get a feel for the situation surrounding the problem. They analyze the company, its market, its competition, and the industry in general. The **situation analysis** is a background investigation that helps refine the research problem. This step involves obtaining information about the company and its business environment by means of library research and extensive interviewing of company officials.

In the situation analysis, researchers also try to refine the problem definition and develop hypotheses for testing. A research **hypothesis** is a tentative supposition that, if supported, would suggest a possible solution to a problem. An example of a testable hypothesis is: More women than men use the Internet. If research supports this hypothesis, it would likely lead to changes in large Internet portals such as Yahoo! and MSN to make sure their entry sites and banner ads are appealing to the correct audiences.[6] The project then turns to generating data that can be used to test the correctness of the hypotheses.

Conduct an Informal Investigation

Having developed a feel for the problem, the researchers are now ready to collect some preliminary data. This **informal investigation** consists of gathering readily available information from people inside and outside the company—middlemen, competitors, advertising agencies, and consumers.

The informal investigation is a critical step in a research project because it will determine whether further study is necessary. Decisions can frequently be made with information gathered in the informal investigation. For example, hotels hire professional "mystery shoppers" to check in and act like typical guests when in fact they are evaluating the hotel's service. For as little as $1,500, a hotel can have its operation completely examined. And the examinations are thorough! For example, one hotel-rating company evaluates 50 items between a hotel's front door and the completion of check-in.[7] If the results of such a test are very positive, a hotel might decide that additional research is not needed. Alternatively, a poor result may dictate some immediate changes or more research.

Plan and Conduct a Formal Investigation

If the project warrants continued investigation, the researcher must determine what additional information is needed and how to gather it.

Select Sources of Information

Primary data, secondary data, or both can be used in an investigation. **Primary data** are new data gathered specifically for the project at hand. When researchers at a midwestern supermarket chain watched 1,600 shoppers move through the store, and discovered that 80% of the traffic was in 20% of the store (the produce, dairy, and meat sections), they were collecting primary data. **Secondary data** are available data, already gathered for some other purpose. For example, the data in a study by the Food Marketing Institute, an industry trade group, that reported the differences in food preference and shopping behavior of men and women, are secondary data.

One of the biggest mistakes made in marketing research is to collect primary data before exhausting what can be learned from information available in secondary sources. Ordinarily, secondary information can be gathered much faster and at far less expense than primary data. This is especially true today with so much data available over the Internet. For example, the U.S. Census Bureau has created the American FactFinder website to assist researchers in locating population data down to the community level. Statistics on housing, income, transportation, employment, and education are readily accessible at this site.

www.census.gov

Sources of Secondary Data. Excellent sources of secondary information are available to marketing researchers. One source is the many records and reports *inside* the firm itself. For example, the daily call reports completed by sales people are used primarily to keep track of how they are spending their time. However, if they are examined over several months or years, they can provide a firm with important information on how its mix of customers is changing. Similarly, a contest with mail-in entries might be a good promotional tool. It also can be a source of information. Consumers who enter contests have indicated by their behavior that they are interested in particular products. Examining the geographic origins of these responses might indicate where the best potential markets are.

Shown here is a sample of the results of the first U.S. census conducted in 1790. It took 18 months to complete and served as the basis (as it does today) for the number of seats allocated to each state in the House of Representatives. The decennial census continues to be one of the most important sources of population data available in the United States.

The Return for SOUTH CAROLINA having been made fince the foregoing Schedule was originally printed, the whole Enumeration is here given complete, except for the N. Weftern Territory, of which no Return has yet been publifhed.

DISTICTS	Free white Males of 16 years and upwards, including heads of families.	Free white Males under fixteen years.	Free white Females, including heads of families.	All other free perfons.	Slaves.	Total.
Vermont	22435	22328	40505	255	16	85539
N. Hampfhire	36086	34851	70160	630	158	141885
Maine	24384	24748	46870	538	NONE	96540
Maffachufetts	95453	87289	190582	5463	NONE	378787
Rhode Ifland	16019	15799	32652	3407	948	68825
Connecticut	60523	54403	117448	2808	2764	237946
New York	83700	78122	152320	4654	21324	340120
New Jerfey	45251	41416	83287	2762	11423	184139
Pennfylvania	110788	106948	206363	6537	3737	434373
Delaware	11783	12143	22384	3899	8887	59094
Maryland	55915	51339	101395	8043	103036	319728
Virginia	110936	116135	215046	12866	292627	747610
Kentucky	15154	17057	28922	114	12430	73677
N. Carolina	69988	77506	140710	4975	100572	393751
S. Carolina	35576	37722	66880	1801	107094	249073
Georgia	13103	14044	25739	398	29264	82548
	807094	791850	1541263	59150	694280	3893635

Total number of Inhabitants of the United States exclufive of S. Weftern and N. Teiritory.	Free white Males of 21 years and upwards.	Free Males under 21 years of age.	Free white Females.	All other Perfons.	Slaves.	Total
S. W. territory	6271	10277	15365	361	3417	35691
N. Ditto	—	—	—	—	—	—

Outside the firm there are also a number of excellent secondary data sources. The federal government is the largest provider of demographic market information. For example, the American Community Survey (ACS) being developed by the U.S. Census Bureau for nationwide implementation will provide annual demographic, economic, and housing data on all communities in the country. Rather than rely on the decennial (once every 10 years) census of the population, community planners, businesspeople, and government officials will have current data on which to base decisions. Other sources include the websites of firms and trade and professional organizations, private research firms, universities, business publications, and, of course, any good library. Some useful Web sources are described in Table 7.2.

www.census.gov/acs/www

Researchers must be aware that there is risk associated with using secondary data. Because the users have no control over how, when, by whom, or why the data were collected, they may not meet the objectives of the research. For example, some projects are undertaken to prove a preconceived point. The results of this so-called advocacy research often get considerable publicity, but may in fact be quite misleading. Thus researchers should check the source, motivation for the study, and definitions of key terms before relying on secondary data.

Sources of Primary Data.   After exhausting all the available secondary sources considered pertinent, researchers may still lack sufficient data. If so, they must turn to primary sources and gather or purchase the information. In a company's research project, for instance, a researcher may interview the firm's sales people, middlemen, or customers to obtain the market information needed.

Select a Primary Data-Gathering Method   There are three widely used methods of gathering primary data: observation, survey, and experimentation. Because each method has strengths and weaknesses, more than one may be used at different stages of a project. For example, observation may be used to develop hypotheses about

TABLE 7.2

Print and Electronic Sources of Secondary Data

Business and marketing publications and directories
Sales & Marketing Management magazine: <www.salesandmarketing.com>
American Demographics magazine: <www.marketingtools.com>
Advertising Age magazine: <www.adage.com>
Quirk's Marketing Research Review: <www.quirks.com>
The New York Times Business section: <www.nytimes.com/pages/business>
BrandWeek's list of top American brands: <www.brandweek.com> click on Superbrands
Executive Gateway to the Internet: <www.ceoexpress.com>

Marketing and research company websites
Gallup Poll: <www.gallup.com>
Nielsen Retail index: <www.acnielsen.com>
Roper Starch Reports: <www.roper.com>
Fuld & Co.: <www.fuld.com> Click on Internet Intelligence Index for over 600 competitive intelligence-related sites

Government agencies and publications
Directory to all government agencies: <www.house.gov/house/govsites.html>
U.S. Census Bureau: <www.census.gov>
Statistical Abstract of the U.S.: <www.census.gov/statab/www>
CIA World Factbook: <www.odci.gov/cia/publications/factbook/index.html>
Fed Stats—statistics from over 100 federal government agencies: <www.fedstats.gov>
Federal Trade Commission: <www.ftc.gov>

Marketing roundtables, discussion groups, and other resources
Web Digest for Marketers: <www.wdfm.com>
Marketing Tracks—sources and commentary: <www.nsns.com/MouseTracks>
Web Marketing Today Info Center: <www.wilsonweb.com/marketing>

Professional association sources
American Marketing Association: <www.ama.org>
Direct Marketing Association: <www.the-dma.org>
Sales and Marketing Executives International: <www.smei.org>

shoppers' behavior and a survey may then be conducted to test those hypotheses. However, in many situations the researcher must select from among them. The choice of which to use depends on the nature of the problem, but it will also be influenced by how much time and money are available for the project.[8]

Observation Method.   The **observation method** involves collecting data by observing the actions of a person. In observation research there is no direct interaction with the subjects being studied.

Information may be gathered by *personal observation* or *mechanical observation.* In one kind of personal observation, the researcher poses as a customer. This technique is used by retailers, for example, to get information about the performance of sales people or to determine what brands the sales people emphasize. Mechanical observation takes many forms. One, described earlier, is the scanner used in retail stores to record purchases. Other, more dramatic forms are eye cameras that measure pupil dilation to record a person's response to a visual stimulus such as an ad, and brain wave monitors to test whether reactions to an object, such as a commercial, are primarily emotional or logical.

Internet "cookies" permit a special kind of observation. In Web jargon, a **cookie** is an inactive data file placed on a person's computer hard drive when that person visits a particular website. A cookie can record the visitor's activities while connected to the site. For example, it can keep track of which pages on the site are opened, how long the visitor remains at the site, the links the visitor makes to other sites, and the site from which the visitor came. If the site offers products for sale, purchases can also be recorded on a cookie. The cookie also allows the visitor (or more accurately, the visitor's computer) to be identified. All the information stored in the cookie is transferred to the host the next time the person connects to its website. The information from a cookie is used, for example, to develop a profile of an individual so that on subsequent visits to the host site the visitor can be greeted by name or offered particular products based on past purchases.[9] Through the cookies it places on visitors' computers Amazon.com individually tracks millions of shoppers and book-buying customers and offers suggestions about titles they might enjoy based on what they have considered or purchased on past visits.

The observation method has several merits. It can provide highly accurate data about behavior in given situations. Usually the parties being observed are unaware that they are being observed, so presumably they behave in a normal fashion. Thus the observation technique eliminates bias resulting from the intrusion of the research process into the situation. Also, because there is no direct interaction with the subject, there is no limit to how many times or for how long a subject can be observed. However, observation provides only information about *what* happens, it cannot tell *why*. Observation cannot delve into motives, attitudes, or opinions. To illustrate, what might explain why the ratio of shoppers' visits to purchases is much higher for the bakery department than for any other department in a supermarket? Interviews would be necessary to test your possible explanations.

Survey Method. A **survey** consists of gathering data by interviewing people. Surveys can be conducted in person, or by telephone, by mail, or via the Internet. The advantage of a survey is that information comes directly from the people you are interested in. In fact, it may be the only way to determine the opinions or buying plans of a group. Surveys have several potential limitations:

- There are opportunities for error in the construction of the survey questionnaire and in the interviewing process.
- Surveys can be expensive and time-consuming.
- Desired respondents sometimes refuse to participate, and those who do respond often cannot or will not give true answers.

As we will see below, careful design and execution of a survey can reduce the effects of these limitations.

Face-to-face interviews are more flexible than phone or mail interviews because interviewers can probe more deeply if an answer is incomplete. Ordinarily, more information can be obtained by personal interviews than by other survey methods. They also have the advantage of being able to use various stimuli such as products, packages, and ads. Rising costs and other problems associated with door-to-door interviewing have prompted many market researchers to conduct surveys in locations that attract large numbers of people, such as shopping centers, airports, and parks. Because this approach was first used in shopping centers, it is generally called a *mall intercept* interview. However, there is growing concern about whether or not people interviewed in these settings are "typical" consumers.

In addition to their high cost and time-consuming nature, personal interviews also face the possible limitation of interviewer bias. An interviewer's appearance, style in asking questions, and body language can all influence a respondent's answers.

Another popular face-to-face type of personal interview is the **focus group.** In a focus group, a moderator leads 6 to 12 people in a discussion. Typically the participants are strangers before the session. They are contacted, screened for suitability, and invited to attend. Because focus group sessions require that participants gather

Teenage Research Unlimited, a Chicago research firm, tracks teenage trends through a variety of techniques including focus groups and face-to-face interviews. By completing drawings, such as the one shown here, teens provide clues that are useful to marketers. Interpreting the data is the challenge. Is there a recent trend reflected in this actual example?

at a particular time and place, and often last for two to three hours, participants are usually rewarded with cash or merchandise. General questions are posed by the moderator to prompt participants into freely discussing the topic of interest.

The strength of focus groups is found in the interaction of the participants. A comment by one person triggers thoughts and ideas in others, and the ensuing interaction can produce valuable insights. Focus groups generate ideas and hypotheses that can be tested using other research methods. However, when several independent focus group sessions conducted on the same topic produce a common theme, managers will sometimes act on the information without additional validation.

Telephone surveys can usually be conducted more rapidly than either personal or mail surveys. Because a few interviewers can make many calls from a central location, this method is easy to administer. A telephone survey can also be timely. For instance, to determine the impact of a particular TV commercial, viewers are contacted by phone within hours of the commercial's appearance, while the experience is still fresh. Telephone surveys have been used successfully with executives at work. When preceded by a letter introducing the study and a short call to make an appointment for the actual interview, these surveys can elicit a high cooperation rate.

One limitation of telephone surveys is that the interview must be short or the respondent becomes impatient. Also, about 30% of households have unlisted numbers, have moved since the latest directory was printed, or have no telephone. To lower the cost of telephone interviewing and reduce the problems of unlisted numbers and outdated directories, some surveys are done with the aid of computers. To ensure that all telephone owners, even those with unlisted numbers, have an equal chance of being called, researchers use a method called *random digit dialing* in which computers randomly select and dial numbers.

A **mail survey** involves sending a questionnaire to potential respondents, asking them to complete it, and having them return it. Traditionally mail surveys have used

MARKETING IN THE INFORMATION ECONOMY

For which kinds of consumer surveys is the Internet appropriate?

The Internet has been used in a wide variety of consumer research settings. For example, M&M Mars invited consumers to vote for a new color of its well-known candy (purple won), and Pepsi asked consumers to vote for a favorite, among five, commercials, with the winner to be run on the Superbowl broadcast. Some would argue that these are really promotional activities disguised as research.

What about test marketing? Procter & Gamble has found that offering new products on a dedicated website is a quick, cost-effective way to judge demand. For example, when the company was concerned that consumers and retailers might balk at the $44 price on its Crest Whitestrips tooth-bleaching product, it offered the product on a website called *whitestrips.com.* When 144,000 kits were sold in 8 months, the company felt it had a winner as well as the evidence it needed to convince reluctant retailers.

And then there are straightforward surveys in which consumers are asked questions about themselves and their behavior. When Polaroid conducted an e-mail survey, a higher proportion of respondents indicated that they had scanned a Polaroid picture than the proportion in the general population who had even taken a Polaroid photograph. As a result, company officials were skeptical about who the sample in the survey actually represented.

For now it seems the rule should be to use the Internet with caution when doing surveys. It can be faster and less expensive than traditional methods, but those should not be the primary considerations in designing a study.

Sources: "Marketing Hits & Misses," *Sales & Marketing Management,* April 2002, p. 12; Erin White, "Market Research on the Internet Has Its Drawbacks," *The Wall Street Journal,* Mar. 2, 2000, p. B4; John Gaffney, "How Do You Feel about a $44 Tooth-Bleaching Kit?" *Business 2.0,* October 2001, pp. 126–127.

the post office to deliver and return questionnaires; however, e-mail is growing in popularity as a distribution method. Because interviewers are not used, this type of survey is not hampered by interviewer bias or problems connected with managing a team of interviewers. In addition, because there is no interviewer present, the respondent can remain anonymous. As a result, answers are more likely to be frank and honest.

A major problem with mail surveys is the compilation of an appropriate mailing list. In some cases lists are readily available. However, many studies require a sample for which there is no readily available mailing list. For example, if Toys "Я" Us wants to survey a nationwide sample of parents expecting the birth of their first child, it might have a difficult time compiling an up-to-date list. Fortunately, there are businesses, called list brokers that develop and maintain mailing lists. Another problem is the reliability of the information in the completed questionnaires. In a mail survey, researchers have no control over who actually completes the questionnaire or how carefully it is done.

One more problem is that a mail survey usually gets a low response rate, often less than 30% of those contacted. This is more than a numbers problem. If the respondents have characteristics that differentiate them from nonrespondents on important dimensions of the survey, the results will be invalid. For example, in a community survey about interest in the local PBS television station, the people willing to take the time to respond are likely to be highly interested in public television and therefore not representative of the entire community. Techniques for improving mail response rates include prenotification by phone, offering a reward, duplicate mailings and postcard reminders, and keeping the survey short and the questions simple.

Increasingly the Internet is being used to conduct research. In an **Internet survey**, questionnaires can be posted on a firm's website or e-mailed to prospective respondents. Everything from short surveys to lengthy focus groups are being tried online. Two of the most important advantages of this tool are speed and cost. An Internet survey can be done more quickly than any other method, and because all transmissions are electronic, there are significant personnel and material savings. However, the primary advantage is the flexibility of a multimedia environment. Online surveys can include images that can be manipulated, streaming video, sounds, and other features that would be impractical with alternative data collection methods.

Internet surveys have many of the same disadvantages as mail surveys, namely, verification of the identity of the respondent is not possible, good lists from which samples can be drawn are often difficult to find, and provision of an incentive to encourage response is difficult because there is not yet a reliable method of electronic delivery. Until Internet usage becomes more widespread, probably the greatest single concern in using the Internet for surveys is how well users represent the general population.[10]

Experimental Method. An **experiment** is a method of gathering primary data in which the researcher is able to observe the results of changing one variable in a situation while holding all other conditions constant. Experiments are conducted in laboratory settings or in the field. In marketing research, a "laboratory" is an environment in which the researcher has control over all the relevant conditions.

Consider this example: A small group of consumers is assembled and presented with a brief product description (called a *product concept*) and proposed package for a new breakfast cereal. After they examine the package, the people are asked whether they would buy the cereal, and their responses are recorded. Next, a similar group of consumers is brought together and presented with the identical package and product information, except that a nutritional claim for the cereal is printed on the package. Members of this group are also asked if they would buy the product. The researcher has complete control over the test environment, and the only thing changed is the nutritional claim on the package. Therefore, any difference in buying intentions between the groups can be attributed to the claim.

Laboratory experiments can be used to test many components of marketing strategy. For example, ads can be tested to determine how well the intended message is understood and various bundles of product features can be compared to see which is preferred. However, recognize that the laboratory setting is not an actual purchase, so consumers' responses may be influenced by the situation. To overcome this problem, some experiments are conducted outside the controlled conditions of the lab, or in the field. A *field experiment* is similar to a laboratory experiment but is conducted under more realistic conditions. For example, the owner of a chain of retail stores might try a traffic-building promotional program in one or two stores and then compare sales results with results in similar stores without the promotion. Certainly not everything in the stores can be controlled. However, if researchers believe all relevant conditions in the stores remained similar, any differences in sales can be credited to the promotion.

A common experiment is test marketing. In **test marketing** the researcher duplicates real market conditions in a limited geographic area to measure consumers' responses to a strategy before committing to a major marketing effort. Test marketing is undertaken to forecast sales for a particular marketing mix or to compare the performance of different marketing mixes. For example, McDonald's test-marketed pizza in selected areas for over two years before deciding not to add it to the menu of their traditional outlets.

The advantage of test marketing over a survey or a lab experiment is that it informs marketers how many people *actually buy* a product, instead of how many say they *intend to buy* it. However, duplicating the entire marketing effort on a small scale has several disadvantages. Test marketing is expensive; spending $500,000 to $1 million is not uncommon. It is also time-consuming. Testing frequently lasts 9 to 12 months. Lever Bros. kept Lever 2000 deodorant soap in test for two years before going national. Another problem is the researcher's inability to control the situation. Tests are impossible to keep secret from competitors, who may intentionally disrupt the test by temporarily changing their marketing mixes. When Pepsi tested Mountain Dew Sport drink in Minneapolis, Quaker Oats, the maker of Gatorade, flooded the market with coupons and advertising. (Apparently, however, Pepsi learned quite a lot because it subsequently purchased Quaker Oats to obtain the Gatorade brand!)

Because of the inherent limitations of the kind of test marketing just described, researchers have tried to find faster, less visible alternatives. One of these combines surveys, product trial, and an extensive database to forecast sales. It works like this. A group of selected volunteers is shown ads and possibly other information about the new product, including the proposed price. They are then asked a number of questions about how well they like it, whether or not they'd buy it, and if it seems like a good value. Some of the consumers who indicate they like the product are given samples to test and are interviewed again. Finally, the researcher takes all this information, combines it with the marketer's planned strategy for distribution and promotion, and compares it to information on similar, previously marketed products that are stored in a database. Using a statistical model, the researcher then forecasts sales for the new product. Probably the best known of these procedures is called Bases by the research firm ACNielsen.

www.bases.com

The potential benefits of such a simulated test market include:

- Results can be produced quickly, often in as little as eight weeks.

- The tests can be done secretly, without competitor knowledge or interference.

- The cost may be lower than a traditional test market.

The drawbacks are:

- The procedure is suitable only for consumer packaged goods and some over-the-counter pharmaceuticals.

- Because the forecasting models are based on historical sales of similar products, it may not be appropriate for unique new products.

- It is expensive, and testing alternative marketing mixes adds to the cost.

Sometimes this approach is used to refine a marketing strategy that is then followed by traditional test marketing, The time, effort, and expense that go into researching new products indicates how important they are and how difficult it is to anticipate how consumers will respond to a marketing effort.

International marketers sometimes use a few countries as a test market for a continent or even the world. Colgate-Palmolive introduced Palmolive Optims shampoo and conditioner in the Philippines, Australia, Mexico, and Hong Kong. When sales proved satisfactory, distribution was expanded to large portions of Europe, Asia, Latin America, and Africa.

Prepare Forms for Gathering Data
Whether interviewing or observing subjects, researchers use a questionnaire or form on which there are instructions and spaces to record observations and responses. It is not easy to design a data-gathering form that elicits precisely the information needed. Here are several fundamental considerations:

- *Question wording.* If a question is misunderstood, the data it produces are worthless. Questions should be written with the potential respondent's vocabulary, reading level, and familiarity with jargon in mind.

- *Response format.* Questions are designed for either check mark responses (such as yes-no, multiple-choice, agree-disagree scales) or open-ended replies. Open-ended questions are often easier to write and frequently produce richer answers, but they require more effort from the respondent and therefore lower the level of cooperation.

- *Questionnaire layout.* The normal procedure is to begin with easier questions and move to the more difficult or complicated questions. Possibly sensitive topics (for example, personal hygiene) or private matters (age, income) are normally placed at the very end of a questionnaire.

- *Pretesting.* All questionnaires should be pretested on a group of respondents to identify problems and make corrections and refinements prior to the actual study.

Complete books are available on questionnaire design. Extreme care and skill are needed to produce a questionnaire that maximizes the likelihood of getting a response while minimizing bias, misunderstanding, and respondent irritation.

Plan the Sample   It is unnecessary to survey or observe every person who could shed light on a research problem. It is sufficient to collect data from a sample if it is *representative* of the entire group. We all make use of sampling. For example, we often form opinions of people based on a few interactions. However, if the interactions include only one aspect of a person's life, for example work interactions, and ignore home life or recreation, they may not be representative. The key in these personal issues *and* in marketing research is whether the sample provides an accurate representation. Representativeness has been an issue in using the Internet to collect data. As attractive as it is for data collection, many researchers are concerned about how well Internet users represent the general population.

The fundamental idea underlying sampling is that a small number of items—a sample—if properly selected from a larger number of items—a universe—will have the same characteristics and in about the same proportion as the larger number. Obtaining reliable data with this method requires the right technique in selecting the sample.

Improper sampling is a source of error in many studies. One firm, for example, selected a sample of calls from all the calls made to its 800 number and used the information to make generalizations about its customers. Would you be comfortable saying these callers are representative of all the firm's customers or even all the dissatisfied ones? Although numerous sampling techniques are available, only by using a random sample can a researcher confidently make generalizations about a universe. A *random sample* is selected in such a way that every member of the universe has an equal chance of being included.

All other (nonrandom) samples are known as *convenience samples*. Convenience samples are quite common in marketing research, for two reasons. First, random samples are very difficult to get. Even though the researcher may *select* the subjects in a random fashion, there is no guarantee that they all will participate. Some will be unavailable and others will refuse to cooperate. As a result, researchers often resort to carefully designed convenience samples that reflect the characteristics of the universe as closely as possible. Second, not all research is done with the objective of generalizing to a universe. For example, to confirm the judgment of the advertising department, a researcher may be satisfied with the finding that a small group of respondents all take a similar message away from an ad.

A common question regarding sampling is: How large should a sample be? With random methods, a sample must be large enough to be truly representative of the universe. Thus the size will depend on the diversity of characteristics within the universe. All basic statistics books contain general formulas for calculating sample size. In the case of nonrandom samples, because the objective is not to make generalizations, researchers can select any size sample they and the managers using the data feel comfortable with.

Collect the Data   Collecting primary data by interviewing, observation, or both can be done by people or machines. Unfortunately, it is often the weakest link in the research process. A research project can be designed with great care, but the fruits of these labors may be lost if the data gathering is inadequately conducted.

It is often difficult to motivate people who collect data. Because they frequently are part-time workers doing what is often a monotonous task for relatively low pay, proper training and supervision are essential to avoid problems. For instance, poorly trained data gatherers may fail to establish rapport with respondents or may change the wording of questions. In extreme cases, there have even been instances where interviewers faked the responses and filled out the questionnaires themselves!

Mechanical data collection includes such devices as retail scanners (described earlier), video cameras, audiotapes, and computer terminals (often found in malls, airport terminals, and hotel lobbies). The human element of the data collector is eliminated with these devices, but there are new issues that can affect data quality such as equipment reliability, how participants' responses and behavior are affected by the mechanical device, and the conversion of the raw data into useable form.

Analyze the Data and Present a Report

The value of research is determined by its results. And because data cannot speak for themselves, analysis and interpretation are key components of any project. Computers allow researchers to tabulate and process masses of data quickly and inexpensively. This tool can be abused, however. Managers have little use for reams of computer printouts. Researchers must be able to identify pivotal relationships, spot trends, and find patterns—that's what transforms data into useful information.

The end product of the investigation is the researcher's conclusions and recommendations. Most projects require a written report, often accompanied by an oral presentation to management. Here communication skill becomes a factor. Not only must researchers be able to write and speak effectively, they must adopt the perspective of the manager in presenting research results.

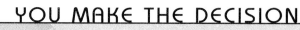
Conduct a Follow-up

Researchers should follow up their studies to determine whether their results and recommendations are being used. Management may choose not to use a study's findings for several reasons. The problem that generated the research may have been misdefined, become less urgent, or even disappeared. Or the research may have been completed too late to be useful. Without a follow-up, the researcher has no way of knowing if the project was on target and met management's needs or if it fell short. As a result, an important source of information for improving research in the future would be ignored.

Competitive Intelligence

A research area that is only recently receiving widespread, serious attention is competitive intelligence. U.S. marketers have learned from their foreign counterparts that closely monitoring competitors can be extremely useful. Japanese firms in particular have made a science out of watching and learning from their rivals.

Although it sounds intriguing, **competitive intelligence** is simply the process of gathering and analyzing available public information about the activities and plans of competitors. The data used to study competitors come from a variety of internal and external sources. The most common are databases created and sold by research firms. The simplest of these are newspaper and magazine clipping services that monitor a large number of publications for articles on particular industries or companies. There are several thousand of these competitive database services available today.

Another source is government reports, produced and made available by U.S. and foreign government agencies. For example, the Japan Center for Information and Cultural Affairs provides government documents, statistics on Japan, and information on various Japanese industries. Along the same line, the European Union provides competitive and financial information on European commerce.

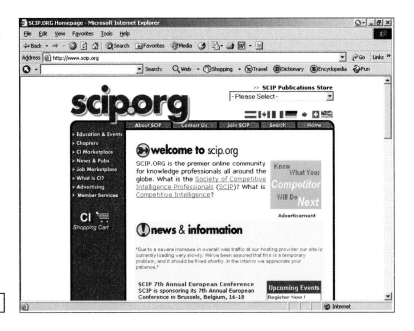

www.scip.org

Employees, particularly sales people, are the primary internal source of competitive data. It has become a standard practice for firms to incorporate space for competitive information in the reporting forms used by sales people. Other employees, such as engineers, service personnel, and purchasing agents, can pick up and report helpful information—if they are trained to be alert.

It is relatively common to use various observation techniques to collect competitive information. For example, representatives of consumer product manufacturers regularly shop retail stores to monitor competitors' prices and promotions. And it is not uncommon for a firm to buy a competitor's new product and take it apart in order to examine and test it—a procedure called *reverse engineering*.

One of the newest sources of competitive intelligence is the Internet. In an attempt to please current or potential customers, firms put information on their websites that a few years ago would have been considered highly proprietary. Price lists, suppliers' and distributors' names, plans for the future, and new-product information are commonly posted. Other website information may be less direct but still valuable. For example, firms proud of their research and development efforts, often list research papers produced by their technical people. These papers can provide insights into the direction the firm is headed.[11] There are also firms that specialize in conducting intelligence gathering. For some, the information collected becomes the attraction that draws visitors to their websites. They, in turn, sell advertising space on the sites. An example is Company Sleuth.

www.companysleuth.com

Clearly there is the potential for legal and ethical abuses in gathering competitive intelligence. Incidents of sifting through trash, electronic eavesdropping, and hiring competitors' employees to learn their plans are unfortunately not uncommon. Despite trade secret laws that make it illegal to acquire data through "improper means" such as theft, there are many unclear situations. Based on court opinions, attempts to get information when a competitor is taking reasonable care to conceal it from public exposure are unethical and may be illegal.

Many firms take elaborate precautions to protect the security of confidential information. Common techniques include the use of paper shredders, alerting employees to the importance of discretion, and limiting the circulation of sensitive documents. Of particular concern is the ease with which a thief can extract information from a careless sales person's or other employee's misplaced briefcase or personal computer.

Ethical Issues in Marketing Research

As the desire for better information grows and the technology for gathering data improves, marketers are faced with an increasing variety of ethical issues related to the collection and use of research information. Typical of the growing concerns are the following:

www.ftc.gov

- *Privacy in data collection.* It is possible to observe people with hidden cameras, identify an individual's purchase behavior by combining scanner data and credit card or check-cashing records, and track Internet activity with cookies. At what point does data collection became an invasion of privacy? The Federal Trade Commission is the primary government agency charged with consumer protection. From the number of issues it is addressing—including the conditions under which firms can share credit histories and purchasing information of customers, the disposition of medical records, and the protection of the privacy of children on the Internet—it's apparent this is a growing concern. Unfortunately, the temptation to misuse access to private information has proven too strong for some mangers to resist.

- *Privacy in data use.* In the routine process of business, firms often gather a considerable amount of information about their customers. This information, if linked to an individual's name and address, could be highly valuable to other businesses. For example, airlines have information about travel behavior that a travel magazine publisher would find useful. Does the airline have the right to sell that information?

- *Intrusiveness.* All marketers want information. The problem is that gathering that information can be annoying and inconvenient for the respondent. Telephone surveys conducted around dinnertime, extraneous (to the transaction) data collected at the time of a purchase, and questionnaires sent to people at work can all be intrusive. The issue here is: At what point does requesting information become excessively intrusive?

- *Deceptive implementation.* On occasion, researchers use deception to gather data. For example, phoning a business and falsely representing oneself as a potential customer in order to collect data, or intentionally misleading respondents about the sponsor or objective of the research are deceptions. Some researchers intentionally don't disclose to respondents that they are research subjects participating in a study. For example, a researcher in a grocery store pretending to be a shopper and asking fellow shoppers their opinions of products or brands is nondisclosure. In most cases, these deceptions are harmless and are actually viewed by researchers as essential to gathering candid responses. However, at what point is extracting information from a person under false or misleading pretenses inappropriate?

- *False representation.* Practices called "sugging" (selling under the guise of research) and "frugging" (fund raising under the guise of research) are unfortunately so common that they are negatively affecting the ability of legitimate researchers to gain respondents' cooperation. Practitioners of these techniques use the ruse that they are researchers conducting a survey. After securing the cooperation of the unsuspecting consumer and posing a few questions, they attempt a sale or ask for a donation. Some argue that research and selling or fund raising should never be combined in the same presentation. Others contend that the issue is whether the consumer is misled, not what is presented.

There have been several reactions to practices such as these. One is efforts by professional associations such as the American Marketing Association and the Advertising Research Foundation to discourage such practices among their members and other practitioners.

Status of Marketing Research

Significant advances have been made in both quantitative and qualitative research methodology, and researchers are making effective use of the behavioral sciences, mathematics, and statistics. Still, many companies invest very little in determining market opportunities for their products. Several factors account for the less-than-universal acceptance of marketing research:

- *Predicting behavior is inexact.* Because of the many variables involved, marketing research often cannot predict future market behavior accurately. AT&T's missed opportunity with cellular technology, described in the chapter-opening case, indicates that, even with information, firms still make misjudgments. When dealing with consumer behavior, the researcher may be hard pressed to determine present attitudes or motives (for reasons that were explained in Chapter 4), much less what they will be next year.

- *Conflicting objectives between researchers and managers.* The manager is frequently required to make quick decisions in the face of uncertainty, often with incomplete information. Researchers, on the other hand, are prone to approach problems in a cautious, scientific manner. This leads to disagreements about the research that should be conducted, how long it should take, and the way in which the results should be presented.

- *A project orientation to research.* Many managers do not treat marketing research as a continuous process. Too often marketing research is viewed in a fragmented, one-project-at-a-time manner. It is used only when management realizes that it has a marketing problem. The growth in the use of MkIS, DSS, and data mining will likely improve this situation.

Making research more "actionable"–that is, on target and of value to managers–is a challenge. However, it is far from impossible. In examining the issue in interviews with both researchers and managers, communications proved to be the key. When managers and researchers communicate continuously and consistently at every stage of the research process, the likelihood of research leading to effective action increases greatly.

Summary

Competitive pressure, the cost of making a mistake, and the complexity of both domestic and foreign markets all contribute to the need for marketing research. For a company to operate successfully today, management must engage in marketing research: the development, interpretation, and communication of decision-oriented information. Three tools used in research are marketing information systems, decision support systems, and the research projects.

A marketing information system (MkIS) is an ongoing set of procedures designed to generate, analyze, disseminate, store, and retrieve information for use in making marketing decisions. An MkIS provides a manager with a regularly scheduled flow of information and reports. As firms develop global MkISs, they are faced with problems of timing, accuracy of data, and terminology and measurement differences.

A decision support system (DSS) differs from an MkIS in that the manager, using a personal computer, can interact directly with data. The DSS adds speed and flexibility to the MkIS, but requires considerable investment to create and maintain.

Data used in an MkIS or DSS come from databases, which are organized sets of data pertinent to a particular topic stored and updated in a computer. Retail scanners are major sources of data that go into databases.

When data sets grow beyond simply a "base" of information, they are referred to as data warehouses. These enormous collections of data are probed for patterns and meaningful relationships in a process called data mining.

A marketing research project is undertaken to help resolve a specific marketing problem. The problem must first be clearly defined. Then a researcher conducts a situation analysis and an informal investigation. If a formal investigation is needed, the researcher decides which secondary and primary sources of information to use. Secondary data already exist. Primary data are gathered for the problem at hand. Primary data are gathered using observation, surveys, or experiments. Observation is unintrusive, but cannot provide explanations for the behavior observed. Surveys are conducted in person, by phone, or through the mail. The Internet and e-mail are growing in popularity as tools for doing surveys. The challenges in survey research are selecting a sample, designing a questionnaire, and generating an adequate response. The research project is completed when data are analyzed and the results reported. Follow-up provides information for improving future research.

Researchers have recently developed a stronger interest in competitive intelligence, or finding out what competitors are currently doing and forecasting what they are likely to do in the future. The news media, government, the Internet, and a company's own sales people are important sources of competitive intelligence information.

Among the ethical issues in marketing research are protecting the privacy of respondents when collecting and using data, being overly intrusive, deceiving respondents, and selling or fund raising under the guise of research.

Some managers are not highly supportive of research because its task, predicting behavior, is inexact and very difficult to accomplish; researchers and managers often operate with different objectives; and research is conducted sporadically. These problems can be reduced and research made actionable if researchers and managers remain in close contact.

More about the **Census Bureau**

The Census Bureau is a wealth of valuable information for marketers, much of it current and all of it free. But how easy is it to use raw data, such as you found on its website?

Some companies have recognized the challenge marketers face and have stepped in to solve it, by combining census data with other demographic and psychographic data in order to provide useful information. One of these companies is the research firm Claritas, which has developed a method called *geodemographic clustering,* based on zip codes, demographic data from the U.S. Census, and household data collected by Claritas itself. The trade name for the resulting product is PRIZM (short for Potential Rating Index for ZIP Markets).

Using census data on education, income, occupation, housing, ethnicity, urbanization, and other variables, Claritas groups the 36,000 U.S. zip codes into 62 clusters or segments. The firm relies on the principle that people with similar demographic and lifestyle characteristics tend to live near each other. Each cluster is then further examined for similarities in lifestyles and consumption behavior, and each is given a descriptive name such as "kids and cul-de-sacs," "gray power," and "shotguns and pickups." Among other things, PRIZM can tell marketers how consumers in these clusters are likely to spend their leisure time, what kinds of products they frequently purchase and the types of vehicles they drive, and how likely they are to adopt the latest technology. Marketers use this information to identify zip codes for direct-mail promotions, to select locations for retail outlets, and to determine the best mix of products and brands to offer in particular store locations.[12]

www.claritas.com

1. How important is the data from the Census Bureau to a geodemographic clustering technique such as PRIZM?

2. What kind of market research questions do you think a firm like Claritas is best suited to answer?

Key Terms and Concepts

Marketing research (175)
Marketing information system (MkIS) (176)
Decision support system (DSS) (178)
Database (180)
Data warehouse (180)
Data mining (180)
Retail scanners (181)
Single-source data (182)

Situation analysis (183)
Hypothesis (183)
Informal investigation (184)
Primary data (184)
Secondary data (184)
Observation method (186)
Cookie (186)
Survey (187)
Face-to-face interviews (187)

Focus group (187)
Telephone survey (188)
Mail survey (188)
Internet survey (189)
Experiment (190)
Test marketing (190)
Competitive intelligence (194)

Questions and Problems

1. Explain how a marketing information system (MkIS) differs from a decision support system (DSS).

2. Should the task of marketing research go beyond providing data to marketing managers?

3. Evaluate surveys, observation, and experimentation as methods of gathering primary data in the following projects:

   a. A sporting goods retailer wants to determine college students' brand preferences for skis, tennis rackets, and golf clubs.
   b. A supermarket chain wants to determine shoppers' preferences for the physical layout of fixtures and traffic patterns, particularly around checkout counters.
   c. A manufacturer of conveyor belts wants to know who makes buying decisions for his product among present and prospective users.

4. Using the steps in the research process from the text, describe how you would go about investigating the feasibility of a copy shop adjacent to your campus.

5. Examine the procedure that Consumers Union uses in formulating the evaluations of automobiles presented in *Consumer Reports*. (The method is described in the magazine.) Based on the discussion of sampling in the chapter, comment on the procedure.

6. Shortly after a patient used a credit card to pay a bill at a dentist's office, she received a telephone solicitation for dental insurance. This suggests that the credit card company is developing a database using the specific purchasing activity of cardholders and selling it. Does this raise an issue of invasion of privacy?

7. If you were designing an academic program for the marketing researcher of the future, what areas of study would you include?

Interactive Marketing Exercises

1. Assume you work for a manufacturer of a liquid glass cleaner that competes with Windex and Glass Wax. Your manager wants to estimate the amount of product that can be sold throughout the country. To help the manager in this project, prepare a report that shows the following information for your state and, if possible, your home city or county. Carefully identify the sources you use for this information.

   a. Number of households or families.
   b. Income or buying power per family or per household.
   c. Total retail sales in the most recent year for which you can find reliable data.
   d. Total annual sales of food stores, hardware stores, and drug stores.
   e. Total number of food stores.

2. Interview the manager of the bookstore that serves your school about the marketing information system it uses (keep in mind that it may be a very informal system).

   a. What are the data sources?
   b. What are the data collected?
   c. What reports are received and on what schedule?
   d. What problems arise with the MkIS?
   e. How could the MkIS be improved?

Cases for Part 2

CASE 1 — The Gap

Fashioning a New Merchandising Strategy

When businesses all across America began allowing their employees to wear "business-casual" clothes in the 1990s, The Gap was well positioned to capitalize on the new fashion trend. Its classic line of khaki pants and cotton button-down shirts were the epitome of the updated office dress code, and The Gap quickly became the nation's largest specialty apparel retailer. Its sales rose dramatically, from $1.93 billion in 1990 to $11.64 billion in 1999, as the number of Gap stores around the United States (and the rest of the world) grew in number.

But other retailers soon followed The Gap's example of offering simple lines of casual clothes and, in 2000, sales began declining as the company was unable to sustain its momentum. In response, The Gap tried to change its fortunes by offering trendier fare but wound up alienating its core customer base of 20- to 30-year-olds instead. The company's CEO, Mickey Drexler, reflected on the failed strategy by saying, "We probably got a little bored at being consistent and simple. Big mistake."

"Gap was never trendy. Gap was very traditional," agreed one retail analyst. The Gap's trademark style of simple, traditional clothing catapulted it from a single, privately owned store to a retail giant and fashion phenomenon. Its subsequent inability to follow that strategy with one of equivalent impact ultimately cost Drexler his job and has left its customers, employees, and stockholders wondering if The Gap can overcome a muddled position.

Designing a Retail Success Story

Donald Fisher founded The Gap in 1969, when he became frustrated by a store that would not allow him to return a pair of Levi jeans that were too short. He located his first Gap store in San Francisco, and stocked it with Levi's in a wide variety of sizes. The Gap quickly expanded across the country, supported by a fixed 50% markup that Levi Strauss required of all retailers selling its merchandise. However, the Federal Trade Commission ruled that manufacturers such as Levi Strauss could not fix retail prices for their products, and jeans became a discounted product overnight.

The Gap responded by adopting a back-to-basics merchandise strategy, stocking its stores with all-cotton apparel in a deep assortment of colors. The Gap acquired Banana Republic in 1983, a chain of stores featuring safari styles that were popularized by a number of successful movies, such as the *Indiana Jones* series. That trend had waned by 1988, however, and the Banana Republic chain was repositioned as an upscale Gap with more adventurous fashions. Gap branched out even more when it introduced GapKids in 1986 and babyGap fashions in 1990. The company tried to further expand its customer base in 1994 with Old Navy Clothing Co., a chain that carries specially designed apparel and accessories targeted at consumers with incomes of $20,000 to $50,000. Its wide selection offers a department store–style assortment of items for men, women, children and babies, and is priced 20% to 25% below The Gap's merchandise. Along the way, The Gap also became a publicly traded company, making the Fisher family extremely wealthy.

Falling into the Gap

Millard "Mickey" Drexler was appointed president of Gap, Inc., in 1987 and later promoted to CEO. He was credited with anticipating the khaki craze of the 1990s and successfully guiding The Gap's merchandising strategy by accurately predicting the whims of fickle shoppers. As sales at The Gap took off in the early 1990s, Drexler made plans for aggressive expansion, more than doubling the number of company stores between 1996 and 2001. By October of 2001, The Gap boasted 2,759 stores, followed by Old Navy with 732, and Banana Republic with 422. The total number had risen to more than 4,100 by February of 2002.

However, The Gap's increase in sales began to depend on new store openings because sales at existing stores were not increasing. In 2000, The Gap posted revenue of $13.67 billion and profits of $877 million. Sales were barely higher in 2001 ($13.8 billion) but the company lost $7.8 million. That was because sales at stores open at least one year began falling in mid-2000, dropping 5% for the year, followed by an 11% decline in 2001. Despite this downturn, which showed no signs of stopping as late as June of 2002, The Gap continued expanding, adding as much as 25% more square footage in the late 1990s and 2000. Drexler proposed adding another 10% in 2002, but scaled that figure back to 3% in March of that year. "Who in their right mind would have expanded like The Gap in the face of such terrible results?" asked one retail consultant.

Trying On a Trendier Style

A number of factors were blamed for The Gap's problems, including a weak economy and more intense competition. As it turns out, manufacturing khakis and button-down shirts and T-shirts isn't all that difficult, and a number of other retail chains tried on The Gap's merchandising strategy for size. Discounters such as Target, Wal-Mart, and Kohl's were particularly successful in luring loyal customers from The Gap and Old Navy. One study found that prices for comparable items at Target were an average of 27% less than at Old Navy.

In an attempt to increase sales by attracting a new market segment, The Gap began offering trendier fashions to appeal to the country's population of 31.3 million teens, a group that spent $153 billion on clothes in 1999. But the teen market is a fickle one, and predicting what they will purchase at any given time is a gamble. In addition, they are extremely price sensitive and will sacrifice quality for economy because they tend to wear their clothes for only one season. According to a retail consultant, "Quality of the clothes doesn't mean anything—that's a parent thing. It's cool as long as their friends are wearing it."

By courting teens, The Gap began to more aggressively compete with a new array of retail chains, including Abercrombie & Fitch, American Eagle, Gadzooks, Rave, and Deb Shops. However, these stores are very clear in their mission: They want those teen bucks and their fashions are not meant to appeal to many adults. The Gap, on the other hand, continued to try to attract 20- to 30-year-olds while appealing to the high school set as well. This led to some unfortunate decisions, including capri pants and polo shirts in every conceivable color followed by low-rise jeans and sparkly T-shirts and then a plethora of beige sweaters and brown pants. These styles alienated The Gap's core audience of twentysomethings while failing to appeal to teens. Even Drexler was critical of his company's "fashion don'ts," describing one line of jeans as being "very strange looking with patches on the back that are very wrong." He also conceded "We changed too much, too quickly in ways that weren't consistent with our brands."

Banana Republic and Old Navy made their own share of merchandising blunders. Old Navy was criticized for being too trendy and responded by developing the Old Navy Collection, a line designed to appeal to older shoppers. Banana Republic went through a purple faze in 2000 that apparently made its customers very blue because the line was a failure.

In addition, these sibling chains began cannibalizing The Gap's sales. As the economy weakened, customers defected from The Gap to Old Navy. And as The Gap began introducing trendier fare, some of its loyal customers upgraded to Banana Republic. "Right now I just go to Gap for jeans," commented one 27-year-old Gap shopper. "I don't really go there for work wear—that's where Banana Republic comes into play." Other Gap shoppers were put off when Old Navy stores began opening. Its lower-cost merchandise was similar to that being sold at The Gap, but of lesser quality, and some people felt that translated into poorer quality at The Gap stores as well. In addition, The Gap introduced a line of clothes in 2001 that featured unfinished edges on its jackets and jeans and these styles contributed to the quality complaints. "It looks incomplete instead of avant-garde," complained another 27-year-old consumer. Management at The Gap denied the quality criticism however, and one spokesperson maintained very clearly, "We've not reduced the quality we put into our merchandise."

Another factor that hurts The Gap when competing against smaller chains is its sheer size. It takes The Gap nine months, twice as long as Abercrombie & Fitch, for example, to introduce a new line of merchandise, making it much harder to respond to the fickle tastes of teenagers. In contrast, Zara, a hot retail clothing chain in Europe, needs a mere three weeks to take its clothes from conception to display. At Zara, store managers are given the ability to interact directly with fashion designers and product managers via the Internet. The ideas are swiftly turned into actual designs and are then manufactured at nearby plants.

Instead of relying on Third World countries for its labor pool, as most clothing manufacturers do, Zara decided to keep its operations closer to its customers. "We need to give consumers what they want, and if I go to South America or Asia to make clothes, I simply can't move fast enough," explained Jose Maria Castellano, CEO of Inditex, Zara's corporate parent. While Zara's fashions are more like those found in Banana Republic than The Gap, its prices are more comparable to Old Navy's. It keeps its prices down while achieving an astonishingly fast time to market by limiting its advertising and reliance on sales promotions. Because it is capable of responding to its customers' desires so quickly, Zara rarely marks down prices and is capable of refreshing its stores' offerings twice a week. In fairness, Zara is much smaller than The Gap, which contributes to its nimbleness, but its type of market responsiveness defines a challenge for The Gap.

Tightening Its Belt

In 2001, management of The Gap began taking steps to get the company back on track. John Lillie, a member of the company's board of directors, was appointed vice chairman. He made the tough decision to lay off 1,040 employees in July and later announced that The Gap would reduce its capital spending to $400 million in 2002, down from $1 billion in 2001. And despite continued plans for expansion, albeit on a much smaller scale than in previous years, 51 of The Gap's less successful stores were closed in 2001.

The Gap continued to sell items over the Web, however. It introduced its first site, *www.gap.com* in 1997, followed by *www.gapkids.com* and *www.babygap.com* in 1998. Soon after, *www.bananarepublic.com* went online in 1999, and *www.oldnavy.com* went live in 2000. On The Gap's site shoppers often can find online coupons and significantly discounted prices. In addition, maternity clothes are offered only via the Web and not in Gap stores. Shoppers at *www.gap.com* also note that the website features a larger selection of basic items, such as belts and socks, than its sister stores.

In the spring of 2002, The Gap unveiled a new series of television commercials directed by such popular Hollywood directors as Cameron Crowe and the Coen brothers. The ads were shot in black and white and starred a variety of hot actors, including Dennis Hopper, Orlando Bloom, and Christina Ricci. Billboard and print ads featured Kiefer Sutherland, Danny Glover, and Matthew Broderick. (Several of the company's current print ads can be seen at The Gap's corporate site, *www.gapinc.com*.) It's clear that these star-studded spots are an attempt to recapture the magic of a previous, award-winning campaign The Gap produced in 1988 called, "Individuals of Style." This series of ads featured athletes, musicians, actors, and other celebrities simply wearing Gap fashions and looking cool. Of the new ads, one Gap executive explained, "These spots convey a sense of summer that's fun for everyone to imagine, featuring iconic Gap clothes that everyone loves to wear."

That last part is still open to debate. The Gap's 2002 spring line was indeed reminiscent of its original back-to-basics strategy, and yet did not sell particularly well. This led to an announcement by Drexler in May 2002 that he would be retiring later in the year as soon as a new CEO could be appointed. He explained his imminent departure by saying, "I believe Gap, Old Navy, and Banana Republic are now in a position to offer the product assortments our customers expect and that reflect what our brands have always stood for. The time is right for me to move on, and for the company to bring in new leadership to take the business forward." Only time will tell whether the company's new CEO can help The Gap find a way not to lose its proverbial shirt.

Questions

1. What social influences in consumer behavior are likely to have an effect on The Gap's future marketing strategy?

2. How would you segment the markets for The Gap, Banana Republic, and Old Navy?

3. Is it possible to define three distinct target markets for these chains?

4. What role has The Gap's original position played in its subsequent performance? Is it possible to reposition a store such as The Gap?

www.gap.com

CASE 2

UPS versus FedEx versus USPS

Delivering New Services for Their Customers

United Parcel Service (UPS) was founded in 1907 by Jim Casey after he borrowed $100 from a friend to start a parcel-delivery and messenger service in Seattle, Washington. Hired to deliver packages from local department stores to shoppers' homes, UPS's early "fleet" of delivery vehicles included a Model T and a few motorcycles. As UPS approaches its centennial, it has a fleet of 150,000+ trucks and over 500 planes, and serves every company in *Fortune* magazine's list of the 1,000 largest companies in the U.S.

UPS had very little private-sector competition in the package delivery market until Frederick Smith started Federal Express (now FedEx) in 1971. Whereas UPS was known for its reliable, albeit somewhat slow, delivery of parcels via ground transportation, FedEx invested in an extensive fleet of planes in order to "absolutely, positively" deliver its clients' documents and parcels overnight. Although FedEx charged a premium for its speedy service and sophisticated tracking system, businesses large and small willingly paid for this previously unavailable expedience.

Both companies succeeded in luring business away from the ubiquitous and once dominant United States Postal Service (USPS). This federal agency was officially established in 1775, with Ben Franklin as the first postmaster general. USPS mail carriers became famous for their tenacious delivery of mail despite rain, snow, or other bad weather. Today, USPS is responsible for more than 46% of the world's card and letter deliveries.

By the 1980s, the preferred suppliers of parcel-delivery duties had become clear for commercial and residential customers. For less important packages that required no tracking and that could be left in a mailbox or at the front door, USPS was fine. UPS was the favored choice for parcels via slower, ground transportation when some tracking capabilities were required. FedEx was most often used for critical documents and packages that had to be received the next day.

Since then, a variety of factors have dramatically changed the parcel-delivery business. Globalization and advancements in technology, including the Internet, have created new opportunities and challenges for shipping suppliers as well as their customers. Thus, in order to remain competitive, UPS, FedEx, and USPS have been forced to rethink their core businesses. As a result, they have all begun offering competing services, at times even partnering together to meet the needs of their customers. However, each of the three remains dominant in its core niche and has successfully expanded into other areas of shipping as well.

Boxing Up the Competition

Just as it was in 1907, UPS's primary business is ground transportation. No other company, or even the USPS, is as adept, reliable, and economical at moving packages to any address, residential or commercial. For years, UPS has relied on a tightly defined business model that prescribes everything from how the firm's drivers should dress (for example, shirts can't be unbuttoned below the top button) to how they should walk (briskly, but without running).

Most of UPS's executives began their careers in the driver's seat, learning to adhere to these policies.

UPS moves over 14 million packages each day, and almost 11 million of those are via ground transportation. But Big Brown, as the company is often called, has also expanded its air express business to compete head-to-head with FedEx, often performing the task in a more efficient and less costly manner than its competitor. For example, UPS utilizes trucks instead of airplanes to deliver packages up to 500 miles overnight. This translates into an average cost per package of $6.65, compared to $11.89 for FedEx. Another challenge for FedEx is that its large corporate clients have the power to negotiate lower prices. UPS still caters to the small business market and, thus, is less affected by large corporate discounts. One analyst observed, "FedEx for years had been turning up its nose on the small-parcel business, and it has hurt them."

The differences in operations are reflected in the firms' performance. For the 2002 fiscal year, UPS reported net income of over $3 billion on revenue (sales volume) of more than $31 billion. By comparison, FedEx had revenues of just over $20 billion and earnings of $700 million. USPS, as a federal agency, does not issue comparable figures, but typically has been plagued by large annual losses.

To further compete with FedEx's overnight delivery service, UPS upgraded its own tracking system so that as a customer signs to accept a delivery, the information is immediately transmitted to UPS's computers. Senders can go online to receive real-time status reports about their shipments, including the time of delivery. These services are critical in a time when companies are under intense pressure to deliver goods to their clients in a timely manner. UPS now delivers over 1 million air express packages each day, compared to almost 3 million for FedEx.

Retaliating, FedEx is challenging UPS on the ground. Between 1999 and 2001, FedEx spent about $4 *billion* on the purchase and upgrade of delivery companies with trucking operations. It wasn't an easy transition, however, and it is taking considerable time for FedEx to integrate the new services into its existing operations. The company still utilizes two different fleets for air and ground deliveries. "UPS moved quicker into FedEx's turf than FedEx moved into that of UPS," explained a former consultant for FedEx.

In 2000, FedEx made about 1.5 million ground deliveries, and captured 11% of the market. Its capabilities were sorely tested, however, when the terrorist attacks on September 11, 2001, shut down the nation's commercial airspace. FedEx immediately began to acquire additional trucks to move its cargo all over the country. Amazingly, every package reached its final destination within two days, even those that were sent from Seattle to New York.

Such efficiencies by UPS and FedEx have hurt USPS. Although it provides confirmation of delivery for priority mail and tracking and confirmation services for express (or overnight) mail, a report issued by the Office of the Consumer Advocate berated USPS for "not providing the priority service promised." But, as a government monopoly, USPS does not have the ability to operate like a regular business. It cannot freely raise or lower prices or add new services. "It is not good business to take up to two years to be able to change your prices in response to the marketplace," a USPS senior vice president stated.

With more than 900,000 employees, the USPS spends 76% of its revenues on labor, compared to 56% for UPS and 42% for FedEx. The agency lost about $3 billion in 2001. Unlike its competitors, USPS must deliver to 134 million addresses and an additional 20 million post office boxes each day. And those numbers are growing by 2 million every year. In addition, it is not allowed to unilaterally shut down any post offices, despite the fact that only one-quarter of them are profitable. As a result, it is asking Congress for expanded powers, an idea that has met fierce resistance from its competitors. "We are very concerned [they] will willingly undercut the competition, and lose money, in order to gain volume," contended a UPS spokesperson. The USPS has even hinted that it is willing to forgo its protected position as a federally controlled monopoly in order to institute new business practices.

Being on Time with an Internet Strategy

Another challenge facing USPS is the Internet, which has facilitated the use of e-mail and online bill-paying systems. Bank mailings have decreased 18% since 1996, and first-class mail volume is down. In response, USPS is taking advantage of the Internet to give its customers an alternative form of document distribution. UPS is also allowing customers to electronically transmit documents via a secure website. Encryption technology is used so that only the document's sender and recipient can access it, an attractive feature for companies such as law offices and brokerage houses that often need to send "sensitive" materials. Because overnight deliveries of such documents comprise 40% of FedEx's overnight deliveries, such services might eventually cut into its bottom line. For now, the impact is minimal, but as businesses begin to embrace this technology in the future, one transportation consultant warned, "FedEx is exposed."

The Web has also given rise to a number of e-tailing companies that require a means for shipping their goods to customers. With its dominance in ground shipping in the late 1990s, UPS was well positioned to establish a foothold in this market. By 2001, the company was responsible for 55% of all online shipments. By comparison, FedEx had 10% of the business, with USPS somewhere in between.

Trucking into New Markets

Besides shipping packages for e-tailing enterprises, UPS has begun to help these same clients streamline their operations by handling a variety of their physical distribution tasks. This new venture is capable of handling warehousing, picking and packing, product repair, and customer service. To support these endeavors, UPS invested over $11 *billion* in technology during the 1990s. UPS's chief executive officer at the time stated, "We're becoming a logistics company because we have many customers who don't want to do certain things themselves any longer, customers who are saying, 'I want to produce a product, and after that I want you to take care of it.'" Validating the substantial investment, UPS's logistics business is increasing by 40% each year.

FedEx has also ventured into logistics, but with mixed results. It built a warehouse in Singapore to handle National Semiconductor's chip inventory, but lost the business to UPS in 1999. UPS is also helping Ford coordinate its car deliveries to dealerships, and in just one year, reportedly saved the company $240 million. A vice president of logistics for Ford said, "Speed is the mind-set at UPS. They'll meet a deadline at any cost."

UPS is hoping to lure additional customers to its warehouse in Singapore and is intent on further expanding its international presence. It was recently awarded six air routes between the U.S. and China, cracking FedEx's dominance in that particular market. FedEx has between 10% and 15% of the international overnight market, and UPS accounts for between 8% and 12%. The leaders are DHL and TNT Post Group. Currently, overnight deliveries comprise only 10% of international shipments, so both companies see potential opportunities for growth. So too does USPS, which now offers expedited delivery service from the U.S. to other countries.

Parceling Up the Workload

As FedEx and UPS continue to battle each other in the air and on the ground, both are finding unique ways to strengthen their own positions. In 2001, USPS agreed to pay FedEx a little less than $1 billion a year to carry airmail on its extensive fleet of aircraft. By doing so, USPS is hoping to reduce its own fleet and its reliance on commercial airlines for mail transportation, as well as improve Express (next-day) and Priority Mail (several-day) services. Conversely, FedEx is paying more than $100 million to place its collection boxes at post office locations around the country. "This is a lot like the U.S. Department of Transportation building roads for the exclusive use of Chrysler vehicles to the exclusion of all other vehicles," complained a spokesperson from UPS.

U.S. businesses spend about $15 billion each year preparing their mailings so that they qualify for bulk-mail discounts. Thus, in 2001, UPS began picking up first-class mail bound for the USPS from small businesses to help them realize volume discounts by combining the items into bulk shipments. UPS charges about $2 a mail sack, and in return, customers save a little money and their mail reaches the local post office more quickly. UPS may have very ambitious goals with respect to first-class mail. "If Congress were ever to open up mail delivery to competition, UPS would be the first one in the door," observed the executive director of the Mailers Council.

Exhibiting a willingness to do everything from taking over a company's physical distribution function to just picking up a customer's outgoing mail and delivering it to the post office, UPS is seeking to retain its leadership position in the business of delivering letters and packages. In turn, FedEx and USPS are constantly scrambling to protect their positions and to find additional ways in which to help individuals, companies, and other organizations meet their delivery needs.

Questions

1. a. Would the purchase of delivery services for letters and packages always be the same buy class for a large company?
    b. How would buy class affect the buying-decision process for this particular product?
2. How, if at all, would the motives and decision processes used in selecting delivery services for letters and packages differ between individual consumers and business users?

3. What type(s) of target-market strategies are being used by UPS, FedEx, and USPS?

www.ups.com

www.fedex.com/us

www.usps.com

Sources

Case 1: The Gap *www.gapinc.com*, May 2002; Miguel Helft, "Fashion Fast Forward," *Business 2.0*, May 2002, pp. 60–66; Marc Graser, "H'wood Talent Boosts Clothier's Star Wattage," *Variety*, Apr. 29, 2002, p. 9; Julie Creswell, "Gap Got Junked," *Fortune*, Mar. 18, 2002, p. 93; Victoria Colliver, "Gap Pins Loss on Poor Fashion Sense," *The San Francisco Chronicle*, Feb. 27, 2002, p. B1; Louise Lee and Nanette Byrnes, "More than Just a Bad Patch," *BusinessWeek*, Feb. 11, 2002, p. 36; Amy Merrick, "Analysts Are Divided on Gap's Actual Value," *The Wall Street Journal*, Jan. 11, 2002, p. C2; Michael Totty, "The Consumers' Choice," *The Wall Street Journal*, Dec. 10, 2001, p. R6; Amy Merrick, "Gap's Image Is Wearing Out," *The Wall Street Journal*, Dec. 6, 2001, p. B1; Louise Lee, "Gap: Missing That Ol' Mickey Magic," *BusinessWeek*, Oct. 29, 2001, pp. 86–88; Amy Merrick, "CEO Concedes Gap Made Errors, Promises Senior-Level Oversight," *The Wall Street Journal*, Sep. 10, 2001, p. B6; Calmetta Coleman, "Gap Keeps Struggling Amid Myriad Turnaround Plans," *The Wall Street Journal*, Mar. 5, 2001, p. B4; Lorrie Grant, "Like, Be Hip or Be Gone in Teen Clothes Market," *USA TODAY*, July 5, 2000, p. 8B.

Case 2: UPS versus FedEx versus USPS
www.hoovers.com, accessed Feb. 7, 2002; Charles Haddad, "FedEx: Gaining on the Ground," *Business Week*, Dec. 16, 2002, p. 126; Michael Liedtke, "Eskew Hustles to Keep Brown in the Black," St. Louis Post-Dispatch, Nov. 29, 2002, pp. C18–C19; David Hannon, "Logistics: What's Hot," *Purchasing*, Apr. 18, 2002, p. 43; "US Postal Service Puts on the Moves," *Transportation & Distribution*, February 2002, p. 11; Mark Tatge, "Start the Ground War," *Forbes*, Nov. 26, 2001, p. 146; Abbey Klaassen, "UPS: Dale Hayes," *Advertising Age*, Oct. 8, 2001, p. S16; Rick Brooks, "Got Mail?" *The Wall Street Journal*, June 22, 2001, p. B1; Charles Haddad and Jack Ewing, "Ground Wars," *Business Week*, May 21, 2001, pp. 64–68; Marianne Lavelle, "Why the Postman Can't Deliver Profits," *U.S. News & World Report*, Apr. 9, 2001, p. 46; Rick Brooks, "Outside the Box," *The Wall Street Journal*, Feb. 12, 2001, p. R20; Randolph Schmid, "Post Office, FedEx Reach Agreement to Work Together," *St. Louis Post-Dispatch*, Jan. 11, 2001, p. C1; Brian O'Reilly, "They've Got Mail!" *Fortune*, Feb. 7, 2000, pp. 100–101+; Kelly Barron, "Logistics in Brown," *Forbes*, Jan. 10, 2000, pp. 78–83; and *www.usps.com*, accessed June 15, 2002.

8 Product Planning and Development

"The Segway HT 'will be to cars what the car was to the horse and buggy.'"

Will the **Segway HT** Start Rolling?

The next big revolution in transportation might have no seats, steering wheel, roof, air conditioner, or radio—not even cup holders. It does, however, have two motors, five solid-state gyroscopes, and two tilt sensors—along with a top speed of 12 miles per hour.

The Segway™ Human Transporter (HT), sometimes called "Ginger" and "IT," is a battery-powered one-person scooter. Its inventor, Dean Kamen, expects IT will revolutionize short-distance travel. Looking like a cross between a lawn mower and the popular kids' scooter, the Razor, the Segway HT has been compared—perhaps with some exaggeration—to the Internet in terms of its potential to change the world. According to Kamen, the Segway HT "will be to cars what the car was to the horse and buggy." He pictures urban centers from which cars have been banished to make room for millions of "empowered pedestrians" riding the Segway HT.

Kamen, a self-taught physicist who holds more than 150 patents, has spent $100 million to give birth to a completely new product. Kamen is president of DEKA Research and Development Corp. and chairman of Segway LLC, which can produce 40,000 Segway HTs a month.

Kamen anticipates—or at least hopes—that college students, police forces, letter carriers, and vast numbers of third-world families will line up to buy the two-wheeled transporter. It's cheap to run and easy to maneuver. With the ability to travel 11 to 17 miles on one battery charge (which costs about 10 cents), the commercial version of the Segway HT can carry a 250-pound passenger and 75 pounds of cargo.

The scooter's computers monitor the user's center of gravity 100 times a second. When the rider leans forward, the Segway HT moves in that direction; and the opposite is true as well. Those who have ridden it describe the human–machine interface as resembling a form of mind reading. Says Kamen, "When you use a Segway HT, there's a gyroscope that acts like your inner ear, a computer that acts like your brain, motors that act like your muscles, wheels that act like your feet."

Even before the nature of the product was widely known, the project generated much publicity. The hype notwithstanding, Kamen wants the machine to be taken seriously, viewed as a viable solution to worldwide problems of overcrowding, poor transportation infrastructure, pollution, and the high cost of fuel.

Kamen is first targeting commercial customers such as the U.S. Postal Service, GE Plastics, Disney, and the National Parks Service, all organizations that can afford the $5,000 price tag for the industrial model. The Postal Service has purchased 20 Segway HTs and is evaluating them with respect to different routes, climates, and personnel needs. Rumors and skepticism have surrounded the development of the Segway HT. A consumer model of the Segway HT will eventually sell for about $3,000. Kamen's hope is that selling first to major corporations and

 www.segway.com

government agencies first will pave the way to the consumer marketplace.

A tireless inventor, Kamen isn't done tinkering with his newest creation. Rumor, which he has exploited so well in the past, now has it that the Stirling engine—created 200 years ago to run quietly, efficiently, and without exhaust—is about to find its first large-scale commercial application in the next version of the Segway Human Transporter.[1]

Can Kamen and Segway LLC make the Segway HT a success? Why or why not?

Three factors stand out in the Segway case. First, both relatively small entrepreneurs like Dean Kamen and giant companies like General Motors need to develop new products in order to attain success in the marketplace. Second, the nature of new products is as extensive as one's imagination. And third, success with new products is not guaranteed, as numerous failures (including costly flops such as the Edsel automobile, the Premier "smokeless" cigarette, and Corfam artificial leather) indicate.

This chapter will provide you with insights regarding each of these important issues. Specifically, after studying this chapter, you should be able to explain:

Chapter Goals

- The meaning of the word *product* in its fullest sense.
- What a "new" product is.
- The classification of consumer and business products.
- The relevance of these product classifications to marketing strategy.
- The importance of product innovation.
- The stages in the new-product development process.
- Criteria for adding a product to a company's line.
- Adoption and diffusion processes for new products.
- Organizational structures for product planning and development.

The Meaning of Product

In a *narrow* sense, a product is a set of basic attributes assembled in an identifiable form. Each product is identified by a commonly understood descriptive (or generic) name, such as steel, insurance, tennis rackets, or entertainment. Features such as brand name and postsale service that appeal to consumer emotions or add value play no part in this narrow interpretation. According to this interpretation, an Apple and a Compaq would be the same good—a personal computer. And Disney World and Six Flags would be equivalent—both are amusement parks.

In marketing we need a broader definition of product to indicate that customers are not really buying a set of attributes, but rather benefits that satisfy their needs. Thus users don't want sandpaper; they really want a smooth surface. To develop a sufficiently broad definition, let's start with *product* as an umbrella term covering goods, services, places, persons, and ideas. Throughout this book, when we speak of products, we are using this broad connotation.

Thus a product that provides benefits can be something other than a tangible *good*. Red Roof Inn's product is a *service* that provides the benefit of a comfortable night's rest at a reasonable price. The Hawaii Visitors Bureau's product is a *place* that provides sun and sand, relaxation, romance, cross-cultural experiences, and other benefits. In a political campaign, the Democratic or Republican Party's product is a *person* (candidate) whom the party wants you to buy (vote for). The American Cancer Society is selling an *idea* and the benefits of not smoking. In Chapter 11 we discuss in more detail the marketing of intangible products such as services and ideas.

www.visit.hawaii.org

To further expand our definition, we treat each *brand* as a separate product. In this sense, two Internet service providers, America Online and MSN, for example, are different products. Squibb's aspirin and Bayer aspirin are also separate products, even though the only physical difference may be the brand name on the tablet. But the brand name suggests a product difference to the consumer, and this brings the concept of want-satisfaction into the definition. Going a step further, some consumers prefer one brand (Squibb's) and others favor a different brand (Bayer) of a similar product.

Any change in a feature (design, color, size, packaging), however minor, creates another product. Each such change provides the seller with an opportunity to use a new set of appeals to reach what essentially may be a new market. Pain relievers (Tylenol, Ascriptin) in capsule form are a different product from the same brand in tablet form, even though the chemical contents of the tablet and the capsule are identical. Seemingly minor product changes can be the key to success (or failure). On the minus side, what seemed like a relatively small change in the formula for Coke in 1985 turned out to be a huge mistake. On the plus side, after the Arby's sandwich chain reworked its "BLT" by adding more bacon and switching to honey wheat bread, stores that sold this item enjoyed a 6% sales increase.[2]

We can broaden this interpretation still further. A Sony big-screen TV bought in a discount store on a cash-and-carry basis is a different product than the identical model purchased in a department store. In the department store, the customer may pay a higher price for the TV but buys it on credit, has it delivered free of charge, and receives other store services. Our concept of a product now includes the services that accompany it when purchased. A prime example is the warranty that assures a buyer of free replacement or repair of a defective product during a specified period of time.

We're now ready for a definition that is useful to marketers. As shown in Figure 8.1, a **product** is a set of tangible and intangible attributes, which may include

FIGURE 8.1

The Attributes Comprising a Product.

A product is much more than a set of physical attributes.

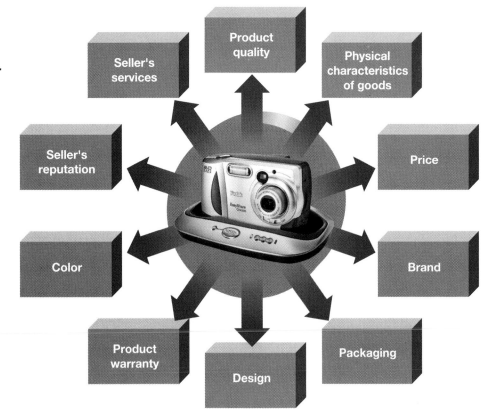

packaging, color, price, quality, and brand, plus the seller's services and reputation. A product may be a good, service, place, person, or idea. In essence, then, customers are buying much more than a set of attributes when they buy a product. They are buying want-satisfaction in the form of the benefits they expect to receive from the product.

Classifications of Products

To design effective marketing programs, organizations need to know what kinds of products they are offering to potential customers. Thus it's helpful to separate *products* into homogeneous categories. First we will divide all products into two categories—consumer products and business products—that parallel our description of the total market. Then we will subdivide each category.

Consumer and Business Products

Consumer products are intended for personal consumption by households. **Business products** are intended for resale, for use in producing other products, or for providing services in an organization. Thus the two types of products are distinguished on the basis of *who will use them* and *how they will be used.*

The position of a product in its distribution channel has no bearing on its classification. Kellogg's cornflakes are categorized as consumer products, even if they are in the manufacturer's warehouses, in a freight line's trucks, or on retailers' shelves, *if ultimately they will be used in their present form by households.* However, Kellogg's cornflakes sold to restaurants and other institutions are categorized as business products no matter where they are in the distribution system.

Often it is not possible to place a product in only one class or the other. Seats on a United Airlines flight from Chicago to Phoenix may be considered a consumer product if purchased by students or a family going on vacation. But a seat on the same flight bought by a sales rep on a work-related trip is categorized as a business product. United Airlines, or any other company in a similar situation, recognizes that its product falls into both categories and therefore develops separate marketing programs for each market.

These distinctions may seem like "splitting hairs," but they are necessary for the strategic planning of marketing programs. Each major category of products ultimately goes to a distinctive type of market and thus requires different marketing methods.[3]

Classification of Consumer Goods

For marketing purposes, distinguishing consumer goods from business goods is helpful but only a first step. The range of consumer goods is still too broad to be useful. Consequently, as shown in Table 8.1, they are further classified as convenience goods, shopping goods, and specialty goods, and also as unsought goods (not in table). This classification is not based on intrinsic differences in the products themselves. Rather, it is based on how consumers go about buying a particular product. Depending on the buying behavior of different consumers, a single product—such as wine or software—can fall into more than one of the four categories.

Convenience Goods   A tangible product that the consumer feels comfortable purchasing without gathering additional information and then actually buys with a minimum of effort is termed a **convenience good.** Normally the advantages resulting from shopping around to compare price and quality are not considered worth the required time and effort. A consumer is willing to accept any of several brands and thus will buy the one that is most accessible. For most buyers, convenience goods

TABLE 8.1

Categories of Consumer Goods: Characteristics and Marketing Considerations

	Type of Product*		
	Convenience	**Shopping**	**Specialty**
Examples	Canned fruit	Furniture	Expensive suits
Characteristics			
Time and effort devoted by consumer to shopping	Very little	Considerable	As much as necessary to find desired brand
Time spent planning the purchase	Very little	Considerable	Considerable
How soon want is satisfied after it arises	Immediately	Relatively long time	Relatively long time
Are price and quality compared?	No	Yes	No
Price	Usually low	Usually high	Usually high
Purchase frequency	Usually frequent	Infrequent	Infrequent
Marketing Considerations			
Length of channel	Long	Short	Short to very short
Retailer	Relatively unimportant	Important	Very important
Number of outlets	As many as possible	Few	Few; often only one in a market
Stock turnover	High	Lower	Lower
Gross margin	Low	High	High
Responsibility for advertising	Producer's	Joint responsibility	Joint responsibility
Point-of-purchaser display	Very important	Less important	Less important
Brand or store name	Brand name	Store name	Both
Packaging	Very important	Less important	Less important

*Unsought products are not included. See text explanation.

include many food items, inexpensive candy, drug sundries such as aspirin and tooth-paste, and staple hardware items such as light bulbs and batteries.

Convenience goods typically have a low unit price, are not bulky, and are not greatly affected by fad and fashion. They usually are purchased frequently, although this is not a necessary characteristic. Items such as Christmas tree lights or Mother's Day cards are convenience goods for most people, even though they may be bought only once a year.

Because a convenience good must be readily accessible when consumer demand arises, a manufacturer must be prepared to distribute it widely and rapidly. However, because most retail stores sell only a small volume of the total output of a convenience good (such as a particular brand of candy bar), it is not economical for the manufacturer to sell directly to all retail outlets. Instead the producer relies on wholesalers to sell the product to selected retailers.

Retailers usually carry several brands of the same type of convenience item, because consumers frequently have a brand preference (even though they will accept a substitute). However, retail outlets are not inclined to advertise convenience goods because many other stores carry the same brands (such as General Electric and Sylvania light bulbs). Thus any advertising by one retailer would help its competitors. As a result, much of the advertising burden is shifted to the manufacturer.

Shopping Goods

A tangible product for which a consumer wants to compare quality, price, and perhaps style in several stores before making a purchase is considered a **shopping good.** Examples of shopping goods—at least for most consumers—are fashionable apparel, furniture, major appliances, and automobiles. The process of searching and comparing continues as long as the customer believes that the potential benefits from more information are worth the additional time and effort spent shopping. A *better* purchase might be saving several hundred dollars on the purchase of a new car or finally finding a software package that prepares financial statements in the manner desired by the buyer.

With shopping goods, buying habits affect the distribution and promotion strategies of both manufacturers and middlemen (such as retail stores). Shopping-goods manufacturers require fewer retail outlets because consumers are willing to look around for what they want. To facilitate comparison shopping, manufacturers often try to place their products in stores located near other stores carrying competing items. Similarly, department stores and other retailers that carry primarily shopping goods like to be near each other. Further, many retailers carry several brands of the same shopping good to allow shoppers to make in-store comparisons.

Manufacturers usually work closely with retailers in marketing shopping goods. Because manufacturers use fewer retail outlets, they are more dependent on those they do select. Retail stores typically buy shopping goods in large quantities, and it's common for manufacturers to distribute directly to retailers. To buyers of a shopping good, the reputations of the stores carrying the product often are more important than the images of the manufacturers. For example, a consumer may be more loyal to a Circuit City store than to various brands of audio and video equipment, such as JVC and Sanyo.

Specialty Goods

A tangible product for which a consumer has a strong brand preference and is willing to expend substantial time and effort in locating the desired brand is called a **specialty good.** The consumer is willing to forgo more accessible substitutes to search for and purchase the desired brand. Examples of products usually categorized as specialty goods include expensive men's suits, stereo sound equipment, health foods, photographic equipment, and, for many people, new automobiles and certain home appliances. Various brands, such as Armani, Nikon, and BMW, have achieved specialty-good status in the minds of some consumers.

www.giorgioarmani.com

Attaining specialty-good standing in consumers' minds, as Cole Haan has done, is highly desirable. Shoppers exert added effort to locate a specialty good, and they tend to be less concerned about price than other features of this type of product. Of course, becoming a specialty good requires not just outstanding quality or value but also large expenditures on advertising to build a distinctive brand image.

www.colehaan.com

Because consumers *insist* on a particular brand and are willing to expend considerable effort to find it, manufacturers can use few retail outlets. Ordinarily the manufacturer deals directly with these retailers. The retailers are extremely important, particularly if the manufacturer uses only one in each geographic area. And where the opportunity to handle the product is highly valued, the retailer may be quite willing to abide by the producer's policies regarding the amount of inventory that needs to be maintained, how the product should be advertised, or other marketing factors.

Because relatively few outlets are used *and* the product's brand name is important to buyers, both manufacturer and retailer advertise the product extensively. Often the manufacturer pays a portion of the retailer's advertising costs, and the name of the store carrying the specialty good frequently appears in the manufacturer's ads.

Unsought Goods

There's one more, quite different category of goods. In fact, it's so unlike the other three categories that we have not included it in Table 8.1. Nevertheless, because some firms sell unsought goods, this category deserves brief discussion.

An **unsought good** is a new product that the consumer is not yet aware of *or* a product that the consumer is aware of but does not want right now. A battery-powered one-person scooter, as described in the chapter-opening case, might be an unsought good for most people, either because they are unaware of it or do not want one after learning about it. Bathroom tissue made strictly from cotton fiber, including the Cottonelle brand, would seem to be an unsought good. Despite a commercial in which a roll of tissues says, "I've got a silk gentle touch you can actually feel," few consumers know about the product and fewer still seek it out at the store.[4] Other unwanted products might include gravestones for those who have not lost a loved one, and snow tires in the summer.

As the name suggests, a firm faces a very difficult, perhaps impossible, advertising and personal selling job when trying to market unsought goods. The best approach may be to make consumers aware of the product and continue to remind them of it, so they will buy the advertised brand when the need arises. Marketers of unsought goods try to build familiarity with their offerings by placing ads on bus stop benches or in church bulletins.

Classification of Business Goods

As with consumer goods, the general category of *business goods* is too broad to use in developing a marketing program. Consequently, as shown in Table 8.2, we separate business goods into five categories: raw materials, fabricating materials and parts, installations, accessory equipment, and operating supplies. This classification is based on the product's broad *uses*. For example, a business good may be used in producing other products, in operating an organization, and in other ways we will discuss.

Raw Materials

Business goods that become part of another tangible product prior to being processed in any way (except as necessary to assist in handling the product) are considered **raw materials**. Raw materials include:

- Goods found in their natural state, such as minerals, land, and products of the forests and the seas.

- Agricultural products, such as cotton, fruits, livestock, and animal products, including eggs and raw milk.

Because of their distinctive attributes, these two groups of raw materials usually are marketed differently. For instance, the supply of raw materials in their natural state is limited, cannot be substantially increased, and often involves only a few

TABLE 8.2

Categories of Business Goods: Characteristics and Marketing Considerations

	Type of Product				
	Raw Materials	**Fabricating Materials and Parts**	**Installations**	**Accessory Equipment**	**Operating Supplies**
Examples	Iron ore	Engine blocks	Blast furnaces	Storage racks	Paper clips
Characteristics					
Unit price	Very low	Low	Very high	Medium	Low
Length of life	Very short	Depends on final product	Very long	Long	Short
Quantities purchased	Large	Large	Very small	Small	Small
Frequency of purchase	Frequent delivery; long-term purchase contract	Infrequent purchase, but frequent delivery	Very infrequent	Medium frequency	Frequent
Standardization of competitive products	Very much; grading is important	Very much	Very little; custom-made	Little	Much
Quantity of supply	Limited; supply can be increased slowly or not at all	Usually no problem	No problem	Usually no problem	Usually no problem
Marketing Considerations					
Nature of channel	Short; no middlemen	Short; middlemen only for small buyers	Short; no middlemen	Middlemen used	Middlemen used
Negotiation period	Hard to generalize	Medium	Long	Medium	Short
Price competition	Important	Important	Varies in importance	Not main factor	Important
Presale/postsale service	Not important	Important	Very important	Important	Very little
Promotional activity	Relatively little	Moderate	Sales people very important	Important	Not too important
Brand preference	None	Generally low	High	High	Low
Advance buying contract	Important; long-term contracts	Important long-term contracts	Not usual	Not usual	Not usual

large producers. Further, such products generally are of a commodity nature, must be carefully graded, and, consequently, are highly standardized. Consider coal as an example; it is extracted in great quantities and then is graded by hardness and sulfur content.

The characteristics of raw materials in their natural state affect how they are marketed. For example:

- Prices are normally set by supply and demand, approximating the conditions of perfect competition. As a result, individual producers have little or no control over the prevailing market price.

- Because of their great bulk, low unit value, and the long distances between producer and business user, transportation is an important consideration for natural raw materials.

- As a result of the same factors, natural raw materials frequently are marketed directly from producer to business user with a minimum of physical handling.

- Not much effort is expended on product differentiation for this type of product. It is tough, for example, to distinguish one producer's coal from another producer's. However, some producers have been successful in developing and promoting their own brands of agricultural products (such as the famous Chiquita bananas).

Agricultural products are supplied by small producers as well as larger corporate farms, typically located some distance from their markets. The supply is largely controllable by producers, but it cannot be increased or decreased rapidly. The product is perishable and is not produced at a uniform rate throughout the year. Most citrus fruits, for example, ripen in late winter and thus are readily available at that time of year and become less available in subsequent months. Standardization and grading are commonplace for agricultural products. Also, transportation costs are likely to be high relative to the product's unit value.

Middlemen are ordinarily needed to market agricultural products because many producers are small and numerous and markets are distant. Transportation and warehousing greatly influence effectiveness *and* efficiency of distribution. Typically, there is relatively little promotional activity with agricultural products, as compared to other types of business goods.

Fabricating Materials and Parts   Business goods that become part of the finished product after having been processed to some extent fit into the category of fabricating materials and parts. The fact that they have been processed distinguishes them from raw materials. **Fabricating materials** undergo further processing; examples include pig iron going into steel, yarn being woven into cloth, and flour becoming part of bread. **Fabricating parts** are assembled with no further change in form; they include such products as zippers in clothing and semiconductor chips in computers.

Fabricating materials and parts are usually purchased in large quantities. Normally, buying decisions are based on the price and the service provided by the seller. To ensure an adequate, timely supply, a buyer may place an order a year or more in advance. Because consumers are concerned about price, service, and reliability of

Some products, including Talon zippers, are purchased by both business and consumer markets. For apparel makers, zippers are a fabricating part in a clothing item. Most consumers view a zipper as a convenience good, purchased as easily as possible. However, consumers who sew their own clothes may view a Talon zipper as a specialty good and, if so, will expend extra effort to locate and buy Talon rather than accepting another brand.

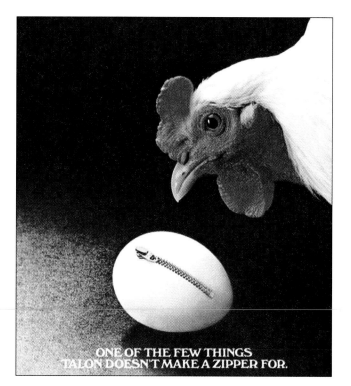

ONE OF THE FEW THINGS TALON DOESN'T MAKE A ZIPPER FOR.

supply, most fabricating products are marketed directly from producer to user. Middlemen are used most often when the buyers are small in size and/or when buyers have small fill-in orders (after the large initial order) requiring rapid delivery.

Branding fabricating materials and parts is generally unimportant. However, some firms have successfully pulled their business goods out of obscurity by branding them. Talon zippers and the NutraSweet brand of sweeteners are examples.

www.nutrasweet.com

Installations
Manufactured products that are an organization's major, expensive, and long-lived equipment are termed **installations.** Examples are large generators in a dam, a factory building, diesel engines for a railroad, and blast furnaces for a steel mill. The characteristic of installations that differentiates them from other categories of business goods is that they directly affect the scale of operations in an organization producing goods or services. Adding 12 new Steelcase desks will not affect the scale of operations at American Airlines, but adding 12 Boeing 757 jet aircraft certainly will. Therefore, jet aircraft are categorized as installations, but desks normally are not.

The marketing of installations presents a real challenge, because each unit sold represents a large dollar amount. Often each unit is made to the buyer's detailed specifications. Also, much presale and postsale servicing is essential. For example, an elevator or an escalator requires installation, maintenance, and—inevitably—repair service. Sales are usually made directly from producer to business user; no middlemen are involved. Because installations are technical in nature, a high-caliber, well-trained sales force is needed to market installations. Because installations require careful, detailed explanation, promotion emphasizes personal selling.

Accessory Equipment
Tangible products that have substantial value and are used in an organization's operations are called **accessory equipment.** This category of business goods neither becomes an actual part of a finished product nor has a significant impact on the organization's scale of operations. The life of accessory equipment is shorter than that of installations but longer than that of operating supplies. Some examples are point-of-sale terminals in a retail store, small power tools, forklift trucks, and office desks.

It is difficult to generalize about how accessory equipment should be marketed. For example, for some products in this category, it is suitable for a manufacturer to sell directly to a final customer. This is true particularly when an order is for several units or when each unit is worth a lot of money. A manufacturer of forklift trucks may sell directly to customers because the price of a single unit is large enough to make this form of distribution profitable. Normally, however, manufacturers of accessory equipment use middlemen—for example, office equipment distributors. The reasons: Typically, the market is geographically dispersed, there are many different types of potential users, and individual orders may be relatively small.

Operating Supplies
Business goods that are characterized by low dollar value per unit and a short life and that contribute to an organization's operations without becoming part of the finished product are called **operating supplies.** Examples are lubricating oils, pencils and stationery, and heating fuel. Purchasers want to buy operating supplies with fairly little effort. Thus operating supplies are the convenience goods of the business sector.

As with the other categories of goods, the characteristics of operating supplies influence how they should be marketed. Because they are low in unit value and are bought by many different organizations, operating supplies—like consumer convenience goods—are distributed widely. Thus, the producing firm uses wholesaling middlemen extensively. Also, because competing products are quite standardized and there is little brand insistence, price competition is normally stiff.

Importance of Product Innovation

A business exists to satisfy customers while making a profit. Fundamentally, a company fulfills this dual purpose through its products. New-product planning and development are vital to an organization's success. This is particularly true now, given (1) rapid technological changes, which can make existing products obsolete, and (2) the practice of many competitors to copy a successful product, which can neutralize an innovative product's advantage. Thus, as emphasized by a top executive at Pillsbury, "In the end, the company with the most new products wins."[5] Of course, these new products must be satisfying to customers and profitable for the firm.

Requirement for Growth

Sooner or later, many product categories and individual brands become outdated. Their sales volume and market shares drop because of changing consumer desires and/or superior competing products. Once successful products that are now in much less demand include audiocassettes, 35-millimeter cameras, VHS videotapes, and electric typewriters. Some brands that no longer exist or have been relegated to remote locations in stores include Munsingwear shirts, White Cloud bathroom tissue, Oldsmobile and Plymouth autos, and Royal Crown Cola.[6]

Thus a guideline for management is "innovate or die." For many companies a substantial portion of this year's sales volume and net profit will come from products that did not exist 5 to 10 years ago. Introducing a new product at the right time can help sustain a firm. In fact, companies that are leaders in terms of profitability and sales growth obtain 39% of their revenues from products introduced during the preceding 5 years; the corresponding figure for the least successful companies is 23%.[7]

Some firms that were successful innovators for long periods—familiar names such as Rubbermaid, McDonald's, H. J. Heinz, The Gap, and Procter & Gamble—haven't maintained a steady flow of new products in recent years. Some of their competitors have been more successful. For example, Total toothpaste, which fights gum disease, helped Colgate-Palmolive surpass P&G's market share in this competitive market. Perhaps with this situation in mind, the head of P&G stated, "The core business is innovation. If we innovate well, we will ultimately win."[8]

High Failure Rates

For many years, the "rule of thumb" has been that about 80% of new products fail. However, because of dissimilar definitions of *new product* and *failure*, the statistics often vary from one study to another. According to one study, even the best companies suffer 35% mortality for new products. An examination of 11,000 new goods and services discovered that 56% are still on the market five years after being introduced. Of course, some of those products still on the market undoubtedly are on the brink of failure whereas others are hugely successful.[9]

Why do new products fail? The most common problem is not being different than existing products. Among the numerous examples are Smucker's ketchup, Cracker Jack Cereal, and Miller clear beer. A new product is also likely to fail if it does not deliver on its promise. Beech Aircraft's Starship plane was supposed to perform like a jet at the price of a propeller plane. Instead, the finished product wound up performing like a propeller plane (indeed it was a turboprop) at the price of a jet![10]

Further, a product is subject to failure if it is perceived as offering poor value in relation to its price. Priced at $4 to $7 apiece, the General Foods Culinova refrigerated dinners did not pass consumers' value tests. Other factors that can undermine new products include poor positioning and lack of marketing support.

To gain market share in a well established market, a company may need to take a big risk with a product that runs counter to consumers' normal behavior. Using that approach, Kimberly-Clark decided to introduce pre-moistened toilet paper on a roll. Do you think this product will be the biggest advancement (in the bathroom, not for society as a whole) since toilet paper was first placed on a roll? Or do you think it will be just another product failure?

www.cottonelle.com

Considering how vital new products are to a company's growth, the large number of new-product introductions, and the high failure rates, product innovation deserves special attention. Given that a product introduction by a large company often costs from $20 million to $50 million,[11] firms that are inattentive to their new products may face financial ruin because of the high cost of product failure. Organizations that effectively manage product innovation can expect to reap a variety of benefits—differential advantage, higher sales and profits, and a solid foundation for the future.

Development of New Products

It's often said that nothing happens until somebody sells something. This is not entirely true. First there must be something to sell—a good, service, person, place, or idea. And that "something" must be developed.

What Is a "New" Product?

www.tourguideusa.com

www.pepsiblue.com

Just what is a "new" product? Are annual models of autos new products? Would a guided tour on an audio CD for use in your car (Tour Guide USA) qualify as new in your view? Or, how about a cola beverage infused with berry flavors (Pepsi Blue) or a clear beerlike beverage (Coors' Zima)? Does an online auction of prospective employees run by Monster.com qualify as new?[12] Or must a product be revolutionary, never before seen, before we can class it as *new*? Does this last description apply to the Segway HT scooter? Or to a GPS (global positioning system) device that pinpoints the user's location? How new a product is affects how it should be marketed.

There are numerous connotations of "new product," but we will focus our attention on three distinct categories of **new products:**

- Products that are *really innovative*—truly unique. Notable innovations during the 20th century range from the zipper to the photocopy machine and, or course, the computer. A recent example is a security device that electronically compares a photo of a person's face against a security database to assure proper identification; a similar product uses fingerprints.[13] Still-to-be-developed products in this category would be a cancer cure and, easily, inexpensively repaired automobiles. Any new product in this category satisfies a real need that is not being satisfied at the time it is introduced.

- Replacements that are *significantly different* from existing products in terms of form, function, and—most important—benefits provided. Notable successes from the past century include cellophane, sterile bandage strips, and ballpoint

Will consumers ever be ready for e-books?

In the late 1990s, the convergence of several technologies created optimism about the commercial prospects for paperless books—better termed *electronic books* or *e-books*. This product is, in effect, a single-purpose handheld computer, which can be linked to the Internet. The early brands included SoftBook, Rocket eBook, Franklin eBookman, and EveryBook.

An e-book actually has two parts, the storage unit (or reader) and the content of the book. After purchasing the storage unit, a reader chooses content from a selection spanning best sellers, obscure or foreign-language books, journals, and textbooks. The content is delivered via the Internet—for a fee, of course.

A reader can store the contents of at least 10 books on a device that is about the same size as a paperback book and also can electronically underline content and write notes in the margin. Rather than buying five or so separate paper textbooks, a college student might buy or lease an e-book that is loaded with all the textbooks needed for the upcoming term. Publishers expected (or hoped) that paperless books would pare such costs as paper, printing, and shipping. Of course, e-books could create conflicts between publishers and book stores if publishers decide to bypass retailers and sell the content of books through their websites.

For a brief period in 2000, it looked as though the market for e-books had taken off. In a bold experiment, best-selling author Stephen King posted his short novel, *Riding the Bullet,* on the Internet for downloading at $2.50 a copy. Unavailable anywhere in print form, the 66-page story was purchased by a half million consumers in two days.

As it turned out, the writer's popularity rather than the public's acceptance of the technology accounted for King's successful experiment. Overall, there have been relatively few buyers of e-books. Marketers have discovered that several challenges with electronic books need to be addressed:

- Before they permit their books to be electronically delivered, publishers are insistent on enacting safeguards to prevent consumers from copying and passing on the content of e-books.

- Incompatible technologies prevent millions of handheld computer users from downloading most publishers' paperless books.

- The prices of e-books is an issue for some (perhaps many) consumers because they typically cost as much as or more than conventional paperbacks.

- And some observers say relatively few readers will abandon "that emotional connection people have with their (paper) books."

Thus the jury is still out as to whether e-books turn out to be a product that meets the needs of a sufficient number of consumers or a technology in search of a viable business opportunity.

Sources: John Mark Eberhart, "E-Books Proved Hard to Hold on to," *The Kansas City Star,* July 28, 2002, p. J7; David D. Kirkpatrick, "Forecasts of an E-Book Era Were, It Seems, Premature," *The New York Times,* Aug. 28, 2001, pp. A1, C2; "Online Focus—Larry Kirshbaum," March 2001, *www.pbs.org/newshour/media/ebooks/kirchbaum.html;* "Online Focus—The Business of E-Books," Mar. 16, 2000, *www.pbs.org/newshour/bb/media/jan-june00/ebookssidebar.html;* "Online Focus—E-Books Take Off," Mar. 16, 2000, *www.pbs.org/newshour/bb/media/jan-june00/e-books 3-16 html;* and Martha Mendoza, "Electronic Books Aren't Flying off the Screen," *St. Louis Post-Dispatch,* Aug. 31, 1999, p. C6.

pens. Disposable contact lenses, digital cameras, and electric or hybrid autos are replacing predecessors because the newer products deliver new or added benefits desired by buyers.

- *Imitative* products that are new to a particular company but not new to the market. Usually, annual models of autos and new versions of cereals are appropriately placed in this category. In another situation, a firm may simply want to capture part of an existing market with a "me too" product. To maximize company-wide sales, makers of cold and cough remedies routinely introduce imitative products, some of which compete with a nearly identical product *from the same company.* That's the case with Robitussin Severe Congestion, Robitussin Multi-Sympton Cold and Flu, Advil Cold and Sinus, and Advil Flu and Body Ache, all put out by Wyeth Consumer Healthcare.

Ultimately, of course, whether or not a product is new depends on how the intended market perceives it. If buyers consider it to be significantly different from competitive products in some relevant characteristic (such as appearance or performance), then it is indeed a new product. Lately, marketers have found that anything labeled *digital* is especially appealing to numerous consumers. Thus "digital" has been attached to not just telephones and televisions, but also lights, music, and even a KitchenAid toaster priced at $89.99. Even though not all of these products are technically digital, many buyers prefer them to regular or analog versions.[14] As in other situations, *perception is reality*!

New-Product Strategy

To achieve strong sales and healthy profits, every producer of business goods or consumer goods should have an explicit strategy with respect to developing and evaluating new products. This strategy should guide every step in the process of developing a new product.

A **new-product strategy** is a statement identifying the role a new product is expected to play in achieving corporate and marketing goals. For example, a new product might be designed to protect market share, meet a specific return-on-investment goal, or establish a position in a new market. Or a new product's role might be to maintain the company's reputation for innovation or social responsibility. The last outcome appears to have been a primary aim of General Motors when it introduced the EV1 electric vehicle. Although EV1 may have helped GM rebut criticism about not being environmentally sensitive, it has failed with respect to achieving sufficient sales.[15]

A new product's intended role also will influence the *type* of product to be developed. To illustrate:

Company Goal		Product Strategy		Recent Examples
To defend market share	→	Introduce an addition to an existing product line or revise an existing product	→	Pizza Hut's "Big New "Yorker" and Stuffed Crust" pizzas
To strengthen a reputation as an innovator	→	Introduce a *really* new product—not just an extension of an existing one	→	Digital cameras offered by Sony, Canon, and other firms

A new-product strategy can also help a firm avoid the problem of having numerous products under development but few actually becoming ready for the market.[16] The priorities in the strategy can be used to determine which prospective products should receive special attention, which should go on the "back burner," and which should be scrapped. Only in recent years have many companies consciously identified new-product strategies. The process of developing new products has become more efficient *and* more effective for firms with strategies because they have a better sense of what they are trying to accomplish.

Stages in the Development Process

FIGURE 8.2

Major Stages in the New-Product Development Process.

Guided by a company's new-product strategy, a new product is best developed through a series of six stages, as shown in Figure 8.2. Compared to unstructured

development, the formal development of new products provides benefits such as improved teamwork, less rework, earlier failure detection, shorter development times, and—most important—higher success rates.[17]

At each stage, management must decide whether to proceed to the next stage, abandon the product, or seek additional information.[18] Here's a brief description of what should happen at each stage of the **new-product development process:**

1. *Generating new-product ideas.* New-product development starts with an idea. A system must be designed for stimulating new ideas within an organization and then reviewing them promptly. In one study, 80% of companies pointed to customers as their best source for new-product ideas. A growing number of manufacturers are encouraging—in some cases, requiring—suppliers to propose innovations. And franchise systems frequently turn their owner–managers' ideas into highly successful products, such as the Egg McMuffin sandwich at McDonald's and annual club memberships at Moto Photo film-processing shops.[19]

A GLOBAL PERSPECTIVE

Can new-product ideas be found on other continents?

Seeking added sales and perhaps a differential advantage, a growing legion of companies are scanning foreign markets for new-product ideas. Various products introduced in the U.S.—including Whiskas cat food from Mars Inc., the Symphony chocolate bar from Hershey Foods, and Colgate Fresh Confidence toothpaste from Colgate-Palmolive—originated in foreign markets.

Several factors prompt U.S. companies to look abroad for new-product ideas:

- Bored with mere imitations, consumers are willing to accept novel products.

- Truly innovative products, even potential breakthroughs, might be uncovered in foreign markets where problems are approached from a different perspective. For instance, Shaman Pharmaceuticals of San Francisco tapped the knowledge of "medicine men" in Ecuador to identify tropical plants and trees that may contain curative compounds. This approach helped the company develop several drugs.

- Marketing a foreign product in the firm's home country can be much cheaper than starting the development process from scratch. With that in mind, Prince, the sporting goods company, acquired the U.S. distribution rights for a high-tech tennis ball machine that can fire 10 types of shots at 8 degrees of difficulty.

- An existing foreign product may be the best way of satisfying an ethnic market segment in the home country. For example, Colgate-Palmolive was confident the lighter texture and pleasing smell of its Fabuloso cleaner, developed abroad, would appeal to Hispanics in the U.S.

An established foreign product is not guaranteed success here. The following guidelines can help:

- Stick to products that coincide with American trends. A greater interest in healthful foods helped Kellogg's achieve success in the U.S. with Mueslix, a cereal combining grains, nuts, and fruits that was invented in Switzerland.

- Don't just rely on the product's newness, but ensure it has a significant benefit.

- Concentrate on products that have achieved widespread success in foreign markets. In 1997, Häagen-Dazs successfully brought a very sweet, butterscotch-like flavor from Buenos Aires to the U.S.

Some products introduced recently in other countries are likely to find their way to the U.S., perhaps in slightly adapted form or carrying a different brand. Do you see promise in Mr. Proper, cleaning tissues infused with thyme (the spice), offered in Germany? Or how about a product from the United Kingdom, the Sushi Made Easy kit that contains all the necessities except the fresh fish?

Sources: Nanette Byrnes, "Brands in a Bind," *Business Week*, Aug. 28, 2000, p. 236, Allyson L. Stewart-Allen, "Innovative Products Introduced in Europe," *Marketing News*, Apr. 10; 2000, p. 19; David Leonhardt, "It Was a Hit in Buenos Aires—So Why Not Boise?" *Business Week*, Sept. 7, 1998, pp. 56, 58; Frederick C. Klein, "New Aussie Giant Serves Up Aces; Our Man Is Bushed," *The Wall Street Journal*, May 26, 1995, p. B8; Thomas M. Burton, "Drug Company Looks to 'Witch Doctors' to Conjure Products," *The Wall Street Journal*, July 7, 1994, p. A1; Michael J. McCarthy, "More Companies Shop Abroad for New-Product Ideas," *The Wall Street Journal*, Mar. 14, 1990, pp. B1, B6; and Bob Hagerty, "Unilever Scours the Globe for Better Ideas," *The Wall Street Journal*, Apr. 25, 1990, p. A11.

2. *Screening ideas.* At this stage, new-product ideas are evaluated to determine which ones warrant further study.[20] Typically, a management team relies on its experience and judgment, rather than on market or competitive data, to screen the pool of ideas.

3. *Business analysis.* A surviving idea is expanded into a concrete business proposal. During the stage of **business analysis,** management (a) identifies product features; (b) estimates market demand, competition, and the product's profitability; (c) establishes a program to develop the product; and (d) assigns responsibility for further study of the product's feasibility.

4. *Prototype development.* If the results of the business analysis are favorable, then a prototype (or trial model) of the product is developed. In the case of services, the facilities and procedures necessary to produce and deliver the new product are designed and tested. That certainly is a necessary step in developing a new roller-coaster ride for an amusement park!

    In the case of goods, a small quantity of the trial model is manufactured to designated specifications. Technical evaluations are carried out to determine whether it is practical to produce the product. A firm may construct a prototype and subject it to lab tests in order to judge whether the proposed product will endure normal—even abnormal—usage. Apple Computer puts new models through various durability tests that range from pouring a soft drink onto the computer to subjecting the screen to over 100 pounds of pressure.[21]

5. *Market tests.* Unlike the internal tests conducted during prototype development, **market tests** involve actual consumers. A new tangible product may be given to a sample of people for use in their households (in the case of a consumer good) or their organizations (a business good). Following the trial, users are asked to evaluate the product.

Virtually all products, ranging from Barbie dolls to Goodyear tires, undergo various tests before and also after being introduced to the market. Some producers do the testing themselves; others outsource the testing to specialized firms. Here, a new Goodyear tire is tested under simulated conditions in a laboratory.

www.goodyear.com

This stage in new-product development often entails test marketing, in which the product is placed on sale in a limited geographic area. Market-test findings, including total sales and repeat purchases by the same customers, are monitored by the company that developed the product (and perhaps by competitors as well). Some companies seek to interrogate shoppers as they examine a product in a store. Quaker State, for instance, used that approach to gauge purchase likelihood and other factors during a test market for a Slick 50 engine-treatment product.[22]

The product's design and production plans may be adjusted as a result of test findings. Following market tests, management must make a final "go–no go" decision about introducing the product.

6. *Commercialization.* In this stage, full-scale production and marketing programs are planned and then implemented. Up to this point in development, management has virtually complete control over the product. However, once the product is "born" and made available for purchase, the external competitive environment becomes a major determinant of its destiny.

Note that the overall new-product strategy guides the first two stages—idea generation and screening. This strategy can provide a focus for generating new-product ideas *and* a basis for evaluating them.

In the six-stage process, the first three stages are particularly critical because they deal with ideas and, as such, are the least expensive.[23] More important, many products fail because the idea or the timing is wrong—and the first three stages are intended to identify such situations. Each subsequent stage becomes more costly in terms of the dollars and human resources necessary to carry out the required tasks.

New-product development used to be a lengthy process, typically taking almost a year for minor revisions and more than three years to complete the process for a major breakthrough. Now, because of competitive pressures and other factors such as globalization and rapid technological change, new-product development is typically accomplished in months, rather than years. Still, even with a mandate for rapid development, it took a team of 7-Eleven and Frito-Lay employees more than a year to develop a new "Frito pie" to the point where it was ready for test marketing. In order to bring new products to market faster and faster, some companies skip stages in the development process. The most common omission is the fifth stage, market tests.[24] Without this stage, however, the company lacks the most telling reactions to the proposed product.

Historically, the marketing of goods has received more attention than the marketing of services. Thus it is not surprising that the new-product development process is not as advanced in services fields as it is in goods industries.[25] Thus service firms can (oftentimes, must) devise a new-product development process that suits their distinctive circumstances.

www.fritolay.com

Producer's Criteria for New Products

When should a company add a new product to its current assortment of products? Here are guidelines that some producers use in answering this question:

- There must be *adequate market demand.* Too often management begins with the wrong question, such as, "Can we use our present sales force?" or "Will the new item fit into our production system?" The necessary first question is, "Do enough people really want this product?" A product is destined to fail if it fills a need that isn't important to consumers or doesn't even exist.

- The product must *satisfy key financial criteria.* At least three questions should be asked: "Is adequate financing available?" "Will the new item reduce seasonal and cyclical fluctuations in the company's sales?" And most critical, "Can we make a sufficient profit with the product?"

- The product must be *compatible with environmental standards*. Key questions include "Does the production process avoid polluting the air or water?" "Will the finished product, including its packaging, be friendly to the environment?" And, "After being used, does the product have recycling potential?"

- The product must *fit into the company's present marketing structure*. The Donna Karan brand that features women's clothing probably could be applied to a new line of designer sheets and towels, whereas the Sherwin Williams paint company would likely find it more difficult to add sheets and towels to its product mix. Specific questions related to whether or not a new product will fit the company's marketing expertise and experience include "Can the existing sales force be used?" "Can the present channels of distribution be used?"

Besides these four issues, a proposed product must satisfy other criteria. For instance, it must be in keeping with the company's objectives and image. The product also must be compatible with the firm's production capabilities. And it must satisfy any pertinent legal requirements.

Middleman's Criteria for New Products

In considering whether to buy a new product for resale, middlemen such as retailers and wholesalers should apply all the preceding criteria except those related to production. In addition, a middleman should apply the following guidelines:

- The middleman must have *a good working relationship with the producer*. By distributing a new product, a middleman should stand to benefit from (a) the producer's reputation, (b) the possibility of getting the right to be the only company to sell the product in a given territory, and/or (c) the promotional and financial help given by the producer.

- The producer and middleman must have *compatible distribution policies and practices*. Pertinent questions include "What kind of selling effort is required for the new product?" "How does the proposed product fit with the middleman's policies regarding repair service, alterations (for clothing), credit, and delivery?" "Does the product complement existing products?"

- As in the case of producers, the product must *satisfy key financial criteria*. One question is especially pertinent to middlemen: "If adding a new product necessitates eliminating another product because of a shortage of shelf or storage space, will the result be a net gain in sales?" And the fundamental question always is: "Can we make a sufficient profit with the product?"

New-Product Adoption and Diffusion

The likelihood of achieving success with a new product, especially a really innovative product, is increased if management understands the adoption and diffusion processes for that product. Once again, we stress that organizations need to understand how prospective customers behave. The **adoption process** is the set of successive decisions an *individual person or organization* makes before accepting an innovation. **Diffusion** of a new product is the process by which an innovation spreads throughout a *social system* over time.[26]

By understanding these processes, an organization can gain insight into how a product is or is not accepted by prospective customers and which groups are likely to buy a product soon after it is introduced, later on, or never. This knowledge of buying behavior can be valuable in designing an effective marketing program.

Stages in the Adoption Process

A prospective buyer goes through six **stages in the adoption process**—deciding whether to purchase something new:

Stage	Activity in That Stage
Awareness	Individual is exposed to the innovation; becomes a prospect.
Interest	Prospect is interested enough to seek information.
Evaluation	Prospect judges the advantages and disadvantages of a product and compares it to alternatives.
Trial	Prospect adopts the innovation on a limited basis. A consumer tries a sample, if the product can be sampled.
Adoption	Prospect decides whether to use the innovation on a full-scale basis.
Confirmation	After adopting the innovation, prospect becomes a user who immediately seeks assurances that decision to purchase the product was correct.

Adopter Categories

Some people will adopt an innovation soon after it is introduced. Others will delay before accepting a new product, and still others may never adopt it. Research has identified five **innovation adopter categories,** based on when in the life of a product individuals adopt a given innovation. Nonadopters are excluded from this categorization. Characteristics of early and late adopters are summarized in Table 8.3. We should add that it's unlikely an individual will be in the same category, such as early adopter, for all products. It's possible a person may fall in one category for a specific product (like audio equipment) but go into another category for a much different product (like clothing).

Innovators   Representing about 3% of the market, **innovators** are venturesome consumers who are the first to adopt an innovation. For example, some consumers buy the newest electronic products before they are introduced in the U.S. They do this by ordering from one of two online vendors that offer Japanese products that have not yet been exported by their manufacturers.[27]

In relation to later adopters, innovators are likely to be younger, have higher social status, and be in better financial shape. Innovators also tend to have broad social relationships involving various groups of people in more than one community. They are likely to rely more on nonpersonal sources of information, such as advertising, rather than on sales people or other personal sources.

Early Adopters   Comprising about 13% of the market, **early adopters** purchase a new product after innovators but sooner than other consumers. Unlike innovators,

TABLE

8.3

Characteristics of Early and Late Adopters of Innovations

	Early Adopters	Late Adopters
Key Characteristics		
Venturesome	Innovators	
Respected	Early adopters	
Deliberate	Early majority	
Skeptical		Late majority
Tradition-bound		Laggards
Other Characteristics		
Age	Younger	Older
Education	Well educated	Less educated
Income	Higher	Lower
Social relationships: within or outside community	Innovators: outside Others: within	Totally local
Social status	Higher	Lower
Information sources	Wide variety; many media	Limited media exposure; limited reliance on outside media; reliance on local peer groups

www.wherifywireless.com

who have broad involvements *outside* a local community, early adopters tend to be involved socially *within* a local community. Early adopters are greatly respected in their social system; in fact, other people are interested in and influenced by their opinions. Thus the early adopter category includes more opinion leaders than any other adopter group. Sales people are probably used more as information sources by early adopters than by any other category.

In the process of diffusion, a **change agent** is a person who seeks to accelerate the spread of a given innovation. In business, the person responsible for introducing an innovative new product must be a change agent. Consider a new security device that combines global-positioning and digital-wireless technologies in a three-ounce bracelet. When worn by a child, the bracelet allows a parent to monitor a child's location by Internet or phone. Marketers of this device must be effective change agents, convincing consumers that it is worthwhile to spend about $400 to purchase the bracelet and then about $30 per month in service fees for this type of added safety.[28]

A change agent focuses the initial persuasive efforts, notably targeted advertising campaigns, on people who fit the demographic profile of early adopters. Other consumers respect—often request—the opinions of early adopters and eventually will emulate their behavior. Thus, if a firm can get early adopters to buy its innovative product and they are satisfied by it, then they will say good things about the new offering. This is called *word-of-mouth communication*. In turn, the broader market eventually will accept the product as well. Of course, unlike advertising that is controlled by the firm, word of mouth can be influenced through advertising but is still largely uncontrolled. And sometimes, it turns out to be unfavorable and harmful rather than favorable and helpful.[29]

Early Majority The **early majority**, representing about 34% of the market, includes more deliberate consumers who accept an innovation just before the "average" adopter in a social system. This group is a bit above average in social and economic measures. Consumers in the early majority group rely quite a bit on ads, sales people, and contact with early adopters.

Late Majority

The **late majority,** another 34% of the market, is a skeptical group of consumers who usually adopt an innovation to save money or in response to social pressure from their peers. They rely on members of the early and late majorities as sources of information. Advertising and personal selling are less effective with this group than is word-of-mouth communication.

Laggards

Laggards are consumers who are bound by tradition and, hence, are last to adopt an innovation. They comprise about 16% of the market. Laggards are suspicious of innovations and innovators; they wonder why anyone would pay a lot for a new kind of safety device, for example. By the time laggards adopt something new, it may already have been discarded by the innovators in favor of a newer concept. Laggards typically are older and usually are at the low end of the social and economic scales.

We are discussing only *adopters* of an innovation. For most innovations, there are many people who are *not* included in our percentages. They are **nonadopters;** they never adopt the innovation.

Characteristics Affecting Adoption Rate

The speed or ease with which a new product is adopted is termed its **adoption rate.** Five characteristics affect the adoption rate, especially in the case of truly innovative products:[30]

- *Relative advantage:* the degree to which an innovation is superior to currently available products. Relative advantage may be reflected in lower cost, greater safety, easier use, or some other relevant benefit. Safest Stripper, a paint and varnish remover introduced by 3M, has several advantages and thus scores high on this characteristic. The product contains no harmful chemicals, has no odor, and allows the user to refinish furniture indoors rather than having to work outdoors.

- *Compatibility:* the degree to which an innovation coincides with the values and lifestyles of prospective adopters. Because many consumers want to save time *and* satisfy their desires now rather than later, microwave popcorn certainly satisfies this characteristic.

- *Complexity:* the degree of difficulty in understanding or using an innovation. The more complex an innovation is, the more slowly it will be adopted—if it is adopted at all. Combined shampoo and conditioners certainly are simple to use, so adoption of them was not impeded by complexity. However, some consumer electronics products and various services on the Internet have problems with this characteristic.

- *Trialability:* the degree to which an innovation may be sampled on some limited basis. Setting aside the other characteristics, the greater the trialability, the faster will be the adoption rate. For instance, a central home air-conditioning system is likely to have a slower adoption rate than a new seed or fertilizer, which may be tried on a small plot of ground. In general, because of this characteristic, costly products will be adopted more slowly than will inexpensive products. Likewise, many services, such as insurance, are difficult to use on a trial basis, so they tend to be adopted rather slowly.

- *Observability:* the degree to which an innovation actually can be demonstrated to be effective. In general, the greater the observability, the faster the adoption rate. For example, a new weed killer that works on existing weeds probably will be accepted sooner than a product that prevents weeds from sprouting. The reason? The latter product, even if highly effective, produces no dead weeds to show to prospective buyers!

SOURCE: *Malden Mills*/**AP**

Malden Mills has developed a jacket that can heat up to 114 degrees. The jacket's technology relies on ultra-thin stainless-steel fibers that conduct heat and can survive normal washing. Two light-weight rechargeable batteries heat the jacket for up to five hours. Considering the five characteristics that affect the pace at which a new product is adopted, is this new product likely to get off to a hot start?

A company would like an innovative product to satisfy all five characteristics as previously discussed. But few do. One-time cameras come close, however. Procter & Gamble hopes that a kit for dry cleaning clothes at home also does.[31] A moist cleaning cloth from the Dryel kit and the dirty clothes are placed in a nylon bag, then run through a heated cycle in the clothes dryer, a process that minimizes *complexity*. Considering that it can be used at home at any time, time-short consumers probably would give the product high marks for *compatibility*. Dryel and Custom Cleaner, a competing brand, cost about $10, a price level that contributes to *trialability*. Each manufacturer claims that its brand produces clean clothes at a fraction of the cost of so-called professional dry cleaning. If so, home dry-cleaning kits also possess *relative advantage* and *observability*, the final two characteristics that accelerate the adoption rate for new products.

Organizing for Product Innovation

For new-product programs to be successful, they must be supported by a strong, long-term commitment from top management. This commitment must be maintained even when some new products fail. To implement this commitment to innovation effectively, new-product efforts must be soundly organized.

Types of Organization

There is no "one best" organizational structure for product planning and development. Many companies use more than one structure to manage these activities. Some widely used organizational structures for planning and developing new products are:

- **Product-planning committee.** Members include executives from major departments—marketing, production, finance, engineering, and research. In small firms, the president and/or another top-level executive often serve on the committee.
- **New-product department or team.** These units are small, consisting of five or fewer people. The head of the group typically reports to the company president. In a large firm, this may be the president of a division.
- **Brand manager.** This individual is responsible for planning new products as well as managing established products. A large company may have many brand managers who report to higher marketing executives.

Product innovation is too important of an activity to handle in an unorganized, nonchalant fashion, figuring that somehow the job will get done. What's critical is to make sure that some person or group has the specific responsibility for new-product development—and is backed by top management.

As the new product is completed, responsibility for marketing it usually is shifted either to an existing department or to a new department established just for this new product. In some cases the team that developed the product may continue as the management nucleus of the new unit.

Integrating new products into departments that are already marketing established products carries two risks, however. First, executives who are involved with ongoing products may have a short-term outlook as they deal with day-to-day problems of existing products. Consequently, they may not recognize the long-term importance of new products and, as a result, neglect them. Second, managers of successful existing products often are reluctant to assume the risks inherent in marketing new products.

Shifting Arrangements

Beginning in the 1950s, many companies—Procter & Gamble, Pillsbury, and General Foods, to name a few—assigned the responsibility for planning new products as well as coordinating the marketing efforts for established ones to a brand manager. Essentially, a brand manager, sometimes called a *product manager*, plans the complete marketing program for a brand or group of products. Specific tasks include setting marketing goals, preparing budgets, and drafting plans for advertising and personal selling activities. Developing new products along with improving established products may also be part of the job description.

The biggest drawback of this structure is that a company often saddles brand managers with great responsibility but provides them with little authority. For instance, brand managers are expected to develop the plan by which the sales force will market the product to wholesalers and retailers, but they have no real authority over the sales force. Their effectiveness depends largely on their ability to influence other executives to cooperate with their plans.

The pace of technological change since the early 1990s has placed a premium on rapid decision making. For this reason and others, such as lack of authority, one observer went so far as to state that brand managers were an "endangered species." Over time, the brand manager structure was modified in some companies. For instance, Ford turned to brand managers, General Motors dropped them, and Procter & Gamble added *category managers* who oversee the activities of a related group of brand managers.[32]

Despite these prominent examples, many firms are now relying on team efforts—such as the product-planning committee discussed earlier—to develop new products. Typically, these are *cross-functional* teams, consisting of representatives from not only market research and marketing but also product design, engineering, and manufacturing. The rationale has been explained as follows, "Cross-functional teams offer the benefits of different perspectives and skill sets, and . . . a functionally diverse team can improve the quality of products developed and reduce the cycle time necessary to launch new products."[33]

Summary

The first commandment in marketing is "Know thy customer," and the second is "Know thy product." The relative number and success of a company's new products are a prime determinant of its sales, growth rate, and profits. A firm can best serve its customers by producing and marketing want-satisfying goods or services.

To manage its products effectively, a firm's marketers must understand the full meaning of *product,* which stresses that customers are buying want-satisfaction. Products can be classified into two basic categories—consumer products and business products. Each category is then subdivided, because a different marketing program is required for each distinct group of products.

There are many views as to what constitutes a *new* product. For marketing purposes, three categories of new products need to be recognized—innovative, significantly different, and imitative.

A clear statement of the firm's new-product strategy serves as a solid foundation for the six-stage development process for new products. At each stage, a firm needs to decide whether to proceed to the next stage or to halt the project. The early stages in this process are especially important. If a firm can make an early *and correct* decision to stop the development of a proposed product, a lot of money and labor can be saved.

In deciding whether or not to add a new product, a producer or middleman should consider whether there is adequate market demand for it. The product also should fit in with the firm's marketing, production, and financial resources.

Management needs to understand the adoption and diffusion processes for a new product. A prospective user goes through six stages in deciding whether or not to adopt a new product. Adopters of an innovation can be divided into five categories, depending on how quickly they accept an innovation such as a new product. These categories are innovators, early adopters, early majority, late majority, and laggards. In addition, there usually is a group of nonadopters. Five characteristics of an innovation seem to influence its adoption rate: relative advantage, compatibility, complexity, trialability, and observability.

Successful product planning and development require long-term commitment and strong support from top management. Furthermore, new-product programs must be soundly organized. Most firms use one of three organizational structures for new-product development: product-planning committee or team, new-product department, or brand manager. Recently, the trend has been away from brand managers and toward team efforts for developing new products.

More about **Segway HT**

Perhaps this section should be titled "More about Dean Kamen" because as advanced and possibly revolutionary as it is, the Segway HT is certainly not Kamen's only invention. He has also devised a number of medical devices, including a pump that gives patients small doses of medicine on an ongoing basis and the first portable dialysis machine. Still, neither these devices nor the Segway is Kamen's most innovative creation. That honor belongs to the IBOT, a high-tech wheelchair.

In a shopping mall one day, Kamen saw a man in a wheelchair being helped up a curb by his struggling friends. Some time later, Kamen slipped in the shower and whirled to keep himself from falling. Put those two seemingly unrelated events together, and most of us wouldn't come up with much. Kamen envisioned a wheelchair that uses gyroscopes and electronic sensors to keep its balance (which it does better than a human, according to its inventor). The IBOT's two pairs of midsize wheels are set on a swivel so it can climb curbs and even stairs. Its sensors send thousands of instructions per second to the chair's computer to keep it stable when the occupant moves. The chair can swivel and balance on two of its wheels to raise the seated occupant to standing height. It can even move through sand and other soft surfaces as well as rocky terrain.

"This changes everything," says Sandi Tagliareni, a former figure skater who needs a wheelchair as a result of multiple sclerosis. "I would take it up into the White Mountains to [do] some hiking on the trails," said George St. Hilaire, who has used a wheelchair for several years.

Recognizing that 2 million Americans rely on wheelchairs, which translates to a $1 billion industry, Johnson & Johnson saw the potential in Kamen's IBOT. After acquiring the rights to the technology developed by Kamen, J&J began clinical trials of the wheelchair, now named the Independence 3000 IBOT Transporter. The intent is to gain the approval of the Food and Drug Administration for sale to the public. With a retail price around $25,000, the IBOT will be more expensive than other customized, motorized wheelchairs. Although some competing wheelchairs have a number of the same features at the IBOT, none has the ability to climb stairs.[34]

1. As a new product, does the IBOT differ from the Segway HT in important ways?

2. How does the IBOT score with respect to the five characteristics that affect the rate at which innovations are adopted?

3. Who are likely to be the innovators and early adopters of the IBOT? Who will be among the late majority and laggards, and why?

Key Terms and Concepts

Questions and Problems

1. In what respects are the products different in each of the following cases?

   a. A Whirlpool refrigerator sold at an appliance store and a similar refrigerator sold by Sears under its Kenmore brand name. Assume that Whirlpool makes both refrigerators.
   b. A CD by the singer Jewel purchased online from Amazon.com and the same CD sold by a Blockbuster store.
   c. An airline ticket purchased through a travel agent and an identical ticket purchased directly from the airline via the Internet.

2. a. Explain the various interpretations of the term *new product*.
   b. Give some examples, other than those cited in this chapter, of products in each of the three new-product categories.

3. "Because brand preferences are well established with regard to many items of women's clothing, these items—traditionally considered shopping goods—will move into the specialty-goods category. At the same time, however, other items of women's clothing can be found in supermarkets and variety stores, thus indicating that some items are convenience goods."

   a. Explain the reasoning in these statements.
   b. Do you agree that women's clothing is shifting away from the shopping-goods classification? Explain.

4. Compare the elements of a producer's marketing mix for a convenience good with those of the mix for a specialty good.

5. In which of the five categories of business goods should each of the following be included? And which products may belong in more than one category?

   a. Trucks
   b. Medical X-ray equipment
   c. Typing paper
   d. Copper wire
   e. Printing presses
   f. Nuts and bolts
   g. Paper clips
   h. Land

6. In developing new products, how can a firm make sure that it is being socially responsible with regard to scarce resources and our environment?

7. Assume that the following organizations are considering additions to their product lines. In each case, does the proposed product meet the criteria for adding a new product? Explain your decisions.

   a. McDonald's—salad bar
   b. Safeway supermarkets—automobile tires
   c. Exxon—personal computers
   d. Banks—life insurance
   e. Amazon.com—life insurance

8. Several new products from foreign countries are described in the Global Perspective box. In your opinion, which ones will enjoy the greatest success in the U.S.? Explain your choices.

9. Describe the kinds of people who are most likely to be found in (a) the innovator category of adopters and (b) the late-majority category.

10. Why are many firms relying more on cross-functional teams and less on product managers for new-product development?

Interactive Marketing Exercises

1. Arrange a meeting with the manager of a large retail outlet in your community. Discuss two topics with the manager:

   a. What recently introduced product has been a failure or appears destined to fail?
   b. Did this product, in retrospect, satisfy the criteria for adding a new product? (Remember to consider not just the middleman's criteria but also applicable producer's criteria.)

2. Design, either in words or drawings, a new product that fits into one of the first two categories of newness—that is, a really innovative product or a significant replacement, not just an imitative product. Then evaluate how your proposed product rates with respect to the five characteristics of an innovation that influence the adoption rate.

"Palm Inc. is still the leading supplier of PDAs, but finds itself in a tight spot."

Can **Palm** Get a Better Grip on Its Market?

After you sell millions of personal digital assistants (PDAs), what do you do for an encore? Market leader Palm Inc. is struggling to address that question.

Having achieved faster success in the marketplace than the IBM PC, the Sony Walkman, color TV, or cell phone, the PDA (now often called a handheld computer) has become something of a cultural icon. Nevertheless, Palm faces formidable competitors, some of whom are even licensing Palm's innovative operating system.

Basic PDAs keep your contact list, your calendar, and your notes readily accessible in a small lightweight package. PDAs have actually traveled a rocky road to their current popularity. Several early models came onto the market and quickly disappeared; Apple's Newton was a notable and much-publicized failure in the early to mid-1990s. The Newton's heralded function, handwriting recognition, was intended to free users from the keyboard, but it didn't work very well. Consumers responded to the high price and hype by staying away from the product.

Then in 1996, Palm—which had been designing the software for handheld computers made by other firms—finally wrapped its own hardware design around the program it was licensing. Thus the Palm Pilot, later known as the Palm, was born. This "new and improved" PDA delivered on the promise of doing a few simple tasks with ease and dependability. The Palm didn't change the world; rather, according to *Fortune* magazine, it "just made life easier."

Many business executives, students, entrepreneurs, and homemakers found the "new and improved" PDA to be indispensable. Approximately 16 million people own PDAs now. Enjoying surging sales, Palm Inc. became a huge success. With more accessories coming out all the time and the promise of greater capabilities always on the horizon, it appeared that handheld users would always have something new and exciting to purchase and that, as a result, Palm Inc. would have a very rosy future.

But that hasn't quite materialized. Palm Inc. is still the leading supplier of PDAs, but finds itself in a tight spot. Now that it is in both the software and the hardware businesses, Palm must add new technical features *and,* at the same time, ensure that its product remains light and small and looks stylish. In addition, the company needs to engage in aggressive and effective marketing. Doing all three of these tasks simultaneously and well enough to fend off stiff competition has been difficult for Palm.

For one thing, the slumping economy of the late 1990s hit sales hard. Shares of Palm's stock fell by nearly half when the company announced it would take an operating loss early in 2001. Palm compounded its difficulties with several missteps of its own. For example, the firm missed the deadlines it had announced for delivering new and better Palm models, including one with a color screen. Consumers continued to buy, but they purchased the cheaper models stores had on their shelves, thereby reducing

www.palm.com

profit margins and harming the company's financial performance. Palm also overreacted to supply problems and wound up with excess inventories of component parts, further damaging its financial results. Then in mid-2002, it admitted—with considerable embarrassment that its m130 model displays far fewer than the 65,000+ colors that Palm said it did. Palm compounded the problem by refusing to offer a refund along with its public apology. Eventually, facing criticism and a possible class action lawsuit, Palm relented and offered a full refund to any disgruntled m130 owners.

Palm has ridden the wave with its PDA, from birth through popularity to what might be its moment of truth.[1] What can the firm expect in terms of customer demands and competitive pressures in the next several years?

Chapter Goals

Palm Inc., like most firms, faces the challenges of protecting its competitive position as well as building sales and profits with new products as a market evolves. This case illustrates that, over time, a company must make numerous decisions about its array of products. Whether the correct decisions are made—and made at the right time—greatly affects a company's degree of success, not just for a single year but for many years to come.

At any given time, a firm may be marketing some new products and some old ones while others are being planned and developed. This chapter covers a number of strategic decisions pertaining to an organization's assortment of products. After studying this chapter, you should be able to explain:

- The difference between product mix and product line.
- Major product-mix strategies—positioning, expansion, alteration, and contraction.
- Trading up and trading down.
- Managing a product throughout a life cycle.
- Planned obsolescence.
- Style and fashion.
- The fashion-adoption process.

Product Mix and Product Line

www.carma-labs.com

Red Hat Inc. markets only Linux software, Carma Laboratories, Inc. sells just lip balm (and one other item), and WD-40 Co. concentrates on a single brand of spray lubricant. These examples notwithstanding, few firms rely on a single product; instead, most sell many products. A **product mix** is the set of all products offered for sale by a company. The structure of a product mix has both breadth and depth. Its **breadth** is mea-sured by the number of product lines carried, its **depth** by the variety of sizes, colors, and models offered within each product line. A product-mix structure is illustrated in Figure 9.1.

A broad group of products, intended for essentially similar uses and having similar physical characteristics, constitutes a **product line**. Firms may delineate a product line in different ways. For Wyeth Consumer Healthcare, its various forms of Robitussin cough remedies (such as Pediatric and Maximum Strength syrups and cherry-flavored drops) represent a product line. However, for a large drugstore or supermarket, all brands of cough suppressants—not just Robitussin products—comprise one of the store's many product lines.

FIGURE 9.1

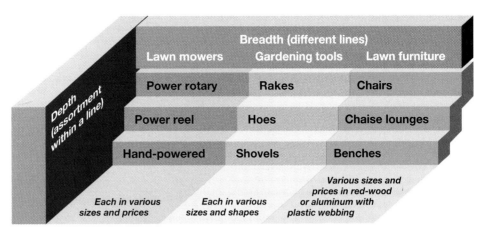

Product Mix—Breadth and Depth in a Lawn and Garden Store.

Product-Mix Strategies

At one time, Anheuser-Busch Companies offered snack foods, baked goods, adventure park entertainment, and about 25 brands of beer to consumers. Did this diverse assortment of products develop by accident? No—it reflected a planned strategy, as did the company's subsequent decision to dispose of the snack foods and baked goods divisions. To be successful in marketing, producers and middlemen need carefully planned strategies for managing their product mixes, as we'll see next.

Positioning the Product

Management's ability to bring attention to a product and to differentiate it in a favorable way from similar products goes a long way toward determining that product's revenues. Thus management needs to engage in *positioning*. Recall from the discussion in Chapter 6 that positioning entails developing the image that a product projects in relation to competitive products and to the firm's other products.

Regardless of which positioning strategy is used, the needs of the target market always must be considered. For example, Six Continent Hotels has developed multiple (perhaps too many) offerings to satisfy diverse target markets. Thus, besides its traditional hotels, the lodging firm now has Holiday Inn full-service, Express, Select, Garden Court, Family Suites Resort, and SunSpree Resort properties as well as Staybridge Suites and Inter-Continental and Crowne Plaza hotels and resorts. Likewise, to satisfy different consumers' desires, Anheuser-Busch has both regular and light beers at multiple price levels, several brands of nonalcoholic brews, and now a beer that is low in carbohydrates.[2]

www.sixcontinentshotels.com

Marketing executives can choose from a variety of positioning strategies. Sometimes they decide to use more than one for a particular product. Here are several major positioning strategies.

Positioning in Relation to a Competitor
For some products the best position is directly against the competition. This strategy is especially suitable for a firm that already has a solid differential advantage or is trying to solidify such an advantage. After nine years of relying on a single (but successful) model, General Motors' Saturn division finally brought out larger models. The L (for "larger") series is intended to attract customers from Saturn's primary competitors, Honda and Toyota. To fend off rival makers of microprocessors, Intel Corp. has used the slogan, "Intel Inside," and a long-running advertising campaign to convince buyers that its product is superior to competitors'.[3]

www.saturnbp.com

For other products, head-to-head positioning is exactly what *not* to do, especially when a competitor has a strong market position. In women's professional basketball, the American Basketball League and the Women's National Basketball Association competed directly against each other, including overlapping seasons. Ultimately, the ABL lost out to the WNBA, which has the financial backing of the men's NBA.[4]

One view is that underdogs should try to be the opposite of—or at least much different than—the market leader. Southwest Airlines positioned itself effectively as the low-fare alternative to full-service airlines. In fact, larger competitors as well as start-ups, such as JetBlue and Frontier, have been trying to emulate Southwest's practices, which satisfy a sizable segment of travelers and generate profits.[5]

Positioning in Relation to a Product Class or Attribute Sometimes a company's positioning strategy entails associating its product with (or distancing it from) a product class or attribute. For example, some companies try to place their products in a desirable class, such as "Made in the USA."

Other firms promote their wares as having an attractive attribute, such as "low energy consumption" or "environmentally friendly." This strategy is widely used now for food products. Libby's, Campbell Soup, Kellogg's, and competing companies, for instance, have introduced lines of foods with one common denominator—

they contain no or very little salt. These items are positioned against products that are packed with the conventional amounts of salt. Sometimes what's in, rather than left out of, the product is emphasized. That's the case with Volvo, which constructed a steel frame around the passenger compartment in order to be positioned as *the* safe automobile.

Positioning by Price and Quality   Certain producers and retailers are known for their high-quality products and high prices. In the retailing field, Saks Fifth Avenue and Neiman Marcus are positioned at one end of the price–quality continuum. Discount stores such as Kmart and Dollar General are at the other end. We're not saying that discounters ignore quality; rather, they stress low prices.

In recent years, both Ford and General Motors have sold large numbers of sport-utility vehicles (SUVs). Now, virtually every automaker has introduced or is preparing to launch its own SUV, most of which feature four-wheel drive and other high-quality, but expensive amenities. In a market filled with 25 or more models of SUVs, ranging from the familiar Ford Explorer and Chevy Suburban to the obscure Mitsubishi Outlander and Toyota Sequoia, producers are struggling to differentiate their particular model from all the others. Without differentiation, particularly with respect to positioning on the price–quality continuum, some models are likely to fail.

Product-Mix Expansion

Product-mix expansion is accomplished by increasing the depth within a particular line and/or the number of lines a firm offers to customers. Let's look at these options.

When a company adds a similar item to an existing product line with the same brand name, this is termed a **line extension.** For illustrations, pull the coupons insert out of your Sunday newspaper. You'll probably see examples such as Pillsbury promoting about 10 variations of its well-known biscuits and rolls; Vaseline announcing new versions of Intensive Care lotions; and Log Cabin advertising its sugar-free, as well as regular, syrups.

The line-extension strategy is also used by organizations in services fields. For example, some years ago the Roman Catholic Church broadened its line of religious services by adding Saturday and Sunday evening masses, and universities offer programs to appeal to prospective older students.

There are many reasons for line extensions. The main one is that the firm wants to appeal to more market segments by offering a wider range of choices for a particular product. Line extensions have been one of the more prominent—and debatable—practices during the past 15 or so years. As discussed in the "You Make the Decision" box, line extensions have become so common as to raise questions about their effectiveness.

Another way to expand the product mix, referred to as **mix extension,** is to add a new product line to the company's present assortment. Jell-O pudding pops and Bic disposable lighters, both successes, and Bic pantyhose and adidas colognes, both failures, are examples of mix extension. As described in the case at the beginning of Chapter 6, the maker of Swatch watches went far afield to create the very small and inexpensive Smart Car—so much so that eventually Daimler (the maker of Mercedes Benz autos) took the project over.

In order to gain a competitive advantage, generate more sales, and build customer satisfaction, Kimberly-Clark Corp. has extended its line of diapers in several ways. For example, as shown in the ad, the company not only offers a line of training pants under the Pull-Ups brand but also has separate versions for boys and girls.

www.pull-ups.com

Clothes make the man, but underpants make the kid.

Nothing makes a little kid feel like a big kid quite like a pair of real underpants. Which is why Pull-Ups training pants have fun designs that make them look just like underwear. There are even blue sides for boys and pink for girls. Pull-Ups training pants. When your child feels like a big kid, he'll stay dry like one.

Pull-Ups I'm a Big Kid Now.
TRAINING PANTS

Johnson & Johnson's products illustrate the distinction between mix extension and line extension. When J&J introduced a line of Acuvue disposable contact lenses, that's *mix* extension because it added another product to the company's product mix. In contrast, line extension adds more items within the same product line. When J&J adds new versions of Tylenol pain reliever, that's *line* extension.

Under a mix-extension strategy, the new line may be related or unrelated to current products. Furthermore, it may carry one of the company's existing brand names or may be given an entirely new name.

Typically, the new line is related to the existing product mix because the company wants to capitalize on its strengths and experience. Given the success of Reese's peanut butter cups, Hershey's thinks the brand says "peanut butter" to consumers, so it introduced a line of Reese's peanut butters. Hunt-Wesson holds a similar view about its Swiss Miss brand and chocolate, so it developed Swiss Miss puddings in chocolate and other flavors. In both cases, the new lines carry one of the company's popular brands to benefit from consumers' familiarity with and good feelings toward that brand. We'll consider this approach in more detail when *brand equity* is discussed in the next chapter.

Alteration of Existing Products

Rather than developing a completely new product, management might do well to take a fresh look at the organization's existing products. Often, improving an established product, termed **product alteration,** can be more profitable and less risky than developing a completely new one. The substitution of NutraSweet for saccharin in diet sodas increased sales of those drinks. Redesigning the product itself can sustain its appeal or even initiate its renaissance. For example, Kimberly-Clark redesigned its disposable diapers so that they are less bulky and also come in separate styles for girls and boys.

Product alteration is not without risks, however. When Coca-Cola Co. modified the formula for its leading product and changed its name to New Coke, sales plunged. As a result, the old formula was brought back three months later under the Coca-Cola Classic name.

Alternatively, especially for consumer goods, the product itself is not changed but its packaging is altered. For example, Pillsbury developed a unifying background for the package of most of its dessert mixes, a royal blue field with small white polka dots.[6] To gain a small differential advantage, companies are offering a variety of food products (such as sliced and shredded cheeses) in packages that reseal using zipper-like devices. Thus packages can be altered to enhance appearance or to improve the product's usability.

Product-Mix Contraction

Another strategy, **product-mix contraction,** is carried out either by eliminating an entire line or by simplifying the assortment within a line. Thinner and/or shorter product lines or mixes can weed out low-profit and unprofitable products. The intended result of product-mix contraction is higher profits from fewer products. General Mills (Wheaties, Betty Crocker, Gold Medal flour) decided to concentrate on its food business and, consequently, sold its interest in Izod (the "alligator" apparel maker) and its lines of children's toys and games. In services fields, some travel agencies have shifted from selling all modes of travel to concentrate on specialized tours and trips to exotic places. And, to reduce their liability risks and insurance costs, many physicians have stopped offering obstetrical services.

During the early 1990s, most companies expanded—rather than contracted—their product portfolios. Numerous line extensions document this trend. Lately, some firms that wound up with an unmanageable number of products or multiple unprofitable items or lines engaged in product-mix pruning. As a result, many organizations now have fewer product lines, and the remaining lines are thinner and shorter. There are myriad examples of product-mix contraction, sometimes involving well-known firms. For example, Procter & Gamble pruned its food business by selling the Jif brand of peanut butter and the Crisco brand of cooking oils

AN ETHICAL DILEMMA?

In May 2000, the 3M Co. dropped its highly successful Scotchgard product that protected fabrics from stains. The decision was motivated by research findings that minuscule amounts of a key ingredient in Scotchgard were found in the blood of people all over the country. This finding raised many troubling questions, notably: How did the chemical (perfluorooctane sulfonate, or PFOS for short) get into people's blood? Could such small amounts of PFOS cause harm to humans?

In laboratory tests, enormously large doses of PFOS killed monkeys and rats. Although there was no evidence that the chemical was harmful to humans, 3M decided to drop Scotchgard. The company realized that dropping the product before a substitute was in place could hurt its financial performance. In contrast, the Environmental Working Group claimed that 3M knew for at least 25 years that PFOS caused bodily harm and, as such, the firm's decision should have been made much earlier.

Does a company have an ethical responsibility to eliminate a product as soon as preliminary research results show potentially harmful effects from it? Or does a company's leadership have a responsibility to continue to build sales and profits (and shareholder value) while seeking conclusive research results regarding whether or not a product is indeed harmful?

Sources: Kara Sissell, "3M Defends Scotchgard Phaseout," *Chemical Week,* Apr. 11, 2001, p. 33; and Joseph Weber, "3M's Big Cleanup," *Business Week,* June 5, 2000, pp. 96–98.

This ad shows how a company, Giorgio Armani in this case, can develop a separate and somewhat lower-price offering in order to appeal to a new segment of the market. As such, Armani Exchange is a good example of the marketing practice called trading down.

www.armaniexchange.com

www.smucker.com

to J. M. Smucker Co. According to P&G's CEO, the sale would help the company concentrate on "building big brands in core categories." Smucker's president saw the acquired brands as "providing opportunity for greater top- and bottom-line growth" for the firm.[7]

Trading Up and Trading Down

The product strategies of trading up and trading down involve a change in product positioning *and* an expansion of the product line. **Trading up** means adding a higher-price product to a line in order to attract a broader market. Also, the seller intends that the new product's prestige will help the sale of its existing lower-price products.

Consider some examples of trading up. To its line of inexpensive sport watches, Swatch added an $80 Chrono stopwatch and other upgraded watches. Home-improvement retailers, including both Home Depot and Lowe's, are now offering more expensive products, all the way up to $39,500 chandeliers.[8] And even pet food manufacturers have traded up to "superpremium" lines, as illustrated by Pedigree from Kal Kan and Purina One from Ralston Purina.

Trading down means adding a lower-price product to a company's product line. The firm expects that people who cannot afford the original higher-price product or who see it as too expensive will buy the new lower-price one. The reason: The lower-price product carries some of the status and some of the other more substantive benefits (such as performance) of the higher-price item.

The Marriott Corp. followed a trading-down strategy when it started (1) Courtyard by Marriott hotels, targeted at the midprice market long dominated by chains such as Holiday Inn and Ramada Inn, and (2) Fairfield Inns, to compete in the economy-price market. Even some designers of highly fashionable women's clothing, such as Donna Karan and Bill Blass, are trading down by introducing lower-price lines. The new lines are priced between $100 and $900 per item, typically less than one-half the price of their top lines.[9]

Trading up and trading down are perilous strategies because the new products may confuse buyers, resulting in negligible net gain. It is equally undesirable if sales of the new item or line are generated at the expense of the established products. When *trading down,* the new offering may permanently hurt the firm's reputation and that of its established high-quality product. To reduce this possibility, new lower-price products may be given brand names unlike the established brands. That's why Hewlett-Packard Co. established a separate Apollo label for a new line of low-price printers, and Williams-Sonoma Inc. chose West Elm as the label for its lower-price furniture catalog.[10] With this approach, a company forfeits the benefits of a well-known brand name but still can capitalize on its experience in distributing and promoting the successful product.

www.westelm.com

In *trading up,* on the other hand, the problem depends on whether the new product or line carries the established brand or is given a new name. If the same name is used, the firm must change its image enough so that new customers will accept the higher-priced product. At the same time, the seller does not want to lose its present customers. The new offering may cloud the established image, not attracting new customers but driving away existing customers. To avoid that problem, Sears used the Great Indoors name for a new chain of stores that sells comparatively expensive brands that are not found in Sears' traditional stores.[11]

www.thegreatindoors.com

If a different brand name is used, either for trading down or trading up, the company must create awareness for it. Of course, promotion and other steps must be taken to stimulate consumers to buy the new product or to shop at the new store.

The Product Life Cycle

As we saw in Chapter 8, a product's life cycle can have a direct bearing on a company's survival. The life cycle of a product consists of four stages: introduction, growth, maturity, and decline. The concept of product life *applies to a generic category of product* (microwave ovens and microprocessors, for example) and not to specific brands (Sharp and Intel, respectively). A **product life cycle** consists of the aggregate demand over an extended period of time for all brands comprising a generic product category.

A life cycle can be graphed by plotting aggregate sales volume for a product category over time, usually years. It is also worthwhile to accompany the sales volume curve with the corresponding profit curve for the product category, as shown in Figure 9.2. After all, a business is interested ultimately in profitability, not just sales.

The *shapes* of these two curves vary from one product category to another. Still, for most categories, the basic shapes and the relationship between the sales and the profit curves are as illustrated in Figure 9.2. In this typical life cycle, the profit curve for most new products is negative, signifying a loss, through much of the introductory stage. In the latter part of the growth stage, the profit curve starts to decline while sales volume is still rising. Profits decline because the companies in an industry usually must increase their advertising and selling efforts and/or cut their prices to sustain sales growth in the face of intensifying competition during the maturity stage.

Introducing a new product at the proper time will help maintain a company's desired level of profit. Striving to maintain its dominant position in the wet-shaving market, the Gillette Company faces that challenge often. A while back, a large French firm cut into Gillette's market share by introducing the highly successful Bic disposable razors. After considerable research and development, Gillette counterattacked with the Sensor razor, featuring independently suspended blades. The strategy worked, as many consumers left the convenience of low-price disposable razors in

FIGURE 9.2

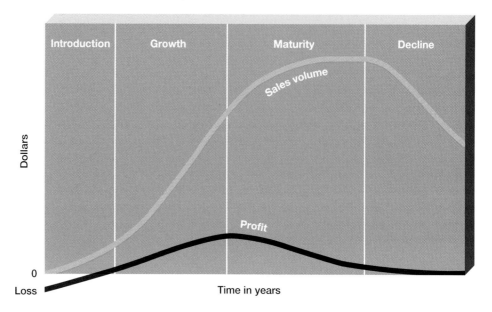

Typical Life Cycle of a Product Category.

During the introduction stage of a life cycle, a product category—and virtually all brands within it—is unprofitable. Total profits for the product category are healthy during the growth stage but then start to decline while a product's sales volume is still increasing.

favor of the better shaves provided by the higher-price Sensor razor. Gillette then traded up again, introducing the triple-blade Mach3 razor, priced about 35% higher than the Sensor.[12]

If a new product lacks competition and is particularly appealing to consumers, a firm can charge a fairly high price and achieve strong profits. That was the case with Mach3, so Gillette was able to reap healthy profits from the wet-shaving market soon after the new product was introduced. Intel Corp. has sought a measure of control over prices by introducing new generations of microprocessors only two or three years apart, even while demand is still growing for its current version. In recent years, though, Intel has had to rely more on price cuts to maintain its share of the market for microprocessors used in personal computers.[13]

The product life-cycle concept has been criticized as lacking empirical support and being too general to be useful in specific cases.[14] Admittedly, the product life cycle is not perfect and it must be adapted to fit different circumstances. Nevertheless, it is both straightforward and powerful. A company's marketing success can be affected considerably by its ability to determine and adapt to the life cycles for each of its product categories.

Characteristics of Each Stage

Management must be able to recognize what part of the life cycle its product is in at any given time. The competitive environment and marketing strategies that should be used ordinarily depend on the particular life-cycle stage. Table 9.1 contains a synopsis of all four stages. Each stage is highlighted below.

Introduction   During the **introduction stage**, sometimes called the *pioneering stage*, a product is launched into the market in a full-scale marketing program. It has gone through product development, including idea screening, prototype, and market tests. The entire product may be new, such as the zipper, the videocassette recorder, and the fat substitute for prepared foods. Or it may be well-known but have a significant novel feature that, in effect, creates a new-product category; microwave ovens and in-line skates are examples.

For really new products, normally there is very little direct competition. However, if the product has tremendous promise, numerous companies may enter the industry early on. That has occurred with digital TV, introduced in 1998. Despite disappointing sales through 2001, the category is viewed as having enormous potential because of the product's enhanced picture quality. Consequently, major producers such as Zenith and Sony are placing more and more emphasis on digital TVs. Mitsubishi's American division, in fact, decided to stop producing the old kinds of TVs and concentrate entirely on digital sets.[15]

Because consumers are unfamiliar with the innovative product or feature, a pioneering firm's promotional program is designed to stimulate demand for the entire product category rather than a single brand. Introduction is the most risky and expensive stage because substantial dollars must be spent not only to develop the product but also to seek consumer acceptance of the offering. Many, perhaps most, new products are not accepted by a sufficient number of consumers and fail at this stage.

Growth   In the **growth stage,** or *market-acceptance stage,* sales and profits rise, frequently at a rapid rate. Competitors enter the market, often in large numbers if the profit outlook is particularly attractive. Mostly as a result of competition, profits start to decline near the end of the growth stage.

As part of firms' efforts to build sales and, in turn, market share, prices typically decline gradually during this stage. In high-tech fields, such as microprocessors, prices tend to fall sharply even as the industry is growing rapidly. According to a top executive at Eastman Kodak, "The only thing that matters is if the exponential growth of your market is faster than the exponential decline of your prices."[16] Appropriate marketing strategies for this stage, as well as the other three, are summarized in Table 9.1.

Maturity   During the first part of the **maturity stage,** sales continue to increase, but at a decreasing rate. When sales level off, profits of both producers and middlemen decline. The primary reason: intense price competition.

TABLE 9.1 Characteristics and Implications of Different Product Life-Cycle Stages

	Stage			
	Introduction	**Growth**	**Maturity**	**Decline**
Characteristics				
Customers	Innovators	Mass market	Mass market	Loyal customers
Competition	Little if any	Increasing	Intense	Decreasing
Sales	Low levels, then rising	Rapid growth	Slow/no annual growth	Declining
Profits	None	Strong, then at a peak	Declining annually	Low/none
Marketing Implications				
Overall strategy	Market development	Market penetration	Defensive positioning	Efficiency or exit
Costs	High per unit	Declining	Stable or increasing	Low
Product strategy	Undifferentiated	Improved items	Differentiated	Pruned line
Pricing strategy	Most likely high	Lower over time	Lowest	Increasing
Distribution strategy	Scattered	Intensive	Intensive	Selective
Promotion strategy	Category awareness	Brand preference	Brand loyalty	Reinforcement

Source: Adapted from material provided by Professor David Appel, University of Notre Dame.

Seeking to differentiate themselves, some firms extend their product lines with new models; others come up with a "new and improved" version of their primary brand. During this stage, the pressure is greatest on those brands that trail the #1 and #2 brands. During the latter part of this stage, marginal producers, those with high costs or no differential advantage, drop out of the market. They do so because they lack sufficient customers and/or profits.

Decline For most products, a **decline stage**, as gauged by sales volume for the total category, is inevitable for one of the following reasons:

- A better or less expensive product is developed to fill the same need. Microprocessors made possible many replacement products such as handheld calculators (which made slide rules obsolete) and video games (which may have pushed the category of board games, such as Monopoly and Clue, into their decline stage).

- The need for the product disappears, often because of another product development. For example, the broad appeal of frozen orange juice virtually eliminated the market for in-home mechanical or electrical fruit squeezers. (However, renewed interest in fresh foods has recently boosted sales of fruit squeezers.)

- People simply grow tired of a product (a clothing style, for instance), so it disappears from the market.

Seeing little opportunity for revitalized sales or profits, most competitors abandon the market during this stage. However, a few firms may be able to develop a small market niche and remain moderately successful in the decline stage. Some manufacturers of wood-burning stoves have been able to do this.

Length of Product Life Cycle

The total length of the life cycle—from the start of the introduction stage to the end of the decline stage—varies across product categories. It ranges from a few weeks or a short season (for a clothing fashion) to many decades (for autos or telephones). And it varies because of differences in the length of individual stages from one product category to the next. Furthermore, although Figure 9.2 suggests that all four life-cycle stages cover nearly equal periods of time, the stages in any given product's life cycle usually last for different periods.

Three variations on the typical life cycle are shown in Figure 9.3:

- In one, the product gains widespread consumer acceptance only after an extended introductory period (see part *a*). Fat substitutes, such as Olestra, can

FIGURE 9.3

Product Life-Cycle Variations.

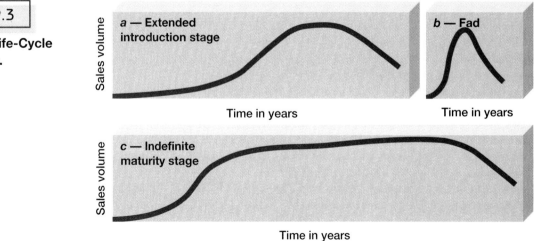

be used in making foods ranging from potato chips to ice cream. However, this product category appears to be stuck in the introduction stage of its life cycle, perhaps because of shifts in consumer attitudes regarding fat in foods and/or concerns about possible side effects such as abdominal cramps.[17]

- In another variation, the entire life cycle begins and ends in a relatively short period of time (part *b*). This variation depicts the life cycle for a **fad,** a product or style that becomes immensely popular nearly overnight and then falls out of favor with consumers almost as quickly. Hula hoops and lava lamps are examples of past fads. Nasal dilators (such as Breathe Right strips), "virtual pets," and "power bead" bracelets (which purport to provide benefits based on the bead colors) are likely to be classified as fads from the last few years of the 20th century.[18]

- In a third variation, the product's mature stage lasts almost indefinitely (part *c*). This life cycle is illustrated by canned, carbonated soft drinks, portable stereos (such as the Walkman and now MP3 players),[19] and also the automobile with a gasoline-powered, internal-combustion engine. Electric- and hybrid-powered cars have been introduced, but the automobile as we know it remains dominant.

Setting aside fads, which represent a special case, product life cycles are getting shorter generally. If competitors can quickly introduce a "me too" version of a popular product, it may move swiftly into the maturity stage. Or rapid changes in technology can make a product obsolete virtually overnight. Some said that would occur in the audio field, with digital audiotapes replacing compact discs (CDs), but that didn't happen. The latest forecast is that even newer formats, notably DVD-audio and direct download from the Internet, will turn the CD into a dinosaur.[20]

Moreover, a number of product categories do not make it through all four stages of the life cycle. Some fail in the introductory stage. That occurred a while back with a product that played laserdiscs rather than videotapes. The product suffered from several shortcomings (such as limited storage capacity) and thus never caught on, superseded by the digital versatile disc (DVD) player.

Also, because the life cycle refers to product categories rather than individual brands, not every brand proceeds through all four life-cycle stages. For instance, some brands fail early in the cycle. That's what happened with Cord and LaSalle, both of which failed during the introduction stage of the life cycle for automobiles. Other brands are not introduced until the market is in the growth or maturity stage. The Saturn is a very successful example in the automotive field.

Life Cycle Is Related to a Market

When we say a product is in a specific stage of its life cycle, implicitly we are referring to a specific market. A product may be well accepted (growth or maturity stage) in some markets but still be striving for acceptance in other markets. At the time Ortho Pharmaceuticals introduced Retin-A as a treatment for acne, existing products already served this purpose. Thus the acne-treatment category probably was in the maturity stage. However, it was discovered that Retin-A might be effective in reducing facial wrinkles. In effect, it created a new product category. Hence, Retin-A fit into both the acne-treatment category that was in the maturity stage among teenagers, and into the wrinkle-remover category that was in the introductory or perhaps early growth stage among middle-aged people.

In terms of geographic markets, a product may be in its maturity stage in one country and its introductory stage or perhaps even unknown in another country. For example, steel-belted radial tires were in their maturity stage in western Europe well before they were available across the U.S. In contrast, so-called fast foods are a mature product category in America, but are less common in some other parts of the world. And finally, chilled coffee in cans and bottles is widely accepted in Japan—at least $4 *billion* in annual sales. Yet sales of this beverage in the U.S. are paltry—perhaps

if it's not the future of business.

it's a fiscally sensible present.

With ads such as this one, Palm, Inc. seeks to establish its personal digital assistant as an important business tool that allows mobile communications and delivers results.

10% of the level in Japan. However, seeing growth potential for this product in North America, PepsiCo and Starbucks Coffee are collaborating to market chilled coffee-based beverages. Frappuccino, a product of the joint venture, has been very well received by consumers, commanding an 80% market share in this still small category.[21]

Life-Cycle Management

To some degree, the collective actions of firms offering competing products in the same category affect the shape of the sales and profit curves over the course of a life cycle. Even single companies can have an impact. A giant firm may be able to shorten the introductory stage by broadening the distribution or increasing the promotional effort supporting the new product.

Generally, however, companies cannot substantially affect the sales and profit curves for a product category. Thus their task is to determine how best to achieve success within the life cycle for a category. For an individual firm, successful life-cycle management depends on (1) predicting the shape of the proposed product's cycle even before it is introduced and (2) successfully adapting marketing strategies at each stage of the life cycle.

Entry Strategies
A firm entering a new market must decide whether to plunge in during the introductory stage. Or it can wait and make its entry during the early part of the growth stage, after innovating companies have proven there is a viable market.

The strategy of entering during the introductory stage is prompted by the desire to build a dominant market position right away, and thus lessen the interest of potential competitors and the effectiveness of actual competitors. This strategy worked for Sony with the Walkman, Amana and Litton with microwave ovens, and recently

USRobotics (now Palm Inc.) with personal digital assistants, Intuit with Quicken financial software, and eBay with online auctions.

According to one line of thinking, there is a benefit, called a **first-mover advantage** (or *pioneer advantage*), to getting a head start in marketing a new type of product. The premise is that the company that introduces a new product can target the highest potential market segments and can determine how to produce the good or service at lower and lower costs, to mention just a couple of specific benefits. However, pioneering requires a large investment, and the risks are great—as demonstrated by the high failure rate among new products. In fact, in the PDA category, Apple's Newton was the pioneer, but soon failed. Many dot-com failures, such as eToys, Kozmo, and Garden.com, were pioneers in their categories, but failed nevertheless—raising doubts about whether there really is a first-mover advantage.[22]

Large companies with the marketing resources to overwhelm smaller innovating firms are most likely to be successful with a delayed-entry strategy. In one such case, Coca-Cola introduced Tab and then Diet Coke, and Pepsi-Cola introduced Diet Pepsi, and the two giants surpassed Kirsch's No-Cal Cola, the pioneer.

A study of 50 product categories concluded that the first-mover advantage is temporary, not lasting. The pioneer remains the market leader in only four of the categories (cola soft drink, color television, shortening, and telephone). In contrast, delaying entry until the market is proven can sometimes pay off. According to this same study, being an "early leader" can be advantageous over the long run. An early leader, which is a firm that enters a product category many years after the first mover but then gains market leadership during the growth stage of the cycle, is the current leader in more than one-half the 50 product categories.[23]

Managing on the Rise

When sales are growing strongly and profits are robust in a product category, you might think marketing managers have little to do except tally up their anticipated bonuses. That's not the case. Decisions made during the growth stage influence (1) how many competitors enter the market and (2) how well the company's brand within a product category does both in the near and distant future.

During the growth stage of the life cycle, a company has to devise the right strategies for its brand(s) in that product category. Target markets have to be confirmed or, if necessary, adjusted. Product improvements must be formulated, prices assessed and perhaps revised, distribution expanded, and promotion enhanced.

Home video games were introduced in the 1970s, but the more captivating (perhaps addictive) Nintendo brand, in effect, created a new product category in the 1980s. As described in a case following this part of the text, this product appeared to be in the growth stage of its life cycle as the 1990s began. However, video game sales stagnated in the mid-1990s. Since then, to stimulate sales, Nintendo, Sony, and now Microsoft have been engaged in "technological leap frog." That is, the three competitors are constantly striving to gain a differential advantage, even if only temporary, by building more video, audio, and graphics capabilities into their systems, while controlling prices.[24]

Managing during Maturity

Common strategies to maintain or boost sales of a product during the maturity stage of its life cycle include not just implementing line extension, but also modifying the product, designing new promotion, and devising new uses for the product.[25] Such steps may lead to added purchases by present customers and/or may attract new customers.

To reach a new market, Time Inc. extended its *Sports Illustrated* line, introducing separate editions for women (publication halted at end of 2000) and kids. As sales flattened out, some cruise lines modified their services by adding fitness programs and offering special theme cruises (sometimes in conjunction with a professional sports team). In the public sector, the U.S. Mint is considering redesign of all coins except the quarter, perhaps to spur interest among coin collectors.[26]

The DuPont Co. appears to be particularly adept at sustaining mature products, such as Teflon protective coating and Lycra fiber. Lycra is a brand of spandex, a fiber DuPont invented in 1959. DuPont's primary strategy to generate continuing interest in Lycra has been to develop improved versions of it. The product now is used in a variety of clothing, ranging from hosiery to women's and men's fashions to cycling shorts. DuPont also backs Lycra with aggressive promotion, such as a $40 million global ad campaign stressing that clothes made with Lycra help consumers "look better, feel better."[27]

www.lycra.com

Surviving the Decline Stage   Perhaps it is in the decline stage that a company finds its greatest challenges in life-cycle management. For instance, condensed milk was developed prior to the Civil War when there was no electrical refrigeration to prevent food from spoiling. Now, with refrigerators in almost all U.S. homes, this product is in its decline stage. Borden sold its brand of condensed milk to Eagle Family Foods, which is trying to reinvigorate the product. Eagle launched a "Make Magic in Minutes" campaign to show consumers that condensed milk can help them make various food treats, easily and year-round.[28]

When sales are declining, management has the following alternatives:

- Ensure that marketing and production programs are as efficient as possible.
- Prune unprofitable sizes and models. Frequently this tactic will *decrease* sales but *increase* profits.
- "Run out" the product; that is, cut all costs to the bare minimum to maximize profitability over the limited remaining life of the product.
- Best (and toughest) of all, improve the product in a functional sense, or revitalize it in some manner. Some publishers are working hard to maintain the appeal of the dictionary. St. Martin's Press, for instance, has introduced a dictionary that includes workplace slang and also bios of celebrities. As part of a collaboration with Microsoft, the new dictionary will be available on a CD-ROM for use on personal computers and also in the traditional printed format.[29]

If one of these alternatives doesn't work, management will have to consider **product abandonment.** The expense of carrying profitless products goes beyond what shows up on financial statements. For example, there is a very real cost to the managerial time and effort that is diverted to terminally ill products. Management often is reluctant to discard a product, however, partly because it becomes attached to the product over the years. Knowing when and how to abandon products successfully may be as important as knowing when and how to introduce new ones.

Either before or after abandoning a declining product, a company may redefine its mission to concentrate on a more promising venture. That's what Fluke Manufacturing did when its traditional test and measurement devices started to become obsolete because of computing technology. Thus it was no fluke that the company came up with the following mission statement: "To be the leader in compact professional electronic test tools."[30]

www.fluke.com

Planned Obsolescence and Fashion

American consumers seem to be constantly searching for "what's new" but not "*too new.*" They want newness—new products, new styles, new colors. However, they want to be moved gently out of their habitual patterns, not shocked out of them. Consequently, many manufacturers use a product strategy of planned obsolescence. The intent of this strategy is to make an existing product out of date and thus increase the market for replacement products. Consumers often satisfy their thirst for newness through fashion. And producers of fashions rely heavily on planned obsolescence, as we'll see.

Nature of Planned Obsolescence

The term **planned obsolescence** is used to refer to either of two developments:

- **Technological obsolescence.** Significant technical improvements result in a more effective product. For instance, cassette tapes made vinyl phonograph records outmoded, and then compact discs rendered cassettes virtually obsolete. This type of obsolescence is generally considered to be socially and economically desirable, because the replacement product offers more benefits and/or a lower cost.

- **Style obsolescence.** Superficial characteristics of a product are altered so that the new model is easily differentiated from the previous model. Style obsolescence, sometimes called "psychological" or "fashion" obsolescence, is intended to make people feel out-of-date if they continue to use old models. Products subject to this type of obsolescence include clothing, furniture, and automobiles.

Normally, when people criticize planned obsolescence, they mean style obsolescence. Still, technological (or functional) obsolescence is sometimes criticized. For example, Microsoft has been chided for its periodic revisions of Windows and related products. As one critic said sarcastically, "New versions of software are often little more than 'bug fixes,' . . . and you're given the privilege of paying for those fixes."[31] In our discussion, when we speak of planned obsolescence, we will mean *only* style obsolescence, unless otherwise stated.

Nature of Style and Fashion

Although the words *style* and *fashion* are often used interchangeably, there is a clear distinction. A **style** is a distinctive manner of construction or presentation in any art, product, or endeavor (singing, playing, behaving). Thus we have styles in automobiles (sedans, station wagons), in bathing suits (one-piece, bikini), in furniture (early American, French provincial), and in music (jazz, rap).

A **fashion** is any style that is popularly accepted or purchased by successive groups of people over a reasonably long period of time. Not every style becomes a fashion. To be considered a fashion, or to be called "fashionable," a style must be accepted by many people. All styles listed in the preceding paragraph, except perhaps rap music, qualify as fashions. All past societies, including ancient Egypt and medieval Europe, had fashions and so does contemporary America.

Fashion is rooted in sociological and psychological factors. Basically, most of us are conformists. At the same time, we yearn to look and act a *little* different from others. We probably are not in revolt against custom; we simply wish to be a bit distinctive but not be accused of having bad taste or disregarding norms. Fashion furnishes the opportunity for self-expression.

Fashion-Adoption Process

The fashion-adoption process reflects the concepts of (1) cultural, social-class, and reference-group influences on consumer buying behavior, as discussed in Chapter 4, and (2) the diffusion of innovation, as explained in Chapter 8. People usually try to imitate others at the same or the next higher socioeconomic level. One way of doing this is to purchase a product that is fashionable in the group you want to be like.

Thus the **fashion-adoption process** is a series of buying waves that arise as a particular style is popularly accepted in one group, then another group, and another, until it finally falls out of fashion. This movement, representing the introduction, rise, popular culmination, and decline of the market's acceptance of a style, is referred to as the **fashion cycle**. A case can be made that synthetic fibers such as polyester in clothing and the convertible model of automobile are two products that have run the full fashion cycle.

There are three theories of fashion adoption, as depicted in Figure 9.4:

- **Trickle-down,** where a given fashion cycle flows *downward* through several socioeconomic levels.
- **Trickle-across,** where the cycle moves *horizontally* and *simultaneously within* several socioeconomic levels.
- **Trickle-up,** where a style first becomes popular at lower socioeconomic levels and then flows *upward* to become popular among higher levels.

Traditionally, the *trickle-down* theory has been used to explain the fashion-adoption process. As an example, designers of women's apparel first introduce a style to opinion leaders in the upper socioeconomic groups. If they accept the style, it quickly appears in leading fashion stores. Soon the middle-income and then the lower-income markets want to emulate the leaders, and the style is mass marketed. As its popularity wanes, the style appears in bargain-price stores and finally is no longer considered fashionable.

The *trickle-up* process also explains some product-adoption processes. Consider how styles of music such as jazz and rap became popular. Also look at blue denim pants and jackets, athletic footwear, even pasta in the 1990s, and so-called urban clothing over the past several years.[32] They all have one thing in common: They were popular first with lower socioeconomic groups, and later their popularity "trickled up" to higher-income markets.

Today the *trickle-across* theory best explains the adoption process for most fashions. It's true that there is some flow downward, and obviously there is an upward flow. But, by means of modern production, communication, and transportation, companies can disseminate style information and products so rapidly that all social levels can be reached at about the same time.

Recognizing this accelerated adoption process, most apparel manufacturers produce a wide *variety* of essentially one style. They also produce distinct *qualities* of the same basic style so as to appeal to different income groups.[33] For example, within a few weeks of the beginning of the fall season, the same style of dress (but at different quality levels) appears in (1) small, exclusive dress shops appealing to the upper social class, (2) large department stores aiming at the middle class, and (3) discount

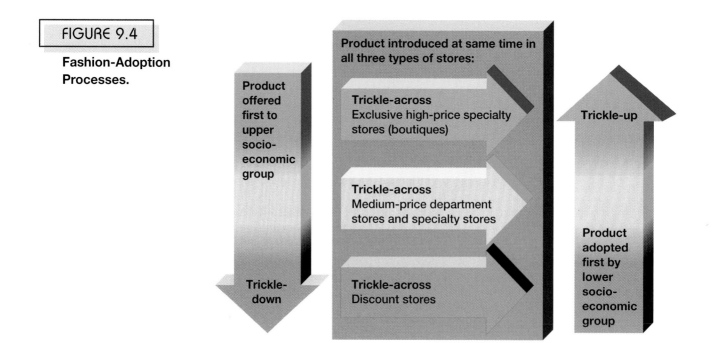

FIGURE 9.4

Fashion-Adoption Processes.

How do new fashions make it so quickly from Europe to the U.S.?

Many—but certainly not all—fashion trends in clothing start in Europe and then find their way to the U.S. Sometimes, "knockoffs" of new styles show up in department stores and discount houses *before* the original, high-price version reaches exclusive dress shops. This can happen if a competitor pays attention to public fashion shows that some designers still use to announce their fall fashion lines or otherwise obtains information about upcoming styles. Then the competing firm hurries through the production process, perhaps paying less attention to quality, and rushes the knockoff dresses into distribution channels.

The Internet is also contributing to the rapid dispersion of fashion trends. For one thing, Yves Saint Laurent and some other designers of *haute couture* (which roughly translates to very expensive, fashionable clothing) are running their periodic fashion shows live on the Net. As such, anyone can see what high-end fashion houses are promoting as "new and hot." For another, relatively new services allow subscribers to see not only what fashion models are wearing on runways around the world but also photos of what

products are being featured in the display windows of leading retail chains and what young people in large cities are wearing. The Worth Global Style Network, founded by two English brothers, sells subscriptions to its Web-based trend-monitoring service for about $3,000 per year.

Designers for clothing manufacturers and merchandise buyers for retail chains that are located in North America still need to travel occasionally to Europe and other parts of the world in order to see styles—live and in person—and detect trends in various locales. However, the Internet has made it much easier and cheaper for people in the fashion industry to monitor what's happening around the world, thereby reducing the amount (and expense) of extensive travel and speeding fashions from limited to widespread availability.

Sources: Teri Agins, "To Track Fickle Fashion, Apparel Firms Go Online," *The Wall Street Journal,* May 11, 2000, pp. B1, B14; William Echikson, "Designers Climb onto the Virtual Catwalk," *Business Week,* Oct. 11, 1999, pp. 164, 168; and Mike Bosworth, "Gavels Pound on Knockoff Vendors," *Apparel Industry Magazine,* April 1999, pp. 86–90.

houses and low-price women's ready-to-wear chain stores, where the target is the portion of the lower class that has some disposable income.

Within each class, the dresses are purchased early in the season by the opinion leaders—the innovators. If the style is accepted, its sales curve rises as it becomes popular with the early adopters and then with the late adopters. Eventually, sales decline as the style loses popularity. This cycle is a horizontal movement, occurring virtually simultaneously within each of several socioeconomic levels.

Marketing Considerations in Fashion

Accurate forecasting is critical to success in fashion merchandising. This is extremely difficult, however, because the forecaster must deal with complex sociological and psychological factors. On-target forecasting—indeed, effective marketing—has become increasingly difficult in the clothing industry in recent years. One reason: Smaller numbers of female consumers are responding to annual style changes; many women are simply buying fewer clothes. Another reason: The trend in which firms allowed—even encouraged—casual dress by workers may be waning. In fact, sales of business suits and other tailored wear were up 12% in 2001 compared to 2000. The reversal is attributed to a more serious state of mind in the United States, brought about by the soft economy and the terrorist attacks of September 11, 2001.[34]

When a firm's products are subject to the fashion cycle, management must know what stage the cycle is in at all times. Managers must decide at what point to get into the cycle and when to get out. Frequently a manufacturer or a retailer of fashionable items operates largely on intuition and inspiration, tempered by considerable experience.

Ordinarily a retailer cannot participate successfully in all stages of the fashion cycle at the same time. Thus a specialty apparel store—whose stocks are displayed in limited numbers without price tags—should get in at the start of a fashion trend. And a department store appealing to the middle-income market should plan to enter the cycle in time to mass-market the style as it is climbing to its peak of popularity. For example, given its middle-income target market, Sears is striving to have its clothing stay within one year of the latest styles. Fundamentally, retail executives must keep in mind the product's target market in deciding at which stage(s) of the life cycle its stores should offer fashionable apparel.[35]

Summary

Many strategic decisions must be made to manage a company's assortment of products effectively. To start, a firm must select strategies regarding its product mix. One decision is how to position the product relative to competing products and other products sold by the firm.

Another strategic decision is whether or how to expand the product mix by adding items to a line and/or introducing new lines. Altering the design, packaging, or other features of existing products is still another option among the strategies of selecting the best mix. The product mix also can be changed by eliminating an entire line or by simplifying the assortment within a line. Alternatively, management may elect to trade up or trade down relative to existing products.

Executives need to understand the concept of a product life cycle, which reflects the total sales volume for a generic product category. Each of the cycle's four stages—introduction, growth, maturity, and decline—has distinctive characteristics that have implications for marketing. Managing a product as it moves through its life cycle presents a number of challenges and opportunities. Eventually, a product category may lack adequate acceptance; at that point, all or most companies should abandon their versions of this product.

Planned obsolescence is a controversial product strategy, built around the concepts of style, fashion, and the fashion cycle. Fashion—essentially a sociological and psychological phenomenon—follows a reasonably predictable pattern. With advances in communications and production, the fashion-adoption process has moved away from the traditional trickle-down pattern. Today the process is better described as trickle-across. There also are examples of fashions trickling up. Managing a product, such as expensive apparel, through a fashion cycle may be even more challenging than adjusting another type of product's strategies during its life cycle.

More about **Palm**

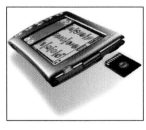

In about five years, PDA capabilities have improved, and the competitive landscape has come to resemble a full-scale battleground. New firms have entered the fray, and others such as European heavyweights Nokia and Ericsson are doing so. At the same time, the growth in annual sales has dropped to about 20%, still substantial but far below the earlier rates of over 100% per year.

Late in 2001, Palm's founders left the company to start a competing firm, Handspring, which licenses Palm's software for its own, increasingly popular PDA called the Visor. Then Microsoft brought out a slimmed-down version of Windows for PDAs, called Pocket PC, which includes versions of Word and Excel as well as e-mail and Web browser capabilities. Compaq, HP, Casio, Toshiba, and Audiovox have licensed Pocket PC for their own new PDAs. To further complicate Palm's situation, the company's CEO resigned.

Meantime, Palm seeks to maintain a leadership position in the handheld computer market. It still holds the largest market shares—almost 50% in the U.S. and about 40% around the world. Despite being the first mover, Palm is now viewed as lagging behind other firms, notably Sony and Hewlett-Packard, with respect to product innovation. Seeking more flexibility with regards to business relationships, among other factors, Palm announced plans to split itself into separate enterprises—one focused on hardware for handhelds and the other on developing and licensing software for these devices.

Personal digital assistants (PDAs) such as the Palm are steadily evolving into a new kind of product with more and more capabilities such as full-color screens, faster processors, and multimedia. Sometimes called "hybrids," these devices combine mobile phones, wireless e-mail, and Web browsers along with the same contact and planning capabilities of the original PDAs.

Some of the latest-generation products, like Handspring's Treo, flip open like cell phones; the BlackBerry allows the user to receive and send e-mail with a real, if tiny, built-in keyboard. Palm is fighting back with an enhanced operating system and also new models like the i705, which retails for about $450. Featuring a wireless modem like the BlackBerry's, the i705 handles both e-mail and attachments to such electronic messages.

Devices powered by Microsoft's Pocket PC operating system, with their portable versions of Word and Excel, also will battle for sales and market share, while seeking the most important factor of all—profits. All of the manufacturers in the handheld computer field are counting on innovations like wireless technology to justify prices of at least several hundred dollars and to build demand in the marketplace. In time, prices may come down, either because the technology will be cheaper to produce or because the firms will resort to a price war. If or when that happens, having a superior product, channels, and/or promotion will be essential for viability—and profitability.[36]

1. What stage of its life cycle is the PDA in?

2. As the PDA proceeds through its life cycle, how will target markets shift and how should Palm's marketing strategies change?

Key Terms and Concepts

Product mix (236)
Breadth (236)
Depth (236)
Product line (236)
Product-mix expansion (239)
Line extension (239)
Mix extension (239)
Product alteration (240)
Product-mix contraction (241)
Trading up (242)

Trading down (242)
Product life cycle (243)
Introduction stage (244)
Growth stage (245)
Maturity stage (245)
Decline stage (246)
Fad (247)
First-mover advantage (249)
Product abandonment (250)
Planned obsolescence (251)

Technological obsolescence (251)
Style obsolescence (251)
Style (251)
Fashion (251)
Fashion-adoption process (251)
Fashion cycle (251)
Trickle-down theory (252)
Trickle-across theory (252)
Trickle-up theory (252)

Questions and Problems

1. "It is inconsistent for management to follow concurrently the product-line strategies of *expanding* its product mix and *contracting* its product mix." Discuss.

2. "Trading up and trading down are product strategies closely related to the business cycle. Firms trade up during periods of prosperity and trade down during recessions." Do you agree? Why?

3. Name one category of goods and one category of services you believe are in the introductory stage of their life cycles. For each product, identify the market that considers your examples to be truly new.

4. Does the Internet accelerate or delay the movement of a new product category through the introduction stage and into later stages of its life cycle?

5. What are two products that are in the decline stage of the life cycle? In each case, point out whether you think the decline is permanent. What recommendations do you have for rejuvenating the demand for either of these products?

6. How might a company's advertising strategies differ, depending on whether its brand of a product is in the introduction stage or the maturity stage of its life cycle?

7. What products, other than apparel and automobiles, stress fashion and style in marketing? Do styles exist among business products?

8. Is the trickle-across theory applicable to the fashion-adoption process in product lines other than women's apparel? Explain, using examples.

9. Planned obsolescence is criticized as a social and economic waste because we are urged to buy things we do not like and do not need. What is your opinion? If you object to planned obsolescence, what are your recommendations for correcting the situation?

Interactive Marketing Exercises

1. Select a product category in which you are interested. Go to either the Internet or the library, and identify the national or state trade association for this product category. Then obtain from the association sales figures for this product over its history and other information that will allow you to plot the life cycle for this product. What stage of the life cycle is this product in? Explain.

2. Arrange a meeting with a supermarket manager or a department manager in a supermarket. Discuss how the manager handles the challenge of line extensions. In which product category are line extensions most common? When new items are added to the line, how does the manager find space for the new entries—by giving more space to this category, dropping other items carrying this same brand, pruning other brands in this category, or some other means? What criteria are used in making this decision?

10

Brands, Packaging, and Other Product Features

PART 3

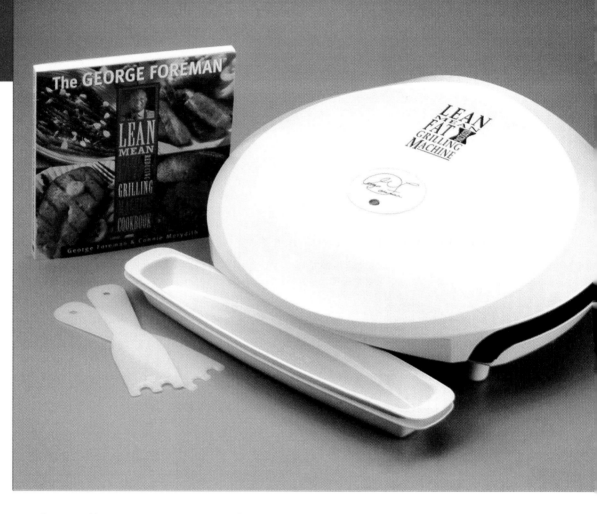

"The grill's success not only is a result of having a good product but also 'should be attributed to George Foreman and the credibility he has with the public.'"

Is George Foreman the Champion in Another Ring?

A junior high school dropout from a poor Houston neighborhood, George Foreman came to the public's attention by winning an Olympic gold medal in the boxing ring in 1968. He then built a successful career as a professional heavyweight boxer, eventually retiring in 1977 to become an evangelical minister. Ten years after that, he returned to the boxing ring, but lost a bout to Evander Holyfield. But in 1994, Foreman won back the heavyweight championship at age 46, the oldest man to do so.

A rugged, ornery fighter in his younger years, Foreman eventually became a cheerful, self-deprecating man who seemed unimpressed by his achievements. His new popularity led to many opportunities to endorse products, ranging from hamburgers to mufflers. But what Foreman is likely to be best remembered for, outside the boxing ring, is the line of grills that carries his name.

Grills? Yes, the ex-boxer collaborated with Salton, Inc., an Illinois-based firm, to introduce George Foreman's Lean, Mean, Fat Reducing Grilling Machine. With sales approaching $1 billion, Salton designs, markets, and distributes small appliances and other products for the home. The company places great emphasis on its array of brands. Its small appliances carry a variety of labels, including Toastmaster, Farberware Melitta, and Juiceman. The company also has other lines of tabletop, time, lighting, personal care, and wellness products, with brands such as Block China, Westclox, and Stiffel.

Resembling a waffle iron, the grill cooks the top and bottom of foods at the same time, so cooking time is faster. The grill is tilted, so fat runs off the food and collects in a small tray. The grill was introduced in 1995; the now well-known celebrity promoted it through infomercials on TV and personal appearances. Looking back, Foreman says the first customers were "old people and the blind, because it's easy to operate, and older people are very concerned about fat." Sales of the grill took off after a couple of years. It has now earned the status of the biggest-selling household appliance—ever.

Salton has launched other products bearing Foreman's name, including a countertop appliance that can roast whole chickens or beef or pork roasts. The Foreman family of appliances now includes over 100 items and accounts for nearly one-half the company's sales volume.

To gain the worldwide, perpetual rights to the George Foreman name for branding purposes, Salton entered into one of the largest endorsement contracts any celebrity ever signed. The company agreed to pay a total of $137.5 million for the perpetual rights to the "George Foreman" name. This payout far exceeded George's largest boxing payday, which was $12.5 million for the Holyfield fight. Salton's management is quick to point out that this contract actually saved the firm considerable money because the original contract gave Foreman almost 60% of the profits from all products carrying his name.

For its investment, Salton received a strong brand built on the Foreman name and, perhaps equally important, the former fighter's charming personality and his willingness to promote the products at any opportunity. Salton's chief executive, Leon Dreimann, admitted that at

www.saltoninc.com

first, he "did not recognize the love that the public had for George." Now he realizes that the grill's success not only is a result of having a good product but also "should be attributed to George Foreman and the credibility he has with the public."

When the economy softened at the start of the new century, sales of many products—including small appliances—sagged or at least leveled off. As Salton called on its marketing expertise in efforts to build sales, some observers wondered whether the firm had overpaid Foreman. Salton's president, Bill Rue, remained confident that the brand would have longevity. "We never regretted this deal with Foreman," he said. "Without doing it we couldn't expand the brand. . . . Foreman is a brand to us. It's not a grill."[1]

What does Salton need to do to assure that the George Foreman brand keeps a smile on the face of consumers?

As the George Foreman case illustrates, a brand can be all-important for many products. Otherwise, how do you account for some consumers wanting Bayer aspirin and others preferring or at least accepting Walgreen's brand, when both are physically and chemically the identical product? Other consumers' choices are influenced not only by the brand but also by the package, design, or another product feature. Because these product features are important elements in a marketing program, we devote this chapter to them. After studying this chapter, you should be able to explain:

Chapter Goals

- The nature and importance of brands.
- Characteristics of a good brand name.
- Branding strategies of producers and middlemen.
- Why and how a growing number of firms are building and using brand equity.
- The nature and importance of packaging and labeling.
- Major packaging strategies.
- The marketing implications of other product features—design, color, and quality—that can satisfy consumers' wants.

Brands

The word *brand* is comprehensive; it encompasses other narrower terms. A **brand** is a name and/or mark intended to identify the product of one seller or group of sellers and to differentiate the product from competing products. *Brand* is also used, not really correctly, to refer to a specific product, as in "sales of the brand."[2]

A **brand name** consists of words, letters, and/or numbers that can be vocalized. A **brand mark** is the part of the brand that appears in the form of a symbol, design, or distinctive color or lettering. A brand mark is recognized by sight but cannot be expressed when a person pronounces the brand name. Crest, FUBU, and Bearing Point (formerly KPMG Consulting) are brand names. Brand marks are the distinctively lined globe of AT&T and the Nike "swoosh." Green Giant (canned and frozen vegetable products) and Arm & Hammer (baking soda) are both brand names and brand marks. Sometimes the term *logo* (short for *logotype*) is used interchangeably with brand mark or even brand name, especially if the name is written in a distinctive, stylized fashion.

www.fubu.com

A **trademark** is a brand that has been adopted by a seller and given legal protection. (A trademark for a service has come to be called, not surprisingly, a *service* *mark*. Our use of *trademark* also covers *service mark*.) A trademark includes not just the brand mark, as many people believe, but also the brand name. The Lanham Act of 1946 permits firms to register trademarks with the federal government to protect them from use or misuse by other companies. The Trademark Law Revision Act, which took effect in 1989, is intended to strengthen the registration system to the benefit of U.S. firms. In Europe, companies can now submit a single application to obtain trademark registration and protections throughout the European Union.[3]

Companies strive vigorously, even filing law suits, to protect their trademarks. Recent instances include Gateway, the computer maker, filing suit against a company for imitating its black-and-white cow pattern on another product. Also, the World Wrestling Federation and the World Wildlife Fund grappled over the initials WWF. Eventually, a court ruled in favor of the wildlife group; subsequently, the wrestling enterprise changed its initials to WWE, with "E" representing Entertainment.[4]

One method of classifying brands is on the basis of who owns them. Thus we have **producers' brands** and **middlemen's brands,** the latter being owned by retailers or wholesalers. Florsheim (shoes), Prozac (Eli Lilly & Company's antidepressant drug), Courtyard by Marriott (lodging), and Qantas (an Australian airline) are producers' brands; Lucerne (Safeway), Craftsman (Sears), and St. John's Bay (JCPenney) are middlemen's brands.

The terms *national* and *private* have been used to describe producer and middleman brand ownership, respectively. However, marketing people prefer the *producer–middleman* terminology. To say that a brand of poultry feed marketed in three states by a small Birmingham, Alabama, manufacturer is a *national* brand, or that the brands of Wal-Mart and Sears are *private* brands, stretches the meaning of these two terms.

A GLOBAL PERSPECTIVE

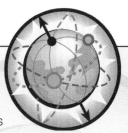

Who's got the Bud?

A company trying to establish a global brand may find another firm using the same brand in some countries. For example, Anheuser-Busch Companies (A-B), the St. Louis–based brewery, isn't the only company placing the Budweiser brand on beer. A century-old brewery in the Czech Republic, Budejovicky Budvar, sells a Budweiser brew in parts of eastern Europe as well as Germany. The American brand is sold throughout most of the rest of the world. Further, the Czech brand is called "the beer of kings," and the American brand "the king of beers."

What's the problem? Essentially, both brewers lay claim to the Budweiser trademark. A-B began making Budweiser beer in the U.S. in 1876. Then in 1895, Czechs in a community called Budweis started a brewery to make and sell its own Budweiser beer. When the two enterprises began to expand into other countries, the dispute over the Budweiser trademark erupted.

Eventually, in 1939, the two competitors agreed to divide up the world market with respect to where each concern could use the Budweiser brand. Thus A-B affixes various names on its product in European countries—the well-known Budweiser in some, but Bud, American Bud, and Anheuser-Busch B in others. The only area in which both brewers use the Budweiser brand is Great Britain.

Wanting to develop its version of Budweiser as a global brand, A-B persisted in seeking an agreement with Budvar. In late 1995, A-B offered to pay the Czech brewery $200 million for the worldwide rights to the Budweiser name. Because the name is so well known, the Czech brewery saw added sales potential for its own Budweiser brand and, consequently, rejected A-B's proposal.

The two breweries seem to have arrived at an unannounced truce. Both companies continue their marketing efforts around the world. In fact, the Czech beer is now available in the U.S. under the Czechvar brand.

Sources: Al Stamborski, "Czech Beer Comes Back to the U.S. after 60-Year Hiatus," *St. Louis Post-Dispatch*, Mar. 9, 2001, pp. E1, E7; "Czechs Drop Attempt to End Bud War," *St. Louis Post-Dispatch*, Nov. 12, 1997, p. 1D; Robert L. Koenig, "Bud War," *St. Louis Post-Dispatch*, Oct. 22, 1995, p. 1A; and Roger Thurow, "The King of Beers and Beer of Kings Are at Lagerheads," *The Wall Street Journal*, Apr. 3, 1992, p. A1.

Reasons for Branding

For consumers, brands make it easy to identify goods or services. They aid shoppers in moving quickly through a supermarket, discount outlet, or other retail store and in making purchase decisions. Brands also help assure consumers that they will get consistent quality when they reorder.

For sellers, brands can be promoted. They are easily recognized when displayed in a store or included in advertising. Branding reduces price comparisons. That is, because brands are another factor to be considered in comparing different products, branding reduces the likelihood of purchase decisions that are based solely on price. The reputation of a brand also influences customer loyalty among buyers of services as well as business and consumer goods. Finally, branding can differentiate commodities (Sunkist oranges, Morton salt, and Domino sugar, for example). A wholesaler is even trying to establish a Hearts on Fire brand for diamonds.[5]

Not all brands are widely and favorably recognized by their target markets. And among those that are, many are unable to maintain a position of prominence. However, as a result of such activities as aggressive promotion and careful quality control, a few brands (Chevrolet autos and Gillette razors) retain their leadership positions over a long time. Consequently, enormous amounts of money are spent to acquire companies that have widely recognized brands. Italy's Gucci Group bought another firm in order to acquire several well-known brands, including Yves Saint Laurent (luxury fashion accessories) and Van Cleef & Arpels (fragrances). Recently, Nestlé paid over $15 *billion* to purchase two companies and a controlling interest in a third, acquiring such popular brands as Hot Pockets, Edy's, and Purina.[6]

Reasons for Not Branding

Two responsibilities come with brand ownership: (1) promoting the brand and (2) maintaining a consistent quality of output. Many firms do not brand their products because they are unable or unwilling to assume these responsibilities.

Some items remain unbranded because they cannot be physically differentiated from other firms' products. Clothespins, nails, and raw materials (coal, cotton, wheat) are examples of goods for which product differentiation, including branding,

Despite the difficulty of differentiating a commodity, Morton International succeeded in creating a well-known, favored brand of salt. Some Morton ads, including this one, have been aimed at reinforcing the brand name; others promote new uses for the product.

www.mortonsalt.com

is generally unknown. The perishable nature of products such as fresh fruits and vegetables works against branding. However, well-known brands such as Dole pineapples and Chiquita bananas demonstrate that even agricultural products can be branded successfully.

Selecting a Good Brand Name

Some brand names are so good that they contribute to the success of products. Consider, for example, DieHard batteries and the Roach Motel (which is a pest-eradication device, not a discount motel). But it takes more than a clever brand name to ensure success in the marketplace. Witness Trans World Airlines, the aptly named airline that eventually faltered and was acquired by a competitor. Other brand names are so poor that they are a factor in product failures. Occasionally products achieve success despite poor brand names—consider Exxon, which had no meaning when it was first introduced.

Choosing a name for a product may appear trivial, but it's not. One consultant went so far (perhaps too far) as to say, "The most important element in a marketing program—and the one over which marketing managers can exert the most control—is the naming of a product."[7]

The Challenge Nowadays, selecting a good brand name for a new product is especially challenging. The reason? We're running out of possibilities. On the one hand, about 10,000 new products are launched annually; on the other hand, only 50,000 words comprise the standard desk-size dictionary.[8] Further, many words either already adorn products (such as Pert Plus, Cascade, and Veryfine) or are unsuitable as brand names (such as obnoxious, hypocrite, and deceased).

One solution is to combine numbers with words, numbers, and/or letters to form a brand name. Examples include Net2Phone (an Internet telecommunications service), Formula 409 (household cleaner), WD-40 (lubricant and protectant), and Lotus 1-2-3

web.net2phone.com

Ralston Purina devised the brand name of Beneful for a line of dog food. Does this brand pass the test of suggesting what the product's benefits or uses are? If you think "beneficial" or "benefit" when you see Beneful, then it certainly does. Also, the ad's last line is "Healthful. Flavorful. Beneful," placing a thought in consumers' minds about the last part of the name. Does the brand have the other four characteristics of a desirable brand name?

www.beneful.com

It reads like a Who's Who of ingredients.

PURINA
Beneful
brand DOG FOOD

You've never seen anything like this before. Beneful® brand dog food from Purina has wholesome grains for energy, protein-rich beef that helps build strong muscles and vegetables with vitamins and minerals. You'll love the complete nutrition. Your dog will love the taste. He'll only think he's getting spoiled. Beneful from Purina.

HEALTHFUL. FLAVORFUL. BENEFUL.

www.beneful.com

(software). Another possibility is to create a brand name that isn't part of the English language. Examples of so-called *morphemes* include Ameritrade stock brokerage, Lexus autos, and Compaq computers.[9]

Desirable Characteristics Various characteristics determine the desirability of a brand name for either a good or a service.[10] It's difficult to find a brand name that rates well on every attribute. Still, a brand name should have as many of the following five characteristics as possible:

- *Suggest something about the product, particularly its benefits and use.* Names connoting benefits include Beautyrest, Mr. Goodwrench, and Minute Rice. Product use is suggested by Dustbuster, Ticketron, and La-Z-Boy chairs.

- *Be easy to pronounce, spell, and remember.* Simple, short, one-syllable names such as Tide, Ban, Aim, and Surf are helpful. However, even some short names, such as Aetna and Inacom, aren't easily pronounced by some consumers. Other brands that may not meet this criterion, at least not in the U.S., include Frusen-Glädje (ice cream), Au Bon Pain (bakeries), and Asahi (beer).

- *Be distinctive.* Brands with names like National, Star, Ideal, United, Allied, or Standard fail on this point. Many services firms begin their brand names with adjectives connoting strength and then add a description of the business, creating brands such as Allied Van Lines and United Parcel Service. But are these really distinctive?

- *Be adaptable to additions to the product line.* A family name such as Kellogg, Lipton, or Ford may serve the purpose better than a highly distinctive name suggesting product benefits. When fast-food restaurants added breakfasts to their

To protect its famous brand name, Xerox ran humorous ads to make a serious point, namely that Xerox is a brand name. The ads stressed that Xerox is neither a verb nor a common noun. Also note that the ad indicated that "Xerox" should be used in conjunction with a noun, such as "copier."

"But Mr. Carruthers, you said you needed forty Xeroxes."

Mr. Carruthers used our name incorrectly. That's why he got 40 Xerox copiers, when what he really wanted was 40 copies made on his Xerox copier.

He didn't know that Xerox, as a trademark of Xerox Corporation, should be followed by the descriptive word for the particular product, such as "Xerox duplicator" or "Xerox copier."

And should only be used as a noun when referring to the corporation itself.

If Mr. Carruthers had asked for 40 copies or 40 photocopies made on his Xerox copier, he would have gotten exactly what he wanted.

And if you use Xerox properly, you'll get exactly what you want, too.

P.S. You're welcome to make 40 copies or 40 photocopies of this ad. Preferably on your Xerox copier.

XEROX

www.xerox.com

menus, McDonald's name fit better than Burger King or Pizza Hut. Likewise, names like Alaska Airlines and Southwest Airlines may inhibit geographic expansion more than a name such as United Airlines.

- *Be capable of registration and legal protection.* Brand names are covered under the Lanham Act, its 1989 revision, and other laws.

The naming process isn't cheap, costing $25,000 and up for the name itself. Then an organization typically has to spend much more than that to promote the new brand.

Protecting a Brand Name

A firm with a well-known, successful brand name needs to actively safeguard it. Otherwise, this valuable asset can be damaged—or even lost entirely—in either of two ways.

Product Counterfeiting
Some unscrupulous manufacturers engage in **product counterfeiting** by placing a highly regarded brand on their offering, disregarding the basic fact that they do not own the rights to the brand. If you have ever been to New York City, you probably have been offered "genuine" Rolex or Gucci watches for $10 to $20 by a street vendor. Counterfeiting can be found in many categories, including leather goods, athletic footwear, software, toys, video games, and automobile replacement parts.

According to the latest estimates, imitation products cost American companies as much as $200 *billion* annually. One study concluded that over 100,000 jobs in the U.S. were lost as a result of piracy in a single category, namely software. Because it's relatively easy to do and because law enforcement agencies do not vigorously pursue violators, a top FBI official called product counterfeiting "the crime of the 21st century."[11]

Counterfeiters can't be eliminated, but companies can—and should—battle knockoffs. First, they need to watch for counterfeit goods carrying one of their brands. Second, producers—perhaps through their trade association—can offer cash rewards for information about piracy. Third, when imitations are identified, legal action should be taken against the violators. Firms cannot afford to ignore this illegal practice because it can diminish the worth of a trademark owner's products. In that vein, Lego, the Danish toy maker, recently won a legal judgement against a Chinese firm that was producing and selling a counterfeit version of the famous building blocks.[12]

Generic Usage
Over a period of years, some brand names become so well accepted that they are commonly used instead of the generic names of the particular product categories.[13] Examples follow:

Generic Terms That Formerly Were Brand Names

aspirin	escalator	linoleum	thermos
brassiere	harmonica	nylon	yo-yo
cellophane	kerosene	shredded wheat	zipper

Originally these names were trademarks that could be used only by the owner. What happened? Well, a brand name can become generic in two primary ways:

- There is no simple generic name available, so the public uses the brand name as a generic name. This occurred with shredded wheat, nylon, and cellophane. The Formica Corporation wages an ongoing struggle, thus far successful, to retain the legal status of its Formica brand of decorative laminate.[14]

www.formica.com

- As contradictory as it appears, sometimes a firm is too effective in promoting a brand name. Although not yet legally generic, names such as Levi's, Band-Aid, Scotch Tape, and Kleenex are on the borderline. These brand names have been promoted so heavily and so successfully that many people use them generically. To illustrate, which terms do you use in conversation—adhesive bandage or Band-Aid, facial tissue or Kleenex? We suspect the latter in both cases

There are various means to prevent the generic use of a brand name:

- Right after the brand name, place the ® symbol (if the brand is a registered trademark for a good), TM (if it is not registered), or SM (for a service).

- Better yet, use the brand name together with the generic name—Dacron brand polyester, for instance.

www.rollerblade.com

- Call attention to and challenge improper use of your brand name. Rollerblade Inc. has gone so far as to sue competitors who use "rollerblade" as a generic word. Thus the maker of Rollerblades disdains a statement like "I broke my neck rollerblading" and prefers the term in-line skating.[15]

Branding Strategies

Both producers and middlemen face strategic decisions regarding the branding of their goods or services.

Producers' Strategies

Producers must decide whether to brand their products and whether to sell any or all of their output under middlemen's brands.

Marketing Entire Output under Producer's Own Brands
Companies that rely strictly on their own brands usually are very large, well financed, and well managed. Maytag and IBM, for example, have broad product lines, well-established distribution systems, and large shares of the market. The reasons why a producer relies strictly on its own brands were covered in the earlier section on the importance of branding to the seller.

A small proportion of manufacturers rely strictly on this strategy, refusing to produce items to be sold as retailers' or wholesalers' brands. Gillette is one such company. The firm's top executive said that manufacturing so-called private-label products would be "a sign of weakness." A company vice president was more blunt, "If any manager did that, he should be shot by the shareholders."[16] This stubbornness will not eliminate competition from middlemen, however. Many middlemen want to market under their own brands. If one manufacturer refuses to sell to them, they simply go to another.

It's particularly difficult for a new firm to produce only for its own brands. Only a minority of manufacturers employ this strategy, and the number seems to be decreasing. A primary reason is that there are lots of opportunities to make products to which middlemen apply their own brands.

Branding of Fabricating Materials and Parts
Some producers use a strategy of *branding fabricating materials and parts* (manufactured goods that become part of another product following subsequent manufacturing).[17] This strategy is used in marketing Dan River cottons, Acrilan fabrics, and many automotive parts such as spark plugs, batteries, and oil filters. DuPont has consistently and successfully used this strategy, notably with its Lycra spandex fiber and Stainmaster stain repellant for carpets.

www.dolby.com

With this strategy, the seller seeks to develop a market preference for its branded parts or materials. Dolby Labs seeks to create a market situation in which buyers insist that a stereo sound system include a Dolby noise-reduction component. This firm wants to convince manufacturers that their stereo sound systems will sell better if they contain Dolby noise-reduction units.

This strategy is most likely to be effective when the particular type of fabricating parts or materials has two characteristics:

- The product is also a consumer good that is bought for replacement purposes—Champion spark plugs and Delco batteries, for example.

Intel Corporation produces processors that are an integral fabricating part in computers. The company has used an "Intel Inside" branding strategy and extensive advertising to convice numerous manufacturers and buyers of computers that its processor is superior to competing products.

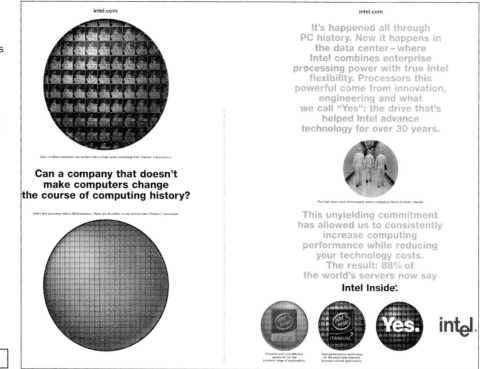

www.intel.com

www.onstar.com

- The item is a key part of the finished product—an integral part of an automobile, for instance. Johnson Controls and General Motors are trying to build recognition for, respectively, the HomeLink control pad and the OnStar navigation system. Other manufacturers are likely to follow suit, considering that 44% of consumers said they will take branded auto parts into account when choosing the next brand and model of car they will buy.[18]

Marketing under Middlemen's Brands A widespread strategy among manufacturers is to sell part or all of their output to middlemen for branding by these customers. Firms such as Borden, Keebler, and Reynolds Metals have their own well-known brands, and they also produce goods for branding by middlemen.

This approach allows a manufacturer to "hedge its bets." A company employing this strategy hopes its own brands will appeal to some loyal customers, whereas middlemen's brands are of interest to other, perhaps more cost-conscious shoppers. Moreover, for a manufacturer, the output produced for middlemen's brands ordinarily represents additional sales. This strategy also helps a manufacturer fully utilize its plant capacity.

One drawback of this strategy is that the manufacturer may lose some customers for its own brands. Another drawback to marketing under middlemen's brands is that the producer's revenues depend on the strength of the middleman's marketing campaign for that brand. This problem grows as the proportion of a producer's output going to middlemen's brands increases.

Middlemen's Strategies

The question of whether to brand must also be answered by middlemen.

Carry Only Producers' Brands Most retailers and wholesalers follow this policy. Why? They do not have the finances or other resources to promote a brand and maintain its quality.

Carry Both Producers' and Middlemen's Brands   Many large retailers and some large wholesalers stock popular producers' brands and also have their own labels. Sears, for instance, offers an assortment of manufacturers' brands such as Healthtex children's clothing and Firestone tires as well as its own brands such as Kenmore appliances and Craftsman tools.

Middlemen may find it advantageous to market their own brands, in place of or in addition to producers' brands, because it increases their control over their target markets. A retailer's brand can differentiate its products. If customers prefer a given retailer's brand, sometimes called a *store brand*, they can get it only from that retailer. Examples include:

Some Retailers' Brands of Apparel

Nordstrom: Classiques Entier
Lord & Taylor: Identity, Kate Hill
Saks Fifth Avenue: Real Clothes, SFA Collections

---

www.saks.com

Prices on producers' brands sometimes are cut drastically when retail stores carrying these brands compete with each other. For an extended time, clothing carrying the labels of designers such as Ralph Lauren and Liz Claiborne was subject to price cutting. A retailer might avoid at least some of this price competition by establishing its own appealing brands. Department stores, ranging from Famous-Barr to JCPenney, are placing more emphasis on store brands. One consultant estimated that store brands will soon account for about 35% of department stores' volume, compared to about 12% less than 10 years ago.[19]

Furthermore, middlemen usually can sell their brands at prices below those of producers' brands and still earn higher gross margins. For example, in dry cereals, a store brand may provide up to twice as much gross profits as a producer's brand.[20] This is possible because middlemen often can acquire merchandise carrying their own brands at lower costs than similar merchandise carrying producers' brands. Costs may be lower because manufacturers have to pay to advertise and sell their own brands, but these expenses are not included in the prices of products sold for branding by middlemen. In some cases, but fewer than in the past, costs may be lower because the quality of the products carrying middlemen's brands is lower than the quality of competing products bearing producers' brands. Also, producers may offer good prices in this situation because they are anxious to get the extra business.

Middlemen have to be careful in pricing their own brands. According to one study, if store brands of groceries are not priced at least 10% below producers' brands, many consumers will not buy them. However, if the store brand is more than 20% lower in price, some consumers become suspicious about quality. In contrast, another study concluded that other factors such as relative quality are more important than price level in determining the success of middlemen's brands versus producers' brands.[21]

Middlemen's brands have had their greatest impact in the marketing of consumer packaged goods, such as groceries and personal care products. The Safeway supermarket chain has long relied on Lucerne and other brands it owns. Loblaw's, the largest supermarket chain in Canada, has found great success with its President's Choice (PC) brand. Wal-Mart, the largest retailer, is multiplying its store brands as well, led by its Sam's American Choice label. When Wal-Mart introduced its own laundry detergent, some observers thought the move was intended in part to pressure Procter & Gamble into reducing its wholesale prices.[22]

Middlemen's brands are now on about one of every five items sold in supermarkets, drug stores, and discount outlets in the U.S. The outlook for middlemen's brands is strong, with one study indicating that 60% of retailers plan to place more emphasis on middlemen's brands. According to one forecast, the private-brand food business will account for $100 billion in volume in North America by 2005, which would be about three times the volume for private brands *in all product categories* just 10 years earlier.[23]

To counter middlemen's brands, some leading manufacturers, including Procter & Gamble and Philip Morris, cut prices on a number of their well-known brands, including Pampers diapers, Tide detergent, and Marlboro cigarettes. Other manufacturers, including Gillette, concentrate on convincing consumers of the superiority of their brands in relation to private brands. All factors considered, neither producers' brands nor middlemen's brands have demonstrated a convincing competitive superiority over the other in the marketplace. Consequently, the "battle of the brands" shows every indication of remaining intense.[24]

Strategies Common to Producers and Middlemen

Producers and middlemen alike must choose strategies with respect to branding their product mixes, branding for market saturation, and joint branding activity with another company.

Branding within a Product Mix
At least three different strategies are used by firms that sell more than one product:

- *A separate name for each product.* This strategy is employed by Lever Brothers and Procter & Gamble. Citigroup, the largest financial services firm in the U.S., still emphasizes some of its individual brands (such as Travelers and Diners Club) while also using the "Citi" part of its corporate identity in other brand names (such as Citibank and Citimortgage). To reduce brand confusion, Bass Hotels & Resorts (now Six Continents Hotels) removed the Holiday Inn name from its upscale Crowne Plaza establishments.[25]

- *The company name combined with a product name.* Examples include Johnson's Pledge and Johnson's Glo-Coat, and Kellogg's Rice Krispies and Kellogg's Corn Pops.

- *The company name alone.* Today few companies rely exclusively on this policy. However, it is followed for the most part by Heinz and Libby in the food field as well as by General Electric in various industries.

www.armorall.com/prodcat

Using the company name for branding purposes, often termed **family branding,** makes it simpler and less expensive to introduce new, related products to a line.[26] Also, the prestige of a brand can be spread more easily if it appears on several products rather than on only one. Armor All Products took advantage of the smashing success of Armor All Protectant by adding other car care products, such as Armor All Cleaner and Armor All Car Wax. The company name is best suited for marketing products that are related in quality, in use, or in some other manner.

Branding with the company name places a greater burden on the firm to maintain consistent quality among all products. One bad item can reflect unfavorably, even disastrously, on all other products carrying the same brand. For this reason, many companies prefer to let each individual product succeed or fail on its own—the first branding strategy in the list above.

Branding for Market Saturation
With increasing frequency, firms are employing a **multiple-brand strategy** to increase their total sales in a market. They have more than one brand of essentially the same product, aimed either at the same target market or at distinct target markets. Suppose, for example, that a company has built one type of sales appeal around a given brand. To reach other segments of the market, the company may use other appeals with other brands. Two Procter & Gamble detergents, Tide and Dreft, illustrate this point. Some people feel that if Tide is strong enough to clean soiled work clothes, it should not be used on lingerie and other fine clothing. For these people P&G has Dreft, a detergent promoted as being gentler than Tide.

Not surprisingly, Chattem, Inc., is interested in capitalizing on the widespread recognition of its Gold Bond brand. As indicated by this insert distributed in Sunday newspapers, the Gold Bond name has been applied to several personal-care products.

 www.goldbond.com/
info.asp

Sometimes, multiple brands are necessary to penetrate separate target markets. For instance, Black & Decker (B&D) tools have strong appeal to do-it-yourselfers but not to professional tradespeople. Hence, B&D removed its company name from power tools aimed at tradespeople and switched to DeWalt, the name of a maker of high-quality stationary saws that was acquired by Black & Decker years ago.[27]

Cobranding   More and more often, two separate companies or two divisions within the same company agree to place both of their respective brands on a particular product or enterprise. This arrangement is termed **cobranding,** or *dual branding.*

Cobranding is increasingly evident in the food products field and also in franchising. Boxes of Duncan Hines brownies mix proclaim that the product contains M&M's. Heath Bars, Sunkist lemons, and Ocean Spray cranberries are all frequently promoted ingredients of other products, such as Betty Crocker's Sunkist Lemon Bars mix. In franchising, cobranding occurs when two or more companies—often in the restaurant field—agree to share the same or adjacent retail space. As one example, Yorkshire Global Restaurants uses cobranding for two of its divisions in order to maximize drawing power and space efficiency. The rationale is that Long John Silver's has a particularly strong following for lunch while A&W does better at dinner time.[28]

As with any marketing strategy or tactic, cobranding has potential benefits and drawbacks. This form of cooperation can result in a differential advantage over competitors. Cobranding can provide added revenues for one or both of the participating firms. When two franchises cooperate, they may ring up greater combined sales than if they were in separate locations. The biggest potential drawbacks to cobranding are possible overexposure of a brand name and, even more significant, the risk of damaging a brand's reputation if the cooperative endeavor fails.

Building and Using Brand Equity

In the minds of many consumers, just having a brand name such as Sprint, Nabisco, Hilton, or Hallmark adds value to a product. In particular, brands like these connote favorable attributes (such as quality or economy). What we're talking about is **brand equity,** which is the value a brand adds to a product.[29]

The leading brands, according to three different studies, are shown in Table 10.1. The Harris Poll asked consumers which brands they "consider the best," whereas EquiTrend ranking is based on consumer perceptions of overall quality. In contrast, the Interbrand-*Business Week* project judged the worth of a brand to be the present value of future earnings that can be attributed to the brand itself.[30]

There is little overlap across the top-10 lists. In fact, only two brands—Coca-Cola and General Electric—were on two of the three lists. Also note that only four services—two television channels, Disney, and McDonald's—were on any of the lists. Finally, and perhaps not surprising considering that two of the studies polled consumers in the U.S., just three of the leading brands (Honda, Mercedes-Benz, and Nokia) are from outside the U.S.

Brands, however they are judged or ranked, are very important assets for a company. The former head of Quaker's food business stated it this way: "If this company were to split up, I would give you the property, plant and equipment and I would take the brands and the trademarks, and I would fare far better than you."[31]

If you're not convinced that a brand name by itself can have much value, consider some research results. In one study, the proportion of subjects choosing corn flakes cereal jumped from 47% when the brand was not known to 59% when the brand was identified as Kellogg's. In another study, when samples of computer buyers were asked how much more or less they would pay for particular brands rather than a relatively unknown brand, there was a range of $339. Brands commanding a premium—that is, possessing substantial equity—included IBM, Compaq, Hewlett-Packard, and Dell.[32]

We tend to think of brand equity as a positive aspect of a product. Occasionally a brand will have negative equity. In such a situation, a brand creates unfavorable impressions about a product in a consumer's mind. For example, after Bridgestone/Firestone Inc. had to recall millions of defective tires, one analyst stated, "You have a serious risk of the Firestone brand imploding." In the services field, Trans World Airlines was

TABLE 10.1 The Leading Brands—Based on Different Criteria

Rank	Harris Poll	EquiTrend	Interbrand-*Business Week*
1.	Discovery Channel	Sony	Coca-Cola
2.	Craftsman Tools (Sears)	Dell Computer	Microsoft
3.	Hershey's Kisses	Ford Motor	IBM
4.	Bose (stereos/speakers)	Kraft Foods	General Electric
5.	WD-40 spray lubricant	Coca-Cola	Intel
6.	Crayola (crayons/markers)	General Electric	Nokia
7.	Reynolds Wrap aluminum foil	Pepsi-Cola	Disney
8.	The Learning Channel	Tide	McDonald's
9.	Neosporin ointment	Honda	Marlboro
10.	M&M's chocolate candies	General Motors	Mercedes-Benz

Sources: Deborah L. Vance, "A Name You Can Trust," *Marketing News,* Sept. 16, 2002, p. 3; "Sony Retains #1 Position in the Harris Poll Annual 'Best Brand' Survey for Third Year in a Row," *PR Newswire,* July 17, 2002; and Gerry Khermouch, "The Best Global Brands," *Business Week,* Aug. 5, 2002, pp. 92–96+.

plagued by financial problems and uneven customer service for many years. As a result, in the minds of many air travelers, the TWA brand had negative equity. Not surprisingly, Trans World eventually agreed to be acquired by the parent company of American Airlines, which eliminated the TWA name.[33]

Building a brand's equity consists of developing a favorable, memorable, and consistent image—no easy task.[34] Product quality and advertising play vital roles in this endeavor. However, if substantial brand equity can be achieved, the organization that owns the brand can benefit in several ways:

www.craftsman.com

- The brand itself can become an edge over competition, what we call a *differential advantage*, influencing consumers to buy a particular product. Examples include Craftsman (Sears' brand for hand tools and gardening equipment), BMW, and Häagen-Dazs.

- Because it is expensive and time-consuming to build brand equity, it creates a barrier for companies that want to enter the market with a similar product.

- The widespread recognition and favorable attitudes surrounding a brand with substantial brand equity can facilitate international expansion. For example, a top executive at McDonald's described what happens when the company brings the Golden Arches to a new country: "It is a huge event. It is a happening. . . . We time and again set new sales records."[35]

- Brand equity can help a product survive changes in the operating environment, such as a business crisis or a shift in consumer tastes.

www.oceanspray.com

Brand equity is often used to expand a product mix, especially by extending a product line. Examples include Ocean Spray drinks in flavors other than the original cranberry, and Wesson olive and canola oils. Similarly, all or part of a strong brand name can be applied to a new product line. For instance, there are now Olay cosmetics, Ann Taylor personal care products, Starbucks ice cream, Courtyard by Marriott motels, and Marquis by Waterford crystal ware.[36] The rationale for using an existing, strong brand name on a new item or line is that the brand's equity will convey a favorable impression of the product and increase the likelihood that consumers will at least try it.

If a brand has abundant equity, that does not necessarily mean it should be applied to other products. Procter & Gamble decided its hugely successful Crest name should be used on different kinds of toothpaste but not on other product categories such as mouthwash. In developing a spaghetti sauce, Campbell determined its popular brand name would not convey an Italian image, so it selected Prego as the name for its new sauce. Also, strong equity does not guarantee success for new items or lines using the well-regarded brands. Even with their famous brand names, Harley-Davidson cigarettes, Levi's tailored men's clothing, Dunkin' Donuts cereal, and Swatch clothing did not pass the test of continuing consumer acceptance.

Trademark Licensing

Products with considerable brand equity have strong potential for **trademark licensing,** also called *brand licensing*. For example, Polo/Ralph Lauren licenses its popular brand to numerous companies for their use on various items of apparel. Under a licensing arrangement, the owner of a trademark grants permission (a license) to other firms to use its brand name and brand mark on their products. A licensee, which is the company that receives a license, ordinarily pays a royalty of about 5% to 10% of the wholesale price of each item bearing the licensed trademark. The royalty percentage varies depending on the amount of equity connected with the brand offered by a licensor, which is the company that owns it.

This branding strategy accounted for under $20 billion in retail sales in the early 1980s and now racks up about $100 *billion* in annual volume in the U.S. However, sales of licensed merchandise fluctuate from year to year, primarily as a result of economic conditions. One popular area for licensing is toys, especially those that feature characters from popular movies and books such as the Harry Potter series. But the biggest category of licensed merchandise is apparel. Recognizing that women account for the majority of purchases of licensed items, some manufacturers are designing licensed sports apparel to suit female sizes and tastes. Perhaps surprisingly, a growing area of licensing involves products displaying companies' brands and trademarks.[37]

Strategic decisions must be made by both the licensor and the licensee. For instance, a licensor such as Pierre Cardin must ask, "Should we allow other firms to use our designer label?" In turn, a potential licensee such as a manufacturer of eyeglass frames must ask, "Do we want to put out a line of high-fashion frames under the Pierre Cardin name?"

Owners of well-known brands are interested in licensing their trademarks for various reasons:

- *It can be very profitable.* There is little expense for the licensor. However, to protect the reputation of its trademark, the licensor must set criteria for granting licenses and monitoring licensing arrangements.

- *There is a promotional benefit.* The licensor's name gets circulation far beyond the original trademarked item. As phrased by the licensing director at Timberland Co., licensing generates both "cash and cachet."[38]

Licensing also offers promise to potential licensees. Specific reasons for acquiring a trademark license are:

- *The likelihood of new-product success may be improved.* It's a lot easier for an unknown firm to get both middlemen and consumers to accept its product if it features a well-known trademark.

- *Marketing costs may be reduced.* One licensee explained that licensing is "a way of taking a name with brand recognition and applying it to your merchandise without having to do the advertising and brand building that is so expensive."[39] Any savings may exceed the royalty fees paid to the licensor.

Packaging and Labeling

Even after a product is developed and branded, strategies must still be devised for other product-related aspects of the marketing mix. One such product feature, and a critical one for some products, is packaging. Closely related to packaging, labeling is another aspect of a product that requires managerial attention.

Purposes and Importance of Packaging

Packaging consists of all the activities of designing and producing the container or wrapper for a product. Packaging is intended to serve several vital purposes:

- *Protect the product on its way to the consumer.* A package protects a product during shipment. Furthermore, it can prevent tampering with products, notably medications and food products, in the warehouse or the retail store. The design and size of a package can also help deter shoplifting. That's why small items, such as compact discs, come in larger-than-needed packages.

- *Protect the product after it is purchased.* Compared with bulk (that is, unpackaged) items, packaged goods generally are more convenient, cleaner, and less susceptible to losses from evaporation, spilling, and spoilage. Also, "childproof" closures thwart children (and sometimes adults) from opening containers of medications and other potentially harmful products.

- *Help gain acceptance of the product from middlemen.* A product must be packaged to meet the needs of wholesaling and retailing middlemen. For instance, a package's size and shape must be suitable for displaying and stacking the product in the store. An odd-shaped package might attract shoppers' attention, but if it doesn't stack well, the retailer is unlikely to purchase the product.

- *Help persuade consumers to buy the product.* Packaging can assist in getting a product noticed by consumers. Here's why that is important: "The average shopper spends 20 minutes in the store, viewing 20 products a second."[40] At the point of purchase—such as a supermarket aisle—the package can serve as a "silent sales person." In the case of middlemen's brands, which typically are not advertised heavily, packaging must serve as the means of communicating with shoppers.

Historically, packaging was intended primarily to provide protection. Today, with its marketing significance fully recognized, packaging is a major factor in gaining distribution and customers. For example, to get consumers to buy more Kleenex tissues, Kimberly-Clark developed a set of Expressions boxes featuring various designs such as Amish quilts. The company's rationale is that attractive boxes will encourage consumers to place Kleenex in various rooms of the house.[41] In the cases of convenience goods and operating supplies, most buyers consider one well-known brand about as good as another. Thus these types of products might be differentiated by a package feature—no-drip spout, reusable jar, or self-contained applicator (liquid shoe polish and glue, for example).

Ultimately, a package may become a product's differential advantage, or at least a significant part of it. That was certainly true with Coca-Cola and its distinctive contour glass bottle, so much so that the firm replicated the contour shape in bottles made of other materials, such as plastic. Recently the soft drink company introduced the Fridge Pack, a carton that holds 12 cans, has an opening in the front for access, and fits nicely on a refrigerator shelf. This seemingly small packaging improvement boosted Coke sales in markets where the Fridge Pack was introduced, reportedly because it allows consumers to keep more soft drink cans cold.[42]

Packaging Strategies

In managing the packaging of a product, executives must make the following strategic decisions.[43]

Packaging the Product Line
A company must decide whether to develop a family resemblance when packaging related products. **Family packaging** uses either highly similar packages for all products or packages with a common and clearly

A package with an attractive appearance and a useful function can boost a product's sales, as Dean Foods' "chug" container has shown. The single-serving package is used for pints of various milk products and even orange juice in different sizes. The package has helped make milk "cool" to some teenagers, which is critical to the dairy industry in its constant battle with carbonated beverages, juices, and bottled water.

www.deanfoods.com

noticeable feature. Campbell's Soup, for instance, uses visually similar packaging for all of its condensed-soup cans, although minor changes (such as adding pictures of the prepared product) are made in the labels occasionally. When new products are added to a line, recognition and images associated with established products extend to the new ones. Family packaging makes sense when the products are of similar quality and have a similar use.

Multiple Packaging For many years there has been a trend toward **multiple packaging,** the practice of placing several units of the same product in one container. Dehydrated soups, motor oil, beer, golf balls, building hardware, candy bars, towels, and countless other products are packaged in multiple units. Test after test has proved that multiple packaging increases total sales of a product.

Changing the Package When detected, a company needs to correct a poor feature in an existing package, of course. Unless a problem was spotted, firms stayed with a package design for many years. Now, for competitive reasons, packaging strategies and tactics are reviewed annually along with the rest of the marketing mix.[44]

Firms need to monitor—and consider—continuing developments, such as new packaging materials, uncommon shapes, innovative closures, and other new features (measured portions, metered flow). All are intended to provide benefits to middlemen and/or consumers and, as a result, are selling points for marketers.

To increase sales volume, many companies find it costs much less to redesign a package than to conduct an expensive advertising campaign. To attract the teen market, Dean Foods Co. introduced a new single-serving "chug" container that can be resealed and fits in a car's drink holder. Although milk consumption didn't get a boost from the familiar "milk mustache" advertising campaign, milk sales jumped markedly following the introduction of the chug container.[45]

Redesign of packaging is neither easy nor inexpensive, however. This task can cost from $20,000 for a simple, single product to $250,000 for a project that entails a product line and requires consumer research and testing. And these figures do not include the expense of promoting the new package design.[46]

Criticisms of Packaging

Packaging is in the public eye today, largely because of environmental issues. Specific concerns are:

- *Packaging that depletes natural resources.* This problem is magnified by firms that prefer larger-than-necessary containers. This criticism has been partially addressed through the use of recycled materials in packaging. A point in favor of packaging is that it minimizes spoilage, thereby reducing a different type of resource waste.

- *Forms of packaging that are health hazards.* Government regulations banned several suspect packaging materials, notably aerosol cans that used chlorofluorocarbons as propellants. Just as important, a growing number of companies are switching from aerosol to pump dispensers.

- *Disposal of used packages.* Consumers' desire for convenience in the form of throwaway containers conflicts with their stated desire for a clean environment. Some discarded packages wind up as litter, others add to solid waste in landfills. This problem can be eased by using biodegradable materials in packaging.

- *Deceptive packaging.* A common problem is that the package size conveys the impression of containing more than the actual contents. Government regulations plus greater integrity on the part of business firms regarding packaging have alleviated this concern to some extent.

- *Expensive packaging.* Even in seemingly simple packaging, such as for soft drinks, as much as one-half the production cost is for the container. Still, effective packaging reduces transportation costs and spoilage losses.

Marketing executives are challenged to address these criticisms. At the same time, they must retain or even enhance the positive features of packaging, such as product protection, consumer convenience, and marketing support.

Labeling

A **label** is the part of a product that carries information about the product and the seller. A label may be part of a package, or it may be a tag attached to the product. Obviously there is a close relationship among labeling, packaging, and branding.

Types of Labels   There are three primary kinds of labels:

- A **brand label** is simply the brand alone applied to the product or package. Some oranges are stamped Sunkist or Blue Goose, and some clothes carry the brand label Sanforized.

- A **descriptive label** gives objective information about the product's use, construction, care, performance, and/or other pertinent features. On a descriptive label for a can of corn, there will be statements concerning the type of corn (golden sweet), style (creamed or in niblet kernels), can size, number of servings, other ingredients, and nutritional contents.

- A **grade label** identifies the product's judged quality with a letter, number, or word. Canned peaches are grade-labeled A, B, and C, and corn and wheat are grade-labeled 1 and 2.

Brand labeling is an acceptable form of labeling, but it does not supply sufficient information to a buyer. Descriptive labels provide more product information but not necessarily all that is needed or desired by a consumer in making a purchase decision.

Statutory Labeling Requirements Labeling has received its share of criticism. Consumers have charged, for example, that labels contained incomplete or misleading information and there were a confusing number of sizes and shapes of packages for a given product.

The public's complaints about false or deceptive labeling and packaging have led to a number of federal labeling laws. The Fair Packaging and Labeling Act of 1966 provides for (1) *mandatory* labeling requirements; (2) an opportunity for business to *voluntarily* adopt packaging standards that can limit the proliferation of the same product in different weights and measures; and (3) administrative agencies, notably the Food and Drug Administration and the Federal Trade Commission, with the *discretionary* power to set packaging regulations.

More recently, the Nutrition Labeling and Education Act (NLEA), which was enacted in 1994, established a set of **nutrition labeling** standards for processed foods. The intent of this law is to ensure full disclosure of foods' nutritional contents. Labels must clearly state the amount of calories, fat, cholesterol, sodium, carbohydrates, and protein contained in the package's contents. In addition, the amounts must be stated as a percentage of a daily intake of 2,000 calories. Vitamin and mineral content also must be expressed as a percentage of the recommended daily allowance.[47]

As part of the NLEA, the Food and Drug Administration issued standard definitions for key terms used in labeling, such as *light, lean,* and *good source.* To be labeled *light,* for example, a brand ordinarily has to contain one-half the fat or one-third fewer calories than standard products in this category. The NLEA allows firms to include on labels some health claims, such as fiber's value in preventing heart disease. And companies are permitted to list on labels endorsements of their products from health organizations such as the American Heart Association.

The nutrition labeling changes mandated by the NLEA apply to about 200,000 packaged foods, including meat and poultry products. Supporters of this law argue that the labeling requirements promote improved nutrition, thereby reducing health care costs. Of course, these savings occur only if consumers read the labels and use the information in choosing foods. The results of one study suggest that shoppers obtained and understood more nutrition information following the introduction of nutrition labeling.[48]

Recently, as so-called organic foods grew to about $10 billion in sales, the U.S. Department of Agriculture decided it was necessary to define what qualified as *organic.* For example, animals that are the sources of organic meat, eggs, and dairy products cannot have had any growth hormones or antibiotics. Products certified as organic can display a green-and-white USDA label on their packages.[49]

An amendment to the Fair Packaging and Labeling Act that was implemented in 1994 mandates that metric weights and measures along with traditional American weights and measures (such as inches, pounds, and pints) be shown on the labels of selected products. Rather than replacing the American system, as many companies feared, the metric information is supplementary.[50]

Design, Color, and Quality

A well-rounded program for product planning and development will include strategies and policies on several additional product features. Design, color, and quality are covered in this chapter. Two more features, warranties and postsale service, are covered in Chapter 21 because they closely relate to the implementation of a company's marketing program.

Design

One way to satisfy customers and gain a differential advantage is through **product design,** which refers to the arrangement of elements that collectively form a good or service. Good design can improve the marketability of a product by making it easier

Here, designers with Samsung Electronics Co. consider alternative formats for a new product. Samsung is now placing as much emphasis on design as on technology in creating new products, ranging from MP3 players to liquid-crystal displays, for both consumer and business markets.

www.samsung.com

to operate, upgrading its quality, improving its appearance, and/or reducing production costs. For instance, computer programmers are supposed to assure that any new software is very user-friendly.

According to an IBM executive, design is "a strategic marketing tool."[51] Design is receiving more and more attention for several reasons:

- Rapidly advancing technologies are generating not only new products (such as desktop computer cameras for videoconferencing) that need attractive, yet functional designs, but also new materials that can enhance design capabilities.

- A growing number of firms have turned to low prices as a competitive tool. In turn, designers have been asked to rework some of their companies' products and lower the costs of making them as one way of maintaining profit margins.

- A distinctive design may be the only feature that significantly differentiates a product. Perhaps with that in mind, Samsung appears to be paying particular attention to product design—with excellent results. No corporation won more Industrial Design Excellence Awards over a five-year period than Samsung. Its winners range from a DVD player that is less than 1 inch thick to the "Smart Cooker," a cooking pad with a sensor that measures cholesterol and other attributes of foods so a chef or homemaker can adjust recipes as desired.[52]

Companies are also being called upon to design products that are easily used by all consumers, including disabled individuals, the burgeoning number of senior citizens, and others needing special considerations. This approach is termed **universal design**. As one example, the Kohler Co. designed a bathtub with a door, eliminating the danger of having to climb into the tub. And some home builders are featuring wider halls and doors in selected models, in order to accommodate wheelchairs. Occasionally, products designed for the disabled or seniors also appeal to other consumers. Responding to concerns expressed by older passengers, the public transit agency in Paris simplified its routes map; the new version has been a big hit with passengers of all ages.[53]

For most consumer and business goods, ranging from furniture to electronic equipment, design has long been recognized as important. According to estimates, design accounts for only 2% of the total cost of producing and marketing a product. As a result, a design that's a hit with consumers can produce a giant return on invest-

278   Chapter Ten

ment for a firm. Consider, for example, Volkswagen's Beetle. Decades ago, the car's odd shape generated a great deal of attention and attracted many buyers. It eventually fell out of favor, largely because of safety and environmental reasons. In 1998, Volkswagen of America introduced the New Beetle, featuring a familiar design including a front end that resembles a "happy face." This time around, a variety of new technology was added to complement the Beetle's appealing design. Volkswagen hopes to duplicate that "retro" success by reintroducing its microbus in 2005.[54]

Color

Like design, **product color** often is the determining factor in a customer's acceptance or rejection of a product, whether it is a dress, a table, or an automobile. In fact, color is so important that the U.S. Supreme Court confirmed in 1995 that the color of a product or its packaging can be registered as part of a trademark under the Lanham Act. Color by itself can qualify for trademark status when, according to the Court's ruling, it "identifies and distinguishes a particular brand, and thus indicates its source." The case under review involved greenish-gold dry-cleaning press pads manufactured by the Qualitex Company. Other distinctive colors that help identify specific brands are Owens-Corning's pink insulation and Kodak's gold color-film boxes.[55]

As with other marketing-mix elements, a differential advantage might be gained by identifying the most pleasing color and in knowing when to change colors. In the late 1990s, for example, Apple Computer used fruit-inspired colors, such as grape and tangerine, for its iMac PC. Apple's color decisions were backed by a survey indicating that over half of consumers disdained drab colors for high-tech products.[56] Of course, bright colors would probably be a disadvantage for PCs or other electronic products aimed at executives. Thus poor color choices can result in a differential *dis*advantage. For instance, if a garment manufacturer or the person responsible for purchasing merchandise for a retail store guesses wrong on what will be the fashionable color in women's clothing, disaster may ensue.

Color can be extremely important for packaging as well as for the product itself. Color specialists say it's no coincidence that Nabisco, Marlboro, Coca-Cola, Campbell, and Budweiser are all top-selling brands. In each case, red is the primary color of their packaging or logo. Red may be appealing because it "evokes feelings of warmth, passion and sensuality." As described in the You Make the Decision box, it appears that blue has become a very popular color among American companies for their brands.[57]

For some products, such as clothing and autos, color is a critical ingredient. For many others, it would seem to be less important. Recently, however, rainbow colors have proved to be an appealing feature for a variety of other products, ranging from personal computers to household appliances, including the George Foreman grill.

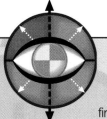

Quality

There's no agreement on a definition of product quality, even though it is universally recognized as significant. One professional society defines **product quality** as the set of features and characteristics of a good or service that determine its ability to satisfy needs.[58] Despite what appears to be a straightforward definition, consumers frequently disagree on what constitutes quality in a product—whether it be a cut of meat or a performance by a rock musician. Personal tastes are deeply involved; what you like, another person may dislike. It is important to recognize, therefore, that quality—like beauty—is to a large extent "in the eyes of the beholder."

Besides personal tastes, individual expectations also affect judgments of quality. That is, a consumer brings certain expectations to a purchase situation. Sometimes you have high expectations, as with a movie about which you read rave reviews. Other times you have modest expectations, as with a course for next semester that is described by a current student as "not too boring." Your evaluation of a product's quality depends on whether the actual experience with the good or service exceeds, meets, or falls short of your expectations.

For some companies, *optimal* quality means that the product provides the consumer with an experience that meets, but does not exceed, expectations. The rationale is that there's no sense in incurring added costs to provide what amounts to *excessive* quality. Some firms that adopt this viewpoint supplement adequate product quality with superior customer service. According to one survey of personal computer users, this approach can be effective in generating repeat customers.[59] Other businesses, however, strive to exceed consumers' expectations in order to produce high levels of customer satisfaction and, in turn, brand loyalty.

For many years, there was substantial room for improved quality in many American-made products. For instance, German and Japanese automakers beat their American competitors by turning out better-performing, more-reliable cars. Hence, since the 1980s, U.S. industry has paid more and more attention to product quality. One sign of progress is that domestic automakers have narrowed—but not entirely eliminated—the quality gap with foreign manufacturers.[60] As will be discussed in Chapter 11, product quality should be a primary consideration not only for manufacturers of goods but also for producers of services.

Recently, quality was called "the single most critical factor for businesses to survive in the ever expanding and competitive global market place." For instance, General Motors discovered that Chinese consumers thought that products made in their own country were inferior to imports. Hence, GM's advertising in China stressed the high quality of Buicks that were made in Shanghai. At first, the cars sold as fast as GM could make them, but then sales slowed to the point that the GM-Chinese joint venture decided to introduce new models and cut prices.[61]

Because it is not easily duplicated, many organizations seek to boost product quality to gain a differential advantage. At the least, an enterprise needs to avoid a differential *dis*advantage related to product quality.

To seize an advantage or avert a disadvantage, a number of businesses, government agencies, and nonprofit entities have implemented **total quality management (TQM)** programs. TQM entails not just specific policies and practices, but a philosophy that commits the organization to continuous quality improvement in all its activities. In recent years, TQM has received some criticism for not improving financial performance as much as would be expected given the necessary investment of time and effort. However, according to one study, the introduction of TQM creates distinctive competencies for a firm, which in turn can have a favorable effect on performance.[62]

Another noteworthy quality-related development is called **ISO 9000** (pronounced ICE-o nine thousand). ISO 9000 is a set of related standards of quality management that have been adopted by about 60 countries, including the U.S. Companies that meet ISO 9000 standards are awarded a certificate, which often puts them in a favorable position with large customers. Worldwide, about 400,000 companies have earned ISO 9000 certification. Now some firms are seeking and earning ISO 14001 certification, demonstrating implementation of an environmental management system.[63]

Some critics say that the standards place too much emphasis on documenting what a producer is doing and pay too little attention to whether what's being done results in satisfactory products. As one skeptic observed, "You can certify a manufacturer that makes life jackets from concrete, as long as those jackets are made according to the documented procedures." Perhaps with such criticism in mind, new ISO 9001:2000 standards emphasize customer-related processes as well as ongoing improvement.[64]

Summary

Effective product management involves developing and then monitoring the various features of a product—its brand, packaging, labeling, design color, quality, warranty, and postsale service. A consumer's purchase decision may take into account not just the basic good or service, but also the brand and perhaps one or more of the other want-satisfying product features.

A brand is a means of identifying and differentiating the products of an organization. Branding aids sellers in managing their promotional and pricing activities. The dual responsibilities of brand ownership are to promote the brand and to maintain a consistent level of quality. Selecting a good brand name—and there are relatively few really good ones—is difficult. Once a brand becomes well known, the owner may have to protect it from product counterfeiting and from becoming a generic term.

Manufacturers must decide whether to brand their products and/or sell under a middleman's brand. Middlemen must decide whether to carry producers' brands alone or to establish their own brands as well. Both producers and middlemen must set policies regarding branding groups of products and branding for market saturation. The use of cobranding, placing two brands on a product or an enterprise, is growing.

An increasing number of companies are recognizing that the brands they own are or can be among their most valuable assets. They are building brand equity—the added value that a brand brings to a product. Although it's difficult to build brand equity, doing so successfully can be the basis for expanding a product mix. Products with abundant brand equity also lend themselves to trademark licensing, a popular marketing arrangement.

Packaging is becoming increasingly important as sellers recognize the problems, as well as the marketing opportunities, associated with it. Companies must choose among strategies such as family packaging, multiple packaging, and changing the package. Labeling, a related activity, provides information about the product and the seller. Many consumer criticisms of marketing relate to packaging and labeling. As a result, there are several federal laws regulating these activities.

Companies are now recognizing the marketing value of both product design and quality. Good design can improve the marketability of a product; it may be the only feature that differentiates a product. Projecting the appropriate quality image and then delivering the level of quality desired by customers are essential to marketing success. In many cases, firms need to enhance product quality to eliminate a differential disadvantage; in others, firms seek to build quality as a way of gaining a differential advantage.

More about **George Foreman**

Salton, Inc., is now marketing the Foreman line as well as its other brands internationally. In 2001, in order to gain distribution in Europe, Salton acquired a firm based in the United Kingdom and another located in France.

On the basis of his boxing career, George Foreman has a measure of name recognition around the world, which will help the company build awareness and recognition for the Foreman grills and other Foreman products. But effective marketing also requires that Salton convey to consumers the brand's attributes—such as quality, convenience, state-of-the-art design, and value price. In addition, as often occurs in international marketing, there may be cross-cultural issues to deal with—for example, the views of a country's residents toward meat or toward different methods of food preparation.

Even expanding the product line at home will present challenges for Salton and its star spokesperson. Entering the outdoor gas grill market with a George Foreman grill placed the brand in the same ring with such entrenched competitors as Weber and Sunbeam. That endeavor proved unsuccessful, and Salton accepted defeat.

Domestically or internationally, Salton is counting on Foreman still having a strong endorsement punch. The company believes in the strength of the brand as well as the affection people feel for the man who became a brand name. As explained by Salton's CEO, "We saw what his name could do for us."[65]

1. What are some of the advantages and disadvantages of basing a brand on the name and reputation of a celebrity?

2. What else can Salton, Inc., do to benefit from its well-established George Foreman brand?

Key Terms and Concepts

Brand (260)
Brand name (260)
Brand mark (260)
Trademark (260)
Producer's brand (261)
Middleman's brand (261)

Product counterfeiting (265)
Family branding (269)
Multiple-brand strategy (269)
Cobranding (270)
Brand equity (271)
Trademark licensing (272)

Packaging (273)
Family packaging (274)
Multiple packaging (275)
Label (276)
Brand label (276)
Descriptive label (276)

Questions and Problems

1. Evaluate each of the brand names in Table 10.1 in relation to the characteristics of a good brand, indicating the strong and weak points of each name.

2. Do the following e-commerce brands possess the characteristics of a good brand?

   a. Fogdog Sports (sporting goods)
   b. CareerBuilder.com (job search and employee recruiting)
   c. Peapod, Webvan, and HomeGrocer.com (all of which are or were grocery shopping and delivery services)
   d. HotBot (search engine for the Web)
   e. FreeRealTime.com (stock quotes and financial information at no charge)

3. Identify one brand that is on the verge of becoming generic.

   a. Why should a company protect the separate identity of its brand?
   b. What course of action should a company take to do so?

4. In which of the following cases should the company use its name as part of the product's brand name?

   a. A manufacturer of men's underwear introduces women's underwear.
   b. A manufacturer of hair care products introduces a line of portable electric hair dryers.

5. A manufacturer of snow skis sold under a brand that has built up substantial equity acquires a company that markets ski boots carrying a brand that enjoys about the same amount of equity. What branding strategy should the acquiring organization adopt? Should all products (skis and boots) now carry the ski brand? The boot brand? Is there some other alternative that you think would be better?

6. Why do some firms sell identical products under more than one of their own brands?

7. Assume that a large department store chain proposed to the manufacturers of Maytag washing machines that Maytag supply the department store with machines carrying the store's brand. What factors should Maytag's management consider in making a decision? If the situation instead involved a supermarket chain and General Foods' Jell-O, to what extent should different factors be considered?

8. An American manufacturer plans to introduce its line of camping equipment (stoves, lanterns, ice chests) in several European Union countries. Should management select the same brand for all countries or use a different brand in each country? What factors should influence the decision? How should brand equity enter into the decision?

9. Select one product and indicate how you would improve its design.

10. Give examples of products for which the careful use of color has increased sales. Can you cite examples to show that poor use of color may hurt a product's salability?

Interactive Marketing Exercises

1. Visit a large local supermarket and:

   a. Obtain the store manager's opinions regarding which products are excellently packaged and which are poorly packaged. Ask the manager for reasons.
   b. Walk around the store and compile your own list of excellent and poor packages. What factors did you use to judge quality of packaging?

2. Ask five students who are not taking this course to evaluate the following names for a proposed expensive perfume: Entice, Nitespark, At Risk, and Foreglow. For evaluation purposes, share with the students the characteristics of a good brand name. Also ask them to suggest a better name for the new perfume.

Chapter

11

Services Marketing

"Enterprise tries to make its service offering more tangible. For example, ads touting the company's 'We'll pick you up' slogan feature pictures of a gift-wrapped car."

Can **Enterprise Rent-A-Car** Stay in the Fast Lane?

Enterprise Rent-A-Car began as an auto-leasing business in 1957. The company's founder, Jack Taylor, was a new-car salesperson who realized that leasing offered advantages to certain customers. With the financial support of the dealership he worked for, Taylor began a leasing business that, by the early 1960s, had evolved into a car-rental business. Starting with 17 cars at one location in St. Louis, the business has grown to well over 600,000 vehicles and over 5,000 locations in the U.S., Canada, Germany, the United Kingdom, and Ireland. Enterprise earned first place for customer service, ahead of Hertz, Avis, and National, in a 2000 J. D. Power and Associates survey.

Like good marketers in every industry, Enterprise began by segmenting the potential market and selecting a particular target. In examining the rental market, Taylor noted that the established firms specialized in renting cars at airports to business and leisure travelers. Rather than go head-to-head with the likes of Hertz and Avis, he looked for other user segments. What he found was individuals in temporary need of cars because their vehicles were in the shop for repairs or had been stolen. However, serving this market requires a marketing mix that is quite different from the one used by the traditional car-rental firm.

The first issue is price. A consumer with a car in the garage for repairs can be in a pinch for transportation. And in cases of accidents or theft, insurers are responsible for insured motorists' economic losses from being without a car. But unlike many business travelers, price is a key consideration for both of these segments. To keep its prices down, Enterprise has to find ways to keep its costs lower than the competition. One tactic is to keep its rental cars for up to 15 months before selling them. Other major rental companies turn their cars over in about six months.

Another significant factor is distribution of the service, or in Enterprise's case, retail locations. Firms pursuing the leisure and business air travelers tend to have expensive downtown and airport locations. Enterprise selects suburban store fronts and shopping-strip locations that are less expensive but yet accessible to its target markets. As a result of these tactics, Enterprise can offer rental rates as much as 30% below those of other firms.

Promotion is another difference. Hertz and Avis do a lot of expensive mass-media advertising. Enterprise recognizes that the insurance and repair replacement markets are largely controlled by two groups. One is auto insurance adjusters, who approve payments for their clients' rental cars. The other is auto repair shop operators, who are frequently asked for rental recommendations by customers. In addition to doing some advertising, local Enterprise managers develop close ties with these businesses in their areas, making reputation and referrals a key ingredient of their success. When it does advertise, Enterprise tries to make its service offering more tangible. For example, ads touting the company's "We'll pick you up" slogan feature pictures of a gift-wrapped car.

 www.enterprise.com/
car_rental

Surviving tough economic times also requires effective marketing decisions. The car-rental industry was already suffering in the downturn of the late 1990s, which slowed business travel and therefore kept many potential car renters at home. Because its strategy is to cater to the consumer market rather than the business traveler, Enterprise fared better than some. It still gets about 95% of its business from its neighborhood locations, despite having opened offices at many airports in the last few years. After the terrorist attacks of September 11, 2001, however, a glut of cars and a dearth of travelers left at least two competitors, ANC Rental Corp. (owner of Alamo and National) and Budget, in bankruptcy protection and the industry in general in a severe slide.

Additional unexpected problems that arose in the wake of the attacks tested firms' resiliency. For example, most car renters, including Enterprise, temporarily waived their one-way rental drop-off fees (up to $100 for leaving a rented car in a remote location) as stranded travelers flooded their offices. The firms then found themselves hiring extra employees or even paying for tow trucks to get thousands of cars back. Enterprise announced it would likely sell many of the vehicles rather than recover them.[1]

As a services firm, how does Enterprise's marketing program differ from a goods marketer?

Enterprise is marketing a service—use of a vehicle. Recall that our definition of a product in Chapter 8 includes goods *and* services. This distinction is much more than a matter of semantics. Services are fundamentally different from goods in ways that affect their marketing. Recognizing what those differences are and understanding their implications are essential in developing effective services.

Chapter Goals

After studying this chapter, you should be able to explain:

- The importance of services in advanced economies.
- The special situation of nonbusiness services marketing.
- The characteristics of services and their marketing implications.
- How a services marketing mix is designed.
- The challenge of managing services quality.
- The productivity and performance challenges faced by services marketers.

Nature and Importance of Services

The U.S. has moved beyond the stage where goods production is its main economic activity to the stage where it has become the world's largest services economy. Over two-thirds of the nation's gross domestic product (GDP) is accounted for by services, and just over one-half of all consumer expenditures are for services. Projections to the year 2005 indicate that services will attract an even larger share of consumer spending.

Services are also the major source of employment. More than 80% of the non-farm labor force is employed in service industries. According to U.S. Department of Labor predictions, virtually all the fastest-growing occupations between 1996 and 2008 are in services. The industries in which job growth will be the fastest are data and information management, institutional and in-home health care, education, and financial services.[2]

That services account for over one-half of consumer expenditures is impressive, but it still grossly understates the economic importance of services. These figures do not include the vast amounts spent for business services. And by all indications, spending for business services will continue to grow. As commerce has become increasingly complex and competitive, managers have found that calling on specialized service providers is effective and efficient. The result is that many tasks formerly performed by regular employees, from research and training to advertising and distribution, are increasingly being "outsourced" to specialists.

Definition of Services

What should be classified as a service? The answer isn't always apparent because invariably services are marketed in conjunction with goods. Virtually all services require supporting goods (you need an airplane to provide air transportation service), and goods require supporting services (to sell even a shirt or a can of beans calls for at least a cashier's service). Furthermore, a company may sell a combination of goods and services. Thus, along with repair service for your car, you might buy spark plugs or an oil filter. Therefore, it may be helpful to think of every product as a mix of goods and services located on a continuum ranging from mostly goods to mostly services, as shown in Figure 11.1.

For marketing purposes, it is useful to separate services into two categories. In the first are services that are the main *purpose or object* of a transaction. Suppose you rent a car from Enterprise. The company makes a car available (a tangible good), but what you are purchasing is accessibility to transportation (a service). Because you are buying the use of the car, not the car itself, this is a service transaction. In the second category are services that *support or facilitate* the sale of a good or another service. Thus, when you rent the car from Enterprise, you can also obtain collision insurance, the use of a cellular phone, and an electronic navigational device. These are called supplementary or support services because you obtain them only in conjunction with renting the car.

Considering these distinctions, we define **services** as identifiable, intangible activities that are the main object of a transaction designed to provide want-satisfaction to customers. This definition excludes supplementary services that support the sale of goods or other services. Even though we are excluding supplementary services from our discussion, we don't want to underestimate their importance. In industries where there are few differences among the primary products of competitors, supplementary services can be the basis for a differential advantage.

Scope of Services

Using a broad definition of transactions and customers, it is appropriate to recognize both for-profit and nonbusiness services organizations. **For-profit services firms** sell to consumers or other businesses with profitable operations as a primary goal. This category is reflected in the following examples, classified by industry:

- *Housing and other structures:* Rental of offices, warehouses, hotels, motels, apartments, houses, and farms.
- *Household operations:* House maintenance and repairs, security, landscaping, and household cleaning.

FIGURE 11.1

A Goods–Services Continuum.

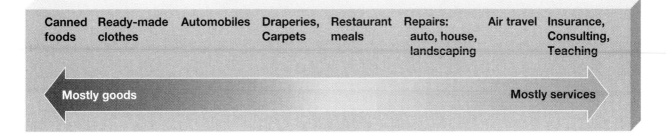

Canned foods | Ready-made clothes | Automobiles | Draperies, Carpets | Restaurant meals | Repairs: auto, house, landscaping | Air travel | Insurance, Consulting, Teaching

Mostly goods ← → Mostly services

- *Recreation and entertainment:* Theaters, spectator sports, amusement parks, participation sports, restaurant meals, and resorts.
- *Personal care:* Laundry, dry cleaning, personal grooming care, and spas.
- *Medical and health care:* Physical and mental medical services, dental, nursing, hospitalization, optometry, and physical therapy.
- *Private education:* Vocational schools, nursery schools, charter schools, and some continuing education programs.
- *Professional business services:* Legal, accounting, advertising, marketing research, public relations, and management consulting.
- *Financial services:* Personal and business insurance, banking, credit and loan service, brokerage service, and investment counseling.
- *Transportation:* Freight and passenger service on common carriers, automobile repairs and rentals, and express package delivery.
- *Communications:* Broadcasting, telephone, fax, computer, and Internet services.

These groups are not separated into business and consumer services as we did with goods because most of these services are purchased by both market groups.

Nonbusiness services organizations are of two types. One type is **not-for-profit (N-F-P) services organizations,** which have a profit goal because growth and continued existence depend on generating revenue in excess of its costs. However, profit (which may be referred to by a different name, such as "surplus") is secondary to the N-F-P's primary objective. This services sector has tripled since 1980 and now includes more than 1.5 million organizations that generate and spend billions of dollars and employ thousands of people.[3] In many cases N-F-Ps operate in a fashion very similar to for-profit businesses. Examples, organized by primary focus, include:

- *Educational:* Private grade schools, high schools, colleges, and universities.
- *Cultural:* Museums, opera and theater groups, zoos, and symphony orchestras.
- *Religious:* Churches, synagogues, temples, and mosques.
- *Charitable and philanthropic:* Charities, service organizations (Salvation Army, Red Cross), research foundations, and fund-raising groups (United Way).
- *Social concerns:* Organizations dealing with family planning, civil rights, termination of smoking, environmental concerns, the homeless, those for or against abortion, or those for or against nuclear energy.
- *Professional and trade:* Labor unions, certification groups, professional associations (American Marketing Association, American Medical Association), trade associations, and lobbying groups.
- *Social:* Fraternal organizations, civic clubs, special interest clubs.
- *Health care:* Hospitals, nursing homes, health research organizations (American Cancer Society, American Heart Association), health maintenance organizations.
- *Political:* Political parties, individual politicians.

You may note some overlap in the preceding two lists. For example, private education appears on both lists because some educational institutions are profit seeking, whereas others are not-for-profit. Also, most museums and hospitals are not-for-profit, but some are profit seeking.

Finally, the scope of services is further broadened by including a second type of nonbusiness organization. A **nonprofit organization** provides services but does not have a profit or surplus objective. Federal, state, and local government agencies fall into this category. They provide services, often charging for them, and may even operate in competition with for-profit businesses. For example, the U.S. National Park Service competes with private forms of outdoor recreation.

Many nonprofit organizations are heavily involved in some form of marketing. For example, the U.S. Postal Service annually spends over $100 million on advertising aimed at consumers and businesses that includes television, radio, and print media as well as direct mail and point-of-purchase materials.[4]

If nonbusiness organizations do an ineffective marketing job, the costs are high. Empty beds in hospitals and empty classrooms constitute a waste of resources a society can ill afford. There are additional social and economic costs of ineffective nonbusiness marketing. If the death rate from smoking rises because the American Cancer Society and similar organizations cannot persuade people that smoking is harmful, we all lose. When antilitter organizations fail to convince people to control their solid-waste disposal, society suffers. Thus, marketing by nonbusiness organizations should be treated as a serious undertaking with important consequences.

The Development of Services Marketing

Traditionally, many service industries—both business and nonbusiness—have not been market-oriented. There are several reasons why they lagged behind sellers of goods in accepting the marketing concept and in adopting marketing techniques.

Some services providers enjoy monopoly status. Until very recently most public utilities (telephone, electricity, water, natural gas) were operated as geographic monopolies under the supervision of government agencies. Quite naturally, when an organization is the only supplier of a necessity in a market, the focus of attention is on production and efficient operations, not marketing.

In some cases marketing activities are externally constrained. A number of large services industries are subject to substantial restrictions by federal and state governments or professional associations. Until recently, for example, all major forms of interstate transportation services were severely restricted in marketing practices such as pricing, distribution, market expansion, and product introduction. In the fields of law, accounting, and health care, various state laws and professional-association regulations prevented and, to varying degrees, still prevent their members from engaging in advertising, price competition, and other marketing activities.

Many nonbusiness services providers are uncomfortable with a business image. These organizations attempt to distance themselves from business and its profit objective. As a result, they do not employ many business techniques, including marketing. In some professional-service industries, tradition suggests that the focus should be on producing the service, not on marketing it. Proud of their abilities to conduct an orchestra, diagnose an illness, or give legal advice, these professionals historically have not considered themselves businesspeople.

More recently, several developments have contributed to a growing awareness of marketing among services organizations:

- The success of services companies such as Marriott hotels and Disney theme parks serve as examples of the power of good marketing.

- Consumer protests, changes in laws, and court decisions have removed many of the governmental and professional-association restrictions on marketing in some services industries. These changes, along with increased competition, have generated a growing awareness of marketing challenges and opportunities.

- Reductions in federal aid, tax law changes that discourage gift giving, competition for funds from a new generation of social causes, and a slowdown in corporate contributions have squeezed the budgets of many nonbusiness services organizations. Consequently, many have begun to adopt modern business techniques, including marketing with a customer orientation.

Developing a Services Marketing Program

Marketing business and nonbusiness services includes the same basic elements as marketing goods. Whether its focus is goods or services, every organization should first define and analyze its markets, identify segments, and select targets. Then attention should turn to designing a coordinated marketing mix—the goods or services offering, the price structure, the distribution system, and the promotional activities—around a differential advantage that will create the position the organization desires. However, some important differences between goods and services influence these marketing decisions. The most important differences are described below.

Characteristics of Services

The four characteristics that differentiate services from goods—**intangibility, inseparability, heterogeneity,** and **perishability**—are major factors driving the differences between goods and services marketing.

Intangibility   Because services are intangible, it is impossible for prospective customers to sample—feel, see, hear, taste, or smell—a service before they buy it. Consequently, a company's promotional program must be explicit about the benefits to be derived from the service, rather than emphasizing the service itself. Four promotional strategies that may be used to suggest service benefits and reduce the effect of intangibility are:[5]

www.carnival.com

- *Visualization.* For example, Carnival Cruise Lines depicts the benefits of its cruises with ads that show happy people dancing, dining, playing deck games, and visiting exotic places.

- *Association.* By connecting the service with a tangible good, person, object, or place, a particular image can be created. Professional sports teams are linked with cities or regions to give them an identity. Prudential Insurance suggests stability and security with its Rock of Gibraltar. Merrill Lynch uses the symbol of a bull to imply strength and leadership.

- *Physical representation.* American Express uses color—gold or platinum—for its credit card services to symbolize wealth and prestige. Enterprise, the auto rental firm, depicts a car wrapped as a package in its TV ads to emphasize its unique delivery feature. The United Way depicts its role with a helping hand and a rainbow, symbols of support and a brighter future.

- *Documentation.* There are two forms of documentation—*past performance* and *future capability.* A hospital can document its past performance, for example, by pointing out in its ads how many babies have been born and cared for in its obstetrics department. Another hospital might choose to stress its capability by highlighting the specialized equipment it has available should an emergency arise during the delivery of a baby.

Websites are a valuable tool in reducing the intangibility of a service. They make it possible for marketers to present extensive information, use animation and sound, and answer a site visitor's specific questions via e-mail. By expanding the marketer's communications arsenal, the Web increases the quantity and quality of available information and thereby improves the customer's understanding of the service. An example is Royal Caribbean Cruise Line.

Inseparability   Services typically cannot be separated from the creator–seller of the service. Moreover, many services are created, dispensed, and consumed simultaneously. For example, dentists create and dispense almost all their services at the same time, *and* they require the presence of the consumer for the services to be performed. The same is true of a fast-food drive-up window employee, a physical therapist, and even an automatic teller machine.

A service's inseparability means that services providers are involved concurrently in the production and the marketing efforts. One physician can treat only so many medical patients in a day. This characteristic limits the scale of operation in a services firm. And the customers receive and sometimes consume the services at the production site–in the firm's "factory," so to speak. Consequently, customers' opinions regarding a service frequently are formed through contacts with the production-sales personnel and impressions of the physical surroundings in the "factory." In the case of education, this would be the teacher and the classroom.

From a marketing standpoint, inseparability limits distribution. It frequently means that direct sale is the only possible channel of distribution, and an individual seller's services can be sold only where direct contact is possible.

There is an exception to the inseparability feature. Some services are sold by a person who is representing the creator–seller. A travel agent, insurance broker, or rental agent, for instance, represents, promotes, and sells services that will be provided at a later time by the institutions producing them. In these situations, the customer's opinion of the service can be influenced by the intermediary's appearance and behavior. Thus services marketers should be particularly careful in selecting agents and brokers.

Heterogeneity   It is difficult if not impossible for a service firm, or even an individual seller of services, to standardize output. Each unit of the service is somewhat different from every other unit of the same service because of the human factor in production and delivery. Regardless of its efforts, Delta Airlines does not give the same quality of service on every flight, or even to each passenger on the same flight. All performances of the Boston Pops Orchestra, or all haircuts you get, are not of equal quality.

For the buyer this condition means it is difficult to forecast quality in advance of consumption. You pay a fixed amount to see the Atlanta Braves baseball team play without knowing whether it will be an exciting or a dull game. For some services it

Unused services capacity, such as these empty chairlift seats, is lost forever. In response to this perishability feature, services marketers develop strategies, such as offering discounts during slow periods, to balance supply and demand.

may even be difficult to judge the quality after it has been received, such as when you receive a diagnosis from a physician or get advice from a minister or rabbi.

To offset heterogeneity, services companies should pay special attention to the product-planning and implementation stages of their marketing programs. From the beginning, management must do all it can to ensure consistency of quality and to maintain high levels of quality control. Service quality will be given special attention later in this chapter.

Perishability Services are highly perishable because the existing capacity cannot be stored or inventoried for future use. A cruise ship that sails with unoccupied staterooms, empty seats at a church service, and idle house painters represent available supply that is lost forever. Perishability creates potential imbalances in supply and demand. Furthermore, the demand for many services fluctuates considerably by season, by day of the week, and by hour of the day. Ski lifts can sit idle all summer, whereas golf courses in some areas go unused in the winter. The ridership of city buses fluctuates greatly during the day.

Perishability and the resulting difficulty of balancing supply with fluctuating demand poses promotion, product-planning, scheduling, and pricing challenges to services executives. Some organizations have developed new uses for idle capacity during off-seasons. During the summer, ski resorts operate their ski lifts for hikers and sightseers. Advertising and creative pricing are also used to stimulate demand during slack periods. Marriott Hotels, for example, offer lower prices and family packages on weekends, when there are fewer business travelers.

The Services Customer

Like goods marketers, service businesses should define a target market consisting of present and potential customers. They then direct their marketing only in the direction of these prospective buyers.

In contrast, nonbusiness services organizations must aim at two markets. One is the **provider market**—the contributors of money, labor, materials, or other resources to the organization. The second is the **client market**—the recipients of money or services from the organization. This recipient market is much like the customer market for a business. However, nonbusiness institutions—such as churches, hospitals, or universities—don't refer to their clients as customers. Instead, they call them parishioners, patients, or students. Because a nonbusiness organization must deal with two different markets, it must develop two different marketing programs—one directed at its resource providers, the other aimed at its clients.

Selecting Target Markets

Selecting target markets is essentially the same whether a firm is marketing goods or services. From Chapters 4 through 6, we know that services marketers need to understand how geographic and demographic factors of the market affect the demand for a service. Marketers also must try to determine their customers' buying behavior—their buying motives and patterns. The psychological determinants of buying behavior—motivation, perceptions, attitudes, personality—become more important when marketing services rather than goods. This is because we cannot touch, smell, or taste the service offered. For the same reasons, the sociological factors of social-class structure and reference groups are significant determinants of buying behavior in services markets.

In the course of selecting target markets, the concept of market segmentation has been adopted by many services marketers. There are apartment complexes for students, and others for the over-55 crowd. Some car-repair shops target owners of foreign cars. Limited-service motel chains (Motel 6, Days Inn) cater to the economy-minded segment. Hotels providing only suites (Embassy Suites, Residence Inn) seek to attract families and business travelers who prefer a "home away from home."

Segmentation strategies are also useful for nonbusiness marketers. Remember, they have two quite separate markets to analyze—resource providers and clients. Each of these two markets usually needs to be further segmented in some detail. A broad (nonsegmented) appeal to the provider market is likely to produce poor results. Likewise, trying to be all things to all people in the client market may mean being "nothing to anybody" and going broke in the process.

Many nonbusiness organizations segment their client markets, although they probably do not consider it market segmentation. For instance, country clubs develop different programs for golfers, tennis players, swimmers, and card players. Symphony orchestras design special programs for children, and arrange bus transportation and matinee performances for senior citizens.

Product Planning

The planning and development of goods has its counterpart in the marketing of services—by both business and nonbusiness organizations. The nonbusiness institution, however, requires one product-planning program for its provider market and one for its client market. Intangibility, inseparability, and high perishability present significant product-planning challenges in services marketing. In terms of product planning, a marketer of services must make strategic decisions concerning:

- What services to offer.
- What product-mix strategies to adopt.
- What features, such as branding and support service, to provide.

Services Offering
Many service firms have become successful by identifying—and then satisfying—a previously unrecognized or unsatisfied consumer want. Consider the cellular phone producers that have entered the expanding market for immediate access to communications. These firms provide a familiar service but overcome the constraint of the fixed-base telephone. In the process they had to create a signal transfer infrastructure and an easy-to-use, highly portable cellular phone.

Like goods marketers, service firms seek ways to *differentiate* their offerings. This is particularly important for services because of the intangibility characteristic. In the absence of physical differences, competing services may appear very similar to the customer. One option is to expand the product, preferably by adding attractive, promotable features. For example, in the highly competitive financial services industry, banks are trying to lure new retail customers. For example, J. P. Morgan Chase has greeters meet customers as they enter the bank and escort them to the area they wish to visit, and Woodforest National Bank in Texas has opened branches in grocery and other retail stores. Its branches in Wal-Mart stores are open 24 hours, seven days a week. Other banks are opening their branches on Sundays.[6] Ideally, added features should be ones that cannot be easily duplicated by competitors or they will be quickly neutralized. In the case of banks, reducing the fee for checking accounts or ATM usage, for example, is easily copied. On the other hand, improving the customer interaction skills of bank employees would likely produce a more durable difference.

The lesson here is that service features should be added with caution. For example, a service feature that is difficult for competitors to duplicate is the Ritz-Carlton's "technology butler." Having a skilled computer technician available around the clock to assist guests with large and small software and hardware problems is viewed as highly valuable by traveling executives. However, finding people to fill the position and justifying the salaries will likely prevent most hotels from copying the Ritz.[7]

In most nonprofit organizations the "product" offered to *clients* typically is a service (education, health care, religion, culture), a person (in politics), a cause (stop smoking or don't do drugs), or a cash grant (research foundation). Some nonprofits offer goods such as food and clothing to clients, but usually these goods are incidental to the main services provided by the organization.

The key to selecting the services to offer is for an organization to decide (1) what "business" it is in and (2) what client markets it wants to reach. If a church views its mission only as providing religious services, its assortment will be limited. If this church views its mission broadly—as providing fellowship, spirituality, and personal development—it will offer more services to more markets. The church may then offer family counseling services, day-care services, religious education courses, and social activities for single people.

Planning the services offering to the *provider* market is more difficult. An organization asks people to contribute money, time, skills, or other resources to a cause. The contribution is the price paid in order to make the organization's services available. But what is the contributor getting for this price? What are the contributors buying with their donations? In the case of donations, the donors can receive an assortment of benefits that may include:

- Feeling good about themselves or relieving guilt.
- Helping an organization provide a worthwhile service to others.
- Receiving a tax deduction.
- Contributing to their social status.
- Supporting their social or religious beliefs.

The challenge for the marketer is to understand what particular benefits motivate a potential provider, communicate those benefits, and ensure that the provider actually receives them following the donation.

Product-Mix Strategies

Several of the product-mix strategies discussed in Chapter 9 can be employed by services marketers. Consider the strategy of *expanding the line*. Disney added parks in Tokyo and Paris and is developing a theme park in Hong Kong, following on its success in the U.S., France, and Japan. Although not identical, the parks will be sufficiently similar to benefit greatly from the worldwide recognition of the Disney name, as described in the case following this chapter.

www.disney.com

In the nonprofit field, symphony orchestras expand their line by offering children's concerts and pop concerts for teenagers and college students. Universities have added adult night classes, distance learning utilizing the Internet, and concentrated between-semester courses.

Carnival Cruise Lines *contracted its services mix* by selling a casino hotel in the Bahamas—part of a series of moves designed to get the cruise ship company out of the resort business. Because of the high cost of malpractice insurance, some physicians have contracted their product mix by discontinuing the practice of obstetrics.

In response to the growing success of Internet brokerage firms such as Charles Schwab Corp., Merrill Lynch, the largest full-service securities firm in the U.S., is *altering its services offering*. The firm introduced online trading for its 5 million customers, a dramatic change for a firm that takes great pride in the personal service provided by its brokers.

Having accomplished its original mission, the virtual eradication of polio, the March of Dimes could have declared victory and disappeared. However, that would have wasted its recognized brand, established organization, and solid base of providers or donors. So, the agency has redefined its "product" as protecting children in many different ways.

www.marchofdimes.com

Managing the life cycle of a service is another strategy. Recognizing that the credit card industry is in the maturity stage, VISA sought ways to maintain its growth. The answer was new uses for the card, rather than issuing cards to more people. For starters, VISA targeted dentists, physicians, supermarkets, theaters, and even fast-food outlets, trying to get them to encourage their customers to pay with a VISA card. Likewise, amusement parks such as Knott's Berry Farm in California, Six Flags, and Great America have avoided the sales-decline stage of the life cycle by periodically adding new attractions.

Product Features

The emphasis in product planning is different for services than for goods. For example, packaging is nonexistent in services marketing. However, other features—branding and quality management, for instance—present greater challenges for services industries.

Branding of services is a problem because maintaining consistent quality, a responsibility of brand ownership, is difficult. Also, the intangibility characteristic means a brand cannot be physically attached to the service itself.

A services marketer's goal should be to create an effective brand image. The strategy to reach this goal is to develop a total theme that includes more than just a good brand name. To implement this strategy, the following tactics frequently are employed:[8]

- Use a *tangible object* to communicate the brand image or difference. The "gift-wrapped" car of Enterprise and the permanence and stability of Prudential's "rock" symbolize what these firms feel make them stand out.

- Develop a *memorable slogan* to accompany the brand. "We'll leave the light on for you" by Motel 6 and the Yellow Pages' "Let your fingers do the walking" are appealing and easily remembered slogans.[9]

- Use a *distinctive color scheme* on all tangible aspects of the brand. Southwest Airline's planes and Hertz's black and gold office décor, shuttle vans, and uniforms are highly recognizable.

Nonbusiness organizations have been slow to exploit branding. The little that has been done suggests that brands can provide effective marketing support. Colleges not only use nicknames (a form of brand name) primarily for their athletic teams, but

Smart cards: blessing, curse, or just not necessary?

It looks like a credit card but it includes a microprocessor and memory chip, and that makes all the difference in the world. Called a "smart card," this technology was hailed as a major breakthrough for shopping on the Internet and generally replacing cash for most purchases. And it has been a hit in Europe and Asia. So much so that in Hong Kong, 95% of the residents between the ages of 15 and 65 use one. In contrast, a survey of U.S. Internet users found that only 2% had smart cards.

The smart card has two primary features. A consumer can load money into its "electronic wallet" to be used anywhere the card is accepted. In Hong Kong that includes all forms of mass transit, grocery stores, fast-food outlets, telephones, and even parking meters. The second feature is validation and identification information stored on the card that prevents theft or misuse and can also be used to control access to dormitories, offices, and apartment buildings.

Smart cards became popular in Europe and Asia because there was a high incidence of credit card fraud and inexpensive and reliable authorization equipment for use by retailers was not widespread. In the United States, magnetic-stripe credit cards and photo IDs have largely controlled the problem of misuse so consumers saw little need for another card to replace cash.

There's another issue with smart cards. Depending on how they are set up, everything from individual medical records to the purchases made with the card can be collected, stored, and transmitted. As a result, there are concerns about invasion of privacy when they are used. To expand the international success of smart cards to the United States, proponents must identify a need they can satisfy better than alternatives. Any ideas?

Sources: Stacy Forster, "Smart Cards Escape the U.S. Mind," *The Wall Street Journal*, July 16, 2002, p. D2; Mark Fischetti, "Safety at a Cost," *Scientific American*, August 2002, pp. 86–87; Bruce Einhorn, "Hong Kong's Savvy Use of Smart Cards," *Business Week Online*, June 24, 2002, at *www.businessweek.com/technology*.

also to identify their students and alumni. Most universities have school colors—another feature that helps increase the market's recognition of the school. Among health research organizations, the Lung Association has registered as a trademark its double-barred Christmas Seal cross. Likewise, the trademarks of the American Red Cross and the YMCA are readily recognized by many people.

Pricing Structure

In services marketing there is a great need for managerial skill in pricing. Because services are perishable, they cannot be stored, and demand for them often fluctuates considerably. Each of these features has significant pricing implications. To further complicate pricing, customers often have a "do-it-yourself" alternative, as in auto or home repairs. There are two tasks in designing a *pricing structure*: determine the base price and select strategies to adjust the base price.

Price Determination in For-Profit Firms
Services marketers set their prices by adding a markup to their costs (called cost plus) or by estimating what target customers are willing to pay, regardless of cost. Electric power and telephone companies, for example, use a cost basis to set prices that will generate a predetermined rate of return on investment. Painters, plumbers, and electricians frequently price their services on a cost-plus basis. Airlines, on the other hand, tend to meet competitors' prices, especially on routes served by two or more airlines, even if those prices result in a financial loss.

The perishability characteristic of services suggests that the demand for a service should influence its price. Interestingly enough, sellers often do recognize situations of strong demand and limited supply. For example, ticket prices are raised significantly for the farewell tours of popular musical groups, and hotels located near sports stadiums raise their room rates for the dates of championship events. The opposite situation, excess supply, has created an industry on the Internet. Firms such as Priceline allow a buyer to specify a price he or she is willing to pay for a service such as a plane ticket on a particular day. If an airline flying the route is willing to sell a seat at that price, they have a deal. Other services offered on Priceline include hotel rooms, cars, home mortgages, and long-distance phone service.

Price Determination by Nonprofits   Pricing in nonbusiness organizations is different from pricing in a for-profit firm. In the first place, pricing becomes less important when profit making is not a goal. Also, a nonbusiness organization is faced with special forms of pricing in the provider market and in the client market.

In the *provider* market, nonbusiness organizations do not set the price—the amount of the resource contributed. That price is set by contributors when they decide how much they are willing to pay (donate) for the benefits they expect to receive. However, a price is often suggested—for example, donate one day's pay or volunteer for one day a month. And the suggested price is often translated into a client benefit (for example, the amount of food or clothing $100 will provide in an underdeveloped country) to provide the donor with a basis for valuing the contribution.

In the *client* market, some nonbusiness organizations face the same pricing situation, and can use the same methods, as profit-seeking firms. Museums and opera companies, for example, must decide on admission prices; fraternal organizations must set a dues schedule; and colleges must determine how much to charge for tuition. But most nonbusiness organizations cannot use the same pricing methods employed by business firms. These nonbusiness organizations know that they cannot cover their costs with prices charged to clients. The gap between anticipated revenues and costs must be made up by contributions. As yet, there simply are no real guidelines for nonbusiness pricing.

Also, some nonbusiness groups tend to believe there are no pricing considerations with regard to clients because there is no monetary charge to the client. Actually, the goods or services received by clients rarely are free—that is, without a price of some kind. The client almost always pays a price—in the form of travel and waiting time and, perhaps, embarrassment or humiliation—that a money-paying client would not have to pay.

Pricing Strategies   Several common pricing strategies are applicable in services marketing—in both profit-seeking and nonbusiness organizations. *Discounts,* for example, are widely used in marketing services. A season pass for the Metropolitan Opera or the Los Angeles Philharmonic Orchestra costs less per performance than tickets purchased for individual performances. Daily rates charged by Hertz or Avis are lower if you rent a car for a week or a month at a time. These are forms of quantity discount.

A *flexible-price* strategy is used by many service organizations. Museums and movie theaters offer lower prices for children and senior citizens. In some cities, bus transportation costs less during off-peak hours. The University of Colorado charges a higher tuition in its business and engineering colleges than in arts and sciences. On the other hand, the University of Notre Dame and many other universities typically follow a *one-price* strategy. That is, all students pay the same tuition for a full load of course work.

Databases that allow a company to examine an individual's purchase history, can be combined with real-time supply information that indicates how much of a service remains unsold. Using this information a firm can engage in *dynamic pricing,* or adjusting price to meet individual circumstances. For example, an airline can calculate the value of each of its customers based on their individual purchase histories. It can also compute the likelihood of selling the remaining inventory of seats on a particular flight at any time, using historical data. Combining the two pieces

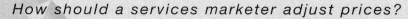
How should a services marketer adjust prices?

There was a time when the price of attending college was a fixed amount, payable by check or cash. A few of the most qualified students were able to reduce the cost by qualifying for scholarships or defer payment by getting a loan. But things have changed at some colleges and universities. Now many schools accept payment by credit card. The students or their parents benefit by using premium-related credit cards that permit them to earn points toward airline flights or other retail purchases. The schools, on the other hand, pay service fees to the credit card companies of as much as 2%. Boston College, for example, quit accepting credit card payment when its annual service fees reached $1.5 million, whereas Colorado State University recently paid over $1 million in credit card fees.

Even more dramatic are the discounts students are able to wrangle by playing one school's offer against another's. According to a national association, about 70% of first-year students receive discounts that average $7,000 per student from the 330 private colleges surveyed.

How should a services marketer go about determining changes in its payment method or price discounts?

Sources: June Knonholz, "On Sale Now: College Tuition," *The Wall Street Journal,* May 16, 2002, pp. D1+ ; Michael Booth, "Colorado Colleges Get Nicked with Credit-Card Fees," *The Denver Post,* Apr. 26, 2002, p. A1.

of information, an individual can be offered a price that considers the value of retaining the person's loyalty, maximizes the probability of a ticket being purchased, and optimizes the revenue from the flight.

Price competition among service providers varies by industry. Where it has become more common, the use of price competition seems to exist at three levels:

- Price is rarely mentioned as organizations attempt to compete on other dimensions. For example, a health maintenance organization (HMO) will run an ad explaining its services, but will not dwell much on price.

- The seller uses a segmentation strategy and targets a given market at a specific price. A law firm, for example, may prominently advertise its low prices for divorce proceedings or the preparation of a will.

- Intense price competition occurs as firms stress comparative prices in their advertising. Credit card companies and cellular phone service providers have engaged extensively in advertising that compares their prices with those of competitors.

Price competition is particularly intense in service industries where the products are viewed as highly interchangeable, such as fast food. Interestingly, in areas where the products should be fairly easy to differentiate, such as professional services, price competition seems to be increasing. This would suggest that professional services marketers are not effectively using the other components of the marketing mix to differentiate their offerings.

Distribution System

Designing a distribution system for a service (whether in the for-profit or nonbusiness context) involves two tasks. One is to select the parties through which ownership will pass (called the channel of distribution), and the other is to provide facilities for physically distributing the services.

Channels of Distribution   The ownership channel for most services is short and quite simple because of the inseparability characteristic. That is, a service usually cannot be separated from its producer.

The only other frequently used channel includes one agent middleman. For example, an agent or broker often is used when marketing securities, travel arrangements, or housing rentals.

Short channels usually mean more control on the part of the seller. With direct distribution or only a single middleman, it would seem that service marketers should be able to reduce the heterogeneity or variance in the service from one transaction to another. However, because the service provider is also creating the service, a single firm may operate a large number of virtually identical short channels. For example, McDonald's has over 30,000 outlets in 121 countries, all producing and distributing the product. Thus, the control problems are in the *number* of middlemen to be managed, not the length of the channel.

Distribution Facilities   A good location is essential when the distribution of a service requires personal interaction between producer and consumer, especially today because consumers are so convenience-oriented. Some services marketers have broadened their distribution by extending their accessibility, thus offsetting to some extent the limitations imposed by the inseparability factor. Zoots, a dry-cleaning chain with operations in nine eastern states, is using technology to improve distribution convenience. In addition to home or office pick-up and delivery service, Zoots has drive-through locations. By providing customers with bar-coded garment bags, soiled clothing can be dropped off at one of its outlets, cleaned, and picked up by the customer at any time from lockers outside the store. Preapproved charges are made to the customer's credit card and the customer is sent an itemized statement monthly. By eliminating all personal interaction, Zoots makes the transaction more convenient.

The Internet has greatly broadened the distribution of some services, making it easier for buyers and sellers to establish contact. Bank One and other U.S. banks are faced with competition from Canadian banks that can offer consumers Internet-based accounts virtually anywhere in North America the banking laws permit. Like Bank One, all services retailers need to examine how the Internet impacts the inseparability characteristic of their businesses.

Not-for-profit organizations try to provide arrangements to make donor contributions easy and convenient. Besides cash and checks, charities use payroll deductions, installment plans, and credit cards. If you are contributing used goods, the Disabled American Veterans may collect them at your residence.

Location is also critical when dealing with nonbusiness client markets. Libraries have branches; blood banks conduct blood drives on location in factories and schools; Goodwill Industries locates its stores in low-income neighborhoods; and big-city museums arrange for portable exhibits to be taken to small towns.

Promotional Program

Several types of promotion are used extensively in services marketing—in both profit-seeking and nonprofit organizations. In fact, promotion is the one part of the marketing mix with which services marketers are most familiar and adept. Unfortunately, many services firms, especially nonbusiness organizations, believe that promotion is marketing and overlook the other mix elements.

Personal Selling   Because of the inseparability characteristic, personal selling plays a pivotal role in promotional programs for most services. Face-to-face contact between buyer and seller is required in order to make a transaction. Thus, it is important that a service employee be skilled at customer relations as well as capable of producing a quality service.

Personal selling is frequently employed by not-for-profit organizations in soliciting donations. Potentially large donors may be approached by fundraisers (sales people). Many nonprofit organizations also use personal selling to reach their

www.zoots.com

Some for-profit, nonprofit, and not-for-profit organizations have identified ways to work together to achieve their individual goals. For example, once a year law enforcement officials become celebrity servers in Red Lobster restaurants, talking to guests about Special Olympics and accepting donations. Recently, the program called "Cops & Lobsters" raised more than $1.2 million for the Special Olympics' cause.

www.redlobster.com/
fun/cops.asp

clients. For example, all branches of the military make use of recruiters. For centuries, religious missionaries recruited new members by personal contact. Colleges send admissions officers, alumni, and current students to talk to high school students, their parents, and their counselors. These representatives may not be called sales people, but that is exactly what they are.

Whether they realize it or not, all employees of a service provider who come in contact with a customer are, in effect, part of that organization's sales force. In addition to a regular sales force, customer-contact personnel might include airline counter attendants, law office receptionists, package delivery people, bank tellers, ticket takers, and ushers at ballparks or theaters.

The term **service encounter** is used to describe a customer's interaction with any service employee, or with any tangible element such as a service's physical surroundings (bank, theatre, medical office). A large part of a customer's evaluation of an organization and its service is made on the basis of service encounters. Consequently, management must prepare its contact personnel and physical surroundings. The approach to this preparation is often called *internal marketing* to emphasize the idea that a services organization should view its employees as customers to whom it markets customer-contact jobs. When an organization adopts this perspective, it will go to great lengths to select the right people for these jobs, train them, and make the jobs interesting and fulfilling. The net effect is satisfying service encounters for customers and success for the organization. Unfortunately, many service organizations do not think in these terms and, as a result, have not developed the orientation necessary to produce outstanding customer-contact employees.[10]

Advertising   For years, advertising has been used extensively in many service fields—transportation, recreation, and insurance, for example. At one time, advertising by professional-services providers including attorneys, physicians, and accountants was prohibited by their professional associations on the grounds that it was unethical. However, the Supreme Court has ruled that prohibiting a professional firm from advertising is restraint of trade and thus a violation of antitrust laws. Some associations still try to impose constraints on advertising, but the restrictions continue to be eased.

Nonbusiness organizations use advertising extensively to reach their donor markets. Mass media (newspapers, television, radio) frequently are used in annual fund-raising drives. Direct-mail and telephone solicitation can be especially effective in reaching particular donor-market segments, such as cash contributors, religious or ethnic group members, or college alumni. However, telephone contact is coming under fire under the broad heading of telemarketing. Because some firms have abused this form of communication, several states have passed laws allowing consumers to place themselves on "no-call" lists, with organizations that ignore the lists risking severe penalties. The relatively low cost of a website on the Internet has provided nonprofits such as colleges and universities, and organizations like the Special Olympics and Mothers Against Drunk Driving (MADD) with an opportunity to communicate more information than was possible in the past.

Forming an alliance with a for-profit organization can be another valuable source of promotion for nonbusiness organizations. Called *cause-related marketing*, it involves developing a relationship that generates sales for the firm and publicity (along with donations) for the nonprofit organization. A survey of young people found that two-thirds consider the causes that may be affected when they shop for clothing and other items. And more than one-half would switch to a brand or retailer that is associated with a good cause if price and quality are equal.[11] An example of cause-related marketing is the Avon Breast Cancer Crusade, begun by the firm in 1993. Its stated mission is funding access to care and finding a cure for breast cancer. Through its various activities the firm has raised over $165 million in the U.S. alone.

Large and small nonbusiness groups also can communicate with client markets through advertising. The military branches are heavy users of marketing, with over $265 million budgeted for advertising in 2001. Utilizing what it describes as a "corporate" model, the Pentagon is reducing its reliance on traditional, network television ads and is moving toward alternatives. For example, short spots on youth-oriented cable channels and information booths at NASCAR events are part of today's recruitment advertising.[12] In another kind of recruiting, a Midwestern women's religious order with a budget of less than $200,000, developed a marketing plan and is using advertising to help attract prospective members.[13]

Other Promotional Methods Various forms of sales promotion are frequently used by services marketers. Laundry and dry-cleaning firms, opticians, and auto-repair shops include reduced-price offers in telephone directories and coupon books mailed periodically to local households. Travel agents, ski resorts, and landscaping services have displays at sports shows or home shows. These displays show the beneficial results of using the service.

Other promotional tools used by not-for-profit organizations include front-end premiums (a gift or incentive such as sheets of personalized return address labels that accompany direct-mail solicitations), back-end premiums (gifts such as mugs, T-shirts, CDs, or videos offered for donations of various amounts), and virtual incentives (coupons that can be redeemed at online retailers).[14]

Many service firms, especially in the recreation and entertainment fields, benefit considerably from free publicity. Sports coverage by newspapers, radio, and television provides publicity, as do newspaper reviews of movies, plays, and concerts. Travel sections in newspapers help sell transportation, housing, and other services related to the travel industry.

Managing Service Quality

In Chapter 10, we noted the elusiveness of product quality. Service quality is particularly difficult to define, measure, control, and communicate. Yet in services marketing, the quality of the service is critical to a firm's success. Two airlines each fly Boeing 737s and charge the same fare; two auto-repair shops each use factory-authorized parts and charge the same price; and two banks make home mortgage loans at identical interest rates. Assuming similar times and locations, quality of the service is the only factor that differentiates what is offered by these firms.[15]

Services providers must understand two attributes of **service quality:** First, quality is defined by the customer, not by the producer-seller. Your hairstylist may be delighted with the job done on your hair, but if you think your hair looks terrible, then the service quality is poor. Second, customers assess service quality by comparing their expectations to their perceptions of how the service is performed. In this process, there is no guarantee that expectations will be reasonable, nor is there any assurance that a customer's perception of performance will be based on more than a single experience.

Consequently, to effectively manage quality, a services firm should:

1. Help customers formulate expectations.
2. Measure the expectation level of its target market.
3. Strive to maintain consistent service quality at or above the expectations level.

Expectations are based on information from personal and commercial sources, promises made by the service provider, and experience with the particular service as well as other similar services. Firms have an opportunity through their formal and informal communications to influence customers' expectations. Because of the intangibility of services, providers tend to exaggerate performance. Extravagant claims for education programs, weight-loss regimens, and vacation packages that contribute to unrealistic expectations are unfortunately too commonplace.

A services firm must conduct research to measure expectations. Gathering data on the target market's past behavior, existing perceptions and beliefs, and exposure to information can provide the basis for estimating expectations.

With the desired level of service keyed to expectations, the next challenge is standardizing service performance—that is, maintaining consistency in service output. Service performance typically varies even within the same organization. This is true in such diverse fields as opera, legal services, landscaping, baseball, hospital care, and marketing courses. The reason is simple: services are most often performed by people and their behavior is very difficult to standardize.

As part of managing service quality, an organization should design and operate an ongoing quality assessment and improvement program. The foundation of quality improvement is monitoring the level and consistency of service quality. Holding to the idea that service quality is defined by customers, a firm must regularly measure customer satisfaction—that is, customers' perceptions of the quality of an organization's services. The Ritz-Carlton hotel chain, a two-time winner of the Malcolm Baldrige National Quality Award, emphasizes employee training and measuring customer satisfaction.

www.ritzcarlton.com

One proposal for standardizing the quality of service delivery is to substitute machines for people whenever possible. At least in theory, an ATM machine or a website on the Internet treats every interaction in the same fashion. Although it's a fact that a machine will not suffer from fatigue, forgetfulness, or stress, this argument ignores the variability on the customer side of the exchange. If a consumer is not adept at surfing the Internet, forgets the required ATM personal identification number, or gets impatient with the branching process on a recorded telephone answering system, the quality of the service encounter is likely to be inconsistent. This possible shortcoming, despite the standardization and reliability of machines, is one factor that may explain why Internet shopping accounts for only 2% of total retail sales.[16]

To standardize the quality of their local operations, some nonbusiness organizations are copying the operating structures used by commercial franchise systems. For example, Camp Fire Girls and Boys and United Way provide local units with managerial expertise, performance evaluation, marketing guidance, and purchasing assistance in exchange for a fee. This arrangement provides the local unit with policies to

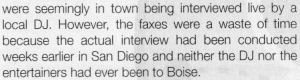

Should radio listeners in smaller markets such as Boise, Idaho, have access to the same on-air talent as big markets like San Diego? What if they are led to believe that the DJ is a local resident? Clear Channel Communications, a conglomerate of nearly 50 stations made possible by a federal law that liberalized the number of stations one company could control, thinks so. Using a technique called "voice tracking" the programs of popular radio personalities can be customized to sound as if they are actually local shows and broadcast on more than one of Clear Channels' stations. The attraction for the company is the ability to sell advertising to national advertisers in many different markets, providing economies of scale to both the broadcaster and the advertiser. But are listeners being unfairly misled? Recently, listeners to a Boise station (owned by Clear Channel Communications) were invited to fax the station with questions for a pop duo who were seemingly in town being interviewed live by a local DJ. However, the faxes were a waste of time because the actual interview had been conducted weeks earlier in San Diego and neither the DJ nor the entertainers had ever been to Boise.

Is it unethical to mislead listeners about when or where a broadcast is taking place?

Sources: Anna Wilde Mathews, "A Giant Radio Chain Is Perfecting the Art of Seeming Local," *The Wall Street Journal*, Feb. 25, 2002, pp. A1+; Chris Baker, "Rockville Disc Jockey Spins Tale of Two Cities," *The Washington Times*, May 25, 2002, p. A1.

achieve consistency in all its operations, a high level of managerial expertise, and valuable operating economies.

The Future of Services Marketing

Until recently, many services industries enjoyed growth, supported by government and professional-association regulations, the absence of significant foreign competition, and a strong economy. But the environment is changing, bringing with it a focus on increasing productivity and customer-satisfying performance.

The Impact of Technology

Technology has dramatically changed some services industries and created others. The most immediate impact is being felt by firms that act as agents or brokers for services providers. The Internet offers firms in the travel, accommodations, recreation, and insurance industries a cost-effective way to bypass intermediaries. As a result, travel agents, insurance brokers, and other types of middlemen are being confronted with a new type of competition. In another industry, interactive telecommunications technology has created a distance learning capability that is changing the way training and education are distributed. These and other developments on the horizon will force many services firms to redefine what they do. For example, facsimile machines have diminished the need for overnight delivery of documents, causing FedEx to reinvent itself as an information company rather than a delivery service.

Need for Increased Productivity

The changing services environment has exposed inefficiency and poor management in many services industries, clearly demonstrating the need for restructuring. At the same time, inefficiency provides competent services firms with a tremendous opportunity to increase productivity. This opportunity is being seized by services chains and franchise systems that are replacing small-scale, independent services firms and professionals in many fields. Examples include Kaiser Permanente and Humana in health care; Midas Muffler and Jiffy Lube in auto repairs and maintenance; Pearle

Vision and LensCrafters in vision improvement; and Re/Max and Century 21 in real estate.

Not long ago, attempts to increase services productivity were focused on a manufacturing-based approach. For example, Burger King and McDonald's adopted assembly line techniques and increased their output per worker. The most widely adopted technology was some form of computer-based information system that increased the efficiency of operations. And for several years this manufacturing-based model for increasing service productivity was successful.

However, the basic premise of the manufacturing model is that machines and technology are the primary keys to increased productivity, that the people who deliver the services are not as important. But this premise no longer works in the services environment. Instead, a model is needed that combines technology and customer-contact workers, and designs the business operations around the needs of the customer.

Performance Measurement

Profit-seeking service firms can evaluate their performances by using quantitative measures such as profitability, market share, or return on investment, and then can compare these figures with industry averages and trends. However, for most non-business organizations, because their objectives are so varied, there are few generally accepted performance measures. Consequently, measuring marketing performance in the nonbusiness sector requires some imagination and creativity.

Nonbusiness organizations can quantify the contributions they receive, but the result reflects only their fund-raising abilities. It does not measure the services rendered to their clients. How do you quantitatively evaluate the performance of, say, the Red Cross? Perhaps by the number of people the organization houses and feeds after a hurricane or some other natural disaster. Or by the number of people trained in first aid and life-saving techniques. Churches, museums, and YMCAs can count their attendance, but how do they measure the quality of the services and benefits they provide to their clients?

The analysis and management of customer complaints is an evaluation tool that can be used by both nonbusiness and profit-seeking organizations. The complaint-management process involves keeping track of (1) customer complaints, (2) how they are resolved, and (3) whether the complaint handling was satisfactory, so the complaining customer ends up as a returning customer.

Prospects for Growth

Services will continue to take an increasing share of the consumer dollar, just as they have done over the past 40 years. Time pressure and a reevaluation of priorities are contributing factors. This forecast seems reasonable even for periods of economic decline. History shows that the demand for services is less sensitive to economic fluctuations than the demand for goods.

The demand for commercial services should also continue to expand as business becomes more complex and as management further recognizes its need for specialized support services and the value of outsourcing. In professional services especially, the use of marketing programs is expected to continue growing. This expansion will occur as physicians, lawyers, and other professionals come to understand the economic benefits they can derive from an effective marketing program.

The significance of nonbusiness marketing will increase as the people in these organizations understand what marketing is and what it can do for them. As noted earlier in this chapter, many nonbusiness organizations have a limited concept of marketing, even though they engage in some efforts without calling it marketing. The marketing activities they do perform (usually promotion) often are not well coordinated, and the people in charge of them usually have other duties and titles. In a university, for example, personal selling may be managed by the director of admissions, fund raising coordinated by a director of development, and advertising done through an office of public information. For a more effective marketing job, most nonbusinesses need a more formal, recognizable marketing structure.

Summary

The scope of services marketing is enormous. About 50% of what consumers spend goes for services, and more than 80% of nonfarm jobs are in services industries. Services purchased by businesses constitute another major segment of the economy. The nonbusiness services field includes thousands of organizations spanning educational, cultural, religious, charitable, social, health care, and political activities. Services marketers can be divided into for-profit businesses and nonbusiness organizations, made up of not-for-profits and nonprofits. The not-for-profit organizations have a profit (or surplus) objective, but it is secondary to some other goal. Nonprofits do not have a profit objective.

Most product offerings are a mix of tangibles (goods) and intangibles (services), somewhere between pure goods and pure services. To distinguish between goods and services, we define services as separately identifiable, intangible activities that are the main object of a transaction designed to provide want-satisfaction.

Services are intangible, usually inseparable from the seller, heterogeneous, highly perishable, and widely fluctuating in demand. These characteristics that differentiate services from goods have several marketing implications.

The growth in services has not been matched by service management's application of the marketing concept. Monopoly status, external constraints, and a nonbusiness orientation have caused many services marketers to be slow in adopting marketing techniques that, in goods marketing, have brought satisfaction to consumers and profits to producers and middlemen. However, that is changing as constraints and restrictions are removed, and service producers observe the benefits of effective marketing.

Developing a program for marketing services is much the same as for goods, but takes into account the characteristics of services. Management first identifies its target market, making use of market segmentation strategies, and then designs a marketing mix around a differential advantage to provide want-satisfaction for the market.

Many nonbusiness services organizations must deal with two markets: donors, the contributors to the organization; and clients, the recipients of the organization's money or services. Consequently, a nonbusiness organization must develop two separate marketing programs: one to attract resources from donors and one to provide services to clients.

In the product-planning stage, services enterprises use various product-mix strategies, and they should try to brand their services. Service firms must determine base prices and select appropriate pricing strategies. Pricing in nonbusiness organizations often is quite different from pricing in profit-seeking businesses.

Channels of distribution are quite simple in services marketing, and middlemen are not often used. The main physical distribution challenge is to locate the services organization where it can most effectively serve its markets. Regarding promotion, services firms often use personal selling and advertising extensively and quite effectively. These organizations are recognizing the importance of service encounters and the need to engage in internal marketing directed at customer-contact personnel.

Consistently maintaining a level of quality that the customer expects is critical to a company's success. Managing customers' expectations is an important services issue.

The expanding services arena has exposed inefficiency in services industries. Key issues in improving services marketing are the effective use of technology, the need to increase productivity, and the development of useful performance measures.

More about Enterprise Rent-A-Car

Enterprise prides itself on going well beyond the expected when it comes to customer service. One of its founding principles is that satisfied customers drive business growth. The tag line "We'll pick you up" means just what it says, for instance, even though bringing rental cars to customers can present special scheduling challenges for employees. Everyone at Enterprise knows, however, that because the firm dedicates itself to the local market, customers are not likely to be the anonymous business travelers passing through airports who make up competitors' customer bases. They are people in the neighborhood who will be coming back to rent another car if they are satisfied—or go elsewhere if they are not.

High customer-satisfaction ratings are a prerequisite for employee promotions, and if ratings for a branch fall below the corporate average, no one at that branch can be promoted until the score improves. However, customer satisfaction is not the only performance criterion at Enterprise. Addition-

ally, nearly everyone in the firm is paid compensation that is tied to profits. Thus, employees are challenged to make a profit while pleasing customers.

Enterprise also looks after its business customers. To insurance companies like GEICO that link their claims systems to Enterprise's automated car-rental system, the firm provides access to real-time reservation information. That in turn allows insurers to offer their customers a valuable service and makes them look good, keeping them happy with Enterprise so they keep coming back.[17]

1. Like all service firms, Enterprise must adapt to the characteristics of intangibility, inseparability, heterogeneity, and perishability.

   a. What elements of Enterprise's marketing strategy reflect a sensitivity to these characteristics?

   b. What else could Enterprise do to adapt to these characteristics of services?

2. Should Enterprise change its marketing efforts if it decides to pursue other auto-rental market segments, such as business travelers at airports, to a greater extent than it has?

Key Terms and Concepts

Services (287)
For-profit services firms (287)
Not-for-profit (N-F-P) services organizations (288)
Nonprofit organization (288)

Intangibility (290)
Inseparability (290)
Heterogeneity (290)
Perishability (290)
Provider market (292)

Client market (292)
Service encounter (300)
Service quality (302)

Questions and Problems

1. Collect several pieces of letterhead stationery from different departments at your school and business cards from administrators and professors. Are the colors, logos, symbols, type styles, and other layouts similar or different? Make the same comparison for the websites of several units of the school. Which of the four characteristics of services do your findings support or contradict?

2. Services are highly perishable and are often subject to fluctuations in demand. In marketing an amusement park, how can a company offset these factors?

3. Cite some examples of large service firms that seem to be customer-oriented, and describe what these firms have done to create this impression. (A good resource is *www.fastcompany.com/themes*.)

4. Identify three segments of your school's donor market and the benefits offered to them in return for their donations.

5. Present a brief analysis of the market for each of the following service firms. Make use of the components of a market discussed in Chapters 4 and 5, and the concepts of market segmentation in Chapter 6.

a. Hospital in your city
b. Hotel near a large airport
c. Indoor tennis club
d. Regional airline

6. What are some ways in which each of the following service firms might expand its product mix?

   a. Certified public accountant (CPA)
   b. Hairstyling salon
   c. Bank

7. A financial consultant for a private university suggested a change in the school's pricing methods. He recommended that the school discontinue its present one-price policy, under which all full-time students pay the same tuition. Instead, he recommended that the tuition vary by departments within the university. Thus, students majoring in high-cost fields of study, such as engineering or a laboratory science, would pay higher tuition than students in lower-cost fields, such as English or history. Should the school adopt this recommendation?

8. Explain how the components of the marketing mix (product, price, distribution, promotion) are applicable to marketing the following social causes:

   a. The use of returnable bottles, instead of the throwaway type
   b. The prevention of heart ailments
   c. A campaign against smoking
   d. Obeying the speed limit

9. "When used by consumers for making purchases, the Internet seems to offset the service characteristics of inseparability and heterogeneity." Explain whether or not that statement is true.

10. How would you measure the marketing performance of each of the following?

    a. adidas website
    b. Your school
    c. The Republican Party
    d. A group in favor of gun control

Interactive Marketing Exercises

1. Grade the marketing performance of a sample of five profit-seeking services firms in your college community by asking 10 of your friends to rate each of them on a scale of 10 (excellent performer) to 1 (very poor performer). Compute an average "performance score" for each firm. On the basis of your survey, identify those that are doing a good marketing job and those that are not. In your report, explain briefly the reasons that contribute to the ratings of the best and worst performers.

2. Examine the websites of three nonbusiness services organizations (for example, a charity, a college or university, and a professional or trade association). Report the evidence you find that indicates the organizations are focused on a need, have identified a target market, and have developed a complete marketing mix.

Cases for Part 3

Walt Disney Co.

Continuing to Expand into Tomorrowland

Once known exclusively for its revolutionary animated movies, U.S. amusement parks, and children's television programming, the Walt Disney Co. has rapidly expanded during the last two decades. Its vast empire now includes foreign theme parks, several movie production companies, special-effects firms, professional sports franchises, cable and network television, publishing companies, retail stores, a cruise line, theater productions, and even real estate holdings.

In 2002, the year that Walt Disney would have turned 100 years old, the company used this anniversary to refocus attention on its amusement parks. It chose "100 Years of Magic" as a theme and heavily promoted the celebration with special ads, new parades, and commemorative merchandise. It also opened Walt Disney Studio in Paris to complement Disneyland Paris, which opened in 1992. Both domestically and abroad, Disney continues to make the point, "It's a small world after all."

Opening the First House of Mouse

The first Disney park was conceived and funded by Walt Disney himself. After mortgaging his house and selling part of his company to the ABC network, Walt purchased 182 acres of land in Anaheim, California, for $17 million. The spread became the site of Disneyland, which opened in 1955.

However, Walt had even bigger plans and felt rather landlocked by this location. So he ensured there would be enough room for his next theme park by buying 28,000 acres in Orlando, Florida. The Magic Kingdom at Walt Disney World opened on this site in 1971, followed by Epcot in 1982, Disney-MGM Studios in 1989, and Disney's Animal Kingdom in 1998. Disney managed to acquire another 55 acres of land in Anaheim, and Disney's California Adventure debuted in 2001.

The California complex now has more of the same resortlike feel found in its Florida counterpart, albeit on a much smaller scale. With three hotels and a shopping and restaurant area known as Downtown Disney, the hope is that visitors will stay longer and spend more money at the California property. Guests at Disney's parks in Orlando stay an average of seven days, compared with two days in Anaheim. "The Orlando philosophy is to get you there, keep you there, and to make sure you spend all your money with them," commented a former Disney executive. "In Anaheim, we needed a reason for folks to stick around."

There were high hopes for the new California Adventure park, especially because attendance at Disneyland decreased by 8% in the early 1990s. Disney World's attendance also fell by 4%, and the theme park unit as a whole saw a subsequent 30% decline in earnings. With all new roller coasters, popular attractions from other Disney parks, and an emphasis on the California lifestyle, one analyst predicted that the new park would increase attendance at Disneyland by 50%—to 20 million people annually. To encourage guests to visit both parks in Anaheim, Disney created a three-day dual-park pass and priced it at $99 compared to a one-day pass at either park for $43.

The early results for California Adventure have been weak, at best. In mid-2002, attendance at this venue was down 10% compared to 2001, which was judged to be a poor start. A drawback of the park, according to some patrons, is the scarcity of activities for young children. To remedy that problem, California Adventure is working on a new kids' area and a thrill ride similar to one in the Disney-MGM Studios park in Orlando. Meanwhile, prices are being discounted to lure more customers through the park's turnstiles.

Walt Disney World has also been seeking more visitors. It continues to add attractions, most recently Disney's Animal Kingdom and a spectacular Animal Kingdom Lodge. However, it is also trying another tactic. "We knew we had something here that offered a wide variety of people great joy, but many people perceived that we were just for families," explained a marketing executive for the company. "We're reinventing the brand by making it relevant to various life stages." Four markets are being targeted: younger couples and older couples with grown children as well as families with young children and families with teens. By emphasizing its golf courses, Pleasure Island (a nightclub-type atmosphere located in Downtown Disney,) and fine dining options, Disney World is trying to attract everyone from honeymooners to retirees, with the latter group hopefully bringing their grandchildren.

With a variety of attractions, more than 26,000 hotel rooms, and a reputation as "the happiest place on Earth," Disney World continues to be the most popular vacation spot in the U.S. The Walt Disney Co. is hoping to duplicate this success in Europe and in Asia.

Spreading the Magic Overseas

Disneyland and Disney World attract tourists from around the world, especially Asians. As a result, Disney entered into a licensing agreement with a Japanese company called Oriental Land and opened Tokyo Disneyland in 1983. In exchange for a small initial investment of $20 million, Disney continues to receive between 5% and 10% of the park's revenues. The park was a huge success, so much so that one Japanese professor referred to it as "the greatest cultural event in Japan during the '80s." But attendance began to fall in 1999, as did spending per guest and net profits. One analyst in Tokyo explained, "Over the past decade, Tokyo Disneyland has managed to shield itself from [Japan's ailing] economy. But the drop in guest spending suggests those days may be ending."

The second park to be opened overseas, in 1992, was Euro Disneyland. Located outside Paris, the park initially had to deal with criticism from some people and apathy from many others. Some French intellectuals characterized it as a cultural wasteland. The park lost close to $2 *billion* in its first several years of operation.

Disney executives threatened to close the park unless costs were slashed and revenues increased. Financing was rearranged, ticket prices were cut, and attractions were added. The park also changed its name to Disneyland Paris. Largely because of these changes, park attendance jumped 21% from 8.8 million visitors in 1994 to 10.7 million in 1995; hotel occupancy increased as well. Perhaps most important, the park turned a profit of $23 million in 1995. It is now the number one tourist attraction in France—drawing even more visitors than either the Louvre or the Eiffel Tower.

Tokyo DisneySea was opened in 2001. Much like its California Adventure counterpart, it was expected to help increase attendance at Tokyo Disneyland—perhaps from 17 million visitors a year to 25 million. It is targeting a slightly older crowd with wilder rides, a full-service spa, and alcoholic beverages. However, its $46 price tag is steep in a depressed economy. In addition, the Tokyo parks face stiff competition from Universal Studios, which opened its own theme park in Osaka in 2001.

Soon after adding a second park in Japan, Disney did likewise in France. Walt Disney Studio Paris, similar to MGM Studios in Orlando, opened in 2002. It replicates many of that park's most successful attractions, and features a variety of rides and shows that have a distinct European flavor. It too faces competition, this time from Warner Brothers, which has its own parks in Germany and Spain. Unlike the Tokyo complex, however, Disney owns 39% of the two parks in France.

Final plans are being made for a Disneyland park that will open in Hong Kong in 2006. Disney's chief executive officer, Michael Eisner, referred to the Hong Kong site as "the most spectacular park location we have anywhere in the world," and also as "a beachhead for the Disney brand in the most populous nation on earth." With a 43% stake in the new park, it is understandable that Eisner has a special interest in this enterprise.

In mid-2002, the *Hong Kong Economic Times* reported that Disney had taken an important first, but nonbinding step to open a second park in China, this one in Shanghai. According to observers, the two parks would compete for the same customers. Disney, not surprisingly, had a different view. In late 2002, Disney reversed course and said it would not build another park in China, besides the one in Hong Kong, until at least 2010. Instead, Disney will concentrate on attaining its forecast of 5.6 million annual customers for the Hong Kong park, with one-third coming from mainland China. Eventually, Disney wants 10 million guests to enter Hong Kong Disneyland each year.

With the addition of each new theme park, the Parks and Resorts business unit contributes more and more money to the company. By 2002, this unit accounted for more than one-quarter of the company's total revenues.

Diversifying Mickey's Holdings

Disney's theme parks are very much related to the rest of the firm's holdings. Within the parks' boundaries, you can find a wealth of Disney merchandise, a subset of which can be found in its Disney Stores in various cities. The parks also feature shows that promote its network and cable programs, such as the popular Disney Channel cartoons, *Stanley* and *Rolie Polie Olie*. Other attractions, such as "Beauty and the Beast," were developed as offshoots of popular Broadway musicals. There are also Radio Disney hubs and Internet kiosks that feature Disney websites. And the ESPN Zone is a popular restaurant within several parks, especially on game days. The sports-themed Zones are also a reminder to customers that

Disney owns TV and radio enterprises as well as two professional sports franchises, hockey's Mighty Ducks of Anaheim and baseball's Anaheim Angels.

The man responsible for Disney's broad holdings is Eisner. When he took over as CEO in 1984, the company was devoted to its theme parks and G-rated movies. Eisner judged that long-term success required diversification of the company's operations and expansion into fast-growing international markets. With a vision of building a global entertainment company, he embarked on a series of acquisitions and ventures that transformed Disney into the entertainment powerhouse it is today. One of Eisner's most significant decisions was to purchase Capital Cities/ABC Inc., one of the broadcast TV networks, for $19 billion in 1995.

Some critics argue that Disney is too diversified and that Eisner is too involved in every aspect of the company's business. From reading movie scripts to choosing furniture for new hotels, he is notoriously hands-on and not at all apologetic. "I consider myself the chief creative officer. My value is in the area of making sure that everything we do is ethical, moral, and creatively of the highest quality." This attitude initially worked well for Eisner, as Disney's stock increased by 27% annually until 1997. That year, before-tax profits climbed to over $4 billion, but subsequently fell almost $1 billion over the next five years.

Despite all the diversification, Disney's good fortune often depends on the success of its animated pictures or even a single television show. *The Lion King* was one of the biggest-grossing films ever and generated an additional $1 billion in merchandise sales. When ABC was suffering in the TV ratings, the network reintroduced the prime-time game show genre. *Who Wants to Be a Millionaire* debuted in 1999 and was a phenomenal hit, boosting the network's ratings and generating more than a half billion dollars in profits for ABC. However, the network overexposed the show, running it several times a week, and severely diluted its appeal. By fall 2001, ABC was in fourth place in the prime-time ratings.

While trying to get its network back on track, Disney is also reformulating its retail strategy. More than 500 Disney Stores, offering several product lines including clothes, toys, and videos, opened in U.S. malls in the 1990s. But sagging sales in the late 1990s caused the company to scale back and make plans to close between 100 and 200 of the stores. The survivors are being recast as either Disney Play or Disney Kids at Home outlets, designed to attract specific target markets. Focused on 4- to 10-year-old children, Disney Play offers princess costumes, plush items, and other games and toys. Aimed at parents of kids aged 3 to 10, Disney Kids at Home features apparel, furniture, electronics, and a few toys. The makeover, which will cost approximately $200 million, was tested in two malls located in California and New Jersey. Meanwhile, Disney's largest retail competitor, Warner Bros., announced plans to close all of its stores.

Trying to Write a Happy Ending

As Disney's 2001 fiscal year neared conclusion on September 30, park attendance was suffering because of a weak economy and the company expected a net loss of around $150 million for the year. Disney was in the midst of laying off about 4,000 employees when the terrorist attacks occurred on September 11th. With fears about traveling and/or being in crowded public places, compounded by economic concerns, countless customers canceled or at least postponed their plans to visit large amusement parks.

In response, Disney began offering unprecedented discounts on park passes and hotel rooms. For example, for a limited time, Southern California residents were able to purchase two-day multiple-park passes for just $49. Nevertheless, by December 2001, attendance had dropped as much as 25% at Disney parks.

The September 11th tragedy and the resulting attendance problems complicated Disney's plans for its "100 Years of Magic" celebration. The company withheld advertising for several weeks after the attacks, but then resumed its promotion for the centennial celebration. Visitors who had initially canceled their travel plans began rebooking their trips.

Eisner noted (or hoped), "When the economy does come back, and as confidence in America's safety continues to grow, there is every reason to believe the performance at our parks will be stronger than ever." However, in mid-2002, traffic at Disney's theme parks was still below year-earlier levels. In particular, the number of foreign customers was off sharply. Still, like the popular space ranger Buzz Lightyear in the movie *Toy Story*, Eisner hopes Disney's amusement parks will continue to play an integral role in propelling the company "to infinity and beyond!"

Questions

1. How does Disney address the unique challenges and opportunities posed by the four distinguishing characteristics of a service?

2. How has Disney attempted to increase the brand equity associated with its Disney World resort?

3. Do you agree with Disney's decision to split its retail locations into adult- and kid-focused stores? Why or why not?

4. What product-mix strategy is Disney pursuing with the development of the new park in Hong Kong? What product-mix strategy is it pursuing with Walt Disney Studio Paris, Tokyo DisneySea, and California Adventure?

Nintendo versus Sony versus Microsoft

Positioning Their Products for a Big Score

A new product category was born in 1976 when Fairchild unveiled the Video Entertainment System. The product featured 21 different video games that could be played using a television as the monitor. The most popular of these games was Pong. Compared to today's fast-paced, supergraphics video games, Pong was merely a simplistic version of video Ping-Pong. But millions of users found it to be addictive, and the video game market took off. Enthusiasm for home video games soared in 1977, when Atari introduced the Video Computer System. By 1978, hardware and software sales totaled $200 million.

Today, home video games represent a $20 *billion* market worldwide. However, the enormity of this market could not save the industry's pioneers, Fairchild and Atari, which were doomed by a lack of product innovation and by the intense competition in the field. Recently, another hardware manufacturer was forced out of the game, and even the market leaders are continuously striving to improve the capabilities of their brands in order to win (or retain) the favor of consumers.

The Industry's Top Players

The rise of personal computers in the mid-1980s spurred interest in computer games, which caused a crash in the home video game market. Video games rebounded when a number of different companies developed hardware consoles that provided graphics superior to the capabilities of computer games. By 1990, the Nintendo Entertainment System dominated the product category, only to be usurped by Sega when it introduced its Genesis system. By 1993, Sega commanded almost 60% of the U.S. video game market, and was one of the most recognized brand names among American kids.

Sega's success was short-lived, however. In 1995, Saturn launched a new 32-bit system (*bit,* as you probably know, is a unit of computer memory). The product was a dismal failure for a number of reasons. As the primary software developer for Saturn, Sega did not support efforts by outside game developers to design compatible games. In addition, Sega's games were often delivered late to retailers. Finally, the price of a Saturn system was greater than other comparable machines.

Nintendo and Sony benefited greatly from Saturn's missteps. Unveiled in late 1994, Sony's Play-Station was installed in 70 million homes worldwide by the end of 1999. Its "open design" encouraged the

efforts of outside developers, resulting in a vast array of games—almost 3,000 in all—that were compatible with the PlayStation. It too featured 32-bit graphics, which appealed to an older audience. As a result, at one time, more than 30% of PlayStation owners were over 30 years old.

Nintendo 64, introduced in 1996, had eye-popping 64-bit graphics and could be found in more than 28 million homes by 1999. Its primary users were between the ages of 6 and 13, a result of Nintendo's efforts to limit the amount of violent and adult-oriented material featured on games that can be played on its systems. Because the company exercises such control over software development, Nintendo 64 had only one-tenth the number of compatible games as PlayStation did.

By 1999, Sony commanded 56% of the video game console market, followed by Nintendo with 42%; Sega's share had fallen all the way to 1%. Hence, Sega either had to concede defeat or introduce an innovative video game machine that would ring up huge sales—and it had to do so before either Nintendo or Sony could bring their next-generation console to market. The Sega Dreamcast arrived in stores in September 1999 with an initial price tag of $199. Anxious gamers placed 300,000 advance orders, and initial sales were promising. A total of 1.5 million Dreamcast machines were purchased within four months, and initial reviews of the system were positive. The 128-bit system was capable of generating 3-D visuals, and 40 different games were available within three months of Dreamcast's introduction.

By the end of the year, Sega had boosted its market share to 15%. But the Dreamcast couldn't sustain its momentum. Although its game capabilities were impressive, the system didn't deliver all the functionality Sega had promised. A 56K modem (which used a home phone line) and a Web browser were meant to allow access to the Internet so gamers could play each other online, surf the Web, and visit the Dreamcast Network for product information and playing tips. Unfortunately, these features either weren't immediately available or were disappointing in their execution.

More than Just Fun and Games

Sega wasn't alone in having a strategy of adding functionality beyond games. Sony and Nintendo adopted the same philosophy for the machines they introduced in 1999. Both Nintendo's Neptune system and

Sony's PlayStation 2 (PS2) were built on a DVD (digital versatiledisc) platform and featured a 128-bit processor. Analysts applauded the move to DVD because it is less expensive to produce and allows more storage than CDs. It also gives purchasers the ability to use the machines as CD music players and DVD movie players. As a Sony marketing director commented, "The full entertainment offering from PlayStation 2 definitely appeals to a much broader audience. I have friends in their 30s who bought it not only because it's a gaming system for their kids, but also a DVD player for them." In addition, PlayStation 2 is able to play games developed for its predecessor, which was CD-based. This gave the PS2 an enormous advantage in the number of compatible game titles that were immediately available.

Further enhancing the PS2's appeal is its high-speed modem so users can access the Internet through digital cable as well as over telephone lines. This gives Sony the ability to distribute movies, music, and games directly to PS2 consoles. "We're positioning this as an all-around entertainment player," commented Ken Kutaragi, the head of Sony Computer Entertainment. However, some prospective customers were put off by the console's initial price of $360.

Shortly after the Neptune was introduced, Nintendo switched strategies and announced the impending release of its newest game console, the GameCube. However, unlike the Neptune, the GameCube would not run on a DVD platform nor would it initially offer any online capabilities. However, it would be more attractively priced at $199. A marketing vice president for Nintendo of America explained the company's change in direction, "We're the only competitor whose only business is video games. We want to create the best gaming system." Nintendo also made the GameCube friendly for outside game developers and began trying to add games, such as sports titles, to attract an older audience. Best known for its monstrous successes with games aimed at the younger set, such as *Donkey Kong, Super Mario Bros,* and *Pokemon,* Nintendo sought to attract older users, especially because the average video game player is 28. However, youthful Nintendo users were pleased to hear that they could use their handheld Game Boy Advance systems as controllers for the GameCube.

Nintendo scrambled to ensure there would be an adequate supply of GameCubes on the date in November 2001, when they were scheduled to go on sale. It also budgeted $450 million to market its new product, anticipating stiff competition during the holiday shopping season. With more than 20 million PlayStation 2 systems sold worldwide, the GameCube as a new entry in the video game market would make the battle for market share even more intense.

Microsoft Gets in the Game

For almost a decade, the video game industry had just three main players—Nintendo, Sega, and Sony. Because of strong brand loyalty and high product-development costs, newcomers faced a daunting task in entering this race and being competitive. One company was undeterred, however. Microsoft began selling its new Xbox in November 2001, three days before the GameCube made its debut. Some observers felt the Xbox was conceived to rival PlayStation 2, which has functions that rival Microsoft's WebTV system and even some lower-level PCs.

Like the PS2, the Xbox was built on a DVD platform, but it was constructed using a processor from Intel. This open design allowed Microsoft to develop the Xbox in just two years, and gave software developers the option of using standard PC tools for creating compatible games. In addition, Microsoft solicited the advice of successful game developers and even incorporated some of their feedback into the design of the console and its controllers. As a result of their efforts, Microsoft had about 20 games ready when the Xbox became available. The GameCube, by contrast, had only eight.

Further differentiating the Xbox from the GameCube was Microsoft's online strategy. Whereas Nintendo had no immediate plans for Web-based play, the Xbox came equipped with an Ethernet port for broadband access to the Internet. Microsoft announced its own Web-based network on which gamers can come together for online head-to-head play as well as for organized tournaments. Subscribers to this service pay a small monthly fee and must have high-speed access to the Internet, a potential drawback considering that only 12% of U.S. households currently have broadband connections.

By contrast, Sony promoted an open network that allows software developers to manage their own games, including associated fees charged to users. However, interested players must purchase a network adapter for an additional $39.99. Although game companies are not keen on the prospect of submitting to the control of a Microsoft-controlled network, it would require a significant investment for them to manage their own servers on the Sony-based network.

The Price of Winning the Video Game Wars

Microsoft's Xbox was priced initially at $299. Prior to the Xbox's introduction, Sony dropped the price of the PlayStation 2 to $299 as well. Nintendo's GameCube maintained a significant price advantage, selling for $100 less than either competitor's product.

Gamers eagerly snapped up the new consoles, making 2001 the best year ever for video game sales. For the first time, U.S. consumers spent more money, $9.4 billion, on video game equipment than they did at the box office. By the end of the 2001 holiday season, 6.6 million PS2 consoles had been sold in North America, followed by 1.5 million Xbox units and 1.2 million GameCubes.

What ensued was an all-out price war, beginning when Sony decided to put even more pressure on the Xbox by cutting the PS2's price to $199. Microsoft quickly matched that price. Wanting to maintain its lower-price status, Nintendo reduced the price of the GameCube by $50, to $149.

By mid-2002, Microsoft's Xbox had sold between 3.5 and 4 million units worldwide, but Nintendo had surpassed Microsoft by selling 4.5 million GameCubes. With the benefit of a lengthy head start, Sony had shipped 32 million PS2s. However, seven years after being introduced, the original PlayStation was being sold in retail outlets for a mere $49. It had a significant lead in terms of number of units in homes around the world, however, with a 43% share. As shown in the graph, Nintendo 64 was second with 30%, followed by the Sony PlayStation 2 with 14%. The Xbox and GameCube each claimed about 3% of the market, with Sega's Dreamcast comprising the last 7%.

Game Consoles in Homes as of June 2002

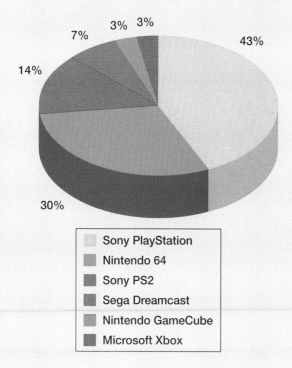

Legend:
- Sony PlayStation
- Nintendo 64
- Sony PS2
- Sega Dreamcast
- Nintendo GameCube
- Microsoft Xbox

Source: Byron Acohido, "Will Microsoft's Xbox Hit the Spot?" *USA Today*, June 4, 2002, p. 2B.

Other Players Jockey for Position

Once an industry leader, Sega announced in 2001 that it would stop producing the Dreamcast and other video game hardware components. The company said it would develop games for its competitors' consoles. Thus Sega slashed the price of the Dreamcast to $99 in an effort to liquidate its inventory of more than 2 million units and immediately began developing 11 new games for the Xbox, four for the PS2, and three for Nintendo's GameBoy Advance.

As the prices of video game consoles have declined, consoles and games have become the equivalent of, respectively, razors and blades. That is, the consoles generate little if any profit, but the games are very profitable. The profit margins on games are attractive, affected to some degree by whether the content is developed by the console maker (such as Sony) or by an independent game publisher (such as Electronic Arts). Thus the competition to develop appealing, perhaps even additictive, games may be even more intense than the battle to produce the best console. In particular, Nintendo, Sony, and Microsoft want games that are exclusive to their own systems. With that in mind, they not only rely on large in-house staffs that design games but they also pay added fees to independent publishers for exclusive rights to new games.

Sales of video games rose 43% in 2001, compared to a modest 4% increase for computer-based games. But computer game players are a loyal bunch, and they see many advantages in playing games on their computers rather than consoles. For one thing, they have access to a mouse and a keyboard, which allow them to play much more sophisticated games. In addition, they have been utilizing the Internet for years to receive game updates and modifications and to play each other over the Web.

Sony and Microsoft are intent on capturing a portion of the online gaming opportunity, however, and even Nintendo has decided to sell a modem that will allow GameCube users to play online. As prices continue to fall and technology becomes increasingly more sophisticated, it remains to be seen whether these three companies can keep their names on the industry's list of "high scorers."

Questions

1. Where is the video game console with regards to the product life cycle?

   a. How about online gaming?

   b. What are the implications of each product's life-cycle stage?

2. Should video game companies:
   a. Continue to alter their products to include functions besides games?
   b. Move aggressively into online gaming?
3. Does Microsoft's Xbox have the desired attributes of a brand name?

Sources

Case 1: Walt Disney Co.
www.disney.com, accessed on May 8, 2002; "Disney to Focus on Hong Kong Theme Park," *The Famous Columbia Daily Tribune*, Dec. 9, 2002, p. 2B; "The Best Managers: Ken Kutaragi," *Business Week*, Jan. 13, 2003, p. 64; Eryn Brown, "Sony's Big Bazooka," *Fortune*, Dec. 30, 2002, pp. 111, 112, and 114; Bruce Orwall, "Disney Theme-Park Business Isn't Rebounding as Forecast," *The Wall Street Journal*, Aug. 5, 2002, p. B3; Bruce Orwall and Karby Leggett, "Disney Signs Letter of Intent to Build Shanghai Theme Park," *The Wall Street Journal*, July 22, 2002, p. A3; Bruce Orwall, "Disney Stores Get New Script," *The Wall Street Journal*, Mar. 1, 2002, p. B1; Lisa Gubernick, "The Full Mickey—at a Discount," *The Wall Street Journal*, Mar. 1, 2002, p. W10; Matthew Benz, "Disney Assets Ready to Shine in 2002," *Amusement Business*, Jan. 14, 2002, p. 8; Tim O'Brien, "Q&A: Weiss Speaks Out on Future of Disney," *Amusement Business*, Jan. 14, 2002, pp. 3–8; Marc Gunther, "Has Eisner Lost the Disney Magic?" *Fortune*, Jan. 7, 2002, pp. 64–69; Juliana Koranteng, "Euro Disney Preparing to Unwrap $600 Mil Walt Disney Studio Park," *Amusement Business*, Dec. 17, 2001, p. 12; Johnnie Roberts, "Disney's Lost Magic," *Newsweek*, Dec. 10, 2001, p. 52; Erika Rasmusson, "Brand New World, *Sales & Marketing Management*, December 2001, p. 56; "Now Playing at Disney: Twofers," *Business Week*, Nov. 19, 2001, p. 50; Chester Dawson, "Will Tokyo Embrace Another Mouse?" *Business Week*, Sept. 10, 2001, p. 65; and Ronal Grover, "Now Disneyland Won't Seem So Mickey Mouse," *Business Week*, Jan. 29, 2001, pp. 56–58.

Case 2: Nintendo versus Sony versus Microsoft
Rebecca Buckman, Khanh Tran, and Robert Guth, "Secret Project at Microsoft Features an Xbox with Extras," *The Wall Street Journal*, July 1, 2001, p. B1; Byron Acohido, "Will Microsoft's Xbox Hit the Spot?" *USA Today*, June 4, 2002, p. 1B; Khanh Tran, "Sony to Cut Price of PlayStation 2 by a Third in U.S.," *The Wall Street Journal*, May 14, 2002, p. D8; Khanh Tran, "Consoles Outrun Computers," *The Wall Street Journal*, Apr. 19, 2002, p. A 13; Khanh Tran, "Sony, Microsoft: The Online Games Begin," *The Wall Street Journal*, Apr. 10, 2002, p. B3; Khanh Tran, "U.S. Videogame Industry Posts Record Sales," *The Wall Street Journal*, Feb. 7, 2002, p. B5; Kenneth Hein, "Nintendo Grows Up," *BrandWeek*, Jan. 7, 2002, pp. 12–15; Steve Hamm and Jay Greene, "In This Game, Microsoft Is More David than Goliath," *Business Week*, Nov. 19, 2001, p. 46; Khanh Tran, "Sega to Make Xbox Games for Microsoft," *The Wall Street Journal*, Mar. 30, 2001, p. B3; Khanh Tran, "How Microsoft Hopes to Win with Xbox," *The Wall Street Journal*, Jan. 31, 2001, p. B1; Steven Levy, "Here Comes PlayStation 2,"*Newsweek*, Mar. 6, 2000, pp. 54–59; Dean Takahashi, "'Sonic' Boom Marks Sega's Comeback in Video Games," *The Wall Street Journal*, Jan. 13, 2000, p. B6; Rachel Beck, "Dreamcast Goes on Sale Today; Players Already Seem to Love It," *St. Louis Post-Dispatch*, Sept. 9, 1999, p. C1; Ben Pappas, "From Pong to Kingpin," *Forbes*, May 31, 1999, p. 54; Maryanne Murray Buechner, "The Battle Has Just Begun," *Time Digital*, Apr. 12, 1999, pp. 28–31; Benjamin Fulford, "Killer Sequel," *Forbes*, Apr. 5, 1999, pp. 52–53; Reiji Yoshida, "Sega Plays Survival Game with Dreamcast," *Japan Times Weekly International Edition*, Dec. 14–20, 1998, p. 13; "The Interactive Digital Software Association Report on Video and Computer Game Software," *Billboard*, Apr. 4, 1998, p. 56; and information from *www.emuunlim.com*, accessed Oct. 15, 1999.

Chapter

12

Price Determination

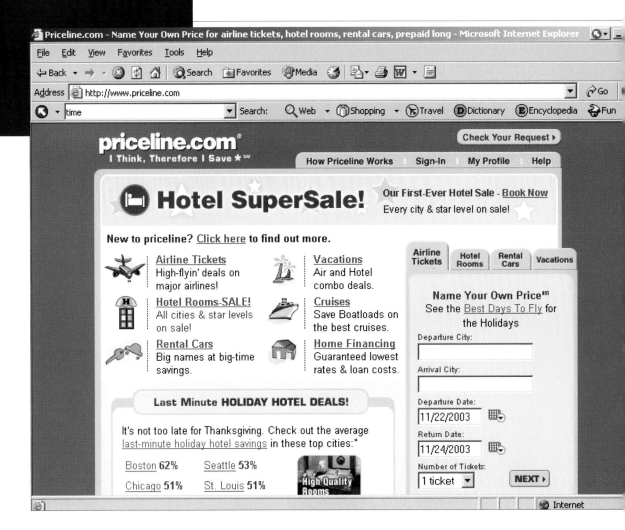

"According to . . . the founder of Priceline.com Inc., his company's approach to pricing is 'absolutely revolutionary.'"

With Priceline.com, Is the Price Always Right?

You've probably seen or heard the ads in which William Shatner, the former star of *Star Trek,* urges consumers to visit Priceline.com to "name your own price" for various products, including airline tickets, cars, and home mortgages. According to Jay Walker, the founder of Priceline.com Inc., his company's approach to pricing and selling these products is "absolutely revolutionary."

So what is Priceline all about? And, more important than whether or not it is revolutionary, will it generate profits over the long haul? Walker raised more than $100 million in venture capital to launch Priceline, his vision of "buyer-driven commerce." Priceline began by selling otherwise vacant airline seats to price-conscious leisure travelers who were willing to fly at inconvenient times in exchange for a price they deemed to be acceptable.

Walker developed and patented a business process that begins when a prospective traveler logs on to Priceline.com. The consumer fills out a form specifying desired departure and arrival cities and travel dates as well as the maximum acceptable ticket price. A person submitting a bid agrees to accept any departure time between 6 A.M. and 10 P.M. on the stipulated travel date. The information submitted by a hopeful traveler is then compared against a database maintained by Priceline to determine whether or not a match is available. The information contained in the database includes prices the airlines are willing to accept for unsold seats. If there's a match (that is, the desired travel dates and cities at a mutually acceptable price), the customer is notified by e-mail. If a match is made, the traveler has to purchase the ticket.

At the request of participating airlines, Priceline has instituted a number of other restrictions to ensure that it sells tickets to people, typically leisure travelers, who probably would not purchase an airline ticket without a special inducement. Thus the consumer cannot pick a particular airline, ask to change the flight schedule, or receive frequent-flier miles. Often, the flights include a change of planes with one or more stops. As a result, it's possible that a traveler could fly from Chicago to New York via Miami. All of the bookings are round-trip. A customer who cannot take the flight is not allowed to request a refund.

Unfortunately, in Priceline.com's first year of business, only 7% of the requests submitted by prospective travelers wound up in a match. A big reason for the low match rate was that only two airlines, TWA (subsequently acquired by American Airlines) and America West, initially signed up for Priceline's service. In addition, Priceline subsidized many of the bids and wound up losing about $30 on each ticket it sold. Considering that Priceline makes its money by keeping the difference between the consumer's bid and the amount it paid for the product, this was a costly approach that was deemed necessary to build a customer base.

However, Priceline recorded its first-ever profits in the second and third quarters of 2001. Under the direction of a new president and CEO, the firm cut costs, reined in advertising spending, and

www.priceline.com

focused more tightly on travel discounts—mainly for airline seats, hotel rooms, and rental cars.

Not surprisingly, the new CEO expressed optimism about the company's prospects, particularly inasmuch as Priceline had just weathered a difficult battle with Expedia, a competing name-your-own-price hotel-reservations site run by Microsoft. To resolve a patent-infringement suit filed by Priceline, Microsoft agreed to pay royalties to Priceline.

The terrorist attacks of September 11, 2001, hit the entire travel industry very hard. Many of Priceline's customers, mostly leisure travelers, stayed home immediately after the attacks. Hence, airlines cut down on the number of available empty seats in the short term by canceling dozens of flights. Further, the airlines cut air fares on a widespread basis in order to stimulate sales. In the aftermath of the travel crisis, Priceline reverted to a losing quarter at the end of 2001.

Analysts then wondered whether or not Priceline was well equipped to survive an extended slowdown in travel at the same time that it battled with other competitors such as Travelocity and Expedia. Priceline remains confident. Following the severe disruption caused by the events of September 11, the firm's CEO stated, "People's desire to save money is, if anything, higher as they step up their level of travel."[1]

In this situation, who actually determines the price for the airline seats offered through Priceline? Is it the consumer, Priceline, or the airlines that contract with Priceline?

"How much should we charge for airline seats?" "How does price fit into our marketing mix?" Airlines—in fact, all organizations—face these questions constantly. These kinds of questions are asked any time an enterprise introduces a new product or considers changing the price on an existing one.

In this chapter we cover the role of price in the marketing mix—what price is, how it can be used, and how it is set relative to such factors as product costs, market demand, and competitors' prices. After studying this chapter, you should be able to explain:

Chapter Goals

- The meaning of price.
- The significance of price in our economy, in a consumer's mind, and to an individual firm.
- The concept of value and how it relates to price.
- Major pricing objectives.
- Key factors influencing price.
- The types of costs incurred in producing and marketing a product.
- Approaches to determining prices, including cost-plus pricing, marginal analysis, and setting prices in relation only to other prices in the market.
- Break-even analysis.

In this chapter we will discuss major methods used to determine a price. Before being concerned with actual price determination, however, executives—and you—should understand the meaning and importance of price.

Meaning of Price

Some pricing difficulties occur because of confusion about the meaning of *price*, even though the concept is easy to define in familiar terms. Simply, **price** is the amount of money and/or other items with utility needed to acquire a product. Recall that *utility* is an attribute with the potential to satisfy wants.

Based in Connecticut, Barter Business Unlimited (BBU) brings together organizations that want to barter. BBU clients use trade dollars, rather than cash, to make a transaction. For example, if a hotel that is a BBU client trades 10 hotel rooms worth $1,000, the hotel earns that amount of trade dollars for use in acquiring needed goods and/or services from other BBU clients.

www.bbu.com

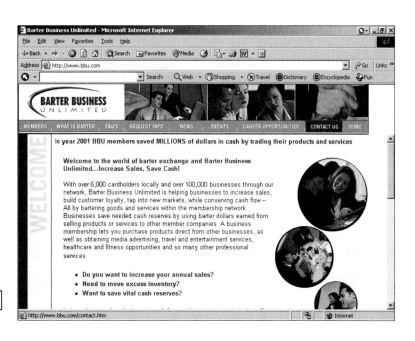

Thus price may involve more than money. To illustrate, the price of a rare Alex Rodriquez baseball card may be (1) $500; (2) the rookie cards for 10 players, including Barry Bonds and Pedro Martinez; or (3) some combination of dollars and baseball cards. Exchanging goods and/or services for other products is termed **barter.** Because our economy is not geared to a slow, ponderous barter system, we typically state price in monetary terms and use money as our medium of exchange.

In socially undesirable situations, there are prices called blackmail, ransom, and bribery. Here are prices under various names and the products with which they are associated in normal situations:[2]

Price Is What You Pay . . .		For What You Get
Tuition	→	Education
Interest	→	Use of money
Rent	→	Use of living quarters or a piece of equipment for a period of time
Fare	→	Taxi ride or airline flight
Fee	→	Services of a physician or lawyer
Retainer	→	Lawyer's or consultant's services over a period of time
Toll	→	Long-distance phone call or travel on some highways
Salary	→	Services of an executive or other white-collar worker
Wage	→	Services of a blue-collar worker
Commission	→	Sales person's services
Dues	→	Membership in a union or a club

Practical problems arise when we try to state simply the price of a product. Suppose you paid $395 for a desk, but your instructor paid only $295 for one of similar size. At first glance, it looks as if the instructor taught the student a lesson! But consider this: Your desk—which has a beautiful finish—was delivered to your apartment, and you had a year to pay for it. The instructor, a do-it-yourself buff, bought a partially assembled, unfinished desk. It had to be put together and then stained and varnished. The seller provided neither delivery nor credit. Now, even with the differences in price, who got the better deal? The answer is not as easy as it first appeared.

This example indicates that the definition depends on determining exactly what is being sold. A seller usually is pricing a combination of (1) the specific good or service that is the object of the transaction, (2) several supplementary services (such as a warranty), and (3) in a very real sense, the want-satisfying benefits provided by the product. Sometimes it is difficult even to define the price of the predominant good or service itself. On one model of automobile, a stated price may include radio, power steering, and power brakes. For another model of the same brand, these three items may be priced separately. So, to know the real price of a product, you need to look at the identifiable components that make up that product.

Importance of Price

Price is significant in our economy, in the consumer's mind, and in an individual firm. Let's consider each situation.

In the Economy

A product's price influences wages, rent, interest, and profits. Price is a basic regulator of the economic system because it influences the allocation of the factors of production: labor, land, and capital. High wages attract labor, high interest rates attract capital, and so on. As an allocator of resources, price determines what will be produced (supply) and who will get the goods and services produced (demand).

Criticism of the American system of reasonably free enterprise and, in turn, public demand for added restraints on the system are often triggered by negative reactions to prices or pricing policies. To reduce the risk of government intervention, businesses need to establish prices in a manner and at a level that consumers and government officials consider socially responsible.

In the Customer's Mind

Some prospective customers are interested primarily in low prices, whereas another segment is more concerned with other factors, such as service, quality, value, and brand image. It's safe to say that few, if any, customers are attentive to price alone *or* are entirely oblivious to price. One study identified four distinct segments of shoppers: *brand loyals* (relatively uninterested in price), *system beaters* (prefer certain brands but try to buy them at reduced prices), *deal shoppers* (driven by low prices), and *uninvolveds* (seemingly not motivated by either brand preferences or low prices).[3]

An important question is whether consumer price sensitivity can be predicted. There is no clear-cut answer. The four shopper segments mentioned above are not distinguished by demographic factors. Rather, according to the study's results, the segments' differing degrees of price sensitivity are more likely to be related to psychographic factors, such as lifestyle, or to which product categories are involved. In contrast, a major study of sales data for 18 product categories in a chain of 83 supermarkets concluded that consumers' relative interest in price does vary across demographic groups. According to this research, consumers with particular attributes—such as low income level, small house, or large family—are likely to be price sensitive.[4]

Another consideration is that some consumers' perceptions of product quality vary directly with price. Typically, the higher the price, the better the quality is perceived to be. In the words of an engineering consultant, "Many consultants have told me that when they raised their prices, their sales went up." The explanation was that with higher prices, clients felt more comfortable regarding the quality of the advice.[5]

Haven't you been concerned about product quality—such as when you are looking at ads for compact disc players—if the price is unexpectedly low? Or, at the other extreme, have you selected a restaurant for a special dinner because you heard it was fairly high priced so you expected it to be very nice? Consumers' perceptions of quality may be influenced not just by price but also by such factors as store reputation and advertising.

In this ad, Toshiba's Electronic Imaging Division stresses important features—high speed, small size, and sharp color resolution—as well as an affordable price. The notion of value is captured well by a phrase in the ad that says the Toshiba FC22 is "a whole lot of copier for very little coin."

www.toshiba.com

www.extstay.com

Price is also important as a component of value. In recent years customers, both in consumer and business markets, have come to expect—and have sought—better value in the goods and services they purchase. **Value** is the ratio of perceived benefits to price and any other incurred costs. Examples of *other incurred costs* for consumers include time associated with shopping for the product, gasoline used traveling to the place of purchase, and perhaps aggravation assembling the product. Online shopping can reduce some of these other costs, such as the effort of traveling from one store to another; however, it may amplify some costs, such as the perceived risk of buying a product without seeing it in person.

When we say a product has ample value, we don't necessarily mean it is inexpensive or has a very low price. Rather, good value indicates that a particular product has the kinds and amounts of potential benefits—such as quality, image, and purchase convenience—consumers expect at a particular price level.

Many businesses are responding to calls for more value by devising new products. For instance, since the mid-1990s, the number of extended-stay hotels has grown tremendously. The target market for this product consists of people who need or want to stay in the same locale for several days, weeks, or even months. Given surging demand for this type of lodging as well as the success of Residence Inns by Marriott, many new chains—Candlewood Suites, Extended Stay America, and InTown Suites, to mention several—entered this field. They offer value by providing relatively low rates as well as amenities that are important to extended-stay guests, such as spacious rooms, kitchenettes, and free buffet breakfasts. To pare expenses, this type of hotel reduces or eliminates less important amenities, such as room service and daily housekeeping.[6]

Other businesses are striving for better value with existing products. ABB Ltd., a manufacturer of power transformers and other large, expensive equipment, has worked hard to enhance product quality *and* pare production costs. With lower costs, the urge to increase prices in order to maintain profits is lessened. Another avenue to enhanced value is to give customers more at the same price. Although they are dissimilar in many respects, both Little Caesar's and California Pizza Kitchen have used that approach by providing larger portions and holding the line on prices.[7]

Attention to value was certainly heightened by the recessions of the early 1990s and the start of the new century. However, the increased emphasis on value probably reflects a more fundamental shift in attitudes. Consumers' greater interest in the ratio of benefits to price has created a new approach to pricing, not surprisingly called "value pricing," which we will discuss in Chapter 13.

In the Individual Firm

A product's price is a major determinant of the market demand for it. Through prices, money comes into an organization. Thus price affects a firm's competitive position, revenues, and net profits. According to a McKinsey consultant, "Pricing is extremely important because small changes in price can translate into huge improvements in profitability." In fact, in a study of 1,000 companies, the McKinsey firm found that a 1% increase in price would improve profits by 7%, assuming no change in sales volume.[8]

Some businesses use higher prices to convey an image of superior quality. This approach will have a positive impact only on consumers who consider quality important. It's most likely to work well in the case of services and certain goods for which consumers have difficulty judging quality on an objective basis. To be highly effective in signaling superior quality, the high price should be combined with other conspicuous elements of the marketing mix, such as a compelling advertising message and an appealing package design.[9]

Prices are important to a company most of the time—but not always. Several factors can limit how much effect pricing has on a company's marketing program. Differentiated product features, a favorite brand, high quality, convenience, or some combination of these and other factors may be more important to consumers than price. As we saw in Chapter 10, one object of branding is to *decrease* the effect of price on the demand for a product. Thus we need to put the role of pricing in a company's marketing program in its proper perspective: It is only one of four marketing-mix elements that must be skillfully combined—and then adapted over time—to achieve business success.

Pricing Objectives

Every marketing activity—including pricing—should be directed toward a goal. Thus management should decide on its pricing objective before determining the price itself.[10] Yet, as logical as this may sound, few firms consciously establish a pricing objective.

To be useful, the pricing objective management selects must be compatible with the overall goals set by the firm and the goals for its marketing program. Let's assume that a *company's goal* is to increase return on investment from its present level of 15% to 20% within three years. It follows that the primary *pricing goal* during this period should be to achieve some stated percentage return on investment. It would be questionable, in this case, to adopt a primary pricing goal of maintaining the company's market share or of stabilizing prices.

We will discuss the following **pricing objectives:**

- Profit-oriented:
  - To achieve a target return
  - To maximize profit
- Sales-oriented:
  - To increase sales volume
  - To maintain or increase market share
- Status quo–oriented:
  - To stabilize prices
  - To meet competition

Recognize that all these objectives can be sought—and hopefully attained—through pricing that is coordinated with other marketing activities such as product design and distribution channels. And all these objectives are ultimately aimed at satisfactory performance over the long run. For a business, that requires ample profits.

Profit-Oriented Goals

Profit goals may be set for the short or long term. A company may select one of two profit-oriented goals for its pricing policy.

Achieve a Target Return   A firm may price its product to *achieve a target return*—a specified percentage return on its *sales* or on its *investment*. Many retailers and wholesalers use a target return *on sales* as a pricing objective for short periods such as a year or a fashion season. They add an amount to the cost of the product, called a *markup,* to cover anticipated operating expenses *and* provide a desired profit for the period. Safeway or Kroger's, for example, may price to earn a net profit of 1% on a store's sales. A chain of men's clothing stores may have a target profit of 6% of sales, and price its products accordingly. (Markup and other operating ratios are discussed fully in Appendix A following this chapter.)

Achieving a target return *on investment* is measured in relation to a firm's net worth (its assets minus its liabilities). This pricing goal is often selected by the leading firm in an industry. Target-return pricing is used by industry leaders such as DuPont, Alcoa, and ExxonMobil because they can set their pricing goals more independently of competition than smaller firms in the industry. The leaders may price so that they earn a net profit that is 15% or 20% of the firm's net worth.

Maximize Profits   The pricing objective of making as much money as possible is probably followed more than any other goal. The trouble with this goal is that to some people, *profit maximization* has an ugly connotation, suggesting profiteering, high prices, and monopoly. Where prices are unduly high and entry into the field is severely limited, public criticism can be expected. If market conditions and public opinion do not bring about reasonable prices, government may intervene.

In both economic theory and business practice, however, there is nothing wrong with profit maximization. Theoretically, if profits become high in an industry because supply is short in relation to demand, new capital will be attracted to increase production capacity. This will increase supply and eventually reduce profits. In the marketplace it is difficult to find many situations where profiteering has existed over an extended period of time. Substitute products are available, purchases are postponable, and competition can increase to keep prices at a reasonable level.

A profit-maximization goal is likely to be far more beneficial to a company if it is pursued over the *long term.* To do this, however, firms may have to accept modest

Pharmaceutical companies have introduced various drugs to fights AIDS or the HIV virus. Inevitably, the firms have been criticized for charging excessive prices for these drugs—prices that are beyond the means of the majority of those infected with HIV or AIDS. The original price of AZT was about $8,000 for a one-year supply *per patient;* the corresponding price for Sustiva was $4,800. The companies have responded to the criticism by saying that high prices are necessary in order to recover the enormous costs of developing the complex drugs. In 2001, however, Merck announced that its prices for two HIV-suppressing drugs in impoverished parts of the world, such as sub-Saharan Africa, would be about one-tenth of the price charged in the U.S.

Is it ethical to charge a seemingly high price for a product that could be a life or death necessity?

Sources: John Carey and Amy Barrett, "Drug Prices: What's Fair?" *Business Week,* Dec. 10, 2001, pp. 60–64+; Lori Hinnant, "Merck Slashes AIDS Drug Prices for the World's Poor," *Pittsburgh Post-Gazette,* Mar. 19, 2001, p. D4; and Charles W. Henderson, "AIDS Groups Protest Pricing of New Du Pont Drug," *AIDS Weekly Plus,* Oct. 5, 1998.

profits or even losses over the short term. For example, a company entering a new geographic market or introducing a new product frequently does best by initially setting low prices to build a large clientele. Repeat purchases from this large group of customers may allow the firm to maximize its profits over the long term.

The goal should be to maximize profits on *total output* rather than on each single product. In fact, a company may maximize total profit by setting low, relatively unprofitable prices on some products in order to stimulate sales of others. The Gillette Company frequently promotes razors at very low prices. The firm hopes that once customers acquire its razors, they will become loyal customers for Gillette blades, which generate healthy profits for the company. The same would appear to be true for Hewlett-Packard with regards to its printers and, in turn, print cartridges.

Sales-Oriented Goals

In some companies, management's pricing is focused on sales volume. The pricing goal may be to increase sales volume or to maintain or increase the firm's market share.

Increase Sales Volume
This pricing goal of *increasing sales volume* is typically adopted to achieve rapid growth or to discourage other firms from entering a market. The goal is usually stated as a percentage increase in sales volume over some period, say, one year or three years.

Management may seek higher sales revenues by discounting or by some other aggressive pricing strategy. Periodically, the Monsanto Co. has lowered the prices of its popular Roundup brand of herbicide. For some time, the intent of these price cuts seemingly was to stimulate more farmers to use the product, and on more acres of land. Following the expiration of the U.S. patent on Roundup, further price reductions were necessary to fend off generic competitors.[11]

Occasionally companies are willing to incur a loss *in the short run* to expand sales volume or meet sales objectives. Clothing stores run end-of-season sales, and auto dealers offer rebates and below-market loan rates on new cars. Many vacation spots, such as golf courses and resorts, reduce prices during off-seasons to increase sales volume.

Maintain or Increase Market Share
In some companies, both large and small, the pricing objective is to *maintain or increase market share.* Why is market share protected or pursued so vigorously? In growing fields, such as computers and other technology-based products, companies want large shares in order to gain added

clout with vendors, drive down production costs, and/or project a dominant appearance to consumers. In order to gain a foothold in the marketplace, many electronic-commerce firms emphasized market share or sales volume over profits, at least in the short run. Perhaps that's one reason why so many of these "dot-coms" went out of business.[12]

Most industries today are not growing much, if at all, *and* have excess production capacity. Many firms need added sales to utilize their production capacity more fully and, in turn, gain economies of scale and better profits. Because the size of the "pie" isn't growing in most cases, businesses that need added volume have to grab a bigger "slice of the pie"—that is, greater market share. The U.S. auto and retail grocery industries illustrate these situations.

Other firms are also intent on maintaining their market shares. In the mid-1990s, for instance, the Japanese yen rose considerably in relation to the American dollar, making Japanese products more expensive in American dollars. To maintain their market shares, Toyota, Nissan, and Honda accepted smaller profit margins and reduced their costs so that they could lower the selling prices of their autos in the U.S. The situation changed when the yen weakened in the first years of the new century. Then U.S. automakers charged that their Japanese counterparts manipulate the yen in order to gain a cost advantage that allows lower prices without hurting profit margins.[13]

Status Quo Goals

Two closely related goals—*stabilizing prices* and *meeting competition*—are the least aggressive of all pricing goals. They are intended simply to maintain the firm's current situation—that is, the status quo. With either of these goals, a firm seeks to avoid price competition.

Price stabilization often is the goal in industries where (1) the product is highly standardized (such as steel or bulk chemicals) *and* (2) one large firm, such as Phelps Dodge in the copper industry, historically has acted as a leader in setting prices. Smaller firms in these industries tend to "follow the leader" when setting their prices. What is the reason for such pricing behavior? A price cut by any one firm is likely to be matched by all other firms in order to remain competitive; therefore, no individual firm gains, but all may suffer smaller profits. Conversely, a price boost is unlikely to be matched. But the price-boosting firm faces a differential disadvantage, because other elements of a standardized product such as gasoline are perceived to be fairly similar.

Even in industries where there are no price leaders, countless firms deliberately price their products to meet the prevailing market price. This pricing policy gives management an easy means of avoiding difficult pricing decisions.

Firms that adopt status quo pricing goals to avoid price competition are not necessarily passive in their marketing. Quite the contrary! Typically these companies compete aggressively using other marketing-mix elements—product, distribution, and especially promotion. This approach, called *nonprice competition,* will be discussed in Chapter 13.

www.phelpsdodge.com

Factors Influencing Price Determination

Knowing its pricing objective, a company can move to the heart of price management: determining the base price of a product. **Base price,** or *list price,* refers to the price of one unit of the product at its point of production or resale. This price does not reflect discounts, freight charges, or any other modifications such as leader pricing, all of which will be discussed in the next chapter.

The same procedure is followed in pricing both new and established products. Pricing an established product usually is less difficult than pricing a new product, however, because the exact price or a narrow range of prices may be dictated by the market.[14]

According to one consultant, failing to consider the various interrelated factors that affect pricing is "the most common mistake made by small businesses."[15] Thus other factors, besides objectives, that influence price determination are discussed next.

Estimated Demand

In pricing, a company must estimate the total demand for the product. This is easier to do for an established product than for a new one. The steps in estimating demand are: (1) determine whether there is a price the market expects and (2) estimate what the sales volume might be at different prices.

The **expected price** of a product is the price at which customers consciously or unconsciously value it—what they think the product is worth. Expected price usually is expressed as a *range* of prices rather than as a specific amount. Thus the expected price might be "between $250 and $300" or, for another product, "not over $20."

A producer must also consider a middleman's reaction to price. Middlemen are more likely to promote a product if they approve its price. Sometimes they don't. For instance, retailers—notably Wal-Mart—complained when Rubbermaid Inc. tried to raise prices. The manufacturer thought it needed to, after the cost of resin (a major ingredient in its various plastic housewares and toys) more than doubled. However, rather than antagonize retailers, Rubbermaid settled for smaller increases, which hurt the company's profits.[16]

It's possible to set a price too low. If the price is much lower than what the market expects, sales may be lost. For example, it probably would be a mistake for L'Oreal, a well-known cosmetics maker, to put a $1.49 price tag on its lipstick or to price its imported perfume at $3.49 an ounce. In all likelihood, shoppers would be suspicious about product quality, or their self-concept would not let them buy such low-priced products.

After raising a product's price, some organizations have experienced a considerable increase in sales. When this occurs, it indicates that customers infer better quality from the higher prices. This situation is called **inverse demand**—the higher the price, the greater the unit sales. Inverse demand usually exists only within a given price range and only at low price levels. At some point (see Figure 12.1), inverse demand ends and the usual-shaped curve is evident. That is, demand declines as prices rise.

How do sellers determine expected prices? One restaurant in London, rather than putting prices in its menus, lets patrons decide how much to pay after they have completed their meals. With this unconventional approach, customers pay an amount they think is equal to the value received from the dining experience. The restaurant owner claims that patrons pay about 20% more than he would charge![17]

Typically, to gauge expected prices, sellers may submit products to experienced retailers or wholesalers to gauge the selling price the market will accept for a particular item. Or they may go to customers. A business goods manufacturer, for instance, might get price estimates by showing models or blueprints to engineers working for prospective customers. Another alternative is to ask a sample of consumers what they would expect to pay for the product, or which item in a list of alternatives with known prices is most similar to the test product. Using such methods, a seller can determine a reasonable range of prices.

It is extremely helpful to estimate what the sales volume will be at several different prices. By doing this, the seller is, in effect, determining the demand curve for the product. Moreover, the seller is gauging *price elasticity of demand*, which refers to the responsiveness of quantity demanded to price changes. (Price elasticity of demand is covered in more detail in Appendix A following this chapter.)

www.loreal.com

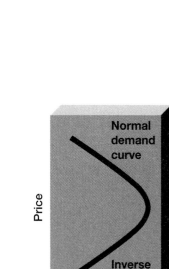

FIGURE 12.1

Inverse Demand.

Sellers can choose from several methods to estimate sales at various prices. Recall some of the demand-forecasting methods discussed in Chapter 6—survey of buyer intentions, test marketing, executive judgment, and sales-force composite, for example. These methods can be used in this situation as well.[18]

Competitive Reactions

Competition greatly influences base price. A new product is distinctive only until competition arrives, which is inevitable. The threat of potential competition is greatest when the field is easy to enter *and* profit prospects are encouraging. Competition can come from these sources:

- *Directly similar products:* Nike versus adidas or Reebok running shoes.
- *Available substitutes:* DHL air express versus Schneider National truck shipping or Union Pacific rail freight.
- *Unrelated products seeking the same consumer dollar:* DVD (digital versatile disc) player versus a bicycle or a weekend vacation.

For directly similar products, it is important to learn what consumers think about competing products. Thus a marketer at DuPont stressed, "Understanding customer perceptions of the organization's and competitors' offerings is the first step in developing good pricing decisions."[19]

For similar or substitute products, a competitor may adjust its prices. In turn, other firms have to decide what price adjustments, if any, are necessary to retain their customers. In the photographic-film industry, for instance, Fuji used lower prices to build its market share at the expense of Kodak. Although it held a 70% share of the market, Kodak cut its prices to combat Fuji. Now both film companies need to be concerned about the declining prices of a product that is a threat to photographic film, namely the digital camera.[20]

Other Marketing-Mix Elements

A product's base price is influenced considerably by the other ingredients in the marketing mix.

Product   We've already observed that a product's price is affected by whether it is a new item or an established one. Over the course of a life cycle, price changes are necessary to keep the product competitive. A product's price is also influenced by whether (1) it may be leased as well as purchased outright, (2) a trade-in is involved, and (3) it may be returned by the customer to the seller for a refund or an exchange. For example, a firm that has a liberal return policy may compensate by having higher initial prices.

The end use of the product must also be considered. For instance, there is little price competition among manufacturers of packaging materials or producers of industrial gases, so their price structure is stable. These business products are only an incidental part of the final article, so customers will buy the least expensive product consistent with the required quality.

Distribution Channels   The channels and types of middlemen selected will influence a producer's pricing. A firm selling both through wholesalers and directly to retailers often sets a different factory price for these classes of customers. The price to wholesalers is lower because they perform services that the producer would have to perform—such as providing storage, granting credit to retailers, and selling to small retailers.

Promotion   The extent to which the product is promoted by the producer or middlemen and the methods used are added considerations in pricing. If major promotional responsibility is placed on retailers, they ordinarily will be charged a lower price for a product than if the producer advertises it heavily. Even when a producer promotes heavily, it may want retailers to use local advertising to tie in with national advertising. Such a decision must be reflected in the producer's price to retailers.

Cost of a Product

Pricing of a product also should consider its cost. A product's total unit cost is made up of several types of costs, each reacting differently to changes in the quantity produced. In many industries, especially those based on leading-edge technologies such as microprocessors and optic fibers, a product's costs are viewed—and treated—in much different ways than they were just a decade or so ago.

Consider a couple of examples. In the software field, there are substantial up-front research and development costs, but the costs of producing each unit of the finished product are relatively small. Thus some software developers give away hundreds of thousands of copies of their product when it is introduced in order to gain favorable word-of-mouth publicity and, in turn, sales of related software and future upgrades of this product. Red Hat Inc. essentially gives away Linux operating-systems software but then sells technical support services to Linux users. In another industry, Teleport Communications (a provider of local network services that is now part of AT&T Corp.) installed more optic fibers than a customer requested—and did so without additional charge. Why? As technology surely advances, the customer will want more capacity. Therefore, the company installed more capacity than was needed because the cost of extra fibers is far less than the cost of labor to do the job again in the future.[21]

www.redhat.com

The following cost concepts are fundamental to our discussion of pricing:

Various Kinds of Costs

- A **fixed cost,** such as rent, executive salaries, or property tax, remains constant regardless of how many items are produced. Such a cost continues even if production stops completely. It is called a fixed cost because it is difficult to change in the short run (but not in the long run).
- **Total fixed cost** is the sum of all fixed costs.
- **Average fixed cost** is the total fixed cost divided by the number of units produced.
- A **variable cost,** such as labor or materials, is directly related to production. Variable costs can be controlled in the short run simply by changing the level of production. When production stops, for example, all variable production costs become zero.
- **Total variable cost** is the sum of all variable costs. The more units produced, the higher is this cost.
- **Average variable cost** is the total variable cost divided by the number of units produced. Average variable cost is usually high for the first few units produced. And it decreases as production increases because of such things as quantity discounts on materials and more efficient use of labor. Beyond some optimum output, it increases because of such factors as crowding of production facilities and overtime pay.
- **Total cost** is the sum of total fixed cost and total variable cost for a specific quantity produced.
- **Average total cost** is total cost divided by number of units produced.
- **Marginal cost** is the cost of producing and selling one more unit. Usually the marginal cost of the last unit is the same as that unit's variable cost.

These concepts and their interrelationships are illustrated in Table 12.1 and Figure 12.2. The interrelationship among the various *average costs per unit* from the table is displayed graphically in the figure. It may be explained briefly as follows:

- The **average fixed cost curve** declines as output increases, because the total of the fixed costs is spread over an increasing number of units.
- The **average variable cost curve** usually is U-shaped. It starts high because average variable costs for the first few units of output are high. Variable costs per unit

TABLE 12.1 **An Example of Costs for an Individual Firm**

Total fixed costs do not change in the short run, despite increases in quantity produced. Variable costs are the costs of inputs—materials and labor, for example. Total variable costs increase as production quantity rises. Total cost is the sum of all fixed and variable costs. The other measures in the table are simply methods of looking at costs per unit; they always involve dividing a cost by the number of units produced.

(1) Quantity Produced	(2) Total Fixed Costs	(3) Total Variable Costs	(4) Total Costs (2) + (3)	(5) Marginal Cost per Unit	(6) Average Fixed Cost (2) ÷ (1)	(7) Average Variable Cost (3) ÷ (1)	(8) Average Total Cost (4) ÷ (1)
0	$256	$ 0	$256		Infinity	Infinity	Infinity
1	256	84	340	$ 84	$256.00	$84	$340.00
2	256	112	368	28	128.00	56	184.00
3	256	144	400	32	85.33	48	133.33
4	256	224	480	80	64.00	56	120.00
5	256	400	656	176	51.20	80	131.20

FIGURE 12.2

Unit Cost Curves for an Individual Firm.

This figure is based on data in Table 12.1. Here we see how *unit* costs change as quantity increases. Using cost-plus pricing, two units of output would be priced at $184 each, whereas four units would sell for $120 each.

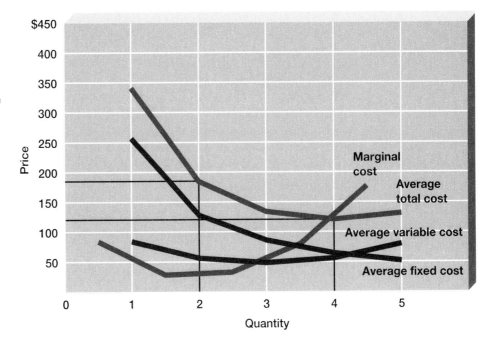

then decline as the company realizes efficiencies in production. Eventually the average variable cost curve reaches its lowest point, reflecting optimum output with respect to variable costs (not total costs). In Figure 12.2 this point is at three units of output. Beyond that point the average variable cost rises, reflecting the increase in unit variable costs caused by overcrowded facilities and other inefficiencies. If the variable costs per unit were constant, then the average variable cost curve would be a horizontal line at the level of the constant unit variable cost.

- The **average total cost curve** is the sum of the first two curves—average fixed cost and average variable cost. It starts high, reflecting the fact that total *fixed* costs are spread over so few units of output. As output increases, the average total cost curve declines because unit fixed cost and unit variable cost are decreasing. Eventually the point of lowest total cost per unit is reached (four units of output in the figure). Beyond that optimum point, diminishing returns set in and average total cost rises.

- The **marginal cost curve** has a more pronounced U-shape than the other curves in Figure 12.2. The marginal cost curve slopes downward until the second unit of output, at which point the marginal costs start to increase.

Note the relationship between the average total cost curve and the marginal cost curve. The average total cost curve slopes downward *as long as the marginal cost is less than the average total cost.* Even though marginal cost increases after the second unit, the average total cost curve continues to slope downward until the fourth unit. This occurs because marginal cost—even when going up—is still less than average total cost.

The two curves—marginal cost and average total cost—intersect at the lowest point of the average total cost curve. Beyond that point (the fourth unit in the example), the cost of producing and selling the next unit is higher than the average cost of all units. The data in Table 12.1 show that producing the fifth unit reduces the average fixed cost by $12.80 (from $64 to $51.20), but causes the average variable cost to increase by $24. From then on, therefore, the average total cost rises. This occurs because the average variable cost is increasing faster than the average fixed cost is decreasing.

Cost-Plus Pricing

We are now at the point in price determination to talk about setting a *specific* selling price. Most companies establish their prices based on:

- *Total cost plus a desired profit,*
- *Marginal analysis*—a consideration of both market demand and supply; and/or
- *Competitive market conditions.*

According to a survey that examined the approaches used to price new products, 9% of companies "guesstimate" what the base price for a new product should be, whereas 37% match what competitors charge for similar offerings. One-half the responding firms charge what the market will bear, if conditions allow. The most common approach, used by 52% of the companies, is to choose a price that is intended to cover costs and provide a fair profit. Because the total is more than 100%, evidently most firms use more than one approach. That's true, according to a survey by the Professional Pricing Society, which found that the majority of companies use a combination of methods to set price.[22]

Let's first discuss the most popular method, **cost-plus pricing**, which means setting the price of one unit of a product equal to the total cost of the unit plus the desired profit on the unit. Suppose that King's Kastles, a contractor, figures the labor and materials required to build and sell 10 condominiums will cost $750,000, and other expenses (office rent, depreciation on equipment, management salaries, and so on) will be $150,000. The contractor wants to earn a profit of 10% on the total cost of $900,000. This makes cost plus desired profit $990,000. So, using the cost-plus method, each of the 10 condos is priced at $99,000.

Although it is an easily applied method, cost-plus pricing has limitations. One is that it does not recognize various types of costs or the fact that these costs are affected differently by changes in level of output. In our housing example, suppose that King's Kastles built and sold only eight condos at the cost-plus price of $99,000 each. As shown in Table 12.2, total sales would then be $792,000. Labor and materials chargeable to the eight condos would total $600,000 ($75,000 per unit). Because the contractor would still incur the full $150,000 in overhead expenses, the total cost would be $750,000. This would leave a profit of $42,000, or $5,250 per condominium instead of the anticipated $9,000. On a percentage basis, profit would be only 5.6% of total cost rather than the desired 10%.

TABLE 12.2 **King's Kastles: An Example of Cost-Plus Pricing**

Actual results often differ from planned outcomes because various types of costs react differently to changes in output.

King's Kastles' Costs, Selling Price, and Profit	Number of Condominiums Built and Sold by King's Kastles	
	Planned = 10	Actual = 8
Labor and materials costs ($75,000 per condo)	$750,000	$600,000
Overhead (fixed) costs	150,000	150,000
Total costs	$900,000	$750,000
Total sales at $99,000 per condo	990,000	792,000
Profit: Total	$ 90,000	$ 42,000
Per condo	$ 9,000	$ 5,250
As percent of cost	10%	5.6%

A second limitation of this pricing approach is that market demand is ignored. That is, cost-plus pricing assumes that cost determines the value of a product, or what customers are willing to pay for it. But what if the same number of units could be sold at a higher price? Using cost-plus pricing, the seller would forgo some revenues. Conversely, if fewer units are produced, each would have to sell for a higher price to cover all costs and show a profit. But if business is slack and output must be cut, it's not wise to raise the unit price. Another limitation of this method is that it doesn't recognize that total unit cost changes as output expands or contracts. However, a more sophisticated approach to cost-plus pricing can consider such changes.

Prices Based on Marginal Costs Only

Another approach to cost-plus pricing is to set *prices based on marginal costs only*, not total costs. Refer again to the cost schedules shown in Table 12.1 and Figure 12.2, and assume that a firm is operating at an output level of three units. Under marginal cost pricing, this firm could accept an order for one more unit at $80 or above, instead of the total unit cost of $120. The revenue from a unit sold at $80 would cover its variable costs. However, if the firm can sell for a price above $80—say, $85 or $90—the balance contributes to the payment of fixed costs.

Not all orders can be priced to cover only variable costs. Marginal cost pricing may be feasible, however, if management wants to keep its labor force employed during a slack season. It may also be used when one product is expected to attract business for another. Thus a department store may price meals in its café at a level that covers only the marginal costs. The reasoning is that the café will bring shoppers to the store, where they will buy other, more profitable products.

Pricing by Middlemen

At first glance, cost-plus pricing appears to be widely used by retailing and wholesaling middlemen. A retailer, for example, pays a given amount to buy products and have them delivered to the store. Then the merchant adds an amount, called a markup, to the acquisition cost. This markup is estimated to be sufficient to cover the store's expenses and provide a reasonable profit. Thus a building materials outlet may buy a power drill for $30 including freight, and price the item at $50. The $50 price reflects a markup of 40% based on the selling price, or 66⅔% based on the merchandise cost. Of course, in setting prices, middlemen also should take into account the expectations of their customers.

Various types of retailers require different percentage markups because of the nature of the products handled and the services offered. A self-service supermarket has lower costs and thus can have a lower average markup than a full-service delicatessen. Figure 12.3 shows examples of markup pricing by middlemen. (Markups are discussed in more detail in Appendix A.)

FIGURE 12.3

Examples of Markup Pricing by Retailers and Wholesalers.

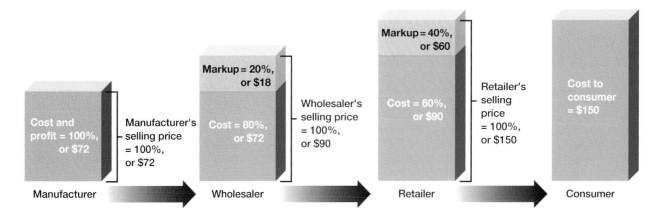

Is cost-plus pricing really used by middlemen? For the following reasons, it's safe to say that cost-plus pricing is *not* used widely by middlemen:

- Most retail prices are really just offers. If customers accept the offer, the price is fine. If they reject it, the price usually will be changed quickly, or the product may even be withdrawn from the market. Prices thus are always on trial.

- Many retailers don't use the same markup on all the products they carry. A supermarket, for instance, may have a markup of 10% to 15% on sugar and soap products, 15% to 25% on canned fruit and vegetables, and 10% to 45% on fresh meats and produce, depending on the particular item. These different markups for distinctive products reflect competitive considerations and other aspects of market demand.

- A middleman usually doesn't actually set a base price but only adds a percentage to the price already set by the producer. The producer's price is set to allow each middleman to add a reasonable markup and still sell at a competitive retail price. The key price is set by the producer, with an eye on the final market. Thus what seems to be cost-plus pricing by middlemen is usually market-influenced pricing.

Evaluation of Cost-Plus Pricing

A firm should be market-oriented and cater to consumers' wants, so why are we considering cost-plus pricing? Simply, cost-plus pricing must be understood because it is straightforward, easy to explain, and—as a result—used by numerous firms. In fact, although not commonplace among traditional middlemen, a recent study found that cost plus is the most common pricing method among *e-commerce* companies.[23]

The traditional perspective has been that costs should be a determinant of prices, but not the only one. Costs are a floor for a company's prices. If goods are priced below this floor for a long time, the firm will be forced out of business.

In recent years, inflation has diminished and firms have had great difficulty raising prices. As a result, a new perspective is that price should determine costs. That is, a firm may not have much flexibility in setting its price so costs must be reduced if profits are to be realized. If this perspective is accepted, production processes and marketing activities must be revamped to squeeze out costs wherever possible. After cutting prices in its battle with Fuji, Eastman Kodak started a major effort to cut costs by about $750 million.[24] The appropriate conclusion is that used by itself, cost-plus pricing is a weak and unrealistic method because it ignores market conditions, notably demand and competition.

Break-Even Analysis

One way to consider both market demand and costs in price determination is using **break-even analysis** to calculate break-even points. A **break-even point** is that quantity of output at which total revenue equals total costs, *assuming a certain selling price*. There is a different break-even point for every selling price. Sales exceeding the break-even point result in a profit on each additional unit. The more sales are above the break-even point, the larger will be the total and unit profits. Sales below the break-even point result in a loss to the seller.

Determining the Break-Even Point

The method of determining a break-even point is illustrated in Table 12.3 and Figure 12.4. In our example, Futon Factory's fixed costs are $25,000, and variable costs are constant at $30 per unit. In our earlier example (Table 12.1 and Figure 12.2), we

TABLE 12.3 — Futon Factory: Computation of Break-Even Point

At each of several prices, we wish to find out how many units must be sold to cover all costs. At a unit price of $100, the sale of each unit contributes $70 to cover overhead expenses. The Futon Factory must sell about 357 units to cover its $25,000 in fixed costs. See Figure 12.4 for a depiction of the data in this table.

(1) Unit Price	(2) Unit Variable Costs	(3) Contribution to Overhead (1) − (2)	(4) Overhead (Total Fixed Costs)	(5) Break-even Point (Rounded) (4) ÷ (3)
$ 60	$30	$ 30	$25,000	833 units
80	30	50	$25,000	500 units
100	30	70	$25,000	357 units
150	30	120	$25,000	208 units

assumed that unit variable costs are *not* constant but fluctuate. To simplify our break-even analysis, we now assume that variable costs *are* constant.

The total cost of producing one unit is $25,030—Futon Factory obviously needs more volume to absorb its fixed costs! For 400 units, the total cost is $37,000 ($30 multiplied by 400, plus $25,000). In Figure 12.4 the selling price is $80 a unit and variable costs of $30 per unit are incurred in producing each unit. Consequently, any revenue over $30 contributes to covering fixed costs (sometimes termed *overhead*). When the price is $80, that would be $50 per unit. At a price of $80, the break-even point is 500 units, because a $50 per-unit contribution will just cover overhead of $25,000.

Stated another way, variable costs for 500 units are $15,000 and fixed costs are $25,000, for a total cost of $40,000. This amount equals the revenue from 500 units sold at $80 each. So, at an $80 selling price, the break-even volume is 500 units. Figure 12.4 shows a break-even point for an $80 price. However, it is highly desirable to calculate break-even points for several different selling prices.

The break-even point may be found with this formula:

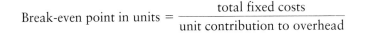

$$\text{Break-even point in units} = \frac{\text{total fixed costs}}{\text{unit contribution to overhead}}$$

FIGURE 12.4

Break-Even Chart for Futon Factory with an $80 Selling Price.

If this company sells 500 units, total costs are $40,000 (variable cost of 500 × $30, or $15,000, plus fixed costs of $25,000). At a selling price of $80, the sale of 500 units will yield $40,000 revenue, and costs and revenue will equal each other. At the same price, the sale of each unit above 500 will yield a profit.

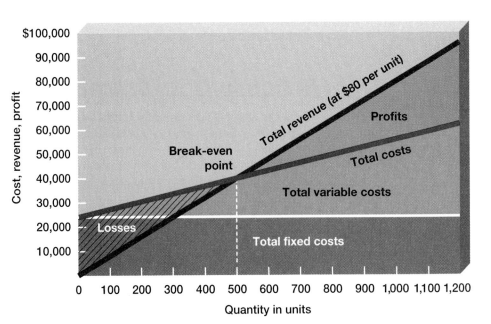

Because unit contribution to overhead equals selling price less the average variable cost, the working formula becomes:

$$\text{Break-even point in units} = \frac{\text{total fixed costs}}{\text{selling price} - \text{average variable cost}}$$

Evaluation of Break-Even Analysis

A drawback of break-even analysis is that it cannot tell us whether or not we *can* actually sell the break-even amount. Table 12.3, for example, shows what revenue will be at the different prices *if* the given number of units can be sold at these prices. The amount the market will buy at a given price could be below the break-even point. If that happens, the firm will not break even—it will show a loss.

Two basic assumptions underlie simple break-even analysis: (1) Total fixed costs are constant, and (2) variable costs remain constant per unit of output. Actually, fixed costs may change (although usually not in the short term) and average variable costs normally fluctuate.

Despite these limitations, management should not dismiss break-even analysis as a pricing tool. Even in its simplest form, break-even analysis is helpful because in the short run many firms experience reasonably stable cost and demand structures.[25]

Prices Based on Marginal Analysis

Another pricing method, marginal analysis, also takes account of both demand and costs to determine the best price for profit maximization. Firms with other pricing goals might use *prices based on marginal analysis* to compare prices determined by different means.

Determining the Price

To use marginal analysis, the price setter must understand the concepts of average and marginal revenue as well as average and marginal cost. **Marginal revenue** is the income derived from the sale of the last unit. **Average revenue** is the unit price at a given level of unit sales; it is calculated by dividing total revenue by the number of units sold.

Referring to the hypothetical demand schedule in Table 12.4, we see that Limos for Lease can sell one unit (that is, lease one limousine for a two-hour period on a weekend night) at $80. To attract a second customer and thereby lease two limos on

TABLE 12.4

Limos for Lease: Demand Schedule for an Individual Firm

At each market price a certain quantity of the product—in this example, a two-hour rental of a limousine on a weekend night—will be demanded. Marginal revenue is simply the amount of additional money gained by selling one more unit. Limos for Lease gains no additional marginal revenue after it has rented its fourth limo at a price of $53.

Units Sold (Limos Leased)	Unit Price (Average Revenue)	Total Revenue	Marginal Revenue
1	$80	$80	
2	72	144	$64
3	63	189	45
4	53	212	23
5	42	210	−2
6	34	204	−6

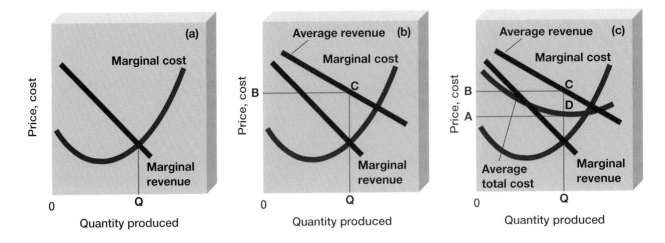

FIGURE 12.5

Price Setting and Profit Maximization through Marginal Analysis.

the same night, it must reduce its price to $72 for each unit. Thus the company receives an additional $64 (marginal revenue) by selling a second unit. After the fourth unit, total revenue declines each time the unit price is lowered in order to sell an additional unit. Hence, there is a negative marginal revenue.

Marginal analysis is illustrated in Figure 12.5. We assume that a company—a services firm, like Limos for Lease, or a manufacturer—will continue to produce and sell its product as long as revenue from the last unit sold exceeds the cost of producing this last unit. That is, output continues to increase as long as marginal revenue exceeds marginal cost. At the point where they meet, production theoretically should cease. Ordinarily a company will not want to sell a unit at a price less than its out-of-pocket (variable) costs of producing it. The optimum volume of output is the quantity level at which *marginal cost equals marginal revenue*, or quantity Q in Figure 12.5a.

Thus the unit price is determined by locating the point on the average revenue curve that represents an output of quantity Q—the level at which marginal cost equals marginal revenue. Remember that average revenue represents the unit price. Referring to Figure 12.5b, in which the average revenue curve has been added, the unit price at which to sell quantity Q is represented by point C—that is, price B.

The average total cost curve has been added in Figure 12.5c. It shows that for output quantity Q, the average unit cost is represented by point D—that is, unit cost A. Thus, with a price of B and an average unit cost of A, the company enjoys a unit profit given by B minus A in the figure. Total profit is quantity Q times the unit profit.

Evaluation of Marginal Analysis Pricing

Marginal analysis has been used sparsely as a basis for price setting. According to businesspeople, it can be a help in studying past price movements. However, many managers think marginal analysis *cannot* serve as a practical basis for setting prices unless accurate, reliable data can be obtained for plotting the curves.

On the brighter side, management's knowledge of costs and demand is improving. Computerized databases are bringing more complete and detailed information to management's attention all the time. And experienced management can do a fairly accurate job of estimating marginal and average costs and revenues.

Prices Set in Relation to Market Alone

Cost-plus pricing is one extreme among pricing methods. At the other extreme is *prices set in relation to the market alone*. The seller's price may be set right at the market price to meet the competition, or it may be set above or below the market price.

Pricing to Meet Competition

Pricing to meet competition is simple to carry out. In a situation with multiple suppliers, a firm should ascertain what the prevailing market price is and, after allowing for customary markups for middlemen, arrive at its own selling price. To illustrate, a manufacturer of women's shoes knows that retailers want to sell the shoes for $70 a pair and have an average markup of 40% of their selling price. Consequently, after allowing $28 for the retailer's markup, the producer's price is $42. This manufacturer then has to decide whether $42 is enough to cover costs and provide a reasonable profit. Sometimes a producer faces a real squeeze if its costs are rising but the market price is holding firm.

One situation in which management might price a product right at the market level is when competition is keen and the firm's product is not differentiated significantly from competing products.[26] To some extent, this pricing method reflects the market conditions of **perfect competition**. That is, product differentiation is absent, buyers and sellers are well informed, and the seller has no discernible control over the selling price. Most producers of agricultural products and small firms marketing well-known, standardized products use this pricing method. As explained in the Marketing in the Information Economy box, the Internet is moving some industries toward perfect competition.

MARKETING IN THE INFORMATION ECONOMY

Who gets a price advantage from the Internet?

The Internet facilitates **dynamic pricing,** in which prices are adjusted instantly and frequently in line with what the market will bear. Dynamic pricing is evident in various forms of electronic commerce. The most popular, or at least the most visible, is online auctions. The auction can be initiated by a seller, who offers a product for sale online, or by a buyer, who announces the desire to purchase a particular good or service online. To learn about variations on the basic method, review the eBay, FreeMarkets, and Bluefly cases elsewhere in this book and the Priceline.com case at the beginning of this chapter.

It's widely believed that dynamic pricing will result in lower prices. However, one study concluded that the prices of three online booksellers were virtually identical for over one-half the items examined. In contrast, a late-1990s research project determined that prices for the two products examined, books and music CDs, were 9% to 16% lower online than at conventional retailers. A more recent study concluded that prices for term life insurance dropped as Internet usage grew.

The reasons for lower prices? First, comparison shopping is easier on the Internet, helped greatly by "shopping robots" (more on this type of electronic search engine in the next chapter). Of course, consumers may gather price information through the Internet and then use it to negotiate a lower price from a conventional "offline" seller such as a retail store. In addition, online buyers may be able to design a product to meet their particular needs, thereby assuring

maximum value from the purchase. Dell Computer stressed that advantage in order to build its online sales volume.

However, the Internet also should, or could, benefit sellers' pricing activities. The reasons? For one thing, it's much easier for a seller to change prices online than to retag every item in an actual retail store. In addition, because shoppers have to provide various information in order to make an online purchase and their transactions can be compiled and analyzed, e-commerce firms can tailor special offerings for individual customers. For example, if a customer's several purchases of decorating accessories at PotteryBarn.com were all related to the living room, the company could provide the customer with a special incentive (such as a 25% discount) for a purchase related to a different room in the home.

In a real sense, the Internet fosters conditions approaching perfect competition. That is, nearly identical products are available from numerous suppliers, and prospective buyers have ample information for making purchase decisions. Thus the Internet has had—and probably will continue to have—a tremendous impact on pricing, perhaps affecting this element of marketing more than any other element.

Sources: David P. Hamilton, "The Price Isn't Right," *The Wall Street Journal*, Feb. 12, 2001, pp. R8, R10; Gene Koretz, "E-Commerce: The Buyer Wins," *Business Week*, Jan. 8, 2001, p. 30; Robert D. Hof, "Going, Going, Gone," *Business Week*, Apr. 12, 1999, pp. 30–32; and Amy E. Cortese, "Good-Bye to Fixed Pricing?" *Business Week*, May 4, 1998, pp. 71–73+.

The sharp drop in revenue occurring when the price is raised above the prevailing market level indicates that the individual seller faces a **kinked demand** (see Figure 12.6). The prevailing price is at A. Adjusting this price is not beneficial to the seller for the following reasons:

- Above the prevailing price, demand for the product drops sharply, as indicated by the fairly flat average revenue curve beyond point P. Above price A, demand is highly elastic and, as a result, total revenue declines.

- Below price A, demand for the product increases very little, as shown by the steeply sloping average revenue curve and the negative marginal revenue curve below point P. Demand is highly inelastic and, as a result, total revenue still declines.

In the case of kinked demand, total revenue decreases each time the price is adjusted from the prevailing price, A in Figure 12.6. The prevailing price is well established. Consequently, when a single firm reduces its price, its unit sales will not increase very much—certainly not enough to offset the loss in average revenue.

So far in our discussion of pricing to meet competition, we have observed market situations that involve *many* sellers. Oddly enough, this same pricing method is often used when the market is dominated by a *few* firms, each marketing similar products. This type of market structure, called an **oligopoly**, exists in such industries as copper, aluminum, soft drinks, breakfast cereals, auto tires, and even among barber shops and grocery stores in a small community. When the demand curve is kinked, as in Figure 12.6, oligopolists should simply set prices at a competitive level and leave them there. Typically they do.

Pricing below Competition

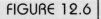
www.drugemporium.com

A variation of market-based pricing is to set a price *below* the level of your main competitors. **Pricing below competition** is done by discount retailers, such as Wal-Mart, Target, and Drug Emporium, which stress low markup, high volume, and few customer services (including sales people). They price heavily advertised, well-known brands 10% to 30% below the suggested list price, which is normally charged by full-service retailers. Even retailers that offer an assortment of customer services may price below the competitive level by eliminating some services. Some gas stations offer a discount to customers who pay with cash instead of a credit card, for instance.

The risk in pricing below competition is that consumers begin to view the product (or an entire retail store) as an undifferentiated commodity, such as coal and bulk

FIGURE 12.6

Kinked Demand Curve.

This type of curve faces firms selling well-known, standardized products as well as individual firms in an oligopolistic market structure. The kink occurs at the point representing the prevailing price, A. At prices above A, demand declines rapidly. A price set below A results in very little increase in volume, so revenue is lost; that is, marginal revenue is negative.

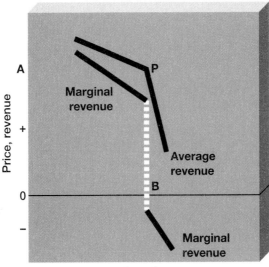

Can you deal with a kinked demand curve?

Intense price competition has characterized the airline industry in the U.S. since it was deregulated. In an attempt to increase the number of passengers, an airline such as United may cut its price on a heavily traveled route—New York to Los Angeles, for example. However, competitors on this route, such as American and Delta, usually match that lower fare immediately. As a result, there is no significant shift in the market share held by each airline on that route. But another result is that the market price settles—at least temporarily—at the lower level. Unless the number of passengers increases substantially, the profits of all airlines flying this route and matching the cut-rate prices are likely to suffer.

What marketing strategies might an airline use to avoid having to match a competitor's price cut?

salt, with the entire focus on price differences. If that happens, and some would say it already has in fields such as personal computers, then consumers choose the brand with the lowest price. In turn, competing firms are likely to wind up in a price war that diminishes or eliminates profits. One observer asked a question that applies to any industry in which firms rely on price as a way to gain an edge over competitors: "How can restaurant chains ever expect to charge top dollar again after relentlessly pushing . . . [low] prices?"[27]

Pricing above Competition

Producers or retailers sometimes set their prices *above* the prevailing market level. Usually, **pricing above competition** works only when the product is distinctive or when the seller has acquired prestige in its field. Most communities have an elite

Rolex positions its watches as top quality. This ad provides few details about the product's attributes but rather seeks to create a favorable image for the Cestello model. Rolex watches carry high prices, often $2,000 or more; in fact, the suggested retail price for the watch in this ad is $19,550. Hence, the company distributes this product through a limited number of outlets to reach a relatively small segment of the total market. Retailers that sell this brand are expected to provide superior service, especially knowledgeable sales people.

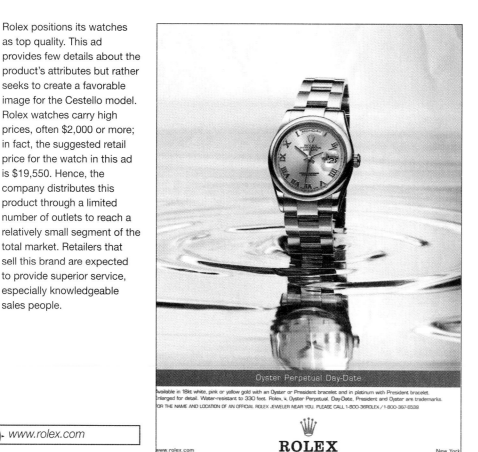

www.rolex.com

A GLOBAL PERSPECTIVE

How is a new currency affecting pricing in Europe?

As explained in Chapter 3, all but three of the countries in the European Union have adopted a common currency, called the euro. (Denmark, Great Britain, and Sweden chose to retain their national currencies, at least for the time being.) The new bills and coins were introduced at the start of 2002, replacing francs, marks, pesetas, and other currencies.

The adoption of a common currency has significant implications for firms doing business in these 12 countries, which collectively have about 300 million citizens and represent about one-sixth of the global economy. Among them are:

- With a single currency, resulting in what's called price transparency, marketers will find it more difficult to use different price levels in different countries because consumers can easily compare prices. Prior to the euro, companies would vary prices from country to country, taking into account such factors as competition and consumers' price sensitivity in a particular region. For example, in the late 1990s, a bottle of Gatorade cost almost four times as much in Germany as in Spain. However, with the euro in place, price convergence—a reduction in the range of prices—should occur over time.

- Facing added price competition, retailers and wholesalers are likely to seek lower prices from their suppliers.

Coinciding with the euro's introduction, many companies modified—or considered modifying—their pricing strategies. Here are some options:

- Determining whether a single "pan-European" price is necessary or price differences are still plausible. As one executive commented, "The common currency doesn't erase 2,000 years of historical and cultural differences."

- Designing innovative products that address specific needs and, as a result, are not subject to constant price comparisons.

- Establishing a pan-European marketing program, consisting of a common product, package, price, and promotional program across this entire region of the world. Procter & Gamble is very interested in this approach.

Some European shoppers and consumer organizations claimed that companies saw the introduction of the euro as an opportunity to raise prices. Specifically, many consumers thought that prices have been "rounded up" during the conversion from the national currency to the euro. However, any such increases evidently were offset by price reductions on other products. According to the president of the European Central Bank, "Overall, there is no evidence that the euro changeover has had a significant effect on the average price level."

Sources: David Fairlamb, "Has the Euro Unleashed a Wave of Price Gouging?" *Business Week,* Sept. 16, 2002, p. 43; Daniel Dombey, Tony Major, and Hugh Williamson, "Euro Is Widely Blamed for Price Increases," *Financial Times,* June 1, 2002, p. 6; Michael R. Sesit, "Shopping Around—Euro Adds Momentum to Price Comparisons," *The Wall Street Journal,* Jan. 11, 2002, p. 27; Andrea Know, "Pricing in Euroland," *World Trade,* January 1999, pp. 52–56; and Maricris G. Briones, "The Euro Starts Here," *Marketing News,* July 20, 1998, pp. 1, 39.

clothing boutique and a prestigious jewelry store where prices are noticeably above the level set by other stores with seemingly similar products. However, a gas station that has a strong advantage based on a superior location (perhaps the only such station for many miles on an interstate highway) may also be able to use above-market pricing.

Above-market pricing often is employed by manufacturers of prestige brands of high-cost goods such as autos (Ferrari, Bentley), crystal (Waterford), leather products (Gucci, Fendi), and watches (Breguet, Rolex). Patek Philippe, a Swiss firm, makes only about 30,000 watches per year, but they are priced from about $4,000 to over $1 million—per watch! Above-market pricing also is used for business goods. Sometimes it can be effective for relatively low-cost goods. Premier Industrial, for example, prices its fasteners and tubing at least 10% higher and occasionally much higher than competing products. Premier, an industrial distributor, can do

www.waterford.com

www.patekphilippe.com

this because—unlike competitors—it accepts small orders and ships an order within 24 hours.[28]

Some services firms also price above their competitors. In the hotel industry, the Ritz Carlton and Fairmont chains have used this approach successfully. In the airline industry, the supersonic Concorde may be the best example. British Airways flies this aircraft between London and New York, and Air France does likewise between Paris and New York. The Concorde flies at about twice the speed of sound, over 1,300 miles per hour, which is more than two times the speed of a regular commercial jet. As a result, a flight between Paris and New York takes about 3½ hours, compared to a regular flight time of 8 hours. The reduced travel time comes with a steep price, with a round-trip fare typically costing at least $12,500.[29]

Summary

In our economy, price influences the allocation of resources. In individual companies, price is one significant factor in achieving marketing success. And in many purchase situations, price can be of great importance to consumers. However, it is difficult to define price. A general definition is: Price is the amount of money and/or other items with utility needed to acquire a product.

Before setting a product's base price, management should identify its pricing objective. Major pricing objectives are to (1) earn a target return on investment or on net sales, (2) maximize profits, (3) increase sales, (4) hold or gain a target market share, (5) stabilize prices, and (6) meet competition's prices.

Besides the firm's pricing objective, other key factors that influence price setting are: (1) demand for the product, (2) competitive reactions, (3) strategies planned for other marketing-mix elements, and (4) cost of the product. The concept of elasticity refers to the effect that unit-price changes have on the number of units sold and on total revenue.

Three major methods used to determine the base price are cost-plus pricing, marginal analysis, and setting the price only in relation to the market. For cost-plus pricing to be effective, a seller must consider several types of costs and their reactions to changes in the quantity produced. A producer usually sets a price to cover total cost. In some cases, however, the best policy may be to set a price that covers marginal cost only. The main weakness in cost-plus pricing is that it completely ignores market demand. To partially offset this weakness, a company may use break-even analysis as a tool in price setting.

In actual business situations, price setting is influenced by market conditions. Hence, marginal analysis, which takes into account both demand and costs to determine a suitable price for the product, is helpful in understanding the forces affecting price. Price and output level are set at the point where marginal cost equals marginal revenue. The effectiveness of marginal analysis in setting prices depends on obtaining reliable cost data.

For many products, price setting is relatively easy because management simply sets the price at the level of competition. Pricing at prevailing market levels makes sense for firms selling well-known, standardized products and sometimes for individual firms in an oligopoly. Two variations of market-level pricing are to price below or above the levels of primary competitors.

More about Priceline.com

After establishing its website as a place to bid on airline tickets, Priceline.com had much bigger ambitions. According to Jay Walker, the company's founder (who has since left the firm), "There is no [product] category we won't be in."

The hotel industry was a natural area of expansion for Priceline. Walker explained, "Until now, hotels have been faced with the worst of two possible worlds. If they lower prices for some rooms, they risk angering guests who paid higher prices. If they keep prices static, there is the opportunity risk, where rooms go unsold."

By allowing consumers to name their own price, Priceline sells rooms to travelers who otherwise would not book rooms with the participating hotel chains. Just months after its launch in October 1998, Priceline was booking more than 4,000 rooms per month in 200 cities in the U.S. By mid-2001, the enterprise was selling more than 50,000 room nights monthly.

Less successful was the company's move into groceries and gasoline. In a venture called WebHouse Club Inc., Priceline attempted to entice shoppers to buy their cereal, soft drinks, and other groceries online instead of at a "bricks and mortar" supermarket. Shoppers specified the prices they would pay for items in 149 different categories, using an account they activated at the website after obtaining an identification card at a participating store. A $3 monthly fee entitled consumers to make bids and instantly find out whether or not the products' manufacturers accepted them. After paying online with a credit card, the customer then went to one of the participating local supermarkets, walked the aisles, and picked out the items purchased. To counter criticism that the process was time-consuming, Priceline's management stated that many shoppers already spend time clipping and organizing manufacturers' coupons from newspaper inserts and then going to a store to redeem them.

The new operation failed, however. Basically, many large consumer product companies refused to participate, leaving WebHouse to subsidize the discounts it had promised shoppers. Firms like Kimberly-Clark were reluctant to give discounts to WebHouse because they did not want to endanger their brands or other distribution channels.

The gasoline venture failed for similar reasons. Large gasoline marketers balked because of Web-House's refusal to tell retailers which of their competitors had joined the program. Also, as one major marketer pointed out, "Gasoline is partly a convenience purchase. People don't want to search across town to save $2 a month."[30]

1. What issues did Priceline's WebHouse venture overlook in attempting to apply the name-your-own-price concept to groceries?

2. What other product categories might be suitable for Priceline's business model?

Key Terms and Concepts

Price (318)
Barter (319)
Value (321)
Pricing objectives (323)
Base price (list price) (325)
Expected price (326)
Inverse demand (326)
Fixed cost (329)
Total fixed cost (329)
Average fixed cost (329)
Variable cost (329)

Total variable cost (329)
Average variable cost (329)
Total cost (329)
Average total cost (329)
Marginal cost (329)
Average fixed cost curve (329)
Average variable cost curve (329)
Average total cost curve (330)
Marginal cost curve (330)
Cost-plus pricing (331)
Break-even analysis (333)

Break-even point (333)
Marginal revenue (335)
Average revenue (335)
Pricing to meet competition (337)
Perfect competition (337)
Dynamic pricing (337)
Kinked demand (338)
Oligopoly (338)
Pricing below competition (338)
Pricing above competition (339)

Questions and Problems

1. a. Explain how a firm's pricing objective may influence the promotional program for a product.
   b. Which of the six pricing goals involves the largest, most aggressive promotional campaign?

2. What marketing conditions might logically lead a company to set "meeting competition" as a pricing objective?

3. What is your expected price for each of the following articles? How did you arrive at your estimate in each instance?

   a. An Internet service that would send you, via e-mail, daily news from two cities of your choosing (e.g., your hometown, a city where you might like to live in the future).
   b. A new type of cola beverage that holds its carbonation long after it has been opened; packaged in 12-ounce (355-milliliter) and 2-liter bottles.
   c. A nuclear-powered 23-inch table-model television set, guaranteed to run for 10 years without replacement of the original power-generating component; requires no battery or electric wires.

4. Name three products, including at least one service, for which you think an inverse demand exists. For each product, within which price range does this inverse demand exist?

5. In Figure 12.2, what is the significance of the point where the marginal cost curve intersects the average total cost curve? Explain why the average total cost curve is declining (slightly) to the left of the intersection point and rising (again, slightly) beyond it. Explain how the marginal cost curve can be rising while the average total cost curve is still declining.

6. What are the merits and limitations of the cost-plus method of setting a base price?

7. In a break-even chart, is the total *fixed* cost line always horizontal? Is the total *variable* cost line always straight? Explain.

8. Referring to Table 12.3 and Figure 12.4, what would be Futon Factory's break-even points at prices of $50 and $90, if variable costs are $40 per unit and fixed costs remain at $25,000?

9. A small manufacturer sold ballpoint pens to retailers at $8.40 per dozen. The manufacturing cost was 50 cents for each pen. Expenses, including all selling and administrative costs except advertising, were $19,200. How many dozen must the manufacturer sell to cover these expenses and pay for an advertising campaign costing $6,000?

10. In Figure 12.5, why would the firm normally stop producing at quantity Q? Why is the price set at B rather than at D or A?

Interactive Marketing Exercises

1. Select three goods (new or used nonfood items in the price range of $10 to $100) that you are considering buying. Determine the price of each of these items in your local community by checking with one or more retail outlets. Then go to an online auction site such as eBay.com or Amazon.com, and check the prices of each of these items. Which are cheaper—the online or in-store prices? Where would you buy each item? What reasons underlie your decisions?

2. Identify one store in your community that generally prices *below* the levels of most other firms and one that prices *above* prevailing market levels. Arrange an interview with the manager of each store. Ask both managers to explain the rationale and procedures associated with their pricing approaches. Also ask the manager of the store with below-market prices how profits are achieved with such low prices. Ask the manager of the store with above-market prices how customers are attracted and satisfied with such high prices.

Appendix A | Marketing Math

Marketing involves people—customers, middlemen, and producers. Much of the business activity of these people is quantified in some manner. Consequently, knowledge of certain concepts in economics, accounting, and finance is essential for decision making in many areas of marketing. With that in mind, this appendix presents an overview—or, for many of you, a review—of (1) price elasticity of demand, (2) the operating statement, (3) markups, and (4) analytical ratios.

Price Elasticity of Demand

Price elasticity of demand refers to the responsiveness of quantity demanded to price changes. Specifically, it gauges the effect that a change in the price of a product has on amount sold and on total revenue. (Total revenue—that is, total sales in dollars—equals the unit price times the number of units sold.)

We say demand is **elastic** when (1) reducing the unit price causes an increase in total revenue *or* (2) raising the unit price causes a decrease in total revenue. In the first case, the lower price results in a boost in quantity sold that more than offsets the price cut—hence, the increase in total revenue. In the second case, the higher price results in a large drop in quantity sold that more than counters the potential gain from the price rise—hence, the decrease in total revenue.

These elastic demand situations are illustrated in Figure A.1. We start with a situation where, at $5 a sandwich, the Campus Sandwich Company sells 100 units and the total revenue (TR) equals $500. When the firm lowers price to $4, the quantity sold increases to 150 and total revenue also goes up—to $600. When the price is boosted to $6, however, the quantity sold drops off so much (to 70 sandwiches) that total revenue also declines (to $420). Thus demand is *elastic* when the price change (either up or down) and total revenue change move in the *opposite* direction.

Demand is **inelastic** when (1) a price cut causes total revenue to decline *or* (2) a price rise results in an increase in total revenue. In each of these situations, the changes in unit price more than offset the relatively small changes in quantities sold. That is, when the price is cut, the increase in quantity sold is not enough to offset the price cut, so total revenue goes down. And when the unit price is raised, it more than counters the decline in quantity sold, so total revenue goes up. Simply, demand is *inelastic* when the price change and the resulting change in total revenue go in the *same* direction.

Inelastic demand situations are illustrated in Figure A.2. Again we start with a unit price of $5, Paperbacks and More sells 100 units, and total revenue is

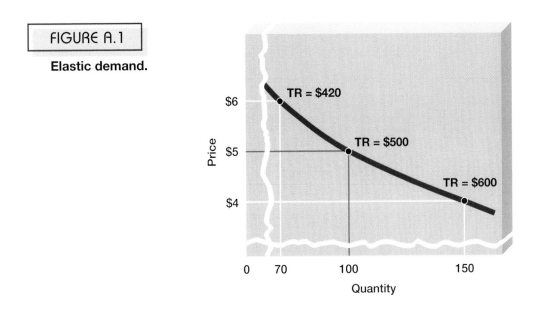

FIGURE A.1

Elastic demand.

Inelastic demand.

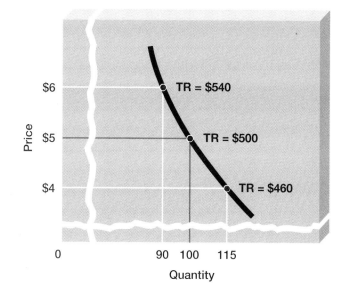

$500. When the store lowers the unit price to $4, the quantity of books sold increases to 115. But this is not enough to offset the price cut, so total revenue declines to $460. When the unit price is raised to $6, the quantity sold falls off to 90. But the price increase more than offsets the drop in quantity sold, so total revenue goes up to $540.

In general, the demand for necessities (salt, sugar, cigarettes, gasoline, telephone service, gas and electric service) tends to be inelastic. If the price of gasoline goes up or down, say 10 or 15 cents a gallon, the total number of gallons sold does not change very much. Simply, consumers need gasoline for their cars. Conversely, the demand for products purchased with discretionary income (luxury items, large appliances, furniture, autos) typically is much more elastic. That is why the demand for new electronics products often soars as prices decline in the early stages of the life cycle.

Moreover, the demand for individual *brands* is more elastic than is the demand for the broader *product* category. If consumers encounter an unsatisfactory price on an individual brand, they ordinarily can purchase an alternative brand. However, if they are displeased with the prices in an entire product category, they may not be able to find an alternative type of product to meet their needs. Thus the demand for Continental Airlines or Hertz rental cars is far more elastic (price sensitive) than is the demand for air travel or rental cars in general.

Price elasticity of demand is not just a theoretical concept in economics. It has practical value. By gauging whether demand for a product is elastic or inelastic, marketing executives are better able to establish suitable prices for their products.

The Operating Statement

A company prepares two main financial statements—a balance sheet and an operating statement. A **balance sheet** shows the assets, liabilities, and net worth of a company at a given time—for example, at the close of business on December 31, 2002.

The focus of our attention here, however, is the operating statement. Often called a *profit-and-loss statement* or an *income statement,* an **operating statement** is a summary of the firm's income and expenses over a period of time—for example, the 2002 calendar year. The operating statement shows whether the business earned a net profit or suffered a net loss during the period covered.

An operating statement can cover any period of time. To fulfill income tax requirements, virtually all firms prepare a statement covering operations during a calendar year or another 12-month period called a fiscal year. It is also common for businesses to prepare monthly, quarterly, and/or semiannual operating statements.

Table A.1 is an operating statement for a hypothetical firm, the Alpha-Zeta Company, which could be either a wholesaler or a retailer. The major difference between the operating statement of a middleman and that of a manufacturer is the cost-of-goods-sold section. A manufacturer shows the cost of goods *manufactured,* whereas the middleman's statement shows net *purchases.*

The essence of business is very simple. A company buys or makes a product and then (hopefully)

An Operating Statement for a Wholesaler or a Retailer

The Alpha-Zeta Company
Operating Statement for Month Ending December 31, 2002

Gross sales		$87,000	
Less: Sales returns and allowances	$ 5,500		
Cash discounts allowed	1,500	7,000	
Net sales			$80,000
Cost of goods sold			
Beginning inventory, December 1 (at cost)		$18,000	
Gross purchases	$49,300		
Less: Cash discounts taken on purchases	900		
Net purchases	$48,400		
Plus: Freight in	1,600		
Net purchases (at delivered cost)		50,000	
Cost of goods available for sale		$68,000	
Less: Ending inventory December 31 (at cost)		20,000	
Cost of goods sold			48,000
Gross margin			$32,000
Expenses			
Sales-force salaries and commissions		$11,000	
Advertising		2,400	
Office supplies		250	
Taxes (except income tax)		125	
Telepone and fax		250	
Delivery expenses		175	
Rent		800	
Heat, light, and power		300	
Depreciation		100	
Insurance		150	
Interest		150	
Bad debts		300	
Administrative salaries		7,500	
Office salaries		3,500	
Miscellaneous expenses		200	
Total expenses			27,200
Net profit before taxes			$ 4,800

sells it for a higher price. From the sales revenue, the seller intends to cover the cost of the merchandise and the expenses of the business and have something left over, which is called **net profit**. These relationships form the basic structure of an operating statement:

- Sales minus cost of goods sold equals gross margin.

- Gross margin minus expenses equals net profit.

An example based on the Alpha-Zeta Company in Table A.1 follows:

	Sales	$80,000
less	Cost of goods sold	48,000
equals	Gross margin	32,000
less	Expenses	27,200
equals	Net profit	$ 4,800

Now let's look at the primary components in an operating statement.

Sales

The first line in an operating statement records **gross sales**—the total amount sold by an organization, stated in dollars. From this figure the Alpha-Zeta Company (hereafter, A-Z) deducts sales returns and sales allowances. A-Z also deducts discounts granted to employees when they purchase merchandise or services.

In virtually every firm at some time during an operating period, customers want to return or exchange merchandise. In a **sales return,** the customer is refunded the full purchase price in cash or credit. In a **sales allowance,** the customer keeps the merchandise but is given a reduction from the selling price because of some dissatisfaction. The income from the sale of returned merchandise is included in a company's gross sales, so returns and allowances must be deducted to calculate net sales.

Net Sales

The most important figure in the sales section of the statement is **net sales,** which represents the net amount of sales revenue, out of which the company will pay for the products and all its expenses. The net sales figure is also the one on which many operating ratios are based. It is designated as 100% (of itself), and the other items are then expressed as a percentage of net sales.

Cost of Goods Sold

As we work toward determining A-Z's net profit, we deduct from net sales the cost of the merchandise. To calculate the **cost of goods sold** in a retail or wholesale operation, we start with the value of any merchandise on hand at the beginning of the period. To this we add the net cost of what is purchased during the period. From this total we deduct the value of whatever remains unsold at the end of the period.

In Table A.1 the firm started with an inventory worth $18,000, and during the course of the month, it purchased goods that cost $50,000. Thus A-Z had a total of $68,000 worth of goods available for sale. If all were sold, the cost of goods sold would have been $68,000. At the end of the month, however, there was still $20,000 worth of merchandise on hand. Thus, during the month, A-Z sold goods that cost $48,000.

We just spoke of merchandise *valued at* a certain figure or *worth* a stated amount. Actually, the problem of inventory valuation is complicated and sometimes controversial. The rule of thumb is to value inventories at cost or market, whichever is lower. The application of this rule in the real world may be difficult. Assume

that a store buys six beach balls at $5 each and the following week buys six more at $6 each. The company places all 12, jumbled, in a basket display for sale. Then one is sold, but there is no marking to indicate whether its cost was $5 or $6. Thus the inventory value of the remaining 11 balls may be $60 or $61. If we multiply this situation by thousands of purchases and sales, we begin to see the depth of the problem.

A figure deserving some comment is the **net cost of delivered purchases.** A company starts with its gross purchases at billed cost. Then it must deduct any purchases that were returned or any purchase allowances received. The company should also deduct any discounts taken for payment of the bill within a specified period of time. Deducting purchase returns, allowances, and discounts gives the net cost of purchases. Freight charges paid by the buyer (called **freight in**) are added to net purchases to determine the net cost of *delivered* purchases.

In a manufacturing concern, the cost-of-goods-sold section has a slightly different form. Instead of determining the cost of goods *purchased*, the firm determines the cost of goods *manufactured*, as in Table A.2. Cost of goods manufactured ($50,000) is added to the beginning inventory ($18,000) to ascertain the total goods available for sale ($68,000). Then, after the ending inventory of finished goods has been deducted ($20,000), the result is the cost of goods sold ($48,000).

To find the cost of goods *manufactured*, a company starts with the value of goods partially completed (beginning inventory of goods in process—$24,000). To this beginning inventory figure is added the cost of raw materials, direct labor, and factory overhead expenses incurred during the period ($48,000). The resulting figure is the total goods in process during the period ($72,000). By deducting the value of goods still in process at the end of the period ($22,000), management finds the cost of goods manufactured during that span of time ($50,000).

Gross Margin

Gross margin is determined by subtracting cost of goods sold from net sales. Gross margin, sometimes called *gross profit*, is a key figure in the entire marketing program. When we say that a certain store has a *margin* of 30%, we are referring to the gross margin.

Expenses

Operating expenses are deducted from gross margin to determine net profit. The operating expense section includes marketing, administrative, and miscellaneous expenses. It does not, of course, include the cost of goods purchased or manufactured, because these costs have already been deducted.

TABLE A.2 Cost-of-Goods-Sold Section of an Operating Statement for a Manufacturer

Beginning inventory of finished goods (at cost)			$18,000
Cost of goods manufactured:			
Beginning inventory, goods in process		$24,000	
Plus: Raw materials	$20,000		
Direct labor	15,000		
Overhead	13,000	48,000	
Total goods in process		$72,000	
Less: Ending inventory, goods in process		22,000	
Cost of goods manufactured			50,000
Cost of goods available for sale			$68,000
Less: Ending inventory, finished goods (at cost)			20,000
Cost of goods sold			$48,000

Net Profit

Net profit is the difference between gross margin and total expenses. Obviously, a negative net profit is a loss.

Markups

Many retailers and wholesalers use markup percentages to determine the selling price of an article. Normally the selling price must exceed the cost of the merchandise by an amount sufficient to cover operating expenses and still leave the desired profit. The difference between the selling price of an item and its cost is the **markup**, sometimes referred to as the *mark-on*.

Typically, markups are expressed in percentages rather than dollars. A markup may be expressed as a percentage of either the cost or the selling price. Therefore, we must first determine which will be the *base* for the markup. That is, when we speak of a 40% markup, do we mean 40% of the *cost* or 40% of the *selling price*?

To determine the markup percentage when it is based on *cost*, we use the following formula:

$$\text{Markup \%} = \frac{\text{dollar markup}}{\text{cost}}$$

When the markup is based on *selling price*, the formula to use is:

$$\text{Markup \%} = \frac{\text{dollar markup}}{\text{selling price}}$$

All interested parties must know which base is being used in a given situation. Otherwise there can be considerable misunderstanding. To illustrate, suppose that Allan Aaron runs a clothing store and claims he needs a 50% markup to make a small net profit. Blanche Brister, who runs a competitive store, says she needs only a 33⅓% markup and that Aaron must be either inefficient or a big profiteer.

Actually, both merchants are using identical markups, but they are using different bases. Each seller buys hats at $6 apiece and sets the selling price at $9. This is a markup of $3 per hat. Aaron is expressing his markup as a percentage of cost—hence the 50% figure ($3 ÷ $6 = 0.5, or 50%). Brister is basing her markup on the selling price ($3 ÷ $9 = 0.333, or 33⅓%).

It would be a mistake for Aaron to try to get by on Brister's 33⅓% markup, as long as Aaron uses cost as his base. If Aaron used the 33⅓% markup, but *based it on cost*, the markup would be only $2. And the selling price would be only $8. This $2 markup, averaged over the entire hat department, would not enable Aaron to cover his usual expenses and make a profit. *It is conventional to state markup percentages as a percentage of selling price.*

Markup Based on Selling Price

The following diagram shows the relationships among selling price, cost, and markup. It can be used to calculate these figures regardless of whether the markup is stated in percentages or dollars, and whether the percentages are based on selling price or cost:

		Dollars	Percentage
	Selling price		
less	Cost	———	———
equals	Markup		

As an example, suppose a merchant buys an article for $90 and knows the markup based on selling price must be 40%. What is the selling price? By filling in the known information in the diagram, we obtain:

		Dollars	Percentage
	Selling price		100
less	Cost	90	
equals	Markup		40

The percentage representing cost must then be 60%. Thus the $90 cost is 60% of the selling price. The selling price is then $150. That is, $90 equals 60% of the selling price. Then $90 is divided by 0.6 (or 60%) to get the selling price of $150.

A common situation facing merchants is to have competition set a ceiling on selling prices. Or possibly the sellers must buy an item to fit into one of their price lines. Then they want to know the maximum amount they can pay for an item and still get their normal markup. Assume that the selling price of an article is set at $60—set by competition or by a $59.95 price line. The retailer's normal markup is 35%. What is the most the retailer should pay for this article? Again let's fill in what we know in the diagram:

		Dollars	Percentage
	Selling price	60	100
less	Cost		
equals	Markup		35

The dollar markup is $21 (that is, 35% of $60). So by simple subtraction we find that the maximum cost the merchant will want to pay is $39.

Series of Markups

Markups are figured on the selling price at *each level of business* in a channel of distribution. A manufacturer applies a markup to determine its selling price. The manufacturer's selling price then becomes the wholesaler's cost. The wholesaler must determine its own selling price by applying its usual markup percentage based on its—the wholesaler's—selling price. The same procedure is carried out by the retailer, using the wholesaler's selling price as its—the retailer's—cost.

The following calculations illustrate this point:

Producer's cost $7   } Producer's markup =
Producer's selling price $10 } $3, or 30%

Wholesaler's cost $10 } Wholesaler's markup =
Wholesaler's selling price $12 } $2, or 16⅔%

Retailer's cost $12 } Retailer's markup =
Retailer's selling price $20 } $8, or 40%

Markup Based on Cost

If a firm customarily deals in markups based on cost—and sometimes this is done among wholesalers—the same diagrammatic approach may be employed. The only change is that cost will equal 100%. The selling price will be 100% plus the markup based on cost. As

an example, a firm bought an article for $70 and wants a 20% markup based on cost. The markup in dollars is $14 (in other words, 20% of $70). The selling price is $84 (that is, $70 + $14):

		Dollars	Percentage
	Selling price	84	120
less	Cost	70	100
equals	Markup	14	20

The relationship between markups on cost and markups on selling price is important. For instance, if a product costs $6 and sells for $10, there is a $4 markup. This is a 40% markup based on selling price, but a 66⅔% markup based on cost. The following may be helpful in understanding these relationships and in converting from one base to another:

If selling price = 100%   If cost = 100%

$10 = 100% $\begin{cases} 60\% \rightarrow \text{Cost} = \$6.00 \leftarrow 100\% \\ 40\% \rightarrow \text{Markup} = \$4.00 \leftarrow 66\frac{2}{3}\% \end{cases}$ $\}$ $10 = 166⅔%

The relationships between the two bases are expressed in the following formulas:

$$\% \text{ markup on selling price} = \frac{\% \text{ markup on cost}}{100\% + \% \text{ markup on cost}}$$

$$\% \text{ markup on selling price} = \frac{\% \text{ markup on selling price}}{100\% - \% \text{ markup on selling price}}$$

To illustrate the use of these formulas, let's say that a retailer has a markup of 25% on *cost*. This retailer wants to know what the corresponding figure is, based on selling price. In the first formula we get:

$$\frac{25\%}{100\% + 25\%} = \frac{25\%}{125\%} = 0.2, \text{ or } 20\%$$

A markup of 33⅓% based on *selling price* converts to 50% based on cost, according to the second formula:

$$\frac{33\frac{1}{3}\%}{100\% - 33\frac{1}{3}\%} = \frac{33\frac{1}{3}\%}{66\frac{2}{3}\%} = 0.5, \text{ or } 50\%$$

The markup is closely related to gross margin. Recall that gross margin is equal to net sales minus cost of goods sold. Looking below gross margin on an operating statement, we find that gross margin equals operating expenses plus net profit.

Normally the initial markup in a company, department, or product line must be set a little higher than the overall gross margin desired for the selling unit. The reason? Some reductions will be incurred before all the articles are sold. Because of one factor or another, certain items will not sell at the original price. They will have to be marked down—reduced in price from the original level. Some pilferage, damages, and other shortages also typically occur.

Analytical Ratios

From a study of the operating statement, management can develop several ratios to evaluate the results of its marketing program. In most cases net sales is used as the base (100%). In fact, unless specifically mentioned to the contrary, all ratios reflecting gross margin, net profit, or any operating expense are stated as a percentage of net sales.

Gross Margin Percentage

The ratio of gross margin to net sales is termed simply **gross margin percentage**. In Table A.1 the gross margin percentage for A-Z is $32,000 ÷ $80,000, or 40%.

Net Profit Percentage

The ratio called **net profit percentage** is determined by dividing net profit by net sales. For A-Z this ratio is $4,800 ÷ $80,000, or 6%. This percentage may be calculated either before or after federal income taxes are deducted, but the result should be labeled to show which it is.

Operating Expense Ratio

When total operating expenses are divided by net sales, the result is the **operating expense ratio.** Using the figures in Table A.1, this ratio for A-Z is $27,200 ÷ $80,000, or 34%. In similar fashion we may determine the expense ratio for any given cost. Thus we note in the table that rent expense was 1%, advertising 3%, and sales-force salaries and commissions 13.75%.

Stockturn Rate

Management often measures the efficiency of its marketing operations by means of the **stockturn rate.** This figure represents the number of times an amount equal to the average size of the firm's inventory is *turned over*, or sold, during the period under study. The rate is calculated on either a cost or a selling-price basis. Both the numerator and the denominator of the fraction must be expressed in the same terms, either cost or selling price.

On a *cost* basis, the formula for stockturn rate is:

$$\text{Stockturn rate} = \frac{\text{cost of goods sold}}{\text{average inventory at cost}}$$

The average inventory is determined by adding beginning and ending inventories and dividing the result by 2. In Table A.1 the average inventory is

($18,000 + $20,000) ÷ 2 = $19,000. The stockturn rate then is $48,000 ÷ $19,000 = 2.53. Because inventories usually are abnormally low at the first of the year in anticipation of taking physical inventory, this average may not be representative. Consequently, some companies find their average inventory by adding the book inventories at the beginning of each month and then dividing this sum by 12.

Now let's assume inventory is recorded on a *selling-price* basis, as is done in most large retail organizations. Then the stockturn rate equals net sales divided by average inventory at selling price. Sometimes the stockturn rate is computed by dividing the number of *units* sold by the average inventory expressed in *units*.

Wholesale and retail trade associations in many types of businesses publish figures showing the average stockturn rate for their members. A firm with a low rate of stockturn is not generating sufficient sales volume or is carrying too much inventory. In either case, it is likely to be spending too much on storage and inventory. The company runs a high risk of obsolescence or spoilage.

If the stockturn rate gets too high, the company's average inventory may be too low. Often a firm in this situation is using hand-to-mouth buying (that is, buying small quantities and selling all or most of them before replenishing inventory). In addition to incurring high handling and billing costs, the company is likely to be out of stock on some items.

Markdown Percentage

Sometimes retailers are unable to sell products at the originally stated prices. When this occurs, they often reduce these prices to move the products. A **markdown** is a reduction from the original selling price. The size of an individual markdown is expressed as a percentage of the original sales price. To illustrate, a retailer purchases a hat for $6 and marks it up 40% to sell for $10. The hat does not sell at that price, so it is marked down to $8. Now the seller may advertise a price cut of 20% (which is $2 ÷ $10).

Management frequently finds it helpful to determine the markdown percentage. Then the size and number of markdowns and the reasons for them can be analyzed. Retailers, particularly, analyze markdowns.

Markdown percentage is calculated by dividing total dollar markdowns by total net sales during a given period. Two important points should be noted. First, the markdown percentage is determined in this fashion whether the markdown items were sold or are still in the store. Second, the percentage is calculated with respect to total net sales, and not only in connection with sales of marked-down articles. As an example, assume that a retailer buys 10 sports hats at $6 each and prices them to sell at $10. Five hats are sold at $10. The other five are marked down to $8, and three are sold at the lower price. Total sales are $74 and total markdowns are $10. The retailer has a markdown ratio of $10 ÷ $74, or 13.5%.

Markdowns do not appear on the operating statement because they occur *before* an article is sold. The first item on an operating statement is gross sales. That figure reflects the actual selling price, which may be the selling price after a markdown has been taken.

Return on Investment

A commonly used measure of managerial performance and of the operating success of a company is its rate of return on investment. We use both the balance sheet and the operating statement as sources of information. The formula for calculating **return on investment** (ROI) is as follows:

$$ROI = \frac{net\ profit}{sales} \times \frac{sales}{investment}$$

Two questions may come to mind. What do we mean by "investment"? Why do we need two fractions? It would seem that the sales component in each fraction would cancel out, leaving net profit divided by investment as the meaningful ratio.

To answer the first query, consider a firm whose operating statement shows annual sales of $1,000,000 and a net profit of $50,000. At the end of the year, the balance sheet reports:

Assets	$600,000	Liabilities		$200,000
		Capital stock	$300,000	
		Retained earnings	100,000	400,000
	$600,000			$600,000

The ROI figure is obviously affected by which figure we use. But is the investment $400,000 or $600,000? The answer depends on whether we are talking to the stockholders or to the company executives. Stockholders are more interested in the return on what they have invested—in this case, $400,000. The ROI calculation then is:

$$ROI = \frac{\$50,000}{sales\ \$1,000,000} \times \frac{sales\ \$1,000,000}{investment\ \$400,000} = 12\frac{1}{2}\%$$

Management, on the other hand, is more concerned with total investment, as represented by total assets ($600,000). This is the amount that the executives must manage, regardless of whether the assets

were acquired by stockholders' investment, retained earnings, or loans from outside sources. Within this context the ROI computation becomes:

$$ROI = \frac{net\ profit\ \$50,000}{sales\ \$1,000,000} \times \frac{sales\ \$1,000,000}{investment\ \$600,000} = 8\frac{1}{3}\%$$

Regarding the second question, we use two fractions because we are dealing with two separate elements—the rate of profit on sales and the rate of capital turnover. Management really should determine each rate separately and then multiply the two. The rate of profit on sales is influenced by marketing considerations—notably, sales volume, price, product mix, and advertising effort. Capital turnover is a financial consideration that is not involved directly with costs or profits—only with sales volume and assets managed.

To illustrate, say our company's profits doubled with the same sales volume and investment because of an excellent marketing program this year. In effect, we doubled our profit rate with the same capital turnover:

$$ROI = \frac{net\ profit\ \$100,000}{sales\ \$1,000,000} \times \frac{sales\ \$1,000,000}{investment\ \$600,000} = 16\frac{2}{3}\%$$
$$\underbrace{\hspace{2cm}}_{10\%} \times \underbrace{\hspace{2cm}}_{1\frac{2}{3}} = 16\frac{2}{3}\%$$

As expected, this 16⅔% is twice the ROI calculated above.

Now assume that we earned our original profit of $50,000 but did it with an investment of only $500,000. We cut the size of our average inventory, and we closed some branch offices. By increasing our capital turnover from 1.67 to 2, we raised the ROI from 8⅓% to 10%, even though sales volume and profits were unchanged:

$$ROI = \frac{\$50,000}{\$1,000,000} \times \frac{\$1,000,000}{\$500,000} = 10\%$$
$$\underbrace{\hspace{2cm}}_{5\%} \times \underbrace{\hspace{2cm}}_{2} = 10\%$$

Finally, let's say that we increased our sales volume—we doubled it—but did not increase our profit or investment. The cost-profit squeeze has brought us "profitless prosperity." The following results occur:

$$ROI = \frac{\$50,000}{\$2,000,000} \times \frac{\$2,000,000}{\$600,000} = 8\frac{1}{3}\%$$
$$\underbrace{\hspace{2cm}}_{2\frac{1}{2}\%} \times \underbrace{\hspace{2cm}}_{3\frac{1}{3}} = 8\frac{1}{3}\%$$

The profit rate was cut in half, but this was offset by a doubling of the capital turnover rate. The result was that the ROI was unchanged.

Questions and Problems

1. Construct an operating statement from the following data and compute the gross margin percentage:

Purchases at billed cost	$15,000
Net sales	30,000
Sales returns and allowances	200
Cash discounts given	300
Cash discounts earned	100
Rent	1,500
Salaries	6,000
Opening inventory at cost	10,000
Advertising	600
Other expenses	2,000
Closing inventory at cost	7,500

2. Prepare a retail operating statement from the following information and compute the markdown percentage:

Rent	$ 9,000
Closing inventory at cost	28,000
Sales returns	6,500
Cash discounts allowed	2,000
Salaries	34,000
Markdowns	4,000
Other operating expenses	15,000
Opening inventory at cost	35,000
Gross sales	232,500
Advertising	5,500
Freight in	3,500
Gross margin as percentage of sales	35

3. What percentage markups on cost correspond to the following percentages of markup on selling price?
   a. 20%
   b. 37½%
   c. 50%
   d. 66⅔%

4. What percentage markups on selling price correspond to the following percentages of markup on cost?
   a. 20%
   b. 33⅓%
   c. 50%
   d. 300%

5. A hardware store bought a gross (12 dozen) of hammers, paying $602.40 for the total order. The retailer estimated operating expenses for this product to be 35% of sales, and wanted a net profit of 5% of sales. The retailer expected no markdowns. What retail selling price should be set for each hammer?

6. Competition in a line of sporting goods limits the selling price on a certain item to $25. If the store owner feels a markup of 35% is needed to cover expenses and return a reasonable profit, what is the most the owner can pay for this item?

7. A retailer with annual net sales of $2 million maintains a markup of 66⅔% based on cost. Expenses average 35%. What are the retailer's gross margin and net profit in dollars?

8. A company has a stockturn rate of five times a year, a sales volume of $600,000, and a gross margin of 25%. What is the average inventory at cost?

9. A store has an average inventory of $30,000 at retail and a stockturn rate of five times a year. If the company maintains a markup of 50% based on cost, what are the annual sales volume and cost of goods sold?

10. From the following data, compute the gross margin percentage and the operating expense ratio:

   Stockturn rate = 9

   Average inventory at selling price = $45,000

   Net profit = $20,000

   Cost of goods sold = $350,000

11. A ski shop sold 50 pairs of skis at $90 a pair, after taking a 10% markdown. All the skis were originally purchased at the same price and had been marked up 60% on cost. What was the gross margin on the 50 pairs of skis?

12. A women's clothing store bought 200 suits at $90 each, The suits were marked up 40%. Eighty were sold at that price. The remaining suits were each marked down 20% from the original selling price, and all were sold. Compute the sales volume and markdown percentage.

13. An appliance retailer sold 60 portable cassette players at $40 each after taking markdowns equal to 20% of the actual selling price. Originally all the cassette players had been purchased at the same price and were marked up 50% on cost. What was the gross margin percentage earned in this situation?

14. An appliance manufacturer produced a line of small appliances advertised to sell at $30. The manufacturer planned for wholesalers to receive a 20% markup, and retailers a 33⅓% markup. Total manufacturing costs were $12 per unit. What did retailers pay for the product? What were the manufacturer's selling price and percentage markup?

15. A housewares manufacturer produces an article at a full cost of $4.80. It is sold through a manufacturers' agent directly to large retailers. The agent receives a 20% commission on sales, the retailers earn a margin of 30%, and

the manufacturer plans a net profit of 10% on the selling price. What is the retail price of this article?

16. A building materials manufacturer sold a quantity of a product to a wholesaler for $350, and the wholesaler in turn sold it to a lumberyard. The wholesaler's normal markup was 15%, and the retailer usually priced the item to include a 30% markup. What is the selling price to consumers?

17. From the following data, calculate the return on investment, based on a definition of *investment* that is useful for evaluating managerial performance:

Net sales	$800,000
Gross margin	280,000
Total assets	200,000
Cost of goods sold	520,000
Liabilities	40,000
Average inventory	75,000
Retained earnings	60,000
Operating expenses	240,000
Markup	35%

Chapter

13

Pricing Strategies

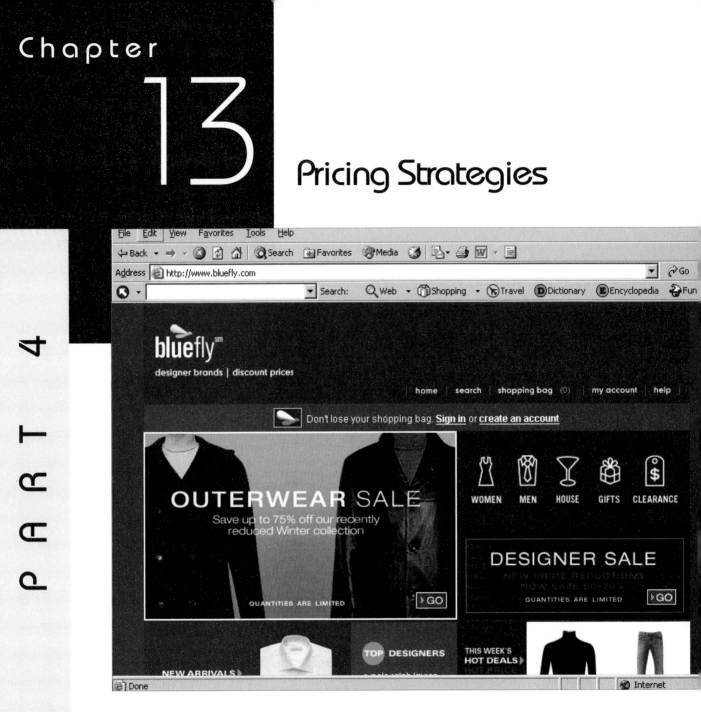

"In addition to low prices, Bluefly's average customer values convenience, designer brands, and top-quality customer service."

Can **Bluefly** Soar High with Low Prices Online?

Like many—perhaps most—online enterprises, Bluefly Inc. has struggled to satisfy its shareholders. However, as an important step in that direction, the online clothing retailer may have come up with a way of pleasing its target market of price- and fashion-conscious shoppers. If so, the firm may be able to please both consumers and investors over the long run.

Bluefly, founded in 1998, promotes itself as an online outlet store that specializes in end-of-season, excess, and closeout products. The "e-tailer's" offerings consist of well-known brands of clothing with prices that are substantially below normal retail levels. Although thin by ordinary standards, Bluefly's gross margin of about 28% actually compares favorably to those of many other e-tailers. As in a bricks-and-mortar clothing outlet, the online merchant has an ever-changing inventory. Despite a sometimes incomplete range of sizes, Bluefly has managed to attract some loyal customers.

Surveys and focus groups revealed that although both genders visit the Bluefly.com website, the core shopper is a thirty-something woman with higher-than-average income and a keen interest in fashion. In addition to low prices, Bluefly's average customer values convenience, designer brands, and top-quality customer service.

To meet customers' needs and expectations, Bluefly has revamped its website several times. New features were added to allow shoppers to check out "recent arrivals" easily; to build a personalized online catalog from their preferred styles, brands, and sizes; to focus on a particular category of clothing; to locate items from a specific designer; or to go directly to items with clearance prices. A user survey found that about two-thirds of the visitors to Bluefly.com check in once a month, and fully 25% log on every day to scan the latest finds from Prada, Gucci, Polo, Fendi, or Calvin Klein, all carrying prices below what would be found in stores.

Bluefly's CEO says that its online activities have been aided by successful catalog operations such as Lands' End and Eddie Bauer. That is, these firms have accustomed consumers to buying clothes without the benefit of touching the fabric or trying the garment on, paving the way for the next step, choosing a suit or top with the click of a mouse. To allay any consumer concerns about buying online, the New York–based Bluefly.com allows returns within 90 days of purchase. It even includes a preaddressed shipping label with every order for customer convenience in returning an item, if necessary.

There's no question that low prices represent Bluefly.com's primary drawing card. The firm stresses that its combination of merchandise and prices represents exceptional values. For example, one shopper was delighted to pay $396 for a black leather Fendi bag that carried a suggested retail price of $900. According to one consumer, "Price point was the No. 1 reason" for becoming a loyal Bluefly customer.

The CEO of Bluefly summarized the firm's strategy as follows, "Bluefly sells designer fashions at outlet store prices, and we are attempting to become the first retailer to offer the best of the shopping experience at a department

www.bluefly.com

store combined with the best of the catalog shopping experience combined with the best of the off-price shopping experience." Considering the wide-ranging, intense competition in clothing retailing, "off-price"—that is, deeply discounted—may be the most important variable in Bluefly's formula.[1]

Do you think that Bluefly's emphasis on low prices is a viable long-term strategy?

Fundamentally, in managing the price element of a company's marketing mix, management of a firm—whether it operates in cyberspace like Bluefly or in physical space—first must decide on its pricing goal and then set the base price for a good or service. The final task, as shown in Figure 13.1, is to design pricing strategies that are compatible with the rest of the marketing mix. Many strategic questions related to price must be answered—not just by Bluefly as in the preceding case, but by all firms. These questions include: Will our company compete primarily on the basis of price, or on other factors? What kind of discount schedule should be adopted? Will we occasionally absorb shipping costs? Are our approaches to pricing ethical and legal?

In this chapter we primarily discuss ways in which a firm adjusts a product's base price to coincide with its overall marketing program. After studying this chapter, you

Chapter Goals

should be able to explain:

- Price competition, notably value pricing, and nonprice competition.
- Pricing strategies for entering a market, especially market skimming and market penetration.
- Price discounts and allowances.
- Geographic pricing strategies.
- Special pricing situations, notably one-price and flexible-price approaches, leader pricing, everyday low pricing and high-low pricing, and reactive and proactive changes.
- Legal issues associated with pricing.

FIGURE 13.1

The Price-Determination Process.

The first two steps were discussed in Chapter 12. The third step is the subject of this chapter.

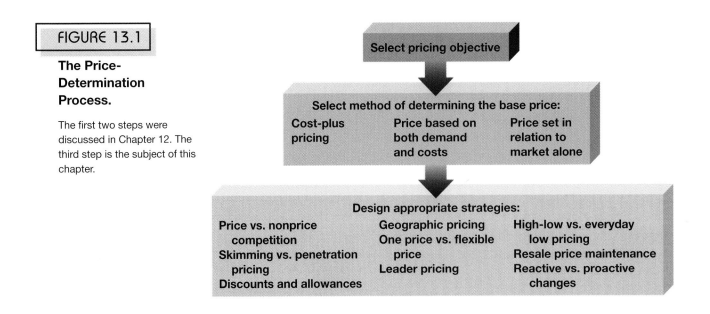

We will use the term *strategy* frequently in this chapter, so let's explain its meaning. A **strategy** is a broad plan of action by which an organization intends to reach a particular goal. To illustrate, a company may adopt a strategy of offering quantity discounts to achieve the goal of a 10% increase in sales this year.

Price versus Nonprice Competition

In developing a marketing program, management has to decide whether to compete primarily on the basis of price or the nonprice elements of the marketing mix. This choice obviously affects other parts of the firm's marketing program.

Price Competition

A company engages in **price competition** by regularly offering products priced as low as possible and typically accompanied by few if any services. Consumer electronics, computers, and air travel are among the myriad industries characterized by rigorous price competition at the present time. Start-up airlines have intensified price competiton in both the U.S. and Europe recently.[2]

In the retail sector, large discount chains, including Wal-Mart and Kmart, compete largely on the basis of price. Smaller chains, such as Dollar General and Family Dollar Stores, offer so-called deep discounts and thus depend even more on low prices. Deep discounters have been expanding rapidly by "enticing consumers with a wide range of food and household products in clean, well-organized and heavily stocked stores."[3]

Price competition has been spreading to other parts of the world as well. For example, price reductions are becoming more common throughout Europe. This switch in competitive strategy was due to the elimination of various trade barriers and, for a while, the continent's economic woes. Some online retailers, both in the U.S. and abroad, have used price competition in their efforts to lure buyers and establish a foothold in the market.

 www.dollargeneral.com

Dollar Tree Stores, Inc., which has over 2,000 outlets under the Dollar Tree and other banners, sells all of its merchandise for $1 per item. To make a profit, "deep discounters" such as Dollar Tree must control both operating expenses and cost of goods sold. One approach is finding suppliers willing to sell closeout merchandise and excess inventory at very low costs.

 www.dollartree.com

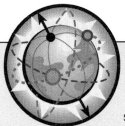

A GLOBAL PERSPECTIVE

Does the Wal-Mart way work around the globe?

In becoming the world's largest retailer, Wal-Mart adhered to a basic formula—selling consumables (such as health and beauty aids), soft goods (such as apparel), and hard goods (such as gas-powered outdoor grills) at sharply discounted prices. The formula, emphasizing price competition, has been phenomenally effective in the U.S. However, the company is a novice internationally; its initial foray into a foreign country did not occur until 1991. Wal-Mart established a partnership with Cifra SA, a discount retail chain in Mexico in that year. The first joint effort, a Sam's Club, was hugely successful from the outset.

Despite its first triumph in Mexico, Wal-Mart has found it difficult to attain success, much less blockbuster performance, outside the U.S. In every new country, the American chain has encountered cultural differences and/or unfamiliar regulations; the company has also made some mistakes. In China, for example, Wal-Mart tried to sell items (such as extension ladders) that wouldn't fit into the residents' tiny apartments. In Germany, the firm underestimated the resolve of trade unions and more than a dozen well-entrenched competitors. In fact, the arrival of Wal-Mart precipitated a price war (*preiskreig* in German).

Wal-Mart's top management is "learning by doing" in the international arena. For example, it has determined that giving local managers ample authority with regards to merchandising decisions is preferable to centralized buying. The American retailer also outlasted a regulation in Germany prohibiting prices that are "too low."

Many consumers in the countries that Wal-Mart enters are pleased about the broad collections of low-price merchandise in the newcomer's stores. But some consumers, executives, and government officials are not enthralled with the invader from America. For example, a common refrain in Europe has been that Wal-Mart's arrival will force small retailers out of business as a result of stepped-up price competition.

Wal-Mart now has over 1,250 stores in eight foreign countries, ranging from Argentina to China, and the U.S. commonwealth of Puerto Rico. It is the largest retailer in both Canada and Mexico. The retail behemoth is opening more than 100 stores outside the U.S. annually. In 2002, it put its toe into a new market by purchasing part of a supermarket chain in Japan. By 2005, Wal-Mart's sales outside the U.S. are likely to be about $50 billion—to go along with perhaps $250 billion in sales in its home market!

Of course, Wal-Mart's ultimate success outside the U.S. is far from assured. In fact, the firm even closed two unsuccessful stores (out of about 100) in Germany. However, given its huge size and winning track record, the company founded by Sam Walton probably has a better chance for worldwide success, if not domination, than any other foreign invader.

 www.walmart.com

Sources: Tony Czuczka, "Wal-Mart to Close First Two Stores in Germany since Entering European Continent," *Associated Press Newswires*, July 10, 2002; David Luchnow, "How NAFTA Helped Wal-Mart Reshape the Mexican Market," *The Wall Street Journal*, Aug. 31, 2001, pp. A1, A2; Barbara Thau, "Wal-Mart Takes On the World," *HFN*, Sept. 3, 2001, p. 8; Yumiko Ono and Ann Zimmerman, "Wal-Mart Enters Japan with Seiyu Stake," *The Wall Street Journal*, Mar. 15, 2002, p. B5; and Ernest Beck and Emily Nelson, "As Wal-Mart Invades Europe, Rivals Rush to Match Its Formula," *The Wall Street Journal*, Oct. 6, 1999, pp. A1, A6.

In Chapter 12 we discussed how more and more consumers are seeking better value in their purchases. In response, many companies are using what's called **value pricing.** This form of price competition aims to improve a product's value—that is, the ratio of its benefits to its price and related costs. To implement value pricing, a firm typically (1) offers products with lower prices but the same, or perhaps added, benefits and, at the same time, (2) seeks ways to slash expenses so profits do not suffer.

Value also can be improved by introducing a much better product with a somewhat higher price than competing entries. Gillette's Mach3Turbo razor, Intel's Itanium 2 microprocessor chip, and Goodyear's Eagle F1 tire all illustrate this approach.[4] Despite these notable examples, this approach is not that common today.

During the 1990s, value pricing became a pivotal marketing trend in diverse fields, ranging from personal computers to fast food. Consider an example. Taco Bell trimmed prices on some of its mainstays such as tacos and burritos and tried, but then dropped, cheaper snack-size items. Equally important, the chain attacked its cost structure, particularly labor costs. Its employees "assemble" tacos and other items from meats and vegetables cooked, sliced, and otherwise prepared by outside suppliers and delivered to the outlets.[5]

Value pricing certainly emphasizes the price element of the marketing mix. But that's not enough. A top executive of a computer company stated it in this way: "If all you have to offer is price, I don't think it's a successful long-term strategy."[6] Consequently, value pricing depends on creatively combining all elements of the marketing mix in order to maximize benefits in relation to price and other costs.

With a value-pricing strategy, products often have to be redesigned to expand benefits and/or shave costs. Relationships with customers have to be strengthened to generate repeat sales. Steps toward this end include frequent-buyer programs, toll-free customer service lines, and hassle-free warranties. And advertising has to be revamped to provide more facts and fewer emotional appeals. Finally, firms that desire to stress value need to negotiate aggressively with suppliers. What was said about one deep discounter applies rather well to all firms relying on value pricing, ". . . to sell merchandise at Family Dollar's low price points, you had to first buy it at the right price."[7]

Nonprice Competition

In **nonprice competition,** sellers maintain stable prices and attempt to improve their market positions by emphasizing other aspects of their marketing programs. Of course, competitors' prices still must be taken into consideration, and price changes will occur over time. Nevertheless, in nonprice competition, the emphasis is on something other than price.

Using terms familiar in economic theory, we can differentiate price and nonprice competition. In *price* competition, sellers attempt to move up or down their individual demand curves by changing prices. In *nonprice* competition, sellers attempt to shift their demand curves to the right by means of product differentiation, promotional activities, or some other technique. In Figure 13.2, the demand curve faced by the producer of a given model of skis is DD. At a price of $350, the producer can sell 35,000 pairs a year in the European market. On the basis of price competition alone, sales can be increased to 55,000 if the producer is willing to reduce the price to $330. The demand curve is still DD. However, the producer is interested in boosting sales without any decrease in selling price. Consequently, the firm embarks on a fresh promotional program—a form of nonprice competition. Suppose that enough new customers

FIGURE 13.2

Shift in Demand Curve for Skis.

Nonprice competition can shift the demand curve for a product. A company selling skis in the European market used a promotional program to sell more skis at the same price, thereby shifting DD to D'D'. Volume increased from 35,000 to 55,000 units at $350 (point X to point Y). Besides advertising, what other devices might this firm use to shift its demand curve?

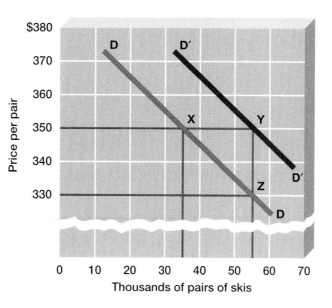

are persuaded to buy at the original $350 price that unit sales increase to 55,000 pairs a year. In effect, the firm's entire demand curve has been shifted to position D'D'.

With price competition, many consumers "learn" to buy a brand only as long as it has the lowest price. There is little customer loyalty when price is the only feature differentiating products from each other. As one consultant advised retailers, "Long-term price competition can take a devastating toll on profits."[8] With nonprice competition, however, a seller retains some advantage through its differentiation on other features (such as stylish design), even when another company decides to undersell it. Thus many firms stress nonprice competition, and others would like to rely on it rather than price competition. Wanting to be masters of their own destinies, companies believe they have more control in nonprice competition.

The best approach in nonprice competition is to build strong—if possible, unassailable—brand equity for the firm's products. Two methods of accomplishing this are to develop distinctive, hopefully unique, products and to create a novel, appealing promotional program. In addition, some firms emphasize the variety and quality of the supplementary services they offer to customers.[9]

Market-Entry Strategies

In preparing to enter the market with a new product, management must decide whether to adopt a skimming or a penetration pricing strategy.

Market-Skimming Pricing

Setting a relatively high initial price for a new product is referred to as **market-skimming pricing.** Ordinarily the price is high in relation to the target market's range of expected prices. That is, the price is set at the highest possible level that the most interested consumers will pay for the new product. For example, L'Oréal started with a relatively high price for Niosôme, a wrinkle-fighting facial cream.[10]

With a suggested retail price between $1,995 and $2,495, did the producer of the Voloci motorbike use market-skimming or market-penetration pricing when it introduced this product? The Voloci has many desirable features, including a top speed of 30-miles-per-hour, disc brakes, a 25-mile range on a battery charge, and a recharging time of only 3 hours. Is this set of features sufficient to justify a market-skimming strategy?

www.voloci.com

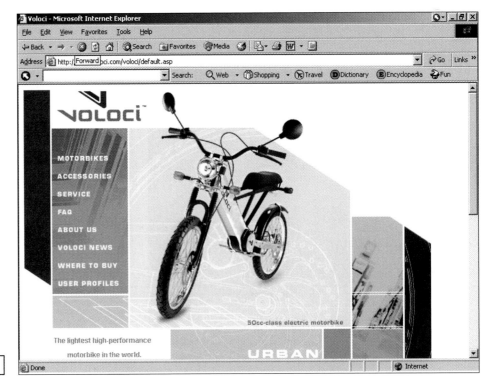

Market-skimming pricing has several purposes. Because it should provide healthy profit margins, it is intended primarily to recover research and development costs as quickly as possible. Lofty prices can be used to connote high quality. Market-skimming pricing is likely to curtail demand to levels that do not outstrip the firm's production capacities. Finally, it provides the firm with flexibility, because it is much easier to lower an initial price that meets with consumer resistance than it is to raise an initial price that has proven to be too low to cover costs. Even though the price may be lowered gradually, the high initial prices associated with market skimming are subject to criticism from consumers and government officials.

Market-skimming pricing is suitable under the following conditions:

- The new product has distinctive features strongly desired by consumers.
- Demand is fairly inelastic, most likely the case in the early stages of a product's life cycle. Under this condition, lower prices are unlikely to produce greater total revenues.
- The new product is protected from competition through one or more entry barriers such as a patent.

www.bellagio.com

Market skimming is used for various products, notably in pricing new technological goods such as high-definition TVs. Some new hotels and resorts, such as the Bellagio in Las Vegas, use market-skimming pricing. And in a much different industry, the original price of the LASIK vision-correction procedure was more than $2,000 per eye. As a result of growing competition, LASIK prices started dropping, however.[11]

Market-Penetration Pricing

www.pandg.com

In **market-penetration pricing,** a relatively low initial price is established for a new product. The price is low in relation to the target market's range of expected prices. The primary aim of this strategy is to penetrate the mass market immediately and, in so doing, generate substantial sales volume and a large market share. At the same time, starting with a low price is intended to discourage other firms from introducing competing products. When it launched the SpinBrush, a battery-powered toothbrush, Procter & Gamble chose penetration pricing for these reasons. However, P&G's entry was so successful that despite the low price, directly competing products such as Gillette's Oral–B CrossAction Power have been introduced.[12]

Market-penetration pricing makes the most sense under the following conditions:

- A large market exists for the product.
- Demand is highly elastic, typically in the later stages of the life cycle for a product category.
- Substantial reductions in unit costs can be achieved through large-scale operations. In other words, economies of scale are possible.
- Fierce competition already exists in the market for this product or can be expected soon after the product is introduced.

Some software companies have used the ultimate in penetration pricing—giving away their products for a limited time or up to a stipulated quantity. Computer Associates, for example, gave away the first million copies of its Simply Money accounting program! What motivates such a giveaway? Some firms want to create favorable word of mouth to motivate later buyers and to stimulate purchases of upgrades and complementary software by the recipients of the giveaways. Others intend to generate revenue from such sources as training, technical support, and even advertising at their websites for various firms.[13]

Referring to penetration pricing, two consultants stated, "Extended use of this offensive tactic inevitably leads to kamikaze pricing and calamity in markets as competitors respond, cost savings disappear, and customers learn to ignore value."[14] Thus, to avoid triggering intense price competition that erodes profits, firms typically need to use penetration pricing selectively.

In an extreme case, penetration pricing might violate federal antitrust laws. If a company gives away its products or charges a price that is below its cost and plans to raise prices later on in order to recoup earlier losses, such **predatory pricing** is likely to be illegal. Microsoft was charged with this practice when it gave away its Web browser, Internet Explorer, allegedly to obtain a dominant position in the market. Critics charge that predatory pricing can drive firms out of a market, thereby reducing competition, in which case the surviving firm(s) can raise prices substantially. Other observers say that low prices, whatever the seller's purpose, benefit buyers. In any event, following an early-1990s Supreme Court decision that rejected a charge of harmfully low prices, it has become very difficult to prove predatory pricing in a court case.[15]

Discounts and Allowances

Discounts and allowances result in a deduction from the base (or list) price. The deduction may be in the form of a reduced price or some other concession, such as free merchandise or advertising allowances. Discounts and allowances are common in business dealings.

Quantity Discounts

Quantity discounts are deductions from a seller's list price intended to encourage customers to buy in larger amounts or to buy most of what they need from the seller offering the deduction. Discounts are based on the size of the purchase, either in dollars or in units.

A **noncumulative discount** is based on the size of an *individual order* of one or more products. A retailer may sell golf balls at $2 each or at three for $5. A manufacturer or wholesaler may set up a quantity discount schedule such as the following, used by a manufacturer of industrial adhesives:

Boxes Purchased in a Single Order	% Discount from List Price
1–5	None
6–12	2.0
13–25	3.5
Over 25	5.0

Noncumulative quantity discounts are intended to encourage large orders. Many expenses, such as billing, order filling, and salaries of sales people, are about the same whether the seller receives an order totaling $10 or one totaling $500. Consequently, selling expense as a percentage of sales decreases as orders grow in size. With a noncumulative discount, a seller shares such savings with a purchaser of large quantities.

A **cumulative discount** is based on the total volume purchased *over a specified period*. This type of discount is advantageous to a seller because it ties customers closely to that firm. The more total business a buyer gives a seller, the greater the discount.

Cumulative discounts can be found in many industries. Airline frequent-flyer and hotel frequent-guest programs are one example. In a much different field, Monsanto Co. offered a form of cumulative discount in order to gain more purchases of Posilac, a drug that stimulates milk production in cows. To qualify for the discount,

POSILAC HELPS MAKE COWS MORE PROFITABLE REGARDLESS OF AGE, COLOR, OR BREED.

farmers had to agree to purchase the drug for at least six months.[16] Cumulative discounts also are common in selling perishable products. These discounts encourage customers to buy fresh supplies frequently so that the buyer's merchandise will not become stale.

Quantity discounts can help a producer achieve real economies in production as well as in selling. On the one hand, large orders (motivated by a noncumulative discount) can result in lower production and transportation costs. On the other hand, frequent orders from a single customer motivated by a cumulative discount can enable the producer to make much more effective use of production capacity. Thus the producer might benefit even though individual orders are small and do not generate savings in marketing costs.

Trade Discounts

Trade discounts, sometimes called *functional discounts,* are reductions from the list price offered to buyers in payment for marketing functions the buyers will perform. Storing, promoting, and selling the product are examples of these functions. A manufacturer may quote a retail price of $400 with trade discounts of 40% and 10%. The retailer pays the wholesaler $240 ($400 less 40%), and the wholesaler pays the manufacturer $216 ($240 less 10%). The wholesaler is given the 40% and 10% discounts. The wholesaler is expected to keep the 10% to cover costs of wholesaling functions and pass on the 40% discount to retailers. Sometimes, however, wholesalers keep more than the 10%—and it's not illegal for them to do so.

Note that the 40% and 10% discounts do not constitute a total discount of 50% off list price. They are not additive because the second discount (in this case, 10%) is computed on the amount remaining after the preceding discount (40%) has been deducted.

Cash Discounts

A **cash discount** is a deduction granted to buyers for paying their bills within a specified time. The discount is computed on the net amount due after first deducting trade

FIGURE 13.3

Parts of a Cash Discount.

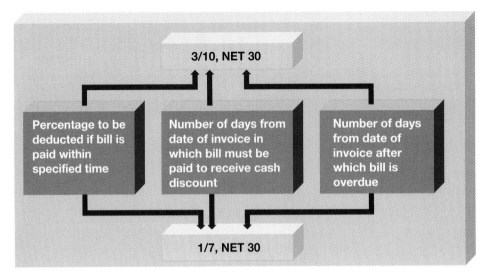

and quantity discounts from the base price. Every cash discount includes three elements, as indicated in Figure 13.3:

- The percentage discount.
- The period during which the discount may be taken.
- The time when the bill becomes overdue.

Let's say a buyer owes $360 after other discounts have been granted and is offered terms of 2/10, n/30 on an invoice dated October 8. This means the buyer may deduct a discount of 2% ($7.20) if the bill is paid within 10 days of the invoice date—by October 18. Otherwise the entire (net) bill of $360 must be paid in 30 days—by November 7.

There are almost as many different cash discounts as there are industries. For example, in women's fashions, large discounts and short payment periods have been common; thus a cash discount of 5/5, n/15 would not be surprising. Such differences persist not so much for business reasons but because of tradition in various industries.

Most buyers are eager to pay bills in time to earn cash discounts. The discount in a 2/10, n/30 situation may not seem like very much. But this 2% is earned just for paying 20 days in advance of the date the entire bill is due. If buyers fail to take the cash discount in a 2/10, n/30 situation, they are, in effect, borrowing money at a 36% annual rate of interest. Here's how we arrived at that rate: In a 360-day business year, there are 18 periods of 20 days. Paying 2% for one of these 20-day periods is equivalent to paying 36% for an entire year.

Other Discounts and Allowances

To stimulate sales, some sellers offer rebates to prospective customers. A **rebate** is a discount on a product that a customer obtains by submitting a form or certificate provided by the seller. There are two kinds of rebates:

- A *coupon*, which is a small printed certificate that the customer presents when purchasing the product in order to obtain a discount equal to the value shown on the certificate.
- A *mail-in rebate*, in which the customer fills out a short form, encloses proof of the purchase, and sends the paperwork to a specified address. If all goes well, a rebate check arrives in the mail a short while later. Marketers favor mail-ins not only because they stimulate sales and can be offered for quite short periods, but

also because few consumers, seldom more than 10%, actually submit them for redemption.[17]

Marketers' use of mail-in rebates has been growing whereas the distribution of *printed* coupons has been stagnant or even on the decline. But a relatively new technique, called e-coupons or virtual coupons, is emerging. A company places an e-coupon on its website or sends a coupon to a consumer via e-mail. A shopper can redeem this kind of coupon in cyberspace and/or at a physical store that sells the firm's products, depending on the conditions attached to the offer.[18]

The intent of **price customization** is to establish various prices on the basis of how much value is attached to a product by different people. It's important, though, to build a "fence" to keep customers who value a product highly from taking advantage of low prices. Quantity discounts are one fencing mechanism that can be used in conjunction with price customization. Others include multiperson pricing (such as "companion fares" offered by airlines) and a less expensive alternative (which involves developing a lower-price line of products).[19]

A manufacturer of goods such as air conditioners or toys purchased on a seasonal basis may consider granting a **seasonal discount.** This discount of, say, 5%, 10%, or 20% is given to a customer who places an order during the slack season. Off-season orders enable manufacturers to better use their production facilities and/or avoid inventory-carrying costs. Many services firms also offer seasonal discounts. For example, Club Med and other vacation resorts lower their prices during the off-season.

A **promotional allowance** is a price reduction granted by a seller as payment for promotional services performed by buyers. To illustrate, a producer of builders' hardware gives a certain quantity of free goods to dealers who prominently display its line. Or a clothing manufacturer pays one-half the cost of a retailer's ad featuring its product.

www.clubmed.com

The Robinson-Patman Act and Price Discrimination

The discounts and allowances discussed here may result in various prices for different customers. Such price differentials represent **price discrimination.** In certain situations price discrimination is prohibited by the Robinson-Patman Act, one of the most important federal laws affecting a company's marketing program. (Any federal law regulating pricing is applicable only in cases where there is *interstate* trade. However, many states have pricing statutes that cover sales *within* the state—that is, *intrastate* trade.)

Main Provisions of the Act
The **Robinson-Patman Act,** passed in 1936, was intended to curb price discrimination by large retailers. It was written in very general terms, so over the years it has also become applicable to manufacturers.

Not all price differentials are illegal under the act. Price discrimination is unlawful only when the effect *may be* to substantially injure competition. In other words, a price difference is allowed if it does not substantially reduce competition. This law does *not* apply to sales to ultimate household consumers, because presumably they are not in business competition with each other.

Defenses and Exceptions
Price discrimination is legal in response to changing conditions that affect the marketability of products. For instance, differentials are allowed in cases of seasonal obsolescence (for products such as Christmas decorations), physical deterioration (fruits and vegetables), and going-out-of-business sales. Competitive considerations also are relevant. For example, about a decade ago, retailers selling prescription drugs accused pharmaceutical companies of illegal discrimination. The retailers claimed that the manufacturers had two tiers of prices, with hospitals and mail-order pharmacies being charged only a small fraction of

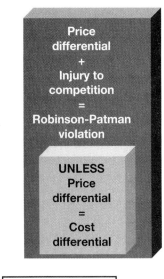

FIGURE 13.4

The Robinson-Patman Act.

what retail pharmacies must pay for identical products. Each manufacturer said the differentials are necessary—and legal—because hospitals and HMOs choose other manufacturers' products if they are not given significant price concessions. A judge dismissed the case, however, ruling that the retail pharmacies had not documented the existence of a pricing conspiracy.[20] All factors considered, typically a price differential is allowable if it is needed to meet competitors' prices.

Price differentials also are permissible if they do not exceed differences in the cost of manufacture, sale, or delivery of the product (see Figure 13.4). Cost differences may result from (1) variations in the quantity sold or (2) various methods of sale or delivery of the product. Thus, if selling a large quantity of a product directly to Safeway is more efficient than selling a small quantity through wholesalers to a neighborhood grocery store, the producer can legally offer Safeway a lower price per unit of the product. Such differentials are allowable even though there is a reasonable probability of injuring competition.

Under the Robinson-Patman Act, a buyer is as guilty as the seller if the buyer *knowingly* induces or receives an unlawful price differential. This provision is intended to restrain large buyers from demanding discriminatory prices. The American Booksellers Association (ABA) filed a lawsuit alleging that the two largest retail book chains place "pressure on publishers to make secret and illegal deals that put independent bookstores at a serious competitive disadvantage." According to the trade association, Barnes & Noble and Borders obtain discounts from publishers that violate federal laws. From a practical standpoint, however, it is difficult to prove that a buyer coerced or knowingly received an unlawful price differential from a supplier. Thus, in the book-retailing case, it was not surprising that the ABA opted for an out-of-court settlement, even though the $4.7 million payment by the two large chains was modest, at best.[21]

Quantity discounts result in different prices to various customers. Consequently, these discriminatory prices could be illegal under the Robinson-Patman Act if it is shown that they injure competition. To justify price differentials stemming from its quantity discount schedule, a firm must rely on the cost defense provided in the act. In a nutshell, quantity discounts are legal if the resulting price differentials do not exceed differences in the cost of manufacturing, selling, or delivering the product.

Trade discounts are not addressed in the Robinson-Patman Act or in its predecessor, the Clayton Act. However, court cases many years ago established that separate discounts could be given to distinct classes of buyers. That is, one discount could be granted to wholesalers and another to retailers, as long as all buyers within a given group were offered the same discount.

Various types of promotional allowances are lawful *only* if they are offered to all competing customers on proportionally equal terms. For example, assume that a large chain receives promotional support valued at $15,000 when it purchases $750,000 of goods from a manufacturer. Another retailer should not expect the same dollar amount of support on a much smaller (say, $40,000) order. However, the second retailer is entitled to the same percentage amount of support as given to the large chain, 2% in this case. The $40,000 order should yield promotional services and materials valued at $800. Despite the straightforward math, disputes frequently arise over what is meant by "proportionally equal terms."

Geographic Pricing Strategies

In pricing, a seller must consider the costs of shipping goods to the buyer. These costs grow in importance as freight becomes a larger part of total variable costs. Pricing policies may be established whereby the buyer pays the entire freight expense, the seller bears the whole burden, or the seller and buyer share this expense. The strategy chosen can influence the geographic limits of a firm's market, locations of its production facilities, sources of its raw materials, and its competitive strength in various geographic markets.

Point-of-Production Pricing

In a widely used geographic pricing strategy, the seller quotes the selling price at the point of production, and the buyer selects the mode of transportation and pays all freight costs. **FOB factory pricing** (or *FOB mill pricing*) is the only geographic pricing strategy in which the seller does not pay any of the freight costs. The seller pays only for loading the shipment aboard the freight carrier—hence the term *FOB*, which stands for *free on board*.

Under FOB factory pricing, the seller nets the same amount on each sale of similar quantities. The delivered price to the buyer varies according to the freight costs. In purchasing goods from a manufacturer in Columbia, Missouri, differences in freight costs surely will provide a customer in St. Louis with a lower delivered price than a customer in Pittsburgh.

The Federal Trade Commission has considered FOB factory pricing to be legal. However, this pricing strategy has serious marketing and financial implications. In effect, FOB factory pricing makes a given seller more attractive to nearby customers and much less attractive to distant customers. The reason? Because the customers bear the freight costs, they prefer to deal with suppliers located close to them, rather than far away. Thus the firm in Pittsburgh mentioned above probably would seek suppliers in Pennsylvania or nearby Ohio and West Virginia as alternatives to the supplier in Missouri. Of course, this assumes that alternative suppliers are comparable with respect to other important factors, such as product quality.

Uniform Delivered Pricing

Under **uniform delivered pricing**, the same delivered price is quoted to all buyers regardless of their locations. This strategy is sometimes referred to as *postage stamp pricing* because of its similarity to the pricing of first-class mail service. Of course, just like first-class mail, freight costs go up as weight of the shipment increases. Using our same example, if the Missouri-based manufacturer adopted uniform delivered pricing, the delivered cost of goods would be the same for the businesses in Pittsburgh, St. Louis, and elsewhere across the country, assuming of course that the shipments weigh the same amounts.

Uniform delivered pricing is typically used where freight costs are a small part of the seller's total costs. This strategy is also used by many retailers who believe "free" delivery is an additional service that strengthens their market position.

With a uniform delivered price, the net revenue to the seller varies depending on the freight cost involved in each sale. In effect, buyers located near the seller's factory pay some of the costs of shipping to more distant locations. Critics of FOB factory pricing usually favor a uniform delivered price. They maintain that the freight cost should not be charged separately to customers any more than other single marketing or production expenses.

Zone-Delivered Pricing

Zone-delivered pricing divides a seller's market into a limited number of broad geographic zones and then sets a uniform delivered price for each zone. The freight charge built into the delivered price is an average of the charges to all points within a zone. An eastern firm that quotes a price and then says "Slightly higher west of the Rockies" is using a two-zone pricing system. Zone-delivered pricing is similar to the *distance-based pricing* used by package-delivery services, notably UPS and Federal Express. In switching from flat-rate to distance-based prices, FedEx divided the U.S. into eight zones.[22] Of course, even with zone-delivered pricing, freight costs vary on the basis of the weight of the shipment.

For many years, FedEx charged the same flat rate for shippping a particular weight of package in the mainland U.S.—irrespective of whether the destination was nearby or far away. Now FedEx uses geographic zones as the basis for charging different rates. This approach, in contrast to uniform delivered pricing, relates the shipping fee to the anticipated expense of moving the package to the intended destination.

www.fedex.com/us/ rates/zone

When using this strategy, a seller must be careful to avoid charges of illegal price discrimination. Under a strict interpretation, the zones must be drawn so that all buyers who compete for a particular market are in the same zone. This condition is almost impossible to meet in densely populated areas, such as the East, which means that zone-delivered pricing is not practical everywhere.

Freight-Absorption Pricing

To penetrate distant markets, a seller may be willing to pay part of the freight cost. Thus, under **freight-absorption pricing,** a manufacturer quotes to the customer a delivered price equal to its factory price *plus* the shipping costs that would be charged by a competitive seller located near that customer. In our continuing example, let's assume the manufacturing firm in Missouri agreed to freight absorption. Then the customer in Pittsburgh would not be charged full freight costs, but only the costs that would be charged by a competing supplier located close to the customer—say, in Youngstown, Ohio.

A freight-absorption strategy is adopted to offset competitive disadvantages of FOB factory pricing. With an FOB factory price, a firm is at a price disadvantage when trying to sell to buyers located in markets near competitors' plants. The reason? Because buyers pay the shipping costs under FOB factory pricing, these charges will grow as the distance between supplier and customer increases. A nearby supplier has an advantage over more distant suppliers, at least with respect to shipping costs. Freight absorption erases any price advantages that are due to differences in shipping costs.

A seller can continue to expand its geographic market as long as its net revenue after freight absorption is larger than its marginal cost for units sold. If a manufacturer's cost of producing, selling, and shipping one more unit—that is, its marginal cost—is $75, then freight-absorption pricing makes sense so long as the revenue received by the manufacturer exceeds $75. The firm's revenue would consist of the selling price of the product plus any freight costs charged to the buyer.

Freight absorption is particularly useful to a firm that has (1) excess capacity, (2) high fixed costs, and (3) low variable costs per unit of product. In these cases, management must constantly seek ways to cover fixed costs. Freight-absorption pricing is one means of generating additional sales volume to do that.

Freight absorption is legal if it is used independently and not in collusion with other firms. Also, it must be used only to meet competition. In fact, if it is practiced properly, freight absorption can strengthen competition by breaking down geographic monopolies.

Special Pricing Strategies and Situations

To be effective in setting initial prices, evaluating existing prices, and adjusting them as necessary, a firm needs to be aware of a variety of special pricing strategies and situations.[23]

One-Price and Flexible-Price Strategies

Early in its pricing deliberations, management should decide whether to adopt a one-price or a flexible-price strategy. Under a **one-price strategy**, a seller charges the *same* price to all similar customers who buy identical quantities of a product. Under a **flexible-price strategy**, also called a *variable-price strategy*, similar customers may pay *different* prices when buying identical quantities of a product. Although you may think otherwise, this practice is normally legal.

In the U.S., most organizations follow a one-price policy. This strategy shifts the focus from price to other factors, such as product quality. A one-price strategy can build customer confidence in a seller—whether at the manufacturing, wholesaling, or retailing level—because the buyer does not have to worry that other customers paid lower prices. Thus, with a one-price strategy, weak bargainers need not think they are at a disadvantage.

Several airlines, Continental and US Airways for example, have used aggressive flexible pricing to enter new markets and to increase their market shares on existing routes. (However, this strategy hasn't produced consistent profits for either enterprise.) Their new business comes from two sources—passengers now flying on other airlines and passengers who would not fly at higher prices. Especially in the second group, demand for air travel is highly elastic. The trick is to keep apart the segment of pleasure travelers (in which demand tends to be elastic) and the segment of business travelers (in which demand is typically inelastic). Airlines separate these segments by placing restrictions on lower-price tickets—requiring advance purchase and a Saturday night stay in the destination city, for example. Flexible pricing is also used in many other fields.

A variable-price strategy abounds in buying situations involving trade-ins. With flexible pricing, buyer-seller bargaining often determines the final price.[24] Both factors, trade-ins and bargaining, are common in automobile retailing. Thus, even though window-sticker prices may suggest a one-price policy, variable pricing has been the norm in selling cars.

In launching the Saturn model, General Motors urged its dealers to set fixed prices so as to minimize haggling between consumer and sales person. That pricing approach set Saturn apart from other brands, with car shoppers responding favorably to Saturn's one-price approach. Thus, in recent years, a number of automakers have encouraged their dealers to at least try a one-price strategy for new-car sales. Of course, as independent firms, dealers can decide whether to use a one-price ("no-haggle") strategy or a variable-price ("let's make a deal") strategy. In the same industry, used-car superstores such as AutoNation and CarMax chose a one-price strategy.[25]

Flat-rate pricing, a variation of the one-price strategy, received some attention lately. Under such an arrangement, a purchaser pays a stipulated single price and then can consume as little or as much of the product as desired. An example of highly successful flat-rate pricing is the single admission fee charged by the Walt Disney Co. at its amusement parks. Some years ago, America Online switched to a flat rate of

$19.95 per month (later raised to $23.90) for unlimited time online. Flat-rate pricing should be used only for products with a low marginal cost and, as one writer stated, "for which there's a natural limit to demand—like all-you-can-eat salad. Or bus trips."[26]

A **single-price strategy** is an extreme variation of the one-price strategy. Not only are all customers charged the same price, but all items sold by the firm carry a single price! This approach, which originated many decades ago, involves offering frugal shoppers a variety of merchandise ranging from grocery items to cosmetics at a single price of $1.

Typically a store that adopts a single-price strategy purchases discontinued products as well as production overruns from a variety of sources at a small fraction of their original costs. Low prices cannot sell unappealing merchandise for long; therefore, single-price stores cannot get by with merchandise that is outdated and/or shoddy. Several single-price chains, including 99¢ Only and Everything for a Buck, are growing rapidly because they provide shoppers with exceptional values.[27]

Price Lining

Price lining involves selecting a limited number of prices at which a business will sell related products. It is used extensively by retailers of apparel. The Athletic Store, for instance, sells several styles of shoes at $39.88 a pair, another group at $59.95, and a third assortment at $79.99.

For the consumer, the main benefit of price lining is that it simplifies buying decisions. For the retailer, price lining helps in planning purchases. The buyer for The Athletic Store can go to market looking for shoes that can be sold at one of its three price points.

Rising costs can put a real squeeze on price lines. That's because a company hesitates to change its price line every time its costs go up. But if costs rise and prices are not increased accordingly, profit margins shrink and the retailer may be forced to seek products with lower costs.

Odd Pricing

Earlier, we briefly discussed pricing strategies that might be called *psychological* pricing: pricing above competitive levels, raising an unsuitably low price to increase sales, and price lining. All these strategies are intended to convey desirable images about products.

Odd pricing, another psychological strategy, is commonly used in retailing. **Odd pricing** sets prices at uneven (or odd) amounts, such as 49 cents or $19.95, rather than at even amounts. Autos are priced at $13,995 rather than $14,000, and houses sell for $119,500 instead of $120,000. Odd pricing is often avoided in prestige stores or on higher-priced items. Expensive men's suits, for example, are priced at $750, not $749.95.

The rationale for odd pricing is that it suggests lower prices and, as a result, yields greater sales than even pricing. According to this reasoning, a price of 98 cents will bring in greater revenue than a $1 price for the same product. Research has indicated that odd pricing can be an effective strategy for a firm that emphasizes low prices. According to another study, many consumers look only at the first two digits in a price. If so, companies should choose a price such as $1.99, rather than $1.95 or $2.09, in order to maximize sales and profits for a particular product.[28]

Leader Pricing and Unfair-Practices Acts

Many firms, primarily retailers, temporarily cut prices on a few items to attract customers. This strategy is called **leader pricing**. The items on which prices are cut are termed **leaders**; if the leader is priced below the store's cost, it's a **loss leader.**

www.amazon.com

Leaders should be well-known, heavily advertised products that are purchased frequently. For example, for a while, Amazon.com cut the base price of currently popular books by 50%. As stated in one article, "Amazon may be able to treat best-selling books as loss leaders that attract customers into its online store where they can be tempted by other merchandise that isn't priced so cheaply."[29] But, to improve profit margins, Amazon and other booksellers eventually scaled back the discounts on best sellers.

More than 20 states have **unfair-practices acts,** sometimes called *unfair-sales acts,* to regulate leader pricing. Typically, these laws prohibit a retailer or wholesaler from selling an item below invoice cost *plus* some stipulated amount. Varying from state to state, "cost plus" is usually defined as either a markup of several percent or the firm's cost of doing business.

In a widely publicized test of this type of law, three Arkansas drugstores charged that Wal-Mart's pharmacies sold some prescription drugs below cost in order to drive small competitors out of business. The giant discounter admitted it sold some products below cost but did so to provide value to customers rather than to destroy competitors. Ultimately, the Arkansas Supreme Court sided with Wal-Mart, stating, "Drugstores are far from destroyed. There is simply enhanced competition in the area." More recently, Wal-Mart was not as fortunate; these state laws prevented the chain from selling gasoline at the "everyday low prices" it had in mind."[30]

According to their supporters, unfair-practices acts eliminate price cutting intended to drive other products or companies out of business. However, such laws permit firms to use leaders—if their price is *above* the stipulated minimum. According to critics, these laws reduce retailers' freedom to set prices. Going a step further, the purpose of a business is to make a profit on the *total* enterprise, not necessarily on each transaction. Thus unfair-practices acts limit retailers' ability to determine how best to generate profits. Also, the minimum prices stipulated by these laws may result in higher prices, which hurts consumers' pocketbooks. In some states these laws have been declared unconstitutional.

High-Low Pricing and Everyday Low Pricing

Many retailers, especially supermarkets and department stores, that want to engage in price competition rely on **high-low pricing.** This strategy entails alternating between regular (high) and "sale" (low) prices on the most visible products offered by a retail firm. Frequent price reductions are combined with aggressive promotion to convey an image of very low prices. By starting with relatively high prices, retailers can boost their profits through sales to the segment of shoppers that really wants the product and is not very price sensitive. Then prices can be cut by various amounts on the basis of quantities of remaining inventory for various products. The practice of high-low pricing is common; in fact, according to one study, over 60% of transactions in department stores involved "sale" (that is, lower than original) prices.[31] JCPenney, with its numerous and heavily promoted sales, is a prime example of a retailer that relies on high-low pricing.

Given the need to change prices frequently, high-low pricing can be costly. It also may cause some consumers to not purchase products at regular prices, but always wait for reduced prices. Further, some consumer advocates have criticized high-low pricing, asserting that it misleads shoppers. The concern is that most transactions are made at decreased prices, which means that the so-called low prices are normal rather than real bargains.[32]

For a retailer that intends to compete on the basis of price, the alternative to high-low pricing is everyday low pricing (EDLP). Basically, **everyday low pricing** involves consistently low prices and few if any temporary price reductions. This strategy is featured by some large discounters, such as Wal-Mart and Family Dollar, and warehouse clubs, such as Costco. In 1998, "Jeden Tag Tefpreise!" signs proclaiming everyday

Wal-Mart emphasizes everyday low pricing and thus promotes its "Always Low Prices" on signs throughout its stores. When it moved into Germany, the new store signs read "Jeden Tag Tiefpreise!" which is German for everyday low prices.

www.steinmart.com

low prices were hung in German retail outlets that were acquired by Wal-Mart. EDLP has also been adopted by numerous other retailers, including such diverse chains as Linens 'n Things, Stein Mart, and Men's Wearhouse.[33]

There are several reasons for EDLP. Retailers expect (or at least hope) that it will improve their profit margins because the average sales price will be higher than would be the case with high-low pricing. Further, retailers can point to their use of EDLP when negotiating lower purchase prices from suppliers. And operating expenses should be lessened, with profits boosted, because of lower levels of advertising.[34]

A manufacturer ordinarily gives retailers a variety of discounts and allowances to stock and promote its brands. In addition, many manufacturing firms engage in high-low pricing by providing short-term "special deals" involving larger deductions and perhaps even free merchandise. In the 1990s, Procter & Gamble (P&G) switched course and substituted consistently low prices for most special deals on about one-half of its products, such as Oxydol detergent. Among the reasons for the shift was the belief that with steady retail prices, consumers might be less price-oriented and more loyal to P&G's well-known brands. However, with its modified pricing strategy, the consumer-goods giant lost substantial market share across 24 categories using the modified pricing strategy; hence, P&G abandoned EDLP.[35]

Which is better—EDLP or high-low pricing? A controlled experiment compared the effects of the two pricing strategies on 26 product categories in a chain of 86 grocery stores. EDLP increased sales, whereas high-low pricing resulted in slightly lower volume. More important, profits fell 18% with EDLP but jumped almost as much with high-low pricing.[36] Unaware of or ignoring this research, or with contrary evidence in hand, numerous firms rely on everyday low pricing.

Resale Price Maintenance

Some manufacturers want to control the prices at which middlemen resell their products; this is termed **resale price maintenance**. Manufacturers seek to do this to protect the brand's image. Publicly, they state that their control of prices—and avoidance of discounted prices—provides middlemen with ample profit margins. In turn, consumers should be able to expect sales help and other services when they buy the manufacturers' products from middlemen. Critics, however, claim that control over prices leads to inflated prices and excessive profits.

Most, perhaps nearly all, retailers use electronic systems in which a checkout clerk scans bar codes on products to automatically ring up prices. Now, some stores are experimenting with similar self-scanning systems that allow shoppers to check out on their own.

Both systems have the potential for ethical problems, but let's focus here on store-controlled (rather than self-scanning) electronic systems. According to a tabulation of mid-1990s pricing-accuracy studies in nine states, the price charged for 3.9% of the almost 150,000 items examined was in error. However, perhaps surprisingly, undercharges outnumbered overcharges by a ratio of almost 3 to 2. The error rate was much lower in grocery stores (2.7%) than in other retail outlets (6%).

Retailers say any mispricing is due to human error, specifically clerks failing to put price reductions into the scanning system's computer. Some consumers and their advocates charge that retailers put price increases into the system before price decreases. That means the store is in an advantageous position compared to consumers when price changes are made.

Is it ethical for retail chains to use electronic checkout scanning systems?

Sources: Guy Richard Clodgelter, "Pricing Accuracy at Grocery Stores and Other Retail Stores Using Scanners," *International Journal of Retail & Distribution Management,* 1998, pp. 412–420; and Catherine Yang, "Maybe They Should Call Them 'Scammers,' " *Business Week,* Jan. 16, 1995, pp. 32, 33.

One way in which producers can gain a bit of control, and perhaps provide guidance to retailers, is with a **suggested list price.** This price is set by a manufacturer at a level that provides retailers with their normal markups. To illustrate, a producer sells to, say, a hardware store a certain product for $6 a unit. It recommends a retail price of $9.95, which would furnish the store with its normal markup of 40% of selling price. This is only a *suggested* retail price. Retailers have the right to sell the product for less or more than the suggested price.

Other manufacturers try even harder to control their products' retail prices. Such effort is worthwhile only for a producer selling to relatively few retailers that want very much to carry the product. A manufacturer may even threaten to stop shipment of products to retailers that price products substantially below suggested list prices.

Is it legal to act aggressively in order to control retail prices? From about 1930 to 1975, a set of state and federal laws permitted manufacturers to set minimum retail prices for their products. The state laws became known as *fair-trade laws.* However, such price controls were prohibited by the federal Consumer Goods Pricing Act of 1975. According to this law, a producer no longer can set resale prices and impose them on resellers.[37]

The struggle over resale price maintenance never seems to end, however. Recently, the focus has been on whether or not a supplier can set a *maximum* price without violating antitrust laws. In what turned out to be a significant case, the owner of a Unocal 76 gas station charged that the supplier stipulated the maximum retail price, thereby limiting the station owner's ability to compete and be profitable. After hearing this case, the U.S. Supreme Court ruled that a supplier's setting maximum prices was not automatically illegal but had to be considered on a case-by-case basis. The key issue is whether or not fixing a maximum price enhances or inhibits competition.[38] This ruling did not affect the fixing of *minimum* prices, a practice that remains automatically illegal.

Sometimes manufacturers are charged with violating antitrust laws as a result of their efforts to control resale prices. For example, Nine West Group Inc., a large women's shoe company, was charged by the Federal Trade Commission with taking actions to restrict competition among shoe retailers, in order to obtain higher prices for its shoe brands. Eventually Nine West agreed to cease the controversial practices and made a $34 million payment to put the matter to rest, thereby averting future legal action.[39]

Pricing Strategies **373**

Reactive and Proactive Changes

After an initial price is set, a number of situations may prompt a firm to change its price. As costs increase, for instance, management may decide that raising price is preferable to maintaining price and either cutting quality or promoting the product aggressively. According to a pricing consultant, "Small companies are more reluctant to raise prices than their large counterparts."[40] Obviously, it's wise to raise prices gradually and with little fanfare. The "art" of raising pricing is discussed further in the nearby You Make the Decision box.

Temporary price cuts may be used to sell excess inventory or to introduce a new product. Also, if a company's market share is declining because of strong competition, its executives may react initially by reducing price. Small firms' price cuts typically are not matched by large competitors, unless they significantly diminish the larger firm's sales. Decreasing price makes the most sense when enough new customers are attracted to offset the smaller profit margin per sale.[41] Nevertheless, for many products, a better long-term alternative to a price reduction is improving the overall marketing program.

Any firm can safely assume that its competitors will change their prices—sooner or later. Consequently, every firm should have guidelines on how it will react. If a competitor *boosts* price, a short delay in reacting probably will not be perilous. However, if a competing firm *reduces* price, a prompt response normally is required to avoid losing customers.

YOU MAKE THE DECISION

Is it no longer possible to raise prices?

Outright price increases are less common now than they were in the 1990s. Instead, Broadway theaters add a $1.25 "renovation fee" to the price of a ticket, an auto dealer in Georgia charges for document preparation, and a Florida resort adds a daily fee of $12 to cover amenities ranging from local calls to housekeeping. Even Microsoft, judged several years ago to be abusing its pricing power, devised a way to boost revenues and improve margins. The software giant announced a new subscriptionlike plan that included automatic software upgrades and that, according to some disgruntled customers, increased the cost of Microsoft products.

Why are firms taking such disguised or circular measures rather than simply raising prices across the board or at least selectively? Three factors, in particular, are reducing marketers' pricing flexibility:

- During a soft economy, which characterized the U.S. in recent years, consumers are particularly price sensitive. Further, they are willing to spend extra time searching for "good deals," with price receiving the most scrutiny. Under these circumstances, businesses keep their base prices (typically the figure that is advertised and otherwise communicated to consumers) as low as possible.

- It's particularly difficult to boost prices when inflation is very low, the situation during the first part of the new century. Rather, firms must build or maintain profits by cost-cutting and economies of scale.

- The Internet has also affected pricing for products sold online as well as those sold in more traditional ways. Essentially, a growing number of consumers are using search engines (we'll discuss these *shopping robots* more in Chapter 16) to make price comparisons and identify the lowest available price for a product. These search engines tend to focus on base prices rather than a total price including any special fees.

Decisions about the frequency and amount of price increases, whether hidden or visible, ordinarily are based on several factors. Among the factors are likely reactions of the target market and the degree to which executives are comfortable taking risks (such as losing customers alienated by a price hike). Although difficult to do at this time, periodic price increases may still be attempted in order to augment or maintain profit margins.

When are visible, rather than hidden, price increases worth the risk of lost customers?

Sources: Rebecca Buckman, "New Microsoft Pricing Looms," *The Wall Street Journal*, June 24, 2002, p. B8; Barbara Hagenbaugh, "Low Inflation Has Officials Worried," *USA Today*, May 10, 2002, p. B6; and Lisa Gubernick, "The Little Extras That Count (Up)," *The Wall Street Journal*, July 12, 2001, pp. B1, B4.

In the absence of collusion, occasional price reductions occur even in an oligopoly with relatively few firms, because the actions of all sellers cannot be controlled. Every so often some firm will cut its price, especially if sales are flat. From a seller's standpoint, the big disadvantage in price cutting is that competitors will retaliate—and not let up. A **price war** may begin when one firm decreases its price in an effort to increase its sales volume and/or market share. The battle is on if other firms retaliate, reducing price on their competing products. Additional price decreases by the original price cutter and/or its competitors are likely to follow until one of the firms decides it can endure no further damage to its profits. Most businesses would like to avoid price wars.

Always part of business, price wars have been even more common since the early 1990s. Low prices often are the primary weapon in numerous disparate fields, such as computer microprocessors, cigarettes, air travel, and ready-to-eat cereals. Even ski resorts, at least those in Colorado, compete intensely through low prices by offering "buddy passes" and other discounts. With large inventories on hand, a price war erupted in the personal-computer industry in 2002, with competitors promoting not only rock-bottom prices but also free accessories. Fast-food chains also began competitive price-cutting in 2002. According to one consultant, price wars often are "overreactions to threats that either aren't there at all or are not as big as they seem."[42]

Price wars can be harmful to a firm, especially one that is financially weak. One article listed the damages as follows: "Customer loyalty? Dead. Profits? Imploding. Planning? Up in smoke." In the music retailing business, for example, consumer-electronics chains such as Best Buy decided to use compact discs and now DVDs as leaders to attract shoppers. Record store chains such as Camelot and Musicland retaliated with price cuts of their own. The consumer-electronics retailers could afford leader pricing because they earned profits on other items like TVs and DVD players, but the record stores didn't have another major generator of profits. As a result, a number of record store chains either shut down or had to reorganize under bankruptcy laws.[43] After extended price wars, companies in other industries as different as groceries and personal computers have gone out of business.

In the short term, consumers benefit from price wars through sharply lower prices. But over the longer term, the net effects on consumers are not clear-cut. Ultimately, a smaller number of competing firms might translate to fewer product choices and/or higher prices for consumers.

www.bestbuy.com/about

Summary

After deciding on pricing goals and setting the base (or list) price, marketers must establish pricing strategies that are compatible with the rest of the marketing mix. A basic decision facing management is whether to engage primarily in price or nonprice competition. Price competition establishes price as the primary, perhaps the sole, basis for attracting and retaining customers. A growing number of businesses are adopting value pricing to improve the ratio of benefits to price and, in turn, lure customers from competitors. In nonprice competition, sellers maintain stable prices and seek a differential advantage through other aspects of their marketing mixes. Common methods of nonprice competition include offering distinctive and appealing products, promotion, and/or customer services.

When a firm is launching a new product, it must choose a market-skimming or a market-penetration pricing strategy. Market skimming uses a relatively high initial price, market penetration a low one.

Strategies also must be devised for discounts and allowances—deductions from the list price. Management has the option of offering quantity discounts, trade discounts, cash discounts, and/or other types of deductions. Decisions on discounts and allowances must conform to the Robinson-Patman Act, a federal law regulating price discrimination.

Freight costs must be considered in pricing. A producer can require the buyer to pay all freight costs (FOB factory pricing), or a producer can absorb all freight costs (uniform delivered pricing). Alternatively, the two parties can share the freight costs (freight absorption).

Management also should decide whether to charge the same price to all similar buyers of identical quantities of a product (a one-price strategy) or to set different prices (a flexible-price strategy). Many organizations, especially retailers, use at least some of the following special strategies: price lining—selecting a limited number of prices at which to sell related products; odd pricing—setting prices at uneven (or odd) amounts; and leader pricing—temporarily cutting prices on a few items to attract customers. Some forms of leader pricing are illegal in a number of states. A company must also choose between everyday low pricing, which relies on consistently low prices and few if any temporary price reductions, and high-low pricing, which involves alternating between regular and "sale" prices on the most visible products offered by a firm.

Many manufacturers are concerned about resale price maintenance, which means controlling the prices at which middlemen resell products. Some approaches to resale price maintenance are more effective than others; moreover, some methods may be illegal.

Market opportunities and/or competitive forces may motivate companies to initiate price changes or, in different situations, to react to other firms' price changes. A series of successive price cuts by competing firms creates a price war, which can harm the profits of all participating companies.

More about **Bluefly**

After showing that it can generate sales online and develop loyal customers for its low-price, high-fashion clothing, Bluefly needs to demonstrate that it can be profitable over the long term. One challenge is, ironically, the pricing strategy that is so attractive to its customers.

Essentially, in order to keep its prices relatively low, Bluefly must keep its markups relatively small. Whereas Bluefly marks up a pair of pants or shoes by, say, $10, a department store like Macy's is likely to have a markup of $14 and a catalog giant like Lands' End might have a markup of $17 on a similar private-brand item. As a result, Bluefly's gross margins—the dollars available to cover operating expenses and provide a profit—have tended to be about 28%. In contrast, gross margins for Macy's, Lands' End, and similar firms are likely to be 10 or more percentage points larger.

To avoid price increases and the associated risk of losing some of its price-conscious customers, Bluefly has made efforts to pay less for the merchandise it resells. Higher sales volume would give the firm more leverage in seeking quantity discounts from vendors. In addition, to compensate for its relatively small gross margins, the company has trimmed some expenses, even laying off part of its work force and cutting back on marketing activities. Other expenses are more difficult to pare. One way or another, the e-tailer needs to store its inventory; further, it must cover various costs associated with shipping and merchandise returns. In addition, Bluefly believes it must retain ample staff to assure good customer service.

Bluefly's business model, like that of some defunct Internet firms such as Garden.com and Webvan, is still unproven. The model has several premises:

- Merchandise that carries the names of well-known designers and is priced low will attract customers.

- Low prices and small margins will discourage online competition.

- Relatively small gross margins can still provide profits because Bluefly.com does not have (1) some forms of overhead such as rent or mortgage payments for physical stores, (2) a lot of expensive employees, and (3) the costs of printing and mailing catalogs.

Other dot-coms, both those that have failed and many that still survive, have found it is far easier to attract online customers than to keep them and to earn a profit. The jury is still out as to whether or not Bluefly will be able to do that.[44]

1. Do you think Bluefly's pricing strategy is sound given that the firm needs profits to survive and, beyond that, to satisfy shareholders?

2. What should Bluefly do to improve its gross margins and, in turn, earn a profit?

Key Terms and Concepts

Questions and Problems

1. For each of the following products, should the seller adopt a market-skimming or a market-penetration pricing strategy? Support your decision in each instance.

   a. High-fashion dresses styled and manufactured by Yves St. Laurent
   b. An exterior house paint that lasts twice as long as any competitive brand
   c. A by-subscription website that sends you daily e-mails containing information about up to five topics of your choosing
   d. A tablet that converts a gallon of water into a gallon of automotive fuel

2. As economic unification was attained and trade barriers were removed throughout the multination European Union (EU), numerous companies deliberated how best to achieve sales and profits in all or part of this huge market. Name two U.S. brands that might benefit from adopting a market-skimming pricing strategy in the EU, and two others that should use a market-penetration strategy.

3. Carefully distinguish between cumulative and noncumulative quantity discounts. Which type of quantity discount has the greater economic and social justification? Why?

4. A manufacturer of appliances quotes a list price of $800 per unit for a certain model of refrigerator and grants trade discounts of 35%, 20%, and 5%. What is the manufacturer's selling price? Who might get these various discounts?

5. The Craig Charles Company (CCC) sells to all its customers at the same published price. One of its sales managers discerns that Jamaican Enterprises is offering to sell to one of CCC's customers, Rocky Mountain Sports, at a lower price. CCC then cuts its price to Rocky Mountain Sports but maintains the original price for all other customers. Is CCC's price cut a violation of the Robinson-Patman Act?

6. "An FOB point-of-production price system is the only geographic price system that is fair to buyers." Discuss.

7. An eastern firm wants to compete in western markets, where it is at a significant disadvantage with respect to freight costs. What pricing alternatives can it adopt to overcome the freight differential?

8. Under what conditions is a company likely to use a variable-price strategy? Can you name firms that employ this strategy other than when a trade-in is involved?

9. On the basis of the topics covered in this chapter, establish a set of price strategies for the manufacturer of a new glass cleaner that is sold through middlemen to supermarkets. The manufacturer sells the cleaner at $15 for a case of a dozen 16-ounce bottles.

10. Friends of yours are entering the world of electronic commerce, intent on selling college-related merchandise and memorabilia on the Internet. On the basis of your reading of this chapter, what three points of advice would you offer them about pricing strategies?

Interactive Marketing Exercises

1. Talk to the owner or a top executive of a firm in your community regarding whether this company emphasizes price or nonprice competition and the reasons for following this course. Also ask whether its approach is similar to or dissimilar from the normal approach used by competitors to market the primary product sold by this firm.

2. Identify a firm in your community that is selling products online. Arrange an interview with the person who directs the company's marketing. Ask the executive which of the following pricing strategies the online firm is using as well as the rationale for the choices:

   a. Price or nonprice competition

   b. Market-skimming or market-penetration pricing

   c. Noncumulative or cumulative discounts

   d. One-price or flexible-price strategy

   e. Everyday low pricing or high-low pricing

Cases for Part 4

CASE 1 — Southwest Airlines

Staying on Course through Turbulent Times

At the end of 2002, Southwest Airlines announced its 30th consecutive year of profitability—a remarkable feat for an American airline even during the best of times. The company's basic strategy of providing no-frills service at low fares to pleasure travelers (rather than business travelers) on relatively short flights has helped Southwest maintain its position as the leading low-cost airline in the U.S.

Southwest's fiscal accomplishment is even more amazing considering that Southwest had to deal with a significant change in leadership as its charismatic founder and CEO, Herb Kelleher, stepped down in June 2001. In addition, the terrorist attacks on September 11, 2001, had an enormous negative impact on the airline industry.

Getting off the Ground

The groundwork for Southwest Airlines was laid in 1966 when Kelleher sketched his plans to launch a low-fare airline on the back of a cocktail napkin. Southwest officially took off in 1971, with three planes serving three Texas cities; the airline began interstate service in 1978. Eventually, Southwest spread its wings to serve about 60 airports in 30 states. The company's revenues now surpass $5.5 billion. As the fourth-largest U.S. airline, Southwest completely dominates the low-fare market and has 10% of air traffic in the U.S. At the end of 2002, Southwest reported a profit of just under $200 million, disappointing by its standards. However, at least Southwest is operating in the black; the other major air carriers lost a combined $13 billion in 2001 and 2002.

Much of Southwest's success has been attributed to Kelleher and his quest to provide low fares and high levels of customer service. His vision has been carried out, as evidenced by five "triple crown" awards in the 1990s, an industry measure that tracks customer complaints, on-time arrivals, and lost baggage. *Fortune* magazine placed Southwest on its list of the 10 most admired companies as well as its list of the best companies for which to work.

The core of Southwest's marketing strategy remains short-flight, domestic routes; thus 85% of its flights are 750 miles or less. In addition, Southwest serves airports that are readily accessible, rather than large, crowded international airports. In this way, the airline reduces long delays that arise because of congested air traffic, a problem that has been compounded at larger airports as a result of post–September 11 security measures.

Flying in the Wake of Terror

All airlines, not just the two with hijacked aircraft, were drastically affected by the unprecedented events of September 11, 2001. As soon as flights were allowed to resume, the entire industry—including Southwest—experienced sharp drops in passenger traffic. However, unlike the other major carriers, Southwest did not cut the number of its flights or lay off any of its employees. This strategy was particularly risky for Southwest because it primarily flies shorter routes and more people opted to drive rather than fly these lesser distances. "We are willing to suffer some damage, even to our stock price, to protect the jobs of our people," stated the company's new CEO, James Parker.

According to Southwest's president and chief operating officer, Colleen Barrett, "No one could have anticipated the horrible events of September 11, but Southwest entered this event with the strongest balance sheet in the industry." With an operating cost per available seat mile of about 7.5 cents, the company does indeed have a sizable advantage in that the industry average is 9.5 cents. Barrett added, "Southwest has always managed its business in good times as though they were bad times, so that our financial conservatism would help us when revenues were thin."

For several weeks, Southwest's passenger load was about one-third of normal. To try to fill its empty seats, Southwest launched a major advertising campaign on September 19, 2001. The first U.S. airline to resume full-scale advertising, Southwest did so cautiously. Instead of taking its traditionally humorous approach, the spots featured the air carrier's employees vowing to help get America flying again.

Southwest then relied on its favorite marketing strategy by announcing lower fares. By September 30, Southwest was flying at 52% of its capacity, compared to 38.5% of capacity the week before. By November, industry capacity had fallen 16% from the previous year, but Southwest's had grown by 7%.

Staying on Course with a New Crew

The employee unity demonstrated in Southwest's post–September 11 ads was real. Southwest has enjoyed a relatively good working relationship with its about 35,000 employees. In 1973, it was the first airline to develop a profit-sharing initiative. Kelleher believed strongly in his employees and made them a priority above all else.

During his years at the helm of Southwest, Kelleher encouraged his employees to have a good time at work and to inject humor into their daily activities. Employees' uniforms are more casual than on other airlines, and Southwest reports noteworthy accomplishments of individual employees in its in-fight magazine.

High employee morale means low turnover, which in turn helps maintain low costs. It also leads to exceptional levels of customer service. Says Barrett, "We are not an airline with great customer service. We are a great customer service organization that just happens to be in the airline business." Company policy even dictates, "No employee will ever be punished for using good judgment and good old common sense when trying to accommodate a customer—no matter what our rules are."

Even Southwest encounters turbulence, though. During its rapid expansion in the late 1990s, the airline experienced operational delays and employee problems typical of its larger competitors. The outcomes were lower on-time rankings and more lost luggage. With employees demanding higher wages and the company flying all over the country, it became harder to maintain Southwest's unique culture and friendly work environment.

Fueling the Competition

Other airlines have attempted to duplicate Southwest's success with low-fare, low-cost, short-hop operations. Launched in 1994, Shuttle by United operated primarily on the West Coast. It was unable to compete with Southwest, however, and is now defunct. Delta Express emerged in 1995, but its operations were eventually slashed by 50%. And US Airways eliminated its MetroJet unit.

Parker doesn't seem surprised by these failures. "They want to be Southwest, but they also want to assign seats, or offer a first class or serve hot meals," he says. "We've been very disciplined about what we are and we stick to it, evolving our vision."

Even start-up airlines in Europe want to emulate Southwest. Ryanair, an Irish airline, as well as easyJet and Go, both based in London, offer cheap tickets to compete with Europe's state-owned, high-price carriers. Michael O'Leary, the head of Ryanair, declared Kelleher a genius. "Kelleher was the one who brought air travel within the pockets of average people," O'Leary commented. But the service on Ryanair and the other European start-ups make a Southwest flight seem like first class. Not only do they not offer food, Go even charges for water. And you can forget about frequent–flyer benefits and sometimes even refunds for canceled flights.

In the U.S., one executive who appears to have been paying attention to Kelleher is Gordon Bethune of Continental Airlines. In 1993, the carrier ranked last in baggage handling and on-time performance. Worse, when Bethune became CEO in 1994, Continental lost $600 million. Like Kelleher, Bethune believes that happy employees translate to happy customers. Thus he offered employees incentives for high levels of job performance. Now employee turnover at Continental is less than 5%, and the company booked 25 profitable quarters before the streak ended in the fourth quarter of 2001.

A new start-up, JetBlue, is also showing promise. Since its founding in 2000, the airline has attracted customers with Southwest-like fares for travel between 17 cities, first on the East Coast and then on the West Coast. Other ways in which JetBlue satisfies customers are leather seats and live satellite TV, with individual screens for each passenger. JetBlue, along with Southwest, may be very well positioned considering one analyst's forecast that as much as one-half of air travel will be handled by discount airlines within 10 years. Perhaps with that in mind, Delta Air Lines decided to launch another low-cost carrier, named Song.

Avoiding Soaring Costs and Fare Wars

The events of September 11th forced many airlines to make cost-cutting decisions that would have previously been unthinkable. But Southwest had been controlling expenses since its inception. It offers cheaper snacks than most other airlines, and operates a single type of aircraft, the Boeing 737, to reduce employee training costs and spare parts inventories. By turning its planes around in 20 to 30 minutes from the time they arrive at the airport gate to the time they back away with a new load of passengers, Southwest's aircraft are in the air for an average of 11 hours per day, compared to 8 hours for other airlines.

Southwest has also been utilizing the Internet to save money. In 1996, it was the first major carrier to sell tickets directly to consumers. Considering that it typically costs an airline $10 to sell a ticket through a travel agency and $5 through its own toll-free reservations number, a $1 online selling cost amounts to impressive savings. By 2000, 25% of its revenue was generated online, primarily by its own website, saving Southwest $80 million for the year. Other airlines were generating only 6% to 7% of their revenues online.

Post–September 11, managing costs became increasingly difficult for the entire airline industry. The threat of future attacks dramatically increased insurance premiums and the need for additional security measures. Southwest cut travel agency commissions from 8% to 5% and even delayed deliveries of aircraft it had ordered from Boeing.

After reducing capacity, U.S. airlines struggled to fill their available seats. Even prior to September 11, the economy was faltering, and business travelers were more price conscious. After the attacks, some travelers abandoned planes for their own cars or a train. The number of air travelers dropped 8% in the first nine months of 2002, compared to the same period in 2001.

To stimulate demand, the airlines cut their fares, sometimes to levels below Southwest's prices. As one response, Southwest tried to make it more difficult for consumers to compare its fares with those of other airlines. For instance, Southwest refused to allow online travel agencies, such as Orbitz and Travelocity, to sell its travel services or even to access its fares. Some industry analysts speculated that Southwest did this because its prices were being beaten by its competitors and, as a result, Southwest was losing credibility as the low-fare leader.

Flying into the Future

The combination of too few passengers and too much debt forced both US Airways Group and United Airlines to file for Chapter 11 bankruptcy protection in 2002. All of the unprofitable major airlines have been forced to rethink business models, and changes—both large and small—are occurring. For example, American Airlines said it would switch its focus from revenues to efficiency, altering its route structure and capacity to do so.

Southwest has had to adapt as well. With more stringent security requirements, the suitability of Southwest's plastic boarding passes was questioned. Traditional paper boarding passes include information about checked bags and avoid the possibility of passengers being able to board a flight without having undergone a security check.

Whereas most carriers are still struggling to recover from the terrorist attacks, Southwest is expanding. It continues to add longer routes, such as Chicago to Oakland. In addition, in February 2002, Southwest announced plans to hire 4,000 more employees. "With our low-cost, low-fare structure, we feel we're pretty recession-resistant," Parker remarked in July 2001. Nobody could have predicted the terrorist attacks that rocked the entire country, including the airline industry. But Parker's prescient remarks and Southwest's subsequent performance indicate that this particular airline is prepared to weather even very severe storms.

Questions

1. What pricing strategies does Southwest Airlines employ to compete against other airlines?

2. What types of costs must Southwest and other airlines control to remain competitive? Are they fixed or variable costs?

3. How is the Internet affecting Southwest's pricing strategy as it relates to its competition?

www.southwest.com/
about_swa

CASE
2

Dell Computer Corp.

Keeping Prices as Low as Dell

Most college students just want to pass their midterms. Michael Dell wanted to take on IBM. That's a pretty ambitious goal for a student selling made-to-order personal computers (PCs) over the phone out of his dorm room at the University of Texas. In 1984, Dell decided to pursue this quest full-time, so he dropped out of school even though he had only $1,000 in seed money.

Only 12 years later, Dell Computer's share of the domestic PC market was larger than IBM's. By 2001, Dell was *the* leader with over 25%, surpassing Compaq (13%), Hewlett-Packard (10%), Gateway (8%), and Dell's original target, IBM (6%). Still CEO of the company he founded, Dell has amassed a personal fortune that—according to a recent estimate—placed him among the 20 wealthiest Americans.

Dell Computer's climb to the top has revolutionized the industry. Instead of focusing on product innovation, the customary strategy for computer firms, Dell created a new business model. In order to keep prices low and delivery times short, Dell purchases components directly from manufacturers, assembles them to meet a customer's specifications, and then ships the final product in record time. Instead of selling through retail outlets, Dell relies on a direct-sales approach and catalogs; in addition, the industry leader has embraced the Internet like no other company. Today, Dell sells over $50 million of computer equipment via the Web *every day*.

Dell's success has caused its competitors to rethink their business strategies. In order to compete with Dell, other PC makers have been forced to lower their prices and, however possible, cut costs. With profit margins diminishing across the industry, many analysts wonder (a) whether Dell will be able to continue slashing prices to gain market share and (b) whether any of its competitors will go out of business trying to keep pace.

Booting Up a New Computer Company

By adopting a direct sales model, Michael Dell was able to eliminate middlemen, keep prices low, and deliver products more quickly than his competitors. In 1988, the company achieved annual revenues of $159 million, and began selling its stock publicly. By 1993, Dell Computer had captured 4% of the market for PCs in the U.S. and became one of the top-five PC manufacturers in the world. Its stock, which was sold originally for $8.50 per share, was worth $100 in 1995.

One of the first companies to begin selling products over the Internet, Dell introduced www.dell.com in 1996. Meanwhile, Dell continued to expand into foreign markets, such as China and Central America, and introduced new products, such as workstations and network servers. Dell, which became the top sellers of PCs in 2001, now has revenues exceeding $30 billion.

The advent of the Internet facilitated Dell's direct-sales approach by giving it another means for reaching clients and suppliers. Dell uses the Web not only to promote and sell its products, but also to order components and parts from numerous suppliers—sometimes placing orders on an hourly basis. Using the Internet for procurement helps Dell keep its inventory low and deliver custom-made PCs with preloaded software in as little as three days. Because computers are made to order, customers receive what they want and Dell isn't struck with unwanted computers that were built according to inaccurate sales forecasts.

Dell's inventory levels are especially low compared to the rest of the PC industry. Dell maintains stock for just four days of operations; by comparison, Compaq carriers 24 days' worth of stock. This difference represents an enormous cost advantage for Dell. In addition, because it can deliver finished products so quickly to customers, Dell typically collects payment from clients long before it pays suppliers. In other words, the company would make money as a result of its positive cash cycle, even if it didn't turn a profit on its product sales.

By maintaining close contact with suppliers, Dell Computer is also able to pass along cost savings to customers in as little as one day. As a Dell executive explained, "Michael focuses relentlessly on driving low-cost material from the supplier through the supply chain to our customers." As a small example, when Michael Dell noticed that one supplier had brought pastries to a meeting, he complained, "Take those back and let's knock the price off the next shipment of materials you bring in. We don't need food. We want a better price." Dell's emphasis on cost control translates to expense ratios that are much smaller than competitors'. In fact, Dell's ratio of 10 cents for every sales dollar compares favorably to 21 cents for Hewlett-Packard (HP).

Deleting the Competition

In an attempt to gain more market share, Dell decided to leverage its cost advantage and challenge competitors to a price war in late 2000. The market leader slashed prices up to 20%, forcing competitors either to follow suit or lose sales. Several competitors tried to match Dell's prices, only to change tactics within a few months. Most were forced to lay off employees. By late 2001, the market shares of Compaq, HP, and Gateway had eroded, whereas Dell's share increased by almost one-third.

Compaq was determined to stabilize its share in relation to Dell's. A company executive stated, "Compaq will not allow Dell to win our customers away." Prior to the price war, Compaq was the market leader and had been aggressively cutting prices as well as reducing its inventory and increasing its direct-sales efforts. But, unable to keep up with Dell, Compaq was acquired by HP in September 2001. "We're in for a round of consolidation, and only the fittest will survive," observed an HP executive.

Gateway has been especially persistent in trying to match Dell. After returning to profitability in 2001 by focusing on higher-margin products, Gateway decided to aggressively pursue the market share it had lost in the PC sector. Thus, in early 2002, Gateway announced another round of price cuts on its brand of PCs. "We did the math. If we sell more PCs we'll [also] sell more of our value-added products and services," explained a Gateway vice president. The underdog sold more units but because of the lower prices, generated less dollar revenue and, in turn, big losses.

HP and IBM both declared the price war "irrational," electing to concede market share rather than lower prices and harm profitability. Dell's assault was well timed. The economy and stock market were declining, making investors and analysts more willing to accept lower earnings reports. In addition, consumers were more price sensitive and were very eager to find the best deal. By late 2001, a year after firing the initial salvo in the PC price war, Dell was still profitable with earnings of $1.8 billion for the year. The rest of the industry lost more than $2 billion, causing Michael Dell to proclaim, "When we sell these products, we make money. When our competitors sell them, they lose money."

Taking a Byte out of Profit Margins

Despite Dell's apparent gains on its competitors, some observers believe the company may have paid a heavy price to do so. Profit margins fell to less than 6% of sales for Dell; competitors that tried to match Dell's prices experienced similar declines. An industry analyst pointed out. "All Dell is accomplishing is to drain gross profit dollars out of the PC segment for everybody." Eventually, Dell was forced to cut 5,000 jobs.

Back in 1992, when the PC was still in its growth stage, Compaq slashed prices in its quest to be the leading supplier of PCs in the U.S. The company achieved its goal and boosted revenues, but profitability suffered and never returned to its original levels. Today, the PC appears to be in the maturity stage of its life cycle, making it more difficult to increase sales. The PC sector is saturated to a great extent, and corporate users are keeping their larger computers for longer periods of time before upgrading them. "It used to be that you could cut prices and people would buy more. There aren't customers for this stuff at any price," explained one industry analyst.

Significant product innovations would be one way to spur sales, but declining profits are curbing investments in technology. Compaq's research and development (R&D) spending fell from 6% of revenues in 1991 to 3.5% in 2000. Two years later, Compaq suspended development of its Alpha chip as a result of budget constraints. Dell traditionally spends only 1.5% of revenues on R&D. "Dell has made this a cost game," complained Compaq's CEO. "Price compression is killing innovation."

Dell Computer executives contend that the firm is being very innovative by developing new cost-containment practices. Others in the industry disagree. The CEO of Sun Microsystems put it bluntly, "Dell is a grocery store. They're not in the PC business any more than Safeway is in the food manufacturing business."

Keying In on New Markets

Indeed, much like a grocery store, Dell is counting on selling other companies' product innovations. Microsoft and Intel, two of Dell's suppliers, will continue to put substantial dollars into R&D. Dell plans to incorporate the advances they come up with in products with higher profit margins, such as servers, storage units, and other networking components. In a much different move, Dell decided to offer an unbranded desktop PC to dealers that primarily serve small enterprises in the U.S.

Dell is careful about selecting new product entries. For example, when it first evaluated the emerging market for handheld computers (previously called personal digital assistants or PDAs), Dell decided to steer clear of this product for two reasons. The market potential was judged to be insufficient, and there are no clearly defined industry standards. However, in late 2002, Dell changed its mind and announced a move into this product category.

Dell Computer is always interested in expanding its share of the PC market. When it had about one-quarter of the domestic market, and 16% of the global market, Dell began looking for new ways to increase revenues. Traditionally a strong player in the corporate sector, many consumers discovered Dell for the first time when it slashed prices in 2001.

Capitalizing on this momentum, Dell began running a new series of slick commercials featuring "Steven" and the tag line, "Dude, you're gettin' a Dell." Also known as "The Dell Guy," Steven (played by actor Benjamin Curtis) became a popular spokesman for the company. Michael Dell even started personally pitching his company's wares on QVC, the home-shopping channel. On December 2, 2001, Dell rang up more sales than on any other day in its history, totaling $80 million. Not coincidentally, more than 33,000 PCs were sold on QVC that day.

These efforts have helped Dell more than double its share of the global *consumer* PC market from 7% in 2000 to 16% in 2002. Of course, Dell was acquiring a larger share of a smaller pie as industry sales fell by 31% during the year.

Trying to improve profitability, several of Dell's competitors (including HP, IBM, and Compaq) are using new pricing approaches for products other than PCs. For instance, much like a utility company, some computer suppliers are attaching meters to servers installed at a customer's location and then sending monthly bills based upon usage. The customer benefits by paying less for servers, and the computer makers receive guaranteed revenues on a regular basis. But Dell is active on many fronts. For example, in the area of distribution, the firm has added in-mall kiosks and, most recently, selling space within the stores of major retailers such as Sears. As Dell establishes new distribution methods, readies new products, and targets new markets, other firms in the computer industry may have to get even more creative with their pricing strategies in order to remain competitive.

Questions

1. a. Which pricing objectives is Dell pursuing?
   b. What type of long-term impact will Dell's pricing strategy have on the computer industry?
2. How are Dell's prices influenced by the other elements in its marketing mix?
3. When entering new markets, what type of pricing strategy does Dell employ?

Sources

Case 1: Southwest Airlines Wendy Zellner,
"Holding Steady," *Business Week,* Feb. 3, 2003, pp. 66–68; Nicole Harris, "Delta to Launch Low-Cost Carrier with Florida, Northeast Flights," *The Wall Street Journal,* Jan. 29, 2003, P. A3. "Flight Tickets Drop Off," *Columbia Daily Tribune,* Oct. 21, 2002, p. 3B; Dan Reed, "Southwest

Challenges Grow . . . as Airline Widens Its Reach," *USA Today,* Oct. 17, 2002, pp. 1B, 2B; Scott McCartney, "American Airlines to Retrench in Bid to Beat Discount Carriers," *The Wall Street Journal,* Aug. 13, 2002, pp. A1, A8; Susan Carey, "US Airways Files Chapter 11 to Help Its Restructuring," *The Wall Street Journal,* Aug. 12, 2002, pp. A1, A6; Michael Arndt, "American Draws a Bead on JetBlue," *Business Week,* June 24, 2002, p. 48; David Koenig, "Southwest Stays above Turbulence with Plan for 4,000 New Hires," *St. Louis Post-Dispatch,* Feb. 19, 2002, p. C9; Scott McCartney, "Continental Airlines Keeps Little Things and It Pays Off Big," *The Wall Street Journal,* Feb. 4, 2002, p. A1; Cynthia Wilson, "Low-Cost Carriers Add Aircraft in Ripe Markets," *St. Louis Post-Dispatch,* Feb. 3, 2002, p. F1; Cynthia Wilson, "Southwest Will End Plastic Boarding Passes," *St. Louis Post-Dispatch,* Jan. 22, 2002, p. C12; Adam Bryant, "Who's Next: James Parker, CEO, Southwest Airlines," *Newsweek,* Dec. 31, 2001/Jan. 7, 2001, pp. 84–85; Erika Rasmusson, "Flying High," *Sales & Marketing Management,* December 2001, p. 55; Brad Foss, "Low-Fare Airlines Have Advantage in the Skies and on Wall Street," *St. Louis Post-Dispatch,* Dec. 15, 2001, p. 1BIZ; Betsy Cummings, "Smooth Takeoff," *Sales & Marketing Management,* October 2001, pp. 35–40; Melanie Trottman, "Amid Crippled Rivals, Southwest Again Tries to Spread Its Wings," *The Wall Street Journal,* Oct. 11, 2001, p. A1; Michelle Conlin, "Where Layoffs Are a Last Resort," *Business Week,* Oct. 8, 2001, p. 42; JoAnn Greco, "Southwest's Second Act Takes the Stage," *The Journal of Business Strategy,* September/October 2001, pp. 28–29; Chris Woodyard, "Southwest's Fares Aren't Always Lowest," *USA Today,* July 31, 2001, p. 1B. Shaun McKinnon, "New Faces, Old Methods," *The Arizona Republic,* July 29, 2001, p. D1; Jennifer Rewick, "Flying High," *The Wall Street Journal,* Feb. 12, 2001, p. R36; Ernest Beck, "London to Frankfurt, $28," *The Wall Street Journal,* Oct. 6, 2000, p. W10; Daniel Michaels, "No-Frills Irish Airline Flies High," *The Wall Street Journal,* Sept. 6, 2000, p. B1; and Alan Rosenspan, "Airline Soars to New Heights," *Direct Marketing,* December 1998, pp. 18–21.

Case 2: Dell Computer Corp. Gary McWilliams,
"Dell Plans to Peddle PCs inside Sears, Other Large Chains," *The Wall Street Journal,* Jan. 30, 2003, pp. B1, B3; "The Best Managers: Michael Dell," *Business Week,* Jan. 13, 2003, p. 62; David Kirkpatrick, "The PC's New Tricks," *Fortune,* Oct. 28, 2002, pp. 88–90+; Arlene Weintraub, "Gateway: Picking Fights It Just Might Lose," *Business Week,* Sept. 9, 2002, p. 52; Gary Mc Williams, "In About Face, Dell Will Sell PCs to Dealers," *The Wall Street Journal,* Aug. 20, 2002; p. B1; Andrew Park, "Whose Lunch Will Dell Eat Next?" *Business Week,* Aug. 12, 2002, pp. 66–67; Sandra Bolan, "Price War Helps Canadian Economy," *Computing Canada,* Apr. 12, 2002, p. 16; Scott Van Camp, "Dell Hawks Hardware on Shopping Channel," *Adweek Magazine's Technology Marketing,* April 2002, p. 4; Tom Mainelli, "Gateway Country Goes to War," *Network World,* Feb. 8, 2002, no pages given; Andy Serwer, "Dell Does Domination," *Fortune,* Jan. 21, 2002, pp. 70–75; Suzanne Vranica, "Another Advertising Star Is Born as Viewers Embrace Dell's Pitchman," *The Wall Street Journal,* Jan. 20, 2002, p. B1; Aliza Pilar Sherman, "The Idol LIfe," *Entrepreneur,* January 2002, pp. 55–56; "Dell, the Conqueror," *Business Week,* Sept. 24, 2001, p. 92; "The Mother of All Price Wars," *Business Week,* July 30, 2001, p. 32; J. William Gurley, "Why Dell's War Isn't Dumb," *Fortune,* July 9, 2001, p. 134; Gary McWilliams, "How Dell Fine-Tunes Its PC Pricing to Gain Edge in a Slow Market," *The Wall street Journal,* June 8, 2001, p. A1; Bob Brewin, "Dell Declares PC Price War," *Computerworld,* May 28, 2001, p. 8; Janice Revell, "The Price Is Not Always Right," *Fortune,* May 14, 2001, p. 240; and "How Dell Keeps from Stumbling," *Business Week,* May 14, 2001, p. 38B.

"The company's boldest decision was to sell its products through new channels in addition to its independent reps."

Can AVON PRODUCTS Use Distribution for a Makeover?

Avon Products, Inc., was founded in 1886, when David McConnell hired a housewife to sell perfume door to door in Winchester, New Hampshire. For the next 100 years the company's marketing formula remained essentially the same: Hire women who want flexible hours and extra income to sell cosmetics to their neighbors. The concept was successful, largely because of the personal contact in the sales process. With her regular visits to homebound women, the "Avon lady" made friends who became loyal customers. Over time, Avon's sales force grew to more than 3 million reps around the world, and annual revenues were in the vicinity of $6 billion.

However, times change. As the number of working women has increased, fewer potential customers can be found at home. These same women have more disposable income to spend on beauty products, but less time to do so. Thus the challenge for the direct-selling firm has been to update its corporate image and reach the tens of millions of women in the U.S. who don't know an Avon rep and have never used one of the company's products. Of course, Avon has to do this without alienating its current sales force and customers. At the same time, Avon is developing a separate product line that will be aimed at trend-motivated female teens.

To reach these groups, Avon adopted a more contemporary logo as well as classier product packaging and sales brochures. Next, it more than doubled the budget for advertising that used slogans like "Dare to change your mind about Avon." Large increases in research and development expenditures are intended to yield highly successful new products, such as Anew Retroactive. The skin cream, launched in 2000, became Avon's biggest-ever product launch with first-year sales of almost $100 million.

But the company's boldest decision was to sell its products through new channels in addition to its independent sales reps. In 1995, Avon distributed a direct-mail catalog and started accepting mail, telephone, and fax orders directly from consumers. Soon after, it added a website for two purposes—to generate online sales and to help its reps manage their businesses. Within several years, the website had 300,000 registered users. Consumers who visit the website can also request a visit from an Avon sales person.

Avon also struck agreements to have an upscale cosmetics line, beComing, distributed through JCPenney and Sears stores. However, this new channel hasn't worked out well. Sales of the line of lipstick, nail polish, and perfume have not met expectations. Sears soon dropped the beComing line, and Penney later did likewise.

To complete its facelift, Avon decided to open some company-owned stores around the country, including a glitzy showcase in the Trump Tower in New York City. Next, about 50 Beauty Center kiosks popped up in malls. The new outlets reach women who hadn't considered Avon for their cosmetic purchases. In fact, new customers account for over 90% of sales at the stores and kiosks. As one convert at a mall in Peabody, Massachusetts, explained, "I wouldn't take the time to order out of an Avon brochure, but I'll buy it if it's here." Avon can also recruit new reps at these outlets.

www.avon.com

Results from the website and retail outlets have been encouraging to Avon's upper management and to at least some of the firm's reps. Numerous consumers visiting the kiosks and Avon.com requested visits from an Avon rep. In addition, market research revealed that brand awareness increased and the company's image improved in areas in which an Avon Beauty Center was located. In the words of a rep in the state of New York, "We felt a pinch when Avon announced the retail venture. But now I look at Avon's beComing as an advertisement for the Avon line I carry."

However, Avon's additional channels were troubling to other reps. And considering that they still account for the lion's share of sales, the reps certainly cannot be ignored. According to a senior executive at the firm, "Managing channel conflict is probably our number one concern right now." To placate its sales force, Avon at first limited the number of products it sold online and at its kiosks to less than 10% of its 5,000–item assortment and gave reps exclusive use of product discounts and promotions.

The head of Avon, Andrea Jung, is committed to the new channels and, in her words, "a far more significant move into retail." Thus, while implementing the new distribution arrangements, Jung may also have to reassure the other Avon reps that she is looking out for their best interests.[1]

What are the advantages and disadvantages of Avon's using multiple ways to reach consumers?

Even before a product is ready for market, management should determine what methods and routes will be used to get it there. This means establishing strategies for the product's distribution channels and physical distribution. Then, as illustrated by Avon's situation, distribution activities and relationships need to be monitored and adjusted over time.

The area of distribution is in a state of flux, perhaps even transformation, in large part because of the widespread usage of the Internet, the growth of electronic commerce, and the resulting competition and conflict among channels and members of supply chains. Consider, for instance, the titles of two articles: "Merrill Lynch Shakes Up Industry by Going Online" and "Off-Line Dealers Push for Legal Protection."[2] Given the dynamic—some would say chaotic—situation in distribution, this element of the marketing mix should command substantial attention from business owners and executives.

www.ml.com

Managing a distribution channel often begins with a producer. Therefore, we will discuss channels largely from a producer's vantage point. As you will see, however, the problems and opportunities that middlemen face in managing their channels are similar to those faced by producers. After studying this chapter, you should

Chapter Goals be able to explain:

- The nature and importance of middlemen and distribution channels.
- The sequence of decisions involved in designing a channel.
- The major channels for goods and services.
- Vertical marketing systems.
- How to choose specific channels and middlemen.
- Intensity of distribution.
- The nature of conflict and control within distribution channels.
- Legal considerations in channels.

Middlemen and Distribution Channels

Ownership of a product has to be transferred somehow from the individual or organization that makes it to the consumer who needs and buys it. Goods also must be physically transported from where they are produced to where they are needed. Services ordinarily cannot be shipped but rather are produced and consumed in the same place. As explained in Chapter 2, the companies that add value to a product that is eventually bought by an individual or an organization comprise a *value chain*. In this chapter and the following two, we pay special attention to the role of middlemen and selected other facilitating organizations as members of the value chain.

Distribution's role within a marketing mix is getting the product to its target market. The first critical activity in getting a product to market is arranging for its sale and the transfer of title from producer to final customer. Other common activities (or functions) are promoting the product, storing it, and assuming some of the financial risk during the distribution process.

A producer can carry out these functions in exchange for an order—and payment—from a customer. Or producer and customer can share these activities. Typically, however, firms called middlemen perform some of these activities on behalf of the producer or the customer.

A **middleman** is a business firm that renders services related *directly* to the sale and/or purchase of a product as it flows from producer to consumer. (Note that in business, *middleman* is an accepted, gender-neutral term.) A middleman either owns the product at some point or actively aids in the transfer of ownership. Often, but not always, a middleman takes physical possession of the product.

Middlemen are commonly classified on the basis of whether or not they take title to the products being distributed. **Merchant middlemen** take title to the products they help to market. The two groups of merchant middlemen are wholesalers

Timepieces International relies on direct sales through this website and also through ads that promote purchases by mail or by phone. Note that the firm says it can offer high-quality watches at low prices by not using middlemen. What activities does Timepieces International have to perform or forgo if it doesn't use middlemen?

www.timepiecesusa.com/catalog/powerstore.cgi

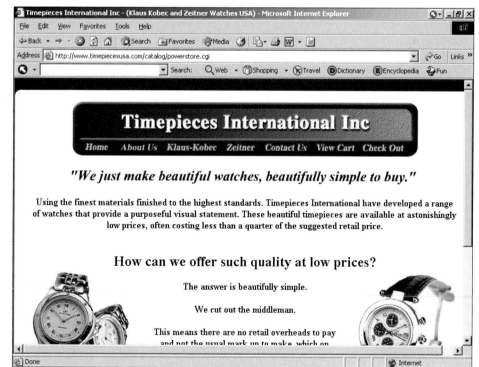

and retailers. **Agent middlemen** never own the products, but they do arrange the transfer of title. Real estate brokers, manufacturers' agents, and travel agents are examples of agent middlemen.

How Important Are Middlemen?

Critics say prices are high because there are too many middlemen performing unnecessary or redundant functions. Some manufacturers draw this conclusion, especially during a recession, and seek to cut costs by eliminating wholesaling middlemen. Although middlemen can be eliminated from channels, a practice called **disintermediation**, lower costs may not always be achieved.[3] The outcome is not predictable because of a basic axiom of marketing: *You can eliminate middlemen, but you cannot eliminate the essential distribution activities they perform.*

Activities such as creating assortments and storing products can be shifted from one party to another in an effort to improve efficiency and/or effectiveness. However, someone has to perform the various activities—if not a middleman, then the producer or the final customer.[4] It is usually not practical for a producer to deal directly with ultimate consumers. Think for a moment how inconvenient your life would be if there were no retail middlemen—no supermarkets, gas stations, or ticket sales outlets, for instance.

Middlemen may be able to carry out distribution activities better or more cheaply than either producers or consumers. Even huge firms sometimes conclude that using middlemen is better than a "do-it-yourself" approach to distribution. For example, financially troubled Kmart Corp. relied primarily on Fleming Companies to supply grocery products to its over 1,800 stores. Kmart entered into this arrangement in order to obtain benefits such as better grocery assortments and lower wholesale prices. Nevertheless, with Kmart in bankruptcy protection and Fleming facing financial and other problems, the firms ended their relationship in early 2003. Kmart said it would obtain groceries from other sources.[5]

www.lotuslight.com

Middlemen act as sales specialists for their suppliers. Conversely, they serve as purchasing agents for their consumers. Consider the sales role performed by Lotus Light Enterprises, a distributor that represents about 500 vendors and their 14,000 different teas, herbal products, and related items. According to a Lotus Light manager, "Our most important service is providing a forum for our customers' products. We show their products to retailers and exhibit them at trade shows."[6] As illustrated in Figure 14.1, middlemen also provide financial services for both suppliers and customers. And their storage services, capability to divide large shipments into smaller ones for resale, and market knowledge benefit suppliers and customers alike.

What Is a Distribution Channel?

A **distribution channel** consists of the set of people and firms involved in the transfer of title to a product as the product moves from producer to ultimate consumer or business user. A channel of distribution always includes both the producer and the final customer for the product in its present form as well as any middlemen such as retailers and wholesalers.

The channel for a product extends only to the last person or organization that buys it without making any significant change in its form. When its form is altered and another product emerges, a new channel is started. When lumber is milled and then made into furniture, two separate channels are involved. The channel for the *lumber* might be lumber mill → broker → furniture manufacturer. The channel for the *finished furniture* might be furniture manufacturer → retail furniture store → consumer.

Besides producer, middlemen, and final customer, other institutions aid the distribution process. Among these *intermediaries* are banks, insurance companies, storage firms, and transportation companies. However, because they do not take title to

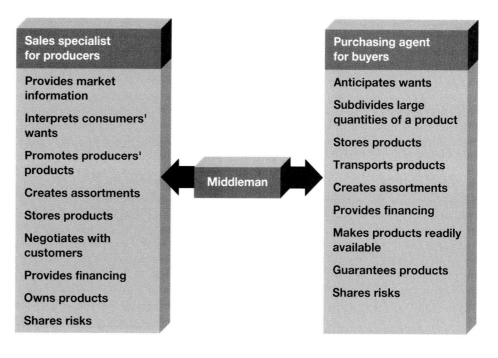

FIGURE 14.1

Typical Activities of a Middleman.

Sales specialist for producers

Provides market information

Interprets consumers' wants

Promotes producers' products

Creates assortments

Stores products

Negotiates with customers

Provides financing

Owns products

Shares risks

Middleman

Purchasing agent for buyers

Anticipates wants

Subdivides large quantities of a product

Stores products

Transports products

Creates assortments

Provides financing

Makes products readily available

Guarantees products

Shares risks

the products and are not actively involved in purchase or sales activities, these intermediaries are not formally included in the distribution channel.

This chapter focuses on the flow (or transfer) of *ownership* for a product, whereas part of Chapter 16 examines the *physical* flow of goods. These flows are distinct; consequently, different institutions may carry them out. For example, a contractor might order roofing shingles from a local distributor of building materials. To minimize freight and handling costs, the product might be shipped directly—that is, shingles manufacturer → contractor. But the channel for transfer of ownership would be manufacturer → distributor → contractor.

Designing Distribution Channels

Similar firms often have dissimilar channels of distribution. For instance, large sellers of auto insurance use different channels. To reach prospective customers, Aetna relies on independent agents who typically sell several brands of insurance. In contrast, State Farm markets through agents who sell only its brand of insurance products. Like virtually all firms, insurance providers have tried to determine whether or how to incorporate the Internet into their distribution strategies. Some have proceeded slowly for fear of alienating long-time middlemen. State Farm, for example, quotes rates online. In several states, shoppers can purchase insurance via the Internet; in most areas, however, State Farm refers these prospects to local agents.[7]

A company wants a distribution channel that not only meets customers' needs but also provides a differential advantage. With that in mind, Caterpillar uses construction equipment dealers that provide customers with many valued services, ranging from rapid fulfillment of order for repair parts to advice about equipment financing. Installers' Service Warehouse, which sells auto parts, seeks an advantage by employing former mechanics to provide expert advice to parts managers or mechanics at dealerships or repair shops who call to place orders or ask questions about a particular part.[8]

To design channels that satisfy customers and outdo competition, an organized approach is required. As shown in Figure 14.2, we suggest a sequence of four decisions:

1. *Specify the role of distribution.* A channel strategy should be designed within the context of the entire marketing mix. First, the firm's marketing objectives are reviewed. Next, the roles assigned to product, price, and promotion are specified. Each element may have a distinct role, or two elements may share an assignment. For example, a manufacturer of pressure gauges may use middlemen, direct-mail advertising, and website announcements to convince prospective customers that it is committed to servicing the product following the sale.

2. *Select the type of channel.* Once distribution's role in the overall marketing program has been agreed on, the most suitable type of channel for the company's product must be determined. At this point in the sequence, a firm needs to decide whether middlemen will be used in its channel and, if so, which types of middlemen.[9]

   To illustrate the wide array of institutions available, as well as the difficulty of channel selection, consider a manufacturer of DVD (digital versatile disc) players. If the firm decides to use middlemen, it must choose among many different types. At the retail level, the range of institutions includes consumer electronics outlets, department and discount stores, mail-order firms, and e-tailers.

3. *Determine intensity of distribution.* The next decision relates to intensity of distribution—that is, the number of middlemen used at the wholesale and retail levels in a particular territory. As we will see later, the target market's buying behavior and the product's nature have a direct bearing on this decision. Because of the desires of prospective customers, Goodyear found it necessary to extend its distribution beyond its own stores and, as a result, now sells most of its tire lines through Sears and various discount outlets.

4. *Choose specific channel members.* The last decision concerns the selection of specific firms to distribute the product. Sometimes, a company—often a small one trying to market a new product—has little choice regarding which channel members to use. In this case, the company has to go with those middlemen that are willing (and hopefully able) to distribute the product. Typically, though, a company that is designing a channel has various companies from which to choose for each type of institution that will form the channel.

Some insurance companies use agents, and others sell only online. Among insurance providers that rely on agents, some sell their products through offices that sell multiple brands. Others, such as State Farm, use agents that sell only its brand. Which approach is best? That depends on company-specific factors, including the needs and desires of the firm's target markets as well as the role of distribution within the complete marketing mix.

www.statefarm.com/quote/quote.htm

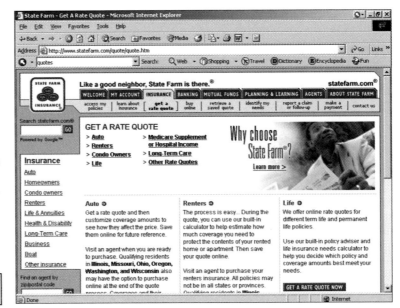

FIGURE 14.2

Sequence of
Decisions to Design a
Distribution Channel.

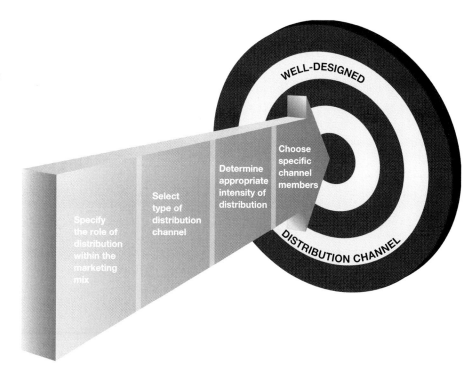

Assume that the manufacturer of DVD players prefers two types of middle-men: department stores and specialty outlets. If the DVD players will be sold in Chicago, the producer must decide which department stores—Marshall Field's and/or Sears—will be asked to distribute its product line. Also, one or more consumer electronics chains—from a group including Tweeter and Circuit City—might be selected. Similar decisions must be made for each territory in the firm's market.

www.tweeter.com

When selecting specific firms to be part of a channel, a producer should consider whether the middleman sells to the customers that the manufacturer wants to reach and whether the middleman's product mix, pricing structure, promotion, and customer service are all compatible with the manufacturer's needs.

In this design sequence, the first decision relates to broad marketing strategy, the second and third to channel strategies, and the last to specific tactics. In the next two major sections, we cover these channel strategies in more detail. First we will look at the major channels traditionally used by producers and at two special channels. Then factors that most influence a company's choice of channels can be discussed. After that, we will consider how many middlemen should be used by a firm.

Selecting the Type of Channel

Firms may rely on existing channels, or they may devise new channels to better serve current customers and to reach new prospects. A small company named New Pig (its real name) decided not to use conventional middlemen such as supermarkets and hardware stores to sell a dust cloth with special dirt-attracting properties. Instead, to reach a primarily female target market, this firm chose to distribute its product through beauty salons.[10] Of course, many manufacturers are using the Internet to sell their wares directly to customers. For instance, besides selling through various types of retailers, Clinique Laboratories, Inc., is selling its cosmetics and hair-care products online.

www.clinique.com

A GLOBAL PERSPECTIVE

Why do gray markets give producers and middlemen gray hair?

Occasionally items are sold through distribution channels that are not authorized by the manufacturer. It's been estimated that this practice, called **gray marketing** or sometimes *export diversion,* may account for about $10 billion in sales annually in the U.S. It usually involves products made in one country and destined for sale in another country. Cameras, computer disk drives or entire PCs, perfumes, cars, and liquor are among the diverse products sold through gray markets.

Ordinarily, gray marketing arises when a product with a well-known brand name carries different prices under different circumstances. For example, a product's wholesale price may vary depending on the country in which it is sold or the quantity purchased. In one form of gray marketing, a wholesaling middleman purchases a product made in one country and agrees to distribute it in a second country, but instead diverts the product to a third country (often the U.S.). Because the product typically is sold at a discount in a reputable outlet, not on the "black market" or from the trunks of cars, it isn't apparent that normal distribution has not been used.

So what's wrong with gray marketing? According to manufacturers, gray marketing disrupts their distribution and pricing strategies. Also, after spending time and money to promote the product, authorized distributors lose sales to the gray market. Producers then have to placate their authorized distributors. Moreover, when consumers buy products through the gray market, they may wind up without warranties or service contracts.

Still, some parties see benefits in gray marketing. Unauthorized distributors are able to sell products they normally cannot acquire. To sell excess output, some manufacturers allow gray marketing. Consumers pay lower prices for popular products and may also find them at more outlets. Based on a rationale of potentially lower prices for consumers, the European Union enacted a law to prohibit automakers from restricting gray market sales.

Some manufacturers have concluded that it's too difficult and costly to fight gray marketing. But other producers try to minimize it through various means, such as taking unauthorized distributors to court. General Motors, for example, won't honor warranties on new vehicles intended for the Canadian market that are diverted to the U.S. The automaker has also told its dealers that participating in gray marketing will subject them to fines or reduced supply of new cars. Further, some law enforcement agencies, at least in the U.S., continue to prosecute individuals and firms engaged in gray marketing.

Because it continues, gray marketing represents one more challenge for both producers and wholesaling middlemen as they seek to manage the distribution of their products.

Sources: Peter Brieger, "GM Fights Grey-Market Sales: To Void Car Warranties," *National Post,* July 18, 2002, p. FP3; "Car Makers Lose Power to Stop Gray Market," *Canada News Wire,* July 17, 2002, no pages given; Amy Borrus, "Exports That Aren't Going Anywhere," *Business Week,* Dec. 4, 1995, pp. 121, 124; and Gert Assmus and Carsten Wiese, "How to Address the Gray Market Threat Using Price Coordination," *Sloan Management Review,* Spring 1995, pp. 31–41.

Most distribution channels include middlemen, but some do not. A channel consisting only of producer and final customer, with no middlemen providing assistance, is called **direct distribution**. ServiceMaster uses a direct approach to sell its cleaning services to both residential and commercial customers. Displeased with slow sales of a line of personal–computer servers, IBM switched from an indirect method involving distributors to a direct approach using its own sales force to call on big accounts.[11]

A channel of producer, final customer, and at least one level of middlemen represents **indirect distribution**. Marshall amplifiers, which have been used by legendary guitarists including Eric Clapton and Jimi Hendrix, are distributed indirectly. Specifically, this manufacturer uses a legion of distributors located in over 150 countries.[12]

www.marshallamps.com

One level of middlemen—retailers but no wholesaling middlemen, for example— or multiple levels may participate in an indirect channel. (For consumer goods, sometimes a channel in which wholesalers are bypassed but retailers are used is incorrectly termed *direct*, rather than indirect, distribution.) With indirect distribution a producer must determine the type(s) of middlemen that will best serve its needs. The range of options at the wholesale and retail levels will be described in the next two chapters.

Major Channels of Distribution

Diverse distribution channels exist today. The most common channels for consumer goods, business goods, and services are described next and summarized in Figure 14.3.

Distribution of Consumer Goods Five channels are widely used in marketing tangible products to ultimate consumers:

FIGURE 14.3

Major Channels of Distribution for Different Categories of Products.

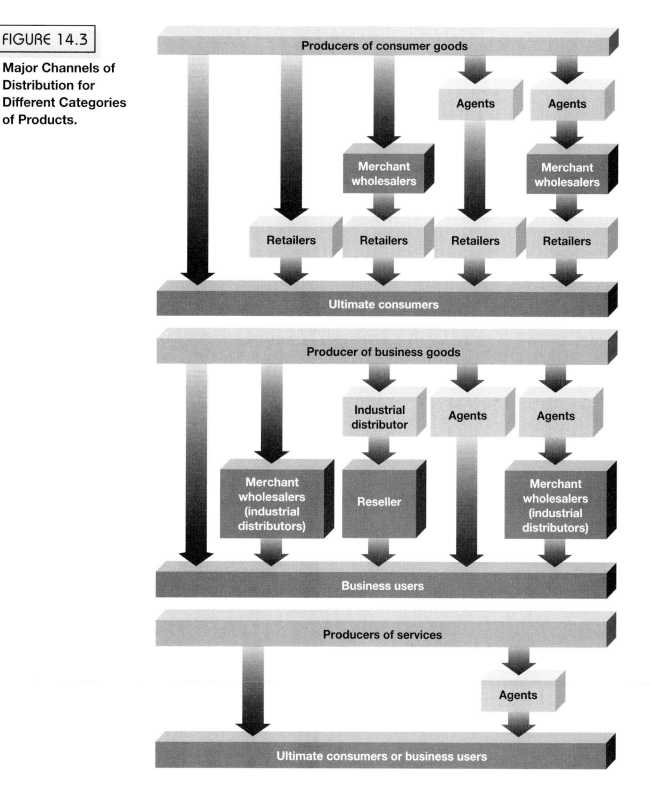

- *Producer → consumer.* The shortest, simplest distribution channel for consumer goods involves no middlemen. The producer may sell from door to door or by mail. For instance, the Southwestern Company uses college students to market its books on a house-to-house basis.

- *Producer → retailer → consumer.* Many large retailers buy directly from manufacturers and agricultural producers. To the chagrin of various wholesaling middlemen, Wal-Mart has increased its direct dealings with producers.

- *Producer → wholesaler → retailer → consumer.* If there is a traditional channel for consumer goods, this is it. Small retailers and manufacturers by the thousands find this channel the only economically feasible choice.

- *Producer → agent → retailer → consumer.* Instead of using wholesalers, many producers prefer to rely on agent middlemen to reach the retail market, especially *large-scale* retailers. For example, Clorox uses a sales and marketing agency (such as Acosta) to reach retailers (such as Dillon's and Schnucks, both large grocery chains), which in turn sell Clorox's cleaning products to consumers.

- *Producer → agent → wholesaler → retailer → consumer.* To reach *small* retailers, producers often use agent middlemen, who in turn call on wholesalers that sell to large retail chains and/or small retail stores. Working as an agent on behalf of various grocery products manufacturers, Acosta sells to some wholesalers (such as Supervalu) that distribute a wide range of products to retailers (such as Dierberg's, a supermarket chain in the St. Louis area). In turn, Dierberg's offers its assortment of products to final consumers.

Distribution of Business Goods

A variety of channels is available to reach organizations that incorporate the products into their manufacturing process or use them in their operations.[13] In the distribution of business goods, the terms *industrial distributor* and *merchant wholesaler* are synonymous. The five common channels for business goods are:

- *Producer → user.* This direct channel accounts for a greater *dollar* volume of business products than any other distribution structure. Large installations, such as jet engines, helicopters, and elevators (all of which are made by divisions of United Technologies), are usually sold directly to users.

- *Producer → industrial distributor → user.* Producers of operating supplies and small accessory equipment frequently use industrial distributors to reach their markets. Manufacturers of building materials and air-conditioning equipment are two examples of industries that make heavy use of industrial distributors.

- *Producer → industrial distributor → reseller → user.* This channel has been common for computer products and related high-tech items. Distributors, which usually are large, national companies, buy various products from manufacturers and then bundle them with related products for resale. Resellers, which usually are smaller, local firms, work closely with end users to meet the buyers' needs. With direct distribution growing, particularly sales through the Internet, distributors and resellers are seeking new ways to add value through their roles. Resellers of computer products, for example, are offering technology solutions such as network installation.[14]

- *Producer → agent → user.* Firms without their own sales departments find this channel desirable. Also, a company that wants to introduce a new product or enter a new market may prefer to use agents rather than its own sales force.

- *Producer → agent → industrial distributor → user.* This channel is similar to the preceding one. It is used when, for some reason, it is not feasible to sell through agents directly to the business user. For example, the order size may be too small to justify direct selling. Or decentralized inventory may be needed to supply users rapidly, in which case the storage services of an industrial distributor are required.

Distribution of Services
The intangible nature of services creates special distribution requirements. There are only two common channels for services:[15]

- *Producer → consumer.* Because a service is intangible, the production process and/or sales activity often require personal contact between producer and customer. Thus a direct channel is used. Direct distribution is typical for many professional services, such as health care and legal advice, and personal services, such as weight-loss counseling and hair cutting. However, other services, including travel and insurance, may also be sold and distributed directly.

- *Producer → agent → consumer.* Although direct distribution often is necessary for the performance of a service, producer–customer contact may not be required for distribution activities. Agents frequently assist a services producer with transfer of ownership (the sales task). Many services, notably travel, lodging, advertising media, entertainment, and insurance, are sold through agents. However, various advances in computing and communications technologies have made it easier for customers to deal directly with service providers, thereby threatening the role of agents.[16]

Multiple Distribution Channels

Many, perhaps most, producers are not content with only a single distribution channel. Instead, for reasons such as reaching two or more target markets or avoiding total dependence on a single arrangement, they employ **multiple distribution channels**. For example, Sherwin-Williams paints and Goodyear tires are distributed through wholesalers, independent retailers, large retail chains, and the manufacturers' own stores. Thus far, neither firm has added the Internet as another channel. (Similarly, many companies establish multiple *supply* channels to ensure that they have products when needed.)

Use of multiple channels occurs in several distinct situations.[17] A manufacturer is likely to use multiple channels to reach *different types of markets* when selling:

- The same product (for example, sporting goods or insurance) to both consumer and business markets.[18]

- Unrelated products (education and consulting; rubber products and plastics).

Multiple channels are also used to reach different segments within a single market when:

- Size of the buyers varies greatly. An airline may sell directly to travel departments in large corporations, but rely on travel agents to reach small businesses and ultimate consumers.

- Geographic concentration differs across parts of the market. A manufacturer of industrial machinery may use its own sales force to sell directly to customers that are located close together, but may employ agents in sparsely populated markets.

A significant trend involves selling the *same brand to a single market* through channels that compete with each other; this is sometimes called *dual distribution*. Many independent insurance agents are concerned, even angry, because insurance companies (including Allstate Corp.) are arranging for banks to sell their products and/or are experimenting with Internet selling.[19] When they are not satisfied with the market coverage provided by existing retail outlets, producers may open their own stores, thereby creating dual distribution. Or they may establish their own stores primarily as testing grounds for new products and marketing techniques.

Although multiple distribution channels provide benefits to the producer, they can aggravate middlemen—as Avon has learned. In another industry, many owners of franchised Carvel Ice Cream Bakery Stores rebelled when faced with multiple channels. The franchisees (who are middlemen) claimed their marketing efforts were

Pizzeria Unos' restaurants, featuring "original Chicago-style deep dish pizza," have been quite successful. In fact, some customers prefer this brand of pizza so much that they want to prepare it at home. As a result, the company developed a line of products for sale in grocery stores, notably supermarkets. Now, Pizzeria Uno reaches consumers through multiple distribution channels.

 www.pizzeriauno.com

undermined and sales and profits reduced when the producer decided to sell its ice cream in supermarkets as well as in franchised stores.[20]

Sometimes multiple channels can be arranged in such a way that a firm's middlemen do not get upset. One approach, which is difficult to achieve, is to develop separate marketing strategies for each channel. For example, the Scotts Company sells some of its lawn-care products to large discount chains but reserves other products only for smaller stores.[21]

Vertical Marketing Systems

Historically, distribution channels stressed the independence of individual members. That is, a producer used various middlemen to achieve its distribution objectives. However, the producer typically was not concerned with middlemen's needs. Conversely, wholesalers and retailers were more interested in preserving their freedom than in coordinating their activities with a producer. These priorities of conventional distribution channels provided an opportunity for a new type of channel.

During the past several decades, the vertical marketing system (VMS) has become *the* dominant form of distribution channel. A **vertical marketing system** is a tightly coordinated distribution channel designed specifically to improve operating efficiency and marketing effectiveness. A VMS illustrates the concept of function shifting that was discussed earlier in this chapter. In a VMS, no marketing function is sacred to a particular level or firm in the channel. Instead, each function is performed at the most advantageous position in the channel.

The high degree of coordination or control characterizing a VMS is achieved through one of three means: common ownership of successive levels of a channel, contracts between channel members, or the market power of one or more members. Table 14.1 shows these three distinct forms of vertical marketing systems.

In a **corporate vertical marketing system**, a firm at one level of a channel owns the firms at the next level or owns the entire channel. Nike (athletic shoes and sports wear) and Swatch (watches), for example, own retail outlets. Of course, there's no assurance that a corporate system, or any other channel, will work out well. Several years ago, automakers (notably General Motors and Ford) started buying back and operating some of their previously franchised dealerships. However, the new arrangement evidently didn't improve efficiency or effectiveness and thus was abandoned rather quickly. "It's a costly lesson for us, but nevertheless I think we have learned that our dealers are our partners for life," explained a Ford Division manager.[22]

Middlemen may also engage in this type of vertical integration. For example, many grocery chains, including Kroger's, own food-processing facilities, such as dairies, which supply their stores. And various large retailers, including Sears, own all or part of manufacturing facilities that supply their stores with many products.

In a **contractual vertical marketing system**, independent producers, wholesalers, and retailers operate under contracts specifying how they will try to improve the effectiveness and efficiency of their distribution. Three kinds of contractual systems have developed: wholesaler-sponsored voluntary chains (for example, Supervalu grocery stores); retailer-owned cooperatives (Ace hardware stores); and franchise systems (Domino's pizza and Midas automotive maintenance and repairs). All will be discussed in Chapter 15.

An **administered vertical marketing system** coordinates distribution activities through (1) the market and/or economic power of one channel member or (2) the willing cooperation of channel members. Sometimes the brand equity possessed by a manufacturer's product is strong enough to secure the cooperation of retailers in matters such as inventory levels, advertising, and store display. Manufacturers such as Corning in ovenware, Rolex in watches, and Kraft in food products typically are able to coordinate various aspects of the channels they use. For instance, given

www.supervalu.com

TABLE 14.1

Types of Vertical Marketing Systems

Type of System	Control Maintained by	Examples
Corporate	Ownership	Singer (sewing machines), Goodyear (tires), Tandy Corp. (electronics)
Contractual:		
Wholesaler-sponsored voluntary chain	Contract	Western Auto stores, IGA stores
Retailer-owned cooperative	Stock ownership by retailers	True Value hardware stores
Franchise systems:	Contract	
Manufacturer-sponsored retailers		Ford, DaimlerChrysler, and other auto dealers
Manufacturer-sponsored wholesalers		Coca-Cola and other soft drink bottlers
Marketers of services		Wendy's, Midas Muffler, Holiday Inn, National car rentals
Administered	Economic power	Hartman luggage, General Electric, Kraft foods

Kraft's strong brands and large marketing budgets, some grocery chains allow the manufacturer to decide which products are placed where on retail shelves—not just Kraft items, but also competitors' products.[23]

It's important to note that retailers, especially giant ones, are more likely to dominate channel relationships now than in prior years. Thus, even a huge manufacturer such as Procter & Gamble decided that one step toward satisfying Wal-Mart was to establish an office in Bentonville, Arkansas, the location of the largest retailer's headquarters. More than 400 other manufacturers have also set up outposts in Bentonville.[24]

In the distant past, competition in distribution usually involved two different conventional channels. For instance, two producer → retailer → consumer channels tended to compete with each other. Eventually, competition pitted a conventional channel against some form of VMS. Thus a traditional producer → retailer → consumer channel, such as Van Heusen shirts sold through various department stores, battled an administered VMS for business, such as cooperative merchandising efforts between Polo Ralph Lauren and a specific chain of department stores.

Now the most common competitive battles are between different forms of vertical marketing systems. For example, a corporate system (stores owned by Goodyear) competes with a contractual system (Firestone's franchised dealers). Considering the potential benefits of vertical marketing systems with respect to both marketing effectiveness and operating efficiencies, they should continue to grow in number and importance.

Factors Affecting Choice of Channels

If a firm is customer-oriented—and it should be if it hopes to prosper—its channels are determined by consumer buying patterns. As stated in a study about the insurance industry, "It's time to stop battling about distribution channels and listen to what the customer wants."[25] Thus the nature of the market should be the key factor in management's distribution decisions. Other considerations are the product, the middlemen, and the company itself.

Market Considerations

A logical starting point is to consider the target market—its needs, structure, and buying behavior:

- *Type of market.* Because ultimate consumers behave differently than business users, they are reached through different distribution channels. Retailers, by definition, serve ultimate consumers, so they are not in channels for business goods.

- *Number of potential customers.* A manufacturer with few potential customers (firms or industries) may use its own sales force to sell directly to ultimate consumers or business users. Boeing uses this approach in selling its jet aircraft. Conversely, a manufacturer with many prospects would likely use middlemen. Reebok relies on numerous middlemen, notably retailers, to reach the millions of consumers in the market for athletic footwear. A firm that uses middlemen does not need as large a sales force as a company, such as Avon, that depends primarily on direct sales to final consumers.

- *Geographic concentration of the market.* When most of a firm's prospective customers are concentrated in a few geographic areas, direct sale is practical. This situation is found in the textile and garment manufacturing industries. When customers are geographically dispersed, direct sale is likely to be impractical because of high travel costs. Instead, sellers may establish sales branches in densely populated markets and use middlemen in less concentrated markets. Some small American manufacturers turn to specialized middlemen, called *trade intermediaries,* to crack foreign markets. Manufacturers sell their goods to these firms at lower-than-normal wholesale prices in exchange for the intermediaries' ability to secure distribution in markets around the globe.[26]

- *Order size.* When either order size or total volume of business is large, direct distribution is economical. Thus a food products manufacturer would sell directly to large supermarket chains. The same manufacturer, however, would use wholesalers to reach small grocery stores, whose orders are too small to justify direct sale.[27]

Product Considerations Although there are numerous product-related factors to consider, we will highlight three:

www.3m.com/us/ index.jhtml

- *Unit value.* The price attached to each unit of a product affects the amount of funds available for distribution. For example, a company can afford to use its own employee to sell a printing-press part that costs more than $10,000. But it would not make sense for a company sales person to call on a household or a business firm to sell a $2 ballpoint pen. Thus 3M Company avoided online sales because the typically low unit value and small quantity ordered made the transaction unprofitable for the firm.[28] Products with low unit values usually are distributed through one or more levels of middlemen. There are exceptions, however. For instance, if order size is large because the customer buys many units of a product at the same time from the company, then a direct channel may be economically feasible.
- *Perishability.* Some goods, including many agricultural products, physically deteriorate fairly quickly. Other goods, such as clothing, perish in a fashion sense. As was discussed in Chapter 11, services are perishable because they cannot be held in inventory. Perishable products require direct or very short channels.
- *Technical nature.* A highly technical *business* product is often distributed directly to business users. The producer's sales force must provide considerable presale and postsale service; wholesalers normally cannot do this. *Consumer* products of a technical nature pose a real distribution challenge. Ordinarily, because of other factors discussed in this section, producers cannot sell highly technical products directly to the consumer. As much as possible, they sell them directly to retailers, in which case product servicing often poses problems.

For a variety of technical products, such as golf clubs (which, believe it or not, are technical because of the myriad sizes, materials, grips, and features), some consumers do preliminary shopping in "bricks and mortar" stores. Then they go to the Internet to seek the lowest price for the specific brand and model they want. The purchase might be made online or from the store, often depending on whether the store is willing to match an online vendor's lower price.

Middlemen Considerations Here we begin to see that a company may not be able to arrange exactly the channels it desires:

- *Services provided by middlemen.* Each producer should select middlemen offering those marketing services that the producer either is unable to provide or cannot economically perform. For instance, firms from other countries seeking to penetrate business markets in the U.S. commonly utilize industrial distributors. This kind of middleman furnishes needed capabilities such as market coverage, sales contacts, and storage of inventories.[29]
- *Availability of desired middlemen.* The middlemen preferred by a producer may not be available. They may carry competing products and, as a result, not want to add another line. Some years ago, when Wally Amos wanted to expand the distribution for his Famous Amos Chocolate Chip Cookies, he was unable to get the product on the shelves of a sufficient number of supermarket chains. Hence, the Famous Amos company boosted sales by relying on alternative middlemen—warehouse clubs, vending machines, and even fast-food restaurants.[30]
- *Producer's and middleman's policies.* When middlemen are unwilling to join a channel because they consider a producer's policies to be unacceptable, the

producer has fewer channel options. Some retailers or wholesalers, for example, will carry a producer's line only if they receive assurance that no competing middlemen will carry the line in the same territory. A growing number of small manufacturers have become very frustrated with the demands for lower prices and other concessions that are placed on them by giant retailers such as Wal-Mart and Home Depot. Thus makers of various products ranging from children's clothing to garden products decided, very reluctantly, to not do business with these retailers.[31]

Company Considerations Before choosing a distribution channel for a product, a company should consider its own situation:

- *Desire for channel control.* Some producers establish direct channels because they want to control their product's distribution, even though a direct arrangement may be more costly than an indirect one. By controlling the channel, producers can achieve more aggressive promotion, assure the freshness of merchandise stocks, and set their products' retail prices. Seeking to break the dominance of department stores in the distribution of upscale cosmetics, The Limited's Intimate Brands division decided to establish its own retail cosmetics chains, beginning with Victoria's Secret Beauty. With this move, Intimate Brands hopes to have more control over the marketing mix, including prices and sales staff, and also allocation of the marketing budget.[32]

www.limitedbrands.com/
about/vs/vsb

- *Services provided by seller.* Some producers make decisions about their channels based on the distribution functions desired (and occasionally demanded) by middlemen. For instance, numerous retail chains will not stock a product unless it is presold through heavy advertising by the producer.

- *Ability of management.* The marketing experience and managerial capabilities of a producer influence decisions about which channel to use. Many companies lacking marketing know-how turn the distribution job over to middlemen.

- *Financial resources.* A business with adequate finances can establish its own sales force, grant credit to its customers, and/or store its own products. A financially weak firm uses middlemen to provide these services.

In a few cases, virtually all factors point to a particular length and type of channel. However, there often is not a single "best" channel. In most cases, the guiding

In the mid-1990s, Michael Dell, the founder of Dell Computer Corp., saw the Internet as a way to deal directly with computer buyers. The company's site is organized for different groups of customers. Note that shoppers can place an order online or by calling a toll-free number. Today, about 50% of Dell's sales are made online, which represents approximately $50 million in Internet volume *daily*.

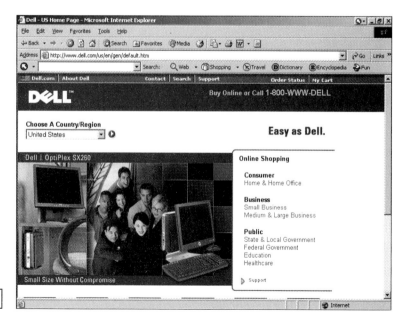

www.dell.com

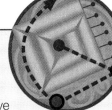

MARKETING IN THE INFORMATION ECONOMY

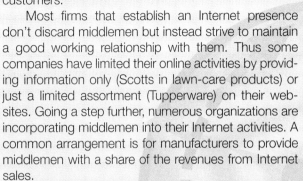

Will the growth of the Internet be the demise of middlemen?

Many producers of diverse goods and services reach customers through the Internet. Dell Computer, Merrill Lynch, Tupperware, and all American air carriers are among the legion of firms that have established websites as one more way to sell their products. In the airline industry, online travel booking services such as Travelocity and Expedia first took business away from traditional travel agents. Then, led by Southwest Airlines, the air carriers decided to eliminate middlemen to the extent possible by using their own websites to sell directly to customers.

Will direct contact between producers and ultimate consumers or end users eliminate middlemen in many industries? The potential benefits of bypassing middlemen and perhaps even a company's own sales force through online selling can be captivating. According to one estimate, selling through a website can cut expenses related to sales commissions and paperwork by as much as 15%. In addition, there may be savings from reducing or eliminating middlemen's markups.

Some companies, such as Amazon.com, locate on the Internet to gain a differential advantage. Others, such as Merrill Lynch, go online to avoid a disadvantage which for Merrill Lynch would be an inability to serve customers online. And still other firms, such as Tupperware and Avon, add the Internet as a channel in order to reach new customers.

But let's not write off middlemen in this Internet era. Most companies continue to use middlemen. For one thing, few manufacturers are geared up to ship very small quantities to numerous buyers, whereas middlemen are. Further, many consumers and end users still want to see the actual product, or at least talk with a real

person, prior to making a purchase. Various types of wholesaling middlemen and retailers offer these services to prospective customers.

Most firms that establish an Internet presence don't discard middlemen but instead strive to maintain a good working relationship with them. Thus some companies have limited their online activities by providing information only (Scotts in lawn-care products) or just a limited assortment (Tupperware) on their websites. Going a step further, numerous organizations are incorporating middlemen into their Internet activities. A common arrangement is for manufacturers to provide middlemen with a share of the revenues from Internet sales.

It's quite possible that middlemen will benefit, rather than suffer, from the move to online sales. They may be called upon to provide the services that producers with online enterprises either cannot or do not want to provide. Consider a prominent example. Most large "bricks and mortar" bookstores use a publisher → retailer → consumer channel. In contrast, Amazon.com tends to rely on a longer channel of publisher → wholesaler → retailer → consumer.

Sources: "Web Sites Force Middlemen to Redefine Markets," *The Wall Street Journal,* June 11, 2002, p. B4; Dana Hedgpeth, "Out of the Picture?" *The Washington Post,* May 19, 2002, p. H1; Paula Saunders, Herbert Brown, Roger Brucker, and Richard Bloomingdale, "Disintermediation and the Changing Distribution Landscape," *Marketing Management Journal,* Fall 2001, pp. 51+; Andrea Isabel Flores, "Tupperware to Launch Online Sales, Creating Rival to Own Representatives," *The Wall Street Journal,* Aug. 10, 1999, p. B8; "Merrill Lynch Shakes Up Industry by Going Online, *St. Louis Post-Dispatch,* June 2, 1999, pp. C1, C2; and George Anders, "Some Big Companies Long to Embrace Web but Settle for Flirtation," *The Wall Street Journal,* Nov. 4, 1998, pp. A1, A14.

factors send mixed signals. If a company with an unproven product having low profit potential cannot place its product with middlemen, it may have no other option but to try to distribute the product directly to its target market.

Determining Intensity of Distribution

At this point in designing a channel, a firm knows what role has been assigned to distribution within the marketing mix, and which types of middlemen will be used (assuming indirect distribution is appropriate). Next the company must decide on the **intensity of distribution**—that is, how many middlemen will be used at the wholesale and retail levels in a particular territory. Optimal intensity, from the standpoint of a producer, is just enough middlemen to meet the desires of the target market. Extra intensity boosts the producer's marketing expenses, but does not really help the firm. Of course, like so many tasks in marketing (and life), achieving this optimum is easier said than done.[33]

FIGURE 14.4

The Intensity-of-Distribution Continuum.

Intensive	Selective	Exclusive
Distribution through every reasonable outlet in a market	Distribution through multiple, but not all, reasonable outlets in a market	Distribution through a single wholesaling middleman and/or retailer in a market

There are many degrees of intensity. As shown in Figure 14.4, we will consider the three major categories—ranging from *intensive* to *selective* to *exclusive*. Distribution intensity ordinarily is thought to be a single decision. However, if the channel has more than one level of middlemen (wholesaler and retailer, for example) or the firm is using multiple channels, the appropriate intensity must be selected for each level and channel.

Different degrees of intensity may be appropriate at successive levels of distribution. A manufacturer can often achieve intensive retail coverage with selective, rather than intensive, wholesale distribution. Or selective intensity at the retail level may be gained through exclusive intensity at the wholesale level. Of course, the wholesaling firm(s) will determine which retail outlets actually receive the product. Despite this lack of control, a producer should plan the levels of intensity needed at both the wholesale and retail levels.

Intensive Distribution

Under **intensive distribution**, a producer sells its product through every available outlet in a market where a consumer might reasonably look for it. Ultimate consumers demand immediate satisfaction from convenience goods and will not defer purchases to find a particular brand. Thus intensive distribution is often used by manufacturers of this category of product. For example, some ice cream makers such as Häagen-Dazs eventually decided they needed intensive, rather than selective, distribution; as such, they supplemented their own outlets with distribution through grocery chains. Likewise, shortly after acquiring the Iams brand of pet food, Procter & Gamble concluded that sales were being lost by relying only on veterinary clinics and pet store chains at the retail level of the channel. As a result, P&G added supermarkets and discount stores to its retail channel members.[34]

Retailers often control whether a strategy of intensive distribution actually can be implemented. For example, a new manufacturer of toothpaste or a small producer of potato chips may want distribution in all supermarkets, but these retailers may limit their assortments to, say, four fast-selling brands.

Except when they want to promote low prices, retailers are reluctant to pay to advertise a product that is sold by competitors. Therefore, intensive distribution places much, perhaps most, of the advertising and promotion burden on the producer. Many producers offer cooperative advertising, in which they reimburse middlemen for part of the cost of ads featuring the producer's product.

Selective Distribution

In **selective distribution**, a producer sells its product through multiple, but not all possible, wholesalers and retailers in a market where a consumer might reasonably look for it. Selective distribution is appropriate for consumer shopping goods, such as various types of clothing and appliances, and for business accessory equipment, such as office equipment and handheld tools. The relative ease of online selling has prompted firms in many industries to shift from selective to more intensive distribution.

In contrast, a company may choose to be more selective after some experience with intensive distribution. The decision to change usually hinges on the high cost of intensive distribution or the unsatisfactory performance of middlemen. Some middlemen always order in small, unprofitable amounts; others may be poor credit risks. Eliminating such marginal channel members may reduce the number of outlets *but* increase a company's sales volume. Many companies have found this to be the case simply because they were able to do more thorough selling with a smaller number of accounts.

A firm may move toward more selective distribution to enhance the image of its products, strengthen customer service, improve quality control, and/or maintain some influence over its prices. For instance, the Step2 Company, a manufacturer of large, plastic toys, decided its products would not be distributed through discount stores. Instead, the firm reaches consumers through other retailers as well as a Step2 Direct page on its website.[35] Whether or not Step2's efforts to control its prices at the retail level in order to protect its image and profit margins are fruitful is open to question.

www.step2.com/direct

Exclusive Distribution

Under **exclusive distribution**, the supplier agrees to sell its product only to a single wholesaling middleman and/or retailer in a given market. At the wholesale level, such an arrangement is normally termed an exclusive *distributorship* and, at the retail level, an exclusive *dealership*. A manufacturer may prohibit a middleman that holds an exclusive distributorship or dealership from handling a directly competing product line. However, that type of restriction is becoming less common. Thus, even under an exclusive distributorship, many middlemen handle directly or, at least, indirectly competing products (for example, high-price and economy-price power mowers).

Producers often adopt an exclusive distribution strategy when it is essential that the retailer carry a large inventory. Thus, exclusive dealerships are frequently used in marketing consumer specialty products such as expensive suits. This strategy is also desirable when the dealer or distributor must furnish installation and repair service. For this reason, manufacturers of farm machinery and large construction equipment grant exclusive distributorships.

Exclusive distribution helps a manufacturer control the last level of middleman before the final customer. A middleman with exclusive rights is usually willing to promote the product vigorously. Why? Interested customers will have to purchase the product from this middleman because no other outlets in the area carry the same brand. However, a producer suffers if its exclusive middlemen in various markets do not serve customers well. Essentially a manufacturer has "all its eggs in one basket."

An exclusive dealer or distributor has the opportunity to reap all the benefits of the producer's marketing activities in a particular area. However, under exclusive distribution, a middleman may become too dependent on the manufacturer. If the manufacturer fails, the middleman also fails (at least for that product). Another risk is that once sales volume has been built up in a market, the producer may add other dealers or, worse yet, drop all dealers and establish its own sales force.

Conflict and Control in Channels

Distribution should be—and often is—characterized by goals shared by suppliers and customers and by cooperative actions. But conflicts as well as struggles for control are increasingly common in this Internet age. To manage distribution channels effectively requires an understanding of both conflict and control, including techniques to (1) decrease conflict, or at least its negative effects, and (2) increase a firm's control within a channel.

Channel conflict exists when one channel member perceives another channel member to be acting in a way that prevents the first member from achieving its distribution objectives. Firms in one channel often compete vigorously with firms in other channels; this represents horizontal conflict. Even within the same channel, firms disagree about operating practices and try to gain control over other members' actions; this illustrates vertical conflict.

A by-product of the rise of the Internet has been added channel conflict, both horizontal and vertical in nature. For example, Home Depot decreed that its suppliers should not sell their products online. A letter from the chain to suppliers stated, "We, too, have the right to be selective in regard to vendors we select, and . . . a company may be hesitant to do business with its competitors." Perhaps trying to win favor with these same vendors, Lowe's encouraged its suppliers to go online. Lowe's stated its interest in linking websites and maybe even sharing revenues with its suppliers.[36]

Another practice, chargebacks by middlemen, has created severe vertical conflict in many channels. A **chargeback** is a penalty that a retailer or wholesaler assesses to a vendor that actually or allegedly violates an agreed-upon distribution policy or procedure. The bases for chargebacks are wide-ranging, including improperly boxed merchandise, mistimed shipments, and damaged merchandise. Producers say the charges are excessive with respect to frequency or amount and, worse yet, often are without justification. Very upset by chargebacks, an executive with a home-furnishings manufacturer described retailers as follows, "They are all cheaters and are stealing from us." In another industry, some manufacturers of grocery products have claimed that Flemings Cos., the huge wholesaler, abuses chargebacks and other deductions. Middlemen defend chargebacks as legitimate assessments for noncompliance with reasonable policies and procedures. What is undeniable is that chargebacks have created serious tension and ill will in some channels.[37]

Horizontal Conflict

Horizontal conflict occurs among firms on the same level of distribution. The cellular telephone field provides an excellent example. Cell phone equipment and services can be bought seemingly everywhere. Consider the range of competitors: office-supply outlets, department stores, warehouse clubs, and consumer electronics retailers as well as the telecommunications providers (such as Sprint) with their own outlets, toll-free telephone lines, and websites.

Basically, horizontal conflict is a form of business competition. It may occur among:

- *Middlemen of the same type:* Maryvale Hardware (an independent retailer) versus Fred's Friendly Hardware (another independent retailer), for example.

www.dunnedwards.com/oz.html

- *Different types of middlemen on the same level*: Fred's Friendly Hardware (an independent retailer) versus Dunn-Edwards Paint (one unit in a large chain) versus Lowe's paints area (a single department in a store within a giant chain).

A primary source of horizontal conflict is **scrambled merchandising**, in which middlemen diversify by adding product lines not traditionally carried by their type of business. Supermarkets, for instance, expanded beyond groceries by adding health and beauty aids, small appliances, snack bars, and various services. Retailers that originally sold these lines became irritated both at supermarkets for diversifying and at producers for using multiple distribution channels. Banks selling insurance, mutual funds, and trust services is another example of scrambled merchandising in the previously tradition-bound world of financial services.

Scrambled merchandising and the resulting horizontal competition may stem from consumers, middlemen, or producers. Many *consumers* prefer convenient, one-stop shopping, so stores broaden their assortments to satisfy this desire. *Middlemen* constantly strive for higher gross margins and more customer traffic, so they increase

Some supermarket chains in Europe engage in scrambled merchandising to the point of offering autos for sale. This photo depicts a joint promotion between Porsche and Coca-Cola in a Carrefour store in Warsaw, Poland.

the number of lines they carry. Perhaps with that in mind, a supermarket chain in France began to sell Korean-made Daewoo autos at discount prices in its stores, much to the chagrin of regular Daewoo dealers.[38] *Producers* seek to expand their market coverage and to reduce unit production costs through economies of scale, so they add new means of distribution. Such diversification intensifies horizontal conflict.

Vertical Conflict

Perhaps the most severe conflicts in distribution involve firms at different levels of the same channel. **Vertical conflict** typically occurs between producer and wholesaler or between producer and retailer.

Producer versus Wholesaler   A producer and a wholesaler may disagree about aspects of their relationship. For instance, Anheuser-Busch instituted a set of incentives to encourage its wholesalers to stock only A-B products and, conversely, to drop other brands. Channel friction is likely to develop between A-B and any wholesaler that desires to carry other profitable brands but does not want to miss out on the financial incentives that are part of A-B's "100% share of mind" program.[39]

Why do conflicts arise? Basically, manufacturers and wholesalers have differing points of view. On the one hand, manufacturers think that wholesalers neither promote products aggressively nor hold sufficient inventories. And they contend that wholesalers' services cost too much. On the other hand, wholesalers believe that producers either expect too much, such as requiring an extensive inventory of the product, or do not understand the wholesaler's primary obligation to customers.

Channel conflict sometimes stems from a manufacturer's attempts to bypass wholesalers and deal directly with retailers or consumers. Direct sales occur because either producers or customers are dissatisfied with wholesalers' services or because market conditions invite or require this approach. With the rise of the Internet, battles about direct sales are increasingly common.

To bypass wholesalers, a producer has two alternatives:

• *Sell directly to consumers.* Producers may employ door-to-door, mail-order, or online selling. They may also establish their own distribution centers in various

As the saying goes, there's strength in numbers. Thus relatively small retailers of ten band together to gain the benefits of size. In the case of Ace Hardware, the retailers own the wholesale operation. Ace, founded in the mid-1920s, now numbers over 5,000 stores in all 50 states plus more than 60 other countries.

areas or even their own retail stores in major markets. Many clothing and shoe manufacturers, such as Phillips-Van Heusen and adidas America, own and operate numerous factory outlets. Sunbeam Corp., now named American Household Inc., also tried this alternative (more on factory outlets in the next chapter).[40] Typically, manufacturers use this approach as a supplementary, rather than sole, form of distribution.

• *Sell directly to retailers.* Under certain market and product conditions, selling directly to retailers is feasible and advisable. An ideal retail market for this option consists of retailers that buy large quantities of a limited line of products. Luxottica Group of Italy, which makes more eyeglass frames than any other company, eliminated most of its wholesale distributors (and also bought two retail chains that sell eyeglasses and sunglasses). According to the firm, a shorter channel not only boosted its profit margins but also improved service to optical shops that buy frames from Luxottica for resale.[41]

Direct distribution—a short channel—places a financial and managerial burden on the producer. The manufacturer must operate its own sales force and handle physical distribution of its products. Further, a direct-selling manufacturer faces competition from its former wholesalers, which no doubt will begin distributing competitive products.

To avoid being bypassed in channels or to respond when they are bypassed, wholesalers need to improve their competitive positions. Their options include:

• *Improve internal performance.* Many wholesalers have modernized their operations. Functional, single-story warehouses have been built outside congested downtown areas, and mechanized materials-handling equipment has been installed. Computers have improved order processing, inventory control, and billing.

- *Provide management assistance to customers.* Wholesalers have realized that improving customers' operations benefits all parties. Thus many of them offer programs to assist their customers in areas such as layout, merchandise selection, promotion, and inventory control. For instance, Graybar Electric, a distributor with annual sales in the vicinity of $5 billion, decided to spend $90 million on a new system for storing and analyzing sales data and to provide the reports to both suppliers and customers.[42]

www.iga.com/aboutIGA/
international.html

- *Form a voluntary chain.* In this form of vertical marketing system, a wholesaler contractually agrees to furnish management services and volume buying power to a group of retailers. In turn, the retailers promise to buy all, or almost all, their merchandise from the wholesaler. Examples of wholesaler-sponsored voluntary chains include IGA (groceries) and Western Auto (automotive products).

- *Develop middlemen's brands.* Some large wholesalers have successfully established their own brands. Supervalu has developed its Flavorite brand for groceries and Super Chill for soft drinks. A voluntary chain of retailers provides a built-in market for the wholesaler's brands.

Producer versus Retailer

Conflict between manufacturers and retailers—in fact, between any two parties—is likely to intensify during tough economic times. Conflict is also bound to occur when producers compete with retailers by selling through producer-owned stores or over the Internet. A number of apparel makers, including Polo, have opened retail outlets. Doing so aggravated department stores and specialty retailers that carry the manufacturers' brands.[43]

Producer and retailer may also disagree about terms of sale or conditions of the relationship between the two parties. In recent years large retail chains have demanded not only lower prices but also more service from suppliers. Producers sometimes find it costly, if not nearly impossible, to comply with the retailers' new policies. The policies cover the gamut, including larger contributions to advertising and other promotion expenses and even the quality of hangers on which apparel is hung (so that the retailer doesn't have to pay for hangers and rehang the merchandise when it is received at the store).[44]

Conflict also has occurred as some large retailers, especially in the grocery field, have demanded a so-called **slotting fee** (also called a *slotting allowance*) to place a manufacturer's product on store shelves. An examination by a federal agency indicated that a typical fee would be as much as $5,000 per store for each version of the product. Manufacturers with popular brands can often negotiate lower fees. According to one

AN ETHICAL DILEMMA?

In exchange for shelf space in their stores, many supermarket chains require manufacturers to pay slotting fees (as discussed in the text). Part or all of the revenues a chain receives from this policy might be passed on to consumers in the form of lower prices. Or the chain can retain these revenues to cover added labor costs associated with shelving new products and/or to boost profits. Critics claim that such charges stifle the introduction of new products, particularly those developed by small producers lacking the resources to pay the mandated fees. Supermarkets contend they must recoup the costs of reviewing the flood of new products, stocking some of them, and removing failures.

Assume that you are a supermarket-chain vice president who is responsible for establishing policies regarding supply chain management. Is it ethical for your chain to demand slotting fees from manufacturers?

Sources: "GAO Says Grocers Offered Little Help in Investigation," *St. Louis Post-Dispatch*, Sept. 15, 2000, p. C6; and Paul N. Bloom, Gregory T. Gundlach, and Joseph P. Cannon, "Slotting Allowances and Fees: Schools of Thought and the Views of Practicing Managers," *Journal of Marketing*, April 2000, pp. 98–108.

estimate, the slotting allowances paid by manufacturers total to about $9 billion annually. Because profit margins on grocery products are small at the retail level, these fees represent a significant share, perhaps one-quarter or more, of supermarket chains' profits. Given the controversy (see the Ethical Dilemma box), the Federal Trade Commission launched a study of slotting allowances before judging whether this practice should be regulated in some way.[45]

Both producers and retailers have methods to gain more control. Manufacturers can:

- *Build strong consumer brand loyalty.* Meeting and surpassing customers' expectations is a key in creating such loyalty.

- *Establish one or more forms of a vertical marketing system.* Procter & Gamble uses the administered type of VMS whenever possible.

- *Refuse to sell to uncooperative retailers.* This tactic may not be defensible from a legal standpoint.

- *Arrange alternative retailers.* Squeezed by large retail chains, some producers are building their distribution strategy around smaller specialty stores. Although risky, a number of apparel makers have taken this course of action.

Effective marketing weapons are also available to retailers. They can:

- *Develop store loyalty among consumers.* Skillful advertising and strong store brands are means of creating loyal customers.

- *Improve computerized information systems.* Information is power. Knowing what sells and how fast it sells is useful in negotiating with suppliers.

- *Form a retailer cooperative.* In this type of vertical marketing system, a group of relatively small retailers bands together to establish and operate a wholesale warehouse. The primary intent is to obtain lower costs on merchandise and supplies through volume buying power. For example, the owner of Rapid Transmissions in Escondido, California, formed a cooperative with other auto repair shops to secure better prices from parts suppliers.[46]

Of course, no approach assures that a producer, wholesaler, or retailer will remain competitive. Any of these paths can become rocky. For instance, the TruServ cooperative suffered financial problems in the late 1990s that affected its ability to serve members, mostly True Value hardware stores. As a result, some members fled TruServ and joined other cooperatives.[47]

www.truevalue.com

Who Controls Channels?

Every firm would like to regulate the behavior of the other members in its distribution channel. A company that is able to do this has **channel control.** In many situations, including distribution channels, power is a prerequisite for control. **Channel power** is the ability to influence or determine the behavior of another channel member.

There are various sources of power in distribution channels. They include:

- *Expertise*—for example, possessing vital technical knowledge about the product or valuable information about customers.

- *Rewards*—providing financial benefits to cooperative channel members.

- *Sanctions*—penalizing uncooperative firms or even removing them from the channel.

Interestingly, power doesn't have to be exercised to provide control. A firm might be able to gain control just by making other channel members aware that it has, for example, sanctioning power. Not surprisingly, the types of power used to influence distributors have a strong effect on their levels of satisfaction.[48]

Historically, manufacturers were viewed as controlling channels—that is, they made the decisions regarding types and number of outlets, participation of individual middlemen, and business practices to be followed by a channel. Considering the enormous size and strong customer loyalty that some middlemen—particularly retailers—now possess, this point of view is one-sided and outdated.

Middlemen now control many channels. Certainly the names Safeway, Target, and Nordstrom mean more to consumers than the names of many producers' brands sold in these stores. Large retailers are challenging manufacturers for channel control, just as many manufacturers seized control from wholesalers years ago. Not surprisingly, powerful retail chains—most notably Wal-Mart—squeeze low prices and other forms of support from producers. Even small retailers can be influential in local markets because their reputations may be stronger than their suppliers' prestige.

Manufacturers contend they should assume the channel leader's role because they create the new products and need greater sales volume to benefit from economies of scale. Retailers also stake a claim for leadership, because they are closest to ultimate consumers and, as a result, are best able to know consumers' wants and to design and oversee channels to satisfy them. Various factors contributed to retailers' growing ability to control channels. Perhaps most notably, many retailers implemented electronic scanning devices, giving them access to more accurate, timely information about sales trends of individual products than producers have.[49]

A Channel Viewed as a Partnership

It is myopic to see a channel as a fragmented collection of independent, competing firms. Instead, suppliers and middlemen should view a channel as a partnership aimed at satisfying end users' needs rather than as something they "command and control." The head of Sutter Home Winery attributes the company's success to its good distributors and cooperative working relationship with them: "I have always felt it was a real partnership."[50]

In a distribution channel, a partnership can entail a variety of cooperative activities that benefit both parties. For instance, a supplier may be asked to get involved in a customer's new-product development efforts. Bailey Controls, a division of ABB Automation that makes control systems for large manufacturing plants, even allowed one of its suppliers, Arrow Electronics, to have a warehouse at Bailey's factory. An increasingly common occurrence is for a firm to provide a supplier with information about past or projected sales and/or existing inventory levels so the supplier can better schedule its production and fill the customer's orders in a timely manner. For example, Wal-Mart decided to allow each of its thousands of suppliers to examine two years of sales figures for that vendor's products across the giant retail chain.[51] In Chapter 16, we'll discuss *collaborative planning, forecasting, and replenishment,* which emphasizes this type of data sharing in a channel.

There are various potential benefits of partnering. Lower inventory and operating costs, improved quality of products and service, and more rapid filling of orders are all possible, but by no means assured. There are risks as well. A close working relationship often requires sharing sensitive information, which may be misused by the other party; worse yet, it may wind up in a competitor's hands. Because firms entering a partnership often reduce the number of other suppliers or customers with which they do business, they may have few options if the relationship doesn't work out.[52]

To increase coordination and facilitate partnerships within channels, many large firms have pared the number of suppliers with which they do business. Some observers suggest, however, that the resulting "preferred vendor" lists are a means for sizable customers to dominate relatively small suppliers. As implied, channel partners are not necessarily equals. Still, given the potential sales volume that comes with being a preferred vendor, most suppliers are willing to meet the demands of powerful customers.[53]

Another growing practice that fosters partnerships is **category management,** in which a retailer allows a large supplier to manage an entire product category (such as carbonated beverages in a supermarket or cook books in a bookstore). Under category management, the supplier designated as "captain" decides which items will be placed on a retailer's shelves and in what quantities and locations. Advocates contend that category management boosts sales and pares expenses for retailers; opponents state that retailers are giving up opportunities for autonomy and differentiation.[54]

Many channel partnerships really are part of a broader, significant trend called *relationship marketing* (introduced in Chapter 1). In the context of distribution channels, relationship marketing refers to a concerted effort by a company not only to work closely with customers to better understand and satisfy their needs but also to develop long-term, mutually beneficial relationships with them. Conversely, customers can seek to engage in relationship marketing with their suppliers.[55]

Legal Considerations in Managing Channels

Attempts to control distribution are subject to legal constraints. The legal aspects of four control methods that are sometimes employed by suppliers, usually manufacturers, warrant consideration. Each method is limited by the Clayton Antitrust Act, Sherman Antitrust Act, or Federal Trade Commission Act. None of the four methods is automatically illegal. Distribution control becomes unlawful when it is judged to (1) substantially lessen competition, (2) create a monopoly, or (3) restrain trade.

Exclusive Dealing

A manufacturer that prohibits its dealers from carrying products offered by the producer's competitors is engaged in **exclusive dealing.** If a manufacturer stipulates that any store carrying its Perfecto Gas Grill *not* carry competing brands of outdoor barbecue grills, this is exclusive dealing. Such an arrangement is likely to be *illegal* when:

- The manufacturer's sales volume is a substantial portion of total volume in a given market. Competitors are thus excluded from a major part of the market.

- The contract is between a large manufacturer and a much smaller middleman. Given the size imbalance, the supplier's power may be considered inherently coercive and thus in restraint of trade.

  However, some court decisions have held that exclusive dealing is *permissible* when:

- Equivalent products are available in a market *or* the manufacturer's competitors have access to equivalent dealers. Exclusive dealing may be legal in these cases if competition is not lessened to any large degree.

- A manufacturer is entering a market *or* its total market share is so small as to be negligible. An exclusive-dealing agreement may actually strengthen the producer's competitive position if the middlemen decide to back the product with a strong marketing effort.

  Likewise, a middleman that uses its clout to force a manufacturer to stop selling products to another middleman may be guilty of illegal exclusive dealing. In fact, Toys "Я" Us was accused first by the Federal Trade Commission and later by state agencies of coercing manufacturers, such as Mattel and Hasbro, to withhold popular toys from warehouse clubs, such as Costco and Sam's Club, that would sell the products at discount prices. Although Toys "Я" Us argued that the practice was not illegal, the chain eventually agreed to pay $50 million to settle the state claims.[56]

Tying Contracts

When a supplier sells a product to a middleman only under the condition that the middleman buy another (possibly unwanted) product from the supplier, the two companies have entered into a **tying contract.** If Paramount Products requires middlemen to purchase unpopular, old models of compact disc players in order to be able to buy popular, new models of DVD players, that's a tying contract.

A manufacturer pushes for a tying agreement in several situations. When there are shortages of a popular product, a supplier may see an opportunity to unload other, less desired products. When a supplier relies on exclusive dealers or distributors (in appliances, for example), it may want them to carry a full line of its products. Or when a company grants a franchise (as in fast foods), it may see the franchisees as captive buyers of all the equipment and supplies needed to operate the business.

In general, tying contracts are considered a violation of antitrust laws. There are exceptions, however. Tying contracts may be *legal* when:

- A new company is trying to enter a market.
- An exclusive dealer or distributor is required to carry the manufacturer's full product line, but is not prohibited from carrying competing products.

According to a lawsuit filed by some Domino's franchisees, their franchise rights were tied to a requirement that they make purchases only from the parent company or approved vendors. The franchisees claimed that as a result of a tying contract, they paid excessive prices for products that were essential to their operations. However, an appeals court ultimately decided that a tying contract was not harmful in the context of franchising.[57]

Refusal to Deal

To select and perhaps control its channels, a producer may refuse to sell to certain middlemen. This practice is called **refusal to deal.** A 1919 court case established that manufacturers can select the middlemen to whom they will sell, so long as there is no intent to create a monopoly. In the mid-1990s, independent service companies charged Eastman Kodak Co. with trying to monopolize the business of repairing its brand of photocopiers. A federal jury agreed, deciding that Kodak illegally refused to sell parts for its photocopiers to independent service companies. Under the verdict, the 11 companies were awarded more than $70 million in damages from Kodak.[58]

A manufacturer's decision to end or diminish a relationship with a wholesaler or retailer may not be legal. Generally it is *illegal* to drop or withhold products from a middleman for (1) carrying competitors' products, (2) resisting a tying contract, or (3) setting prices lower than desired by the manufacturer. Some years ago, the New York attorney general charged that Stride Rite Corp. held back Keds shoes from retailers that did not abide by the manufacturer's "suggested" retail prices. Eventually, Stride Rite agreed to pay over $7 million to resolve the claim.[59]

Exclusive-Territory Policy

Under an **exclusive-territory policy,** a producer requires each middleman to sell *only* to customers located within an assigned territory. In several court cases, exclusive (also called *closed*) sales territories were ruled unlawful because they lessened competition and restrained trade. The courts sought to encourage competition among middlemen handling the *same* brand.

Exclusive territories may be *permitted* when:

- A company is small *or* is a newcomer in the market.
- A producer establishes a corporate vertical marketing system and retains ownership of the product until it reaches the final buyer.

- A producer uses independent middlemen to distribute the product under consignment, in which a middleman does not pay the supplier until after the merchandise is sold.

As you can see, these conditions certainly are subject to interpretation. Thus it is not uncommon for conflicts to be settled by the courts.

Summary

The role of distribution is getting a product to its target market. A distribution channel carries out this assignment, with middlemen performing some tasks. A middleman is a business firm that renders services directly related to the purchase and/or sale of a product as it flows from producer to consumer. Middlemen can be eliminated from a channel, but some organization or individual still has to carry out their essential functions.

A distribution channel is the set of people and firms involved in the flow of title to a product as it moves from producer to ultimate consumer or business user. A channel includes producer, final customer, and any middlemen that participate in the process.

Designing a channel of distribution for a product occurs through a sequence of four decisions: (1) delineating the role of distribution within the marketing mix; (2) selecting the appropriate type of distribution channel; (3) determining the suitable intensity of distribution; and (4) choosing specific channel members.

A variety of channels are used to distribute consumer goods, business goods, and services. Firms often employ multiple channels to achieve broad market coverage, although this strategy can alienate some middlemen. Vertical marketing systems, which are tightly coordinated channels, have become widespread in distribution. There are three forms of vertical marketing systems: corporate, contractual, and administered.

Numerous factors need to be considered in selecting a distribution channel. The primary consideration is the nature of the target market. Other considerations relate to the product, the middlemen, and the company itself.

Distribution intensity refers to the number of middlemen a producer uses at the wholesale and retail levels in a particular territory. To increase distribution intensity, which ranges from intensive to selective to exclusive, some channel members have set up Internet sites that sell products to current and/or new customers.

Firms that distribute goods and services sometimes clash. There are two types of conflict: horizontal (between firms at the same level of distribution) and vertical (between firms at different levels of the same channel). Scrambled merchandising is a prime cause of horizontal conflict. Vertical conflict typically pits producer against wholesaler or retailer. Manufacturers' attempts to bypass middlemen, perhaps through online selling, are a prime cause of vertical conflict.

Channel members frequently strive for some control over one another. Depending on the circumstances, either producers or middlemen can achieve the dominant position in a channel. Members of a channel are served best if they all view their particular network as a partnership requiring coordination of distribution activities. Channel partnerships are part of a significant trend called relationship marketing.

Attempts to control distribution may be subject to legal constraints. In fact, some practices, such as exclusive dealing and tying contracts, may be ruled illegal.

More about AVON PRODUCTS

Avon remains committed to—and dependent upon—its army of independent sales reps. In fact, the direct-selling firm intends to have 750,000 reps in the U.S. by 2007, which would represent an increase of more than one-third over five years. Beyond its time-tested sales methods, Avon recognizes that adding channels and appealing to new market segments are also critical to the company's success. With about three-quarters of U.S. women in the work force instead of at home and the widespread use of the Internet for commercial purposes, direct selling has become an entirely new business. At the same time, demographic and economic trends have established female teenagers and young women as a viable market segment for cosmetics marketers.

Like so many enterprises, Avon is working hard to capitalize on the power of the Web. The firm's website was launched in 1997, in a rather low-key manner.

The caution was intentional, in order to avoid a backlash from Avon reps who felt their sales would be diminished as a result of the Internet. However, this cautious approach may have cost Avon the chance to get a lead in the online cosmetics business. Smaller e-business ventures that didn't face Avon's constraints soon captured the bulk of the online market, worth nearly $1 billion a year.

Redesigned in 2000 with a $60 million budget, www.avon.com now allows customers to search for products, place an order, and take advantage of special offers and promotions—once the exclusive province of Avon's reps. Online shoppers can also obtain information about becoming a sales representative. Avon has even made reps a part of its website. With one click, Internet shoppers can contact an "e-representative" who sells online (with lower order-processing costs than for door-to-door sales). This new type of sales rep earns a 20% to 25% commission while paying the company a fee of only $15 a month. E-reps can offer their customers exclusive features such as access to Avon's full product line, special promotions and new-product offerings, and information about women's health and beauty. Customers also have e-mail access to the rep, which personalizes the shopping experience to some degree.

Avon is using a more personal approach to tap into the teenage female market, which spends about $25 *billion* annually on beauty-related products. A cornerstone of the strategy is to recruit reps ages 16 to 24 to sell Avon's products to their peers beginning in late 2003. Rather than going door to door, the "junior reps" will make their sales pitches in social settings, even slumber parties.

One reason why Avon is using young people as sales reps is to overcome teens' perceptions that the company's products are for their mothers and grandmothers, but not for them. Toward that same end, Avon has developed an entirely new teen-focused product line, carrying the Mark label.

Avon is now using a variety of methods to reach its traditional market of women ages 25 to 55 as well as female teenagers and young women. In addition, the cosmetics marketer has added retail stores, an Internet presence, and younger sales reps to its long-standing middle-aged sales force. With these moves, Avon believes it has completed its makeover—at least until its appearance becomes weary at some point in the future.[60]

1. After adding channels, can Avon avoid serious conflict with its sales reps?

2. Is Avon's direct-sales model, including sales reps of different ages, still a viable channel for this type of product?

Key Terms and Concepts

Middleman (389)
Merchant middleman (389)
Agent middleman (390)
Disintermediation (390)
Distribution channel (390)
Gray marketing (394)
Direct distribution (394)
Indirect distribution (394)
Multiple distribution channels (397)
Vertical marketing system (VMS) (399)
Corporate vertical marketing system (399)

Contractual vertical marketing system (399)
Administered vertical marketing system (399)
Intensity of distribution (403)
Intensive distribution (404)
Selective distribution (404)
Exclusive distribution (405)
Channel conflict (406)
Chargeback (406)
Horizontal conflict (406)

Scrambled merchandising (406)
Vertical conflict (407)
Slotting fee (409)
Channel control (410)
Channel power (410)
Category management (412)
Exclusive dealing (412)
Tying contract (413)
Refusal to deal (413)
Exclusive-territory policy (413)

Questions and Problems

1. Which of the following institutions are middlemen? Explain.

   a. Girl Scout cookie seller
   b. Electrical wholesaler
   c. Real estate broker
   d. Railroad
   e. Advertising agency
   f. Grocery store
   g. Online stockbroker
   h. Internet bank

2. Which of the channels illustrated in Figure 14.3 is most apt to be used for each of the following products? Justify your choice in each case.

   a. Fire insurance
   b. Single-family residences
   c. Farm hay balers
   d. Washing machines
   e. Hair spray
   f. An ocean cruise

3. "The great majority of business sales are made directly from producer to business user." Explain why this occurs, first in terms of the nature of the market, and then in terms of the product.

4. "You can eliminate middlemen, but you cannot eliminate essential distribution activities." Discuss how this statement is supported or refuted by vertical marketing systems.

5. A small manufacturer of fishing lures is faced with the problem of selecting its channel of distribution. What reasonable alternatives does it have? Consider particularly the nature of its product and the nature of its market.

6. Is a policy of intensive distribution consistent with consumer buying habits for convenience goods? For shopping goods? Is intensive distribution normally used in marketing any type of business goods?

7. From a producer's viewpoint, what are the competitive advantages of exclusive distribution?

8. A manufacturer of a well-known brand of men's clothing has been selling directly to one dealer in a Southern city for many years. For some time the market has been large enough to support two retailers very profitably. Yet the present dealer objects strongly when the manufacturer suggests adding another outlet. What alternatives does the manufacturer have in this situation? What course of action would you recommend?

9. "Manufacturers should always strive to select the lowest-cost channel of distribution." Do you agree? Should they always try to use the middlemen with the lowest operating costs? Why or why not?

10. A new company is designing and making stylish—in fact, very trendy—women's clothing. Should the firm establish a website to sell its products?

Interactive Marketing Exercises

1. Arrange an interview with either the owner or a top-level manager of a small manufacturing firm. Inquire about (a) the distribution channel(s) the company uses for its primary product, (b) the factors that were the greatest influences in arriving at the channel(s), (c) whether the company would prefer some other channel, and (d) the firm's strategy regarding online selling.

2. Visit with either a supermarket manager or a buyer for a supermarket chain to learn more about slotting fees and any other charges they levy on manufacturers. Inquire whether such charges have led to channel conflict and how the supermarket chain is handling this type of situation. Also ask whether any grocery products manufacturers refuse to pay slotting fees and whether the chain ever waives the fees.

"Many pet owners are exceedingly devoted to their animals, and some of them are not particularly price sensitive."

Can PETsMART Be Top Dog?

About 60% of U.S. homes have pets, making the pet supply business both large and potentially profitable. Annual U.S. expenditures on pet supplies are at least $20 billion, with a small but increasing percentage being spent online. Pet owners, many of whom are devoted to their animals and are not particularly price sensitive, tend to buy the same brands over and over. When they shop, they like convenience, expert advice, and an atmosphere of care and concern to match their own. But many of them seem to want something more, and Phoenix-based PETsMART believes it knows what that is.

The revenues of PETsMART, which is the #1 pet-supply retail chain in the U.S., have been increasing steadily since the company adopted a new strategy with an emphasis on service. Not only will pet owners find the same big selection of food, supplies, and accessories for their animals in PETsMART's 560 North American stores, but now they can also come in for pet training, grooming, and styling. Further, veterinary care is provided through an alliance with Banfield, The Pet Hospital. Shoppers can even take home a stray; PETsMART has placed more than 1 million homeless animals from its in-store adoption centers.

The chain is also sprucing up its stores, removing warehouse-style steel shelving and instead trying to create a warm, open, and brightly colored environment. Pet-training classes are held front and center, where other shoppers can see them. And products are grouped by pet type rather than by category, so cat owners, for instance, can find all their product needs in the same area of the store.

PETsMART increased its advertising budget by about $3 million, helping support the in-store changes that brought revenues up about 10% as operating expenses declined. PETsMART revamped its inventory policy, too, choosing to supply stores more often with fast-moving items rather than trying to keep a full range of items in stock in every store. An overhaul of its employee training program and an incentive bonus program were put in place to support PETsMART's new emphasis on providing service and enhancing the shopping experience.

PETsMART's success has not gone unnoticed. Its chief rival, Petco, based in San Diego, has made similar changes in its approximately 580 stores. In addition to grouping products by pet type and installing hundreds of new signs containing information about diet, exercise, grooming, and habitat for pets, Petco is moving its displays of small pets from the back to the front of the store. Emphasizing live animals in a can't-miss location is a way of making the shopping experience friendlier and more interactive, Petco management believes. "It showcases live pets without exploiting them," says one regional supervisor, "which is why they're not in the windows."

Petco makes strategic use of store windows, however. Owners can look through the glass in the waiting area to watch their pets being groomed in "salons" right near the store entrance. Or a shopper or waiting pet owner can check out

www.petsmart.com
www.petco.com

the birds on display, now in the high-profile spot in the center of the store instead of out of sight along the back and side walls where they used to be.

It's evident that both chains have chosen to focus more on services such as grooming and training—and are finding it highly profitable. "We found our current format to be very effective," said a Petco spokesperson. "We've had double-digit sales increases, and we're meeting our targets. Why are we doing it? We felt we should take a good thing and make it better, not because it wasn't working."

The pet supply market is enormous and, very important, has proven to be relatively immune to economic downturns. But as PETs-MART and Petco have discovered, the needs and wants of even the most loyal customers can change over time.[1]

What will be the keys to long-term success for PETsMART or for its competitors in the retailing of pet supplies?

Distribution of consumer products begins with the producer and ends with the ultimate consumer. Between the two, there is usually at least one middleman—a retailer. The many types of retail institutions and their marketing activities are the subjects of this chapter.

You have abundant experience with retailing—as a consumer. And perhaps you also have worked in retailing. This chapter builds on that experience and provides insights about retail markets, different types of retailers, and key strategies and trends in retailing, notably the growing volume of retail sales through the Internet. After studying this chapter, you should be able to explain:

Chapter Goals

- The nature of retailing.
- What a retailer is.
- Types of retailers classified by form of ownership.
- Types of retailers classified by marketing strategies.
- Forms of nonstore retailing, including online sales to final consumers.
- Trends in retailing.

Nature and Importance of Retailing

www.crateandbarrel.com/aboutus/default.asp

For every successful large retailer like Publix supermarkets, Crate & Barrel stores, and of course Wal-Mart, thousands of tiny retailers serve consumers in very small areas. Despite their differences, all have two common features: They link producers and ultimate consumers, and they perform valuable services for both. In all likelihood, all of these firms are retailers, but not all of their activities may qualify as retailing. Let's see how that can be.

Retailing and Retailers

If a Winn-Dixie supermarket sells floor wax to a gift shop operator to polish the shop's floor, is this a retail sale? Can a wholesaler or manufacturer engage in retailing? When a service such as Aamco transmission repair is sold to an ultimate consumer, is this retailing? Obviously, we need to define some terms, particularly *retailing* and *retailer,* to answer these questions and to avoid misunderstandings later.

Retailing (or *retail trade*) consists of the sale, and all activities directly related to the sale, of goods and services to ultimate consumers for personal, nonbusiness use. Although most retailing occurs through retail stores, it may be done by any institution. A Tupperware rep selling plastic containers at lunchtime meetings at a factory is engaged in retailing, as is a farmer selling vegetables at a roadside stand.

Any firm—manufacturer, wholesaler, or retailer—that sells something to ultimate consumers for their nonbusiness use is making a retail sale. This is true regardless of *how* the product is sold (in person, online, or by telephone, mail, or vending machine) or *where* it is sold (in a store, at the consumer's home, at another physical location, or on the Internet). However, a firm engaged *primarily* in retailing is called a **retailer.** In this chapter we will concentrate on retailers rather than on other types of businesses that make only occasional retail sales.

In the past few years, it has become common to differentiate *bricks-and-mortar* retailers (that is, those with physical stores) from *clicks-and-modem* retailers (those that operate online). The latter type, also referred to as *e-tailers,* is covered at various places in the chapter. Further, although this chapter focuses primarily on retailers of *goods,* much of what is said—particularly regarding marketing strategies—also applies to retailers of *services* (as covered in Chapter 11).

Economic Justification for Retailing

As discussed in Chapter 14, all middlemen basically serve as purchasing agents for their customers and as sales specialists for their suppliers. To carry out these roles, retailers perform many activities, including anticipating customers' wants, developing assortments of products, acquiring market information, and financing.

It is relatively easy to become a retailer. No large investment in production equipment is required, merchandise can often be purchased on credit, and store space can be leased with no down payment or a simple website can be set up at modest cost. Considering these factors, perhaps it's not surprising that there are just over 1.1 million retail firms in the U.S.[2] This large number of companies, many of which are trying to serve and satisfy the same market segments, results in fierce competition and better values for shoppers.

To enter retailing is easy; to fail is even easier! To survive in retailing, a firm must do a satisfactory job in its primary role—catering to consumers. Stanley Marcus, the former chairman of Neiman Marcus, described a successful retailer as "a merchant who sells goods that won't come back to customers who will."[3] Of course, a retail firm also must fulfill its other role—serving producers and wholesalers. This dual role is both the justification for retailing and the key to success in retailing.

www.neimanmarcus.com

Size of Market and Firms

Retail sales in 2001 totaled almost $3.2 *trillion* (see Figure 15.1). The increase in total sales volume has been tremendous—more than sixfold from the early 1970s to 2001. Even adjusting for the rise in prices, total retail sales and per capita retail sales have gone up considerably.

There is a high degree of concentration in retailing. As depicted in Figure 15.2, three-quarters of retail firms have fewer than 10 employees. These small merchants ring up about one-eighth of all sales to consumers. Conversely, a small number of companies account for a large share of retail trade. Just 0.3% of all retailers had 500 or more employees, but these firms accounted for about 45% of total retail sales.

Figure 15.2 does not tell the full story of large-scale retailing because it represents a tabulation of individual *store* sales and not *company* sales volume. A single company may own many stores, as in the case of chains. When retail sales are analyzed by companies, the high degree of concentration becomes even more evident. As shown in Table 15.1, the sales of the 10 largest retailers summed to over $572 billion in 2001, which comprised about 18% of total retail trade.

Stores of different sizes face distinct challenges and opportunities. Buying, promotion, staffing, and expense control are influenced significantly by whether a store's sales volume is large or small. Size of a retail business creates certain advantages and

FIGURE 15.1

Total Retail Trade in the United States.

Retail sales have increased steadily over the past three decades.

Sources: http://landview.census.gov/ mrts/www/data/pdf/annpub01.pdf; 1997 Economic Census, Retail Trade—Geographic Area Series, U.S. Census Bureau, Washington, DC, 2000, p. United States 7; and corresponding censuses from prior years.

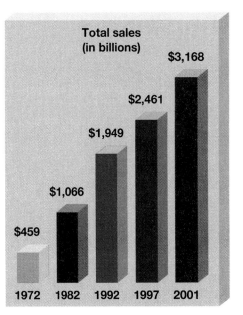

FIGURE 15.2

Distribution of Retail Stores and Sales by Number of Employees.

Sources: Statistical Abstract of the United States: 1999, 119th edition, U.S. Bureau of the Census, Washington, DC, 1999, p. 556.

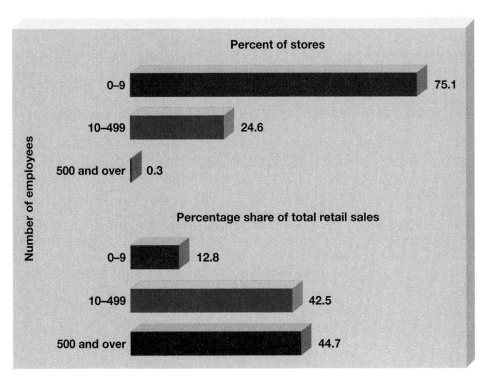

disadvantages, several of which are described in Table 15.2. Considering these factors, large stores ordinarily—but not always—have a competitive advantage over small stores.

Small retailers face a variety of difficulties, and many fail. Of course, a strong economy helps small merchants hold their own. In fact, the number of retail failures in 1998 (the latest year for which this information is available) was one-sixth lower than the prior year and just below the level at the start of the 1990s.[4]

TABLE 15.1

Total Sales of 10 Largest Retailers Based in the United States

Retailer	2001 Sales (billions)	% Change in Sales, 2000–2001	2001 Net Profit as % of Sales
1. Wal-Mart	$217.8	+ 12.2	3.1
2. Home Depot	53.6	+ 14.6	5.7
3. Kroger	50.1	+ 2.2	2.1
4. Sears	41.1	+ 0.3	1.8
5. Target	39.9	+ 7.5	3.4
6. Albertson's	37.9	+ 3.1	1.3
7. Costco	34.8	+ 7.6	1.7
8. Safeway	34.3	+ 6.8	3.7
9. JCPenney	32.0	+ 0.5	0.3
10. Kmart	31.1	− 2.4	(6.9)
Total	$572.6		
Average for top 10 firms		+ 5.2	1.6

Note: In some cases, total sales may include nonretail revenues. Total volume in 2000 for these 10 firms was $528.5 billion.
Sources: Mike Duff, "Top North American Retail Companies: Big Got Bigger and Take On the World," *Discount Store News*, July 8, 2002, p. 18.

TABLE 15.2

Competitive Positions of Large and Small Retailers

Selected Bases for Evaluation	Who Has the Advantage?
Division of labor and specialization of management	Large-scale retailers—their biggest advantage.
Flexibility of operations—merchandise selection, services offered, store design, reflection of owner's personality	Small retailers—their biggest advantage.
Buying power	Large retailers buy in bigger quantities and thus get lower wholesale prices.
Access to desirable merchandise	Large retailers promise suppliers access to large numbers of customers, whereas a single small retailer may be viewed as insignificant.
Development and promotion of retailer's own brand	Large retailers.
Efficient use of advertising, especially in city-wide media	Large retailers' markets match better with media circulation.
Ability to provide top-quality personal service	Small retailers, if owners pay personal attention to customers and also to selecting and supervising sales staff.
Opportunity to experiment with new products and selling methods	Large retailers can better afford the risks.
Financial strength	Large retailers have resources to gain some of the advantages noted above (such as private brands and experimentation).
Public image	Small retailers enjoy public support and sympathy. However, the public often votes with its wallet by shopping at big stores.

How do small retailers succeed? They understand their target markets very well. Then, in seeking to satisfy their consumers, they need to differentiate themselves from large retailers.[5] Here are two possible avenues not just to survival but to success:

- Many consumers seek benefits that small stores often provide better than large stores. For instance, some people seek high levels of shopping convenience. Small outlets located near residential areas offer such convenience. Other consumers desire abundant personal service. A small store's highly motivated owner–manager and customer-oriented sales staff may surpass a large store on this important shopping dimension.

- Numerous small retailers have formed or joined contractual vertical marketing systems, as explained in Chapter 14. These entities—called retailer cooperatives, voluntary chains, or franchise systems—give members some of the advantages of large stores, such as specialized management, buying power, and a well-known name.

Operating Expenses and Profits

Total operating expenses for retailers average 28% of retail sales. In comparison, wholesaling expenses run about 11% of *wholesale* sales or 8% of *retail* sales.[6] Thus, roughly speaking, retailing costs are about 2½ times the costs of wholesaling when both are stated as a percentage of the sales of the specific type of middleman.

Higher retailing costs are the result of dealing directly with ultimate consumers—answering their questions, showing them different products, and so on. Compared to wholesale customers, ultimate consumers typically expect more convenient locations with nicer décor, both of which drive up retailers' costs. Also, relative to wholesalers, retailers typically have lower total sales and lower rates of merchandise turnover. Retailers buy smaller quantities of merchandise, again compared to wholesalers, so their overhead costs are spread over a smaller base of operations. Furthermore, retail sales people often cannot be used efficiently because customers do not come into stores at a steady rate.

Retailers' costs and profits vary depending on their type of operation and major product line. Assorted kinds of retailers earn wide-ranging gross margins—the difference between net sales and cost of goods sold. For instance, gross margins for auto dealers and gasoline service stations are in the vicinity of 15%, whereas margins for retailers of clothing, shoes, and jewelry are around 40%.

Healthy gross margins do not necessarily translate into high levels of net profits. Some retailers have large gross margins but incur heavy operating expenses, resulting in meager profits. Conversely, other retailers with small gross margins are able to serve customers well with low operating expenses, thereby winding up with substantial net profits. For example, e-tailers have substituted new technology for physical stores and, to a large extent, for retail sales people. As a result, online stores should have lower operating expenses compared to traditional stores, if they can (1) reach a point where they do not have to advertise very heavily in order to attract customers and (2) handle the fulfillment of orders in an efficient manner.

Just as retail firms' gross margins range widely, so do their net profits. Supermarkets typically earn a profit of less than 1% of sales, compared to as much as 10% for some specialized retailers. In general, retailers' net profits average about 3% of sales. This modest figure may surprise people who suspect that retailers make enormous profits.

Physical Facilities

Later in this chapter we will classify retailers according to their product assortments, price strategies, and promotional methods. Here, we'll look at **physical facilities**, which represent the distribution element of a retailer's marketing mix.

Some firms engage in *nonstore* retailing—by selling through catalogs or door to door, for example—but many more firms rely on retail *stores*. Retailers that operate physical (or bricks-and-mortar) stores must consider four aspects of physical facilities:

- *Location.* It is frequently stated that there are three keys to success in retailing: location, location, and location! Although overstated, this axiom does underscore that a store's site should be the first decision made about facilities. Considerations such as surrounding population, traffic, and cost determine where a store should be located.

- *Size.* This factor refers to the total square footage of the physical store, not the magnitude of the firm operating it. A firm may be quite large with respect to total sales, but each of its outlets may be only several thousand square feet in size. Even though a 7-Eleven store is quite small, the more than 21,000 of them around the globe ring up over $27 billion in annual sales.[7]

- *Design.* This factor refers to a store's appearance, both exterior and interior.

- *Layout.* The amount of space allocated to various product lines, specific locations of products, and a floor plan of display tables and racks comprise the store's layout.

As would be expected, the location, size, design, and layout of retail stores are based on where consumers live and how they like to go about their shopping. Consequently, the bulk of retail sales occur in urban, rather than rural, areas. And in urban areas, suburban shopping areas have become dominant, whereas many downtown areas have declined.

Shopping centers are the principal type of retail location in most suburban areas. A **shopping center** consists of a planned grouping of retail stores that lease space in a structure that is typically owned by a single organization. Shopping centers can be classified by such attributes as size, market served, and types of tenants. In order of increasing size, there is the *convenience center, neighborhood center, community center,* and *regional center.*

Another kind, a *power center,* can be of various sizes. Its distinguishing attribute is a tenant mix that includes several large, popular limited-line stores that stress value (such as Circuit City, Home Depot, and Toys "Я" Us), but not a department store anchor. The rise of power centers that began in the early 1990s subsided at the end of the decade because of saturation in some markets.[8]

Another kind, a *life-style center,* has become more widespread in the past several years. Substantially smaller than a regional center, a life-style center combines the feel of a village square with fountains and extensive landscaping and a collection of retail stores (such as Talbots and Williams-Sonoma) that are well known and appeal to upscale shoppers.[9]

The largest kind of shopping center, a *regional center,* is anchored by one or more department stores and complemented by many smaller retail outlets. Typically, regional shopping centers are enclosed, climate-controlled, and gigantic. The biggest, Mall of America in suburban Minneapolis, opened in 1992. Under one roof, it combines over 500 retail stores with an amusement park, two lakes, 50 restaurants, and more than a dozen movie theaters—all adjacent to 17,000 free parking spaces. This "megamall" draws over 40 million shoppers and tourists annually, and most retailers with stores there are generating satisfactory levels of sales. Steps are being taken to greatly expand the size of Mall of America![10]

Starting in the mid-1950s, regional centers became the hub of shopping and social activities in many communities. Eventually, though, many shoppers grew too time conscious to spend much time shopping or socializing at a huge mall. From the early 1980s to late 1990s, the average amount of time consumers spent in malls on a monthly basis dropped from 12 hours to under 5 hours. Some observers are pessimistic about the future of regional centers, especially those that are several decades

The gigantic Mall of America created a powerful magnet for consumers by combining shopping with a variety of entertainment. This photo shows how entertainment (the Lego Imagination Center) is located adjacent to retailers (note the Banana Republic store) in this mall. The fact that a shopper spends three hours at the Mall of America, three times the national average for malls, has influenced the design and renovation of other large shopping centers.

www.mallofamerica.com

old. One real estate executive went so far as to predict that the number of malls in the U.S. would drop from a peak of 2,000 in the mid-1990s to 1,200 prior to 2010. Older regional centers that are of medium size (400,000 to 800,000 square feet) and are located closer to downtown rather than the suburbs are in the greatest jeopardy.[11]

With such forecasts, it's not surprising that relatively few regional centers are being built now. Instead, many enclosed malls are being renovated and modernized to enhance their appeal to shoppers. Sometimes, entertainment is taking center stage in today's malls. Other enclosed malls and often the space surrounding them are being revamped for mixed uses, combining retail stores, office space, and/or residential units. According to one estimate, more than 400 mixed-use developments have been created around the country.[12]

The growth of suburban shopping led to vacant stores and decreased retail sales in many downtown areas. Now some retail firms see opportunities in the urban core. To mention a couple of examples, Sterling Optical and Athlete's Foot have opened nonmall locations in urban neighborhoods. Some cities have worked to revitalize their downtown shopping districts. Enclosed shopping centers featuring distinctive designs—including Water Tower Place in Chicago—and new mixed-use projects—including Minzer Park in Boca Raton, Florida—are successful in some downtown areas.[13]

Wherever they are located, most retail stores have gotten larger and larger, perhaps because the overhead of operating a store doesn't vary much on the basis of size. Many outlets such as Sports Authority, Lowe's, and Best Buy are called "big boxes," alluding to their enormous sizes as well as their rather plain designs. Because some consumers do not want to devote the necessary time and energy to shop at very large stores, a few chains are experimenting with smaller formats. For example, Wal-Mart is now opening Neighborhood Markets, each about 50,000 square feet, about one-quarter the size of the chain's supercenters. Home Depot Inc. is trying out a format, about two-thirds the size of its regular stores, that is located in and merchandised for urban neighborhoods.[14]

Classification of Retailers

We will classify retailers on two bases: form of ownership and marketing strategies. Any retail firm can be classified according to both bases. For example, Sears is a corporate chain of department stores with broad, relatively deep assortments, moderate prices, and levels of personal service that vary across departments. In contrast, a neighborhood paint store operates as an independent limited-line store that has narrow, relatively deep assortments, tries to avoid price competition, and provides extensive personal service.

Retailers Classified by Form of Ownership

The major forms of ownership in retailing are corporate chain, independent, and contractual vertical marketing system (VMS). The VMS category includes several different types.

Corporate Chains

A **corporate chain** is an organization of two or more centrally owned and centrally managed stores that generally handle the same lines of products. Three factors differentiate a chain from an independent store and the contractual form of VMS:

- Technically, two or more stores constitute a chain. Many small merchants that open several stores in shopping centers and newly populated areas do not think of themselves as chains, however. Perhaps with that in mind, the U.S. Bureau of the Census considers 11 stores to be the minimum size for a chain.

- A corporate chain has central ownership; as we'll see soon, a contractual VMS does not.

- Because of centralized management, individual units in a chain typically have little autonomy. Strategic decisions are made at headquarters, and operations typically are standardized for all the units in a chain. Standardization assures consistency, but it often results in inflexibility. And that means a chain sometimes cannot adjust rapidly to local market conditions.

Corporate chains are tremendously significant in retailing, accounting for about 40% of total retail trade. Chains are especially prevalent in the department store business, but are less common among auto and home supply stores or eating places.[15] Essentially, chains are large-scale retail institutions. As such, they possess the comparative strengths and weaknesses outlined in Table 15.2.

Independent Stores

An **independent retailer** is a company with a single store that is not affiliated with a contractual vertical marketing system. Most retailers are independents, and most independents are quite small. Independents usually have the characteristics of small retailers presented in Table 15.2.

Independent retailers typically are viewed as having higher prices than chain stores. However, because of differences in merchandise and services, it is difficult to compare the prices of chains and independents directly. For instance, chains often have their own private brands that are not sold by independents. Also, independents and chain stores frequently provide customers with different levels—and perhaps quality—of services. Many customers are willing to pay extra for services they consider valuable, such as credit, delivery, alterations, installation, a liberal return policy, and friendly, knowledgeable personal service.

Contractual Vertical Marketing Systems

In a **contractual vertical marketing system,** independently owned firms join together under a contract specifying how they will operate. The three types of contractual VMS are discussed below.

Retailer Cooperatives and Voluntary Chains
The main difference between these two types of systems is who organizes them. A **retailer cooperative** is formed by a group of small retailers that agree to establish and operate a wholesale warehouse. In contrast, a **voluntary chain** is sponsored by a wholesaler that enters into a contract with interested retailers.

Historically these two forms of contractual VMS have been organized for defensive reasons—to enable independent retailers to compete effectively with large, strong chains. They do this by providing their retail members with volume buying power and management assistance in store layout, employee and management training programs, promotion, accounting, and inventory control systems.

www.iga.com

Retailer cooperatives are declining, but still have strong representatives in groceries (Certified Grocers) and hardware (TruServ and Ace). Voluntary chains are prevalent in the grocery field (IGA, Supervalu); they are also found in auto supplies (Western Auto) stores.

Franchise Systems
Franchising involves a continuing relationship in which a parent company provides management assistance and the right to use its trademark in return for payments from the owner of the individual business unit. The parent company is called a *franchisor,* whereas the owner of the unit is called a *franchisee.* The combination of franchisor and franchisees comprises a *franchise system.*

www.franchise.org

This type of contractual VMS is growing steadily, generating an estimated $1 *trillion* in annual sales and accounting for as much as two-fifths of all retail sales in the U.S. According to the International Franchise Association, about 320,000 retail units are affiliated with about 1,500 franchise systems.[16]

There are two kinds of franchising:

- **Product and trade name franchising.** Historically the dominant kind, product and trade name franchising is prevalent in the automobile (Ford, Honda) and petroleum (Chevron, Texaco) industries. It is a distribution agreement under which a supplier authorizes a dealer to sell a product line, using the parent company's trade name for promotional purposes. The franchisee agrees to buy from the franchisor and also to abide by specified policies. The focus in product and trade name franchising is on *what is sold.*

- **Business format franchising.** Much of franchising's growth and publicity over the past four decades has involved the business format kind (used by firms such as Taco Bell, Midas, and H&R Block). This kind of franchising covers an entire method (or format) for operating a business. A successful retail business sells the right to operate the same business in another geographic area. The franchisee expects to receive from the parent company a proven method of operating a business; in return, the franchisor receives from each business owner payments and also conformance to policies and standards. The focus here is on *how the business is run.*

The franchisor has applied its business format to the retailing of five different types of used goods. Computer Renaissance, which sold used computer equipment, is no longer offered by Winmark, but the other four franchises are still viable.

www.
winmarkcorporation.com

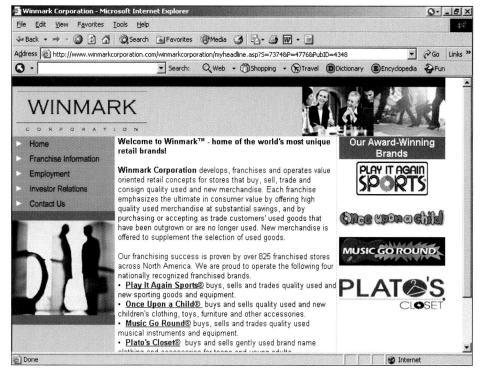

Selling franchises can be attractive to a successful retail business that wants to expand. Among the advantages:

- Rapid expansion is expedited, because franchisees provide capital when they purchase franchises. Ambitious, successful retailers and service firms, such as Berlitz in language training, are employing franchising as an offensive tool.
- Because they have an investment at risk, franchisees typically are highly motivated to work hard and adhere to the parent company's proven format.

Buying a franchise can offer protection to a prospective new retail store or to an independent store that faces stiff competition from chains. Among the benefits:

- Franchisees can use the parent company's well-known trade name, which should help attract customers. Nestlé's franchised cookie outlets should have good name recognition.
- Various forms of management assistance—including site-selection and store-layout guidance, technical and management training, promotional programs, and inventory control systems—are provided to franchisees prior to as well as after opening the business. Because of such aids, franchising has been referred to as "entrepreneurship with a safety net."[17]

Franchising is not without problems. Some franchisees criticize franchisors for practices such as the following: (1) not providing franchisees with the promised levels of business support; (2) locating too many of the company's outlets in the same market; or (3) unjustifiably terminating or not renewing the franchise agreement. Some franchisees work long hours but do not earn an adequate return on their personal efforts or their financial investment.[18] Even worse, a number of franchises that were based on poor products or unsound business practices have failed. Franchisors have

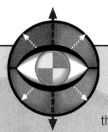
their own complaints, notably some franchisees deviate from the system's policies and practices.

Despite some challenges, continued growth in franchising is expected. For one thing, 92% of existing franchisees consider themselves successful, a statistic that is widely publicized by franchisors. (Of course, this statistic ignores franchisees that fail.) Further, some franchisors are working more closely with their franchisees. GNC, for instance, accepted a franchisee's suggestion that smoothie bars be added to the vitamin and nutrition stores.[19]

Numerous products, especially services, lend themselves to franchising. Growth areas in franchising often coincide with demographic and social trends. At this time, therefore, services designed to aid either an aging population or time-starved individuals and families have potential as franchises. One such franchise is Home Instead, which provides companionship and assistance to senior citizens.[20]

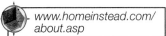
www.homeinstead.com/about.asp

Retailers Classified by Marketing Strategies

Whatever its form of ownership, a retailer must develop marketing-mix strategies to succeed in its chosen target markets. In retailing, the marketing mix emphasizes product assortment, price, location, promotion, and customer services designed to aid in the sale of a product. Such services include credit, delivery, gift wrapping, product installation, merchandise returns, store hours, parking, and—very important—personal assistance.

Table 15.3 classifies retail stores on the basis of three elements of the marketing mix:

- Breadth and depth of product assortment.
- Price level.
- Amount of customer services.

We will now consider, in very brief fashion, key factors associated with each type of retail store. There are examples of highly successful operations within each of these store types (none more successful than Wal-Mart in the category of discount stores). Likewise, other chains (Kmart, for example) and some store types (department stores, for instance) are under severe competitive pressures and, as such, are modifying some strategies. You will see that certain retailers are similar to others because new or modified institutions have filled the "strategic gaps" that once separated different types of institutions.

Department Stores

www.filenes.com

Long a mainstay of retailing in the U.S., a **department store** seeks a differential advantage through a combination of distinctive, appealing merchandise and numerous customer services, such as alterations, credit plans, and bridal registry. Familiar department store names include Filene's, Dillard's, Foley's, Rich's, Marshall Field's, Sears, and JCPenney.

Some department store chains, notably Montgomery Ward, have gone out of business in recent years. The surviving chains face serious challenges. Because of their prime locations and abundant customer services, their operating expenses are considerably higher than most other retailers. Many producers' brands that used to be available exclusively through department stores are now widely distributed and available at discounted prices. And the quality of sales help has deteriorated in many department stores.[21]

Other retail institutions, such as discount houses and category-killer stores, are aggressively trying to lure shoppers away from department stores by offering lower

TABLE 15.3 Retail Stores Classified by Key Marketing Strategies

Type of Store	Breadth and Depth of Assortment	Price Level	Amount of Customer Services
Department store	Very broad, deep	Avoids price competition	Wide array
Discount store	Broad, shallow	Emphasizes low prices	Relatively few
Limited-line store	Narrow, deep	Traditional types avoid price competition; new kinds emphasize low prices	Varies by type
Specialty store	Very narrow, deep	Avoids price competition	At least standard; extensive in some
Off-price retailer	Narrow, deep	Emphasizes low prices	Few
Category-killer store	Narrow, very deep	Emphasizes low prices	Few to moderate
Supermarket	Broad, deep	Some emphasize low prices; others avoid price competition	Few
Convenience store	Narrow, shallow	High prices	Few
Warehouse club	Very broad, very shallow	Emphasizes very low prices	Few (open only to members)

prices. The convenience of buying from catalogs or online represents still more competition. Department stores' share of total retail trade has dropped about 5 percentage points since the early 1990s.[22]

Striving to gain an advantage or at least remain competitive, many department stores are adjusting some of their strategies and tactics. Among the changes, Federated is adding amenities (such as technology-equipped customer lounges) to appeal to upscale shoppers, Penney's has moved to centralized checkout areas, Sears sought to improve its image and apparel lines by acquiring Lands' End, and May is experimenting with smaller stores. Despite their problems, department stores as a group still account for a huge amount of retail sales. Moreover, this type of institution has success stories, perhaps none more prominent than Kohl's. This rapidly growing chain is attracting customers through a combination of leading brands, cheaper locations, customer-friendly store layout, lower prices, and very tight inventory control.[23]

www.kohls.com

Discount Stores

Discount retailing involves comparatively low prices as a major selling point combined with reduced costs of doing business. Several institutions, including off-price retailers and warehouse clubs, rely on discount retailing as their main marketing strategy.

The prime example of discount retailing is the **discount store,** a large-scale retail institution that normally carries a broad assortment of soft goods (particularly apparel) and hard goods (including popular brands of appliances and home furnishings). Wal-Mart, Target, and Kmart are the largest discount chains, although Kmart

Various manufacturers and retailers, ranging from Nike to Tommy Hilfiger, have opened huge "flagship" stores. This photo shows the interior of the 110,000-square-foot Toys "Я" Us store in downtown New York that has, among other features, a 60-foot Ferris wheel. The toy retailer expects the store to generate favorable public relations *and* to be profitable. However, perhaps because of how costly they are to construct and operate, the success of retailers' flagship stores has been mixed.

www.toysrus.com

has been struggling mightily to regain financial solvency.[24] In recent years, other discount chains with smaller stores, including Dollar General and Family Dollar, have been growing rapidly. Discount stores have had a major impact on retailing, causing many merchants to lower their prices.

The leading discount chains are also committing substantial resources to a much expanded discount store, called a **supercenter.** Basically, it is a combined discount store and grocery store. Wal-Mart's more than 1,250 supercenters are different than discount stores in several noteworthy ways: larger size, wider aisles, more attractive decor, broader assortment of merchandise, and added customer services. A company executive surmised that all or most regular Wal-Mart stores could be supercenters in the future.[25]

Limited-Line Stores

Much of the "action" in retailing in recent years has been in **limited-line stores,** which typically sell products such as clothing, baked goods, and furniture and seek to maintain full, or nondiscounted, prices. New types of limited-line retailers have gained a foothold by emphasizing low prices.

The breadth of assortment varies somewhat across limited-line stores. A store may choose to concentrate on several related product lines (shoes, sportswear, and accessories), a single product line (shoes), or part of one product line (athletic footwear). We identify limited-line stores by the name of the primary product line—furniture store, hardware store, or clothing store, for example. Some retailers such as grocery stores and drugstores that used to be limited-line stores now carry much broader assortments because of scrambled merchandising, a strategy described in the preceding chapter.

Specialty Stores
A **specialty store** concentrates on a particular product line (baked goods) or even part of a product line (cinnamon rolls). Examples of specialty stores are athletic footwear stores, meat markets, and dress shops. (Specialty *stores* should not be confused with specialty *goods.* In a sense, specialty stores are misnamed, because they may carry not just specialty goods but any of the categories of consumer goods that were discussed in Chapter 8.)

Most specialty stores strive to maintain manufacturers' suggested prices, although they may offer their own store brands at lower prices. The prosperity of specialty stores depends on their ability to attract and then satisfy consumers who especially want deep assortments and perhaps extensive, top-quality services as well.

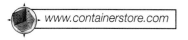
www.batteriesplus.com/
aboutus.html

Successful specialty store chains include Zany Brainy, which concentrates on learning toys that stimulate children's creativity and thinking; Batteries Plus, which specializes in various types of batteries; and the Old Navy clothing chain. Sunglass Hut International, which squeezes hundreds of different pairs of sunglasses into its tiny outlets, decided to add a complementary assortment of watches.[26]

www.containerstore.com

Forecasts for specialty stores are mixed. Many in malls are coping with a shrinking number of shoppers drawn to shopping centers. However, some theme-oriented specialty chains are prospering. For example, the Container Store is attracting numerous consumers who want to have "a place for everything."[27]

www.paylessinfo.com/
corporate_info/company

Off-Price Retailers
When some discount stores started to trade up during the 1980s, **off-price retailers** positioned themselves below discount stores with lower prices on selected product lines. Off-price retailers are most common in the areas of apparel (Ross Dress for Less, for example) and footwear (Payless ShoeSource).

To the extent possible, off-price retailers concentrate on well-known producers' brands. They often buy manufacturers' excess output, inventory remaining at the end of a fashion season, or irregular merchandise (called *seconds*) at lower-than-normal wholesale costs.

Factory outlets are a special type of off-price retailer. They usually sell a single company's merchandise. This type of institution gives manufacturers another channel for their products—one over which they have complete control. Many popular brands, such as Polo Ralph Lauren, Nike, Crate & Barrel, and Dansk, are featured in factory outlets.

A few of these stores are located adjacent to a company's manufacturing facility—hence, the name. However, typically they are grouped together in *outlet centers*, usually some distance from major malls and downtown shopping areas. Outlet centers grew rapidly from the inception of the concept in the early 1980s until the mid-1990s. At that time, some shoppers retreated from outlets because a growing number of retailers in regional shopping centers turned to value pricing. In the latter half of the past decade, the number of outlet centers in the U.S. shrunk from about 325 to 275. Recently, some developers altered their outlet center strategies by adding more upscale brands (such as Coach) as well as various amenities (such as valet parking and spacious restrooms) in order to attract more affluent consumers.[28]

Category-Killer Stores A phenomenon of the 1980s, a **category-killer store** aims to capture a large portion of sales in a specific product category and, in so doing, "kill" the competition. What distinguishes a category killer is the combination of low prices *and* many different sizes, models, styles, and colors of the products. For example, a Borders or a Barnes & Noble bookstore ordinarily carries over 100,000 titles, perhaps 10 times the assortment of the typical mall bookstore.[29]

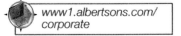
www.ikea-usa.com

Successful category killers include Ikea in home furnishings, Circuit City in consumer electronics, Home Depot and Lowe's in building supplies, Bed Bath & Beyond in soft goods for the home, and Toys "Я" Us. Other product areas with category killers are housewares, recorded music, and sporting goods. Category-killer stores took sales and customers away from long-standing retailers, especially specialty stores and department stores. The format has been extended to other products. For example, CarMax and AutoNation established "megastores" featuring very large inventories of used cars and trucks. However, CarMax has opened only about three dozen outlets, and AutoNation has closed its used-car megastores. Other category-killer chains have also stumbled; for instance, Jumbo Sports wound up in bankruptcy.[30]

Seeing the problems experienced by some category killers, one executive predicted that category killers "will be a diminishing force," mainly as a result of the size and effectiveness of large discount chains. Still, the combination of deep assortments and low prices is appealing to many consumers. Thus the impact of this type of retail store is expected to expand.[31]

Supermarkets

As with *discount*, the word *supermarket* can be used to describe a method of retailing *and* a type of institution. As a method, **supermarket retailing** features several related product lines, a high degree of self-service, largely centralized checkout, and competitive prices. Supermarket retailing is used to sell various kinds of merchandise, including building materials, office products, and especially groceries.

As a type of institution, a **supermarket** offers a moderately broad, moderately deep product assortment spanning groceries and some nonfood lines. Some supermarkets use price *offensively*, featuring low prices to attract customers. Others use price *defensively*, relying on leader pricing to avoid a price disadvantage. Having very thin gross margins, supermarkets need high levels of inventory turnover to achieve satisfactory returns on invested capital.

www1.albertsons.com/ corporate

A grocery shopper can choose among not only many brands of supermarkets (Publix, Safeway, Albertson's, and Kroger, to name several), but also various types of institutions (warehouse clubs, meat and fish markets, and convenience stores). Competition has intensified further, as Wal-Mart and the other giant discount chains have made major moves into grocery retailing, opening supercenters and/or regular-size supermarkets.[32]

Reacting to competitive pressures, some supermarkets cut costs and stressed low prices, offering more private brands and few customer services. Others expanded their store size and added more nonfood lines and groceries (ethnic foods, for example) attuned to a particular market area. They also added various service departments, including video rentals, delicatessens, financial institutions, and pharmacies. Loblaw dominates grocery retailing in Canada, with one differential advantage being wide-ranging supplementary services—to the point of putting a fitness club in one of its new supermarkets.[33]

Convenience Stores

To satisfy consumers' increasing desire for convenience, particularly in suburban areas, the **convenience store** emerged in the latter half of the past century. Besides selected groceries and nonfoods (especially beverages, snacks, and cigarettes), gasoline, fast foods, and selected services (such as car washes and automated teller machines) can be found in many convenience stores. Its label reflects the institution's appeal and explains how its higher prices are justified. Examples of convenience store chains are 7-Eleven, Circle K, and Convenient Food Mart.

Convenience stores compete to some extent with both supermarkets and fast-food restaurants. Furthermore, petroleum companies have modified many of their service stations by phasing out auto repairs and adding a convenience section and perhaps a fast-food counter as well. To mention a few examples, Arco has AM/PM Mini Marts, Texaco has Star Marts, and Mobil is partnering with both Blimpie and Pizza Hut.[34]

To boost their competitiveness, convenience stores have adjusted their marketing mixes. For example, the 7-Eleven chain has added fresh foods, notably sandwiches, and is experimenting with in-store kiosks for financial services and limited online purchases. According to a consulting firm, convenience stores could better live up to their names by accepting e-mails from consumers and then having their orders, including groceries, rental videos, and perhaps dry cleaning, ready for pickup at a designated time.[35]

Warehouse Clubs

An institution that has mushroomed since the mid-1980s, the **warehouse club**, is a combined retailing and wholesaling operation. Warehouse clubs are open only to members who pay an annual fee of about $25 to $50. Their target markets are small businesses (some purchasing merchandise for resale), select groups (such as government personnel and credit union members), and—to an increasing degree—individual consumers.

A warehouse club carries about the same breadth of assortment as a large discount store, but in much less depth. It is housed in a warehouse-type building with tall metal display and storage racks. The primary advantage of a warehouse club is its extremely low prices. (Prices for household consumers typically are about 5% higher than prices offered to business members.) This institution has some drawbacks. To mention a couple, the clubs' assortments are limited and skewed toward large quantities and huge packages, and customers ordinarily must load their purchases in their vehicles.

The leading warehouse clubs are Costco, Sam's Club (owned by Wal-Mart), and BJ's Wholesale. As with other retail institutions, warehouse clubs continue to modify and refine their strategies. For example, Costco has added "big ticket" items such as diamond engagement rings and its own Kirkland brand of appliances. In the words of a Costco executive, "We want to surprise people at every turn. Even if you don't buy the Waterford crystal, it makes an impact on you." Not surprisingly, Sam's has followed suit, even offering fine wines.[36]

The owner of a small independent bookstore runs short of best-sellers during the peak Christmas season. Obtaining more inventory from the store's normal supplier, a wholesaler in another city, takes several days. In the meanwhile, thousands of dollars of sales could be lost. A warehouse club about 5 miles from the bookstore carries a limited selection of books, and they are priced at about the bookstore's wholesale cost. By buying best-sellers at the warehouse club, substituting new price stickers, and getting the books on the store's shelves within a couple of hours rather than several days, the independent bookstore builds sales during this critical selling period *and* satisfies its customers.

Considering that customers do not know the bookstore acquired some of its best-sellers from a warehouse club and then resold them, is this ethical business behavior on the part of the bookstore owner?

Nonstore Retailing

A large majority, about 80%, of retail transactions are made in stores. However, a growing volume of sales is taking place away from stores. Retailing activities resulting in transactions that occur away from a physical store are called **nonstore retailing**. It is "guesstimated" that sales volume through nonstore retailing is in the vicinity of $400 billion annually.[37] On the basis of this figure, nonstore sales account for about one-eighth of total retail trade.

We will consider five types of nonstore retailing: direct selling, telemarketing, automatic vending, online retailing, and direct marketing. (Rather than worrying about the confusing names, we suggest that you focus on the features and competition across the five types.) Each type may be used not just by retailers, but by other types of organizations as well.

Direct Selling

In the context of retailing, **direct selling** is defined as personal contact between a sales person and a consumer away from a store that results in a sale. Annual volume of retail direct selling in the U.S. was almost $27 billion in 2001. These transactions were rung up by about 11 million independent sales people, only 10% of whom devote full time to direct selling. Direct selling is also widespread in Japan, which accounts for about 29% of the worldwide volume of this form of nonstore retailing. The U.S. represents almost 34% of the total, and all other countries the rest.[38]

The two kinds of direct selling are door to door and party plan. Many well-known direct-selling companies, including Mary Kay, Amway, Shaklee, Pampered Chef, Creative Memories, and Excel Telecommunications, market diverse products through direct selling. This channel is particularly well suited for products that require extensive demonstration. Home/family care (such as cookware and cleaning products) and personal care (such as cosmetics) account for the largest volumes of direct selling.[39]

With so many women—more than one-half—now working outside the home, reps of direct-selling firms call on employees in the workplace or give sales parties at lunchtime in offices. Some employers take a dim view of such selling in the workplace. As discussed in the Chapter 14 case, to gain added customers, Avon has turned to new channels. So too has Tupperware, which is distributing its products (primarily plastic food storage containers) not only by direct selling, but also at kiosks in shopping malls, through large retail chains, and on the Internet.[40]

Direct selling has drawbacks. Commissions, paid when a sale is made, run as high as 50% of the retail price. Recruiting, training, motivating, and retaining sales

www.creativememories.com/profile.asp

The Pampered Chef, Ltd., markets a wide variety of kitchen tools using party-plan selling. Each year, independent sales reps hold over 1 million Pampered Chef "kitchen shows" in the homes of friends and neighbors to present the company's line of products, such as a measuring cup that has a built-in plunger to remove the contents. Using only direct selling, Pampered Chef rings up over $700 million in annual sales.

www.pamperedchef.com

people are difficult tasks. To counter occasional problems with high-pressure sales tactics, nearly all states have "cooling off" laws that permit consumers to nullify a party-plan or door-to-door sale within several days of the transaction.

Direct selling also offers significant benefits. Consumers can buy at home or at another convenient nonstore location that provides the opportunity for personal contact with a sales person. For the seller, direct selling represents the boldest method of trying to persuade ultimate consumers to make a purchase.

Telemarketing

Sometimes called *telephone selling*, **telemarketing** refers to a sales person initiating contact with a prospective customer and closing a sale over the telephone. Products that can be bought without being seen are suitable for telemarketing. Examples are pest-control services, magazine subscriptions, credit cards, and athletic club memberships. One estimate places the total annual volume of telemarketing in the retail sector at about $275 billion.[41]

Telemarketing is not problem free. Often encountering hostile people on the other end of the line and experiencing many more rejections than closed sales, most telephone sales reps last just a short while in the job. Further, some telemarketers rely on questionable and/or unethical practices, such as implying that the call is for other than selling purposes. In addition, some telemarketing involves outright fraud—for example, attempts to obtain a person's credit card number for illegal use. It's estimated that such fraud costs consumers $40 *billion* annually.[42]

Both states and federal agencies have enacted rules to constrain telemarketers' activities. One rule, for instance, bans calls before 8 A.M. and after 9 P.M. Also, over 15 states have passed laws that prohibit many, but not all, telemarketers from calling residents who sign up for a "no-call" list. The Federal Trade Commission is working on a national no-call list. These rules also empower government officials to seek stiff fines against violators.[43]

Despite these problems, telemarketing sales have increased in recent years. Fundamentally, some people appreciate the convenience of making a purchase by phone. The future of telemarketing is sure to be affected by the degree to which the problems are dealt with *and* by the surge of online retailing.

Automatic Vending

The sale of products through a machine with no personal contact between buyer and seller is called **automatic vending**. The appeal of vending is convenient purchase. Products sold by automatic vending are usually well-known brands of foods and beverages with a high rate of turnover. It's estimated that vending rings up approximately $30 billion in annual sales, which represents about 1% of all retail trade.[44]

Vending machines can expand a firm's market by reaching customers where and when they cannot come to a store. Thus vending equipment is found almost everywhere. Automatic vending has high operating costs because of the need to replenish inventories frequently. The machines also require maintenance and repairs.

The difficulties mentioned above may hinder future growth. However, vending innovations give reason for some optimism. For starters, there is a continuing flow of new products for vending machines, including movie soundtracks (sold in theater lobbies), freshly squeezed orange juice, heatable diet dinners, office supplies, and even live bait for fishing. Vending machines that accept credit or debit cards or even charge a purchase to the customer's cell phone account are being tested and, in some cases, introduced. Technological advances also allow operators to monitor vending machines from a distance, thereby reducing the number (and lost revenues) of out-of-stock or out-of-order machines. Of course, the benefits of these advances have to be weighed against their costs.[45]

Online Retailing

When an enterprise uses its website to offer products for sale and then individuals or organizations use their computers to make purchases from this company, the parties have engaged in *electronic transactions* (also called *online selling* or *Internet marketing*). Many electronic transactions involve two businesses, but this chapter focuses on sales by firms to ultimate consumers. Thus we are interested in **online retailing,** which consists of electronic transactions in which the purchaser is an ultimate consumer.

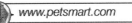

www.fogdog.com

Online retailing has attracted numerous new enterprises, such as Fogdog Sports, Buy.com, and CDNow.com. It has also drawn existing retailers, such as Nordstrom, Lands' End, and PETsMART, into operating either on their own or in alliances with Internet firms. Not all retailers have embraced online selling, however. According to one study, 95% of the leading bricks-and-mortar merchants have a website, but only

PETsMART exemplifies "bricks-and-clicks" retailing in which a major online site is combined with a network of physical stores, with the dual approaches intended to generate substantial sales and satisfactory profits. Note that besides promoting various products for online purchase, the firm's home page also helps consumers locate a nearby PETsMART physical store.

www.petsmart.com

45% of the firms allow shoppers to make online purchases. The overriding reason why some retailers do not add a clicks-and-modem option are the high costs of establishing a secure e-commerce site and then processing and shipping the orders.[46]

Some websites, especially those launched by general-merchandise retailers such as Wal-Mart and Target, feature broad assortments. Other Internet-only firms, notably Amazon.com, are using various methods to broaden their offerings. However, most e-tailers concentrate on one or two product categories that are often reflected in their names—wine.com, 1-800-Flowers.com, and Furniture.com are several examples.

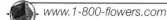
www.1-800-flowers.com

Whatever their differences, e-tailers are likely to share an attribute: They are unprofitable or, at best, barely profitable. Of course, there are substantial costs in establishing an online operation. Aggressive efforts to attract shoppers and retain customers through extensive advertising and low prices are also expensive. The substantial losses racked up by online enterprises used to be accepted, with the rationale being that all available funds should be used to gain a foothold in this growing market. Now investors expect e-tailers to deliver profits in the near term. Fortunately, there is progress in that regard. According to a study, 56% of retail firms

MARKETING IN THE INFORMATION ECONOMY

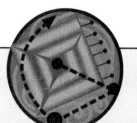

Have "bots" changed shopping and pricing on the Internet?

Many, probably most, consumers engage in comparison shopping—that is, searching for the lowest price on a particular item. Before the Internet, such comparisons required a store-to-store search or a series of price-checking telephone calls. With the advent of e-commerce, price comparisons became much easier. Still, moving from website to website and then locating the desired item and its price was somewhat time-consuming.

Online price comparisons became much easier when comparison-shopping engines made their debut in 1995. They were devised to help consumers do comparison shopping on the Internet. These shopping robots, nicknamed "bots," do this by searching the Web for a particular item and then furnishing the interested consumer with a list of merchants who offer it, including the prices they charge. For example, within seconds, BizRate.com can examine several million products and a couple of thousand online merchants and furnish a shopper with a list of the best prices offered by reputable Internet firms for a specific item.

Bots are becoming increasingly popular and widespread. According to one survey, 85% of American shoppers use a bot at least some of the time they shop online; 8% use one every time. There are many competing bots now: PriceGrabber.com, mySimon, PriceScan.com, and BizRate.com, to name several. Shopping robots are also increasingly common in other parts of the world. Examples include BuyCentral and Kelkoo in Europe as well as DealTime.com, which has sites in Europe and Asia besides the U.S. And future growth is predicted. According to one research firm, bots will be part of 10% of total online sales in 2005, compared to less than 4% in 2000.

Nothing's perfect, so shopping robots have some shortcomings:

- For one thing, they don't automatically have access to every online merchant's prices. Some e-tailers have blocked bots from their sites because they are concerned about being forced into a price war with competitors. In addition, a few online merchants don't disclose hidden costs, such as shipping and handling.

- Also, to generate revenues, some bots give preferential, top-of-the-list placement to online merchants that pay a fee. Hence, the comparison-shopping results may not be listed strictly according to price levels.

These circumstances make it difficult for potential buyers to make informed purchase decisions, even with price comparisons from bots.

Nevertheless, it appears that bots (and other factors) are forcing e-tailers and also traditional retailers to monitor and adjust their prices more frequently. As a professor stated, "After all, fixed prices have been around only for a couple hundred years."

Sources: "According to BizRate.com, Comparison Shopping Bots Are Coming of Age," *Business Wire*, Mar. 14, 2002, no pages given; Jeanette Borzo, "A Consumer's Report—Searching: Out of Order?" *The Wall Street Journal*, Sept. 24, 2001, p. R13; Chris Taylor, "Bot till You Drop," *Time*, Oct. 11, 1999, pp. 52–53; and Scott Kirsner, "The Bots Are Back," *CIO Web Business*, May 1, 1999, pp. 26–28.

report that their e-commerce activities were profitable in 2001, an improvement from 43% in 2000.[47]

According to various estimates, online retailing registered sales in the vicinity of $70 billion in 2002. Despite various challenges, this form of nonstore retailing is expected to grow rapidly and significantly for the foreseeable future. Online sales represented less than 1% of retail spending in 1999, but one analyst estimated that the figure would climb to 5% by 2005. Even as online sales rise, the number of e-tailers could decline if the recent "dot–com shakeout" continues.[48]

Which product categories are consumers most likely to buy on the Internet in the future? The categories in which online retailing accounts for the largest portions of total retail volume include books, music and videos, computer hardware and software, travel, toys, and consumer electronics. Of course, given that change on the Internet occurs at warp speed, these categories soon may be surpassed by others—perhaps health and beauty aids, auto parts, pet supplies, or even groceries.[49]

Direct Marketing

There is no consensus on the exact nature of direct marketing. In effect, it comprises all types of nonstore retailing other than direct selling, telemarketing, automatic vending, and online retailing. In the context of retailing, we define **direct marketing** as using advertising to contact consumers who, in turn, buy products without visiting a retail store. (Be careful to distinguish among the terms direct *marketing,* direct *selling,* and direct *distribution*!) As denoted by the preceding section, we have chosen to treat online retailing, which involves computer contact, as a separate type of nonstore retailing.

Direct marketers contact consumers through one or more of the following media: radio, TV, newspapers, magazines, catalogs, and mailings (direct mail). Consumers order by telephone or mail. Some direct marketers offer a wide variety of product lines; others carry only one or two lines such as books or fresh fruit. Direct marketing is big business, accounting for perhaps $200 billion in annual retail sales![50]

Under the broad definition, the many forms of direct marketing include:

- *Direct mail,* in which firms mail letters, brochures, and even product samples to consumers, and ask them to purchase by mail or telephone. This approach works best for selling various services, such as credit cards and athletic club memberships, and well-known goods, such as magazines and recorded music. Some small retailers use direct mail in creative ways. For example, Zane's Cycles, in Branford, Connecticut, sends postcards to selected customers offering a special price on a child's bike. This promotion is directed at customers who, according to the firm's database, purchased a baby seat for a bicycle three years earlier.[51]

- *Catalog retailing,* in which companies mail catalogs to consumers or make them available at retail stores. After expanding at an annual rate of 10% during the 1980s, the growth of catalog retailing flattened out during the first half of the 1990s but then picked up again in the second half of the decade. Firms engaged in catalog retailing suffered a temporary sales slowdown following September 11, 2001, as a result of delays in delivering catalogs.[52]

  The number of catalogs distributed in the U.S. nearly doubled between 1980 and 2000—to about 15 *billion* each year. Recently, though, some companies have cut back on their assortment of catalogs, reduced the number of copies of each catalog they distribute, or even exited this field. An encouraging factor for catalog firms, however, is that some of their competencies, such as maintaining large customer databases and shipping small orders, transfer very well to online retailing.[53]

- *Televised shopping,* in which various categories of products are promoted on dedicated TV channels and through *infomercials,* which are TV commercials that run for 30 minutes or even longer on an entertainment channel. The leading shopping channels, QVC and the Home Shopping Network, sell jewelry, consumer electronics, home décor, and other products at relatively low prices. Infomercials have been used to sell various items, including cutlery and home-based businesses. Televised shopping burgeoned during the 1980s, but has slowed down in recent years, perhaps as a result of the inroads made by online retailing.[54]

Direct marketing has drawbacks. Consumers must place orders without viewing or touching the actual merchandise (although they may see a picture of it). To offset this, direct marketers must offer liberal return policies. Furthermore, catalogs and, to some extent, direct-mail pieces are costly and must be prepared long before they are issued. Price changes and new products can be announced only through supplementary catalogs or brochures.

On the plus side, like other types of nonstore retailing, direct marketing provides shopping convenience. In addition, direct marketers enjoy comparatively low operating expenses because they do not have the overhead of physical stores. Direct marketing's future is difficult to forecast, given the rise of the Internet. The issue is whether or not firms relying on direct marketing can achieve and sustain a differential advantage in a growing competition with online enterprises.

Institutional Change in Retailing

As consumers change, so do forms of retailing. Executives would like to anticipate major changes before they occur. When the change is as revolutionary as the sudden, dramatic emergence of online retailing, that's difficult to do. However, evolutionary changes in retailing often follow a pattern in which an established institution trades up to attract a broader market and achieve higher margins. Sooner or later, high costs and, ultimately, high prices (as perceived by its target markets) make the institution vulnerable to new retail types, most likely a low-cost, low-price store.[55]

To illustrate, discount stores have been trading up recently. Target has been successful in becoming, as contradictory as it sounds, an "upscale discounter."[56] If trading up by discount stores is pervasive, an opening may be created for a new low-cost, low-price institution. Maybe that's already here, in the form of "deep" discounters such as Dollar General and/or e-tailers such as Amazon.com, which continues to broaden its offerings while emphasizing low prices.

How will retail institutions or, more broadly, retailing change during the next several years? On the negative side, some analysts think that retailers have overbuilt and that a "shakeout" is likely to occur. Under this scenario, some large chains and numerous small independents would fail, and other retailers would be acquired by stronger firms. On the positive side, it has been suggested that there will be more blending of physical stores and online retailing, with this practice labeled "bricks and clicks." More and more conventional retail businesses are establishing their own websites as another avenue for sales. Further, some stores have installed or are experimenting with Internet-linked kiosks that allow shoppers to obtain more information about desired products or to order out-of-stock items. Conversely, a number of Internet companies are establishing alliances with traditional retailers. In addition, some online merchants are making arrangements with third-party firms (for example, a private postal center) to accept shipments of merchandise for customers for whom home delivery is impractical.[57]

Retail firms must identify and respond to significant trends that affect retailing. According to one study, six major trends (for instance, the growing number of households with nontraditional composition) have changed the nature of the consumer market. Retailers need to recognize and understand these trends and adapt their strategies in order to satisfy shoppers. In particular, companies in the retail arena will have to provide consumers with substantial value that takes into account not just price, but also the quality of products and the shopping experience.[58]

A GLOBAL PERSPECTIVE

Are all retailers moving into foreign countries?

Considering that the large majority of retail firms are tiny, the simple answer is no. Most retailers are doing well to prosper in their own community, without thinking about global success.

Nevertheless, numerous firms based in the U.S. have expanded their retail operations into other countries. For instance, Tupperware's biggest market is Europe. Perhaps surprisingly, Wal-Mart has a relatively small international presence (about 10 nations) but grand global plans. Conversely, many merchants from elsewhere have significant operations in the U.S. To mention two examples, Ahold, a Netherlands-based company, owns several American grocery chains (including Giant, Stop & Shop, and the Peapod online operation) and Ikea, a Swedish firm, has ambitious plans to expand its furniture outlets in this country. And 7-Eleven, the majority of which is owned by a Japanese firm, has 6,000 stores in the U.S. and 17,000 more in other nations.

Of course, merchants can expand geographically without leaving their home base by engaging in e-tailing on the Internet. Thus, as retailers consider how to compete effectively against other retail types (department stores against category killers, for instance), what to do online, and what institutional changes are likely to occur, they also need to be aware of global challenges and opportunities.

Sources: Andy Reinhardt, "E-Commerce Starts to Click," *Business Week,* Aug. 26, 2002, p. 56; Delbert Ellerton, "Joining the Party," *St. Louis Post-Dispatch,* July 21, 2002, pp. G20-G21; and David Koenig, "7-Eleven Toast 75 Years with Free Slurpees," *St. Louis Post-Dispatch,* July 10, 2002, p. C7.

Summary

Retailing is the sale of goods and services to ultimate consumers for personal, nonbusiness use. Any institution (even a manufacturer) may engage in retailing, but a firm engaged primarily in retailing is called a retailer. Retailers serve as purchasing agents for consumers and as sales specialists for producers and wholesaling middlemen. They perform many specific activities, such as anticipating customers' wants, developing product assortments, and financing.

There are about 1.1 million retail firms in the U.S.; collectively they generated almost $3.2 trillion in sales during 2001. Most retail firms are small—either single stores or several stores under common ownership. Small retailers can survive—and even prosper—if they remain flexible and pay careful attention to personally serving customers' needs. Retailers' profits are usually a tiny fraction of sales, generally about 3%.

Besides making decisions about product, price, promotion, and customer services, retailers also must devise strategies related to physical facilities. Specific decisions concern location, size, design, and layout of the store. Downtown shopping areas declined as suburban shopping centers grew. Now regional shopping centers are feeling competitive pressures from many sources, including Internet firms.

Retailers can be classified by (1) form of ownership, including corporate chain, independent store, and various kinds of contractual vertical marketing systems (notably franchising), and (2) key marketing strategies. Types of retailers, distinguished according to product assortment, price levels, and customer service levels, include department stores, discount stores, limited-line stores (notably specialty stores, off-price retailers, and category-killer stores), supermarkets, convenience stores, and warehouse clubs. Mature institutions such as department stores, discount stores, and supermarkets face strong challenges from new competitors, particularly chains of category-killer stores in various product categories.

Although the large majority of retail sales are made in physical stores, perhaps 20% occur away from stores. And this proportion is growing steadily. Five major forms of nonstore retailing are direct selling, telemarketing, automatic vending, online retailing, and direct marketing. Each type has advantages as well as drawbacks. Online retailing, in particular, is growing dramatically.

Retail owners and executives must try to anticipate changes in retail institutions. Often, evolutionary change begins when one type of institution begins to trade up. To succeed, retailers need to identify significant trends and ensure that they develop marketing strategies to satisfy consumers.

More About PETsMART

Besides competing through bricks-and-mortar stores, PETsMART, Petco, and other pet supply retailers went online to satisfy consumers and beat competitors. Some consumers prefer cyberstores, such as PETsMART.com, because they offer an extensive product assortment and, in some respects, greater convenience than is found in physical stores. Pet supplies are suitable for e-tailing because, among other reasons, fit and color are seldom an issue, so merchandise returns are minimal. Total online sales of pet supplies exceed $200 million.

At least a dozen pet supply companies launched new websites in the late 1990s. Among them were Pets.com, which was partially funded by Amazon.com, and Petopia, Petco's online venture. Despite its quirky ad campaign featuring the Sock Puppet mascot, Pets.com folded, as did Petopia and Petstore. PETsMART.com, however, remains an integral part of PETsMART's strategy to sell its products through three different channels— stores, catalogs, and the Web. The company cross-promotes the three and works hard to overcome any conflicts among them.

PETsMART.com's brand awareness certainly benefits from its parent company's numerous retail stores and established catalog. It also has the merchandise-buying and pricing expertise to complement its warehousing and order-fulfillment systems. But PETsMART.com still faces problems. Distribution, in particular, is a significant concern for pet supply e-tailers. After all, how efficient is it to ship a 40-pound bag of dog food? Some online retailers, hoping to attract orders, charged negligible amounts for shipping and handling, thereby cutting into potential profits.

In fact, when it folded in late 2000, the heavily promoted Pets.com site was estimated to be several years away from profitability. The demise of Pets.com and several rivals could help PETsMART.com survive and prosper. But PETsMART needs a set of marketing strategies that produce customer satisfaction—and profitability—over the long term.

With that in mind, PETsMART.com is featuring both breadth and depth of merchandise assortment, products at various price levels, and special departments for popular pets. A free online magazine and a community section on the site (with pet care tips, links to local charities, and photo contests) are all intended to create a shopper-friendly Internet experience. With these strategies in place, PETsMART.com might be on its way to becoming "top dog" on the Web.[59]

1. To what extent does PETsMART.com take sales away from PETsMART bricks-and-mortar stores?

2. How can online retailers compete with bricks-and-mortar stores with respect to customer service?

Key Terms and Concepts

Retailing (retail trade) (420)
Retailer (421)
Physical facilities (424)
Shopping center (425)
Corporate chain (427)
Independent retailer (427)
Contractual vertical marketing system (428)
Retailer cooperative (428)
Voluntary chain (428)
Franchising (428)

Product and trade name franchising (428)
Business format franchising (428)
Department store (431)
Discount retailing (432)
Discount store (432)
Supercenter (433)
Limited-line store (433)
Specialty store (433)
Off-price retailer (433)
Category-killer store (434)

Supermarket retailing (434)
Supermarket (434)
Convenience store (435)
Warehouse club (435)
Nonstore retailing (436)
Direct selling (436)
Telemarketing (437)
Automatic vending (438)
Online retailing (438)
Direct marketing (440)

Questions and Problems

1. In each of the following situations, is the seller a *retailer* and is the transaction a *retail sale*?

   a. Independent contractor selling lawn-care services door to door.
   b. Farmer selling produce door to door.
   c. Farmer selling produce at a roadside stand.
   d. Sporting goods store selling uniforms to a professional baseball team.
   e. Fogdog Sports selling running shoes online to a college student.

2. What recommendations would you offer to a department store chain for reducing retailing costs? What would you recommend to discount stores in this regard?

3. Support or refute the following statements, using facts and statistics where appropriate:

   a. "Retailing is typically small-scale business."
   b. "There is a high degree of concentration in retailing today; the giants control the field."

4. The ease of entry into retailing undoubtedly contributes to the high failure rate among retailers, which—in the view of some—creates economic waste. Should entry into retailing be restricted? If so, how could this be done?

5. Do you agree that there are three keys to success in retailing—location, location, and location? How do you reconcile this perspective with the fact that there is so much price competition in retailing at the present time?

6. What can specialty stores do to strengthen their competitive positions?

7. "The supermarket, with its operating expense ratio of 20%, is the most efficient institution in retailing today." Do you agree with this statement? In what ways might supermarkets further reduce their expenses?

8. "Direct selling is the most efficient form of retailing because it eliminates wholesalers and retail stores." Discuss.

9. What new retail institutions might we see in the future?

10. Of the types of retail stores discussed in the chapter, which ones do you think have been or would be most successful in foreign countries? Which ones have been or would be unsuccessful in other countries? Explain your answers.

Interactive Marketing Exercises

1. Arrange an interview with a small retailer. Discuss with this merchant the general competitive positions of small and large retailers, as covered in this chapter. Which, if any, of these points does the small retailer disagree with, and why? Also ask what courses of action this merchant takes to achieve or maintain a viable competitive position. Interview a second small retailer, ask the same questions, and compare your answers.

2. Choose two retail franchise systems, and send a letter or an e-mail to their headquarters requesting information that is provided to prospective purchasers of a franchise. (Local units of the franchise systems should be able to supply you with the headquarters' mailing addresses; or go to the International Franchise Association website, *www.franchise.org,* to obtain franchisors' names and addresses.) Once you have received the information, evaluate whether you would like to own either of these franchises. What criteria did you use in making this evaluation?

Wholesaling and Physical Distribution

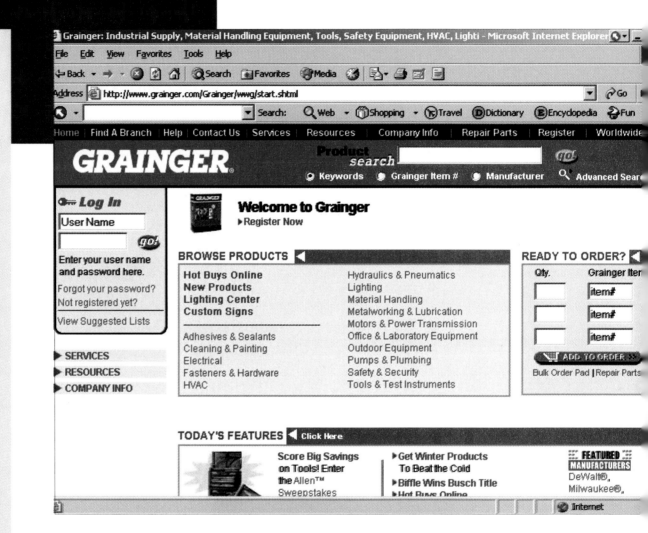

"Customers rely on Grainger to make their businesses run more cheaply and efficiently."

Can W.W. Grainger Harness Every Distribution Channel?

In 1927, Chicago businessman William Grainger spotted a business opportunity. When a firm needed a replacement electric motor, the only option was to order a new one and wait days or even weeks for delivery. To solve the problem, Grainger started a wholesale business that stocked an inventory of electric motors of different sizes made by various manufacturers. To advertise the motors, he created and distributed an eight-page catalog.

More than 75 years later, W.W. Grainger, Inc., has become a $5 billion business with more than 15,000 employees and an inventory of over 500,000 products and repair parts. The company has nine regional distribution centers and almost 600 branches that put its products within 20 minutes of 70% of U.S. businesses. And its catalog contains nearly 100,000 items.

Grainger has a relatively narrow but very deep product assortment, stocking only maintenance, repair, and operations (MRO) products and reselling them to other businesses. Its inventory includes hand and power tools, cleaning equipment, light bulbs of all sizes and shapes, every kind of fastener, and almost anything else you can imagine that would be used to keep a business operating. In fact, according to company legend, Grainger is the only supplier of bear repellent needed by workers on the Alaskan oil pipeline. Its customers range from factories to military bases to schools.

Grainger is the largest company of this type, conducting more than 100,000 transactions a day. Its 2 million customers rely on Grainger to make their businesses run more cheaply and efficiently. Most MRO products are commodities, and about 40% of their cost lies in the labor-intensive purchasing process. So, Grainger's value proposition is powerful: It reduces the search and processing costs for items, allowing companies to order multiple items from a single distributor and pay one invoice.

The success of the company is attributed to its outstanding reputation for customer service. To meet and exceed customers' expectations, Grainger created a "no excuses" guarantee and empowered its employees to assure customer satisfaction. "It's the service that builds our brand and our national presence," says the company's head of marketing, sales, and service. "Customers consistently tell us that. And that's why we've invested so heavily in multiple channels."

Those channels (actually, methods of learning about the company's products and then placing orders) include:

- Telephone, which accounts for more than one-half of Grainger's orders.

- Almost 600 branch offices around the country, which account for another one-third.

- The Internet, which takes in about 10% of orders. Customers can also search or browse the company's website to locate thousands of items by product category, description, or manufacturer.

- A massive catalog, available both on paper and on CD-ROM. To illustrate Grainger's depth of offerings, the catalog includes 46 pages of socket wrenches!

www.grainger.com

Sales slipped recently for the first time, which Grainger attributes more to cost cutting by its recession-sensitive customers than to the efforts of the dozens of smaller competing firms in the MRO business. Grainger is taking various steps to build revenues. For example, larger branches are being opened, with more floor space for showcasing seasonal and impulse-purchase items. The company is also collecting purchase data from each customer order, and consolidat- ing it into databases designed around products, customers, and transactions. Compiling purchase data "enables our people to lead the conversation toward a solution rather than just responding to a series of customer inquiries," says a Grainger executive.[1]

How can Grainger continue to coordinate the activities of its many distribution channels, including the Internet, as it strives to stay on top?

Chapter Goals

Although consumers shop regularly at the stores of retailers, they rarely see the establishments of wholesaling middlemen such as W.W. Grainger. Also, beyond noticing transportation carriers such as trucks and trains, consumers have little exposure to how products actually are moved from the point of production to the point of final sale. As a result, wholesaling and physical distribution are too often ignored or misunderstood by consumers.

Nevertheless, wholesaling middlemen can be essential members of a distribution channel, and physical distribution is an integral aspect of marketing most goods. And with the rise of the Internet, all aspects of distribution are receiving more attention as online enterprises try to figure out how to procure merchandise for sale and then deliver it to customers after it is sold. This chapter will provide you with insight into how wholesale markets, wholesaling institutions, and physical distribution activities relate to marketing. After studying this chapter, you should be able to explain:

- The nature and economic justification of wholesaling.
- The role of wholesaling middlemen in the distribution process.
- Differences across three categories of wholesaling middlemen.
- Major types of merchant wholesalers, agent wholesaling middlemen, and manufacturers' sales facilities, and the services they render.
- The nature and purpose of physical distribution.
- The systems approach to physical distribution.
- How physical distribution can strengthen a marketing program and reduce marketing costs.
- The five subsystems within physical distribution: order processing, inventory control, inventory location and warehousing, materials handling, and transportation.

Nature and Importance of Wholesaling

Wholesaling and retailing enable what is produced to be purchased for consumption. We already know that retailing involves sales to ultimate consumers for their personal use. Now we'll see what the role of wholesaling is in the marketing system.

Wholesaling and Wholesaling Middlemen

Wholesaling (or *wholesale trade*) is the sale, and all activities directly related to the sale, of goods and services to businesses and other organizations for (1) resale, (2) use in producing other goods or services, or (3) operating an organization. When a business firm sells shirts and blouses to a clothing store that intends to resell them to final consumers, this is wholesaling. When a mill sells flour to a large bakery for making bread and pastries, this is also a wholesale transaction. And when a firm sells uniforms to an organization for its employees to wear in carrying out their duties, this is wholesaling as well.

Sales made by one producer to another are wholesale transactions, and the selling producer is engaged in wholesaling. Likewise, a discount store is involved in wholesaling when it sells calculators and office supplies to a business firm. Thus wholesaling includes sales by any firm to any customer *except* an ultimate consumer who is buying for personal, nonbusiness use. From this perspective, all sales are either wholesale or retail transactions—distinguished only by the purchaser's intended use of the good or service.

In this chapter we will focus on firms engaged *primarily* in wholesaling. This type of company is called a **wholesaling middleman.** We will not focus on retailers involved in occasional wholesale transactions or on manufacturers and farmers because they are engaged primarily in production rather than wholesaling. Keep in mind, then, that *wholesaling* is a business *activity* that can be carried out by various types of firms, whereas a *wholesaling middleman* is a business *institution* that concentrates on wholesaling.

Economic Justification for Wholesaling

Most manufacturers are small and specialized. They don't have the capital to maintain a sales force to contact the many retailers or final users that are (or could be) their customers. Even for manufacturers with sufficient capital, some products or lines generate such a small volume of sales that it would not be cost-effective to establish a sales force to sell them.

At the other end of the distribution channel, most retailers and final users buy in small quantities and have limited knowledge of the market and sources of supply. Thus there is often a gap between the seller (producer) and the buyer (retailer or final user).

A wholesaling middleman can fill this gap by providing services of value to manufacturers and/or retailers. For example, this type of middleman pools the orders of many retailers and/or final users, thereby creating a market for the small producer. At the same time, a wholesaling middleman selects various items from among many alternatives to form its product mix, thereby acting as a buying service for retailers and final users. Essentially, the activities of a wholesaling middleman create time, place, and/or possession utility.

Let's look at two situations, one specific and the other broad, to see how wholesaling middlemen serve producers and retailers. A manufacturer of modular office dividers, Pleion Corp., replaced most of its sales force with independent dealers. The switch allowed Pleion to expand into new regions quicker and halved the company's marketing expenses. Taking a broader perspective, there were numerous predictions that the rise of electronic commerce would harm distributors, perhaps even eliminate many of them. Thus far, many wholesaling middlemen are thriving by furnishing needed services to online enterprises. For instance, many e-tailers rely upon distributors to assemble and, in some cases, even ship customers' orders.[2]

From a broad point of view, wholesaling brings to the distribution system the economies of skill, scale, and transactions:

- Wholesaling *skills* are efficiently concentrated in a relatively few hands. This saves the duplication of effort that would occur if many producers had to perform wholesaling functions themselves. For example, one wholesaler's warehouse in Memphis, Tennessee, saves many manufacturers from having to build their own warehouses to provide speedy service to customers in this area.

- Economies of *scale* result from the specialization of wholesaling middlemen performing functions that might otherwise require several small departments run by producing firms. Wholesalers typically can perform wholesaling functions more efficiently than can most manufacturers.

- *Transaction* economies come into play when retailers and/or wholesaling middlemen are introduced between producers and their customers. Assume that four manufacturers want to sell to six retailers. As shown in Figure 16.1, *without* a middleman, there are 24 transactions; *with* one wholesaling middleman, the number of transactions is cut to 10. Four transactions occur when all the producers sell to the middleman, and another six occur when the middleman sells to all the retailers.

Size of the Wholesale Market

The total annual sales volume of wholesaling middlemen was more than $4 *trillion* in 1997 (the year of the last published national census of wholesale trade). As shown in Table 16.1, this level of sales represents an increase of almost 60% over 1987 and close to 800% over 1967. Even if the effects of inflation are taken into account, these figures still reflect a major increase in wholesale trade.

You might be surprised that total wholesale trade exceeds total retail trade by a wide margin. How can this be, especially considering that a product's retail price is higher than its wholesale price? We can find an explanation by considering the customers of wholesaling middlemen. About 75% of the sales of wholesaling middlemen are made to organizations *other than* retailers.[3] For example, some products sold to nonretailers are *business* goods (such as large printing presses or iron ore) that, by definition, are never sold at retail. Others may be *consumer* goods (such as groceries or toys) that are sold more than once at the wholesale level, with all such transactions counted as part of total wholesale trade. Thus total wholesale trade is greater than total retail trade because wholesale trade includes sales of business goods and successive sales of consumer goods at the wholesale level.

At last count, 450,000 wholesaling middlemen were conducting business in the U.S. According to Table 16.1, the number of such establishments rose substantially—by one-half, between 1967 and 1987 but has declined slightly since then. Despite the

FIGURE 16.1

The Economy of Transactions in Wholesaling.

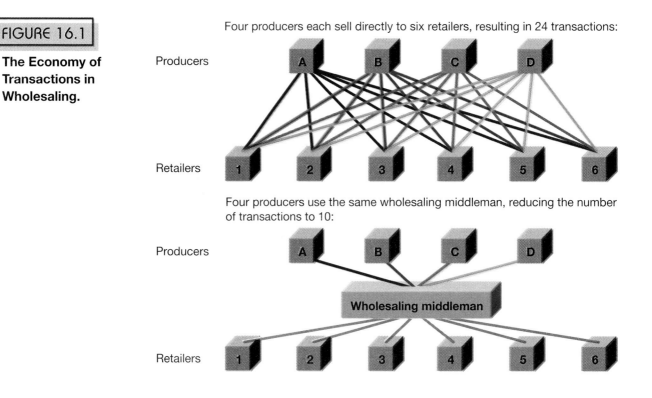

Four producers each sell directly to six retailers, resulting in 24 transactions:

Producers

Retailers

Four producers use the same wholesaling middleman, reducing the number of transactions to 10:

Producers

Wholesaling middleman

Retailers

TABLE
16.1

Total Wholesale Trade versus Total Retail Trade in the United States

Total wholesale sales (in current dollars) increased almost 60% between 1987 and 1997, although the number of wholesaling middlemen declined. Compare these figures with the growth in retail sales over the same period.

Year	Number of Wholesaling Middlemen	Wholesale Sales (billions)	Retail Sales (billions)
1999	450,000	n/a	$2,868
1997	453,000	$4,060	2,461
1987	470,000	2,525	1,540
1977	383,000	1,258	723
1967	311,000	459	310

Note: n/a indicates that this statistic is not yet available.
Sources: *Statistical Abstract of the United States: 2001,* U.S. Bureau of the Census, Washington, DC, 2001, pp. 648, 658; *http://landview.census.gov.mrts/www/data/pdf/annpub01.pdf; 1997 Economic Census,* Retail Trade—Geographic Area Series, U.S. Census Bureau, Washington, DC, 2000, p. United States 7, *www.census.gov/prod/ec97/97r44-US.pdf;* and corresponding censuses from prior years.

drop, these statistics document that wholesaling middlemen remain viable members of distribution channels.

Profile of Wholesaling Middlemen

A producer or retailer considering the use of wholesaling middlemen must know what options are available, whom these middlemen serve, and how they operate.

Major Categories Wholesaling middlemen vary greatly in products carried, markets served, and methods of operation. We will discuss about 10 different types. Nevertheless, all fit into three categories developed by the U.S. Bureau of the Census (see Figure 16.2). Brief descriptions follow, with more details presented later in the chapter:

- A **merchant wholesaler** is an independently owned firm that engages primarily in wholesaling and takes title to (that is, owns) the products being distributed.

FIGURE 16.2

Types of Wholesaling Institutions.

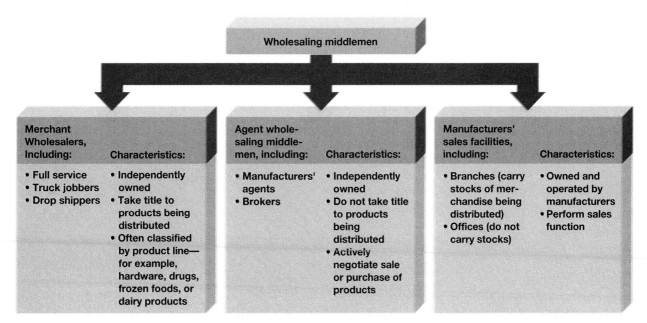

Sometimes these firms are referred to simply as *wholesalers, jobbers,* or *industrial distributors.*[4] Merchant wholesalers form the largest segment of wholesaling firms when measured by either number of establishments or sales volume.

- An **agent wholesaling middleman** is an independently owned firm that engages primarily in wholesaling by actively negotiating the sale or purchase of products on behalf of other firms but that does *not* take title to the products being distributed.

- A **manufacturer's sales facility** is an establishment that engages primarily in wholesaling and is owned and operated by a manufacturer but is physically separated from manufacturing plants.[5] These facilities are common in fields ranging from major appliances to plumbing equipment to electrical supplies. The two major types are similar except in one important respect. A **manufacturer's sales branch** carries an inventory of the product being sold, but a **manufacturer's sales office** does not.

Although wholesaling middlemen are not part of every distribution channel, they are present in most. According to one survey, 32% of business goods manufacturers rely on merchant wholesalers. Another 42% use agent wholesaling middlemen, and the remaining 26% distribute their products directly (perhaps using sales branches or offices) to final customers.[6]

The statistics in Figure 16.3 (the latest available census data) indicate that merchant wholesalers account for the majority of sales made through wholesaling middlemen. Between 1967 and 1987, merchant wholesalers continually increased their share of wholesale trade, whereas the other two categories declined. Since then, manufacturers' sales facilities have taken a small amount of market share from merchant wholesalers.[7]

Operating Expenses and Profits
Total operating expenses for wholesaling middlemen average about 11% of *wholesale* sales; expenses for retailers run about 28% of *retail* sales. Therefore, generally speaking, the expenses of wholesaling middlemen take about 8% of the ultimate consumer's dollar.[8]

Operating expenses vary widely across the several categories of wholesaling middlemen:

- Merchant wholesalers have the highest average expenses, at 14% of sales. However, the range is wide. For example, expenses for wholesalers of a complete assortment of grocery products typically are below 10% of sales, compared with as much as 30% for office equipment wholesalers.

- Agent wholesaling middlemen have fairly low costs, around 4.5% of sales, largely because they do not have to carry inventories.

- The two types of manufacturers' sales facilities generally have much different cost structures. Sales offices' operating expenses are about 4% of sales; sales branches' expenses are around 11%, because of the costs incurred in storing merchandise.

FIGURE 16.3

Share of Wholesale Trade, by Category of Institution.

Sources: *1997 Economic Census,* Wholesale Trade, Geographic Area Series, U.S. Census Bureau, Washington, DC, 2000, p. United States 7, *www.census.gov/prod/ec97/97w42.US.pdf;* and corresponding censuses from prior years.

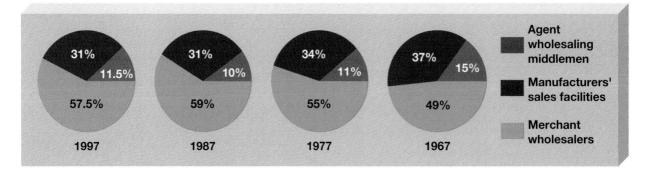

We should not conclude that agent wholesaling middlemen are highly efficient and merchant wholesalers inefficient because of the disparity in their expenses. The differences in costs are partially traceable to differences in the services they provide. Also, because of factors such as perishability, value in relation to bulk, and special storage requirements, there are tremendous variations in the expenses connected with wholesaling various products. For example, jewelry has much higher value in relation to bulk than furniture, so this factor would suggest lower storage costs for jewelry as a percentage of value. However, any savings on this factor might be offset by the added expenses of providing adequate security for jewelry in inventory.

Net operating profit expressed as a percent of net sales is rather modest for wholesaling middlemen and is considerably lower than for retailers (except for large grocery stores). Generally, wholesaling profits range from 1.5% to 4% of sales.

Merchant Wholesalers

Wholesaling middlemen that take title to products—that is, merchant wholesalers—are common in the marketing of both consumer goods and business goods. We'll examine several types next.

Full-Service Wholesalers

An independent merchant middleman that performs a full range of wholesaling functions is a **full-service wholesaler.** This type of middleman may handle consumer and/or business products that may be manufactured or nonmanufactured (such as grown or extracted), and are imported, exported, or made and sold domestically.

www.supervalu.com

The forms of assistance offered by full-service wholesalers are summarized in Table 16.2. W.W. Grainger, the subject of the chapter-opening case, is a prime example of this type of middleman. Supervalu Inc. illustrates how a full-service wholesaler operates. As the largest wholesaler of groceries and related products, Supervalu helps independent grocery stores remain viable by providing them with the

TABLE 16.2	Full-Service Wholesalers' Typical Services to Customers and to Producers

Service	Description
Buying	Act as purchasing agent for customers.
Creating assortments	Buy from many suppliers to develop an inventory that matches customers' needs.
Subdividing	Buy in large quantities (such as a truckload) and then resell in smaller quantities (such as a dozen).
Selling	Provide a sales force for producers to reach small retailers and other businesses, at a lower cost than producers would incur by having their own sales forces.
Transportation	Make quick, frequent deliveries to customers, reducing customers' risks and investment in inventory.
Warehousing	Store products in facilities that are nearer customers' locations than are manufacturing plants.
Financing	Grant credit to customers, reducing their capital requirements. Aid producers by ordering and paying for products before purchase by customers.
Risk taking	Reduce a producer's risk by taking title to products.
Market information	Supply information to customers about new products and producers' special offers and to producer–suppliers about customers' needs and competitors' activities.
Management assistance	Assist customers, especially small retailers, in areas such as inventory control, allocation of shelf space, and financial management.

business tools that large grocery chains have. Supervalu's services include construction, design, and equipment services for grocery stores, advertising support, and three tiers of private brands.[9]

www.skechers.com/international

Manufacturers in various industries distribute their products directly, thereby eliminating wholesalers in their channels. Amana Refrigeration, a maker of home appliances, decided to deal directly with appliance retailers. Obviously, this action displeased many wholesalers that had carried the Amana line. On the international front, rather than working through wholesalers, Skechers decided to open its own retail stores in Europe for its trendy footwear.[10]

To remain competitive and boost profits, full-service wholesalers are striving to improve their operations. Three common avenues are enhanced quality, advanced technology, and value-added services. Distributors of semiconductor chips and related products, for example, now assist manufacturers by doing some product assembly and providing inventory management and rapid delivery of orders.[11]

Partnerships between wholesalers and either producers or customers are increasingly common. Ordinarily, these arrangements represent the administered type of vertical marketing system (discussed in Chapter 14). To cite one example, Nabisco formed a partnership with a major customer, Wegmans Food Markets. Instead of Nabisco estimating the amount of, say, Planters cashews the grocery chain will need in an upcoming period, the two firms exchange sales forecasts via the Internet and then agree on a suitable order. To reduce shipping costs, Nabisco even agrees to ship the packaged cashews to Wegmans along with competitors' orders.[12]

Full-service wholesalers comprise the majority of merchant wholesaling middlemen. They have held their own in competitive struggles with other forms of indirect distribution, including manufacturers' sales facilities and agent middlemen.[13]

At some point, the total number of merchant wholesalers may decline significantly because of increasing mergers and acquisitions. In the wholesaling of computer-related electronics parts, for instance, mergers and acquisitions reduced the number of distributors by almost one-half between 1995 and 2000.[14] A growing number of distributors believe they need to be bigger to maintain their competitive edge. Smaller wholesalers will have to decide whether they intend to acquire, be acquired, or somehow insulate themselves from this trend—perhaps by serving small market niches.

Other Merchant Wholesalers

Two types of merchant wholesalers with distinctive operations also warrant brief description:

- A **truck jobber**, also called a *truck distributor,* carries a limited line of perishable products (such as candies, dairy products, or potato chips, and delivers them by truck to stores. Jobbers furnish fresh products so frequently that retailers can buy perishable goods in small amounts to minimize the risk of loss.

- A **drop shipper**, also known as a *desk jobber,* sells merchandise for delivery directly from the producer to the customer but does not physically handle the product. They are common in only a few product categories, including coal, lumber, and building materials, that are typically sold in very large quantities and that have high freight costs in relation to their unit value.

Agent Wholesaling Middlemen

As distinguished from merchant wholesalers, agent wholesaling middlemen (1) do *not* take title to products and (2) typically perform fewer services. As shown in Table 16.3, product characteristics and market conditions determine whether a distribution channel should include agent or merchant wholesaling middlemen. For their

TABLE
16.3

Factors Suggesting Which Type of Wholesaling Middlemen Should Be Used in a Channel

Factors	Favoring Agent Wholesaling Middlemen	Favoring Merchant Wholesalers
Nature of product	Nonstandard, perhaps made to order	Standard
Technicality of product	Simple	Complex
Product's gross margin	Small	Relatively large
Number of customers	Few	Many
Concentration of customers	Concentrated geographically and in a few industries	Dispersed geographically and in many industries
Frequency of ordering	Relatively infrequently	Frequently
Time between order and receipt of shipment	Customer satisfied with relatively long lead time	Customer requires or desires shorter lead time

Source: Adapted from Donald M. Jackson and Michael F. d'Amico, "Products and Markets Served by Distributors and Agents," *Industrial Marketing Management,* February 1989, pp. 27–33.

assistance, agent middlemen receive a commission, which is a percentage of sales volume, to cover their expenses and to (hopefully) provide a profit. Commission rates vary from about 1% to 10%, depending mainly on the nature of the product and the services performed.

Agent wholesaling middlemen lost one-third of their share of wholesale trade between 1967 and 1987. In the case of agricultural products, agent middlemen were replaced by merchant wholesalers or by direct sales to food-processing companies and grocery stores. Likewise, for manufactured goods, agent middlemen were supplanted by merchant wholesalers or direct distribution. Since then, agents have fought back. In fact, their share of total wholesale trade grew between 1987 and 1997, the most recent year for which final census statistics are available.[15]

On the basis of sales volume, the most significant types of agent wholesaling middlemen are manufacturers' agents and brokers. Each is described next.

Manufacturers' Agents

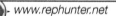
www.rephunter.net

An independent agent wholesaling middleman that sells part or all of a manufacturer's product mix in an assigned geographic territory is a **manufacturers' agent,** or *manufacturers' representative*. According to census data, just under 30,000 manufacturers' reps operate in the U.S.[16] Agents are not employees of the manufacturers; they are independent business firms. Although technically independent, agents have little or no control over prices and terms of sale, which are established by the manufacturers they represent.

Because a manufacturers' agent sells in a limited territory, each producer uses multiple agents to cover its total market. Manufacturers' reps have year-round relationships with the companies (often called *principals*) they represent. Each agent usually serves several noncompeting manufacturers of related products. For example, a manufacturers' agent may specialize in toys and carry an assortment of noncompeting lines in dolls, learning materials, and outdoor play equipment.

Manufacturers' agents are used extensively in distributing many types of consumer and business goods, ranging from sporting goods to heating and air-conditioning vents and ductwork. Their main service to manufacturers is selling. Because a manufacturers' agent does not carry nearly as many lines as a full-service wholesaler, an agent can be expected to provide knowledgeable, aggressive selling.

Manufacturers' agents are most helpful to:

- A small firm that has a limited number of products and no sales force.
- A business that wants to add a new, possibly unrelated line to its existing product mix, but its present sales force lacks familiarity with either the new line or the new market.
- A firm that wants to enter a new market that is not yet sufficiently developed to warrant the use of its own sales force.

A manufacturers' agent can be cost-effective because its major expenses (such as travel and lodging) are spread over a number of manufacturers' lines. Also, because producers pay them a commission, reps are paid only for what they actually sell. Some agents operate on a commission as low as 2% of net sales, whereas others earn as much as 20%; the average is about 5%.[17] Depending on how difficult the product is to sell and whether it is stocked by the agent, operating expenses of reps can vary greatly.

There are limitations to what manufacturers' agents do. Agents *usually* do not carry an inventory of merchandise, do not install machinery and equipment, and are not equipped to furnish customers with repair service. However, to remain viable, manufacturers' reps are adding new services. Because they have direct contact with customers, some are able to assist their principals in developing new products. Others offer telemarketing and direct-mail programs. Perhaps most important, manufacturers' agents are the "eyes and ears" in local markets for their principals.[18]

Brokers

www.foodbrokerusa.com

A **broker** is an independent agent wholesaling middleman that brings buyers and sellers together and provides market information to one party or the other. It furnishes information about many topics, including prices, products, and general market conditions. Typically, a broker does not physically handle the products being distributed. In recent years, manufacturers' agents and brokers have become more similar with respect to attributes and services. In fact, in the groceries industry, what used to be a food broker is now referred to as a sales and marketing agency.

Most brokers work for sellers, although some represent buyers. Brokers are used in selling real estate and securities, but they are most prevalent in the food field. For example, a seafood broker handles the output from a salmon cannery, which operates only about three months each year. The canner employs a broker to find buyers among retail stores, wholesalers, and other institutions such as government agencies.

Brokers have no authority to set prices. They simply negotiate a sale and leave it up to the seller to accept or reject the buyer's offer. Brokers receive relatively small commissions, with the average being 3.5%.[19]

Other Agent Wholesaling Middlemen

Three additional types of agent wholesaling middlemen account for smaller shares of wholesale trade than manufacturers' reps and brokers. Nevertheless, they are very important for certain products and in specific markets. These middlemen are:

- A **selling agent** essentially substitutes for a marketing department by marketing a manufacturer's entire output. Selling agents play a key role in distributing textile products and coal and, to a lesser extent, apparel, food, lumber, and metal products.
- An **auction company** helps assembled buyers and sellers complete their transactions. Traditional auction companies provide auctioneers who do the selling, and physical facilities for displaying the sellers' products. This type of auction company is extremely important in the wholesaling of used cars and certain agricul-

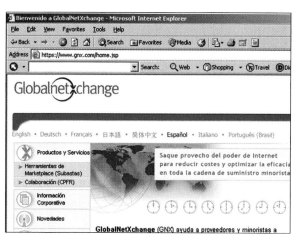

www.gnx.com

www.dovebid.com

www.liquidation.com

tural products such as tobacco, livestock, and fruit. In the mid-1990s, Internet-based auction companies started to appear, providing a website at which sellers offer products for sale and both consumers and organizations search for bargains or rare products. Now, according to one source, there are 2,500 Internet-based auction sites, including FreeMarkets, Liquidation.com, DoveBid, and others focused on business markets.[20]

- An **import–export agent** brings together sellers and buyers from different countries. Export agents work in the country in which the product is made; import agents are based in the country where the product will be sold.

Nature and Importance of Physical Distribution

After a company establishes its channels of distribution, it must arrange for actually moving its tangible products through these channels. **Physical distribution,** which we use synonymously with *logistics,* consists of all activities involved in moving the right amount of the right products to the right place at the right time. According to various estimates, total annual spending on logistics is between $600 billion and

AN ETHICAL DILEMMA?

As explained in Chapter 14, through gray marketing, products wind up being distributed outside a manufacturer's authorized distribution channels. For example, an export agent (or some other type of wholesaling middleman) may establish a relationship with a European manufacturer to distribute its line of stereo equipment in South America, but not in the U.S. However, without the manufacturer's knowledge, the agent diverts a large shipment for sale in the U.S. Assume that you're the stereo equipment buyer for a chain of discount stores. The export agent contacts you about purchasing some stereos at prices substantially below the normal wholesale price.

Would it be ethical to buy these stereos for resale in your stores? Would your view depend on whether you knew for sure that the stereos were indeed gray market goods?

From this "nerve center" at the headquarters of Schneider National, Inc., about 450 employees use satellite technology to keep track of the company's more than 40,000 pieces of trucking equipment. The system cut Schneider's internal costs by nearly one-quarter and boosted on-time deliveries from under 90% to about 99%.

www.schneider.com

$1 *trillion* in the U.S.; worldwide, the total is approximately $2 trillion. For an individual firm, the cost of logistics can be equivalent to 10% to 15% of sales.[21]

In its full scope, physical distribution for manufacturers includes the flow of *raw materials* from their sources of supply to the production line *and* the movement of *finished goods* from the end of the production line to the final users' locations. Middlemen manage the flows of goods *onto* their shelves as well as *from* their shelves to customers' homes, stores, or other places of business.

The activities comprising physical distribution are order processing, inventory control, inventory location and warehousing, materials handling, and transportation. A decision regarding any one of these activities affects all the others. Location of a warehouse influences the selection of transportation methods and carriers; the choice of a carrier influences the optimum size of shipments.

Increasing Attention to Physical Distribution

As described in one article, "Virtually the entire economy depends on the arcane and complex science of logistics to get billions of parts and supplies into U.S. manufacturing plants on time and to distribute finished products efficiently to consumers."[22] Without effective logistics, a business is likely to have mismatches such as an out-of-stock part that shuts down an assembly line *or* a warehouse full of patio furniture in Atlanta but unsatisfied customers in New Orleans. These examples underscore that the appropriate assortment of products must be in the right place at the right time to maximize the opportunity for profitable sales. Further, the movement of goods from one place to another must be accomplished in a cost-effective manner.

Physical distribution is one area of marketing with substantial opportunities for cost cutting. And the potential savings are great. For some products, such as furniture and building materials, physical distribution represents the largest operating expense. Profits are paper-thin for many businesses, so any savings are appreciated. A supermarket, for instance, typically earns a net profit of about 1% of sales. Thus every $1 a supermarket saves in physical distribution costs has the same effect on profit as a $100 increase in sales!

Effective logistics also can be the basis by which a firm gains and sustains a differential advantage. On-time delivery, which requires competent physical distribu-

Can the locations of over 50,000 truck tractors and trailers be pinpointed?

In years past, trucking companies and other freight carriers often didn't know the locations of their equipment (trucks, railcars). As a result, carriers either could not inform customers about the status of their shipments or, at best, could do so only sometimes.

That has changed. Most transportation firms can pinpoint the locations of their equipment, and many monitor shipments on a real-time basis. Schneider National, based in Green Bay, Wisconsin, started this movement in 1988. Today Schneider, the largest trucking company, knows within 100 feet where all of its over 14,000 tractors (the front part of the truck that contains the engine) are at any time.

How is this done? A number of carriers have equipped their tractors with tracking devices and onboard computers that permit two-way communication between truck and company office through a satellite. Recently, Schneider decided to add similar devices to its trailers. By doing so, it knows where they are even when they are not tethered to a tractor—in trailer staging areas or on railcars, for example. Tracking systems are also used by railroads and other modes of transportation.

Real-time monitoring pleases customers because they can know not only the precise location of a shipment but also its expected arrival time. A carrier benefits too. For instance, a tracking system helps a trucking company reroute rigs to avoid delays and to locate empty trailers when extra capacity is needed. Such steps increase the efficiency of expensive transportation equipment. As a Schneider executive commented, "Most of the payback will come from greater asset utilization." Tracking both tractors and trailers could produce annual savings of $5 billion, according to one transportation consultant.

A tracking system produces intangible benefits as well. For example, following the attacks of September 11, 2001, Schneider used its tracking system to determine that the drivers of its 18 trucks that were in Manhattan were unharmed.

Sources: *www.schneider.com/aboutschneider/media.html;* Daniel Machalaba and Carrick Mollenkamp, "Companies Struggle to Cope with Chaos, Breakdowns and Trauma," *The Wall Street Journal,* Sept. 13, 2001, p. B1; Wendy Leavitt, "Relocating the Edge," *Fleet Owner,* July 1999, p. 110; Daniel Machalaba, "Schneider National to Outfit Trailers with Tracking Devices to Map Locations," *The Wall Street Journal,* May 7, 1999, p. A2; and Warren Cohen, "Taking to the Highway," *U.S. News & World Report,* Sept. 18, 1995, pp. 84–87.

---

tion, can provide an edge. With that in mind, Sun Microsystems' unit in Asia is able to deliver replacement parts on time for 99.7% of all orders.[23]

Opportunities to better satisfy customers, cut costs, and/or gain a competitive edge expanded greatly in 1980. During that year, two new federal laws (the Motor Carrier Act and the Staggers Act) completed the deregulation of marketing activities related to *interstate* transportation. Previously, pricing by railroads, airlines, and trucking companies had been subject to restrictive regulations. By the beginning of 1995, *intrastate* trucking was basically deregulated as well.

Following deregulation, transportation firms could decide which rates (prices) and levels of service would best satisfy their target markets. For example, relatively soon after deregulation, Landair Transport Inc. gained recognition by promising on-time deliveries; in fact, 99% of its shipments arrived within 15 minutes of the scheduled time.[24] Deregulation also benefited shippers, who could shop around for rates and service levels that met their needs.

In the past several years, the surge of electronic commerce has underscored the importance of physical distribution. The challenge relates to **fulfillment,** which entails having the merchandise that is ordered by a customer in stock and then packing and shipping it in an efficient, timely manner. Manufacturers typically are adept at filling large orders for a small number of customers, and conventional retailers are used to shoppers coming to their bricks-and-mortar stores and then carrying home their purchases. However, many manufacturers and retailers that engage in e-commerce are encountering difficulties in filling and shipping small orders for a large number of customers.

Even purely Internet retailers "are discovering that if they don't control their own warehouses and shipping, their reliability ratings with customers can turn dismal." If there are problems with fulfillment, the likelihood of repeat purchases drops sharply. Some firms engaged in electronic commerce are doing their own fulfillment, but many—perhaps most—are outsourcing the fulfillment task to firms such as Lenmar and New Roads. Other distributors, such as Alliance Entertainment and GSI Commerce, serve as an **online category manager** by handling e-commerce fulfillment in a particular product area for manufacturers and conventional retailers.[25]

Supply Chain Management

Occasionally we have referred to marketing as a *total system* of business activities rather than a series of fragmented operations. **Supply chain management** represents a total system perspective of distribution, combining distribution channels and physical distribution. The core of supply chain management (SCM) is coordinated logistics.

Traditionally, logistics activities were fragmented and, in many firms, they still are. If you ask, "Who's in charge of physical distribution?" the answer should not be "No one." Moreover, responsibility for it should not be delegated to various units that may have conflicting goals. The production department, for instance, is interested primarily in long production runs to minimize unit manufacturing costs, even though the result may be high inventory costs. In contrast, the finance department wants a minimum of funds tied up in inventories. At the same time, the sales department desires to have a wide assortment of products available at locations near customers.

Uncoordinated conditions like these preclude a flow of products that satisfies the firm's goals. To alleviate this problem, a number of firms have established separate departments responsible for all logistics activities. Even when this occurs in large firms, physical distribution usually is separated from the marketing department. This separation causes problems when a company is trying to formulate and implement coordinated marketing strategies, including logistics. With supply chain management, individual logistics activities are brought together in a unified way. More and more, the Internet is being used to allow supply chain members to monitor—on a real-time bases—key factors such as the status of orders and inventory levels.[26]

The **total cost concept** is integral to effective supply chain management. A company should determine the set of activities that produces the best relationship between costs and profit for the *entire* physical distribution system. This approach is superior to focusing strictly on the separate costs of individual distribution activities.

Sometimes a company attempts to minimize the cost of only one aspect of physical distribution—transportation, for example. Management might be upset by the high fees for air freight. But the expense of this mode of transportation may be more than offset by savings from (1) lower inventory costs, (2) less insurance and interest expense, (3) lower crating costs, and (4) fewer lost sales because of out-of-stock conditions. The point is not that air freight is the best mode of transportation; which mode is best varies with the situation. The key point is that physical distribution should be viewed as a *total system*, with all related costs being analyzed.

Effective supply chain management can improve several aspects of performance. A consultant estimated that superior SCM can (1) improve on-time deliveries by about 20%, (2) reduce necessary inventory levels by about 50%, and (3) boost the firm's profits by an amount equal to 3% to 6% of sales. To cite a specific example, Autoliv, a Swedish company that produces auto-safety equipment, was able to reduce the hours needed to oversee vendors and to pare its inventory by 75% when it turned to Web-based management of its supply chain.[27]

As part of supply chain management, some companies are contracting out, or *outsourcing*, their physical distribution function. It's more and more common for logistics companies to manage firms' distribution processes under a multiyear contract. The growth of **contract logistics,** also called *third-party logistics* or simply *3PL,*

Recognizing companies' willingness to outsource various logistics-related activities, CNF Inc. established Menlo Worldwide in 2001. By offering contract logistics and a variety of other services (such as order fulfillment, packaging assistance, and shipping services), Menlo Worldwide seeks to help its customers "attain operational excellence across their global supply chains."

 www.menloworldwide.
com

www.vectorscm.com

reflects a broader trend in the U.S. whereby firms are outsourcing various business tasks ranging from payroll to public relations. An independent firm that contracts to manage another company's entire supply chain is being called a *4PL*, which signifies it does even more than a 3PL provider.[28]

Companies are turning to contract logistics for essentially the same reasons they outsource other business tasks. Basically, by delegating one or more physical distribution tasks to a third party, a firm can concentrate on its core business (for example, producing power hand tools or fine lingerie). Further, it expects to become more effective (as indicated by greater customer satisfaction) and/or more efficient (as indicated by lower costs and greater return on investment) in the area of logistics.[29]

The scope of contract logistics becomes evident in the examination of a single industry, automobiles. In early 2000, Ford Motor Co. hired UPS to oversee movement of new cars from the end of the assembly line to dealer showrooms. General Motors Corp. went a big step further, forming a joint venture with CNF Inc., a transportation company, to handle all of GM's logistics activities.[30]

According to a survey of executives involved in supply chain activities in 11 countries, over 75% of companies are outsourcing part of their physical distribution activities. Contract logistics comprises at least a $50 billion business annually, three times its size in 1994, and has been on a growth curve. The logistics activities that are most often outsourced include management of warehouses and distribution centers; Web-based communications related to physical distribution; and transportation management.[31]

Strategic Use of Physical Distribution

Viewing and using physical distribution strategically may enable a company to strengthen its competitive position by providing more customer satisfaction and/or by reducing operating costs. The management of physical distribution can also affect a firm's marketing mix—particularly distribution channels. Each opportunity is described below.

Improve Customer Service
A well-run logistics system can improve the service a firm provides its customers—whether they are middlemen or ultimate users. Further, the level of customer service directly affects demand. This is true especially

in marketing undifferentiated products (such as chemicals and most building materials) where effective service may be a company's only differential advantage. For example, Batesville Casket is committed to delivering any one of 300 models to its funeral home customers within 48 hours.[32]

To ensure reliable customer service, management should set standards of performance for each subsystem of physical distribution. These standards should be quantitatively measurable. The goal of Fairchild Semiconductor, for instance, is to deliver 95% of its products directly from factories to customers within two days and 99% within three days.[33] Here are other hypothetical examples:

- *Sporting goods wholesaler:* Fill 99.5% of orders accurately, without increasing the size of the order-fulfillment staff.

- *Industrial distributor:* Fulfill at least 85% of orders received from inventory on hand, but maintain an inventory turnover ratio of 12 times per year.

Reduce Distribution Costs

Many avenues to cost reductions may be available through effective physical distribution management. For example, inventories—and their attendant carrying costs and capital investment—can be reduced through more accurate forecasting of demand for various goods. According to one estimate, better demand forecasts could reduce total inventory in the U.S. by 25%, which would pare inventory levels by over $150 *billion.*[34]

When National Semiconductor applied the total cost concept, it committed to a major investment, building a distribution center in Singapore. The company decided that all computer chips assembled in East Asia would be shipped to this facility, sorted there, and then sent by air freight to customers around the world. National Semiconductor contracted with FedEx Corp. to manage this distribution process. Over a two-year period, logistics costs shrank from 2.6% to 1.9% of sales. On a sales base of a couple of *billion* dollars, that's a considerable savings.[35]

Create Time and Place Utilities

Storage, which is part of warehousing, creates *time utility* by correcting imbalances in the timing of production and consumption. An imbalance can occur when there is *year-round consumption* but only *seasonal production*, as in the case of agricultural products. For instance, time utility is created and value is added when apples are harvested and stored in the fall for sale and consumption months later. In other situations, warehousing helps adjust *year-round production* to *seasonal consumption*. A manufacturer may produce lawn mowers on a year-round basis; during the fall and winter, the mowers are stored for sale in the spring and summer.

Transportation adds value to products by creating *place utility*. A fine suit hanging on a manufacturer's rack in Hong Kong has less value than an identical suit ready for sale in a retailer's store in Baltimore. Transporting the suit from Hong Kong to Baltimore creates place utility and adds value to it.

Stabilize Prices

Careful management of warehousing and transportation can help stabilize prices for an individual firm or for an entire industry. If a market is temporarily glutted with a product, sellers can store it until supply and demand conditions are better balanced. Such use of warehousing facilities is common in the marketing of agricultural products and other seasonally produced goods.

The judicious movement of products from one market to another may enable a seller to (1) avoid a market with depressed prices or (2) take advantage of a market that has a supply shortfall and/or higher prices. If demand for heating oil is stronger in Akron, Ohio, than in Des Moines, Iowa, a producer should be able to achieve greater revenues by shifting some shipments from Des Moines to Akron.

Influence Channel Decisions

Decisions regarding inventory management have a direct bearing on a producer's selection of channels and the location of middlemen. Logistical considerations may become paramount, for example, when a company decides to decentralize its inventory. In this case, management must determine (1) how many sites to establish and (2) whether to use wholesalers, the company's own warehouses, or public warehouses. One producer may select merchant wholesalers that perform storage and other warehousing services. Another may prefer to use a combination of manufacturers' agents for aggressive selling and public warehouses for assembling and shipping orders.

Control Shipping Costs Managers with shipping responsibilities need to ensure that their companies enjoy the best combination of delivery times *and* shipping rates for whatever methods of transportation they deem to use. The pricing of transportation services is one of the most complicated parts of American business. The rate (or tariff) schedule is the carrier's price list; typically it is complex. To cite one example, shipping rates vary for different types of goods, depending on many factors including not only distance to the destination, but also the bulk and weight of the products. Therefore, being able to interpret a tariff schedule properly is a money-saving skill for a manager with shipping responsibilities.

Tasks in Physical Distribution Management

Physical distribution refers to the actual physical flow of products. In contrast, **physical distribution management** is the development and operation of processes resulting in the effective and efficient physical flow of products.

Irrespective of whether a firm handles physical distribution on its own or partners with one or more other firms to carry out this function, effective physical distribution management requires careful attention to five interrelated activities:

*   Order processing
*   Inventory control
*   Inventory location and warehousing
*   Materials handling
*   Transportation

Each of these activities must be carefully coordinated with the others.

Order Processing

The starting point in a physical distribution system is *order processing*, which is a set of procedures for receiving, handling, and filling orders promptly and accurately. This activity should include provisions for billing, granting credit, preparing invoices, and collecting past-due accounts. Customer ill will results if a company makes mistakes or is slow in filling orders. In addition, inefficient order processing can lead to unnecessarily large inventories. That's why virtually all firms rely on computers to execute most of their order-processing activities. At the same time, some suppliers provide customers with computer technology to use in placing orders.

There have been various technology-facilitated advances in order processing. One of the more notable is **electronic data interchange (EDI),** in which orders, invoices, and perhaps other business information are transmitted by computer rather than by mail. As such, EDI speeds up the process and markedly reduces paperwork.

Originally, EDI required a direct computer link between supplier and customer. Now EDI is being conducted via the Internet, which has lowered the costs of the process and, in turn, expanded the number of firms that can transmit orders and other distribution-related information electronically. For instance, many small retailers are

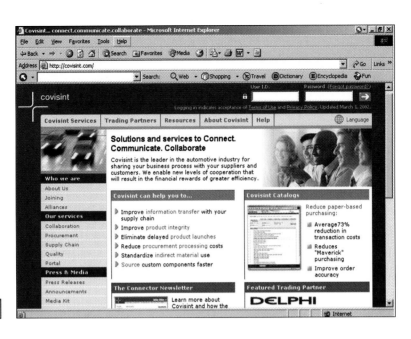

DaimlerChrysler, Ford, and General Motors agreed, in early 2000, to collaborate on a single online supplier exchange for the auto industry. A key goal of Covisint is to reduce redundancies in procurement processes, thereby lowering product costs and operating expenses for both the automakers and their suppliers. Participating firms carry out various aspects of physical distribution management at the Covisint site.

www.covisint.com

using e-mail to place orders with suppliers. At the other end of the size spectrum, Wal-Mart has stipulated that all of its suppliers use the Internet for EDI.[36]

Some of the largest manufacturers, led by automakers, intend to use the Internet for virtually all of their purchasing. In 2000, three automakers established an Internet-based enterprise, now named Covisint, for parts procurement, supply chain management, and other purposes. Online auctions will be part of the new purchasing arrangements. Likewise, Boeing has cooperated with Oracle Corp. to establish an online procurement system for the aircraft industry. Internet-based purchasing is supposed to lower purchase prices, as a result of increased competition among suppliers, and reduce the cost of order processing significantly.[37]

Inventory Control

Managing the size and composition of inventories, which represent a sizable investment for most companies, is essential to any physical distribution system. The goal of *inventory control* is to satisfy the order-fulfillment expectations of customers while minimizing both the investment and fluctuations in inventories.

Customer-Service Requirements   Inventory size is determined by balancing costs and desired levels of customer service. Different customers have varying needs regarding order fulfillment. In today's acutely competitive environment, most individuals or organizations expect the order to be filled, accurately and completely, almost immediately. The rare customer is one who is less demanding and will accept an occasional out-of-stock item or a slight delay in receiving an order. Management must identify and respond to differences in expected levels of customer service.

When a company knows its customers' expectations regarding order fulfillment, it then must decide what percentage of orders it intends to fill promptly from inventory on hand. Out-of-stock conditions result in lost sales, erosion of goodwill, even departure of customers. Yet to be able to fill 100% of orders promptly may require an exceedingly large and costly inventory.

Economic Order Quantity   Management must establish the optimal quantity for reorder when it is time to replenish inventory. The **economic order quantity (EOQ)** is the volume at which the sum of inventory-carrying costs and order-processing costs are at a minimum. Typically, as order size increases, (1) inventory-carrying cost goes

Will RFID replace bar codes?

Most products contain bar codes that are read by scanners for purposes of transactions and inventory control. Now after 30 years in which bar codes have been paramount, a new technology is on the horizon. A radio frequency identification (RFID) tag consists of a tiny memory chip equipped with a minuscule radio antenna. The theory of RFID is that the tags will allow constant monitoring of the whereabouts of products in various locations, including manufacturing plants, warehouses, and retail storerooms and selling floors. At the time of a transaction, an RFID tag could also trigger automatic replenishment.

Currently, RFID tags are fairly expensive, about $1 apiece. Hence, they don't make sense for lower-cost items found in retail outlets. In addition, the underlying technology is still being perfected to overcome limitations such as radio waves not being able to go through metal.

Given its financial might and forward thinking, it's not surprising that Wal-Mart Stores anticipates that RFID will yield substantial benefits in supply chain management. Hence, the huge retailer is already testing RFID technology.

On what kinds of merchandise will RFID tags first be cost-effective?

Sources: Amy Helen Johnson, "35 Years of IT Leadership: A New Supply Chain Forged," *Computerworld,* Sept. 30, 2002, pp. 38–39; Heather Green, "The End of the Road for Bar Codes," *Business Week,* July 8, 2002, p. 76B; and Mark Roberti, "Your Inventory Wants to Talk to You," *Business 2.0,* May 2002, pp. 84–87.

up because the average inventory is larger and (2) order-processing cost declines because there are fewer orders.

In Figure 16.4, point EOQ represents the order quantity having the lowest total cost. Actually, the order quantity that a firm considers best (or optimal) often is larger than the EOQ. That's because management must try to balance the sometimes conflicting goals of low inventory costs and responsive customer service. For various reasons, such as gaining a differential advantage, a firm may place a higher priority on customer service than on inventory costs. To completely fill orders in a timely manner may well call for a larger order quantity than the EOQ—for example, quantity X in Figure 16.4.

Just-in-Time First widely used in Japan, **just-in-time** (JIT) integrates inventory control, purchasing, and production scheduling. Applying JIT, a firm buys in small quantities that arrive *just in time* for production and then it produces in quantities

FIGURE 16.4

Economic Order Quantity.

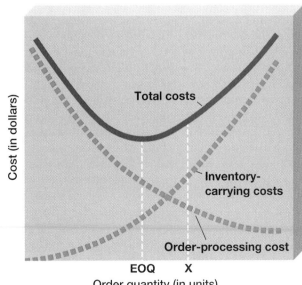

just in time for sale. When effectively implemented, the just-in-time concept has many benefits. By purchasing in small quantities and maintaining low inventory levels of parts and finished goods, a company can achieve dramatic cost savings because fewer items are damaged, stolen, or otherwise become unusable. Production and delivery schedules can be shortened and made more flexible and reliable. When order quantities are relatively small and deliveries frequent, a company can quickly spot and correct a quality problem in the products received.[38]

During the 1980s, the JIT philosophy was adopted in the American auto industry and then was implemented gradually by other leading firms such as IBM, Xerox, and General Electric. An organization that relies on JIT tends to use fewer suppliers because a high level of coordination is needed. JIT puts pressure on a supplier to meet a manufacturer's needs in a very timely fashion. In some instances, it has created friction between vendor and customer.

www.bose.com

An updated version of JIT was developed by the Bose Corp., the maker of high-end audio equipment. Under *JIT II*, a company provides a supplier with sales forecasts and other useful information, some of which may be confidential. In turn, a supplier often places one of its employees at the customer's plant to handle all or part of the purchasing function. As with any business practice, there are potential problems with JIT II, such as sharing of confidential data. Hence, some companies are using JIT or JIT II, whereas many others are not convinced the improvements in customer service are sufficient to justify the additional costs.[39]

Market–Response Systems

JIT's focus tends to be on production and the relationship between a producer and its suppliers. There's a parallel trend, however, involving producers or wholesalers of finished goods and their customers. Several labels have been used to describe this counterpart to JIT; we prefer **market-response system**. The central idea is that expected or actual purchases by final customers, those who intend to consume the product, should activate a process to produce and deliver replacement items. In this way, a product is pulled through a channel on the basis of demand rather than on short-term price reductions or other inducements that often result in excess inventories.

The intent of a market–response system is similar to that of JIT, namely to have just the right amount of goods in stock to satisfy demand and then to replenish exhausted stocks rapidly. By minimizing the quantity of inventory that languishes in middlemen's warehouses, a market–response system can shrink the funds that channel members tie up in inventory. Consumer prices may also drop, or at least not rise much.

Essentially, with a market–response system, a retailer's computer knows when a product is sold and, in turn, notifies the supplier's computer that a replacement is needed. Numerous retailers, including some e-tailers, have adopted some kind of market–response system. For example, various retailers, including Penney's and Wal-Mart, have their computers linked to those of VF Corp., an apparel maker based in Greensboro, North Carolina. Each night a store's computer sends to VF's computer precise information about which of the manufacturer's products, including Lee and Wrangler jeans and Vanity Fair women's underwear, were sold that day. Then VF ships replacements, either from existing inventory or as soon as they are produced. Store shelves are replenished as soon as two days later.[40]

www.vfc.com

More recently, the scope of market–response systems has expanded beyond automatic replenishment. **Collaborative planning, forecasting, and replenishment (CPFR)** is a method by which a producer or a wholesaler and a customer, ordinarily a retail chain, jointly and interactively develop sales forecasts through a shared website and cooperatively design marketing plans. The intent of CPFR is to supply the right amount of products—neither too many nor too few—in response to demand. The outcomes of CPFR are not just decision rules related to replenishment but also a full program for marketing a specific product. CPFR requires sharing of confidential information between the participating channel members, so it depends on trust in the relationship.[41]

An early test of CPFR involving Warner-Lambert, Inc., which makes Listerine mouthwash, and Wal-Mart produced very promising results. Of particular interest was a 25% reduction in inventories of Listerine. Subsequent tests, involving other firms, have generated sales gains and/or reductions in out-of-stock situations. These results notwithstanding, most retailers (with Wal-Mart being one exception) are still in the early stages of CPFR. One prerequisite for widespread usage that is being addressed is the development of user-friendly software that assures secure exchanges of sensitive information over the Internet.[42]

CPFR is very much related to company-wide initiatives that are intended to integrate by means of computer programs the various business functions of an organization. The functions include sales, manufacturing, purchasing, distribution, financial management, and human resources. These efforts are commonly called **enterprise resource planning systems,** or simply *ERP* or *enterprise software.* As ERP has evolved, increased attention is being given to what has been labeled *supply chain optimization* and *customer relationship management,* both of which are directly linked to distribution.[43]

Inventory Location and Warehousing

Management must make critical decisions about the size, location, and transportation of inventories. These areas are interrelated, often in complex ways. The number and locations of inventory sites, for example, influence inventory size and transportation methods. One key consideration in managing inventories is *warehousing,* which embraces a range of functions, such as assembling, dividing, and storing products and preparing them for reshipping. The importance of this function is underscored by the fact that the part of supply chain management receiving the largest share of information technology expenditures in 2002 was warehouse management systems.[44]

Types of Warehouses
Any producer, wholesaler, or retailer has the option of operating its own private warehouse or using the services of a public warehouse. A **private warehouse** is more likely to be an advantage if (1) a company moves a large volume of products through a warehouse, (2) there is very little, if any, seasonal fluctuation in this flow, and (3) the goods have special handling or storage requirements.

A **public warehouse** offers storage and handling facilities to individuals or companies. Public warehousing costs are a variable expense. Customers pay only for the space they use, and only when they use it. Public warehouses can also provide office and product display space, and accept and fill orders for sellers.

Distribution Centers
An effective inventory-location strategy may involve the establishment of one or more **distribution centers.** This type of facility, typically very large in size, is planned around markets rather than transportation requirements. The idea is to develop under one roof an efficient, fully integrated system for the flow of products—taking orders, filling them, and preparing them for delivery to customers.[45]

Distribution centers have been established by many well-known firms. W.W. Grainger, the wholesaler profiled at the beginning of the chapter, has invested $200 million to replace or completely refurbish its distribution centers in order to reduce the number of shipments the branches have to make and to improve customer service. In an entirely different industry, Nintendo of America has a 380,000-square-foot distribution center in North Bend, Washington, where products are received in large, sealed containers from Japan. From there, video games and accessories are shipped to 10,000 stores nationally. Orders are filled with an accuracy rate that translates to less than one item misshipped per every 10,000 shipped.[46]

At the start of the new century, ambitious e-commerce firms such as Amazon, eToys, and Webvan spent very large sums to construct distribution centers at carefully selected locations. Amazon, for example, established centers in Kansas, Kentucky, and Nevada to serve as the hubs of its physical distribution system. The other two firms, however, were among the many e-tailers that went out of business as a result of insufficient sales and/or exorbitant expenses.[47]

Distribution centers can cut costs by reducing the number of warehouses, pruning excessive inventories, and eliminating out-of-stock conditions. Companies are in business to sell goods, not to store or ship them, so warehousing and delivery times must be cut to a minimum. Distribution centers can help in this regard as well.

Materials Handling

Selecting the proper equipment to physically handle products, including the warehouse building itself, is the *materials handling* subsystem of physical distribution management. Equipment that is well matched to the task can minimize losses from breakage, spoilage, and theft. Efficient equipment can reduce handling costs as well as time required for handling.

Modern warehouses typically are huge one-story structures located in outlying areas where land is less expensive and loading platforms are easily accessed by trucks and trains. Conveyor belts, forklift trucks, and other mechanized equipment are used to move merchandise. In some warehouses the order fillers are even outfitted with in-line skates!

Containerization is a cargo-handling system that has become standard practice in physical distribution. Shipments of products are enclosed in large metal or wood containers. A container is transported and remains unopened from the shipper's facil-

A GLOBAL PERSPECTIVE

How large can container ships be?

Containerization is prevalent in shipping merchandise across an ocean. Container ships navigate the Pacific Ocean between Asia and the U.S., traveling at up to 25 knots per hour. They also move between Asia and Europe by way of the Suez Canal.

Container ships are huge. Imagine three football fields laid end to end, and that's roughly the surface area of a container ship. Typically, the containers used in international transit are about 40 feet long. A few years ago, about 2,200 containers would fit onto a ship. Then one company, Maersk Sealand, built a dozen even larger vessels that cost at least $100 million apiece. Each of these ships holds about 3,300 containers, which would span 27 miles if placed end to end. A British shipping organization is now designing an "ultralarge" ship that would have a capacity of 9,000 or more containers.

Why are container ships getting bigger and bigger? The answer lies in economies of scale. Operating expenses, such as fuel and labor, do not go up commensurate with capacity. Thus larger ship size means that it costs less to transport a single container overseas.

Another company is taking a different approach, testing the premise that some shippers will pay more for faster deliveries of containers. FastShip Inc. is working on a vessel that would cut the transit time for a container ship in half (from seven days down to three or four days, for example). Of course, the ships will be more costly (perhaps $250 million apiece), and they will have much higher operating expenses. Thus shipping fees will be substantially above those charged by companies such as Maersk Sealand that rely on huge ships. But FastShip is generating some excitement. According to a professor, the speedier container ship could "do for ocean service what Federal Express has done for package delivery." Of course, the unanswered question is whether there are sufficient customers willing to pay a premium for more rapid delivery of containers.

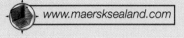

www.maersksealand.com

Sources: "Supersize Cargo Ships," *Popular Mechanics,* March 2002, p. 25; Philip Siekman, "The New Wave in Giant Ships," *Fortune,* Nov. 12, 2001, pp. I182[I]+; and Daniel Machalaba, "Is This Boat the FedEx of the Seas?" *The Wall Street Journal,* Mar. 15, 2000, p. B1.

ity (such as a manufacturer's plant) to its destination (such as a wholesaler's warehouse). Containerization minimizes physical handling, thereby reducing damage, lessening the risk of theft, and allowing for more efficient transportation.

Transportation

A major function of the physical distribution system in many companies is *transportation*—shipping products to customers. Management must decide on both the mode of transportation and the particular carriers. In this discussion we will focus on *intercity* shipments.

In arranging transportation, firms are trying to satisfy customers while controlling expenses. To do so, many small companies are forming or joining *shippers' cooperatives*. This type of organization, which is run by the members, pools the shipping needs of a group of firms in order to obtain volume discounts from various carriers, such as railroads. One small business, Marshmallow Products Inc. of Cincinnati, was pleased that its shipping costs dropped 40% after joining a shippers' cooperative. A number of small Internet merchants as well as customers of online auctions go to a website, such as iShip.com, to use software that allows them to display the current rates charged by various transportation firms for different types of service.[48]

www.iship.com

Major Modes Railroads, trucks, pipelines, water vessels, and airplanes are the leading modes of transportation. In Table 16.4 these five methods are compared on the basis of criteria likely to be used by physical distribution managers in selecting a mode of transportation. Of course, the ratings of alternative modes of transportation can vary from one manager in a buying center to the next manager, even within the same buying organization.[49]

Virtually all *intracity* shipping is done by motor truck. The relative use of four of the major modes, along with trends for *intercity* shipping, are shown in Table 16.5. (Airplanes are not included in the table inasmuch as air freight comprises less than 1%

| TABLE 16.4 | **Comparison of Transportation Methods** |

	Transportation Method				
Selection Criteria	**Rail**	**Water**	**Highway**	**Pipeline**	**Air**
Speed (door-to-door time)	Medium	Slowest	Fast	Slow	**Fastest**
Cost of transportation	Medium	**Lowest**	High	Low	Highest
Reliability in meeting delivery schedules	Medium	Poor	Good	**Excellent**	Good
Variety of products carried	**Widest**	**Widest**	Medium	Very limited	Somewhat limited
Number of geographic locations served	Very many	Limited	**Unlimited**	Very limited	Many
Most suitable products	Long hauls of carload quantities of bulky products, when freight costs are high in relation to product's value	Bulky, low-value nonperishables	Short hauls of high-value goods	Oil, natural gas, slurried products	High-value perishables, where speed of delivery is all-important

TABLE 16.5

Distribution of Intercity Freight Traffic in the United States Based on Ton Miles

Specific Mode	% of Total			
	2000	1990	1970	1950
Railroads	41	38	40	56
Trucks	29	25	21	16
Pipelines	17	20	22	12
Water vessels	13	16	17	15
Total	100	100	100	100

Notes: These data do not cover *intracity* freight traffic or ocean coastal traffic between U.S. ports. A *ton mile* refers to 1 ton of freight being transported 1 mile. Air freight accounts for less than 0.5% of total intercity shipping, as measured in ton miles. The 1950 and 1990 columns do not total to 100% due to rounding.

Source: "Overview of U.S. Freight Railroads," Association of American Railroads, January 2002, *www.aar.org/ PubCommon/Documents/AboutTheIndustry/Overview/pdf;* and *Railroad Facts,* 1999 edition, Association of American Railroads, Washington, DC, 1999, p. 32.

of the total.) By the way, virtually all *intracity* shipping is done by motor truck. As indicated in the table, the use of trucks has expanded greatly since 1950. Even as the relative position of railroads slipped between 1950 and 1970, the absolute amount of rail freight increased considerably. The railroads' position has stabilized since 1970.

For several years in the late 1990s, the future of railroads was clouded as a result of various factors, including problems of the railroads' own making, such as congested tracks and poor monitoring systems. After considerable efforts and sizable expenditures on new equipment, facilities, and technology, railroads are getting back on track. Recently, trucking firms have been suffering as a result of what's been called "the perfect storm." Specifically, a record number of trucking companies failed in 2000 and 2001 because they couldn't cope with the combination of higher labor, fuel, and insurance costs along with the economic slowdown that reduced demand for trucking services.[50]

Intermodal Transportation   Using two or more modes of transportation to move freight is termed **intermodal transportation.** This approach is intended to seize the advantages of multiple forms of transportation. Continued strong growth is forecast for intermodal transportation, largely because of the ongoing globalization of business, stimulated by compacts such as the North American Free Trade Agreement. In fact, intermodal is overtaking coal as the largest single revenue source for railroads.[51]

So-called *piggyback service* involves carrying truck trailers on railroad flatcars. For example, a shipment of auto glass is loaded on J. B. Hunt Transport trucks at the Pilkington Libbey-Owens-Ford plant near Toledo, Ohio. The truck trailers are placed on a Burlington Northern Santa Fe train in Chicago for a trip to Los Angeles. There, Hunt trucks take the glass to its destination in Fontana, California. This intermodal arrangement provides (1) more flexibility than railroads alone can offer, (2) lower freight costs than trucks alone, and (3) less handling of goods.[52] Another form of intermodal transportation, *fishyback service,* combines ships or barges with either railroads or trucks, or both.

With the trend toward intermodal methods, more companies that have goods to move are interested in **one-stop shipping,** which consists of one transportation firm offering multiple modes of transportation to customers. Typically, the carrier owns the various modes (such as a truck line, cargo ships, and even airplanes); sometimes, however, they will turn to an outside firm if they need to use a mode of transportation they don't own.[53]

www.jbhunt.com

Seeking economies of scale, container ships that carry goods across oceans have been getting larger and larger. This giant ship crosses the Pacific—often between Hong Kong and Long Beach, California—in about 11 days, moving at a speed of up to 25 knots (about 29 miles) per hour. The Carsten Maersk (shown here), which is owned by Maersk Sealand, is too large to go through the Panama Canal but it can traverse the Suez Canal.

www.maersksealand.com

www.jesforwarding.com

Freight Forwarders   A specialized intermediary serving firms that ship in less-than-full-load quantities is called a **freight forwarder.** Its main function is to consolidate less-than-carload or less-than-truckload shipments from several shippers into full-load quantities. The complexities of foreign shipments have prompted many companies to rely on forwarders.

A freight forwarder picks up the merchandise at the shipper's place of business and arranges for delivery at the buyer's door. A small shipper benefits from the speed and minimum handling associated with large shipments. It may also cost less to use a freight forwarder than to deal directly with a carrier because of the volume discounts that forwarders obtain from airlines, railroads, and other carriers. A freight forwarder also provides its customers with traffic management services, such as selecting the best transportation mode(s) and route(s).

Package-Delivery Firms   For more than 30 years, **package-delivery firms** have been on the rise. These companies deliver shipments of small packages and high-priority mail. In contrast to freight forwarders, which do not own their own transportation equipment, package-delivery firms do. Companies such as Airborne Express and United Parcel Service (UPS), in effect, use intermodal transportation. In the case of FedEx, for example, a package is picked up by truck, shipped intercity or overseas by plane, and delivered locally by truck. The surge in both just-in-time purchasing and electronic commerce, particularly where the shipment is headed to a consumer, has contributed to the continuing growth of this type of transportation company.

www.airborne.com

Package-delivery firms compete vigorously not only among themselves but also with the U.S. Postal Service (as described in Case 2 following Part 2). The competition is particularly intense in the overnight-delivery market, where FedEx and UPS go head-to-head. Each giant tries to surpass the other with respect to delivery times, technology that helps customers prepare and then track their shipments, and—of course—low prices. Now most transportation firms view each other as adversaries. In the words of the head of Yellow Corp., the country's biggest trucking firm, "Our competitors today are the UPSs and the FedExs of the world."[54]

Here, a FedEx employee uses a handheld device to record data that enable the tracking of a customer's shipment. Some technological advances pose threats for package-delivery firms. For instance, many documents previously shipped overnight are now being transmitted via e-mail. But technology also brings opportunities. For example, the growth of e-commerce has markedly increased the quantity of small packages being shipped from vendor to buyer.

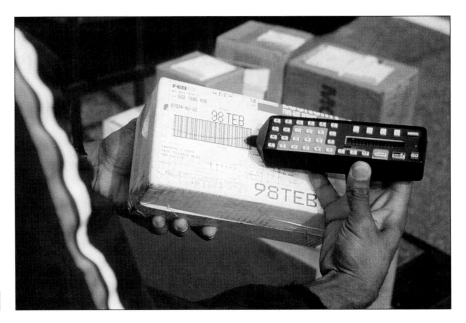

www.fedex.com

Summary

Wholesaling consists of the sale, and all activities directly related to the sale, of goods and services for resale, use in making other products, or operation of an organization. Firms engaged primarily in wholesaling, called wholesaling middlemen, provide economies of skill, scale, and transactions to other firms involved in distribution.

Three categories of wholesaling middlemen are merchant wholesalers, agent wholesaling middlemen, and manufacturers' sales facilities. The first two are independent firms; the third is owned by a manufacturer. Merchant wholesalers take title to products being distributed; agent wholesaling middlemen do not. In recent years, the shares of total wholesale trade captured by the three categories have stabilized, with merchant wholesalers accounting for the majority share.

Merchant wholesalers, which account for the majority of wholesale trade, include both full-service and limited-service wholesalers. Of the three major categories of wholesaling middlemen, merchant wholesalers offer the widest range of services and thus incur the highest operating expenses.

Agent wholesaling middlemen lost ground to merchant wholesalers for at least a couple of decades. The main types of agent middlemen are manufacturers' agents and brokers. Because they perform more limited services, agent middlemen's expenses tend to be lower than merchant wholesalers'.

Physical distribution is the flow of products from supply sources to a firm and then from that firm to its customers. The goal of physical distribution is to move the right amount of the right products to the right place at the right time. The costs of trying to do this are a substantial part of total operating costs in many firms. Moreover, physical distribution is a potential source of substantial cost reductions in many companies.

Physical distribution activities are still fragmented operationally and organizationally in many firms. To overcome these shortcomings, supply chain management takes a total system perspective of distribution. The total cost concept should be applied to physical distribution. That is, management should strive *not* for the lowest total cost of a single physical distribution activity, but for the best balance between customer service and total cost. Effective management of physical distribution can help a company gain an advantage over competitors through better customer service and/or lower operating costs. To improve their physical distribution, more and more firms are turning to contract logistics.

The operation of a physical distribution system requires management's attention and decision making in five areas: order processing, inventory control, inventory location and warehousing, materials handling, and transportation. They should not be treated as individual activities but as interrelated components within a physical distribution system. Effective management of these five activities requires an understanding of electronic data interchange; economic order quantity; just-in-time processes; market–response systems such as collaborative planning, forecasting, and replenishment (CPFR); distribution centers; and intermodal transportation.

More about **W.W. Grainger**

The Grainger company took to the Internet early and wholeheartedly. In an effort to meet the needs of its varied customers, the firm has had a series of websites. TotalMRO.com was a catalog site designed to aggregate the catalogs of many suppliers, including Grainger's competitors. MROverstocks.com was an online auction site for discontinued and surplus supplies. FindMRO.com was a sourcing venture for hard-to-find items. All three were eventually consolidated into *Material Logic,* which failed to find enough investors or participating distributors to keep it afloat. A similar Grainger venture, OrderZone.com, was intended to increase the firm's customer base by appealing to small and medium-sized customers. But too many visitors to the site were browsers instead of buyers, and the venture was sold.

Clearly, some of Grainger's Internet ventures were not fruitful. Undaunted, the firm developed Grainger.com, with the intent of saving money for big customers. Weyerhauser Inc., for instance, can buy two-thirds of its safety and general mill supplies from Grainger online for about $300,000. Purchasing the remaining one-third from 1,300 small distributors would cost the timber and paper products company about $2.4 million. Seeing a mutually beneficial opportunity, Grainger is working with Weyerhauser to switch all of its maintenance, repair, and operations (MRO) product purchases to Grainger's website. Even as it seeks to capitalize on such opportunities, Grainger.com has become the largest business-to-business operation in e-commerce, and it recently expanded to include a repair parts center.

Grainger continues to seek innovative ways to use the Internet. For example, the firm is planning to place online (1) "explosion diagrams" showing the interiors of products such as motors and (2) pop-up videos that demonstrate installation procedures for various products. "We're still investing in e-procurement systems," says a company vice president. "But the industry's rate of transition is slower than we thought it would be. It's still a matter of when, not if."[55]

1. Will online purchases of MRO products continue to grow? What are some of the advantages to (a) vendors and (b) customers of online procurement?

2. What can Grainger do to assure that it is prepared, whether or not online purchases of MRO products become prevalent?

Key Terms And Concepts

Wholesaling (448)
Wholesaling middleman (449)
Merchant wholesaler (451)
Agent wholesaling middleman (452)
Manufacturer's sales facility (452)
Manufacturer's sales branch (452)
Manufacturer's sales office (452)
Full-service wholesaler (453)
Truck jobber (454)
Drop shipper (454)
Manufacturers' agent (455)
Broker (456)
Selling agent (456)
Auction company (456)

Import–export agents (457)
Physical distribution (457)
Fulfillment (459)
Online category manager (460)
Supply chain management (460)
Total cost concept (460)
Contract logistics (460)
Physical distribution management (463)
Electronic data interchange (EDI) (463)
Economic order quantity (EOQ) (464)
Just-in-time (JIT) (465)
Market–response system (466)

Collaborative planning, forecasting, and replenishment (CPFR) (466)
Enterprise resource planning (ERP) systems (467)
Private warehouse (467)
Public warehouse (467)
Distribution center (467)
Containerization (468)
Intermodal transportation (471)
One-stop shipping (471)
Freight forwarder (471)
Package-delivery firms (471)

Questions and Problems

1. Which of the following are wholesaling transactions?

   a. Color Tile sells wallpaper to an apartment building contractor and also to the contractor's wife for her home.

   b. General Electric sells motors to Whirlpool for its washing machines.

   c. A shrimp "farmer" sells fresh shrimp to a local restaurant.

d. A family orders carpet from a friend, who is a home decorating consultant, at 50% off the suggested retail price. The carpet is delivered directly to the home.

2. As shown in Figure 16.3, agent wholesaling middlemen and manufacturers' sales facilities have lost part of their share of wholesale trade to merchant wholesalers over the past several decades. But then this erosion stopped. What could the two types of wholesaling middlemen do to combat merchant wholesalers in the future?

3. Why is it that manufacturers' agents often can penetrate a market faster and at a lower cost than a manufacturer's sales force?

4. Which type of wholesaling middleman, if any, is most likely to be used by each of the following firms? Explain your choice in each instance.

   a. A small manufacturer of a liquid glass cleaner to be sold through supermarkets.
   b. A small canner in Vermont packing a high-quality, unbranded fruit product.
   c. A small-tools manufacturing firm that has its own sales force selling to the business market and now wants to add backyard barbecue equipment to its product mix.
   d. A textile mill in Malaysia producing unbranded towels, sheets, pillowcases, and blankets.

5. Looking to the future, which types of wholesaling middlemen do you think will increase in importance, and which ones will decline? Explain.

6. "The goal of a modern physical distribution system in a firm should be to operate at the lowest possible *total* costs." Do you agree?

7. Name some products for which you think the cost of physical distribution constitutes at least one-half the total price of the goods at the wholesale level. Can you suggest ways of decreasing the physical distribution cost of these products?

8. "A manufacturer follows an inventory-location strategy of concentration rather than dispersion. This company's inventory size will be smaller, but its transportation and warehousing expenses will be larger than if its inventory were dispersed." Do you agree? Explain.

9. "The use of public warehouse facilities makes it possible for manufacturers to bypass wholesalers in their channels of distribution." Explain.

10. For each of the following products, determine the best transportation method for shipment to a distribution center in the community where your school is located. In each case the buyer (not the seller) will pay all freight charges, and, unless specifically noted, time is not important. The distribution center has a rail siding and a dock for loading and unloading trucks.

    a. Disposable diapers from Wisconsin. Total shipment weight is 112,000 pounds.
    b. A replacement memory card for your computer, which is now inoperative. Weight of shipment is 1.5 pounds, and you need this card in a hurry.
    c. Blank payroll checks for your company. (There is a sufficient number of checks on hand for the next two weekly paydays.) Shipment weight is 100 pounds.
    d. Ice cream from St. Louis. Total shipment weight is 42,000 pounds.

Interactive Marketing Exercises

1. Interview the owner or a manager at a firm that is a type of merchant wholesaler (such as a full-service wholesaler). Ask the owner or manager to describe the firm's activities, its differential advantage or disadvantage at the present time, and the company's prospects for the future. Conduct a similar interview with the owner or a manager of a firm that is a type of agent wholesaling middleman (such as a broker). How do you explain any discrepancies between the interview results and the content of this chapter (other than saying that the chapter must be wrong)?

2. A manufacturer of precision lenses used in medical and hospital equipment wants to ship a 5-pound box of these lenses from your college town to a laboratory in Stockholm, Sweden. The lab wants delivery in five days or less. The manufacturer wants to use a package-delivery service but is undecided as to which shipper to choose. Compile and compare the types of services provided and prices charged by FedEx, United Parcel Service, and one other package-delivery firm.

Cases for Part 5

CASE 1

Target Corp.

Hitting the Bull's-Eye in Discount Retailing

For many years after its first discount store opened in 1962, Target proceeded cautiously. It followed a plan for modest growth, locating new stores throughout the Midwest. But when Bob Ulrich was appointed Target's new chief executive officer in 1994, he had bigger plans for the company. He envisioned nationwide expansion, with Target becoming a powerful brand, on par with labels such as Disney and Apple.

To fulfill this vision, Target's top management needed to design a set of strategies to distinguish the chain in the minds of consumers. "We had three strategic choices," said Target's vice chairman. "To specialize, to become the low-cost producer, or to differentiate ourselves." Wal-Mart is already the recognized low-cost leader in discount retailing, and specialization was deemed too narrow an approach. So Target decided to differentiate itself within the industry by blending *designer* with *discount* and *fashion* with *frugality*. The chain hired successful designers, such as Todd Oldham, Michael Graves, and Mossimo Giannulli, to develop economically priced lines of housewares and fashions that would be sold only in Target stores. And it opened new outlets all across the country, with the intention of growing its parent company's revenues from $40 billion in 2001 to at least $65 billion in 2005.

Aiming to Harness the "Power of One"

Target was the creation of The Dayton Company, a century-old, conservative department store chain based in Minnesota. In 1902, George Dayton opened Goodfellows, a large department store, in downtown Minneapolis. By 1910, the corporation had adopted The Dayton Company name. Over time, new stores were opened throughout the Midwest, including the world's first enclosed, two-story shopping mall in suburban Minneapolis in 1956. Six years later, Target made its debut in Roseville, Minnesota, and was promoted as "a new idea in discount stores."

In 1969, The Dayton Company merged with the J. L. Hudson Company, another midwestern department store company, which was based in Detroit, Michigan. The outcome was The Dayton Hudson Corporation (DHC). In 1978, DHC purchased Mervyn's, a West Coast chain of midprice stores, thereby becoming the nation's seventh-largest retailer.

By 1979, Target was contributing more revenues to DHC than any of its other entities. Corporate sales exceeded $10 billion in 1987. Given its size, DHC was able to acquire the prestigious, Chicago-based Marshall Field's department stores in 1990.

Since Ulrich assumed the helm of DHC, all of the firm's department stores (including 19 Dayton's locations and 21 Hudson's locations) have been renamed Marshall Field's. This rebranding decision rankled both employees and customers in Minneapolis and Detroit. One company spokesperson explained the decision, "We selected Marshall Field's name because it is known worldwide and represents our largest business."

An even more significant name change took place in January 2000 when DHC became Target Corporation. The change is understandable considering that the Target unit accounts for 80% of the entire firm's revenues. It is expected that if Target Corporation achieves its sales goal of at least $65 billion by 2005, Target stores alone will account for $57 billion or more of total revenues. While Mervyn's (now called Mervyn's California) and Marshall Field's struggle to achieve consistent sales performances and have no plans for new stores in the near future, Target continues to build revenues and expand throughout the U.S.

Some industry analysts have questioned whether one company can adequately address the distinctive demands of a discount chain (Target,) a midpriced operaton (Mervyn's California,) and a department store chain (Marshall Field's). But Ulrich believes these three entities can benefit from each other. The company adopted a strategy, called the "Power of One," which seeks to infuse each division's best practices throughout the entire organization. The divisions also share valuable information and data. For instance, fashion trends being observed by Marshall Field's department stores help Target's merchandising department predict which styles will be popular each season.

Focusing on Fashion

Target's strategies to become the designer discount chain also include brightly lit, clutter-free store interiors and edgy advertising campaigns that feature Target's ubiquitous bull's-eye logo. But the merchandise is what truly distinguishes Target from its rivals.

Michael Graves' line of housewares has transformed mundane objects, such as tea kettles and spatulas, into art deco pieces. Mossimo's line of adult apparel incorporates the latest trends into clothing basics, providing updated looks for budget-minded consumers. And Todd Oldham, a renowned woman's clothing designer, was hired to develop a line of home fashions that reflect his preference for big prints and bright colors. "Target and I have very similar views about what's important in design," Oldham said. "We both believe that consumers crave design that's smart and interesting, while at the same time is accessible and affordable." Oldham's words certainly coincide with Target's slogan, "Expect More/Pay Less."

Part of Target's strategy is to concentrate on "soft lines," such as apparel and bedding, which are susceptible to style updates. (It's a bit more difficult to make a power tool, for instance, fashionable.) Also, if a category or line doesn't work out well, Target's executives are not reluctant to abandon it. "They're smart at selectively bailing out of categories early," commented a former Target executive.

Soft lines also have the potential for good profit margins. All factors considered, it was no surprise when Target stopped selling personal computers in the mid-1990s. PCs require a great deal of personal selling, have small profit margins, and suffer from high rates of customer returns. Target continues to sell software, however. "They've had a tough time in hard lines, but so many specialty retailers are in hard lines," explained one retail consultant. "The key place to win is in apparel, and Target is going to win it in soft lines."

Target has also updated its distribution strategy. In the past, it had a difficult time keeping hot items adequately stocked in its stores. To remedy this situation, it has implemented a new shelf tag system to identify the chain's top 1,000 items *and* a system to expedite the flow of these items from its regional distribution centers to Target stores. The company also said it would double its number of regional distribution centers by 2005. "We believe these steps are critical to our ability to increase market share and profitability," explained the company president.

Targeting Kmart and Wal-Mart

Whereas Wal-Mart touts its low prices and Target promotes its fashion sense, Kmart has been unable to develop and maintain a consistent and effective appeal to shoppers. Forced into bankruptcy, many Kmart stores have fallen into disarray, with erratic inventory levels and outdated layouts and décor. In contrast, Target stores are clean and uniform in appearance, with 12-foot aisles and no boxes of unshelved merchandise in sight.

Target rang up sales of almost $44 billion in fiscal 2002, producing earnings in excess of $1.5 billion. Kmart generated more than $30 billion in revenues, but *lost* over $2 billion. Target's recent expansion into the northeast portion of the country has been especially threatening to Kmart. On Long Island, New York, for instance, a Kmart saw its sales decrease by 25% when a new Target opened in the same area.

Although Target has supplanted Kmart as the #2 discount chain in the U.S., it continues to run far behind Wal-Mart. In fact, as measured by sales, Target is less than one-fifth the size of its Arkansas-headquartered competitor. Target avoids head-to-head clashes with Wal-Mart by stressing fashion and using promotional discounts, whereas Wal-Mart emphasizes well-known items and everyday low prices. But Target is intent on matching Wal-Mart's prices when they compete directly in the same market. However, Target rounds up its prices to the nearest 99 cents (e.g., $18.99), but Wal-Mart doesn't (e.g., $18.76).

Wal-Mart is not only the largest discount chain in the U.S., but also the largest company in the entire world as measured by sales volume. It amassed more than $244 *billion* in sales for the fiscal year ending in January 2003—more than the combined revenues of the next nine largest discount retailers (including Target and Kmart). As of early 2003, Wal-Mart had more than 2,800 stores in the U.S. whereas Target had over 1,100.

But Target is looking to aggressively expand in the near future. It already has stores in 47 states, although its major markets remain in the Midwest, especially Chicago, Minneapolis, and Detroit. In 2001, Target committed $3.5 billion in capital spending to expand even further, and used some of that money to take over 35 locations previously occupied by the now defunct Montgomery Ward chain. Target is adding square footage at a rate of 10% to 12% per year, which translates to about 65 store openings annually. About one-third of these new stores are SuperTargets, designed to compete with Wal-Mart's Supercenters.

Taking a Shot at New Formats

Wal-Mart originally developed the supercenter format as a way to get people into its stores on a more regular basis. Eventually, Target saw the huge potential of the hybrid stores. "Consumer preferences were changing, with folks being pressed for time," said Target's president. "The combination of general merchandise and food was growing in popularity." Thus the first Target supercenter opened in Omaha, Nebraska, in 1995, and offered typical Target merchandise plus groceries. By late 2002, 82 SuperTargets had been opened, compared to 1,243 Wal-Mart Supercenters.

Adding groceries to the merchandise mix dramatically increases the complexity of a store's operations, and the profit margins are significantly smaller on food than on nonfood items. Wal-Mart's ownership of 25 grocery warehouses throughout the U.S. as well as its volume of business give it significant price and cost advantages over Target. It's estimated that Target's grocery prices are 8% below supermarket chains' prices, but Wal-Mart's are at least 20% lower.

Both companies are fully committed to the format. Target intends to have 310 supercenters in operation by 2010, whereas Wal-Mart plans to have about 2,700 by then. Noting Wal-Mart's much more aggressive expansion plans for supercenters, a wholesaling middleman commented, "If Target was winning [in supercenters], they would speed it up."

Target opened another type of store in 1998 when it launched its own website. But the company couldn't keep up with the growing Internet sales volume. Hence, Target arranged for Amazon to handle a number of website-related tasks, such as software development and order fulfillment. Besides offering a subset of the physical store's merchandise, as many other retailers do, www.target.com features items not available at its bricks-and-mortar locations. The distinctive offerings include oversized products, such as Little Tikes furniture, and items the company wants to test-market, such as a $200 Graco jogging stroller. A wide assortment of merchandise from Mervyn's and Marshall Field's will be offered at the website as well.

In addition to its website, Target has been promoting its new Target Visa card, the first "smart card" to be offered by a retailer in the U.S. "This revolutionary new card offers our guests a credit vehicle with greater convenience, broader utility, increased value and expanded rewards programs," stated Target's vice chairman. With an embedded chip, each card contains 64 kilobytes of memory that enables users to download special promotional offers from the Internet and from readers located at Target stores.

The smart card can track purchases for the company's loyalty program and for its Take Charge of Education School Fundraising Program. In this loyalty program, customers who charge a certain amount of merchandise on the Target Visa card receive a coupon for 10% off a day's purchases at the chain. In the Take Charge program, Target donates a small percentage of a cardholder's purchases to a school selected by the customer.

Smart cards have proven to be quite popular in Europe, and Target hopes they will catch on in the U.S. According to a top executive at Target, "Adding a smart chip and providing chip readers in our stores underscores our commitment to introduce creativity and excitement to our guests." And when it comes to being creative and exciting, this company seems to be right on target.

Questions

1. Besides other discount chains such as Wal-Mart and Kmart, what types of retailers represent serious competition for Target?

2. What else can Target do to differentiate itself from Wal-Mart?

3. What are the advantages and disadvantages to Target of operating superstores?

www.targetcorp.com

CASE 2

Costco versus Sam's Club

Making Sure Membership Has Its Privileges

In 1977, Sol Price opened his first store in San Diego and named it the Price Club. His last name was the perfect choice for this outlet, the first warehouse club, which offered individuals and small businesses the opportunity to purchase a variety of merchandise at rock-bottom prices.

Buying in bulk directly from manufacturers, keeping the stores as simple as possible, and requiring small annual membership fees allowed Price Club to charge prices that were just a bit above wholesale prices. In fact, although the majority of warehouse clubs' transactions are with consumers, a substantial portion of their annual sales volume comes from organizations that are making purchases for resale or for use in their own enterprises. Thus, although classified as retailers, warehouse clubs really are a hybrid retail–wholesale operation.

Seeing Price Club's success, other retail firms decided to develop their own brand of warehouse club. Wal-Mart opened its first three Sam's Clubs in 1983, and Kmart tried to keep pace with, of course, the Pace chain. Soon, the market became saturated to some extent, resulting in a number of store closings and acquisitions. Sam's bought Pace, and later Costco took over the Price Club organization. Before long, these two retailers—Sam's and Costco—accounted for 85% of the volume rung up by warehouse clubs. BJ's Wholesale Club is #3, but far behind the leaders.

For a time, the two chains remained separated to a large degree by geography. But as they continued to expand, Costco and Sam's began to compete directly against each other more frequently. Today, the rivalry is fierce, with each merchant continually looking for new and innovative merchandise and services to offer shoppers. One industry analyst noted, "The idea is to give members as much value as you can, not only to keep renewal rates high, but to attract new members."

Keeping Prices Low

The basic premise of a warehouse club is simple. As described by Costco's chief executive officer, James Sinegal, "Costco is able to offer lower prices and better values by eliminating virtually all the frills and costs historically associated with conventional wholesalers and retailers, including sales people, fancy buildings, delivery, billing and accounts receivable. We run a tight operation with extremely low overhead which enables us to pass on dramatic savings to our members." The same is true for Sam's Club.

Both chains target two groups for membership:

- Budget-minded individuals who want to buy groceries and other product categories at deep discounts. Many shoppers are likely to buy some products, such as packaged foods and paper goods, in bulk. Other consumers are looking for a "treasure," such as a big-screen television or a piece of jewelry at a very attractive price.

- Small and medium-size businesses that often resell items purchased at warehouse clubs or use them in their day-to-day operations.

Membership fees are fairly consistent across the industry. As of late 2002, Costco charged $45 annually, for both groups, whereas Sam's fees were $35 for individuals and $30 for organizations. Sam's own website even admits, "Profits are primarily derived from membership sales." So keeping membership rates as high as possible is absolutely imperative to being successful.

Keeping prices low is another priority. Sinegal never allows his stores' merchandise to be marked up by more than 14%. Costco's senior vice president, explained the policy, "The members count on us to deliver the best deal. Jim doesn't cheat on that." Sinegal elaborated, "We (at Costco) have a product selection of about 4,000 items; if you went into Target or Wal-Mart, you'd find around 100,000 items. We may only select two toasters to sell, or two types of peanut butter, but those will be the best values that we can find at that moment."

Bulking Up on Higher-Price Goods

Costco, which opened its first warehouse club in Seattle in 1983, differentiated itself from other warehouse clubs by offering some upscale merchandise in addition to multiple-unit packages of batteries, paper towels, and cereal. Throughout the aisles of Costco stores, shoppers can find "treasures" ranging from TaylorMade golf clubs to Prada and Coach purses. Furthermore, Costco buys and resells more Bordeaux wines than any other U.S. retailer, and has sold 50,000 carats of diamonds in a year. Costco will give customers a refund plus $100 if their diamond is appraised for less than twice what they paid for it. In 2002, Costco began carrying merchandise from Nautica, Kitchen Aid, and Ralph Lauren.

Costco works very hard to avoid out-of-stock situations, often relying on "vendor-managed inventory." For example, Kimberly-Clark receives data each day from every Costco store in the country regarding their supply of, say, Huggies diapers. It is Kimberly-Clark's responsibility to monitor the data to ensure that each store has just enough diapers so it doesn't run out of stock. A larger supply would take up scarce space and reduce the funds available for other merchandise.

Kimberly-Clark, which manages inventory for 44 different retailers, says it has been able to save $200 million in two years and benefits by keeping its clients happy. Ultimately, these savings (or at least a part of the savings) are passed on to consumers, which is one reason why prices for general merchandise have not been increasing much in the U.S.

Not to be outdone, Sam's has added more expensive items to its merchandise mix. The Wal-Mart unit recently sponsored "a diamond extravaganza," featuring high-quality gems priced as high as $1 million, which traveled to various Sam's locations around the country. From a case of Courvoisier cognac with custom-designed labels that sold for $10,000 to a 10-foot-tall Remington statue worth about the same amount, Sam's has been working to noticeably upgrade its merchandise.

But Costco doesn't appear to be worried. One of the chain's executives stated, "You don't bring in a pallet of fancy merchandise and think you can cultivate a certain customer. They might bring in a pallet of Ralph Lauren shirts for $37. But while our customers will buy five of them, their customers won't spend $37 on a shirt." Perhaps this is a reference to Sam's parent company being Wal-Mart, a retailer that appeals to consumers with moderate incomes. Wal-Mart's chief executive conceded, "Costco's membership base is a little more affluent, so it allowed them to get to a better merchandise mix faster than Sam's."

As part of the Wal-Mart corporation, Sam's has access to employee training seminars and other support programs. "We also leverage best practices in store planning and construction," commented Sam's vice president of operations.

Introducing a Pallet of New Services

High-quality merchandise at low prices isn't the only attraction of warehouse clubs to shoppers. Both Sam's and Costco offer an array of services, including pharmacies, optical shops, food courts, and discounts on travel and automobiles. For example, Sam's customers can purchase an "elite" membership for $100 that provides roadside towing and a dental plan. Costco's "Executive" members pay a higher fee for access to financial services, such as insurance and mortgage applications, long-distance service, and even a 401K plan. "A lot of our business members have 10 employees or less, so the cost for them to enroll in a traditional 401K plan is prohibitive," said one of Costco's vice presidents.

These services differentiate warehouse clubs from other types of competitors, such as Target and Wal-Mart, and build customer loyalty. Both companies boast a membership renewal rate of about 85%. Sam's and Costco continue to add services as they expand aggressively and compete directly with one another with increasing frequency.

Taking Some of the Warehouse Out of the Clubs

By early 2003, Costco had over 300 U.S. stores, and Sam's had about 525. Reflecting its higher-price merchandise, Costco's sales-per-store figure was significantly higher than Sam's. Whereas Sam's reported revenues of $31.7 billion for the year ended January 31, 2003, Costco rang up $38 billion in sales for its fiscal year that ended August 31, 2002. These totals translate to $125 million per store for Costco compared to $60 million for Sam's.

To increase per-store sales, Sam's is working to improve the appearance and flow of its outlets. It opened a prototype in Plano, Texas, featuring a more open floor plan and colorful signs to help shoppers find what they're looking for. A café allows members to enjoy a leisurely lunch or snack, and a Sam's Sound area features large televisions that run advertising snippets, in-store messages, and video clips. Merchandise is grouped into more distinct sections, instead of being arranged in almost endless rows of shelving units. Electronic kiosks guide buyers in their selection of fine wines, a digital media center has computers available to give access to Sam's website, and the jewelry display has been significantly upgraded.

Each company is expected to continue opening new stores at a rapid rate. By the end of the 2003 fiscal year, Sam's target was to have 555 domestic stores compared to 326 for Costco. In some cases, aggressive expansion has taken these merchants out of their comfort zones. For instance, although Sam's has been the dominant warehouse club in Texas for many years, Costco added 10 new locations in the Lone Star State in a two-year period. Analysts worry about saturating the domestic market, but according to a Sam's vice president, "We don't necessarily see, looking into the future, that saturation will occur. We just continue to see good growth and markets for this format." Indeed, these firms are finding that some smaller, more rural communities are able to adequately support the introduction of a warehouse club.

Neither chain is overlooking the international arena—and all of its unique challenges and opportunities. Heading into 2003, Sam's had about 65 international stores, located in Mexico, China, and Brazil. Costco was operating 105 clubs in Canada, Mexico, the United Kingdom, and Asia. Both firms have had to adjust to foreign tastes and shopping styles. Sinegal believes, however, that the warehouse club concept is viable for any country. But he was surprised by how consumers' preferences varied across countries. For instance, shoppers in the U.K. snapped up cranberry juice, a beverage previously unavailable to them. Olive oil, basketball hoops, and doughnuts proved to be wildly popular in Japan.

Some issues had to be overcome in Japan. As described by one analyst, "The high price of land and the difficulty in finding it is the primary reason you don't see many big retailers over there." As a result, Costco splits its 140,000-square-foot stores into two levels. Surprisingly, although Japanese consumers tend to live in relatively small dwellings with limited storage space, Costco nevertheless sells numerous items in multiple-unit packages. "Customers buy things together, then divide them up," stated a Costco executive. "You see people in the parking garage all the time tearing open packages, splitting them up and going their separate ways."

One out of every six American adults now belongs to a warehouse club. When the global economy was hit hard in 2001, the retailing and wholesaling sectors suffered. However, even in the face of economic slowdowns, warehouse clubs continue to thrive and are expected to increase sales by an impressive annual rate of 15%. Thus the spirited competition between Costco and Sam's Club will continue—and perhaps intensify.

Questions

1. What are the pros and cons of operating a retail-wholesale outlet that requires shoppers to be members?

2. What is Costco's differential advantage in relation to Sam's? How about Sam's compared to Costco's?

3. In what ways, if any, do warehouse clubs have to deal differently with ultimate consumers than with wholesale buyers?

4. Should a warehouse club add new services that might increase its costs and, in turn, its prices in order to attract new members? Or should it seek to identify possible cost savings in order to maintain or even lower prices? Explain.

www.costco.com

www.samsclub.com

Sources

Case 1: Target Corp.
www.targetcorp.com, accessed Mar. 13, 2003; *www.walmartstores.com,* accessed Mar. 13, 2003, *www.hoovers.com,* accessed Mar. 13, 2003; Robert Berner, "Target: The Cool Factor Fizzles," *Business Week,* Feb. 24, 2003, pp. 42, 44; Amy Merrick and Ann Zimmerman, "Target, J.C.Penney, Nordstrom Post Higher 4th-Quarter Profits," *The Wall Street Journal,* Feb. 21, 2003, p. A2. Robert Berner, "Has Target's Food Foray Missed the Mark?" *Business Week,* Nov. 25, 2002, p. 76; Chana Schoenberger, "Bull's-Eye," *Forbes,* Sept. 2, 2002, p. 76; Kemp Powers, "Kitchen-Sink Retailing," *Forbes,* Sept. 2, 2002, p. 78; Mike Duff, "Top North American Retail Companies," *DSN Retailing Today,* July 8, 2002, pp. 18–24; "Target: 40 Years of Retailing," *Home Textiles Today,* May 27, 2002, pp. 16–17; "Target: Product Development Excellence," *Home Textiles Today,* Apr. 12, 2002, p. 85; Laura Heller, "The Super Growth Leaders—Target," *DSN Retailing Today,* Dec. 10, 2001, pp. 20+; "Target Taps Designer Todd Oldham," *Home Textiles Today,* Sept. 10, 2001, p. 1; Ken Clark, "A Smarter Target," *Chain Store Age,* August 2001, p. 92; "On Target" *The Economist,* May 5, 2001, p. 6; Susan Chandler, "Target Corp. Makes Field's Day," *Chicago Tribune,* Jan. 13, 2001, sec. 2, p. 1; Gerry Khermouch, "Target Hits Bullseye," *Brandweek,* June 5, 1995, pp. 22–26.

Case 2: Costco versus Sam's Club
www.walmartstores.com, accessed Mar. 13, 2003; *www.samsclub.com,* accessed Sept. 24, 2002; *www.costco.com,* accessed Sept. 24, 2002; Nanette Byrnes, "The Bargain Hunter," *Business Week,* Sept. 23, 2002, p. 82; "Sam's Upgrades New Club Prototype," *DSN Retailing Today,* Aug. 12, 2002, p. 5; "Warehouse Format Fetes Milestone and Makeover," *Chain Store Age,* August 2002, pp. 70–72; Suzanne Woolley, "Costco? More Like Costgrow," *Money,* August 2002, pp. 44–46; Mike Duff, "Clubs Look to Build on Successful Initiatives," *DSN Retailing Today,* May 20, 2002, p. S5; Doug Desjardins, "Costco Forges Ahead with Clubs No. 3 and 4," *DSN Retailing Today,* May 6, 2002, p. 4; Doug Desjardins, "Clubs Benefit by Adding New Member Perks," *DSN Retailing Today,* April 22, 2002, p. 5; Ken Clark, "Two Strategies, One Popular Segment," *Chain Store Age,* November 2001, pp. 56–58; Ann Zimmerman, "Taking Aim at Costco, Sam's Club Marshals Diamonds and Pearls," *The Wall Street Journal,* Aug. 9, 2001, p. A1; and Emily Nelson and Ann Zimmerman, "Kimberly-Clark Keeps Costco in Diapers, Absorbing Costs Itself," *The Wall Street Journal,* Sept. 7, 2000, p. A1.

**Ducks lose feathers in autumn and are unable to fly for two weeks.
So they know a little something about being out of work.**

ASK ABOUT IT AT WORK.™

Employees who are out of work need money to cover expenses. When you make AFLAC insurance available, you providing just that. AFLAC gives employees access to extra protection from lost wages that can help aid them dur recovery. And AFLAC makes direct payments to whomever policyholders choose regardless of other insurance bene All at little or no direct cost to you. Call 1-800-99-AFLAC or visit www.aflac.com.

*"The high level of name recognition the duck
has wrought is only one element of AFLAC's
continuing promotional campaign to raise
brand awareness and U.S. sales."*

When **AFLAC's** Duck Squawks, Who's Listening?

If you don't know what supplemental insurance is or don't know whether you will ever need it, you are not alone. It is "extra" insurance covering the financial consequences of, say, accidents or major illnesses, sold directly to consumers or to employers that offer it as an employee benefit in the form of a voluntary payroll deduction plan. Whereas medical insurance will cover doctor visits and hospital stays, supplemental insurance provides for the costs of travel, lodging, child care, phone and utility payments, rent or mortgage, and even lost income that an individual or family may incur.

Selling supplemental insurance may not sound like a very exciting business, but for the last 50 years it has created a steady profit for the family-run firm of AFLAC and healthy returns to equity of about 20% for its shareholders. And it's not limited to the U.S. In fact, its supplemental insurance sold in Japan earns AFLAC, headquartered in Columbus, Georgia, about three-quarters of its $9.7 billion in sales every year. AFLAC insures about 25% of the Japanese population, and this Fortune 500 company is the third-largest U.S. firm doing business in Japan.

Before 2000, few people outside Columbus were aware of AFLAC's existence, however, much less its success. Then a white duck with a yellow beak and blue bandana began to appear on U.S. television, vainly squawking "Aaaaaa-flaaack" to roller-coaster riders, figure skaters, hikers, zoo visitors, and other consumers oblivious to its raucous call. As the consumers in the ads discussed their insurance problems, the duck waddled after them, unheard by them but spectacularly memorable to television audiences. If creating brand awareness is a goal, the ads seem to be successful. AFLAC certainly thinks so, spending $35 million a year on broadcast advertising alone.

The high level of name recognition the duck has wrought is only one element of AFLAC's continuing promotional campaign to raise brand awareness and U.S. sales. Besides the duck, an image developed by a company that worked on *Jurassic Park*, AFLAC utilizes several other promotional tools. Broadcast and print advertising are supported by a highly successful website that not only educates consumers about the company but also allows prospective sales associates to apply for employment opportunities that offer attractive earning potential (pay is solely on a commission basis).

Once on board, these independent sales associates can also use the website to present information to prospects and clients. There they find a point-of-sale policy enrollment system with such state-of-the-art features as electronic signature capture and a benefits presentation that corporate clients can deliver to their employees. Training and support from AFLAC ensure that its 40,000 licensed agents deliver a consistent message about the firm's products to the marketplace.

The website also offers other promotional tools the firm has developed in the wake of the duck's fame. For example, visitors can buy merchandise bearing the company logo, including clothing and a plush squawking duck, whose proceeds are donated to cancer care. AFLAC's

www.aflac.com

philanthropic efforts support the pediatric oncology unit at Children's Healthcare of Atlanta.

Other promotional activities include AFLAC's sponsorship of a National Assistant Coach of the Year recognition, which is awarded to 500 male and female assistant coaches at colleges and high schools around the country. Winners must exemplify longevity, knowledge, long-term success, special contributions to the school and community, and a record of overcoming obstacles. Although the duck may seem an unlikely symbol for an insurance company, there's no question that it has brought AFLAC's visibility to new heights and improved the effectiveness of its other promotional tools. Over the last five years, the company's U.S. sales have grown 21% a year.[1]

Besides visibility, what else is AFLAC accomplishing with its promotion program, and what challenges is it likely to face in using that prominence to get its message to its sales organization and prospective customers?

Like all marketers, AFLAC is faced with deciding how much and what types of promotion to undertake. These decisions are complicated by the fact that there are many forms of promotion and no two marketing situations are exactly alike. This chapter will help you understand how the various forms of promotion can be brought together in an integrated marketing communications effort that contributes to a firm's total marketing program. After studying this chapter, you should be able to explain:

Chapter Goals

- The role of promotion.
- The forms promotion can take.
- The concept of integrated marketing communications.
- How the process of communicating relates to effective promotion.
- Key considerations in developing a promotion mix.
- Alternative promotional budgeting methods.
- The major types of promotion regulation.

The Role of Promotion in Marketing

A feature of a free-market system is the right to use communication as a tool of influence as well as information. In the U.S. socioeconomic system, that freedom is reflected in the promotional efforts by businesses to affect the awareness, feelings, beliefs, and behavior of prospective customers. Let's examine how promotion works from an economic perspective and from a marketing perspective.

Promotion and Imperfect Competition

The American marketplace operates under conditions of imperfect competition, characterized by incomplete market information, product differentiation, and emotional buying behavior. As a result, companies use promotion to provide information for the decision maker's buying-decision process, to assist in differentiating their products, and to persuade potential buyers.

In economic terms, the role of promotion is to change the location and shape of the demand (revenue) curve for a company's product. (See Figure 17.1 and recall the discussion of nonprice competition in Chapter 13.) Through promotion a company strives to increase its product's sales volume at any given price (Figure 17.1a); that is, the firm seeks to shift its demand curve to the right. Simply stated, promotion is intended to make a product more attractive to prospective buyers.

FIGURE 17.1

The Goals of Promotion.

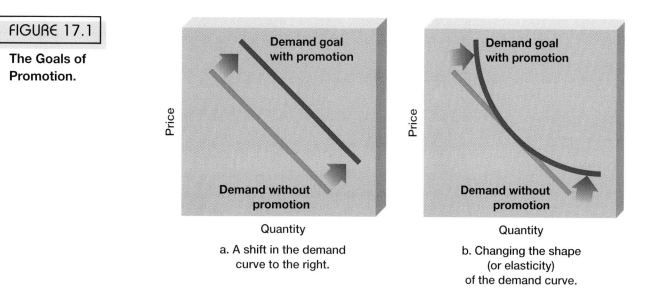

a. A shift in the demand curve to the right.

b. Changing the shape (or elasticity) of the demand curve.

A firm also hopes that promotion will affect the demand elasticity for its product (Figure 17.1b). Recall from Appendix A that elasticity is the responsiveness of demand to a change in price. The intent is to make the demand more inelastic when price increases and more elastic when price decreases. In other words, management wants promotion to increase the attractiveness of a product so the quantity demanded will decline very little if price goes up (inelastic demand), and sales will increase considerably if price goes down (elastic demand).

Promotion and Marketing

From a marketing perspective promotion is intended to further the objectives of an organization. It makes use of various tools to perform three essential promotional roles—informing, persuading, and reminding target audiences. The relative importance of these roles depends on the circumstances faced by the firm. Let's consider each of them separately.

The most useful product will be a failure if no one knows it exists, so the first task of promotion is to *inform*. Beyond simply being aware of a product or brand, customers must understand what benefits it provides, how it works, and how to get it. These are just a few examples of the information promotion provides channel members and consumers. In the electronic appliance industry, for example, Palm uses advertising to educate the market about the operation and features of each new generation of handhelds. In another instance, when a small Canadian firm was faced with consumers who couldn't understand its toy called X-zylo, a gyroscopic cylinder that can be thown 100 yards, the inventor informed retailers and consumers about it with demonstrations at fairs, in company parking lots, and on school playing fields.[2]

Another purpose of promotion is *persuasion*. Intense competition among firms puts tremendous pressure on the promotional programs of sellers. In an economy with an abundant supply of products, consumers have many alternative ways of satisfying even basic physiological needs. As a result, persuasive promotion is essential. Campbell Soup Company has been marketing condensed soup for over 100 years, and accounts for 80% of all soup sales in the U.S. It is one of the most recognized brands and packages in the country. Studies show that virtually every household has some Campbell's soup in the pantry. Yet the firm spends over $100 million a year advertising soup. Why? Partly because it regularly introduces new flavors but, more important, because its primary products are condensed soups that require some minimal preparation. And as one industry analyst quipped, "If you're under 70 years old,

Promotion takes many forms. To reach younger consumers who tend to avoid traditional media, BMW created eight-minute action films accessible via the Internet. Though the films utilize well-known directors and actors, the real "stars" are the BMWs. In less than a year, 11 million consumers had logged on and seen the cars go through their paces.

www.BMWfilms.com

you buy ready-to-serve soup."[3] Thus, Campbell's, faced with intense competition from alternative easier-to-prepare foods, uses promotion to persuade soup buyers.

Consumers also must be *reminded* about a product's availability and its potential to satisfy. Sellers bombard the marketplace with thousands of messages every day in hopes of attracting new consumers and establishing markets for new products. Given the intense competition for consumers' attention, even an established firm must constantly remind people about its brand to retain a place in their minds. It is unlikely that a day goes by, for example, in which you don't see some form of promotion (an in-store display, counter sign, vending machine, billboard, or imprinted T-shirt) for Coca-Cola. In fact, the company spends over $200 million a year in the U.S. just advertising Coca-Cola and Diet Cola soft drinks.[4] Because there is little new to inform consumers about Coke, much of this promotion is intended simply to offset competitors' marketing activity by keeping its brand in front of the consumer.

Recognizing that it is both important and varied, we define **promotion** as all personal and impersonal efforts by a seller or the seller's representative to inform, persuade, or remind a target audience.

Promotion Methods

Promotion, to whomever it is directed, is an attempt to influence. There are four forms of promotion: personal selling, advertising, sales promotion, and public relations. Each has distinct features that determine the role it can play in a promotion program:

In 2001, the Oscar Mayer Wienermobile celebrated its 65th anniversary. The 27-foot long vehicles (there are nine of them) tour the U.S. visiting fairs, carnivals, store openings, and other events promoting the company's products. Wienermobiles are also touring in Hawaii, Puerto Rico, Canada, Spain, and Japan. They are driven by recent college graduates hired to serve as "hot dog ambassadors of goodwill." You can see the inside of a Wienermobile on the Oscar Mayer website.

www.kraftfoods.oscarmayer.com

- **Personal selling** is the direct presentation of a product to a prospective customer by a representative of the organization selling it. Personal selling takes place face-to-face or over the phone, and it may be directed to a business person or a final consumer. We list it first because, across all organizations, more money is spent on personal selling than on any other form of promotion.

- **Advertising** is nonpersonal communication paid for by a clearly identified sponsor promoting ideas, organizations, or products. The most familiar outlets for ads are the broadcast (TV and radio) and print (newspapers and magazines) media. However, there are many other advertising vehicles, from billboards to T-shirts and, more recently, the Internet.

- **Sales promotion** is sponsor-funded, demand-stimulating activity designed to supplement advertising and facilitate personal selling. It frequently consists of a temporary incentive to encourage a sale or purchase. Many sales promotions are directed at consumers. The premiums offered by fast-food outlets in conjunction with popular movies are examples. The majority, however, are designed to encourage the company's sales force or other members of a distribution channel to sell products more aggressively. When sales promotion is directed to the members of the distribution channel, it is called *trade promotion*. Included in sales promotion are a wide spectrum of activities, such as event sponsorships, frequency programs, contests, trade shows, in-store displays, rebates, samples, premiums, discounts, and coupons.

- **Public relations** encompasses a wide variety of communication efforts to contribute to generally favorable attitudes and opinions toward an organization and its products. Unlike most advertising and personal selling, it does not include a specific sales message. The targets may be customers, stockholders, a government agency, or a special-interest group. Public relations can take many forms, including newsletters, annual reports, lobbying, and support of charitable or civic events. The Fuji and Goodyear blimps and the Oscar Mayer Wienermobiles are familiar examples of public relations devices.

Publicity is a special form of public relations that involves news stories about an organization or its products. Like advertising, it consists of an impersonal message that

www.goodyear.com/us/blimp

reaches a mass audience through the media. But several features distinguish publicity from advertising: It is not paid for, the organization that is the subject of the publicity has little or no control over it, and it appears as news and therefore has greater credibility than advertising. Organizations actively seek good publicity and frequently provide the material for it in the form of news releases, press conferences, and photographs. When a picture of a company's CEO appears on the cover of a business publication and is accompanied by a flattering article in the magazine, it is often attributable to the efforts of the firm's public relations department. There also is, of course, bad publicity, which organizations try to avoid or deflect.

Integrated Marketing Communication

Marketers have a variety of promotional tools at their disposal. To make effective use of them, a company's personal selling, advertising, and other promotional activities should form a coordinated promotional program within its total marketing plan. However, these activities are fragmented in many firms, with potentially damaging consequences. For example, advertising directors and sales-force managers may come into conflict over resources, or the sales force may not be adequately informed about the details of a particular sales promotion effort. This wouldn't happen if the elements comprising promotion were part of an **integrated marketing communication (IMC)** effort, a strategic business process used to plan, develop, execute, and evaluate coordinated communication with an organization's public.[5]

IMC begins with a strategic planning effort designed to coordinate promotion with product planning, pricing, and distribution, the other marketing-mix elements. Promotion is influenced, for instance, by how distinctive a product is and whether its planned price is above or below the competition. A manufacturer or middleman must also consider its promotional links with other firms in the distribution channel. For example, Toyota recognizes that its success is closely tied to the performance of its independent dealers. Therefore, in addition to advertising its automobiles directly to consumers, the firm asks recent Toyota purchasers to complete an extensive questionnaire on dealer performance that includes everything from how promptly they were greeted on the first visit to the showroom to how well the new car's features were explained at delivery. A dealership's results on the survey influence its subsequent allocation of the most popular Toyota models.

An Audience Perspective

An IMC approach adopts the position that a customer or prospect is exposed to many bits and pieces of information about a company or brand. Certainly some of these are designed and presented by the marketer, but many, possibly the majority, come from other sources. These sources can include personal experiences, the opinions of friends, and comparisons made by competitors in their advertising. On the basis of all this information, an individual makes an evaluation and forms a judgment. With so little control over the information an audience uses, or how the information is used, a marketer's promotional efforts must be highly coordinated and complementary to have an impact. That means anticipating the opportunities when the target audience will be exposed to information about the company or brand, and effectively communicating the appropriate message in those "windows of opportunity." Usually this involves utilizing several promotional methods, and requires a high degree of coordination.

IMC Elements

The use of an IMC approach to promotion is reflected in how managers think about the information needs of the message recipients. Organizations that have adopted an IMC philosophy tend to share several characteristics, notably:

- An awareness of the target audience's information sources, as well as their media habits and preferences.
- An understanding of what the audience knows and believes that relates to the desired response.
- The use of a mix of promotional tools, each with specific objectives but all linked to a common overall goal.
- A promotional effort in which personal selling, advertising, sales promotion, and public relations are coordinated in order to communicate a consistent message.
- A carefully timed, continuous flow of information adapted to the audience's information needs.

Implementing IMC

By definition, IMC embraces the entire promotional program. In developing integrated communications, a company coordinates its advertising, personal selling, sales promotion, public relations, and direct marketing to accomplish specific objectives. For example, Kraft Foods teamed with Universal Pictures for a major cross-brand promotion to coincide with the studio's rerelease of the movie *E.T.* on its twentieth anniversary. Virtually every American home has some Kraft food product in the cupboard (examples include Maxwell House, Oscar Mayer, Alpha-Bits, Jell-O, and all the Nabisco cookies and crackers). And research indicated that *E.T.* is very popular with mothers and kids. The challenge for Kraft was to make the most of the opportunity with an IMC program that met the schedule of the movie's release. The promotion involved: [6]

- Featuring E.T. on 100 million packages of Kraft and Nabisco products across 29 brands in eight different product categories.
- Designing and implementing E.T.-related in-package premiums that included E.T. figurines, phone cards, temporary tattoos, and fingertip flashlights.
- Conducting a sweepstakes with prizes including 10 trips to Universal Studios and 15,000 E.T. bicycles and PC games.
- Providing point-of-purchase stand-alone displays, end-of-aisle displays, and floor graphics for use by retailers.
- Organizing store-specific E.T. promotional programs and local sweepstakes offers.
- Developing five television ads linking the movie, the sweepstakes, and Kraft products.
- Producing a print ad campaign for placement in various magazines as well as an extensive Internet marketing program on Kraft and Nabisco websites.

To be successful the promotion required the coordinated efforts of dozens of internal and external departments and functions.

An IMC program may incorporate several different promotional campaigns, with some even running concurrently. Depending on objectives and available funds, a firm may undertake simultaneous local, regional, national, and international programs. Moreover, a firm may have one campaign aimed at consumers, and another at wholesalers and retailers.

Evaluating IMC

The last step in an IMC program is evaluation. A program can be evaluated in a number of ways. One approach is to examine how it is implemented. For example, if the promotion by a large manufacturer of consumer goods is being carried out in a manner consistent with the notion of IMC, we would expect to find:

- An advertising program consisting of a series of related, well-timed, carefully placed ads that reinforce personal selling and sales promotion efforts.

- A personal selling effort that is coordinated with the advertising program. The firm's sales force would be fully informed about the advertising portion of the campaign—the theme, media used, and the schedule for the appearance of ads. The sales people would be able to explain and demonstrate the product benefits stressed in the ads, and be prepared to transmit the promotional message and supporting material to middlemen so they can take part in the campaign.

- Sales promotional devices, such as point-of-purchase display materials, that are coordinated with other aspects of the program. Incentives for middlemen would be clearly communicated and understood. Retailers would be briefed about consumer promotions and adequate inventories would be in place.

- Public relations efforts scheduled to coincide with the other mix components and emphasizing the same theme.

More rigorous evaluation examines the results of the program. The outcome of each promotional component is compared with the objectives set for it to determine if the effort was successful. Listed below are some typical promotion objectives and some common measures associated with each of them:[7]

- *Awareness of a company or a brand:* competitive brand position studies, focus groups with distributors at trade shows, and website "hits."

- *Interest in a product or brand:* number of brochures or other company publications distributed, attendance at company-sponsored seminars, and website traffic on specific pages.

- *Action:* usage of sales support tools by distributors and retailers, responses to direct mail, customer inquiries or store visits, and sales.

This is an example from a Samsung IMC campaign designed to create the brand awareness enjoyed by rivals Sony, Panasonic, and Hitachi. The $70 million effort played off the word "DigitAll" to emphasize the range of products the company offers. The campaign included coordinated ads utilizing television, radio, magazines, outdoor, and the Internet, and redesigned product packages, brochures, and point-of-purchase displays to carry a consistent message at the retail level.

www.samsungusa.com

www.army.mil

To be meaningful, most of these measures need to be taken before and after the promotional effort, with the difference between the two measures indicating its effect. For example, the U.S. Army uses a number of promotional tools in its recruiting efforts including mass-media advertising, a website, and sponsorships. Included among the sponsorships are Arena Football and the National Hot Rod Association (NHRA). To assess the value of its NHRA sponsorship, the Army tracks the number of leads generated from visitors to its booths at drag-racing events, and the proportion of those leads that actually become recruits. By comparing the relative productivity of these promotional tools over time, the Army can maximize the productivity of its resources.[8]

Barriers to IMC

Despite its intuitive attractiveness, an IMC approach to promotion is not universally supported. In some organizations the promotional functions are in different departments. For example, the sales force may be in a unit apart from where advertising decisions are made. As a result, there is a lack of internal communication and coordination. In other companies there is a belief that promotion is such an imprecise activity that efforts to carefully design objectives and coordinate efforts would be unproductive. In still other firms there is a history of relying on a particular form of promotion and a resistance to consider alternatives.

Fully utilizing an IMC approach would likely require a firm to make several changes. One involves restructuring internal communication to ensure that all relevant parties involved in promotion are working together. Some firms have approached this by creating a marketing communications (or marcom) manager who oversees the planning and coordination of promotional efforts. A second change entails conducting research to gather the necessary information about the target audience. Firms utilize extensive customer databases for this purpose, but they are costly to create and expensive to maintain. Finally, and most important, top management must support the effort to integrate promotion. Strong leadership is essential in order to gain commitment from the entire organization.

Next we'll examine how communication, the core of promotion, actually works. Then we'll move to the key managerial issues in a promotion program.

The Communication Process and Promotion

Communication is the verbal or nonverbal transmission of information between someone wanting to express an idea and someone else expected or expecting to get that idea. Because promotion is a form of communication, much can be learned about structuring effective promotion by examining the communication process.

Fundamentally, communication requires only four elements: a message, a source of the message, a communication channel, and a receiver. In practice, however, important additional components come into play. Figure 17.2 illustrates these components of a communication process, and relates them to promotion activities.

Consider this hypothetical example of what happens when a teenager sees an ad for the U.S. Army.

- The information that the sender wants to share must first be encoded into a transmittable form. In marketing this means transforming an idea ("The Army involves individual commitment and unwavering teamwork") into words ("An Army of One"), or pictures (a group of soldiers working together to accomplish a difficult mission), or a combination of the two.

- Once the message has been *transmitted* through some communication channel, the symbols must be *decoded*, or given meaning, by the receiver. The received

FIGURE 17.2

The Communication Process in Promotion.

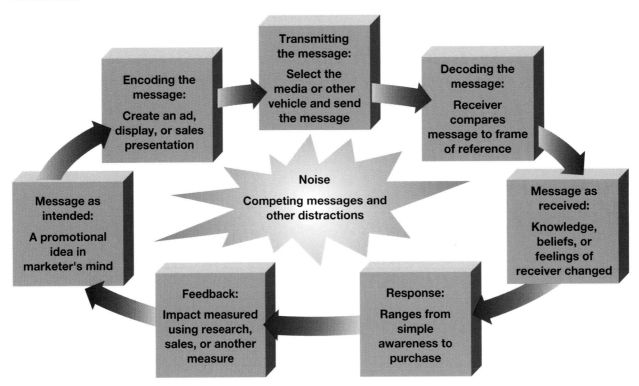

MARKETING IN THE INFORMATION ECONOMY

Are you ready for advergames that become viral objects?

What do Jeep, Martha Stewart, Microsoft, and Boise Cascade Office Products Division have in common? If you guessed they are all trying to communicate with hard-to-reach target markets, you would be right. Traditional media advertising has not been particularly effective in reaching young adults (for Jeep and Martha Stewart) or middle-level, white-collar workers (for Microsoft and Boise Cascade). So these firms, and others with a similar problem, are trying advergames—games specifically designed as part of a firm's online advertising program. An Internet research firm claims advertisers spent over $8 billion on interactive gaming in 2002. For example, visitors to the Jeep site can take a Wrangler Rubicon SUV on a virtual off-road test drive and submit their performance scores in a sweepstakes.

Boise Cascade has office employees complete a personality questionnaire online and then responds with a description of that personality type and some suggestions for effective behavior. Makers of these interactive "games" claim they give sellers lengthy, uninterrupted, voluntary interaction with prospects. And what about the "viral" aspect? Most games are designed so the players will involve their friends so the seller also benefits from word-of-mouth communication.

Sources: Keith Ferrazzi, "Advertising Shouldn't Be Hard Work," *The Wall Street Journal*, Apr. 30, 2002, p. B4; Tobi Elkin, "Digital Gamesscapes Lure Major Marketers," *AdAge.com*, May 28, 2002; Jean Halliday, " 'Ultimate' Off-Roader Pushed with Online Game," *AdAge.com*, May 13, 2002.

---

message may be what the sender intended ("In the Army I can be part of an important team") or something else that is possibly less desirable ("The Army is overpromising in order to get recruits"), depending on the recipient's frame of reference.

- If the message has been transmitted successfully, there is some change in the receiver's knowledge, beliefs, or feelings. As a result of this change, the receiver formulates a *response*. The response could be nonverbal (making a mental note to ask a high school counselor about the opportunities that exist in the military), verbal (asking friends if they have ever considered joining), or behavioral (visiting a recruiting office).

- The response serves as *feedback*, telling the sender whether the message was received and how it was perceived by the recipient. Through feedback the sender can learn what a communication accomplished. Then a new message can be formulated and the process begun again.

- All stages of the process can be affected by *noise*—that is, any external factor that interferes with successful communication. (Anything competing for the attention of the prospect, but particularly messages about career opportunities, are noise for the U.S. Army.)

What does the communication process tell us about promotion? First, the act of encoding reminds us that messages can take many forms. Messages can be physical (a sample, a premium) or symbolic (verbal, visual), and there are a myriad of options within each of these categories. For example, the form of a verbal message can be factual, humorous, or even threatening.

Second, the number of channels or methods of transmitting a message are limited only by the imagination and creativity of the sender. Consider that promotional messages are transmitted by the voice of a sales person, the airwaves of radio, the mail, the side of a bus, a website on the Internet, and the lead-in to a feature in a movie theater. Each channel has its own characteristics in terms of audience reach, flexibility, permanence, credibility, and cost. In selecting a channel, a marketer must have clearly defined objectives and a familiarity with the features of the many alternatives. For example, how would you promote organic foods and beverages? Acrica, a small firm competing with food-marketing giants, faces two problems. First, it has

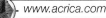 www.acrica.com

To reach the users of its products, mainly administrative assistants in businesses, Boise Cascade Office Products developed an award winning interactive promotion. By filling out a short self-administered personality-typing questionnaire (mailed with the company's catalog or found on its website), these potential customers had some fun, learned a little about themselves and their co-workers and, in the process, a little about Boise's products.

to get noticed by consumers. Because competitors have millions more to spend on communications it is easy for the firm's messages to be overlooked. Second, Acrica has to educate consumers about the benefits of its products because most have little more than a general awareness of what organic means. To gain attention and provide information, the firm has created "organic gardens" on 20-foot flatbed trucks that visit schools, corporate campuses, fairs, and various retail sites to explain the concept and hand out samples. In a year the trucks have made it possible for the firm to put samples in the hands of a million consumers.[9]

Third, how the message is decoded or interpreted depends on its form (encoding and transmission) and the capability and interest of the recipient. In designing and sending messages, marketers must be sensitive to the audience. What is their vocabulary and level of verbal sophistication? What other messages have they received? What experiences have they had? What will get and hold their attention?

Finally, every promotion should have a measurable objective. The response and feedback provided by the recipients can be used to determine if the objective is accomplished. Feedback may be collected in many forms—changes in sales, recall of advertising messages, more favorable attitudes, increased awareness of a product or an organization—depending on the objective of the promotion. For some promotional activities the objective may be modest—for example, an increase in the audience's awareness of a brand. For others, such as a direct-mail solicitation, the objective would be a particular level of sales. Without objectives, there is no way of evaluating the effectiveness of a message.

Determining the Promotional Mix

A **promotion mix** is an organization's combination of personal selling, advertising, sales promotion, and public relations. An effective promotional mix is a critical part of virtually all marketing strategies. Product differentiation, positioning, trading up and trading down, and branding all require effective promotion. Designing an effective promotional mix involves a number of strategic decisions about five factors: (1) target audience, (2) objective of the promotion effort, (3) nature of the product, (4) stage in the product's life cycle, and (5) amount of money available for promotion.

Target Audience

As is true for most areas of marketing, decisions on the promotional mix will be greatly influenced by the target audience. The target may be final consumers, who could be further defined as existing customers or new prospects. Some marketers (notably toy and fast-food firms) direct much of their efforts at decision makers rather than the actual purchasers. In some cases the target consists of middlemen in order to gain their support in distributing a product, or in the case of a company about to make a stock offering, the investment community.

Final consumers and middlemen sometimes buy the same product, but they require different promotion. To illustrate, 3M Company sells its blank CDs to final consumers through computer and office-supply stores. Promotion to dealers includes sharing the cost of yellow pages ads and advertising in specialized business magazines such as *Office Products Dealer*. Different ads aimed at final consumers are run in magazines such as *Personal Computing, Fortune*, and *Business Week*.

A promotion program aimed primarily at middlemen is called a **push strategy,** and a promotion program directed primarily at end users is called a **pull strategy.** Figure 17.3 contrasts these two strategies.

Using a push strategy means a channel member directs its promotion primarily at the middlemen that are the next link forward in the distribution channel. The product is "pushed" through the channel. Take the case of a hardware producer that sells its tools and replacement parts to household consumers through wholesalers and retailers such as Ace and True Value. The producer will promote heavily to wholesalers, which then also use a push strategy to retailers. In turn, the retailers promote to consumers. A push strategy usually involves a lot of personal selling and sales promotion, including contests for sales people and displays at trade shows. This promotional strategy is appropriate for many manufacturers of business products, as well as for consumer goods that are undifferentiated or do not have a strong brand identity.

With a pull strategy, promotion is directed at end users—usually ultimate consumers. The intention is to motivate them to ask retailers for the product. The retailers, in turn, will request the product from wholesalers, and wholesalers will order it from the producer. In effect, promotion to consumers is designed to "pull" the product through the channel. This strategy relies on heavy advertising and sales promotion such as premiums, samples, or in-store demonstrations.

FIGURE 17.3

Push and Pull Promotional Strategies.

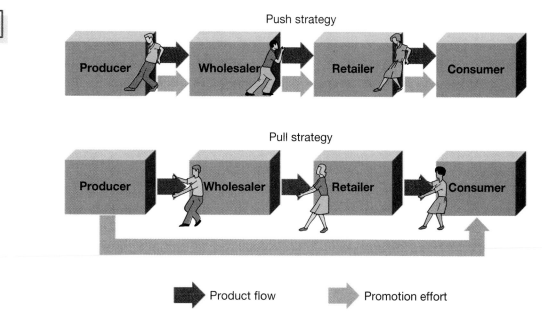

Promotion campaigns should have defined targets and objectives. This award-winning ad for Volkswagen is targeted at a young audience as part of a campaign to strengthen the brand's image. It shows a VW owner so "into" his car that when everyone else at a rock concert is flicking their lighters in the dark, he holds up the lighter from his vehicle.

Retailers have little incentive to provide shelf space for minor variations of existing brands unless they are confident the products will sell. So manufacturers of consumer packaged goods often use a pull strategy to get new products stocked on supermarket shelves. For example, when Dr. Pepper introduced Red Fusion, the first new flavor addition in the company's 117-year history, it employed television, radio, outdoor, and Internet advertising in addition to point-of-sale materials and in-store sampling. In the crowded soft drink category, this type of pull strategy gives retailers needed reassurance that the brand has a reasonable chance of success.

Promotion Objective

A target audience can be in any one of six stages of buying readiness. These stages—awareness, knowledge, liking, preference, conviction, and purchase—are called the **hierarchy of effects** because they represent stages a buyer goes through in moving toward a purchase, with each also describing a possible goal or effect of promotion. The objective of promotion is to get the prospect to the final, or purchase stage, but in most cases that is not possible until the person has moved through the earlier stages. Thus, a promotion effort may have what appears to be a modest but essential objective, such as creating knowledge about a product's advantages.

www.nutrisoy.com

Awareness At the *awareness* stage the seller's task is to let the buyers know that the product or brand exists. Here the objective is to build familiarity with the product and the brand name. The government has recently endorsed the health claim that soy protein helps reduce the risk of heart disease. However, few consumers know what food products contain soy. To increase awareness, Archer Daniel Midland Company, the world's leading processor of soy, has formed an alliance with food makers to label products that contain its soy protein. The logo, similar to the one used to indicate the presence of NutraSweet in a product, is employed to make consumers aware of the presence of soy as an ingredient.

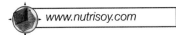

www.netjets.com

Knowledge *Knowledge* goes beyond awareness to learning about a product's features. The concept of fractional aircraft ownership is unfamiliar to many potential buyers, so NetJets, one of the firms in the industry, has developed a *Buyer's Guide*

booklet to explain it. Because the booklet is more extensive than an advertisement, a prospect can gain a considerable amount of knowledge and have many basic questions answered.

Liking   *Liking* refers to how the market feels about the product. Promotion can be used to move a knowledgeable audience from being indifferent to liking a brand. A common technique is to associate the item with an attractive symbol or person. The sporting goods company, adidas, has partnering relationships with the athletic programs of seven universities including Arizona State, Northwestern, University of Tennessee, and the University of Notre Dame, as well as the New York Yankees major league baseball team. By providing uniforms and equipment to the players and coaches that include its company's logo, adidas hopes to create a favorable impression on the fans of these teams.

Preference   Creating *preference* involves distinguishing among brands such that the market finds your brand more attractive than alternatives. It is not uncommon to like several brands of the same product, but the customer can't make a decision until one brand is preferred over the alternatives. Ads that make a comparison with the competition are intended to create a preference. In the auto-rental business, Avis has made a not-so-subtle comparison for over 40 years with the ad slogan "We Try Harder." In a recent attempt to demonstrate what trying harder involves, Avis has extended the campaign with several "-er" themes (safe-er, fast-er, new-er, etc.), each describing a specific feature that Avis contends differentiates it from the competition.

Conviction   *Conviction* entails the actual decision or commitment to purchase. A student may prefer the IBM PC over a clone, but not yet be convinced to buy a computer. The promotion objective here is to increase the strength of the buyer's need. Trying a product and experiencing the benefits that come from using it are very effective in strengthening the conviction to own it. Radio Shack encourages consumers to visit its stores and try its computers, and auto dealers invite consumers to test-drive new cars.

Purchase   *Purchase* can be delayed or postponed indefinitely, even for customers who are convinced they should buy a product. The inhibitor might be a situational factor such as not having enough money at the moment, or a natural resistance to change. Action may be triggered through a temporary price reduction or the offer of additional incentives. For example, according to a survey conducted in 2001, 76% of shoppers reported using a reduced-price coupon to make a purchase during the year.[10]

Promotional efforts are also aimed at obtaining repeat purchases or building loyalty among customers who have purchased a product. A credit card company's database that indicates a cardholder has not made a purchase using the credit card for an unusual length of time might trigger a direct-mail piece or a personal phone call.

Nature of the Product

Several product attributes influence the promotion mix. We will consider three that are especially significant: unit value, customization, and service requirements.

Unit Value   A product with low unit value is usually relatively uncomplicated, involves little risk for the buyer, and must appeal to a mass market to survive. As a result, advertising would be the primary promotional tool. In contrast, high-unit value products often are complex and expensive. These features suggest the need for personal selling. BMW dealers are being encouraged to have sales people get out of the showroom and call on prospects. By increasing the personal selling effort through techniques such as delivering cars to potential customers for test-drives, BMW hopes to stimulate declining U.S. sales.

Degree of Customization   The benefits of most standardized products can be effectively communicated with advertising. However, if a product must be adapted to the individual customer's needs, personal selling is typically necessary. Thus you would expect to find an emphasis on personal selling in the promotion mix for something like home remodeling or an expensive suit of clothing. As customization finds its way into more product categories, personal selling grows in importance. For example, Levi Strauss pioneered individual, custom-fit jeans with its "Original Spin" concept. At a Levi company store, individual body measurements are taken using an imaging process, the data are transmitted to the Levi factory, and a custom-fit pair of jeans is delivered. In this customizing situation, the communication and interaction role of the retail clerk increases substantially.

Although the principle of relying on advertising for standard products and personal selling for customized items holds in most instances, it is being challenged by firms searching for efficient ways to implement mass customization. For example several firms are offering customization via the Internet. Customatix produces customized shoes and Lands' End allows a consumer to design a pair of chinos using interactive systems on their websites.[11]

www.cmax.com

www.landsend.com

Presale and Postsale Service   Products that must be demonstrated, for which there are trade-ins, or that require frequent servicing to stay in good working order lend themselves to personal selling. Typical examples are riding lawn mowers and powerboats.

Stage in the Product Life Cycle

Promotion strategies are influenced by a product's life-cycle stage. When a new product is introduced, prospective buyers must be informed about its existence and its benefits, and middlemen must be convinced to carry it. Thus both advertising (to consumers) and personal selling (to middlemen) are critical in a product's introductory stage. At introduction a new product also may be something of a novelty, offering excellent opportunities for publicity. Later, if a product becomes successful, competition intensifies and more emphasis is placed on persuasive advertising. Table 17.1 shows how promotional strategies change as a product moves through its life cycle.

Funds Available

Regardless of the most desirable promotional mix, the amount of money available for promotion is often the ultimate determinant of the mix. A business with ample funds can make more effective use of advertising than a firm with limited financial resources. For example, television advertising can carry a particular promotional message to far more people and at a lower cost per person than most other media. Yet a firm may have to rely on less expensive options, such as yellow pages advertising or a website.

One low-budget approach is only limited by the imagination of the marketer. Called **viral marketing** it involves creating a situation in which consumers spread information about a company or brand to other people. Viral marketing differs from word-of-mouth advertising only in that the company intentionally stimulates the communication flow. An example of viral marketing is the electronic greetings Blue Mountain Arts allows its website visitors to send to anyone with an Internet connection.

www.bluemountain.com

TABLE 17.1

Promotional Strategies for Different Product Life-Cycle Stages

Market Situation	Promotional Strategy
Introduction Stage	
Customers are not aware of the product's features, nor do they understand how it will benefit them.	Inform and educate potential customers that the product exists, how it might be used, and what want-satisfying benefits it provides. In this stage, a seller must stimulate primary demand—the demand for a type of product—as contrasted with selective demand—the demand for a particular brand. For example, producers had to sell consumers on the value of compact discs in general before they considered it feasible to promote a particular brand. Normally, heavy emphasis must be placed on personal selling. Exhibits at trade shows are also used extensively in the promotional mix. A trade show gives a new product broad exposure to many middlemen. Manufacturers also rely heavily on personal selling to attract middlemen to handle a new product.
Growth Stage	
Customers are aware of the product's benefits. The product is selling well, and middlemen want to handle it.	Stimulate selective (brand) demand as competition grows. Increase emphasis on advertising. Middlemen share more of the total promotional effort.
Maturity Stage	
Competition intensifies and sales level off.	Advertising is used more to persuade rather than only to provide information. Intense competition forces sellers to devote larger sums to advertising and thus contributes to the declining profits experienced in this stage.
Decline Stage	
Sales and profits are declining. New and better products are coming into the market.	All promotional efforts are cut back substantially. The focus moves to reminding remaining customers.

The Promotion Budget

Establishing promotion budgets is extremely challenging because management lacks reliable standards to determine how much to spend altogether on advertising, personal selling, and the remainder of the promotion mix, or how much of the total budget to allocate to each mix component. A firm may have the alternative of adding three sales people or increasing its trade show budget by $200,000 a year, but it cannot determine precisely what increase in sales or profits to expect from either expenditure.

Promotional activities generally are budgeted as current operating expenses, implying that their benefits are used up immediately. However, it's been suggested that advertising (and presumably other promotional efforts) should be thought of as a capital investment, even if it must be treated as an expense for accounting purposes. The reason is that the benefits and returns on promotional expenditures are like investments, often not immediately evident, instead accruing over several years. For example, several advertising slogans including "The ultimate driving machine"

(BMW), "Finger lickin' good" (KFC), and "Because I'm worth it" (L'Oreal) were recently inducted into the Advertising Slogan Hall of Fame because of their enduring impact. Regularly repeating messages such as these builds awareness and familiarity, sometimes for years, before actual sales are produced. Taking a longer-term, investment perspective on promotion would likely lead to greater consistency in the amounts spent, and the manner in which the budget is allocated across the types of promotion.

Rather than one generally accepted approach to promotion budgeting, there are four common **promotional budgeting methods:** percentage of sales, all available funds, following the competition, and budgeting by task or objective. These methods are frequently discussed in connection with the advertising budget, but they may be applied to any promotional activity as well as being used to determine the total promotional budget.

Percentage of Sales

The promotional budget may be related in some way to company income, as a percentage of either past or anticipated sales. A common approach for determining the sales base is to compute an average between the previous year's actual sales and expected sales for the coming year. Some businesses prefer to budget a fixed amount of money per unit of past or expected future sales. Manufacturers of products with a high unit value and a low rate of turnover (automobiles or appliances, for example) frequently use the unit method.

Because the percentage-of-sales method is simple to calculate, it is probably the most widely used budgeting method. Moreover, it sets the cost of promotion in relation to sales income, making it a variable rather than a fixed expense.

There are two important limitations to basing promotional expenditures on past sales. First, management is effectively making promotion a result of sales when, in fact, it is a cause of sales. Second, using the percentage-of-past-sales method reduces promotional expenditures when sales are declining—just when promotion usually is most needed.

All Available Funds

A new company or a firm introducing a new product frequently plows all available funds into its promotional program. The objective is to build sales and market share as rapidly as possible during those early, critical years. After a time, management generally finds it necessary to invest in other things, such as new equipment, expanded production capacity, or warehouses and distribution centers (as Internet marketing firms are now doing), so the method of setting the promotional budget is changed.

Following Competition

A weak method of determining the promotional budget, but one that is used occasionally, is to match the promotional expenditures of competitors or to spend in proportion to market share. Sometimes only one competitor is followed. In other cases, if management has access to industry average expenditures on promotion through a trade association, these become company benchmarks.

There are at least two problems with this approach. First, a firm's competitors may be just as much in the dark regarding how to set a promotional budget. Second, a company's promotional goals may be quite different from its competitors' because of differences in strategic marketing planning.

Task or Objective

The best approach for establishing the promotional budget is to determine the tasks or objectives the promotional program must accomplish and then decide what they will

Drug makers are well known for giving gifts to physicians as a method of sales promotion. In 2001, the drug industry spent $19 billion on advertising and promotion, more than double what was spent in 1996. About 50% of the total consists of free drug samples given to doctors. The rest includes traditional advertising, the cost of sales reps, and gifts. Concerns about the increasing cost of drugs has led several states to pass or consider passing laws requiring disclosure of gifts or payments over a small amount (typically $25 to $50).

The American Medical Association (AMA) and the Pharmaceutical Research and Manufacturers Association (PhRMA) have ethical policies about giving and receiving gifts. Both associations believe their policies are adequate if they are more strictly followed.

Some pharmaceutical reps have never known an environment in which gift giving was not the norm. By the same token, some physicians virtually demand gifts in exchange for prescribing a firm's drugs.

Are there any conditions under which gift giving by a drug company to a physician is an ethical sales promotion technique?

Sources: Scott Hensley, "AMA, Prescription-Drug Makers Agree Ethics Policy Needs Better Implementation," *The Wall Street Journal*, Jan. 21, 2002, p. B4; Melody Petersen, "Vermont Requires Drug Makers to Disclose Payments to Doctors," *The New York Times*, June 13, 2002, pp. C1+; Jon Chesto, "Laws Aim at Gifts by Drug Makers," *The Boston Herald*, June 12, 2002, p. 31; John Sanko, "Health Calls for Doctors to Disclose Gifts, Trips," *Rocky Mountain News*, July 13, 2002, p. 3C.

cost. The task method forces management to realistically define the goals of its promotional program and view them outside the confines of a defined budgetary period.

This is often called the buildup method because of the way the budget is constructed. For example, a company may elect to enter a new geographic market. Management determines this venture will require five additional sales people. Compensation and expenses of these people will cost a total of $350,000 per year. Salary for an additional sales supervisor and expenses for an extra office and administrative needs will cost $80,000. Thus in the personal selling part of the promotional mix, an extra $430,000 must be budgeted. Similar estimates can be made for the anticipated costs of advertising, sales promotion, and other promotional tools. The promotional budget is built up by summing the costs of the individual promotional tasks needed to reach the goal of entering the new territory.

Regulation of Promotion

Because a primary objective of promotion is to sell something through persuasion, the potential for abuse always exists. As a result, some firms must be discouraged or prevented from intentional or unintentional misrepresentation. In addition, some consumers, because they lack particular knowledge or skills, need protection from being misled. Thus, there is a need for regulation to discourage the occurrence of abuses and to correct those that do occur.

Regulations have been established by the federal government and most state and local governments in response to public demand. In addition, professional associations and individual businesses have established promotion guidelines.

Federal Regulation

Federal regulation of promotional activities applies to firms engaged in interstate commerce. It is authorized by three major pieces of legislation: the Federal Trade Commission Act and the Robinson-Patman Act, both administered by the Federal Trade Commission (FTC), and the Lanham Trademark Act.

The measure that has the broadest influence on promotional messages is the **Federal Trade Commission Act.** The act prohibits unfair methods of competition. And, according to FTC and federal-court decisions, one area of unfair competition is false, misleading, or deceptive advertising.

www.ftc.gov

Under the original Federal Trade Commission Act, false or misleading advertising had to injure a competitor before a violation could be charged. This loophole led to the enactment of the **Wheeler-Lea Amendment** to the FTC Act in 1938. This amendment considerably strengthened the original act by specifying that an unfair competitive act violates the law if it injures the public, regardless of the effect it may have on a competitor. Thus, consumer protection also became a concern of the FTC.

The FTC has plenty of clout—particularly in the case of ads or other promotion activities deemed false or deceptive. For example, the commission may require a company to substantiate its advertising claims by submitting test results or other supporting evidence. If the commission concludes that an ad is, in fact, deceptive it can have it removed from circulation with a consent decree or a cease and desist order. In extreme cases, if the commission concludes that a firm's deceptive ads have created an incorrect impression on the public, it can order the firm to run corrective advertising to offset the misinformation.

Some other areas of consumer protection that have drawn the attention of the FTC include lending and credit granting practices, privacy and identity theft, telemarketing, and franchising. The Internet, as an emerging tool of communication and selling, is attracting special attention. Recently, for example, the FTC notified the operators of online search engines that they must disclose if sites they list have paid to be suggested to consumers.

The **Robinson-Patman Act,** which is best known for outlawing price discrimination, has two sections relating to promotional allowances offered to wholesalers and retailers. These sections state that a seller must offer promotional services or payments for them, on a proportionally equal basis to all competing wholesalers or retailers. Thus, if a manufacturer wants to furnish in-store demonstrators, advertising support, or any other type of promotional assistance, it must make it available proportionally to all firms competing in the resale of the product. "Proportionally equal" has sometimes been hard to define. Generally the courts have accepted the amount of the product purchased as a basis for allocation. Say, for example, that Martin's, a regional supermarket chain, buys $150,000 worth of merchandise per year from a grocery wholesaler, and Hank's, a neighborhood grocery store, purchases $15,000 worth from the same wholesale firm. The wholesaler may legally offer Martin's promotional allowances valued at 10 times those offered to Hank's.

The 1946 **Lanham Trademark Act** made false claims about one's own products illegal. It was broadened in 1988 by the **Trademark Law Revision Act** to encompass comparisons made in promotional activity. This law regulates claims about where a product is manufactured, for example, use of the phrase "Made in the U.S.A.," and it also protects firms from false comparisons made by competitors.

www.fcc.gov

Several other federal agencies are involved in the regulation of promotion. The Federal Communications Commission (FCC) licenses radio and television stations. Its mandate, to ensure that public interest is considered, combined with its authority to remove or deny the renewal of licenses, gives the FCC considerable power over the content of advertising. In addition, the FCC oversees the telephone industry and enforces the **Telephone Consumer Protection Act** of 1991. Among other things, this law requires telemarketers to keep a "do-not-call" list of consumers who request that they not receive telephone solicitations, and it restricts the indiscriminant use of automatic telephone dialing systems.

www.fda.gov

The Food and Drug Administration (FDA) is responsible for regulating the ingredients, labeling, packaging, branding, and advertising of packaged food, cosmetic, and drug products. It is the FDA that is responsible for warning labels that appear on food and drug packages and in advertising. Recently the agency forbade the sale of water containing nicotine without federal approval, ruling that it qualifies as a drug. The FDA also is the agency that established the legal definitions for

In promotion, will the EU stitch together a regulatory blanket or a crazy quilt?

A fundamental principle of the European Union is the free movement of goods and services across borders. However, the member countries face some challenges in determining how that applies to marketing communications. What follows are some recent issues and complicating exceptions:

- The volume of spam, unsolicited commercial e-mail, in the EU increased from 500,000 to 4.5 million messages in one year, prompting officials to introduce restrictions. Companies in member countries cannot send promotional e-mail to consumers unless they agree to receive it. However, the ban can only apply to e-mail originating in EU countries. Thus, spam from the U.S. or other countries is not restricted.

- EU regulators agreed that in disputes between consumers and businesses, the laws of the country where the injury took place apply. In cross-border disputes, that means the laws of the consumer's nation would take precedence. However, for online marketing the laws where the supplier or website is located apply.

- An EU directive called "TV Without Frontiers" is designed to permit broadcasters to beam adver-

tising messages into any country when the message conforms to the laws of the country of origin. However, because of existing laws in several member countries (for example, Sweden bans ads to children, Germany prohibits "two for the price of one" offers, France does not permit advertising of alcoholic beverages, and Belgium requires that auto ads include warnings against dangerous driving), the rules may be changed to force ads to meet the standards of the destination country.

The development of regulations is of special concern to firms designing integrated marketing communication efforts that utilize a variety of promotional tools to reach multinational audiences.

For more on this issue, see the website *www.europa.eu.int* and search "advertising regulation."

Sources: Paul Meller, "International Business: Europe Proposes Dual Plan on Disputes in Commerce," *The New York Times*, May 4, 2002, p. C2; "Spam Is Officially Canned," Global News Wire, Financial Times Information, May 30, 2002; Malcolm Earnshaw, "Brands and Consumer Protection," *Media Week*, Global News Wire, April 19, 2002; Brandon Mitchener, "EU Panel Suggests Banning E-Mail That's Unsolicited," *The Wall Street Journal*, May 31, 2002, p. B2.

terms such as "natural," "light," and "low fat" when they are used in advertising or promotion.

The U.S. Postal Service regulates advertising done through the mail. Of particular concern is the use of the mail to commit fraud or distribute obscene material. The Postal Service also oversees sales promotions such as premiums, contests, coupons, and samples that are sent through the mail.

State and Local Regulation

Legislation at the state level is intended to regulate promotional activities in intrastate commerce. Most of these state statutes are patterned after a model developed by *Printers' Ink* magazine in 1911 to establish truth in advertising. Today 44 states have what are known as **Printers' Ink statutes** to punish "untrue, deceptive, or misleading" advertising. Several states have established separate state agencies to handle consumer protection, and some states' attorneys general have taken a very proactive stance in regulating promotional activity of tobacco and alcoholic beverages as well as telemarketing.

A general type of local legislation that affects personal selling is the so-called **Green River ordinance** (so-named because Green River, Wyoming, was one of the first towns to enact such a law). Green River ordinances restrict sales people who represent firms located outside the affected city and who sell door-to-door or call on business establishments. To operate in a community with a Green River ordinance, a sales person is typically required to register locally and purchase a license. Supposedly passed to protect local citizens from fraudulent operators, the measures also serve to insulate local businesses from outside competition.

Regulation by Private Organizations

Numerous private organizations exert considerable control over the promotional practices of business. For example, the Council of Better Business Bureaus and several advertising trade associations joined forces to create a self-regulation process. Two agencies have come out of this collaboration: the Council's National Advertising Division (NAD) and its Children's Advertising Review Unit (CARU). Both investigate complaints of false and misleading advertising brought by competitors, consumers, and local Better Business Bureaus. If NAD or CARU find an ad unsatisfactory, they negotiate with the advertiser to discontinue or modify the ad. Despite the fact that neither NAD nor CARU can force compliance or sanction an advertiser in any way, they have been very successful in getting objectionable ads changed or dropped.

www.caru.org
www.nadreview.org

The media also serve a regulatory role. Virtually all publications and broadcasters have established standards for acceptable advertising. For example, in ads directed at children, the three major networks have specified that the words "just" and "only" cannot be used in reference to price. Standards in the print media tend to vary by the size and type of publication. Some are quite strict. For example, *Good Housekeeping* and *Parent* magazines test products to substantiate the claims before ads are accepted. Finally, some professional associations have established codes of ethics that include standards for communications. For example, the American Marketing Association specifies that the promotional efforts of its members avoid using false or misleading advertising, high-pressure or misleading sales tactics, and sales promotions that use deception or manipulation.

www.marketingpower.com

Summary

Promotion is the fourth component of a company's total marketing mix. In economic terms, the role of promotion is to change a firm's demand curve—either shifting it to the right or changing its shape to make demand inelastic when prices increase and elastic when prices decrease. In marketing terms it means informing, persuading, and reminding existing or prospective customers. The primary methods of promotion are personal selling, advertising, sales promotion, and public relations.

Integrated marketing communication (IMC) describes a coordinated promotional effort that includes planning, developing, executing, and evaluating communication with an organization's publics. An IMC approach to promotion adopts a customer perspective, selects from the alternative promotional tools to produce a defined response, coordinates all promotional efforts, and evaluates the effectiveness of promotion activity.

Promotion is communication. Fundamentally, the communication process consists of a source sending a message through a channel to a receiver. The success of communication depends on how well the message is encoded, how easily and clearly it can be decoded, and whether any noise interferes with its transmission. Feedback, the response created by a message, is a measure of how effective a communication has been.

When deciding on the promotional mix (the combination of advertising, personal selling, and other promotional tools), management should consider (1) the target audience, (2) the objective of the promotion effort, (3) the nature of the product, (4) the stage of the product's life cycle, and (5) the funds available for promotion.

There are several methods involved in setting a total promotional budget. The most common method is to set the budget as a percentage of past or anticipated sales. Other methods include using all available funds and following the competition. The best approach is to set the budget by establishing the promotional objectives and then estimating how much it will cost to achieve them.

In response to the desire to protect consumers and curb abuses, there are a number of federal laws and agencies regulating promotion. Promotional practices also are regulated by state and local legislation, by private organizations, and by industry.

More About **AFLAC**

Competitors have, of course, noticed the effectiveness of AFLAC's promotional efforts (even though the purported duck is really a goose!). In Japan, not only has a troubled economy challenged business at all levels, but government deregulation of the financial services sector has also begun catching up with the insurance industry. Local industry giants like Nippon Life and Tokio Marine & Fire began to compete with AFLAC for the first time. Fear that the marketing by these domestic Japanese firms will be aggressive—and that their current customers will prefer to buy supplemental insurance from them rather than split their coverage among different firms—brought AFLAC's stock price down temporarily. AFLAC rebounded, however, and is counting on its competitors' high operating costs and overhead to help it maintain its price advantage in Japan. AFLAC has also acquired a new sales force of 50,000 door-to-door reps in Japan, thanks to an agreement it signed before deregulation with Japan's number two life insurance provider, Dai-ichi Mutual. The Dai-ichi reps market both their firm's and AFLAC'S products.

Then there is the competition at home. AFLAC's chief rival in supplemental coverage, Colonial Life & Accident Insurance Co., is rolling out its own national media campaign starting with 30-second commercials, followed by print, radio, and billboard ads. Although it has only one-third the market share of AFLAC, Colonial's $1 million campaign may succeed in making its name better known. "We need to be out there more so that consumers better understand the value" of supplemental insurance benefits, says Colonial's CEO.[12]

1. Now that AFLAC is facing more competition both at home and abroad, what can it do to make its promotion program more effective and efficient?

2. How influential do you think Colonial's campaign will be, given AFLAC's head start? What could Colonial do to gain more exposure within the limits of its budget?

Key Terms and Concepts

Promotion (486)	Promotion mix (494)	Wheeler-Lea Amendment (502)
Personal selling (487)	Push strategy (495)	Robinson-Patman Act (502
Advertising (487)	Pull strategy (495)	Lanham Trademark Act (502)
Sales promotion (487)	Hierarchy of effects (496)	Trademark Law Revision Act (502)
Public relations (487)	Viral marketing (498)	Telephone Consumer Protection Act (502)
Integrated marketing communication (IMC) (488)	Promotional budgeting methods (500)	Printers' Ink statutes (503)
Communication (492)	Federal Trade Commission Act (501)	Green River ordinance (503)

Questions and Problems

1. Integrated marketing communications is just another way to say, "Keep everyone informed about what is going on." Comment.

2. Relate each of the components of the communication process model to the following situations:
   a. A college student trying to convince her father to buy her a used car.
   b. A sales person describing the same car to the college student.

3. How might the message on a company's website differ from the message it would use in a magazine advertisement?

4. The promotional budget for many products would be divided between a push strategy and a pull strategy. For the product below, give an example of who might be in the push strategy audience and who might be in the pull strategy audience:
   a. Contact lenses
   b. Golf balls
   c. Home insulation
   d. Personal computers
   e. Frozen pizza

5. Would it be appropriate for a firm to use advertising to create awareness of its brand at the same time that it

uses sales promotion to stimulate purchase? Explain using an Internet portal such as America Online as an example.

6. Explain how the nature of the following products would likely affect its promotional mix.

   a. Automobile tires
   b. Use of a tanning salon
   c. Light bulbs
   d. Ten-minute automobile oil changes
   e. College education
   f. Individual Retirement Account (IRA)

7. How does the life-cycle stage of the automobile industry explain the promotional efforts carried out on behalf of most brands?

8. Assume you are marketing a liquid that removes creosote (and the danger of fire) from chimneys in home fireplaces. Briefly describe the roles you would assign to advertising, personal selling, sales promotion, and direct marketing in your promotional campaign.

9. Do you think additional legislation is needed to regulate advertising? To regulate personal selling? If so, explain what you would recommend.

Interactive Marketing Exercises

1. An ad should have a particular objective that should be apparent to a careful observer. For each of the following promotional objectives, find an example of a print ad:

   a. Primarily designed to inform.
   b. Primarily designed to persuade.
   c. Primarily designed to remind.

2. An integrated promotional program is a coordinated series of promotional efforts built around a single theme and designed to reach a predetermined goal. It often includes several of the promotional methods described in the chapter. For an important event at your school (such as a homecoming, the recruitment of new students, or a fund-raising effort), describe the promotional tools used and evaluate their appropriateness based on the criteria in the chapter for designing a promotional mix.

Chapter

18

Personal Selling and Sales Management

"The ASG division of Johnson Controls depends on its sales force to carry its message to customers."

Has **Johnson Controls** Found a New Road to Sales?

Johnson Controls is a diversified company with annual sales over $18 billion. It produces batteries, security systems, heating and air-conditioning regulators, and plastic bottles, among other products. The company's largest and most successful division, the Automotive Systems Group (ASG), is a supplier to automobile and truck manufacturers.

ASG has enjoyed a 20% annual growth rate since 1995. Its success is partly due to the way the division approaches marketing and sales. It begins with a recognition that success demands more than just meeting requirements. As one Johnson executive put it, "The most significant strength we have is the ability to translate [customer] knowledge into innovative products and technologies that add value to automakers by increasing brand differentiation and customer satisfaction." The ASG division of Johnson Controls depends on its sales force to carry its message to customers, a job it has done so well that it has been ranked among *Sales & Marketing Management*'s 25 best sales forces.

ASG's strength has several sources:

- Rather than rely on the carmakers for direction on auto interiors, ASG goes directly to the final customers and does its own extensive customer research. Drivers and passengers are interviewed, videotaped, probed in focus groups, and asked to photograph the interior features they like and dislike in their cars. As a result, the company develops new products that are supported by detailed data for its sales people to present to the auto manufacturers. "Our sales people . . . can go to customers with product plans that cus-

tomers didn't even ask for because we've done the research and know what customers want," says the division's president of marketing and business development worldwide.

- ASG has redefined the role of its sales people. With few potential customers (because there are only a handful of automakers) and very large purchases, ASG sales people must have the confidence and trust of the manufacturers. They need to combine their knowledge of the customer with information about the market's needs and solid new-product ideas. In other words, ASG needs to have its marketing team and sales people working closely together. To encourage this collaboration, ASG combines sales and marketing under one executive.

- ASG has broken down a major barrier between sales people and other employees by eliminating sales commissions that disproportionately reward sales people. Now sales people are paid year-end performance bonuses, and engineers, marketing managers, and product designers receive bonuses based on the division's performance. Because everyone benefits from the division's common success, support of the sales effort is undertaken with enthusiasm.

- Because of its market focus, ASG recognizes that sales people need to develop relationships with customers. However, management is also aware of the value of team interaction at every level. For example, it's

www.johnsoncontrols.com

not uncommon for representatives from sales, engineering, product design, and marketing to visit a customer, or for a similar group to host a customer team when they visit ASG to see a product test or discuss a new concept. The division's director of advanced development, who often accompanies sales people on sales calls, says of his role, "I'm there to help customers visualize what a new product will look like and how it will function."

- Personal selling at ASG is about much more than generating transactions. It also includes saving the customer money. With a new Internet-based product data management program, ASG sales reps all over the world can conduct an online search when a customer makes a new-product request to determine whether the company has already developed a similar product. If it has, Johnson Controls can save its customers millions of dollars by customizing the existing design to the automaker's preference.

ASG's broader, integrated approach to the sales function is characteristic of a growing number of firms. On the basis of the success of ASG and others that have adopted a similar perspective, this may be the model that puts organizations in the fast lane. [1]

What would a business need to do in order to establish a sales culture like the one at Johnson Controls' ASG division ?

The importance of personal selling and the need for its integration with marketing can seldom be understated. The cooperation fostered at Johnson Controls and the success it has produced certainly support this position. ASG's innovations in sales-force management have established a new standard in its industry and left the competition scrambling to catch up.

Chapter Goals
After studying this chapter, you should be able to explain:

- The role of personal selling in a promotion program.
- When a firm is likely to utilize personal selling.
- The forms of personal selling and the variety of personal selling jobs.
- Important developments in how personal selling is performed.
- The personal selling process.
- The strategic role of sales-force management.
- The challenges in staffing, operating, and evaluating a sales force.

Nature of Personal Selling

Personal selling is involved when a student buys a Honda motorcycle or an Ann Taylor store sells a dress to a businesswoman. But you should recognize that some personal selling also occurs when (1) Citicorp recruits a graduating senior who majored in marketing or, conversely, a student tries to convince Citicorp to hire her; (2) a minister talks to a group of students to encourage them to attend church services; (3) a lawyer tries to convince a jury that her client is innocent; or even (4) a boy persuades his mother to buy him something from Toys "Я" Us. The point is that a form of personal selling occurs in nearly every human interaction.

The goal of all marketing effort is to increase profitable sales by providing want-satisfaction to consumers over the long run. Therefore, in a business context **personal selling** is the personal communication of information to persuade somebody to buy something. It is by far the major promotional method used to reach this goal. To illustrate, the number of people employed in advertising is below 500 *thousand*. In personal selling, the number is close to 16 *million*.[2] In many companies, personal selling is the largest single operating expense, often equaling 8% to 15% of sales. In contrast, advertising costs average 1% to 3% of sales.

Personal Selling as a Form of Promotion

Personal selling is the direct, *personal* communication of information, in contrast to the indirect, *impersonal* communication of advertising, sales promotion, and other promotional tools. This means that personal selling can be more flexible than these other tools. Sales people can tailor their presentations to fit the needs and behavior of individual customers. They can see their customers' reactions to a particular sales approach and make adjustments on the spot.

Also, personal selling can be focused on individuals or firms that are known to be prospective customers if an organization has done an adequate job of segmenting and targeting its market. As a result, wasted effort is minimized. In contrast, advertising messages are often wasted on people who are not realistic prospects.

Another advantage of personal selling is that its goal is to actually make a sale. Advertising usually has a less ambitious goal. It is often designed to attract attention, provide information, and arouse desire, but seldom does it stimulate buying action or complete the transfer of title from seller to buyer.

On the other hand, a full-fledged personal selling effort is costly. Even though personal selling can minimize wasted effort, the cost of developing and operating a sales force is high. Another disadvantage is that a company may find it difficult to attract the quality of people needed to do the job. At the retail level, many firms have abandoned their sales forces and shifted to self-service for this very reason.

In Chapter 17 we discussed five factors that influence an organization's promotional mix—the target market, the objective, the product, the product's life-cycle stage, and the money available for promotion. Referring to those five factors and its nature, personal selling is likely to carry the bulk of the promotional load when:

- The market is concentrated geographically, in a few industries, or in several large customers.
- The value of the product is not readily apparent to the prospect.
- The product has a high unit cost, is quite technical in nature, or requires a demonstration.
- The product must be fitted to an individual customer's need, as in the case of securities or insurance.
- The product is in the introductory stage of its life cycle.
- The organization does not have enough money to sustain an adequate advertising campaign.

Types of Personal Selling

In business situations, there are two types of personal selling, as shown in Figure 18.1. One is where the customers come to the sales people. Called **inside selling**, it primarily involves retail sales. In this group, we include the sales people in stores and the sales people at catalog retailers such as Lands' End or L. L. Bean, who take telephone orders. Also included are the telephone order takers at manufacturers and wholesalers, most of whom take existing customers' routine orders over the telephone. By far, most sales people in the U.S. fall into this first category, but some are being replaced by purchasing done over the Internet.

In the other kind of personal selling, known as **outside selling**, sales people go to the customer. They make contact by telephone or in person. Most outside sales forces usually represent producers or wholesaling middlemen, selling to business

FIGURE 18.1

**Scope of Personal
Selling.**

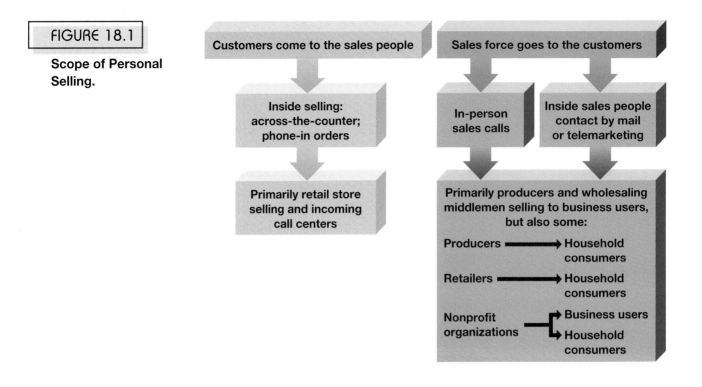

users and not to household consumers. However, in our definition of an outside sales force, we also include (1) producers whose representatives sell directly to household consumers—for example, insurance companies such as State Farm or Northwestern Mutual and in-home sellers such as Kirby Vacuum cleaner distributors; (2) representatives of retail organizations who go to consumers' homes to demonstrate a product, give advice, or provide an estimate, such as sales people for some furniture stores and home heating and air-conditioning retailers; and (3) representatives of nonprofit organizations—for example, charity fund raisers, religious missionaries, and workers for political candidates.

Wide Variety of Sales Jobs   The types of sales jobs and the activities involved in them cover a wide range. Consider the job of a Coca-Cola driver–sales person who calls routinely on a group of retail stores. That job is in another world from the IBM rep who sells a computer system for managing reservations to Delta Airlines. Similarly, a sales rep for Avon Products selling door to door in Japan or China has a job only remotely related to that of a Cessna airplane rep who sells executive-type aircraft to Dow Chemical and other large firms in the U.S.

A typical sales job includes three activities: order taking, customer support, and order getting. The relative emphasis on these functions is what distinguishes one sales job from another. The range of sales jobs is represented by the following six categories:[3]

• *Delivery–sales person.* In this job the sales person primarily delivers the product—for example, soft drinks or fuel oil—and services the account. The order-getting responsibilities are secondary, although most of these sales people are authorized to and rewarded for finding opportunities to increase sales to existing accounts.

• *Inside order taker.* This is a position in which the sales person takes orders and assists customers at the seller's place of business—for example, a retail clerk on the sales floor at a JCPenney store or a telephone representative at a catalog retailer such as Eddie Bauer or L. L. Bean. Many customers have already decided

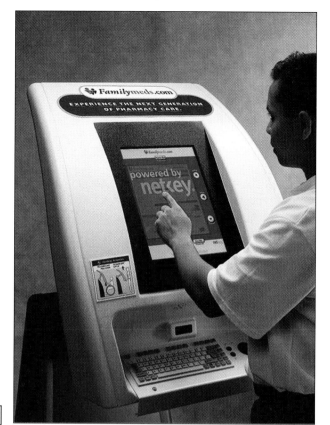

Stand-alone Internet kiosks in retail stores that permit shoppers to use a modified version of the retailer's website are increasing in popularity. A retailer can provide shoppers with many services through a kiosk including purchase suggestions, product inventory information, item searches, and even credit-card scanning. Viewed as a way of reducing retailers' costs, the question remains whether kiosks can adequately replace retail sales clerks.

www.netkey.com

to buy. The sales person's job is to answer customers' questions, serve them efficiently, and engage in suggestion selling.

- *Outside order taker.* In this position the sales person goes to the customer in the field and requests an order. An example is a John Deere sales person calling on a farm equipment dealer, or a sales rep for a radio station selling advertising time to local businesses. The majority of these sales are repeat orders to established customers, and much of the sales person's time is devoted to support activities such as assisting the distributors with promotion and training their sales people. Typically outside order takers also are assigned goals that require them to seek new customers and introduce new products to existing customers.

- *Missionary sales person.* This type of sales person is expected to provide information and other services for existing or potential customers, perform promotional activities, and build goodwill. A missionary sales person does not solicit orders. An example of this job is a detail sales person for a pharmaceutical firm such as Merck or Eli Lilly.

- *Sales engineer.* In this position the major emphasis is on the person's ability to explain the product to a prospective customer, and also to adapt the product to the customer's particular needs. The products involved here typically are complex, technically sophisticated items. As technical experts, sales engineers frequently assist regular sales reps with a particular problem or opportunity on an "as-needed" basis.

- *Consultative sales person.* This involves the creative selling of goods and services. This category contains the most complex, difficult selling jobs—especially the creative selling of services, because you can't see, touch, taste, or smell them. Customers often are not aware of their need for a seller's product. Or they may not realize how that product can satisfy their wants better than the product they are now using. Consultative selling requires that a relationship of trust be established with the customer. It often involves designing a system to fit the needs of a particular customer to get an order.

A classification with several categories of jobs helps dispel the notion that all sales jobs are alike. However, it is worth noting that some richness is lost in the creation of any classification. In fact, there is considerable diversity in sales because firms design jobs to fit their particular situations. A study in the 1980s identified over 120 specific and reasonably exclusive tasks performed by at least some sales people.[4] A more recent study identified nearly 50 more tasks, many associated with the use of technology in selling.[5] So even though it is possible to classify sales jobs in a general way, it's important to note that specific sales jobs are tailored to the needs of the market and the sales organization.

The Professional Sales Person

As suggested by the opening case, the business-to-business sales job of today is quite different from the stereotype of the past. The images of high pressure, false friendship, and glibness are largely outdated, as is the notion of a price-cutting order chaser. Even the stereotype of the sales *man* is much less evident as more and more women enter selling.

The sales rep that has emerged is the professional sales person. Today these reps are fully responsible for a designated market, which may be a geographic area or a category of customers. They frequently engage in a total selling job identifying prospects, servicing their customers, building goodwill, selling their products, and training their customers' sales people. Professional reps act as a mirror of the market by relaying market information back to the firm. They organize much of their own time and effort. They often take part in recruiting new sales people, sales planning in their territories, and other managerial activities.

Greater sales professionalism also is more commonplace among retailers who view personal selling as a major component of their promotion strategy. Sales people are carefully selected to ensure they have the proper aptitude and are thoroughly trained to instill the necessary skills. They fully understand the products they are selling and are well versed in providing customer service. The Tattered Cover, a Denver bookstore, is successful in a highly competitive industry because of the quality of the service it delivers. The founder, Joyce Meskis, attributes the service to the store's professional staff.[6]

www.tatteredcover.com

The Cost of Personal Selling

The cost of a sales call depends on the sales approach used. For firms selling commodities and emphasizing price, the cost is about $85. On the other hand, when the sales approach is to identify and design solutions for customers' problems, the cost of a call is $190.[7] Add to this the fact that it typically takes from three to six calls to make a sale to a new customer, and it becomes apparent that personal selling is expensive.

The Uniqueness of Sales Jobs

Several features differentiate sales jobs from other jobs in an organization:

- The sales force is largely responsible *for implementing a firm's marketing strategies*. Moreover, it's the sales reps who *generate the revenues* that are managed by the financial people and used by the production people.

- Sales people are typically the most *visible representatives of their company* to customers and to society in general. Many sales jobs require the rep to socialize with customers who frequently are upper-level executives in their companies. Opinions of the firm and its products are formed on the basis of impressions made by sales people in their work and in outside activities. The public ordinarily does not judge a company by its factory or office workers, and customers can't judge products until after they are purchased and used.

- Sales reps operate with *limited direct supervision.* For success in selling, a sales rep must work hard physically and mentally, be creative and persistent, and show considerable initiative. This combination requires a high degree of self-motivation.

- By the nature of the job, sales people *have more rejections than acceptances;* that is, more prospects choose not to buy than to buy. A sales person who internalizes the rejection will quickly become discouraged.

- Sales jobs frequently involve considerable *traveling and time away from home.* To reduce sales travel time, some firms redesign sales territories, route sales trips better, and rely more on telemarketing and electronic ordering. Nevertheless, being in the field, sales people deal with a seemingly endless variety of people and situations. These stresses, coupled with long hours and traveling, require mental toughness and physical stamina. Personal selling is hard work!

Changing Patterns in Personal Selling

Traditionally, personal selling was a face-to-face, one-on-one situation between a sales person and a prospective buyer. This situation existed both in retail sales involving ultimate consumers and also in business-to-business transactions. In recent years, however, some very different selling patterns have emerged. These new patterns reflect a growing purchasing expertise among consumers and business buyers, which, in turn, has fostered more sophistication in personal selling. Several of these patterns are described as follows.

Selling Centers

To match the expertise of the buying center (described in Chapter 5) in business markets, an increasing number of firms on the selling side have adopted the organizational concept of a **selling center.** A selling center is a group of people representing a sales department as well as other functional areas in a firm such as finance, production, and research and development brought together to meet the needs of a particular customer. This is sometimes called a *sales team* or *team selling.*

Team selling is expensive, and is therefore usually restricted to accounts that have a potential for high sales volume and profit. Procter & Gamble, for example, has selling teams assigned to large retailers such as Wal-Mart. The opening case described how Johnson Controls uses sales teams. When AT&T sells to a large multinational firm such as Nestlé, AT&T will send a separate selling team to deal with each of Nestlé's major divisions.

Most sales teams are ad hoc groups, assembled to deal with a particular opportunity. Except for the sales person, the team members have other responsibilities in the firm. This creates several managerial issues. For example, who directs a team—the most senior person involved, the sales person who organizes the team, or the most experienced member? What happens if the buying center decides it prefers to work with a senior manager on the team or the technical expert who "speaks their language" rather than the sales person? Also, how should team members be evaluated and compensated? Despite these challenges, the increasing complexity of sales has made team selling increasingly popular.

Systems Selling

The concept of **systems selling** means selling a total package of related goods and services—a system—to solve a customer's problem. The idea is that the system will satisfy the buyer's needs more effectively than selling individual products separately. Xerox, for example, originally sold individual products, using a separate sales force for each major product line. Today, using a systems-selling approach, Xerox studies a customer's office information and operating problems. Then Xerox provides a total automated system of machines and accompanying services to solve that customer's office problems.

System selling has several benefits. The most obvious is that it produces a larger initial sale because a system rather than a product is purchased. Second, it reduces compatibility problems because all parts of the system come from the same supplier. Third, it often means that the supplier is also retained to service the system because of its familiarity with it. Finally, if the system performs effectively, the system provider is in an excellent position to propose upgrades as they are needed.

Systems selling is not right for every situation. For example, the components that make up some systems, such as Internet routing equipment, are so complex that they require the expertise of several firms.

Global Sales Teams

As companies expand their operations to far-flung corners of the globe, they expect their suppliers to do the same. Having products readily available, understanding local conditions, and providing quick service are essential to maintaining global customers. To service their largest and most profitable global customers, sellers are forming **global sales teams**. Such a unit is responsible for all of a company's sales to an account anywhere in the world. For example, IBM, with annual sales of $85 billion, supplies information technology products and services using global sales teams that are organized by industry.

By focusing on a specific industry such as aerospace, automotive, or pertoleum, team members develop specialized expertise. A senior sales executive usually serves as team manager, and is located at or very close to the customer's headquarters. As a result, the teams are prepared to deal with issues and opportunities on short notice wherever they may occur.

Relationship Selling

Developing a mutually beneficial relationship with selected customers over time is **relationship selling**. It may be an extension of team selling, or it may be developed by individual sales reps in their dealings with customers. In relationship selling, a seller discontinues the usual practice of concentrating on maximizing the number and size of individual transactions. Instead, the seller attempts to develop a deeper, longer-lasting relationship built on trust with key customers—usually larger accounts.

Unfortunately, often there is little trust found in buyer–seller relationships, either in retailer–consumer selling or in business-to-business selling. In fact, in some circles selling is viewed as adversarial, with one side winning and the other side losing. For example, a buyer may try to squeeze the last penny out of the seller in price negotiations, even with the knowledge that the agreed-on price may make it difficult for the seller to perform adequately.

How do sellers build trust? First and foremost, there must be a customer orientation. The seller must place the customers' needs and interests on a par with its own. From that will follow a shared vision of success, an expanded time horizon that looks beyond the immediate sale, and a perspective that the parties to a transaction are partners not adversaries.

A selling center in a sales organization complements the buying center in a buying organization. Designed as an *ad hoc* group of functional specialists brought together to meet the needs of a particular customer, a selling center can improve the service provided to the customer, and help overcome some of the barriers and misunderstanding that often exist between functions in the selling firm.

Many large companies—Procter & Gamble, Hyatt Hotels, and Kraft Foods to name just a few—have realigned their sales forces to engage in relationship selling.

Telemarketing

Telemarketing is the innovative use of telecommunications equipment and systems as part of the "going to the customer" category of personal selling. Under certain conditions, telemarketing is attractive to both buyers and sellers. Buyers placing routine reorders or new orders for standardized products by telephone use less of their time than with in-person sales calls.

Many sellers find that telemarketing increases selling efficiency. With the high costs of keeping sales people on the road, telemarketing reduces the time they spend on routine order taking. Redirecting routine reorders to telemarketing allows the field sales force to devote more time to creative selling, major account selling, and other more profitable selling activities.

Here are examples of selling activities that lend themselves nicely to a telemarketing program:

- Seeking leads to new accounts and identifying potentially good customers that sales reps can follow up with in-person calls.

- Processing orders for standardized products. Cryovac, a firm that produces packaging material for food processors and supermarkets among other things, operates an inbound call center that allows customers to place routine orders without having to contact a sales rep.

- Dealing with small-order customers, especially where the seller would lose money if field sales calls were used. Red Wing Shoe Company, a manufacturer of work boots and outdoor footwear, sells its products through many retailers all over the country. The company cannot afford to have sales reps visit small retailers more than once or twice a year in, for example, Idaho mining towns or

For many consumers telemarketing has a negative image. They see it as intrusive and annoying. Unfortunately, its reputation has also been damaged by some unscrupulous practitioners. However, in many B-2-B situations it is a highly professional, cost effective way to meet the routine and standard needs of buyers.

farming communities in Arkansas. Between visits these small stores are encouraged via telemarketing to replenish their inventories.

- Improving relations with middlemen. Manufacturers use telemarketing to answer dealers' questions about inventory management, service, and replacement parts. This gives the dealers an immediate source for assistance, saving them the time and effort of trying to track down a sales person.

Internet Selling

www.baxter.com

Most sales efforts over the Internet would not be considered personal, and therefore would not be part of a discussion about *personal* selling. For example, Baxter International (a seller of hospital supplies) makes it very easy for customers to place orders through its website, creating many impersonal transactions. In fact, the impersonal nature of the process is one of its strengths, because it speeds up purchasing and reduces the frequency of errors. However, one category of **Internet selling,** the business-to-business auction, qualifies as personal selling because of its interactive nature.[8]

www.PurchasePro.com

Using the traditional auction format, a seller (working through an intermediary such as PurchasePro.com that provides the linking technology) notifies potential bidders of a product available for sale. Typically the item for sale is a discontinued model of a product or excess inventory of some raw material. According to a predetermined schedule, bids are submitted electronically in round-robin fashion in real time. Both the seller and all the bidders see each bid and have the opportunity to respond.

www.freemarkets.com

Another version is called a reverse auction. (Recall the FreeMarkets, Inc. description at the beginning of Chapter 5.) The prospective buyer notifies potential sellers of its willingness to purchase a specified product and an electronic auction is held to select a seller. In both auction formats, there is an interchange of information between buyers and sellers, negotiation of terms, and intense price competition.

www.propurchase.com

Internet auctions began selling commodities or standardized goods. For example, a state bought salt for use on icy roads, and a computer memory chip maker sold microprocessors. However, as the technology improves Internet auctions are becoming more broadly applied. ProPurchase.com has facilitated auctions for firms in 245 industries including automotive, construction, education, energy, hospitality, printing, and real estate.

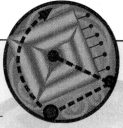
Sales-Force Automation

In recent years organizations have equipped their sales people with an increasing array of electronic tools. Pagers, laptop computers, fax machines, and cellular phones allow sales people access to the Internet, e-mail, and various company databases. They also allow sales people to electronically communicate with their managers, marketers, and others in their organization by providing such things as market intelligence, call reports, credit applications, and customer questions.

Today organizations are moving beyond using these tools only for communication to integrating them with software that allows a sales person to create customized reports for customers, develop proposals with prices, discounts, delivery dates, and other information critical to making a sale, estimate costs for particular orders, and develop forecasts for customers and territories. This capability of using electronic tools to combine company and client information in real time to enhance the sales function is known as **sales force automation (SFA).**

SFA has the potential to create better-informed sales people who can more effectively respond to the needs of customers. According to a sales executive at Owens Corning, with SFA "They (sales people) become the real managers of their own business and their own territories."[9]

Automating a sales force is an expensive proposition that is likely to require frequent upgrades as new, more sophisticated tools become available. The experience of firms indicates that implementing SFA involves several challenges:

- Identifying which parts of the sales process can benefit the most from automation.
- Designing a user-friendly system.
- Gaining the cooperation of the sales force so they incorporate the technology in their jobs.[10]

Experience with automation has been mixed as firms sort out what works and what doesn't. Typical problems include unrealistic expectations by management because of the large investments required, attempting to implement too much at once instead of phasing in a program, and resistance by sales people. However, on the basis of a recent survey in which 83% of the responding companies indicated plans to upgrade their systems, it is safe to say the sales role of the future will include a significant electronic component.[11]

The Personal Selling Process

The **personal selling process**, depicted in Figure 18.2, is a logical sequence of four steps that a sales person takes in dealing with a prospective buyer. This process is designed to produce some desired customer action, and ends with a follow-up to ensure customer satisfaction. The desired action usually is a purchase by the customer.

Prospecting

The first step in the personal selling process is really two related steps. Prospecting consists of identifying possible customers and then qualifying them—that is, determining whether they have the necessary potential to buy. They are combined as a single step because they are typically done at the same time.

Identifying Prospective Customers
The identification process is an application of market segmentation. By analyzing the firm's database of past and current customers, a sales rep can determine characteristics of an ideal prospect. Comparing this profile to a list of potential customers will produce a set of prospects.

A list of potential customers can be constructed using suggestions from current customers, trade associations and industry directories, the customer lists of related but noncompeting businesses, and mail-in or telephone responses to ads.

A little thought often will suggest logical prospects. Homestead House (a furniture store chain) and AT&T find prospects in lists of building permits issued. Insur-

FIGURE 18.2

The Personal Selling Process.

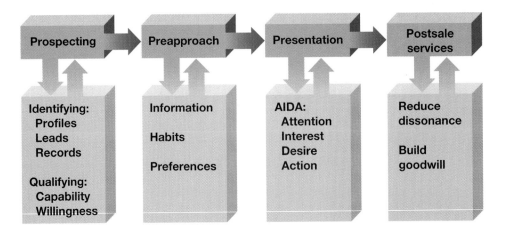

ance companies (Northwestern Mutual or Prudential), real estate firms (Re/Max, Century 21), and even local diaper services use marriage and birth announcements in newspapers as sources.

Qualifying Prospects   After identifying prospective customers, a seller should qualify them—that is, determine whether they have the necessary willingness, purchasing power, and authority to buy. To determine willingness to buy, a seller can seek information about any changes in the prospect's situation. For example, a business firm or a household consumer may have had a recent problem with an insurance provider. In this case there may be an opportunity for a sales person from a competing insurer to get that prospect's business.

To determine a prospect's financial ability to pay, a seller can refer to credit-rating services such as Dun & Bradstreet. For household consumers or small businesses in an area, a seller can get credit information from a local credit bureau. Identifying who has the authority to buy in a business or a household can be difficult, as we saw back in Chapters 4 and 5. In a business, the buying authority may rest with a committee or an executive in a distant location. Besides determining the buying authority, a seller also should identify the one or more persons who influence the buying decision. A purchasing agent may have buying authority, but what he or she buys may depend on the recommendation of an office secretary, a factory engineer, or a vice president.

www.dnb.com

Preapproach to Individual Prospects

Before calling on prospects, sales people should conduct a preapproach—learning all they can about the persons or companies to whom they hope to sell. This might include finding out what products the prospects have used in the past, what they are now using, and their reactions to these products. In business-to-business selling, a sales person or selling team should find out how buying decisions are made in the customer's organization. A sales rep can target the right people if he or she knows who is the gatekeeper, who influences and/or makes the buying decision, and who actually makes the purchase.

Finding out something about the prospect's personal life—interests, activities, and habits—as well as gathering some insights into the preferred business practices of the prospect can be useful. Sales people should try to get all the information they can, so they will be able to tailor their presentations to individual buyers.

Presenting the Sales Message

With the appropriate preapproach information, a sales person can design a sales presentation that will attract the prospect's attention. The sales person will then try to hold the prospect's interest while building a desire for the product and, when the time is right, attempt to stimulate action by closing the sale. This approach, called **AIDA** (an acronym formed by the first letters of Attention, Interest, Desire, and Action), is used by many organizations.

Attract Attention—the Approach   The first task in a sales presentation is to attract the prospect's attention and to generate curiosity. In cases where the prospect is aware of a need and is seeking a solution, simply stating the seller's company and product may be enough. However, more creativity often is required.

For instance, if the sales person was referred to the prospect by a customer, the right approach might be to start out by mentioning this common acquaintance. Or a sales person might suggest the product benefits by making some startling statement. One sales training consultant suggests greeting a prospect with the question, "If I can cut your selling costs in half, and at the same time double your sales volume, are you interested?"

Hold Interest and Arouse Desire
After attracting the prospect's attention, the challenge for the sales rep is to hold it and stimulate a desire for the product with a sales presentation. There is no universal format here, but when it is practical, a product demonstration is invaluable. Whatever format is followed in the presentation, the sales person must always show how the product will benefit the prospect.

Some companies train their sales people to use a canned sales talk—a memorized presentation designed to cover all points determined by management to be important. Companies engaging in telemarketing typically use scripted sales talks. They may be appropriate if the sales person is inexperienced or knows very little about the customer, but a presentation with more flexibility can be personalized and tailored to individual customers' needs.

Meet Objections and Close the Sale
After explaining the product and its benefits, a sales person should try to close the sale—that is, obtain action on the customer's part. Periodically in a presentation, the sales person may venture a trial close to test the prospect's willingness to buy. One method is posing an "either-or" question that presumes the prospect has decided to buy. For example, "Would you prefer that the installation be done immediately or would it be better to have it done next week?"

The trial close tends to uncover the buyer's objections. The toughest objections to answer are those that are unspoken. Thus, a sales person should encourage buyers to state their objections. Then the sales person has an opportunity to meet the objections and bring out additional product benefits or reemphasize previously stated points.

Postsale Services

An effective selling job does not end when the order is written up. The final stage of a selling process is a series of postsale activities that can build customer goodwill and lay the groundwork for future business. An alert sales person will follow up sales to ensure that no problems occur in delivery, financing, installation, employee training, and other areas that are important to customer satisfaction.

Postsale service reduces the customer's postpurchase cognitive dissonance—the anxiety that usually occurs after a person makes a buying decision (discussed in Chapter 4). In this final stage of the selling process, a sales person can minimize the customer's dissonance by (1) summarizing the product's benefits after the purchase, (2) repeating why the product is better than alternatives not chosen, (3) describing how satisfied other buyers have been with the product, and (4) emphasizing how satisfied the customer will be with the product.

Strategic Sales-Force Management

Managing the personal selling function is a matter of applying the three-stage management process (planning, implementation, and evaluation) to a sales force and its activities. Sales executives begin by setting sales goals and planning sales-force activities. This involves forecasting sales, preparing sales budgets, establishing sales territories, and setting sales quotas. Then a sales force must be organized, staffed, and operated to implement the strategic plans and reach the goals that were set. The final stage involves evaluating the performance of individual sales people as well as appraising the total sales performance.

Effective sales-force management starts with a qualified sales manager. Finding the right person for this job is not easy. In many organizations the common practice when a sales management position becomes available is to reward the most productive sales person with a promotion. The assumption is that, as a manager, an effective sales person will be able to impart the necessary wisdom to make others equally successful.

However, the qualities that lead to effective sales management are often the opposite of the attributes of a successful sales person. Probably the biggest difference in the positions is that sales people tend to be self-motivated and self-reliant. They often work independently, receiving all the credit or blame for their successes or failures. In contrast, sales managers must work through and depend on others, and must be prepared to give recognition rather than receive it.

It is an unusual person who can be a successful sales manager without previous selling experience. To be effective, a sales manager must understand customers, appreciate the role of the sales person, and have the respect of the sales force. These attributes can only be acquired by spending time in sales. The resolution may come in not using the sales management position as a reward for outstanding sales performance. Rather, the criteria for sales management should be respectable sales performance coupled with the necessary attributes of management.

Staffing and Operating a Sales Force

Because most sales executives spend the bulk of their time in staffing and operating their sales forces, we will discuss these activities in some detail. Figure 18.3 shows what's involved.

Recruitment and Selection

Selecting personnel is the most important management activity in any organization. This is true whether the organization is an athletic team, a college faculty, or a sales force. No matter what the caliber of sales management, if a sales force is distinctly inferior to that of a competitor's, the rival firm will win.

Sales-force selection involves three tasks:

1. Determining the type of people needed by preparing a written job description.
2. Recruiting an adequate number of applicants.
3. Selecting the most qualified persons from among the applicants.

Determining Hiring Specifications   There have been many attempts to identify a general set of personality attributes that explain selling success.[12] However, these lists tend to be of little practical value because they consist of common sense characteristics such as assertiveness and empathy, don't account for motivation, and fail to recognize the differences in sales jobs.

Some companies analyze the personal histories of their existing sales representatives in an effort to determine the traits common to successful (and unsuccessful) performers. Even when a firm thinks it knows what the important attributes are, measuring the degree to which each quality should be present or the extent an abundance of one can offset the lack of another is difficult.

A better approach is to identify the specifications for the particular job, just as if the company were purchasing equipment or supplies rather than labor. This calls for a detailed job analysis and a written job description. The description then becomes the basis for identifying the aptitude and skills a person needs to perform

FIGURE 18.3

Staffing and Operating a Sales Force.

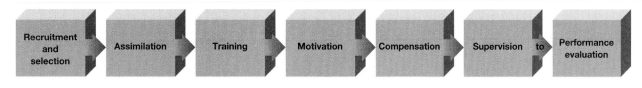

Recruitment and selection → Assimilation → Training → Motivation → Compensation → Supervision → Performance evaluation

the job. Later, this written description will be invaluable in training, compensation, and supervision.

Recruiting Applicants   A planned system for recruiting a sufficient number of applicants is the next step in selection. A good recruiting system:

- Operates continuously, not only when sales-force vacancies occur.
- Is systematic in reaching all appropriate sources of applicants.
- Provides a flow of more qualified applicants than is needed.

To identify recruits, large organizations often use placement services on college campuses or professional employment agencies. Smaller firms that need fewer new sales people may place classified ads in trade publications and daily newspapers. Many firms solicit recommendations from company employees, customers, or suppliers.

Matching Applicants with Hiring Specifications   Sales managers use a variety of techniques—including application forms, interviews, references, credit reports, psychological tests, aptitude tests, and physical examinations—to determine which applicants possess the desired qualifications. Virtually all companies ask candidates to fill out application forms. In addition to providing basic screening information, the application indicates areas that should be explored in an interview.

No sales person should be hired without at least one personal interview. And it is usually desirable to have several interviews conducted by different people in different physical settings. Pooling the opinions of a number of people increases the likelihood of discovering any undesirable characteristics and reduces the effects of one interviewer's possible bias.

The individuals involved in the selection process need to be aware of the laws against discrimination in order to avoid inadvertent violations. For example, it is illegal to ask on an application or in an interview a person's age or marital status. Testing for intelligence, attributes, or personality, although legal under the proper conditions, is somewhat controversial. Some companies avoid testing for fear that they will be accused of discrimination. However, employment tests are legitimate selection tools as long as the attributes measured can be shown to predict job performance.

Assimilating New Sales People

After sales people are hired, management should integrate them into the company. Because selling by its nature involves a considerable amount of rejection by prospects, the new sales person needs support in order to avoid becoming discouraged. A wise sales manager will recognize that the new people must be made comfortable with the details of the job, their fellow workers, and their status in the firm if they are to be successful.

Training a Sales Force

Virtually all companies put new and inexperienced sales people through an orientation and sales training program, often lasting weeks or months. Recognizing that the recent college graduates it hires into its sales force are unlikely to have much experience with its appliances, Whirlpool devised an unusual training experiment.[13] Eight new hires spent two months living in a house together, using the products the company sells. Under the supervision of trainers, they cooked, cleaned, baked, and washed using their employer's products. At the end of the program the trainees had the experience and confidence to go out into the field and teach retail sales clerks how to sell Whirlpool appliances.

Even experienced sales people need continual training to improve their selling skills, learn about new products, and improve their time- and territory-management

Most professional sales people are comfortable with pagers, faxes, and e-mail, but using a computer to analyze a customer's database to prepare for a sales call, as shown here, or taking advantage of sales presentation software remains relatively uncommon. Barriers to use include a high level of comfort with existing sales methods and the cost of training required to learn new approaches.

practices. A recent survey found that 65% of companies give experienced sales people 1 to 10 days of training a year, with a primary focus on improving product knowledge.[14] One of the primary training areas for experienced sales people is in the use of sales-force automation tools described earlier in the chapter.

Motivating a Sales Force

Sales people, especially outside sales forces, require a high degree of motivation. Think back to our earlier discussion about the uniqueness of sales jobs—how sales people often work with little or no direct supervision and guidance from management, and how they must deal with frequent rejection by customers. In addition, outside sales people work most of the time away from the support and comfort of home office surroundings.

Consequently, management faces a challenge in motivating sales people. One key is to determine what motivates the sales reps—is it a need for money, status, control, accomplishment, or something else? People differ in what motivates them, and the motivations change over a person's life. A young sales person is more likely to be motivated by money, whereas an older sales person may be more interested in recognition.

Sales executives can draw from a wide assortment of specific motivational tools. Financial incentives—compensation plans, expense accounts, fringe benefits—serve as basic motivators, but they don't always push people to exceptional performance. Nonfinancial rewards—job enrichment, praise from management, recognition and honor awards (pin, trophy, certificate)—may stimulate some reps. Sales meetings and sales contests are often-used alternatives. Many firms provide cruises, resort trips, and other travel incentives as rewards to top-performing sales reps. The importance of finding ways to motivate sales people is reflected in the attention it receives in the sales management literature.[15]

Compensating a Sales Force

Financial rewards are by far the most widely used tool for motivating sales people. Consequently, designing and administering an effective sales compensation plan is a big part of a sales manager's job. Financial rewards may be direct monetary payments

Apparently some sales people are less than candid. For example, several sales people at WorldCom lied to their employer by double-booking sales in order to increase their incomes. In a survey of sales managers commissioned by *Sales & Marketing Management* magazine nearly half the managers suspected that their sales people lied to customers, and only 16.5% had never heard one of their reps make an unrealistic promise to a customer. The reasons for lying range from a desire to make more money to pressure from management to reach sales quotas.

Should a sales manager ever tolerate lying by a sales rep?

Sources: Erin Strout, "To Tell the Truth," *Sales & Marketing Management,* July 2002, pp. 40–47; Yochi J. Dreazen, "Pressure for Sales Fostered Abuses at WorldCom," *The Wall Street Journal,* May 16, 2002, p. B1+.

(salary, commission) or indirect monetary compensation (paid vacations, pensions, insurance plans).

Establishing a compensation system calls for decisions concerning the level of compensation as well as the method of compensation. The level refers to the total dollar income that a sales person earns over a period of time. Level is influenced by the type of person required for the job and the competitive rate of pay for similar positions. The method is the system or plan by which the sales person will reach the intended level.

The three widely used **methods of sales-force compensation** are straight salary, straight commission, and a combination plan. A *salary* is a fixed payment for a period of time during which the sales person is working. A *salary-only plan* (called a straight salary) provides security and stability of earnings for a sales rep. This plan gives management control over a rep's effort, and the reps are likely to spend time on nonselling activities that cater to the customer's best interests. The main drawback of a straight salary is that it does not offer an incentive for sales people to increase their sales volume. Also, a straight salary is a fixed cost for the firm, unrelated to sales volume or gross margin.

Straight-salary plans typically are used when:

- Compensating new sales people or missionary sales people.
- Opening new territories.
- Selling a technical product that requires a lengthy period of negotiation.

A *commission* is a payment tied to a specific unit of accomplishment. Thus a rep may be paid 5% of every dollar of sales or 8% on each dollar of gross margin. A *straight-commission plan* (commission only) tends to have just the opposite merits and limitations of a straight salary. A straight commission provides considerable incentive for sales people to sell, and it is a variable cost related directly to a rep's sales volume or gross margin. On the other hand, it is difficult to control straight-commission people. And it is especially difficult to get them to perform tasks for which no commission is paid.

Straight-commission plans may work well when:

- A strong incentive is needed to generate sales.
- Very little nonselling work is required, such as setting up displays in retail stores.
- The company is financially weak and must relate its compensation expenses directly to sales or gross margins.

A heavy emphasis on commissions can cause employees to lose sight of the importance of the customer. Kirby Company, for example, has sold vacuum cleaners door to door for 70 years using distributors paid on straight commission. The com-

Should organizations use special incentives to motivate sales people?

Regardless of the compensation method used, many organizations also offer additional incentives to motivate their sales people. These incentives are typically cash or some other type of reward (merchandise or travel) over and above normal compensation for meeting a defined goal in a specified period of time. For example, Isuzu loaded money into special debit cards for sales people who met sales goals (and the recipients were reminded of the incentive every time they used their cards). Others argue that if an organization has a sound compensation program, added incentives are not necessary and may actually lead to problems. For example, Oracle offered

its sales people much higher commissions for sales made during the last few days of a quarter than for sales at the beginning of a quarter (to improve the appearance of results presented to the investment community). However, the incentive led sales people to focus more on timing sales than meeting customers' needs. For more information on incentives see *www.incentivecentral.org.*

What would justify using sales-force incentives?

Sources: Ian Mount, "Out of Control," *Business 2.0,* August 2002, pp. 38–44; "SMM's Best of Sales & Marketing—Best Incentive Plan: GM Isuzu Trucks," *Sales & Marketing Management,* September 2001, pp. 27–32.

pany is highly successful, selling about $1 billion worth of machines a year. Its long history suggests that most of its distributors are ethical. However, over 1,000 consumer complaints nationwide suggest the lure of commissions has caused some distributors to take advantage of elderly and disadvantaged consumers.[16]

The ideal method of compensation is a *combination plan* that has the best features of both the straight-salary and the straight-commission plans, with as few of their drawbacks as possible. To reach this ideal, a combination plan must be tailored to a particular firm, product, market, and type of selling. Today about three-quarters of the firms in the U.S. use some kind of combination plan.

Supervising a Sales Force

Supervising a sales force is difficult because sales people often work independently at far-flung locations where they cannot be continually observed. And yet supervision serves both as a means of ongoing training and as a device to ensure that company policies are being carried out.

An issue that management must resolve is how closely to supervise. If too close, it can unduly constrain the sales person. One of the attractions of selling is the freedom it affords sales people to develop creative solutions to customers' problems. Close supervision can stifle that sense of independence. Conversely, too little supervision can contribute to a lack of direction. Sales people who are not closely supervised may not understand what their supervisors and companies expect of them. They may not know, for example, how much time to spend servicing existing accounts and how much developing new business.

The most effective supervisory method is personal observation in the field. Typically, at least half a sales manager's time is spent traveling with sales people. Other supervisory tools are reports, e-mail, and sales meetings.

Evaluating a Sales Person's Performance

Managing a sales force includes evaluating the performance of sales people. Sales executives must know what the sales force is doing in order to reward them or make constructive proposals for improvement. By establishing performance standards and studying sales people's activities, managers can develop new training programs to upgrade the sales force's efforts. And, of course, performance evaluation should be the basis for compensation decisions and other rewards.

Performance evaluation can also help sales people identify opportunities for improving their efforts. Employees with poor sales records know they are doing something wrong. However, they may not know what the problem is if they lack objective standards by which to measure their performance.

Both quantitative and qualitative measures should be used to formulate a complete picture of performance. **Quantitative evaluation bases** generally have the advantage of being specific and objective. **Qualitative evaluation bases** often reflect broader dimensions of behavior, but are limited by the subjective judgment of the evaluators. For either type of appraisal, management faces the difficult task of setting standards against which a rep's performance can be measured.

Quantitative Bases

Sales performance should be evaluated in terms of inputs (efforts) and outputs (results). Together, inputs such as number of sales calls per day or direct selling expenses, and outputs such as sales volume or gross margin, provide a measure of selling effectiveness.

Useful quantitative input measures include:

- Call rate—number of calls per day or week.
- Number of formal proposals presented.
- Nonselling activities—number of promotion displays set up or training sessions held with distributors or dealers.

Some quantitative output measures useful as evaluation criteria are:

- Sales volume by product, customer group, and territory.
- Sales volume as a percentage of quota or territory potential.
- Gross margin by product line, customer group, and territory.
- Orders—number and average dollar amount.
- Closing rate—number of orders divided by number of calls.
- Accounts—percentage of existing accounts retained and number of new accounts opened.

An increasing number of firms, among them IBM and Hallmark, are using customer satisfaction as a performance indicator. Satisfaction is measured a number of different ways, from detailed questionnaires that customers complete to counting the number of complaints received from customers.

Assessing satisfaction reflects a recognition by companies that there is more to selling than making a sale. Firms have discovered that finding a new customer is much more difficult and expensive than keeping an existing one. As a result, they have shifted their emphasis from a single-minded focus on sales volume to satisfaction. This allows a sales person to nurture a small account with considerable potential rather than always go for the big order. And it discourages sales people from engaging in detrimental actions such as loading up customers with unneeded inventory in order to meet a sales quota.

Qualitative Bases

In some respects, performance evaluation would be much easier if it could be based only on quantitative criteria. The standards would be absolute, and the positive and negative deviations from the standard could be measured precisely. Quantitative measures would also minimize the subjectivity and personal bias of the evaluators.

However, many qualitative factors must be considered because they influence a sales person's performance. Some commonly used factors are:

- Knowledge of products, company policies, and competitors.
- Time management and preparation for sales calls.
- Quality of reports.
- Customer relations.
- Personal appearance.

A successful evaluation program will appraise a sales person on all the factors that can be related to performance. Otherwise management may be misled. A high daily call rate may look good, but it tells us nothing about how many orders are being written up. A high closing rate may be camouflaging a low average order size or a high sales volume on low-profit items.

Summary

Personal selling is the main promotional method used in American business, regardless of whether it is measured by number of people employed, by total expenditures, or by expenses as a percentage of sales. The total field of personal selling comprises two broad types. One covers selling activities where the customers come to the sales people—primarily retail store or retail catalog selling, but also includes the order takers at manufacturers and wholesalers. The other includes all selling situations where the sales people go to the customer—primarily outside sales forces.

Sales jobs today range from order takers through support sales people (missionary sellers, sales engineers) to order getters (consultative sellers). The sales job has evolved. A new type of sales rep—a professional sales person—has been developing over the past few decades. But this new breed of sales rep still faces the unique characteristics of selling: implementing the firm's marketing strategy, representing the company, little direct supervision, frequent rejection by prospects, and considerable travel.

Some changing patterns in personal selling have emerged in recent years—patterns such as selling centers (team selling), systems selling, global sales teams, relationship selling, telemarketing, Internet selling, and sales force automation.

The personal selling process consists of four steps, starting with prospecting for potential buyers and then preapproaching each prospect. The third step is the sales presentation, which includes attracting attention, arousing buyer interest and desire, meeting objections, and then hopefully closing the sale. Finally, postsale activities involve follow-up services to ensure customer satisfaction and reduce dissonance regarding the purchase.

The sales management process involves planning, implementing, and evaluating sales-force activities within the guidelines set by the company's strategic marketing plan. The tasks of staffing and operating a sales force present managerial challenges in several areas. The key to successful sales-force management is to do a good job in selecting sales people. Then plans must be made to assimilate these new people into the company and to train them. Management must set up programs to motivate, compensate, and supervise a sales force. The final stage in sales-force management is to evaluate the performance of the individual sales people.

More about **Johnson Controls**

There is yet another way of selling auto parts looming on Johnson Controls' horizon. Billed as the biggest electronic commerce initiative in the world, an online auction called Covisint could revolutionize the way automakers purchase parts. Car companies have invested about $200 million in the new enterprise to date, hoping that it will be easier and cheaper for them to buy what they need. Some estimate that this online "parts catalog" could take as much as $3,000 off the production costs of a $20,000 automobile.

Covisint was begun as two separate efforts conducted by Ford Motor Co. and General Motors Co., both of whom tried to buy auto parts over the Internet beginning in 1999. After struggling with two different sets of online instructions and purchasing codes, one for each firm, parts suppliers suggested the two companies consolidate their efforts. The result was Covisint. (*www.covisint.com*)

In addition to reducing their costs, car manufacturers also hope to realize time savings from the new system, in view of the fact that they can request design changes instantly and indicate production volumes on the site as well. This makes Covisint a potential information clearinghouse for parts suppliers and their own supply chains as well. Confusion and paperwork could be reduced, too, shaving more time off the production cycle and leading to further savings.

Johnson Controls sees Covisint as another sales tool, but not necessarily the only one. "If our customers want us to channel through Covisint, we will," says its director of e-business speed. "But some of our customers . . . will not use Covisint, so we must have a dual strategy." Thus, personal selling is likely to continue as one of the company's strongest avenues for sales.[17]

1. How can Johnson Controls and its ASG division prepare its sales force to operate in the new Covisint environment, with information flowing freely along the supply chain?

2. Should ASG be in favor of an operation like Covisint? Why or why not?

Key Terms and Concepts

Personal selling (510)
Inside selling (511)
Outside selling (511)
Selling center (515)
Systems selling (516)
Global sales teams (516)

Relationship selling (516)
Telemarketing (517)
Internet selling (518)
Sales force automation (SFA) (519)
Personal selling process (520)
AIDA (521)

Methods of sales-force
  compensation (526)
Quantitative evaluation bases (528)
Qualitative evaluation bases (528)

Questions and Problems

1. The cost of a two-page, four-color advertising spread in one issue of *Sports Illustrated* magazine is more than the cost of employing two sales people for a full year. A sales-force executive is urging her company to eliminate a few of these ads and, instead, to hire more sales people. This executive believes that for the same cost, a single good sales person working for an entire year can sell more than one ad in an issue of *Sports Illustrated*. How would you respond?

2. Would systems selling make more sense for a soft drink bottler or a plumbing supplies distributor? Why?

3. Refer to the classification of sales jobs from delivery–sales person to creative seller and answer the following questions:

   a. In which types of jobs are sales people most likely to be free from close supervision?
   b. Which types are likely to be the highest paid?
   c. For which types of jobs is the highest degree of motivation necessary?

4. What type of business should consider replacing inside telephone sales people with a Web-based ordering system?

5. What are some sources you might use to acquire a list of prospects for the following products?

   a. Bank accounts for new area residents.
   b. Dental X-ray equipment.
   c. Laptop computers.
   d. Contributors to the United Way.
   e. Baby furniture and clothes.

6. If you were preparing a sales presentation for the following products, what information about a prospect would you seek as part of your preparation?

   a. Two-bedroom condominium.
   b. New automobile.
   c. Carpeting for a home redecorating project.

7. What sources should be used to recruit sales applicants in each of the following firms? Explain your choice in each case.

   a. A Marriott Hotel that wants companies to use the hotel for conventions.
   b. IBM, for sales of software to manage parts inventories for automakers.
   c. Johnson Controls' Automotive Systems Group.

8. Compare the merits of straight-salary and straight-commission plans of sales compensation. What are two types of sales jobs in which each plan might be desirable?

9. How might a firm determine whether a sales person is using high-pressure selling tactics that might damage customer satisfaction?

10. How can a sales manager evaluate the performance of sales people in getting new business?

Interactive Marketing Exercises

1. Review your activities of the past few days and identify those in which:
   a. You did some personal selling.
   b. People tried to sell something to you.

   Select one situation in each category where you thought the selling was particularly effective, and explain why.

2. Interview three students from your school who recently have gone through the job interviewing process conducted by companies using your school's placement office. Use the personal selling process described in the chapter to evaluate the students' sales efforts. Prepare a report covering your findings.

Chapter
19
Advertising, Sales Promotion, and Public Relations

"Convincing a substantial share of the 89% of U.S. consumers who have never taken a cruise that it can be the vacation of their dreams is the goal of the cruise marketers."

Can Royal Caribbean Cruise to a Profitable Harbor?

In an industry adding 70% more capacity while four competitors go under because of insufficient demand, what is the best way to stay afloat? The cruise industry in general and Royal Caribbean International in particular are hoping the answer isn't just lowering prices. New shipboard amenities include ice rinks, rock-climbing walls, extensive children's facilities and programs, conference centers, basketball courts, gaming arcades, theaters, and entertainment complexes with state-of-the-art broadcasting and recording facilities. These costly features in addition to dozens of themed restaurants and bars suggest what cruise lines may need to offer in order to succeed.

Convincing a substantial share of the 89% of U.S. consumers who have never taken a cruise that it can be the vacation of their dreams is the goal of cruise marketers. To fill nearly 17 million berths (the worldwide capacity expected by 2006) with passengers, cruise lines are building new ships and refitting existing ones on the basis of a redefined concept of the cruise experience. One approach is to appeal specifically to people who, in the words of an ad agency creative director, want to "stay as young as possible as long as they can," regardless of their age.

Royal Caribbean launched the first-ever ship incorporating an ice rink and a rock-climbing wall, and quickly followed it with two others. It annually spends around $40 million on media advertising to inform and attract consumers, and nearly the same amount on an integrated marketing campaign that includes direct mail, trade promotion, and interactive and print advertising. Number two in the industry, the company hopes to see its sales revenue grow steadily over the next few years to $3 billion.

In the wake of the recent weakened economy, Royal Caribbean did cut prices, along with its competitors (not just those in the cruise business but in the travel industry in general, including resorts and hotels). But it was viewed as a short-term, tactical response to a temporary condition. Standard & Poor's analysts foresee that as baby boomers become a major part of the customer mix in coming years, the industry will be able to avoid supply running ahead of demand in the long term. In fact, Royal Caribbean's television ads are aimed squarely at this demographic group, with 1970s soundtracks and a "lust for life" theme. Also, new destinations and new departure points are being added to make it even easier and more attractive to get away on one of its ships.

The firm is keeping a high public relations profile as well. The first major cruise ship to visit New York harbor after September 11, 2001, was its new 142,000-ton *Adventure of the Seas,* which was christened by the city's mayor and took its first (ceremonial) cruise with members of the city's fire and police departments on board. In another public relations effort, specific websites for the firm's individual ships feature information about its efforts to protect the environment.

Among its other promotional activity, Royal Caribbean supports efforts to raise demand for tourism in general. For example, it is a member

www.royalcaribbean.com

of the Travel Industry Association of America, a national nonprofit organization that represents the U.S. travel industry. Recently the association undertook a three-year international marketing campaign called See America in an attempt to reverse a 24% drop in the U.S.'s share of world tourism.

Cruise lines, including Royal Caribbean, also court travel agents with commissions of 10% to 16%, as well as free or discounted vacations to let them personally experience particular ships and destinations. Booking a cruise requires making many difficult choices, which is where travel agents demonstrate their worth. However, some experienced consumers are venturing online to book for themselves. So Royal Caribbean also hosts its own website to make the process as convenient and easy as possible.[1]

How important are advertising and other forms of promotion in marketing cruise lines and other vacation products?

Advertising, sales promotion, and public relations are the mass-communication tools available to marketers. As the name suggests, *mass* communication uses the same message for everyone in an audience. The mass communicator trades off the advantage of personal selling, the opportunity to deliver a tailored message in person, for the advantage of reaching many people at a lower cost per contact.

The term mass communication does not imply indiscriminate efforts to reach large audiences. As we saw with Royal Caribbean in the opening case, marketers are constantly seeking refinements that will allow them to present their messages to more specifically defined target audiences.

This chapter examines *nonpersonal*, mass-communication promotional tools—advertising, sales promotion, and public relations. After studying this chapter, you should be able to explain:

Chapter Goals

- The nature and scope of advertising, sales promotion, and public relations.
- Characteristics of the major types of these mass communication tools.
- How advertising campaigns are developed and advertising media are selected.
- The alternative ways firms organize their advertising efforts.
- How sales promotion is managed to maximize its effectiveness.
- The role of public relations in the promotional mix.

Nature and Scope of Advertising

All advertisements (ads, for short) have four features:

- A verbal and/or visual nonpersonal message.
- An identified sponsor.
- Delivery through one or more media.
- Payment by the sponsor to the medium carrying the message.

Advertising, then, consists of all the activities involved in presenting through the media a nonpersonal, sponsor-identified, paid-for message about a product or organization.

Advertising in one form or another is used by most organizations. The significance of advertising is indicated by the amount of money spent on it. In 2001, total U.S. advertising expenditures were over $231 *billion,* over four times the amount spent in 1980. A slightly smaller amount, $214 *billion*, was spent in the rest of the world during 2001. Table 19.1 shows the relative importance of the major U.S. advertising media over the past 30 years. Until 1999, newspapers were the most widely used medium, based on total advertising dollars spent. However, television is now the most heavily used medium. As newspapers' share has declined, the proportions accounted for by direct-mail advertising and the newcomer, the Internet, have increased.

Advertising as a Percentage of Sales

The amount of advertising that businesses do seems daunting. For example, Procter & Gamble spends more than $4.5 *billion* a year worldwide.[2] However, it's important to put the expenditure in context. When you consider that Procter & Gamble has 250 brands that it sells in more than 140 countries and that those brands are targeted at more than 5 billion consumers, the amount to get its message out (less than $1 per prospect per year) seems more reasonable. Table 19.2 shows the 10 companies with the largest dollar expenditures for advertising in the U.S. Not surprisingly, these are companies with which we are all familiar. The table also indicates the percentage of sales each of the companies spends on advertising. The data suggest that frequently purchased convenience goods require more advertising to generate a dollar's worth of sales than infrequently purchased durable goods.

Industry averages can be misleading. How much an individual firm spends on advertising is influenced by its resources and objectives more than by what other firms in the industry are doing. In the U.S., Ford Motor Co. spends slightly more than 2% of its sales on advertising, whereas Mitsubishi's U.S. ad budget is 4% of its sales. Despite this proportional difference, Ford spends about $8 on advertising for every dollar spent by Mitsubishi.[3]

TABLE 19.1

Advertising Expenditures in the United States by Medium

In 2001, the amount spent on advertising declined for the first time in a decade. The decline was attributed to an economic recession and the failure of many Internet companies that spent lavishly on advertising in 1999 and 2000.

Medium	2001 Expenditures (in billions)	2000 (%)	1990 (%)	1980 (%)	1970 (%)
Television	54	24	22	21	18
Direct mail	45	18	18	14	14
Newspapers	$ 44	20	25	28	29
Radio	18	8	7	7	7
Yellow pages	14	5	7	—	—
Magazines	11	5	5	6	7
Internet	6	3	—	—	—
Other*	40	17	15	24	25
Total percentage†	___	100	100	100	100
Total dollars (in billions)	$232	$247	$128	$55	$20

*Before 1988 this category included yellow pages. Also includes outdoor, transportation advertising, weekly newspapers, regional farm publications, and point-of-sale advertising.

†Percentages have been rounded.

Sources: Robert J. Coen, "McCann's Insider's Report," Universal McCann Erickson, Dec. 6, 1999; Robert J. Coen, "More Gains Forseen for '95 Ad Spending," *Advertising Age*, May 8, 1995, p. 36; 1980 figures from *Advertising Age*, Mar. 22, 1982, p. 66. Others adapted from *Advertising Age*, Nov. 17, 1975, p. 40; "Bob Coen's Insider Report," McCann-Erickson World Group, *www.mccann.com*, accessed on Sept. 1, 2002.

TABLE
19.2

Top Ten National Advertisers in 2001, Based on Total Expenditures in the United States

Company	Advertising Expenditures	
	Dollars (in billions)	As Percentage of U.S. Sales
1. General Motors	3.4	2.5
2. Procter & Gamble	2.5	12.6
3. Ford Motor Co.	2.4	2.2
4. PepsiCo	2.2	13.0
5. Pfizer	2.2	12.3
6. DaimlerChrysler	2.0	2.7
7. AOL Time Warner	1.9	6.2
8. Philip Morris Cos.	1.8	4.1
9. Walt Disney Co.	1.8	8.3
10. Johnson & Johnson	1.6	8.0

Source: "100 Leading National Advertisers, 2002 Edition," *Advertising Age,* June 24, 2002, accessed from the website *www.adage.com.*

Advertising Cost versus Personal Selling Cost

Although there are no accurate figures for the cost of personal selling, we do know it far surpasses advertising expenditures. Only a few manufacturing industries, such as drugs, toiletries, cleaning products, tobacco, and beverages, spend more on advertising than on personal selling. Advertising runs 1% to 3% of net sales in many firms, whereas the expenses of recruiting and operating a sales force are typically 8% to 15% of sales.

At the wholesale level, advertising costs are very low. Personal selling expenses for wholesalers, however, may run 10 to 15 times more than their expenditures for advertising. Even among many retailers, including some with self-service operations, the total cost of their customer-contact employees is substantially higher than what they spend on advertising.

Types of Advertising

Advertising can be classified according to (1) the target audience, either consumers or businesses; (2) the objective sought, the stimulation of primary or selective demand; and (3) what is being advertised, a product versus an institution. To fully appreciate the scope and types of advertising, it is essential to understand these three classifications.

The Target: Consumer or Business
An ad is directed at consumers or businesses; thus it is either **business-to-consumer advertising** or **business-to-business advertising.** Retailers by definition sell only to consumers; therefore, they are the only type of business not faced with this decision. On the other hand, many manufacturers and distributors must divide their advertising between business customers and consumers. For example, DaimlerChrysler advertises to fleet buyers such as the car rental companies and to final consumers; similarly, Marriott Corp. advertises its resorts and hotels to corporate clients and to households.

The Type of Demand: Primary or Selective
Primary-demand advertising is designed to stimulate demand for a generic category of a product such as coffee, electricity, or garments made from cotton. In contrast, **selective-demand advertising** is intended to stimulate demand for individual brands such as Folgers coffee, American Electric Power electricity, and Liz Claiborne sportswear.

Primary-demand advertising is used in either of two situations. The first is when the product is in the introductory stage of its life cycle. This is called *pioneering advertising*. The objective of pioneering advertising is to inform, rather than persuade, the target market. Recall from Chapter 4 that a consumer must first be made aware of a product before becoming interested in or desiring it. To inform engineers about microprocessors, Intel ran pioneering ads.

The other use of primary-demand advertising occurs throughout the product life cycle and therefore is considered *demand-sustaining advertising*. It is usually done by trade associations trying to stimulate or sustain demand for their industry's product. Thus, the National Fluid Milk Processor Promotion Board encourages us to consume more milk with its campaign depicting celebrities with milk "mustaches."

Selective-demand advertising is essentially competitive advertising. It pits one brand against the rest of the market. This type of advertising is employed when a product is beyond the introductory life-cycle stage and is competing for market share with several other brands. Selective-demand advertising emphasizes a brand's special features and benefits—its differential advantage.

A special case of selective-demand advertising that makes reference to one or more competitors is called **comparison advertising**. In this kind of advertising, the advertiser either directly, by naming the rival brand, or indirectly, through inferences, claims some point of superiority over the rival. Recent examples include Papa John's "Better Ingredients, Better Pizza" campaign, and Apple's "Real People" series of ads depicting computer users who have switched from Windows PCs to Apple MacIntosh machines. Comparison advertising is encouraged by the Federal Trade Commission as a means of stimulating competition and disseminating useful information to customers. Advertisers must be careful that any comparative claims can be substantiated.

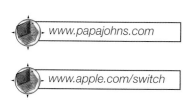

www.papajohns.com

www.apple.com/switch

The Message: Product or Institutional

All selective advertising may be classified as product or institutional. **Product advertising** focuses on a particular product or brand. It is subdivided into direct-action and indirect-action product advertising:

- *Direct-action* advertising seeks a quick response. For instance, a magazine ad containing a coupon or an 800 number may urge the reader to send or call immediately for a free sample, or a supermarket ad in a local newspaper stresses specials available for only a few days.

- *Indirect-action* advertising is designed to stimulate demand over a longer period of time. It is intended to inform or remind consumers that the product exists and to point out its benefits. The "lonely repairman" who has appeared in television and print ads for Maytag appliances for over 35 years is an example. Most network television advertising is indirect action, whereas much local television advertising is direct action.

Institutional advertising presents information about the advertiser's business or tries to create a favorable attitude—that is, build goodwill—toward the organization. In contrast to product advertising, institutional advertising is not intended to sell a specific product. Its objective is to create a particular image for a company. United Airlines, for example, spent millions over the years communicating its corporate philosophy with the "Fly the Friendly Skies" campaign.

The Source: Commercial or Social

The focus here is on commercial messages but the most valued form of endorsement is noncommercial, for instance, when a trusted friend or relative recommends a product. Commonly referred to as *word-of-mouth advertising*, technically it doesn't fit our definition of advertising. In fact, the very reason that it doesn't conform to the definition is what makes it so prized. That is, the recommender is not paid. Word-of-mouth recommendations are highly credible because the recommender has only the best interests of the recipient as the motivation for sharing an opinion. So despite the fact that it is not strictly a type of advertising, word of mouth deserves our consideration.

Firms try to *stimulate* word-of-mouth endorsements. Probably the most successful in history was a program created by MCI called "Friends and Family." It offered a person and a circle of specified individuals reduced rates when they called each other if they all subscribed to the long-distance calling plan. Alternatively, some firms try to *simulate* word-of-mouth endorsements. For example, Sony Erickson is getting consumers to try its mobile phone that doubles as a digital camera by having trained actors visit tourism attractions, pretending to be tourists and asking strangers to take their pictures with the phone/camera. The ensuing conversation often ends in an endorsement of the product by the actor. Not surprisingly, consumer activists object to what they consider a deceptive practice.[4]

www.newgate.com

The Internet has generated increasing interest in personalized messages. Though they are transferred electronically and not by "word of mouth," they can have the same effect. And because messages can move rapidly through an ever-expanding network of Internet users, the benefits of a positive message (and the damage of a negative one) can be very substantial. In the electronic setting, the term word of mouth has been replaced by *viral marketing*, depicting how a message is passed from one person to another through a social system.[5] Viral marketing has the same advantages as word-of-mouth endorsements. First, it frequently has no direct cost because the message originates with a customer. Second, a person's social network is quite homogeneous, so the message likely reaches members of the target market. Finally, because it arrives as a message from a friend or acquaintance it is usually read by the recipient unlike much advertising, which is simply ignored.

Developing an Advertising Campaign

An **advertising campaign** consists of all the tasks involved in transforming a theme into a coordinated advertising program to accomplish a specific goal for a product or brand. Typically a campaign involves several different advertising messages, presented over an extended period of time, using a variety of media. For example, after a seven-year run, Coca-Cola replaced its "Always Coca-Cola" campaign with a message intended to be more of an invitation than a command. Using the slogan "Coca-Cola.enjoy," the company was suggesting that the soft drink goes along with relaxing. The new campaign, which was introduced in the U.S. in early 2000, was dropped in 2001 in favor of one built around the message "Life tastes good."[6]

An advertising campaign is planned within the framework of the overall strategic marketing plan and as part of a broader promotional program. The framework is established when management:

- Identifies the target audience.
- Establishes the overall promotional goals.
- Sets the total promotional budget.
- Determines the overall promotional theme.

With these tasks completed, the firm can begin formulating an advertising campaign. The steps in conducting a campaign are defining objectives, establishing a budget, creating a message, selecting media, and evaluating effectiveness.

Defining Objectives

The purpose of advertising is to sell something—a good, service, idea, person, or place—either now or later. This goal is reached by setting specific objectives that are reflected in individual ads incorporated into an advertising campaign. For example, in 1999 Avon launched a mutimillion-dollar television and print ad cam-

With a tight budget and an unfamiliar brand, an unorthodox advertising strategy was used to launch the Mini Cooper in the U.S. Rather than television, the typical medium for announcing a new automobile, the Mini made use of billboards, posters, and other more localized tools, For example, "Minis" were mounted on Ford Excursion SUVs, and when people asked about the vehicle they were directed to the brand's website.

www.miniusa.com

paign in 26 markets worldwide. The campaign, dubbed "Let's Talk" was intended to support the company's direct sales force of 2.8 million Avon ladies while the firm introduced new lines of cosmetics in retail stores. As the campaign unfolded, the specific objectives shifted from heightening awareness of the Avon brand to a greater emphasis on introducing some new cosmetic products.[7]

Typical advertising objectives are to:

- *Support personal selling.* Advertising may be used to acquaint prospects with the seller's company and products, easing the way for the sales force, as Avon is doing.

- *Improve dealer relations.* Wholesalers and retailers like to see a manufacturer support its products with advertising.

- *Introduce a new product.* Consumers need to be informed even about line extensions that make use of familiar brand names.

- *Expand the use of a product.* Advertising may be used to lengthen the season for a product (as Lipton did for iced tea); increase the frequency of replacement (as Fram did for oil filters); or increase the variety of product uses (as Arm & Hammer did for baking soda).

- *Counteract substitution.* Advertising reinforces the decisions of existing customers and reduces the likelihood that they will switch to alternative brands.

Establishing a Budget

Once a promotional budget has been established (discussed in Chapter 17), it must be allocated among the various activities comprising the overall promotional program. In the case of a particular brand, a firm may wish to have several ads, as well as sales promotion and public relations activities, directed at different target audiences all at the same time. In addition to its "Let's Talk" campaign, Avon has professional tennis players Venus and Serena Williams under contract to appear in ads, launched a "Kiss Goodbye to Breast Cancer" campaign that includes a donation to breast cancer research for purchases of certain products, sponsored a charity concert and a fund-raising auction of celebrities' dresses, and continues to support launches of new products tailored to specific ethnic and demographic markets around the

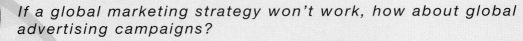
If a global marketing strategy won't work, how about global advertising campaigns?

The notion of a global marketing strategy—using the same marketing mix everywhere a company does business—has proven to be impractical. Even marketing icons such as McDonald's and Coca-Cola adapt their product assortments and distribution methods to particular markets. But what about advertising? With differences in language, culture, and customs, it would seem to be a difficult marketing-mix element to globalize. However, several companies are moving in that direction. Exxon developed a campaign for its portfolio of petroleum brands that presents the same message regardless of the country in which they appear. To accomplish its goal the firm produced numerous versions of the ad, all with the same story lines but in 25 different languages. Consumer goods maker Mars, best known for its candy products, conducted a global campaign encouraging consumers to guess what color the new

M&M's candy would be, and using the Internet to respond. As a result, the firm gathered the names of a million interested customers worldwide. Range Rover is another brand with a global advertising campaign. Executives from ad agencies all over the world who handle the local Range Rover accounts gathered in England to formulate the campaign. According to one participant, "It's in Ford's (the parent company) interest to try and gain economies of scale with a similar platform for positioning. . . . Obviously, the costs can be amortized by agreeing to the positioning centrally and competing in any market in the world."

Sources: Vanessa O'Connell, "Exxon 'Centralizes' New Global Campaign," *The Wall Street Journal,* July 11, 2002, p. B6; Paul McIntyre, "Mars Raises the Bar in Its Latest Campaigns," *The Australian,* Aug. 29, 2002, p. M11; Paul McIntyre, "Global Grunt from Range Rover," *The Australian,* Aug. 29, 2002, p. M11.

world.[8] Because all these efforts must be paid for from the promotional budget, the potential value of each must be weighed and allocations made accordingly.

One method that firms use to extend their budgets is **cooperative advertising,** which is a joint effort by two or more firms intended to benefit each of the participants. There are two types of cooperative ads— vertical and horizontal. *Vertical cooperative advertising* involves firms on different levels of distribution. For example, a manufacturer and a retailer share the cost of the retailer's advertising of that manufacturer's product. Frequently the manufacturer prepares the actual ad, leaving space for the retailer's name and address. Then the manufacturer and retailer share the media cost of placing the ad. Many local retail ads in newspapers, radios, and on television involve co-op funds.[9]

Another type of vertical cooperation is an *advertising allowance*, or cash discount offered by a manufacturer to a retailer, to encourage the retailer to advertise or prominently display a product. In cooperative advertising the manufacturer has control over how the money is actually spent, but that is not the case with an advertising allowance.

Cooperative arrangements benefit retailers by providing them with extra funds for promotion. Manufacturers also benefit because cooperative advertising provides them with local identification for their products. In addition, a manufacturer's ad dollars go further because rates charged by local media (such as a daily newspaper) are typically lower for ads placed by local firms than for ads placed by national advertisers.

Horizontal cooperative advertising is joint advertising in which two or more firms on the same level of distribution, such as a group of retailers, share the costs. The chapter-opening case includes an illustration of horizontal cooperative advertising. Royal Caribbean has joined with other members of the Travel Industry Association of America, a national nonprofit organization made up of firms in the tourism business, to fund advertising intended to stimulate demand for tourism in general.

Making changes now.
Making waves soon.

We're changing to Shell. Please enjoy what these changes will bring. **Bright new facilities · Deposit preventing gasoline · A commitment** to service and convenience. Waves of change are coming soon.

Waves of change™

Shell, a unit of Royal Dutch/Shell, recently acquired several thousand Texaco service stations across the U.S. As the company converts the appearance of the stations to Shell's yellow and red design, it must also inform consumers of the change. The message is built on an attention getting theme of "waves of change" accompanied by an explanation.

The principal benefit is that by pooling their funds, the firms achieve greater exposure or impact than if they advertised individually.

Creating a Message

Whatever the objective of an advertising campaign, to be successful the individual ads must get and hold the *attention* of the intended audience, and *influence* that audience in the desired way. Attention can be achieved in many ways. (Recall our discussion of perception in Chapter 4.) Television makes possible special visual effects, as for example the flying cans in the Mountain Dew ads and the talking lizards in the Anhueser-Busch ads. Radio can use listeners' imaginations to create mental images that would be impossible to actually produce. Surprising, shocking, amusing, and arousing curiosity are all common techniques to gain attention. Thus a print ad might be mostly white space, or a billboard might show the product in an unusual setting.

If the ad succeeds in getting the audience's attention, the advertiser has a few seconds to communicate a message intended to influence beliefs and/or behavior. The message has two elements, the *appeal* and the *execution*. The appeal in an ad is the reason or justification for believing or behaving. It is the benefit that the individual will receive as a result of accepting the message.

Some advertisers mistakenly focus their appeal on product features or attributes. They either confuse attributes with benefits, or assume that if they present the product's attributes, the audience will infer the correct benefits. Telling consumers that a breakfast cereal contains fiber (an attribute) is much less meaningful than telling them that because it contains fiber, consuming it reduces the likelihood of colon cancer (the benefit).

Execution is combining in a convincing, compatible way the feature or device that gets attention with the appeal. An appeal can be executed in different ways. Consider, for example, the many characters advertisers have created to get messages across—the Pillsbury Doughboy and Green Giant, Eveready's Energizer Bunny, the Michelin man, Ronald McDonald, and Kellogg's Tony the Tiger. Great care must be taken to ensure that the execution doesn't overwhelm the appeal. Taco Bell developed an execution that featured a Chihuahua obsessed with the company's products. After a two-year campaign and $200 million of advertising, the company decided to

In 1997 the rules on direct-to-consumer (DTC) advertising of prescription drugs on television were relaxed by the Food and Drug Administration. As a result, prescription drug advertising to the general public increased from $1 billion in 1997 to nearly $2.5 billion in 2000. Prior to the rules' revision, the advertising for prescription drugs was directed at health care professionals.

DTC ads are not required to provide detailed information on the potential side effects or the proper use of the drugs. They must, however, include toll-free numbers or websites where consumers can get detailed information about the advertised drug.

Consumers seem to be influenced by the ads. One study found that 25% of respondents said they had been prompted by DTC ads to call or visit a doctor to discuss the product being advertised. Consumer welfare advocates are concerned that consumers, influenced by the persuasive techniques of advertising but without a complete understanding of a drug, will pressure physicians to prescribe it.

Should DTC prescription drug advertising meet a higher ethical standard than advertising for products such as soft drinks or fast food?

Sources: Stuart Elliot, "Pharmaceutical Makers and Ad Agencies Fight to Preserve Campaigns for Prescription Drugs," *The New York Times,* July 12, 2002, p. C2; Steven Findley, "Do Ads Really Drive Pharmaceutical Sales?" *Marketing Health Services,* Spring 2002, pp. 21+; Michael Waldholz, "Patients Need to View Drug Ads with Some Healthy Skepticism," *The Wall Street Journal,* July 1, 2002, p. D6.

reduce the dog's role in its ads and focus more on the food. According to a Taco Bell franchisee, the dog, which had become a pop-culture icon, appearing on the cover of *TV Guide* magazine and in a music video, became the focus. Meanwhile, the food was receiving too little attention. The evidence was in the results. Although many people were familiar with the Chihuahua, Taco Bell sales increased only 2% during the campaign.[10]

Selecting Media

In describing the steps involved in developing an advertising campaign, we discussed the creation of an advertising message before selection of the **advertising media** in which to place the ad. In actuality these decisions are usually made simultaneously. Both the message and the choice of media are determined by the nature of the appeal and the intended target audience.

Advertisers need to make decisions at each of three successive levels in selecting the specific advertising medium to use:

1. Which *type(s)* will be used—newspaper, television, radio, magazine, or direct mail? What about the less prominent media of billboards, the Internet, and yellow pages?

2. Which *category of the selected medium* will be used? Television has network and cable; magazines include general-interest *(Newsweek, People)* and special-interest *(Popular Mechanics, Runner's World)* categories; there are national as well as local newspapers; and the Internet offers portals as well as individual websites.

3. Which *specific media vehicles* will be used? An advertiser that decides first on radio and then on local stations must determine which stations to use in each city.

Here are some general factors that will influence media choice:

- *Objectives of the ad.* The purpose of a particular ad and the goals of the entire campaign influence which media to use. For example, if the campaign goal is to generate appointments for sales people, the company may rely on direct mail. If an advertiser has a short lead time, local newspaper or radio may be the medium to use.

- *Audience coverage.* The audience reached by the medium should match the geographic area in which the product is distributed. Furthermore, the selected medium should reach the desired types of prospects with a minimum of wasted coverage—that is, reach people who are not prospects for the product. Many media, even national and other large-market media, can be targeted at small, specialized market segments. For example, *Time* magazine publishes regional editions with different ads in the East, Midwest, and West. Large metropolitan newspapers publish suburban editions as well as regional editions within the city.

- *Requirements of the message.* The medium should fit the message. For example, magazines provide high-quality visual reproductions that attract attention along with printed messages that can be carefully read and evaluated. As a result, they are well suited to business-to-business advertising.

- *Time and location of the buying decision.* If the objective is to stimulate a purchase, the medium should reach prospective customers when and where they are about to make their buying decisions. This factor highlights one of the strengths of point-of-purchase advertising (such as ads placed on shopping carts and in the aisles of supermarkets), which reach consumers at the actual time of purchase.

- *Media cost.* The cost of each medium should be considered in relation to the amount of funds available to pay for it and its reach or circulation. For example, the cost of network television exceeds the available funds of many advertisers. To compare various media, advertisers use a measure called **cost per thousand (CPM)**, which is the cost of reaching a thousand people, one time each, with a particular ad.

Beyond these general factors, management must evaluate the advertising characteristics of each medium it is considering. We have carefully chosen the term *characteristics,* instead of advantages and disadvantages, because a medium that works well for one product is not necessarily the best choice for another product. To illustrate, a characteristic of radio is that it makes its impressions through sound and imagination. The roar of a crowd, the rumbling of thunder, or screeching tires can be used to create mental images quickly and easily. But radio will not do the job for products that require a specific visual image. Let's examine the characteristics of the major media.

Television   Virtually every U.S. household has a television, and on average viewers watch more than seven hours a day.[11] Television combines motion, sound, and special visual effects. Products can be demonstrated as well as described on TV. It offers wide geographic coverage, and flexibility in when the message can be presented. However, TV ads lack permanence, so they must be seen and understood immediately. As a result, TV does not lend itself to complicated messages.

Television can appear to be a relatively expensive medium, but it has the potential to provide a large audience. For example, a single 30-second spot on the 2002 Super Bowl telecast cost $2.2 million to reach an audience of 138 million viewers. Table 19.3 shows how the cost of a network ad in prime time has increased over the years. Television ads are also expensive to produce. It's not unusual for a firm to spend $500,000 to create a 30-second commercial. As a result, fewer ads are being made, and they are being kept on the air longer.

The share of the television audience in prime time that is held by the networks has declined from 70% in 1985 to about 35% today.[12] The major reason is the growing popularity of cable and direct-broadcast satellite television. Over 65% of American homes (80% with household incomes over $50,000) have cable, with an average of 62 stations per household. The result is more fragmented markets and specialized programming, making it difficult to reach a mass market. On the positive side, the specialization of cable channels such as MTV, CNBC, and ESPN offers an advertiser a more homogeneous group of viewers at a lower price (because the audience is smaller) than broadcast networks.

Advertisers are also using *place-based* television to reach attractive target audiences—young professionals, teenagers, working women—who have become less accessible through traditional media. Firms such as Whittle Communications and CNN put TVs in classrooms, waiting rooms, supermarkets, airports, health clubs, and other places where "captive audiences" are likely to gather.

Direct Mail Over 60 *billion* pieces of direct-mail advertising are distributed in the U.S. each year.[13] It can be sent in the traditional fashion, using the Postal Service or an overnight delivery, or electronically by fax or e-mail.

Direct mail has the potential of being the most personal and selective of all media. Highly specialized direct-mail lists can be developed from a firm's own customer database or purchased from list suppliers (among the thousands available are lists of air traffic controllers, wig dealers, college professors, pregnant women, and disc jockeys). Because direct mail goes only to the people the advertiser wishes to contact, there is almost no wasted coverage. However, even with carefully selected mailing lists, a direct-mail effort with a response rate of 1% to 2% is often viewed as successful.[14] Traditional direct mail also allows for the distribution of product samples. Printing and postage fees make the cost per thousand of direct mail quite high compared with other media.

www.the-dma.org

The technological alternative, electronic direct mail or e-mail, is less expensive to send. However, the low cost has led to indiscriminate distribution of unsolicited commercial e-mail (called spamming). It has become so commonplace and annoying that a number of public agencies and private groups are seeking ways to regulate it.

Reaching the prospect does not ensure that the message is communicated. Direct mail is pure advertising. It is not accompanied by editorial matter (unless the advertiser provides it). Therefore, a direct-mail ad must attract its own readers. This is critical when you consider that the average American home receives more

TABLE 19.3 The Cost of Prime-Time Advertising on Network Television

Year	Program	Type of Ad	Cost
1980	M*A*S*H	30 seconds	$150,000
	Dallas	30 seconds	145,000
1992	Murphy Brown	30 seconds	310,000
	Roseanne	30 seconds	290,000
1995	Seinfeld	30 seconds	490,000
	Home Improvement	30 seconds	475,000
1999	Ally McBeal	30 seconds	450,000
	ER	30 seconds	750,000
2000	Will & Grace	30 seconds	480,000
	Friends	30 seconds	540,000
2002	Survivor	30 seconds	420,000
	Everybody Loves Raymond	30 seconds	300,000

Sources: "50 Years of TV Advertising: The Buying and Selling," *Advertising Age*, Spring 1995, p. 29; Joe Mandese, "Seinfeld Is NBC's $ 1M/Minute Man," *Advertising Age*, Sept. 18, 1995, p. 11; Joe Mandese, "'ER' Tops Price Chart, Regis Wears the Crown," *Advertising Age*, Oct. 2, 2000, pp. 1+; David Goetzl and Wayne Friedman, "'Friends' Tops Ad Price List," *Advertising Age*, Sept. 30, 2002, pp. 1+; and personal contacts.

than 10 direct-mail pieces a week, and that half of all direct-mail pieces are discarded unopened.[15]

Newspapers

As an advertising medium, newspapers are flexible and timely. Ads can be inserted or canceled on very short notice and can vary in size from small classifieds to multiple pages. Pages can be added or dropped, so the space in newspapers is not limited in the way time is constrained on TV and radio. Newspapers can be used to reach an entire city or, where regional editions are offered, selected areas. Cost per thousand is relatively low.

On the other hand, the life of newspapers is very short. Typically, they are discarded soon after being read. A metropolitan newspaper provides coverage of about one-half the households in a local market. However, in many large cities, circulation of daily newspapers is decreasing. Also, the growth of the Internet has created a new source of competition for newspapers. Especially hard hit is classified advertising, which accounts for about 40% of newspaper ad revenue.[16] Finally, because newspapers don't offer much format variety, it is difficult to design ads that stand out.

Radio

When interest in television soared after World War II, radio audiences (especially for network radio) declined so dramatically that some people predicted radio's demise. However, radio has enjoyed a rebirth as an advertising and cultural medium, with the number of stations increasing at a steady rate. Today there are over 11,000 stations in the U.S. (60% of them FM).

Radio is a low-cost per thousand medium because of its broad reach. Nearly 80% of Americans listen to the radio daily, and on average, adults 18 year of age and over listen more than 20 hours a week. With programming ranging from all-talk to sports to country music, certain target markets can be pinpointed quite effectively. Radio commercials can be produced in less than a week, at a cost far below television.

Because radio makes only an audio impression, it relies entirely on the listener's ability to retain information heard and not seen. Also, audience attention is often at a low level, because radio is frequently used as background for working, studying (Is your radio on now?), or some other activity.

Yellow Pages

A printed directory of local business names and phone numbers organized by type of product, the yellow pages has been around since the late 1800s. The breakup of the Bell System telephone monopoly in 1983 led to an increase in the number of yellow pages directories. Today there are over 6,000 in the U.S., with large metropolitan areas commonly having four or five competing directories.[17] The yellow pages are a source of information with which most consumers are familiar. And they are used by consumers at or very near the buying decision. On the negative side, yellow page ads are difficult to differentiate, and an advertiser's message is surrounded by the messages of competitors. In addition, traditional printed yellow pages directories are receiving competition from electronic yellow pages on the Internet.

Magazines

Magazines are the medium to use when high-quality printing and color are desired in an ad. Magazines can reach a national market at a relatively low cost per reader. In recent years, the rapid increase in special-interest magazines and regional editions of general-interest magazines has made it possible for advertisers to reach a selected audience with a minimum of wasted circulation. Business and trade magazines, many of which are given away to readers, can be effective in reaching specialized industry audiences. The number of different magazines in the U.S. has increased from just over 14,000 in 1993 to nearly 18,000 today.[18]

Magazines are usually read in a leisurely fashion, in contrast to the haste in which other print media are read. This feature is especially valuable to the advertiser with a lengthy or complicated message. A variety of production innovations have made it possible to enliven magazine ads. Over-sized, foldouts, pullout sections, and poly-wrapped samples are becoming common. Magazines have a relatively long life, anywhere from a week to a month, and a high pass-along readership.

With less flexible production schedules than newspapers, magazines require that ads be submitted several weeks before publication. In addition, because they are published weekly or monthly, it is difficult to use timely messages. Magazines are often read at times or in places—on planes or in doctors' offices, for instance—far removed from where a buying impulse can be acted on.

Out-of-Home Advertising

Spending on out-of-home advertising is growing at about 10% a year, amounting to over $5 billion today.[19] At one time the category was dominated by billboards, and was called outdoor advertising. However, *out-of-home* is more descriptive today because billboards now are in malls, arenas, airports, and other indoor locations as well as outdoors.

www.oaaa.org

There have been other changes in billboards as well. One is the computer-painting technology that makes it possible to create high-quality visual reproductions. Another development is the capability built into the boards themselves, including three-dimensional structures, special lighting effects, digital tickers, and continuous motion. Low cost per thousand is the chief advantage of out-of-home media, although prices vary by the volume of traffic passing a site.

Most out-of-home advertising is for local businesses, but it is increasingly being used for national brand-building ads. Because it is seen by people "on the go," billboard advertising is appropriate only for brief messages. The rule of thumb is six words or less.

Billboards can provide intense market coverage within an area. However, unless the advertised product is a widely used good or service, considerable wasted circulation will occur, because many of the passersby will not be prospects. Finally, the landscape-defacing criticism of outdoor advertising may be a consideration for some advertisers.

Interactive Media

Interactivity refers to a feature that permits the advertising message recipient to respond immediately using the same medium. For example, a person receiving an e-mail message can reply with the click of a mouse. The fastest-growing interactive medium is the World Wide Web, which gives millions of organizations and individuals direct, electronic access to one another.

Until recently access to the Web required a personal computer. Now "Internet appliances" are available. Less sophisticated (and less expensive) than a PC, Internet appliances provide only the capability to traverse the Internet and to exchange e-mail messages. These devices are likely to contribute to an even faster diffusion of the Internet among consumers around the world.

The opportunity the Web has created has not been lost on marketers who can use it to communicate advertising messages. This medium requires the recipient to take the initiative and tap into the sender's message. Once the connection is established, the recipient controls the flow of information, selecting with mouse clicks the pages to examine and how long to remain connected. For example, a consumer interested in buying a car might begin by using the Web to find out which companies make minivans. From there, the consumer could move on to information about performance, safety features, technical specifications, and prices of specific makes. The next step might be to locate a page that identifies dealers in the area, their respective inventories, and financing alternatives.

As an advertising medium, the Internet is particularly popular with companies selling products that involve extensive decision making. Ford Motor Co. shifted a significant portion of its national magazine advertising budget to interactive media, including

www.iab.net

How should "unconventional" advertising media be evaluated?

Conventional media (radio, television, magazines, newspaper, billboards) are very important outlets for advertising as are some of the newer vehicles such as e-mail and websites with banner and pop-up ads. But marketers are constantly on the alert for new ways and places to put their messages in front of prospects. You may be familiar with television monitors with advertising in airport waiting areas, grocery stores, and other places people wait in line or congregate. You've also seen ads on buses, taxis, blimps, hot air balloons, shopping carts, racing cars, the clothing of professional athletes, and in sports arenas. Even the uniforms of college athletes carry the logos of sponsoring equipment makers.

Marketers continue to look for places where they can put ads with the knowledge that these places are visited by their target customers. Some recent examples of unconventional placements include advertising:

- Stenciled on sidewalks.
- On popcorn bags in theaters, airsickness bags on planes, automatic pinsetters in bowling alleys, and stall doors of public restrooms.

- At gasoline pumps via small television monitors that also present news clips.
- At the bottom of the cups used for holes on golf courses.
- Imprinted in the sand on beaches (created by a roller towed behind a tractor).
- On the sides of buildings projected with lasers.
- At ATM machines while transactions are being processed.
- On recycling bins, trash receptacles, and storage units.

An important consideration in selecting a place to put advertising is the cost versus the benefit. How would you go about evaluating one of these unconventional media sites?

Source: www.advertising.utexas.edu/world/Unconventional.asp.

---

the Internet. The company's primary site (*www.ford.com*) provides information about all the brands and directs customers to other sites including one where they can shop for a car and another where Ford owners can receive service reminders as well as recall information. The websites produce over a half million leads for Ford dealers a year, with some dealers claiming that 30% of their sales are now initiated on the Internet.[20]

Some small companies with limited promotional budgets have discovered that the Internet allows them to reach a broader geographic market. For example, Barbecue Renew, a Kirkland, Washington, retailer of barbecue-grill replacement parts, turned to the Internet after local newspaper ads proved unsuccessful. It now generates sales from all over the U.S. from its website.[21]

www.grillparts.com

Interactivity creates a very different environment for advertisers. On the plus side, the audience has demonstrated its interest by logging on, and the technology makes it easy to track the number of visitors to the site, how long they stay connected, and what areas of the site they visit. On the other hand, using this medium requires some proficiency with the technology on the part of recipients. Also, with hundreds of thousands of websites only a mouse click away, holding a visitor's attention is difficult.

Media decision makers abroad are faced with different conditions that require local knowledge. For example, the move toward greater democracy has created new media options in some eastern European countries, where private radio and television stations now can run up to four times as much advertising as was permitted on state-owned stations. On the other hand, print media in most of the world cannot offer the special editions and narrowly targeted audiences available in highly developed countries.

Evaluating the Advertising Effort

Top executives want proof that advertising is worthwhile. They want to know whether dollars spent on advertising are producing as many sales as could be reaped from the same dollars spent on other marketing activities. On the other

Gillette used a combination of out-of-home ads and viral marketing to introduce its Venus razor. Trucks such as this one at spring break sites informed women about the product. Visitors to the truck were invited to enter a sweepstakes and to send electronic greeting cards to friends that included an opportunity to also enter the contest. Since 20% of the sweepstakes' entries came from card recipients, Gillette felt the viral component of the campaign significantly expanded the audience.

hand, advertisers promise only that a certain number of people will be exposed to an ad. They do not guarantee a certain level of sales and, in most instances, would even find it impossible to indicate the portion of sales that are attributable to advertising.

Difficulty of Evaluation It is hard to measure the sales effectiveness of advertising. By the very nature of the marketing mix, all elements—including advertising—are so intertwined that it is nearly impossible to measure the effect of any one by itself. Factors that contribute to the difficulty of measuring the sales impact of advertising are:

- *Different objectives.* Although all advertising is ultimately intended to increase sales, individual ads may not be aimed at producing immediate results. For example, some ads simply announce new store hours or service policies. Other ads are designed to build corporate goodwill or contribute to a brand's position.

- *Effects over time.* Even an ad designed to have an immediate sales impact may produce results weeks or months after it appears. An ad may plant in the prospect's mind a seed that doesn't blossom into a sale for several weeks.

MARKETING IN THE INFORMATION ECONOMY

Is what you see what's really there?

The use of virtual television advertising, inserting images into live broadcasts or existing film so that they appear to be part of the actual or original setting, is becoming increasingly commonplace. For example, if an advertiser wants a can of a particular brand of soft drink to appear on a table in a scene of a previously filmed sitcom, it can be done. This is called virtual product placement.

The technology is similar to what has been used to make the puck more visible in televised hockey games or to highlight the first-down line in televised football games. Firms such as General Motors, Kodak, Tecate beer, and others are now arranging to have virtual signs with their names and logos appear on athletic fields, on scoreboards, and on stadium walls for television viewers to see.

One attraction of virtual advertising is that it can be inserted selectively so an advertiser can have its message seen only by consumers in certain broadcast areas. So, for example, with the Super Bowl, which is seen by a worldwide audience, the advertiser could select only the countries in which it does business. In addition to their use with the National Football League, virtual ads are appearing on broadcasts of major league baseball, professional soccer, motor racing, and horse racing.

Sources: Chris Zelkovich, "High-Tech Blamed for Bowl Glitches," *Toronto Star,* Feb. 5, 2002, p. E3; Michael Bartlett, "Virtual, Interactive Ads on Cubs–Padre Game Tonight," *News Bytes News Network,* July 31, 2001, accessed at *www.newsbytes.com,* item CX2001212U0899; Shelley Emling, "Virtual Product Placement Ads Coming to a Television Set Near You," *Austin-American Statesman,* Sept. 26, 2002, p. C1.

Starch Readership Service measures consumers' recollections of seeing or reading magazine ads. The tabs on this Stouffer's ad provide scores indicating what proportion of a sample of magazine readers recall noticing the ad, associating it with the brand, reading some of the copy, and reading most of the copy. An advertiser can compare the scores of its ads against those of other ads as an indication of effectiveness.

• *Measurement problems.* Consumers cannot usually say when or if a specific ad influenced their behavior, let alone if it caused them to buy. Human motivation is too complicated to be explained by a single factor.

In spite of these problems, advertisers try to measure advertising effectiveness because they must—and some knowledge is better than none. An ad's effectiveness may be tested before it is presented to the target audience, while it is being presented, or after it has completed its run.

Methods Used to Measure Effectiveness

Ad effectiveness measures are either direct or indirect. **Direct tests,** which compile the responses to an ad or a campaign, can be used only with a few types of ads. Tabulating the number of redemptions of a reduced-price coupon incorporated in an ad, for example, will indicate its effectiveness. Coupons frequently are coded so they can also be traced to the publications in which they were run. Another direct test of an ad's effectiveness is the number of inquiries received from an ad that offers additional information to prospects who call or write in.

Most other measures are **indirect tests** of effectiveness, or measures of something other than actual behavior. One of the most frequently used measures is advertising recall. Recall tests are based on the premise that an ad can have an effect only if it is perceived and remembered. Three common recall tests are:

• *Recognition*—showing people an ad and asking if they have seen it before.
• *Aided recall*—asking people if they can recall seeing any ads for a particular brand.
• *Unaided recall*—asking people if they can remember seeing any ads within an identified product category.

Refinements are constantly being made in advertising testing. Developments in areas such as laboratory test markets and computer simulations hold promise for the future. However, the complexity of decision making, combined with the multitude of influences on the buyer, will continue to make measuring the effectiveness of advertising a difficult task.

Organizing for Advertising

There are three ways a firm can manage its advertising:

• Develop an internal advertising department.
• Use an outside advertising agency.
• Use a combination of an internal department and an outside advertising agency.

Regardless of which alternative is selected, generally the same specialized skills are necessary to do the advertising job. Creative people are needed to prepare the copy, generate audio and/or video material, and design the formats. Media experts are required to select the appropriate media, buy the time or space, and arrange for the scheduled appearance of the ads. And managerial skills are essential to plan and administer the entire advertising program.

Internal Departments

All these advertising tasks, some of them, or just overall direction can be performed by an internal department. A company whose advertising is a substantial part of its marketing mix will usually have its own advertising department. Large retailers, for example, have their own advertising departments, and many do not use advertising agencies at all. If a company has adopted the marketing concept, the advertising department head will report to the organization's top marketing executive.

Advertising Agencies

Many companies, especially producers, use advertising agencies to carry out some or all of their advertising activities. An **advertising agency** is an independent company that provides specialized advertising services. Many large agencies have expanded the services they offer to include sales promotion, public relations, and even broader marketing assistance. As a result, they are frequently called upon to assist in strategic planning, marketing research, new-product development, package design, and selection of product names.

Advertising agencies plan and execute entire advertising campaigns. They employ more advertising specialists than their clients do, because they spread the cost over many accounts. A client company can benefit from an agency's experience gained from other products and campaigns.

Inside Department and Outside Agency

Many firms have their own advertising department and also use an advertising agency. The internal department acts as a liaison with the agency, giving the company greater control over this major expenditure. The advertising department approves the agency's plans and ads, is responsible for preparing and administering the advertising budget, and coordinates advertising with personal selling. It may also handle direct marketing, dealer displays, and other promotional activities if they are not handled by the agency.

Sales Promotion

Sales promotion is one of the most loosely used terms in the marketing vocabulary. We define **sales promotion** as demand-stimulating devices designed to supplement advertising and facilitate personal selling. Examples of sales promotion devices are coupons, premiums, in-store displays, sponsorships, trade shows, samples, in-store demonstrations, and contests.

Sales promotions are conducted by producers and middlemen. The target for producers' sales promotions may be middlemen, end users—households or business users—or the producers' own sales forces. Middlemen direct sales promotion at their sales people or prospects further down the channel of distribution.

Nature and Scope

Sales promotion is distinct from advertising or personal selling, but these three forms of promotion are often used together in an integrated fashion. For example, prospective customers may be generated from people who enter a contest to win a copier at the Canon website and at a Canon exhibit at an office equipment trade show. These prospects might be sent some direct-mail and e-mail advertising and then be contacted by a sales person.

There are two categories of sales promotion: *trade promotions*, directed to the members of the distribution channel, and *consumer promotions*, aimed at consumers. It may surprise you to learn that manufacturers as a group spend about twice as much on trade promotion as they do on advertising, and an amount about equal to their expenditures on consumer promotions.[22]

The magnitude of sales promotion activities is mind-boggling. Although no statistics are available on total expenditures, the trade publication *PROMO Magazine*, compiles an annual estimate that places the figure at about $100 billion in 2001, an increase of about 100% since 1990.[23]

Several factors in the marketing environment contribute to the popularity of sales promotion:

- *Short-term results.* Sales promotions such as couponing and trade allowances produce quicker, more measurable sales results than brand-building advertising.
- *Competitive pressure.* If competitors offer buyers price reductions, contests, or other incentives, a firm may feel forced to retaliate with its own sales promotions.
- *Buyers' expectations.* Once they are offered purchase incentives, consumers and channel members get used to them and soon begin expecting them.
- *Low quality of retail selling.* Many retailers use inadequately trained sales clerks or have switched to self-service. For these outlets, sales promotion devices such as product displays and samples often are the only effective promotional tools available at the point of purchase.

One problem management faces is that many sales promotion techniques are short-run, tactical actions. Coupons, premiums, and contests, for example, are designed to produce immediate (but short-lived) responses. As a result, they tend to be used as stopgap measures to reverse unexpected sales declines rather than as parts of an integrated marketing program.

Sales promotion should be included in a company's promotion plans, along with advertising and personal selling. This means setting sales promotion objectives and strategies, determining a sales promotion budget, and selecting appropriate sales promotion techniques.

Determining Objectives and Strategies
Three broad objectives of sales promotion were suggested when the term was introduced in Chapter 17:

- Stimulating business user or household demand for a product.
- Improving the marketing performance of middlemen and sales people.
- Supplementing advertising and facilitating personal selling.

A single sales promotion technique may accomplish one or two—but probably not all—of these objectives.

Determining Budgets
The sales promotion budget should be established as a specific part of the budget for the total promotional mix. If sales promotion is included in an advertising or public relations budget, it may be overlooked or poorly integrated with the other components of promotion. Setting a separate budget for sales promotion forces a company to recognize and manage it.

Within the concept of developing an integrated marketing communications strategy, the amount budgeted for sales promotion should be determined by the task or objective method. This forces management to identify specific objectives and the sales promotion techniques that will be used to accomplish them.

Directing the Sales Promotion Effort Many marketers plan and implement their sales promotion efforts internally. Others rely on specialized agencies. Sales promotion agencies fall into two primary categories. The first category is called *promotional service agencies*. They specialize in executing sales promotion programs such as sampling and couponing.

The other type of organization, called a *promotional marketing agency*, provides management advice and strategic planning of sales promotion as well as execution of the resulting program. As the use of sales promotion has increased, more organizations have turned to promotional marketing agencies for guidance. Rather than treat sales promotion as a periodic, single-shot sales stimulator, more firms are now integrating it into a planned strategy with long-term goals.

Selecting the Appropriate Techniques A key step in sales promotion management is deciding which devices will help the organization reach its promotional goals. Factors that influence the choice of promotional devices include:

- *Nature of the target audience.* Is the target group loyal to a competing brand? If so, a high-value incentive or coupon may be necessary to disrupt customers' purchase patterns. Is the product bought on impulse? If so, an eye-catching point-of-sale display may be enough to generate sales.
- *Nature of the product.* Does the product lend itself to sampling, demonstration, or multiple-item purchases?
- *Cost of the device.* Sampling to a large market may be prohibitively expensive.
- *Current economic conditions.* Coupons, premiums, and rebates are good options during periods of recession or inflation, when consumers are particularly price conscious.

Common sales promotion techniques are shown in Table 19.4, where they are divided into three categories based on the target audience: business users or households, middlemen, and producers' sales forces. To illustrate the significance of sales promotion, several of these techniques are described below.

Sampling. Sampling is the only sure way of getting a product in the hands of potential customers. And it would seem to be a powerful motivator. In a national survey of consumers, 89% of the respondents said they "feel better" about purchasing a product after sampling it, and 69% believed samples and demonstrations influence their purchase decisions more than radio or television ads.[24]

TABLE 19.4	**Major Sales Promotion Devices, Grouped by Target Audience**	
Business Users or Households	**Middlemen and Their Sales Forces**	**Producers' Own Sales Forces**
Coupons	Trade shows and exhibitions	Sales contests
Cash rebates	Point-of-purchase displays	Demonstration model of product
Premiums (gifts)	Free goods	Sample of product
Free samples	Advertising allowances	
Contests and sweepstakes	Contests for sales people	
Point-of-purchase displays	Training middlemen's sales forces	
Product demonstrations	Product demonstrations	
Trade shows and exhibitions	Advertising specialties	
Advertising specialties		

Sampling is not a new technique. A New Jersey promotions firm has been assembling samples of relevant products and distributing them to new mothers for over 45 years. However, in order to get the product in the right hands, creativity has increased. For example, marketers that share the same target markets are teaming up. Some west coast luxury resorts are offering guests a no-strings-attached opportunity to take a $150,000 Aston Martin convertible for a two-hour drive, a British Columbia hotel provides guests with a gift basket of new products, and the Ritz-Carlton in New York supplies guests with Burberry raincoats to use during their stay.[25] S. C. Johnson, the maker of Off! insect repellent, placed samples of its product in a million new Sunbeam barbecue grills. And snack food makers have joined with Blockbuster to give video renters samples of new products.

Sampling is most commonly done through the mail. Other methods include newspaper inserts and direct person-to-person handouts on the street or in stores or malls. Some firms are experimenting with sampling through their websites on the Internet. The advantage is that the people requesting a sample are most likely very interested in the product. However, the interest could wane while they wait for the sample to be delivered.

The cost per thousand of sampling is much higher than advertising. However, the conversion rate (the proportion of people exposed who buy the product) is typically around 10% for sampling, which is considerably better than advertising.[26]

Couponing. The volume of manufacturers' coupons directed to consumers is staggering. In 2001 nearly 240 *billion* were distributed, but only 4 billion (less than 2%) were redeemed. Despite the low level of redemption, consumers saved over $3 billion by using coupons.[27]

Most coupons are distributed as freestanding inserts (FSI) in newspapers, which explains why the Sunday paper is so heavy! Other methods of distribution are direct mail, in magazines, and coupons packaged in or on products. An increasing number of coupons are being distributed in retail stores. One technique is to offer coupons in a dispenser attached to the retail shelf where a product is displayed. The rationale is that consumers, at the point of purchase, may be influenced to select a particular brand if a coupon is readily available. Not surprisingly, these coupons have redemption rates as much as nine times higher than coupons included in newspapers. Another method growing in popularity is to electronically dispense coupons at the checkout counter on the basis of the items a consumer purchases. Thus, when a shopper buys a particular brand of a product, a coupon might be issued for a competing alternative. This approach is designed to encourage brand switching on the consumer's next shopping trip. Also, consumers who are members of retailers' frequent-shopper programs are given coupons when they make purchases.

A small but growing number of coupons are being distributed on the Internet. Combining the Internet and coupons provides access to hard-to-reach audiences. For example, college students can log onto coolsavings.com, become registered members, and download coupons for redemption at campus-area restaurants and retail stores.

Although most coupons are for frequently-purchased convenience items, they are used by marketers of other products as well. When its share of new car sales were down in 1999, GM mailed millions of $500 coupons to U. S. consumers.

Critics of coupons point out that they are expensive. The average face value of a coupon for a packaged good is 74 cents.[28] Another problem is that they may undermine brand loyalty. Coupons may teach consumers to seek out the best bargains rather than consistently select a particular brand. Finally, some marketers are discouraged by the low redemption rate. Procter & Gamble discontinued couponing for its Luvs disposable diapers after only 5 million were redeemed out of 500 million distributed. The company explained on its website (*www.luvs.com/faqs*) that rather than spend money on coupons it was going to lower the everyday price of the diapers.

www.popai.org

www.coolsavings.com

Black & Decker received an award from the industry's professional association for this point-of-purchase promotion.

www.popai.com

However, after receiving numerous complaints from mothers, the company reinstated coupons but only for consumers who register to receive them.

Couponing has increased in other parts of the world, but the methods of distribution are different from those in the U.S. Whereas the bulk of coupons in the U.S. are FSIs, in Canada, coupons are most often included as a part of ads. Spanish and Italian marketers place coupons in or on packages. And in several other European countries, coupons are distributed door to door.

Sponsorships and Event Marketing. Corporate sponsorship of events has become a major promotional activity. Worldwide expenditures exceed $24 billion, with $9.5 billion of the total spent in North America.[29] Most corporate sponsorships are for sports events and charitable causes. Auto racing draws the greatest amount of corporate sponsorships, estimated at $1.35 billion in 2000.[30] The remainder includes concerts and entertainment tours, festivals and fairs, and the arts. Considering that there are over 50,000 festivals and events in the U.S. each year, the range of sponsorship opportunities is almost unlimited.

Sponsorship is typically viewed as a long-range image-building activity; for example, the U.S. Postal Service sponsors a bicycle racing team and its star, Lance Armstrong, a multiple winner of the Tour de France. But it can also have an effect on sales. When Eddie Cheever won the Indianapolis 500 race in a car sponsored by Rachel's Gourmet Snacks, the small Minnesota firm was able to sign up new distributors all over the country.[31]

Unlike advertising time or space in which the advertiser is in complete control, sponsorship is sometimes shared. As a result, a sponsor has to be very explicit about what will be provided and what is expected. Reebok withdrew its $6.4 million sponsorship of the 2000 Sydney Olympics when organizers arranged for other sportswear firms to provide hats and rugby shirts.[32]

The principal difficulty in justifying sponsorship expenditures is measuring their effectiveness. Because sales are usually not the primary objective, the value of a sponsorship is frequently determined by the amount of publicity it generates for the sponsor (and comparison of that to the cost of an equivalent amount of advertising). An alternative approach is a survey of attendees before and after an event to determine awareness and brand preference.

www.ussponsorship.com

Trade Shows.   Associations in industries as diverse as computers, sporting goods, food, and broadcasting sponsor trade shows. There are 5,000 trade shows a year in Canada and the U.S. alone. About half restrict attendance to business representatives, whereas the remainder allow consumers to attend. In a typical year, trade shows host about 1.3 million exhibitors and attract 85 million visitors.[33]

The appeal of a trade show is efficiency. In one place and in a compressed amount of time, trade shows allow buyers and sellers to see and interact with many of their counterparts.

On the other hand, trade shows are expensive for exhibitors. In addition to the cost of the booth and the living expenses of the company representatives during the show, transporting equipment and display material is costly. As a result, firms are selective about the trade shows they attend, often requiring the sponsors to provide demographic profiles of the attendees.

The trade show industry is on track to continue growing. Much of the growth has come from offshoots of existing broad-based events. Like advertising, trade shows are seeking out narrower market segments and offering more specialized topics.

Product Placements.   For many years firms have paid fees to have their products used as props in movies, and the practice is growing. Among the most notable are *Back to the Future* (for the sheer number of placements), *E.T.* (for the impact placement had on the sales of Reese's Pieces) and *Cast Away* (for the prominence of the product, Federal Express, in the movie). With the exception of game shows such as *Wheel of Fortune*, television has been less open to product placements because paid placements must be disclosed to the audience. However, that may be changing. For example, participants in the *Survivor* shows on CBS are seen consuming the sponsors' products. Some examples of product placements are shown in Table 19.5. Product placements also occur in novels and video games.

Placements have proved very beneficial to some products, taking them from virtual obscurity to national prominence. You may have noticed product placements, but if you're like most consumers these props simply added to the realism of the experience, and that is the strength of a product placement. It displays the product in a noncommercial way, sometimes linking it with the show's characters and creating a positive association for the audience.

www.upp.net

TABLE 19.5 Examples of Product Placements

Movie or TV Show	Product(s)
GoldenEye	IBM computers, BMW, Perrier, and Omega
Baywatch	Hawaiian Tropic suntan products
Seinfeld	*TV Guide,* Snapple, Mars candy bars, Junior Mints
You've Got Mail	America Online
Deep Impact, Object of My Affections, 3rd Rock from the Sun	Avalon bottled water
The Horse Whisperer	EquiSearch.com, Range Rover
Risky Business, Men in Black	RayBan sunglasses
Flubber, He Got Game	RAM Sports (balls)
Chicago Hope	Heartstream Inc. (heart defibrillator)
Ace Ventura: Pet Detective	Gatorade

Sources: Dale D. Buss, "Making Your Mark in Movies and TV," *Nation's Business,* December 1998, pp. 28+; Wayne Friedman and Jean Halliday, "BMW's MGM Promotional Deal Puts 007 in Z8 Driver's Seat," *Advertising Age,* Mar. 1, 1999, p. 8; *www.upp.net/hall-of-fame.html.*

As noted earlier, technology has made "virtual product placement" in films possible. This greatly increases opportunities for product placements. For example, newer products can replace older ones or simply be added to remakes of movies or syndicated television shows. Or different brands can be displayed in a show broadcast in different parts of the country or the world. Advertisers, concerned with the implications of video recorders that can be programmed to automatically eliminate commercials during playback, are enthusiastic about increasing product placements.

Public Relations

Public relations is a management tool designed to favorably influence attitudes toward an organization, its products, and its policies. It is an often overlooked form of promotion. In most organizations this promotional tool is typically a stepchild, relegated far behind personal selling, advertising, and sales promotion. There are several reasons for management's lack of attention to public relations:

www.instituteforpr.com

- *Organizational structure.* In most companies, public relations is not the responsibility of the marketing department. If there is an organized effort, it is usually handled by a small public relations department that reports directly to top management.

- *Inadequate definitions.* The term public relations is used loosely by both businesses and the public. There are no generally accepted definitions of the term. As a result, what actually constitutes an organized public relations effort often is not clearly defined.

- *Unrecognized benefits.* Only recently have many organizations come to appreciate the value of good public relations. As the cost of promotion has gone up, firms are realizing that positive exposure through the media or as a result of community involvement can produce a high return on the investment of time and effort.

Nature and Scope

Public relations activities typically are designed to build or maintain a favorable image for an organization with its various publics—customers, prospects, stockholders, employees, labor unions, the local community, and the government. We're aware that this description is quite similar to our definition of institutional advertising. However, unlike advertising, public relations need not use the media to communicate its message.

Good public relations can be achieved in many ways. Some examples are supporting charitable projects (by supplying volunteer labor or other resources), participating in community service events, sponsoring nonprofessional athletic teams, funding the arts, producing an employee or customer newsletter, and disseminating information through exhibits, displays, and tours. Major firms such as ExxonMobil and Archer Daniels Midland sponsor shows on public television (PBS) as part of their public relations effort.

Publicity as a Form of Public Relations

Publicity is any communication about an organization, its products, or policies through the media not paid for by the organization. Publicity usually takes the form of a news story appearing in the media or an endorsement provided by an individual, either informally or in a speech or interview. This is good publicity.

There is also, of course, bad publicity—a negative story about a firm or its product appearing in the media. In a society that is increasingly sensitive about the environment and in which news media are quick to report mistakes, organizations tend to focus on this negative dimension of publicity. As a result, managers are so concerned with avoiding bad publicity that they overlook the potential of good publicity.

There are three means for gaining good publicity:

- *Prepare and distribute a story (called a news release) to the media.* The intention is for the selected newspapers, television stations, or other media to report the information as news.

- *Personal communication with a group.* A press conference will draw media representatives if they think the subject or speaker has news value. Company tours and speeches to civic or professional groups are other forms of individual-to-group communications.

- *One-on-one personal communication, often called lobbying.* Companies lobby legislators or other powerful people in an attempt to influence their opinions, and subsequently their decisions.

Publicity can help accomplish any communication objective. It can be used to announce new products, publicize new policies, recognize employees, describe research breakthroughs, or report financial performance. But to receive coverage, the message, person, group, or event being publicized must be viewed by the media as newsworthy. This is what distinguishes publicity from advertising—publicity is not "forced" on the audience. This is also the source of its primary benefit. The credibility of publicity typically is much higher than advertising. If an organization tells you its product is great, you may well be skeptical. But if an independent, objective third party says on the evening news that the product is great, you are more likely to believe it.

Other benefits of publicity are:

- *Lower cost.* Publicity usually costs less than advertising or personal selling because there are no media space or time costs for conveying the message and no sales people to support.

- *Increased attention.* Many consumers are conditioned to ignore advertising or at least pay it scant attention. Publicity is presented as editorial material or news, so it is more likely to be watched, listened to, or get read.

- *More information.* Because it is presented as editorial material, publicity can contain greater detail than the usual ad. More information and persuasive content can be included in the message.

- *Timeliness.* A company can put out a news release very quickly when some unexpected event occurs.

Of course, publicity has limitations:

- *Loss of control over the message.* An organization has no guarantee that a news release will appear in the media. In addition, there is no way to control how much or what portion of a story the media will print or broadcast.

- *Limited exposure.* The media will typically use news releases to fill space when there is a lack of other news and only use them once. If the target audience misses the message when it is presented, there is no second or third chance.

- *Publicity is not free.* Even though there are no media time and space costs, there are expenses in generating ideas for publicity and in preparing and disseminating news releases.

www.microsoft.com/ presspass/ todaysnews.htm

Recognizing the value of publicity, some organizations have one or more staff members who generate news releases. These stories are sent to the media and are typically made available to anyone via the company's website. For example, Microsoft provided an extensive collection of releases useful in learning about the company's perspective on its recent antitrust case as well as other issues.

Summary

Advertising, sales promotion, and public relations are the nonpersonal, mass-communications components of a company's promotional mix. Advertising consists of all the activities involved in presenting to an audience a nonpersonal, sponsor-identified, paid-for message about a product or organization. The total advertising expenditure in a firm is typically 1% to 3% of sales, considerably less than the average cost of personal selling. Most advertising dollars are spent on television, newspapers, and direct mail. Other frequently used media are radio, magazines, yellow pages, and out-of-home displays. The Internet is increasing in importance as an ad medium.

Advertising can be directed to consumers or businesses. Ads are classified according to whether they are intended to stimulate primary or selective demand. Primary demand is demand for a generic category of a product. Primary demand ads are used to introduce new products and to sustain demand for a product throughout its life cycle. Selective-demand ads emphasize a particular brand or company. They are divided into product ads, that focus on a brand, or institutional ads, that focus on an organization. Product ads are further subdivided into direct action ads, which call for immediate action, and indirect-action ads, which are intended to stimulate demand over a longer period of time. A selective-demand ad that makes reference to one or more competitors is called a comparative ad. Finally, ad messages are transmitted through commercial or social sources. Although not strictly advertising, social sources are very effective when they can be stimulated or simulated by advertisers.

An advertising campaign involves transforming a theme into a coordinated advertising program. Designing a campaign includes defining objectives, establishing a budget, creating new messages, selecting media, and evaluating the effort. Objectives can range from creating awareness of a brand to generating sales. Advertising budgets can be extended through vertical and horizontal cooperative arrangements. An advertising message—consisting of the appeal and the execution of the ad—is influenced by the target audience and the media used.

A major task in developing a campaign is to select the advertising media—the general type, the particular category, and the specific vehicle. The choice should be based on the characteristics of the medium, which determine how effectively it conveys the message, and its ability to reach the target audience. Each of the media that carry advertising have characteristics that make them more or less suitable for a particular advertising objective.

A difficult task in advertising management is evaluating the effectiveness of the advertising effort—both the entire campaign and individual ads. Some methods of advertising allow for direct measures of effect, but most can only be evaluated indirectly. A commonly used technique measures recall of an ad. To carry out an advertising program, a firm may rely on its own advertising department, an advertising agency, or a combination of the two.

Sales promotion consists of demand-stimulating devices designed to supplement advertising and facilitate personal selling. The amount of sales promotion increased considerably in the past two decades, as management sought measurable, short-term sales results.

Sales promotion should receive the same strategic attention that a company gives to advertising and personal selling, including setting objectives and establishing a budget. Sales promotion can be directed toward final consumers, middlemen, or a company's own employees. Management can choose from a variety of sales promotion devices. Some of the most common are samples, coupons, sponsorships, trade shows, and product placements. Like advertising, sales promotion performance should be evaluated.

Public relations is a management tool designed to favorably influence attitudes toward an organization, its products, and its policies. It is a frequently overlooked form of promotion. Publicity, a part of public relations, is any communication about an organization, its products, or policies through the media that is not paid for by the organization. Typically these two activities are handled in a department separate from the marketing department in a firm. Nevertheless, the management process of planning, implementation, and evaluation should be applied to these activities in the same way it is applied to advertising, sales promotion, and personal selling.

More about Royal Caribbean

Royal Caribbean allows travelers to book reservations through its own website, and a few of them do; about 1.5% of all U.S. cruise tickets are currently sold online. But the company also uses its site to build and protect business for its highly valued travel agent partners, who book about 95% of all cruises. The site refers travelers to agents at several points in the booking process in the section, "Travel Agents: A Great Resource," and it will even help site visitors find a local agent by ZIP code if the customer decides to turn the transaction over to a real person. If so, Royal Caribbean pays the agent the full commission no matter how much of the transaction was completed online. And Royal Caribbean makes sure that no cruise discounts are available anywhere, including on the Internet, that are better than those its travel agents are able to offer.

Still, the cruise industry faces a challenge when it comes to working with travel agents. In the late 1990s Renaissance Cruises decided to pursue direct-mail, telemarketing, and website promotions, thus bypassing agents, some of whom retaliated by actively discouraging customers from booking Renaissance vacations. The company ended up shutting down its consumer online booking service, which is now available only to travel agents, and disbanding its telemarketing team. The money it had saved in travel agents' commissions was more than offset by the cost of the direct promotions and the price cuts Renaissance had to offer to gain back the business that travel agents were sending away.

Royal Caribbean has never committed so serious an error, but it may still have some catching up to do where travel agents are concerned. A recent "Cruise Week" poll rated the firm near the bottom of its industry category (Major Cruise Lines) in terms of day-to-day dealings with agents, prices, and commitment to the distribution channel. Smaller and medium-sized agencies were particularly dissatisfied, and the firm's overall rating was 6.4 out of a possible 10. So the company will have to improve its relationships with its distribution channel even as it continues to woo new customers through promotion.[34]

1. Are the significant promotional and distribution roles travel agents play in Royal Caribbean's marketing effort typical of other services firms? Why or why not?

2. Would it be wise for Royal Caribbean to attempt to gain more direct control of its promotion to consumers? If so, what promotional tools should it consider using?

Key Terms and Concepts

Advertising (534)
Business-to-consumer advertising (536)
Business-to-business advertising (536)
Primary-demand advertising (536)
Selective-demand advertising (536)

Comparison advertising (537)
Product advertising (537)
Institutional advertising (537)
Advertising campaign (538)
Cooperative advertising (540)
Advertising media (542)
Cost per thousand (CPM) (543)

Direct tests (549)
Indirect tests (549)
Advertising agency (550)
Sales promotion (550)
Public relations (556)
Publicity (556)

Questions and Problems

1. How do you account for the variation in advertising expenditures as a percentage of sales among the different companies in Table 19.2?

2. Select a general type of advertising medium for each of the following products and explain your choice.

   a. Internet-based investment service
   b. Hanes pantyhose
   c. Tax-preparation service
   d. Mortuary
   e. Toys for young children
   f. Plastic clothespins

3. Many grocery product and candy manufacturers earmark a good portion of their advertising budgets for use in magazines. In contrast, department stores use newspapers more than local radio stations as an advertising medium. Are these media choices wise for these industries and firms? Explain.

4. Why is it worthwhile to pretest ads before they appear in the media? How could a test market be used to pretest an ad? (You may want to refresh your memory with a review of test marketing in Chapter 7.)

5. What procedures can a firm use to determine how many sales dollars resulted from a direct-mail ad?

6. What type of sales promotion would be effective for selling expensive consumer products such as houses, automobiles, or cruise trips? How about expensive business products?

7. What advantage would sampling have over advertising for a new brand of sunscreen lotion?

8. Should virtual product placement raise any ethical concerns for the media?

9. Bring to class an article from a daily newspaper that appears to be the result of a firm's publicity efforts. Summarize the points made in the article that may benefit the firm. Could advertising create the same benefits?

Interactive Marketing Exercises

1. Common appeals or benefits and examples of product categories in which they are frequently used include:
   - Physical well-being (food, nonprescription drugs)
   - Social acceptance (cosmetics, health and beauty aids)
   - Material success (automobiles, investments)
   - Recognition and status (clothing, jewelry)
   - Sensory pleasure (movies, candy)
   - Time savings (websites)
   - Peace of mind (insurance, tires)

Find print ads that make use of five of these appeals. Comment on the effectiveness of the execution (the compatability of the appeal and the method of gaining attention).

2. Visit a supermarket, drugstore, or hardware store, and make a list of all the sales promotion tools you observe. Describe how each one relates to the sales promotion objectives described in the chapter. Which do you think are particularly effective, and why?

Cases for Part 6

<table>
<tr><td>CASE
1</td><td>Nike</td></tr>
</table>

Maintaining a Promotional Edge

When Nike was launched in the 1960s, athletic shoes were seen as primarily functional, not fashionable. There was very little competition, and most manufacturers of athletic footwear occupied a particular market niche. For instance, basketball players wore Converse, track athletes and football players wore adidas and Puma, and Keds appealed to those desiring casual styles. Nike's founders, Phil Knight and Bill Bowerman (Knight's former track coach at the University of Oregon) also had a niche in mind. They wanted to provide competitive athletes with a high-performance shoe and, along the way, unseat adidas as the market leader for running shoes.

Almost 40 years later, Nike has achieved its goal and more. It is now in first place with a 42% share of the athletic footwear market. Knight helped his company become the industry's front-runner by expanding his original vision to include casual, as well as competitive athletes. Nike also designs shoes for a multitude of sports besides just running, and has begun marketing sporting equipment and clothing. Along the way, Nike adopted one of the most memorable catch phrases in advertising by encouraging potential customers to "Just Do It."

Despite these successes, Nike faces some significant hurdles, including a flat market, intense competition, a dicey public relations issue, and changing trends in footwear styles.

Getting into the Race

Because they had limited resources and unlimited confidence in their product, Knight and Bowerman did very little marketing initially. Their approach was to persuade top runners to wear their shoes, and let the athletes promote Nike products by word of mouth. The approach worked and sales grew rapidly, reaching $14 million by 1976. Coincidentally a physical fitness revolution was taking place in the U.S. and the number of "weekend warriors" who needed athletic shoes was growing. Even more important, athletic shoes became fashionable wardrobe staples. Nike was well positioned to take advantage of these developments, and during the next five years, sales and profits surged at an astonishing rate of 75% per year.

Nike stumbled in the 1980s. Symptomatic of its problem was a failure to recognize the aerobics boom. Thinking it was a fad, Nike virtually ignored this market segment and the women who were its major participants. When it finally did produce a shoe for aerobics, it was functional, but not attractive. By not keeping in touch with current market trends, Nike's market share declined from 50% in 1980 to 22% in 1986 as competitors such as Reebok and L.A.Gear did a better job of giving customers what they wanted. To reverse this trend, Nike adjusted by recognizing consumers' desires for appearance, style, and image, as well as functional performance. The company's new sense for the market was best reflected in signing Michael Jordan to an endorsement contract in 1985. Air Jordans, a shoe focused on the basketball category, eventually accounted for 25% of the total sales of athletic footwear. Ads for the shoe emphasized fashion and lifestyle along with performance, redefining how Nike products would be marketed. The "Just Do It" campaign debuted in 1988 appealed to every person's desire to improve, regardless of his or her athletic abilities.

During the 1990s, Nike expanded its product mix to include apparel, equipment, and accessories. Nike also began sponsoring a variety of sporting events, including golf tournaments and soccer matches. It continued to sign famous athletes as endorsers and began sponsoring professional and collegiate teams. The trademark Nike "swoosh" became ubiquitous, making the company highly visible to spectators and television audiences. In addition, Nike began utilizing a promotional tactic now known as *guerrilla marketing*. By running ads in and around events it hadn't paid to sponsor, Nike was able to garner much of the goodwill that sponsorship generates. It became so adept at this that during the 1998 Winter Olympics, 73% of people surveyed mistakenly thought Nike was an official sponsor. The result of all these efforts was a sales explosion, from $3.8 billion in 1994 to $9.2 billion in 1997. That same year, Nike's market share climbed back to 48% and the company achieved $796 million in earnings, its highest ever.

Sweating Out Some Challenges

Nike found it could not sustain this growth, however, and sales remained flat for the next three years, hovering around $9 billion a year. In addition, earnings began to decline, reaching only $451 million in 2001. Apparently not learning from its previous mistakes, Nike missed out on a new market trend when "brown" shoes began to become popular in the late 1990s. Timberland, the leading manufacturer of brown shoes and hiking boots, benefited greatly from this new fashion direction. New Balance responded by purchasing Dunham, another maker of muted footwear. But Nike was slow to react, and passed up on an opportunity to acquire North Face Inc., a company well known for its outdoor clothing and equipment. "It would have doubled the business overnight and made Nike a dominant player," complained a former Nike executive. Nike did eventually introduce a line of "all-conditions" footwear, but by that time, its market share had slipped subtantially.

Nike was also late in getting onboard with extreme sports enthusiasts. Once a very small niche, extreme sports have exploded in popularity, particularly with affluent, suburban kids. Extreme footwear isn't just functional, it's fashionable, and it's also one of the fastest-growing segments in athletic shoes. A sign of the times is the fact that a recent market research survey of teenage boys found that they admire Tony Hawk (a *retired* skateboarder) more than Michael Jordan.

Nike has had difficulty breaking into this market because the company was viewed as being too traditional by the antiestablishment participants and fans of the X-Games. Some of them even displayed bumper stickers reading, "Don't Do It." Now Nike has a skateboard division that recently partnered with a company called Savier to introduce a new line of skate shoes. It also purchased Hurley International, Inc., a company that makes skate and surfer fashions.

Also contributing to its falling market share was Nike's emphasis on high-priced footwear, despite the fact that consumers were balking at the prices for athletic shoes. Nike reintroduced its classic Air Jordans in 2001, with a not-so-classic price of $200. Although the shoes were gussied up in a metallic box and accompanied by a CD, sales failed to meet Nike's expectations. Nike's other pricey offerings included its Shox line ($143 a pair) and Presto slip-ons (ranging up to $95 a pair.) "They put too much emphasis on new technologies like Shox and lost market share

in the midpriced arena," pointed out the CEO of a large footwear retail chain.

Committing a Foot Fault

The firm suffered a public relations setback when it was accused of working with subcontractors who used child labor in Third World "sweatshops" to manufacture Nike products. Its image was further tarnished when Knight withdrew funding for the University of Oregon after students there protested these practices. The company responded to the accusations by conducting audits at each of its factories to ensure children were not working at the plants, but the damage had been done.

One college student decided to press Nike about the issue by ordering a pair of personalized sneakers from Nike's website with the word "sweatshop" printed where most buyers would put their initials or nickname. Nike refused to fill his order, and the student shared the incident with friends and family via e-mail. To his surprise, his e-mail message was widely circulated across the Internet. But instead of generating negative publicity for Nike, his story spurred interest in the personalized sneakers. One Nike manager commented, "Certainly, this has been a more effective marketing campaign than we could have launched on our own."

Staying Ahead of the Competition

When Nike failed to capitalize on new trends, such as brown shoes and extreme sports, it opened doors to other competitors. New Balance's share of the market increased from 3.7% in 1999 to 11% in 2001, and its revenues grew 42% to $813 million. It did that by spending a relatively modest $13 million on advertising, compared to $155 million for Nike and $49 million for Reebok. Although it ranks number four in market share behind Nike, adidas, and Reebok, New Balance has the highest level of brand loyalty among its competitors. It accomplished this by targeting a slightly older group (ages 25 to 45), and by providing a variety of width sizes. Paul Heffernan, vice president for global marketing at New Balance, commented, "I can't tell you how many people tell me that we make the only shoes they can wear."

In 2001, adidas replaced Reebok as the number two athletic shoe company in the U.S., as Reebok's market share fell under 12%. However, Reebok's once wildly successful aerobics shoes were experiencing a comeback because 1980s fashion suddenly became hip again. In an effort to court the edgy, urban market, Reebok signed tennis-playing Venus Williams and basketball star Allen Iverson to lucrative endorsement contracts, then watched as demand for their tennis and basketball shoes rose more than 50%.

On the other hand, adidas put its money into the 2002 World Cup. It spent $36.8 million on this single soccer event and hoped to succeed in promoting its new $200 "Predator Mania" shoe. The high-end soccer shoe market is virtually owned by adidas, with a 70% share, although Nike has its own $200 shoe, called the "Mercurial Vapor." Nike, is trying to capture some of adidas's market share, and spent more than it ever had before in promoting its soccer shoes during the World Cup. By doing so, it is hoping to increase its marketing presence overseas, where soccer is the number one sport.

The granddaddy of all the athletic shoe companies filed for bankruptcy in 2001. Converse announced it would shut three plants and lay off 1,000 employees because it had not had a successful new product since it introduced Chuck Taylor All-Star basketball shoes in the 1950s. In 1995, Converse stopped making shoes for running, walking, tennis, and football, to concentrate solely on basketball, but even reintroducing the classic Chuck Taylors couldn't stop the company's slide. One industry analyst explained, "Converse has steadfastly refused to make itself popular. Nike and Reebok own the market. They've done whatever they could to create a product that was novel and exciting."

Reformulating Its Game Plan

One of Nike's most exciting new products has been the Presto, which is available in six different styles and a mind-boggling 150 color combinations. Most of the styles are slip-ons without laces, and they range in price from $36 for infants to $95. For $95, consumers can go to Nike's website and choose a style and the colors, and even have the shoes personalized. (Just don't ask for "sweatshop.") Nike positioned the Presto as a fashion item instead of an athletic shoe, and did not hire a celebrity athlete to endorse the product. Instead it bought commercial time on MTV and Comedy Central, and placed ads in teen magazines. Nike budgeted $15 million to advertise the

Presto line, but that didn't matter once people started telling their friends about the cool new shoes. Initial inventory sold out across the country and one Foot Locker manager said, "If I could have a million pairs of them, I'd give my left arm."

In addition to its new "brown" shoes, skate shoes, and slip-ons, Nike is introducing baseball gloves and golfing equipment (including balls and clubs to complement Nike's already successful line of "swoosh" apparel). It signed up a number of professional athletes to promote the new products, including Tiger Woods, who recently began using the Nike golf balls and one of its drivers.

Nike also formed a new business unit to direct its women's division. Nike sales of women's footwear and apparel were $1.4 billion in 2000, comprising only 16% of the company's total revenues. Considering the fact that women's clothes account for almost half the total $36.4 billion U.S. market, it represents an area with significant opportunities for growth. To support this new venture, Nike is opening a number of retail stores devoted to women, and is creating "concept shops" within department stores to focus attention on its products. It even hired a designer to create a line of maternity fashions. Nike hopes to attract female buyers by combining hip fashion with athletic functionality. For instance, some of the clothes feature pockets for keys or CD players.

With the introduction of these new product lines, Nike seems determined not to miss out on any significant market trends, as it has in the past. But as it continues to delve into additional product areas and face tougher competition, promotion will play a major role in determining whether Nike will remain the industry's front-runner. Perhaps it is predestined, however. After all, Knight named his company Nike after the Greek goddess of victory.

Questions

1. What is the role of promotion in a consumer product company such as Nike?

2. What are some appropriate promotional objectives for Nike?

3. Are there other promotional methods Nike should consider in its quest to remain the market leader?

www.nike.com

Steering the Promotional Strategy of the Newest Civilian Hummer

The first civilian Hummer, known as the H1, was launched by AM General in 1992. It received a great deal of publicity as a result of the "parent" vehicle's role in the Gulf War and because it was prominently featured in several of Arnold Schwarzenegger's movies. However, AM General put very little muscle into promoting the vehicle, only spending about half a million dollars on advertising in the year 2000. This limited promotional effort, combined with a high sticker price, kept sales figures for the H1 well below 1,000 units on an annual basis.

Hoping to improve sales of the civilian Hummer, AM General entered into an agreement with General Motors (GM) to introduce a new, less expensive version, the H2. Unlike its predecessor, the new Hummer has a sleek, well-funded advertising campaign designed to leave prospects anxious to find out if the newest version really is as the ads say "Like nothing else."

Getting the "Off-Road" Hummer on Road

In 1979, the U.S. Army developed specifications for a High Mobility Multi-purpose Wheeled Vehicle (HMMWV) that could forge its way through unforgiving terrain while carrying troops and a wide variety of military equipment and hardware. Six firms submitted proposals for consideration, three were selected to produce prototypes, and AM General was ultimately chosen to manufacture 55,000 vehicles for the Army. The company simplified the name to Humvee, and the vehicle proved successful enough that the Army ordered another 48,000 units. AM General realized that the U.S. military market would soon be saturated, and began targeting foreign militaries and other commercial applications such as oil exploration companies, the U.S. Forest Service, and the border patrol. A few thousand additional Hummers were sold, but AM General wanted to explore additional alternatives.

Then a fortuitous event occurred. When Arnold Schwarzenegger watched news footage from the Gulf War in the early 1990s, he saw the U.S. Army's tough-as-nails Humvee (it eventually became known as the Hummer) and he wanted to own one. For years, he claims, he had been looking for a vehicle "that looked different, that looked powerful, that looked special."

Convinced he had found it, he contacted the Hummer's manufacturer, AM General, and talked its management into making and selling him a custom-built version. That started the wheels turning for a new version of the Hummer, targeted at the consumer market.

When Schwarzenegger approached AM General about building a highway-suitable Hummer for his own use, the company's CEO was enthusiastic. "Although AM General is first and foremost a defense contractor," he explained, "the defense industry is now changing and defense contractors must respond by looking for applications for existing products and reinvesting in new businesses." Besides, this was hardly a novel idea. The Jeep made its debut in World War II and became a military mainstay for over 50 years. When it was made available to the civilian market, the Jeep quickly became a familiar sight on American roads, and still boasts a loyal following of Jeep enthusiasts.

The H1 Hits the Road

Basically the same as the military version, the civilian H1 was 6 feet tall and 7 feet wide, with a diesel V-8 engine and 16 inches of ground clearance. It had the same drivetrain, chassis, engine, and body as the military version, but had been adapted with exterior lighting and markings to comply with federal highway standards. Off the highway, it could still get over rocks that were almost 2 feet high and make its way through 40 inches of water. In addition, its driver had the ability to change its tires' pressure from inside the cab for smoother transitions between different types of terrain. So, how much was this unique vehicle? Well, as they say, if you had to ask you probably couldn't afford a price tag that could easily exceed $100,000.

About 50 dealers throughout the U.S. were granted franchises to sell the H1. These dealers had existing car or truck dealerships and were interested in adding the Hummer as a noncompeting extension of their current product lines. They received an 18% gross margin on the selling price of each vehicle. The franchise agreement specified that the dealership's service manager and two mechanics be factory-trained by AM General, and required the purchase of special factory tools and a modest inventory of spare parts.

Despite the fact that it never sold more than 1,000 units in a year, the Hummer became a popular novelty. It remained a perennial favorite at automobile trade shows and the Dallas-based department store Neiman Marcus even featured a pair of his-and-her Hummers as its "supergift" in one of its holiday catalogs. A minimal amount of money was invested in promoting the H1, although there were some print and television ads produced that described it as the "world's most serious 4 × 4." The H1 received its best publicity when it was positively reviewed in car magazines, but even the good reviews couldn't overcome the car's high sticker price.

Shifting into High Gear with a New Partnership

In 1998, General Motors decided to test the viability of a new, heavy-duty, sport-utility vehicle (SUV) code-named "Chunk." Market research was conducted and focus groups were surveyed to determine Chunk's design and features. Mike DiGiovanni, who later became Hummer general manager, recalled, "We put Chunk in a variety of clinics, first with a GMC name-badge on it and reaction was so-so, and then with different import badges on it and reaction was still so-so. Finally, before giving up, we put the Hummer name on it and reaction went through the roof."

GM approached AM General to see if the manufacturer of the H1 would consider selling the Hummer brand name to GM while continuing to build and assemble Hummers at its facility near South Bend, Indiana. AM General quickly agreed to the alliance, and a prototype of the new vehicle, the H2, was unveiled at the Detroit Auto Show in 2000.

That same year, GM decided to find a new advertising agency to handle the account. AM General had never allocated much money to promote the H1, but GM reportedly budgeted $20 million for the launch of the 2003 H2. Modernista!, a small ad agency in Boston won the coveted account, and Liz Vanzura was appointed GM's advertising director for the Hummer. Vanzura had previously been responsible for the 1998 launch of Volkswagon's restyled Beetle, and had been listed as one of *Advertising Age*'s Marketing 100 in 1999 for overseeing the new Beetle's successful introduction. "I feel lucky," she explained. "It's the second time I get to work on a cool brand."

Vanzura and Modernista! wasted no time in developing a new brand image and surrounding advertising campaign for the Hummer. They started with a "bridge" campaign for the H1 in order to raise awareness of the Hummer line prior to the introduction of the H2. One analyst explained that the "Hummer has to overcome some of its military heritage. They have to go into upscale SUV territory to capture more units." So instead of focusing on the H1's military lineage by continuing to tout it as "The world's most serious 4 × 4," a new tag line was developed, proclaiming Hummers to be "Like nothing else." The new ads were funded by AM General at a cost of $3 million, because the manufacturer remains financially responsible for the H1. This was a large jump in the Hummer's advertising budget, considering the fact that AM General traditionally spent less than $1 million annually to promote the H1.

Four different ads were created within the campaign, although they all contain common copy that reads, "Sometimes you find yourself in the middle of nowhere. And sometimes in the middle of nowhere you find yourself. The legendary H1." Vanzura hopes the new ads will strike a chord with "rugged individualists." "Do they get that yacht? Do they get the vacation house in Aspen?" she asked and went on to explain, "This is what we're competing with: people's time and what they do with their money. We're really not competing in an automotive category." Another industry analyst described the ads by saying that, "With the copy in these ads, they are clearly trying to get you to feel some other emotions you wouldn't normally associate with Hummer and create a stronger emotional aspiration." The new ads began appearing in August of 2001, less than one year before the H2 would make its debut.

Lining Up to Kick Its Tires

Although the H2 wasn't available for purchase until June of 2002, prospective buyers were given the opportunity to hold a spot in the anticipated waiting line by making a deposit that averaged $1,000. The anticipation was such that some of those consumers then turned around and auctioned their positions on eBay for several thousand dollars or, in one case, $15,100. (That was only for the privilege to buy one of the first units produced!)

GM funded the construction of a new plant to accommodate the manufacture of the H2 SUV, and began assembling test models in January 2002. Total plant capacity is around 45,000 units per year, and if all goes well, GM plans to unveil another model, the H2 Sport-Utility Truck, in 2004 or 2005. GM plans to sell around 25,000 H2s in its first year. The H2 SUV sports the front of a Chevy Suburban and the rear of a Chevy Tahoe, although it's about 6 inches shorter and 5 inches wider than the Tahoe for better four-wheel drive performance.

Although it retains the flattened, boxy shape of the H1, the H2 is about half a foot longer, but not as tall (by 6 inches). It will still climb 16-inch rocks and cross water that is almost 2 feet deep, however. And the H2 is much quieter than the H1, although it will achieve only about 11 or 12 miles per gallon of gas. Whereas the H1 was designed to seat four people, the H2 can accommodate five and offers an optional third row that provides space for a sixth person as long as he or she doesn't mind sharing the space with a very large spare tire.

With a starting price of $48,800, GM hopes the H2 will be more price comparable to other luxury SUVs than the H1. However, sales for the luxury SUV market were down more than 24% in June 2001. In addition, a market research survey revealed that around this same time, 44% of those polled had strong brand awareness of the Hummer but only 5% would consider buying one. Then the war on terrorism that was precipitated by the events of September 11, 2001, once again brought the military version, and therefore the entire Hummer line, back into the spotlight.

Targeted at "rugged individualists" who appreciate the H2's unique off-road performance and "successful achievers" who want to make a statement with their choice of vehicle, the H2 remains something of a novelty. Its ads continue to carry the tag line, "Like nothing else" and continue to position the Hummer line as being an extreme sort of SUV. For example, one ad proclaims, "When the asteroid hits and civilization crumbles, you'll be ready." Another states, "Threaten the men in your office a whole new way." Typically, H1 owners were men who earned in excess of $200,000 and were an average of 50 years old. The new ads are targeted at prospective buyers in their early forties who earn more than $125,000 a year. But women are in no way left behind with copy that recommends the H2 as being "Perfect for rugby moms."

If the H2 SUV and sport-utility truck prove to be successful, GM has plans to manufacture an H3 itself. It will be a midsize SUV based on the Chevy Trailblazer and will sport a sticker price in the $30,000 range. GM has high expectations and hopes to sell between 80,000 and 100,000 units annually, which would make the latest Hummer product one humdinger of a success.

Questions

1. Why would GM want the Hummer brand name when it already has an established line of SUVs?

2. Following the new mass media advertising campaign for the H2 (that is, ads in national magazines and on television), what other promotion tools should GM consider using to sell the H2 to its intended target markets?

3. Do you agree with GM's decision to downplay the Hummer's military heritage in its promotion effort? Why or why not?

www.hummer.com

Sources

Case 1: Nike   Hilary Cassidy, "Players Stay on Toes, Jump High to Get Ahead," *Brandweek,* June 17, 2002, p. S56; Gabriel Kahn, "adidas Knows the Whole World Is Watching Cup," *The Wall Street Journal,* June 5, 2002, p. A6; Maureen Tkacik, "As Extreme Goes Mass, Nike Nips at Skate-Shoe Icon," *The Wall Street Journal,* Apr. 24, 2002, p. A1; "Nike Goes After Rawlings' Strong Hold on Gloves," *The Wall Street Journal,* Apr. 1, 2002, p. A1; "Woods Wields Nike Driver," *USA Today,* Feb. 1, 2002, p. 7C; Hilary Cassidy, "Brand Builders," *Brandweek,* Mar. 25, 2002, pp. 19–20; John Gaffney, "Shoe Fetish," *Business 2.0,* March 2002, pp. 98–99; Chuck Stogel, "It's Easier Being Green," *Brandweek,* Jan. 28, 2002, pp. 16–20; Hilary Cassidy, "Chasing a Retail Brand," *Brandweek,* Jan. 21, 2002, pp. 18–20; Paula Stepankowsky, "Nike Tones Up Its Marketing to Women with Concept Shops, New Apparel Lines," *The Wall Street Journal,* Sept. 5, 2001, p. B19; Alex Wong, "Back to the 'Classics': Old Shoes Give Reebok New Life," *The Wall Street Journal,* Aug. 9, 2001, p. B4; Douglas Robson, "Just Do . . . Something," *Business Week,* July 2, 2001, pp. 70–71; Erin White, "Word of Mouth Makes Nike Slip-On Sneakers Take Off," *The Wall Street Journal,* June 7, 2001, p. B1; Kathy Chen, "Nike Gets Traction from Sweatshop Spat," *The Wall Street Journal,* Feb. 28, 2001, p. B14; Maxine Clayton, "Converse Files for Bankruptcy," *St. Louis Post-Dispatch,* Jan. 23, 2001, p. C7; Tania Mason, "The Importance of Being Ethical," *Marketing,* Oct. 26, 2000, p. 27. Louise Lee, "Can Nike Still Do It?" *Business Week,* Feb. 21, 2000, pp. 120–128; James Pilcher, "Extreme Sports Dominate Gear Market," Associated Press Online, Feb. 11, 2000; Lee Gomes, "Nike Forecasts Disappointing Sales as Outlets for Sneakers Dwindle," *The Wall Street Journal,* Feb. 9, 2000, p. B10; Matt Carmichael, "Nike Integration on TV, Online a Strong Lesson," *Advertising Age,* Jan. 31, 2000, p. 74; Pila Martinez, "Nike Asks UA Protestors to Tour Oversees Shoe Factories," *The Arizona Daily Star,* Nov. 7, 1999, p. 4B; Julie Schmit, "Nike's Image Problem after Global Outcry, Company Makes Strides to Improve," *USA Today,* Oct. 4, 1999, p. 1B; William Symonds and Louise Lee, "They're Running as Fast as They Can," *Business Week,* July 12, 1999, pp. 106–108; Joan O'Hamilton, "A Shoe of One's Own," *Business Week,* May 24, 1999, pp. 62–64; and Dottie Enrico, "Nike Hopes to Regain Sales Footing with New Ads," *USA Today,* Dec. 29, 1997, p. 3B.

Case 2: The Hummer   "Hummer Launches Edgy Campaign," Associated Press Online, July 1, 2002; James Healey, "If You're Driving, Hummer 2 is a Humdinger," *USA Today,* June 14, 2002; Jim Matega, "GM Takes H2 from 'Chunk' to SUV Hunk," *Chicago Tribune,* June 14, 2002; Jim Matega, "Little Hummer Does Family Name Proud," *Chicago Tribune,* June 7, 2002; Ann Job, "Home-Grown H1 is Bold, Brawny and Expensive," *South Bend Tribune,* Mar. 31, 2002, Automotive p. 1; Keith Benman, "Gearing Up for H2 Production," *South Bend Tribune,* Dec. 12, 2001, p. B1; Fred Ricart, "It's a Jungle out There," *Automotive News,* Aug. 13, 2001, p. 4; Ted Evanoff, "GM Blazes a New Trail with Its Marketing Strategy for Upscale Hummer,"

Bend Tribune, Dec. 12, 2001, p. B1; Fred Ricart, "It's a Jungle out There," *Automotive News,* Aug. 13, 2001, p. 4; Ted Evanoff, "GM Blazes a New Trail with Its Marketing Strategy for Upscale Hummer," *Indianapolis Star,* Aug. 12, 2002; Jean Halliday, "Of Hummers and Zen," *Advertising Age,* Aug. 6, 2001, p. 29; Jean Halliday, "Auto Engineer Having More Fun in Marketing," *Advertising Age,* June 4, 2001, p. 8; Michael Green, *HUMMER,* Motorbooks International, Osceola, WI, 1992; Paul Dodson, "Hummer Maker Targets Fleet Sales," *South Bend Tribune,* Feb. 28, 1993, pp. D1+; Greg Johnson, "Demand for Hummer Has Dealers Humming a Happy Tune," *Los Angeles Times,* Oct. 13, 1992, pp. D1+.

Strategic Marketing Planning

"Our goal is to make our coffee available where people shop, travel, play, and work so it bursts into the national consciousness."

Can **Starbucks** Continue to Brew Plans for Profitable Growth?

Seattle, long known for its rainy weather, is now also acclaimed as the home of the best coffee in the U.S. This distinction is due in no small part to Starbucks, which opened its first coffee bar in Seattle in 1971. Named after the first mate in *Moby Dick*, the chain attacked the retail coffee market with all the enthusiasm of the original Starbuck and his fellow crew members. Within 10 years, it had expanded to five outlets, a roasting plant, and a local wholesaling business. The outlets feature a variety of coffees, including blends of the day, lattés, mochas, and cappuccinos. The coffee can be iced or flavored with syrups, whatever suits the customer.

The company's mission is "to establish Starbucks as the premier purveyor of the finest coffee in the world while maintaining our uncompromising principles as we grow." Those principles relate to high standards for its coffee, a great work environment, diversity, satisfied customers, profitability, and giving back to the community and the environment. In addition, the company set the objective of being the most recognized and respected brand in the world. To achieve this ambition, Starbucks plans to add more retail locations and develop new products and channels that capitalize on the Starbucks name.

The chain's CEO, Howard Schultz, seemed to place as much emphasis on human resource management as on marketing. He began by creating an enviable package of employee training and benefits, including a free pound of coffee per week, all available to every worker. Schultz believes that happy employees lead to satisfied customers and repeat business. According to one analyst, "Ten percent of their customers come in twice a day. That's a pretty remarkable figure for a retailer."

On the marketing front, Starbucks aimed to capture the majority of a city's retail coffee market before moving on to the next locale. Schultz explained the company's strategy by saying, "Our goal is to make our coffee available where people shop, travel, play, and work so it bursts into the national consciousness." While spreading gradually throughout North America, Starbucks began overseas expansion, beginning with East Asia. It opened its first locations in Tokyo and Singapore in 1996, and acquired the United Kingdom's leading specialty coffee retailer, Seattle Coffee Company, in 1998.

The chain continually takes steps to better satisfy its existing customer base and to capitalize on its strong brand equity by expanding into new markets. For example, although coffee-drink sales make up about 75% of the company's revenue, the dollar amount brought in by other merchandise—such as coffee makers, a line of premium teas, compact discs, and stuffed bears—is substantial ($90 million in 2001). Looking for ways to attract more customers at lunchtime and later in the day, Starbucks expanded its menu to include sandwiches and salads. However, this move has not been very successful.

Recognizing that lines at its stores can discourage new patrons from coming into an outlet, Starbucks created a "swipeable," prepaid card that cuts the time to pay for a purchase. The card,

www.starbucks.com

which was introduced in late 2001, comes in denominations between $5 and $500. Thus far, the Starbucks Card has been very popular, accounting for over 5% of transactions. Improved employee training and automatic espresso machines are also helping to speed service.

A heavily used website, www.starbucks.com, lets patrons find the nearest Starbucks, subscribe to a newsletter, purchase CDs and coffee, of course, as well as sign up for and then manage a Starbucks smart card. Tapping into another trend, wireless Internet access is available for customer use in upwards of 2,000 Starbucks outlets in the U.S. and Europe.

As 2002 ended, Starbucks had more than 6,000 outlets in the U.S. and about 30 other countries. The chain has been expanding so rapidly that *The Onion* ran a satirical headline stating, "A New Starbucks Opens in Rest-room of Existing Starbucks." Satire aside, Starbucks' strategy evidently has been effective, with the chain's sales surpassing $3 billion worldwide.[1]

Over the years, has Starbucks developed sound and consistent plans?

Chapter Goals

In this chapter we'll examine how a company, including Starbucks, plans its total marketing program. After studying this chapter, you should be able to explain:

- The nature and scope of planning and how it fits within the management process.
- Similarities and differences among mission, objectives, strategies, and tactics.
- How strategic company planning differs from strategic marketing planning.
- The steps comprising strategic marketing planning.
- The purpose and contents of an annual marketing plan.
- Similarities and differences as well as weaknesses and strengths across several models used in strategic planning.

As the Starbucks case suggests, success for any organization requires skillful marketing management. The *marketing* part of the term *marketing management* was defined in Chapter 1, but what about the *management* part? **Management** is the process of planning, implementing, and evaluating the efforts of a group of people working toward a common goal. In this chapter we provide an overview of the management process and examine planning in some detail. In the next chapter, we will cover implementation and evaluation, the other two steps in the management process.

Planning as Part of Management

The management process, as applied to marketing, consists basically of (1) planning a marketing program, (2) implementing it, and (3) evaluating its performance. This process is depicted in Figure 20.1.

The *planning* stage includes setting goals and designing both strategies and tactics to reach these goals. The *implementation* stage entails designing and staffing the marketing organization and then directing the actual operation of the organization according to the plan. The *evaluation* stage consists of analyzing past performance in relation to organizational goals.[2] This third stage indicates the interrelated, ongoing nature of the management process. That is, the results of this stage are used in *planning* goals and strategies for future periods. So the cycle continues.

FIGURE 20.1

The Management Process in Marketing.

PLANNING:
Analyze situation
Set goals
Select strategies and tactics

IMPLEMENTATION:
Organize
Staff
Direct

EVALUATION:
Compare performance with goals

Feedback, so management can adapt future plans and their implementation to the changing environment

The Nature of Planning

"If you don't know where you're going, any road will get you there." The point of this axiom is that all organizations need both general and specific plans to fulfill their purposes. Management should first decide what it intends to accomplish as a total organization and develop a strategic plan to achieve these results. Based on this overall plan, each division of the organization should determine what its own plans will be. Of course, the role of marketing in these plans needs to be considered.

If planning is so important, exactly what is it? Simply, **planning** is deciding now what we are going to do later, including how and when we are going to do it. Without a plan, we cannot get anything done effectively and efficiently, because we don't know what needs to be done or how to do it.

In **strategic planning,** managers match an organization's resources with its market opportunities over the long run. A long-run perspective does not mean that plans can be developed or executed in a sluggish manner. The term **strategic window** describes the limited amount of time in which a firm's resources coincide with a particular market opportunity.[3] Typically, the "window" is open only for a relatively short period. Thus a firm must be able to move rapidly and decisively when a strategic window opens.

An Internet enterprise, eCompanyStore.com, saw a strategic window in which it could multiply its sales volume. The firm, which sells promotional products such as

For decades, a small firm, Idus-Howard Inc., used advertising and personal selling to market custom logo merchandise. It received orders by phone and fax. But then the company changed its name and approach. Now, as eCompanyStore, it focuses on larger accounts and sells online. The firm seeks to "help our customers manage and procure their promotional products and uniforms with unprecedented speed and accuracy."

www.ecompanystore.com

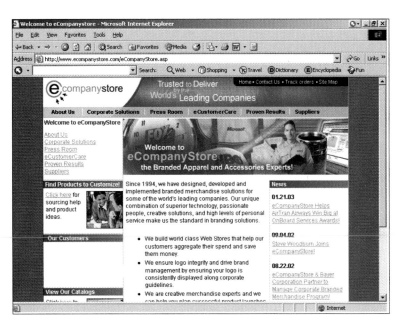

clothing and glassware with company logos imprinted on them, switched from traditional methods to a reliance on online selling. To concentrate on large customers, eCompanyStore.com even made the painful decision to not serve its existing small customers. In two years, the firm secured 30 relatively large customers for which it built customized websites that each customer uses to purchase substantial quantities of various promotional products displaying its own organization's logo.[4]

Essential Planning Concepts

You need to be familiar with not only the terms already introduced, but also other basic terms used in discussing marketing management, especially in the planning phase.

Mission   An organization's **mission** states what customers it serves, what needs it satisfies, and what types of products it offers. A mission statement indicates, in general terms, the boundaries for an organization's activities.

To be useful, a mission statement cannot be either too broad and vague or too narrow and specific. To say that a firm's mission is "to benefit American consumers" is vague; to state that its purpose is "to make tennis balls" is overly narrow. Neither statement outlines meaningful benefits for customers or provides much guidance to management. Unless the firm's purpose is clear to executives, strategic planning is likely to result in disagreement and confusion.

In the past, companies tended to state their missions in product-oriented terms, such as "We make furnaces" (or telephones, or tennis rackets). Today, a firm abiding by the marketing concept expresses its mission in customer-oriented terms that reflect the needs it is striving to satisfy and the benefits it is providing. Thus, instead of "We make furnaces," Lennox Industry's mission is "to create indoor comfort products that make your home or office a better place."[5] Recall that Table 1.1 illustrated marketing-oriented ways of stating a company's mission.

Objectives and Goals   Although they are sometimes differentiated, we treat *objectives* and *goals* as synonyms. An **objective** is simply a desired outcome. Effective planning must begin with a set of objectives that are to be achieved by carrying out plans. To be worthwhile and workable, objectives should be:

- Clear and specific.
- Stated in writing.
- Ambitious, but realistic.

Lennox International Inc. was founded more than 100 years ago in Iowa by a machine-shop operator who invented a new type of coal-fired furnace. Over the years, the company added new product lines and brands. With annual sales of over $3 billion, Lennox now has a mission of providing "indoor comfort products that make your home or office a better place."

www.lennox.com

- Consistent with one another.
- Quantitatively measurable when possible.
- Tied to a particular time period.

Consider these examples:

Weak (too general)		Workable
Increase our market share.	→	Increase our market share to 25% next year from its present 20% level.
Improve our company's image.	→	Receive favorable recognition awards next year from at least three consumer or environmental groups.

Strategies and Tactics The term *strategy* was originally associated with military operations. In business, a **strategy** is a broad plan of action by which an organization intends to reach its objectives and, in turn, to fulfill its mission. In marketing, the relationship between objectives and strategies may be illustrated as follows:

Objectives		Possible Strategies
Increase sales next year by 10% over this year's figure.	→	1. Intensify marketing efforts in domestic markets. 2. Expand into foreign markets.

Two organizations might have the same objective but use contrasting strategies to reach it. For instance, both firms might aim to increase their market shares by 20% over the next three years. To do that, one firm in, say, the packaged-foods industry might intensify its efforts in household markets; a competing firm might concentrate on expanding into institutional markets (for example, food-service organizations). Conversely, two organizations might have different objectives but select the identical strategy to reach them.

A **tactic** is a means by which a strategy is implemented. A tactic is a more specific, detailed course of action than a strategy. Moreover, tactics generally cover shorter time periods than strategies. Here's an illustration:

Strategy		Tactics
Direct our promotion to males, ages 25–40.	→	1. Advertise in magazines read by this market segment. 2. Sponsor events attended in person and/or watched on TV by this group.

To be effective, a tactic must coincide with and support the strategy with which it is related. That's sometimes difficult to do, as Planet Hollywood found out. A key strategy for the restaurant chain was a theme built around celebrities, many of whom were investors in the business. A related tactic was frequent appearances at the restaurants by stars and other well-known personalities. However, most celebrities didn't want to interact with the public. Equally damaging, the restaurants' food was generally poor. The post–September 11 decline in tourism also hurt the chain. As a result, Planet Hollywood filed for Chapter 11 bankruptcy protection and is in danger of disappearing from this planet.[6]

www.planethollywood.com

Key Questions for an Organization The concepts of mission, objectives, strategies, and tactics raise important questions that must be answered by an organization seeking success in business or, more specifically, in marketing. These questions can be summarized as follows:

Concept		Question
Mission	→	What business are we in?
Objectives	→	What do we want to accomplish?
Strategies	→	In *general* terms, how are we going to get the job done?
Tactics	→	In *specific* terms, how are we going to get the job done?

Scope of Planning

Planning may cover long or short periods. Strategic planning is usually long range, spanning three, five, or even more years. It requires the participation of top management and often involves a planning staff.

Long-range planning deals with company-wide issues such as expanding or contracting production, markets, and product lines. For example, all firms in the home appliance industry must look ahead for perhaps as long as a decade to identify key markets, plan new products, and update production technologies.

www.whirlpool.com

Short-range planning typically covers one year or less and is the responsibility of middle- and lower-level managers. For example, presumably the Whirlpool Corporation annually considers such issues as which target markets it will concentrate on and whether its marketing mixes for each of these markets need to be changed. Naturally, short-range plans must be compatible with the organization's long-range intentions.

Planning a firm's marketing strategies should be conducted on three different levels:

- *Strategic company planning.* At this level management defines an organization's mission, sets long-range goals, and formulates broad strategies to achieve the goals. Company-wide goals and strategies then become the framework for planning in the firm's different functional areas, such as production, finance, human resources, research and development, *and* marketing.

- *Strategic marketing planning.* The top marketing executives set goals and strategies for an organization's marketing effort. Strategic *marketing* planning obviously should be coordinated with *company-wide* planning.

- *Annual marketing planning.* Short-term plans should be prepared for a firm's major functions. Covering a specific period, usually one year, an annual marketing plan is based on the firm's strategic marketing planning.

Attitudes toward strategic planning seem to run in cycles. During the 1970s, strategic planning was highly valued in large corporations. Then, during the 1980s and most of the 1990s, the focus shifted to implementation and evaluation—especially efforts to boost efficiency and profitability. Strategic planning seems to have come back into favor—particularly as it relates to global expansion. In fact, according to one survey, 27% of high-level corporate executives ranked strategic planning as the most important business function. Only product development, placed on top by 29% of the participants, ranked higher.[7]

Now, one expert is urging executives to adjust their thinking about strategic planning. A basic premise, according to this new perspective, is that the macroenvironment can be influenced in some respects, such as by establishing new business models. Fairly recent start-ups, including eBay, E*Trade, and Amazon.com, have done this.[8]

us.etrade.com

Strategic Company Planning

Strategic company planning consists of four essential steps:

1. Define the organizational mission.
2. Analyze the situation.

3. Set organizational objectives.

4. Select strategies to achieve these objectives.

The process is shown in the top part of Figure 20.2.[9] The first step, *defining the organizational mission*, influences subsequent planning. For some firms, all that needs to be done is to review the existing mission statement and confirm that it is still suitable. However, this straightforward step is too often ignored.

Conducting a situation analysis, the second step, is vital because strategic planning is influenced by many factors beyond and within an organization. A **situation analysis** consists of gathering and studying information pertaining to one or more specified aspects of an organization. We'll talk more about conducting a situation analysis in an upcoming section.

The third step in strategic company planning, *deciding on a set of objectives*, guides the organization in fulfilling its mission. Objectives also provide standards for evaluating performance.

By this point in its strategic planning, the organization has determined where it wants to go. The fourth step, *selecting appropriate strategies*, indicates how the firm is going to get there. **Organizational strategies** represent broad plans of action by which an organization intends to fulfill its mission and achieve its goals. Strategies are selected either for the entire company if it is small and/or has only a single product *or* for each division if the company is large and/or has multiple products or units.

Do companies actually engage in strategic planning and then prepare a written plan? The results of one survey indicated that almost 70% of firms had strategic plans in place; among them, nearly 90% believed their strategic plans had been effective. However, according to more recent data, only 12% of relatively small firms (defined as those with fewer than 500 employees) had a long-range plan in writing. In fact, almost 60% of these companies had no written plans.[10]

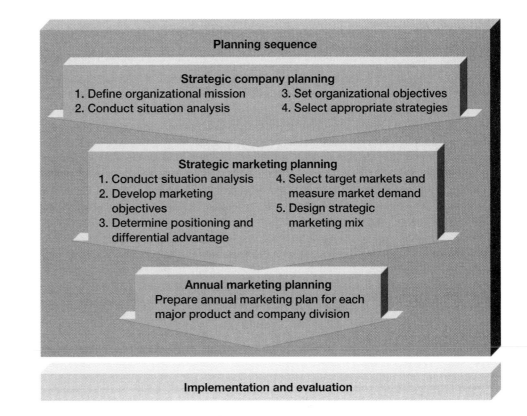

FIGURE 20.2

Three Levels of Organizational Planning.

Strategic Marketing Planning

After planning for the organization as a whole, management needs to lay plans for each major functional area, such as marketing or production. Of course, planning for each function should be guided by the organization-wide mission and objectives.

Strategic marketing planning is a five-step process:

1. Conduct a situation analysis.
2. Develop marketing objectives.
3. Determine positioning and differential advantage.
4. Select target markets and measure market demand.
5. Design a strategic marketing mix.

These five steps are shown in the middle of Figure 20.2, indicating how they relate to the four steps of strategic company planning. Each step is discussed below.

Situation Analysis

The first step in strategic marketing planning, **situation analysis,** involves analyzing where the company's marketing program has been, how it has been doing, and what it is likely to face in the years ahead. Doing this enables management to determine if it is necessary to revise the old plans or devise new ones to achieve the company's objectives.

Situation analysis normally covers external environmental forces and internal nonmarketing resources that were discussed in Chapter 2. A situation analysis also considers the groups of consumers served by the company, the strategies used to satisfy them, and key measures of marketing performance. Due attention should be given to identifying and assessing competitors that are serving the same markets. Also, as stressed by two consultants, it's important to "get out of the box"—that is, to develop new perspectives on the organization's core activities and to question assumptions about how it does business (assumptions such as "we must offer competitive prices").[11]

Situation analysis is critical, but it can be costly, time-consuming, and frustrating. For example, it is usually difficult to extract timely, accurate information from the "mountains" of data compiled during a situation analysis. Moreover, some valuable information, such as sales or market-share figures for competitors, is often unavailable.

As part of a situation analysis, many organizations perform a **SWOT assessment.** In this activity, a firm identifies and evaluates its most significant *s*trengths, *w*eaknesses, *o*pportunities, and *t*hreats. To fulfill its mission, an organization needs to capitalize on its key strengths, overcome or alleviate its major weaknesses, avoid significant threats, and take advantage of promising opportunities.[12]

We're referring to strengths and weaknesses in an organization's own capabilities. For example, a strength of Sears is its large size, which gives it—among other things—clout in dealing with suppliers. However, a weakness is its comparatively high operating expenses, which makes it difficult for Sears to compete on the basis of low prices.

Opportunities and threats often originate outside the organization. According to RadioShack's chief executive, advances in computing and telecommunications technologies presented the chain with the opportunity to "demystify technology in every neighborhood in America." With more than 7,000 stores, RadioShack Corp. intends to be the "most trusted specialty retailer" of various high-tech products and also provide installation and support services. But a threat is the variety of competitors, ranging from competing chains such as CompUSA to telecommunications giants such as AT&T, that to some degree have similar intentions.[13]

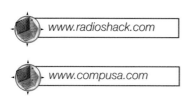

www.radioshack.com

www.compusa.com

Marketing Objectives

The next step in strategic marketing planning is to *determine marketing objectives*. Marketing goals should be closely related to company-wide goals and strategies. In fact, a *company strategy* often translates into a *marketing goal*. For example, to reach an organizational objective of a 20% return on investment next year, one organizational strategy might be to boost marketing efficiency by 10%. This company strategy could become a marketing goal. In turn, a strategy of converting all sales people from salaried compensation to a commission basis might be adopted to achieve this marketing goal.

We already know that strategic planning involves matching an organization's resources with its market opportunities. With this in mind, each marketing objective should be assigned a priority on the basis of its urgency and its potential impact on an area of focus and, in turn, the organization. Then resources should be allocated in line with these priorities.[14]

Positioning and Differential Advantage

The third step in strategic marketing planning actually involves two complementary decisions: *how to position a product in the marketplace* and *how to distinguish it from competitors*. As described in Chapters 6 and 9, **positioning** refers to a product's image in relation to competing products as well as other products marketed by the same company. For example, a Canadian company is trying to win over U.S. consumers by promoting the dreadful taste of its cough syrup! Because Buckley's Mixture doesn't use sugar or alcohol to overcome the chemical taste, the product's slogan is: "It tastes awful. And it works."[15]

After the product is positioned, a viable differential advantage has to be identified. **Differential advantage** refers to any feature of an organization or brand perceived by customers to be desirable and different from those of the competition. Some dry cleaning outlets have sought an advantage by using petroleum-based solvents rather than the traditional cleaning agent, which may cause cancer.[16]

Besides striving for an advantage, a company has to avoid a **differential disadvantage** for its product. Returning to the dry cleaning example, the outlets using the "new and improved" cleaning agents still need to offer competitive prices. Otherwise, they risk having a price *dis*advantage, which could negate the advantage gained by using an alternative cleaning method.

The concepts of differential advantage and differential disadvantage apply to both goods and services and—in areas such as retailing—to entire firms. One consultant believes that retailers can gain a differential advantage by developing one or more of four *est* dimensions—the low*est* prices, the bigg*est* assortments, the hott*est* (most fashionable) merchandise, and the easi*est* store to shop in. Nordstroms, which is on the rebound from two years of declining earnings, doesn't compete on the basis of low prices but has excelled in the other three areas. Conversely, a firm risks a differential *dis*advantage if it is only average or "pretty good" on these four dimensions.[17]

In contrast to large cruise ships, Windjammer Barefoot Cruises positions its product as a more informal, less crowded vacation. Windjammer's "tall ships," each an actual working ship with a unique history, accommodate either 64 or 128 vacationers. The ships meander throughout the Caribbean Sea, sailing primarily at night and stopping at various islands in the region during the day.

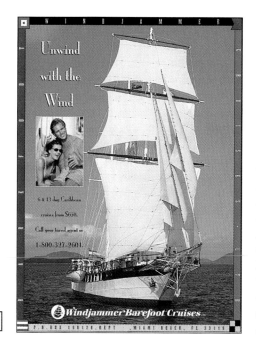

Target Markets and Market Demand

Selecting target markets is the fourth step in marketing planning. As covered in earlier chapters, a **market** consists of people or organizations with needs to satisfy, money to spend, and the willingness to spend it. For example, many people favor air travel *and* are both able and willing to pay for it. However, this large group is made up of a number of segments (that is, parts of markets) with various preferences. Because an organization typically cannot satisfy all segments with different needs, it is wise to concentrate on one or more of these segments.

A **target market** refers to a group of people or organizations at which a firm directs a marketing program. To choose one or more target markets, a firm must forecast demand (that is, sales) in market segments that appear promising. As discussed in Chapter 6, the results of demand forecasting represent valuable information in deciding whether a specific segment is worth pursuing, or whether alternative segments need to be considered.

Marketing Mix

For each target market, management must design a **marketing mix,** which is the combination of multiple aspects of the following four elements: a product, how it is distributed and promoted, and its price. These four elements, which were covered in detail in Chapters 8 through 19, are intended to please the target market(s) and, equally important, achieve the organization's marketing objectives.

Each marketing-mix element contains numerous options. Further, decisions regarding one element affect the others. Marketing decision makers need to consider these options and relationships when designing a marketing mix for a particular target market. Here's an illustration of a customer–satisfying marketing mix. Midwest Express Airlines, which focuses on business travelers, offers several enhancements, including leather seats, full in-flight dinners, and fresh-baked chocolate chip cookies served on afternoon flights. Midwest uses the industry's standard methods for promoting and distributing its service, and it matches competitors' coach fares—while providing what amounts to business-class service. As a result, since it was founded in the mid-1980s, Midwest has grown steadily to become the 22nd largest carrier in the U.S.[18]

www1.midwestexpress.com/corporate

Annual Marketing Planning

Besides strategic planning for several years into the future, more specific, shorter-term planning is also vital. Thus, as shown in the bottom part of Figure 20.2, preparation of an annual plan follows planning of a strategic nature. An **annual marketing plan** is the blueprint for a year's marketing activity for a specified organizational division or major product. It should be a written document, not just kept in mind.

A separate plan normally should be prepared for each major product and company division. Sometimes separate plans are even developed for key brands and important target markets. As the name implies, an annual marketing plan usually covers one year. There are exceptions, however. Because of the seasonal nature of some products or markets, it may be advisable to prepare plans for shorter time periods. For fashionable clothing, plans are made for each season, lasting just several months. The planning horizon is even shorter in today's information economy. As noted in one article, "On the Internet, companies have to be ready to change goals or strategies virtually overnight."[19]

Purposes and Responsibilities

An annual marketing plan serves several purposes:

- It summarizes the marketing strategies and tactics that will be used to achieve specified objectives in the upcoming year. Thus it becomes the "how-to-do-it" guide for executives and other employees involved in marketing.

AN ETHICAL DILEMMA?

Assume you are the product manager responsible for a line of cellular telephones. In the past year, your brand has fallen from second to third in terms of sales. You attribute the decline to an unfair comparative advertising campaign run by the new second-place firm. The company used ads that pointed to alleged shortcomings in your cell phones. Unexpectedly, you are presented with an opportunity to regain the upper hand when one of your sales people brings you a copy of that competitor's marketing plan for next year. The sales person found it on a chair following a seminar attended by representatives from a number of companies that make cell phones and related products. After studying this document, you could adjust your plans to counter the other firm's strategies.

Even though you didn't buy or steal the plan, is it ethical to read and use it?

- The plan also points to what needs to be done with respect to the other steps in the management process—implementation and evaluation of the marketing program.
- Moreover, the plan outlines who is responsible for which activities, when they are to be carried out, and how much time and money can be spent.

The executive responsible for the division or product covered by the plan typically prepares it. Of course, all or part of the task may be delegated to subordinates. Preparation may begin nine months or more before the start of the period covered by the plan. Early work includes necessary research and arranging other information sources. The bulk of the work occurs one to three months prior to the plan's starting date. The last steps are to have the plan reviewed and approved by upper management. Revision may be necessary before final approval is granted. The finished version of the plan, or relevant parts of it, should be shared with all employees who will be involved in implementing the agreed-upon strategies and tactics.

Recommended Contents

Annual marketing planning follows a sequence similar to strategic marketing planning. However, annual planning has a shorter time frame and is more specific—especially with respect to the plans laid. Still, as shown in Table 20.1, the major sections in an annual plan give due attention to topics covered in strategic marketing planning.[20]

In an annual plan, more attention can be devoted to tactical details than is feasible in other levels of planning. As an example, strategic marketing planning might stress personal selling within the marketing mix. If so, the annual plan might recommend increased college recruiting as a source of additional sales people.

An annual marketing plan actually relates to all three steps of the management process, not just planning. Sections 5 through 7 of Table 20.1 deal with implementa-

TABLE 20.1

Contents of an Annual Marketing Plan

1. *Executive Summary.* In this one- or two-page section, the thrust of the plan is described and explained. It is intended for executives who desire an overview of the plan but need not be knowledgeable about the details.
2. *Situation Analysis.* Essentially, the marketing program for a major division of a company (called a strategic business unit) or product covered by the plan is examined within the context of pertinent past, present, and future conditions. Much of this section might be derived from the results of strategic marketing planning. Additional information of particular relevance to a one-year planning period may be included in this section.
3. *Objectives.* The objectives in an annual plan are more specific than those produced by strategic marketing planning. However, annual objectives must help achieve organizational goals and strategic marketing goals.
4. *Strategies.* As in strategic marketing planning, the strategies in an annual plan should indicate which target markets are going to be statisfied through a combination of product, price, distribution, and promotion.
5. *Tactics.* Specific activities, sometimes called action plans, are devised for carrying out each major strategy included in the preceding section. For ease of understanding, strategies and tactics may be covered together. Tactics specifically answer the question of *what, who,* and *how* for the company's marketing efforts.
6. *Financial Schedules.* This section normally includes two kinds of financial information: projected sales, expenses, and profits in what's called a pro forma financial statement; and the amounts of resources dedicated to different activities in one or more budgets.
7. *Timetable.* This section, often including a diagram, answers the question of *when* various marketing activities will be carried out during the upcoming year.
8. *Evaluation Procedures.* This section addresses the questions of *what, who, how,* and *when* connected with measuring performance against goals, both during and at the end of the year. The results of evaluations during the year may lead to adjustments in the plan's strategies and/or tactics or even the objectives to be achieved.

tion, and section 8 is concerned with evaluation. To increase the likelihood of careful review, some firms limit annual plans to a specified length, such as 20 pages.

Selected Planning Models

For more than three decades, a number of frameworks or tools—we'll call them *models*—have been designed to assist with strategic planning. Most of these models can be used with both strategic company planning *and* strategic marketing planning. In this section, we briefly discuss several planning models that have received ample attention. First, however, you need to be familiar with a form of organization, the strategic business unit, that is integral to both planning and organizational structure in companies.

Strategic Business Units

Most large and medium-sized companies—and even some smaller firms—consist of multiple units and market numerous products. In such firms, company-wide planning cannot serve as an effective guide for executives who oversee the organization's various divisions. The Altria Group, Inc. (formerly Philip Morris Company) provides an example. The mission, objectives, and strategies in its tobacco division are—and must be—quite different from those in its packaged food division.

Consequently, for more effective planning and operations, a multidivision or multiproduct organization should be divided according to its major markets or products. Each such entity is called a **strategic business unit (SBU)**. Each SBU may be a major division in an organization, a group of related products, or even a single major product or brand.

To be considered an SBU, an entity should: be a separately identifiable business; have a distinct mission; have its own competitors; and have its own executive team with profit responsibility.

One challenge in setting up SBUs in an organization is to arrive at the *optimum* number. Too many can bog down top management in details associated with planning, operating, and reporting. Too few SBUs can result in each one covering too broad an area for meaningful planning.

SBUs for two giant corporations and a nonprofit organization are as follows:

- *The Boeing Company:* commercial airplanes, integrated defense systems, Boeing Capital Corporation, Connexion by Boeing, and air traffic management.

As stated in this ad, "The McGraw-Hill Companies provides information that is critical to every part of our lives." It does so through three strategic business units: education (including publishing of textbooks such as this one), financial services, and information and media services.

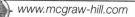

FIGURE 20.3

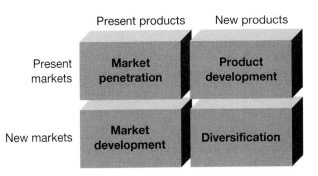

Product-Market Growth Matrix.

• *Your university or college:* different schools (such as business and engineering) *or* different delivery systems (such as on-campus curricula and distance learning).

Let's now consider several well-known planning models.

Product-Market Growth Matrix

Most organizations want or need to get bigger and, therefore, objectives often focus on growth—that is, a desire to increase revenues and profits. In seeking growth, a company has to consider *both* its markets and its products. Then an enterprise has to decide whether to sustain, and perhaps enhance, what it is now doing *or* to establish new ventures. The **product-market growth matrix** depicts these options.[21]

As shown in Figure 20.3, there are four fundamental product-market growth strategies:

• *Market penetration:* A company tries to sell more of its present products to its present markets. Supporting tactics might include greater spending on advertising or personal selling. For example, the William Wrigley Jr. Co. relies on this strategy, encouraging smokers to chew gum where smoking is prohibited. Or a company tries to become a single source of supply by offering preferential treatment to customers who will concentrate all of their purchases with that company.

www.wrigley.com

Garmin Ltd. markets navigation and communications equipment for the aviation and consumer markets. The company's Global Position System (GPS) products, which pinpoint a user's location, have been especially successful. Garmin's consumer products stress the advantage of having turn-by-turn directions from a starting point to a destination. Which product-market growth strategy is Garmin Ltd. using?

www.garmin.com

One of the four product-market growth strategies is to offer the firm's goods and services for sale in new markets. In this context, the additional market could be a demographic group, type of organization, or region of the world not served by the company.

Numerous North American and European firms have chosen China as a desirable market for expansion. They have experienced wide-ranging degrees of success. On the minus side, a Dutch supermarket chain, Ahold, has pulled out of China, and Park 'n' Shop, owned by a Hong Kong conglomerate, has significantly cut back its operations there. On the plus side, Coca-Cola has 30,000 employees and 31 bottling plants after just two decades of operation in China. The most successful foreign businesses in China may be operators of giant discount stores. Carrefour from France and Wal-Mart each have several dozen stores placed around this giant country. Both chains have exceeded their performance expectations in China and thus are moving forward ambitiously in this market.

Here are some aspects of the Chinese market that are likely to dictate strategic adjustments:

- Chinese consumers in major urban areas like Western goods and the convenience of giant stores that allow one-stop shopping. Although over 90% of the Chinese population live in rural areas, Coca-Cola is generating one-half of its sales from urban markets in this country.

- Getting products to rural areas is made difficult by the immense distances and the poor roads.

- Local Chinese brands are entrenched in rural areas. When P&G entered China in 1988, there were only 30 hair-care brands in the entire country. Having witnessed P&G's success, more than 1,800 local brands have sprung up, many of them knock-offs of P&G products.

- Obtaining economies of scale is particularly important in China because operating costs, especially physical distribution, are much higher than in most Western countries. That's another reason why 100,000-square-foot "hypermarkets" have done well in urban areas.

Of course, some strategies and techniques are useful anywhere. Thus Coca-Cola is building a database identifying every potential retailer in the country that does or could sell soft drinks, how much they sell, and at what price. And the hypermarkets have introduced centralized purchasing and computerized inventory tracking to Chinese retailing.

Sources: Leslie Chang, "Western Stores Woo Chinese Wallets," *The Wall Street Journal*, Nov. 26, 2002, pp. B1, B6; Gabriel Kahn, "Coke Works Hard at Being the Real Thing in Hinterland," *The Wall Street Journal*, Nov. 26, 2002, pp. B1+; and "Not So Fuzzy," *The Economist*, Feb. 23, 2002, pp. 66+.

- *Market development:* A firm continues to sell its present products, but to a new market. Firms that depend to a large degree on just a few customers often engage in market development to spread their risk. Exline Inc., a machine shop in Salina, Kansas, was forced to do that when Enron Corp. and other big customers in the energy industry imploded. In the context of consumer products, cruise lines such as Carnival and Royal Caribbean have been concentrating their marketing efforts on the almost 90% of Americans who have never taken a cruise.[22]

- *Product development:* An organization develops new products to sell to its existing markets. Some ski resorts, for example, built steep, dangerous slopes in order to appeal to thrill-seeking "extreme" customers. The Wrigley company also used this strategy by introducing mint-flavored gum aimed at teenagers. Medical Center Pharmacy in Scottsbluff, Nebraska, expanded by offering new product lines—first, wheelchairs and hospital beds for in-home use and, subsequently, on-site repair and even custom building of these products. Such moves are intended to better satisfy, and generate more revenues from, existing customers.[23]

- *Diversification:* A company develops new products to sell to new markets. To cite one example, at various points in its history, the Boeing Company moved far away from aircraft to market other vehicles (light rail systems, hydrofoils) and disparate services (urban planning, desalination of water supplies). This approach is risky because it doesn't rely on either the company's successful products or its established

MARKETING IN THE INFORMATION ECONOMY

Does the Internet foster cannibalization?

With the surge of the Internet, more and more companies face the issue of cannibalization. Recalling a case from an earlier chapter, Petsmart.com is surely pulling at least some shoppers away from the namesake physical stores. Online selling can result in cannibalization, as can the sale of Internet-based products that move earlier products toward obsolescence. For instance, new VoIP (voice-over Internet protocol) communications systems are replacing traditional PBX (private branch exchange) systems in some organizations.

Cannibalization becomes more controversial when the new efforts, online or otherwise, are taking or might take sales away from independent channel members. Recall the Chapter 14 case in which Avon's sales reps expressed concern that the company's addition of a website (and other channels) will take sales away from them, thus reducing their incomes. Car and truck dealerships reacted in much the same way to the Internet forays launched—and now abandoned—by the auto manufacturers. A Chevrolet dealer probably spoke for many of his colleagues when he said, "If they [GM] build cars and let us sell them, we'll be one big happy family."

If added sales and profits from new products more than offset reductions experienced by existing products, then cannibalization can be beneficial. One business writer concluded, "Traditional retailers have realized that the benefits of joining the dot–com community far outweigh any potentially competitive cannibalization." With that in mind, Krause's Furniture, based in southern California, has added a website featuring an extensive electronic catalog as another channel for its merchandise.

For firms facing online competition, cannibalization is essential. According to one observer, "Companies that learn to cannibalize themselves today will rule tomorrow's business jungle. Those that don't will find themselves in someone else's pot."

Sources: "VoIP: More than Long-Distance Savings," *Communication News,* January 2002, p. 10; Connie Robbins Gentry, "When Worlds Collaborate," *Chain Store Age,* April 2001, pp. 101+; Joseph B. White and Fara Warner, "Auto Brass Seeks to Rebuild Ties with Irked Dealers," *The Wall Street Journal,* Jan. 24, 2000, p. A12; and Jerry Useem, "Internet Defense Strategy: Cannibalize Yourself," *Fortune,* Sept. 6, 1999, pp. 121–122+.

---

position in one or more markets. Sometimes it works, but sometimes it doesn't. According to research conducted by the Bain & Co. consulting firm, diversified enterprises do not perform as well financially as relatively focused organizations.[24]

As market conditions change over time, a company may shift product-market growth strategies. For example, when its present market is fully saturated, an organization may have no choice other than to pursue new markets. That's the path followed by Liz Claiborne Inc., which earned a reputation for making stylish clothing for women engaged in professional careers. Eventually, the apparel firm added new brands in order to serve a variety of target markets, especially economy-minded female shoppers. Today, Claiborne labels, such as Villager and Crazy Horse, can be found in a wide range of retail outlets, including Mervyn's, Kohl's, and JCPenney.[25]

www.lizclaiborne.com/lizinc

In pursuing one or more product-market growth strategies, a company seeks to build its sales and profits, of course. However, in the case of product development, it's possible that revenues rung up by new products may come at the expense of other products sold by that firm. This situation is called **cannibalization.** Eastman Kodak Co. realized that sales of its traditional films might suffer when it introduced digital-imaging products. The case introducing Chapter 6 alludes to potential cannibalization—the prospect of the Smart Car taking sales away from full-size, higher-price autos sold by DaimlerChrysler. And the Claiborne clothing firm, discussed above, accepted some degree of cannibalization.

Why does a company take actions that could result in cannibalization? Very simply, if it doesn't introduce new products or channels to better serve existing customers, one or more competitors almost surely will. If that occurs, the passive firm will lose customers and, in turn, revenues. A study that focused on high-tech industries cast a favorable light on cannibalization, concluding that success with truly innovative new products requires a willingness to cannibalize in order to achieve substantial gains in the future.[26]

BCG Matrix

Developed by a management consulting firm, the Boston Consulting Group, the **BCG matrix** dates back 30 years.[27] Using this model, an organization classifies each of its SBUs (and, sometimes, major products) according to two factors: its market share relative to competitors *and* the growth rate of the industry in which the SBU operates. When the factors are divided simply into high and low categories, a 2 × 2 grid is created, as displayed in Figure 20.4.

In turn, the four quadrants in the grid represent distinct categories of SBUs or major products. The categories differ with respect not only to market share and industry growth rate, but also to cash needs and appropriate strategies:

- *Stars.* High market shares and high industry growth rates typify SBUs in this category. However, an SBU with these attributes poses a challenge for companies because it requires a lot of cash to remain competitive in growing markets. Aggressive marketing strategies are imperative for stars to maintain or even build market share. The leading brands of "luxury" autos—such as BMW, Lexus, and Mercedes Benz—are currently viewed as stars. Although none of these brands has a commanding market share on an absolute basis, each is doing relatively well in an expanding segment of the new-car market.[28]

- *Cash cows.* These SBUs have high market shares and do business in mature (low-growth) industries. When an industry's growth diminishes, stars move into this category. Because most of their customers have been with them for some time and are still loyal, a cash cow's marketing costs are not high. Consequently, it generates more cash than can be reinvested profitably in its own operations. As a result, cash cows can be "milked" to support other SBUs that need more resources. Marketing strategies for cash cows seek to defend market share, largely by reinforcing customer loyalty. As examples, consider Campbell's canned soups and Gillette's "3 B's," namely blades for razors, brushes for teeth, and batteries.[29]

www.gillette.com/products

- *Question marks* (sometimes called *problem children*). SBUs characterized by low market shares but high industry growth rates fit in this category. A question mark has not achieved a foothold in an expanding, but highly competitive, market. The question surrounding this type of endeavor is whether it can gain adequate market share and be profitable. If management answers "no," then the SBU should be divested or liquidated. If management instead answers "yes," the firm must

FIGURE 20.4

The BCG Matrix.

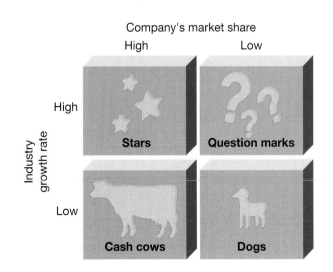

come up with the cash to build market share—more cash than the typical question mark generates from its own profits. Appropriate marketing strategies for question marks focus on establishing a strong differential advantage and, thereby, building customer support. Blockbuster Inc. is using the proceeds from its long-standing cash cow, video and now DVD rentals, to enter a growing area—the sale of both movies and games on DVDs. However, this effort is a question mark because of the presence of larger, entrenched competitors, particularly Wal-Mart, which prices DVDs very low to generate store traffic. Blockbuster believes its advantages lie in rewarding DVD purchasers with a free rental and in allowing DVD rental customers to buy a copy of the movie.[30]

www.blockbuster.com/bb/about

- *Dogs.* These SBUs have low market shares and operate in industries with low growth rates. A company normally would be unwise to invest substantial funds in SBUs in this category. Marketing strategies for dogs are intended to maximize any potential profits by minimizing expenditures *or* to promote a differential advantage to build market share. The company can say "Enough's enough!" and divest or liquidate a dog. Even Wal-Mart has had to deal with some dogs, selling its Deep Discount Store and Helen's Arts and Craft divisions.

The portfolios of most organizations with numerous SBUs or major products include a mix of stars, cash cows, question marks, and dogs. Consider one company's situation. The flagship brands of PepsiCo Inc.—Frito's, Pepsi, Quaker Oats, and Mountain Dew—can be described as cash cows. A joint venture with Lipton produced a line of stars: Lipton bottled and canned iced teas. The company also hopes that its Aquafina bottled water is another star. Pepsi's sports drink, All Sport, was a question mark at the time that PepsiCo acquired the competing Gatorade brand. Subsequently, PepsiCo sold the All Sport brand. Finally, Pepsi has had some dogs, such as Crystal, a clear cola that attracted few customers and thus failed.[31]

www.pepsico.com/company/brands/shtml

In the financial arena, an investor needs a balanced portfolio with respect to risks and potential returns. Likewise, a company should seek a balanced portfolio of SBUs. Certainly, cash cows are necessary, perhaps indispensable. Stars and question marks are also integral to a balanced portfolio, because products in growing markets determine a firm's long-term performance. Although dogs are undesirable, it's a rare company that doesn't have at least one.

A single firm typically cannot affect the growth rate for an entire industry. (An exception might be the dominant firm in a fairly new, rapidly growing industry. Recent examples include Microsoft in operating-systems software, and Rollerblade, Inc., in in-line skates.) If growth rate cannot be influenced, companies must turn to the other factor in the BCG matrix—market share. Hence, strategies based on the BCG matrix tend to concentrate on building or maintaining market share, depending on which of the four SBU categories is involved. Various strategies require differing amounts of cash, which means that management must continually allocate the firm's limited resources (notably cash) to separate marketing endeavors.

www.rollerblade.com/about_us

GE Business Screen

On the surface, the **GE business screen** appears to be very similar to the BCG matrix. This planning model, developed by General Electric with the assistance of the McKinsey consulting firm, also involves two factors and results in a grid.[32] But, as we shall see, the two models are different in significant respects.

Management can use the GE business screen to classify SBUs or major products on the basis of two factors: market attractiveness and business position. Each factor is rated according to several criteria. *Market attractiveness* should be judged with respect to market growth rate (similar to the BCG matrix), market size, degree of difficulty in entering the market, number and types of competitors, technological requirements, and profit margins, among other criteria. *Business position* encompasses market share (as in the BCG matrix), SBU size, strength of differential advantage, research and development capabilities, production capacity, cost controls, and strength of management, among others.

The criteria used to rate market attractiveness and business position are assigned different weights because some criteria are more important than others. Then each SBU is rated with respect to all criteria. Finally, overall ratings (usually numerical scores) for both factors are calculated for each SBU. On the basis of these ratings, each SBU is labeled as high, medium, or low with respect to (1) market attractiveness and (2) business position. For example, an SBU may be judged as having high market attractiveness but medium business position.

Following the ratings, an organization's SBUs are plotted on a 3 × 3 grid, as depicted in Figure 20.5. The best location for an SBU is the upper left cell because it points to (1) the most attractive market opportunity and (2) the best business position to seize that opportunity. In contrast, the worst location is the lower right cell, for the opposite reasons. The nine cells have implications with respect to how resources are allocated and, in turn, what marketing strategies are suitable.

Every organization has to make decisions aimed at using its limited resources most effectively. That's where these planning models can help—determining which SBUs or major products should be stimulated for growth, which ones maintained in their present market positions, and which ones eliminated. An SBU's evaluation, as indicated by its location on the GE business screen, suggests how it should be treated:

www.sgi.com/products

www.kodak.com

- *Invest strategy.* SBUs in the three cells in the upper left of the grid should receive ample resources. To strengthen or at least sustain such SBUs, bold, well-financed marketing efforts are needed. Several years ago, Silicon Graphics, Inc. announced that it would concentrate on producing powerful server computers that are well suited for challenging technical and Internet applications. The firm's decision seemed to be based on an assessment indicating high market attractiveness and a midrange business position. Eastman Kodak Co. is following this strategy with respect to digital cameras, as are several competitors.[33]

- *Protect strategy.* Resources should be allocated selectively to SBUs along the diagonal running from the lower left to the upper right of the grid. This somewhat defensive approach helps an SBU maintain its present market position while it generates cash needed by other SBUs. For example, while investing in digital cameras, Kodak has also spent large sums on extensive advertising campaigns to protect its position in the color film industry.[34]

- *Harvest strategy.* Because they lack an attractive market and a strong business position, SBUs in the two cells just below the three-cell diagonal should not receive substantial new resources. Instead, expenditures should be curtailed to

FIGURE 20.5

The GE Business Screen.

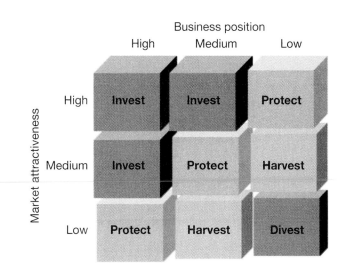

maximize any remaining profits. An alternative is to sell these SBUs. A case can be made that General Motors has been following this strategy with some of its brands, such as Oldsmobile (being phased out by 2005) and Buick, or even some models, such as full-size sedans.[35]

- *Divest strategy.* SBUs in the lower right cell do not have much going for them. Hence, an SBU in this location should not receive any resources. The best approach probably is to eliminate it from the organization's portfolio by selling it or, failing that, shutting it down. When the Gerber Products Company failed to convince senior citizens about the benefits of Singles, pureed single-serving meals such as turkey in mornay sauce, it dropped the line.[36]

www.kraft.com

Firms typically employ more than one of these four strategies and adjust them over time. To illustrate, after assessing its portfolio, Kraft Foods Inc. employed a *harvest* strategy by selling some divisions, such as specialty oils and food service, that had small profit margins and/or did not fit into the firm's core activities. A Kraft executive labeled the divested businesses "hippopotamuses" rather than the preferred "greyhounds." The funds derived from the transactions were used to support a *protect* strategy for key brands such as Maxwell House, Oscar Mayer, and Jell-O. More recently, Kraft followed an *invest* strategy by acquiring Nabisco and its stable of strong brands and by expanding its presence in the frozen-pizza area with brands such as Jack's and DiGiorno.[37]

Assessment of the Planning Models

These planning models have been praised and criticized.[38] Although each model is somewhat distinctive, all share some limitations:

- The primary limitation is probably oversimplification. The models base the assessment of market opportunities and subsequent decisions on only two or three key factors. In this regard, the GE business screen, which uses multiple criteria for assessing market attractiveness and business position, is an improvement over the BCG matrix. Still, the GE model lacks precision, in that what constitutes *high*, *medium*, and *low* for each of the two factors is largely a matter of judgment.

- There is also the possibility of placing an SBU on a grid or choosing a strategy without relevant, reliable information. For example, whether market share is critical to a product's profitability is still debated.

- Another potential limitation is that the results from a planning model might be used to override the critical business judgments made by line managers such as a marketing vice president. A better approach to decision making is to take into account the results from the model *and* the judgments of executives who are well informed about the particular situation.

However, these models also produce noteworthy benefits:

- Most important, they encourage careful, consistent assessment of market and product opportunities, allocation of resources, and formulation of strategies. Without planning models, these activities might be haphazard—for example, using one set of criteria this month and, with no good reason, another set next month.

- Another benefit is straightforward classification. Each model permits an organization to examine its entire portfolio of SBUs or major products in relation to criteria that influence business performance.

- The models can also point to attractive business opportunities and suggest ventures to avoid.

The search for helpful planning aids is ongoing. A while back, for instance, two consultants urged firms to develop their organizational strategies in terms of *value disciplines*. According to this framework, a firm must increase the value offered to customers by cutting prices, improving products, or enhancing service. Doing so requires choosing—and effectively implementing—one of three value disciplines: operational excellence, product leadership, or customer intimacy.[39]

Dell Computer and Wal-Mart exemplify operational excellence. Illustrations of product leadership include Nike (footwear and now sporting goods, such as golf clubs) and Jupiter Networks (top-of-the-line routers for directing Internet traffic, until the telecommunications industry slumped badly and the company had to redirect its activities). Customer intimacy emphasizes delivering precisely what specific customers really want and cannot find elsewhere. It appears that Amazon.com is trying to do this, as it provides customers with their own "store" (a record of their shopping experiences and additional recommendations related to a recent purchase) as well as allowing hopeful consumers to post "wish lists" that can be accessed by friends and family members.[40]

Overall, we believe planning models can help management allocate resources and also develop sound business and marketing strategies. Of course, any planning model should supplement, rather than replace or override, managers' judgments and decisions.

Summary

The management process consists of planning, implementation, and evaluation. Planning provides direction to an organization by deciding now what we are going to do later, including when and how we are going to do it. Strategic planning is intended to match an organization's resources with its market opportunities over the long run.

In any organization, there should be three levels of planning: strategic company planning, strategic marketing planning, and annual marketing planning. In strategic company planning, management defines the organization's mission, assesses its operating environment, sets long-range goals, and formulates broad strategies to achieve the goals. This level of planning guides planning in different functional areas, including marketing.

Strategic marketing planning entails five steps: conduct a situation analysis, develop marketing objectives, determine positioning and differential advantage, select target markets and measure market demand, and design a marketing mix. On the basis of strategic marketing plans, an annual marketing plan lays out a year's marketing activities for each major product and division of an organization. An annual plan includes tactics as well as strategies. It is typically prepared by the executive responsible for the division or product.

Management can rely on one or more of the following models for assistance with strategic planning: The product-market growth matrix, the BCG matrix, and the GE business screen. In seeking growth through new products, an organization may need to deal with the matter of cannibalization. A planning model helps management see how best to allocate its resources and to select effective marketing strategies.

More about Starbucks

Starbucks is still expanding, and in more than one direction. In 1996, the coffee purveyor formed an alliance with Dreyer's to create Starbucks ice cream, which quickly became the best-selling brand of coffee ice cream in the U.S. Starbucks also partnered with PepsiCo to produce and market Frappuccino® a bottled, ready-to-drink iced coffee that became a runaway success in North America. Now the joint venture is targeting canned DoubleShot, which has "the delicious intensity of rich espresso mellowed by a sweet touch of cream," at a younger market segment than the bottled Frappuccino. Starbucks sees it as a morning drink, also differentiating it from the afternoon break or pick-me-up market for Frappuccino.

Starbucks has also built a network of relationships with other firms that allow it to reach new markets. For instance, food service companies and grocery chains, warehouse clubs, coffee distributors, hotels, airlines, retailers, and restaurants are among the 5,500 food service accounts that bring in about one-third of the company's specialty revenues. The company also has a long-term agreement with Kraft Foods to market and distribute whole-bean and ground coffees in retail stores in the U.S. The Starbucks-PepsiCo collaboration distributes Frappuccino and DoubleShot to 200,000 supermarkets, convenience stores, and drugstores in the U.S. and Canada.

Starbucks has become a very familiar brand in many parts of the world. In fact, in a mid-2002 ranking compiled by *Business Week*, Starbucks was included among the fastest-growing global brands. Beyond North America and the United Kingdom, you can find Starbucks in many distant locales, including Thailand, Australia, Bahrain, Israel, Japan, Austria, and China. Starbucks' latest destinations include Greece, Germany, and Spain. The company now operates over 1,200 stores outside the U.S., most of them operated with local partners. Despite some initial resistance to Starbucks' outlet in Beijing's Forbidden City, the president of Starbucks Coffee International said at the time, "So far, we've been very fortunate; we've been embraced everywhere we've gone without exception."

To sustain its enviable record of sales and profits, Starbucks must address at least four major challenges:

- According to some reports, the number of Starbucks' outlets in the U. S. will soon reach the point of saturation.

- Whereas numerous "baby boomers" are enamored with the Starbucks concept, some members of Generations X and Y disdain the "expensive, fancy coffees" and New Age music that characterize the outlets.

- The employee harmony that Howard Schultz, the head of Starbucks, worked so hard to create has been eroding. Evidently, some store managers and counter workers have tired of the relatively low pay and odd working hours (such as arriving very early in the morning to open an outlet).

- Beyond different taste preferences, each foreign market has other distinctive attributes that need to be dealt with, such as various employment-related regulations in France, lower coffee prices in Italy, and an anti–U.S. sentiment in some parts of the world.

Ultimately, Starbucks envisions that its green-and-white logo will be on 25,000 outlets and dozens of products in millions of retail outlets around the world. Of course, past achievements do not assure future success. For that to happen, and for the chain to remain as famous as the first mate in *Moby Dick*, Schultz and his management team need to meet the preceding challenges while seeking new opportunities for growth.[41]

1. Where in the product-market growth matrix does Starbucks' expansion into grocery stores fall? What about ice cream? Frappuccino? Expansion around the globe?

2. Which of the above ventures are in line with the company's mission statement: "to establish Starbucks as the premier purveyor of the finest coffee in the world while maintaining our uncompromising principles as we grow"?

3. What strategies should Starbucks use in seeking success in countries such as Italy and France that have long-established traditions of independent coffee bars? What about in Asian countries that have long-standing tea-drinking traditions?

Key Terms and Concepts

Questions and Problems

1. Should a small firm (a manufacturer, a traditional retailer, or an online enterprise) engage in formal strategic planning? Why or why not?

2. Every organization needs to define its mission. Using a customer-oriented approach (benefits provided or wants satisfied), answer the question "What business are we in?" for each of the following companies:
   a. Holiday Inns (which is part of the Six Continents PLC organization)
   b. Amazon.com
   c. Dell Computer
   d. Universal (movie) Studios
   e. Goodyear Tire and Rubber Co.

3. In the situation-analysis step of strategic marketing planning, what specific external environmental factors should be analyzed by a firm that manufactures equipment used for backpacking in the wilderness?

4. Can a product have a differential advantage and a differential disadvantage at the same time?

5. Identify and explain the differential advantage or disadvantage for the primary product for one of the following organizations:
   a. United Airlines
   b. Your university or college

   c. Victoria's Secret
   d. The United Way in your community
   e. Major-league baseball
   f. eBay

6. For one of the six organizations listed immediately above, describe its target market(s).

7. Use an example to explain the concept of a strategic business unit.

8. a. What's the basic difference between the BCG matrix and the GE business screen?
   b. Which do you think is better, and why?

9. If you were the vice president of marketing for a large airline, which of the three planning models would you find most useful? Why?

10. "The European Union (EU), which has a goal of the economic unification of Europe, means absolute chaos for American firms targeting consumers in countries that belong to the EU. For a number of years, the situation will be so dynamic that U.S. executives should not waste their time on formal strategic planning related to European markets." Do you agree with this statement?

Interactive Marketing Exercises

1. Either go online or to your school's library and obtain a copy of an annual report for a major corporation. On the basis of your examination of the year-end review, which of the following product-market growth strategies is being used by this company: market penetration, market development, product development, and/or diversification?

2. Talk with the owner or manager of a local firm about its marketing strategies. Considering the information you have obtained, determine the differential advantage or disadvantage for the firm's primary product. Then indicate how the advantage could be strengthened or how the disadvantage could be alleviated.

Chapter
21

Marketing Implementation and Evaluation

PART 7

". . . perhaps no fashion-focused firm executes rapidly better than Zara."

Can Anyone Catch **Zara** in the Fashion Race?

Zara is the fashion world's fastest-growing retailer of moderately priced, stylish women's clothing, and the company seeks to move with lightning speed. In an industry where come-and-go fads are the norm, rapid implementation of strategies make sense—in fact, it may be necessary in order to survive. And perhaps no fashion-focused firm executes rapidly better than Zara, which is the cornerstone of Inditex Group, a privately held Spanish retail firm.

Its high-speed design, production, and distribution methods allow Zara to bring new merchandise to market in just three weeks, compared with six months or more for comparable retailers (nine months for Gap Inc., for instance). Instead of making changes once or twice a season, Zara delivers new styles to its 450 stores twice a week and carries no style for more than a month. In this way, Zara responds to customers' changing tastes during the course of a fashion season. Because its energetic designers take real-time information from store managers to create more than 12,000 new items each year, the clothing chain also offers the degree of variety that brings customers back week after week just to see what's new. Merchandising mistakes, when they occur, simply don't last long enough to hurt sales, and markdowns and clearance sales aren't necessary.

The first Zara store opened more than 25 years ago in La Coruña, Spain, which is still the company's corporate headquarters. Over the years, Zara has grown to be the largest unit of Inditex. The parent company also includes five smaller fashion chains selling such lines as lingerie, teen styles, and upscale men's clothing.

Collectively, the Inditex units sell more than 90 million garments a year.

Once Zara decided to make speed in implementation and responsiveness to fashion-conscious shoppers its hallmarks, its overall strategy fell into place. For example, most of its products are made in Spain whereas competitors typically use producers in developing countries in order to obtain lower labor costs. But as Inditex's CEO explains, "The fashion world is in constant flux and is driven not by supply but by customer demand. We need to give consumers what they want, and if I go to South America or Asia to make clothes, I simply can't move fast enough."

The same rationale guides operations at the company's 5-million-square-foot warehouse (the size of about 90 football fields). This enormous space is connected to 14 Zara factories by tunnels that carry merchandise on rails and cables to separate staging areas for every Zara store. "The vast majority of the items are in here only a few hours," says Inditex's logistics director. Managers and technical specialists monitor the physical distribution system constantly, considering details such as the sequence and size of deliveries, departure times, and shipping routes.

Deliveries are scheduled by time zone; orders for the Americas and Asia are packed and shipped in the morning, and orders for Europe in the afternoon. "We are always fine-tuning things, with the same objectives: flexibility and speed," says the logistics director. The aim is to deliver

www.zara.com

merchandise to stores before they open, when trucks can more easily cope with downtown traffic and store managers can readily accept and process the deliveries. A new warehouse that will double Inditex's capacity is being built northeast of Madrid, Spain.

Zara does almost no advertising or other promotion. What little it does announces new stores and reminds customers about a new fashion season a couple of times yearly. None of Inditex's chains, including Zara, sells through the Internet or catalogs. "The center of it all is the store," explains the group's managing director.

A combination of good fashion sense, real-time information from consumers, tightly controlled production, and carefully designed logistics—along with rapid implementation, of course—has helped triple Inditex's revenues in recent years. "No one can replicate their model," says one analyst.[1]

What does Zara do especially well in implementing its marketing strategies? What aspects of its implementation might be improved?

The Zara case illustrates not just inventive strategic plans but also ongoing implementation of strategies and tactics and periodic evaluation of results. In Chapter 20 we defined the management process in marketing as planning, implementing, and evaluating marketing in an organization. Most of this book has dealt with **planning** a marketing program. For example, we discussed how to select one or more target markets and how to design an integrated marketing program that satisfies the desires of a particular market.

Now in this chapter we discuss the implementation and evaluation of a marketing program. **Implementation** is the stage in the management process during which an organization attempts to carry out its strategic plan. At the end of an operating period (or even during the period) management should conduct an **evaluation** of the organization's performance. This stage involves determining how well the company or division is achieving the goals set forth in its strategic planning and then, as necessary, preparing new or modified plans.

Chapter Goals

After studying this chapter, you should be able to explain:

- The role of implementation in the management process.
- Organizational structures used to implement marketing programs.
- Warranties and other postsale services as means of assuring customer satisfaction.
- The nature of a marketing audit and the meaning of misdirected marketing effort.
- The steps comprising the evaluation process in marketing.
- Analyses of sales volume, market share, and marketing costs.
- How findings from sales and cost analyses can be used by managers.

Implementation in Marketing Management

There should be a close relationship among planning, implementation, and evaluation. Without strategic planning, a company's operational activities—its implementation tactics—can go off in any direction, like a team without a game plan. As stressed recently, "Implementation . . . is a critical link between the formulation of marketing strategies and the achievement of superior organizational performance."[2]

Sparked by management consulting firms, there was tremendous interest in strategic planning a couple of decades ago. Then disenchantment set in, because

In this ad, the Principal Financial Group stresses that it assembles a set of financial products to meet the specific needs of an individual customer rather than the same "cookie cutter" solution for everyone. Effective implementation will be challenging for the company, however. In particular, Principal will need to recruit, hire, and train representatives who can—as the ad promises—"analyze your current situation and arrive at smart business solutions."

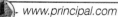
www.principal.com

many companies came to realize that strategic *planning* alone was not enough to ensure success. These plans had to be *effectively implemented*. Experience has shown that good planning cannot offset poor implementation, but effective implementation sometimes can overcome deficient planning.

In recent years, therefore, much attention has been devoted to implementing a company's strategies. Consider airlines and hotels that set objectives and then develop strategies related to prices. These enterprises are likely to be interested in the degree of price competition, the percentage of seats or rooms sold, and total revenue. Computer programs can assist service firms in this area of yield management. Omni Hotels Corp., for example, uses a program called OmniCHARM (Centralized Hotel Automated Revenue Management) to estimate demand on the basis of historical sales patterns. The demand estimates, along with data about the number of unsold rooms for different dates, are helpful in setting specific prices that coincide with the firm's pricing objectives and strategies.[3]

Implementation comprises three activities:

- *Organizing the marketing effort.* The relationship between marketing and the other functions of the firm must be defined. Once a company has developed its strategic marketing plan, an early activity is to organize the people within the marketing department who will implement it.

- *Staffing the organization.* For plans to produce the intended results, a company or a nonbusiness concern needs skilled, dedicated employees to carry them out well. Thus selection of people is all-important—whatever the type of organization. A college coach's success depends greatly on his or her ability to recruit the right players. According to one article, the most common reason for failure among top executives is not putting the right people in the right jobs. Thus a CEO who intends to be successful should adopt the motto, "People first, strategy second."[4] Likewise, a sales manager's success depends in great measure on the people who are selected for selling positions.

- *Directing the execution of marketing plans.* In this third phase of implementation, revenues are generated by carrying out the firm's strategies and tactics. To do so, management needs to direct the work of the people who have been selected and organized as the marketing team. Success in this phase depends to a large extent on four important aspects of managing employees—delegation, coordination, motivation, and communication.

Detailed discussion of staffing and directing an organization can be found in management textbooks. However, in this text, it is appropriate to consider how organizational structures are used to implement marketing programs.

Organizing for Implementation

Organizational structures are receiving increasing attention because executives in both American and foreign companies recognize that yesterday's arrangements may hinder operations in today's dynamic environment.[5] Traditional structures isolate different business functions and have many managerial layers between customers and decision makers. That runs counter to satisfying customers profitably, which requires talking with—and listening to—customers. Teamwork across business functions such as marketing and production is also essential.

Procter & Gamble, General Motors, Eastman Kodak, Siemens (the huge German electronics concern), and Donna Karan International (the clothing maker) are among many firms that have made significant organizational changes fairly recently.[6] In a very real sense, traditional vertical structures are being replaced by horizontal organizations.[7] Several specific trends are noteworthy:

- *Fewer organizational levels.* The intent is to aid communication among executives who develop strategic plans, the employees who have continuing contact with the market, and customers.

- *Employee empowerment.* Granting more authority to middle-level executives in decentralized locations can stimulate innovation and generate faster responses to market shifts. And empowering customer-contact personnel can boost both customer satisfaction and repeat business. With that in mind, Enterprise Rent-A-Car allows an employee to take special actions to satisfy a customer. Likewise, any staff member at a Ritz-Carlton hotel is empowered to spend up to $2,000 on a solution to a customer's problem.[8]

www.enterprise.com/about

www.ritzcarlton.com

- *Cross-functional teams.* By having personnel from various departments work on a project, not only are barriers among functions broken down but the best combination of expertise and experience is dedicated to an assignment. Among the believers is a vice president of Nestlé USA, who stated, "Cross-functional teams in almost every instance will come up with a better solution than an individual." This type of team is strongly recommended for developing new products, particularly in high-technology industries.[9]

Revising an organizational structure is challenging, because employees must give up long-standing, comfortable arrangements. But the results often justify the effort. Modicon, a manufacturer of automation-control equipment, once considered product development strictly an engineering task. Now it is carried out by a 15-person team representing marketing, manufacturing, and finance in addition to

www.modicon.com

engineering. Under the new arrangement, the time required to develop software packages was cut by two-thirds.[10]

Company-Wide Organization

In Chapter 1 we stated that one of the three components of the marketing concept is to coordinate all marketing activities. In product-oriented or sales-oriented firms, marketing activities are likely to be fragmented. The sales force is separate from advertising, and sales training may be under the human resources department. In a market-oriented enterprise, all marketing activities are coordinated under one executive, as shown in Figure 21.1. The marketing chief, who usually is a vice president, reports directly to the president, and is equivalent to top executives in finance, production, and other major functions.

Another aspect of organizational coordination is to establish effective working relationships between marketing and each of the other major functional areas. Marketing can help production, for example, by providing accurate sales forecasts. Production can return the favor by providing defect-free finished products precisely when needed to fill customers' orders. Marketing and finance specialists can work together to establish pricing and credit policies.

Sales Organization within a Marketing Department

Within a marketing department, especially in large firms, the selling function may account for a significant share of resources. Thus, a sales force frequently is specialized in some organizational fashion. The intent is to effectively implement the company's strategic marketing plan. Most often, the sales force is specialized in one of three ways—by geographic territory, product line, or customer type. Sometimes a hybrid form is created by combining the best features of two forms.

Geographic Specialization
Perhaps the most widely used method of specializing selling activities is on the basis of **geographic specialization.** Each sales person is assigned a specific territory in which to sell. Several sales people representing contiguous territories are placed under a district or regional sales manager. As shown in Figure 21.2A, these territorial supervisors report directly to the general sales manager.

FIGURE 21.1

Company Organization Embracing the Marketing Concept.

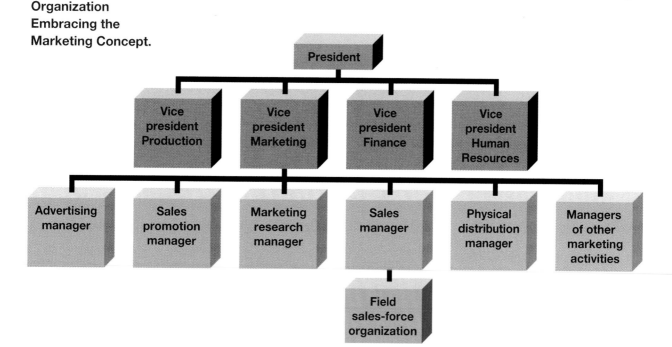

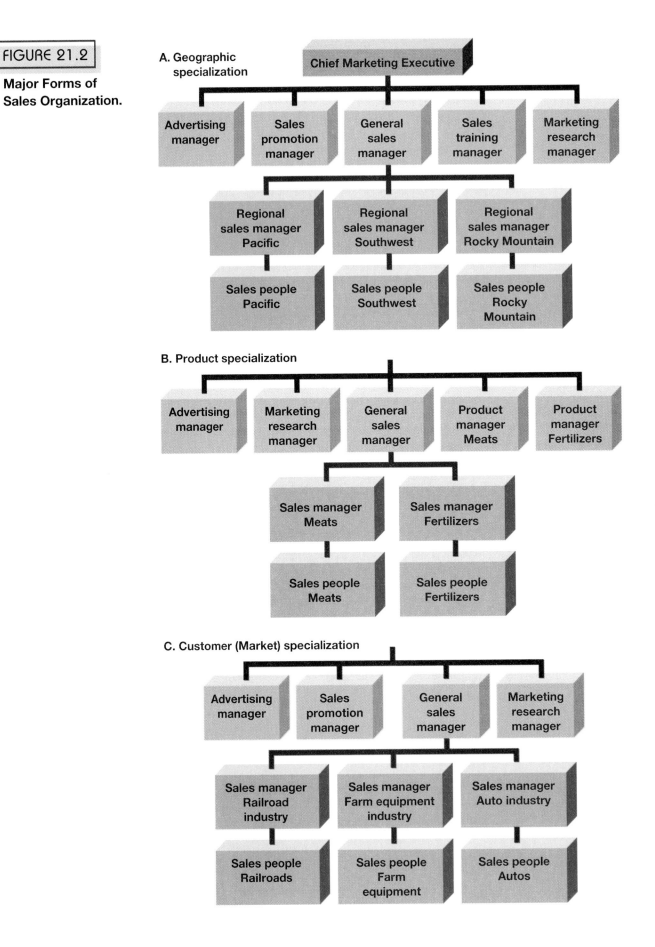

FIGURE 21.2

Major Forms of
Sales Organization.

A. Geographic specialization

Chief Marketing Executive

- Advertising manager
- Sales promotion manager
- General sales manager
- Sales training manager
- Marketing research manager

General sales manager:
- Regional sales manager Pacific → Sales people Pacific
- Regional sales manager Southwest → Sales people Southwest
- Regional sales manager Rocky Mountain → Sales people Rocky Mountain

B. Product specialization

- Advertising manager
- Marketing research manager
- General sales manager
- Product manager Meats
- Product manager Fertilizers

General sales manager:
- Sales manager Meats → Sales people Meats
- Sales manager Fertilizers → Sales people Fertilizers

C. Customer (Market) specialization

- Advertising manager
- Sales promotion manager
- General sales manager
- Marketing research manager

General sales manager:
- Sales manager Railroad industry → Sales people Railroads
- Sales manager Farm equipment industry → Sales people Farm equipment
- Sales manager Auto industry → Sales people Autos

A geographic organization is supposed to result in excellent implementation of sales strategies in each local market and strong coordination of the sales force. Customers can be serviced quickly and thoroughly, and local sales reps can respond better to competitors' actions in a given territory.

As its major drawback, a geographic organization does not provide the product expertise or other specialized knowledge that some customers may want. To address that problem, some time ago the professional imaging division of the Eastman Kodak Company switched from a geographic alignment of its sales force to one that takes into account sales people's expertise *and* customer needs. Rather than calling on all kinds of customers in a territory such as Atlanta, a Kodak rep now works with certain types of customers, say commercial color labs, in a somewhat larger geographic area.[11]

Product Specialization

Another basis for organizing a sales force is **product specialization,** as illustrated in Figure 21.2B. A company such as a meat packer may divide all of its products into two lines—meat products and fertilizers (made from the by-products of meat packing). One group of sales reps sells only meats and another group sells the fertilizers. Each group reports to its own product sales manager who, in turn, reports to the general sales manager.

This type of organization is especially well suited for companies that are marketing:

- Complex technical products, such as a manufacturer of several electronic products.
- Unrelated or dissimilar products, including a company marketing luggage, folding tables and chairs, and toy building blocks.
- Thousands of items, such as a hardware wholesaler.

The main advantage of a product-focused sales organization is the attention each line can get from the sales force. A drawback is that more than one sales rep from a company may call on the same customer. This duplication not only is costly but also may irritate customers. In 2000, FedEx Corp. converted to a unified sales force for its airfreight and ground-delivery services. The move was made in order to reduce duplication and to facilitate cross-selling of the distinct services. Several years after switching a sales force to customer specialization, Eastman Kodak adopted a product-focused arrangement for the entire company. The intent was to give executives more flexibility in managing product groups.[12]

Customer Specialization

In recent years, many companies have divided their sales departments on the basis of **customer specialization.** In this arrangement, customers are grouped by type of industry or by channel of distribution. An oil company may categorize its markets by industry, such as railroads, auto manufacturers, and farm-equipment producers, as shown in Figure 21.2C. A firm that specializes its sales operations by channel of distribution may have one sales force selling to wholesalers and another dealing directly with large retailers.

As more companies fully implement the marketing concept, the customer-focused type of organization is likely to increase. This arrangement is consistent with the customer-oriented philosophy that underlies the marketing concept. That is, the organizational emphasis is on customers and markets rather than on products. One author maintains that an organization must be structured around customer groups if integrated marketing communications is to be effective.[13]

A variation of customer specialization is the **major accounts organization.** Companies adopt this structure as a better way to deal with large, important customers. A major accounts organization usually involves team selling, a concept introduced in Chapter 18. Under this arrangement, a selling team—consisting perhaps of a sales rep, a technical specialist, a financial executive, and a manufacturing person—negotiates with a buying team from a customer's organization. Procter & Gamble, for example, established a series of selling teams, each specializing in a broad category (such as cleaning products) to better service key accounts, including Wal-Mart.

Postsale Follow-Through

It is shortsighted to think that marketing ends when a sale is made. In line with the marketing concept, a firm should be committed to ensuring that customers are fully satisfied. If that is accomplished, organizational objectives (including the desired level of profits) probably will be achieved. In addition, it's likely that loyal customers will be created, thereby contributing to the future vitality of the company.

Some specific elements of a marketing program are implemented largely after a sale is made. Customer satisfaction—as well as future revenues—require that a company provide its customers with suitable warranties and other desired postsale services. Thus we should consider important aspects of these marketing activities.

Warranties

The purpose of a **warranty,** which we use interchangeably with *guarantee,* is to assure buyers they will be compensated if the product does not perform up to reasonable expectations. American companies decide on the terms and length of their product warranties. In contrast, the countries comprising the European Union agreed jointly that the length of guarantees must be at least two years. EU members that stipulate longer mandatory lengths (six years in the United Kingdom, for example) can maintain them. All of the member countries converted an EU directive regarding consumer guarantees into national laws at the start of 2002.[14]

Years ago, courts seemed to recognize only an **express warranty,** which is one stated in written or spoken words. Usually this form of reassurance was quite limited in its coverage and seemed mainly to protect the seller from buyers' claims. As a result, the following caution was appropriate: "Caveat emptor," which means "Let the buyer beware."

But times change. Numerous complaints led to a governmental campaign to protect consumers in many areas, including product warranties. Courts and government agencies have broadened the scope of warranty coverage by recognizing **implied warranty.** This means a warranty was *intended,* although not actually stated, by the seller. Furthermore, producers are being held responsible, even when the sales contract is between a retailer and a consumer. Now the caution is: "Caveat venditor," or "Let the seller beware."

www.hyundaiusa.com/
service/sewar.html

An automaker can differentiate its particular brand in various ways—through styling and/or fuel economy, for example. In 1999, seeking a differential advantage, Hyundai announced the longest warranty in the auto industry. The firm's warranty was extended two years or 24,000 miles beyond the norm. Following the change, Hyundai's sales rose substantially. A related issue is the cost associated with the more generous warranty.

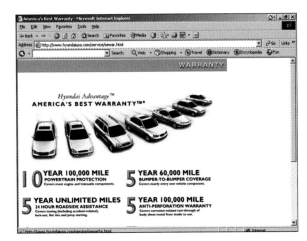

www.cpsc.gov

www.djgusa.com

Product Liability Passage of the Consumer Product Safety Act in 1972 reflected a changed attitude regarding product liability and injurious products. This federal legislation created the Consumer Product Safety Commission (CPSC), which has the authority to mandate safety standards for many consumer products not covered by separate laws or other agencies. The CPSC publishes information regarding injurious products, naming brands and producers. It can ban the distribution of these products without a court hearing. In turn, offending companies and the individuals leading them may face criminal, not just civil, charges. For example, a $1.3 million penalty was levied against Cosco, a manufacturer, for not reporting numerous injuries and at least one death attributed to four flawed products, including a high chair that was very complicated to assemble and thus was sometimes used incorrectly.[15]

Product liability is a legal action asserting that an illness, accident, or death resulted from the named product because it was harmful, faulty, or inadequately labeled. Basically, liability results from one or more of three problems: a flaw in product design, a defect in production, or a deficiency in warning the customer about proper use and potentially harmful misuse of the product.[16]

In the past 20 years, some product-liability claims involved entire categories of goods, including asbestos insulation and breast implants. Other cases focused on specific brands of toys, tampons, pharmaceuticals, birth-control devices, tires, automobiles, acne medication, and chain saws, among others. For instance, claims were brought against the makers of the Ford Explorer sport-utility vehicle and Firestone tires, alleging liability in numerous rollover accidents. Claims have also been filed against firms offering services such as auto repairs and weight loss programs. According to critics, some product-liability suits are groundless or lack compelling evidence. For example, a law professor stated recently, "Asbestos litigation today is, for the most part, a massively fraudulent enterprise."[17]

In many product-liability cases, juries have granted enormous settlements to the plaintiffs—sometimes tens or hundreds of millions of dollars. The most significant recent cases have involved the tobacco industry, with some of these lawsuits going in favor of the tobacco companies and others ending with awards to the plaintiffs. Cigarette makers were concerned about potentially catastrophic judgments from lawsuits filed on behalf of a large group of harmed smokers. Thus they accepted marketing restrictions and made large payments to the government (beyond normal taxes) in exchange for some limits on product-liability lawsuits. In 1998, tobacco companies agreed to pay a total of over $200 *billion* to the states over 25 years. In return, the industry received protection at the state level. A similar arrangement at the federal level has not materialized.[18]

Thousands of product-liability claims are filed every year in the U.S. Thus this issue is of great consequence to companies because of the financial risk as well as the adverse publicity connected with damage claims. It has proven to be difficult to write a federal law that (1) curbs lawsuits related to allegedly defective products and (2) is considered fair and acceptable by groups on both sides of the issue. A recent attempt in Congress sought to place limits on product-liability judgments against small companies, specifically those with fewer than 25 employees.[19]

Lawsuits charging harm from defective products occur around the world. To mention just two examples, a group of British consumers sued three drug companies over adverse side effects from oral contraceptives, and Japanese consumers sought restitution from a milk products company because they fell ill after consuming a tainted product. In mid-2002, South Korea enacted product-liability legislation, joining more than 30 other major countries with such laws. Product-liability problems are likely to increase for companies marketing in western Europe. European laws now provide compensation to consumers in cases of demonstrated bodily injury or property damage from products, even when there has been no negligence on the part of the seller.[20]

To ward off product-liability claims, many manufacturers place expanded labels on their goods, telling consumers to not misuse the product and informing them of almost every conceivable danger associated with using it. Such **warning labels** go so far as to state: "Shin pads cannot protect any part of the body they do not cover." Or: "Do not iron clothes while on body." And, believe it or not, on a chain saw: "Do not attempt to stop chain with hands or genitals." Producers hope such blatant, seemingly obvious warnings protect them against charges that they did not properly inform consumers about a product's use, misuse, and potential dangers.[21]

Benefits versus Costs   Deficient warranties and warning labels that do not protect companies from product-liability claims can be extremely expensive. In another sense, warranties can be very costly if numerous buyers must be compensated when a product fails or is unsatisfactory. Perhaps for that reason, some companies with powerful brands, including Dell Computer and Sony, are curtailing the length of their warranties.[22]

Rather than considering only costs, some organizations see marketing benefits in warranties. Many sellers, for example, promote their warranties in order to stimulate first-time *and* repeat purchases by reducing consumers' risks. With that in mind, more companies are making their warranties understandable and comprehensive—and, therefore, customer-friendly. Further, "underdog" firms, such as computer maker Atlas Micro, are seeking an advantage by offering longer warranties. The Korean manufacturer Hyundai offers a 10-year warranty on its cars' engines and transmissions and 5-year or 60,000-mile (whichever comes first) coverage on the rest of the vehicle.[23]

It is common practice among manufacturers, retailers, and especially service firms (given the intangible nature of services) to offer a full refund of the purchase price to a dissatisfied buyer. A number of hotel chains, for example, give cash, discounts, or even a free night's stay to any customer who reports a problem. In another field, Harry and David, which sells fresh fruit through catalogs and now online, offers the following assurance: "We guarantee your complete satisfaction. If you are not satisfied with this product, just let us know and we'll make it right with either an appropriate replacement or a refund." Occasionally, a customer may abuse a full-refund guarantee (by exaggerating the magnitude of a problem with a hotel room, for example), but the benefits in terms of avoiding customer dissatisfaction and building customer loyalty are compelling.[24]

www.harryanddavid.com

Customer-friendly warranties are absolutely vital in the online environment. According to one study, offering a money-back guarantee is the biggest step an Internet merchant can take in order to reduce the risk that consumers associate with online shopping.[25]

Other Postsale Services

Many companies must provide **postsale service**, notably maintenance and repairs, to fulfill the terms of their warranties. Other firms offer postsale services to fully satisfy their customers or even gain a differential advantage over competitors. Some businesses use postsale services to augment their revenues. For instance, Otis and Montgomery, both of which sell elevators, rely on service contracts for a portion of their revenues *and* profits.

With more complex products, increasingly demanding and vocal consumers, and now the Internet environment, postsale service has become essential. There are distinctive challenges in attaining both efficiency and effectiveness when providing such services. To illustrate, brief profiles of several postsale activities follow.

Merchandise Returns   The best approach is to minimize the need for returns by selling a satisfying product to a customer and, in situations where delivery is involved, getting the shipment to its destination on time. Even under the best of cir-

How could a guarantee be legal in all countries but one?

Like many firms, Lands' End (acquired by Sears in 2002) reassures its American customers by offering a no-questions-asked, money-back guarantee. Although permissible in countries around the world, this guarantee ran into legal problems in Germany. Soon after the clothing marketer started doing business there, competitors complained to the government about the intruder's warranty. According to a German law enacted in the 1930s, no giveaway of significant value can accompany a purchase. The German Supreme Court concluded that the guarantee violated the old law and represented unfair competition.

What could Lands' End do? Shut down its German operations? Drop or dilute the guarantee? The direct marketer stopped promoting the guarantee directly. However, the Lands' End website in Germany displayed a link to the firm's U.S. website, where the warranty is detailed.

Lands' End also ran an ad in Germany that alluded to the guarantee and mocked the ban. The ad pictured a fly, a washing machine, and the Lands' End logo accompanied by a caption that said the guarantees for the three objects were, respectively, one day, six months, and "advertisement forbidden in Germany." The ad brought even more attention to the guarantee and, by so doing, perhaps (1) attracted additional customers and (2) aggravated both competitors and the government in Germany. In the United Kingdom, Lands' End advertised its unconditional guarantee as being "so good, the Germans banned it."

As e-commerce burgeoned, the German government realized that laws restricting competition could put its country's firms at a disadvantage. Hence, legislation prohibiting such practices as substantial price discounts and giveaways were repealed in 2001. When that occurred, Lands' End may have been pleased to be free to promote its guarantee in Germany *or* maybe the firm missed the free publicity generated by the furor over the "illegal giveaways."

Sources: Lisa A. Yorgey, "A Victory for Direct Marketing in Germany," *Target Marketing,* March 2001, p. 28; Peter Girard, "Lands' End Winks at German Ruling," *Catalog Age,* January 2000, p. 6; "Lands' End's Guarantees Are Too True to Be Good for Competitors in Germany," *St. Louis Post-Dispatch,* Sept. 26, 1999, p. E6; and "Lands' End Ads Run Afoul of German Law," *Advertising Age,* Nov. 2, 1998, p. 48.

cumstances, however, some customers want or need to return their purchases. According to one estimate, about 6% of all items purchased at the retail level are returned. Other recent research found that easy return or exchange of merchandise was the third most important consideration for online shoppers of luxury goods, such as expensive shoes and watches.[26]

Recognizing the importance and the cost of returns, a firm should consider how stringent or generous its conditions for accepting merchandise returns will be. Stringent conditions may curtail costs but are unlikely to gain favor with customers; the opposite is true for generous conditions. In 2002, perhaps looking for ways to improve their financial positions, a number of well-known retail firms tightened their return policies. Target, for instance, announced that a purchase receipt must accompany any return request and that a "restocking fee" will be charged on some products in the electronics area.[27]

Merchants that sell over the Internet and also operate retail stores or wholesale branches face the decision of whether or not to accept returns at the physical outlets. If a firm prohibits its bricks-and-mortar outlets from accepting returns of online purchases, it forfeits a built-in advantage it has over strictly online competitors. Thus the trend among "bricks-and-clicks" middlemen is to accept returns at their outlets.

Online-only companies are discovering that making the return process convenient for customers is a special challenge. Typically, customers are asked to send the returns to a warehouse or office operated by the company or to a separate business that handles fulfillment of orders for the online firm. On the basis of its studies, a research agency recommended that one of the top three ways of improving online service is to establish a simple return process. As with many matters, that's easier said than done.[28]

Many, probably most, online marketers now realize that the quality of customer service is at least as important as website design, product assortment, and competitive prices in attracting and then keeping buyers. Further, many online customers strongly prefer to interact with an actual person. Companies that sell on the Internet can provide this type of customer service on their own or they can outsource this task to a vendor such as LivePerson.

www.liveperson.com

www.otis.com

Maintenance and Repairs A recurring concern among consumers is that manufacturers and retailers do not provide adequate maintenance and repair services for the products they sell. A manufacturer can transfer the primary responsibility for such services to middlemen, compensate them for their efforts, and possibly even train their technicians and customer-contact staff members. This approach is evident in the automobile and personal computer industries. Or a manufacturer can establish regional factory service centers, staff them with well-trained company employees, and strive to make maintenance and repairs a profit-generating activity. This approach is found in the appliance industry. Or service, or at least the first point of contact, can be provided centrally. To process requests for various forms of customer service, Otis established a center that handles over 1.5 million calls a year, responding to situations ranging from a broken escalator to people trapped in an elevator.[29]

Some manufacturers of costly computers, office equipment, and medical diagnostic equipment have developed "smart" products. With built-in sensors and microcomputers, such products diagnose themselves and/or allow a technician to conduct a diagnosis from a distance by means of either wired or wireless telecommunications. This innovation expedites repairs and, by so doing, cuts aggravating "downtime" for valuable products. Further, to the extent that labor costs associated with repairs are reduced, the manufacturer's profit margin on service contracts is improved.[30]

Complaint Handling The most common gripes among consumers, as determined by one study, are deficient product quality, deceptive sales methods, and poor repair work. In 2001, the industries with the dubious distinction of prompting the

Can online customer service be personal—and pleasing?

Recognized as an important factor in closing sales and pleasing shoppers after a transaction is made, customer service in cyberspace is receiving more and more attention. Consequently, Internet merchants are seeking the optimal way of dealing with questions and comments from shoppers who are considering a purchase as well as customers who are happy and those who are not so happy for some reason. As in other business endeavors, an optimum would be the most efficient way of achieving a level of effectiveness that is consistent with the company's goals.

Numerous, perhaps most, online enterprises encourage input via e-mail and/or via a toll-free telephone line. Recent advances in technology are helping to improve customer service in cyberspace. New software can scan customers' e-mails for key words. Then, depending on the key word, the e-mail might be routed to the department that is best able to respond to the customer, or a standard reply is automatically sent back via e-mail (an electronic "form letter"). A drawback of e-mail, besides any delayed response, is the lack of actual human interaction. As far back as 1999 (which is a long time ago given the rapid development of the Internet), research indicated that 90% of online customers want to interact with a real person—now.

A relatively new technology allows real-time electronic dialogue between an online shopper and a firm's customer service agent. The consumer initiates the "chat," typically through an icon on the website that has a label such as "Live Help." Then one or more e-mail iterations ensue. The online agent can even synchronize screens with the customer so they are looking at the same images or information. Typically, the agents are expected to chat with several customers at the same time; of course, effectiveness and customer satisfaction may drop as a result of this attempt at boosting efficiency.

Some online enterprises use their own software and employees to handle shoppers' requests for real-time, personal assistance. Thousands of other Internet merchants are outsourcing this task to firms such as LivePerson, Inc., a specialist in live chat technology. Neiman Marcus Group's online retail division and the Intuit software company are among LivePerson's clients. A live chat allows a firm to provide a measure of personal service to online shoppers and customers. At the same time, this approach affords the opportunity to collect a variety of useful data regarding consumers' interests (about product features, for example) and concerns (about matters such as navigating around the website).

Another new technology has the capability of combining a live chat and a toll-free telephone call. Using voice-over-IP (the "IP" stands for Internet protocol), an online shopper whose computer has a built-in microphone would click an icon to initiate a telephone call to a customer service rep. The same telephone line would be used for Internet access and the call. The audio quality of voice-over-IP is still being refined so as to be suitable for widespread usage—and easy communication between a customer and a customer service rep.

As one company executive observed, "The irony is that the primary benefit of online shopping—convenience—is being undermined by a lack of real-time purchasing assistance." Thus effective real-time customer service will be essential for online firms if they are to establish and maintain a differential advantage over traditional businesses *and* their online competitors.

Sources: Mary Ellen Podmolik, "Companies Chatting Up Customers," *Crain's Chicago Business,* Nov. 18, 2002, p. SR4; Phil Hochmuth, "Quality Question Remains for VoIP," *Network World,* Oct. 7, 2002, no pages given; Peter Fuller, "A Two-Way Conversation," *Brandweek,* Feb. 25, 2002, p. 26; "Retailers Use Online Chats for Customer Service," *St. Louis Post-Dispatch,* Dec. 6, 1999, p. A6; "Online Customer Service: Guiding Consumers through the Maze," *Financial Service ONLINE,* November 1999, pp. 24–27+; and Bill Meyers, "Service with an E-Smile," *USA Today,* Oct. 12, 1999, pp. 1B, 2B.

---

largest numbers of consumer complaints are home improvement, household goods, and auto sales. Consumers become particularly aggravated if they cannot voice their complaints and get their problems solved. According to research, "A majority of consumers are dissatisfied with the way their complaints are resolved."[31] Ignored or mishandled complaints can have dire consequences with respect to lost business and/or negative word-of-mouth communication.

Prompt, effective handling of complaints can increase or, if necessary, restore a customer's confidence in a firm, irrespective of whether it operates in physical space or cyberspace. With that in mind, a producer typically provides customers with a toll-free telephone number and an e-mail address for its customer service department. Recent research indicated that about 85% of phoned-in complaints are satisfied in a single call; less than 35% of complaints conveyed by e-mail or another electronic means are resolved so readily.[32]

Postsale follow-through, like more visible elements of the marketing mix, can be either a differential advantage or a disadvantage. Thus the various forms of follow-through certainly should be on the list of matters managers monitor constantly.

Evaluating Marketing Performance

Soon after a firm's plans have been set in operation, the process of evaluation should begin. Without evaluation, management cannot tell whether a plan is working or which factors are contributing to its success or failure. Evaluation logically follows planning and implementation. A circular relationship exists, as illustrated in Figure 21.3. Plans are made, they are put into action, the results of those actions are evaluated, and new plans are prepared on the basis of this evaluation. To illustrate, the Walt Disney Co. launched an Internet portal, Go.com. However, after two years, the giant entertainment firm abandoned the effort because it could not compete effectively with other portals, such as Yahoo!, for customers. Instead, Disney refocused its Internet endeavors on the websites of its core brands, such as ABC News and ESPN along with the Disney online store.[33]

disney.store.go.com

abcnews.com

Previously we discussed evaluation as it relates to individual parts of a marketing program—the product-planning process, the performance of the sales force, and the effectiveness of the advertising program, for instance. Now let's look at the evaluation of the *total marketing effort.*

The Marketing Audit

A marketing audit is an essential element in a thorough evaluation. An audit implies an assessment of some activity, such as an enterprise's finances. Thus a **marketing audit** is a comprehensive review and evaluation of the marketing function in an organization—its philosophy, environment, goals, strategies, organizational structure, human and financial resources, and performance.[34]

As suggested by Figure 21.3, the results of any evaluation—including a marketing audit—represent vital input to an organization's planning. In advocating the value of marketing audits in the banking industry, one writer stressed, "Simply stated, a [strategic] marketing plan should only be written after the completion of an intensive, objective marketing audit."[35]

A complete marketing audit is an extensive, difficult project. That's why it is conducted infrequently, perhaps every several years. However, a company should not delay a marketing audit until a major crisis arises.

The rewards of a marketing audit can justify the effort. By reviewing its strategies, the firm is likely to keep abreast of its changing marketing environment. Management can identify problem areas in marketing. The audit can spot, for instance, lack of coordination in the marketing program, outdated strategies, or unrealistic goals. Successes can also be analyzed, so the company can capitalize on its strong points. Furthermore, an audit should anticipate future situations. It is intended for "prognosis as well as diagnosis. . . . It is the practice of preventive as well as curative marketing medicine."[36]

FIGURE 21.3

The Circular Relationship among Management Tasks.

Misdirected Marketing Effort

One benefit of evaluation is that it helps correct **misdirected** (or misplaced) **marketing effort.**

The 80–20 Principle

In most firms, a large proportion of the total orders, customers, territories, or products accounts for only a small share of total performance. Conversely, a small proportion produces a large share of sales or profit performance. This relationship has been characterized as the **80–20 principle.** That is, the large majority (say, 80%) of the orders, customers, territories, or products contribute only a small fraction (say, 20%) of sales or profit. One professor said, rather harshly, that customers in this group "nag you, call you, and don't add much revenue."[37] On the other hand, a relatively few of the selling units account for the large majority of the volume or profit.

The 80–20 figure is used simply to highlight the misplacement of marketing effort. In reality, of course, the percentage split varies from one situation to another. To give a couple of hypothetical examples, just 5% of customers might provide 90% of an organization's sales, or 70% of a service firm's clientele might lodge just 3% of all complaints (which means, of course, that the other 30% submit the remaining 97%).

The basic reason for the 80–20 (or similar) split is that almost every marketing program includes misdirected effort. Marketing endeavors and costs are proportional to the *numbers* of territories, customers, or products, rather than to their actual sales volume or profit. For example, approximately the same order-filling, billing, and delivery expenses are involved whether a $500 suit *or* a $25 necktie is sold in a May Company department store. A manufacturer such as Xerox may assign one sales person to each territory. Yet usually there are differences in the actual sales volume and profit among the territories. In each example, the marketing expense is not in line with the actual return.

Reasons for Misdirected Effort

Frequently, executives cannot uncover misdirected effort because they lack sufficient information. The **iceberg principle** is an analogy that illustrates this situation. Only the small tip of an iceberg is visible above the water's surface, and the huge submerged part represents the hidden danger. The figures representing total sales or total costs on an operating statement are like the tip of an iceberg. The detailed figures representing sales, costs, and other performance measures for each territory or product correspond to the dangerous submerged part.

Total sales or cost figures are too general to be useful in evaluation; in fact, they often are misleading. A company's overall sales and profit figures may be satisfactory. But when these totals are subdivided by pertinent factors such as geographic territories, products, or time periods, serious weaknesses often are discovered. A manufacturer of audio equipment showed an overall increase of 12% in sales and 9% in net profit on one product line in one year. But in looking below the "tip of the iceberg," the company's executives found that the sales change within territories ranged from an increase of 19% to a decrease of 3%. Profit rose as much as 14% in some territories, but was down 20% in one.

A more basic cause of misplaced marketing effort is that executives must make decisions based on inadequate knowledge of the exact nature of costs. Too often, management lacks useful information about (1) the disproportionate spread of marketing effort, (2) reliable standards for determining what should be spent on marketing, and (3) the results that should be expected from these expenditures.

As an illustration, a company may spend $250,000 more on advertising this year than last year. But management ordinarily cannot state how much sales or profit should rise as a result of the added expenditures. Also, the executives do not know what would have happened if they had spent the same amount on (1) new-product development, (2) training seminars for middlemen, or (3) some other aspect of the marketing program.

The Evaluation Process

Whether a complete marketing audit or only an appraisal of individual components of the marketing program, the evaluation process involves three steps:

1. Find out *what* happened. Compile the facts, compare results with goals and budgets to determine where they differ.

2. Find out *why* it happened. Determine, to the extent possible, which specific factors in the marketing program caused the results.

3. Decide *what to do* about it. Plan the next period's program so as to improve on unsatisfactory performance and capitalize on the aspects that worked out well.

To evaluate a total marketing program, we need to analyze results. Two tools are available to do this—sales volume analysis and marketing cost analysis. We'll discuss both tools using the Great Midwest Company ("the other GM")—a firm that markets office furniture. The company's 14-state market is divided into four sales districts, each with seven or eight sales people and a district sales manager. The firm sells to office equipment wholesalers and directly to large business users. GM's product mix is divided into four groups—desks, chairs, filing equipment, and office accessories (wastebaskets and desk sets, for example). Some of these products are manufactured by GM and some are purchased from other firms.

Analyses of Sales Volume and Market Share

Management should analyze its sales volume in total and by relevant subdivisions such as geographic territories and product lines. The sales figures also should be examined against company goals. But that's not enough. A firm needs to measure its sales against the entire industry in which it competes. Each of these methods is described now.

Sales Volume Analysis

We start with an analysis of Great Midwest's total sales, as shown in Table 21.1. A **sales volume analysis** is a detailed study of the *net sales* section of a company's profit and loss statement (operating statement). Annual sales doubled from $18 million to

TABLE 21.1 — **Annual Sales Volume of Great Midwest Company, Industry Volume, and Company's Share in 14-State Market**

Year	Company Volume (in millions of dollars)	Industry Volume in Company's Market (in millions of dollars)	Company's Percentage Share of Market
1994	18.0	360	5.0
1995	21.8	450	4.8
1996	22.5	465	4.8
1997	24.5	510	4.8
1998	28.0	600	4.7
1999	31.7	705	4.5
2000	30.4	660	4.6
2001	33.1	765	4.3
2002	34.7	825	4.2
2003	36.0	900	4.0

$36 million during the 10-year period ending with fiscal year 2003. Furthermore, sales increased each year, with the exception of 2000. In most years, sales goals were met or surpassed. Thus far in our analysis, the company's situation is encouraging.

A study of total sales volume alone is usually insufficient and may even be misleading. Remember the analogy of an iceberg! To learn what is going on in the "submerged" parts of a market, we need to analyze sales volume by other relevant dimensions—sales territories, for example.

Table 21.2 is a summary of the sales goals and actual results in Great Midwest's four districts. A key measurement is the *performance index* for each district—that is, actual sales divided by sales goal. An index of 100 means that the district did exactly what was expected. From the table we see that Great Lakes and Heartland did better than expected, and Delta surpassed its goal by a wide margin, but High Plains was quite a disappointment.

So far in our evaluation, we know a little about *what* happened in GM's districts. Now management has to figure out *why* it happened and *what should be done* about it. These are the difficult steps in evaluation. In the High Plains district, the fault may lie in some aspect of the marketing program, or competition may be especially strong in that district. GM's executives also should find out the reasons for Delta's success, and whether this information can be used to benefit other districts.

This brief examination of two aspects of sales volume analysis shows how this evaluation tool may be used. However, for a more useful evaluation, GM's management should go much further. They should analyze their sales volume by individual territories within districts and by product lines. Then they should carry their territorial analysis further by examining volume by product line and customer group *within* each territory. For instance, even though Delta did well overall, the iceberg notion may apply here. Despite the fine *total* performance in this district, there may be hidden weaknesses in an individual product line or territory.

Market-Share Analysis

Comparing a company's sales results with its goals is a useful evaluation, but it does not indicate how a company is doing relative to competitors. A **market-share analysis** compares a company's sales with the industry's sales. A company's share of the market should be analyzed in total, as well as by product line and market segment.

Probably the major obstacle encountered in market-share analysis is obtaining industry sales information in total and in sufficient detail. Trade associations and government agencies are possible sources for sales volume statistics in many industries.

The Great Midwest Company situation illustrates the value of market-share analysis. Recall from Table 21.1 that GM's total sales doubled over a 10-year period, with annual increases in nine of those years. But, during this span, the annual sales for all competing firms in this geographic area increased from $360 million to $900 million

TABLE 21.2

District Sales Volume in Great Midwest Company, 2003

District	Sales Goals (in millions of dollars)	Actual Sales (in millions of dollars)	Performance Index (actual ÷ goal)	Dollar Variation (in millions)
Delta	$10.8	$12.5	116	+1.7
Great Lakes	9.0	9.6	107	+0.6
Heartland	7.6	7.7	101	+0.1
High Plains	8.6	6.2	72	−2.4
Total	$36.0	$36.0		

(a 150% increase). Thus the company's market share actually *declined* from 5% to 4%. Although GM's annual sales increased 100%, its market share declined 20%.

The next step is to determine *why* Great Midwest's market position shrank. The number of possible causes is quite large—and this is what makes management's task so difficult. A weakness in almost any aspect of GM's product line, distribution arrangements, pricing structure, or promotional program may have contributed to the loss of market share. Or the culprit might have been competition. There may be new competitors in the market that were attracted by the rapid growth rates. Or competitors' marketing programs may be more effective than Great Midwest's.

Marketing Cost Analysis

An analysis of sales volume is helpful in evaluating and controlling a company's marketing effort. However, management needs to proceed further and assess costs to determine the relative profitability of its territories, product lines, or other marketing units. In the words of one researcher, "As corporate profits turn down and stocks take a plunge, leading companies are looking at marketing cost analysis to lift their bottom lines [profits]." In fact, if marketers' expenditures are not worthwhile, their budgets may be—in fact, should be—reduced.[38]

A **marketing cost analysis** is a detailed study of the *operating expenses* section of a company's profit and loss statement. As part of this analysis, management should examine any variations between budgeted costs and actual expenses.

Types of Marketing Cost Analysis

A company's marketing costs may be analyzed:

- As they appear in its ledger accounts and profit and loss statement.
- After they are grouped into activity classifications.
- After these activity costs have been allocated to territories, products, or other marketing units.

Analysis of Ledger Expenses

The simplest, least expensive approach is a study of the *object of expenditure* costs as they appear in the profit and loss statement. These figures come from the company's accounting ledger records. The simplified operating statement for the Great Midwest Company on the left side of Table 21.3 is the model we will use in this discussion.

The procedure is to analyze each cost item, such as salaries and media space, in detail. We can compare this period's total with the totals for corresponding periods in the past, and observe the trends. In addition, we can examine actual costs against budgeted amounts. We should also compute each expense as a percentage of net sales. Then we should compare these expense ratios with industry figures, which are often available through trade associations.

Analysis of Activity Costs

Total costs should be allocated among the various marketing activities, such as advertising or warehousing. Then management can analyze the cost of each of these activities.

This procedure entails identifying the major activities and then allocating each ledger expense among those activities. As indicated in the expense distribution sheet on the right side of Table 21.3, we have decided on five activity cost groups in the Great Midwest example. Some items, such as the cost of media space, can be apportioned entirely to one activity (advertising). Other expenses must be spread among several activities. So management must decide on a reasonable basis for allocation among these activities. For example, property taxes may be assigned according to the

TABLE 21.3

Profit and Loss Statement and Distribution of Natural Expenses to Activity Cost Groups, Great Midwest Company, 2003

Profit and Loss Statement (in $000)

Expense Distribution Sheet (in $000)

Activity (Functional) Cost Groups

			Personal Selling	Advertising	Warehousing and Shipping	Order Processing	Marketing Administration
Net sales	$36,000						
Cost of goods sold	−23,400						
Gross margin	12,600						
Operating expenses:							
Salaries and commissions	$2,710	→	$1,200	$ 240	$ 420	$ 280	$ 570
Travel and entertainment	1,440	→	1,040				400
Media space	1,480	→		1,480			
Supplies	440	→	60	35	240	70	35
Property taxes	130	→	16	5	60	30	19
Freight out	3,500	→			3,500		
Total expenses	− 9,700		$2,316	$1,760	$4,220	$ 380	$ 1,024
Net profit	$ 2,900						

proportion of total floor space occupied by each activity. Thus the warehouse accounts for 46% of the total square feet of floor space in the firm, so the warehousing and shipping activity is charged with $60,000, which is 46% of the property taxes.

An analysis of marketing costs gives executives more information than they can get from an analysis of ledger accounts alone. Also, an examination of activity expenses in total provides a starting point for management to evaluate costs by territories, products, or other marketing units.

Analysis of Activity Costs by Product or Market

The third and most beneficial type of marketing cost analysis is a study of the expenses and profitability of specific components of a product assortment or total market. This type of analysis breaks out a product assortment by lines or individual items, or divides up a market by territories, customer groups, or order sizes.

By combining a sales volume analysis with a marketing cost study, an executive or staff member can prepare an operating statement for each product or market segment. These statements can then be assessed to determine how they affect the total marketing program. Cost analysis by product or market enables management to pinpoint trouble spots much more effectively than does an analysis of either ledger account expenses or activity costs.

The procedure for a cost analysis by product or market is similar to that used to scrutinize activity costs. The total cost of each activity (the right side of Table 21.3) is allocated on some basis to each product or market segment being studied. Let's consider an example of a cost analysis, by sales districts, for the Great Midwest Company, as shown in Tables 21.4 and 21.5.

First, for each of the five GM activities, we select a reasonable basis for distributing the cost of that activity among the four districts. These bases are shown in the top part of Table 21.4. Then we determine the number of allocation "units" that make up each activity cost, and we find the cost per unit. This completes the allocation method, which tells us how to allocate costs to the four districts:

- Personal selling poses no problem because it is a direct expense, chargeable to the district in which it occurs.

TABLE 21.4

Allocation of Activity Costs to Sales Districts, Great Midwest Company, 2003

Activity		Personal Selling	Advertising	Warehousing and Shipping	Order Processing	Marketing Administration
		Allocation Basis				
Allocation basis		Direct expense per district	Number of ad pages	Number of orders shipped	Number of invoice lines	Equally among districts
Total activity cost		$2,316,000	$1,760,000	$4,220,000	$380,000	$1,024,000
Number of allocation units			88 pages	10,550 orders	126,667 lines	4 districts
Cost per allocation unit			$20,000	$400	$3	$256,000
		Allocation of Costs				
Delta district <	units	—	27 pages	3,300 orders	46,000 lines	—
	cost	$650,000	$540,000	$1,320,000	$138,000	$256,000
Great Lakes district <	units	—	19 pages	2,850 orders	33,000 lines	—
	cost	$606,000	$380,000	$1,140,000	$99,000	$256,000
Heartland district <	units	—	22 pages	2,300 orders	26,667 lines	—
	cost	$540,000	$440,000	$920,000	$80,000	$256,000
High Plains district <	units	—	20 pages	2,100 orders	21,000 lines	—
	cost	$520,000	$400,000	$840,000	$63,000	$256,000

- Advertising costs are allocated on the basis of the amount of advertising run in each district. GM purchased the equivalent of 88 pages of advertising during the year, at an average cost of $20,000 per page ($1,760,000 ÷ 88).

- Warehousing and shipping expenses are apportioned on the basis of the number of orders shipped. Because 10,550 orders were sent out during the year at a total activity cost of $4,220,000, the cost per order is $400.

- Order-processing expenses are allocated according to the number of invoice lines keyed in during the year. Because there were 126,667 lines, the cost per line is $3.

- Marketing administration is a totally indirect expense. Thus it is divided equally among the four districts, with each district being allocated $256,000.

The final step is to compile the amount of each activity cost to be allocated to each district. The results are shown in the bottom part of Table 21.4. We see that $650,000 of personal selling expenses were charged directly to Delta, for example. Regarding advertising, the equivalent of 27 pages of advertising was run in Delta, so that district is charged with $540,000 (27 pages × $20,000 per page). In the case of warehousing and shipping expenses, 3,300 orders were shipped to customers in the Delta district, at an allocated cost of $400 per order, for a total cost of $1,320,000. To allocate order-processing expenses, management determined that 46,000 invoice lines went to customers in the Delta district. At $3 per line (the cost per allocation unit), Delta is charged with $138,000.

After activity costs have been allocated among the four districts, we can prepare a profit and loss statement for each district. These statements are shown in Table 21.5. Sales for each district are known from the sales volume analysis (Table 21.2). Cost of goods sold and gross margin for the respective districts are obtained by assuming that the company's gross margin of 35% ($12,600,000 ÷ $36,000,000) was maintained in each district.

Table 21.5 subdivides Great Midwest's total results into operating statements for each of the four districts. For example, we note that net profit in the Delta area was

TABLE
21.5

Profit and Loss Statements for Sales Districts (in $000), Great Midwest Company, 2003

	Total	Delta	Great Lakes	Heartland	High Plains
Net sales	$36,000	$12,500	$9,600	$7,700	$6,200
Cost of goods sold	23,400	8,125	6,240	5,005	4,030
Gross margin	12,600	4,375	3,360	2,695	2,170
Operating expenses:					
Personal selling	2,316	650	606	540	520
Advertising	1,760	540	380	440	400
Warehousing and shipping	4,220	1,320	1,140	920	840
Order processing, billing	380	138	99	80	63
Marketing administration	1,024	256	256	256	256
Total expenses	9,700	2,904	2,481	2,236	2,079
Net profit (in dollars)	$ 2,900	$ 1,471	$ 879	$ 459	$ 91
Net profit (as percentage of sales)	8.1%	11.8%	9.2%	6.0%	1.5%

11.8% of sales ($1,471,000 ÷ $12,500,000). In sharp contrast, performance in the High Plains was poor, with a profit of only 1.5% of sales ($91,000 ÷ $6,200,000).

At this point in our performance evaluation, we have completed the *what happened* stage. The next stage is to determine *why* the results are as summarized in Table 21.5. As mentioned earlier, this question is difficult to answer. In High Plains, for example, the sales force obtained only about two-thirds as many orders as the Delta force did (2,100 versus 3,300, as shown in Table 21.4). Was this because of poor selling, inadequate sales training, more severe competition in High Plains, or some other reason among a multitude of possibilities?

After a performance evaluation has determined why district results came out as they did, management can move to the third stage in the evaluation process. That final stage is, *what should management do about the situation?* This stage will be discussed briefly after we review two major challenges in marketing cost analysis.

Challenges in Cost Analysis

If done thoroughly, marketing cost analysis takes substantial effort and thus is costly. In particular, the task of allocating costs is often quite difficult.

Allocating Costs   The challenge is associated with apportioning certain types of activity costs among individual territories, products, or other marketing units. Operating costs can be divided into direct and indirect expenses. **Direct costs,** also called *separable expenses,* are incurred totally in connection with one marketing unit such as a sales territory. Thus salary and travel expenses of the sales representative in the Delta district are direct expenses for that territory. The cost of newspaper space to advertise the company's line of desks is a direct cost of marketing that product. Allocating direct expenses is straightforward. They can be charged entirely to the marketing unit that incurred them.

The allocation challenge arises in connection with **indirect costs,** also called *common costs* or *overhead.* These expenses are incurred jointly for more than one marketing unit. Therefore, they cannot be charged totally to one market segment.

Within the category of indirect costs, some expenses are *variable* and others are *fixed.* (These two types of costs were introduced in Chapter 12.) Order filling and shipping, for example, are largely variable. They would *decrease* if some territories or products were eliminated; conversely, they would *increase* if new products or territories were added. Marketing administrative expenses are more fixed. The cost of the chief marketing executive's staff and related costs would remain about the same, whether or not the number of territories or product lines was changed.

Two common methods for allocating *indirect* expenses are to divide these costs (1) equally among the marketing units being studied (territories, for instance) or (2) in proportion to the sales volume in each marketing unit. But each method gives a different result for the total costs for each marketing unit and, as such, may mislead management.

Full Cost versus Contribution Margin

In a marketing cost analysis, two means of allocating expenses are (1) the contribution-margin (also called contribution-to-overhead) method and (2) the full-cost method. A controversy exists regarding which of these approaches is better for purposes of evaluation.

In the **contribution-margin approach,** only direct expenses are allocated to each marketing unit being analyzed. These costs presumably would be eliminated if that unit, such as a product or sales territory, were eliminated. When direct expenses are deducted from the unit's gross margin, the remainder is the amount that unit is contributing to cover total indirect expenses (or overhead).

In the **full-cost approach,** all expenses—direct and indirect—are allocated among the marketing units under scrutiny. By allocating *all* costs, management can estimate the net profit of each territory, product, or other unit.

For any specific marketing unit, these two methods can be summarized as follows:

Contribution Margin	Full Cost
Sales $	Sales $
less	*less*
Cost of goods sold	Cost of goods sold
equals	*equals*
Gross margin	Gross margin
less	*less*
Direct expenses	Direct expenses
equals	*less*
Contribution margin (the amount available to cover indirect expenses plus a profit)	Indirect expenses
	equals
	Net profit

Proponents of the *full-cost* approach contend that a marketing cost analysis is intended to determine the net profitability of the units being examined. They believe that the contribution-margin method does not fulfill this purpose and may be misleading. A given territory or product may be showing a contribution to overhead. Yet, after indirect costs are allocated, this product or territory may actually have a net loss. In effect, say the full-cost supporters, the contribution-margin approach is the iceberg notion in action. That is, the visible tip (the contribution margin) looks good, whereas the submerged part may contain a net loss.

Contribution-margin proponents contend that it is not possible to logically allocate indirect costs among products or market segments. Furthermore, these costs (such as the salary of the vice president of marketing or the expenses associated with a marketing research department) are not all related to any *one* territory or product, but rather pertain to the entire organization. Therefore, the marketing units should not bear any of these costs. Supporters of the contribution-margin approach also say that a full-cost analysis may show a net loss for a product or territory, but this unit may be contributing something to overhead. If the losing unit is eliminated, its contribution to overhead would have to be borne by other units. With the contribution-margin approach, there would be no question about keeping this unit as long as there is no better alternative.

Use of Findings from Volume and Cost Analyses

So far we have been dealing with the first two stages of marketing performance evaluation—finding out what happened and why it happened. Now we're ready to see some examples of how management might use the results from a combined sales volume analysis and marketing cost analysis to improve performance.

Territories

Knowing the net profit *or* contribution to overhead of territories in relation to previously established expectations gives management several possibilities for action. If territorial problems stem from weaknesses in the distribution system, changes related to distribution may be needed. Firms that use manufacturers' agents may find it advisable to establish their own sales forces in growing markets, for instance. Or, a firm may decide that it would be more economical to substitute agents for its own sales people in all or some territories. Technology may be applied to bring about automatic replenishment and/or reordering via the Internet. If intense competition is the cause of unprofitable volume in some districts, modifications in the promotional program may be necessary. Finally, management may decide to adjust (expand or contract) territories in order to obtain greater cost efficiencies.

Of course, a losing territory might be shut down completely. An abandoned region may have been contributing something to overhead, however, even though a net loss was shown. Management must recognize that this contribution must now be carried by the remaining territories.

Products

When the profitability of each product or group of products is known, unprofitable models, sizes, or colors can be eliminated. Sales people's compensation plans may be altered to encourage the sale of high-margin items. Channels of distribution may be changed. For instance, instead of selling all of its products directly to business users, a machine tools manufacturer shifted to industrial distributors for standard products of low unit value. The company thereby improved the profitability of these products.

Management may decide to discontinue a losing product. But it should not do so without first considering the effect this decision will have on other items sold by the company. Often a low-volume or unprofitable product must be carried simply to round out the product assortment. Supermarkets, for example, carry salt and sugar even though these generate very little if any profit for a store. If they are not available at one store, that seller will lose business, because shoppers will go to other stores that do carry a full complement of grocery products.

Customer Classes and Order Sizes

By combining a sales volume analysis with a cost study, executives can determine the profitability of each group of customers.[39] If one market segment is unprofitable or generates too little profit, then changes may be required in the pricing structure when selling to these customers. Or perhaps customers that have been sold to directly by a producer's sales force should be turned over to wholesaling middlemen. A manufacturer of air conditioners made just such a move when it found that direct sales to individual building contractors were not profitable; hence, this firm switched from its own sales staff to several manufacturers' agents.

A difficulty plaguing many firms today is typically referred to as the **small-order problem.** That is, many orders are below the break-even point. Revenue from each of these orders is actually less than allocated expenses. This problem occurs because several costs, such as billing or direct selling, are essentially the same whether the order amounts to $10 or $10,000. However, the problem extends beyond small orders to any customers who are unprofitable to the firm for one or more of various reasons. For example, a client may actually place relatively large orders but then be so demanding following the sale that the seller's cost of servicing the account is inordinately high.

Management's immediate reaction to the small-order problem may be that no order below the break-even point should be accepted. Or small-volume accounts should be dropped from the customer list. Such decisions may be harmful, however. Some of those small-order customers may, over time, grow into large, profitable accounts.

Management should deal with unprofitable customers, including those whose orders are too small, through a two-step process:

- Determine if problem accounts can be made profitable, either by motivating them to place larger orders, pruning discounts available to them, charging them higher prices or special fees, and/or reducing the level of service provided to them. Proper handling can often turn a losing account into a satisfactory one. For example, a small-order handling charge, which some customers would willingly pay, might change the profit picture entirely.

- If all else fails, cease doing business with unprofitable customers. This might be done, preferably gently, by "encouraging" customers to take their business elsewhere. Steps toward that end would include eliminating services they had been receiving and/or by not retaining the account when a purchase contract expires.[40]

Summary

The management process in marketing consists of the planning, implementation, and evaluation of the marketing effort in an organization. Implementation is the stage in which an organization takes steps to carry out its strategic planning. If it is not implemented effectively, strategic planning is virtually useless.

Implementation includes three activities: organizing, staffing, and directing. In organizing, the company should first coordinate all marketing activities into one department whose top executive reports directly to the president. Then, for the selling function within the marketing department, the company should choose a form of organizational specialization based on geographic territories, products, or customer types.

An underappreciated component of a marketing program, namely warranties and other postsale services, are implemented largely after a sale is made. Warranties require considerable management attention these days because of consumer complaints and governmental regulations. Product liability is an issue of great consequence to companies because of the significant financial risk associated with consumers' claims of injuries caused when using a firm's product.

Many companies provide postsale service—such as merchandise returns, maintenance and repairs, and complaint handling—to fulfill the terms of their warranties and/or to augment their revenues. To promote customer satisfaction, a number of firms are improving their methods of inviting and responding to consumer complaints.

The evaluation stage in the management process involves measuring performance results against predetermined goals. Evaluation enables management to determine the effectiveness of its implementation and to plan corrective action where necessary. A marketing audit is a key element in a marketing evaluation program.

Most companies are victims of at least some misdirected marketing effort. That is, the 80–20 and iceberg principles are at work in many firms because marketing costs are expended in relation to the number of marketing units (territories, products, customers), rather than in relation to their profit potential. Too many companies do not know how much they should spend for marketing activities, or what results they should get from these expenditures.

The financial results of marketing endeavors should be analyzed in terms of sales volume, market share, and marketing costs. One challenge in marketing cost analysis is allocating costs—especially indirect costs—to the marketing units. Given detailed assessments, management can study sales volume and marketing costs by territories, product lines, categories of customer, and/or order sizes. The findings from these analyses can help shape decisions regarding a company's marketing program.

More about **Zara**

The Inditex Group, Zara's parent company, has over 1,300 stores in 40 countries. The firm's combined annual revenues are in the vicinity of $3 billion. Zara accounts for more than 75% of Inditex's total sales. The fashion-forward clothing chain has about a 5% market share in its native Spain; international sales account for about 50% of Zara's revenues. Profit margins have been steady at 10%, which compare favorably to the best in the industry.

Zara is especially well known in Europe, the Middle East, and South America. It has about 450 stores in 28 countries, but only 8 in the U.S. Its present expansion is centered in Germany and Italy, although more U.S. stores remain a possibility.

Zara's success to date can be attributed to all three stages of the management process—planning, implementation, *and* also evaluation. Regarding this last stage, careful monitoring of marketing performance ensures that the stores are stocked with clothing that is desired by consumers and that managers are confident will sell quickly. Store managers and sales people, in fact, play a huge role in determining what is stocked in Zara stores. As they work, they carry handheld computers to record customer comments, requests, and likes and dislikes.

"The role of the store manager goes way beyond that of Gap and H&M [a Swedish competitor]," says one industry analyst. Managers' design suggestions are backed by the research of trend spotters who travel around the world looking for inspiration and ideas.

At the close of each business day, managers in every Zara store around the world use e-mail to submit their orders for new merchandise as well as information about trends and customer preferences to the home office. Then the company's 200 designers evaluate the input about styles and colors, decide what new ideas will be appealing and what current designs need to be tweaked or even dropped, and consult the company's specialists about fabrics, production, and pricing. The designers then create patterns that are transmitted to computers in the company's highly automated manufacturing plants. Customer needs and wants, gauged on a real-time basis, are thus largely responsible for the details of Zara's 12,000 new designs a year.[41]

1. Does Zara carry out a systematic evaluation process? That is, does the chain assess what happened, why, and what to do about it?

2. What measures should Inditex use in evaluating Zara's marketing performance?

Key Terms and Concepts

Questions and Problems

1. "Good implementation in an organization can overcome poor planning, but good planning cannot overcome poor implementation." Explain, using examples from business periodicals, such as *Business Week, Forbes, Advertising Age, Brandweek,* and *The Wall Street Journal.*

2. Give some examples of companies that are likely to organize their sales forces by product groups.

3. A manufacturer of small aircraft designed for executive transportation, Cessna for example, has decided to implement the concept of a selling center. Who should be on this company's selling teams? What problems might this manufacturer encounter when it uses team selling?

4. Explain the relationship between a warranty on small electric appliances, such as a Toastmaster waffle maker, and the manufacturer's distribution system for these products.

5. a. Should the primary role of postsale services be to assure customer satisfaction or to generate added revenues for the firm?
   b. Would the way in which postsale services are carried out vary depending on the role given to this element of marketing by the firm's executives?

6. a. What are several ways in which providing postsale services would vary between an e-tailer and a retailer that has physical stores?
   b. Do online-only firms have any advantages with respect to carrying out postsale services?

7. A sales volume analysis by territories indicates that a manufacturer's sales of roofing materials increased 12% a year for the past three years in a territory comprising South Carolina, Georgia, and Florida. Does this statistic indicate conclusively that the company's sales volume performance is satisfactory in that territory?

8. A manufacturer found that one product accounted for 35% to 45% of the company's total sales in all but 2 of the 18 territories. In each of those two territories, this product accounted for only 14% of the company's volume. What factors might explain the relatively low sales of this item in the two districts?

9. What effects might a sales volume analysis by product have on training, supervising, and compensating a company's sales force?

10. Should a company stop selling to an unprofitable customer? Why or why not? If not, then what steps might the company take to make the account a profitable one?

Interactive Marketing Exercises

1. Interview a sales executive (a) in a manufacturing company and (b) in either a securities brokerage or a real estate brokerage firm to find out how they motivate their sales forces. As part of your report, give your evaluation of each motivational program.

2. Interview a marketing executive to find out how total marketing performance is evaluated in that particular company. As part of your report, include your appraisal of this firm's evaluation program.

Chapter

22

Marketing and the Information Economy

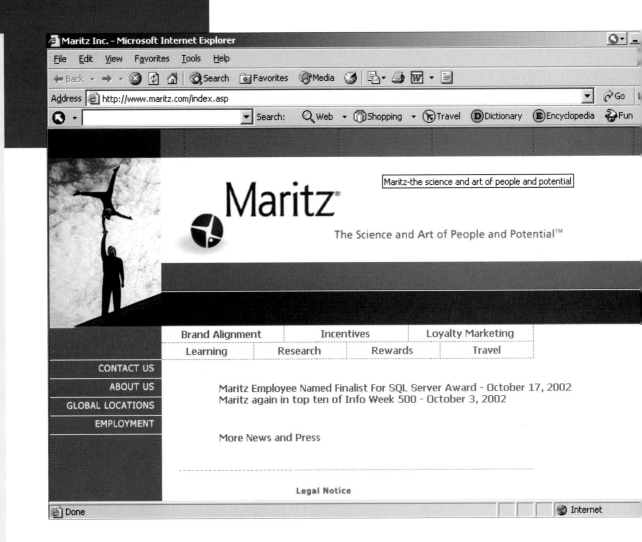

"Maritz's use of technology has grown and now enhances every part of the business."

What's the Incentive for **Maritz** to Use Technology?

When Maritz, Inc., opened for business as a jewelry manufacturer in 1894, its use of technology was limited to some production processes and perhaps a typewriter in its first location, which was founder Edward Maritz's St. Louis home. The situation has changed a great deal in the subsequent 100+ years.

At the height of the economic depression of the 1920s, when consumer purchases of jewelry fell, the firm spun off a new division called Maritz Sales Builders as a survival tactic. The division specialized in selling watches and jewelry to companies that used them for sales performance awards. Then in the 1950s, Maritz expanded its product mix again to include an incentive travel business. By the mid-1970s, the growing firm had entered still another industry, with the acquisition of a marketing research business now known as Maritz Marketing Research, Inc. (MMRI). A business travel planning company was added in 1980, and a business training division was formed in 1989.

Today the firm's revenues are around $1.3 billion a year, and about half its sales come from the travel division. It is still run by a Maritz, a descendant of the founder, and it has 6,500 employees, as well as subsidiaries and business partners all over the world. Corporate travel, performance improvement, and market research remain the firm's three biggest units (it is not in the jewelry industry any longer), but in its 100-year evolution from a small jewelry firm to a major travel and consulting services company, its mission is not the only thing that has changed about Maritz.

The company's use of technology has grown and now enhances every part of the business. The performance improvement unit, Maritz Learning, helps its corporate clients manage training and skills programs for their employees. Customized courses can be delivered through interactive videodisc, CD-ROM, satellite-based distance learning technologies, videoconferencing, and the Internet, offering self-paced learning, assessment, and reinforcement.

Technology also underlies Maritz's employee performance management process, allowing clients to gather the information they need to monitor and reward employee performance. Reports tailored to each level of management can be delivered on the Internet or via e-mail. Another new unit called ONE will use performance management technologies to help client companies align employee performance with their customers' expectations.

The success of the marketing research unit, which designs large-scale customized research studies, has earned the company a spot among the top-10 largest marketing research firms in the U.S. Another product, its MindAbility Browser, measures the ease with which a company's customers can access its websites, tracking the pages viewed, links followed, interaction with the site,

www.maritz.com

and download time during user sessions, and stores the data for the client on a password-protected website for easy access. MMRI recently launched a state-of-the-art Web-based reporting tool, eQuest, that allows users to summarize data and reports from marketing research studies by working directly with the data instead of only viewing them.

In 2001, Maritz transformed its travel management business into a global, high-tech operation when it partnered with firms based in Germany and Australia to form TQ3 Maritz Travel Solutions. The partnership links 1,300 travel offices in over 50 countries. Utilizing electronic technology, Maritz is able to identify schedules and fares, track travel plans, and generate online travel reports for its clients traveling anywhere in the world.

It's all a far cry from the company's early nontechnical days. Maritz has even been recognized for its innovative use of information technology by *Information Week* magazine, and chairman and CEO Steve Maritz, who embraces technology, anticipates acquiring two or three technology companies in the next few years. "It's a great buying time," says the firm's, vice president of international corporate development. Technology could well become the fourth line of Maritz's businesses.[1]

In what ways has Maritz benefited from technology?

Information has always played a major role in marketing. Today, both the quantity and quality of information is increasing at the fastest rate in history. Much of this growth is due to improvements in information technology and the ability of marketers to find creative ways to make use of it. The result is that marketers are entering an information economy in which new ways of doing business are being designed and some existing ways are being reconfigured.

The company described in the chapter-opening case is a good example. For over 70 years, Maritz, Inc., has, among other things, assisted clients in finding ways to motivate and reward employees. Initially the business was built around providing access to tangible incentives such as watches and jewelry. In more recent years, it has evolved into a firm that relies heavily on technology to serve its customers. In all areas of its operations, from performance enhancement to employee training and market research, Maritz has embraced technology as a way of improving its effectiveness and efficiency. Some analysts predict that instead of bricks and mortar (and inventory) defining a business, information and how it is used will be the key attributes of success in the near future.

In this chapter the goal is to examine the role of marketing in this emerging information economy. More specifically, we will look at how information technology is creating new opportunities and challenges and some of the ways marketers are trying to seize these opportunities. On completing this chapter you should:

Chapter Goals

- Appreciate the role of information in marketing.
- Be familiar with the importance of information technology and electronic networking.
- Understand how the Internet has changed how markets function.
- Appreciate some of the ways the Internet is affecting marketing strategy.
- Recognize challenges and opportunities marketers are addressing as they enter the information economy.

The Importance of Information in Marketing

The Industrial Revolution, beginning in the second half of the 19th century, marked the beginning of the widespread application of technology to business. Steam and electric power made it possible to operate large machinery and equipment, conveyors moved products along assembly lines and then into and out of inventory, and individual workers were taught to perform specialized tasks very efficiently. As a result, businesses began to experience substantial improvements in manufacturing productivity. However, the impact of manufacturing technology on marketing was not nearly as dramatic. Although it did result in lower costs and therefore lower prices, the job of the marketer remained largely unchanged, requiring considerable personal interaction before, during, and after most sales.

Significant increases in marketing productivity required a different kind of technology. The job of marketing is to direct the organization in how to most effectively satisfy customers. Providing direction entails learning as much as possible about the customer, and using that information to design need-satisfying strategies. In short, marketing is driven by information. Sellers must learn what buyers like and dislike by monitoring their behavior, asking them questions, and inviting their comments. And all marketers must gather data on current or potential markets to determine their status and to anticipate how they are likely to change.

The effective utilization of information improves the performance of marketing in ways that have been discussed throughout this book. For example, it results in:

- *Better products.* A refined understanding of the buyer allows a marketer to develop products that more closely fit the buyer's needs, requiring fewer compromises and greater satisfaction.

- *Better prices.* What customers are willing to pay for a product depends on how much they value it. Knowing how important a product is to a customer and what resources the customer has available to purchase it helps sellers set attractive prices.

- *Better distribution.* The likelihood of having a product available when and where a customer wants to find it is enhanced if the seller knows the shopping habits and preferences of the buyer.

- *Better promotion.* A product and its benefits can be communicated in many ways. Both the form and the content of advertisements and other promotions can be improved if the marketer understands the buyer's motivations and expectations.

- *Better implementation.* Quicker feedback on marketing programs permits managers to assess their performance and make adjustments before losses mount up or opportunities are missed. Today the response of customers to price changes and promotion programs can be monitored in real time rather than days or weeks after they are introduced.

But recognizing the importance of information and using it effectively are two different things. Except in the smallest businesses, utilization requires technology. In the case of marketing, gathering, analyzing, and storing large amounts of data about markets, competitors, media, distribution, and customer behavior wasn't practical before the widespread availability of computers.

Consider, for example, a supermarket chain with several stores, each with 30,000 different items on its shelves. Without computers, keeping track of the performance of each item, deciding which to keep and which to drop, and determining when and how much to reorder would be an enormous task. However, by today's standards, a relatively small computer can compile a record of all the transactions made at every checkout lane for each store. Utilizing predetermined programs, the computer can use the data to signal when individual items need to be reordered, given more or less shelf space, or even dropped.

Computers can also be used to carry out very complex tasks. Recall the example in Chapter 7 of data mining by Harrah's. The firm profiles gamblers on the basis of their behavior and uses the information to design and target its promotional efforts. Sophisticated analytical techniques and powerful computers allow Harrah's and other firms to sift through millions of bits of consumer-related data and discover patterns that wouldn't be apparent to human observers no matter how much time and effort they invested. Thus the marriage of information and technology has become a fact of life in marketing.

Information Technology in Marketing

Numerous technological developments have had a significant impact on marketing. Certainly television (which provides a mass-market advertising medium), household telephones (which permit easy interaction between buyers and sellers), and personal computers (which increase individual productivity of marketing managers) are examples. Rather than try to discuss all the information technology that is used in marketing, our discussion will focus on recent network applications. We will begin with a brief introduction to the Internet, the backbone of many of these tools, followed by an overview of several levels of electronic networking systems. Then we will return to the Internet for a fuller discussion of how it impacts marketing.

The Internet

In the early 1970s the **Internet** was created as part of a U.S. government project. Its original purpose was to link researchers at many different sites and allow them to exchange information. The procedure for using the Internet served the purposes of the researchers, but it was too cumbersome for broad commercial applications. Then, in 1989 the **World Wide Web** (now simply referred to as the Web) was developed. The Web provides access to a portion of the larger Internet, making it possible for users to share a full range of communications from text to graphics and audio messages. Any individual or organization can create and register a **website,** a collection of Web files beginning with a home page, that is accessible through a unique address. Thus, as we will see, the Web has become the lynchpin for much of the communication that takes place between businesses and between businesses and consumers today.

Electronic Networking

Networks are individuals or organizations linked together to share data, exchange information and ideas, and perform tasks. Some networks are simple, requiring no technology. People have social networks, professional networks, and work group networks. You've probably been advised to develop personal networks and use them when looking for a job. **Electronic networks** are created when the individuals or organizations are linked via some form of telecommunications.[2]

In business, when the personal computers of individuals in a company or department are linked together a local electronic network or **intranet** is created. For example, at an appliance manufacturer, an intranet of designers, engineers, and marketers may be created to share input as a new product is developed. The power of these networks is expanded when they include a server, which is a central, more powerful computer that can store large databases and perform sophisticated analyses. With access to the server through their PCs, the participants in a network can perform

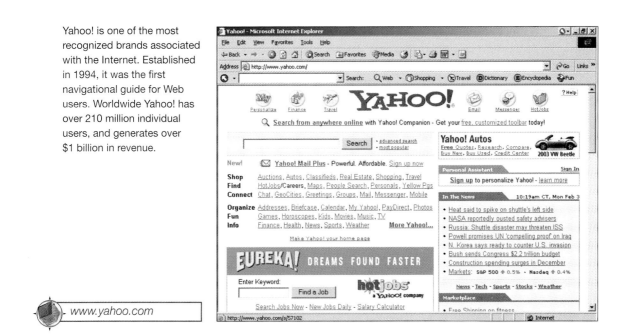

Yahoo! is one of the most recognized brands associated with the Internet. Established in 1994, it was the first navigational guide for Web users. Worldwide Yahoo! has over 210 million individual users, and generates over $1 billion in revenue.

www.yahoo.com

tasks not possible on individual PCs. Several levels of electronic networking exist in the information economy.

Electronic Data Interchange

When electronic networking moves outside the firm, it is known as **electronic data interchange** (**EDI**), which is a proprietary system in which data are exchanged between trading partners, to be used for standardized, preapproved transactions. For example, Kmart stocks Procter & Gamble's Tide detergent in its stores. When the inventory of Tide reaches a predetermined level in Kmart's distribution center, its computer automatically transmits an order to P&G's computer. The P&G computer confirms the order and sets in motion the activities to fill it. Transactions similar to this are carried out thousands of times daily between firms and their suppliers. Doing it electronically saves time, minimizes order-processing expenses, and reduces clerical errors.

Early EDI made use of long-distance telephone lines that allowed the computer in one firm to dial up and "talk" to a supplier's computer. More recent versions utilize the Web. EDI is limited to large firms because of the costs involved in implementation. Because it cannot quickly adjust to price or product availability changes, it is also somewhat inflexible.

Electronic Information Transfer

The Web ushered in another level of networking for marketers. Called **electronic information** (or e-information), this form of networking involves creating a corporate website and posting information on it. Firms are able to make vast amounts of information available on their websites. The information ranges from product descriptions and invitations to suppliers to submit bids on planned purchases to product operating instructions and information about contacting sales personnel. Some e-information websites are open—that is, freely accessible to anyone. Others are restricted—that is, accessible only to those in possession of a password. By applying restrictions, a firm can make the information on its website available selectively to customers, distributors, and/or suppliers.

Many consumer product manufacturers and retailers view an e-information website as a necessary form of communication—like an ad with much more information than possible with traditional media. These sites often include special inducements to attract visitors, such as electronic coupons and contests. For business-to-business marketers, e-information reduces the need for paper-based communication and lowers the costs of working with suppliers and serving distributors because much of the information a customer or supply chain member needs is available 24 hours a day, 7 days a week. As a result, e-information has become the most common use of the Internet for business-to-business marketers.

The postings on an e-information website typically fall into five categories:

- *Background and general information*—primarily the company's history, its mission, corporate philosophy, and general orientation. This category includes financial performance and investor information, the structure of the firm if it is global or has several divisions, and profiles of top managers. Employment opportunities with the firm also are frequently posted here, as are recent press releases. Background and general information pages would be accessible to anyone visiting the site.

- *Current business operations*—for existing and potential business partners. This category typically has information for suppliers (how to contact corporate buyers, invitations to bid on planned purchases, payment terms and conditions, delivery requirements) and customers (product descriptions, dealer contact information, credit terms). Because some of this information is considered confidential, access may be restricted and require a password.

- *Links*—connections to other related sites. For example, a furniture manufacturer's site might make it possible for consumers to link to the website of a retailer located in their area that carries the manufacturer's products. By simply clicking on an icon that describes the related site, the visitor is transferred to it.

- *Attraction and entertainment features*—tools and techniques for engaging site visitors. Attempts to attract and hold visitors to a site often involve weaving the desired promotional message into entertaining features. For example, McDonald's website includes an electronic coloring book, visual tours of McDonald's restaurants around the world, special promotion and contest information, overviews of the firm's environmental efforts, and many more attractions. Entertainment is much more common on the websites of consumer product marketers than business-to-business marketers, but all sites must be attractive and easy to navigate to hold visitors.

- *Contact point*—providing an e-mail link for visitors, permitting them to ask questions or make comments. This opportunity for interaction is a major distinguishing feature for Internet communications in comparison to traditional media advertising. It also requires a high level of attention on the part of the site owner because unanswered inquiries or form letter responses can create substantial ill will.

The benefits marketers are seeking through a website depend on the nature of the organization. The primary benefit to business-to-business firms is greater efficiency in dealing with suppliers and customers. *If* current and potential suppliers and customers can be convinced to search a firm's website, answers to many of their routine questions can be answered without human interaction. When Cisco Systems, a giant maker of routers, switches, and other technical networking equipment, reduced its personal selling effort and moved much of its sales to the Web, it ran into a technical service problem. Customers phoning the service center tied up service engineers, regardless of whether the issue was routine or a significant technical challenge. To relieve the pressure, Cisco put answers to customers' most frequently asked questions (FAQs) on its website. The company found customers liked the approach because they could get answers quickly, 24 hours a day.

www.cisco.com

A website (or portion of a business website) designed for final consumers is intended to build goodwill and strengthen relationships. It is comparable to brand-building advertising, except the opportunity exists to provide much more content and to interact with individual site visitors through e-mail. Virtually all large con-

www.kelloggs.com

www.whirlpool.com

www.artcapitalgroup.com

www.ebay.com

www.freemarkets.com

www.silverfallsseed.com

sumer packaged-goods firms such as Kellogg's, Coca-Cola, and Procter & Gamble maintain e-information sites, as do durable-goods manufacturers such as Whirlpool and Ford Motor Co.

A firm typically attracts visitors through ads placed in other media and by publicizing its website address (called its URL) on its letterhead and on executives' business cards. For both business and consumer marketers, websites offer flexibility, because the content can be changed as frequently as desired, and broad geographic reach, because anyone in the world with access to the Internet is potentially reachable.

Electronic Transactions Note that e-information sites provide information but they are not designed to make transactions. Creating the capability of making purchases directly from a firm's website is known as **electronic transactions** (or e-transactions), the next higher level of electronic networking. E-transactions involve more interaction and feedback than e-information. Both consumer product marketers and business-to-business sellers make use of e-transactions. Because of media coverage, most people are aware that consumers make purchases via the Web—over $51 billion in 2001, and estimated at $72 billion in 2002.[3] However, the dollar volume of so-called B2C (business-to-consumer) online transactions is dwarfed by B2B (business-to-business) sales online. According to the U.S. Census Bureau, consumer purchases on the Web account for only about 5% of the total.[4] Thus, business online purchasing is almost 20-times greater than consumer purchases.

There are two categories of firms that conduct transactions over the Web: (1) new businesses seeking an effective way to reach the market, and (2) existing businesses expanding their access to the market or replacing their current channel. This is an important distinction because the Web has allowed new business models to be created that would be impossible using traditional channels. An example is Art Capital Group, a company that arranges leases of expensive works of art to individuals and businesses that want to display the art but don't want to buy it. The art is actually owned by museums, galleries, and individual collectors around the world. Art Capital Group matches the art owners with prospective customers who are also geographically dispersed. Without the Web it would be virtually impossible to connect such widely distributed groups. Online auctions such as eBay (described in Case 1 at the end of Part 1), and the reverse auctions organized by FreeMarkets (the opening case in Chapter 5) are additional examples of new business models made possible by the Web.

The other category consists of existing firms, both small and large, that want to expand their market access. For example, Silver Falls Seed Company, a wildflower seed and plant company in Silverton, Oregon, could reach only a local clientele prior to going online. Now the firm sells seeds and plants (as well as providing gardening advice, an online newsletter, and some homespun advice on a variety of topics) to a much larger audience. In less than two years its website had nearly 100,000 visitors. Large firms are moving to the Internet as well. Here we find businesses of all types including business services providers such as Maritz, industrial goods suppliers such as W.W. Grainger, and cosmetics firms such as Avon. Wal-Mart, Kmart, Allstate, Toyota, and Office Depot are just a few of the other well-known firms that have broadened their marketing reach through websites designed for e-transactions.

Some firms with e-information sites have avoided moving to e-transactions because of the negative impact selling directly can have on their existing channel members. Another reason for avoiding e-transactions is that even if one or more levels of distribution are removed from a channel, the functions must still be performed. Thus many firms opt to stick with their existing arrangements rather than create the necessary processing, shipping, and customer service required to deal with large numbers of individual orders. According to an industry consultant, "Manufacturers are very good at shipping in bulk to a few distribution points. That's very different than shipping one unit to a person."[5]

Red Envelope, an upscale gift e-tailer, exemplifies firms that have benefited from electronic commerce. The firm shifted its promotional efforts from traditional mass media advertising to e-mail. A half-million bi-weekly e-mails direct prospects to the firm's printed catalog and website. The result has been increased exposure, lowered ordering costs, and increased sales.

www.RedEnvelope.com

Electronic Commerce When a firm reconfigures its marketing operations around the interactions made possible by its Web connections, it is engaging in **electronic commerce** (or e-commerce). This is a sophisticated network that can link a large number of firms at different levels of a distribution channel in what is called an **extranet.** For example, Dow Chemical is linked with over 8,000 customers in 35 countries through an exchange it has created.[6] Customers can review their purchase histories, monitor their orders, and check on the availability of Dow products. In turn, Dow can monitor the customers' purchase patterns and inventory levels and adapt its production and sales efforts accordingly.

Depending on the firm, an extranet might also involve suppliers in the design of products on the website, monitor orders from the time they are taken until the finished products are delivered, and permit customers to examine and make suggestions about the firm's production schedule. Because extranets allow business partners access to highly sensitive data as well as future plans, they require strong relationships and a high level of trust. In return, they speed up decision making with the result that products get to market more quickly and at a lower cost.

The Impact of the Internet on Markets

Transforming the Web into a marketing tool was made possible by several important developments. The most basic is the Web browser. A **browser** provides an Internet visitor with the necessary application program to look at and interact with individual websites. Two of the best known browsers are Netscape Navigator and Microsoft's Internet Explorer. Because a browser acts as a visitor's starting site on any visit to the Web, it has a significant influence on the subsequent sites a Web surfer will visit.

As the number of websites grew, it became apparent that an electronic **directory** (similar in concept to a phone book) was needed. What has become one of the largest and best-known directories was initiated by two graduate students who began compiling a list of sites organized by topics and subtopics. They called it Yahoo! (The letters in the name stand for "Yet another hierarchical officious oracle," reflecting the youthful exuberance of the founders!) It now consists of hundreds of thousands of websites and millions of Web pages.

Even with directories, finding your way around the Web can be difficult. To assist Web visitors, the browser developers and others have created gateway or portal websites. A **portal** is an entrance and a guide to the rest of the Web. Typically a portal offers a directory of websites, a search engine to look for information and other websites, access to e-mail service, news, weather forecasts, and other information designed to attract visitors. Some of the better-known portals are Netscape, Lycos, Excite, and America Online. Browsers, directories, and portals permit easy access to the Web for virtually anyone with a PC and a telephone line connection.

Use of the Internet by businesses and consumers has grown very rapidly. Virtually all of the major firms in the U.S. now have some type of Internet presence, which means that in order to do business with them, their customers and suppliers must also have access. When the former head of IBM, Louis Gerstner, said that the Internet will "transform every important transaction and relationship,"[7] firms of all sizes and types should at least investigate its potential impact on their business.

Among U.S. households, access to the Web grew from 14% in 1996 to over 50% by 2000, but since then the increase in the percentage of households with Internet access has slowed. However, usage by those with access has increased. The number of times per month people log on is increasing, and the amount of total time they are logged on is going up (from 17.5 hours per month to 20.5 hours).[8] Several implications of this phenomenon on how markets operate are described below.

Control of Interactions

The traditional model of marketing communication has the seller largely in control of the information flow. Consumer product firms decide when and where to advertise their products, and business marketers design the messages their sales people will present and plan their visits to clients. Clearly these choices are made with the customer in mind, but they are made by sellers.

In the online environment the interactions are controlled by the recipient. It is the Internet user who must sit down at the computer, search out a website, and decide what pages to examine or ignore. Because these visitors make an effort to get to a site, it is assumed that they are candidates for strong selling messages. For example, besides

Websites such as PriceFarmer allow consumers to compare the prices for the same product from a number of sellers. The eventual result will be more negotiation and fewer fixed prices for all manner of consumer goods and services.

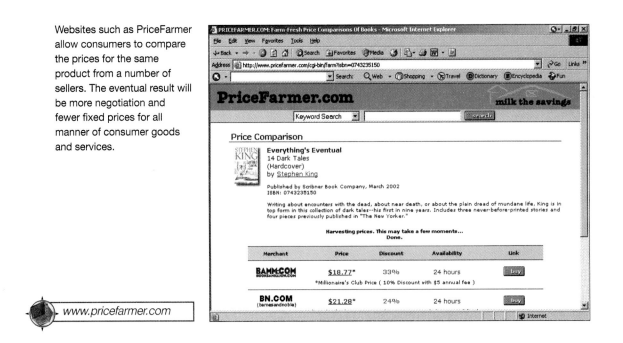

www.pricefarmer.com

www.mentadent.com

offering detailed product information on its website, the maker of Mentadent toothpaste and toothbrushes offers pages that contain an appointment reminder, an oral care quiz, the opportunity to ask an oral hygienist specific questions, and an oral fitness newsletter. And on every page there are direct and indirect promotional messages for the products. In contrast, the mass media advertising for the same brand offers very little beyond reinforcement of the brand name to a passive audience.

More and Better Information

One of the features of the Internet is easy access to more and better information. Customers of FedEx can track the location of a shipment at every stage of its journey because every package is bar-coded and scanned between 15 and 20 times between pickup and delivery. Likewise, consumers can acquire information previously available only to sellers. For example, knowing what a car dealer pays for a particular make of car and the cost to the dealer for specific options can be valuable negotiating tools for a consumer. In 1966, Edmund's began publishing such information in its automobile and truck buyers' guides and selling them in bookstores. However, not many consumers knew about the guides, they quickly became outdated, and consumers had to purchase them. Then in 1995 Edmund's went online. Now free access to constantly updated information about new cars is as close as a mouse click, and 200,000 consumers a day take advantage of it.

www.edmunds.com

Clearly the ability to make comparisons on the Internet forces online firms to be aware of and responsive to the prices charged by other Web marketers. However, it has another implication. Customers can now gather comparison information from the Internet and use it in negotiations with traditional marketers. In the past, many firms had a "geographic monopoly" because they had little or no local competition, and customers were uninformed about the cost of the same product elsewhere. Now there is no reason why a small firm buying printing services or a consumer buying a car need approach the purchase without comparative information.

Customized Products

Customization has been relatively common in business-to-business marketing, although it is generally limited to "big-ticket" purchases with high margins. On the other hand, nearly all consumer products are highly standardized. The reason for the difference is quite simple—the flow of information. Getting the customization details from the buyer to the seller, arranging to have suppliers provide the necessary parts, and sharing the information internally with manufacturing and other functions took too much time. The Internet speeds up that flow and makes customization not only possible but practical. Ford and General Motors have joined Toyota in a commitment to provide customized cars within five days of receiving an order. And the expectation is that customization will quickly spread to consumer electronics and appliances.

One of the advantages of customization is eliminating the investment in inventory. Imagine an automobile dealership with only enough cars and trucks on its lot to permit test-drives. In the auto industry, studies indicate that increased efficiency in production, decreased inventories of parts and finished products, and lower transportation costs as a result of shifting from mass to customized production and marketing could reduce the prices of vehicles by as much as 30%.[9]

Fewer Fixed Prices

Fixed prices are the norm in consumer markets, with only a few exceptions. In business-to-business marketing, negotiated prices are more common, but many prices are fixed there as well. This is likely to change. As the Internet makes real-time auctions possible, fixed prices for business and consumer sales may become rarities. eBay, the dominant firm in consumer and small business Internet auctions, has nearly 40 million registered users bidding on more than 125 million items. Products as diverse as a retired Russian submarine and Barbie dolls are offered on the eBay site.

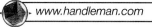
www.freemarkets.com

The reverse auction, as described in the opening case for Chapter 5, is also increasing in popularity. In this situation, the buyer specifies what is desired, and prospective sellers make offers, bidding the price down. Reverse auctions are expected to expand beyond standard, commodity items purchased by businesses to include a wide variety of consumer goods.

Traditional online auctions expand the market, giving sellers access to many more potential buyers. Reverse auctions also give buyers access to more sellers. In both scenarios, prices are determined in real time by the interactions of buyers and sellers.

Restructured Channels

In a traditional arrangement, a manufacturer produces a product and sells it to the next level in the distribution channel (possibly a wholesaler or a retailer). As was described in Chapter 14, firms further down the channel maintain an inventory of the product, promote it locally, possibly provide credit to buyers, take and process orders, distribute the product in smaller quantities to other firms or consumers, and provide a variety of services to the buyers. Many of these activities are related to filling orders, and are captured by the term **fulfillment.**

When a firm sells on the Web and therefore skips one or more channel levels, it must create the systems to provide fulfillment. Even a traditional retailer that goes on the Web must arrange to process orders and get the product to the buyer. One option is to perform these tasks internally. For example, a manufacturer that formerly shipped truckloads of products to wholesalers might start packaging and shipping individual units to consumers. Another option is to outsource fulfillment. Outsourcing may simply involve delivering the purchased product to the customer, or it may include everything from processing the order to postpurchase service issues and everything in-between. For example, JCPenney sells CD players in its stores and on its website, but it sells CDs online through Handleman Company. Handleman, because it fills orders for a number of retailers, can maintain the necessary inventory of music titles (estimated to be at least 200,000), to do this profitably.

www.handleman.com

A number of companies including Lands' End, Ebags.com in cooperation with Timbuk2, and Nike (whose order form is shown here) offer customers the opportunity to customize products via their websites. Even cereal maker General Mills has explored the idea of allowing consumers to select from a list of 100 ingredients to create their own ideal cereal.

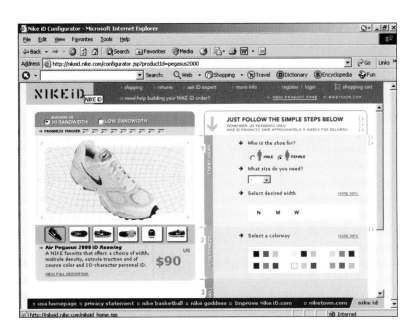

Buyer Communication

Marketers recognize word-of-mouth communication as a potent force because it is seen as an assessment by an objective third party with nothing to gain or lose from a purchase decision. Of course, word of mouth can be negative as well as positive. Thus, firms go to considerable effort to encourage positive word of mouth and to resolve unfavorable impressions that might lead to negative word of mouth.

The Internet has magnified both the speed and the reach of word of mouth. Forums, chat rooms, and individual sites provide a nearly unlimited source of opinions about products and experiences. Even if none of your friends have taken a Carnival cruise, purchased from an L. L. Bean's catalog, or stayed in a hotel in London, you can quickly gather opinions and recommendations of people who have.

Amazon created a forum for word of mouth by inviting its customers to offer reviews and ratings of the books they purchased online. The evaluations are then reproduced on the site for other customers. It is not clear how much influence word-of-mouth reactions from a stranger have on behavior, but their popularity is reflected in the fact that there is at least one site, www.complaints.com, dedicated entirely to negative word of mouth.

www.complaints.com

It's been suggested that many companies have taken advantage of customer ignorance about alternative prices and the relative performance of substitute products. However, the Internet makes information exchange among buyers much easier, shifting power from the sellers to the customers.

The Impact of the Internet on Marketing Strategy

The Internet has created opportunities for firms to create their own websites to communicate with other businesses and consumers, and to conduct transactions. As discussed above, the objectives of these sites are to reduce costs, generate revenue, or both.

In addition to creating new businesses, the Web has changed existing ways of doing business. For example, it has stimulated some unlikely alliances between traditional retailers and Web access providers. America Online and Wal-Mart, Yahoo!

and Kmart, and Microsoft and Best Buy have forged agreements in which the stores promote the Web access provider to their customers in return for promotion of the retailer's online store on the portals. This is just one example of how the Internet has influenced marketing strategy. As the following discussion suggests, many areas have been affected.

Market Research

Like all good marketers, firms making use of the Internet want to segment markets and then concentrate on selected targets. Gathering data about website visits and visitors and relating that data to other information about visitors is a useful place to begin. Online research firm comScore Networks illustrates this approach. It monitors the Internet activities of a panel of 1.5 million Web users. By combining data on their Web browsing, with information on what the panel members buy online, how often, and from what sites, it provides both general and specific insights into the impact of the Internet. Among comScore's recent findings, Web shopping by Hispanics is increasing faster than for the rest of the U.S. population, and Hispanics spend more on average than non-Hispanic online buyers.[10]

www.comscore.com

Traditional marketing research techniques including surveys and focus groups are being conducted on the Web. Clearly using the Web for research doesn't eliminate all the problems of more conventional methods. For example, just as in a mail survey, the researcher can't be sure who completed an Internet survey. But it does offer some unique opportunities. For example, the graphics now possible on the Internet allow respondents in a focus group or survey to look at visual images of a product in motion and from many different angles. Probably the biggest advantages of conducting research over the Internet are the speed with which it can be completed, the comparatively low cost, and the geographic reach. The biggest drawback is that only about half the households in the U.S. have Internet access (which is far more than most other countries in the world), so care must be taken to ensure that respondents represent the group of interest to the researcher.

There are other research techniques to identify segments that involve gathering data through electronic observation of site visitors. One approach, called **clustering,** tracks the pages visited, amount of time at a page, and items purchased by individuals while they navigate a site. It then creates groups or clusters of visitors with very similar patterns. When subsequent visitors display behavior similar to a particular cluster, they can be steered in real time to content or merchandise they are most likely to buy.

Amazon developed a similar technique called **collaborative filtering** that allows it to recommend books or tapes to an individual based on a comparison of the person's selections and the purchases of previous visitors. So, for example, assume that a number of visitors who purchased books on gardening from Amazon.com also examined books on home repairs. When you click on home repairs, in addition to giving you that information, the site would suggest some popular gardening titles.

As the competition intensifies, Internet marketers recognize the importance of segmentation and targeting. As one research analyst observed, "Online services have mostly been competing on selection and price, but now that the playing field is growing, the smart ones are realizing they need to differentiate themselves by offering a relevant, personalized experience to the customer."[11]

Rather than just offering a lower price, Internet marketers are learning to use technology to improve service. For example, NextCard has linked its website to the databases of the major consumer credit bureaus, which allows it to make the process of applying for a Visa credit card much quicker and easier. Another example is the effort of General Motors to add an Internet link to its Onstar system, which combines a car phone and global-positioning equipment to offer travel information and emergency help. The added service allows a driver to listen to an individually designed mix of news, customized traffic reports, and personal e-mail messages.

www.nextcard.com

Channel Relationships

The attraction of the Web for manufacturers is a closer link with the final customer. By selling over the Web and eliminating middlemen, both business and consumer product makers are able to decide which of their products to present, how they will be presented, and what level of service will accompany them. Equally important, the direct connection of the Internet permits manufacturers to obtain unfiltered feedback from the buyers who actually use their products. Firms as diverse as Mattel, Timex, Clinique, Sony, and Kodak are using websites to sell their products.

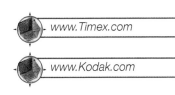

www.Timex.com

www.Kodak.com

For an established firm (other than a retailer), selling on the Web usually means bypassing one or more channel members or even a manufacturer's own sales force. In most instances, this is a source of tension. For example, when General Motors floated the idea of selling cars via the Web in response to the competition of sites such as Autobytel and Cars.com, there was an immediate negative response from its dealers. Closer to home, a firm's own sales force can be affected by Web sales. When Merrill Lynch announced it would offer online trading to its existing clients, its brokers were quick to ask how their commissions would be affected.

The issue is simple. Changing the way a product is sold and distributed has an impact on the individuals and organizations currently selling the product. Anticipating their reaction and insuring they are treated fairly is not as obvious. By moving some of its sales to the Web, a firm risks losing the loyalty and commitment of its existing channel. W.W. Grainger dealt with this by guaranteeing its sales people commissions on all sales made on the Web by customers in their territories. However, paying commissions to sales people or distributors not actually involved in a sale eliminates at least some of the cost savings of selling on the Web.

Because the majority of sales for most manufacturers are still made through traditional channels, the risk of alienating important business partners has affected Web strategies. Some of the approaches used by manufacturers to avoid Internet-related channel conflict are:[12]

- *Use the Web as a lead generator only.* Some manufacturers, notably the auto companies, use their websites to collect sales leads, and then direct potential customers to dealers located near them.

- *Offer different products online.* Mattel offers collectibles online that are not available in stores.

- *Sell online at the retail list price.* To avoid undercutting retail stores, Polaroid sells its digital cameras and photo printers online at the same price consumers find in stores.

- *Involve middlemen in online sales.* When Amway started selling online, it devised a plan to engage and protect its 3 million independent sales representatives. Representatives are encouraged to sign up customers for Amway's website. The sales person then gets a commission for any online purchases made by customers they have registered.[13]

- *Target a different market segment.* Clinique, which offers customized cosmetics and hair-care products on its website, targets consumers who avoid the cosmetics counters in department stores.

Middlemen have devised strategies of their own to add value to their positions in the supply chain. One approach is to take over the final assembly role for products purchased online. The manufacturer ships the product to the distributor in semifinished form, and the distributor completes the assembly and, if appropriate, tests the product before delivery. Called **channel assembly,** this approach allows products to be customized for customers and at the same time shortens the delivery time because many manufacturers, preferring not to disrupt their production processes, postpone custom projects. Another strategy, termed **co-location,** has employees of the distributor stationed at the manufacturer's site to arrange ship-

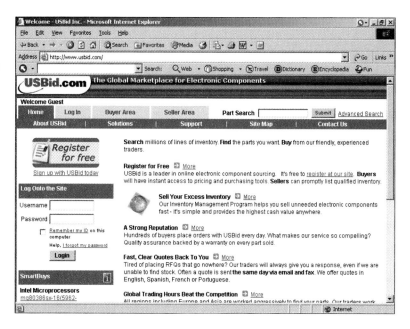

Many websites have been created to serve as intermediaries for business-to-business transactions. This site, usbid.com, specializes in electronic components. Businesses wishing to buy or sell items can tap into a global marketplace to check prices, request bids, or conduct auctions. The result of such sites is more choices for buyers and more prospects for sellers.

ment of the finished product to the customer. Because the product is handled fewer times, co-location shortens delivery time.

The roles of some intermediaries commonly found in traditional channels have been adapted for online selling. For example, as many as 30% of Internet-only retailers use a variation of a business-to-business drop shipper to fill orders.[14] (See Chapter 16 for the description of a drop shipper.) That is, the retailer accepts the customer's order online, then forwards it to a distributor who ships the purchased product directly to the customer with the retailer's name on it. This relieves the Internet retailer of maintaining an inventory as well as the tasks associated with handling, packaging, and transporting the product.

The Internet has also created a new breed of electronic middlemen. These firms make or facilitate transactions through the Internet, but their only investment is a website. The model for this type of operation was created by eBay, the online auction. It has since been copied, modified, and extended to insurance, travel, long-distance phone calls, home repair services, and other industries.

One thing is clear. When a firm uses the Internet for transactions, it has an impact on channel relationships. The resulting channel adjustment may be moderate (redefining the role of middlemen) or drastic (eliminating middlemen).

Promotion

A website without visitors is a waste of money. Equally ineffective is a site without the right visitors—the target audience of the organization. Part of the problem is simply the number of websites and the fact that the search engines can't keep track of them all. Imagine going to a mall with thousands of stores and looking for a particular one using an incomplete directory.

Another complicating factor is that visits to websites are always initiated by the visitor—a customer, supplier, or even a competitor. There is no passive exposure, as occurs with mass media such as television or radio, and very little incidental exposure, as occurs with billboards or walking past a store. These characteristics of the Internet have resulted in some adjustments in how website promotion is carried out.

The first issue is *attracting* the right audience to a website. Several approaches are being used:

- *Banner ads on other websites.* A **banner ad** is a boxed-in promotional message, often appearing at the top of a Web page. A site visitor who clicks on a banner ad is transported to the advertiser's home page. As Web visitors become familiar with banner ads, they tend to ignore them and their effectiveness diminishes. Banner ads are also the least targeted ads. Despite these shortcomings, they account for about one-half of all advertising dollars spent online. The reason is probably the relatively low cost. On average, a banner ad costs about $10 per thousand exposures.

- *Pop-ups and pop-unders.* This is an ad format that creates a new browser window, either atop the browser the visitor to a site is viewing (pop-up) or behind the site currently being viewed (pop-under). Pop-unders fill the screen when the visitor closes a browser. Although pop-ups and pop-unders account for only 2% of Web advertising, they have generated considerable criticism from consumers because they are so intrusive.[15]

- *Portal arrangements.* For a fee, portals give a site a prominent position when a visitor undertakes an appropriately directed search. For example, if K•B Toys has a portal arrangement with Yahoo!, a consumer who uses Yahoo!'s search engine to find toy marketers will find K•B Toys at or near the top of the list.

- *Sponsorship.* For a sponsorship fee, an advertiser is given a permanent place on the host's site. For example, iVillage, a site targeted at women, has a sponsor list that includes Clairol and Kraft. Each sponsor has special offers and advice for the target audience.

- *Targeted e-mail.* With this method, a firm directs e-mail to current or potential customers, inviting them to visit its site. When this approach is not properly targeted, it becomes electronic "junk mail" and can create ill will among the recipients.

- *Affiliate promotion.* Under this approach, a firm includes on its site a link to related sites, usually in exchange for a commission on any sales the arrangement produces. For example, a site selling sporting goods might have as affiliates a sports magazine, a camping equipment site, and a sports memorabilia site. Affiliates are typically identified as such on the site. A recent survey reported that affiliate promotion outperformed all other forms of promotion except targeted e-mail.[16]

Utilizing all of these methods, the volume of Web advertising has increased from $2.8 billion in 1999 to $9.6 billion in 2002.[17] Although this is an impressive growth rate, it is important to keep in mind that it still amounts to less than 4% of total advertising expenditures.

Attracting visitors is only half the battle. The second objective of promotion is *holding* visitors once they click on a site. Internet users are generally viewed as impatient—not surprising, because speed and convenience are major attractions. With a simple mouse click, they can disappear as quickly as they arrived. Thus Internet marketers look for ways to make their sites "sticky."

The holding power of a site is measured in terms of time spent per visit. For example, when Coca-Cola Co. found that visitors spent only an average of 90 seconds at cherrycoke.com, it redesigned the site. In contrast, a site can have excellent holding power but not meet a firm's objective, as Bell Atlantic found out. The firm created an online "soap opera" about a newlywed couple. Episodes were run weekly, and they attracted large audiences, even receiving positive reviews from entertainment critics. However, when consumer surveys showed no change in Bell Atlantic's brand awareness, the feature was discontinued.

There is still much to learn about attracting visitors to online sites and about marketing to them once they arrive. As firms gain experience and more research is conducted, they will develop more savvy about online efforts. In the meantime, some online marketers are willing to go to almost any length to attract customers. For example, in order to build market share, more.com, an online drugstore, allowed

www.cherrycoke.com

customers to lock in the price of an item forever as long as they purchased the item at least once a year. Unfortunately for the company, the tactic didn't build profits along with market share so more.com no longer exists.

Issues and Opportunities in the Information Economy

The information economy and the Internet pose major challenges for marketers. Not only are some traditional strategies and tactics obsolete or quickly becoming so, but entirely new issues are frequently discovered. As always, the firms that find ways to overcome these obstacles are likely to be the most successful in the long run.

Information Quality and Quantity

The Internet demonstrates how valuable information can be. A prospective car buyer who can compare the prices of several sellers has an advantage in negotiations. Similarly, a component supplier to a manufacturer kept informed of the manufacturer's production schedule can minimize inventory costs. However, as the Internet grows, the issues of the quality and quantity of the information provided is becoming a larger issue.

For a little as $75, anyone can register a Web address and create a website. As a result, there are millions of websites in existence and the number is expanding daily. Estimates suggest that there are over 3 billion documents available on the Internet. Visiting the Web is equally easy, requiring only access to a PC and a willingness to pay a monthly connection fee. The problem is that Web users are in danger of being buried by the onslaught of information, and websites risk being lost in the clutter. For example, do consumers want to sift through the terms and conditions of over 300 insurance providers, even if the information is conveniently provided on one website?

Another information issue is quality. There is very little regulation of the Internet and virtually no standards except voluntary guidelines set by professional organizations such as the American Marketing Association. As a result, fraud is quite common. According to the results of a study by the research firm Experian, 97% of online retailers in England have experienced fraud. Furthermore, the reach of the Internet has made this a global problem. Online security experts that monitor chat rooms frequented by credit card thieves report that 5,000 credit card account numbers can be purchased in bulk for as little as $1,000 with guarantees that the numbers are valid![18] How's that for honor among thieves?

www.ama.org

The Web also creates instant critics. Anyone with a website can offer a critique of a company, a product, a book, or anything else, and there is nothing to ensure the credentials of the reviewer or the accuracy of the comments. Some evaluations are given credibility by the sites on which they appear. For example, Amazon has professional critics who review and recommend books and compact discs.

The challenge for marketers using the Internet is to understand their target markets well enough to provide them with the right amount of useful information. Doing any less will frustrate customers in the short term and possibly alienate them in the long run.

Customer Service

Infatuated with the technology and the ability to conduct transactions, some online marketers overlook the importance of service. Presale information, operating instructions, and postsale problem resolution frequently receive too little attention.

Many thought the Web could replace retail stores for consumers or the sales people for business-to-business customers. However, experience indicates that it is difficult to eliminate the services provided by these middlemen. Thus online marketers must address challenges such as returned merchandise, payment problems, and performance complaints. For example, when Amazon began its auction site, it offered a customer satisfaction guarantee. Even though the transactions are between the buyers and sellers, and Amazon only brings them together, Amazon is attempting to avoid the problems eBay experienced when customers were dissatisfied and had nowhere to turn.

Providing service may be the single biggest hurdle for firms comtemplating a move to the Internet. Many of the more successful Internet retailers have found that combining stores with online access is the best formula.[19] Consumers can visit the store to see merchandise firsthand or to return merchandise. Alternatively, consumers can shop from home or use Internet kiosks in the store to obtain detailed information about products or search for items that are not on the store's shelves. In effect, these retailers are offering the best of both worlds to their customers.

Security and Privacy

www.ftc.gov/inforsecurity/

As many as 90% of consumers with Web access have never made an online purchase. The two major reasons are security and privacy.[20] After years of being advised to guard against having credit card numbers stolen, consumers are now asked to freely give those numbers to strangers over the Internet. At the same time, publicity about hackers breaking into merchants' databases to steal account numbers and slip-ups by well-intentioned firms such as Eli Lilly & Co., which accidentally posted the e-mail addresses of nearly 700 users of its antidepressant, Prozac, have made many wary. In addition, efforts by both federal agencies and state legislators to regulate the behavior of Web advertisers and sellers indicate to consumers that problems exist.

Creating a climate of trust on the Internet is difficult. The challenge is compounded by the newness and intangibility of the Internet. Without stores or employees to talk to face-to-face, consumers' hesitancy to share personal or financial information is not surprising. To overcome the fears of potential customers, online buying must develop a reputation as being safe. That means the customers must perceive the system over which they make the transaction and the seller as trustworthy.

www.landsend.com

A seller can create an image of legitimacy in several ways. One approach is to transfer an existing reputation earned in another selling format to electronic commerce. For example, Lands' End, with a proven record as a catalog retailer, simply states on its website, "You have no credit card risk. Period." Another approach is to create associations with trusted brands or firms. For example, a less-well-known firm can increase its credibility and trust by selling only well-established brands on its site.

The Internet has opened international markets for many firms. A visitor to Nintendo's home page can select from 15 different global alternatives in a dozen languages. The Japanese home page is shown here.

www.netmarket.com

Finally, by having a well-known partner or recognizable sponsors, an unknown online merchant can give its site legitimacy.

Online security systems, which involve encryption, digital certification, authentification, virtual account numbers, and other sophisticated technology are not likely to be understood by consumers. However, what they can understand is the assurance of the seller. netmarket.com, for example, briefly describes its elaborate security system and then offers an absolute guarantee of safe shopping.

Privacy concerns focus on how data about Internet visitors are collected and used. Data about Web visitors are gathered in several ways. Some data are provided by visitors when they register on a website. Registration is frequently required in order to gain access to specialized information, games, contests, and other attractive features. Consumers also provide information at the time of a purchase. In addition to some demographic data, the information requested to register on a site or make a purchase often includes a short survey with questions about activities, interests, and other purchase behavior. Data are also gathered without the direct involvement of the visitor. An online firm does this by using a **cookie**, a file placed on the hard drive of the visitor's computer that automatically records where the person goes online, the frequency of visits to a site, and the duration of each visit.

Internet marketers collect the data to better understand their current and potential markets. However, a number of consumer protection concerns have been raised:

- *Gathering information.* Should marketers ever gather information without the express consent of the consumer? Even if permission is granted, should there be limits on the information considered appropriate to gather? Recognizing that children are especially vulnerable, Congress passed the Children's Online Privacy Protection Act, which requires that commercial websites obtain consent from a parent before asking children under 13 years of age for their names, addresses, telephone numbers, or other identifying information. Another challenging question is whether customers should be compensated for the information they provide because it obviously has value to the organizations collecting it.

- *Using information.* Once consumer information is gathered, should its application be constrained? For example, Amazon uses a consumer's profile to suggest books, which few people find objectionable. But should a search engine, assumed by most users to be an objective directory, tailor its recommendations to a searcher's demographics or past purchases? In the U.S. there are few regulations; but in the European Union consumers must be given explicit explanations about how any information they provide will be used.

- *Selling, exchanging, or combining information.* Is it acceptable for a website that has gathered information legitimately to sell it to another firm? For example, an online investment broker or insurance agency would find information about an online bank's customers very valuable. What about combining catalog purchase behavior with online shopping behavior, as several research firms are planning to do? Although these profiles will initially be anonymous, as marketers search for patterns of behavior and target segments, there are questions about what might happen in the future when individuals can be specifically identified.

Marketers prefer self-regulation. However, there are calls for provision of greater control of Internet security and privacy by the government.

International Markets

Theoretically, electronic commerce knows no boundaries. A customer in Taiwan can use the Internet to make a purchase from a Chicago-based firm as easily as can a customer in Milwaukee. The only physical constraint is delivery, and that has been greatly simplified by shipping companies. However, a variety of other issues must be overcome as marketers expand globally.

www.nielsen.com

The model for Web-based marketing has been created in the U.S., relying on the infrastructure that's in place, but many parts of the world lack one or more critical components that have contributed to the rapid growth of online marketing. For example, Nielsen//Net Ratings, an Internet research division of VNU, reports that four countries, the U.S., Germany, England, and Italy, account for half the world's total Internet audience, whereas in China, less than 4% of the population has any access at all and a much smaller proportion can use it to make purchases.[21] Also, few developing countries have national credit card systems, so there is no convenient method of paying for online purchases.

And there's the issue of PC ownership. In countries where per capita income is only a few thousand dollars or less, few people can afford a PC. In some countries, notably Brazil, entrepreneurs are trying to reduce this problem by making the Web accessible in supermarket kiosks for consumers who lack computers.

There are also cultural barriers to the rapid expansion of the Internet. Although English is the standard language for business-to-business transactions, many small-business people are able to communicate only in their native languages. In terms of consumers, local Internet portals have been more successful than larger imported counterparts such as AOL because they provide a rich mix of local content.

Specific legal restrictions imposed by individual governments have added complications to international e-commerce. For example, there is a French requirement that all contracts be written in French, a ban in Finland on mentioning speed as a feature of a car, and a restriction in Sweden on advertising directed at children under 12 years of age. Another complication has been created by the European Union, which has decreed that purchases made by customers in its member countries are subject to sales tax.[22]

In a somewhat surprising turn of events, some laws have actually encouraged international online sales. For example, German consumers find it's cheaper to buy books from websites in Great Britain, and British consumers can get better deals on cars purchased from online dealers in Belgium. In both cases, consumers are reacting to laws that attempt to protect domestic businesses by creating artificially high prices.

Is Covisint a blessing or a curse?

It may depend on who you ask. What was envisioned as a global Internet supply chain with seamless links from a carmaker's suppliers to the final consumer has yet to meet expectations. Covisint was created in 2000 by Ford, General Motors, DaimlerChrysler, Nissan, and Renault as an independent e-business exchange that would facilitate purchasing, reduce inventories, allow consumers to custom-design their cars, and get products to market quicker, all at a lower cost. It has offices in the U.S., Amsterdam, Tokyo, Frankfurt, and Paris.

At the core of the Covisint concept is the Internet. The Internet makes it possible for carmakers, their suppliers, auto dealers, and consumers to communicate and exchange information faster and more efficiently. For example, Covisint arranges reverse auctions in which a carmaker can purchase parts from suppliers in a matter of minutes, a process that took weeks or even months in the past. So far the biggest auction transaction arranged through Covisint was a

$2.6 billion auto parts purchase by DaimlerChrysler. To put that in perspective, the total volume of purchases on eBay, the largest consumer auction website, for an entire quarter were $2.4 billion.

So what's the problem? Suppliers to the automakers believe the system is one-sided. It is being used primarily for reverse auctions in which the suppliers compete against one another on price. As a result, they see all the benefits going to the automakers. That explains why only 7,000 suppliers (out of a potential 50,000) have registered with Covisint. It seems that technology can easily reach across borders but it can't resolve all the challenges that businesses face.

Sources: Peter Loftus, "Making It Work," *The Wall Street Journal,* Feb. 11, 2002, p. R16; David Sedgwick, Ralph Kisiel, and Robert Sherefkin, "Kutner Has Tough Task at Covisint," *Automotive News,* July 1, 2002, p. 1; and Ralph Kisiel, "Low Auction Revenue Plagues Covisint," *Crain's Detroit Business,* July 22, 2002, p. 21.

The Future

The growth of electronic networking in all forms is remarkable. Networks have energized managers, stimulated the development of new business models, and caught the attention of nearly everyone. In the business-to-business sector, electronic networking has added to efficiency and contributed to bottom-line performance. It has been less successful in generating profits for firms that sell to consumers.

Thus far, the most successful Internet marketing sites deal in information. An interesting example is Ancestry.com, a profitable site. It helps people track down their living and deceased family members using a large, searchable database. Because all aspects of a transaction are conducted over the Internet, maximum benefits are achieved. Next in line are the sites that market services such as airline seats or hotel rooms. These marketers have an inventory that becomes obsolete at a definable time—for example, when a plane takes off. The challenge is to develop a yield-management program that adjusts fares over time to fill the largest number of seats at the highest possible price. The most challenging Internet businesses are those handling physical goods that must be inventoried, stored, and distributed. Examples are online marketers of groceries, clothing, furniture, and automobiles. The logistics problems in these businesses consume much of the gains achieved from the online transactions.

Despite its expanding impact, electronic commerce will not replace traditional marketing as we know it. Jeff Bezos, the founder of Amazon.com and one of the leaders of the e-commerce movement, predicted that Internet sellers can attract at most 15% of the world's $5 trillion retail market.[23] Although $750 billion is hardly a trifling amount, Bezos contends that stores will always be around because people enjoy the interaction shopping provides, and some needs must be met more quickly than is possible over the Internet.

Clearly the information economy has arrived. What is yet to be determined is how it will impact each individual industry and business. The challenge for marketers is to determine how information can be most effectively utilized to meet the needs of the customer and satisfy the objectives of the organization. Not surprisingly, determining its value brings us back once again to the marketing concept.

Summary

Information has always played a major role in marketing. The effective utilization of information leads to better products, prices, distribution, and promotion. Technology combined with information is especially powerful.

Although many forms of technology have influenced marketing, the Internet is currently having a major—perhaps unprecedented—impact.

Electronic networks are created when individuals or organizations are linked via some form of telecommunications. Internal electronic networks are called intranets. There are several types of external electronic networks, including electronic data interchanges, electronic information transfer, electronic transactions, electronic commerce, and extranets. All of these now make use of the Internet.

Internet marketing changes the dynamics in markets. The commercial application of the Internet required the development of the World Wide Web and several tools to make it accessible, including browsers, directories, and portals. Now the Web is available to virtually anyone with a PC. Customers gain greater control of interactions with businesses and have the opportunity to compare products and prices. More products are customized, and fewer prices are fixed. New ways are developed to deliver products to buyers, and buyers share more information. The Internet also influences marketing strategy. Areas most affected are marketing research, channel relationships, and promotion.

The information economy poses both challenges and opportunities for marketers. Among the most significant are managing the quality and quantity of information, providing customer service, ensuring the security of transactions and the privacy of customers, and developing international electronic commerce.

The Internet will continue to grow and evolve. At this point companies dealing in information are best able to take advantage of the economies provided by the Internet, whereas those selling goods face the most challenges. Although its impact will be felt by all businesses, it's not likely that the Internet will entirely replace traditional marketing.

More about **Maritz**

Maritz, Inc., has not always experienced success in its efforts to incorporate technology into its businesses. eMaritz, a new online business that allowed client companies to customize sales contests and recognition programs through the Internet, was seen as a way to extend the incentive business to smaller firms. The company broke new ground in that no other firm in the incentive business had a stand-alone Web-based operation, let alone one as comprehensive. Nevertheless, eMaritz did not perform up to expectations.

The service's offerings included program rules, automated promotional and administrative communication, online data-capture tools, and awards that could be put together to create over 180 different incentive programs. Small and medium-sized businesses that are not typical Maritz clients were the first target market for eMaritz. Clients could use eMaritz independently without any need to communicate with a Maritz representative, although the company provided backup support and consulting services.

One motivation for launching the product was to preempt the competition. But in 2002 Maritz, Inc., shut down eMaritz following lower-than-expected profits for the venture.[24]

1. What might explain the market's disappointing response to eMaritz?

2. What general guidelines for the use of technology does the performance of eMaritz suggest?

Key Terms and Concepts

Internet (624)
World Wide Web (624)
Website (624)
Networks (624)
Electronic networks (624)
Intranet (624)
Electronic data interchange (EDI)
   (625)

Electronic information (625)
Electronic transactions (627)
Electronic commerce (628)
Extranet (628)
Browser (628)
Directory (628)
Portal (629)
Fulfillment (631)

Clustering (633)
Collaborative filtering (633)
Channel assembly (634)
Co-location (634)
Banner ad (635)
Cookie (639)

Questions and Problems

1. Two examples of information technology that have had a significant impact on marketing are radio and television. How does the Internet differ from these breakthroughs as a marketing tool?

2. Examine the e-information sites of a fast-food restaurant and a traditional manufacturer (such as Whirlpool or Ford Motor Co.). Using the five categories of information described in the chapter, compare the sites.

3. What key strategic issues are faced by traditional "bricks-and-mortar" retailers such as Wal-Mart, Kmart, and Office Depot when they go online to sell products?

4. Describe one possible marketing implication of each of the following effects of the Internet:
   a. Interaction controlled by customers
   b. More and better information
   c. Fewer fixed prices
   d. New product-delivery methods
   e. More buyer communication

5. Why should firms such as Mattel, Timex, and Sony be concerned about their existing channels when they begin selling products to consumers via the Web?

6. Go to one of the Web portals (Netscape, AltaVista, Lycos), and click through several links. Note the banner ads on each link. What appears to be the objective of the banner ads? What are some factors that may make them effective or ineffective?

7. Providing customer service appears to be one of the primary challenges for Internet marketers. What implications does this have for their "bricks-and-mortar" competitors?

8. There are concerns about Internet marketers using "cookies" to gather data about online customer behavior. Is this different than observing customers as they shop in retail stores?

Interactive Marketing Exercises

1. Interview five students who have shopped on the Web within the last week. Gather the following information:

   a. Why did they choose the Web as a place to shop?
   b. Did they make a purchase? Why or why not?
   c. In the process of shopping, did they make any unplanned site or page visits?
   d. How long did their shopping "trip" take?

   On the basis of this information as well as your own experiences, what do you see as the strengths and weaknesses of the Web as a marketing tool?

2. Talk to the owner or manager of a retail store in a category where online marketing is growing (such as books, recorded music, groceries, videos, or toys). Determine how serious a threat the person considers online marketing to be, and what changes have been made or are planned in response.

Cases for Part 7

McDonald's

Searching for a New Success Recipe

When Ray Kroc founded McDonald's in 1955, his plan was to duplicate a seemingly simple formula in every unit of his growing restaurant chain. And for many years, the McDonald's Corporation's success was the result. The company with the Golden Arches featured a simple menu of hamburgers, french fries, and soft drinks. The food was inexpensive, consistent in quality, and was served speedily from nearly identical establishments that were pleasant and clean.

Kroc's vision and the company's ability to implement it in both company-owned and franchised outlets established McDonald's as the world's most recognized brand and the largest restaurant chain in the U.S. in terms of sales, with revenues over $20 billion in 2002. Along the way, McDonald's introduced products that have remained perennial favorites, such as the Big Mac and the Egg McMuffin. And of course there's the Happy Meal, which is beloved by kids as much for the food as for the toy that comes with it.

But McDonald's has experienced its share of growing pains as well. For example, in attempting to appeal to more adults by providing healthier fare, McDonald's developed the McLean and spent millions to promote the low-fat burger. But sales were disappointing and, in response to customer disinterest, the item was eventually dropped from the menu. Not since Chicken McNuggets were introduced in 1983, has the company had a successful major, new-product launch.

McDonald's also pursued an aggressive expansion strategy in the U.S. This led to a backlash from McDonald's restaurant owners (franchisees) who charged that the company's newer outlets were cannibalizing the sales of existing restaurants. Indeed, revenues in July and August of 2002 were down almost 3% from comparable months in 2001 at U.S. locations that had been open at least a year. In addition, successful franchisees want to weed out some restaurants they consider to be substandard in service, cleanliness, and decor.

These developments have caused management to examine several of Kroc's fundamental policies and formulaic approach. New nonburger food items are being tested, and restaurants are being remodeled in radical (by McDonald's standards) ways. Even the possibility of selling some nonfood items is being explored. In addition, underperforming stores in the U.S. are being closed while outlets are being opened in new locations all over the world.

Beefing Up Its Foreign Operations

Every day, three new McDonald's restaurants open somewhere in the world. However, expansion within the U.S. has slowed considerably, with an estimated 300 new store openings in 2002, compared with 1,100 in 1995. Still, franchisees are grumbling about the saturated domestic market.

Despite the fact that there are more than 30,000 McDonald's worldwide (almost half of which are in the U.S.), the company sees substantial overseas opportunities for growth of its core brand. Since 1996, the number of locations in Asia and Africa has doubled to more than 7,000 restaurants. The same is true of Latin American stores, which now number more than 1,500. In many of these locales, McDonald's has adapted its fare to appeal to local tastes. For instance, Japanese consumers can treat themselves to a Teriyaki Mac Burger. In fact, McDonald's now boasts 46 million customers every day in over 120 countries. But adding new locations is not having the positive impact it once had on performance. In fact, worldwide sales fell by 2% in 2002, forcing executives to address a number of issues in an effort to put the shine back on the Golden Arches.

Confronting Some Supersized Problems

As it continues to strengthen its international presence, McDonald's faces a variety of challenges, some with which it is familiar, and some that are new. Franchisees in Brazil have voiced the same concerns as their American counterparts and have begun to complain loudly about overexpansion. One store owner, who has watched 14 new McDonald's restaurants open near his location, complained, "With every new store that opened, I lost more sales."

In England, sales fell dramatically after dozens of people died of "mad cow" disease. Victims became infected after eating beef that originated from cows with bovine spongiform encephalopathy (although no cases of mad cow disease are believed to have been caused by beef from McDonald's). First appearing in England in 1996, mad cow disease decimated Europe's beef industry. McDonald's initially reacted to the crisis by completely removing beef from its menu and by offering alternative burgers made from pork and ham, as well as grilled cheese sandwiches. It was able to eventually secure beef it felt was disease-free, and even ran an advertising campaign that invited skeptical consumers to tour its meatpacking plants to learn why McDonald's beef is safe. These efforts reversed a 20% decline in burger sales in France in 2001, but many European consumers remain concerned about beef products.

In the U.S. the issue is not avoiding beef, but eating too much of it. Increasing concerns about health and nutrition have led some consumers to move away from fried and grilled fast foods to fresh sandwiches and subs. Not surprisingly, this is coming at a time when obesity rates are rising at an alarming rate. In 2000, about 300,000 Americans died of ailments attributed to being overweight, resulting in health care costs of $117 billion. Adding to the negative picture, several consumers have even sued McDonald's for contributing to their obesity problems.

McDonald's was also challenged in the courtroom when consumers discovered that its french fries were prepared with beef flavoring and were not in fact vegetarian, as the company once claimed. As a result, McDonald's issued a written apology for misleading its customers. The company also donated $10 million to Hindu charitable organizations in an attempt to make amends for misleading Hindus who unwittingly violated their religious practices by eating the fries.

The firm also got caught up in a price war with rival Burger King in 2001. The result was an increase in sales but the first quarterly loss, announced in December, 2002, since McDonald's became a public corporation in 1967.

Efforts to get back on track have followed two routes. One is improving existing operations and the other is exploring new opportunities. In existing establishments, McDonald's executives look for ways to improve customer service and food quality

ratings. Soon after being appointed chief executive officer in 1998, Jack Greenberg introduced new equipment and procedures for food preparation that were meant to eliminate the need for heat lamps and improve taste by cooking food as it is ordered instead of ahead of time. Franchisees made significant financial investments in the new "Made For You" system but have been disappointed by the results. The reaction is captured by a customer who said, "Since they took away the heat lamps, it takes forever—and the food still isn't hot."

Greenberg also commissioned an army of mystery shoppers to frequent McDonald's U.S. restaurants and report back on a variety of factors. These "spies" posed as regular customers and took notes on everything related to quality and service, including whether they were greeted with a smile, how long it took to get their food, and if their order was filled correctly. Apparently the mystery shoppers were needed. A company memo that was issued in July of 2002 reported, "We are meeting our speed of service standard only 46% of the time, and 3 out of 10 customers are waiting more than four minutes to complete their order."

Taking a Bite out of Big Mac

By commissioning more than 100,000 mystery shoppers, Greenberg demonstrated that he understood McDonald's can't afford to be complacent. Competition within the $46 billion U.S. fast-food industry is fierce, and McDonald's 43% market share seems to have stagnated. Sales within the burger category are growing by only 3% annually, versus 12% for custom-made sandwiches. With the exception of Wendy's, other traditional burger rivals are suffering as well. After introducing a new french fry in 1998, Burger King's market share fell by 2 points to 18.5%, prompting the company to announce in 2002 that it would develop yet another french fry recipe.

Subway has benefited greatly from the booming sub sandwich trend and recently surpassed McDonald's in total number of U.S. outlets, making it America's largest restaurant chain with 13,247 as of December of 2001. However, with yearly sales of $40.6 billion worldwide, McDonald's still dwarfs Subway on a global level. "Our size doesn't begin to approach the global bigness of McDonald's, but it still feels pretty darn good to beat them on their home turf," commented a Subway spokesperson.

A new category of restaurants, dubbed "fast casual," has captured the interest of a share of the market. With more than $5 billion in sales in 2001, this segment is growing at a rate of 15% each year. Customers still place their orders at counters, but the atmosphere is cozier, and the ingredients are fresher than those found at traditional fast-food establishments. According to one industry analyst, fast-casual restaurants, such as Panera, are able to charge a premium to people who "want to move beyond fast food but still need food fast." Other fast-casual restaurants include Baja Fresh Mexican Grill (which was purchased by Wendy's in 2002,) Rubio's (home of the fish taco), and Cosi.

Cooking Up New Strategies for the Future

In terms of new opportunities, McDonald's is moving on several fronts. The company is investing in fast-casual chains such as Pret A Manger, Chipotle Mexican, Donatos Pizzeria, Fazoli's Italian, and Boston Market, which was languishing in bankruptcy when McDonald's bought it. One McDonald's executive explained that these investments help the company attract the fast-casual crowd, "No matter what we do, we won't be able to attract those people to the Golden Arches." The firm plans to expand these chains throughout the U.S. and overseas. Existing McDonald's franchisees are excited at the prospect of being able to operate these new restaurants. The company is also testing an outlet that offers Donato's Pizza, Boston Market chicken, and its traditional burgers and fries all under one roof.

McDonald's constantly experiments with other new restaurant concepts, including a diner in Kokomo, Indiana, that offers more than 122 items, in addition to traditional McDonald's fare like McNuggets and Big Macs. Customers place their orders through tableside phones and food is delivered by employees. Coffee afficianados might also discover a McCafé. The test unit opened in Chicago in April of 2001, offering gourmet coffee, tea, and baked goods.

Customers craving a good, old-fashioned McDonald's experience might be surprised the next time they pull into their neighborhood outlet. The company has committed up to $800 million for revamping half of its flagship restaurants within the U.S. These updates are in part a result of a successful campaign that started in France when half the locations there were remodeled in the late 1990s. Each updated restaurant has a new, more sophisticated décor to reflect one of eight different themes, such as music or sports. The familiar red and yellow signs have been replaced with more muted maroon and mustard displays, and the remodeled locations have shown double-digit sales increases. But some American franchisees eschew the idea of installing hardwood floors and televisions that show music videos. One commented, "People are not coming to swoon over the décor. They are coming in and getting out of there. They don't give a rip about what is inside." Considering that suburban locations rack up 60% of their sales at the drive-through window, he may have a point.

But many franchisees are open to new ideas if it means increases in sales. And they are appealing to the corporate offices for help. One response is a continued search for healthier food items. McDonald's now features yogurt and fruit parfaits and is constantly testing low-fat alternatives, such as salads and even veggie burgers. The company announced in September of 2002 a cut in the amount of trans-fatty acids in its french fries, a result of changing the kind of cooking oil it uses. This significantly reduces the amount of cholesterol in each serving of fries.

Unable to restore McDonald's former luster, Jack Greenberg announced his retirement at the end of 2002. His replacement, Jim Cantalupo, a former vice chairman of the corporation, previously headed the company's international operation. One of the challenges he faced was deciding what McDonald's should be. When he took over, customers could get burgers and fries, but also gourmet coffee in Chicago, meatloaf in Kokomo, and fish tacos in Los Angeles, or they could spend a night in one of the company's four-star Golden Arches hotels in Switzerland. One has to wonder if that's what Ray Kroc, the founder, envisioned when he made the observation many years ago, "I don't know what we'll be serving in the year 2000, but we'll be serving more of it than anybody."

Questions

1. Describe several examples from the case that likely reflect strategic marketing planning and several others that represent strategic company planning at McDonald's.

2. Where would you place McDonald's traditional fast-food restaurants on the three planning models presented in Chapter 20? What implications would you draw from the placements?

3. How does the number of McDonald's outlets affect implementation of its marketing efforts?

Booking Sales Online

When Jeff Bezos quit his job on Wall Street in 1994 at age 31 to start a new business selling products over the Internet, he hadn't actually decided what those products would be. But he knew he wanted to provide customers with an enjoyable shopping experience, and he envisioned his company eventually becoming the world's largest "e-tailer" (a term coined to describe an online or electronic retailer). After considering the pros and cons of various options, he chose to sell books, and consistent with his ambition he christened the fledgling business Amazon.com, a reference to the Earth's largest river.

Sales swelled to $3 billion in 2001, but investors were questioning the company's long-term viability. Despite its popularity with Internet shoppers, as of May 2002, Amazon had lost more than $3 billion since opening its virtual doors in 1995. Through it all, Bezos has maintained his positive attitude and grandiose vision. The only thing that seems to elude the firm is sustained profitability.

Making Its Mark in Books and Beyond

In 1996, its first full year of business, Amazon generated more than $10 million in sales. The company utilized the technology of the Web to create a differential advantage over traditional booksellers. For example, unlike most retail stores, an e-tailer is open for business 24 hours a day, seven days a week. Also, Amazon's book business is not constrained by inventory. Shoppers can peruse Amazon's enormous database in search of books by title, author, or subject. When a customer makes a selection, the order is filled by a book wholesaler so Amazon carries only a relatively small inventory of best sellers.

The firm also uses Web technology to personalize its operation. For example, book buyers are given recommendations regarding similar or related works and can receive e-mails notifying them of new releases that may be of interest to them. Amazon even encourages its customers to provide book reviews that are reported on the site. By setting up an interactive, easy-to-use website, Amazon has created an enormous "cyber-community" of book lovers that some feel rivals even the coziest, well-stocked corner bookshop.

Testing Some Novel New Concepts

While still building Amazon's book business, Bezos began adding other product categories. Music CDs and videos were the first. Bezos said that he eventually wanted consumers to be able to purchase "anything and everything" at Amazon. True to his word, he continued to diversify and expand the site's offerings. Within days of its entry into the toy business in 1998, Amazon became the #1 online toy retailer. Tools and hardware, health and beauty aids, kitchen equipment, and electronics soon appeared under the Amazon banner. These categories (called "stores" by Bezos) not only offered Amazon shoppers more merchandise but also necessitated new warehouses and fulfillment infrastructure to handle the added inventory, so costs also increased.

A goal of adding merchandise is to encourage "one-stop" shopping to gain the economies of increased order size. However, the average customer order fell from $31 in early 2000 to $18 in mid-2001. This caused Bezos to seek revenue from other sources. He began to tout Amazon.com as an Internet "incubator" and charged a number of online firms, such as Drugstore.com and Greenlight.com (a car-sales company), to promote their companies on the Amazon website. Unfortunately, many of these failed during the dot–com bust in 2001. Because Amazon's promotional fees were in the form of stock in the companies, the venture provided very little revenue. Bezos soon refrained from referring to Amazon as an incubator.

That misstep didn't stop him from courting additional online partners, however. Bezos simply narrowed his focus to established "brick-and-mortar" retailers like Target, Office Depot, and Circuit City, and adjusted his original vision to include them. "We want to be the place for people to find and discover anything they want to buy online," he maintained. "But we've never said we had to do it all." Besides having their products featured on the heavily trafficked Amazon website, these companies hired Amazon to take over a subset of their online business operation or, in some cases, to run their entire websites. Having Amazon assume responsibility for its website and fulfillment operations helped Toys "Я" Us triple its online sales after a dismal 1999 holiday season during which it missed delivery dates and ran out of inventory. Amazon has even entered into agreements with Borders and Circuit City that allow customers to order goods online and then pick them up at the retailers' locations. These types of service deals added at least $200 million in revenue in 2001, and were actually more profitable than the sale of Amazon's own merchandise.

Bezos' quest for more ways to exploit the potential of the Internet led Amazon to open its own auction site to compete with eBay. However, he quickly amended the strategy to add a new twist. Whereas eBay provides only a forum for buyers and sellers to come together, Amazon allows independent sellers to offer new, used, and refurbished goods on its website right alongside Amazon merchandise. Conduct a search on Amazon.com for the novel *Gone With the Wind,* and you will be offered new editions of the hardcover and paperback titles, as well as a host of used copies from other vendors. The outside merchants pay Amazon a commission when they sell their wares, as well as a listing fee per item.

Called Marketplace by Amazon, this business appears to be counterintuitive; after all, it almost certainly detracts from Amazon's own product sales. Yet Amazon's profits from the sale of Marketplace goods are almost always higher than if the merchandise were from its own warehouse, because Amazon's transaction costs are so low. Some of Amazon's suppliers have balked at the strategy, however. Authors and publishing companies are not thrilled that Amazon has become a used-book reseller since the authors don't receive any royalties from these sales and the publishers don't like to see their new books being sold right next to lower-priced used versions. But customers appreciate having the expanded offering, and Marketplace sales comprised 15% of Amazon's total sales in early 2002.

The fact that consumers purchased $5.2 billion worth of apparel online in 2002 didn't escape Bezos' notice either. That same year, Amazon announced it would begin selling clothing during the holiday season. The strategy was similar to the one Amazon employed with its other bricks-and-mortar partners, but instead of choosing one retailer to represent this particular product category, the company announced that several well-established clothiers would be selling their wares on its website. The online apparel store initially featured more than 400 major clothing brands from a variety of sources, including the Gap and its sister store, Old Navy, as well as Lands' End and Nordstrom. Although Amazon's role is mainly promotional in nature and does not involve any inventory or shipping responsibilities, customers are able to purchase apparel, along with books or any other Amazon product category all in one shopping trip. In return, Amazon receives commissions from the clothing retailers, which makes this an extremely profitable proposition for Amazon.

Going from Best-Seller to the Bargain Bin

Profits became a priority for Bezos in 2001. Sales of books, music, and videos reached $400 million in the third quarter of 2000, but fell to about $351 million in the same quarter of the next year. This greatly concerned investors, precipitating an enormous plunge in the company's stock price. After Amazon stock reached a record high of $113 in December of 2000, it plunged to just $6 per share in late 2001 as investors became jittery about the firm's mounting losses.

Despite the added merchandise lines, its impressive sales growth continued to fall as well, from over 800% in 1997 to about 25% in 2001. Meanwhile, costs associated with offering a greater variety of items increased. Bezos was forced to lay off more than 1,000 employees and close distribution and customer service centers. Although some of Amazon's problems could be blamed on the weakened economy, a number of analysts questioned the company's promotions to stimulate sales and the addition of so many new product categories. But Bezos stuck to his strategy of placing a priority on volume. "A lot of the very best categories are on our website today, and there's a tremendous amount to add inside each category," he pointed out.

To calm investors, Bezos boldly announced in early 2001 that he expected Amazon to turn a profit in the last quarter of that same year. Analysts were doubtful, but Bezos' promise came true when the company reported a net profit of $5 million in the fourth quarter. Bezos was jubilant. "It's a major turnaround for us," he gloated. The company's drive for profitability was fueled by a major cost-cutting initiative that required Amazon to reformulate a number of its operational procedures in order to be more efficient. For instance, a new process was initiated in distribution centers to reduce the number of misplaced items, saving $22 million in fulfillment costs. The company was also able to better manage its inventory levels with new forecasting software, saving another $31 million. In addition, Amazon's arrangements with its Marketplace vendors and other retailers such as Toys "Я" Us produced gross margins that were much higher than the company's normal margins.

Keeping Its Partners and Investors in Suspense

Some of Amazon's retail business partners have grown impatient waiting for their online ventures to become profitable. Toys "Я" Us reported losses of $76 million, from its $277 million in online revenues in 2001, and began pressuring Amazon to renegotiate their original agreement. Two online travel companies, Expedia and Hotwire, soon followed suit. "The fact is the deal right now isn't a winner," commented Hotwire's chief marketing officer. "We're honestly surprised Amazon is not more aggressively promoting the lead e-commerce space, which is travel."

Amazon also faces scrutiny regarding its continual expansion into additional product categories in its quest for greater sales. "Look," commented one Internet analyst, "they've shown us that the book business can be a very nice, profitable business online. So far they have not shown that sales of other merchandise can grow rapidly and be profitable." Bezos continues to passionately defend his company's low-price strategy as well. He stated, "Lowering prices is working for us. Driving unit volume in our business really does reduce costs."

Despite all these concerns, no other e-tailer has been as adept or innovative at finding ways to personalize the very impersonal process of purchasing merchandise online. Amazon introduced the world of e-commerce to "collaborative filtering" technologies. In this high-tech form of upselling, a consumer's purchases are recorded and scrutinized to allow Amazon to make recommendations based on that person's unique tastes. Bezos likes to demonstrate this feature using his own customer account, but this proved to be awkward on one occasion. Amazon suggested he purchase the DVD *Slave Girls from Beyond Infinity*. Embarrassed, he explained to his audience of 500 people that he had recently bought *Barbarella* with Jane Fonda and so it was, in fact, a good recommendation.

The fact that Amazon is still in business when so many other dot–coms have failed is almost certainly a tribute to Bezos' persistence. His unflagging optimism and unique laugh (that was once likened to a "jackass gargling bumblebees") seem to calm the nerves of investors, ensure the cooperation of potential business partners, and reassure stockholders. He is considered an Internet pioneer and, as one analyst put it, "Amazon has proven that e-tailing can work."

Interestingly, Amazon's original products have been its most successful. In the first quarter of 2002, sales of books, music CDs, and videos amounted to $443 million, or more than half of Amazon's total revenue. In comparison, sales of electronics, tools, and kitchen equipment generated just $126 million.

Amazon never stops looking for ways to make e-tailing work better. The company continues to adapt its operations in order to reduce its costs, which once seemed to be spiraling out of control. This has given Amazon the ability to offer special promotions in order to increase sales volume. For instance, as it found more ways to make shipping less expensive, it began giving free delivery for certain purchases over $99. That threshold fell to $49, and then later to $25.

More fundamentally, some see a possible shift in strategy. Amazon has found some success in promoting the goods of brick-and-mortar retailers and providing some or all of their online order fulfillment needs. This approach takes advantage of the firm's strengths—many site visitors and customer service—without an investment in inventory. What remains to be seen is whether Amazon can deliver profits as well as happy online shoppers.

Questions

1. What type of product-market growth strategy is Amazon pursuing? Do you agree with this approach? Why or why not?

2. How does the fact that Amazon is an online operation affect the way the marketing effort is managed?

3. Jeff Bezos has maintained a strategy of offering a broad assortment of products and low prices for shoppers. What is necessary for this approach to produce profits for investors?

Sources

Case 1: McDonald's   *www.mcdonalds.com;* Daniel Eisenberg, "Can McDonald's Shape Up?" *Time,* Sept. 30, 2002, pp. 54–57; Julie Forster, "Thinking outside the Burger Box," *Business Week,* Sept. 16, 2002, pp. 66–67; Shirley Leung, "McHaute Cuisine," *The Wall Street Journal,* Aug. 30, 2002, p. A1+; Shelly Branch, "As Obesity Concerns Mount, Companies Fret Their Snacks, Drinks May Take the Blame," *The Wall Street Journal,* June 13, 2002, p. B1+; Shirley Leung, "Subway Goes Express, Passing McDonald's in the Number of U.S. Restaurant Outlets," *The Wall Street Journal,* Feb. 1, 2002, p. B2; "McSushi?" *Columbia Daily Tribune,* July 23, 2001, p. 1B; John Carreyrou and Geoff Winestock, "In France, McDonald's Takes Mad-Cow Fears by the Horns," *The Wall Street Journal,* Apr. 5, 2001, p. A17; Michael Arndt, "McLatte and Croissant," *Business Week,* Apr. 2, 2001, p. 14; Jennifer Ordonez, "McDonald's to Assess Full-Service Effect on Profit with Launch of Diner Concept," *The Wall Street Journal,* Mar. 16, 2001, p. B5; Andrew Edgecliffe-Johnson, "McDonald's Hit by Beef Safety Fears in Europe," *Financial Times,* Mar. 15, 2001, p. 17; Jennifer Ordonez, "Crunch Time," *The Wall Street Journal,* Jan. 16, 2001, p. A1; Geoff Winestock and Yaroslav Trofimov, "McDonald's Reassures Italians about Beef," *The Wall Street Journal,* Jan. 16, 2001, p. A3; Margaret Studer and Jennifer Ordonez, "The Golden Arches: Burgers, Fries and 4-Star Rooms," *The Wall Street Journal,* Nov. 17, 2000, p. B1; and Miriam Jordan, "McDonald's Heats Up Tempers with Growth in Brazil," *The Wall Street Journal,* Oct. 4, 2000, p. A23.

Case 2: Amazon.com

G. Bruce Knecht, "How Wall Street Whiz Found a Niche Selling Books on the Internet," *The Wall Street Journal,* May 16, 1996, pp. A1, A12; Joshua Cooper Ramo, "Jeffrey Preston Bezos: 1999 Person of the Year," *Time,* Dec. 27, 1999, pp. 56+; Nick Wingfield and Amy Merrick, "Amazon to Offer Retailers' Apparel to Online Buyers," *The Wall Street Journal,* Oct. 30, 2002, p. A3; Stacy Collett, "The Web's Best-Seller," *Computerworld,* Sept. 30, 2002, p. 40; Nick Wingfield, "The Other eBay: Amazon Is Winning over Small Vendors," *The Wall Street Journal,* July 22, 2002, p. B1; Pete Barlas, "Amazon Hopes Free Shipping Delivers," *Investor's Business Daily,* July 19, 2002, p. 4; David Shook, "Remapping Amazon's Course," *Business Week Online,* July 16, 2002; "Amazon Alliances Create Next-gen E-tail Model," *DSN Retailing Today,* May 20, 2002, p. 47; Leslie Kaufman, "Amazon II: Will This Smile Last?" *The New York Times,* May 19, 2002, p. 1; Saul Hansell, "The Markets: Market Place," *The New York Times,* April 24, 2002, p. C1; Nick Wingfield, "Amazon Finds Partners Toys 'R' Us, Expedia, Hotwire Are Growing Restless," *The Wall Street Journal,* March 15, 2002, p. B2; Robert Hof and Heather Green, "How Amazon Cleared That Hurdle," *Business Week,* Feb. 4, 2002, pp. 60–61; Melanie Warner, "Can Amazon Be Saved?" *Fortune,* Nov. 26, 2001, pp. 157–158; Robert Hof, "Amazon: 'We've Never Said We Had to Do It All,' " *Business Week,* Oct. 15, 2001, p. 53; Robert Hof, "Amazon's Go-Go Growth? Gone," *Business Week,* Feb. 12, 2001, p. 39; and Charles Fishman, "Jeff Bezos," *Fast Company,* February 2001, pp. 80–82.

Notes and References

Chapter 1

1. Amy Merrick, "Nordstrom Accelerates Plans to Straighten Out Business," *The Wall Street Journal*, Oct. 19, 2001, p. B4; Stanley Holmes, "Can the Nordstroms Find the Right Style?" *Business Week*, July 30, 2001, pp. 59–60.

2. Robert J. Keith, "The Marketing Revolution," *Journal of Marketing*, January 1960, p. 37.

3. Geraldine E. Williams, "High-Performance Marketing: An Interview with Nike's Phil Knight," *Harvard Business Review*, July–August 1992, pp. 91–101.

4. Tony Jackson, "Reflections of a Knowledge Worker," *Financial Times*, Apr. 27, 1999, p. 12.

5. "The Top 25 Managers," *Business Week*, Jan. 14, 2002, p. 56.

6. The following market-oriented definitions are extracted from the websites and publications of the respective companies. Kodak: We help people share moments and share lives; Amazon.com: We make buying the fastest, easiest, and most enjoyable shopping experience possible; Hewlett-Packard: We engineer and deliver technology solutions that drive business value, create social value, and improve the lives of our customers; Nordstrom's: We offer the customer the best possible selection, quality, and value; Caterpillar: We help our customers build the world's infrastructure and transport its resources.

7. Federal Express website: *www.fedex.com*, May 2002.

8. Barnes & Noble website: *www.barnesandnoble.com*, May 2002.

9. Sonia Reyes, "Pouring On the Sauce for the Home Team," *BrandWeek*, Feb. 4, 2002, p. 30.

10. Sonya S. Hamilton, "You Don't Say," *Sales & Marketing Management*, October, 1994, pp. 111–112.

11. Christopher W. Hart and Michael D. Johnson, "Growing the Trust Relationship," *Marketing Management*, Spring 1999, pp. 9–24; Eric Almquist, Carla Healon, and Nick Hall, "Making CRM Make Money," *Marketing Management*, May/June 2002, pp. 16–21.

12. Harley-Davidson website: *www.harleydavidson.com*, May 2002.

13. John Deere and Company website: *www.johndeere.com*, May 2002.

14. Frederick E. Webster, Jr., "Defining the New Marketing Concept," *Marketing Management 2*, no. 4 (1993), pp. 22–31.

15. Pai-Wing Tam, "Palm, Seeking Business Clients, Targets Corporate Executives," *The Wall Street Journal*, May 13, 2002, p. B6.

16. David A. Aaker, *Building Strong Brands*, The Free Press, New York 1996.

17. Robert C. Blattberg, Gary Getz, and Jacquelyn S. Thomas, *Customer Equity*, Harvard Business School Press, Cambridge, MA, 2001.

18. "Business Ethics' 100 Best Corporate Citizens," *Business Ethics*, March/April 2002, pp. 10–11.

19. Gina Imperator, "New Channels, Old Values," *Fast Company*, October 2000, pp. 364–368; Ron Lieber, "She Reads Customers' Minds," *Fast Company*, February 2001, pp. 54–56.

Chapter 2

1. Elizabeth Kaye McCall, "Radio Enters a New Orbit," *USA Weekend*, Jan. 17–19, 2003, p. 14; Earl Eldridge, "Satellite Radio Transmits Need for Funds," *USA Today*, Aug. 27, 2002, p. 6B; Mike Drummond, "Wall Street, We Have a Problem," *Business 2.0*, July 2002, p. 30; Denis Storey, "A Silver Lining," *Satellite Broadband*, January 2002, p. 44; Adam Rogers, "A Little Space Music," *Newsweek*, Nov. 12, 2001, pp. 67–68; Peter Lewis, "Satellite Radio," *Fortune*, Oct. 15, 2001, pp. 253+; Paige Albiniak, "XM's Downer Upper," *Broadcasting & Cable*, Oct. 2, 2001, p. 12; and Bethany McLean, "Satellite Killed the Radio Star," *Fortune*, Jan. 22, 2001, pp. 94–96+.

2. A set of "ten trend commandments" is contained in Laurie Freeman, "Marketers, Too, Can Keep Ahead of the Curve," *Marketing News*, June 21, 1999, p. 8. Six "waves of change" are discussed in Steven T. Goldberg, "Trend Spotting," *Kiplinger's Personal Finance*, February 2002, pp. 34–39.

3. Ram Subramanian, Nirmala Fernandes, and Earl Harper, "Environmental Scanning in U.S. Companies: Their Nature and Their Relationship to Performance," *Management International Review*, Vol. 33, No. 3 (1993), pp. 271–286.

4. Melanie Wells, "Iced Coffee Market May Get Steamy," *USA Today*, Apr. 24, 1996, p. 2B.

5. Bill Brubaker, "Pfizer Buys Rival Pharmacia for $60 Billion," *Washington Post*, July 16, 2002, p. E1; and Robert Steyer, "Monsanto Marks the Early Success of Celebrex," *St. Louis Post-Dispatch*, July 21, 1999, p. C1.

6. U.S. Census Bureau, *Statistical Abstract of the United States: 2000*, p. 8, at *www.census.gov/epcd/abstract/statistical/statistical-abstract-us.html*, accessed July 24, 2002; and Burney Simpson, "The Future Cardholder," *Credit Card Management*, March 2002, pp. 36–42.

7. Gary L. Berman, "The Hispanic Market: Getting Down to Cases," *Sales & Marketing Management*, October 1991, p. 66.

8. "Ever-Elusive Inflation," *The Economist*, June 19, 1999, p. 24.

9. Margaret Popper, "Inflation's Gone. That's a Good Thing, Right?" *Business Week*, Mar. 4, 2002, p. 60. For an essay that describes price deflation in retailing and recommends strategies for coping with deflation, see Walter K. Levy, "Beware, the Pricing Genie Is out of the Bottle," *Retailing Issues Letter*, November 1994, pp. 1–4.

10. Molly Prior, "TRU Conversions Almost Complete," *DSN Retailing Today*, June 24, 2002, pp. 3, 37; and Monica Roman, "No Fun and Games at Toys 'R' Us," *Business Week*, Feb. 11, 2002, p. 46.

11. James R. Hagerty, "Carpet Makers Confront Era That Extols Wood Floors," *The Wall Street Journal*, Mar. 31, 1998, p. B1.

12. Joseph B. White, "Honda Will Introduce Fuel-Cell Cars," *The Wall Street Journal*, July 25, 2002, p. D4; Jacquelyn Ottman, "Environmental Winners Show Sustainable Strategies," *Marketing News*, Apr. 27, 1998, p. 6; and *www.reclamere.com/our_services_recovery.htm*, accessed on July 16, 2002.

13. Geoffrey A. Fowler, " 'Green' Sales Pitch Isn't Moving Many Products,"

The Wall Street Journal, Mar. 6, 2002, pp. B1, B4; and "Laura Litvan, "Going 'Green' in the '90s," *Nation's Business,* February 1995, p. 31.

14. The contradiction between attitudes and buying behavior was reported in C. Mitchell Adrian and Michael D. Richard, "An Examination of Purchase Behavior versus Purchase Attitudes for Environmentally Friendly and Recycled Consumer Goods," *Southern Business Review,* Spring 1995, pp. 1–15. The plastic cup example was described in Stephen Budiansky, "Being Green Isn't Always What It Seems," *U.S. News & World Report,* Aug. 26, 1996, p. 42.

15. Peter Stisser, "A Deeper Shade of Green," *American Demographics,* March 1994, p. 28.

16. Joseph Pereira, "Women Jump ahead of Men in Purchases of Athletic Shoes," *The Wall Street Journal,* May 26, 1995, p. B1.

17. The statistic regarding working women comes from John Merli, "Working Women Use Radio Heavily," *Broadcasting & Cable,* Aug. 3, 1998, p. 34. The advertising agency study was reported in Stephanie Thompson, "Spin City: 18–49 Women," *Brandweek,* May 10, 1999, pp. S16–S18.

18. Thompson, loc. cit.; and Teri Agins, "Many Women Lose Interest in Clothes, to Retailers' Dismay," *The Wall Street Journal,* Feb. 28, 1995, p. A1.

19. Joan O'C. Hamilton, "A Shoe of One's Own," *Business Week,* May 24, 1999, pp. 62–64.

20. Maria Mallory, Dan McGraw, and Jill Jordan Sieder, "Women on a Fast Track," *U.S. News & World Report,* Nov. 6, 1995, pp. 60+; and Cyndee Miller, "Study Dispels '80s Stereotypes of Women," *Marketing News,* May 22, 1995, p. 3.

21. Diane Crispell, "The New World of Men," *American Demographics,* January 1992, pp. 38–43.

22. Greg Wiles, "Internet Sales Grabbing Bigger Piece of Pie," *National Post,* June 13, 2002, p. FP14; and Lorrie Grant, "Grocery Chore No More," *USA Today,* July 21, 1999, p. 1B.

23. Vanessa O'Connell, "Campbell Decides Its IQ Health Meals May Be Ahead of the Curve for Foods," *The Wall Street Journal,* Apr. 27, 1998, p. B2; and Nikhil Deogun, "Fat-Free Snacks Aren't Wowing Frito Customers," *The Wall Street Journal,* Sept. 12, 1998, pp. B1, B4.

24. Fred Faust, "Smaller Bookstores Challenge Two Chains," *St. Louis Post-Dispatch,* Mar. 19, 1998, p. B1; and Bryan Gruley, "Booksellers Sue Random House on Price Practices," *The Wall Street Journal,* Jan. 15, 1996, p. B10.

25. Melanie Warner, "Oracle and Siebel's Software Hardball," *Fortune,* Oct. 16, 2000, pp. 391+.

26. Eldridge, loc. cit.; Rogers, op. cit.; Lewis, op. cit.; McLean, op cit.; Hiawatha Bray, "Digital Pay Radio Seems Wave of the Future," *St. Louis Post-Dispatch,* Dec. 9, 2001, p. F2.

Chapter 3

1. Charles Fishman, "Why Can't Lego Click?" *Fast Company,* September 2001, pp. 144–157; "Lego's Leap into the Electronic Era," *Toronto Star,* Dec. 24, 2001, p. D03.

2. *International Trade Statistics 2001,* World Trade Organization, Lausanne, Switzerland, 2001.

3. *Statistical Abstract of the United States, 2001,* 121st ed., U.S. Bureau of the Census, Washington, DC, 2001, p. 799.

4. Douglas A. Blackmon and Diane Brady, "Just How Hard Should a U.S. Company Woo a Big Foreign Market?" *The Wall Street Journal,* Apr. 6, 1998, pp. A1+.

5. Miriam Jordan. "Pillsbury Presses Flour Power in India," *The Wall Street Journal,* May 5, 1999, pp. B1+.

6. Mariko Sanchanta, "Wal-Mart Develops a Taste for Japan," *Financial Times,* May 3, 2002, p. 8.

7. Warren J. Keegan, *Global Marketing Management,* 7th ed., Prentice Hall, Upper Saddle River, NJ, 2002.

8. Vanessa Fuhrmans and Gautam Naik, "In Europe, Prescription-Drug Ads Are Banned—and Health Costs Lower," *The Wall Street Journal,* Mar. 15, 2002, p. B1+.

9. Robert Guy Matthews, "Tariffs Impede Trade via Web on Global Scale," *The Wall Street Journal,* Apr. 17, 2000, p. B1.

10. *International Trade Statistics, 2001,* World Trade Organization, Lausanne, Switzerland, 2001, p. 25.

11. Brandon Mitchener, "Increasingly, Rules of Global Economy Are Set in Brussels," *The Wall Street Journal,* Apr. 23, 2002, p. A1+.

12. Charles J. Whalen, Paul Magnusson, and Geri Smith, "NAFTA's Scorecard: So Far, So Good," *Business Week,* July 9, 2001, pp. 54–56.

13. "Amazon Books First-Ever Profits," Deutsche Presse-Agentur, Jan. 22, 2002.

14. *Statistical Abstract of the United States, 2001,* 121st ed., U.S. Bureau of the Census, Washington, DC, pp. 790–791.

15. Hae Won Choi and Gregory L. White, "GM Is Near Deal to Acquire Parts of Daewoo Motor," *The Wall Street Journal,* Apr. 11, 2002, p. D3.

16. Jeffery Ball, Todd Zaun, and Norihiko Shirouzu, "DaimlerChrysler Ponders 'World Engine' in Bid to Transform Scope into Savings," *The Wall Street Journal,* Jan. 8, 2002, pp. A3+.

17. Leigh Gallagher and Melanie Wells, "Bad Fit," *Forbes,* Jan. 8, 2001, p. 210.

18. Richard Johnson, "Crossovers Could Be World Cars, Says Ford Product Boss," *Automotive News Europe,* Jan. 28, 2002, p. 10.

19. Keith Naughton, "Ford's Global Gladiator," *Business Week,* Dec. 11, 1995, pp. 116–117.

20. Leslie Chang, "From KFC to Beauty Spas, Chinese Are Embracing Franchises," *The Wall Street Journal,* Apr. 18, 2002, p. A9.

21. Paulo Prada, "Ja, Ja, Americana's Fabulosa," *The Wall Street Journal,* June 21, 2001, p. B1+.

22. Michael Mann and Edward Alden, "Europe Plans Sanctions on U.S.," *Financial Times,* Apr. 20 & 21, 2002, p. 1.

23. David McHugh, "Euro May Aid Consumers," *South Bend Tribune,* Jan. 27, 2002, p. e3.

24. Sak Onkvisit, "Standardized International Advertising: Some Research Issues and Implications," *Journal of Advertising Research,* November/December 1999, pp. 19–25.

25. Elizabeth Wasserman, "Why Industry Giants Are Playing with Legos," *Fortune/CNET Tech Review,* Winter 2002, pp. 101–106; "Lego Agrees New Games Console Deal with Electronic Arts," *Marketing Week,* Dec. 13, 2001, p. 8; "Lego's Leap into the Electronic Era," loc. cit.

Chapter 4

1. Pat Kiernan and Ali Velshi, "The Money Gang," Cable News Network Inc., Dec. 21, 2001; Fara Warner, "Curb Your Enthusiasm," *Fast Company,* January 2002, pp. 32–36; James P. Miller, "Potent Image Keeps Harley in Hog Heaven," *Chicago Tribune,* Jan. 14,

2001, Sec. 5, pp. 1–2; Leslie Gornstein, "Harley Reaches Crossroads on a Completely New Ride," *St. Louis Post-Dispatch*, July 14, 2001, p. Biz9; Jonathan Fahey, "Love into Money," *Forbes*, January 7, 2001, p. 60+.

2. Unless otherwise noted, the demographic statistics in this chapter come from *Statistical Abstract of the United Sates: 2001*, 121st edition, Bureau of the Census, Washington, DC, 2001.

3. Michael Porter and Anne Habiby, "A Window on the New Economy," *Inc.*, May 1999, pp. 48–49.

4. Several family life-cycle models with marketing implications are compared in Charles M. Schaninger and William D. Danko, "A Conceptual and Empirical Comparison of Alternative Household Life Cycle Models," *Journal of Consumer Research*, March 1993, pp. 580–594.

5. Jacob M. Schlesinger, "Working Full Time Is No Longer Enough," *The Wall Street Journal*, June 29, 2001, pp. A2+.

6. Michael J. Weiss, "Inconspicuous Consumption," *American Demographics*, April 2002, pp. 30–39.

7. Alison Stein Wellner, "The Census Report," *American Demographics*, January 2002, pp. S3–S6.

8. Ibid., p. S5.

9. Gerry Khermouch and Jeff Green, "Buzzzz Marketing," *Business Week*, July 30, 2001, pp. 50–56.

10. Richard P. Coleman, "Continuing Significance of Social Class to Marketing," *Journal of Consumer Research*, December 1983, pp. 265–280.

11. Rebecca Gardyn, "I'll Have What He's Having," *American Demographics*, July 2000, p. 22.

12. James U. McNeal, "Tapping the Three Kids' Markets," *American Demographics*, April 1998, pp. 37–41.

13. A. H. Maslow, *Motivation and Personality*, Harper and Row, New York, 1954, pp. 80–106. Other motivation schemes are presented in most basic psychology texts.

14. Steven Reiss and Susan M. Havercamp, "Toward a Comprehensive Assessment of Fundamental Motivation: Factor Structure of the Reiss Profile," *Psychological Assessment*, June 1998, pp. 97–106.

15. For more details on sensory perception see Eric Arnould, Linda Price, and George Zinkhan, *Consumers*, McGraw-Hill/Irwin, Burr Ridge, IL, 2002.

16. Yumiko Ono, "Marketers Seek the 'Naked' Truth in Consumers' Psyches," *The Wall Street Journal*, June 30, 1997, pp. B1+.

17. Glenn Ruffenach, "Fewer Americans Save for Their Retirement," *The Wall Street Journal*, May 10, 2001, p. A2.

18. Gregory L. White, "Battling the Inferior–Interior Complex." *The Wall Street Journal*, Dec. 3, 2001, p. B1+.

19. This is the classic definition from Gordon W. Allport, "Attitudes," in C. A. Murchinson, ed., *Handbook of Social Psychology*, Clark University Press, Worcester, MA, 1935, pp. 798–844.

20. Jill Carroll and Shirley Leung, "Fries with that Burger? Fewer Consumers Say 'Yes'," *The Wall Street Journal*, Feb. 20, 2002, pp. B1+.

21. Colleen Bazdarich, "In a Buying Mood? Maybe It's the Muzak," *Business 2.0*, March 2002, p. 100.

22. Teresa Dixon Murray, "Slowly Digging Out," *The Plain Dealer*, May 12, 2002, p. G1. Calmetta Coleman, "Debit Cards Look to Give Credit Cards a Run for Consumers' Money," *The Wall Street Journal*, Dec. 3, 2001, p. B1.

23. "Americans' Outlook for the Economy: Neither Best Nor Worst of Times, New Roper ASW Poll Shows," Nov. 29, 2001, at *www.roper.com*.

24. Warner, op. cit.; Gornstein, op. cit.; Fahey, op. cit.

Chapter 5

1. *www.freemarkets.com*, accessed Jan. 8, 2002; Stephanie Franken, "Slump Puts Life into Perspective for Pittsburgh-Based Online Auction Firm," *Pittsburgh Post-Gazette*, Dec. 13, 2001.

2. The statistics on the business market cited in this chapter come from U.S. Census Bureau publications. A particularly useful source is the *Statistical Abstract of the United States*, an annual publication.

3. Wayne Wenzel, "Precision Vision," *Farm Industry News*, July/August 2001, p. 4+.

4. Several interesting case histories of Internet B-2-B buyng and selling can be found on the PurchasePro site, *www.purchasepro.com*.

5. George Anders, "Buying Frenzy," *The Wall Street Journal*, July 12, 1999, pp. R6+.

6. "Diesel Sales Picking Up in American Light Truck Market," Navistar news release dated June 21, 2001, *www.navistar.com*.

7. More information on NAICS (pronounced "Nakes") is available in *North American Industry Classification System—United States, 1997*, U.S. Government Printing Office, Washington, DC, 1997.

8. Al Wrigley, "Maytag Slashing Its Supplier Base 73%," *American Metal Market*, Sept. 8, 1999, p. 1+.

9. Richard G. Jennings and Richard E. Plank, "When the Purchasing Agent Is a Committee: Implications for Industrial Marketing," *Industrial Marketing Management*, November 1995, pp. 411–419.

10. This section is based on Lawrence A. Crosby and Sheree L. Johnson, "Technology: Friend or Foe to Customer Relationships?" *Marketing Management*, November/December 2001, pp. 10–11.

11. Jason Dean and Zach Coleman, "China Airlines to Move Forward with Jet Order," *The Wall Street Journal*, June 5, 2002, p. D3.

12. Jeff Bennett, "Measure of the Auto Industry: Covisint Refines Online Ways to Connect Buyers and Sellers," Feb. 19, 2002, from *www.auto.com* retrieved from the archives of the Detroit Free Press (*www.detroitfree press.com*).

13. *www.freemarkets.com*, accessed Jan. 8, 2002; Stephanie Franken, op.cit.

Chapter 6

1. *www.smart.com* website, press release dated Dec. 10, 2001, entitled "Record Sales and Revenues for 2001"; Scott Miller, "Daimler May Roll Out Its Tiny Car Here," *The Wall Street Journal*, May 9, 2001, p. A21; Jeffrey Ball, "How Can Detroit Top the SUV? Think Golf Carts," *The Wall Street Journal*, July 20, 2001, p. B1, B3; Keith Naughton, "Daimler Thinks Small," *Newsweek*, May 21, 2001, p. 48; Micheline Maynard, "Get Smart," *Fortune*, Mar. 30, 2001, pp. 48–52; Rhoda Miel, "Smart Car's Popularity Gain in Europe Prompts U.S. Study," *Plastics News*, May 14, 2001, p. 19; Michael Harvey, "Ultimate City Slicker," *Financial Times*, Nov. 10, 2001; Judy Feldman et al., "Great Wheels for Every Drive," *Money*, October 2001, p. 146; Will Pinkston and Scott Miller, "DaimlerChrysler Nears Way for U.S. Debut of 'Smart'," *The Wall Street Journal*, Aug. 20, 2001, p. B1.

2. The Hain Food Group 2000 Annual report, *www.thehainfoodgroup.com*.

3. Emily Nelson, "Too many Choices," *The Wall Street Journal*, Apr. 20, 2001, p. B1.

4. Norihiko Shirouzu, "This Is Not Your Father's Toyota," *The Wall Street Journal,* Mar. 26, 2002, p. B1.

5. A good description of social class in marketing can be found in Richard P. Coleman, "The Continuing Significance of Social Class in Marketing," *Journal of Consumer Research,* December 1983, pp. 267–280.

6. From the *www.polo.com* website, June 25, 2002.

7. Paul C. Judge, "Are Tech Buyers Different?" *Business Week,* January 26, 1998, pp. 64–68.

8. Rick Brooks, "Alienating Customers Isn't Always a Bad Idea, Many Firms Discover," *The Wall Street Journal,* Jan. 7, 1999, p. A1.

9. Leslie Gornstein, "Harley Reaches Crossroads on a Completely New Ride," *St. Louis Post-Dispatch,* July 14, 2001, p. BI29.

10. Devon Spurgeon, "Traditional Grocers Feel Vindicated by Webvan's Failure," *The Wall Street Journal,* July 11, 2001, p. B4.

11. Motoko Rich, "Arnold Helps Choice Hotels Woo Travelers," *The Wall Street Journal,* May 2, 2001, p. B6.

12. Emily Nelson, "P&G Tries to Hide Wrinkles in Aging Beauty Fluid," *The Wall Street Journal,* May 16, 2000, p. B1.

13. Andrew E. Serwer, "McDonald's Conquers the World," *Fortune,* Oct. 17, 1994, pp. 103–116.

14. Scott Miller, op cit.; Jeffrey Ball, op cit.; Keith Naughton, op cit.; Micheline Maynard, op cit.; Rhoda Miel, op cit.; Michael Harvey, op cit.; Judy Feldman et al., op cit.; Will Pinkston and Scott Miller, op cit.

Chapter 7

1. "Factfinder for the Nation," U.S. Census Bureau, U.S. Department of Commerce, Washington, DC, May, 2000, accessed at www.census.gov/prod/2000 pubs; "Census 2000 in a Flash," U.S. Census Bureau, U.S. Department of Commerce, Washington, DC, undated, accessed at *www.census.gov/dmd/www/ factsheet.html;* Alison Stein Wellner, "The Census Report," *American Demographics,* January 2002, pp. S1–6; *www.census.gov.*

2. Jack Honomichl, "The Honomichl 50," *Marketing News,* June 10, 2002, pp. H1+.

3. Jack Honomichl, "A Tough Year," *Marketing News,* June 10, 2002, pp. H3+.

4. Joe Ashbrook Nickell. "Big Data's Big Business," *Business 2.Com,* Feb. 20, 2001, pp. 62–63.

5. Joe Ashbrook Nickell, "Welcome to Harrah's," *Business 2.0,* April 2002, pp. 48–54.

6. In fact, a study of Internet users in the U.S. found that as of early 2000 the number of women users exceeded men, but men still log more hours on-line. Brad Reagan, "The Great Divide," *The Wall Street Journal,* Apr. 15, 2002, p. R4.

7. For a dissenting view on the use of mystery shoppers as a research method, see Scott Ahlstrand, "Why Spy?" *Gallup Management Journal,* Winter 2001, pp. 4–6. Other interesting research articles can be found at *www. gallupjournal.com.*

8. Researchers are constantly looking for more effective methods for understanding behavior. For some examples of approaches being used see Melanie Wells, "New Ways to Get into Our Heads," *USA Today,* Mar. 2, 1999, pp. 1B+; Emily Nelson, "Focus Groups: P&G Keeps Cincinnati Busy with All Its Studies," *The Wall Street Journal,* Jan. 24, 2002, pp. A1+; Suzanne Vranica, "Some Focus Groups Use Mensa Members," *The Wall Street Journal,* Feb. 21, 2002, p. B6.

9. Johanna Bennett, "It's My Life," *The Wall Street Journal,* Oct. 29, 2001, p. R9.

10. An experiment comparing the relative effectiveness of mail, fax, e-mail, and the Web for collecting survey data is reported in Rick Weible and John Wallace, "Cyber Research," *Marketing Research,* Fall 1998, pp. 19–24.

11. Adam L. Penenberg, "Is There Snooping on Your Sites?" *Forbes,* May 17, 1999, pp. 322–325.

12. *www.claritas.com,* accessed on Feb. 6, 2002; Deborah D. McManus, "Micro-Marketing," *Broadcasting & Cable,* July 17, 2000, p. 50.

Chapter 8

1. Paul Saffo, "Ginger's Next Trick," *Business 2.0,* February 2002, p. 24; Paul Somerson, "It's Alive! It's Not a Personal Hovercraft Or a Hydrogen-Powered Teleporter. But You'll Want One," *Smart Business for the New Economy,* Jan. 1, 2002, p. 21; Dan Gillmore, "Segway Transporter May Scoot Us into a Brave New World," *St. Louis Post-Dispatch,* Dec. 24, 2001, p. BP 11; John Heilemann, "Reinvent-

ing the Wheel," *Time,* Dec. 10, 2001, pp. 76+.; Jim Krane, "IT's Hip, IT's Hot, IT's New—What Is IT?" *St. Louis Post-Dispatch,* Dec. 4, 2001, p. A1; and Karl Greenberg, "The 'IT' Girl," *Brandweek,* Nov. 12, 2001 p. 37.

2. Bruce Horovitz, "Fast-Food Giants Hunt for New Products to Tempt Consumers," *USA Today,* July 3–4, 2002, pp. 1A, 2A.

3. For a different classification scheme that provides strategic guidelines for management by relating products and prices, see Patrick E. Murphy and Ben M. Enis, "Classifying Products Strategically," *Journal of Marketing,* July 1986, pp. 24–42. Also see Ernest F. Cooke, "The Relationship between a Product Classification System and Marketing Strategy," *Journal of Midwest Marketing,* Spring 1987, pp. 230–240.

4. Christine Bittar, "Kimberly-Clark Adds Cheeky Exposure to Ms. Cottonelle Toilet Paper Rollout," *Brandweek,* May 7, 2001, p. 8.

5. Kathleen Deveny, "Failure of Its Oven Lovin' Cookie Dough Shows Pillsbury Pitfall of New Products," *The Wall Street Journal,* June 17, 1993, p. B1.

6. Vanessa O'Connell and Joe White, "After Decades of Brand Bodywork, GM Parks Oldsmobile—for Good," *The Wall Street Journal,* Dec. 13, 2000, pp. B1, B4; and Stuart Elliott, "The Famous Brands on Death Row," *The New York Times,* Nov. 7, 1993, p. 1F.

7. Barton G. Tretheway, "Everything New Is Old Again," *Marketing Management,* Spring 1998, p. 7.

8. Durk Jager, as quoted in Katrina Brooker, "Can Procter & Gamble Change Its Culture, Protect Its Market Share, and Find the Next Tide?" *Fortune,* Apr. 26, 1999, p. 149. Also see Amy Merrick, "Too Much of a Good Thing?" *The Wall Street Journal,* July 24, 2002, pp. B1, B3; Nanette Byrnes, "Brands in a Bind," *Business Week,* Aug. 28, 2000, pp. 234–236+; and Geoffrey Colvin, "How Rubbermaid Managed to Fail," *Fortune,* Nov. 23, 1998, pp. 32–33.

9. Respectively, Cliff Edwards, "Where Have All the Edsels Gone?" *Pittsburgh Post-Gazette,* May 25, 1999, p. F-7; Tretheway, loc. cit.; and Kuczmarski & Associates, as described in Christopher Power, "Flops," *Business Week,* Aug. 16, 1993, pp. 76–77.

10. The reasons for failure are drawn from the "1995 Innovation Survey," conducted by Group EFO Limited of

Weston, CT. The examples are drawn from Heather Pauly, "Flipping over Flops," *Chicago Sun-Times*, June 29, 1998, p. 43; and Alan Farnham, "It's a Bird! It's a Plane! It's a Flop!" *Fortune*, May 2, 1994, pp. 108–110.

11. Paul Lukas, "The Ghastliest Product Launches," *Fortune*, Mar. 16, 1998, p. 44.

12. Jerry Useem, "*Sold*! Elvis Impersonator for $61.23 an Hour," *Fortune*, Aug. 16, 1999, p. 36.

13. John Simons, "Greed Meets Terror," *Fortune*, Oct. 29, 2001, pp. 145–146.

14. Evan Ramstad, "Products Go Digital . . .Whether They Are or Not," *The Wall Street Journal*, Sept. 7, 1999, p. A11A.

15. Kenneth Cole, "Electric Cars Unlikely to Take Center Stage," *The Detroit News*, Dec. 21, 1998, p. F15.

16. As stressed by a consultant, Philip Himmelfarb, in Roberta Maynard, "The Heat Is On," *Nation's Business*, October 1997, pp. 16, 18.

17. These benefits and a "stage gate system" for new-product development are described in Robert G. Cooper and Elko J. Kleinschmidt, "Stage Gate Systems for New Product Success," *Marketing Management*, Vol. 1, No. 4, 1993, pp. 20–29. For an approach for managing multiple new-product development projects, see Steven C. Wheelwright and Kim B. Clark, "Creating Project Plans to Focus Product Development," *Harvard Business Review*, March–April 1992, pp. 70–82.

18. For a report on the criteria used in making "go–no go" decisions in the product-development process, see Ilkka A. Ronkainen, "Criteria Changes across Product Development Stages," *Industrial Marketing Management*, August 1985, pp. 171–178.

19. The information about customers, suppliers, and franchisees comes, respectively, from "Study: Launching New Products Is Worth the Risk," *Marketing News*, Jan. 20, 1992, p. 2; Neal Templin and Jeff Cole, "Manufacturers Use Suppliers to Help Them Develop New Products," *The Wall Street Journal*, Dec. 19, 1994, pp. A1, A6; and Jeffrey A. Tannenbaum, "Role Model," *The Wall Street Journal*, May 23, 1996, p. R22.

20. For more on the first two stages, termed *opportunity identification*, see Linda Rochford, "Generating and Screening New Product Ideas," *Industrial Marketing Management*, November 1991, pp. 287–296.

21. Faye Rice, "Secrets of Product Testing," *Fortune*, Nov. 29, 1994, pp. 166–171.

22. Jennifer Lach, "Meet You in Aisle Three," *American Demographics*, April 1999, pp. 41–42.

23. Cooper and Kleinschmidt, op. cit., pp. 22–23.

24. Development times are discussed in Pamela Buxton, "Time to Market Is NPD's Top Priority," *Marketing*, Mar. 30, 2000, p. 35. For an in-depth look at the development of the Frito Pie, see Emily Nelson, "Product Development Is Always Difficult; Consider the Frito Pie," *The Wall Street Journal*, Oct. 25, 1999, pp. A1, A22. For insight into one automaker's efforts to develop and bring new models to market more quickly, see David Welch, "Look Who's Finally Stopping Traffic," *Business Week*, Feb. 28, 2000, p. 38. The omission of market tests was described in "Study: Launching New Products Is Worth the Risk," loc. cit.

25. Robert G. Cooper and Scott J. Edgett, "Critical Success Factors for New Financial Services," *Marketing Management*, Fall 1996, pp. 26–37; and Howard Schlossberg, "Services Development Lags Behind New Products," *Marketing News*, Nov. 6, 1989, p. 2.

26. For foundations of diffusion theory and a review of landmark studies on diffusion of innovation, see Everett M. Rogers, *Diffusion of Innovations*, 3d ed., Free Press, New York, 1983.

27. Robert A. Guth and Khanh T. L. Tran, "The Geeks' Secret: Buying Gadgets Direct from Japan," *The Wall Street Journal*, Sept. 4, 2002, pp. D1, D4.

28. "GPS Offers Security," *Columbia Daily Tribune*, Aug. 25, 2002, p. 13A.

29. Denise Smith Amos, "Are You an 'Influential'? Advertisers Want You," *St. Louis Post-Dispatch*, Aug. 6, 1995, pp. E1, E9.

30. Rogers, loc. cit.

31. Tara Parker-Pope, "P&G Puts Two Cleaning Products on Its New Marketing Fast Track," *The Wall Street Journal*, May 18, 1999, p. B6; and Yumiko Ono, "Novel P&G Product Brings Dry Cleaning Home," *The Wall Street Journal*, Nov. 19, 1997, p. B1.

32. The quote about brand managers being an "endangered species" is drawn from Rance Crain, "Brand Management's Decline May Haunt GM," *Advertising Age*, Nov. 6, 1995, p. 16. The shifting arrangements are reported in David Welch, "GM Brand Managers Get the

Boot," *Business Week*, Apr. 22, 2002, p. 14; Jolie Solomon and Carol Hymowitz, "P&G Makes Changes in the Way It Develops and Sells Its Products," *The Wall Street Journal*, Aug. 11, 1987, pp. 1, 12; and Raymond Serafin, "Ford Taps Insiders as Brand Managers," *Advertising Age*, Jan. 1, 1996, p. 3.

33. Various arrangements are discussed in Eric M. Olson, Orville C. Walker, Jr., and Robert W. Ruekert, "Organizing for Effective New Product Development: The Moderating Role of Product Innovativeness," *Journal of Marketing*, January 1995, pp. 48–62. The favorable comment comes from Steve McDougal and Jeff Smith, "Wake Up Your Product Development," *Marketing Management*, Summer 1999, pp. 24–30.

34. Robert M. Metcalfe, "From the Ether," *InfoWorld*, Nov. 22, 1999, p. 90; "Johnson & Johnson Develops Wheelchair That Can Climb Stairs," *St. Louis Post-Dispatch*, July 3, 1999, p. 26OT; Heilemann, loc. cit.; and *www.indetech.com/ibot/index.html*, accessed on Feb. 16, 2002.

Chapter 9

1. "Palm, in Shift, Offers Refund on Flawed Device," *The Wall Street Journal*, Sept. 5, 2002, p. D5; Pui-Wing Tam, "Hand-Held Device Sales Rise 25%, but Growth Rate Trails Past Years," *The Wall Street Journal*, Jan. 31, 2002, p. B9; Erik Sherman, "The 2nd Time Around," *Newsweek*, Nov. 5, 2001, p. 40L; Pui-Wing Tam, "How Palm Tumbled from Star of Tech to Target of Microsoft," *The Wall Street Journal*, Sept. 7, 2001, pp. A1–A4; Tobi Elkin, "Palm Gets Slapped," *Advertising Age*, Sept. 3, 2001, p. 6; Janet Rae-Dupree, "Hand-Held Computers Get Second Life with New Features," *U.S. News & World Report*, June 18, 2001, p. 48; John Simons, "Has Palm Lost Its Grip?" *Fortune*, May 28, 2001, pp. 104–108; and Cliff Edwards, "No Cartwheels for Handspring," *Business Week*, Apr. 2, 2001, pp. 56–58.

2. Christopher Lawton, "Anheuser Tries Low-Carb Beer to Tap Diet Buzz," *The Wall Street Journal*, Sept. 13, 2002, pp. B1, B2.

3. Kathleen Kerwin and Keith Naughton, "A Different Kind of Saturn," *Business Week*, July 5, 1999, pp. 28–29, and Russell Mitchell, "Intel Isn't Taking This Lying Down," *Business Week*, Sept. 30, 1991, pp. 32–33.

4. Michael Goldstein, "Few Leagues of Their Own," *Business Week*, Jan. 18, 1999, pp. 74–76.

5. Cynthia Wilson, "Discount Airlines Fly High," *St. Louis Post-Dispatch*, Sept. 8, 2002, pp. F1, F10. For more on positioning in relation to a competitor, see Jack Trout and Al Ries, "*Don't* Follow the Leader," *Sales & Marketing Management*, February 1994, pp. 25–26.

6. Laura Bird, "Romancing the Package," *Adweek's Marketing Week*, Jan. 21, 1991, pp. 10–11, 14.

7. "J. M. Smucker Acquires Jif, Crisco Brands from P&G," *Nation's Restaurant News*, Oct. 29, 2001, p. 100.

8. James R. Hagerty, "Gilding the Drill Bit? Hardware Giants Go High-End," *The Wall Street Journal*, July 28, 1998, pp. B1, B7.

9. Bianca Riemer and Laura Zinn, "Haute Couture That's Not So Haute," *Business Week*, Apr. 22, 1991, p. 108.

10. Louise Lee, "Williams-Sonoma Tries a New Recipe," *Business Week*, May 6, 2002, p. 36; and Lee Gomes, "H-P to Create a New Subsidiary to Sell Cheap 'Apollo' Brand of Ink-Jet Printers," Jan. 6, 1999, p. B4.

11. Hagerty, loc. cit.

12. William C. Symonds, "Would You Spend $1.50 for a Razor Blade?" *Business Week*, Apr. 27, 1998, p. 46; and Mark Maremont, "Gillette Finally Reveals Its Vision of the Future, and It Has 3 Blades," *The Wall Street Journal*, Apr. 14, 1998, p. A1, A10.

13. Dean Takahashi, "Intel to Unveil Speedier Chips on Monday," *The Wall Street Journal*, Oct. 22, 1999, p. B6; and Andy Reinhardt, "Intel Is Taking No Prisoners," *Business Week*, July 12, 1999, p. 38.

14. The criticisms are summarized in Geoffrey L. Gordon, Roger J. Calantone, and C. Anthony diBenedetto, "Mature Markets and Revitalization Strategies: An American Fable," *Business Horizons*, May–June 1991, pp. 39–50. Alternative life cycles are proposed in Edward D. Popper and Bruce D. Buskirk, "Technology Life Cycles in Industrial Markets," *Industrial Marketing Management*, February 1992, pp. 23–31; and C. Merle Crawford, "Business Took the Wrong Life Cycle from Biology," *The Journal of Product & Brand Management*, Winter 1992, pp. 51–57.

15. Elliot Spagat, "Hit Show of the Season: The Revival of Digital TV," *The Wall Street Journal*, Aug. 1, 2002, pp. D1, D3.

16. Neil Gross and Peter Coy, "The Technology Paradox," *Business Week*, Mar. 6, 1995, p. 77.

17. Michael Booth, "Olestra, Where Art Thou?" *Denver Post*, Mar. 19, 2002, p. F-1.

18. Emily Nelson, "In a Rainbow of Hues, Bracelets Bring a Pot of Gold," *The Wall Street Journal*, Dec. 6, 1999, pp. B1, B4.

19. Eric Adler, "The Walkman at 20: Portable Stereo Has Changed the World," *St. Louis Post-Dispatch*, Sept. 2, 1999, p. G1.

20. The examples in this paragraph and the following one are drawn from "After the Compact Disc," *FT.com*, May 8, 2002; and Sarah Bryan Miller, "In Home Tech, 'Permanent Investments' Have a Short Life Span," *St. Louis Post-Dispatch*, July 7, 2002, pp. F1, F13.

21. Brian Steinberg, "Starbucks, Pepsi Hope Ad Blitz Will Rouse Bottled-Coffee Market," *The Wall Street Journal*, June 19, 2002, p. B6D.

22. Kevin Maney, "Impregnable 'First Mover Advantage' Philosophy Suddenly Isn't," *USA Today*, July 18, 2001, p. 3B. For a discussion of three ways in which pioneers can be "dumb movers," see Gary Hamel, "Smart Mover, Dumb Mover," *Fortune*, Sept. 3, 2001, pp. 191–192+.

23. The concept of "pioneer advantage" and the historical study of the 50 product categories are described in Gerard J. Tellis and Peter N. Golder, "Pioneer Advantage: Marketing Logic or Marketing Legend," *USC Business*, Fall/Winter 1995, pp. 49–53.

24. Reiji Yoshida, "Sega Plays Survival Game with Dreamcast," *Japan Times Weekly International Edition*, Dec. 14–20, 1998, p. 13.

25. Ten distinct strategies are described in Joel R. Evans and Gregg Lombardo, "Marketing Strategies for Mature Brands," *Journal of Product & Brand Management*, vol. 2, no. 1, 1993, pp. 5–19. For a discussion of four strategies—recapture, redesign, refocus, and recast—that are particularly applicable to *business* products, see Paul C. N. Michell, Peter Quinn, and Edward Percival, "Marketing Strategies for Mature Industrial Products," *Industrial Marketing Management*, August 1991, pp. 201–206.

26. Jeannine Aversa, "U.S. Mint Is Looking for a Little Change," *St. Louis Post-Dispatch*, Sept. 10, 2002, p. C1; and Martha Brannigan, "Cruise Lines Look to the Land to Get Boomers on Board," *The Wall Street Journal*, Dec. 6, 1999, p. B4.

27. Sandra Dolbow, "Meet Lycra's New Face," *Brandweek*, Apr. 24, 2000, pp. 1, 89; Becky Ebenkamp, "Lycra Streeetches," *Brandweek*, July 5, 1999, p. 3; and Monica Roman, "How Du Pont Keeps 'Em Coming Back for More," *Business Week*, Aug. 20, 1990, p. 68.

28. Dana James, "Rejuvenating Mature Brands Can Be Stimulating Exercise," *Marketing News*, Aug. 16, 1999, p. 16.

29. Hardy Green, "The Last Word in New Words," *Business Week*, Aug. 30, 1999, p. 6.

30. Bill Saporito, "How to Revive a Fading Firm," *Fortune*, Mar. 22, 1993, p. 80.

31. Joel Dreyfuss, "Planned Obsolescence Is Alive and Well," *Fortune*, Feb. 15, 1999, p. 192[P].

32. Lauren Goldstein, "Urban Wear Goes Suburban," *Fortune*, Dec. 21, 1998, pp. 169–170+.

33. For an example of producing multiple variations of a style, see Riemer and Zinn, loc. cit.

34. Suzanne Smalley, "An Aggressive New Cut," *Newsweek*, June 10, 2002, p. 37; Wendy Bounds, Rebecca Quick, and Emily Nelson, "In the Office, It's Anything Goes," *The Wall Street Journal*, Aug. 26, 1999, pp. B1, B4; Teri Agins, "The Fall of the Jacket Leaves Retailers Torn over Fashion's Future," *The Wall Street Journal*, Aug. 26, 1999, pp. A1, A6; and Teri Agins, "Many Women Lose Interest in Clothes, to Retailers' Dismay," *The Wall Street Journal*, Feb. 28, 1995, pp. A1, A8.

35. Veronica Chambers and Alisha Davis, "Direct from Paris . . . to the Mall," *Newsweek*, Apr. 13, 1998, pp. 64–65.

36. Mark Boslet, "Palm, Faltering, Hopes for Boost from New Gadgets," *The Wall Street Journal*, July 24, 2002, p. D5; Pui-Wing Tam, "For Palm, Splitting in Two Isn't Seamless," *The Wall Street Journal*, June 27, 2002, p. B4; Pui-Wing Tam, "Palm to Speed Launch of System Upgrade," *The Wall Street Journal*, Feb. 5, 2002, p. B6; Walter S. Mossberg, "Palm's New Hand-Held Goes Mano a Mano with a BlackBerry," *The Wall Street Journal*, Jan. 31, 2002, p. B1; and Pui-Wing Tam, "Handspring Plans Line of Hybrid Devices," *The Wall Street Journal*, Oct. 15, 2001, p. B7.

Chapter 10

1. Jonathan Reynolds, "Licensed to Grill," *The New York Times*, Aug. 18, 2002,

pp. 90+; *www.saltoninc.com*, accessed on Mar. 6, 2002; Salton, Inc., 2002 annual report; Shirley Leung, "Grill Sales Slow but Big Payouts Flow to Foreman," *The Wall Street Journal*, Feb. 2, 2001, pp. B1, B4; Thyra Porter, "Salton Supports Growth," *HFN*, Jan. 17, 2000, p. 64; Roy S. Johnson, "Why Retired Sports Pros Make the Best Hucksters," *Fortune*, Feb. 21, 2000, pp. 60–62; and "A Brand New Pitch," *Industry Week*, Mar. 6, 2000, pp. 41–44.

2. Adapted from Peter D. Bennett, ed., *Dictionary of Marketing Terms*, American Marketing Association, Chicago, 1988, p. 18. The incorrect usage is pointed out in John F. Gaski, "Some Troublesome Definitions of Elementary Marketing Concepts—Have You Ever Looked at It This Way?" in D. W. Stewart and N. J. Vilcassim, eds., *1995 AMA Winter Educators' Conference: Marketing Theory and Applications,* American Marketing Association, Chicago, 1995, pp. 425–429.

3. The European procedure is described in Maxine Lans Retsky, "Who Needs the New Community Trademark?" *Marketing News*, June 3, 1996, p. 11. For a description of changes in trademark law and court decisions on trademarks as well as their marketing implications, see Dorothy Cohen, "Trademark Strategy Revisited," *Journal of Marketing,* July 1991, pp. 46–59.

4. "Wrestling Federation Puts the Tag on a New Name," *Brandweek*, May 13, 2002, p. 16; and "Settlement Reached in Gateway Trademark Lawsuit," *Associated Press Newswires*, June 20, 2001.

5. Rodney Ho, "Brand-Name Diamonds: A Cut Above?" *The Wall Street Journal*, June 1, 1998, p. B1; and Betsy Morris, "The Brand's the Thing," *Fortune*, Mar. 4, 1996, pp. 72–75+.

6. Arlene Weintraub, "Can Nestlé Resist This Morsel?" *Business Week*, Sept. 2, 2002, pp. 60, 62; and Thomas Kamm, "Rivalry in Luxury Goods Heats Up as Gucci and LVMH Unveil Deals," *The Wall Street Journal*, Nov. 16, 1999, p. A22.

7. Al Ries, "What's in a Name?" *Sales & Marketing Management*, October 1995, p. 36. This article also discusses eight attributes of a desirable brand name.

8. Material in this paragraph and the following one are drawn from Suein L. Hwang, "Picking Pithy Names Is Getting Trickier as Trademark Applications Proliferate," *The Wall Street Journal*, Jan. 14, 1992, p. B1.

9. For more about morphemes, see Teresa Pavia and Janeen A. Costa, "The Winning Number: Consumer Perceptions of Alpha-Numeric Brand Names," *Journal of Marketing*, July 1993, pp. 85–98; and Casey McCabe, "What's in a Name?" *Adweek's Marketing Week*, Apr. 16, 1990, p. 22.

10. See also Kim Robertson, "Strategically Desirable Brand Name Characteristics," *The Journal of Product & Brand Management*, Summer 1992, pp. 62–72. For a good discussion of the special opportunities and challenges associated with services branding, see Vicki Clift, "Name Service Firms for the Long Haul," *Marketing News*, Dec. 6, 1993, p. 10. Some of the examples in this section are drawn from Leonard L. Berry, Edwin F. Lefkowith, and Terry Clark, "In Services, What's in a Name?" *Harvard Business Review*, September–October 1988, pp. 28–30.

11. "Largest Counterfeit Software Seizure in U.S. History," *PR Newswire*, Nov. 16, 2001; and David Stipp, "Farewell, My Logo," *Fortune*, May 27, 1996, p. 130.

12. Geoffrey A. Fowler, "Copies 'R' Us," *The Wall Street Journal*, Jan. 31, 2003, pp. B1, B4. Alkman Granitsas, "Studios Offer Bounty in Piracy War," *The Wall Street Journal*, July 10, 2002, p. B4; and Russell E. Brooks and Gila E. Gellman, "Combating Counterfeiting," *Marketing Management*, vol. 2, no. 3, 1993, pp. 49–51.

13. An excellent summary of this challenge and a list of safeguards are contained in Maxine S. Lans, "On Your Mark: Get Set or It May Go," *Marketing News*, Sept. 26, 1994, p. 12.

14. Jack Alexander, "What's in a Name? Too Much, Said the FTC," *Sales & Marketing Management*, January 1989, pp. 75, 78.

15. Carrie Goerne, "Rollerblade Reminds Everyone That Its Success Is Not Generic," *Marketing News*, Mar. 2, 1992, p. 1.

16. Patricia Sellers, "Brands: It's Thrive or Die," *Fortune*, Aug. 23, 1993, p. 53.

17. For an excellent discussion of the nature and benefits of this strategy, see Donald G. Norris, "Ingredient Branding: A Strategy Option with Multiple Beneficiaries," *Journal of Consumer Marketing*, Summer 1992, pp. 19–31.

18. Jeff Green, "Hold On—What Make of Alternator Is That?" *Business Week*, Nov. 13, 2000, pp. 203–204; and Morris, op. cit., p. 82.

19. Anne D'Innocenzio, "Big Retailers Steer Brand-Name Makers to Private Labels," *St. Louis Post-Dispatch*, June 2, 2002, p. E8.

20. Greg Burns, "A Froot Loop by Any Other Name," *Business Week*, June 26, 1995, p. 72.

21. The study was conducted by Raj Sethuraman of the University of Iowa, and reported in Richard Gibson, "Store-Brand Pricing Has to Be Just Right," *The Wall Street Journal*, Feb. 14, 1992, p. B1. The second study was summarized in Stephen J. Hoch, "Private Label a Threat? Don't Believe It," *Advertising Age*, May 24, 1993, p. 19.

22. Wal-Mart's approach is summarized in Peter Galuszka and Wendy Zellner, "Soap Opera at Wal-Mart," *Business Week,* Aug. 16, 1999, p. 44. The other examples come from Clyde H. Farnsworth, "Quality: High. Price: Low. Big Ad Budget? Never," *The New York Times*, Feb. 6, 1994, p. F10.

23. The estimated share of store brands in several types of retail stores is from the Store Brands Today page on the Private Label Manufacturers Association website, *www.plma.com*, accessed on July 23, 2002. The proportion of retailers intending to place more emphasis on such products come from Susan Zimmerman, "A Rosy Future," *Progressive Grocer*, November 1998, pp. 45–52. The $100 billion forecast was made by Destination Products International, as reported in Stephanie Thompson, "The New Private Enterprise," *Brandweek*, May 3, 1999, pp. 36+. The estimate of volume in 1995 is based on statistics in Emily DeNitto, "Back into Focus," *Brandweek*, May 29, 1995, pp. 22–26.

24. Recommendations as to how manufacturers can sustain their brands are presented in Susan R. Ashley, "How to Effectively Compete against Private-Label Brands," *Journal of Advertising Research,* January–February 1998, pp. 75+. The examples of price cutting are drawn from Gabriella Stern, "As National Brands Chop Prices, Stores Scramble to Defend Private-Label Goods," *The Wall Street Journal*, Aug. 23, 1993, p. B1.

25. Scheherazade Daneshkhu, "Awareness Becomes the Name of the Game," *Financial Times*, Sept. 9, 1999, p. II; and Paul Beckett and Suzanne Vranica, "Citigroup Spotlights Its Member Brands," *The Wall Street Journal*, June 25, 1999, p. B2.

26. There are potential disadvantages as well as advantages to introducing new

products under the family brand. For more on this, see Barbara Loken and Deborah Roedder John, "Diluting Brand Beliefs: When Do Brand Extensions Have a Negative Impact?" *Journal of Marketing,* July 1993, pp. 71–84.

27. Norton Paley, "Back from the Dead," *Sales & Marketing Management,* July 1995, pp. 30+.

28. D. C. Denison, "Ingredient Branding Puts Big Names in the Mix," *The Boston Globe,* May 26, 2002, p. E2; and Kara LaGrassa, "Entrepreneur of the Year: Sidney Feltenstein, *Franchising World,* Mar. 1, 2001, pp. 8–9.

29. This definition is drawn from the comprehensive examination of brand equity in Peter H. Farquhar, "Managing Brand Equity," *Journal of Advertising Research,* August/September 1990, pp. RC-7–RC-12. For more on brand equity, see David A. Aaker and Erich Joachimsthaler, *Brand Leadership,* The Free Press, New York, 2000; and Don E. Schultz, "Understanding and Measuring Brand Equity," *Marketing Management,* Spring 2000, pp. 8–9.

30. Deborah L. Vance, "A Name You Can Trust," *Marketing News,* Sept. 16, 2002, p. 3; "Sony Retains #1 Position in the Harris Poll Annual 'Best Brand' Survey for Third Year in a Row," *PR Newswire,* July 17, 2002; and Gerry Khermouch, "The Best Global Brands," *Business Week,* Aug. 5, 2002, pp. 92–96+.

31. The quote is from Roger Baird, "Asset Tests," *Marketing Week,* Oct. 1, 1998, pp. 28–31.

32. The Kellogg's example was described by Farquhar, "Managing Brand Equity," op. cit., p. RC-7. The study of personal computers was summarized in Jim Carlton, "Marketing Plays a Bigger Role in Distributing PCs," *The Wall Street Journal,* Oct. 16, 1995, p. B4.

33. David Welch, "Firestone: Is This Brand Beyond Repair?" *Business Week,* June 11, 2001, p. 48; and Christopher Carey, "TWA Boasts Best On-Time Record," *St. Louis Post-Dispatch,* Oct. 7, 1999, p. C2.

34. Farquhar, "Managing Brand Equity," op. cit., pp. RC-8–RC-10.

35. Morris, op. cit., p. 84.

36. The efforts of Oil of Olay to capitalize on its strong brand equity by introducing a new line are described in Tara Parker-Pope, "P&G's Cosmetics Makeover," *The Wall Street Journal,* Apr. 12, 1999, pp. B1, B3. For more on the rationale for the Marquis by Waterford line, see Judith Valente, "A New Brand Restores Sparkle to Waterford," *The Wall Street Journal,* Nov. 10, 1994, p. B1.

37. Statistics in this paragraph come from "Hot Movies Boost Licensing Industry's Hopes for Better Year," *Columbia Daily Tribune,* June 12, 2002, p. 7B. Other material is drawn from "Fashion Plays in Licensing," *Discount Store News,* June 7, 1999, pp. A6–A7.

38. Gerry Khermouch, " 'Whoa, Cool Shirt.' 'Yeah, It's a Pepsi,' " *Business Week,* Sept. 10, 2001, p. 84.

39. Dale D. Buss, "Hot Names, Top Dollars," *Nation's Business,* August 1995, p. 17.

40. Eliot Schreiber, "Retail Trends Shorten Life of Package Design," *Marketing News,* Dec. 5, 1994, p. 7.

41. Raju Narisetti, "Plotting to Get Tissues into Living Rooms," *The Wall Street Journal,* May 3, 1996, pp. B1, B12.

42. Betsy McKay, "Thinking inside the Box Helps Soda Makers Boost Sales," *The Wall Street Journal,* Aug. 2, 2002, pp. B1, B4; and Paul Lukas, "If It Ain't Got Glass, It Ain't Got Class," *Fortune,* Apr. 12, 1999, p. 40. For recommendations on managing the packaging aspect of a company's marketing mix, see Richard T. Hise and James U. McNeal, "Effective Packaging Management," *Business Horizons,* January–February 1988, pp. 47–51.

43. For further discussion of package-design strategies that can boost sales and profit, see Sue Bassin, "Innovative Packaging Strategies," *Journal of Business Strategy,* January–February 1988, pp. 38–42.

44. Schreiber, loc. cit.

45. David Leonhardt, "The Hip New Drink: Milk," *Business Week,* Feb. 16, 1998, p. 44.

46. Laura Bird, "Romancing the Package," *Adweek's Marketing Week,* Jan. 21, 1991, p. 10.

47. Information about the National Labeling and Education Act is drawn from the Food and Drug Administration website: *http://vm.cfsan.fda.gov/,dms/fdnewlab.html.*

48. John Sinisi, "New Rules Exact a Heavy Price as Labels Are Recast," *Brandweek,* Dec. 7, 1992, p. 3. For a study that examines the impact of the NLEA on consumers' processing of nutrition information, see Christine Moorman, "A Quasi Experiment to Assess the Consumer and Informational Determinants of Nutrition Information Processing Activities: The Case of the Nutrition Labeling and Education Act," *Journal of Public Policy & Marketing,* Spring 1996, pp. 28–44. This issue of the journal contains several other articles examining various aspects of nutrition labeling.

49. Eleena de Lisser, "Is That $5 Gallon of Milk Really Organic?" *The Wall Street Journal,* Aug. 20, 2002, pp. D1, D4.

50. Laura M. Litvan, "Sizing Up Metric Labeling Rules," *Nation's Business,* November 1994, p. 62.

51. Bruce Nussbaum, "Is In-House Design on the Way Out?" *Business Week,* Sept., 1995, p. 130. For an overview of how Ikea, the Swedish-based furniture retailer, has made design an integral part of its marketing program, see Lisa Margonelli, "How Ikea Designs Its Sexy Price Tags," *Business 2.0,* October 2002, pp. 106–112.

52. Bruce Nussbaum, "The Best Product Designs of the Year: Winners 2002," *Business Week,* July 8, 2002, pp. 82–89+.

53. "Over 60 and Overlooked—Why Does Business Ignore Older Customers?" *The Economist,* Aug. 10, 2002, no page given; "Business Bulletin," *The Wall Street Journal,* July 13, 2000, p. A1; and Bruce Nussbaum, "What Works for One Works for All," *Business Week,* Apr. 20, 1992, pp. 112–113.

54. The Beetle's comeback was described in Paul Tharp, "VW's Hippie Bus Now for Yuppies," *New York Post,* June 12, 2002, p. 37; and Bill Vlasic, "Bug-Eyed over the New Beetle," *Business Week,* May 25, 1998, p. 88. The figure pertaining to cost of design comes from Brian Dumaine, "Design That Sells and Sells and . . . ," *Fortune,* Mar. 11, 1991, pp. 86, 88.

55. Nancy Arnott, "Shades of Distinction," *Sales & Marketing Management,* June 1995, p. 20; Paul M. Barrett, "Color in the Court: Can Tints Be Trademarked?" *The Wall Street Journal,* Jan. 5, 1995, p. B1; and Junda Woo, "Rulings Clash over Colors in Trademarks," *The Wall Street Journal,* Feb. 25, 1993, p. B1.

56. Cindy Waxer, "Computer Couture," *Yahoo! Internet Life,* November 1999, pp. 144–145.

57. Meera Somasundaram, "Red Packages Lure Shoppers Like Capes Flourished at Bulls," *The Wall Street Journal,* Sept. 18, 1995, p. A13B.

58. Ross Johnson and William O. Winchell, *Marketing and Quality Control,* American Society for Quality Control, Milwaukee, 1989, p. 2.

59. Scott McCartney, "Middling Quality as a Marketing Plus? Survey Finds a Link," *The Wall Street Journal,* May 16, 1994, p. B6.

60. Kevin Schweitzer, "Japanese, European Car Companies Still Lead in Quality, But U.S. Makers Close," *Chicago Tribune,* Oct. 28, 2001, p. 1. For a list of reasons why product quality is so important and for a discussion of the marketing function's role in quality management, see Neil A. Morgan and Nigel F. Pierce, "Market Led Quality," *Industrial Marketing Management,* May 1992, pp. 111–118.

61. James B. Treece, "GM Hustles Compact into Production," *Automotive News,* Dec. 18, 2000, p. 36; "Buick to Lead Price Cuts for China's Auto Industry," *Xinhua News Agency,* Apr. 14, 2000, no page given; and T. S. Raghunathan, S. Subba Rao, and Luis S. Solis, "A Comparative Study of Quality Practices: USA, China and India," *Industrial Management & Data Systems,* May–June 1997, p. 192.

62. Ana Belen Escrig Tena, Juan Carlos Bou Llusar, and Vicenta Roca Puig, "Measuring the Relationship between Total Quality Management and Sustainable Competitive Advantage: A Resource-Based View," *Total Quality Management,* December 2001, pp. 932+.

63. Mark Henricks, "A New Standard," *Entrepreneur,* October 2002, pp. 83–84.

64. Mike Delpha, "ISO 9001:2000 Upgrade: Tips for a Smooth Transition," *Professional Safety,* July 2002, pp. 14, 17. ISO 9000 is covered in Ronald Henkoff, "The Hot New Seal of Quality," *Fortune,* June 28, 1993, pp. 116–118, 120.

65. Salton, Inc., Form 10-K for the fiscal year ended June 29, 2002; Salton, Inc., 2002 annual report; Johnson, loc. cit.

Chapter 11

1. Chris Ayres, "U.S. Car Rental Firms in Chaos in Wake of Attacks," *The London Times,* Business section, Sept. 29, 2001, p. 23; Al Stamborski, "Clayton, Mo.–Based Rental Car Company Gains Customers through Quality Service," *St. Louis Post-Dispatch,* May 24, 2000, p. C1; Kortney Stringer, "Reservations Grow Over Rental-Car Industry's Weak Links," *The Wall Street Journal,* Nov. 14, 2001, p. B4; *www.enterprise.com* accessed on Jan. 21, 2002.

2. Statistics on the economy are from the *Statistical Abstract of the United States: 2001,* 121st ed., U.S. Bureau of the Census, Washington, DC, 2001.

3. Libby Estill, "Sweet Charity," *Incentive,* June 2002, p. 26.

4. Trevor Jensen, "USPS Brings a New Campaign," *Adweek Midwest Edition,* Feb. 25, 2002, p. 2.

5. Based on Leonard L. Berry and Terry Clark, "Four Ways to Make Services More Tangible," *Business,* October–December 1986, p. 53.

6. Michelle Higgins, "Why Banks Are Getting Nicer," *The Wall Street Journal,* May 29, 2002, p. D1.

7. Neal Templin, "For Hotel Guests with Glitches, High-Tech Room Service," *The Wall Street Journal,* Aug. 30, 1999, pp. B1+.

8. Based on Allan C. Reedy, Bruce D. Buskirk, and Ajit Kaicker, "Tangibilizing the Intangibles: Some Strategies for Services Marketing," *Journal of Services Marketing,* no. 3 (1993), pp. 13–17.

9. Visit the Advertising Slogan Hall of Fame at *www.adslogans.co.uk* for examples of memorable slogans from the past.

10. A good description of how one company handles the service encounter is described in Keith H. Hammonds, "Handle with Care," *Fast Company,* August 2002, pp. 102–107.

11. Melinda Ligos, "Mall Rats with a Social Conscience," *Sales & Marketing Management,* November 1999, p 115; Aja Whitaker, "Cause Marketing Gaining Ground," *Management Review,* September 1999, p. 8.

12. Vince Crawley and Rick Maze, "Military Cutting Back on High-Priced Television Commercials," *Navy Times,* Mar. 25, 2002, P. 18; Vince Crawley, "Pentagon Seeks Target Definition in Recruiting Ads," *Navy Times,* Aug. 14, 2000, p. 21.

13. Bree Fowler, "Congregation of Nuns Uses Internet, TV for Recruiting," *South Bend Tribune,* June 10, 2002, p. C3.

14. Estill, loc.cit.

15. Satisfaction with services is based on a customer's perceptions of various types of convenience, most of which are controlled by the seller. Leonard L. Berry, Kathleen Seiders, and Dhruv Grewal, "Understanding Service Convenience," *Journal of Marketing,* July 2002, pp. 1–17, describe how the relationship may work.

16. Ann Grimes, "What's in Store," *The Wall Street Journal,* July 15, 2002, p. R6.

17. Heather Harreld, "Pick-Up Artists," *CIO Magazine,* Nov. 1, 2000, at CIO archives *www.cio.com*; Al Stamborski, loc. cit.

Chapter 12

1. www.priceline.com, accessed on Mar. 9, 2002; Julia Angwin, "Hit by Travel Slump, Priceline Posts a Loss," *The Wall Street Journal,* Feb. 5, 2002, p. B5; Julia Angwin, "After Surviving Dot-Com Rout, Priceline Enters New Storm," *The Wall Street Journal,* Sept. 20, 2001, p. B9; Julia Angwin, "Priceline.com Posts a Profit, Crediting Stringent Cost Cuts, Escalating Demand," *The Wall Street Journal,* Aug. 1, 2001, p. A3; "Priceline.com Replaces Its CEO in Struggle toward Profitability," *St. Louis Post-Dispatch,* May 8, 2001, p. F7; "Priceline and Expedia Bury the Ax," *Business Week,* Jan. 22, 2001, p. 46; Peter Elkind, "The Hype Is Big, Really Big, at Priceline," *Fortune,* Sept. 6, 1999, pp. 193–194+ ; Shari Weiss, "Internet Offers Priceless Marketing, Booking Opportunities," *Hotel & Motel Management,* June 3, 1999, pp. 58, 60; and Heather Green, "Priceline's Bid for the Big Time," *Business Week,* Jan. 18, 1999, p. 43.

2. This list was suggested in part by John T. Mentzer and David J. Schwartz, *Marketing Today,* 4th ed., Harcourt Brace Jovanovich, San Diego, 1985, p. 599.

3. David Meer, "System Beaters, Brand Loyals, and Deal Shoppers: New Insights into the Role of Brand and Price," *Journal of Advertising Research,* May/June 1995, pp. RC2–RC7.

4. Stephen J. Hoch, Byung-Do Kim, Alan L. Montgomery, and Peter E. Rossi, "Determinants of Store-Level Price Elasticity," *Journal of Marketing Research,* February 1995, p. 28.

5. Roberta Maynard, "Taking Guesswork out of Pricing," *Nation's Business,* December 1997, p. 28. For in-depth discussions of the relationship between price levels and perceived quality, see David J. Curry and Peter C. Riesz, "Prices and Price/Quality Relationships: A Longitudinal Analysis," *Journal of Marketing,* January 1988, pp. 36–51; and Valarie A. Zeithaml, "Consumer Perceptions of Price, Quality, and Value: A Means-End Model and Synthesis of Evidence," *Journal of Marketing,* July 1988, pp. 2–22.

6. Stephanie Paterik, "Business Hotels Court the Family Crowd," *The Wall Street Journal,* Aug. 7, 2002, p. D1; and Caroline Wilbert, "What Recession? Extended-Stay Hotels' Business Remains Sweet in a Sour Economy,"

Atlanta Journal-Constitution, Aug. 20, 2002, p. D1.

7. Dean Takahashi, "Little Caesar's Plans 'Big! Big!' Pizzas, while Keeping Price Structure the Same," *The Wall Street Journal,* Sept. 2, 1997, p. B6; and Rahul Jacob, "Beyond Quality and Value," *Fortune* (special issue), Autumn/Winter 1993, pp. 8, 10.

8. Gary H. Anthes, "The Price Had Better Be Right," *Computerworld,* Dec. 21, 1998, pp. 65–66.

9. Frank Alpert, Beth Wilson, and Michael T. Elliott, "Price Signaling: Does It Ever Work?" *Journal of Product & Brand Management,* vol. 2, no. 1, 1993, pp. 29–41.

10. For a list of 21 pricing objectives and a discussion of objectives as part of a strategic pricing program for industrial firms, see Michael H. Morris and Roger J. Calantone, "Four Components of Effective Pricing," *Industrial Marketing Management,* November 1990, pp. 321–329.

11. Caroline Daniel, "Monsanto Enters a Time of Transition, *Financial Times,* Aug. 19, 2002, p. 25; and Robert Steyer, "Monsanto Slashes Roundup Prices," *St. Louis Post-Dispatch,* Sept. 2, 1998, p. C1.

12. Sam Nataraj and Jim Lee, "Dot-Com Companies: Are They All Hype?" *SAM Advanced Management Journal,* July 1, 2002, pp. 10+; and George Anders, "Buying Frenzy," *The Wall Street Journal,* July 12, 1999, pp. R6, R10.

13. Katherine Zachary, "The Yen, Again," *Ward's Auto World,* April 2002, pp. 24–25.

14. For a discussion of new-product pricing, taking into account the product's perceived benefits and entry time, see Eunsang Yoon, "Pricing Imitative New Products," *Industrial Marketing Management,* May 1991, pp. 115–125.

15. Maynard, op. cit., p. 27.

16. Zachary Schiller, "The Revolving Door at Rubbermaid," *Business Week,* Sept. 18, 1995, pp. 80–83.

17. Imogen Wall, "It May Be a Dog-Eat-Dog World, but This Restaurant Won't Prove It," *The Wall Street Journal,* Dec. 11, 1998, p. B1.

18. For a report on how this is done in the business market, see Michael H. Morris and Mary L. Joyce, "How Marketers Evaluate Price Sensitivity," *Industrial Marketing Management,* May 1988, pp. 169–176.

19. George E. Cressman, Jr., "Snatching Defeat from the Jaws of Victory," *Marketing Management,* Summer 1997, p. 15

20. Daniel Eisenberg, "Kodak's Photo Op," *Time,* Apr. 30, 2001, pp. 46–47; and Chanoine Webb, "The Picture Just Keeps Getting Darker at Kodak," *Fortune,* June 21, 1999, p. 206.

21. Steve Hamm, "The Wild and Woolly World of Linux," *Business Week,* Nov. 15, 1999, pp. 130, 134; James Aley, "Give It Away and Get Rich!" *Fortune,* June 10, 1996, pp. 90–92+; and Neil Gross and Peter Coy, "The Technology Paradox," *Business Week,* Mar. 6, 1995, pp. 76–81, 84.

22. Tom Lester, "How to Ensure That the Price Is Exactly Right," *Financial Times,* Jan. 30, 2002, no pages given; and "Pricing Gets Easier (Sort Of)," *Inc.,* November 1993, p. 124.

23. Avraham Shama, "E-Coms and Their Marketing Strategies," *Business Horizons,* September 2001, pp. 14+; and Morris and Calantone, op. cit., p. 323.

24. The perspective that price dictates cost levels is presented in Christopher Farrell and Zachary Schiller, "Stuck!" *Business Week,* Nov. 15, 1993, pp. 146, 148. The magnitude of Kodak's cost-cutting efforts is from Webb, loc. cit.

25. For an approach to break-even analysis that includes semifixed costs and is of more practical value in situations typically faced by marketing executives, see Thomas L. Powers, "Breakeven Analysis with Semifixed Costs," *Industrial Marketing Management,* February 1987, pp. 35–41.

26. G. Dean Kortge and Patrick A. Okonkwo, "Perceived Value Approach to Pricing," *Industrial Marketing Management,* May 1993, p. 134.

27. Dan Koeppel, "Fast Food's New Reality," *Adweek's Marketing Week,* Mar. 30, 1992, pp. 22–23.

28. Margaret Studer, "Patek Philippe Is Luxuriating in Independence," *The Wall Street Journal,* Dec. 11, 2000, p. B18; and Thomas T. Nagle, "Managing Price Competition," *Marketing Management,* vol. 2, no. 1, 1993, p. 41.

29. *www.britishairways.com,* accessed July 30, 2002; and "Air France Celebrates Supersonic Summer," *PR Newswire,* May 19, 1999.

30. Matt Krantz, "Priceline Turns Its First Profit," *USA Today,* Aug. 1, 2001, p. 3B; Julia Angwin, "Priceline Founder Closes Online Bidding Sites for Gas and Groceries," *The Wall Street Journal,* Oct. 6, 2000, p. B1; Nick Wingfield, "New Battlefield for Priceline Is Diapers, Tuna," *The Wall Street Journal,* Sept. 22, 1999, p. B1; and Weiss, loc. cit.

Chapter 13

1. "In the Hot Seat: Q&A with Bluefly's Ken Seiff," *Retailing Today,* Aug. 21, 2000, pp. A10–A12; Rebecca Quick, "Bluefly's Goal: Raise Margins, but Keep Fans," *The Wall Street Journal,* Jan. 25, 2001, pp. B1, B4; Michael Totty, "Making the Sale," *The Wall Street Journal,* Sept. 24, 2001, p. R6; "Bluefly Inc. Streamlines Operations," *Home Textiles Today,* June 25, 2001, p. 6; Paul Miller, "Bluefly.com Enters the Catalog Fray—or Does It?" *Catalog Age,* June 2001, pp. 25; www.bluefly.com, accessed on Mar. 10, 2002.

2. Erin White, "Major Airlines Face Strategy Bind," *The Wall Street Journal,* Oct. 3, 2002, p. B10.

3. Gary Strauss, "99¢ Only Started Trend," *USA Today,* June 22, 1998, pp. 1B, 2B.

4. Don Clark, "Intel to Release Itanium 2 Chip–Company Hopes Entry Will Allow It to Charge High End of Computing," *The Asian Wall Street Journal,* July 9, 2002, p. A7.

5. Patricia Sellers, "Look Who Learned about Value," *Fortune,* Oct. 18, 1993, p. 75; and Bill Saporito, "Why the Price Wars Never End," *Fortune,* Mar. 23, 1992, pp. 68+.

6. Stratford Sherman, "How to Prosper in the Value Decade," *Fortune,* Nov. 30, 1992, p. 98.

7. Anne Faircloth, "Values Retailers Go Dollar for Dollar," *Fortune,* July 6, 1998, p. 166.

8. Albert D. Bates, "Pricing for Profit," *Retailing Issues Newsletter,* September 1990, p. 1.

9. For three recommended forms of non-price competition for retailers, see Bates, op. cit., p. 4.

10. William Echikson, "Aiming at High and Low Markets," *Fortune,* Mar. 22, 1993, p. 89.

11. Sean O'Neill, "Eyes on the Price," *Kiplinger's Personal Finance,* September 2000, pp. 122–123.

12. Charles Forelle, "Do You Really Need a Turbo Toothbrush?" *The Wall Street Journal,* Oct. 1, 2002, pp. D1, D4; and Robert Berner, "Why P&G's Smile Is So Bright," *Business Week,* Aug. 12, 2002, pp. 58–60.

13. Neil Gross and Peter Coy, "The Technology Paradox," *Business Week,* Mar. 6, 1995, pp. 76–77.

14. Reed K. Holden and Thomas T. Nagle, "Kamikaze Pricing," *Marketing Management*, Summer 1998, p. 39.

15. Dan Carney, "Caveat Predator?" *Business Week*, May 22, 2000, pp. 116, 118; and Mike France and Steve Hamm, "Does Predatory Pricing Make Microsoft a Predator?" *Business Week*, Nov. 23, 1998, pp. 130, 132.

16. Robert Steyer, "Monsanto Offers Discounts to Dairy Farmers," *St. Louis Post-Dispatch*, Oct. 22, 1995, p. 1E.

17. William M. Bulkeley, "Rebates' Secret Appeal to Manufacturers: Few Consumers Actually Redeem Them," *The Wall Street Journal*, Feb. 10, 1998, pp. B1, B6.

18. Geoffrey A. Fowler, "Click and Clip," *The Wall Street Journal*, Oct. 21, 2002, p. R8; and Roger O. Crockett, "Penny-Pinchers' Paradise: E-Coupons Are Catching On Fast—and Companies Are Learning to Use Them," *Business Week e.biz*, Jan. 22, 2001, p. EB12.

19. For more about this approach, see Hermann Simon and Robert J. Dolan, "Price Customization," *Marketing Management*, Fall 1998, pp. 10–17.

20. Edward R. Silverman, "Drug Makers Score Startling Victory against Retail Pharmacies," *The Star-Ledger* (Newark, NJ), Dec. 1, 1998, no pages given.

21. David Kipen, "Readers Make or Break Independent Bookstores," *San Francisco Chronicle*, Apr. 25, 2001, p. E1.

22. Douglas A. Blackmon, "FedEx Is to Adopt Rate Structure Based on Distance Package Travels," *The Wall Street Journal*, Jan. 23, 1997, p. B4.

23. For further discussion of pricing strategies and policies, see Gerard J. Tellis, "Beyond the Many Faces of Price: An Integration of Pricing Strategies," *Journal of Marketing*, October 1986, pp. 146–160.

24. For a theoretical model of flexible pricing and discussion of its managerial implications, see Kenneth R. Evans and Richard F. Beltramini, "A Theoretical Model of Consumer-Negotiated Pricing: An Orientation Perspective," *Journal of Marketing*, April 1987, pp. 58–73.

25. "Auto Report," *The Seattle Times*, Aug. 23, 2002, p. F1; Joann Muller, "Old Carmakers Learn New Tricks," *Business Week*, Apr. 12, 1999, pp. 116, 118; and Brian S. Akre, "Restructure of Dealer Networks Will Change Retailing," *Marketing News*, Oct. 26, 1998, p. 10.

26. Julia Angwin, "America Online Faces New Threat from Cut-Rate Internet Services," *The Wall Street Journal*, Feb.

3, 2003, pp. A1, A11; and Peter Coy, "Are Flat Rates Good Business?" *Business Week*, Feb. 10, 1997, p. 108.

27. Strauss, loc. cit.

28. A study of the beneficial effects of odd pricing, if used on a very limited basis, is mentioned in "Why That Deal Is Only $9.99," *Business Week*, Jan. 10, 2000, p. 36. Previously the effectiveness of odd pricing was described in Robert M. Schindler and Lori S. Warren, "Effects of Odd Pricing on Price Recall," *Journal of Business*, June 1989, pp. 165–177. Consumers' paying attention to just the first two digits in a price is examined in Mark Stiving and Russell S. Winer, "An Empirical Analysis of Price Endings with Scanner Data," *Journal of Consumer Research*, June 1997, pp. 57–67.

29. David D. Kirkpatrick, "Chains Raising Book Prices," *Portland Oregonian*, Oct. 10, 2000, p. B1; and George Anders, "Amazon Plans to Offer 50% Discounts on Hardcover, Paperback Bestsellers," *The Wall Street Journal*, May 17, 1999, p. B11.

30. Russell Gold and Ann Zimmerman, "Pumped Out: Wal-Mart's Defeat in Low-Cost Gas Game," *The Wall Street Journal*, Aug. 13, 2001, p. A14; and "Wal-Mart Wins Suit over Low-Price Strategy," *St. Louis Post-Dispatch*, Jan. 10, 1995, p. 7C.

31. Peter J. McGoldrick, Erica J. Betts, and Kathy A. Keeling, "High-Low Pricing: Audit Evidence and Consumer Preferences," *The Journal of Product and Brand Management*, 2000, pp. 316–331; G. S. Bobinski, D. Cox, and A. Cox, "Retail 'Sale' Advertising, Perceived Retailer Credibility and Price Rationale," *Journal of Retailing*, Fall 1996, pp. 291–306; and "Consumers' Reference Prices: Implications for Managers," *Stores*, April 1996, p. RR4.

32. Patrick J. Kaufmann, N. Craig Smith, and Gwendolyn K. Ortmeyer, "Deception in Retailer High-Low Pricing: A 'Rule of Reason' Approach," *Journal of Retailing*, Summer 1994, pp. 151.

33. For an overview of how one chain, Family Dollar Stores, switched from high-low pricing to EDLP, see Michael Friedman, "A Contented Discounter," *Progressive Grocer*, November 1998, pp. 39–41. For information about other chains' use of EDLP, see Duke Ratliff, "Variations on the Theme," *Discount Merchandiser*, March 1996, pp. 24–25. The appearance of EDLP in Germany is covered in Jennifer Negley, "Jeden Tag

Tiefpreise—Sprechen sie EDLP?" *Discount Store News*, June 8, 1998, p. 17.

34. Stuart Hirshfield, "The Squeeze," *Apparel Industry Magazine*, August 1998, pp. 60–64.

35. Tim Ambler, "P&G Learnt the Hard Way from Dropping Its Price Promotions," *Marketing*, June 7, 2001, p. 22.

36. Stephen J. Hoch, Xavier Drpze, and Mary E. Purk, "EDLP, Hi-Lo, and Margin Arithmetic," *Journal of Marketing*, October 1994, pp. 16–27.

37. For a discussion of the legal status of resale price maintenance, plus some steps that manufacturers can take to avoid legal problems when establishing resale price maintenance programs, see Mary Jane Sheffet and Debra L. Scammon, "Resale Price Maintenance: Is It Safe to Suggest Retail Prices?" *Journal of Marketing*, Fall 1985, pp. 82–91.

38. Joel M. Cohen and Arthur J. Burke, "Antitrust: Supreme Court Acts on Maximum Pricing," *International Commercial Litigation*, December 1997/January 1998, p. 43, and Susan B. Garland, "You'll Charge What I Tell You to Charge," *Business Week*, Oct. 6, 1997, pp. 118, 120.

39. "Nine West Settles State and Federal Price Fixing Charges," *M2 Presswire*, Mar. 7, 2000, no pages given.

40. Michael Selz, "Small Firms Use Variety of Ploys to Raise Prices," *The Wall Street Journal*, June 17, 1993, p. B1.

41. Thomas T. Nagle, "Managing Price Competition," *Marketing Management*, vol. 2, no. 1, 1993, p. 45.

42. Scott Kilman, "Diageo Says Industry Price War Is Crimping Its Burger King Sale," *The Wall Street Journal*, Nov. 8, 2002, p. A3. Cliff Edwards, "Everyone Loves a Freebie—except Dell's Rivals," *Business Week*, July 22, 2002, p. 41; and Robert Weller, "Colorado Ski Resorts Give In to Need for Deep Discounts," *St. Louis Post-Dispatch*, Sept. 4, 1999, p.33OT. The statement about price wars, made by a McKinsey consultant, was contained in David R. Henderson, "What Are Price Wars Good For? *Absolutely Nothing*," *Fortune*, May 12, 1997, p. 156.

43. The description of price-war damages is from Andrew E. Serwer, "How to Escape a Price War," *Fortune*, June 13, 1994, pp. 82+. The example about music retailing is based on Tim Carvell, "These Prices Really Are Insane," *Fortune*, Aug. 4, 1997, pp. 109–110+.

44. "In the Hot Seat: Q&A with Bluefly's Ken Seiff," loc. cit.; Quick, op. cit.; Totty, op. cit.; "Bluefly Inc. Streamlines Operations," loc. cit.; Miller, op. cit.; *www.bluefly.com*, accessed on Mar. 10, 2002.

Chapter 14

1. *www.avoncompany.com*, accessed on May 11, 2002; "J.C. Penney Shows Avon the Door," *USA Today*, Feb. 3, 2003, p. 1B. Emily Nelson, "Avon Calls on Good-Looking Research," *The Wall Street Journal*, May 23, 2002, p. B6; "Avon to Target Teens," *Direct Marketing*, November 2001, p. 22; Katarzyna Moreno, "UnbeComing," *Forbes*, June 10, 2001, pp. 151–152; Janet Ginsburg, "Deck the Malls with Kiosks," *Business Week*, Dec. 13, 1999, pp. 86–88; Laura Klepacki, "Avon to Make Stronger Move into Retailing," *WWD*, Dec. 8, 1999, p. 2; Carolyn Edy, "Avon Malling," *American Demographics*, April 1999, pp. 38–40; Leslie Kaufman, "Avon's New Face," *Newsweek*, Nov. 16, 1998, p. 24; and Sharon Machlis, "Beauty Product Sites Facing Channel Clash," *Computerworld*, Nov. 9, 1998, p. 24.

2. Stacy Collett, "Off-Line Dealers Push for Legal Protection," *Computerworld*, Apr. 16, 2001, p. 17; and "Merrill Lynch Shakes Up Industry by Going Online," *St. Louis Post-Dispatch*, July 22, 1999, p. B13. For a discussion of the contention that the Internet is the biggest influence on distribution since the Industrial Revolution, see Leyland Pitt, Pierre Berthon, and Jean-Paul Berthon, "Changing Channels: The Impact of the Internet on Distribution Strategy," *Business Horizons*, March/April 1999, pp. 19–28.

3. For insight regarding whether the Internet will eliminate middlemen in two industries, air travel and groceries, see Eric Clemons, "When Should You Bypass the Middleman?" *Financial Times*, Feb. 22, 1999, p. 14. The term *disintermediation* is explained further in "On-Line Commerce Business Trends," *The Wall Street Journal*, Dec. 12, 1996, p. B4.

4. The concept of shifting activities, the possibility of manufacturers shifting some functions away from their firms, and the opportunity for small wholesalers to perform added functions to maintain their economic viability are all discussed in Ronald D. Michman, "Managing Structural Changes in Marketing Channels," *The Journal of Business and Industrial Marketing*, Summer/Fall 1990, pp. 5–14. The distinctive ways in which electronic channel members carry out distribution-related activities are described in Robert D. Tamilia, Sylvain Senecal, and Giles Corriveau, "Conventional Channels of Distribution and Electronic Intermediaries: A Functional Analysis," *Journal of Marketing Channels*, vol. 9, nos. 3/4, pp. 27–48.

5. Barbara Thau, "Target Inks Deal with Fleming to Supply Food to Stores, Cafes," *HFN*, July 15, 2002, p. 4; and Maria Halkias, "Fleming Shares Plunge," *The Dallas Morning News*, Feb. 5, 2003, p. 1D.

6. *www.lotuslight.com*, accessed on Oct. 25, 2002; and Julie Candler, "How to Choose a Distributor," *Nation's Business*, August 1993, p. 46.

7. *www.statefarm.com/quote/arq.htm*, accessed on Sept. 16, 2002; and Diane Brady, "Insurers Step Gingerly into Cyberspace, *Business Week*, Nov. 22, 1999, p. 160.

8. Karen Roche and Bill O'Connell, "Dig a Wider Channel for Your Products, *Marketing News*, Nov. 9, 1998, p. 10.

9. For guidance on selecting channels for international markets, especially the decision of whether to use middlemen, see Saul Klein, "Selection of International Marketing Channels," *Journal of Global Marketing*, vol. 4, 1991, pp. 21–37.

10. The New Pig example is drawn from "Unconventional Channels," *Sales & Marketing Management*, October 1988, p. 38.

11. Craig Zarley and Edward F. Moltzen, "IBM Takes Direct Route to Small Firms," *Computer Reseller News*, Mar. 1, 1999, p. 2.

12. *www.marshallamps.com*, accessed on Oct. 25, 2002.

13. An excellent discussion of distribution channels for business goods and services is found in Michael D. Hutt and Thomas W. Speh, *Business Marketing Management*, 7th ed., Harcourt, Ft. Worth, TX, 2001, pp. 355–381.

14. Maricris G. Briones, "Resellers Hike Profits through Service," *Marketing News*, Feb. 15, 1999, pp. 1, 14; and Maricris G. Briones, "What Technology Wrought: Distribution Channel in Flux," *Marketing News*, Feb. 1, 1999, pp. 1, 15.

15. For an instructive discussion of this topic, see Donald H. Light, "A Guide for New Distribution Channel Strategies for Service Firms," *The Journal of Business Strategy*, Summer 1986, pp. 56–64.

16. J. C. Conklin, "That's the Ticket," *The Wall Street Journal*, July 12, 1999, p. R45; and George Anders, "Some Big Companies Long to Embrace Web but Settle for Flirtation," *The Wall Street Journal*, Nov. 4, 1998, p. A14.

17. Rowland T. Moriarty and Ursula Moran, "Managing Hybrid Marketing Systems," *Harvard Business Review*, November–December 1990, pp. 146–155.

18. For extensive discussion of this approach to serving distinct markets, see Wim G. Biemans, "Marketing in the Twilight Zone," *Business Horizons*, November/December 1998, pp. 69–76; and John A. Quelch, "Why Not Exploit Dual Marketing?" *Business Horizons*, January–February 1987, pp. 52–60.

19. Deborah Lohse, "Allstate to Launch Online Sales of Car and Home Insurance," *The Wall Street Journal*, Nov. 11, 1999, p. B18; Samuel Schiff, "Agency System Lives but Continued Survival Will Require Adapting to Changes," *Rough Notes*, February 1999, pp. 14–16; and "Dramatic Shift to Multiple Distribution Channels for Property-Casualty Insurance Industry," *Limra's Marketfacts*, March/April 1998, p. 6.

20. Milford Prewitt, "Franchisees' Lawsuits: Chains' Nontraditional Growth Paths Lead to New Encroachment Battles," *Nation's Restaurant News*, Oct. 9, 1995, pp. 118–120; and Jack Hayes, "Carvel, Franchisees Lock Horns over Retail Program, *Nation's Restaurant News*, Sept. 4, 1995, pp. 3, 82.

21. The Scotts example comes from Valerie Reitman, "Manufacturers Start to Spurn Big Discounters," *The Wall Street Journal*, Nov. 30, 1993, p. B1. For further discussion of the advantages and disadvantages of multiple channels as well as ways to minimize conflict resulting from multiple channels, see Martin Everett, "When There's More than One Route to the Customer," *Sales & Marketing Management*, August 1990, pp. 48–50+.

22. "Ford Sells Oklahoma Dealerships," *The Associated Press State & Local Wire*, Apr. 4, 2002; Carol Matlack, "Swatch: Ready for Net Time?" *Business Week*, Feb. 14, 2000, p. 61; Earle Eldridge, "GM Settles Argument with Dealerships," *USA Today*, Jan. 24, 2000, p. 2B; Gregory L. White, "Ford Restarting Move to Buy Stakes in Its Dealers, Albeit More Cautiously," *The Wall Street Journal*, Nov. 22, 1999, p. B22; and Joann Muller, "Meet Your Local GM Dealer: GM," *Business Week*, Oct. 11, 1999, p. 48.

23. For details about Kraft Foods' approach to coordinating (perhaps controlling) distribution activities, see Brandon Copple, "Shelf-Determination," *Forbes*, Apr. 15, 2002, pp. 130–132+.

24. Wal-Mart's dominating power and increasing control in the area of distribution (and, more broadly, the economy and society as a whole) are described in Jerry Useem, "One Nation under Wal-Mart," *Fortune*, Mar. 3, 2003, pp. 65–86+; Jim Hopkins, "Wal-Mart's Influence Grows," *USA Today*, Jan. 29, 2003, pp. 1B+; and Copple, op. cit., p. 140.

25. "Dynamic Shift to Multiple Distribution Channels . . . ," loc. cit.

26. Michael Selz, "More Small Firms Are Turning to Trade Intermediaries," *The Wall Street Journal*, Feb. 2, 1993, p. B2.

27. For more on the idea that market considerations should determine a channel structure, see Louis W. Stern and Frederick D. Sturdivant, "Customer-Driven Distribution Systems," *Harvard Business Review*, July–August 1987, pp. 34–41.

28. Anders, op. cit., pp. A1, A14.

29. Bert Rosenbloom and Trina L. Larsen, "How Foreign Firms View Their U.S. Distributors," *Industrial Marketing Management*, May 1992, pp. 93–101.

30. "Putting the Aim Back into Famous Amos," *Sales & Marketing Management*, June 1992, p. 31.

31. Reitman, op. cit., pp. B1, B2; and Christina Duff, "Nation's Retailers Ask Vendors to Help Share Expenses," *The Wall Street Journal*, Aug. 4, 1993, p. B4.

32. Robert Berner, "Kissing Off the Cosmetics Counter," *Business Week*, Oct. 30, 2000, pp. 108, 112.

33. For an in-depth discussion of differences in distribution intensity, as well as a study of this factor in the context of the consumer electronics industry, see Gary L. Frazier and Walfried M. Lassar, "Determinants of Distribution Intensity," *Journal of Marketing*, October 1996, pp. 39–51.

34. Shelly Branch, "P&G Is out to Fetch Distribution Gains for Iams Pet Food," *The Wall Street Journal*, Jan. 6, 2000, p. A6.

35. *www.step2.com*, accessed on Oct. 26, 2002; and Reitman, op. cit., pp. B1, B2.

36. Sara Nathan, "Defining the Seller in On-Line Market," *USA Today*, Aug. 26, 1999, p. 3B.

37. Ann Zimmerman, "Grocery Distributor Squeezes Suppliers at Bill-Paying Time," *The Wall Street Journal*, Sept. 5, 2002, pp. A1, A10; "Facing Charges," *HFN*, Oct. 8, 2001, pp. 8+; and "Retailers' Defense: Chargebacks Spring from Non-Compliance," *HFN*, Oct. 8, 2001, pp. 11–12.

38. Stephane Farhi, "Eggs, Bread—and a Discount Daewoo," *Automotive News*, June 28, 1999, p. 46.

39. Thomas Lee, "A-B Watches from the Sidelines as Brewery Buyout Frenzy Unfolds," *St. Louis Post-Dispatch*, Apr. 21, 2002, p. E1; and Jakki J. Mohr, Robert J. Fisher, and John R. Nevin, "Communicating for Better Channel Relationships," *Marketing Management*, Summer 1999, p. 40.

40. "Two Outlet Stores Open in Distribution Strategy," *The Wall Street Journal*, Mar. 11, 1997, p. B6; and Teri Agins, "Apparel Makers Are Refashioning Their Operations," *The Wall Street Journal*, Jan. 13, 1994, p. B4.

41. Luisa Kroll, "Tough Guy," *Forbes*, Feb. 4, 2002, pp. 60–61; and Bill Saporito, "Cutting Out the Middleman," *Fortune*, Apr. 6, 1992, p. 96.

42. Rachel Melcer, "Graybar Grows out of Middleman Role," *St. Louis Post-Dispatch*, Sept. 1, 2002, p. E1.

43. "Levi's Plans Own Stores," *Marketing News*, Jan. 30, 1995, p. 1.

44. Laura Bird and Wendy Bounds, "Stores' Demands Squeeze Apparel Companies," *The Wall Street Journal*, July 15, 1997, pp. B1, B12.

45. "Shelf Help?" *Entrepreneur*, October 2002, p. 28; Clayton Kale, "GAO Says Grocers Offered Little Help in Investigation," *St. Louis Post-Dispatch*, Sept. 15, 2000, p. C6; Holman W. Jenkins, Jr., "We ♥ Slotting Fees," *The Wall Street Journal*, Sept. 22, 1999, p. A23; Nahal Toosi, "Congress Looks at the Selling of Shelf Space," *St. Louis Post-Dispatch*, Sept. 15, 1999, p. C1.

46. Nichole L. Torres, "Examine Your Co-Op(tions)," *Entrepreneur*, July 2002, pp. 120, 128.

47. TruServ's travails were described in Jeff Bailey, "Co-ops Gain as Firms Seek Competitive Power," *The Wall Street Journal*, Oct. 15, 2002, p. B5.

48. James E. Zemanek, Jr., and James W. Hardin, "How the Industrial Salesperson's Use of Power Can Affect Distributor Satisfaction: An Empirical Examination," *Journal of Marketing Channels*, vol. 3, no. 1, 1993, pp. 23–45.

49. An early description of the dominance of gigantic retailers and their demands on manufacturers can be found in Zachary Schiller and Wendy Zellner, "Clout!" *Business Week*, Dec. 21, 1992, pp. 66–69+.

50. For a model showing a range of channel relationships, see John T. Gardner, W. Benoy Joseph, and Sharon Thach, "Modeling the Continuum of Relationship Styles between Distributors and Suppliers," *Journal of Marketing Channels*, vol. 2, no. 4, 1993, pp. 11+. The Sutter situation was described in Candler, op. cit., p. 45.

51. "Wal-Mart Expands Access to Product Sales History," *The Wall Street Journal*, Aug. 18, 1999, p. B8; and Myron Magnet, "The New Golden Rule of Business," *Fortune*, Feb. 21, 1994, pp. 60–64. For a discussion of attributes of successful alliances in channels, based on a study of computer dealers, see Jakki J. Mohr and Robert E. Spekman, "Perfecting Partnerships," *Marketing Management*, Winter/Spring 1996, pp. 35–43.

52. Magnet, loc. cit. For more ideas on how to build a good producer-middleman relationship, see James A. Narus and James C. Anderson, "Distributor Contributions to Partnerships with Manufacturers," *Business Horizons*, September–October 1987, pp. 34–42.

53. Agins, loc. cit.

54. Andrew Raskin, "Who's Minding the Store?" *Business 2.0*, February 2003, pp. 70+.

55. John R. Nevin, "Relationship Marketing and Distribution Channels: Exploring Fundamental Issues," *Journal of Marketing Channels*, vol. 23, no. 4, 1995, pp. 327–334.

56. "Toys R Us, Two Toymakers Settle Discounting Suit," *St. Louis Post-Dispatch*, May 26, 1999, p. C9.

57. "Federal Appeals Court Dismisses Antitrust Suit against Domino's," *Associated Press Newswire*, Aug. 27, 1997, no pages given; and Jeffrey A. Tannenbaum, "Franchisees Balk at High Prices for Supplies from Franchisers," *The Wall Street Journal*, July 5, 1995, pp. B1, B2.

58. Jennifer E. Gully, "Image Technical Services, Inc., v. Eastman Kodak Co.," *Berkeley Technology Law Journal*, 1998, pp. 339–353; and Wendy Bounds, "Jury Finds Kodak Monopolized Markets in Services and Parts for Its Machines," *The Wall Street Journal*, Sept. 19, 1995, p. A4.

59. Joseph Pereira, "Stride Rite Agrees to Settle Charges It Tried to Force Pricing by Retailers," *The Wall Street Journal*, Sept. 28, 1993, p. B5.

60. *www.avon.com*, accessed on June 21, 2002; Sally Beatty, "Avon Is Set to Call on Teens," *The Wall Street Journal*, Oct. 17, 2002, pp. B1, B7; Nanette Byrnes, "Avon: The New Calling," *Business Week*, Sept. 18, 2000, pp. 136–148; Erik Gruenwedel, "Kinzan to Launch Branded Homepages for Avon Reps," *Adweek*, Aug. 21, 2000, p. 38; and Erin White, "Ding-Dong, Avon Calling (on the Web, Not Your Door)," *The Wall Street Journal*, Dec. 28, 1999, p. B4.

Chapter 15

1. *www.irconnect.com/petm/pages/faq.html*, accessed on June 10, 2002; "Petsmart's First-Quarter Surge Boosts Yearly Forecast," *St. Louis Post-Dispatch*, June 5, 2002, p. C7; Katherine Hutchison, "Petco Pumps Up 'Millennium' Prototype," *DSN Retailing Today*, Nov. 5, 2001, pp. 3, 46; and Katherine Hutchison, "PetsMart Spruces Up Sales with New Services, Improved Store Format," *DSN Retailing Today*, June 18, 2001, pp. 3, 46.

2. *Statistical Abstract of the United States: 2001*, U.S. Bureau of the Census, Washington, DC, 2001, p. 641.

3. As quoted in Lou Grabowsky, "Globalization: Reshaping the Retail Marketplace," *Retailing Issues Letter*, November 1989, p. 4.

4. *Statistical Abstract of the United States: 1999*, U.S. Bureau of the Census, Washington, DC, 1999, p. 561.

5. For specific ways in which small retailers can remain competitive, see Dale D. Buss, "The Little Guys Fight Back," *Nation's Business*, July 1996, pp. 18–24; and Stanley N. Logan, "The Small Store—a Struggle to Survive," *Retailing Issues Letter*, January 1995, pp. 1–6.

6. *1992 Census of Retail Trade*, Subject Series, U.S. Bureau of the Census, Washington, DC, 1996, p. 2–7; and *1992 Census of Wholesale Trade*, Geographic Area Series—U.S., U.S. Bureau of the Census, Washington, DC, 1995, p. US-9. The 8% figure was calculated by multiplying the 11% representing wholesale operating expenses by 72%, the remainder after the 28% representing retailing operating expenses is subtracted from the 100% representing retail sales (or the consumer's dollar).

7. *www.7-eleven.com/about/history.asp*, accessed on Aug. 26, 2002.

8. "The Plug Gets Pulled on Power Centers," *Building Design & Construction*, April 1997, p. 9; and Ellen Neuborne, "Stores Siphon Shoppers from Regional Malls," *USA Today*, June 13, 1995, p. 1B.

9. Chern Yeh Kwok, "If It's Upscale, Trendy, Affluent and Convenient, It Must Be a Lifestyle Center," *St. Louis Post-Dispatch*, Nov. 12, 2001, p. BP8; and Dean Starkman, "The Mall, without the Haul," *The Wall Street Journal*, July 25, 2001, pp. B1, B8.

10. Eric Slater, "Mall of America Altered Retail Thinking," *The Arizona Republic*, Sept. 16, 2002, p. A7; and Richard Gibson, "Mall of America Considers Expansion That Would More than Double Space," *The Wall Street Journal*, Dec. 30, 1999, p. B8.

11. Dean Starkman, "The Mall Rules," *The Wall Street Journal*, Dec. 18, 2002, pp. B1, B6. Leslie Zganjar, "Mall Makeovers," *The Business Journal*, Feb. 16–22, 2001, pp. 1, 9; and Calmetta Y. Coleman, "Making Malls (Gasp) Convenient," *The Wall Street Journal*, Feb. 8, 2000, pp. B1, B4. The pessimistic forecast was contained in Ellen James Martin, "Mall Blues," *Institutional Investor*, February 1997, p. 119.

12. Chris Penttila, "**Retail**iatory Strike," *Entrepreneur*, December 2002, p. 122; Matt Valley, "The Remalling of America," *National Real Estate Investor*, May 2002, pp. 18–24; John McCloud, "U.S. Shopping Centers Thrive as Hubs of Entertainment," *National Real Estate Investor*, May 1999, pp. 42–55; and Sunil Taneja, "Reinventing the Experience," *Chain Store Age*, November 1998, pp. 153–156.

13. Valley, loc. cit.; and Gabrielle Solomon, "Striking Gold in the Nation's Urban Core," *Fortune*, May 10, 1999, p. 152[J].

14. Mike Troy, "Neighborhood Market Caps Year with Round of New Market Entries," *DSN Retailing Today*, Jan. 27, 2003, pp. 1, 22. *www.walmartstores.com*, accessed Aug. 28, 2002; and Mike Duff, "Home Depot Drops Villager's Hardware for New Concept," *DSN Retailing Today*, Apr. 22, 2002, p. 5.

15. *Statistical Abstract of the United States: 1995*, U.S. Bureau of the Census, Washington, DC, 1995, p. 783.

16. International Franchise Association website, *www.franchise.org/resourcetr/faq*, accessed on Nov. 23, 2002.

17. Bernard Wysocki, Jr., "Start-Up with a Safety Net," Apr. 18, 2001, pp. B1, B6.

18. Peter M. Birkeland, *Franchising Dreams*, University of Chicago Press, Chicago, 2002.

19. Dan Morse and Jeffrey A. Tannenbaum, "Poll on High Success Rate for Franchises Raises Eyebrows," *The Wall Street Journal*, Mar. 17, 1998, p. B2; "Survey Reports 92 Percent of Franchisees Say They Are Successful," *Franchising World*, May/June 1998, pp. 34–36; and Geoff Williams, "Keep Thinking," *Entrepreneur*, September 2002, pp. 100+.

20. Growth areas for franchising are suggested in Dan Morse, "Follow the Demographics, Franchising Experts Advise," *The Wall Street Journal*, Dec. 21, 1999, p. B2; and Dennis Chaplin, "New Partnerships for Franchising," *The Financial Times*, June 22, 1999, p. 2. Factors that have contributed to franchising's growth are outlined in Bruce J. Walker, "Retail Franchising in the 1990s," *Retailing Issues Letter*, January 1991, pp. 1–4.

21. Amy Merrick, Jeffrey A. Trachtenberg, and Ann Zimmerman, "Department Stores Fight an Uphill Battle Just to Stay Relevant," *The Wall Street Journal*, Mar. 12, 2002, pp. A1, A17; and Kevin Helliker, "Montgomery Ward to End 128-Year Run in Retailing," *The Wall Street Journal*, Dec. 29, 2000, p. A3.

22. Brenda Lloyd, "Majors Seek Alternative Retail Formats," *Daily News Record*, Aug. 26, 2002, p. 1; and David Moin, "Differentiate or Die—Retail," *WWD*, June 8, 1998, p. 10.

23. Lloyd, loc. cit.; Anne D'Innocenzio, "Kohl's 'a Terrible Headache,'" *South Bend Tribune*, June 2, 2002, pp. B1, B3; Dave Carpenter, "Sears Forsakes 'Dowdy' Clothes, Buys Lands' End," *St. Louis Post-Dispatch*, May 14, 2002, pp. A1, A9; and Stephanie Anderson Forest, "A Speedy Makeover at Penney's," *Business Week*, Apr. 29, 2002, pp. 92, 94.

24. Lorrie Grant, "Holiday Sales Vital to Kmart Future," *USA Today*, Nov. 8, 2002, pp. 1B, 2B; and Amy Merrick, "Turning Red Ink to Green," *The Wall Street Journal*, Oct. 15, 2002, pp. B1, B3.

25. Jason Roberson, "Supercenter on Horizon; When Wal-Marts Grow Up," *Dayton Daily News*, July 14, 2002, p. F1; and Wendy Zellner, "Look Out, Supermarkets—Wal-Mart Is Hungry," *Business Week*, Sept. 14, 1998, pp. 98, 100.

26. "Sunglass Hut Expands Its Watch Retailing Operations," *Mergers and Acquisitions*, July 2000, pp. 10–11.

27. Gary E. Hoover, "What's in a Store?" *Across the Board*, September 1998, pp. 11+.

28. Glen Creno, "Anthem Outlet Mall Hopes to Buck Trend," *The Arizona Republic*, Nov. 11, 2002, pp. D1, D3; and Ray A. Smith, "Outlet Centers Go Upmarket with Amenities," *The Wall Street Journal*, June 6, 2001, p. B12.

29. Sometimes category killers are referred to as *superstores*. Using this term in this context can create confusion, however, because it is also applied to very large supermarkets. "1982 to 1992: Clubs and Category Killers Arrive on the Scene," *DSN Retailing Today*, August 2002, pp. 21–25; and Babette Morgan, "Borders Enters Big Bookstore Competition Here," *St. Louis Post-Dispatch*, Mar. 20, 1995, p. 3BP.

30. Mike Duff, "IKEA Eyes Aggressive Growth," *DSN Retailing Today*, Jan. 27, 2003, pp. 1, 22. "AutoNation Becomes Largest Retailer," *Automotive News*, Oct. 21, 2002, p. 47; and "Auto News Digest," *Automotive News*, Aug. 19, 2002, p. 32.

31. William M. Bulkeley, "'Category Killers' Go from Lethal to Lame in the Space of a Decade," *The Wall Street Journal*, Mar. 9, 2000, pp. A1, A8.

32. Brian O'Keefe, "Meet Your New Neighborhood Grocer," *Fortune*, May 13, 2002, pp. 93–94, 96.

33. Joel A. Baglole, "Loblaw Supermarkets Add Fitness Clubs to Offerings," *The Wall Street Journal*, Dec. 27, 1999, p. B4; and Len Lewis, "Markets in Motion," *Progressive Grocer*, April 1999, pp. 9–14.

34. *www.mobil.com*, accessed Nov. 24, 2002.

35. David Koenig, "7-Eleven Toasts 75 Years with Free Slurpees," *St. Louis Post-Dispatch*, July 10, 2002, p. C7; "Business Bulletin," *The Wall Street Journal*, Mar. 9, 2000, p. A1; and Joe Dwyer III, "Retail Systems Group Sees Convenience Store of Future," *St. Louis Business Journal*, Feb. 8–14, 1999, p. 32.

36. "Warehouse Format Fetes Milestone and Makeover," *Chain Store Age*, August 2002, pp. 70–72; and Shelly Branch, "Inside the Cult of Costco," *Fortune*, Sept. 6, 1999, pp. 184–186+.

37. This estimate (perhaps better labeled a "guesstimate") of the total annual volume of nonstore retailing represents a sum of the estimates for the five types that are discussed in subsequent sections.

38. The sales figures are drawn from a compilation on the website of the World Federation of Direct Selling Associations: *www.wfdsa.org/statistics*. The estimated number of sales reps is from survey results on the website of the Direct Selling Association: *www.dsa.org/research/numbers.htm*. For seven articles covering various aspects of direct selling, see the *Journal of Marketing Channels*, vol. 2, no. 2, 1992.

39. *www.dsa.org/research/numbers/htm*.

40. Delbert Ellerton, "Joining the Party," *St. Louis Post-Dispatch*, July 21, 2002, pp. G20–G21; and Dennis Berman, "Is the Bell Tolling for Door-to-Door Selling?" *Business Week E.Biz*, Nov. 1, 1999, pp. EB58, EB60.

41. Michael McCarthy and Jayne O'Donnell, "FTC Idea Could Get Telemarketers to Stop Calling," *USA Today*, June 5, 2002, pp. 1B, 2B.

42. Dana Milbank, "Telephone Sales Reps Do Unrewarding Jobs That Few Can Abide," *The Wall Street Journal*, Sept. 23, 1993, pp. A1, A8. The estimated cost of telemarketing fraud is from McCarthy and O'Donnell, loc. cit.

43. Yochi J. Dreazen and Jane Spencer, "Curbing Telemarketers: FTC Moves to Defend Your Dinner Hour," *The Wall Street Journal*, Dec. 19, 2002, pp. D1, D2. Steven C. Bahls and Jane Easter Bahls, "Taking Calls," *Entrepreneur*, January 2002, p. 89.

44. Michael D. Sorkin, "Vending-Machine Sales Slump with the Economy," *St. Louis Post-Dispatch*, July 26, 2002, pp. C1, C2.

45. Michael D. Sorkin, "Wrinkled Bills? No Problem for Today's Vending Machines," *St. Louis Post-Dispatch*, July 21, 2002, pp. A1, A11; Rodney Ho, "Vending Machines Make Change," *The Wall Street Journal*, July 7, 1999, pp. B1, B4; and "Coke Machine Modems Send Distress Signals," *Marketing News*, Oct. 9, 1995, p. 2.

46. Donna Fuscaldo, "No Sale," *The Wall Street Journal*, Dec. 10, 2001, p. R10.

47. "Online Sales in 2001 Generated Profits for More Than Half of All U.S. Retailers Selling Online," *PR Newswire*, June 12, 2002.

48. Ibid.; Heather Green, "Retail: The Cart Is Half Full," *Business Week*, Jan. 13, 2003, pp. 124+. Heather Green, "Lessons of the Cyber Survivors," *Business Week*, Apr. 22, 2002, p. 42; and Greg Wiles, "E-tailers Are Facing Doom, Survey Finds," *St. Louis Post-Dispatch*, Apr. 12, 2000, p. B7.

49. "Online Sales . . . ," loc. cit.; Katy McLaughlin, "Back from the Dead: Buying Groceries Online," *The Wall Street Journal*, Feb. 25, 2003, pp. D1+. and Cristina Lourosa-Ricardo, "Picking the Product," *The Wall Street Journal*, Nov. 22, 1999, pp. R8, R10.

50. Based on figures contained in the *Economic Impact: U.S. Direct & Interactive Marketing Today* study sponsored by the Direct Marketing Association, *www.the-dma.org/cgi/registered/research/libres-ecoimpact2.shtml*, and *www.the-dma.org/cgi/registered/research/charts/dmsales/medium/market.shtml*, accessed Nov. 27, 2002. The estimated sales refer only to direct orders, not to subsequent sales that were based on leads and store traffic generated by telemarketing. Although we considered it separately, telemarketing is sometimes included under the umbrella of direct marketing. Another term often associated with direct marketing, *mail order*, actually refers to the way an order is placed and/or delivered, whereas the types we describe focus on the way contact is made with consumers.

51. Chad Kaydo, "Planting the Seeds of Marketing," *Sales & Marketing Management*, August 1998, p. 73.

52. Bruce Horovitz, "You Ordered It from Horchow? That's Rich!" *USA Today*, Dec. 2, 2002, pp. 1B, 2B; and Steve Jarvis, "A Page-Turner," *Marketing News*, Oct. 8, 2001, p. 3.

53. Jennifer McAlister, "Nonstore: A Growth Slowdown," *Chain Store Age*, Aug. 1, 2002, p. A28; and Sherry Chiger, "Catalog Age 100: Behind the Numbers," Aug. 1, 2002, accessed at *catalogagemag.com*. The number of catalogs is drawn from Calmetta W. Coleman, "Retailers Strive for Shopping Synergy," *The Wall Street Journal*, Dec. 20, 1999, pp. B1, B6.

54. "Nonstore Retailing Gains Favor with Consumers," *Chain Store Age*, August 1999, pp. A29–A32.

55. A theory of institutional change, called the wheel of retailing, was first described in M. P. McNair, "Significant Trends and Developments in the Postwar Period," in A. B. Smith, ed., *Competitive Distribution in a Free, High-Level Economy and Its Implications for the University*, The University of Pittsburgh Press, Pittsburgh, 1958, pp. 17–18.

56. "Target: 40 Years of Retailing," *Home Textiles Today*, May 27, 2002, pp. 16–17; and Gary Strauss, Lorrie Grant, and Michael McCarthy, "Dayton Hudson Hopes Name Change

Hits Bull's-Eye," *USA Today*, Jan. 14, 2000, p. 5B.

57. Ann Grimes, "What's in Store," *The Wall Street Journal*, July 15, 2002, p. R26; Nick Wingfield, "Click and . . . Drive?" *The Wall Street Journal*, July 15, 2002, p. R11; and Robert Berner and Gerry Khermouch, "Retail Reckoning," *Business Week*, Dec. 10, 2001, pp. 72–77.

58. Jay A. Scansaroli and David M. Szymanski, "Who's Minding the Future?" *Retailing Issues Letter*, January 2002, pp. 1–8.

59. Pete Barlas, "Well, Doggone!" *Investor's Business Daily*, Sept. 9, 2002, p. 5. "Petsmart.com," *Catalog Age*, May 2001, p. 47; David Lewis, "As Rivals Perish, PetsMart Increases Online Investment," *Internetweek*, Dec. 4, 2000, p. 106; Pui-Wing Tam and Mylene Mangalindan, "Pets.com's Demise: Too Much Litter, Too Few Funds," *The Wall Street Journal*, Nov. 8, 2000, p. B1; "For Online Pet Stores, It's Dog-Eat-Dog," *Business Week*, Mar. 6, 2000, p. 78.

Chapter 16

1. W.W. Grainger, Inc. website, *investor. grainger.com/downloads/FBpart2.pdf*, accessed Dec. 8, 2002; "Profile— W. W. Grainger, Inc.," *biz.yahoo.com*, accessed June 10, 2002; Dale Buss, "The New Deal," *Sales & Marketing Management*, June 2002, pp. 24–30; "Online Parts Site Gains Popularity," *Industrial Distribution*, December 2001, p. 25; "Junk That Catalog and Get on the Web," *Business Week*, June 26, 2000, p. 28B.

2. Rich Sherman, "Wholesale Distribution—Back in the Chain Game," *Material Handling Management*, April 2001, pp. SCF12–SCF14; J. William Gurley, "Why Online Distributors—Once Written Off—May Thrive," *Fortune*, Sept. 6, 1999, p. 270; and "Making the Switch from Direct to Dealer Sales," *Nation's Business*, July 1996, p. 10.

3. *1992 Census of Wholesale Trade*, Subject Series—Miscellaneous Subjects, U.S. Bureau of the Census, Washington, DC, 1995, p. 42.

4. The terms *merchant wholesaler* and *wholesaler* are sometimes used synonymously with *wholesaling middleman*. This is not accurate, however. *Wholesaling middleman* is the all-inclusive term, covering the three major categories of firms engaged in wholesale trade, whereas *wholesaler* is more restrictive, applying to only one category, namely, merchant wholesaling middlemen.

5. Because manufacturers' sales facilities are owned by manufacturers rather than being truly independent, they could be viewed as a *direct* distribution channel, rather than as distinct middlemen used in indirect distribution. Although this view has merit, we treat manufacturers' sales facilities as a category of middlemen because the Census Bureau does and also because they are separate from manufacturing firms by location, if not by ownership.

6. Donald M. Jackson and Michael F. d'Amico, "Products and Markets Served by Distributors and Agents," *Industrial Marketing Management*, February 1989, p. 28.

7. *1997 Economic Census*, Wholesale Trade, Geographic Area Series, U.S. Census Bureau Washington, DC, 2000, p. United States 7, *www.census.gov/ prod/ec97/97w42-US.pdf*; and corresponding censuses from prior years. For a comprehensive historical analysis of wholesaling, see Robert F. Lusch, Deborah Zizzo, and James M. Kenderine, *Foundations of Wholesaling: A Strategic and Financial Chart Book*, Distribution Research Program, University of Oklahoma, Norman, 1996.

8. Average operating expenses in this paragraph and the following one are based on the *1992 Census of Wholesale Trade*, Geographic Area Series— U.S., U.S. Bureau of the Census, Washington, DC, 1995, p. US-9; and the *1992 Census of Retail Trade*, Subject Series, U.S. Bureau of the Census, Washington, DC, 1996, p. 2–7. The 8% figure was calculated by multiplying the 11% representing wholesale operating expenses by 72%. The remainder after the 28% representing retail operating expenses is subtracted from the 100% representing retail sales (or the consumer's dollar).

9. *www.supervalu.com/home*, accessed on Mar. 14, 2002. For an overview of the challenges faced by a competing full-service wholesaler, the Fleming Companies, see Thaddeus Herrick and Amy Merrick, "End of Kmart Deal Imperils Fleming," *The Wall Street Journal*, Feb. 5, 2003, p. B5.

10. Lara L. Sowinski, "Skechers Puts Its Best Foot Forward," *World Trade*, November 2001, pp. 34–36; and Jeffrey A. Tannenbaum, "Cold War: Amana Refrigeration Fights Tiny Distributor," *The Wall Street Journal*, Feb. 26, 1992, p. B2.

11. Karen Jacobs, "Electronics Distributors Are Reporting Record Profits," *The Wall Street Journal*, July 13,

2000, p. B4. For recommendations on how wholesalers can compete effectively with chains of category-killer stores and warehouse clubs that tend to buy directly from manufacturers, see Robert F. Lusch and Deborah Zizzo, *Competing for Customers*, Distribution Research and Education Foundation, Washington, DC, 1995, pp. 80–108.

12. Faith Keenan, "Logistics Gets a Little Respect," *Business Week E.Biz*, Nov. 20, 2000, pp. EB114–EB115.

13. To gain insight into financial and operating statistics for U.S. and Canadian wholesalers, see Lusch, Zizzo, and Kenderine, loc. cit.

14. Jacobs, loc. cit.

15. *1997 Economic Census*, Wholesale Trade, loc. cit.; and corresponding censuses from prior years.

16. U.S. Economic Census data for 1997, located at *factfinder.census.gov/servlet/ EconSectorServlet?_SectorId=42&_ lang=en*.

17. Ibid.

18. Charles Shaw, "The Rep and the Future—Which Is Now," *Agency Sales*, January 2001, pp. 28–30; and Melissa Campanelli, "Agents of Change," *Sales & Marketing Management*, February 1995, pp. 71–75.

19. U.S. Economic Census data for 1997, loc. cit.

20. The Internet Auction List website, *www.internetauctionlist.com*, accessed on Dec. 8, 2002.

21. Lisa H. Harrington, "Logistics Costs: Good News and Bad," *Transportation & Distribution*, July 2002, p. 9; and Charles Haddad, "A Long Haul to Recovery?" *Business Week*, Jan. 14, 2002, p. 118. The estimate of worldwide spending is from Bill Fahrenwald, "Supply Chain: Managing Logistics for the 21st Century," *Business Week*, Dec. 28, 1998, p. 45. The cost of logistics to an individual firm was estimated by the head of the North American Logistics Association, as reported in Francis J. Quinn, "Logistics' New Customer Focus," *Business Week*, Mar. 10, 1997, p. 54.

22. Jon Bigness, "In Today's Economy, There Is Big Money to Be Made in Logistics," *The Wall Street Journal*, Sept. 6, 1995, pp. A1, A9.

23. Bill McIlvaine, "Going After Value— Logistics Providers Are Offering More Complex Services to Increasingly Demanding Customers," *EBN*, Feb. 25, 2002, pp. 27+. For a discussion of how

firms can achieve a differential advantage through superior physical distribution, see Donald W. Bowersox, John T. Mentzer, and Thomas W. Speh, "Logistics Leverage," *Journal of Business Strategies,* Spring 1995, pp. 36–49.

24. Bruce G. Posner, "Growth Strategies," *Inc.,* December 1989, p. 125.

25. Natalie Hope McDonald, "Under One Roof," *Dealerscope,* July 2002, p. 16; and Faith Keenan, "Warehouse Trouble," *Business Week E.Biz,* Nov. 20, 2000, pp. EB125–EB126. The quote is from George Anders, "Virtual Reality: Web Firms Go on Warehouse Building Boom," *The Wall Street Journal,* Sept. 8, 1999, pp. B1, B8. For more about online category managers, see Bob Sechler, "Behind the Curtain," *The Wall Street Journal,* July 15, 2002, p. R12; and Sandeep Dayal, Thomas D. French, and Vivek Sankaran, "The E-tailer's Secret Weapon," *The McKinsey Quarterly,* 2002, no. 2, no pages given, accessed at *www.mckinseyquarterly.com* on Dec. 8, 2002.

26. Karen Lundergaard, "Bumpy Ride," *The Wall Street Journal,* May 21, 2001, p. R21.

27. Fahrenwald, op. cit., p. 34; and Lundergaard, loc. cit.

28. "Year of the 3PLs," *Journal of Commerce,* Feb. 18, 2002, p. 12; and McIlvaine, loc. cit.

29. The motives for contract logistics are drawn from Quinn, op. cit., p. 69.

30. Alorie Gilbert, "GM Joint Venture to Track In-Transit Inventory," *InformationWeek,* Dec. 18–25, 2000, p. 26; and Daniel Machalaba and Karen Lundegaard, "CNF, GM Plan to Form Logistics Venture to Manage Flow of Vehicle Deliveries," *The Wall Street Journal,* Dec. 14, 2000, p. A6.

31. "Outsourcing of Logistics Is Globally Recognized as a Primary Business Strategy with Significant Value, According to New Study," *Business Wire,* Sept. 30, 2002, no pages given; John Dizard, "The Logistics of Delivering Growth Strategies," *Financial Times,* Jan. 25, 2002, p. 24; McIlvaine, loc. cit.; and "Outsourcing to Drive Growth in Contract Logistics Market," *Logistics Focus,* September 1997, p. 16.

32. Cinda Becker, "An Industry Barometer," *Modern Healthcare,* June 18, 2001, pp. 80–84; and Tom Murray, "Just-in-Time Isn't Just for Show—It Sells," *Sales & Marketing Management,* May 1990, p. 64.

33. McIlvaine, loc. cit.

34. John W. Verity, "Clearing the Cobwebs from the Stockroom," *Business Week,* Oct. 21, 1996, p. 140.

35. Heidi Elliott, "Delivering Competition," *Electronic Business Today,* May 1997, pp. 34–36; and Ronald Henkoff, "Delivering the Goods," *Fortune,* Nov. 28, 1994, pp. 64+.

36. Richard Karpinski, "Wal-Mart Pushes Web EDI," *B to B,* Oct. 14, 2002, p. 15; and Amy Zuckerman, "Should You Do EDI or Internet?" *Transportation & Distribution,* June 1999, pp. 40–42.

37. *www.covisint.com,* accessed on Dec. 10, 2002; David Hannon, "Aircraft Manufacturer Takes E-Buying Bull by the Horns," *Purchasing,* Sept. 20, 2001, pp. S16–S19; and Robert L. Simison, Fara Warner, and Gregory L. White, "Big Three Car Makers Plan Net Exchange," *The Wall Street Journal,* Feb. 28, 2000, pp. A3, A16.

38. Art Raymond, "Is JIT Dead?" *FDM,* January 2002, pp. 30–33. For further discussion of JIT, see Marvin W. Tucker and David A. Davis, "Key Ingredients for Successful Implementation of Just-in-Time: A System for All Business Sizes," *Business Horizons,* May–June 1993, pp. 59–65; and Gary L. Frazier, Robert E. Spekman, and Charles R. O'Neal, "Just-in-Time Exchange Relationships in Industrial Markets," *Journal of Marketing,* October 1988, pp. 52–67.

39. Paulette Thomas, "Electronics Firm Ends Practice Just in Time," *The Wall Street Journal,* Oct. 29, 2002, p. B9; William Atkinson, "Does JIT II Still Work in the Internet Age?" *Purchasing,* Sept. 6, 2001, pp. 41–42; and Fred R. Bleakley, "Some Companies Let Suppliers Work on Site and Even Place Orders," *The Wall Street Journal,* Jan. 13, 1995, pp. A1, A6. Implications of JIT for channels are discussed in Steve McDaniel, Joseph G. Ormsby, and Alicia B. Gresham, "The Effect of JIT on Distributors," *Industrial Marketing Management,* May 1992, pp. 145–149.

40. James A. Cooke, "What's Behind the Curtain?" *Logistics Management,* July 2002, pp. 46–50; Debbie Howell, "12 Hot Issues Facing Mass Retailing—6: Supply-Chain Management," *DSN Retailing Today,* May 20, 2002, p. 33; Jane Hodges, "Supply Chain CEOs," *Chief Executive,* January 2002, pp. 65–66; and Joseph Weber, "Just Get It to the Stores on Time," *Business Week,* Mar. 6, 1995, pp. 66–67.

41. Brian Albright, "CPFR's Secret Benefit," *Frontline Solutions,* October 2002, pp. 30–35.

42. "Vendors Complete CPFR Interoperability Tests," *Transportation & Distribution,* October 2002, p. 18; Carol Sliwa, "CPFR Clamor Persists, but Adoption Remains Slow," *Computerworld,* July 1, 2002, p. 10; Penelope Ody, "Sharing Data Is Just the Beginning of the Process," *Financial Times,* Sept. 1, 1999, p. VI; and John Verity, "Collaborative Forecasting: Vision Quest," *Computerworld,* Nov. 10, 1997, pp. S12–S14.

43. Rod Newing, "Industry Is About to Reinvent Itself," *Financial Times,* Dec. 15, 1999, p. I.

44. "Supply Chain: Keeping It Moving," *Chain Store Age,* October 2002, pp. A26–A28.

45. For case studies about the design of distribution centers by two diverse companies, Jo-Ann Fabrics and Corporate Express, see Mary Aichlmayr, "Design Your Distribution Center Inside Out," *Transportation & Distribution,* November 2002, p. 30.

46. Nintendo's distribution center is detailed in "Nintendo Enhances Performance Conveyor Sortation," *Material Handling Management,* October 2001, pp. 47–51; and Michael Lear-Olimpi, "More than Just Games," *Warehousing Management,* September 1999, pp. 22–30.

47. Robert D. Hof, "What's with All the Warehouses?" *Business Week e.biz,* Nov. 1, 1999, p. EB88.

48. Nick Wingfield, "Iship.com Hopes to Make Shipping Simpler for E-Stores," *The Wall Street Journal,* Sept. 2, 1999, p. B6; and Ken Cottrill, "A Way to Lower Shipping Costs," *Nation's Business,* December 1998, pp. 33–34.

49. For research results indicating that perceptions of different modes vary across members of a buying center, see James H. Martin, James M. Daley, and Henry B. Burdg, "Buying Influences and Perceptions of Transportation Services," *Industrial Marketing Management,* November 1988, pp. 305–314.

50. Charles Haddad, "Transportation: Sharing the Load," *Business Week,* Jan. 13, 2003, pp. 125–126; Philip Siekman, "New Hope for Trucks and Trains," *Fortune,* Dec. 24, 2001, pp. 144[B]+; Robert Johnson, "Record Number of Small Trucking Firms Are Folding," *The Wall Street Journal,* June 25, 2001, pp. A2, A8; and Daniel Machalaba, "Delays and Snafus Grip Rail Freight,"

The Wall Street Journal, May 29, 1998, pp. B1, B2.

51. Daniel Machalaba, "Railroads May Get More Money from Shipping Consumer Goods," *The Wall Street Journal*, Sept. 19, 2002, p. B4; and Sarah Stone, "Intermodal at Global Watershed Point," *Purchasing*, May 20, 1999, pp. 103–105.

52. Joseph Weber, Seth Payne, Kevin Kelly, and Stephanie A. Forest, "The Great Train Turnaround," *Business Week*, Nov. 2, 1992, pp. 56–57; and Sally Solo, "Every Problem Is an Opportunity," *Fortune*, Nov. 16, 1992, p. 93.

53. Anna Wilde Mathews, "More Firms Rely on 'One-Stop' Shipping," *The Wall Street Journal*, Apr. 29, 1997, p. A2.

54. The statement by the Yellow Corp. executive is from Haddad, "A Long Haul to Recovery?" loc. cit. Charles Haddad, "FedEx: Gaining on the Ground," *Business Week*, Dec. 16, 2002, pp. 126+; and "The Man Who's Repackaging UPS," *Business Week*, June 3, 2002, p. 30B.

55. "Grainger Retreats, Closes Material Logic," *Industrial Distribution*, June 2001, pp. 19–20; Kevin Knapp, "Grainger Defends Move; Says OrderZone Equity Swap a Wise Decision," *B to B*, July 3, 2000, p. 6; Buss, loc. cit.; "Online Parts Site Gains Popularity," loc. cit.; and "Junk That Catalog and Get on the Web," loc. cit.

Chapter 17

1. Company brochures; company website, *www.aflac.com*, accessed on January 24, 2002; "Best Marketing Icon: AFLAC's Duck," *Sales & Marketing Management*, September 2001, p. 32; Bethany McLean, "Duck and Coverage," *Fortune*, Aug. 13, 2001, pp. 142–143.

2. Rhea Seymour, "Ideas that Work," *Profit*, June 2002, pp. 66+.

3. Geoff Mulvihill, "Campbell's Earnings Slip Along with Business News," *Associated Press Business News*, Feb. 13, 2002.

4. "The 100 Leaders," *Advertising Age*, Sept. 24, 2001, pp. S19+.

5. This is a condensed version of the definition offered by Don E. Shultz and Heidi F. Shultz, "Transitioning Marketing Communications into the Twenty-First Century," *Journal of Marketing Communications*, March 1998, pp. 9–26.

6. Kate Henry, "Krafting a Retail Return," *Point of Purchase*, March 2002, pp. 22+; Courtney Kane, "Will the

Magic of E.T. Work Again?" *The New York Times*, Mar. 22, 2002, p. 2; Libby Estill, "Promos Phone Home," *Incentive*, February 2002, p. 62.

7. Russ Green, "Making Measuring Simple: Plan Marcomm, Evaluate Criteria," *Advertising Age's Business Marketing*, September 1999, p. 49.

8. Steve Caulk, "Recruiters See Army of Potential at Speedway," *Rocky Mountain News*, July 18, 2002, p. 4B.

9. Stephanie Fagnani, "On the Road Again," *Brandmarketing*, April 2002, p. 12+.

10. "The State of Couponing," *Brandmarketing*, April 2002, pp. 8+.

11. Julie Mitchell, "Customized Clothing Sites Aim for Perfect Shoe Fit," *Investor's Business Daily*, Mar. 6, 2002, pp. 6+.

12. R. Kevin Dietrich, "Columbia, S.C.–Based Insurance Company to Launch TV Ad Campaign Next Year," *The State* (Columbia, SC), Oct. 11, 2001; Bethany McLean, loc. cit.

Chapter 18

1. David Drickhamer, "Peak Performance," *Industry Week*, May 21, 2001; "America's 25 Best Sales Forces," *Sales & Marketing Management*, July 2000, pp. 57–85; "Answer to 'Who Sits Where?' Question, Others Like It Give Johnson Controls a Competitive Edge in Innovation, *PR Newswire*, Jan. 6, 2002; company website, *www.johnsoncontrols.com*, accessed on Apr. 11, 2002; Andy Cohen, "In Control," *Sales & Marketing Management*, June 1999, pp. 32–38; Robert Sherefkin, "GM Seat Deal Would Create New Player," *Automotive News*, Aug. 2, 1999, p. 1; Mark Savage, "Johnson Controls, Lego Team Up with Play Seat," *Milwaukee Journal Sentinel*, Jan. 4, 1999, p. 3; Mark Savage, "Johnson Controls Expects Auto Unit to Grow Rapidly," *Milwaukee Journal Sentinel*, Jan. 28, 1999, p. 1.

2. *Statistical Abstract of the United States, 2001*, 121st ed., U.S. Bureau of the Census, Washington, DC, 2001, pp. 380–382.

3. Several sales job classification schemes have been proposed over the years. See for example: Derek A. Newton, *Sales Force Performance and Turnover*, Marketing Science Institute, Cambridge, MA, 1973.

4. William C. Moncrief, "Selling Activity and Sales Position Taxonomies for

Industrial Salesforces," *Journal of Marketing Research*, August 1986, pp. 261–270.

5. Greg W. Marshall, William C. Moncrief, and Felicia G. Lassk, "The Current State of Sales Force Activity," *Industrial Marketing Management* 28, no. 1, 1998, pp. 87–98.

6. Leonard Berry, *On Great Service*, The Free Press, New York, 1995.

7. Michele Marchetti, "What a Sales Call Costs," *Sales & Marketing Management*, September 2000, pp. 80+. The figures are derived from a study commissioned by *S&MM* magazine and are reported by type of sales approach, industry, size of company, and region.

8. To learn more about how online auctions work visit the website *www.freemarkets.com*. To find out about other auction sites go to *www.internetb2blist.com*.

9. David Prater, "The Third Time's the Charm," *Sales & Marketing Management*, September 2000, pp. 101–104.

10. David Prater, "5 Steps to Salvaging a Failing SFA Program," *Sales & Marketing Management*, September 2000, p. 102.

11. "Get Plugged In," *Sales & Marketing Management*, March 1999, p. 33.

12. For a discussion of efforts to identify characteristics of successful sales people, see Mark W. Johnston and Greg W. Marshall, *Sales Force Management*, McGraw-Hill/Irwin, Burr Ridge, IL, 2003, Chap. 8.

13. Rekha Balu, "Whirlpool Gets Real with Customers," *Fast Company*, December 1999, pp. 74–76.

14. For more details on training practices, see Christine Galea, "2002 Sales Training Survey," *Sales & Marketing Management*, July 2002, pp. 34–37.

15. Recent examples include Becky Meiser, "Show Them the Money," *Sales & Marketing Management*, April 2002, p. 66; Mark McMaster, "The Drive to Strive," *Sales & Marketing Management*, April 2002, p. 67; Christine Galea, "2002 Salary Survey," *Sales & Marketing Management*, May 2002, pp. 32–36.

16. John Taylor, "Program to Examine Kirby Sales Tactics," *Omaha World-Herald*, Apr. 4, 2002, p. 2D.

17. Ted Evanoff, "Concerns Cloud the Future of Web Auto Parts Network," *Indianapolis Star*, June 6, 2001; Ralph Kisiel, "Many Suppliers Still Not Sold in Virtues of Using Covisint," *Crain's*

Detroit Business, Sept. 3, 2001, p. 13; "Covisint Posts Gains in Web-Auction Business," *The Wall Street Journal*, Aug. 13, 2001, p. A6.

Chapter 19

1. *www.almaco.cc/industry.htm*; Hillary Chura and David Goetzl, "Royal Caribbean Christens New Baby Boomer Effort," *Advertising Age*, Jan. 17, 2000; David Goetzl, "Cruise Industry Profits Sink," *Advertising Age*, Nov. 12, 2001; Spud Hilton, "Behind the Building Boom: A Flotilla of New Ships Means New Choices—and Sometimes Bargains," *San Francisco Chronicle*, Apr. 22, 2001, p. T12; Theresa Norton Masek, "Adventure in the Big Apple," *Travel Age West*, Dec. 3, 2001, p. 52; Paula Dobbyn, "U.S. Travel Industry Executives Launch International Marketing Campaign," *Anchorage Daily News*, July 24, 2001; Martha Brannigan, "Cruise Lines Go Online—to Tout Travel Agencies," *The Wall Street Journal*, Aug. 23, 2001, p. B1; Charles Fishman, "Fantastic Voyage," *Fast Company*, March 2000, pp. 170–200; *www.voyageroftheseas.com/index.html*, accessed on Mar. 4, 2002.

2. Laurel Wentz, "P&G Tops $3 Billion Mark in Non–U.S. Ad Spending," *Advertising Age*, Nov. 8, 1999, p. 12.

3. "Revenue per Advertising Dollar Expenditure,"*AdAge.Com*, *www.adage.com/page.cms?pageId=915*, Aug. 31, 2002, pp. 1–4.

4. Suzanne Vranica, "That Guy Showing Off His Hot New Phone May Be a Shill," *The Wall Street Journal*, July 31, 2002, pp. B1+.

5. William M. Bulkeley, "Pass It On," *The Wall Street Journal*, Jan. 14, 2001, pp. R6+.

6. Betty Lui, "Coca-Cola Aims to Recapture the Real Thing," *Financial Times*, Jan. 14, 2000, p. 19; Patti Summerfield, "Global Advertising Isn't Always the Best Strategy," *Strategy*, Apr. 22, 2002, pp. 1+.

7. Christine Bittar, "Advertising Campaigns: Avon Products, Inc." *Brandweek*, Feb. 18, 2002, p. 4.

8. Katarzyna Moreno, "UnbeComing," *Forbes*, June 10, 2002, pp. 151–152; Christine Bittar, "Avon Causes in the Pink: Kissing Cancer Goodbye with Color, Concerts," *Brandweek*, June 3, 2002, p. 26.

9. Examine an issue in your local newspaper. Notice that different retailers feature the same item (supermarkets offer 7-Up at the same time or furniture stores offer the same lounge chair). This is a sign that co-op funds are being used to pay for the ads.

10. Kathryn Kranhold, "Taco Bell Ads to Focus on Food, Not Dog," *The Wall Street Journal*, Oct. 11, 1999, p. B10.

11. "Broadcast TV," *2002 Media Fact Book: A Guide to Competitive Media*, Radio Advertising Bureau, *www.rab.com*, accessed Sept. 1, 2002.

12. "Cable TV," *2002 Media Fact Book: A Guide to Competitive Media*, Radio Advertising Bureau, *www.rab.com*, accessed Sept. 1, 2002.

13. "Direct Mail," *2002 Media Fact Book: A Guide to Competitive Media*, Radio Advertising Bureau, *www.rab.com*, accessed Sept. 1, 2002.

14. Ibid.

15. Ibid.

16. "Newspapers," *2002 Media Fact Book: A Guide to Competitive Media*, Radio Advertising Bureau, *www.rab.com*, accessed Sept. 1, 2002.

17. "Yellow Pages," *2002 Media Fact Book: A Guide to Competitive Media*, Radio Advertising Bureau, *www.rab.com*, accessed Sept. 1, 2002.

18. "Magazines," *2002 Media Fact Book: A Guide to Competitive Media*, Radio Advertising Bureau, *www.rab.com*, accessed Sept. 1, 2002.

19. "Outdoor," *2002 Media Fact Book: A Guide to Competitive Media*, Radio Advertising Bureau, *www.rab.com*, accessed Sept. 1, 2002.

20. Jean Halliday, "Ford Finds E-leads Productive," *Advertising Age*, Jan. 22, 2001, pp. 28+.

21. Nancy J. Wagner, "Picking a Medium for Your Message" *Nations Business*, February 1999, pp. 56–57.

22. Scot Hume, "Trade Promos Devour Half of All Marketing $," *Advertising Age*, Apr. 13, 1992, p. 3.

23. "Introduction: A Half-Full Glass," PROMO 2002 Annual Report, June 1, 2002, accessed on the website *www.promo.com/ar* on Sept. 1, 2002.

24. Libby Estell and Jeanie Casison, "Sampling Sells: A Marketing Strategy that Motivates Consumers," *Incentive*, August 2002, p. 6.

25. Kitty Bean Yancey, "Luxury Hotel Perks Put Guests in the Driver's Seat," *USA Today*, June 7, 2002, p. 9D.

26. Allison Wellmer, "Try It—You'll Like It," *American Demographics*, August 1998, pp. 42+.

27. "Coupons: Wing Clipping," PROMO 2002 Annual Report, June 1, 2002, accessed on the website *www.promo.com/ar* on Sept. 1, 2002.

28. Ibid.

29. "Sponsorship Spending in North America," IEG Sponsorship Report, accessed on the webstie *www.sponsorship.com/learn/northamericaspending*, accessed on Sept. 4, 2002.

30. "Business Bulletin," *The Wall Street Journal*, Feb. 24, 2000, p. A1.

31. Harvey Meyer, "And Now, Some Words about Sponsors," *Nation's Business*, March 1999, pp. 38+.

32. Shawn Doonan and Matthew Garrahan, "Reebok Quits as Olympic Sponsor," *Financial Times*, Dec. 9, 1999, p. 8.

33. William Dunn, "On with the Show," *Marketing Tools*, July/August 1995, pp. 46–55.

34. Martha Brannigan, loc. cit.; "Cruise Week Annual Survey: And How Do You Like the Cruise Lines?" *Cruise Week News*, Jan. 3, 2001, accessed at *www.cruiseweek.com* on July 17, 2001; *www.royalcaribbean.com*.

Chapter 20

1. *www.starbucks.com/aboutus*, accessed June 15, 2002; Michael Krauss, "Starbucks Adds Value by Taking on Wireless," *Marketing News*, Feb. 3, 2003, p. 9; Stanley Holmes, "Planet Starbucks," *Business Week*, Sept. 9, 2002, pp. 100–103+; Shirley Leung, "Starbucks May Indeed Be a Robust Staple," *The Wall Street Journal*, July 26, 2002, p. B4; Greg W. Prince, "Starbucks Pours on Clubby Feeling," *St. Louis Post-Dispatch*, May 28, 2002, pp. C1, C8; Jacqueline Doherty, "Make It Decaf," *Barron's*, May 20, 2002, pp. 20–21; Helen Jung, "Starbucks' Card Smarts," *Business Week*, Mar. 18, 2002, p. 14; George Anders, "Starbucks Brews a New Strategy," *Fast Company*, August 2001, pp. 144–146; Nelson D. Schwartz, "Still Perking after All These Years," *Fortune*, May 24, 1999, pp. 203–210; Tim Moran, "How Starbucks Plunged into Grocery Competition," *Supermarket News*, Apr. 19, 1999, p. 55; David Benady and Lucy Killgren, "Caffeine Hits," *Marketing Week*, May 7, 1998, pp. 28–29; "Making Customers Come Back for More," *For-*

tune, Mar. 16, 1998, p. 156[L]; and Ingrid Abramovitch, "Miracles of Marketing," *Success,* April 1993, pp. 22–27.

2. Many writers and executives use the terms *control* and *evaluation* synonymously. We distinguish between them. To speak of control as only one part of the management process is too restrictive. Rather than being an isolated managerial function, control permeates virtually all other organizational activities. For example, management *controls* its operations through the goals and strategies it selects. Also, the type of organizational structure used in a marketing department determines the degree of *control* over marketing operations.

3. Derek F. Abell, "Strategic Windows," *Journal of Marketing,* July 1978, pp. 21–26.

4. *www.ecompanystore.com.,* accessed Aug. 12, 2002; and Rodney Ho, "Forsaking Sentiment, Small Clients, a Business Grows," *The Wall Street Journal,* Jan. 3, 2000, pp. A11, A13.

5. *www.davelennox.com,* accessed Aug. 12, 2002.

6. Danny Fortson, "Planet Hollywood Goes Bankrupt Again," *The Daily Deal,* Oct. 19, 2001, no pages given; and Richard Gibson, "Fame Proves Fleeting at Planet Hollywood as Fans Avoid Reruns," *The Wall Street Journal,* Oct. 7, 1998, pp. A1, A6.

7. The survey results are reported in Ellen Neuborne, "Mad Ave: A Star Is Reborn," *Business Week,* July 26, 1999, pp. 54–56+. For more on changing attitudes toward strategic planning, see John A. Byrne, "Strategic Planning," *Business Week,* Aug. 26, 1996, pp. 46–52.

8. C. K. Prahalad, "Changes in the Competitive Battlefield," *Financial Times—FT.com,* Aug. 7, 2002, no pages given.

9. Michael A. O'Neil, "A Simple, Effective Approach to the Strategic Planning Process," *Supervision,* March 2001, pp. 3–5.

10. Dan Morse, "Many Small Businesses Don't Devote Time to Planning," *The Wall Street Journal,* Sept. 7, 1999, p. B2; and *Pulse of the Middle Market—1990,* BDO Seidman, New York, 1990, pp. 12–13.

11. For one approach to competitive analysis, see Bruce H. Clark, "Managing Competitive Interactions," *Marketing Management,* Fall/Winter 1998, pp. 8–20. For more about the consultants' recommended reflection process, see Michael Hammer and Steven A. Stanton, "The Power of Reflection," *Fortune,* Nov. 24, 1997, pp. 291+.

12. For more details, see Lili Vianello, "S.W.O.T. Analysis: Plan for Your Business to Be Successful," *Columbia Business Times,* Aug. 3–16, 2002, p. 36.

13. *www.radioshackcorporation.com,* accessed Aug. 13, 2002; and Stephanie Anderson Forest, "Cable, Phone, Internet . . . Who Ya Gonna Call?" *Business Week,* Mar. 1, 1999, pp. 64, 66.

14. Malcolm H. B. McDonald, "Ten Barriers to Marketing Planning," *The Journal of Business and Industrial Marketing,* Winter 1992, p. 15.

15. Joel A. Baglole, "Cough Syrup Touts 'Awful' Taste in U.S.," *The Wall Street Journal,* Dec. 15, 1999, p. B10.

16. Christopher Wanjek, "It's Not Easy Being Clean," *The Washington Post,* Oct. 3, 2000, p. Z6; and "Stacy Kravetz, "Dry Cleaners' New Wrinkle: Going Green," *The Wall Street Journal,* June 3, 1998, pp. B1, B15.

17. Differential advantage in the context of services and retail industries is examined in, respectively, Sundar G. Bharadwaj, P. Rajan Varadarajan, and John Fahy, "Sustainable Competitive Advantage in Service Industries: A Conceptual Model and Research Proposition," *Journal of Marketing,* October 1993, pp. 83–99; and Norman H. McMillan, "EST Retailing: How to Stay out of the Black Hole," *International Trends in Retailing,* Winter 1993, pp. 60–75. Nordstrom's financial results were obtained from *about.nordstrom.com/aboutus/investor,* accessed Dec. 22, 2002.

18. The information about relative size was provided in an e-mail message by Dennis O'Reilly, treasurer of Midwest Express Airlines, on Dec. 20, 2002. David Leonhardt, "Big Airlines Should Follow Midwest's Recipe," *Business Week,* June 28, 1999, p. 40.

19. Marcia Stepanek, "How Fast Is Net Fast?" *Business Week E.Biz,* Nov. 1, 1999, pp. EB52–EB54. An excellent source of information on how various companies prepare their marketing plans is Howard Sutton, *The Marketing Plan,* The Conference Board, New York, 1990.

20. One of many guidebooks for preparing an annual marketing plan is Roman G. Hiebing, Jr., and Scott W. Cooper, *The Successful Marketing Plan,* brief edition, NTC/Contemporary Publishing Group, Lincolnwood, IL, 2000.

21. See H. Igor Ansoff, *The New Corporate Strategy,* Wiley, New York, 1988, pp. 82–85. In this update discussion, Ansoff substituted the term *mission* for *market* in the matrix. We still prefer, and thus retain, the original term.

22. Jeff Bailey, "Reliance on a Few Big Customers Holds Risks," *The Wall Street Journal,* July 30, 2002, p. B5; and Martha Brannigan, "Cruise Lines Look to the Land to Get Boomers on Board," *The Wall Street Journal,* Dec. 6, 1999, p. B4.

23. Julia Boorstin, "Why Is Wrigley So Wrapped Up?" *Fortune,* March 3, 2003, pp. 133–134. Janet Ginsburg, "Not the Flavor of the Month," *Business Week,* Mar. 20, 2000, p. 128; and "Targeting Customer Needs Unveils New Opportunities," *Nation's Business,* September 1998, p. 12.

24. Bill Virgin, "Straying Too Far Can Make Diversification Fail," *The Seattle Post-Intelligencer,* Aug. 27, 2001, p. E1.

25. *www.lizclaiborne.com/lizinc/careers/alt_corpinfo?brands.asp,* accessed on Aug. 13, 2002; and Teri Agins, "Claiborne Patches Together an Empire," *The Wall Street Journal,* Feb. 2, 2000, pp. B1, B4.

26. Rajesh K. Chandy and Gerard J. Tellis, "Organizing for Radical Product Innovation: The Overlooked Role of Willingness to Cannibalize," *Journal of Marketing Research,* November 1998, pp. 474+.

27. *The Experience Curve Reviewed: IV. The Growth Share Matrix of the Product Portfolio,* Boston Consulting Group, Boston, 1973.

28. Jay Palmer, "Taking Off the White Gloves," *Barron's,* Apr. 1, 2002, p. 19.

29. Sara Ellison and Suzanne Vranica, "Campbell Warms Campaign to Heal Soup Sales," *The Wall Street Journal,* Dec. 26, 2002, p. A10. William C. Symonds, "The Big Trim at Gillette," *Business Week,* Nov. 8, 1999, p. 42.

30. Martin Peers, "A New Pitch at Blockbuster: Buy This Movie," *The Wall Street Journal,* Nov. 1, 2002, pp. B1, B4; and Stephanie Anderson Forest, "Blockbuster: The Sequel," *Business Week,* Sept. 16, 2002, pp. 52–53.

31. Nick Roskelly, "Balancing Act: Pursuing New Product Launches While Supporting Core Brands," *Beverage Industry,* October 2002, pp. 96+; and Kenneth

Hein, "New Agers Steal Cola's Hearts," *Brandweek,* June 4, 2001, p. S34.

32. Discussed in Derek F. Abell and John S. Hammond, *Strategic Marketing Planning,* Prentice Hall, Englewood Cliffs, N.J., 1979.

33. Michael Ryan, "Kodak's Big Moment— From Technology Laggard to Innovator Again," *Ziff Davis Smart Business for the New Economy,* July 1, 2001, p. 79; and Lee Gomes, "Silicon Graphics Sets Designs to Ride High-End Computer Line to Turnaround," *The Wall Street Journal,* Nov. 15, 1999, p. B6.

34. Ryan, loc. cit.; and Laurie Freeman, "Shooting for Share," *Supermarket Business,* February 1999, pp. 47+.

35. "Dwindling Ranks," *Automotive News,* Apr. 30, 2001, p. 4; and Kathleen Kerwin, "Reviving GM," *Business Week,* Feb. 1, 1999, pp. 114–120, 122.

36. Paul Lukas, "The Ghastliest Product Launches," *Fortune,* Mar. 16, 1998, p. 44.

37. Bob Garrison, "Building on Success," *Refrigerated & Frozen Foods,* April 2002, pp. 20+; Andrew Edgecliffe-Johnson, "Kraft Looks for More Purchases," *Financial Times—FT.com,* Sept. 3, 2001, no pages given; and Steven Lipin and Yumiko Ono, "Philip Morris's Bakery Unit Is for Sale; Asking Price Is Put at about $1 Billion," *The Wall Street Journal,* July 17, 1995, p. A3.

38. Improvements worth considering are suggested in the following articles: R. A. Proctor and J. S. Hassard, "Towards a New Model for Product Portfolio Analysis," *Management Decision,* vol. 28, no. 3, 1990, pp. 14–17; and Rick Brown, "Making the Product Portfolio a Basis for Action," *Long Range Planning,* February 1991, pp. 102–110.

39. Michael Treacy and Fred Wiersema, "How Market Leaders Keep Their Edge," *Fortune,* Feb. 6, 1995, pp. 88–90+; their ideas are fully described in Michael Treacy and Fred Wiersema, *The Discipline of Market Leaders,* Addison-Wesley, Boston, 1995.

40. For more about Nike's comeback, see Stanley Holmes, "How Nike Got Its Game Back," *Business Week,* Nov. 4, 2002, pp. 129+; and Chuck Stogel, "It's Easier Being Green (If You're Nike)," *Brandweek,* Jan. 28, 2002, pp. 116–118+. For an overview of the strategic shift Jupiter Networks Inc. had to make, see Ben Elgin, "Why Jupiter Must Branch Out," *Business Week,* July 1, 2002, pp. 95–96.

41. Business description of Starbucks Corporation from Multex.com, accessed June 15, 2002; "Starbucks, Pepsi Introduce New Ready-to-Drink Espresso," *Packaging Digest,* May 2002, p. 2; Mark Pendergrast, "Starbucks Goes to Europe . . . with Humility and Respect," *The Wall Street Journal,* Apr. 9, 2002, p. B16; "Doubleshot of Starbucks' Love," *Beverage World,* Mar. 15, 2002, p. 76; Leung, loc. cit.; and Holmes, loc. cit.

Chapter 21

1. Inditex website, *www.inditex.com,* accessed June 15, 2002; Miguel Helft, "Fashion Fast Forward," *Business 2.0,* May 2002, pp. 61–66; Richard Heller, "Galician Beauty," *Forbes,* May 28, 2001, pp. 98+; Benjamin Jones, "Madrid: Zara Pioneers Fashion on Demand," *Europe,* September 2001, pp. 43–44; William Echikson, "The Fashion Cycle Hits High Gear," *Business Week,* Sept. 18, 2000, p. EB66; Jane M. Folpe, "Zara Has a Made-to-Order Plan for Success," *Fortune,* Sept. 4, 2000, p. 80; and William Echikson, "The Mark of Zara," *Business Week,* May 29, 2000, pp. 98–99.

2. Charles H. Noble and Michael P. Mokwa, "Implementing Marketing Strategies: Developing and Testing a Managerial Theory," *Journal of Marketing,* October 1999, pp. 57–73.

3. David Lewis, "Omni Maximizes Revenue," *Internet Week,* Nov. 26, 2001, p. 54; and Neal Templin, "Your Room Costs $250 . . . No! $200 . . . No . . .," *The Wall Street Journal,* May 5, 1999, pp. B1, B16.

4. Ram Charan and Geoffrey Colvin, "Why CEOs Fail," *Fortune,* June 21, 1999, pp. 69–72+.

5. Three developments that have affected organizational structures and, more broadly, the role of management are outlined in Ray Suutari, "Organizing for the New Economy," *CMA Management,* April 2001, pp. 12–13. For a discussion of two organizational forms—a marketing exchange company and a marketing coalition company—that are designed to cope with complex and dynamic business environments, see Ravi S. Achrol, "Evolution of the Marketing Organization: New Forms for Turbulent Environments," *Journal of Marketing,* October 1991, pp. 77–93.

6. For examples, see Brenda Paik Sunoo, "Redesigning the Company at Donna Karan," *Workforce,* July 1998, pp. 27+; and John Hechinger, "Kodak to Reorga-

nize Its Business Again," *The Wall Street Journal,* Nov. 15, 2001, p. B12.

7. Seven elements of a horizontal organization are described in John A. Byrne, "The Horizontal Corporation," *Business Week,* Dec. 20, 1993, pp. 76–81.

8. Dana James, "Lighting the Way," *Marketing News,* Apr. 1, 2002, pp. 1, 11; and Evelyn Theiss, "Research Shows Good Service Is Getting Harder to Find," *St. Louis Post-Dispatch,* June 28, 1999, p. BP22.

9. "Cross-Functional Teams Flourish amid Today's Purchasing Evolution," *Supplier Selection & Management Report,* March 2002, no pages given; Avan R. Jassawalla and Hemant C. Sashittal, "Building Collaborative Cross-Functional New Product Teams," *The Academy of Management Executive,* August 1999, p. 50; and Donald Gerwin, "Team Empowerment in New Product Development," *Business Horizons,* July–August 1999, pp. 29+.

10. The Modicon example is from Byrne, op. cit., p. 80.

11. Melissa Campanelli, "A New Focus," *Sales & Marketing Management,* September 1995, pp. 56, 58.

12. Hechinger, loc. cit.; and Rick Brooks, "FDX Plans Restructuring of Sales Force," *The Wall Street Journal,* Jan. 17, 2000, p. A3.

13. Don E. Schultz, "Structural Straitjackets Stifle Integrated Success," *Marketing News,* Mar. 1, 1999, p. 8.

14. Jennifer Hamilton and Ross D. Petty, "The European Union's Consumer Guarantees Directive," *Journal of Public Policy & Marketing,* Fall 2001, pp. 289–296; and Mike Smith, "Accord Reached on Product Guarantees," *The Financial Times,* Mar. 23, 1999, p. 2.

15. Jayne O'Donnell, "Cosco's History Reads Like Recipe for Recalls," *USA Today,* Apr. 4, 2001, pp. 1B, 3B.

16. J. Joseph Muller, "Three Key Issues in Consideration of Product Liability," *Mid-Missouri Business Journal,* Feb. 16–29, 1995, p. 22.

17. For examples, see Karen Padley, "Ford Wins Appeal of Class Action," *National Post,* May 3, 2002, p. FP16; and Margaret Cronin Fisk, "Suit Probes Acne Drug's Possible Link to Depression," *Miami Daily Business Review,* Apr. 26, 2002, p. A12. The professor's quote was contained in Dan Ackman, "Asbestos Settlements Breaking Out

All Over," *Forbes.com*, Dec. 12, 2002, no pages given.

18. "Big Tobacco Cut Down to Size, Yet Again," *Economist.com/Global Agenda*, Mar. 27, 2002, no pages given; and "Tobacco Takes a Hit," *Time*, July 19, 1999, p. 34.

19. "Curbs on Product Liability Sought," *Chemical Market Reporter*, Aug. 16, 1999, p. 29. For the description of a simulation model of product liability costs, see Conway Lackman and John Lanasa, "Product Liability Cost as a Marketing Tool," *Industrial Marketing Management*, May 1993, pp. 149–154.

20. "Gov't to Encourage Industry Bodies to Set Up PL Centers," *The Korea Herald*, June 15, 2002, no pages given; and Carolyn Aldred, "Suit to Test Europe's Tort Rules," *Business Insurance*, Mar. 18, 2002, pp. 27+.

21. "Group Takes Note of 'Ridiculous' Warning Labels," *Columbia Daily Tribune*, Jan. 18, 2001, p. 6B; and "Seen 'n Heard," *Compliance Reporter*, Nov. 8, 1999, p. 8.

22. Jane Spencer, "Guaranteed to Last a Whole 90 Days," *The Wall Street Journal*, July 16, 2002, pp. D1, D5.

23. Spencer, loc. cit.; Larry Armstrong, "And Now, a Luxury Hyundai," *Business Week*, Feb. 26, 2001, p. 33; and Jerry Edgerton, "Promises, Promises," *Money*, February 1999, p. 173.

24. For an example of an entire promotional campaign based on a service guarantee, see Stephanie Paterik, "Sheraton Plans to Pay Guests for Bad Service," *The Wall Street Journal*, Sept. 6, 2002, pp. B1, B4. For research in the context of services that recommends money-back guarantees, see Glenn B. Voss, A. Parasuraman, and Dhruv Grewal, "The Roles of Price, Performance, and Expectations in Determining Satisfaction in Service Exchanges," *Journal of Marketing*, October 1998, pp. 46+.

25. Dirk Van den Poel and Joseph Leunis, "Consumer Acceptance of the Internet as a Channel of Distribution," *Journal of Business Research*, July 1999, pp. 249–256.

26. Jane Spencer, "The Point of No Return," *The Wall Street Journal*, May 14, 2002, pp. D1, D2; and Ann Zimmerman, "Keep It Simple," *The Wall Street Journal*, Apr. 15, 2002, p. R10.

27. Spencer, "The Point of No Return," loc. cit.

28. "Business Bulletin," *The Wall Street Journal*, Jan. 20, 2000, p. A1; and Lor-

rie Grant, "Online Returns a Hassle, Even with a Storefront," *USA Today*, Oct. 28, 1999, p. 3B.

29. Information about annual number of calls handled was provided by Otis Customer Care via e-mail, December 16, 2002.

30. Jagdish N. Sheth and Rajendra S. Sisodia, "Feeling the Heat," *Marketing Management*, Fall 1995, p. 22; and Scott McCartney, "PC Makers Cure Customer Ills with Virtual House Calls," *The Wall Street Journal*, Mar. 21, 1995, p. B10.

31. David Ho, "Home-Improvement Headaches Rank as the No. 1 Complaint among Consumers," *St. Louis Post-Dispatch*, Nov. 26, 2002, pp. C1, C2; and William Flannery, "Too Many Firms Have Workers Who Think the Customer Isn't Always Right. Training Could Help," *St. Louis Post-Dispatch*, Apr. 18, 1999, pp. E1+. The quote is from Stephen W. Brown, "Service Recovery through IT," *Marketing Management*, Fall 1997, p. 25.

32. "Business Bulletin," *The Wall Street Journal*, Feb. 3, 2000, p. A1. For useful recommendations, see Mary C. Gilly and Richard W. Hansen, "Consumer Complaint Handling as a Strategic Marketing Tool," *The Journal of Product and Brand Management*, Summer 1992, pp. 5–16; and Roland T. Rust, Bala Subramanian, and Mark Wells, "Making Complaints a Management Tool," *Marketing Management*, vol. 1, no. 3, 1992, pp. 41–45.

33. Gary Gentile, "Disney Finds a Way to Make Profits on the Web," *St. Louis Post-Dispatch*, Nov. 12, 2002, pp. C1, C8.

34. For an overview of this technique, see Dennis W. Means, "A Marketing Audit Checklist," *Agency Sales Magazine*, October 1998, pp. 54+.

35. For guidelines about marketing audits, see "How to Kick Off or Pump Up Your Firm's Marketing Plan," *Accounting Office Management & Administration Report*, February 2002, no pages given; and Bill Merrick, "Marketing Committees Evolve as CUs Grow," *Credit Union Magazine*, December 2001, no pages given. The quote is from Dale Terry, "How Does Your Bank's Marketing Size Up?" *Bank Marketing*, January 1995, pp. 53–58.

36. For the original discussion of the marketing audit, see Abe Schuchman, "The Marketing Audit: Its Nature, Purpose, and Problems," in *Analyzing and Improving Marketing Performance: "Marketing Audits" in Theory and Practice*,

American Management Association, New York, Management Report no. 32, 1959, p. 14.

37. Professor Ravi Dhar, as quoted in Diane Brady, "Why Service Stinks," *Business Week*, Oct. 23, 2000, pp. 118–122+.

38. The quote is from Daniel M. Hrisak, "Survey Respondents: Revenue Recognition Has Highest Priority," *Managing the General Ledger*, March 2001, p. 3. Also see John A. Weber, "Managing the Marketing Budget in a Cost-Constrained Environment," *Industrial Marketing Management*, November 2002, pp. 705–717.

39. For a method of determining the value of customers, see Roger Connell, "Calculating the Contribution of Customers—a Practical Approach," *Journal of Targeting, Measurement and Analysis*, September 2002, pp. 13+. For more about examining both sales volume and costs and their links to strategy, see Gordon A. Wyner, "Customer Profitability," *Marketing Management*, Winter 1999, pp. 8–9.

40. Will Morton, "The Unprofitable Customers," *The Wall Street Journal*, Oct. 28, 2002, p. R7.

41. "Stefan Persson: Hennes & Mauritz," *Business Week*, Jan. 13, 2003, p. 63. Inditex website, loc. cit.; Helft, loc. cit.; Heller, loc. cit.; Jones, loc. cit.; Echikson, "The Fashion Cycle Hits High Gear," loc. cit.; Folpe, loc. cit.; and Echikson, "The Mark of Zara," loc. cit.

Chapter 22

1. Jennifer Godwin, "Partings and Performance," *Forbes*, Nov. 27, 2000, *www.forbes.com*; "Maritz Marketing Research, Inc., Launches eQuest," *PR Newswire*, Sept. 28, 2000; company press releases; *www.maritz.com*, accessed on Feb. 14, 2002.

2. The structure for this discussion of electronic networking is based on Ravi Kalakota, Ralph A. Oliva, and Bob Donath, "Move Over E-Commerce," *Marketing Management*, Fall 1999, pp. 22–31.

3. "Online Sales in 2001 Generated Profits for More than Half of All U.S. Retailers Selling Online," news release of Shop.org a division of the National Retail Federation, *www.shop.org/press*, accessed Oct. 7, 2002.

4. Alorie Gilbert, "New Trend Rising after B2B Setbacks," CNET.com, Tech News, *www.news.com.com*, accessed Oct. 7, 2002.

5. Paul Davidson, "Manufacturers Must Alter Strategies for Retail Success," *USA Today*, June 4, 1999, p. 1B.

6. William Hoffman, Jennifer Keedy, and Karl Roberts, "The Unexpected Return of B2B," *McKinsey Quarterly*, no. 3, 2002, accessed at *www.mckinseyquarterly.com*, Oct. 7, 2002.

7. Statement of the chairman of the board, at *www.ibm.com/lvg/* accessed on Oct. 9, 2002.

8. Catharine P. Taylor and Jeff Howe, "Web Disconnect," *Adweek*, Sept. 9, 2002, pp. 22+.

9. Otis Port, "Customers Move into the Driver's Seat," *Business Week*, Oct. 4, 1999, pp. 103–106.

10. Beth Cox, "The E-Commerce Evolution," ecommerce-guide.com, Apr. 25, 2002, accessed at *www.ecommerce.internet.com/news* on Oct. 10, 2002; "Study Reveals Previously Unmeasured Characteristics of U.S. Online Hispanic Population," HispanicAd.com, May 13, 2002, accessed at *www.hispanicad.com/cgi-bin/news* on Oct. 10, 2002.

11. Susan Gregory Thomas, "Getting to Know You.Com," *U.S. News & World Report*, Nov. 15, 1999, pp. 102–112.

12. Paul Davidson, "Manufacturers Squeeze the Hands that Sells Them," *USA Today*, June 4, 1999, p. 1B.

13. Amway Joins Rush to the Net with On-line Store," *St. Louis Post-Dispatch*, Mar. 3, 1999, p. C7.

14. "Can e-Tailers Find Fulfillment?" July 28, 2002, from Knowledge@Wharton, CNET News.com, accessed at *www.news.com* on Oct. 12, 2002.

15. Tim Lemke, "Pop-Ups Strike Out with Internet Advertisers," *The Washington Times*, Sept. 9, 2002, accessed at EBSCO Host, item number 2W60148723187 on Oct. 10, 2002.

16. Dana James, "Linked for Success," *Marketing News*, Jan. 3, 2000, p. 3.

17. Heather Green and Linda Himelstein, "To the Victor Belong the Ads," *Business Week*, Oct. 4, 1999, p. 39; Tom Spring, "Web Ad Explosion," *PC World*, September 2002, pp. 24+.

18. Matt Richtel, "Credit Card Theft Is Thriving Online as Global Market," *The New York Times*, May 13, 2002, p. A1.

19. Ann Grimes, "What's in Store," *The Wall Street Journal*, July 15, 2002, p. R6.

20. Jeff Gelles, "Computer Users Urged to Take Security Precautions," *The Philadelphia Enquirer*, Oct. 8, 2002, accessed at EBSCO Host, item number 2W73374016197 on Oct. 12, 2002.

21. Peter S. Goodman and Mike Musgrove, "China Blocks Web Search Engines," *The Washington Post*, Sept. 12, 2002, p. E1.

22. John Borland, "Europe Takes a Front Seat in Net Rulemaking," CNET News.com, Jan. 15, 2002, accessed at *www.news.com*, Oct. 7, 2002.

23. Abaigail Goldman, "Father of Amazon.com Says e-Tail Will Never Replace Mall," *The Idaho Statesman*, Dec. 27, 1999, p. 6B.

24. "Maritz, Inc., Puts 70 Years of Experience on the Internet with Introduction of eMaritz," *PR Newswire*, July 2, 2001; Peter Shinkle, "Maritz Offers Online Incentive Programs," *St. Louis Post-Dispatch*, July 4, 2001, p. C1; Rick Desloge, "eMaritz Incentives Aim for Small, Mid-Size Firms," *St. Louis Post-Dispatch*, June 22, 2001, p. 3.

Photo Credits

MAYER Rhomboid and Design and WEINERMOBILE are trademarks of Kraft Foods, Inc. and are used with permission.

p. 491 2002 Samsung Electronics America, Inc.

p. 494 Courtesy Boise Office Solutions

p. 496 Courtesy Volkswagen of America

Chapter 18

p. 509 Courtesy Johnson Controls, Inc.

p. 513 Netkey, Inc.

p. 517 Fisher-Thatcher/Getty Images

p. 518 ©R.W. Jones/Corbis

p. 525 ©Tom and Dee Ann McCarthy/Corbis Stock Market

Chapter 19

p. 532 ©AFP/Corbis

p. 539 Courtesy BMW of North America, LLC, used with permission

p. 541 ©Shell Oil Products U.S. and Motiva Enterprises LLC

p. 548 The Gillette Company

p. 549 Courtesy Roper-Starch Worldwide, ©Nestle USA

p. 554 Courtesy Alliance, A Rock-Tenn Company

Chapter 20

p. 568 ©AFP/Corbis

p. 571 Courtesy eCompanystore.com

p. 572 Courtesy Lennox Industries, Inc.

p. 577 Courtesy Windjammer Barefoot Cruises Ltd.

p. 581 ©2002, by The McGraw-Hill Companies, Inc.

p. 582 ©2002 Garmin Ltd.

Chapter 21

p. 592 Jessica Wecker

p. 595 Courtesy Principal Financial Services, Inc.

p. 600 Courtesy Hyundai Motor America

p. 604 Courtesy Liveperson, Inc.

Chapter 22

p. 620 Courtesy Maritz, Inc.

p. 625 Text and artwork copyright ©2002 by Yahoo! Inc. All rights reserved. Yahoo! and the Yahoo! logo are trademarks of Yahoo! Inc.

p. 628 Courtesy RedEnvelope, Inc.

p. 630 Courtesy PriceFarmer.com

p. 632 Courtesy Nike.com

p. 635 Courtesy Usbid, Inc.

Glossary

A

accessory equipment Business goods that have substantial value and are used in an organization's operations.

activity indicator of buying power A market factor that is related to sales and expenditures and serves as an indirect estimate of purchasing power.

administered vertical marketing system An arrangement that coordinates distribution activities through the market and/or economic power of one channel member or the shared power of two channel members.

adoption process The set of successive decisions an individual or organization makes before accepting an innovation.

adoption rate The speed or ease with which a new product is accepted.

advertising All activities involved in presenting to an audience a nonpersonal, sponsor-identified, paid-for message about a product or an organization.

advertising agency An independent company that provides specialized advertising services and may also offer more general marketing assistance.

advertising campaign All the tasks involved in transforming a theme into a coordinated advertising program to accomplish a specific goal for a product or brand.

advertising media The communications vehicles (such as newspapers, radio, and television) that carry advertising as well as other information and entertainment.

agent middleman A firm that never actually takes title to (i.e., owns) products it helps market but does arrange the transfer of title.

agent wholesaling middleman An independent firm that engages primarily in wholesaling by actively negotiating the sale or purchase of products on behalf of other firms but does not take title to the products being distributed.

agribusiness Farms, food-processing firms, and other large-scale farming-related enterprises.

AIDA A sequence of steps in various forms of promotion, notably personal selling and advertising, consisting of attracting Attention, holding Interest, arousing Desire, and generating buyer Action.

annual marketing plan A written document that presents the master blueprint for a year's marketing activity for a specified organizational division or major product.

Asia-Pacific Economic Cooperation forum (APEC) A trade pact among 18 Pacific Rim nations that seeks the elimination of major trade barriers.

Association of Southeast Asian Nations (ASEAN) An agreement creating a free-trade zone among Brunei, Indonesia, Malaysia, the Philippines, Singapore, and Thailand.

attitude A learned predisposition to respond to an object or class of objects in a consistently favorable or unfavorable way.

auction company An agent wholesaling middleman that helps assembled buyers and sellers complete their transactions by providing auctioneers who do the selling and physical facilities for displaying the sellers' products.

automatic vending A form of nonstore retailing where the products are sold through a machine with no personal contact between the buyer and seller.

average fixed cost The total fixed cost divided by the number of units produced.

average fixed cost curve A graph of average fixed cost levels showing a decline as output increases because the total of the fixed costs is spread over an increasing number of units.

average revenue The unit price at a given level of unit sales. It is calculated by dividing total revenue by the number of units sold.

average total cost The total cost divided by the number of units produced.

average total cost curve A graph of average total costs, which starts high, then declines to its lowest point, reflecting optimum output with respect to total costs (not variable costs), and then rises because of diminishing returns.

average variable cost The total variable cost divided by the number of units produced.

average variable cost curve A graph of average variable cost levels, which starts high, then declines to its lowest point, reflecting optimum output with respect to variable costs (not total costs), and then rises.

B

baby boomers Americans born during the 10 years following World War II.

balance of payments The accounting record of all of a country's transactions with all the other nations of the world.

banner ad A boxed-in promotional message often appearing at the top of a Web page.

barter The exchange of goods and/or services for other products.

base price The price of one unit of the product at its point of production or resale. Same as *list price*.

BCG matrix See *Boston Consulting Group (BCG) matrix*.

behavioral segmentation Market segmentation based on consumers' product-related behavior, typically the benefits desired from a product and the rate at which the consumer uses the product.

Boston Consulting Group (BCG) matrix A strategic planning model that classifies strategic business units or major products according to market shares and growth rates.

boycott A refusal to buy products from a particular company or country.

brand A name and/or mark intended to identify and differentiate the product of one seller or a group of sellers.

brand equity The value a brand adds to a product.

brand label The application of the brand name alone to a product or package.

brand licensing See *trademark licensing*.

brand manager See *product manager*.

brand mark The part of a brand that appears in the form of a symbol, design, or distinctive color or type of lettering.

brand name The part of a brand that can be vocalized—words, letters, and/or numbers.

breadth The number of product lines offered for sale by a firm.

break-even analysis A method of calculating the level of output at which total revenue equals total costs, assuming a certain selling price.

break-even point The level of output at which total revenue equals total costs, assuming a certain selling price.

bribes Something given in exchange for services or protection, it is common in foreign markets.

broker An agent wholesaling middleman that brings buyers and sellers together and provides market information to either party and that ordinarily neither physically handles products being distributed nor works on a continuing basis with those sellers or buyers.

browser A program that enables its users to access electronic documents included in the World Wide Web on the Internet.

business analysis One stage in the new-product development process, consisting of several steps to expand a surviving idea into a concrete business proposal.

business cycle The three recurring stages in an economy, typically prosperity, recession, and recovery.

business format franchising An agreement, covering an entire method (or format) for operating a business, under which a successful business sells the right to operate the same business in different geographic areas.

business market The total of all business users.

business marketer A firm performing the activity of marketing goods and services.

business marketing The marketing of goods and services to business users, as contrasted to ultimate consumers.

business product A product that is intended for purchase and resale or for purchase and use in producing other products or for providing services in an organization.

business services market The total set that deals in data and information such as marketing research firms, ad agencies, public utilities, and financial, insurance, legal, or real estate firms.

business-to-business advertising Advertising that is directed at businesses.

business-to-consumer advertising *See consumer advertising.*

business users Business, industrial, or institutional organizations that buy goods or services to use in their own organizations, to resell, or to make other products.

buy classes Three typical buying situations in the business market—namely new-task buying, modified rebuy, and straight rebuy.

buying center In an organization, all individuals or groups involved in the process of making a purchase decision.

buying motive The reason why a person or an organization buys a specific product or makes purchases from a specific firm.

buying roles The users, influencers, deciders, gatekeepers, and buyers who make up a buying center.

C

cannibalization Situation in which a firm introduces new products to stimulate sales but the profit comes at the expense of other products sold by that firm.

cartel A group of companies that produce similar products and act collectively to restrain competition in manufacturing and marketing.

cash discount A deduction granted to buyers for paying their bills within a specified period.

category-killer store A type of retail institution that has a narrow but very deep assortment, low prices, and few to moderate customer services. It is designed to "destroy" all competition in a specific product category.

Category management A distribution practice in which a retailer allows a large supplier to manage an entire product category in a store or chain, with the supplier deciding which items will be placed on a retailer's shelves and in what quantities and locations.

change agent In the process of diffusion, a person who seeks to accelerate the spread of a given innovation.

channel assembly Strategy in which a distributor takes over the final assembly role, which allows products to be customized, thus shortening delivery time because manufacturers often delay custom projects so they don't disrupt their production processes.

channel conflict A situation in which one channel member perceives another channel member to be acting in a way that prevents the first member from achieving its distribution objectives.

channel control The actions of a firm to regulate the behavior of other companies in its distribution channel.

channel power The ability of a firm to influence or determine the behavior of another channel member.

chargeback A penalty that a retailer or wholesaler assesses to a vendor that actually or allegedly violates an agreed-upon distribution policy or procedure.

client market Individuals and/or organizations that are the recipients of a nonprofit organization's money or services. Same as *recipient market.*

clustering Electronic research technique that tracks the pages visited, the amount of time at a page, and the items purchased by individuals as they navigate a site.

cobranding Agreement between two separate companies, or two divisions within the same company, to place both of their respective brands on a particular product or enterprise; also called dual branding.

collaborative filtering Electronic research technique that compares a person's selections and the purchases of previous visitors and enables a site to recommend current products that may be of interest to the visitor.

collaborative planning, forecasting, and replenishment (CPFR) Method by which a producer or wholesaler and a customer, ordinarily a retail chain, jointly and interactively develop sales forecasts through a shared website.

co-location Employees of distributor stationed at the manufacturer's site to arrange shipment of the finished product to the customers.

commercial information environment As contrasted with the social information environment, all communications directed to consumers by organizations and individuals involved in marketing.

Common Market of the South (MERCOSUR) An agreement between Argentina, Brazil, Paraguay, and Uruguay to allow 90% of trade, among these countries, to occur tariff-free.

communication The verbal or nonverbal transmission of information between someone wanting to express an idea and someone else expected or expecting to get that idea. The four elements are a message, a source of the message, a communication channel, and a receiver.

company sales branch See *manufacturer's sales branch.*

comparison advertising A form of selective-demand advertising in which an advertiser either directly (by naming a rival brand) or indirectly (through inference) points out the differences among competing brands.

competitive intelligence The process of gathering and analyzing publicly available information about the activities and plans of competitors.

concentration strategy See *single-segment strategy.*

Consolidated Metropolitan Statistical Area (CMSA) A giant urban center consisting of two or more adjacent Primary Metropolitan Statistical Areas.

consumer advertising Advertising that is directed at consumers.

consumer buying-decision process The series of logical stages, which differ for consumers and organizations, that a prospective purchaser goes through when faced with a buying problem.

consumer product A product that is intended for purchase and use by household consumers for nonbusiness purposes.

Consumer Product Safety Act Federal legislation that created the Consumer Product Safety Commission (CPSC), which has authority to establish mandatory safety standards for many consumer products.

containerization A cargo-handling system in which shipments of products are enclosed in large metal or wood receptacles that are then transported unopened from the time they leave the shipper's facilities until they reach their destination.

contract logistics An arrangement under which a firm outsources various physical distribution activities to one or more independent firms.

contract manufacturing An arrangement in which a firm in one country arranges for a firm in another country to produce the product in the foreign country.

contracting A legal relationship that allows a firm to enter a foreign market indirectly, quickly establish a market presence, and experience a limited amount of risk.

contractual vertical marketing system An arrangement under which independent firms—producers, wholesalers, and retailers—operate under contracts specifying how they will operate in order to improve their distribution efficiency and effectiveness.

contribution-margin approach In marketing cost analysis, an accounting method in which only direct expenses are allocated to each marketing unit being analyzed.

convenience goods A category of tangible consumer products that the consumer has prior knowledge of and purchases with minimum time and effort.

convenience store A type of retail institution that concentrates on convenience-oriented groceries and nonfoods, typically has higher prices than other grocery stores, and offers few customer services.

cookie An inactive data file, placed on the computer's hard drive after the user connects to a particular website, used to record the visitor's activities while connected to the site.

cooperative advertising Advertising promoting products of two or more firms that share its cost.

corporate chain An organization of two or more centrally owned and managed stores that generally handle the same lines of products.

corporate vertical marketing system An arrangement under which a firm at one level of a distribution channel owns the firms at the next level or owns the entire channel.

correlation analysis A statistical refinement of the direct-derivation method, an approach to demand forecasting that takes into account how close the association is between potential sales of the product and the market factor affecting its sales.

cost per thousand (CPM) The media cost of gaining exposure to 1,000 persons with an ad.

cost-plus pricing A major method of price determination in which the price of a unit of a product is set at a level equal to the unit's total cost plus a desired profit on the unit.

countertrade An arrangement under which domestically made products are traded for imported goods.

culture A complex of symbols and artifacts created by a society and handed down from generation to generation as determinants and regulators of human behavior.

cumulative discount A quantity discount based on the total volume purchased over a specified period.

customer relationship management (CRM) An ongoing interaction between a buyer and a seller in which the seller continuously improves its understanding of the buyer's needs, and the buyer becomes increasingly loyal to the seller because its needs are being so well satisfied.

customer specialization One method of organizing selling activities in which each sales person is assigned a specific group of customers, categorized by type of industry or channel of distribution, to which to sell. Same as *market specialization*.

D

database A set of related data that are organized, stored, and updated in a computer.

data mining Method used to identify patterns and meaningful relationships in masses of data that would be unrecognizable to researchers.

data warehouse A collection of data from a variety of internal and external sources, compiled by a firm for use in conducting transactions.

decision support system (DSS) A procedure that allows a manager to interact with data and methods of analysis to gather, analyze, and interpret information.

decline stage The fourth, and final, part of a product life cycle during which the sales of a generic product category drop and most competitors abandon the market.

Delphi method A forecasting technique, applicable to sales forecasting, in which a group of experts individually and anonymously assesses future sales, after which each member has the chance to offer a revised assessment as the group moves toward a consensus.

demand forecasting The process of estimating sales of a product during some future period.

demographic segmentation Subdividing markets into groups based on population factors such as size, age, and growth.

demographics The characteristics of human populations, including such factors as size, distribution, and growth.

department store A large-scale retail institution that has a very broad and deep product assortment, tries not to compete on the basis of price, and offers a wide array of customer services.

depth The relative variety of sizes, colors, and models offered within a product line.

descriptive label The part of a product that gives information about its use, construction, care, performance, and/or other pertinent features.

desk jobber See *drop shipper*.

differential advantage Any feature of an organization or brand perceived by customers to be desirable and different from those of the competition.

differential disadvantage Any feature of an organization or brand perceived by customers to be undesirable and different from those of the competition.

diffusion A process by which an innovation spreads throughout a social system over time.

direct costs Separate expenses that are incurred totally in connection with one market segment or one unit of the sales organization. Same as *separable expenses*.

direct-derivation method An approach to demand forecasting that directly relates the behavior of a market factor to estimated demand.

direct distribution A channel consisting only of producer and final customer, with no middlemen providing assistance.

direct foreign investment A method through which a company can build or acquire production or distribution facilities in a foreign country.

direct investment The actions of a company to build or acquire its own production facilities in a foreign country.

direct marketing A form of nonstore retailing that uses advertising to contact consumers who, in turn, purchase products without visiting a retail store.

direct selling A form of nonstore retailing in which personal contact between a sales person and a consumer occurs away from a retail store. Sometimes called *in-home selling*.

direct tests Measuring or predicting the sales volume attributable to a single ad or an entire advertising campaign.

directory Collection of lists of websites organized by topics and subtopics.

disintermediation The replacement of some traditional intermediaries in a process due to the growth of Internet-based sales.

discount retailing A retailing approach that uses price as a major selling point by combining comparatively low prices and reduced costs of doing business.

discount store A large-scale retail institution that has a broad and shallow product assortment, low prices, and few customer services.

distribution center A facility that has under one roof an efficient, fully integrated system for the flow of products—taking orders, filling them, and preparing them for delivery to customers.

distribution channel The set of people and firms involved in the transfer of title to a product as the product moves from producer to ultimate consumer or business user.

donor market Individuals and/or organizations that contribute money, labor, or materials to a nonprofit organization. Same as *contributor market*.

drop shipper A merchant wholesaler that does not physically handle the product being distributed, but instead sells merchandise for delivery directly from the producer to the customer. Same as *desk jobber*.

dumping The process of selling products in foreign markets at prices below the prices charged for these goods in their home market.

dynamic pricing A form of price adjustment that occurs instantly and frequently in accordance with what the market will bear.

E

early adopters A group of consumers that includes opinion leaders, is respected, has much influence on its peers, and is the second group (following the innovators) to adopt an innovation.

early majority A group of fairly deliberate consumers that adopts an innovation just before the "average" adopter in a social system.

economic environment A set of factors, including the business cycle, inflation, and interest rates, that affect the marketing activities of an organization.

economic order quantity (EOQ) The optimal quantity for reorder when replenishing inventory stocks, as indicated by the volume at which the sum of inventory-carrying costs and order-processing costs are at a minimum.

80–20 principle A situation in which a large proportion of the total orders, customers, territories, or products account for only a small share of the company's sales or profit, and vice versa.

elasticity of demand A price-volume relationship such that a change of one unit on the price scale results in a change of more than one unit on the volume scale.

electronic commerce The buying and selling of goods and services through the use of electronic networks.

electronic data interchange (EDI) Computer-to-computer transmission of orders, invoices, or other business information.

electronic information A form of networking involving the creation of a corporate website to post information about the firm.

electronic networks Individuals or organizations linked via some form of telecommunications.

electronic transactions Purchases made directly from a firm's website.

enterprise resource planning (ERP) systems Strategy in which the various business functions of sales, manufacturing, purchasing, distribution, financial management, and human resources are integrated through the use of computer programs; also called enterprise software.

environmental monitoring The process of gathering information regarding a company's external environment, analyzing it, and forecasting the impact of whatever trends the analysis suggests. Same as *environmental scanning*.

environmental scanning See *environmental monitoring*.

ethics The rules and standards of moral behavior that are generally accepted by a society.

European Union (EU) A political and economic alliance among most of the countries of Western Europe that seeks to liberalize trade among its members.

evaluation The stage of the management process during which an organization determines how well it is achieving the goals set in its strategic planning.

everyday low pricing (EDLP) A pricing strategy that involves consistently low prices and few, if any, temporary price reductions.

exchange The act of voluntarily providing a person or organization something of value in order to acquire something else of value.

exclusive dealing The practice by which a manufacturer prohibits its dealers from carrying products of its competitors.

exclusive distribution A strategy in which a supplier agrees to sell its product only to a single wholesaling middleman and/or retailer in a given market.

exclusive-territory policy The practice by which a producer requires each middleman to sell only to customers located within an assigned territory.

executive judgment A method of sales forecasting that consists of obtaining opinions regarding future sales volume from one or more executives.

expected price The price at which customers consciously or unconsciously value a product—what they think the product is worth.

experiment A method of gathering primary data in which the researcher measures the results of changing one variable in a situation while holding all others constant.

export agent A middleman that operates either in a manufacturer's country or in the destination country and that negotiates the sale of the product in another country and may provide additional services such as arranging for international financing, shipping, and insurance on behalf of the manufacturer.

export merchant A middleman operating in a manufacturer's country that buys goods and exports them.

exporting The activities by which a firm sells its product in another country, either directly to foreign importers or through import–export middlemen.

express warranty A statement in written or spoken words regarding restitution from seller to customer if the seller's product does not perform up to reasonable expectations.

extranet A network that links a large number of firms at different levels of a distribution channel.

F

fabricating materials Business goods that have received some processing and will undergo further processing as they become part of another product.

fabricating parts Business goods that already have been processed to some extent and will be assembled in their present form (with no further change) as part of another product.

face-to-face interview A face-to-face method of gathering data in a survey.

fad A product or style that becomes immensely popular nearly overnight and then falls out of favor with consumers almost as quickly.

family A group of two or more people related by blood, marriage, or adoption living together in a household.

family branding A strategy of using the company name for branding purposes.

family life-cycle stage The series of life stages that a family goes through, starting with young single people, progressing through married stages with young and then older children, and ending with older married and single people.

family packaging A strategy of using either highly similar packages for all products or packages with a common and clearly noticeable feature.

fashion A style that is popularly accepted and purchased by successive groups of people over a reasonably long period of time.

fashion-adoption process A series of buying waves by which a style becomes popular in a market; similar to diffusion of an innovation.

fashion cycle Wavelike movements representing the introduction, rise, popular acceptance, and decline of the market's acceptance of a style.

fashion obsolescence See *style obsolescence.*

Federal Trade Commission Act A federal law, passed in 1914, prohibiting unfair competition and establishing the Federal Trade Commission.

first-mover advantage Strategy of entering a market during the introductory stage of a product in order to build a dominant position; also called pioneer advantage.

fixed cost A cost that remains constant regardless of how many items are produced or sold.

flat-rate pricing Arrangement where a purchaser pays a stipulated single price and then can consume as much or as little of the product as desired.

flexible-price strategy A pricing strategy under which a seller charges different prices to similar customers who buy identical quantities of a product. Same as *variable-price strategy.*

FOB (free on board) factory pricing A geographic pricing strategy whereby the seller quotes the selling price at the point of production and the buyer selects the mode of transportation and pays all freight costs. Same as *FOB mill pricing.*

FOB mill pricing See *FOB factory pricing.*

focus group A preliminary data-gathering method involving an interactive interview of 4 to 10 people.

forecast demand The process of estimating sales of a product during some future period. Same as *demand forecasting.*

foreign exchange Foreign trade— exporting or importing.

for-profit services firms Those that sell to consumers or other businesses with profitable operations as a primary goal.

franchising A type of contractual vertical marketing system that involves a continuing relationship in which a franchiser (the parent company) provides the right to use a trademark plus various management assistance in return for payments from a franchisee (the owner of the individual business unit).

freight absorption pricing A geographic pricing strategy whereby the seller pays for (absorbs) some of the freight charges in order to penetrate more distant markets.

freight forwarder A specialized marketing institution that serves firms by consolidating less-than-carload or less-than-truckload shipments into carload or truckload quantities and arranging for door-to-door shipping service.

fulfillment The act of packing and shipping orders to customers.

full-cost approach In marketing cost analysis, an accounting method in which all expenses—direct and indirect—are allocated to the marketing units being analyzed.

full-service wholesaler An independent merchant middleman that performs a full range of wholesaling functions (from creating assortments to warehousing).

functional discount See *trade discount.*

functional obsolescence See *technological obsolescence.*

G

GE business screen See *General Electric (GE) business screen.*

General Agreement on Tariffs and Trade (GATT) An organization, formed in 1948 and now comprising over 100 countries, that seeks to develop fair-trade practices among its members.

General Electric (GE) business screen A planning model developed by General Electric that classifies strategic business units or major products based on two factors, market attractiveness and business position.

Generation X Those people in the U.S. who were born between approximately 1966 and 1976. Also called *baby busters, twentysomethings,* or *boomerangers.*

Generation Y Those people in the U.S. who were born between either 1976 and 1994, or 1978 and 1982. Also called *echo boomers,* or *millennium generation.*

geographic segmentation Subdividing markets into groups based on their locations.

geographic specialization One method of organizing selling activities, in which each sales person is assigned a specific geographic area—called a territory—in which to sell.

global sales teams A type of personal selling where a team of sales people is responsible for all of its company's sales to an account anywhere in the world.

global strategy A strategy in which essentially the same marketing program is employed around the world.

goal See *objective.*

government market The segment of the business market that includes federal, state, and local units buying for government institutions such as schools, offices, hospitals, and military bases.

grade label The part of a product that identifies the products judged quality (grade) by means of a letter, number, or word.

gray marketing Practice of buying a product in one country, agreeing to distribute it in a second country but diverting it to a third country; also called export diversion.

Green River ordinance Law that restricts door-to-door salespeople by requiring them to register and purchase a license.

growth stage The second part of a product life cycle during which the sales and profits of a generic product category rise and competitors enter the market, causing profits to decline near the end of this part of the cycle.

H

heterogeneity A characteristic of a service indicating that each unit is somewhat different from other units of the same service.

hierarchy of effects The stages a buyer goes through in moving toward a purchase, specifically awareness, knowledge, liking, preference, conviction, and purchase.

high-low pricing A pricing strategy that combines frequent price reductions and aggressive promotion to convey an image of very low prices.

horizontal business market A situation where a given product is usable in a wide variety of industries.

horizontal conflict A form of channel conflict occurring among middlemen (either of the same type or different types) at the same level of distribution.

household A single person, a family, or any group of unrelated persons who occupy a housing unit.

hypothesis A tentative supposition that if proven would suggest a possible solution to a problem.

I

iceberg principle A concept related to performance evaluation stating that the summary data (tip of the iceberg) regarding an activity may hide significant variations among segments of this activity.

implementation The stage of the management process during which an organization attempts to carry out its strategic plans.

implied warranty An intended but unstated assurance regarding restitution from seller to customer if the seller's product does not perform up to reasonable expectations.

import–export agent An agent wholesaling middleman that brings together sellers and buyers in different countries. Export agents work in the country in which the product is made; import agents work in the country in which the product will be sold.

import quota A limit on the amount of a particular product that can be brought into a country.

impulse buying A form of low-involvement decision making; purchases made with little or no advance planning.

independent retailer A company with a single retail store that is not affiliated with a contractual vertical marketing system.

indirect costs Expenses that are incurred jointly for more than one marketing unit and therefore cannot be totally charged to one market segment.

indirect distribution A channel consisting of producer, final customer, and at least one level of middleman.

indirect tests Measuring or predicting the effects of advertising by using a factor other than sales volume.

inflation A rise in the prices of goods and services.

informal investigation The stage in a marketing research study at which preliminary, readily available data are gathered from people inside and outside the company—middlemen, competitors, advertising agencies, and consumers.

infrastructure The country's levels and capabilities with respect to transportation, communications, and energy.

in-home selling See *direct selling*.

innovation adopter categories Groups of people differentiated according to when they accept a given innovation.

innovators A group of venturesome consumers that are the first to adopt an innovation.

inseparability A characteristic of a service indicating that it cannot be separated from the creator–seller of the service.

inside selling Situation where the customer comes to the sales person, includes retail stores and telephone order takers.

installations Manufactured products that are an organization's major, expensive, and long-lived equipment and that directly affect the scale of operations in an organization producing goods or services.

institutional advertising Advertising that presents information about the advertiser's business or tries to create a favorable impression—build goodwill—for the organization.

intangibility A characteristic of a service indicating that it has no physical attributes and, as a result, is impossible for customers to taste, feel, see, hear, or smell before they buy it.

integrated marketing communications (IMC) A strategy in which each of the promotion-mix components is carefully coordinated.

intensity of distribution The number of middlemen used by a producer at the retail and wholesale levels in a particular territory.

intensive distribution A strategy in which a producer sells its product through every available outlet in a market where a consumer might reasonably look for it.

interest rates The percentage amounts either charged to lend money or paid to acquire money.

intermodal transportation The use of two or more modes of transportation to move a shipment of freight.

international market Sales, market potential, or sales potential in foreign (or nondomestic) areas.

international marketing The activities of an organization to market its products in two or more countries.

Internet Global network of networks linking millions of users, originally created to link researchers at many different sites and allow them to exchange information.

Internet selling The offering of goods or services to customers over the Internet.

Internet survey A method of gathering data by posting questionnaires on a firm's website or by e-mailing them to a sample of individuals.

intranet A local electronic network created by linking the personal computers of individuals in a company or department.

introduction stage The first part of a product life cycle during which a generic product category is launched into the market in a full-scale marketing program. Same as *pioneering stage*.

invention In international marketing, the development of an entirely new product for a foreign market.

inverse demand A price-volume relationship such that the higher the price, the greater the unit sales.

ISO 9000 quality standards The International Organization for Standardizations certification to assure that firms conform to specific standards in processes, procedures, operations, controls, and management.

J

joint venture A partnership arrangement in which a foreign operation is owned in part by a domestic company and in part by a foreign company.

just-in-time (JIT) A form of inventory control, purchasing, and production that involves buying parts and supplies in small quantities just in time for use in production and then producing in quantities just in time for sale.

K

kinked demand A condition in which total revenue declines when a product's price is increased or decreased in relation to the prevailing market level.

L

label The part of a product that carries information about the product and the seller.

laggards A group of tradition-bound consumers who are the last to adopt an innovation.

Lanham Trademark Act A federal law passed in 1946 that made it illegal for organizations to make false claims about their own products.

late majority A group of skeptical consumers who are slow to adopt an innovation but eventually do so to save money or in response to social pressure from their peers.

leader In leader pricing, an item on which price is cut.

leader pricing A pricing and promotional strategy in which temporary price cuts are made on a few items to attract customers.

learning Changes in behavior resulting from observation and experience.

level of involvement The amount of effort that is expended in satisfying a need.

licensing A business arrangement whereby one firm sells to another firm (for a fee or royalty) the right to use the first company's brand, patents, or manufacturing processes.

lifestyle Habits that relate to a person's activities, interests, and opinions.

limited-line store A type of retail institution that has a narrow but deep product assortment and customer services that vary from store to store.

line extension One form of product-mix expansion in which a company adds a similar item to an existing product line with the same brand name.

list price See *base price*.

local-content law A regulation specifying the proportion of a finished product's components and labor that must be provided by the importing country.

local operating laws A constraint on how, when, or where retailing can be conducted.

local strategy A strategy used to develop customized marketing programs for each distinct area.

logistics See *physical distribution*.

loss leader In leader pricing, an item on which price is cut to a level that is below the store's cost.

loyalty Faithfulness in a particular brand or retailer so that the consumer purchases that brand or from that retailer without considering alternatives.

M

mail survey A method of gathering data by mailing a questionnaire to potential respondents, and asking them to complete it and return it by mail.

major-accounts organization A variation of customer specialization that usually involves team selling to better service key accounts.

management The process of planning, implementing, and evaluating the efforts of a group of people working toward a common goal.

manufacturers' agent An agent wholesaling middleman that sells part or all of a manufacturer's product mix in an assigned geographic territory. Same as *manufacturers' representative*.

manufacturers' representative See *manufacturers' agent*.

manufacturer's sales branch A manufacturer's sales facility that carries a stock of the product being sold. Same as *company sales branch*.

manufacturer's sales facility An establishment that engages primarily in wholesaling and is owned and operated by a manufacturer but is physically separated from manufacturing plants.

manufacturer's sales office A manufacturer's sales facility that does not carry a stock of the product being sold.

marginal cost The cost of producing and selling one more unit; that is, the cost of the last unit produced or sold.

marginal cost curve A graph of marginal cost levels, which slopes downward until marginal costs start to increase, at which point it rises.

marginal revenue The income derived from the sale of the last unit.

market People or organizations with wants to satisfy, money to spend, and the willingness to spend the money. Alternatively, any person or group with whom an individual or organization has an existing or potential exchange relationship.

market-aggregation strategy A plan of action under which an organization treats its total market as a single segment—that is, as one mass market whose members are considered to be alike with respect to demand for the product—and thus develops a single

marketing mix to reach most of the customers in the entire market. Same as *mass-market strategy* and *undifferentiated-market strategy*.

market factor An item or element that (1) exists in a market, (2) may be measured quantitatively, and (3) is related to the demand for a good or service.

market-factor analysis A sales forecasting method that assumes the future demand for a product is related to the behavior of certain market factors and, as a result, involves determining what these factors are and then measuring their relationships to sales activity.

market-orientation stage The third stage in the evolution of marketing management in which companies identify what customers want and tailor all their activities to satisfy those needs as efficiently as possible.

market-penetration pricing A strategy in which the initial price of a product is set low in relation to the target market's range of expected prices.

market potential The total sales volume that all organizations selling a product during a stated time period in a specific market could expect to achieve under ideal conditions.

market–response system A form of inventory control in which a purchase by a final customer activates a process to produce and deliver a replacement item.

market segmentation The process of dividing the total market for a good or service into several smaller groups, such that the members of each group are similar with respect to the factors that influence demand.

market segments Within the same general market, groups of customers with different wants, buying preferences, or product-use behavior.

market share The proportion of total sales of a product during a stated time period in a specific market that is captured by a single firm.

market-share analysis A detailed analysis of the company's share of the market in total as well as by product line and market segment.

market-skimming pricing A strategy in which the initial price of a product is set high in relation to the target market's range of expected prices.

market specialization See *customer specialization*.

market tests One stage in the new-product development process, consisting of acquiring and analyzing actual consumers' reactions to proposed products.

marketer Any person or organization that desires to stimulate and facilitate exchanges.

marketing A total system of business activities designed to plan, price, promote, and distribute want-satisfying products to target markets to achieve organizational objectives.

marketing audit A comprehensive review and evaluation of the marketing function in an organization—its philosophy, environment, goals, strategies, organizational structure, human and financial resources, and performance.

marketing concept A philosophy of doing business that emphasizes customer orientation and coordination of marketing activities in order to achieve the organization's performance objectives.

marketing cost analysis A detailed study of the Operating Expenses section of a company's profit and loss statement.

marketing information system (MkIS) An ongoing, organized procedure to generate, analyze, disseminate, store, and retrieve information for use in making marketing decisions.

marketing intermediary An independent business organization that directly aids in the flow of products between a marketing organization and its markets.

marketing mix A combination of the four elements—product, pricing structure, distribution system, and promotional activities—used to satisfy the needs of an organization's target market(s) and, at the same time, achieve its marketing objectives.

marketing research The development, interpretation, and communication of decision-oriented information to be used in the strategic marketing process.

markon See *markup*.

Maslow's needs hierarchy A structure of five need levels, arrayed in the order in which people seek to gratify them.

mass customization Developing, producing, and delivering affordable products with enough variety and uniqueness that nearly every potential customer can have exactly what he or she wants.

mass-market strategy See *market-aggregation strategy*.

maturity stage The third part of a product life cycle during which the sales of a generic product category continue to increase (but at a decreasing rate), profits decline largely because of price competition, and some firms leave the market.

merchant middleman A firm that actually takes title to (i.e., owns) products it helps to market.

merchant wholesaler An independently owned firm that engages primarily in wholesaling and takes title to products being distributed. Sometimes called a *wholesaler*.

methods of sales-force compensation The three types of compensation plans are salary, straight commission, and a combination plan.

Metropolitan Statistical Area (MSA) An urban area in the U.S. with a center of population of at least 50,000 and a total MSA population of at least 100,000.

micromarketing The concept of marketing to a small segment of consumers.

middleman A business firm that renders services directly related to the purchase and/or sale of a product as it flows from producer to consumer.

middleman's brand A brand owned by a retailer or a wholesaler.

misdirected marketing effort Marketing endeavors that do not produce results commensurate with the resources expended.

mission An organization's statement of what customers it serves, what needs it satisfies, and what types of products it offers.

mix extension One form of product-mix expansion in which a company adds a new product line to its present assortment.

modified rebuy In the business market, a purchasing situation between a new task and a straight rebuy in terms of time and people involved, information needed, and alternatives considered.

motive A need sufficiently stimulated to move an individual to seek satisfaction.

multinational corporation A truly worldwide enterprise, in which the foreign and the domestic operations are integrated and are not separately identified.

multiple-brand strategy A strategy in which a firm has more than one brand of essentially the same product, aimed either at the same target market or at distinct target markets.

multiple correlation analysis A more sophisticated form of correlation analysis that allows the inclusion of more than one market factor in the calculation.

multiple-distribution channels The use by a producer of more than one channel of distribution for reasons such as achieving broad market coverage or avoiding total dependence on a single arrangement.

multiple packaging The practice of placing several units of the same product in one container.

multiple-segment strategy A plan of action that involves selecting two or more different groups of potential customers as the firm's target markets.

N

net profit percentage The ratio of net profit to net sales.

networks Individuals or organizations linked together to share data, exchange information and ideas, and perform tasks.

new product A vague term that may refer to (1) really innovative, truly unique products, (2) replacement products that are significantly different from existing ones, or (3) imitative products that are new to a particular firm but are not new to the market.

new-product department or team An organizational structure for product planning and development that involves a small unit, consisting of five or fewer people, and that reports to the president.

new-product development process A set of six stages that a new product goes through, starting with idea generation and continuing through idea screening, business analysis, prototype development, market tests, and eventually commercialization (full-scale production and marketing).

new-product strategy A statement identifying the role a new product is expected to play in achieving corporate and marketing goals.

new-task buying In the business market, a purchasing situation in which a company for the first time considers buying a given item.

niche marketers Sellers that pursue single segments within the total market.

niche marketing A strategy in which goods and services are tailored to meet the needs of small market segments.

niche markets A small, targeted segment.

nonadopters Those consumers that never adopt an innovation.

nonbusiness market The total set of churches, colleges and universities, museums, hospitals and other health institutions, political parties, labor unions, and charitable organizations.

noncumulative discount A quantity discount based on the size of an individual order of one or more products.

nonprice competition A strategy in which a seller maintains stable prices and attempts to improve its market position by emphasizing other (nonprice) aspects of its marketing program.

nonprofit organizations Those groups that provide services but do not have a profit objective.

nonstore retailing Retailing activities resulting in transactions that occur away from a retail store.

North American Free Trade Agreement (NAFTA) An agreement among the United States, Canada, and Mexico to eliminate tariffs between the countries.

North American Industry Classification System (NAICS) Coding system similar to the SIC, but has 20 rather than 10 industry sectors, to provide a more detailed and contemporary classification scheme.

not-for-profit services organizations (N-F-P) Those groups that have a profit goal because growth and existence depend on generating revenue in excess of costs.

nutrition labeling The part of a product that provides information about the amount of calories, fat, cholesterol, sodium, carbohydrates, and protein contained in the package's contents.

O

objective A desired outcome. Same as *goal*.

observation method A method of gathering primary data by observing the actions of a person without direct interaction.

odd pricing A psychological pricing strategy that consists of setting prices at uneven (or odd) amounts, such as $4.99, rather than at even amounts, such as $5, in the belief that these seemingly lower prices will result in larger sales volume.

off-price retailer A type of retail institution, often found in the areas of apparel and shoes, that has a narrow and deep product assortment, low prices, and few customer services.

oligopoly A market structure dominated by a few firms, each marketing similar products.

one-price strategy A pricing strategy under which a seller charges the same price to all similar customers who buy identical quantities of a product.

one-stop shipping A transportation firm offers multiple modes of transportation of goods to its customers.

online retailing Electronic transactions made over the Internet in which the purchaser is the ultimate consumer.

operating supplies The "convenience" category of business goods, consisting of tangible products that are characterized by low dollar value per unit and a short life and that aid in an organization's operations without becoming part of the finished product.

organizational strategies Broad plans of action by which an organization intends to achieve its goals and fulfill its mission. These plans are for (1) the total organization in a small, single-product company or (2) each SBU in a large, multiproduct or multibusiness organization.

outside sales The kind of personal selling group in which sales people go to the customers, making contact by mail, telephone, or face-to-face.

P

package-delivery firms Companies that specialize in the delivery of small packages and high-priority mail.

packaging All the activities of designing and producing the container or wrapper for a product.

past sales analysis A method of sales forecasting that applies a flat percentage increase to the volume achieved last year or to the average volume of the past few years.

patronage buying motives The reasons why a consumer chooses to shop at a particular store.

perception The process carried out by an individual to receive, organize, and assign meaning to stimuli detected by the five senses.

perfect competition A market structure in which product differentiation is absent, buyers and sellers are well informed, and the seller has no discernible control over the selling price.

perishability A characteristic of a service indicating that it is highly transitory and cannot be stored.

personal interview See *face-to-face interview.*

personal selling The personal communication of information to persuade somebody to buy something. Alternatively, the direct (face-to-face or over-the-phone) presentation of a product to a prospective customer by a representative of the organization selling it.

personal selling process The logical sequence of prospecting, preapproach, presenting, and postsale services that a sales person takes in dealing with a prospective buyer.

personality An individual's pattern of traits that influences behavioral responses.

physical distribution All the activities involved in the flow of products as they move physically from producer to consumer or industrial user. Same as *logistics.*

physical distribution management The development and operation of processes resulting in the effective and efficient physical flow of products.

physical facilities The building— including its location, design, and layout—that serves as a store for a retail firm.

piggyback service The transporting of loaded truck trailers on railroad flatcars.

pioneering stage See *introduction stage.*

planned obsolescence A strategy that is intended to make an existing product out of date and thus to increase the market for replacement products. There are two forms: technological and style.

planning The process of deciding now what we are going to do later, including when and how we are going to do it.

political and legal forces A set of factors, including monetary and fiscal policies, legislation, and regulations, that affect the marketing activities of an organization.

portal An entrance and guide to the World Wide Web.

position The way a product, brand, or organization is viewed in relation to the competition by current and prospective customers.

positioning A product's image in relation to directly competitive products as well as other products marketed by the same company. Alternatively, a firm's strategies and actions related to favorably distinguishing itself from competitors in the minds of selected groups of consumers. Same as *product positioning.*

postage stamp pricing See *uniform delivered pricing.*

postpurchase cognitive dissonance The anxiety created by the fact that in most purchases the alternative selected has some negative features and the alternatives not selected have some positive features.

postsale service Maintenance and repairs as well as other services that are provided to customers in order to fulfill the terms of a firm's warranty and/or to augment the firm's revenues.

predatory pricing Driving competitors out of the marketplace by giving away products or charging a far-below-the-market price.

price The amount of money and/or other items with utility needed to acquire a product.

price competition A strategy in which a firm regularly offers products priced as low as possible, usually accompanied by a minimum of services.

price customization Method of establishing prices based on how much different people value a product.

price differential The difference in prices of an identical brand from one area to another.

price discrimination A situation in which different customers pay different prices for the same product.

price lining A pricing strategy whereby a firm selects a limited number of prices at which it will sell related products.

price war A form of price competition that begins when one firm decreases its price in an effort to increase its sales volume and/or market share, the other firms retaliate by reducing prices on competing products, and additional price decreases by the original price cutter and/or its competitors usually follow.

pricing above competition One form of market-based pricing in which price is set above the prevailing market level.

pricing below competition One form of market-based pricing in which price is set below the level of your main competitors.

pricing objective The desired outcome that management seeks to achieve with its pricing structure and strategies.

pricing to meet competition A pricing method in which a firm ascertains what the market price is and, after allowing for customary markups for middlemen, arrives at its own selling price.

primary data New data gathered specifically for the project at hand.

primary-demand advertising Advertising that is designed to stimulate demand for a generic category of a product.

Primary Metropolitan Statistical Area (PMSA) A Metropolitan Statistical Area in the U.S. that has a population of at least 1 million.

Printer's Ink statutes State legislation intended to punish "untrue, deceptive, or misleading" advertising.

private warehouse A warehouse that is owned and operated by the firm whose products are being stored and handled at the facility.

producer's brand A brand that is owned by a manufacturer or other producer.

product A set of tangible and intangible attributes, which may include packaging, color, price, quality, and brand, plus the seller's services and reputation. A product may be a good, service, place, person, or idea.

product abandonment A decision and subsequent action by a firm to drop a product that has insufficient and/or declining sales and lacks profits.

product advertising Advertising that focuses on a particular product or brand.

product alteration A strategy of improving an existing product.

product and trade name franchising A distribution agreement under which a supplier (the franchiser) authorizes a dealer (the franchisee) to sell a product line, using the parent company's trade name for promotional purposes.

product color The hue(s) given to a particular product, including its packaging.

product counterfeiting The unscrupulous placement of a brand name on a product without the legal right to do so.

product design The arrangement of elements that collectively form a good or service.

product differentiation A strategy in which a firm uses promotion to distinguish its product from competitive brands offered to the same aggregate market.

product liability A legal action alleging that an illness, accident, or death resulted from the named product because it was harmful, faulty, or inadequately labeled.

product life cycle The aggregate demand over an extended period of time for all brands comprising a generic product category.

product line A broad group of products intended for essentially similar uses and having similar physical characteristics.

product manager An organizational structure for product planning and development that makes one person responsible for planning new products as well as managing established products. Same as *brand manager*.

product-market growth matrix A planning model that consists of four alternative growth strategies based on whether an organization will be selling its present products or new products to its present markets or new markets.

product mix The set of all products offered for sale by a company.

product-mix contraction A strategy in which a firm either eliminates an entire line or simplifies the assortment within a line.

product-mix expansion A strategy in which a firm increases the depth within a particular line and/or the number of lines it offers to consumers.

product-orientation stage The first stage in the evolution of marketing management, in which the basic assumption is that making a good product will ensure business success.

product-planning committee An organizational structure for product planning and development that involves a joint effort among executives from major departments and, especially in small firms, the president and/or another top-level executive.

product positioning See *positioning*.

product quality See *quality*.

product specialization One method of organizing selling activities so that each sales person is assigned one or more product lines to sell.

promotion The element in an organization's marketing mix that serves to inform, persuade, and remind the market of a product and/or the organization selling it in the hope of influencing the recipients' feelings, beliefs, or behavior.

promotion mix The combination of personal selling, advertising, sales promotion, public relations, and publicity that is intended to help an organization achieve its marketing objectives.

promotional allowance A price reduction granted by a seller as payment for promotional services performed by buyers.

promotional budgeting method The means used to determine the amount of dollars allocated to promotion in general and/or to specific forms of promotion.

provider market The contributors of money, labor, materials, or other resources to the organization.

psychoanalytic theory Freudian theory that argues people have subconscious drives that cannot be satisfied in socially acceptable ways.

psychographic segmentation Subdividing markets into groups based on personality dimensions, life-style characteristics, and values.

psychological obsolescence See *style obsolescence*.

public relations Communications efforts that are designed to favorably influence attitudes toward an organization, its products, and its policies.

public warehouse An independent firm that provides for a fee storage and handling facilities for individuals or companies.

publicity A special form of public relations that involves any communication about an organization, its products, or its policies through the media that is not paid for by the sponsoring organization.

pull strategy Promotional effort directed primarily at end users so they will ask middlemen for the product.

push strategy Promotional efforts directed primarily at middlemen that are the next link forward in the distribution channel for a product.

Q

qualitative evaluation bases In sales-force evaluation, subjective criteria for appraising the performance of sales people.

quality The degree to which a product meets the expectations of the customer. Same as *product quality*.

quantitative evaluation bases In sales-force evaluation, specific, objective criteria for appraising the performance of sales people.

quantity discount A deduction from a seller's list price that is offered to a buyer when a large quantity of the product is purchased.

R

raw materials Business goods that become part of another tangible product prior to being processed in any way.

rebate A discount on a product that a customer obtains by submitting a form or certificate provided by the seller.

recipient market See *client market*.

reference group A group of people who influence a person's attitudes, values, and behavior.

refusal to deal A situation in which a producer that desires to select and perhaps control its channels declines to sell to some middlemen.

regional strategy A strategy used to market a product to different regions by recognizing distinctions in climate, custom, or taste.

relationship marketing See *customer relationship management (CRM)*

relationship selling An attempt by a sales

person or organization to develop a deeper, longer-lasting relationship built on trust with key customers—usually larger accounts.

repositioning Reestablishing a product's attractiveness in the target market.

resale price maintenance A pricing policy whereby a manufacturer seeks to control the prices at which middlemen resell their products.

reseller market One segment of the business market, consisting of wholesaling and retailing middlemen that buy products for resale to other organizations or to consumers.

retail scanners The electronic devices at retail checkouts that read the bar code on each item.

retail trade See *retailing*.

retailer A firm engaged primarily in retailing.

retailer cooperative A type of contractual vertical marketing system that is formed by a group of small retailers who agree to establish and operate a wholesale warehouse.

retailing The sale, and all activities directly related to the sale, of goods and services to ultimate consumers for personal, nonbusiness use. Same as *retail trade*.

return on marketing investment A way for firms to measure profit gain from marketing expenditures.

Robinson-Patman Act A federal law passed in 1936 that was intended to curb price discrimination by large retailers and the granting by manufacturers of proportionally unequal promotional allowances to large retailers or wholesalers.

S

sales-force automation (SFA) Strategy of equipping sales people with laptop computers, cellular phones, fax machines, and pagers to give them access to databases, the Internet, and e-mail to help them manage accounts more effectively.

sales-force composite A method of forecasting sales that consists of collecting from all sales people estimates of sales for their territories during the future period of interest.

sales forecast An estimate of probable sales for one company's brand of a product during a stated time period in a specific market and assuming the use of a predetermined marketing plan.

sales-orientation stage The second stage in the evolution of marketing management, in which the emphasis is on using various promotional

activities to sell whatever the organization produces.

sales potential The portion of market potential that a specific company could expect to achieve under ideal conditions.

sales promotion Demand-stimulating devices designed to supplement advertising and facilitate personal selling.

sales team See *selling center*.

sales volume analysis A detailed study of the Net Sales section of a company's profit and loss statement.

scrambled merchandising The main source of horizontal channel conflict, a strategy under which a middleman diversifies by adding product lines not traditionally carried by its type of business.

seasonal discount A deduction from the list price that is offered to a customer for placing an order during the seller's slack season.

secondary data Available data, already gathered for some other purpose.

selective-demand advertising Advertising that is intended to stimulate demand for individual brands.

selective distribution A strategy in which a producer sells its product through multiple, but not all possible, wholesalers and retailers in a market where a consumer might reasonably look for it.

selective perception The process of screening all the marketing stimuli to which an individual is exposed on a daily basis.

self-concept The way a person sees himself/herself. Same as *self-image*.

self-image See *self-concept*.

selling agent An agent wholesaling middleman that essentially takes the place of a manufacturer's marketing department by marketing the manufacturer's entire output.

selling center A group of people representing a sales department as well as other functional areas in a firm (such as finance, production, and research and development) that work cooperatively to achieve a sale. Sometimes called a *sales team* or *team selling*.

separable expenses See *direct costs*.

service An identifiable, intangible activity that is the main object of a transaction designed to provide want-satisfaction to customers.

service encounter In services marketing, a customer's interaction with any service employee or with any tangible element, such as a service's physical surroundings.

service quality The degree to which an intangible offering meets the expectations of the customer.

shopping center A planned grouping of retail stores that lease space in a structure that is typically owned by a single organization and that can accommodate multiple tenants.

shopping goods A category of tangible consumer products that are purchased after the buyer has spent some time and effort comparing the price, quality, perhaps style, and/or other attributes of alternative products in several stores.

single-price strategy An extreme variation of a one-price strategy in which all items sold by a firm carry a single price.

single-segment strategy A plan of action that involves selecting one homogeneous segment from within a total market to be the firm's target market. Same as *concentration strategy*.

single-source data A data-gathering method in which exposure to television advertising and product purchases can be traced to individual households.

situation analysis The act of gathering and studying information pertaining to one or more specified aspects of an organization. Alternatively, a background investigation that helps in refining a research problem.

situational influence A temporary force, associated with the immediate purchase environment, that affects behavior.

slotting allowance A fee that some retailers charge a manufacturer in order to place its product on store shelves.

small-order problem A situation confronting many firms, in which revenue from an order is less than allocated expenses because several costs, such as billing and direct selling, are essentially the same regardless of order size.

social and cultural forces A set of factors, including lifestyles, social values, and beliefs, that affect the marketing activities of an organization.

social class A division of, or ranking within, society based on education, occupation, and type of residential neighborhood.

social information environment As contrasted with the commercial information environment, all communications among family members, friends, and acquaintances about products.

societal marketing concept A revised version of the marketing concept under which a company recognizes that it should be concerned about not only the buyers of its products but also other people directly affected by its operations and with not only tomorrow but also the long term.

specialty goods A category of tangible consumer products for which consumers have a strong brand preference and are willing to expend substantial time and effort in locating and then buying the desired brand.

specialty store A type of retail institution that has a very narrow and deep product assortment (often concentrating on a specialized product line or even part of a specialized product line), that usually strives to maintain manufacturers' suggested prices, and that typically provides at least standard customer services.

stages in the adoption process The six steps a prospective buyer goes through in deciding whether to purchase something new.

standards and certification A requirement that a product contain or exclude certain ingredients or that it be tested and certified as meeting certain restrictive standards.

stimulus-response theory The theory that learning occurs as a person (1) responds to some stimuli and (2) is rewarded with need satisfaction for a correct response or penalized for an incorrect one.

straight rebuy In the business market, a routine, low-involvement purchase with minimal information needs and no great consideration of alternatives.

strategic alliance A formal, long-term agreement between firms to combine their capabilities and resources to accomplish global objectives.

strategic business unit (SBU) A separate division for a major product or market in a multiproduct or multibusiness organization.

strategic company planning The level of planning that consists of (1) defining the organization's mission, (2) analyzing the situation, (3) setting organizational objectives, and (4) selecting appropriate strategies to achieve these objectives.

strategic marketing planning The level of planning that consists of (1) conducting a situation analysis, (2) developing marketing objectives, (3) determining positioning and differential advantage, (4) selecting target markets and measuring market demand, and (5) designing a strategic marketing mix.

strategic planning The managerial process of matching a firm's resources with its market opportunities over the long run.

strategic window The limited amount of time in which a firm's resources coincide with a particular market opportunity.

strategy A broad plan of action by which an organization intends to reach its objectives.

style A distinctive manner of presentation or construction in any art, product, or endeavor.

style obsolescence A form of planned obsolescence in which superficial characteristics of a product are altered so that the new model is easily differentiated from the previous model and people become dissatisfied with it. Same as *fashion obsolescence* and *psychological obsolescence*.

subculture Groups in a culture that exhibit characteristic behavior patterns sufficient to distinguish them from other groups within the same culture.

suggested list price A pricing policy whereby a manufacturer recommends to retailers a final (retail) price that should provide them with their normal markups.

supercenter A combination of a discount house and a complete grocery store.

supermarket A type of retail institution that has a moderately broad and moderately deep product assortment spanning groceries and some nonfood lines, that offers relatively few customer services, and that ordinarily emphasizes price in either an offensive or defensive way.

supermarket retailing A retailing method that features several related product lines, a high degree of self-service, largely centralized checkout, and competitive prices.

suppliers The people or firms that supply the goods or services that an organization needs to produce what it sells.

supply chain management The combination of distribution channels and physical distribution to make up the total marketing system.

survey A method of gathering primary data by interviewing people in person, by telephone, or by mail.

survey of buyer intentions A form of sales forecasting in which a firm asks a sample of current or potential customers how much of a particular product they would buy at a given price during a specified future period.

SWOT assessment Identifying and evaluating an organization's most significant strengths, weaknesses, opportunities, and threats.

systems approach to physical distribution The unification of individual physical distribution activities.

systems selling Providing a total package of related goods and services to solve a customer's problem (needs).

T

tactic A specific means by which a strategy is implemented.

target market A group of customers (people or organizations) for whom a seller designs a particular marketing mix.

tariff A tax imposed on a product entering a country.

team selling See *selling center.*

technological obsolescence A form of planned obsolescence in which significant technical improvements result in a more effective product. Same as *functional obsolescence.*

technology Applications of science for industrial and commercial purposes.

telemarketing A form of nonstore retailing in which a sales person initiates contact with a shopper and also closes the sale over the telephone.

Telephone Consumer Protection Act Federal law that requires telemarketers to keep a "do-not-call" list of consumers who request that they not receive telephone solicitations, it restricts the indiscriminant use of automatic telephone dialing systems, and it prohibits marketers from sending advertising to a facsimile machine without first obtaining the recipient's permission.

telephone survey A method of gathering data by interviewing people over the telephone.

test marketing A method of demand forecasting in which a firm markets its new product in a limited geographic area, measures the sales, and then—from this sample—projects the company's sales over a larger area. Alternatively, a marketing research technique that uses this same approach to judge consumers' responses to a strategy before committing to a major marketing effort.

total cost The sum of total fixed cost and total variable cost for a specific quantity produced or sold.

total cost concept In physical distribution, the recognition that the best relationship between costs and profit must be established for the entire physical distribution system, rather than for individual activities.

total fixed cost The sum of all fixed costs.

total quality management (TQM) A philosophy as well as specific procedures, policies, and practices that commit an organization to continuous quality improvement in all of its activities.

total variable cost The sum of all variable costs.

trade balance In international business, the difference between the value of a nation's imports and the value of its exports.

trade barriers Created by governments to restrict trade and protect domestic industries, these are the most common legal forces affecting international marketers.

trade (functional) discount A reduction from the list price that is offered by a seller to buyers in payment for marketing functions the buyers will perform. Same as *functional discount.*

trademark A brand that has been adopted by a seller and given legal protection.

trademark infringement Act of manufacturing products with names and packaging similar to well-known goods in order to achieve sales.

Trademark Law Revision Act A federal law, passed in 1988, that broadened the Landham Trademark Act to encompass comparisons made in promotional activity.

trademark licensing A business arrangement in which the owner of a trademark grants permission to other firms to use the owner's brand name, logo-type, and/or character on the licensee's products in return for a royalty on sales of those products. Same as *brand licensing.*

trading down A product-line strategy wherein a company adds a lower-priced product to a line to reach a market that cannot afford the higher-priced items or that see them as too expensive.

trading up A product-line strategy wherein a company adds a higher-priced product to a line in order to attract a broader market and, through its added prestige, helps the sale of its existing lower-priced products.

trend analysis A statistical method of forecasting sales over the long term by using regression analysis or over the short term by using a seasonal index of sales.

trickle-across theory In fashion adoption, a fashion cycle that moves horizontally and simultaneously within several socioeconomic levels.

trickle-down theory In fashion adoption, a fashion cycle that flows downward through several socioeconomic levels.

trickle-up theory In fashion adoption, a fashion cycle in which a style first becomes popular with lower socioeconomic levels and then flows upward to become popular among higher levels.

truck distributor See *truck jobber.*

truck jobber A merchant wholesaler that carries a selected line of perishable products and delivers them by truck to retail stores. Same as *truck distributor.*

tying contract The practice by which a manufacturer sells a product to a middleman only under the condition that the middleman also buy another (possibly unwanted) product from the manufacturer.

U

ultimate consumers People who buy goods or services for their own personal or household use in order to satisfy strictly nonbusiness wants.

undifferentiated-market strategy See *market-aggregation strategy.*

unfair-practices acts State laws intended to regulate some forms of leader pricing that are intended to drive other products or companies out of business. Same as *unfair-sales acts.*

unfair-sales acts See *unfair-practices acts.*

uniform delivered pricing A geographic pricing strategy whereby the same delivered price is quoted to all buyers regardless of their locations. Same as *postage stamp pricing.*

universal design The design of products in such a way that they can be used by all consumers, including disabled individuals, senior citizens, and others needing special considerations.

unsought goods A category of consumer tangible products that consists of new products the consumer is not yet aware of or products the consumer is aware of but does not want right now.

utility The attribute in an item that makes it capable of satisfying human wants.

V

value The ratio of perceived benefits to price and any other incurred costs.

value added The dollar value of a firm's output minus the value of the inputs it purchased from other firms.

value chain The combination of a company, its suppliers, and intermediaries, performing their own activities, to add value to a product.

value creation Meeting customers' desires through improved information and technology.

value pricing A form of price competition in which a firm seeks to improve the ratio of a product's benefits to its price and related costs.

values Intangible principles that are a reflection of people's needs, adjusted for the realities of the world in which they live.

variable cost A cost that changes directly in relation to the number of units produced or sold.

variable-price strategy See *flexible-price strategy*.

vertical business market A situation where a given product is usable by virtually all the firms in only one or two industries.

vertical conflict A form of channel conflict occurring among firms at different levels of the same channel, typically producer versus wholesaler or producer versus retailer.

vertical marketing system (VMS) A tightly coordinated distribution channel designed to improve operating efficiency and marketing effectiveness.

viral marketing Strategy of spreading positive information about a company from one person to another,

often utilized by smaller firms.

voluntary chain A type of contractual vertical marketing system that is sponsored by a wholesaler who enters into a contract with interested retailers.

W

warehouse club A combined retailing and wholesaling institution that has a very broad but very shallow product assortment, very low prices, few customer services, and is open only to members. Same as *wholesale club*.

warning label The part of a product that tells consumers not to misuse the product and informs them of almost every conceivable danger associated with using it.

warranty An assurance given to buyers that they will be compensated in case the product does not perform up to reasonable expectations.

website A collection of Web files beginning with a home page that is accessible through a unique address.

Wheeler-Lea Act A federal law, passed in 1938, that amended the Federal Trade Commission Act by strengthening the prohibition against unfair competition, especially false or misleading advertising.

wholesale club See *warehouse club*.

wholesale trade See *wholesaling*.

wholesaler See *merchant wholesaler*.

wholesaling The sale, and all activities directly related to the sale, of goods and services to businesses and other organizations for resale, use in producing other goods and services, or the operation of an organization.

wholesaling middleman A firm engaged primarily in wholesaling.

wholly owned subsidiary A business arrangement in foreign markets in which a company owns the foreign operation in order to gain maximum control over its marketing program and production operations.

World Trade Organization (WTO) Created in 1995, as the governing body of global commerce, consisting of 135-member countries and accounting for 90% of world trade.

World Wide Web Collection of hyperlinked multimedia databases stored all over the world and accessible via the Internet.

Z

zone-delivered pricing A geographic pricing strategy whereby a seller divides its market into a limited number of broad geographic zones and then sets a uniform delivered price for each zone.

Name Index

A

A. C. Nielsen, 176, 191
Aaker, David A., N-1, N-8
ABB Automation, 411
ABB Ltd., 322
ABC, 310, 606
Abell, Derek F., N-21
Abercrombie & Fitch, 201
Abramovitch, Ingrid, N-20
Ace, 399, 428, 495
Achrol, Ravi S., N-21
Ackman, Dan, N-21–N-22
Acohido, Byron, 313–314
Acosta, 396
Acrica, 493–494
Acrilan fabrics, 266
Acuvue, 240
Adidas, 55, 59, 69, 327, 408,
    561–562
Adidas-Salomon AG, 69
Adrian, C. Mitchell, N-2
Advertising Age, 186, 565
Advertising Research
    Foundation, 196
Advertising Slogan Hall of Fame, 500
Aetna, 264
AFLAC, 482–484, 505
Agins, Teri, 253, N-2, N-6, N-13,
    N-20
Ahead Headgear, 160
Ahlstrand, Scott, N-4
Aichlmayr, Mary, N-17
Aim, 264
Air Jordans, 561–62
Airbus, 135
Akre, Brian S., N-11
Alamo, 286
Alaska Airlines, 265
Albertson's, 40, 423, 434
Albiniak, Paige, N-1
Albright, Brian, N-17
Alcoa, 323
Alden, Edward, N-2
Alder, Eric, N-6
Aldred, Carolyn, N-22
Alexander, Jack, N-7
Aley, James, N-10
All Sport, 586
Alley, Kirstie, 102
Alliance Entertainment, 460
Allied Van Lines, 264
Allport, Gordon W., N-3
Allstate Corp., 397, 627
Almega Corp., 165
Almquist, Eric, N-1
Alpert, Frank, N-10
AM General Corporation, 122,
    564–565
AM/PM Mini Marts, 435
Amana, 248, 454
Amazon, 9, 35, 58, 66, 80, 141,
    187, 207, 371, 403, 439, 441,
    468, 477, 574, 589, 633,
    638–639, 641, 647–649
Ambler, Tim, N-11
America Online, 81, 209, 369, 536,
    555, 629, 632, 640

America West, 317
American Airlines, 216, 317, 339,
    381
American Association of Retired
    Persons (AARP), 33
American Basketball League, 238
American Booksellers Association
    (ABA), 41, 366
American Can Company, 140
American Cancer Society, 5, 208,
    288–289
American Community Survey
    (ACS), 185
American Dairy Farmers and Milk
    Processors, 103
American Demographics, 186
American Eagle, 201
American Electric Power, 536
American Express, 35, 149, 180,
    182, 280, 291
American FactFinder, 184
American Heart Association,
    277, 288
American Legacy Foundation, 101
American Marketing Association,
    186, 196, 288, 504, 637
American Medical Association
    (AMA), 288, 501
American Red Cross, 296
Ameritrade, 264
Amgen, 16
Amos, Denis Smith, N-5
Amos, Wally, 401
Amway, 436, 634
Anaheim Angels, 310
Anaheim Mighty Ducks, 310
ANC Rental Corp., 286
Ancestry.com, 641
Anders, George, 403, N-3, N-
    10–N-13, N-17, N-19
Anderson, James C., N-13
Angwin, Julia, N-9–N-10, N-11
Anheuser-Busch Company, 67,
    237, 261, 279, 407, 541
Ann Taylor, 3, 121, 272, 510
Ansoff, H. Igor, N-20
Anthes, Gary H., N-10
Apollo label, 243
Appel, David, 245
Apple Computer, 138, 208, 222,
    235, 249, 279, 475, 537
Aquafina, 83–84
Arby's, 209
Archer Daniels Midland, 496, 556
Ariba Inc., 141, 143
Arizona State, 497
Arm & Hammer, 260, 539
Armor All Products, 269
Armstrong, Lance, 554
Arndt, Michael, 384, 649
Arnott, Nancy, N-8
Arnould, Eric, N-3
Arrow Electronics, 411
Art Capital Group, 627
Ascriptin, 209

Ashai, 264
Ashely, Susan R., N-7
Assmus, Gert, 394
Aston Martin, 553
AT&T Corp., 197, 260, 328, 515,
    520, 576
Atari, 311
Athlete's Foot, 426, 430
Athletic Store, 370
Atkinson, William, N-17
Atlanta Braves, 291
Atlas Micro, 602
Au Bon Pain, 264
Auburn University, 596
Audiovox, 254
Autobytel, 634
Automotive Systems Group (ASG),
    508–510
AutoNation, 369, 434
Avalon bottled water, 555
Aversa, Jeannine, N-6
Avis, 285, 297
Avon, 15, 16, 301, 387–388, 400,
    403, 414–415, 436, 512,
    538–539, 584, 627
Ayres, Chris, N-9

B

BabyGap, 200
Baglole, Joel A., N-15, N-20
Bahls, Jane Easter, N-15
Bahls, Steven C., N-15
Bailey, Jeff, N-13, N-20
Bailey Controls, 411
Bain & Co., 584
Baird, Roger, N-8
Baja Fresh Mexican Grill, 646
Baker, Chris, 303
Ball, Jeffrey, 138, N-2–N-4
Balu, Rekha, N-18
Ban, 264
Banana Republic, 200–202
Band-Aid, 265
Bank of America, 16
Bank One, 299
Barbecue Renew, 547
Barlas, Pete, 650, N-16
Barnes & Noble, 10, 41, 366, 434
Barrett, Amy, 324
Barrett, Colleen, 379–380
Barrett, Paul M., N-8
Barron, Kelly, 205
Bartlett, Michael, 548
Bass Hotels & Resorts, 269
Bassin, Sue, N-8
Bates, Albert D., N-10
Batesville Casket, 462
Batteries Plus, 433
Baxter Healthcare Corporation, 123
Baxter International, 518
Bayer, 142, 160, 209
Bazdarich, Colleen, N-3
Bearing Point, 260
Beatty, Sally, 164, N-14
Beautyrest, 264
Beck, Ernest, 161, 358, 384
Beck, Rachel, 314

Becker, Cinda, N-17
Beckett, Paul, N-7
Bed Bath and Beyond, 434
Beech Aircraft, 217
Beerthon, Pierre, N-12
Bell Atlantic, 636
Bell System, 545
Bellagio, 361
Beltramini, Richard F., N-11
Ben & Jerry's, 178
Benady, David, N-19
Benman, Keith, 567
Bennett, Jeff, N-3
Bennett, Johanna, N-4
Bennett, Peter D., N-7
Bentley, 340
Benz, Matthew, 314
Bergdorf-Goodman, 97
Berman, Dennis, N-15
Berman, Gary L., N-1
Berner, Robert, 480, N-10, N-13,
    N-16
Berry, Leonard L., N-7, N-9, N-18
Berthon, Jean-Paul, N-12
Best Buy, 375, 426, 633
Bethlehem Steel, 127
Bethune, Gordon, 380
Better Business Bureau, 504
Betts, Erica J., N-11
Betty Crocker, 241, 270
Bezos, Jeff, 641, 647–649
Bharadwaj, Sundar G., N-20
Bic, 55, 239
Biemans, Wim G., N-12
Bigness, Jon, N-16
Bill Blass, 243
Bird, Laura, N-6, N-8, N-13
Birkeland, Peter M., N-14
Bittar, Christine, 10, N-4, N-19
BizRate.com, 439
BJ's Wholesale, 435
Black & Decker (B&D), 150, 154,
    161, 270
BlackBerry, 255
Blackmon, Douglas A., N-2, N-11
Blattberg, Robert C., N-1
Bleakley, Fred R., N-17
Bleustein, Jeffrey, 88
Blimpie, 435
Block China, 259
Blockbuster, 553
Bloom, Paul N., 409
Bloomingdale, Richard, 403
Blue Cross & Blue Shield, 280
Blue Fox, 280
Blue Goose, 276
Blue Martini, 280
Blue Moon, 280
Blue Mountain Arts, 498
Blue Pumpkin, 280
Blue Squirrel, 280
Bluefly Inc., 337, 354–356, 376
BlueKite, 280
Bluesocket, 280
BMW, 48, 212, 272, 497–498, 500,
    555, 585
Bobinski, G. S., N-11

Subject Index

Inventory control, 464–467
   customer-service require-
    ments, 464
   economic order quantity,
    464–465
   just-in-time, 465–466
   market-response systems,
    466–467
Inventory location, 467–468
Inverse demand, 326
Invest strategy, 587
Irregular merchandise (seconds), 433
ISO 9000, 281
ISO 14001 certification, 281

J

Jobbers, 452
Joint venture, 32, 66, 68
Just-in-time (JIT), 140, 465–466
Just-in-time II (JIT II), 466

K

Kefauver-Harris Drug Amend-
  ments, 42
Kickbacks, 75
Kinked demand, 338, 339
Knowledge, 496–497

L

Labeling, 276–277
  foreign markets, 71
  warning label, 602
Laboratory experiments, 190
Laggards, 227
Language differences, 58
Lanham Trademark Act of 1946,
  42, 261, 265, 279, 501–502
Late majority, 227
Leader pricing, 370–371
Learning, 107–108
Leasing, 140
Ledger expenses analysis, 610
Legal forces; *see* Political and legal
  forces
Legislation, 41–42
Less developed countries (LDCs), 59
Level of involvement, consumer
  buying-decision process, 95
Licensing, 66–67
Life-cycle management; *see* Product
  life cycle
Life-style, 153
Life-style shopping center, 425
Liking, 497
Limited-line stores, 433–434
Line expansion, 239–240
Links, 626
List price, 325
List of values (LOV), 154
Literacy rate, 58
Lobbying, 557
Local-content law, 60
Local operating laws, 60
Local regulation, promotional
  activities, 503–504
Local strategy, 56
Location, 425, 543
Logistics, 457; *see also* Physical
  distribution
  supply chain management
   and, 460
Logo, 260
Long-range planning, 574

Long run pricing objectives,
  323–324
Loss leader, 370–371
Loss leader pricing, 42
Lower-lower class, 102
Lower-middle class, 101
Loyalty, 59, 95, 136, 360, 410

M

Macro influences, 30
Macroenvironmental forces, 31–32
Magazines, 545–546
Mail-in rebate, 364–365
Mail-order, 407
Mail survey, 188–189
Maintenance, 604
Major accounts organization, 599
Mall intercept interview, 187
Management, 570; *see also* Organi-
  zation structure
  marketing management, 16,
   594–595
  planning as part of, 570–574
Mandatory labeling require-
  ments, 277
Manufactured products, 119
Manufacturers, 212
Manufacturers' agents, 455–456
Manufacturers' representative, 455
Manufacturer's sales branch, 452
Manufacturer's sales facility, 452
Manufacturer's sales office, 452
Manufacturing activity, measures
  of, 130
Marginal analysis, 331
  evaluation of, 336
  prices based on, 335–336
Marginal cost, 329–330, 336
  prices based on, 332
Marginal cost curve, 330
Marginal revenue, 335–336
Mark-on, 348
Markdown percentage, 350–351
Market, 5, 17, 45, 175
  activity costs analysis, 611–613
  channels of distribution and, 400
  defined, 45, 146, 578
  geographic concentration of,
   400
  impact of Internet on, 628–632
  life cycle related to, 247–248
  order size, 401
Market-acceptance stage, 245
Market-aggregation strategy, 158
Market attractiveness, 586
Market demand; *see also* Business
  market demand
  forecasting of, 165–169
  new products and, 223
  target markets and, 578
Market development, 583
Market-entry pricing strategies
  market-penetration pricing,
   361–362
  market-skimming pricing,
   360–361
Market exchange, 5
Market factor, 165
Market-factor analysis, 166–167
Market-orientation stage, 8–9
Market penetration, 582
Market-penetration pricing, 361–362
Market potential, 166

Market research; *see also*
  Marketing research projects
  competitive intelligence, 194–195
  ethical issues in, 196
  Internet and, 633
Market-response system, 466–467
Market saturation, 55, 269–270
Market segment, 17, 147, 175
  businesses; *see* Business market
  consumers; *see* Consumer market
Market segmentation, 147–149; *see*
  also Target-market strategies
  behavioral segmentation,
   154–156
  benefit segmentation, 155
  business markets, 156–158
  business users, 150
  consumers, 150–156
  demographic; *see* Demographic
   segmentation
  geographic segmentation,
   151–152
  overview of, 146–147
  positioning, 162–165
  psychographic; *see* Psychographic segmentation
  subcultures, 100
  target-market strategies,
   158–162, 293
  ultimate consumers, 88, 395
Market share, 165
  pricing objectives and, 324–325
Market-share analysis, 182,
  609–610
Market-skimming pricing, 360–361
Market specialization, 598
Market tests, 222–223
Marketers, 5
Marketing, 6
  company's marketing program,
   17–18
  concept of, 9–16
  consumer cues, 107
  costs of, 21
  direct marketing, 440–441
  in domestic market, 20–21
  evolution of, 6–9
  in fashion, 253–254
  in the global economy, 20
  importance of, 20–25
  in information economy, 13,
   40, 56, 109, 623–634
  legislation affecting, 41
  market-orientation stage, 8–9
  market segment accessibility, 149
  middlemen's brands, 267
  nature and scope of, 4–6
  new products and, 224
  in organizations, 23–24
  product-orientation stage, 7–8
  promotion and, 484–496
  reasons for personal study of,
   24–25
  return on marketing investment, 14
  sales-orientation stage, 8
  technology and, 44
  utility and want-satisfaction,
   21–22
  viral marketing, 498, 538
Marketing audit, 606
Marketing concept, 9–16
  company organization and, 597

components and outcomes of, 11
coordinated marketing activities, 12–14
customer relationship management (CRM), 11
implementation of, 11–12
mass customization, 12
nature and rationale, 10–11
performance metrics, 14–15
societal marketing concept,
  15–16
Marketing cost analysis, 610–614
of activity costs, 610–611
allocating costs and, 613–614
contribution margin
  approach, 614
full cost approach, 614
of ledger expenses, 611
types of, 610–613
use of findings from, 615–616
Marketing department, 597–600
geographic specialization,
  597–599
Marketing environment
external macroenvironment; *see*
  External macroenvironment
external microenvironment,
  44–45
organization's internal environment, 46–47
Marketing exchange, 5
Marketing goal, 577
Marketing information system
  (MkIS), 176–179
characteristics and operation
  of, 176–177
databases, 180–181
decision support system (DSS),
  176, 178–179
designing a, 177
global system, 178
Marketing intermediaries, 45–46
Marketing management, 16,
  594–595
Marketing math, 344–351
analytical ratios; *see* Analytical
  ratios
markups; *see* Markups
operating statement; *see*
  Operating statement
price elasticity of demand,
  344–345
Marketing mix, 17–18, 70–76,
  147
advertising, 75–76
distribution, 17, 73–75, 328
gray marketing, 74
international markets and, 70–76
marketing research, 70, 175
middlemen, 74
physical distribution, 74–75
positioning strategy and, 164
price/pricing, 17, 72–73
product, 17, 328
product planning, 70–72
promotion, 17, 328
retailers and, 431
strategic market planning,
  578–579
Marketing objectives, 577
Marketing program, 17–18
external macroenvironment
  of, 31